Flash 5 Dynamic Content Studio

Philippe Archontakis
David Beard
Eng Wei Chua
Jorge Diogo
Paul Doyle
Brandon Ellis
Justin Everett-Church
Branden Hall
Dan Humphrey
Randy Kato
Nikhil Kilnani
Patricia Lee
Steve Leone
Bryan Mahoney
Andrew Montalenti
Phil Piper
Carlos Ponce
Roger Prideaux
Nicolas S. Roy
Shawn Ryder
Steve Webster

friendsof

DESIGNER TO DESIGNER™

Flash 5 Dynamic Content Studio

First Printed in March 2001

Trademark Acknowledgments

friends of ED has endeavored to provide trademark information about all the companies and products mentioned in this book by the appropriate use of capitals. However, friends of ED cannot guarantee the accuracy of this information.

Published by friends of ED
30 Lincoln Road, Olton, Birmingham, B27 6PA, UK.

Printed in USA

ISBN: 1-903450-06-3

Flash 5 Dynamic Content Studio

Credits

Authors	Philippe Archontakis, David Beard, Eng Wei Chua, Jorge Diogo, Paul Doyle, Brandon Ellis, Justin Everett-Church, Branden Hall, Dan Humphrey, Randy Kato, Nikhil Kilnani, Patricia Lee, Steve Leone, Bryan Mahoney, Andrew Montalenti, Phil Piper, Carlos Ponce, Roger Prideaux, Nicolas S. Ray, Shawn Ryder, Steve Webster
Content Architect	Eleanor Baylis
Editors	Eleanor Baylis, Benjamin Egan, Julia Gilbert, Lisa Stephenson, Douglas Paterson, Ben Renow-Clarke, Andrew Tracy, Alan McCann
Graphic Editors	William Fallon, Katy Freer, Deborah Murray, David Spurgeon
Author Agent	Sophie Edwards
Project Administator	Thomas Stiff
Technical Reviewers	Jason Anderson, Konstantin Bereznyakov, Sudeep Chatterjee, Olivier Debon, Michael D Downing, Larry Drolet, Tobenna T. Ekwueme, Brian Eric Ganninger, Sean Ian Graham, Brandon Houston, Ben Hyland, Steven Izen, Rod Johnson, Ikezi N. Kamanu, James F. Kelly, Daniel Kent, Stephen Kirby, Michael Krisher, Sangyong Lee, Jaap Lous, Jim MacIntosh, Drew McLellan, Monkeymedia.net, Andrew J. Montalenti, Bernard M. Ngassa, Owen Palmer, Kevin Paterson, Timothy Payne, David Schultz, Keyur Shah, Steven Skoczen, Richard Smallwood, Gabrielle Smith, Spiderweb Internet. Jonathan Steer, Andrew Stopford, Kevin Sutherland, William L. Thomson Jr, Michael Walston, Andrew H. Watt, David Whitney, Erik Williams, Benjamin Wong
Index	Martin Brooks, Andrew Criddle
Cover Design	Katy Freer, Deborah Murray
Proof Readers	Joel Rushton, Fionnuala Meacher, Mel Orgee, Luke Brown, Alan McCann, Dan Britton, Joanna Farmer, Thomas Stiff, Ben Renow-Clarke, Catherine O'Flynn, Jez Booker

Flash 5 Dynamic Content Studio

Philippe Archontakis   **www.logient.com**
Having run his own graphic design studio for nine years, Philippe joined the Logient team as a partner, and fell head first in the industry. There he discovered Flash, and immediately fell in love with the idea of blending motion and sound to his graphic skills and his print experience. He still does print design but prefers exploring motion design and studying its advantages for communicating.

David Beard
David is a software developer and technology consultant. He is a founder of Wavelength Releasing llc, where he works with Flash, primarily as a web application medium. David's current efforts are devoted to the development of M.O.D.E – Multi-user Object Development Environment. MODE enables the development of real-time collaboration environments within standard web domains, and will use Flash in various aspects of its user interface and multi-user domain.

Eng Wei Chua   **www.thevisionstudios.com**
Eng Wei is a founding member of the VISION studios, where he has been exploring the wider possibilities for building dynamic and creative Flash sites using middleware applications. With work in their portfolio such as Theme Park Inc (www.themepark.ea.com), Tiberian Sun (www.tiberiansun.com), and Shogun: Total War (www.totalwar.com), the VISION studios are constantly experimenting and pushing the boundaries of dynamic Flash.

Jorge Diogo   **www.blue-pac.com**
Jorge Diogo is a founder member of Blue*Pacific Software. Having trained as a software engineer he has been involved with the Internet industry since its inception, although he has also worked on other fields, most notably video games, wireless internet and performing arts. In the belief that software design is an art form, he tries hard to be a good artist. He'd like to thank Susana and his parents for their constant support, and all his cats for being, well, cats.

Paul Doyle
Based in Glasgow, Scotland, Paul is heavily involved in building web applications with Dreamweaver Ultradev and ASP. Away from this he enjoys watching football and planning his next foreign holiday. Acknowledgments: I would like to dedicate my small part in this book to my girlfriend Claire, for her unlimited patience while I was locked quietly away in another room working. To my family, especially mum – thanks for all your love and support! And thanks to all at friends of ED for their help along the way.

About the Authors

Brandon Ellis   www.aspalliance.com/bellis

Brandon Ellis is a senior web developer at Martin Interactive in Richmond, Virginia. He likes mountain bikes, skateboards, vegetables, cheese pizza, his son Lee, his wife Lynn, hot peppers, beer, computers, sleep, old cars and lots of coffee. You can contact him @ edeveloper@hotmail.com.

Justin Everett-Church   www.infinitumdesign.com

I'm currently Interactive Director at Estudio.com, a studio specializing in Flash shows and games. You can see some of our work at shockwave.com (look for Regurge). When I'm not making games (and other neat stuff) there, I can be found at home playing games (purely for research), making effects for Flashkit, or hanging out in #flashhelp on IRC, a great place to talk to other Flashers. Prior to becoming a Flash devotee, I studied linguistics and foreign policy. This fantastically geekish life takes place in San Jose, California along with my very patient partner and two rather strange looking cats.

Branden Hall   www.figleaf.com   www.neuralust.com

Branden Hall works at Fig Leaf Software where he is the Senior Interactive Developer and a Macromedia Instructor. His work at Fig Leaf, combined with his founding of the Flash 5 ActionScript mailing list, FlashCoders, and his participation in many other lists, conferences and users groups have spawned speculation that Branden cannot possibly be just one man. Amusing though the thought of a host of Branden clones running around may be, his fiancée Patricia Lee guarantees us all that there is, indeed, only one.

Dan Humphrey www.technomedia.co.uk

Dan Humphrey, who lives in Birmingham, UK, is a self taught Flash design and programming wizard, and the owner of TechnoMedia Design & Promotion. Aside form his love of web development, his interests include snowboarding, dance music, women, and beer. Respect to Flashkit.com and all its members - the friendliest and most helpful Flash fanatics on the Internet! Big thanks to my Mum. Contact: dan@technomedia.co.uk

Randy Kato   www.braincraft.com   http://randy.kato.com

Randy Kato wanders and explores, seeking knowledge, experience and wisdom; he's thrilled to be exploring and shaping the digital frontier. He offers immense thanks to Braincraft and all 'Crafters past, present and future. He thanks them for all the knowledge, creativity and brilliance he's absorbed, as well as for all the great times (and hardships) he's been through with them. He also thanks Macromedia for their continued support and devotion to the developer community – adding so much strength to their products. Finally, he thanks all his fellow developers, geeks and freaks. Craft on! *(photo: Matthieu Paley)*

Flash 5 Dynamic Content Studio

Nik Khilnani   http://nuthing.com http://ultrashock.com
Name: Nik Khilnani   **Age:** 23 (30th Jan, 1978)   **Sex:** Male   **Location:** Buffalo/NYC
Occupation: Student/Flasher   **Using Flash Since:** 1998   **Using CGI/Perl Since:** 1998
Likes: Flash and CGI interaction, his guitars   **First Cool Site Remembered:** Kimble.org
Early Inspirational Sites: Praystation, Dextro, Entropy8 **Work Done:** Nuthing.com,
Ultrashock.com, No Fat Communications etc. **Thanks:** Parents, Online Flash community
Sp. Thanks: Patrick Miko, Peter (NRG), Scott Riesett, Scott Stolpmann **Sp. Mentions**:
Scott Winseman, Harish Chawla, Kush Desai

Patricia Lee   www.figleaf.com
Patricia Lee has been working in the web industry ever since her graduate days of 1997
when her biggest challenge was to maintain the pages of her college's School of
Journalism website. Since then she's moved on to Fig Leaf Software, where Patti spends
most of her time developing web based applications using ColdFusion and Spectra,
rounding out her days by teaching ColdFusion classes. And yet, somehow Patti finds
time to get into ActionScript. Perhaps that has something to do with her relationship
with Branden Hall.

Steve Leone   http://home.earthlink.net/~sleone
Hailing from Brooklyn, NY, Leo is an award winning designer and ActionScript junkie;
he has been involved in some of the most innovative Macromedia Flash and Generator
projects to date. Having no background in either programming or design, Leo derives
enjoyment from the challenge. Leo thanks: my beautiful wife for her patience and
support; the talented minds of team Braincraft – Physics professor, Dr. O; Ryan P. for his
infinite ASP wisdom; Chris, Dan, Kevin and Phil for believing in me; Randy and friends
of ED for the opportunity; Bones in Atlanta.

Bryan Mahoney www.GoDynamo.com
Having graduated from McGill University in Montreal, Canada, where he majored in
finance and entrepreneurship major, Bryan promptly founded Dynamo e-Media Inc.
with fellow McGill graduate Alex Nemeroff, and turned his focus to developing
dynamic and innovative web applications. Today, the Dynamo team continues to
experiment with Flash's ability to interact with server-side scripting languages like
ColdFusion.

Andrew J. Montalenti   www.morganth.com
Andrew J. Montalenti is the founder/creator of his own digital playground and online
identity, Morganth.com. At the tender age of 16, he has not only architected numerous
web projects and organizations, but has also helped small businesses in the New York
City and Long Island areas find fresh digital identities. He is currently attending Paul D.
Schreiber High School in New York, and while not at school, or immersed in new
computer technologies, he enjoys hanging out with his friends.

Phil Piper   www.pipey.com

Phil Piper was born in the celtic fairyland that is Cornwall. After completing his physics degree he trained as a science teacher, realized how useless he was at it, and became a programmer instead. After a long spell writing educational software, Phil began developing web applications, and learning about Flash, and eventually bluffed his way into a job with Broadband Communications, UK. **Facetious Job Description**: Mouse Test Pilot. **Likes**: Blue Cheese, Minidisc Players, Puzzle Bobble. **Listens to**: Low, Pavement, The Apples In Stereo, Grandaddy, Calexico. Avoids: Air Travel and Cabbage.

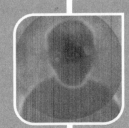

Carlos Ponce   www.logient.com

With ten years experience in print graphic design behind him, and a fascination for new technologies, Carlos began creating for the web three years ago and realized how powerfully communicative electronic media can be. Currently partner and art director at Logient, a Montreal-based web development firm, he and the team work hard to push Flash to its limits and create motion with a message.

Roger Prideaux   http://www.4tex.com

Roger Prideaux is the managing director of 4tex Group. He started out as a computer programmer and has commercial experience in all areas of Internet development: online learning, game production, and web sites. Roger writes regularly for UK computer magazines, and currently specializes in Flash, in persuit of his goal to push the boundaries of Internet development.

Nicolas S. Roy   www.logient.com

Having studied in Computer Science and 3D animation, Nicolas found himself faced with the choice between programming and design. It quickly became clear that his path would be somewhere in the middle, when he discovered his passion in the birth of the graphical web in the early 90s. Nick became a partner in Logient in 1999, where the fusion of creativity and expertise of his teammates help him to push his aspirations to new heights.

Shawn Ryder   www.webryder.com

Shawn Ryder is the owner of Webryder Internet Design and Consulting located in Halifax, Nova Scotia, Canada. Although he took Computer Programming in college, having worked with numerous local and International clients he learned the importance of excellent design skills. Shawn decided that he had to become more creative, and it being the early 1990s, building visually appealing yet purposeful web sites that made good use of Flash seemed the best way to do it. This writing is in memory of Dean Trimper, Janet Irwin, and my Grandmother Alma Sweeny.

Flash 5 Dynamic Content Studio

Steve Webster   www.netbreed.co.uk
Steve Webster is a freelance web developer with several years experience in Flash, scripting and backend development. A keen programmer since the age of 8 [and the good old days of the Sinclair Spectrum 48k], he trained in Software Engineering, and specializes in Flash ActionScripting, PHP and MySQL. He is a moderator in, among others, the Scripting & Backend forum at the excellent FlashKit. Acknowledgments: I would like to thank Nicki Chapple for her overwhelming support and encouragement, without which I would have had a nervous breakdown before finishing my contribution to this book. I'd also like to thank the fine people at friends of ED for giving me my first shot at technical authoring, and for being so understanding.

Palette
and
Table of
Contents

DYNAMIC FRONT END

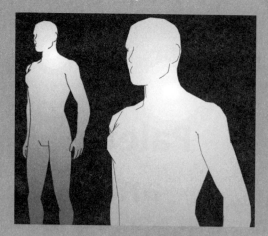

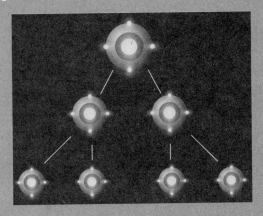

TALKING TO FLASH

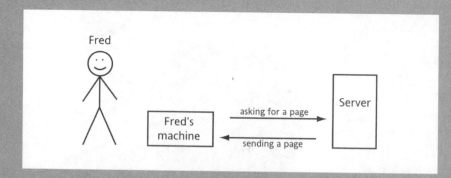

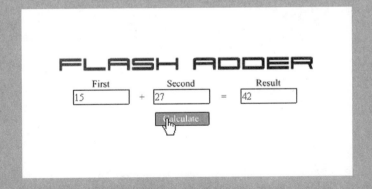

DAN	150
FRED	100
MARK	65

DYNAMIC GENERATION

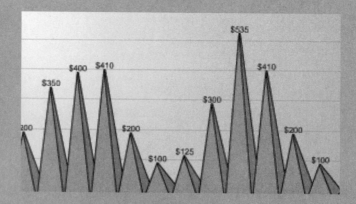

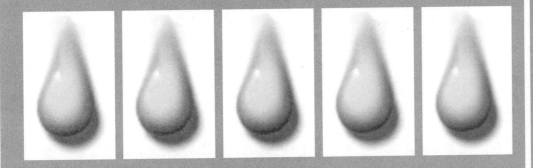

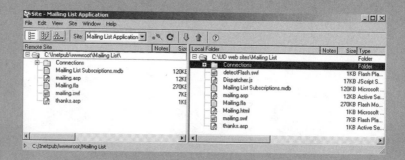

DYNAMIC DATA

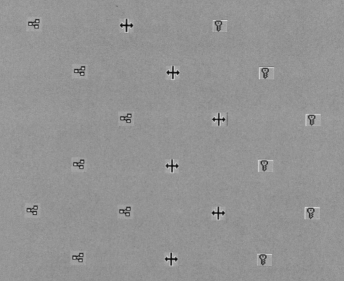

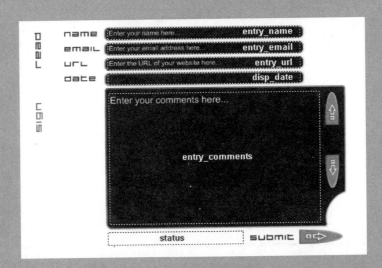

```
<rooms>
        <den>
                <walls>artificial wood paneling</walls>
                <lighting>floor lamps</lighting>
        </den>
                <kitchen>
                <walls>paint over drywall</walls>
                <lighting>recessed lights</lighting>
        </kitchen>
        <dining_room>
                <walls>fine velvet wallpaper</walls>
                <lighting>chandelier</lighting>
        </dining_room>
        <foyer>
                <walls>wall to wall mirrors</walls>
                <lighting>illuminated disco ball</lighting>
        </foyer>
</rooms>
```

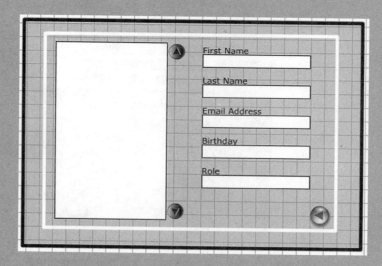

REAL WORLD DYNAMIC CONTENT

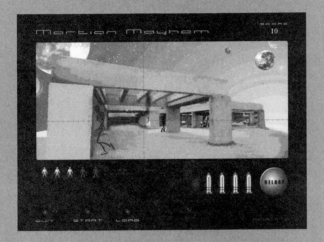

3/26/2001- Information for designers, by designers- John Smith

In a similar incident, a man covered in gold paint attended an emergency room in Kenosha, Wisconsin. Doctors believe that he was afflicted with a gilt complex.

3/26/2001- motion web mind food- Joe Bloggs

A man walked into a doctor's surgery in Greater London today, with a carrot

Flash 5 Studio

Table of Contents

Table of Contents

8 Flash and JavaScript Integration   323

9 Flash and Text Files   353

Table of Contents

13   Using CGI Scripts with Flash   501

Table of Contents

Table of Contents

20 Introduction to Dreamweaver UltraDev   805

21 Integrating UltraDev with Flash   851

Table of Contents

Table of Contents

Introduction

Welcome to the world of Dynamic Flash Content. We've tried to provide everything you could possibly need to know about in order to get going with dynamic Flash development.

'Dynamic Flash?' I hear you say 'sounds good but, well, what do you mean exactly?' We mean Flash that does stuff – really powerful stuff. We mean fabulous front-end Flash interactivity, tied to and exploiting the power of your server.

The key to creating powerful Flash applications is your server. So we've tried to cover everything about the server. We've done this by gearing everything towards a Windows system: we'll show you how to install your desktop server on your Windows machine, and then how to use it – and we mean really use it – with ASP, ColdFusion, Generator, Databases, PHP, MySQL.... Of course, when you get to working with CGI scripts and Perl, we had to loosen the rule a little, so we show you how to upload to a remote server for those chapters. All you need is the CD with all the trial versions of the software, a Windows machine, time, and energy.

Every contributor to this book is a working web designer or coder, and they face the same kind of problems as you every day out there in the trenches, battling with clients, technology, and code, and they've come together to share their hard-won knowledge with you here.

You might find that you want jump around within the book – ASP might lead you straight to relational databases, for example, or you might find that your ActionScripting skills are pretty high, so you can get going on the integration chapters before you need to buff them up further with the higher end things. And then again, you might want to read it cover to cover – all of this is intended, and not the result of a wobbly cohesion of subjects, (honest) but rather the indication of a Studio book. We're hoping that this book will become a pretty important part of your tool kit, and as such, will contain information that you really need to know at some point, but not necessarily linearly.

So what's covered?

The Dynamic Front End
All the back-end skills in the world aren't going to help if your Flash front end just isn't doing the business. You'll create some great looking movies in this section, and round it all of with a full gaming application.

Talking to Flash
We'll start out working with Flash and JavaScript, and then look at updating Flash files with text brought in from outside. And then gear up a notch and start really working with the server: installing a server on your machine, and using the processing power that brings you.

Dynamic Generation
This section is devoted to the tools that make dynamic Flash application development really fast and efficient.

Dynamic Data
Databases are behind every dynamic Flash site. We'll investigate Access and MySQL from beginning to end. And, of course, no discussion of high level Flash, or indeed data, would be complete without an expose on XML, so we'll look at that too.

Real World Dynamic Flash
Finally, we'll put it all together in a couple of real world dynamic Flash case studies

Layout conventions

Firstly, we assume that you're using Expert mode in the Frame/Object Actions windows. We also use the authors' own symbol/variable naming conventions: we don't think that Flash code is yet subject to the more 'formal' constraints of established conventions. This also chimes with the book's principle of laying out the possibilities and letting you make your choices about what suits you best.

We've tried to keep this book as clear and easy to follow as possible, so we've only used a few layout styles to avoid confusion. Here they are...

- Practical exercises will appear under...

Headings in this style

...and they'll have numbered steps like this:

1. Do this first

2. Do this second

3. Do this third etc...

- When we're showing ActionScript code blocks that should be typed into the Actions window, we'll use this style:

```
Mover.startDrag(true);
Mouse.hide();
stop ();
```

- Where a line of ActionScript is too wide to fit on the page, we'll indicate that it runs over two lines by using an arrow-like 'continuation' symbol:

```
if (letters[i].x_pos==letters[i]._x &&
➡ letters[i].y_pos==letters[i]._y){
```

Lines like this should all be typed as a single continuous statement.

- And when we discuss ActionScript in the body of the text, we'll put statements such as `stop` in a code-like style too.

- When we add new code to an existing block, we'll highlight it like this:

```
Mover.startDrag(true);
variable1 = 35
Mouse.hide();
stop ();
```

Pseudo code will appear in this style:

```
If (the sky is blue) the sun is out
    Else (it's cloudy)
```

- In the text, symbol, layer and frame names will use this emphasized style: layer 1, symbol1, this frame while instance names will look like this: instance1.

- Really important points that you ignore at your peril will be highlighted like this:

> *This is a key point, and you should read it really, really carefully.*

- Web addresses will appear in this form: www.friendsofed.com

- New or significant phrases will appear in this **important words** style.

What's on the CD?

The CD in the back of the book contains full support for the book's content. It includes:

- FLAs and SWFs for the worked examples, plus any supporting text/image/code and database files

- Trial versions of key packages, including ColdFusion, Generator, UltraDev, and Perl

Support

If you have any questions about the book or about friends of ED, check out our web site: there are a range of contact email addresses there, or you can just use the generic e-mail address – feedback@friendsofed.com.

There are also a host of other features up on the site: interviews with renowned designers, samples from our other books, and a message board where you can post your own questions, discussions and answers, or just take a back seat and look at what other designers are talking about. So, if you have any comments or problems, write to us, it's what we're here for and we'd love to hear from you.

OK, that's the preliminaries over with. Let's get going on a dynamic adventure!

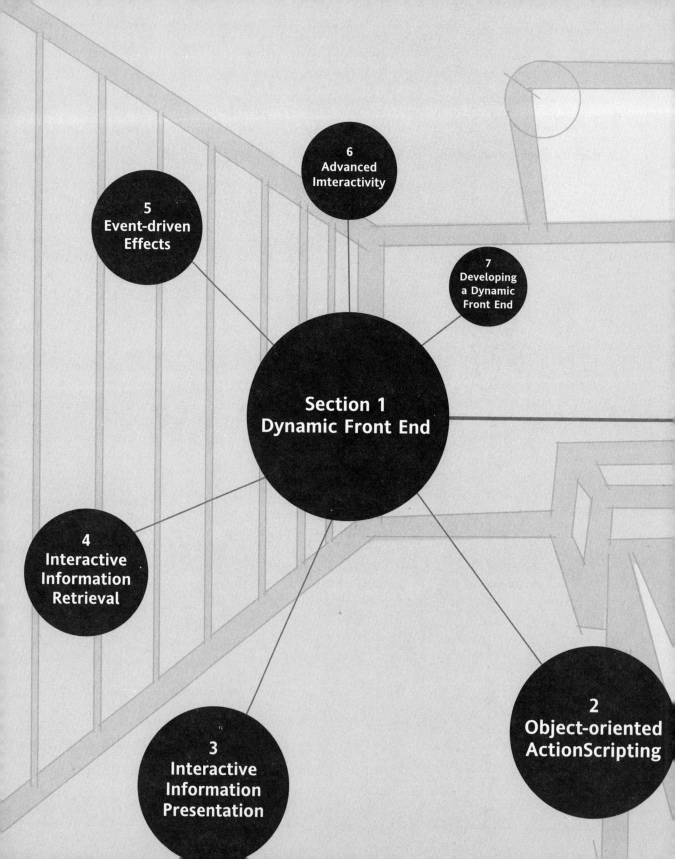

Section 1
Dynamic Front End

6
Advanced
Imteractivity

5
Event-driven
Effects

7
Developing
a Dynamic
Front End

4
Interactive
Information
Retrieval

3
Interactive
Information
Presentation

2
Object-oriented
ActionScripting

Chapter 1
The Web

Before you decide where you're going, it's usually a good idea to pinpoint where you are and where you have come from. This chapter is going to try to put Flash in that perspective. This is important because Flash is a tool with limits, as well as incredible capabilities; it developed to meet the needs and demands of the evolving Web. Truly talented designers will always design to the limits of the tools they are using, as well as to its strengths, so, in order to place Flash effectively, we'll cover:

- The origins of the Web, and where Flash fits in

- Some of the key features and restrictions of Flash

- Some of the essential basic concepts that Flash uses

- Dynamic content and the new mindset of the Flash developer

The origins of the Web

It's funny. About five years ago, plain text was enough to impress me. I used to connect with my 9600-baud modem to this thing called 'the Web'. There were only two really useful things on the web that I knew about then: checking the weather and browsing the book index of Barnes & Noble. Both of these resources were accessed using a protocol called Gopher, which retrieved plain text files across an Internet connection. This protocol is hardly used today.

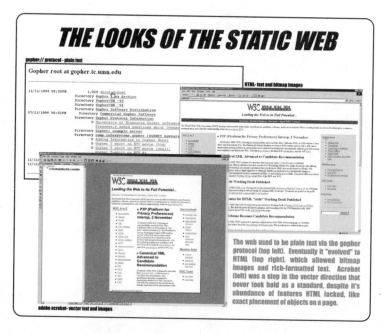

When HTML (HyperText Markup Language) came along, there were those who thought that it would never be of interest to anyone other than the same computer geeks that were involved with the networking concepts hidden deep behind the language – HTTP (HyperText Transfer

Protocol). Maybe it was to do with the fact that these computer programmers and system administrators were busy working with a language which couldn't even produce a screen display to match their own clothing, never mind design a visually pleasing web site!

HTML was the vision of the director of the World Wide Web Consortium (W3C), Tim Berners-Lee, whose idea was to enable academic and research institutions to communicate within their global communities. All that HTML needed to be able to do, for this purpose, was some basic formatting, incorporate the occasional image, and be transferable with HTTP. (It should be noted that HTML and HTTP are *not* synonymous – HTTP supports all sorts of file transfers, including but not limited to, HTML.) As you might imagine, the Web was predominantly about text for a while, until designers began to catch on and started to apply their skills to the Web.

HTML was (and still is) a primitive technology, initially intended to transfer and present information to those who want to find it fast, irrespective of the browser they are using, and with little regard for the way it looked (except for basic formatting). It was intended to deliver content across the Web simply and quickly, and because of this simplicity, HTML has lasted, and is likely to continue to last, as the fastest and most efficient method of delivering text to users. Such simplicity also means though, as anyone who's used HTML will know, that it offers little room for real web design flair and creativity.

HTML is a **markup language**, in that it consists of a number of tags that give you a certain amount of control over the presentation of the information that you are intending to display. So, as you probably already know, you can bold (<B>) and italicize (<I>) words, put them in larger fonts, and so on. This sort of markup was, and still is, very primitive compared to the print-media formats that companies like Adobe and Corel were developing at that time. Although HTML was developed to help present and transfer information, it was never intended to challenge the print-media paradigm. From the designer's point of view, though, it is exactly these humble ambitions of HTML that is its downfall – it doesn't give you precise control over the placement of objects on a page, and any special effects that you might want to use, like slanted text or drop shadows, have to be created as bitmaps and then placed onto an HTML page.

And yet, despite these humble origins, HTML began to catch on. Maybe it was something to do with the way people were beginning to use the web-portable document formats (like Adobe's Acrobat PDFs, which gave full support for vector graphics, print-quality and exact placement of objects on a page), simply didn't provide the speed of information transfer that users wanted; they didn't give users web browsability.

As HTML caught on, so did the designers, and HTML quickly became the web designer's lingo. The language has developed, and as Internet use has flourished far beyond anything anyone might have expected in those early days, so technology has come on a long, long way. Now we have PHP, ASP, JSP, Cold Fusion, JavaScript, and of course, XML, to name but a few. Web sites and web site design have developed all the way from these humble text transfer origins to havens for corporate identities, e-Business, even mobile communication.

Enter Flash

Time moves quickly on the Web. Here we are, about five years on, and the only way to impress some people with a web site is through powerful applications and full audiovisual multimedia presentations. Mere technology and information exchange is not enough anymore, it has to look good, sound good, work well, and impress – all in 20k. So much for plain text. On the other hand, some people breathe a sigh of relief when there's nothing but plain old HTML on an information-driven site. Nowadays, more than ever, web design is about knowing what information users want from the site and serving it up – be it anything from fabulous animations and extraordinary feats of web magic to clean and clear unobtrusive graphics and text. Sometimes, users even want a *choice*.

Macromedia has really been a pioneer in the world of the beautiful Web. Their web presentation tools (Flash and Director) started out as fairly unconventional tools, used by cartoonists and animators to present their work on the Web. It wasn't long, though, before other people started to see the potential of Macromedia's web design arsenal. Full support for vector graphics, and the associated comparatively small file sizes that vector graphics bring you, meant that designers could create full websites, scalable at any resolution, and take advantage of the features that Flash had. Macromedia touted itself as the new Web, with tools such as Fireworks, Freehand and Dreamweaver. Since the Flash files are browser independent, you can visit the same shocked site and watch it run pretty much identically on Netscape or Internet Explorer.

The browser wars

Nowadays HTML is a monstrous beast. When the W3C released version 4 in December `99, Netscape was in a state of limbo (as AOL was taking over), and IE was holding the dominant browser market-share. However, instead of both Netscape and Microsoft trying to fully adapt the standards put forward by the W3C, Microsoft began mixing some of the W3C's standards with their own, creating IE's own browser features. These included the capability to allow MS Word documents to be more viewable when they were saved as HTML, features later used by Frontpage (Microsoft's visual HTML editor).

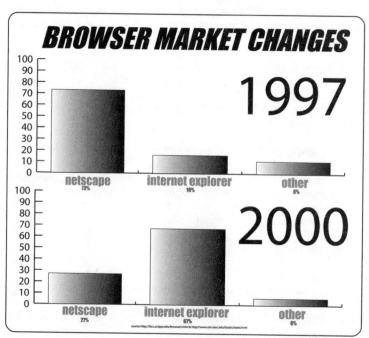

The W3C also brought in the document object model (DOM) standard – essentially an interface that allows scripts to dynamically access and update the content, structure and style of documents on the Web, and return the result of this processing to the presented page. However, neither this standard not the HTML 4 specification were strictly interpreted by Microsoft, and small ambiguities in code started to emerge bringing errors with them. Thus began the endless browser checks for web designers; everyone had to be sure their pages would work in both of the mainstream browsers.

Things didn't stop there, either. Web designers started to like Microsoft's added features, and began implementing IE-only web sites. Microsoft's hold on the browser market proliferated, and now the majority of the Web's current surfers use IE.

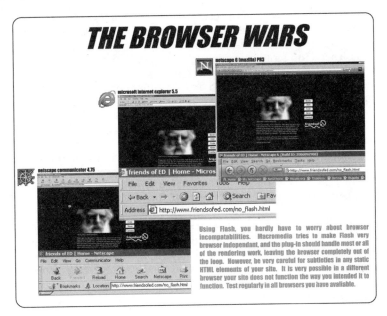

Using Flash, you hardly have to worry about browser incompatabilities. Macromedia tries to make Flash very browser independant, and the plug-in should handle most or all of the rendering work, leaving the browser completely out of the loop. However, be very careful for subtleties in any static HTML elements of your site. It is very possible in a different browser your site does not function the way you intended it to function. Test regularly in all browsers you have available.

Netscape didn't manage to recode parts of their HTML rendering engine to be in compliance with the W3C standards, but has since produced an open-source browser in the form of Mozilla (www.mozilla.org). The open-source community, with the Netscape Gecko engine, is now embracing in full the HTML 4.0 standards set by the W3C. Mozilla can currently be downloaded in developmental builds and preview releases. There is also a lesser-known browser about, Opera (http://www.opera.com), which is lightweight, cross-platform and adheres to the W3C standards.

These browser wars, immensely important though they are to far-reaching sites, and a nuisance to code around, have had virtually no bearing on Flash at all. Thanks to the Flash plug-in, supported by more than 95% of the browser market, designers can rest assured that all they have to do is publish their Flash movie on the Web and it will play on every operating system, and in every browser, that Macromedia says it will.

When Flash got to version 3 it began to get broader acclaim, and web designers began using it for web projects. The version 3 Flash/Director player plug-ins started to come bundled with 4.x versions of Internet Explorer and Netscape. When this happened, designers became confident that users would have the plug-in and that a web site would not force them to download 500k of data (which, at the time, would have taken around 2 minutes).

Big design names started creating short multimedia introductions for companies (most of the time, their own) that really used the full scope of Flash, and demonstrated Flash design skills. Thus began the intro competition that is still going on today (despite deep disapproval from some usability gurus) as Flash designers try and out-cool each other with their intros. It was at about this time that Flash started spreading like wildfire. Surfers who saw Flash wanted to see more, and designers who worked with Flash saw it as the wave of the future.

The version 4 upgrade secured Flash's place as more than an animation tool. As the GUI improved, new tools were incorporated, (new ActionScripting elements, and MP3 audio compression), and movie file sizes shrank, a new breed began to emerge. Some called themselves Flashers, while those who combined other elements into their Flash creations (artistic: Illustrator/Freehand, 3D modeling: 3D Studio Max, Poser, Maya, and filmmaking: Premiere, Final Cut Pro) called themselves New Media Designers. The terms quickly caught on, and Flash found its way into other areas of design. The first really impressive Flash special effects were text effects – what someone could do to make text come on and off the screen and wow the user, but it wasn't long before people began to integrate other media forms into Flash.

Converting 3D models to Flash was (and still can be) a tedious process – importing each frame of a 3D animation, then tracing it manually using Flash's vector tools, and then replacing textures with gradients that look similar. Nonetheless, users began to see 3D interfaces on the web. Flash's ability to import a slew of media formats induced and prompted all sorts of technology integration with Flash – where Flash simply played the role of the web medium to present animation and design created by entirely different products.

And then there's Flash's (initially primitive) scripting language: ActionScript. Flash web sites can interact with the user. Some of the more advanced sites began to look more and more like miniature operating systems or applications than web sites, with buttons, controls, and windows – all inside the browser window. The designer community was maturing; getting really smart, and much, much bigger. Novice and veteran web designers alike were getting into Flash – not just a tool for cool web site intros anymore.

Version 5 has made Flash take it even further. Utilizing an object-oriented language very similar to JavaScript, and a fully integrated development environment, Flash is now a full development suite with a myriad of tools, controls, and functions that make static web designers around the world weep.

What's more, ActionScript has matured into the language it was destined to be – no longer some loose collection of methods that designers had to think long and hard about to make really functional. With a little help, Flash can now talk to a back-end database, using the processing power of a server to do the dirty work, it glitters and shines in the foreground. As ActionScript has developed, so have the possibilities for full-scale Flash web sites; and that is what this book is all about.

Understanding the power of Flash

One tool, so many possibilities; let's look at a simple breakdown of the some of the most powerful and flexible aspects of Flash:

Vector drawing

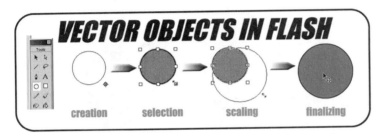

Vector graphic manipulation is not unique to Flash; it's been around for a while. You've probably seen or used vectors in Adobe Illustrator, Macromedia Freehand, Corel Draw or and even Acrobat PDF files. Flash's primary drawing tool uses the flexibility offered by vector graphics.

Fonts, circles, rectangles, lines and even paintbrush strokes are all vectors in Flash. So what are vector graphics? Well, you could say that they're 'the creation of digital images through a sequence of commands or mathematical statements that place lines and shapes in a given two-dimensional or three-dimensional space'. In other words, graphics are created by a set of instructions, rather than a pixel-by-pixel color representation. As you might imagine, instructions are significantly lighter than pixel by pixel representation – while a 50x50 pixel blue circle in bitmap form might get to 10kb in size, stored as 2500 pixels of color information in a file, an infinitely-sized circle in vector/Flash form would be less than 1Kb, as all that would be stored in the file is a command, something like `DrawCircle(color, size)`. This kind of power gives Flash developers who do their drawing in Flash (or in any other vector drawing program) a way to keep the file sizes of their movies relatively small.

This is a pretty important concept. Imagine that you decided to paint a blue circle on your sweater. You pick up your paintbrush, and paint the circle as precisely as your movement allows. Now imagine that your friend, recognizing your flair for fashion, wants to paint exactly the same circle on his sweater as you now have on yours. The simplest thing to do would be to tell him the color of the circle and its radius. You'd be unlikely to tell him all about the hundreds of little blue dots on the sweater that formed the circle, and still less likely to unravel your sweater and give him the long piece of wool with the blue dots on it to copy.

Bitmaps work by storing the color information of every single pixel in a file, which is very useful for storing something true-to-life, like a photograph. There are so many color changes, and few concrete patterns in real life, so it's hard to tell a program how to interpret that photograph as a command or series of commands with parameters – that is, it is hard to make a photograph into a vector graphic. It would be like pulling the sweater apart until there is only one thread with blue dots on it. Using it as a guide, your friend would have to go though every dot of this string of color information (no pun intended), painting a blue dot on the new sweater at the corresponding points. This arduous process would be something akin to rasterization where, in essence, a bitmap program reads a file containing a long string of color information, presenting this color information on the screen. Unlike vector graphics, this color information is resolution dependent, so that the resolution display of the device dictates the dimensions of the bitmap. This is the way your monitor and your TV work.

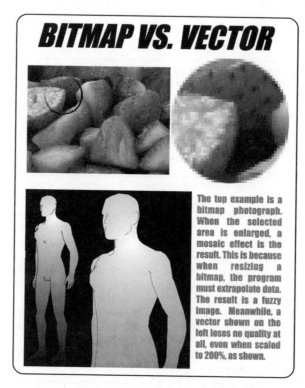

BITMAP VS. VECTOR

The top example is a bitmap photograph. When the selected area is enlarged, a mosaic effect is the result. This is because when resizing a bitmap, the program must extrapolate data. The result is a fuzzy image. Meanwhile, a vector shown on the left loses no quality at all, even when scaled to 200%, as shown.

The string that you hand your friend could well be more than 20 feet long. It's a long string for sure – similarly, a string of color information stored in a file could be 20Kb in file size, which is why bitmaps are so large. There are compression methods implemented in formats like a GIF that work as a kind of shorthand. A pattern of 15 white pixels in a row would be abbreviated – you might have something like "white 15x" instead of "white, white, white, white, white..."

There is, of course, a much simpler way. You could simply tell your friend 'paint a blue circle with a radius of 5 centimeters', which in vector terms might translate as *DrawCircle(blue, 5)*. This statement contains all the data that would be needed, and your friend would handle the processing power. The Flash player plug-in behaves just like this, passing instructions for processing rather than strings of color information – and it's this that helps you to keep your Flash movies so much smaller.

Imports

When you're using Flash, you'll quickly find that there are plenty of other tools around that you'll want to use with it. These are some of the tools widely in conjunction with Flash:

3D Studio Max	3D modeler
Vecta3D	3D Studio Max plug-in that vectorizes 3D models
Swift3D	3D modeler that imports 3D Studio Max models
SoundForge	Sound editor
Swish	Flash text effect creation tool
Quicktime	Compressed movie file format

The beauty lies in the fact that Flash can import practically any file format you would ever think of using. Every common bitmap image type is supported, as are all common sound types (including MP3). You can cut-and-paste directly from Illustrator into Flash or from Freehand into Flash quickly and easily.

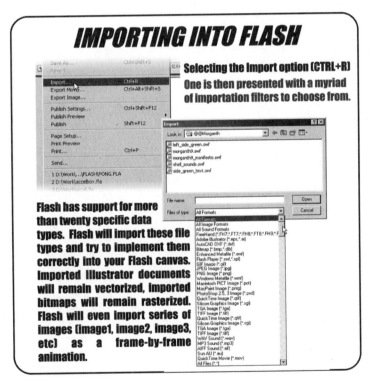

This functionality allows a Flash designer to use other programs to come up with faster, better solutions to what could be complicated problems. For example, using 3D Studio Max and a plug-in like Vecta3D to create 3D Flash animations is much easier and quicker than trying to vector-trace a 3D model in Flash. Print media designers sometimes find drawing certain things much easier in programs like Freehand and Illustrator, so they can do their drawing in another program and perform a simple vector-to-vector import into Flash.

DEFINITION OF TERMS

bitmap: A data file or structure which corresponds bit for bit with an image displayed on a screen, probably in the same format as it would be stored in the display's video memory or maybe as a device independent bitmap. A bitmap is characterised by the width and height of the image in pixels and the number of bits per pixel which determines the number of shades of grey or colours it can represent. A bitmap representing a colored image (a "pixmap") will usually have pixels with between one and eight bits for each of the red, green, and blue components, though other colour encodings are also used. The green component sometimes has more bits that the other two to cater for the human eye's greater discrimination in this component.

raster: The scanning pattern of parallel lines that form the display of an image projected on a cathode-ray tube of a television set or display screen.

vector graphics: A line or movement defined by its end points, or by the current position and one other point; a drawing program that deals with separate shapes such as lines, polygons and text and groups of such objects as opposed to a painting program which stores only bitmaps. The advantage is that it is possible to change any element of the picture at any time since each part is stored as an independent object whereas once something in a bitmap has been overwritten it cannot in general be retrieved.

The timeline

The timeline is a very powerful feature of Flash, and it's sometimes overlooked. The flow of control in conventional programming languages is top-to-bottom. In the Flash environment, however, the timeline handles the flow of control exactly as you tell it to, across multiple layers with many pieces of ActionScript code that can operate simultaneously. This extra layer of control can be pretty complicated, and sophisticated uses have to be well thought out and planned, but it is an extremely powerful feature that can help you do fairly complex things with a lot more ease than you might in conventional programming languages.

Suppose you were a play director, and you're examining two scripts, one for a solo actor, a monologue, and the other for a play with many actors performing simultaneously. The monologue piece is loosely analogous to a normal, top-to-bottom, conventional program. The actor is able to do actions defined by the script, but there is a limit to how much she can say or do at once. Meanwhile, the script for a full play contains stage directions and dialogue for many actors, who are able to speak or do things simultaneously. This is like Flash's method of flow-of-control. Flash represents a normally complicated programming concept, *multi-threading*, in a very intuitive way. By allowing there to be multiple key frames with frame actions in many layers of a timeline, actions can be executed in parallel just as more than one actor can speak simultaneously. This concept adds a whole new dimension to programming.

THE TIMELINE

The Timeline will receive more mouse clicks from you than any other part of Flash. It is how you navigate through your movie, edit chunks of code and control the flow of the movie. There can be many timelines in any given movie, across different movieclips, layers, and scenes. Do not be intimidated by it–learn to master the timeline and stay organized while using it.

For static web designers, the concepts of time and motion in web design may be foreign ones. You may be used to the "create a document that visitors can view" design mentality. However, designing sites in Flash is not just about making 'documents'; it's about making movies, applications, animations, dynamic and interactive elements all weaved into one site.

Flash development is much more difficult than static web design – don't let your old-school colleagues fool you. You have to really plan things, and work with many different elements at design-time. A really good Flash site takes a lot of organization and persistence, but it'll be worth the effort.

It's the timeline that adds this extra dimension to Flash. It allows you to work not only with the look and content of a site, but also how you'll work with and respond to the user, and how you'll help them get what they're looking for from your site. All there really is to understanding how your timeline should work, and your movie flow, is being able to visualize the movie in your mind.

Using the timeline you can organize your movie, place your movie clips, buttons, graphics, sounds, frame labels, and instances, and then manipulate them.

Fully featured ActionScripting

Of course, this is the feature of Flash 5 that makes all the difference: the full and comprehensive ActionScripting language.

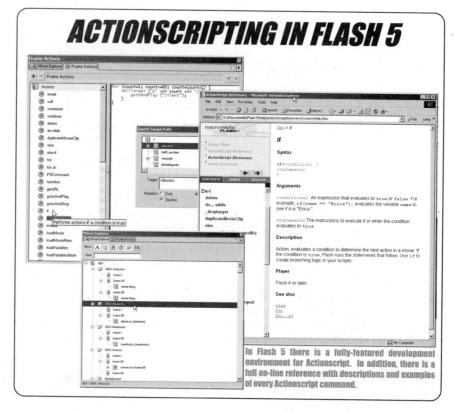

In Flash 5 there is a fully-featured development environment for Actionscript. In addition, there is a full on-line reference with descriptions and examples of every Actionscript command.

With version 5, ActionScript is a powerful language in its own right. If you are familiar with programming, or more specifically with JavaScript, you will feel right at home with ActionScript. And even if you're not, once you've become familiar with ActionScript, you'll find other scripting languages more accessible too.

Because ActionScript is such a powerful feature, we've devoted the first section of the book to it. ActionScript script used with Flash by itself gives you the power to create truly interactive, involving, sticky web sites. Once you can do that it's only a short step to using outside programming languages with ActionScripting as well, like Perl, ASP, ColdFusion, and the rest – which we'll do in the following section of the book. And once you can do that, all you need is a database, and you have a dynamic data-driven website.

Flash on the Web

The powerful features that we've looked at can be used to create original websites with different dynamics and varying levels of interactivity. Many different Flash sites currently exist on the web, most of which use Flash in one of three ways.

Intro sites
These are sites that have only a short introduction when the user enters the site, but then sends the user to a normal, static HTML page. This is the most common implementation of Flash, and was even more common in version 3, when the creation of a full Flash interface was more difficult than it is now.

http://www.fightercombat.com

Fighter Combat International is an example of a site that uses a Flash intro (above) to impress the user initially. After the intro completes its play, the rest of the site takes a fast-loading, static HTML approach (left). This allows for high-bandwidth users to get a "bang for their buck" while the low-bandwidth users still have a usable site in short load times. In addition, the user is provided with a choice of whether or not to watch the intro (top left).

Flash elements

Most of the site is done with static HTML, purely for flexibility and speed of information access, but specific elements of the site, like navigation interface elements, or special effects, are done in Flash. Usually, these types of sites are created because the web designer wants to offer clear, searchable text in the form of HTML, but still take advantage of certain features of Flash.

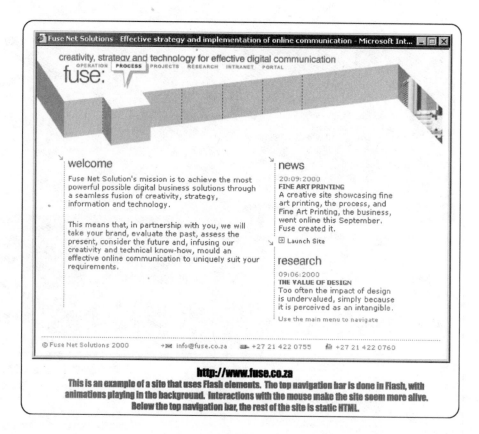

http://www.fuse.co.za
This is an example of a site that uses Flash elements. The top navigation bar is done in Flash, with animations playing in the background. Interactions with the mouse make the site seem more alive. Below the top navigation bar, the rest of the site is static HTML.

Full Flash site

Full Flash sites rely very rarely on static HTML, keeping the user within the Flash environment during their entire stay. They tend to include client-side scripting and server-side scripting, and database power – all of which will soon be second nature to you. When a full Flash site is executed correctly, it is interactive, dynamic, and impressive. But then you know that – it's why you're reading this book.

So what do we mean by dynamic? A dynamic web site is an incredibly powerful one. It works with the user to provide what they're looking for. It's interactive, responsive, and usable. It's what online commerce sites do, and truly powerful information resources. It can display the information it's generating both dynamically and visually – in short, a dynamic Flash web site is a great place to be!

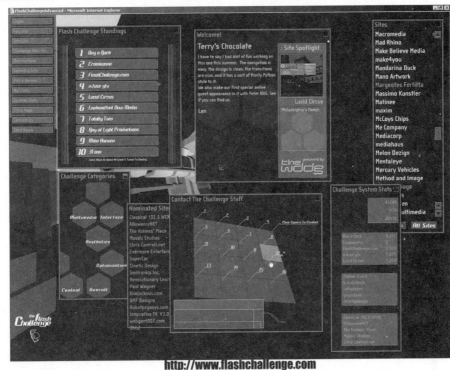

http://www.flashchallenge.com

An excellent example of a full Flash site that feels more like an application than a website. The site goes full-screen and uses a draggable window interface to navigate. It talks] backends that allow users to log in and rate/review websites.

Understanding what Flash can and can't do

Before we go any further, we ought to look at the restrictions Flash brings with it. A good Flash designer knows how to profit from the powerful features of Flash without suffering at the hands of its restrictions. As you get more and more acquainted with Flash, you are going to run into brick walls – you'll find out there are things that you just cannot do without some serious thinking and expertise. Just as the W3C expands the power of HTML, Macromedia will further expand the power of Flash, so you can expect some of these brick walls to evaporate – in the mean time, there are certain things that you simply need to know. This book will try to teach you that by making Flash work with other behind-the-scenes processing powers (back-ends), you can create a Flash site with nearly unlimited flexibility. Before you can reach this status of divinity among Flash designers, you must truly understand what can (and will) frustrate you along the way.

The plug-in

That old problem, you sigh. Well, yes, if anything going is to rain on your parade, it's a site visitor without the plug-in, or with an older version of the plug-in. And it's an unfortunate fact of the web designer's life that even though you and your tech-oriented colleagues know that Flash is the coolest thing since fried rice, this is no guarantee that Joe the web surfer thinks likewise.

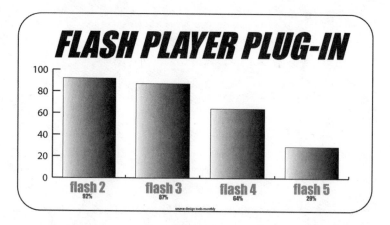

It's an especially pertinent question when you're designing for a client, and it'll come up time and time again. (Things don't get any easier if your client isn't up and running with Flash either – try explaining to a client that in order to visit the site the user has to go to this other site and wait a couple of minutes for a plug-in to download if you fancy a bit of relentless frustration. It's not easy.) So here's that truism that no good web designer can ever afford to forget, especially not one that's going to want to get paid for his or her wizardry - A Good Web Designer Designs For Their Audience.

Clever people have come up with clever ways to do Flash plug-in detection, and even cleverer ways to make users anxious to go and download the plug-in. You're probably already familiar with some of them; you can code your site to check for the plug-in (you'll see how to do this later), and when it's not present show a simple animation or game in HTML, or a previous version of Flash, downloading the latest Flash player in background (although how your customers might feel about this is the next question...).

Helping yourself to the user's processing power

So, Flash takes advantage of the visitor's computer for its processing power. HTML is very easy for most modern computers to handle, needing minimal processing power and memory. Flash allows the designer to take advantage of that extra processing power for animation, special effects, programming power, and the like (albeit at the expense of increased download times). So, the next problem on our list is that Flash movies play differently on different machines.

You what? What's that you say? But just earlier we had mentioned one of the fantastic features of Flash being that it is pretty much browser independent! How can it play differently on different machines? Well, processing power.

Top-of-the-line machines will be able to process heavy Flash movies much more smoothly and more easily than slower machines. RAM, CPU, operating system, video card, and even browser version all play factors in performance. Just as it can take three minutes to do a 3D render on one machine and ten minutes on another, a Flash movie may play at 27 frames per second (fps) on one machine and 12 fps on another. Is there any way around this? No – but you can anticipate such incompatibilities and make sure they do not exist, simply by making sure your movies are as efficient as they possibly can be, and always bearing this factor in mind. There are a few things guaranteed to slow down a Flash movie:

Bitmap images
Generally, once you import a bitmap into Flash you will slow the movie down for the frames in which the bitmap exists. Bitmaps take longer for Flash to animate, so moving them across the screen and fading them in and out may play slowly on slower machines.

Alpha fades
People who are new to Flash tend to overdo Alpha level fading when they first get going. Fading multiple elements of text and images in and out of the movie does, if you use it a lot, chew through processor cycles rapidly.

ALPHA FADING

ALPHA FADE

ALPHA FADE

ALPHA FADE

ALPHA FADE

ALPHA FADE

Shape tweens

As you know, Flash does shape tweening, allowing you to morph vector objects into other vector objects gradually. So, for example, you could put a circle in frame 1, a triangle in frame 20, and a shape tween in between, and Flash fills in the frames in between, gradually converting your circle into a triangle. More complex transformations, especially those large in scale, require a lot of processing power.

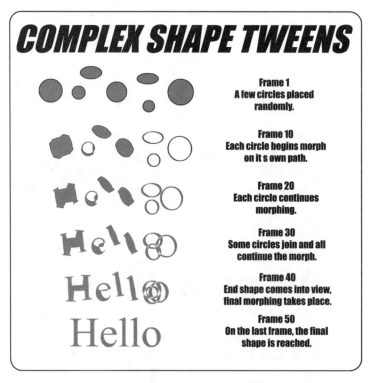

You're probably already developing a keen sense for keeping your Flash movies clean, yet impressive – you know that an impressive special effect isn't that great at 3 fps on someone else's machine. You don't, of course, have to restrict your design to things that a computer way behind the curve can manage, but it's a good idea to use the Bandwidth Profiler a *lot* when you're testing your movie.

What this book will show you is that, wonderful though Flash is, it can't do everything on its own. Nor should it – can you imagine the size the plug-in would have to be to accommodate all the possibilities? ActionScript code is executed client-side, so it would be simply inappropriate if Flash's built-in programming functionality handled complex situations – essentially, your site visitor would need the power of a server on their machine. And this is *the* restriction – the restriction that, in the course of this book, we'll try and help you overcome.

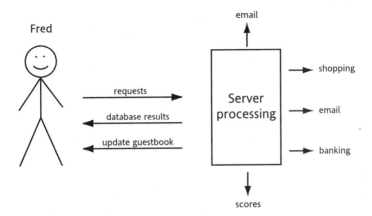

What it breaks down to is that the most powerful Flash solutions are going to get a little help from somewhere else – and the fact that you've picked up this book suggests that you're aware of this! There are things for which you're going to need some server-side code – and that might be anything, ASP, Perl, or something else. Interactivity, fantastic effects and responding to your user belong to Flash and client-side processing. The thing that'll make your Flash applications powerful, though, is your server: you'll be using it for information crunching, generating visuals dynamically, updating records, analyzing records, sending email from your site, and much, much more. Which brings us to the final point:

The coder and the designer

Before version 5 was released, most Flash designers didn't have, or need, programming experience before jumping into website creation. People could really push the Flash envelope without extensive ActionScript.

Those days are long gone now; the new ActionScripting environment has probably already persuaded you that you really need to be a coder and a designer in order to take advantage of all of the features that Flash has to offer. Don't worry if you are completely without programming experience; we'll tell you everything you need to know to make Flash your own dynamic content studio.

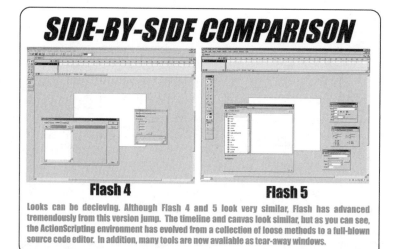

SIDE-BY-SIDE COMPARISON

Flash 4   **Flash 5**

Looks can be decieving. Although Flash 4 and 5 look very similar, Flash has advanced tremendously from this version jump. The timeline and canvas look similar, but as you can see, the ActionScripting environment has evolved from a collection of loose methods to a full-blown source code editor. In addition, many tools are now avaliable as tear-away windows.

I've heard it said that there are Flash 'designers' and Flash 'programmers' – the person who can accommodate both traits really does have control over his or her own design and web site. After all, if you've designed the Flash site in the first place, you know a lot more about how it should really work than anyone else. Although it's common practice in some businesses to split up projects along the lines of art versus technology, a team of developers that can do both will be so much better at creating effective Flash sites.

There is some good news. Most people who get involved with Flash are already designers, and it's much easier to teach someone to code than it is to teach them to design. You can't give someone good "taste", but you can teach him or her to program – especially the sort of programming you'll be using here, with Flash. Very soon you'll be very comfortable with ActionScript, and once you've got a handle on ActionScripting, the other scripting languages, like ASP, JSP, Perl, and other powerful development tools like Generator, are really very accessible. By the time you've finished this book, you'll be Flash coder and designer in one!

The best advice I can give you as you start is to try to see everything in your mind's eye – and don't even *think* "Oh, I'll never understand that. It looks way too complicated". It's not – it's easy! What's more, the class of the coder-designers is a very special group of talented individuals – ever heard of artistic programming? Thought not...

Taking on the Web your own way

By the time you have finished this book, I hope that you will be using Flash expressively and creatively. You may master the specifics of Flash, but you'll never be able to do *everything* that can be done with it. That is the beauty of the technology – so much can be done with it that you are not bound by standards and conventions. Do not be afraid to create something new, for that is how you gain respect in this fast-paced and competitive web world.

It's important that you look in places other than the Web for your inspiration. The ideas you find when you surf the Web are all too often somebody else's. There are loads of great ideas for Flash all around you. When the movie *The Matrix* came out, many people began creating Flash movies that mimicked certain parts of the movie. When you see something in the real world, see if you can't bring it to the Web. That way you'll be creating things that nobody has done before. Many fabulous Flash artists draw their inspiration from all sorts of strands of life and nature. Find things that are uncommon, and recreate them for your audience. If you need an idea, just look around for a few minutes. You are bound to find one lying around somewhere.

This may all seem easier said than done, but once you know how to go about creating original things in Flash, all you need is an original idea. These are all things that you'll learn as a designer, but with the power of programming being added to your belt, there will be so many more possibilities. ActionScript allows you to recreate things like motion and time. The acceleration of an object, for example, can be recreated in Flash using a simple formula. Apply that acceleration to an object, and suddenly it comes alive.

Just observing frustrations or restrictions of everyday living can also help you create practical web applications. Flash is new, and Flash is powerful, and there are many things that people have not done before. Feel free to *invent*.

You also have to start thinking about innovative ways to handle the restrictions of Flash. Creating a full Flash site that efficiently talks to a back-end and has much power and flexibility is a pretty amazing thing!

The bottom line is that you need to stay concentrated, organized, and open-minded. Flash is a powerful tool that can be used not just to create web sites, but stunning audio-visual experiences. It has the power to pull dynamic content from other sources and it integrates well with practically every web technology. It is a creative expression tool that allows designers to not only display their artistic talent, but also bring it to life with time and motion. Look around, come up with new ideas; do things that have never been done before. March to the beat of your own drum; the web is yours for the weaving.

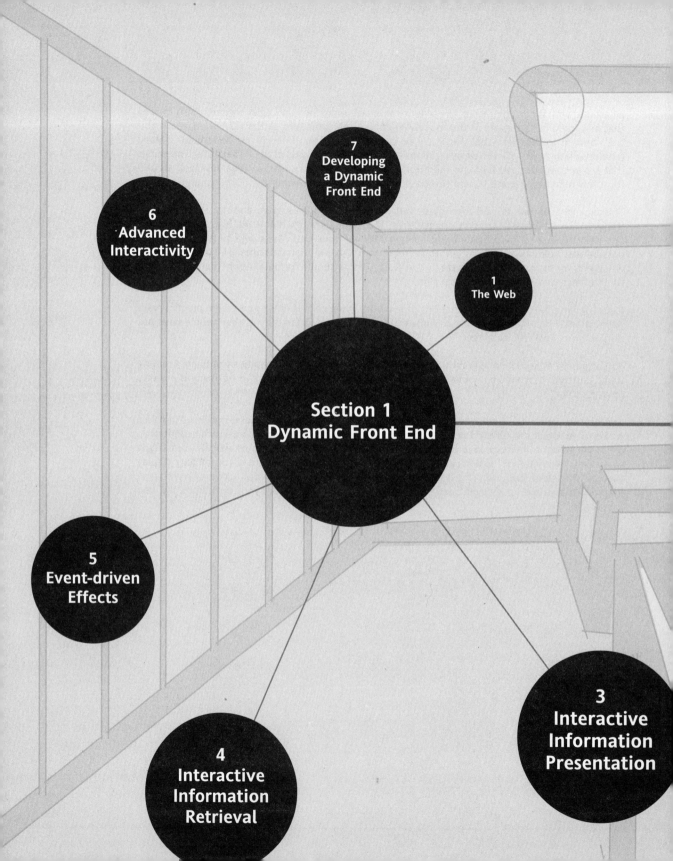

Chapter 2
Object-oriented
ActionScripting

By now, you'll be more than comfortable with simple actions and how they can be attached to a frame in a timeline or to a button, actions that allow you to stop or start a movie, move to a particular frame, or open a new URL in the browser. Back in the days of Flash 3, these actions were (more or less) all that was possible. Flash was still primarily an animator's tool, although a few intrepid pioneers still managed to create quite complex interactivity (and even games!) within those limitations. But generally, developing anything complex in Flash 3 was a bit like digging your way out of prison with a teaspoon.

Version 4 of Flash opened the door to far more complex and entertaining movies. Designers could manipulate the properties of individual movie clips, and use variables and simple expressions. Flash was beginning to look like it had something that resembled a programming language (if you didn't peer too closely), and suddenly everyone was writing games and creating innovative (or crazy) navigation systems. This scripting system soon became known as ActionScript, and those who mastered its quirks quickly became hot property in the career market. With Flash 5 came the ActionScript programming language that Flash 4 had intimated. The syntax of the language now closely resembles JavaScript, so if you've ever written browser scripts using JavaScript, you'll be right at home with the new ActionScript.

We're going to cover a lot in this chapter:

- The principles of object-oriented programming (OO)

- Variables

- Some of Flash's built-in methods

- The `MovieClip` object

- Nesting and paths

- Essential ActionScript: conditional actions, loops, arrays and the `eval` function

- Building your own functions

- Working with movie clips

This chapter will be a fast moving whirlwind tour of OO ActionScripting, and although we'll build some neat little examples, I'll leave a lot of the experimenting up to you. The chapters that follow this one move through ActionScript in much more detail, so you'll find a lot of the concepts and code that we'll use here in more detail and worked into more examples.

I hope that you'll finish this chapter having had a taste of the sorts of things that ActionScripting together with an object-oriented approach makes possible, and ready to start putting it all into practice. I'd really recommend that you get familiar with the ActionScript Reference that comes with Flash 5 to bolster your knowledge, and to seek out the code examples that are available on the Internet – there's a lot to be learnt from them. Finally, before we begin, I suggest that you set your actions window to Expert Mode – there will be a lot of coding further into the chapter, and unless you want to be chasing around inside the action selection panels, the Expert Mode is the Mode to be in.

So, let's get started.

What is object-oriented programming?

(or 'Let's go for a ride in a funny car')

The object-oriented (OO) approach is as much a way of thinking about things as it is a system for programming.

The OO world is made up of things called **objects**. Like a lot of things in programming, it's best introduced with an analogy that has absolutely nothing whatsoever to do with either Flash or programming. So, let's begin with a car.

A car is a fairly distinct type of object (or thing), just as a telephone, a forest and a restaurant menu are types of objects. In OO language, we would call the collection of things that fall under the moniker 'car' a **class** of object. Your car, my car and the police car pulling up outside are all **instances** of cars; that is, they are particular cases of the class of things we call 'car'.

Although cars all belong to the same class of object, there are of course differences between individual cars; the model of the car, the registration, the number of seats and doors, the engine capacity, the dents in the bodywork, these are just a few examples of the attributes we might talk about to build up a picture of a particular car. They are useful attributes to know about any individual car and can be used to make decisions about it (like whether you'd buy it or not, for example).

Properties

In OO language, these attributes of an object are called its **properties**. OO has a special way of writing these properties down, one that we will use later on when we get back to Flash. Suppose I have a car. I can't just call it *car*, because *car* is a class of object, and in the big scheme of things doesn't tell me much about the car in question. When I talk about the car, I want to do so in a way that makes it clear exactly which car I mean, so I could call this car, myCar.

Suppose myCar has two doors and four wheels, and was made by Ford. In OO terms, we could write this set of properties like this:

```
myCar.wheelCount = 4
myCar.doorCount = 2
myCar.manufacturer = Ford
```

This syntax is often called dot syntax (for obvious reasons). The dot is used to indicate that there is a relationship between the entities in the expression, so, in this example, we've said that the number of wheels on the car (wheelCount) is a property of myCar.

Methods

Objects can also have **methods**. A method is an action that we can perform on an object, or cause the object to perform. One method of myCar is that I can turn it on or off, and we can write that in much the same way as we wrote the properties:

```
myCar.startEngine()
```

Or:

```
myCar.stopEngine()
```

These methods are specific sets of actions grouped together and given an appropriate name. There is always something going on 'under the hood', and methods are the convenient shorthand way to deal with those complex underlying processes – just as in the real world I don't really need to understand the details of the electrical system of the car; all I need to know is that if I turn the ignition key, the car will start.

The parentheses (brackets) after the method name are there in case we need to supply some more information. For instance, another method for a car might be drive, and when we drive a car, we're usually going somewhere in particular, for instance to work. So, we'd write this as:

```
myCar.drive(work)
```

work is an example of a **parameter** – something that specifies in more detail what the method should do. The method takes the parameter as input and produces a certain output based upon it. In this case, the parameter is the name of a place (a place, incidentally, would be another kind of object, with its own properties and methods.)

Another example of a method for a car is accelerate. So, if I was driving my car and I wanted to increase its speed by 20 miles per hour, I could use a method that looked like this:

```
myCar.accelerate(20)
```

All the accelerate method does to a car is to increase its speed by a given amount (using some process we don't need to worry about). If we also had a speed property then we'd be able to see the value of this property increase by 20.

Events

The third concept in OO is a thing called an **event**. An event differs from a property or a method in that we don't have direct control over it. An event is something that *happens* to the object, as opposed to something that we *do* to it. It might be something that is triggered by our actions (for example an increase in speed), or it might be something that occurs due to external factors (such as a breakdown or a crash).

When events occur, it's useful to have a course of action already planned. The term used to describe a sequence of actions that will be performed when a particular event occurs is called an **event handler**. Events are (in Flash and JavaScript at least) always prefixed by the word on. So, we might have events called onBreakdown, onCrash or perhaps onAccelerate. Here's an example of an event handler:

```
onCrash() {
     myCar.stopEngine()
}
```

You can see that an event is quite different from a method because we don't have any direct control over when it will occur. The event **handler** is there to provide us with a means to respond to the event when it occurs. The actions (enclosed by curly braces) will be carried out when the event (in this case, a crash) occurs. So, assuming the crash wasn't one of those 80's TV ball-of-flame affairs, it makes sense to turn off the engine.

Another, less worrying example of an event handler might be:

```
onPark() {
     myCar.stopEngine()
     myCar.setHandBrake(true)
     myCar.lockDoors()
}
```

In the onPark event handler, the sequence of actions is as follows: Stop the engine. Set the handbrake. Lock the doors. You'd probably want to get out of the car before locking the doors, but let's not be too fussy. This is, after all, just an analogy.

The OO hierarchy

The power of OO only really starts to show when we begin to look a little deeper, and consider more complicated cases. Let's continue with the car example and extend it a little more.

Remember the first property we gave the car, wheelCount, which defines the number of wheels on the car? Well, as it may have occurred to you at the time, wheels, like cars, are a class of object in their own right. A wheel can also have properties (radius, width, and age, for example). Each of the car's wheels is a distinct instance of the class of things that we call *wheels*.

So, if we wanted to treat the wheels as objects, we need to have some way of identifying each individual wheel. One way to identify them would be to call them wheel1, wheel2, wheel3 and `wheel4`. Which is all very well in theory, but in practice it could get pretty complicated. As soon as we start to look at objects with lots of wheels (trucks or lorries) this individual naming becomes a bit unwieldy.

A better system is to consider the wheels of the vehicle as a group. In OO language this group would be called a collection or an array of wheels. Using this system, the wheels would be identified as `wheel[1]`, `wheel[2]`, `wheel[3]` and `wheel[4]`, where the number in square brackets identifies a particular wheel. This is called the wheel's index. This indexed system is used to deal with a group of objects that make up part of a larger object. It's always easier to deal with numbers rather than words when you're programming.

> *Note: In 'real' programming, an array traditionally starts with index number zero. So if we're employing this example in real code, we would write* `wheel[0]`, `wheel[1]`, `wheel[2]` *and* `wheel[3]` *to describe the same four wheels.*

So whenever I want to refer to one of the wheels of my car, I can refer to it like this:

`myCar.wheel[0]`

Or:

`myCar.wheel[2]`

And so on.

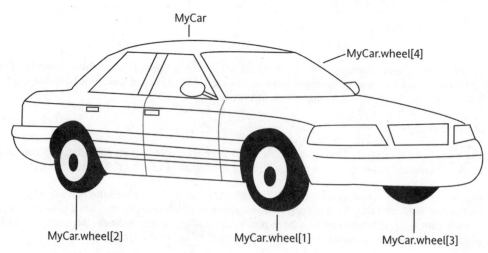

Each wheel is an object in its own right; it has its own set of properties, methods and events. I might refer to the radius of the wheel number 1 of my car like this:

```
myCar.wheel[1].radius
```

The beauty of this OO syntax is that it is hierarchical. The car has wheels. A wheel has a radius. In this syntax you can see immediately that we're talking about the radius of wheel number 1 of myCar. This value is unique in the world since I only have one car, and there is only one wheel number 1. Of course, this example doesn't give us a terribly useful piece of information – unless my car is some kind of dragster, the radius of all the wheels is likely to be the same.

We can extend the concept of a hierarchy even further. A wheel also consists of other objects. A wheel has a tire. The tire has properties such as pressure and tread depth. So, using this hierarchical system, the tread depth of the tire on wheel 4 would be referred to as:

```
myCar.wheel[2].tire.treadDepth
```

Hierarchies in OO always read from left to right and are written in order of ownership. When we talk about hierarchies, we normally use the analogy of a family. As such, myCar is the **parent** of all four wheels. Each wheel is in turn the parent of a tire. Conversely, each tire is the **child** of a wheel. The wheels are all **siblings**, but the tires are not siblings because they don't share the same parent. Family is very important in OO; in that way it's a lot like the Mafia.

Sometimes it's useful for a child object to make a reference in the reverse direction (that is, to refer to its parent). For instance, a wheel might have an onSkid event that occurs whenever that wheel starts to skid. It would be useful if the skid could cause the brakes of the car to release briefly so as to help control the skid (as a matter of fact, this is actually the basis of a simple anti-lock braking system). The event handler for this might look something like:

```
onSkid() {
        parent.releaseBrakes()
}
```

We have an action inside the wheel's onSkid event handler that calls the releaseBrakes() method of its parent object (the car). The parent object is available to every object in OO.

Or, the tires might also have an event handler that deals with blowouts (punctures). In this hierarchy the tire object is two steps (or generations) away from the car object, so we'd write:

```
onBlowOut() {
        parent.parent.applyBrakes()
}
```

This is equally valid. The first parent reference refers to the wheel (the parent of the tire). Since a wheel is an object, it too has a parent (the car), and so it is perfectly valid to write parent.parent. In a true family analogy we could of course say *grandparent*, but as OO only allows parents we make do with referring to the parent of the parent.

> *As you go about your everyday life, think about how objects in our world can be organized into hierarchies, and how the system of properties, methods and events can be applied to different situations. Being able to look at things in this way will not only help you quickly gain expertise in ActionScript programming, but will also help you with many other programming languages.*

I can't emphasise enough how important a clear picture of object-oriented systems is to working with Flash 5. There are four principle reasons that make OO pretty much essential to any programming:

- OO is intuitive. Human beings are naturally used to seeing the world as a set things ('objects') that interrelate hierarchically.

- OO is reliable. The separation of actions (or programming code) into distinct units such as methods and event handlers minimises the impact of errors.

- OO is easily maintained. Again, the subdivision of actions or code into units means that it is easy to locate a problem within the system and resolve or update it without affecting any other part of the system.

- OO is quicker. A clearly defined structure makes it easier to develop and extend your work. Well-designed modular code (such as the methods you create for your objects) can be reused in many different places throughout the system. This is both efficient programming, and saves you a lot of time.

If anything I've said so far isn't clear, then try working out a few more examples for yourself (try applying object-oriented ideas to fairgrounds or movies, for instance). There is also an appendix on object-oriented programming in the back of the book that expands and develops on the principles I've outlined so far, which I recommend you have a look at when you're ready.

In the remainder of this chapter, we'll start applying OO principles to Flash. Provided you've absorbed the simple principles I've outlined in this section, you should have no trouble understanding how Flash can be used to provide structure and interactivity within your movies.

So let's move on to Flash.

Variables and values

Variables are common to every programming language. A variable is like a little labelled box in which you can store information. You can easily access or change this information as long as you know which box it's in. The label on the box is known as the variable's **name**, and the information contained within is called the variable's **value**.

Variables are given values in what is known as a variable **assignment**:

```
x = 10;
```

The value 10 is stored in a variable called x. In Flash there are three categories of information that can be stored in a variable: or – **number**, **string**, and **Boolean**. They are known collectively as **Data Types**, and are significant in that the data type of a variable stipulates what sort of information the variable can hold, and what can be done with it. This one, not surprisingly, is of the number data type, which allows you to do most of the things you could possibly want to do with a number in Flash.

This is a variable assignment where the value is a **string** (that's just programmer's jargon for a piece of text)

```
myString = "This is a string";
```

Notice that when we assign a string variable, the value is enclosed in quotes.

The semicolon (;) at the end of both these variable assignments is used at the end of each instruction. It literally means '*this is the end of the instruction*'. Missing a semicolon at the end of an instruction will usually cause an error in your script – unless, curiously, it is a terminating semicolon, in which case the script will usually compile without an error. A semicolon in ActionScript is a lot like the period (or full-stop) in English punctuation.

Once you have assigned a variable, you can then manipulate it. Here are examples of how we can change the values of the variables that we've just created:

```
x = x + 10;

myString = myString + " and now the string is longer";
```

We've reassigned the value of x to be the current value of x plus 10, so x now equals 20. We've also added another string value onto our existing string, so the value of myString will now be: This is a string and now the string is longer.

The + symbol is known in programming circles as an **operator** since it performs an operation on a variable (in this case addition). The operator is said to be *intelligent* in that it knows how to perform addition with both numbers and strings. In contrast, the minus operator (-) only works with numbers. Subtraction using strings isn't allowed (and doesn't make much sense either when you think about it).

The third type of variable available to you in Flash is the **Boolean** variable (pronounced 'boo-lee-an'). A Boolean variable can only have the value true or false. Here's an example showing Boolean variables in action:

```
isRaining = true;
haveUmbrella = false;
useUmbrella = isRaining && haveUmbrella;
```

The first two lines are just variable assignments with Boolean values. They are used here to indicate two facts about my visit to the supermarket today: for example that it was raining and I didn't have an umbrella.

The third line uses an operator, &&. This operator means *and*. It is only used with Boolean values. The result of any expression that uses the && operator is another Boolean value, which in this instance we assign to the variable useUmbrella.

If both isRaining and haveUmbrella are true, then useUmbrella becomes true. If either (or both) of the values are false, the expression as a whole is false.

In the above case, since one of the values is false (I didn't have my umbrella), the value of useUmbrella becomes false. In plain English, I couldn't use my umbrella because I didn't have one with me. Likewise, if I had taken my umbrella but it hadn't been raining, useUmbrella would again be false (well, I'd look pretty stupid with my umbrella up on a sunny day).

Boolean values are most commonly used when testing for specific conditions and performing actions based on those conditions. We'll look at conditional statements a little later on.

Text field variables

Normally, variables work in the background within your scripts. They don't have any direct correspondence to anything on the movie stage. But there is a special case of a variable that appears as a visible part of the movie. This is when the variable is a **text field**.

Text fields in Flash can be one of three different types, which you select from the Text Options panel. **Static text** fields are just unchanging pieces of text which appear in the movie – these have nothing to do with variables.

The other two types, the **dynamic text** field and the **input text** field, both have a **variable** property. Entering a variable name in this box associates the variable with the text field. In effect, the text field becomes a variable.

Here's an example of text fields being used as variables:

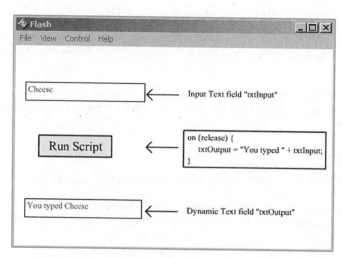

In this movie there are two text fields (labeled). The Run Script button has some ActionScript in its on (release) event handler (the code that runs in response to the user's mouse click). The script takes the string from the txtInput variable (an **Input Text** field) and performs a string operation on it, assigning the result to the **Dynamic Text** field, txtOutput. As you can see, text field variables are treated in scripts just like any other variables. (There's a version on the CD that you can use to experiment with called TextFields)

Dynamic Text fields can help you debug your scripts. By adding a few text fields with variable names corresponding to variables used in your movie, you can watch their values as they change.

Using Flash's built-in methods

Of course, being able to add numbers and join strings is just the tip of the iceberg. There are far more interesting things that we can do with variables, and Flash offers a range of functions that allow us to manipulate variables in many useful ways.

A function is just like a little machine. You put in some raw materials, turn the handle and something useful comes out. This is what a function looks like:

```
myString = "This is a string";
x = length(myString);
```

The function here is called length. This function works out how long a string is. So the variable x ends up with the value 16 (the number of characters in This is a string).

While Flash supports a whole range of functions for all kinds of different purposes, they don't really fit in with the idea of objects that we looked at earlier. By comparison with our earlier analogy, a function is an isolated box with no obvious relationship to anything else.

Fortunately, we can forget about functions for now and use object-oriented syntax instead.

To do this, we simply treat length as a *property* of the string. To find the length of a string in OO, we would write:

```
myString = "This is a string";
x = myString.length;
```

It turns out that every function available in Flash can be used in the form of a *method* of an object, and that's what I'll be doing from this point forward. It's useful however to be aware that most things in ActionScript can be treated in more than one way.

Here's an example of a string method:

```
lowerCaseString = myString.toLowerCase();
```

This method returns the lower-case version of whatever text is stored in the string. There are lots of other methods available for use with string objects.

Unlike strings, numeric variables aren't really treated as objects. To use a mathematical method with a number, we use the Math object, which is a built-in object that comes with Flash. How this works should become clearer with a few examples:

```
myNumber     = 11;
squareRootOfNumber = Math.sqrt(myNumber);
sineOfNumber = Math.sin(myNumber);
```

The sqrt and sin methods are methods of the Math object. Both these methods accept a single input parameter (a number) and return a result (another number).

These are the methods available in the Math object in the ActionScript editor:

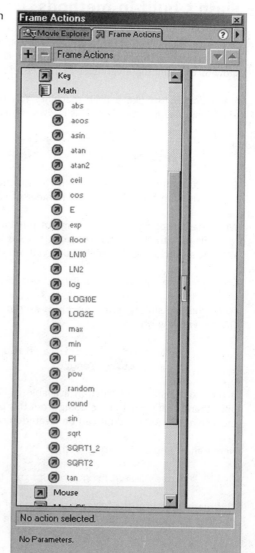

The Math object supplies just about every mathematical function you're likely to need; you can find out more about these in the Flash ActionScript documentation.

The MovieClip object

You've seen how we can use something called the Math object to provide a set of tools for working with numbers, and how strings are also objects with properties such as length. Well, it turns out that these aren't the only objects in Flash. In fact, every single movie clip you create is an instance of the MovieClip object.

When you create a movie clip (by selecting a graphic and converting it to a Movie Clip symbol, or by dragging a clip from the library), you are in fact creating an **instance** of the MovieClip object. Every movie clip has the same set of properties, and you can read these properties into variables or write new values to them.

Suppose you have a movie clip called myClip. That clip comes with a set of properties with values that you can access and change as you need to. These are some of the most frequently used movie clip properties:

myClip._x myClip._y	X and y co-ordinates of the clip
myClip._rotation	Angle of clip rotation of the clip in **radians** (360 degrees = about 6.28 radians)
myClip._alpha	Alpha (or transparency) as a percentage (100 = completely opaque, 0 = completely transparent)
myClip._xscale myClip._yscale	Horizontal and vertical scaling factor of the clip as a percentage (100 = full-size)
myClip._width myClip._height	The width and height of the clip
myClip._currentframe	The current frame of the movie clip (in its internal Timeline)
myClip._visible	Visibility of the clip (a Boolean value: true/false)

So, let's put all this theory into action, fire up Flash and begin working with movie clip properties. You can find the final SWF and FLA that we'll build up here on the CD, called clipProperties.

Flash 5 Dynamic Content Studio

Working with the properties of a movie clip

1. Start by creating a new movie in Flash, with the dimensions 400 by 300. Add a movie clip (anything you like – just use one from the supplied sample libraries if you like). Open the Instance panel and give the clip the name `myClip`. Create a set of six buttons. Make four of them directional arrows (pointing up, down, left and right), label the fifth button `SHOW` and the sixth button `HIDE`. We'll use the buttons to interactively change the properties of `myClip`.

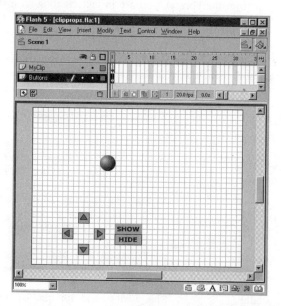

2. Add two Dynamic Text fields. Give these the variable names `xPosition` and `yPosition`. These will be used to display the x and y co-ordinates of the movie clip as they change. Your movie should look something like this:

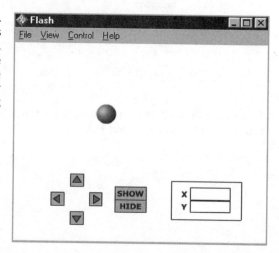

3.   Finally, add some ActionScript to each of the six buttons, using the scripts below:

Left Arrow:
```
on (release) {
    xPosition = myClip._x;
    xPosition = xPosition - 10;
    myClip._x = xPosition;
}
```

Right Arrow:
```
on (release) {
    xPosition = myClip._x;
    xPosition = xPosition + 10;
    myClip._x = xPosition;
}
```

Up Arrow:
```
on (release) {
    yPosition = myClip._y;
    yPosition = yPosition - 10;
    myClip._y = yPosition;
}
```

Down Arrow:
```
on (release) {
    yPosition = myClip._y;
    yPosition = yPosition + 10;
    myClip._y = yPosition;
}
```

Show Button:
```
on (release) {
    myClip._visible = true;
}
```

Hide button:
```
on (release) {
    myClip._visible = false;
}
```

Do these pieces of script look familiar? We've already met event handlers, and now here they are in ActionScript, in the form of mouse event handlers. They allow us to create a set of actions to be carried out in response to a particular mouse event (in this case releasing the left mouse button).

> *Interactive Flash movies are* **event-driven,** *in that they react to the user's interaction with them. There are many other types of event handler in Flash, but mouse events are probably the ones you'll use most often.*

The ActionScript in each of the event handlers on the four movement buttons follows the same basic pattern, which is:

- Get the current x or y value of myClip and assign it to the variable xPosition or yPosition

- Add or subtract 10 depending on the direction of movement we want.

- Set the _x or _y property to the new value of xPosition or yPosition.

The script for the SHOW and HIDE buttons is even simpler, as the value we assign to the _visible property of the clip is always either true or false.

4. Test the movie. Try modifying the values you've set to make different things happen, or adding more buttons that change the rotation or alpha properties of the movie clip.

Nested movie clips: using paths

You'll come across plenty of situations when you'll want to place movie clips inside other movie clips. When you create more complex Flash movies, particularly interactive ones, this is the way to give your movie the structure it needs. A fairly common example is a scrollbar:

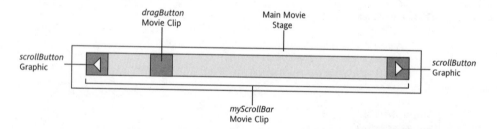

dragButton
Movie Clip

Main Movie
Stage

scrollButton
Graphic

scrollButton
Graphic

myScrollBar
Movie Clip

The entire scrollbar is a movie clip with the instance name myScrollbar, which is placed on the stage of the main movie. Inside the scrollbar movie clip is another movie clip with the instance name dragButton. So, dragButton is the child of myScrollbar, and myScrollbar is the parent of dragButton. Flash's Movie Explorer shows the relationships between movie clips as a tree structure.

There may be more going on here than you expected, but it's really pretty straightforward. The ScrollBar movie clip (with the instance name myScrollBar) contains another movie clip, the ScrollBarDragButton movie clip (with the instance name dragButton) and two copies of the graphic ScrollButton, which make up the two arrows at the ends of the scrollbar. Open up the `Scrollbar` FLA on the CD and see how it works.

> *As you can see from this simple example, movie clips and instance names quickly proliferate when you're developing Flash movies, and so accurate naming is vital to help you (and anyone coming to the movie after you) understand what's what. Try to make a careful distinction between the names of objects in the library (movie clips, graphics and buttons) and the instance names that you give particular instances of these objects within the movie.*

Nesting movie clips has a lot of advantages:

- Easy positioning at design time. In this example, everything contained within the scrollbar can be moved together as a single unit.

- Easy access to the whole object through code. Nesting allows you to manipulate the properties of the whole scrollbar object in your code. For example, you could show or hide the entire scrollbar using some ActionScript in the timeline of the main movie: `myScrollBar._visible = false;`

- The object behaves (to all intents and purposes) as an object in its own right. It can be reused many times within the same movie, or in many different movies, without having to re-design it from scratch each time.

However, there are some even more useful and exciting possibilities that open up when we start to nest movie clips in this way. Every movie clip has its own distinct timeline, independent of everything else. And every timeline has its own set of independent variables.

Variable scope

Suppose that in our scrollbar example the ScrollBar movie clip contained a variable called `value` that changed according to how the user dragged the dragButton movie clip. We could use the `value` variable to store the value of whatever it is that the scrollbar is being used to change in the movie. This `value` would only exist inside instances of the ScrollBar movie clip.

If we then defined another instance of the Scrollbar movie clip on our movie stage, it too would have an internal variable called `value`, but **this** variable would be completely distinct from the variable of the same name in the other movie clip.

Here's an illustration to show what I mean:

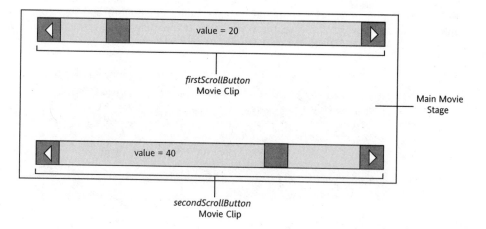

In other words, value is behaving like a property of a scrollbar object. The way in which value exists applies only within each instance of the scrollbar movie clip is what programmers call the variable's **scope**.

Although the variable defined inside a movie clip is only meaningful within that clip, we can find its value from the timeline of the main movie by prefixing the variable name with the name of the movie clip that contains it. The two value variables can be obtained using:

```
value1 = firstScrollBar.value;
```

Or:

```
value2 = secondScrollBar.value;
```

Now suppose we wanted to get the _x property of the dragButton movie clip inside the firstScrollBar movie clip, again from some ActionScript in the main movie timeline. This time we're trying to find out a property of a child movie clip within another movie clip.

Flash follows the OO syntax that we talked about in the car example (well, there's a coincidence). So the x-position property (_x) of dragButton is obtained using something like:

```
dragButtonX = firstScrollBar.dragButton._x;
```

This navigation through the movie clip hierarchy is called a **path**. This term simply describes the sequence of movie clips that we need to traverse to get at a particular property or method. In this case the path is firstScrollBar.dragButton.

More complex paths

When you address a letter to a friend in another country, the address is normally written in a certain order, for example:

> *Street Name,*
> *Town,*
> *Region,*
> *Country.*

OO syntax works in the opposite direction; it starts with the outermost object and works its way down to the innermost child object. So if addresses were written as Flash 5 paths, they'd look like this:

> `Country.Region.Town.Street.`

Note how the order is reversed, and written slightly differently, but that the same information is there. Here's a Flash-specific illustration, showing a nested set of movie clips:

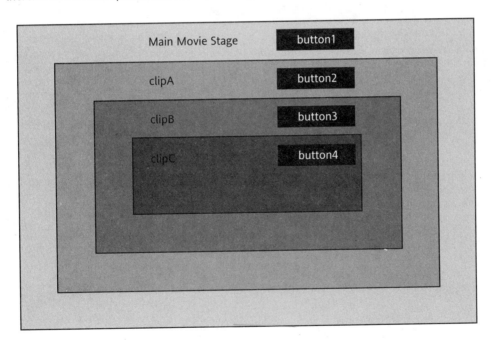

This diagram shows a movie clip, clipA is on the stage of the movie. clipA contains another movie clip with the instance name clipB, which in turn contains a movie clip called clipC.

First, suppose we want to hide clipC when the user clicks on button3 inside clipB. We would add the following code to button3:

```
on (release) {
clipC._visible = false;
}
```

That's fairly straightforward, and we've seen that sort of thing before. The path here is the simplest possible kind of path – a single movie clip name.

Now, if we wanted button2 to be able to hide clipC, we'd use:

```
on (release) {
clipB.clipC._visible = false;
}
```

And to do the same thing from button1, we'd use:

```
on (release) {
clipA.clipB.clipC._visible = false;
}
```

A path is always expressed relative to the current movie clip. What if we wanted to hide clipC using button4, the button inside clipC? Flash uses this to represent the current movie clip, so the ActionScript for button4 would simply be:

```
on (release) {
this._visible = false;
}
```

Suppose that we wanted to move through the hierarchy in the other direction, using a button to hide a movie clip further up the hierarchy, say using button3 to hide clipA? There's another path we can use for this, _parent, which works the same way as the parent object in my car example where a wheel is a parent of a tire. So the ActionScript to hide clipA from button3 would be:

```
on (release) {
_parent._visible = false;
}
```

And to hide clipA from button4, you'd use this:

```
on (release) {
_parent._parent._visible = false;
}
```

_parent can be used to move as far up the hierarchy of movie clips as you like.

Of course, your movie clips aren't always nested one inside another. Sometimes a movie clip has several children. These sibling movie clips can also be made interact by using paths. Time for another diagram:

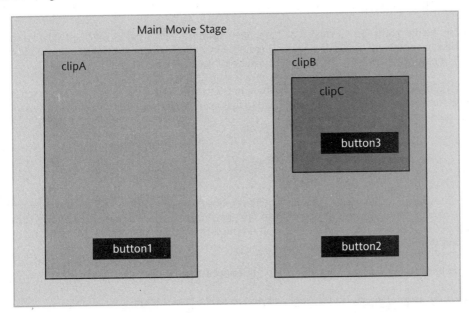

In this example there are three movie clips. clipA and clipB are both children of the main movie, whilst clipC is the child of clipB.

To hide clipA from button2 you use _parent to move one step up the hierarchy to the main movie, then follow that with the path to clipA. So the script for button2 would be:

```
on (release) {
_parent.clipA._visible = false;
}
```

To hide clipC from button1, you use _parent again to move one step up the hierarchy to the main movie, and then follow that with the path two steps down the hierarchy to clipC. Here's the script for button1:

```
on (release) {
_parent.clipB.clipC._visible = false;
}
```

On the other hand, to hide clipA from button3, we have to go two steps up the hierarchy and then one step down:

```
on (release) {
_parent._parent.clipA._visible = false;
}
```

It's possible to access the properties, methods and variables of any clip in a movie from any other; it's just a question of working out the correct path.

Absolute paths: _root

So far, all the paths we've looked at have been **relative** paths; paths specified relative to the movie clip containing the ActionScript. There are times when you might want to use an **absolute** path, a path always relative to the main timeline of your movie.

An absolute path can be used from anywhere in the movie, and it will always be expressed in the same form. To use an absolute path to hide clipA from any of our buttons (in either example), we could use the same script:

```
on (release) {
_root.clipA._visible = false;
}
```

_root is the path that means '*the main movie timeline*'. It is used to specify the absolute path to a movie clip, the path relative to the main timeline. We can refer to any of our movie clips this way: _root.clipA, _root.clipA.clipB (in the first example) or _root.clipB.clipC (in the second example).

Going back to our car example, this is a bit like specifying the car as:

```
universe.milkyWay.solarSystem.earth.UK.myCar
```

Even if (by some crazy coincidence) there is another car on another planet (or in another country) called myCar, the absolute path I've provided ensures that there can be no confusion about which particular myCar I'm talking about. Assuming that there's only one car in the UK called myCar, of course.

When a path is absolute, it doesn't matter where we use it. Unlike _parent, any path beginning with _root always points to the same movie clip.

Paths are key to Flash, that it's very important you're happy with how they work. If my explanations haven't hammered the idea home yet, try it out with some nested movie clips of your own.

Let's move on now, and look at some more advanced ActionScript.

Key ActionScript features

Earlier in this chapter we looked at using variables in Flash to store and manipulate the properties of movie clips, and some of the built-in methods available to you. ActionScript provides a lot more functionality though. Like any other programming language it has features that allow you to:

- Perform different actions depending on the value of one or more variables or properties: **conditional** actions.

- Perform repeated actions: **loops**.

- Create reusable pieces of script to perform specific tasks or calculations: **functions**.

We'll look at each of these in turn now, and then we'll move on to some of the ActionScript features that allow you to access and manipulate movie clips.

Conditional actions

A conditional action is an event or sequence of events that only occurs when some kind of condition exists. In everyday life, conditional actions are things like:

- If you are hungry, then eat some food.

- If it is a weekday, go to work, otherwise, stay at home.

- I want to buy the new *Guided By Voices* CD box set. If I have enough money, buy it; otherwise, go to the bank. If I have enough money in the bank, then draw some out and buy it. Otherwise, don't buy it.

Conditional statements allow decision-making in your movies. A decision statement in Flash follows this format:

```
if (condition) {
    action;
}
```

Where *condition* is an expression requiring that a condition or set of conditions be tested for, and *action* is one or more lines of ActionScript in between the { } braces. These actions will only be carried out if condition is true.

Here's an example of a real conditional statement:

```
if (xPosition < 0) {
    xPosition = 0;
}
```

This code checks to see if the value of xPosition is less than 0, and when it is, resets it to 0. You could use this to prevent a movie clip from being moved off the left side of the stage on a left-arrow button event. We could have used this in the earlier example where we controlled the position of a movie clip with buttons.

Likewise, given that the main movie in that example has a width of 400, we could stop the movie clip from going off the right-hand side when the user clicks the right-arrow button by using:

```
if (xPosition > 400) {
    xPosition = 400;
}
```

If statements can be nested just as movie clips can be. We could make our clip-moving code much more intelligent by using nested conditional statements. Here's some code for the left-arrow button again:

```
on (release) {
    if (myClip._visible == true) {
            xPosition = myClip._x;
            xPosition = xPosition - 10;
    if (xPosition > 0) {
                    myClip._x = xPosition;
            }
        }
    }
```

This might look a little complicated at first, but it's not too difficult to understand if I put it into plain English (in programming we call this an 'algorithm'):

```
When the user has pressed the button {
    If the movie clip is visible {
            Get the x-position of the clip;
            Subtract 10 from the position;
            If the new position is not off the left side of the stage {
                    Move the clip to the new position;
                }
        }
    }
```

(Note that in the code I have checked for the condition (myClip._visible == true). The '==' symbol means '*is equal to*' (or just '*is*'). This is different from the '=' operator which is used elsewhere to assign a value to a variable.)

With a few simple alterations, you could make this code work in all directions. Let's add some similar conditional actions to the movie we created earlier.

Restraining the movie clip to the stage

1. We'll improve the code we used in the moving object example we created earlier, so open it up and make sure the movie's dimensions are 400x300. Then simply add in the code:

Left Arrow:

```
on (release) {
     if (myClip._visible == true) {
          xPosition = myClip._x;
          xPosition = XPosition - 10;
If (xPosition > 0) {
                    myClip._x = xPosition;
          }
}
}
```

Right Arrow:

```
on (release) {
     if (myClip._visible == true) {
          xPosition = myClip._x;
          xPosition = XPosition + 10;
If (xPosition < 400) {
                    myClip._x = xPosition;
          }
}
}
```

Up Arrow:

```
on (release) {
     if (myClip._visible == true) {
          yPosition = myClip._y;
          yPosition = yPosition - 10;
If (yPosition > 0) {
                    myClip._y = yPosition;
          }
}
}
```

Down Arrow:

```
on (release) {
     if (myClip._visible == true) {
          yPosition = myClip._y;
          yPosition = yPosition + 10;
If (yPosition < 300) {
                    myClip._y = yPosition;
          }
}
}
```

2. If you test the movie now, you'll find that the clip myClip is completely constrained.
    The ActionScript calculates the new position of the clip in each button event, and only
    moves the clip if the new position is within the area of the movie's stage. Easy!

Let's make a slightly more mobile example along the same lines. We'll create a little movie clip, myClip, that moves around all by itself. Here's a picture showing the movie clip myClip on the stage. As you can see, there's really nothing to the movie, just a ball. You can find the example that we're about to build on the CD, called MoreClipProperties.file.

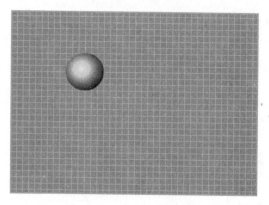

All the important stuff lies in the ActionScript. Let's build the movie and see how it works.

Creating a movie clip with its own momentum

1. Start by creating a movie clip (it doesn't have to be a green ball). Give the clip the instance name myClip in the Instance panel.

2. Next, add a second layer to the timeline, and add two keyframes to the new layer, so that you have three in total. Your timeline should look something like this:

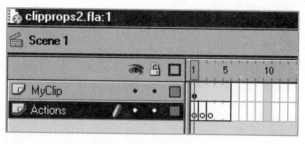

It's a good idea to name your layers intuitively, and keep frame actions separate in their own layer.

3. All the code we need will go into the three keyframes:

    ■   **Keyframe 1 (initialization):** Set two variables for the clip's velocity in the x and y directions. We'll call them xVelocity and yVelocity

- **Keyframe 2 (process):** Get the current x and y co-ordinates of the movie clip, and assign these to variables: $x = myClip._x$, for example

  - Add the x and y velocities to the x and y co-ordinates to get the new position, which we'll call new_x and new_y

  - Check whether the x-position is beyond the left or right sides of the stage, using the or operator '||':
    `if ((new_x < 0) || (new_x > 400))`
    and if so change the value of the x velocity so that the ball reverses its movement along the x-axis: `xVelocity = - xVelocity`

  - Check whether the y-position is beyond the top or bottom sides of the stage:
    `if ((new_y < 0) || (new_y > 300))`
    and if it is change the value of the y velocity so that the ball reverses its movement along the y-axis: `yVelocity = - yVelocity`

  - Set the new position of the clip: `myClip._x = x + xVelocity;` for x

- **Keyframe 3 (loop)**
  Return to the previous frame (using the `prevFrame()` method followed by `play()`) so that the ball moves again.

So to complete the movie, put the following code into the three keyframes in the Actions layer:

Keyframe 1:
```
xVelocity = 5;
yVelocity = 5;
```

Keyframe 2:
```
x = myClip._x;
y = myClip._y;

new_x = x + xVelocity;
new_y = y + yVelocity;

if ((new_x < 0) || (new_x > 400)) {
    xVelocity = -xVelocity;
}

if ((new_y < 0) || (new_y > 300)) {
    yVelocity = -yVelocity;
}
```
and my Clip-y=y+yVelocity for y

```
myClip._x = x + xVelocity;
myClip._y = y + yVelocity;
```

Keyframe 3:
```
prevFrame ();
play();
```

4.   Test the movie. You should find that the movie clip now moves around the stage, bouncing off the four sides.

This movie could, with a little more work, be turned into a 'pong' game, with players controlling paddles on either side of the stage. In this case, you'd want the conditional statement for the x axis to check whether the clip coincided with the position of the paddle, rather than have it bounce off the left and right sides.

Loops

A loop is just a repeated action. There are three kinds of loops in Flash, the while loop, the do...while loop, and the for loop.

While loops

A while loop is a block of code that repeats until a specified condition is met. Here's an example:

```
myNumber = 2;
while (myNumber < 1000) {
    myNumber = myNumber * 10;
}
```

This loop will repeat the actions it contains, multiplying the value of myNumber by 10, for as long as the value of myNumber is less than 1000. So, each time it loops, its value will increase:

Loop1   myNumber = 20
Loop2   myNumber = 200
Loop3   myNumber = 2000

At the start of the fourth loop, the value of myNumber is 2000, which is more than 1000, so the loop won't repeat again and the final value of myNumber will be left at 2000.

You can do exactly the same thing with strings:

```
myString = "";
while (length(myString) < 10) {
    myString = myString + "x";
}
```

This loop will repeatedly add the letter x to myString as long as the length of the string is less than 10 characters. So, when the loop stops, myString will be xxxxxxxxxx.

Do...while loops

A variation of the while loop is the do...while loop, the difference being that the condition is checked at the end of the loop. For this reason, a do...while loop will always be executed at least once.

Here's a do...while loop:

```
myNumber = 5;
do {
    myNumber = myNumber + 5;
} while (myNumber < 3);
```

The value of myNumber will be incremented by 5 before the condition is checked. When the condition is checked, the value of myNumber is, of course, greater than 3, and so the loop does not repeat a second time, leaving myNumber with a value of 10.

do...while and while loops are great for string-replacement. Many languages support a replace string function that will search a string for occurrences of a particular substring and then replace those occurrences with another string. This is what happens when you do a '**find and replace**' in a word processor. I'll show you how to make a little find and replace gadget now. The SWF and FLA are on the CD, and called FindReplace.

A Flash find and replace gadget

1. Start a new movie. Add four text fields, making the first three Input Text fields and calling them txtFind, txtReplace and txtInput, and making txtInput Multiline. Make the fourth text field a Multiline, Dynamic Text field and call it txtOutput. Add a button, and label it Replace.

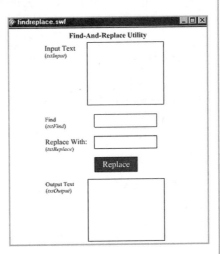

2. That's the interface created. Now we need to add some code to the Replace button, but before we do, a word of warning – there is some stuff in here that will probably

look unfamiliar to you. Don't worry if you don't understand the finer nuances of the script, it's not essential to the subject of the chapter, but it's a nice little example and that's why I've included it. And even if you don't manage to follow it, the great thing about OO is that you can just take it away and use it time and time again, so either way, you win. Here's the code:

```
on (release) {
    processedText = txtInput;
    subStringPos = 0;
    do {
        substringPos = processedText.indexOf(txtFind, subStringPos);
        if (substringPos > -1) {

    processedText = processedText.slice(0, substringPos) +
    txtReplace + processedText.slice(substringPos +
    txtFind.length);

            substringPos = substringPos + txtReplace.length - 1;
        }
    } while (subStringPos > -1);

    txtOutput = processedText;

}
```

3. Publish and experiment.

If you're interested, read the following breakdown of the code. If you're not, just hop on down to the next subsection, 'For Loops'.

So, if you're still here, off we go. Let's first talk about the two new methods we've used here, the `String.indexOf` method and the `String.slice` method.

`String.indexOf` **method**
The syntax for this method looks like this:

```
someString.indexOf(substring, start_position)
```

It takes two parameters:

■ `Substring`, the value of the substring that you're looking for inside `someString`.

■ `start_position`, the number value indicating the position within `someString` that you want to start searching from.

Once you've passed in these two values, the `String.indexOf` method has all it needs to know in order to search the string for a particular value (or substring), starting at the specified position within the string. It returns the character position of the first occurrence of the substring where there is one, and where there isn't one, `indexOf` returns a value of –1.

`String.slice` **method**
The syntax looks like this:

```
someString.slice(start_position, end_position);
```

This method simply takes a slice out of a string from between the two specified positions. The second parameter (end_position) of the slice method is optional, and without this parameter, slice takes the remainder of the string from start_position to the end of the string.

Now you know that, the rest is pretty simple (really!)

■ First we make a copy of the input text when the user presses the Replace button, and assign it to the variable processedText. This is our working copy – we don't want to affect the original text:

```
on (release) {
            processedText = txtInput;
```

■ We also initialize the variable subStringPos to 0. This variable will be used to indicate the position (if any) of the string txtFind in our piece of text:

```
subStringPos = 0;
```

■ Then we use a do...while loop, using the indexOf method and passing in the parameters it needs, and setting the condition that will stop the loop when the value of subStringPos is −1, (because indexOf returns a value of −1 when it can't find a match, and we know that it won't be able to find a match once all the replacements have been made):

```
do {
            substringPos = processedText.indexOf(txtFind, subStringPos);
            if (substringPos > -1) {
```

So, the loop searches for the substring txtFind inside the main string processedText starting from position we initialized earlier, subStringPos.

The loop finishes when indexOf returns −1 (Note that with string functions in Flash, character positions start at 0 for the first character.)

When indexOf returns a number greater than −1, we know there's some text to be replaced, so we continue.

■ When the string is found, we do some string-manipulation with the slice method.

```
processedText = processedText.slice(0, substringPos) +
txtReplace + processedText.slice(substringPos +
     txtFind.length);
```

Or:

1. Take the text from the first character up to the point where we found `txtFind`:

   ```
   ProcessedText = processedText.slice(0, substringPos)
   ```

2. Add to it the new text `txtReplace`:

   ```
   + txtReplace
   ```

3. And add to this the remainder of the string (from `substringPos` + `txtFind.length` to the end):

   ```
   + processedText.slice(substringPos + txtFind.length);
   ```

   The slice method simply returns the rest of the string if we don't pass in the end position parameter, so we leave this off the second time around, as the rest of the string is just what we want.

- The last action inside the loop adds the length of `txtReplace` to the value of `subStringPos`. This means that the next `indexOf` search starts *after* the replacement string:

   ```
   substringPos = substringPos + txtReplace.length - 1;
   ```

The benefit of doing this is that if `txtReplace` is the same as `txtFind`, the loop won't get stuck forever replacing a piece of text with itself. Infinite loops are to be avoided!

Although this string-manipulation script is a little complicated, the beauty of OO programming is that code can be packaged up in various ways for easy re-use. So, once you've written this piece of search-and-replace code, you'll never have to write it again. We'll look at code re-use towards the end of the chapter.

For loops

A `for` loop differs from a `while` or `do...while` loop in that it is controlled by a variable (most commonly used as a counter). Here's an example of a `for` loop:

```
myString = ""
for (n=1; n<=10; n++) {
    myString = myString + n + ",";
}
```

A `for` loop with a counter begins with some code to set up the loop, in this case (n=1; n<=10; n++). This means:

- Let the initial value of the loop variable n be equal to 1 (n=1)

- Loop while n is less than or equal to 10 (n<=10)

- Each time the loop goes round, increment (add to) the value of n.

Note that I have used the syntax n++ to add one to the value of n. This is just a shorthand way of writing n=n+1. Likewise, we can write n– instead of n=n-1. You can use whichever style you prefer.

So, in this example, the loop adds the value of n (plus a comma) to myString each time it loops. The resulting value of myString is therefore:

```
1,2,3,4,5,6,7,8,9,10,
```

Loops can do the same thing in reverse, so:

```
myString = ""
for (n=10; n>0; n–) {
    myString = myString + n + ",";
}
```

Will give you:

```
10,9,8,7,6,5,4,3,2,1,
```

We could have exactly achieved the same result using a while loop, although it would be much less tidy and required two extra lines of code:

```
myString = ""
n = 10;
while (n>0) {
    myString = myString + n + ",";
    n = n - 1;
}
```

In general, whenever you know how many loops you need, use a for loop, and when you can't tell in advance how many loops there'll be (as in my string-replacement example), you'll probably need a do...while or while loop.

Within for...in loops

There is another variation of the for loop, the for...in loop. Instead of having a counter variable, this is a special loop that will go through the list of all children of a particular object. An example of this in pseudo-code would be:

```
        for (each child object in myCar) {
if it is a wheel {
    check the tire pressure;
            }
        }
```

You might use a for...in loop to loop through all the children of a particular movie clip. A child in this context can be a movie clip, a variable, a function or an object. It's useful if you want to perform actions with a set of movie clips in a particular location.

Nesting loops

Loops too can be nested. Here's an example of a nested `for` loop which generates a range of x and y co-ordinates:

```
myString = "";
    for (y=1; y<=5; y++) {
    for (x=1; x<=5; x++) {
        myString = myString + "(" + x + "," + y + "), " ;
    }
    }
```

These nested loops generate every pair of integer co-ordinates from (1,1) to (5,5). It adds each co-ordinate pair to the string variable `myString`. The value of `myString` after the nested loop will look like this:

```
(1,1), (2,1), (3,1), (4,1), (5,1), (1,2), (2,2), (3,2), (4,2),
(5,2), (1,3), (2,3), (3,3), (4,3), (5,3), (1,4), (2,4), (3,4),
(4,4), (5,4), (1,5), (2,5), (3,5), (4,5), (5,5),
```

I'm only listing the values here, but you could use the x and y variables to duplicate a movie clip and create a 5x5 grid of movie clips.

Array objects

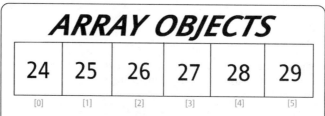

Above, an array object is illustrated. Each block represents one element of the array, and each value inside each box is the value of that element. In this case, this is a 6-element array storing the values 24, 25, 26, 27, 28, and 29. Underneath each value is shown the index of each element. The first index is 0, the last 5.

One of the most powerful and basic features of modern, high-level programming languages is the array. An array is basically a data structure that holds multiple values that are referenced by an index number (remember the car wheels?). Flash 4 developers came up with all sorts of neat tricks to "emulate" arrays, but with Flash 5 came the new `Array` object, that both allows you to create arrays, and offers some additional functionality that makes it easier to work with them. This is how you declare an array in Flash:

```
myArray = new Array();
```

Although Flash allows you to specify the size of the array, you don't have to, because Flash automatically resizes the array based on the number of elements you attempt to access. You can also specify the values of the initial array, like this:

```
myArray = new Array("I", " love", " flash.");
```

This will automatically give `myArray` a length of 3 with the values specified.

So where would you use one? Arrays work very well with counter-controlled loops. For example, if you needed to fill an array with all of the integral values from 1 to 100, you would only need two lines of code:

```
for (i = 0; i < 100; i++)
    myArray[i] = i+1;
```

As you might remember from the discussion of the car wheel array, the first element of an array is at index 0, so this code would fill `myArray[0]` with the value of 1, `myArray[1]` with the value of 2, etc. The last element, `myArray[99]` would have a value of 100 and the loop would be complete. You can use an array to store many values in an easily accessible data structure that can be looped through easily, and therefore modified across-the-board far more easily than if you had stored the values in hundreds of separate variables.

You can also declare an array with a specified length, such as 52 (number of cards in a deck), and initialize the array by setting all values equal to zero.

```
myDeck = new Array(52);
//array initialization
for (i = 0; i < myDeck.length; i++)
    myDeck[i] = 0;
```

Notice the use of the `length` property? This allows you to find out the length of any array object you create — which is useful if you want to run a `for` loop through the whole array. The Array object also has lots of other methods, like `pop`, `push`, `slice`, and `sort`, that allow you to control your arrays without having to manually code functions to deal with the more common elements of array-handling.

ActionScript doesn't support multi-dimensional arrays, which are arrays of arrays.

```
myArray = new Array(); //myArray is one-dimensional
myArray[0] = new Array(); //myArray becomes two-dimensional
myArray[0][0] = new Array(); //myArray becomes three-dimensional
```

You don't usually need anything more than a two-dimensional array, which is most often used to represent rows and columns. For example, you could output the value in the first column, second row of a spreadsheet like this:

```
trace(spreadsheet[0][1]);
```

Arrays are an invaluable programming tool, making coding very much quicker. This next script loops through an array of movie clips, resizing any movie clips in the _root level of the movie (clips in the main timeline). To use it, just put it inside a button on your stage. (You can find an FLA and SWF for this example, called Shrink, on the CD.) Here's the script:

```
for (thisClip in _root) {
    if (typeof (_root[thisClip]) == "movieclip") {
        _root[thisclip]._xscale = 50;
        _root[thisclip]._yscale = 50;
    }
}
```

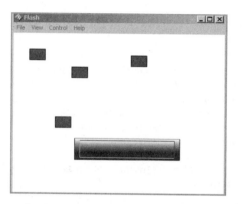 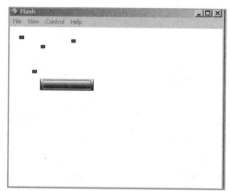

`_root[thisclip]` represents the array, identifying a single element of the array of objects contained in the `_root` movie. Each time the `for` loop loops, `thisClip` is assigned to a reference to the next child object of `_root`. Inside the loop, we use the built-in type of operator to check whether the child object is a movie clip. (We need to make this check because the list of child objects can include strings, movie clips, functions and other objects.) If the particular child object is a movie clip, we set the `_xscale` and `_yscale` properties to 50% (halving the size of the movie clip). The loop repeats for every child of the `_root` movie (including all the child movie clips).

eval – a useful function

The `eval` function is one of the most useful built-in functions in Flash, and as such it warrants its own distinct place in this chapter. So what is it?

The `eval` function takes a string as its input, and *evaluates* that string, meaning that it looks in the movie for anything (a path to a movie clip or a variable, for example) with that name, and returns a reference to that thing.

So suppose you have five movie clips with the instance names clip1, clip2... and so on. You might want to loop through this group of clips and perform the same action on each. The `eval` function can help there. I'll show you an example, and then I'll explain how it works

Using eval to lighten the coding load

1.   Create a new movie 400 by 300, and make a new movie clip (or pull one from the movie clips library that comes with Flash).

2. Create five instances of this movie clip on the stage of your movie. Give them the instance names `clip1`, `clip2`, `clip3`, `clip4` and `clip5`.

3. Add a button to the stage, and hopefully, you'll have something roughly like this:

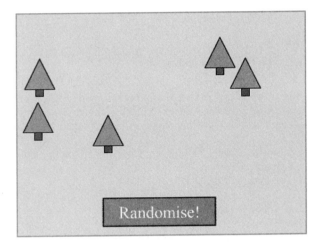

4. Now add the following ActionScript to the button:

```
for (n=1; n<=5; n++) {
    thisClip = eval("clip" + n);
    thisClip._x = Math.random() * 400;
    thisClip._y = Math.random() * 300;
}
```

What we have here is a loop with a counter variable n that ranges from 1 to 5. Inside the loop, we assign `thisClip` to equal `eval("clip" + n)`.

When `n = 1`, `thisClip` becomes a reference to the movie clip `clip1`, so setting the property `thisClip._x` in effect sets the `_x` property of `clip1`. So the loop sets the position of each of the file movie clips to a random position on the 400x300 movie stage.

To set the properties of each clip individually would have required ten lines of code. But by using `eval`, we could randomly place a thousand movie clips as easily as we just did with five.

As I said, useful! Publish your movie and see how it works. (The FLA and SWF for this movie are called `Random` on the CD.)

You could use `eval` to return the value of a variable. For instance:

```
myNumber = 10;
x = eval("MyNumber");
```

In this example, `x` will become equal to `10`. Using `eval` with variables in Flash 5 is rarely necessary, however.

Building your own functions

You have already seen in this chapter that Flash contains many methods used to perform specific tasks. An example is the `length` method of the string object, or the `eval` method that we just looked at. Flash allows you to extend this range of handy tools by creating your own functions.

As we saw earlier on in the chapter, a function is very much like a method. If, for example, you created your own function called `myFunction`, and placed its code inside a movie clip called `myClip`, you could use it by writing:

```
returnedValue = myClip.myFunction();
```

This is exactly the same syntax as the examples we used with the string methods and the methods of the `Math` object. The function behaves exactly like a method of that movie clip because it is contained within the `myClip` movie clip.

So how do we create one of these marvellous functions?

The structure of a user-defined function in Flash is:

```
function function_name (parameter1, parameter2...) {
    actions;
}
```

A function starts with the word `function` (sensibly enough) followed by the name you choose to give the function. Then come the parameters that the function needs (the input), enclosed in parenthesis and separated with commas. You can have as many parameters as you like, or even none at all, in which case the function name is followed by a pair of empty parenthesis. Finally, you put the function's actions within the curly braces. So if you want the function to return a value (like some of the string object's methods), you need to use the `return` action, for example:

```
return (value);
```

Where `value` is the variable or quantity you wish to return from the function.
As is my habit, I'll illustrate the use of user-defined functions with a couple of examples. The first example works out whether a given year is a leap year – it'll make a bit more sense if I tell you what the rules for determining a leap year are:

- If the year is divisible by 400, it is a leap year.

- If the year is divisible by 4, but not divisible by 100, it is a leap year.

So here's the function:

```
function isLeapYear(year) {
    if (year % 400 == 0) {
        return (true);
    }
    else {
        if (year % 4 == 0) {
            if (year % 100 == 0) {
                return (false);
            } else {
                return (true);
            }
        }
        else {
            return (false);
        }
    }

}
```

I've used the modular operator (%) here; this divides one number by another, and returns the remainder. If there is no remainder, then the first value is divisible by the second. So, for example, 5%2 is 1 (five divided by two has a remainder of one).

To use this function, all we need to do is place it in a keyframe in the timeline (usually it makes sense to put the function in the first keyframe of the timeline). Any ActionScript belonging to a function will be ignored (i.e. it won't execute) until we actually use the function. When we want to call the function, it works just like a built-in function.

So, if you define this function in a keyframe on the main timeline, you use it like this:

```
leapYear = _root.isLeapYear(myYear);
```

You could build a little leap year calculator using only the code we've looked at so far, along with two text fields and a button:

In this movie I've just put the function definition in the first keyframe of the main Timeline, then added two text fields (one input field called myYear and one dynamic field called leapYear), and then added the code that calls the function to a button. Hey presto, a leap year calculator. This function would be very useful (in fact, essential) if you ever decide to develop a calendar in Flash. And, of course, you can find it on the CD in working form, called LeapYear.file.

Here's another function, scaleClip. This function will scale any movie clip by a given percentage of its current size:

```
function scaleClip (thisClip, scalePercent) {

    currentXScale = thisClip._xScale;
    currentYScale = thisClip._yScale;

    thisClip._xScale = (currentXScale/100) * scalePercent;
    thisClip._yscale = (currentYScale/100) * scalePercent;

}
```

The first parameter is a reference to a movie clip, thisClip, and the second parameter indicates the percentage by which the movie clip should be scaled, scalePercent.

So for example, if the movie clip is already scaled to 200% in both directions, and we pass 200 as the value for scalePercent, the resulting _xScale and _yScale values for the movie would be (200/100) * 200, or 400 percent.

If you put the scaleClip function into a movie's main timeline (so into the first keyframe's actions), and added a movie clip, giving it the instance name myClip, then you could call the function from a button by simply adding the following code:

```
on(release) {
_root.scaleClip (myClip, 120);
}
```

Each time the button is clicked, the movie clip myClip will be scaled to 120% of its current size. Simple!

So, as you've seen in this section, you can use functions to manipulate movie clips just as easily as you can variables. Note that this function doesn't return a value, and so when you use it there's no need to assign it to a variable.

Re-using your code

Functions are an excellent way to produce well-structured and efficient movies. In general, any action that you need to perform in more than one place in your movie should probably go into a function.

The aim of any programmer is to do as little work as possible. A good programmer will build up a library of useful functions, re-using them in each subsequent project. You can group your functions by placing them inside individual movie clips. By doing this, you are effectively creating new objects for use in Flash. A set of functions placed inside an otherwise empty movie clip will behave just like the built-in Math object, with the functions behaving as methods of your new object.

For example, you might create a movie clip called DateLibrary, and put in it all your date-related functions (such as the leap year calculator). Then, whenever you create a movie that needs to deal with dates, you can just add the `DateLibrary` clip to your movie using the Open As Library menu option. Functions inside movie clips have paths just like nested clips or variables. So you would call my `isLeapYear` function using:

```
x = myDateLibrary.isLeapYear(2000);
```

Where `myDateLibrary` is an instance of the movie clip `DateLibrary`.

Include statements

Creating libraries isn't the only way to store groups of useful functions. You can also store your functions in external text files with the extension `.as` (short for ActionScript). These files can be created using any plain text editor (such as Notepad), so you could create a file called `datelibrary.as` and save it in a directory with your Flash movie (`.swf`) files. Then you can just use the `#include` action in your ActionScript to access your functions:

```
#include "datelibrary.as"
```

This works in much the same way as the command of the same name in HTML. It simply means '*get the contents of the file `datelibrary.as` and insert it here*'. Flash automatically reads from the file when you export, test, or publish a movie, and includes it in the exported form.

For example, you might create an ActionScript file called `sayHello.as` that contains the function `sayHello`:

```
function sayHello() {
        trace("Hello!");
}
```

Then, you would put these two lines of code in the Flash movie:

```
#include "sayHello.as"
sayHello();
```

And, as you'd expect, you'd get "Hello!" outputted, because the function was included into the frame. When the movie was being exported, Flash opened up `sayHello.as` and pasted its content into that frame, replacing the `#include` statement. Then, when the movie actually exported, the frame really *did* contain the function:

```
function sayHello() {
        trace("Hello!");
}
sayHello();
```

It's always a good idea to include everything you need in the first frame of your Flash movie, so that your functions are available throughout the rest of the frames in the movie. When you're working on a large project where the same scripts are used in many different Flash movies, making good use of external `.as` files is a particularly good idea, because if you ever find a mistake in one of your functions, you'll only need to fix it in the external .as file, and not in fifteen different Flash movies.

Reusability is a key feature of the object-oriented philosophy. The best programmers aren't necessarily the ones who work the hardest; it's more likely they've just got a more extensive library of reusable code. It really is that important.

Now that we've spent some time looking at the ins and outs of using ActionScript, we'll take a look at some of the interesting things we can do with movie clips.

Working with movie clips

ActionScript gives you a whole host of methods and actions with which you can manipulate your movie clips – you can duplicate them, create new ones, remove them again, load them, drag and drop them, and more. We're going to look at some of the most useful ways you can work with movie clips in this next section, and although there simply isn't enough room to go through step by step exercises with every one of them, I really recommend that you experiment with the code you'll find here, maybe building on the examples we've built so far within this chapter, or developing your own from scratch.

Duplicating movie clips

Flash allows you to create duplicates of movie clips using ActionScript. This can be particularly useful in applications like games where you might want to generate randomly positioned sprites, or if you are creating a list-box movie clip where the number of items in the list might vary.

If you were to duplicate our old friend the movie clip myClip, to create another copy of this clip from a button while the movie runs, for example, you'd simply use:

```
myClip.duplicateMovieClip("myClip2", 1);
```

The duplicateMovieClip method has three parameters. The first parameter is a reference to the movie clip you wish to duplicate (myclip.), the second parameter provides an instance name for the new clip (myClip2), and the third parameter specifies the **depth**.

The depth parameter tells Flash how to stack the movie clips. The original clip (the one you created at design-time) always has a depth of 0. So by specifying a depth of 1, I specified that myClip2 should be above (in front of) myClip.

If you create more than one copy of a clip, you would normally create each one at a different depth. If you give a new clip the same depth as one you created previously, the new clip will replace the existing one at the same depth.

> *Depths of duplicated movie clips are completely separate from layers or levels in the Timeline, and you should take care not to confuse these concepts. I'll talk more about levels a little further on.*

Creating a new movie clip from the library

Duplicating an existing clip isn't the only way to create new movie clips. It is also possible to create instances of movie clips directly from the library. To do this you use the attachMovie method.

The process here is somewhat different to duplicateMovieClip. Since Flash only exports movie clips from the library if they are used in the movie, you will need to tell Flash to always export this clip. To do this you need to create a **linkage**.

To create a linkage for a movie clip, first open the Library. Then right-click on the clip in the Library and choose the Linkage... menu item. Select the Export this symbol option. You will be prompted for an Identifier. This is the name you will use when you create new instances of the clip.

Suppose you have a movie clip in your library called libraryClip. To prepare the clip, first give it a linkage identifier such as libraryClipID. To create an instance of the clip in the main timeline of your movie, you then use the following code:

```
_root.attachMovie("libraryClipID", "newClip", 1);
```

This method works a lot like duplicateMovieClip, except that there is an additional parameter that specifies the linkage identifier of the clip as it exists in the library. Just as with the duplicateMovieClip method, you also need parameters to specify the name for the new clip and its depth.

I've created an example FLA for you to look at on the CD that utilizes the attachMovie method, together with the scaleClip function we created earlier on in the chapter. It's called AttachScaleClip.file.

Although I have used _root here to make the new movie clip instance a child of the main timeline of the movie, you can use the name of any movie clip. The new instance will be created inside (as a child of) the movie clip you specify. So if you already have a movie clip named containerClip, you can create the new instance inside that clip by using the action:

```
containerClip.attachMovie("libraryClipID", "newClip", 1);
```

Removing duplicated or attached movie clips

Movie clips can be removed completely from your movie using the removeMovieClip method. This action simply removes a named clip from the stage.

The syntax is:

```
MovieClip.target.removeMovieClip();
```

Where target is the name of the clip that you previously created using duplicateMovieClip or attachMovie.

Loading movies from external files

Just as in HTML, you can use Flash to create a hyperlink or redirection script to take the user to another page; in this way you can tell Flash to load a different movie file (.swf file). Different Flash movies can be loaded in to the page as often as you like without loading a new web page.

The action is simply loadMovie.

Loading movies into levels

To understand how this form of loadMovie works, you first need to understand the concept of levels.

Levels

I should emphasize again that levels are not the same as the depths of duplicated movie clips. While depths allow you to create duplicates of movie clips and to determine the order in which they are stacked, levels allow you to stack whole movie files on top of each other in the player. Flash allows you to play several .swf files at once, one on top of another. It does this by placing each movie in a different level. When you create a web page containing a Flash movie, the movie will always start by loading the .swf file specified in the HTML code of the page, and will load this movie into level 0. Level 0 is the bottom level in Flash.

The loadMovie action can then be used within your movie to load additional movies into higher levels. These movies will be stacked on top of the original movie. Any transparent areas in the upper movies will allow parts of lower movies to show through, something like this:

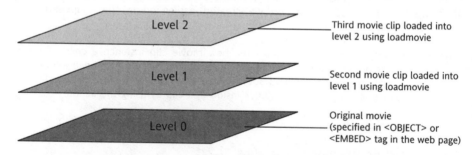

Each movie clip that you load into a level is completely independent of any clip at any other level. The only constraint is that all loaded clips will inherit the movie properties (frame rate, background color and stage size) from the movie playing in level 0. Clips loaded in this way are always aligned with the top-left of the movie area.

Note that if you use duplicateMovieClip or attachMovie to create new movie clip instances in levels 0 or 1 in the diagram above, the duplicates will always remain in that level, and will never overlap anything in the level(s) above, no matter how high you try to stack them.

If you try to load a new clip into a level occupied by another movie clip, the new clip will replace the old one. If you load a new clip into level 0, all loaded movie clips will be removed from all the levels and you will be left with the single (new) clip at level 0.

To use `loadMovie` to load a movie file into a level, you use the action:

```
_level.loadMovie("myfile.swf");
```

Where level is the number of the level into which you want to load the movie. There is no need to use sequential numbers for the levels; indeed, many developers prefer to use multiples of 10. That way there are plenty of empty levels should you find the need later on to load a movie between movies at, say, levels 10 and 20.

If you need to control the timeline of one level from the timeline of another, or handle variables across levels, you just use the `_levelN.` prefix (where N is the number of the level). This provides a path to a movie in a particular level. So to stop the movie in level 3 from actions in a button in any other level, you would use:

```
_level3.stop();
```

And to assign a variable `numberOfChickens` to equal the variable `chickenCount` in level 0, you would use:

```
numberOfChickens = _level0.chickenCount;
```

Loading movies into movie clips

There is another way to use `loadMovie` that does not involve levels at all. The action can be used to load the contents of an `.swf` file into a existing movie clip on the stage.

When you use `loadMovie` in this way, you specify the name of a movie clip in your movie instead of a level. The movie file will load into the specified clip, replacing the existing contents of the clip. For this reason, you'd normally use a completely empty movie clip for this purpose.

Loading movies into movie clips has a lot of advantages over loading them into levels.

- The position and scale of the loaded movie will be inherited from the movie clip into which you load it.
- You can load movies into clips that are hidden, thus allowing you to show a preloader and then display the new movie only after it has loaded.

- You can load the movie into a clip that is part of a hierarchy of nested movie clips, integrating it into the overall organization of your movie.

Here's how you'd use `loadMovie` to replace the contents of the movie clip `myClip` with new content loaded from the file `myfile.swf`:

```
myClip.loadMovie("myfile.swf");
```

Removing movie clips loaded with loadMovie

A movie can be unloaded from a clip or level in two different ways. The first (and most obvious) is to use the `unloadMovie` action. To remove a loaded movie from level 3, for example, you just need the action:

```
_level3.unloadMovie();
```

And to remove a loaded movie from the movie clip `myClip`, you use:

```
myClip.unloadMovie();
```

Note: that after the contents of `myClip` are unloaded, `myClip` continues to exist, albeit empty of content. The other method, which works just as well, is to use an empty `loadMovie` action, such as

```
myClip.loadMovie("");
```

Drag and drop

Drag-and-drop is an intuitive name used to describe what happens when you pick up an item by clicking on a mouse button, drag it to where you want it, and put it down again by releasing the button. In Flash, you can let the user control this process or you can make it happen automatically without the user clicking on anything.

Only a single movie clip can be dragged at any one time. To start a drag, you use:

```
myClip.startDrag();
```

Where `myClip` is the movie clip you want to drag. This is the simplest form of drag. The clip will start to follow the cursor, but will not be centered on the cursor. More often, you would want the clip to remain under the mouse while being dragged. To do this, you use the additional lock parameter thus:

```
myClip.startDrag(true);
```

You can also confine the drag to a particular area on of the stage, by adding four more parameters, left, top, right and bottom:

```
myClip.StartDrag(true, 100, 100, 200, 200);
```

This would confine the clip's drag movement to the region extending from (100,100) to (200,200) on the stage.

If you give the top and bottom parameters the same value, the clip will only be able to be dragged along the horizontal line defined by the left and right parameters. Conversely, if you give the left and right parameters the same value, the clip will only move vertically. This is how you'd go about creating a slider control in Flash.

To drop a clip, use the `stopDrag` method:

```
myClip.stopDrag();
```

Note that there is no need to specify a movie clip; which makes sense, since only one clip can be dragged at any one time.

If you want the movie clip to be dragged without having to start the drag from a separate button, simply put a button inside the movie clip (you would normally use a hidden button, which is a button containing only one graphic placed in the hit frame). For the button action use:

```
this.startDrag(true);
```

In the `on(press)` button event. This will cause the parent clip (the one containing the button) to be dragged.

In the `on(release)` button event, use the `stopDrag` method. The movie clip should now be fully draggable, just like a desktop icon in Windows. Have a look at the example on the CD called `DragDrop.file`.

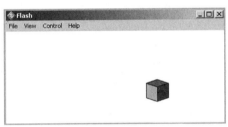

Customizing your cursor

Everyone seems to want to be able to make a custom cursor, and they're really very easy to create in Flash. All you need to is create a movie clip for the cursor, start a drag with this clip, and then hide the default cursor. Flash allows you to hide the default cursor (the `Mouse` object) with the method:

```
Mouse.hide();
```

So a quick way to create a custom cursor would be to create a movie clip called `myCustomCursor` on the main stage, and then add the following actions to the first keyframe of your main Timeline:

```
MyCustomCursor.startDrag(true);
Mouse.hide();
```

If at any time you want to return to the normal cursor, just use the reverse of the above script:

```
MyCustomCursor.stopDrag();
Mouse.show();
```

It's as easy as that.

Clip events

Version 5 introduced a new concept to Flash, the **Clip Event**. A clip event works much like a button event of a button, but applies to a movie clip (and there are many more events for a movie clip than there are for a button.) A clip event is a piece of code that is executed automatically when a certain event occurs involving a movie clip. These events are:

load
: Occurs when a movie clip is loaded (when it first appears in the movie), or when it is created using duplicateMovieClip or attachMovie.

unload
: Occurs when a movie clip is unloaded using unloadMovie or when it is removed from the Timeline.

enterFrame
: Occurs as each frame is played.

mouseMove
: Occurs each time the mouse is moved over the clip.

mouseDown
: Occurs when the left mouse button is pressed over the clip.

mouseUp
: Occurs when the left mouse button is released over the clip.

keyDown
: Occurs when a key is pressed.

keyUp
: Occurs when a key is released.

data
: Occurs when data (loaded with a loadVariables or loadMovie action) arrives in the clip.

Clip events are event handlers (remember those from the car example at the start of the chapter?). To add clip events to a movie clip, we need to create an onClipEvent code block for the clip. Here's how to do it:

Choose a movie clip to which you want to attach a clip event. Right-click on the clip and choose Actions. Then add an onClipEvent handler like the one below:

```
onClipEvent(mouseDown) {
     this._visible=false;
}
```

The code contained in this event handler will be called when the left mouse button is clicked on the movie clip, and the code hides the clip. This has the effect of making the movie clip behave like a button, (but without the hand cursor that you would get if it were a button.)

The load clip event can be used to carry out actions immediately when the clip appears in the movie. You could use this to initialize some variables in the clip.

Going back to my earlier scrollbar example, you could have:

```
onClipEvent(load) {
       min=0;
       max=100;
       value=0;
}
```

This would set some useful default values (or properties) inside the scrollbar movie clip (the maximum, minimum and current values). You could also call a function you have written to perform other initialisation tasks here.

Summary

And that's the end of the tour. I hope that by the time you've got to this point in the chapter you've got a good grasp of the OO approach to programming, the key concepts like class, properties, events, object events, and object hierarchy, and how they apply to the key aspects of Flash; but most importantly, that this understanding will help you in your Flash design and development.

I've tried to emphasise the importance of an object-oriented approach to ActionScript, as well as to Flash more generally. This is not a personal quirk. Flash 5 is object-oriented throughout, and learning to think in an OO way will open a lot of creative doors, as well as helping you solve many of the day-to-day technical challenges involved in 'building stuff' with Flash.

Applying an object-oriented approach to your own Flash programming development will do great things for the flexibility of your Flash projects; the speed at which you can create them, add to them, modify them and maintain them. It'll also make it much simpler for other people to follow your working when they come to a project you've moved on from. Hopefully this short introduction will have given you most of the intellectual tools you need to appreciate, and more importantly use, the techniques demonstrated in the chapters that follow. There's an appendix on the principles of object-oriented programming at the back of the book, which I'd also recommend you have a look at.

But, of course, in the end the secret of learning anything well is to put it into practice as soon and as often as possible. Be adventurous. Set yourself targets and work to achieve them. No pile of textbooks is going to make you an expert; you learn best by doing things. Flash is one of the best construction toys there's ever been, so go ahead and play with it.

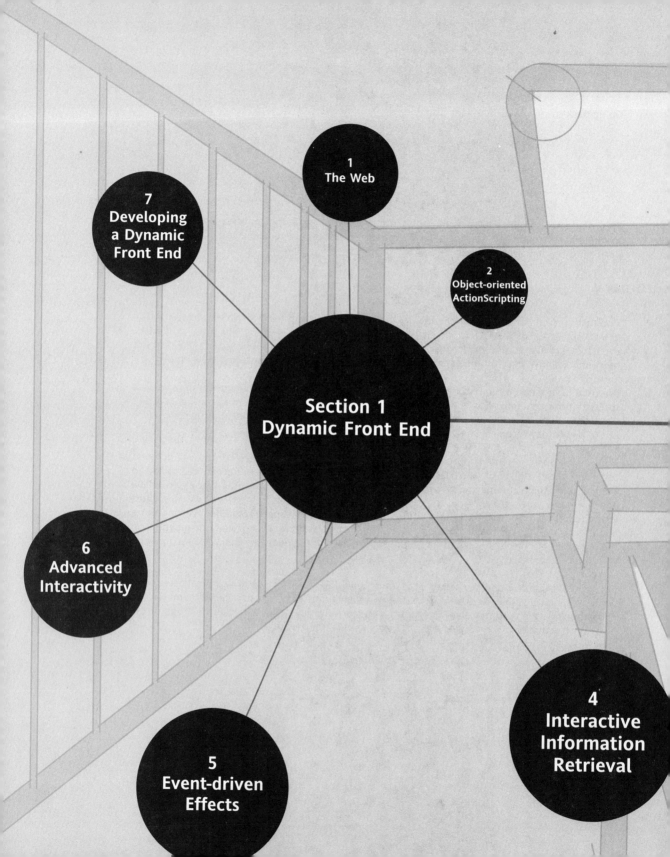

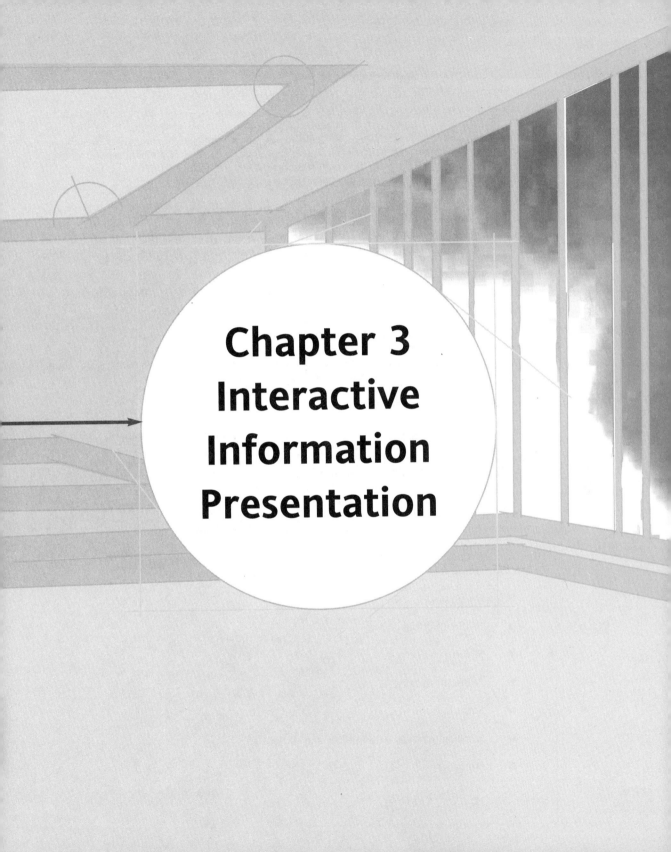

Chapter 3
Interactive
Information
Presentation

In this chapter we'll be covering how to script interface elements – ways of presenting data to users. While one of the goals of this chapter is to teach you how to produce these interface elements, the larger goal is to have you begin to see how the individual commands available in Flash can work together in practical examples. I hope that by the end of the chapter you will see how many effects are built off small modification to the same code, and that large tasks, when broken up into smaller and simpler problems, are much easier to solve.

Along the way, in the next few chapters, we'll be covering some of the dos and don'ts of interface design, especially as it relates to Flash. I've heard a new adjective arise to describe Flash projects whose design or interface style tries to use too many predictable, over-used Flash effects. This adjective is 'flashy', a *double entendre* meaning both the traditional meaning and the Flash-specific meaning above.

This chapter will start off with the fundamental web interactive elements. Anything in this chapter is pretty 'safe'.

That said, an austere design need not dictate an austere functionality. Behind the scenes, you can have powerful scripts that enhance and simplify the user experience. Always keep in mind that this is your main goal, the user experience. No matter how cool your site is to you, if you intend the site to appeal to a certain audience, and it does not, the design has not achieved its goal. This chapter should give you a modest arsenal of interface elements that, at the very least, a web-literate user should be comfortable with.

At the beginning of the chapter I'll cover the components of each ActionScript task bit by bit, but as the chapter goes on, I'll start to pick up the pace a little, making assumptions that you know how to perform tasks covered earlier in the chapter. Since many of these examples build on one another, if something seems confusing, I encourage you to go back and take a look at earlier sections.

As you've been introduced to Expert mode in the previous chapter, we'll continue using it. While you can technically do all of the same things in Normal mode, often you have to do more work, and meanwhile you aren't learning the syntax that is going to save you a lot of time and energy.

Through examples, we'll cover many of the essential interface elements for a Flash movie and a Flash form. More specifically, in this chapter, we'll talk about and build:

- Dialog boxes

- Invisible buttons

- Sliders

- Persistent buttons

- Scroll buttons

- Scrolling mini-app with buttons and slider

- Preloaders

Dialog box

When you want to give feedback to your user, a simple way to do this is to use a dialog box. Dialog boxes are good for displaying confirmations, errors, and short messages. Unlike in HTML, you are not limited to text in your box. You can add graphics, animations, and interactivity. This example will walk through creating a text-based box, but in reality, this is just a concept for creating content that you may want to call up and put away at any point. One client I worked for wanted an environmental site where you could click on buildings and objects to navigate the site, but was worried that its non-traditional style would leave some users stranded. To overcome this, the site starts with a text link console in an over-glorified dialog box.

There are three essential parts to consider when using a dialog box. First there must be a trigger event to tell the box to appear. Then, of course, there must be the box itself, but it must contain the third element, a trigger to make it go away again.

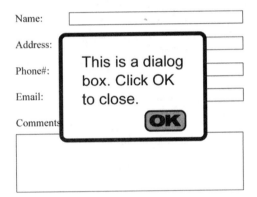

Trigger events can take many forms: from the click of a button, to time-based triggers, or through error-handling scripts. Also, don't be limited by what a dialog box looks like traditionally on the web, a big square with text can be functional, but so can a fun-shaped movie clip playing an animated movie. Let's start by making the simplest dialog box possible, one that just displays a static message when you click a button.

Making a simple dialog box

The source for this example is `DialogBox.fla` on the CD.

1. Start by creating a new document, and draw a large rectangle on the *center* of the stage. Go ahead and write some text on the rectangle using the Text Tool.

This is how your dialog box will look when it pops up.

> This is a dialog box. Click OK to close.

2. Select the rectangle and text, and make it into a new movie clip symbol (F8). Name the symbol dialog box and click OK. Give it an instance name box.

The reason for choosing to make it a movie clip is that we will want to control the symbol to make it go to different frames independently from the main timeline.

> *The only symbol type that can be referenced by scripting, like that we'll be using soon in the button, is the movie clip. The reason it can be scripted is that a movie clip is a type of object, just like an array, sound, color, etc.*

Since the box should appear when we click a button, we need to make sure that it can't be seen until the button has been clicked. This is easy enough to manage.

3. Double-click the dialog box movie clip to access its timeline. Then select frame 1 in the timeline and drag it to frame 2. Now there is nothing in frame 1, and the dialog box won't appear until the second frame of the movie clip; it is, to all intents and purposes, invisible.

If you tried to test the movie right now, you'd get a flashing box, because movie clips, by default, loop through their timelines. A simple stop action will override this.

4. So, go back to frame 1 of the movie clip, and add a stop action to it.

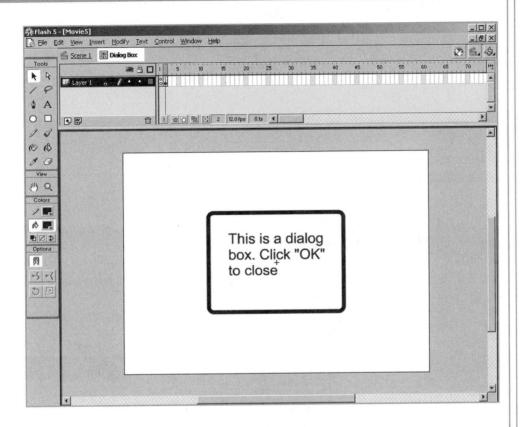

5. Now the box is all set, but it needs a name so that the scripts have something to reference it by. Go back out to the main timeline and pull up the instance panel. Select the movie clip, which should look like a white dot with a black border in the middle of the stage, indicating that there is a movie clip there, but that its first frame is empty.

6. We'll use a button that users can press to bring up the box, so place a button on the stage (either create one, or use one from Flash's included libraries) then add the following actions to the button to bring the dialog box into view:

```
on (release) {
box.gotoAndStop(2)
}
```

7. The final element of the dialog box is the closing trigger. The most common way of dismissing a box is to click a button inside the box, in this case something like an OK message. To do this, double-click on the white dot on the stage of the main movie, to edit the movie clip, and go to frame 2 that holds the box itself.

Add a button to your rectangle, and add the following ActionScript to it:

```
on (release) {
    gotoAndStop(1)
}
```

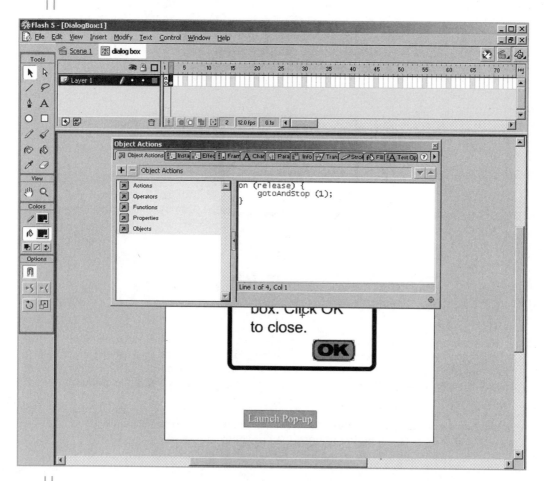

All that's left now is to test it. After you click the first button, if it's on top of your dialog box, you simply need to re-order your movie so that the box movie clip is always on top. There are a number of ways you could do this:

- Add some layers and copy elements to higher and lower layers,

- Using the Bring to Front, Bring Forward, Send Backward, or Send to Back commands within one layer. (Modify > Arrange)

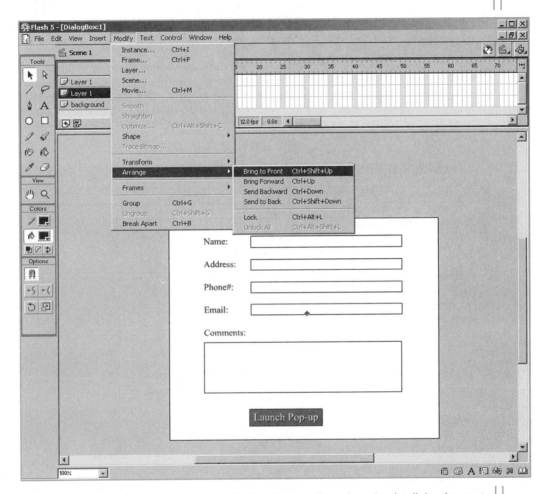

- Using the swapDepths method, which we'll explore in detail in the next chapter. If you are planning on having duplicated movie clips on the main timeline, then you will have to duplicate the dialog box to a depth higher than any other object (just don't forget to change the button to refer to the name of the duplicated movie clip).

After you've mastered simple dialog boxes, try modifying the code to have different effects. Here are a few suggestions that you can explore:

- You might call up several different messages, add each to another frame of the box movie clip and have the triggering buttons go to the appropriate frame. You can also make the text of the box dynamic, setting a variable in the triggering button to recreate the box as needed.

- I usually use dialog boxes to tell the user when Flash is waiting for a response from a database. I then use onClipEvent(data) to trigger the close when the variables have finished loading. Make sure not to use this when you are waiting on two calls since receiving data is not specific to a single call for variables or a movie.

- Add animations that make the boxes appear and disappear in interesting ways. If you decide to go this route, either place the animated sequence in a movie clip on frame 2 of the box movie clip, or animate the sequence directly in the box movie clip and have the triggering button go to frame 2 and play. Below, showing the latter method, is an onion-skin view of animation of a dialog box zooming in.

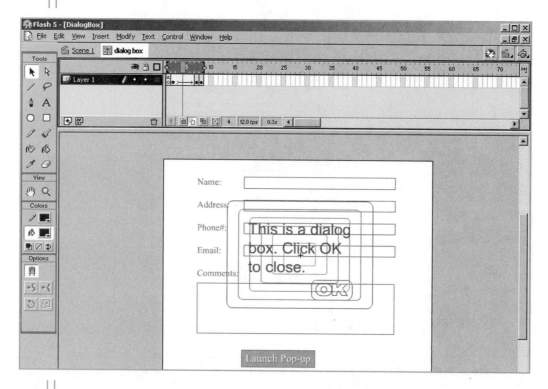

- If you have other buttons on your stage, then you may want a way to make sure that those buttons are non-functional while the box is visible. The simplest way I've found is to add a large invisible button on a layer below the message in the box movie clip – we'll look at invisible buttons next.

There are many uses for dialog boxes; they are an excellent way to give users information, largely because web users are familiar with them. In the rest of the chapter, we will look at several examples that mimic HTML interface elements, and then move to more interesting examples that are Flash specific. In the next section, we'll deal with having a dialog box over other interactive elements.

nvisible buttons

A button is the basic interactive interface element of Flash, but there are times when you'll want your buttons to be inactive under a certain set of conditions. For instance, in the dialog box example, when the box is open, if there is a button underneath the box that button will continue to function even though you may not be able to see it, allowing the user to inadvertently trigger an event you hadn't intended. There is no code for temporarily disabling a button, but there is an easy way to block the button. To demonstrate this, I've changed the transparency of the dialog box to 50% and placed the launch button behind it. Unless you use an invisible button, you could still use the button, to perform its action.

In Flash, when two buttons overlap, the one on the bottom is automatically blocked. All visible buttons have up, over, down and hit states, and what determines whether or not two buttons overlap, is whether or not the hit states overlap. What we mean by an "invisible" button is one with only a hit state, and no visible effect when a user rolls over, presses or releases it. The user's cursor will still turn into a hand, because you are dealing with a button (although in Flash 5 you can even get around this by changing the appearance of the cursor. You were introduced to the code for this in the previous chapter, and we'll examine this in more detail in the next).

To make an invisible button, first create the button shape on the stage, and name it (F8). You now have a regular, if boring, button. Double-click on your button, and drag the frame containing it from the up frame to the hit frame.

When you go back out to the main stage, you will notice that where your button was, there is now a translucent cyan shape. Macromedia was kind enough to leave us a visual clue as to where the hit state is on any button that does not have an up state. It's very similar to the white dot that tells you where a movie clip is when it does not have a first frame. The cyan will disappear when you render the movie, or enable buttons inside Flash.

If you plan on creating any interface that has draggable windows, or any other scheme that will visually block buttons on your stage, you will want to use this effect. It is meant to never be noticed by your users, but could potentially save them from a lot of confusion that could be caused by covered-over buttons.

Slider

Sliders are among the most useful interface elements for representing a continuous range of settings. Any assignable property in Flash is a good candidate for using a slider e.g. transparency.

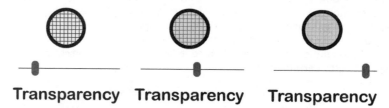

Common uses are for allowing the user to customize an object over a wide range of settings, or as we'll see in the next sections, as a part of the scroller mini-application. The slider we'll be making here is extremely customizable. Instead of hard coding the operations deep down in the slider symbol, we'll be using two of the new Flash 5 features, customizable functions, and onClipEvent to attach the code that may need to change from application to application, to the instance of the slider. This allows us to use the same slider symbol for many purposes with only minimal changes to the instance.

Sliders are composed of four parts:

- The line

- The handle

- Scripting dummy movie clips

- The target

We'll create this in two stages, first dealing with the slider and then constructing a target for it to modify. So, let's begin.

Creating a simple slider

We'll start by making a simple slider that reports a ratio of how far along the line the slider is to its total range, and make a function that turns the ratio into useful information such as an _alpha assignment for a movie clip on the stage. Once we've covered the basics, we'll look at some enhancements you can make to your sliders that will make them function in more customizable ways. Let's start by making the line:

Line movieclip, under the groove (on the bottom layer)

The rounded groove covers over the line movieclip but doesn't affect the scripting of the slider

The line

The line is the track that the handle will follow. While you can certainly use your artistry to make a groove, don't add this drawing here, this line is going to be used for scripting purposes, and should be a simple line made by using the line tool. So:

1. Rename Layer 1 of your movie as slider and draw a straight horizontal line on the stage. You can make the length whatever you want, but don't worry about being very precise right now; it will be easily adjustable later (if you resize the line movie clip on the stage, the slider will automatically use the new length). Select the line, make it a new movie clip symbol (I called mine Line MC), and give it the instance name line.

2. Back on the stage, double-click the line to go inside the movie clip. To make the math easier later, move the line so that its left end is at the registration point in the middle of the stage (the crosshair near the middle). The most accurate way of doing this is to open the Info panel, click on the top left square in the alignment grid, then type 0 in both the X and Y fields and hit enter. The line should now appear to be sticking out to the right of the crosshair.

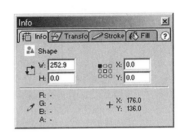

Go back to the main stage, and you have the track ready. Next we'll look at how to make a handle and have it move along the track.

The handle

The handle of the slider has to have the properties of a button as well as those of a movie clip. It needs the button part so that we can tell Flash to start and stop dragging the handle; however, the only thing that can be dragged is a movie clip. The way to solve this problem is to make a button and wrap it in a movie clip. So:

1. On the stage, draw any shape you want as the handle and make it into a new button symbol named handle button. Assign the button states as you like, then return to the main stage. When you've finished, select the button by clicking it once and then make it into a new movie clip symbol called handle with an instance name also of handle.

2. You now have the main structure of the handle setup. Drag the handle onto the line so that it snaps onto the left endpoint of the line. This will assure proper alignment when we test the movie. Now we need to go into the movie clip and assign the script

to the button for dragging, so double click on the `handle` movie clip to go inside it and select the handle button.

3. Bring up the Object Actions panel to add mouse events to the button. To make the slider work as expected, it needs to become draggable once you press on the button, and remain draggable until you let go.

We'll need to add an `on` event. (All the event handlers that deal with button events are inside one of these `on` commands; they can be triggered by either mouse states or key presses.) For the slider, we will only be dealing with the `press`, `release` and `releaseOutside` events of the mouse button.

4. Start with an `on` (press) action. Now add the `startDrag` method inside the `on` statement. The syntax for the `startDrag` action is as follows:

```
startDrag ( target, lockcenter, l, t, r, b );
```

For this example, the target is the current movie clip, so we use the this object.

```
startDrag ( this, lockcenter, l, t, r, b );
```

Since we will want the handle to lock to the mouse, replace lockcenter with `true`.

```
startDrag ( this, true, l, t, r, b );
```

We also want to constrain the dragging to a rectangle, so we will need to add numeric values for each boundary (we actually want to constrain the movement to a line, but we can do that by putting the same value for the top and bottom limits).

The left limit (l) will be the left edge of the line. Since we placed the left edge of the line at the registration mark, all we need to do is find the X position of the line. It's always a good idea to write your code with relative paths whenever possible so that you can change structure easily. So, type `_parent.line._x` to get the x position of the line. (Remember that `_parent` looks up one object level outside the current timeline.)

```
startDrag (this, true, _parent.line._x, t, r, b );
```

The procedure for getting the right limit (r) is very similar. Since the line is the only thing in the movie, accessing the `_width` property of the movie clip will give us the length of the line. Adding this to the x position of the movie clip gives us the right endpoint of the line, and subsequently the right boundary for dragging, so add this code:

```
startDrag (this, true, _parent.line._x, t,
➥ _parent.line._width+_parent.line._x, b);
```

Since we already placed `handle` on the line, we just need to make sure that `handle` can't be moved up or down during the drag. To do that, the top (t) and bottom (b) boundaries are just `_y`, the current y value of the `handle` movie clip.

```
startDrag (this, true, _parent.line._x, _y,
➡ _parent.line._width+_parent.line._x, _y);
```

5. We need to add `on (release, releaseOutside)` to end the dragging. Anytime you drag a button and it's constrained to a rectangle or has the possibility of moving behind a button on a higher level or depth, be sure to add release outside. Otherwise, when you let go outside of the button, the handle will keep dragging until you press the button and release it again.

6. Inside the `on(release, releaseOutside)` statement we need to add a `stopDrag` action. There are no configuration options to `stopDrag`, so we're done with the button script for now.

```
on (release, releaseOutside) {
    stopDrag ();
}
```

Putting all that code together, your Object Actions panel should look like this:

Test the movie to see the slider move!

> *The use of sliders is widespread on the web, because ActionScript can control anything with properties that can be modified, using a slider. You might want to control the _currentFrame of a movie clip, or a variable that is then used by another script. For example, let's say you have looping script that sets the rotation of a movie clip to its current value plus an amount specified by a variable. You can use the slider to set the variable giving the appearance that the slider is controlling the speed the movie clip is turning. In later sections we'll be recycling this technique for a volume and balance controller, scroll bars and a color picker.*

The target

Before we write the script to modify the properties of a target, we need to create it. The target can be any scriptable object – there's a list of some of the many things that can be good targets following this exercise. For now, we'll just create a simple target to illustrate the concept.

1. Add another layer to your main scene and name it transparency target.

2. Draw a shape on the main stage and make it into a new movie clip symbol called alpha target, giving it the instance name target. (The name you use is completely up to you of course, although it will need to be uniform across the movie in order to work with the rest of the script).

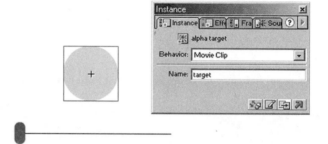

The scripting dummy movie clip

All that's left is to write the script that takes the position of the slider and uses the information in a meaningful way. In Flash 4, it was common to use a looping movie clip to constantly refresh information. In Flash 5 that's not necessary. We'll simply make a movie clip and use one of the new Flash 5 features, onClipEvent to update the data. The reason for making a dummy movie clip to hold the action is so that we can make a later adjustment easily. Otherwise, you could just add these commands directly into the handle movie clip.

1. Go back into the handle movie clip timeline, add a new layer, draw a shape on the new layer and then make it a movie clip symbol called dummy MC. Don't worry what the shape looks like because we'll be deleting it in just a moment. The reason for drawing a shape you are going to delete is that to create a symbol directly on the stage is to select something and convert it to a symbol. If you want a movie clip with absolutely nothing in it, there is nothing to select and convert to a symbol. So you make a shape, convert it to a symbol then go inside it and delete the shape. You could of course make a blank symbol and drag it to the stage, but I find the other way faster.

2. Feel free to delete the shape inside the dummy movie clip then go back out to the handle timeline to continue the scripting (you should now see the dot which represents a blank movie clip).

3. Select the new movie clip and bring up the Object Actions panel. This is where you add onClipEvent actions. An important thing to keep in mind is that as far as targeting is concerned, this code is inside the movie clip. Go ahead and add an onClipEvent action to the dummy movie clip. There are several possible event triggers that you can use, depending on when you want the script to be executed, but

for this example we'll simply choose mouseMove; as the data for a slider only needs to change when you move the slider, mouseMove is both the most computationally efficient and accurate display of the data. Here is where we'll build the script that figures out what point of the line handle is at.

In order to find the percentage of change, we need to find the position of the handle relative to the position of the line, divide it by the length of the line and multiply it by 100. While it would be possible to use one long line of code to do all of the math in one step, it's actually much better coding to break it up into more human-readable chunks. So:

4. Begin by setting the following variables. They represent the length of the line which is also the range that the handle can move in and the current location of the handle. We can use these two pieces of information to determine a ratio of how far the slider has moved in relation to its range.

```
lineLength = _parent._parent.line._width;

handleLoc = _parent._x;
```

You might notice that there are now two _parents in the line's address. This is because the code is part of the dummy movie clip, and therefore a further level removed from the line movie clip.

While the math in those two variables is very simple, it will make the next step a lot easier to follow. With the two variables above, getting the ratio is a very easy matter.

5. Set another variable, ratio with the value handleLoc divided by lineLength. We'll use this in a custom function that will set the appropriate property of the target. To do this, type _parent._parent.doSlide (ratio) into the expression box. This function will be setup using an onClipEvent so that we can change what the slider does without having to create a whole new slider symbol.

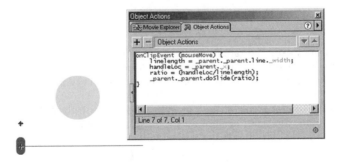

6. Go back to the main stage and select both the line and the handle. Make these into a new movie clip symbol called slider. Select this new movie clip on the main stage, open the Object Actions panel and add an onClipEvent (load) command to it. Inside the clip event, add a function command, calling it doSlide, and giving it a parameter ratio. The parameter is a way of referencing whatever is brought into the function. For instance if you moved the slide exactly half way across the line, it would call _parent._parent.doslide(.5). Inside the function, that value is assigned to a variable called ratio. The code should look like this for now:

```
onClipEvent (load) {
    function doSlide (ratio) {
        }
    }
```

7. Finally, put the code that modifies the properties of the target inside the function, so let the property _alpha with the target, _root.target and give it the value ratio * 100. That's all the code we need – in its entirety, it looks like this:

```
onClipEvent (load) {
    function doSlide (ratio) {
        _root.target._alpha = ratio * 100;
    }
}
```

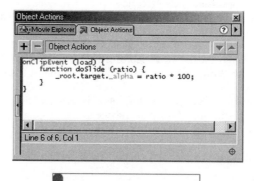

Test the movie to see the target movie clip fade to nothingness as you move the slider to the right. There are plenty of modifications you can make to the slider so that it works in different situations. Rotating it is the most obvious one, and doesn't require any additional work.

If you want the slider to be vertical, or even diagonal, just place it as you'd like to see it. Since when you rotate the slider symbol on the stage, you aren't adjusting anything inside of it, the scripting still works since inside the slider, the handle is still moving horizontally.

Making the computation more efficient

While the scripting is not that intensive on one slider, if you have several on a screen and some animation going on in the background, demand on the processor can add up quickly. We can cut this down by making sure the computation only happens when the user is dragging and moving the mouse, like this:

1. Add a new frame to the handle movie clip. Drag the dummy movie clip along its layer to frame 2, leaving a blank keyframe in frame 1.

2. Add a stop action to frame 1 and then pull up the button actions again. In the on(press), below the startdrag action, add a gotoAndStop(2) Also add a gotoAndStop(1) under the stopDrag action in the other on statement. This code effectively makes the dummy movie clip appear and disappear when you press and release.

```
on (press) {
    startDrag (this, true, _parent.line._x,_y,
➡  _parent.line._width+_parent.line._x, _y);
    gotoAndStop(2)
}
on (release, releaseOutside) {
    stopDrag ();
    gotoAndStop(1);
}
```

Changing the range of the slider

0-100 is not always the optimal range in some applications, and the scale property can do unpredictable things when the scale is set to 0. It's simple enough to change this scale though; to set the scale range from 50% to 100%, you'd simply set up the assignment script in doSlide like this:

```
_root.target._xscale = (ratio * 50) +50
_root.target._yscale = (ratio * 50) +50
```

The multiplier and offset can be changed to fit your individual application.

You could also use the slider with a movie clip of a shape tween animation, for example, using the slider to advance the frames as if it were a movie player. To do this you'd use a value for the multiplier that checked the total frames in the movie clip, rather than a static number. Just make sure you use `int` to make the number an integer; Flash can't go to half frame numbers, like `2.5` for example.

```
_root.target.gotoAndStop(int(ratio * _root.target._totalFrames))
```

Persistent buttons

Buttons are a good way of making something happen once, but there are times when you need the button to keep doing what it's doing until it is released. Buttons by themselves can't do this, but paired up with a looping movie clip they can. In the next example we'll make a movie clip shuttle forward or backward depending on the button the user hits.

Creating a persistent button

The components of the persistent button we'll build here are:

- The target animation (although we'll make a simple one here, you could use one of your own if you'd prefer. Make sure you give it the instance name `SquareCircle`, so that it works with the script later on)

- Creating the `forwards` button

- Duplicating it to create the `backwards` button

- The scripting movie clip

Let's start with the target animation.

The target animation
1.   On layer 1, draw a square on the stage, make it into a movie clip called `squareToCircleAnim` and give it the instance name `squareCircle`. Go into the `squareCircle` movie clip and add 50 or so frames. Add a blank keyframe (F7) to the last frame, and in this frame draw a circle.

2.   Call up the Frame panel in frame 1 and select a shape tween, then add a `stop` action to frame 1 as well.

Now you have a square that morphs into a circle, although if you test it you'll find that it just displays the square because of the stop action in frame 1. We need to add some controls next to allow us to make the animation work.

Creating the button

1. Back on the main stage, add a new layer and create any sort of regular button you like. Place it underneath your square to the right and write Forwards below it on the stage:

Often when I'm creating a button that tells a scripting movie clip what to do, I like to script the button before I make the movie clip. The reason for this is that when I'm building the script I like to test a lot and the only way to call those scripts is with the button. As you'll see in just a moment, the script for the button itself is pretty formulaic anyway.

2. Now we'll add some actions to the button, so add an `on(press)` event. In the `on(press)` statement, we need to add a line telling the scripting movie that we are going to create next, to go to the frame labeled forwards and stop. Type in `script.gotoAndStop("forwards")`.

3. To create the release event script, simply copy the press script we just entered and paste it back into the same window. Then all you need to do is modify the `on` event to `release` and `release outside`, and change the `gotoAndStop` to go to frame 1.

```
Object Actions
 Object Actions                                                              ?
 + -  Object Actions                                                         ▼ ▲
on (press) {
    script.gotoAndStop("forwards");
}
on (release, releaseOutside) {
    script.gotoAndStop(1);
}

Line 7 of 7, Col 1
```

Duplicating the Button

1. Add a third layer to the main scene, copy the button from layer 2, paste it onto the new layer underneath your square to the left, and write Backwards below it.

2. Select this new button and open the Actions panel. Since we copied the previous instance, it contains the code that we just entered. All you need to do is change the reference to the frame label called forwards to one called backwards. This won't affect the forwards button we created to begin with, because scripting attached to buttons is instance-based.

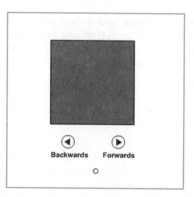

Creating the scripting movie clip

1. This movie clip will hold both the forwards and backwards script. To start it, draw a shape on the stage and make it a movie clip symbol. Our button is going to talk to a movie clip named script, so give the movie clip that instance name, double-click on it and go inside.

2. The movie clip starts out having just one frame currently holding the shape. Add two frames to the timeline and drag the keyframe to frame 2. In frame 1, which is now a blank keyframe, add a stop action.

3. Frames 2 and 3 of the scripting movie clip will house the scripts that make the squareCircle animation move. In frame 2, select the shape and make it a movie clip. Then add an onClipEvent. Select enterFrame as the event so that the script is executed at the movie's frame rate. Inside this statement, add a line telling _parent._parent.squareCircle to go to prevFrame.

    ```
    onClipEvent (enterFrame) {
        _parent._parent.squareCircle.prevFrame();
    }
    ```

4. Make frame 3, which at this point should just be a regular frame, a keyframe. You should now have a new instance of the movie clip from the frame before, with the same scripting in it. In the actions panel, change prevFrame to nextFrame, and, since we don't need it, feel free to go into the movie clip holding the clip event code and delete the shape.

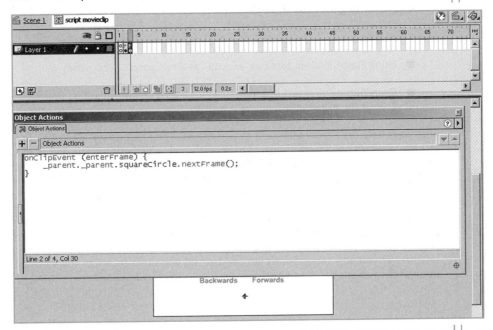

5.   All that's left is to add the frame labels. To do that, use the Frame panel and name as appropriate; in the script movie clip, frame 2 is `backwards` and frame 3 is `forwards`.

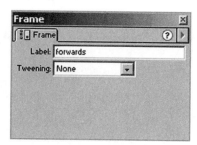

Like the slider, this sort of button/movie clip combination is able to modify any property. In fact, you will often see them together as different ways of controlling the same property. Over the following sections, you'll see it being used as part of a scrolling mini-app.

Also, if you've ever wanted to make a movie play in reverse, the script that we've just created can be easily modified to do just that. Right now, we have a movie clip that plays backwards when you press the backwards button. Instead of doing this by holding down a button, if you used other triggers to tell the script movie clip to go to the backwards frame, the effect would be complete.

Scroll buttons using the scroll property

Scroll buttons take a text box that contain more text than it can show at once and the user to move through the text either by going up or down. Like with most Flash reproductions of standard interface elements, there are different ways to go about setting up the process, as well as there being a lot more interesting things you can do inside the scrolling area, such as including animations and interactivity. This section and the next will cover the two principle methods for scrolling, discussing the pros and cons of each.

These two ways are:

- Using Flash's built-in text box `scroll` and `maxscroll` properties

- Or by putting your text in a movie clip under a mask and adjusting the y position property (`_y`) of the movie clip.

Both ways have their advantages and disadvantages. The first one we'll cover is using the `scroll` technique, which has the advantage of being extremely easy both to code and to fill with dynamic text. The disadvantage to this style is that it moves in whole line increments and is, therefore, not visually smooth. When line two is immediately exactly where line one used to be, it's harder to stay oriented at the point where you are reading.

To use the `scroll` technique, you need a dynamic or input text box with more text than the box allows. Also, the box must be multiline; whether or not it word wraps is up to you. One thing to keep in mind is that in the Flash authoring environment, text boxes automatically grow to hold the lines as you add them. So, to get the text in, you need to assign the value of the textbox through the Actions panel or bring it in using a `loadVariables` action.

Before we get into the nuts and bolts of how to set up the scroll buttons, let me first explain what the properties `scroll` and `maxscroll` are and how they work.

Scroll

To call the `scroll` of a field called `textfield1`, you would type `textfield1.scroll`. The value returned is the number of the line currently at the top of the text box.

Maxscroll

This is the last possible `scroll` for the box. It's not, however, the last line number. Flash will only let you scroll down until the last line of text is on the bottom of the text box; in other words Flash won't let you see blank lines after the text unless there is not enough text to fill the box in the first place. So `maxscroll` is the line number of the top line in the box when the last line is at the bottom of the box.

If that has you a bit confused, try looking at the diagram below.

maxscroll=3   scroll=3

Line 1
Line 2
Line 3
Line 4
Line 5
Line 6

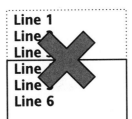

Line 1
Line
Line
Line
Line
Line 6

not possible – no blank
lines at the bottom of the
text box in a scroll system

maxscroll=3   scroll=1

Line 1
Line 2
Line 3
Line 4
Line 5
Line 6

Now that we've covered the basics of `scroll`, let's go ahead and make an example application of a scrolling text box with up and down buttons. For this project, you can use regular buttons or persistent buttons, like the ones we built in the previous section. Normally I'd use persistent buttons, but in order to create this application clearly, I'll use regular buttons. However, if you do it this way you'll have to click them multiple times in order to continue scrolling.

Creating a scrolling text box

For this example, we're going to build:

- A text box to scroll

- Buttons to do the scrolling

The text box

1. Create a multiline dynamic text field with word wrap on the stage. Give it the variable name scrollText so that we can pass the text to it and control it.

2. We'll add the text to the text field using a frame action, so go to frame 1 of the timeline and, in the Actions panel, set the value of the variable, scrollText, to any large amount of text that you can find (how much you need will depend on how big you made the box in the previous step.)

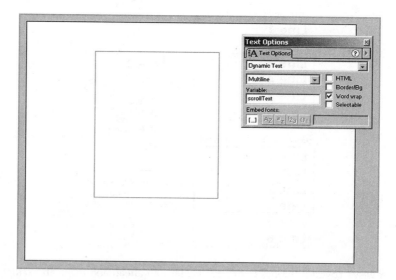

The scroll buttons

The general idea is to scroll in the appropriate direction unless the text is at its limit. The limit for scrolling up using the scroll property will always be 1, and the limit when scrolling down is the maxscroll of the text field. Since you can't go below 1 or above maxscroll, any commands to do that are ignored.

1. Go ahead and create two buttons on the stage, one for each direction.

2. Select the up button, go to the Actions panel and add an on(release) action. Inside we need to add a line that decrements scroll by one.

```
on (release) {
        scrollText.scroll--;
}
```

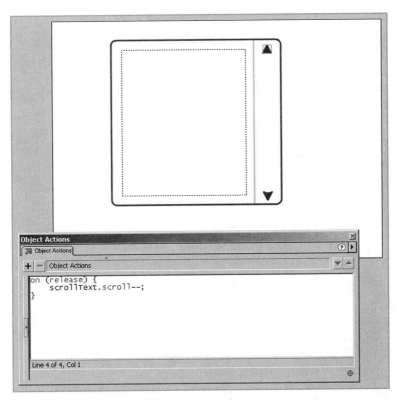

3. The script for the down button is very similar. Instead of decrementing, the script will increment scroll by one:

```
on (release) {
        scrollText.scroll++;
}
```

That's all there is to it. When you test the movie now, you should have a functional scrolling script, albeit quite a choppy one. In the next section we'll go through creating a smooth scrolling system.

buttons or the scroller and the other will still function correctly. There is nothing to say that a scroller must look like this. You should be creative when making your own. Try making effects with the handle movie clip, using the ratio variable to determine how the handle is displayed. For instance, you could have the scale of the handle change as it

Smooth scrolling using the _y property

If you are a developer on tight deadlines, you may want to skip this section. Once your clients realize that this type of scrolling is an option, none of them will want you to use the `scroll` method. There are some very nice advantages to this method - primarily that it just looks better, but also because you can add some really nice subtle effects, like acceleration, into the scrolling process itself. What's more, this type of scrolling is not completely limited to text; anything that can go in a movie clip can go in this scrolling method.

Sounds great right? Well, there are a few down sides. Though it is possible to dynamically call in text for this style, it is rather difficult. Also the script is not quite as straightforward as the earlier scroll box. That said, I always use this style for clients, but for quick projects and internal use, I use the `scroll` scrolling method.

This effect doesn't use a text box, but instead simulates the effect using a movie clip under a mask. So, to create this effect, we need to:

- create the content to be masked

- then the mask

- and the buttons

Masks are a special type of layer, which allow the content of the masked layers to show through only where there is content on the mask layer.

> *There are several limitations to masks that you need to keep in mind when using them. If you are using a symbol as the mask, be sure only to use one. Using more will cause unpredictable results. Also, any movie clip in the mask layer will lose its object qualities. You can't reference or assign any property, or use the goto action on or inside the movie clip.*

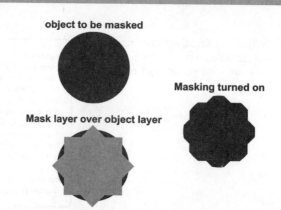

object to be masked

Masking turned on

Mask layer over object layer

To make a layer into mask, right-click on the layer name and choose Mask. The layer immediately below it will be turned into a masked layer. To make any other layer masked by the same mask, drag it between the current masked layer and the mask layer and it will be converted. You can then move the layer below the last masked layer. You can't, however, have any unmasked layers between masked layers and the mask itself.

Even though this effect loses some of its smoothness without persistent buttons, for the sake of clarity, I'll be using regular buttons in this example as well. Feel free to add in some persistent buttons by changing the button actions to clip events in this example if you'd like to see it working smoothly.

A smoother, more complex scroll box

The text box content

1. Make a static text box, write several paragraphs, and then make it a new movie clip symbol with the instance name text. Go into the text movie clip and move the text down until it is just below the pivot mark, then go back to the main stage.

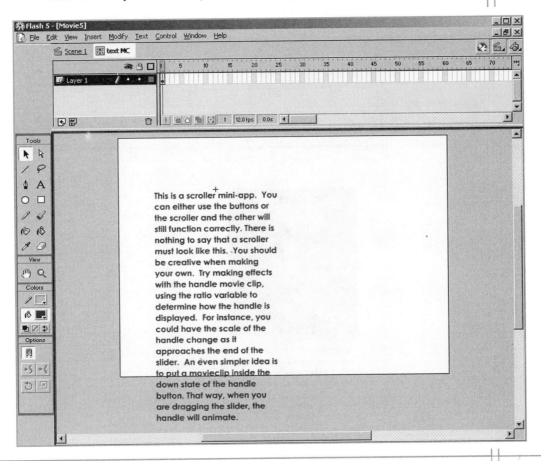

2. When you're moving the text around, you need to specify limits just as you did in the previous scroll example. Positioning the top of the movie clip at zero will make the limits easier to understand.

3. Select the text movie clip and make it into a new movie clip symbol. Name this instance textbox. Like you did before, go into this new symbol and move the text movie clip to just below the pivot. An easy way to do this would be to use the align tool to line up the top of the object with the center of the stage. This way the upper limit will be at the Y position 0.

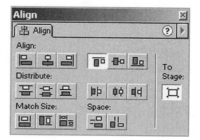

4. To create the illusion of the box, add a new layer above your current one and call it mask (inside the textbox movie clip) and draw a rectangle as wide as your text movie clip, but not as tall. Then position your rectangle so that its top is on the pivot mark. Right-click on the new layer's name in the timeline and select Mask. You should now only see part of your text.

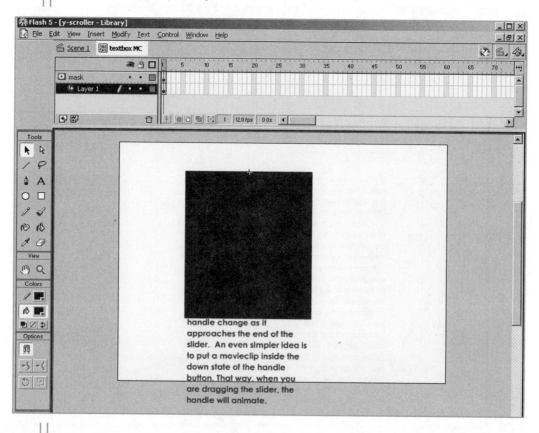

handle change as it
approaches the end of the
slider. An even simpler idea is
to put a movieclip inside the
down state of the handle
button. That way, when you
are dragging the slider, the
handle will animate.

5. Once you are happy with the position of your text, unlock the **masked** layer (not the layer that has the mask, but the layer underneath it), and select it. Draw a line alongside the entire length of the mask, and make that line a movie clip with an instance name `maskLine`. Since you've drawn the line outside the mask, it won't be visible to the user, however it is very important to us. By taking the `_height` of the line, we will know the height of the visible text area.

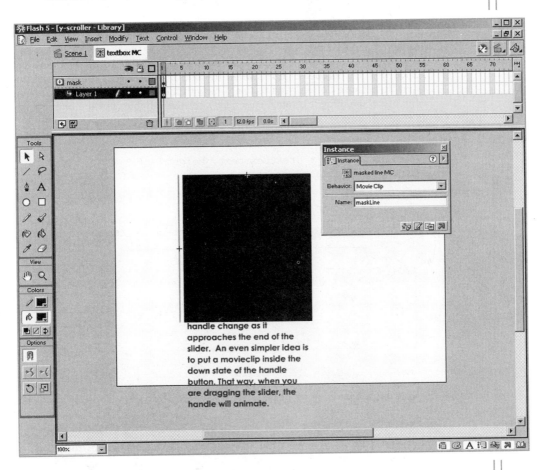

Now we need to determine the lower limit. In general this is just the `_height` of the text movie clip, but it needs to be offset by the height of the mask so that when you scroll to the bottom of the block there is not too much white space. You can make allowances for this by modifying the offset so that it is 80% of what it originally was. Because we placed the mask inside the `textbox` movie clip, we can determine its `height`. Since we can now access all of the appropriate data, we're ready to go ahead and set some variables in frame 1 of the main timeline.

Note: with text, the height property reports the height of the text as if it were broken apart curves instead of the height of the text box (the Info panel will tell you the height of the bounding box for the text).

6. Go into the Actions panel of frame 1 of the main timeline. We need to set three variables: upperLimit, lowerLimit, and scrollVal. The first two have already been discussed, but the third is simply a constant we'll use to move the text movie clip up or down a set number of pixels when the button is pressed. I prefer to set this as a variable because I often need to fine tune with the scrolling speed and by having it in one place, updating it is much easier. Let's set the variables like the ones below:

```
upperLimit = 0;

lowerLimit = -1 * (textbox.text._height - (.8 *
➡ textbox.maskLine._height));

scrollVal = 5;
```

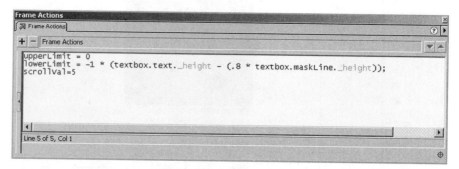

The lowerLimit is multiplied by -1 because Flash's coordinate system is sort of upside down.

In Flash, up goes to negative infinity, and down goes to positive infinity. Multiplying the value of the variable by -1 just reflects that when we are viewing the bottom of the text, the registration point has been pushed up into negative numbers.

The lowerLimit itself is just the height of the text movie clip minus 80% of the mask's height (as determined by the _height of the maskLine).

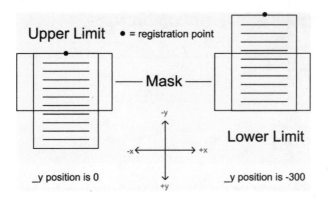

Creating the buttons

1. Create an up and a down button and place them on the stage. At this point, you can either set up the buttons like the example in the persistent effect button section, and use the following code in the script movie clip's onClipEvent, or just add the scripts directly to the buttons. As I said before, for clarity I'll be going through this example just putting the code directly in the buttons.

2. Select the button you'll be using to scroll up so we can add actions. Since we will want the box to move whenever we click on the button, add an on(release) statement. The strategy for moving the text movie clip is by correction, which will move the text whenever you click the button, but if the resulting location is outside the limit, the script will correct it by placing the text movie at the limit. The alternative is to do pretty much the reverse, checking to see if it is possible to move, then move, otherwise set to the appropriate limit.

So the first line inside the on statement for the up button will add scrollVal to the _y property of the text. Doing this will move the text movie clip down, allowing you to see higher lines of text inside the mask.

```
on (release) {
    textbox.text._y += scrollVal;
}
```

We'll use an if statement to check whether the correction is needed. This will compare the y position of text to the upper limit. When the y position is greater than the upper limit, we'll correct it by setting another property that takes variable upperLimit as its value. The if statement looks like this:

```
on (release) {
    textbox.text._y += scrollVal;
    if (textbox.text._y>upperLimit) {
        textbox.text._y = upperLimit;
    }
}
```

```
Object Actions
Object Actions
+ -   Object Actions
on (release) {
    textbox.text._y += scrollVal;
    if (textbox.text._y>upperLimit) {
        textbox.text._y = upperLimit;
    }
}
Line 7 of 7, Col 1
```

The procedure for the down button is mostly the same but with a few small changes. To move the text movie clip up, we need to subtract scrollVal from the y position. The correction script must also change to reflect the lowerLimit. The code should look like this:

```
on (release) {
    textbox.text._y -= scrollVal;
    if (textbox.text._y<lowerLimit) {
        textbox.text._y = lowerLimit;
    }
}
```

And that's all there is to it. Fire up your movie and see how it works. While I've presented this technique as a text scroller, any movie clip could be exchanged for the panel of text. The panorama effect we'll build in the next chapters uses scripts very similar to the ones we used here.

So far we've put together some small but functional interface elements that you can combine in numerous ways to build up mini-applications. In the next section we'll build upon the last three staple elements and create a scrolling mini-app including scroll buttons and a sliding scroll bar that work together. These techniques will work for either scrolling method you choose with only slight modifications.

The full-featured scrolling mini-app: using the slider together with buttons

In this example, we'll build a scroll bar that allows the user to move through some text, using the slider, or the buttons. This is a mini-app and not just two independent interface elements, because while both the elements can control the text box, they also have to work together. In other words, when you use the buttons, the handle of the slider needs to reflect the new position of the text.

As you might expect, then, there are two main elements to this scroll bar: retrofitting the slider, and then adding the script to the buttons to update the slider's handle. I'll cover in general theory what the slider is supposed to do and then outline how to incorporate it into either of the scrolling methods we've discussed.

The scroll bar part 1: updating the slider

be creative when making your own. Try making effects with the handle movie clip, using the ratio variable to determine how the handle is displayed. For instance, you could have the scale of the handle change as it approaches the end of the slider. An even simpler idea is to put a movieclip inside the down state of the handle button. That way, when you are dragging the slider, the

1. Bring in a set of scroll buttons with its text box from either of the two previous examples. Also bring in the generic slider example from several sections ago. As I mentioned in the slider section, the generic slider can be rotated without altering the code. Since most text scrolls from the top down, rotate the slider 90 degrees so that what was the left side of the slider is now the top.

2. Because of the way the slider is set up, there is little that needs to be changed. In fact, only one line of code needs to be altered. The slider we built earlier used a line of script to set the alpha of a movie clip; this is the line that we'll change so that it reflects the scroll position of the text box. For the scroll technique this means applying the ratio to the maxscroll and converting it to an integer.

The `scroll` uses a system that has the lowest possible value of 1, and this ratio is a 0 based system. The code must take this into account. To do this, subtract one from `maxscroll` before it gets multiplied to make it a zero-based number, then add the one back in at the end so it works correctly. This will give you:

```
onClipEvent (load) {
    function doSlide (ratio) {
            _root.scrollText.scroll =
➡ int((ratio*(_root.scrollText.maxscroll-1))+1);
    }
}
```

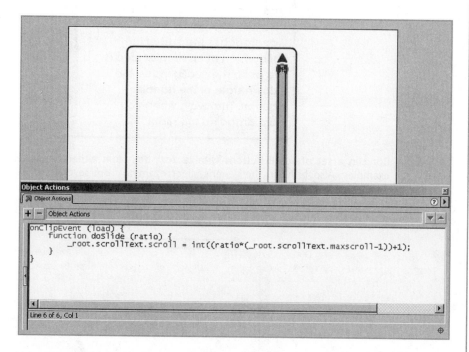

The code for the `_y` technique is just as easy to change. Since the text movie clip has an upper limit of 0, all we need to do is have the slider assign a percentage of the `lowerLimit` to the y position of the `text` movie clip. The code should look like the following:

```
onClipEvent (load) {
    function doSlide (ratio) {
            _root.textbox.text._y= int(ratio*_root.lowerLimit)
    }
}
```

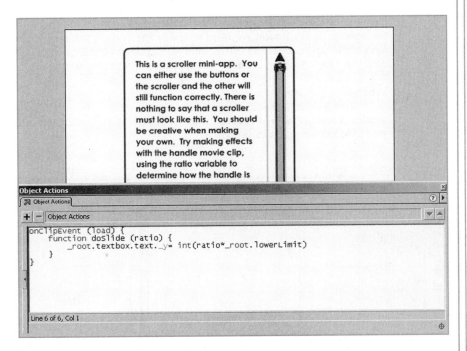

Updating the buttons

Both the buttons and the scroll bar should now allow you to scroll through the text, but the slider, however does not yet reflect clicks on the buttons. We need to add a few lines of code to each button to make this happen:

The handle's button contains a script that currently checks its own location along the bar and assigns a value based on that location which is used to call the doSlide function. This script needs to do the opposite; it will be given a scroll value, or a _y value, from which it should compute a percentage of the total scroll and assign the location of the handle based on that percentage. Since there is nothing specific to the direction of the movement in this, whether it goes up or down, the code will be the same for both buttons.

1. Unlike in the slider example, we will need to send commands into the slider in the scroll bar example. To do this, we need to give the slider an instance name. Let's call it slider.

2. First we need to set a few variables to make the equation easier. We will need the location of the line, lineLoc, and the length of the line, lineLength. These should be defined under the script that scrolls the text, inside the on() statement. Assign the variables like this:

```
lineLoc = slider.line._x;
lineLength = slider.line._width;
```

3. Below these variable assignment lines, we need to add a command to set the _x of the handle. To get a ratio we need to divide the current scroll or y position by the maxscroll or lowerlimit. That ratio is multiplied by the lineLength and added onto the lineLoc. The code for scroll is listed first followed by the code for _y.

```
lineLoc = slider.line._x;
lineLength = slider.line._width;
slider.handle._x = (((scrollText.scroll-1)/(scrollText.maxscroll-
➡ 1))*lineLength)+lineLoc;
```

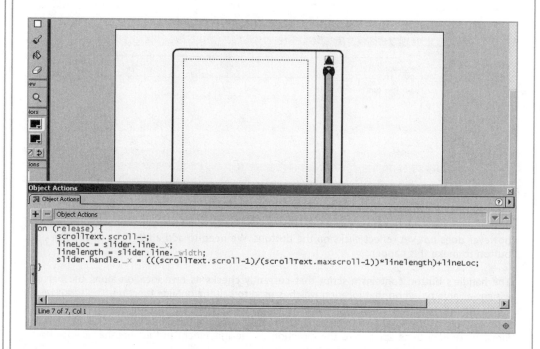

```
on (release) {
    scrollText.scroll--;
    lineLoc = slider.line._x;
    linelength = slider.line._width;
    slider.handle._x = (((scrollText.scroll-1)/(scrollText.maxscroll-1))*linelength)+lineLoc;
}
```

Line 7 of 7, Col 1

```
lineLoc = slider.line._x;
lineLength = slider.line._width;
slider.handle._x =
((textbox.text._y/lowerLimit)*lineLength)+lineLoc;
```

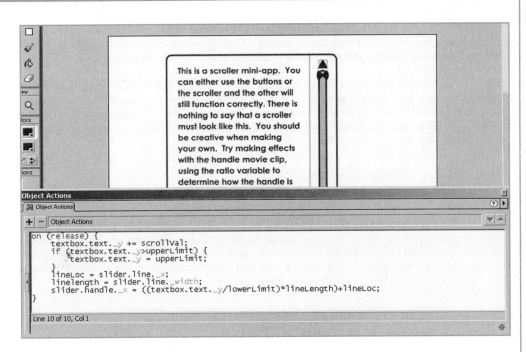

```
on (release) {
    textbox.text._y += scrollVal;
    if (textbox.text._y>upperLimit) {
        textbox.text._y = upperLimit;
    }
    lineLoc = slider.line._x;
    linelength = slider.line._width;
    slider.handle._x = ((textbox.text._y/lowerLimit)*lineLength)+lineLoc;
}
```

Line 10 of 10, Col 1

Dynamic preloader

Flash files can range dramatically in size from less than a kilobyte all the way to many megabytes. Because of this, developers need a way to tell their users how much they have to download and what their progress is so far. In Flash 5 there are two different techniques that you can use, frame- and byte-based preloading.

In Flash 4, the only method of determining the load state of a movie is by the number of loaded frames. For linear animations this was pretty good. For many games and sites though where most of the information can be presented in one frame on the main timeline, this left a lot to be desired.

Now, with Flash 5, the frame method is still available, however you can now also access total bytes and bytes loaded. This technique allows you to show an absolutely accurate snapshot of the download process as well as giving a realistic connection rate when combined with the getTimer function. Though it might seem that the byte preloader would completely replace frame preloading, there are still a few cases where frames can be preferable.

Often, sites sit at a preload screen until the entire file has loaded, ignoring the great streaming abilities of Flash. No matter which method of preloading you use, many times you should not need to download the entire file before displaying content. An argument for frame-based preloading is that if you know a user can't get past a certain frame in a given period of time, then when framesloaded is greater than that frame, there is no reason why you should make the user wait. If you can get the user into your site earlier, it's as if you cut the file size down without having to optimize.

The same is true for the byte-based preloader. After determining the connection speed, you can calculate a buffer period and start the content portion of the file as soon as they get to a point that they should be able to stream the rest in without disruption of the playback.

Let's start by building a basic preloader using the frame method, then modifying it to work with bytes. After that, we'll add a thermometer bar, and finally a connection speed checker. To begin, we'll need to have something to preload. You can either draw a lot of complex shapes, or simply import a large graphic file. Make sure that whatever you add is placed in a frame after the preloader so that it can load in quickly.

Building a basic preloader

Flash will display a frame only after it's finished loading, with the exception of frame 1. That will come in piece by piece either from the top or the bottom, depending on what preference you set in the Publish window. To get rid of this effect, leave frame 1 blank, then wait for Flash to fully load frame 2 before displaying it. Just make sure that whatever frame your preloader script is in has a `stop` action. The source for this example is `basicpreloader.fla` on the CD.

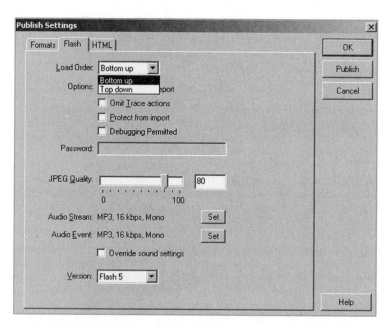

1. Now that we have a large file to preload, go to frame 2 and add a dynamic text field, giving it the variable name `loaded`. Since this frame needs to load quickly, make sure that you only include the font outlines that are necessary. In the text options panel, click on the numbers button and in the space to provide specific characters, type `%` `loade.` (you only need to specify the "d" character once, but don't forget to include the space).

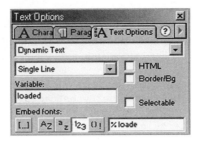

To fill in the `loaded` text field, we need to have a script that updates the percentage loaded constantly. The best way to do this is the `onClipEvent` action for movie clips.

2. Select the field and convert it into a new movie clip symbol called preloader. Give it an instance name of `preloader`. Select the movie clip and bring up the Actions panel. Add an `onClipEvent` action and make the event `enterFrame`.

3. Inside the statement, we need to set the `loaded` variable to say something like 60% loaded. Since the commands that we have access to are frames loaded and total frames, if we divide `_framesloaded` by `_totalframes` and multiply by 100, that will give us the percentage. For the sake of appearance, we'll also want to use the `int` function on the number, so that it displays as a whole number. Let's set the equation above equal to the variable, `percent`. Remember that commands in a clip event are part of the movie clip's timeline; we need to reference the `_root` properties, otherwise we'd get the loading status of the movie clip itself.

```
onClipEvent (enterFrame) {
    percent = int((_root._framesloaded/_root._totalframes)*100);
}
```

4. All that's left then is to put it in the string saying `%` loaded. To do that, set loaded equals `percent + "% loaded"`.

```
onClipEvent (enterFrame) {
    percent = int((_root._framesloaded/_root._totalframes)*100);
    loaded = percent+"% loaded";
}
```

5. If you test now, it should automatically go to 100% since there you are running the file locally without show streaming. You can give Show Streaming a try by selecting it from the View menu. You will notice that it is not a very good preloader since it all of a sudden jumps to 100% after a long time at a very low percentage. This is the weakness of frame-based preloading. If all of the file size is in a few frames, the preload process is inaccurate.

To convert this example, change `_framesloaded` and `_totalframes` to `getBytesLoaded` and `getBytesTotal`. If you test again and show streaming, the effect should be much smoother. Since we now have access to the total bytes, let's change the message from 60% loaded to 60% of 400K loaded. To display this new message, we will need to add the letters f and k to our specific characters in our text box. To find the total file size in Kb instead of B, take the total bytes, divide by 1024 (the number of bytes in a Kb) and use the int function to make it a whole number. Then, add in the string like before. Your code should match the code below.

```
onClipEvent (enterFrame) {
    percent = int((_root.getBytesLoaded()/_root.getBytesTotal())
    ➡ *100);
loaded = percent+ "% of " + int(_root.getBytesTotal()/1024) +
➡ "Kb loaded"
}
```

Adding a thermometer display

Instead of text, it's often nice to represent the preload process graphically. A popular style for this is the thermometer bar approach. In Flash, it's extremely easy. The thermometer is a stopped animation of a sliver of the thermometer tweening into the full bar. In this animation it can have color changes or any secondary animation that's desired. The preloading script will send the tween movie clip to the closest frame that matches the loaded percent times the totalframes property of the tween movie clip. The source for this example is preloaderThermometer.fla on the CD.

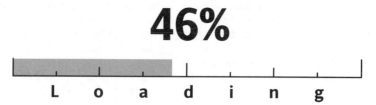

1. To create this effect, go into the movie clip that has the loaded text field. Create a new layer and draw a rectangle the size that you want the final bar to be. To make the shape tween, first add a keyframe at frame 100 (in the new layer) and go back to frame 1. Select the rectangle and use the scale tool to squash it horizontally until it is very thin. Select shape tween from the frame panel and shuttle through the frames to see the rectangle grow to the full bar. Be sure to add a stop action to frame 1 before leaving this movie clip. In your original layer, go to frame 100 and add a regular, non-keyframe. This will make sure that the percentage is viewable at all times.

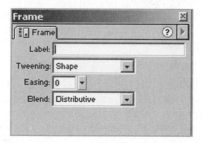

2. Back on the stage, select the movie clip, and go to the Actions panel. Under the action that sets the loaded variable, add a command telling the movie clip to `gotoAndStop` the integer of `percent` divided by `100` multiplied by the total number of frames in this movie. The frame should look like this:

```
onClipEvent (enterFrame) {
    percent =
int((_root._getBytesLoaded()/_root.getBytesTotal())*100);
    loaded = percent+"%";
    gotoAndStop (int(_totalframes*(percent/100)));
}
```

Connection speed detector

Besides being an interesting statistic, connection speed has several uses for a Flash developer. It can be used to dynamically decide when to let a user stop downloading and start viewing content, but it can also be used for movies loaded in by scripting. It's an easy matter to make two SWFs with music rendered out at different compression levels and call one in instead of the other based on the connection speed available to the individual user. The source for this example is `connectionspeed.fla` on the CD.

1. To create a connection speed detector, create a new dynamic text field on the main stage. Make it into a movie clip called speed and give it an instance name of speed. Inside the movie clip, add a new layer to hold the script. In frame 1, add a line that sets a variable named `time1` equal to the `getTimer` function, which will report back the total number of milliseconds that the Flash file has been running. Below `time1`, create `bytes1`, which should equal the total bytes loaded to this point:

```
time1 = getTimer()
bytes1 = _root.getBytesLoaded()
```

These two variables set a starting point for collecting the transfer speed. They will be compared against time and byte value from a few frames later to make the final rate computation.

2. Add a new keyframe in the scripting layer. Put this keyframe at least 5 or 6 frames after the first one. The actual can change based on personal preference, but the longer amount of time between the two samples will give a better average connection rate. In the second keyframe, set the variable time equal to `getTimer` minus `time1` and bytes equal to the current bytes loaded minus `bytes1`. Speed, expressed in Kilobytes per second then, is (bytes/time)*(1000/1024). The 1000 divided by 1024 is the conversion ratio to turn bytes per millisecond into the more common kilobytes per second.

```
//only update the speed variable if the load process is still
//going on.
if(_root.getBytesLoaded() != _root.getBytesTotal()){
    //find the change in time since frame 1
    time = getTimer() - time1
```

continues overleaf

```
            //find the change in load since frame 1
            bytes = _root.getBytesLoaded - bytes1
            //calculate speed by setting a ratio.
            //it may help to change units like we do here
            speed = (bytes/time)*( 1000/1024)
            //this is expressed in B/ms but is converted to Kb/S
            //note: there are 1024 B per Kb
        }
        //if you continued to run this after load stop, the number would
        //go to 0 since there would be no change in bytes (0) but time
        //would keep going.
```

All of the examples above can be used on any timeline in Flash, whether it's the main timeline or a movie loaded in from an external SWF. However you break up the preload, you should always be conscious how to shorten preload time whether it's through optimization or by buffering data and letting some stream in the background. If the download time is still large, you may want to consider the rapidly growing trend of building a preloader game, one that is small but compelling enough to occupy the few minutes of wait.

Summary

In this chapter, we have introduced several useful elements that allow user interaction. We started off with a basic dialog box and then incorporated an invisible button. We then built a simple slider: this is a very useful element that we will reuse again in future exercises. We then had a look at persistent buttons and used them in an exercise to control a shape tween.

We then considered two alternative ways to scroll text with scroll buttons: using scroll and maxscroll properties, and using the _y property with a mask.

By integrating a couple of these elements together (namely the slider and scroll buttons), we were able to create the scrolling mini-app.

We finished off by looking at preloading, both frame-based and byte-based, and ways of displaying loading and connection speed to the user.

Now that we've covered several ways of displaying data to your users, it's time to switch gears and start talking about getting information from your user. In the next chapter, we'll talk about constructing menus based off predefined data either set in Flash, or called by some external means.

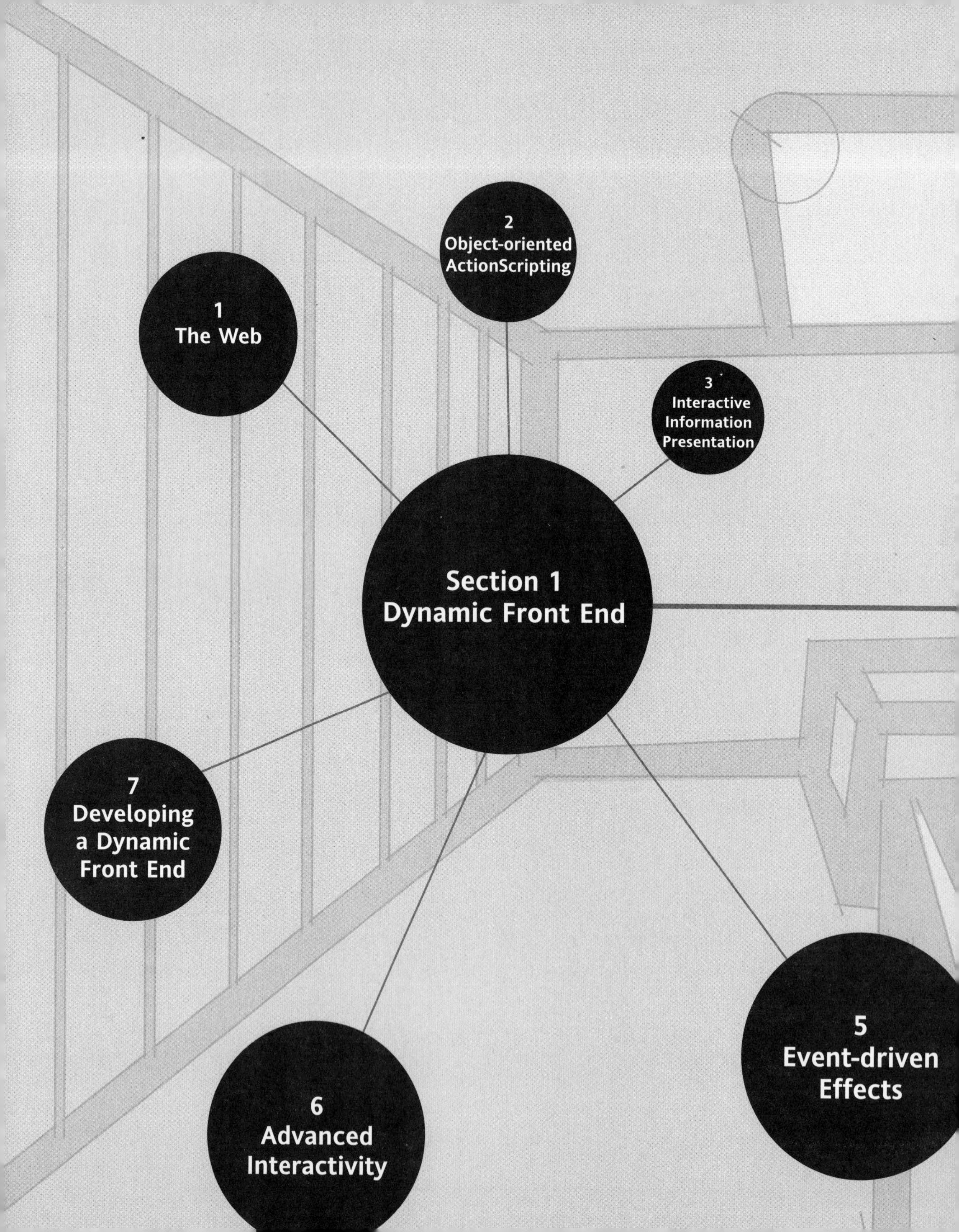

2
Object-oriented
ActionScripting

1
The Web

3
Interactive
Information
Presentation

Section 1
Dynamic Front End

7
Developing
a Dynamic
Front End

6
Advanced
Interactivity

5
Event-driven
Effects

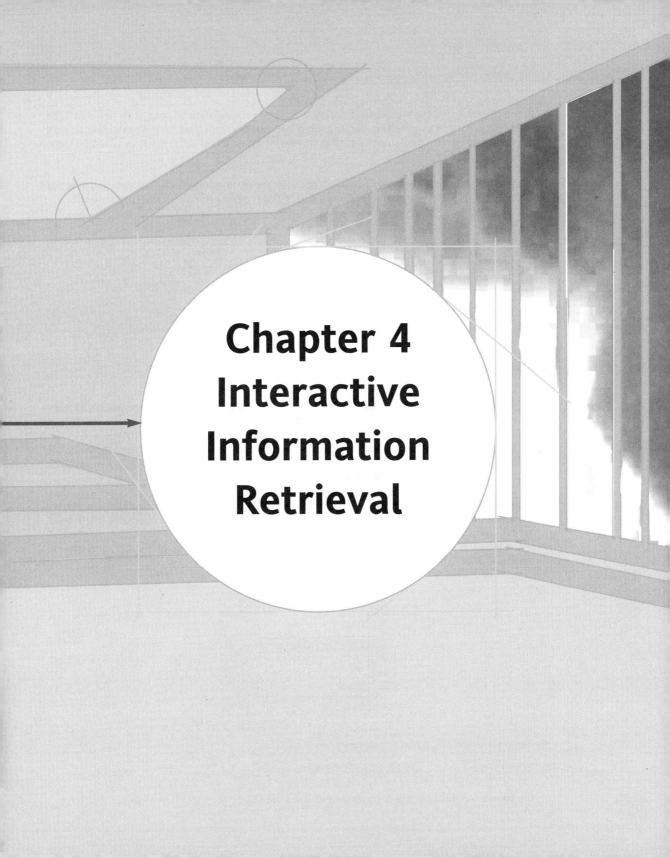

Chapter 4
Interactive
Information
Retrieval

In the previous chapter, we covered several ways of displaying data to your users, it's now time to switch gears and start talking about getting information from your user. In this chapter we'll work through constructing menus based on predefined data either set in Flash, or called by some external means.

Once we've covered all the key form elements, we'll move on to preprocessing and validating the information that you've obtained from the user by considering form checking and parsing.

We'll cover:

- Combo boxes
- Check boxes
- Radio buttons
- Form checking

Dynamic combo box

A combo box is a drop-down box that lets you select from a predefined list of options. It's a handy tool to have for forms, and not all that difficult to create in Flash. A dynamic combo box brings in variables either written in Flash (which we'll be doing here) or loaded from a database, text file, or XML call (using techniques covered in later chapters) and creates the list on the fly. While it's possible to make a static combo box by making each menu item by hand inside a movie clip, making a dynamic combo box once will save you a lot of time down the road.

A combo box consists of several elements. First, there's the main field, which displays a default message until an option is picked. Then there's the drop-down button that opens the list. The list itself is a movie clip containing a choice template that Flash will use to dynamically build the rest of the menu, and finally an invisible button that will close the menu should the user click outside the menu area.

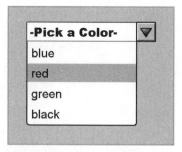

Building a dynamic combo box

The source for this example is `combobox.fla` on the CD.

The data setup

While the data for a combo box is perfectly suited to a data array, I think it's best to work through this example as if this data came from a text file or database call. Unfortunately, this means setting up what in Flash 4 was called a **pseudo-array**. If you're loading variables into a movie, unless you write a script to assign them into an array, they're assigned individually to whatever target or level you choose.

A pseudo-array is a list of variables that have a common name but with a different number at the end of each. An example of this would be `choice1 = 1, choice2 = 2, choice3 = 3`. Since you can't get Flash to tell you how many items are in a pseudo-array, you need to always include a numeric counting variable (or be prepared to write a script that checks for null values). For the example above, a good counter variable would be something like `choiceCount = 3`. It will be very important when programmatically building the menu to use this variable as a limit telling the system when to stop adding menu items.

Let's assume you're making an e-commerce application where the user can pick the color of a T-shirt they want to buy. When the user accesses this particular shirt, there will be a call to the database that brings back available colors, sizes, and the price and places them in `_level0` (the `_root`). Below is a sample stream of data coming back from the database.

```
color1=blue&color2=red&color3=green&color4=black&colorCount=4&
➥ price=19.95&size1=L&size2=XL&sizecount=2
```

To make these variables directly in Flash, add a new layer called variables and the following code to frame 1:

```
colorCount = 4;
color1 = "blue";
color2 = "red";
color3 = "green";
color4 = "black";
price = 19.95;
size1 = L;
size2 = XL;
sizeCount = 2;
```

Now that we know where the data will be, we are going to build the color choice combo box.

Building the menu

The appearance of the combo box can be however you like, but I'll be walking through the construction of one that is very similar in look and function to an HTML version.

1. Start by drawing a long horizontal box that will serve as the main field.

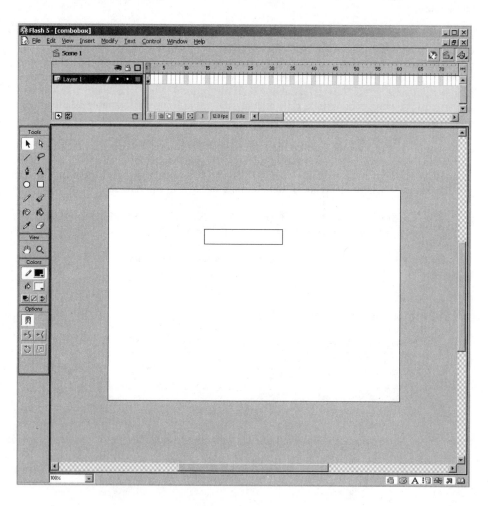

2. Copy the box, paste a new copy onto the stage and drag it out of the way for now.

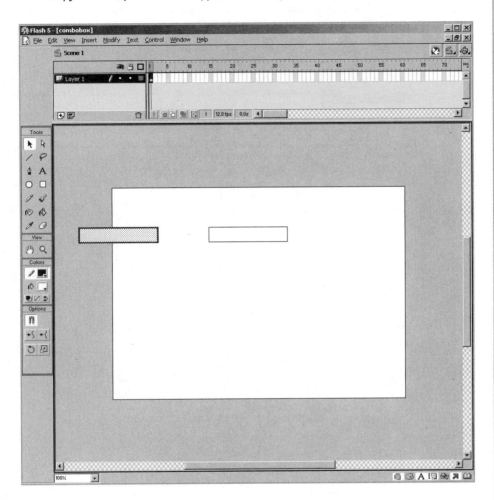

3. Add a square adjacent to the right side of the original rectangle to be the drop-down button. Draw a down arrow in the square, select the whole square and arrow and convert it to a button symbol named show menu button:

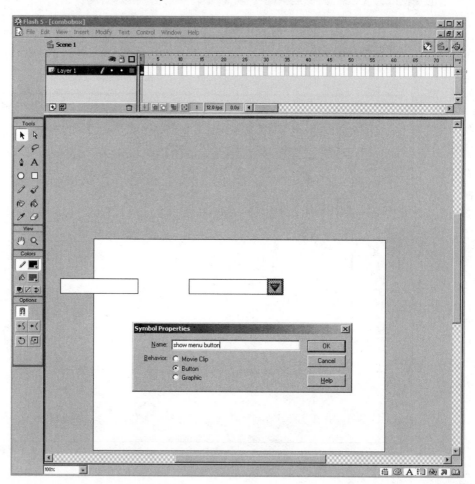

4. Inside the main field rectangle, add a dynamic text field and give it the variable name color. This is the field that the user will use to submit the data. Add some text Pick a Color so the user knows what to do! We're using a dynamic text field so that the user can only select a choice from the list that we will generate, however if you want the user to be able to override your predefined list, you could use an input text field.

5. Now drag the copy of the field rectangle back onto the stage. This is going to act as the drop-down menu segment. The full menu will be composed of several of these segments overlapping to form a contiguous menu. To create this illusion of one drop-down box with many options in it, we need to get rid of the top line of the box. Single-click on it and delete it.

The way this will work is that when a new choice is added on, it will be placed below the previous choice with a slight overlap. That overlap is what will block the bottom line on all the choices that aren't at the bottom. This illustration shows how the menu would look if you shifted each of the menu items over to the right so you can see how the overlapping works:

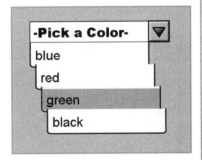

6. Next, select the rectangle, make it into a movie clip called menu MC and give it the instance name list:

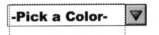

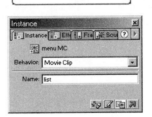

7. Drag the list movie clip to directly under the main field so that it looks like it is sticking out below it:

8.   Go inside the menu MC movie clip, select the field rectangle again, and make it into another movie clip called choice MC. Give this one an instance name `choice1`:

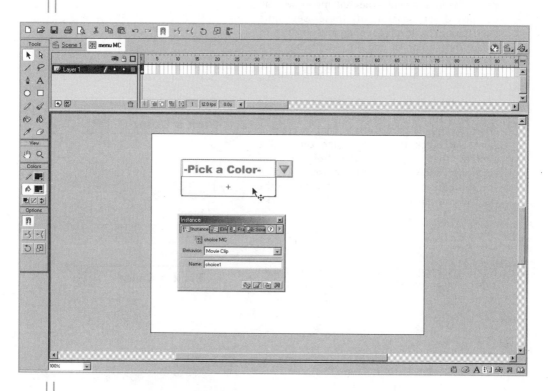

9. Before editing choice1, create a new layer in the menu MC movie clip called invisible button and drag it below Layer 1. On this layer, create a large invisible button named invisible button that covers the whole stage.

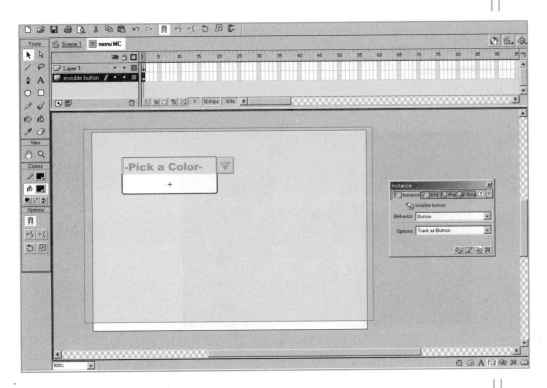

10. In chapter 3, we talked about using an invisible button to block interactivity below the current object earlier. This will do the same, but we'll also be adding code later on so that it also has a function. As before, drag the button's Up frame to the Hit frame.

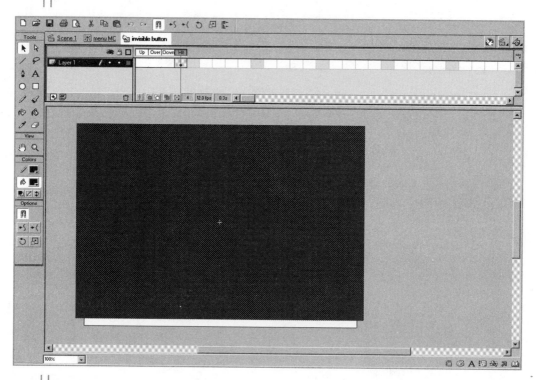

11. choice1 is the movie clip that will be duplicated based on the count variable in the _root. Inside choice1, we need to create a new layer and add a dynamic text field named option. Add the text choice 1 in the box:

12. In choice1, add a layer between the menu background and the text field, and create a button named option button with an Over state that will highlight the choice when you mouseover it. Light or bright colors will work best, so that it doesn't obscure the text that will be on top of it:

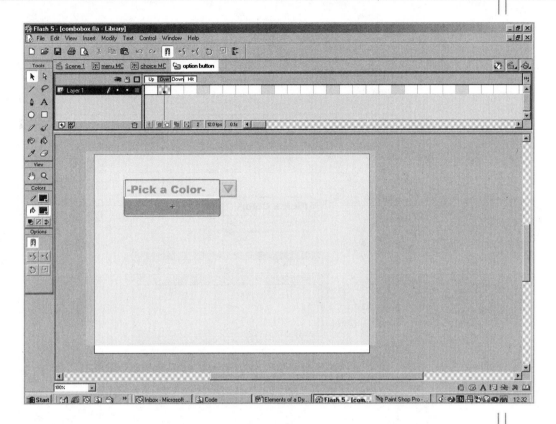

That's it for constructing the architecture of the combo box. All that's left is adding a few lines of code.

Scripting the menu

There are four elements that need to be scripted: the button that makes the drop-down menu appear, the menu creation, the buttons in the choice movie clip, and the invisible button that will close the menu if the user clicks outside the combo box.

The way we'll control the menu's opening and closing is by altering the visibility property of the list movie clip. When a movie has a _visible property of zero, scripts still work inside of it and properties may be changed and accessed, but mouse triggers and drop-targets no longer work.

1. On the main stage, give the button that opens the list menu an on(release) event. Inside that command, set the _visible property of the list movie clip to 1. In Flash, the use of 1 and 0 is the same as the Boolean values true and false. You can use either, but almost always I tend to use the numeric values. There's nothing more that needs to go on in this button since the menu will be closed either by the invisible button or one of the buttons in the choice movie clips.

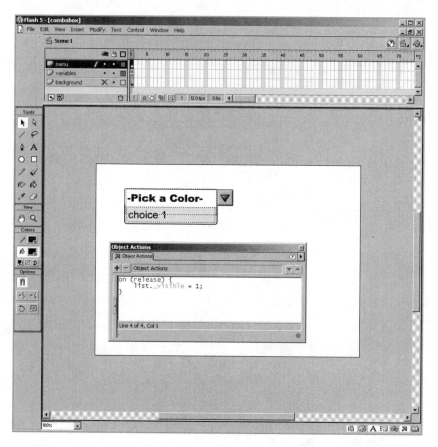

2. To create the menu, click on the `list` movie clip and open the Actions panel. Since
    we should only need to build this once, we can use an `onClipEvent(load)`. We'll
    need to copy the movie clip `choice1` as many times as there are choices, move them
    down so that they form a list, and then fill in the `option` text fields inside the movie
    clips based on the values of the `color` variables.

    ```
    onClipEvent (load) {
    }
    ```

    Since one of the goals of doing a dynamic interface element is the ability to re-purpose
    it easily, we don't really want to hard code the combo box for the pseudo-array `color`.
    Let's instead set a variable called `arrayName` to equal the string "`color`" (the quotes
    are needed around color). This way, when we want to change the combo box to
    something else, size for example, we just have to change this one variable.

    ```
    onClipEvent (load) {
      arrayname = "color";
    }
    ```

Now add a line to change the `_visible` property of the list to 0. This will ensure that the menu is by default off.

```
onClipEvent (load) {
arrayname = "color";
_visible = 0;
}
```

3. To make the rest of the menu, we just need to repeat the process for as many color variables as we have. Tasks like this are best done with an iterative loop. Iterative loops have a series of commands and a condition and as long as the condition is satisfied, the loop continues. Once the condition is not fulfilled, the loop breaks. The key to this is to change an index variable slightly every time it goes through the loop. After a set number of iterations though the loop, the index variable should fail to satisfy the condition that's been set, and break the loop. (If the condition never breaks, you have an infinite loop that will bring up an error in a dialog box when you render the movie.)

We'll use a `for` loop here, which gives you two extra features:

- You can initialize the index variable, which is helpful since most of the time your condition is based on a variable that you need to change. By setting up its initial state, you can make sure that the loop is going to happen exactly as you expect it to.

- You can set an expression instructing the program to do something after a sequence of the loop is completed. This allows you to change the index before running through the loop again.

The syntax of the `for` loop is `for(initialization ; condition ; next) {statements}`. The following diagram demonstrates a simple `for` loop.

Flowchart for the for loop, **for(var i=1; i<3; i++)**

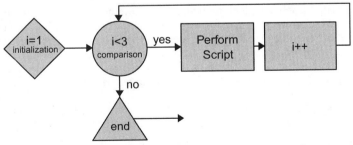

Since we already have `choice1` as a template to create the other menu items, we don't need to create it or move it like the others, but we still need to fill in the variable. Add a line setting the variable `choice1.option` equal to the expression `eval("_root." + arrayname + "1")`. This concatenates the three segments to form `_root.color1` and then evaluates the variable to return the result.

```
onClipEvent (load) {
    arrayname = "color";
    _visible = 0;
    choice1.option = eval("_root."+arrayname+"1");
}
```

Now that we have choice1 set up, we are ready to build the loop that will set up the duplicated movie clips. Let's go ahead and create the for loop starting with the initialization. A common convention in programming is to use the local variable i as the index. Remember that the index needs to start at 2 though, since we already have choice1 taken care of. The syntax for this segment is var i=2.

Then we need to specify the condition that the loop uses. Our condition needs to reflect the fact that we only want to keep duplicating until we've created a choice movie clip for each color variable. Since we have a variable called colorCount that says how many variables there are, we just need to keep looping until the index is no longer less than or equal to the colorCount variable. Since we're not hard wiring this script to color, we just need to again use arrayname to get the job done. When you've finished, the second segment should look like the expression, i <= eval("_root."+arrayname+"Count").

The last segment of the for loop setup says what to do when each sequence of the loop is complete. Since we need to add one onto i, the easiest way to do it is to use the increment operator, ++. The last segment should read i++. All together it should look like this:

```
onClipEvent (load) {
    arrayname = "color";
    _visible = 0;
    choice1.option = eval("_root."+arrayname+"1");
    for (var i = 2; i <= eval("_root."+arrayname+"Count"); i++) {
    }
}
```

Inside the loop, we add the duplication, movement and setting the option variable. The duplicateMovieclip command takes the movie clip and makes a copy, then places it at the exact same spot. Any properties of the movie clip are preserved in the duplication, except for the current frame. Add duplicateMovieclip inside the for loop.

- The target to be duplicated should be choice1.

- The new name needs to be "choice"+i, which is the string choice concatenated with the current index variable.

- The depth should just be i. Depth is internal stacking within the timeline you are already in. It works very much like levels do out on the main timeline, but it's completely internal to the movie clip or level that it's in. For example you can have depths 1-100 in _level0. They will all still be lower than _level1.

```
onClipEvent (load) {
    arrayname = "color";
    _visible = 0;
    choice1.option = eval("_root."+arrayname+"1");
    for (var i = 2; i<=eval("_root."+arrayname+"Count"); i++) {
    duplicateMovieClip ("choice1", "choice"+i, i);
        }
}
```

Once the new movie clip is generated, it needs to be moved into position. Since the new movie clip needs to cover the bottom line of the preceding movie clip, you need to move it down just slightly less than its height. When I was building the example, I just copied the choice1 movie clip onto the stage, adjusted the new one to where I wanted it, and figured out the difference between their _y positions using the Info panel. You should feel free to do it this way or to move it down based on the height of the clip minus some small number. Either way should end up working just fine.

Since this is part of a loop, though, we need to create a rule that will generate positions for all iterations of the choice movie clip. In my case, the difference in _y was 20 pixels. So, to set the location of any movie clip, its _y position should be 20 times the index minus 1 (20 * (i-1)). The reason for subtracting 1 from the index is to account for the fact that choice1 didn't have to move at all. To add this value onto its current position, we can use the += operator which automatically adds whatever is on the right hand side of the operator onto the object's current property.

To synthesize the name of the object that we want to set the _y of, we need to use the eval command. In this case, the eval command returns an object, which we can then append the _y property to.

```
onClipEvent (load) {
    arrayname = "color";
    _visible = 0;
    choice1.option = eval("_root."+arrayname+"1");
    for (var i = 2; i<=eval("_root."+arrayname+"Count"); i++) {
      duplicateMovieClip ("choice1", "choice"+i, i);
      eval("choice"+i)._y +=20*(i-1);
    }
}
```

Now that the movie clip is placed, all that's left is for the item to set the option variable inside the choice movie clip. You'll need to use the eval command again to reference the object, which is a concatenation of "choice" + i + "option". The value should be eval("_root."+arrayname+i).

When it's all done, the `onClipEvent` should look something like the following:

```
onClipEvent (load) {
    arrayname = "color";
    _visible = 0;
    choice1.option = eval("_root."+arrayname+"1");
    for (var i = 2; i<=eval("_root."+arrayname+"Count"); i++) {
        duplicateMovieClip ("choice1", "choice"+i, i);
        eval("choice"+i)._y += 20*(i-1);
        eval("choice"+i+".option") = eval("_root."+arrayname+i);
    }
}
```

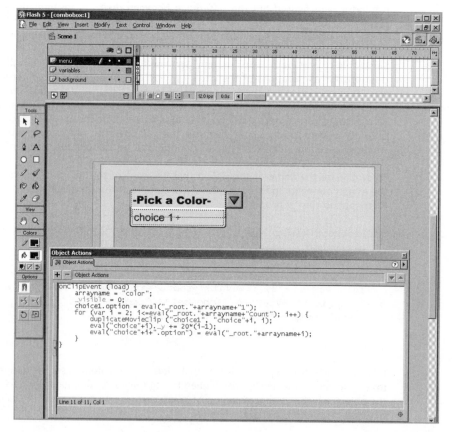

4. Let's move on now to the option button inside the `choice1` movie clip. This button needs to set the main field named `color` on the main stage to the appropriate value, whatever that may be (based on what the user chooses). Since the value is conveniently in the same movie clip, all that needs to happen is to set the main field to the value of `option`. To determine the name of the main field, we'll need to reference the variable `arrayName` in the parent movie clip.

5. Add an `on(release)` command to the button and add a set the variable "`_root.`" + `_parent.arrayname` equal to the variable `option`:

```
on (release) {
    eval("_root."+_parent.arrayname) = option;
}
```

The button will also need to close the menu once the selection has been made. To do that, add a new line setting the `_visible` property of `_parent` back to 0.

```
on (release) {
    eval("_root."+_parent.arrayname) = option;
    _parent._visible = 0;
}
```

To set the action for the transparent button in the parent movie clip, it's essentially the same command. This time, the `on(release)` command should just have a line that sets the `_visible` property of the current object (`this`) to 0.

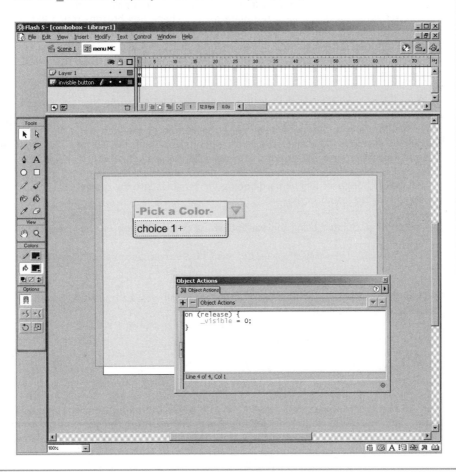

That's all there is to a dynamic combo box. Once this is set up, you should never have to build it again. You can simply make artistic changes to modify the appearance but the underlying commands should not have to change.

If you find that your drop-down box is falling behind other elements on your screen, be sure to take a look at z-ordering (relative stacking of objects in the movie) in Chapter 6, otherwise, put these elements on the top layer and position them in a way that they don't fall behind each other.

Check boxes

Like the combo box, check boxes are a staple of traditional web-based forms. Check boxes are a list of options where you can choose any number of items. These are handy for any time you need the user to "check all that apply", or if you want to limit the selection so that you can check up to a maximum number of items as we'll see in the exercise below.

The setup for a check box is very similar to setting up a menu item in a combo box since we are still dealing with a predefined list. The primary difference here is the way the information is displayed. We'll set up an item template for the check box buttons much like we did in the previous exercise, so that the system can duplicate them and fill them need dynamically with the user's options. Although we'll fill them with variables hard coded into the FLA, you could just as easily use a database or text file to pass in the variables, (but that's a discussion for another chapter.)

For the sake of the example that we'll build up here, let's assume that you've been contracted to create an e-commerce solution for a car dealership. You are in charge of developing the section of the web site that allows customers to select the extra options for their car. Since different cars have different options, you need to make a set of check boxes that is dynamically created each time, based on variables entered in a database (though we will be hard coding the variables into the movie like we did for the combo box).

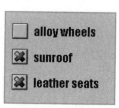

This would be populated using this variable string coming to you on the _root :

```
&extra1=Leather%20Seats&extra2=Sunroof&extra3=Alloy%20Wheels&extra
➡ Count=3
```

To simulate this in Flash without using an external call, you can add the following variables in frame 1 of the main timeline.

```
extra1 = "alloy wheels";
extra2 = "sunroof";
extra3 = "leather seats";
extraCount = 3;
```

To make the check boxes, we'll need to create a generic menu item containing a check box button, and a text box that will hold the item's name. After the template is complete, we'll encase it in a movie clip and write the script that will duplicate and populate the generic menu item much like we did with the combo box example. All that's left then is to use the data in a meaningful way.

A number of things can be done with the data from check boxes. For instance, you might store the indices of the selected check boxes, or you could create a comma-separated variable of all of the names of the selected check boxes. Since it's easier for a human to read the actual names of the checkbox values, we'll make a comma-separated variable on the root of the movie. A sample of the value would be `alloy wheels, sunroof`, provided those two items are checked. The script that does this can be modified in many ways to suit your needs.

In the next exercise, we'll cover the following:

- Making the generic menu item

- Creating and populating the full menu

- Developing a script to record the state of all the check boxes into one variable

- Exploring setting limits on the number of items that can be checked

The source for this example is `checkboxes.fla` on the CD.

Building a dynamic check box

Building the button template
We'll start by building the visual element of the check box itself. Traditionally this is a square that has an x-shape in it when it is selected and is empty otherwise. Once we've created the graphics, we'll then need to organize the structure of the check box symbol so that we can have the x-shape appear and disappear. The easiest way to do that is to make the box the button and have it in a movie clip containing two frames, one with and one without the check.

1. On the stage, draw a square for the empty check box, and make it a button symbol called check box. Then, select it and make it a movie clip symbol called option MC. Make sure that your square has a fill in it so your button is not just the outline of the box. Give the movie clip an instance name choice1, since the whole generic menu item will be inside this movie clip.

2. Inside `choice1`, insert an extra frame in the timeline and then add a new layer. In frame 2 of the new layer, add a blank keyframe and draw an x-shape inside the box. If you toggle back and forth between frames 1 and 2, you should see the x-shape appear and disappear.

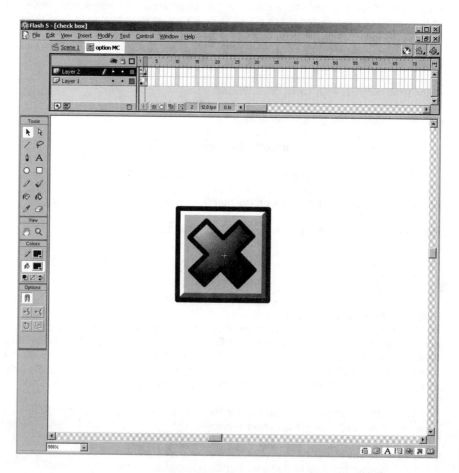

3. To make the movie stop on the frame without the x when you render the movie, add a `stop` action to frame 1. Add a blank keyframe in frame 3 of Layer 2, and a `gotoAndStop(1)` in this frame. Also insert a third frame into Layer 1.

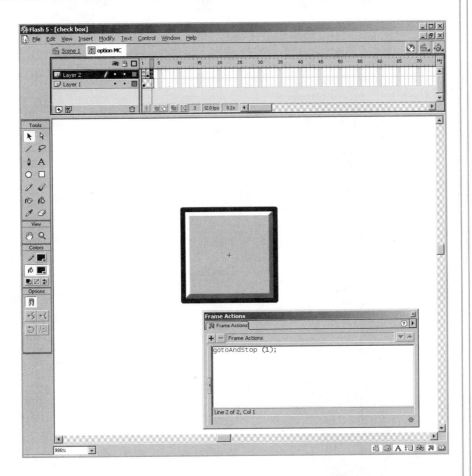

4. Now let's look at the button itself. We need the button to tell its `choice1` movie clip to go to frame 2 if it's in frame 1 and to go to frame 1 if it's in frame 2. While we could do this with `if/else` logic, there is a simpler way, which we'll use here. Add an `on(release)` event to the button and put a `nextframe` action inside it, so if the movie's in frame 1, the button press sends it to frame 2, and if it's in frame 2, then it goes to frame 3 which immediately sends it to frame 1.

If you test the movie now, you should have a check box that appears to function correctly, even though it's not really doing anything.

5. In Layer 2, add a dynamic text field with the variable name `option` and add the text generic option name. (We're using a dynamic text field to prevent the user overwriting the values.) This field will be filled in later in the same way we filled in the combo box example, so make sure you create a large enough text field to handle your longest potential option name.

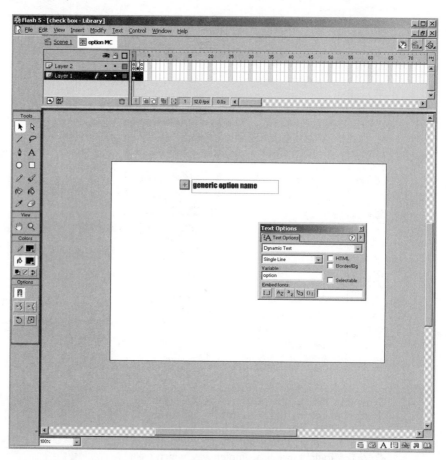

6. Now, go back out to the main timeline and select the `choice1` movie clip. Convert it to a new movie clip symbol called `checkbox array MC`, give it the instance name `list`, and position it wherever you want the check boxes to start building.

We're now ready to start writing the script that will create the populated check boxes.

Scripting the self-creating menu

This script is going to work almost exactly the same way as the combo box script. It will carry out a one-time creation of menu items based on a pseudo-array of variables. The template will be duplicated, moved to the appropriate position and then populated with the correct variable. As with the combo box, there is a template named choice1 that needs to be populated but neither created nor moved by the scripting. The code is so similar, that it would be best to copy it directly from the previous exercise and paste it in the corresponding place on the list movie clip. The code should look like this now:

```
onClipEvent (load) {
        arrayname = "color";
        _visible = 0;
        choice1.option = eval("_root."+arrayname+"1");
        for (var i = 2; i<=eval("_root."+arrayname+"Count"); i++) {
                duplicateMovieClip ("choice1", "choice"+i, i);
                eval("choice"+i)._y = choice1._y+(20*(i-1));
                eval("choice"+i+".option") = eval("_root."+arrayname+i);
        }
}
```

There are only a few changes that we need to make to customize the code to this project.

1. We first need to change arrayname to reflect the new variable names. Since the variables are named extra1, extra2, etc. arrayName should be set to the string "extra".

```
onClipEvent (load) {
        arrayname = "extra";
        _visible = 0;
        choice1.option = eval("_root."+arrayname+"1");
        for (var i = 2; i<=eval("_root."+arrayname+"Count"); i++) {
                duplicateMovieClip ("choice1", "choice"+i, i);
                eval("choice"+i)._y = choice1._y+(20*(i-1));
                eval("choice"+i+".option") = eval("_root."+arrayname+i);
        }
}
```

The next line in the code that set the drop-down menu invisible by default needs to be removed.

```
onClipEvent (load) {
        arrayname = "extra";
        choice1.option = eval("_root."+arrayname+"1");
        for (var i = 2; i<=eval("_root."+arrayname+"Count"); i++) {
                duplicateMovieClip ("choice1", "choice"+i, i);
                eval("choice"+i)._y = choice1._y+(20*(i-1));
                eval("choice"+i+".option") = eval("_root."+arrayname+i);
        }
}
```

The last change is the positioning of the movie clip after it's been duplicated. Before, we were trying to cram them together to form a cohesive list. This time, we need to put a gap between each item. We need to move the item down at least as far as its own height, and preferably a little further to make a gap.

Since all of the items will have the same height, instead of doing the concatenation to get the appropriate object, we can just use the height of the choice1 movie clip. After we get the height of the choice1 movie clip and add a certain number of pixels onto it, we have the relative distance between each item.

Since all of the duplicated movie clips will be starting at choice1's coordinates, we'll need to multiply that value by the index value. Keep in mind, though, that choice1 was never moved, so instead of multiplying by i, we need to multiply by i minus 1. If we didn't subtract 1 from i here, there would be a double gap between choice1 and choice2. Notice also that this amount is a number of pixels that the item needs to be moved, not a static coordinate. So we can add it onto the current _y position using the += operator like we did with the combo box. This will create a vertically stacked set of check boxes.

```
onClipEvent (load) {
    arrayname = "extra";
    choice1.option = eval("_root."+arrayname+"1");
    for (var i = 2; i<=eval("_root."+arrayname+"Count"); i++) {
        duplicateMovieClip ("choice1", "choice"+i, i);
        eval("choice"+i)._y += (choice1._height+5)*(i-1);
        eval("choice"+i+".option") = eval("_root."+arrayname+i);
    }
}
```

If you want any other setup, just change the property and expression to suit your needs. For instance, to do two columns of check boxes, you could set up an if statement to check to see if the index is even, and change the _x position as well as the _y position. This can be made as simple or as complex as you like.

Scripting the data collection

If you tested the movie now, you'd have functional checkboxes, or at least the appearance of them. In reality the checkboxes aren't doing much of use if you are trying to collect data from the user. We need to now go about making a script that will take the states of the checkboxes and do something meaningful with them. In general, it's more helpful to have the data in one place, so we'll use a script that updates a single variable on the root every time a checkbox value is changed. Since the only way to change a checkbox is to click on it, and because we are using a dynamically created check box menu that really only has one button that is replicated through the scripting, we can add the script to the button inside the choice1 movie clip.

1. First, go out to the stage and create a dynamic text box that we will use to display the aggregate data of all the check boxes. Give it the name extraSelection so we can use the arrayName variable to assign the value.

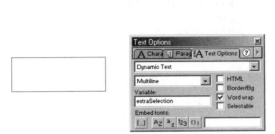

Now go all the way into the choice1 movie clip and bring up the button commands in the Actions panel. It should already contain this code:

```
on (release) {
    nextFrame ();
}
```

To make sure that the extraSelection variable is always up to date, every time we run the script checking each check box and setting the extraSelection's value we'll blank out its value and build it up again. To do this, start by setting the value of extraSelection to the empty string (""). To set extraSelection though, we will want to use the arrayname variable so that we can use this check box symbol in the future without having to go to it and change these sorts of details. Since the variable we want to reset is on the root, the line should look like the following:

```
on (release) {
    nextFrame ();
    eval("_root."+_parent.arrayname+"selection") = "";
}
```

To build the value, we'll set up a loop that will check the status of each check box, and if selected, will add its item name to the extraSelection variable. In a for loop, initialize the index variable to 1 since we need the first check box to be included in the loop. The loop setup itself otherwise has the same properties as the loop that created the check box menu. It should look like this:

```
on (release) {
    nextFrame ();
    eval("_root."+_parent.arrayname+"selection") = "";
    for (var i = 1; i<=eval("_root."+_parent.arrayname+"Count");
    ➡ i++) {
    }
}
```

As a refresher, since this is the second time we are recycling the code, the condition is that the index never exceeds the count variable we created on the root, and after each loop the index is incremented by one.

To determine whether or not a check box is selected, inside the `for` loop, we'll nest an `if` statement. The condition will be whether or not the choice movie clip in question (determined by concatenating the index of the `for` loop to the string `"_parent.choice"`) is in the second frame. In other words, if `eval("_parent.choice" + i)._currentframe == 2`.

```
on (release) {
    nextFrame ();
    eval("_root."+_parent.arrayname+"selection") = "";
    for (var i = 1; i<=eval("_root."+_parent.arrayname+"count");i++) {
        if (eval("_parent.choice"+i)._currentframe == 2) {
        }
    }
}
```

When the `if` statement is satisfied, we need to append the item's `option` variable onto `extraSelection`. We also want a comma separating each item so that they don't run together. This can be done by adding the string `", "` at the end of the line. For the sake of readability, let's make the option variable from the choice movie clip into a variable in this timeline first, then use that variable to set `extraSelection`. Programmatically, this doesn't do much for us, but otherwise it would be a very long, fairly dense line of code.

```
on (release) {
    nextFrame ();
    eval("_root."+_parent.arrayname+"selection") = "";
    for (var i = 1; i<=eval("_root."+_parent.arrayname+"count");i++) {
    if (eval("_parent.choice"+i)._currentframe == 2) {
            addValue = eval("_parent.choice"+i+".option");
            eval("_root."+_parent.arrayname+"selection") +=
        ➡ addValue+", ";
        }
    }
}
```

Notice how the new information was appended to the variable by use of the `+=` operator. In Flash 5, whenever you use `+` and `+=`, if both values are numbers, the operators will produce a number, but if either side is a string, then the result will be a concatenated string.

The `extraSelection` variable is now ready to be used in whatever purpose your form needs.

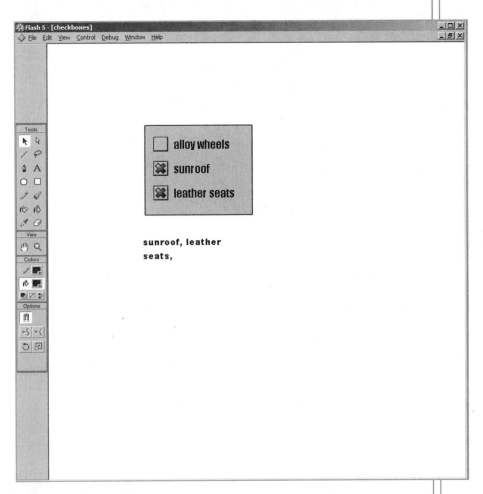

Limiting the number of checked boxes

What if you need to make a form that limits the number of options that can be picked? In the dealership example, imagine they were running a deal that you could pick a bundle of two options for free, you would need to make sure that the user can't click the third item. To do this we need to set up a variable that counts the number of selected items then allows or disallows you to click on an item.

1. Let's first add a limit variable in the _root. This is another variable that would be called in externally, but for now we'll just manually add it. limit would have been assigned along with the values of the check box. Name the variable extraLimit and give it a value of 2. If you don't want to limit the check boxes, you either shouldn't add this section's code to your check boxes, or you will always need to supply a limit variable and make it greater than or equal to your count variable.

```
extraLimit = 2;
```

2. The limit must then be compared to the current number of selected items. Since we already have a process checking the states of each choice movie clip, we could add some code to count the number of selected items quite easily. Go back into the `choice1` movie clip and bring up the button's actions. You should see the following:

```
on (release) {
    nextFrame ();
    eval("_root."+_parent.arrayname+"selection") = "";
    for (var i = 1; i<=eval("_root."+_parent.arrayname+"count");
➡ i++) {
        if (eval("_parent.choice"+i)._currentframe == 2) {
        addValue = eval("_parent.choice"+i+".option");
        eval("_root."+_parent.arrayname+"selection") +=
        ➡ addValue+", ";
        }
    }
}
```

3. Under the line that blanks out the `extraSelection` variable, we need to perform a similar operation for a counter variable. Let's set `_parent.counter` equal to `0`. The reason for adding the `counter` variable to the parent movie clip, is that it's also the parent for all of the choice movie clips. In a moment we'll be adding code that is going to be checking the value of this variable, which means it must be in a convenient place. It's important, though, that this variable isn't on the root so that there won't be conflicts if you use more than one check box series at a time.

```
on (release) {
    nextFrame ();
    eval("_root."+_parent.arrayname+"selection") = "";
    _parent.counter = 0;
    for (var i = 1; i<=eval("_root."+_parent.arrayname+"count");
➡ i++) {
        if (eval("_parent.choice"+i)._currentframe == 2) {
        addValue = eval("_parent.choice"+i+".option");
        eval("_root."+_parent.arrayname+"selection") +=
        ➡ addValue+", ";
        }
    }
}
```

4. Since the `if` statement is already detecting if an item is selected, we can just add a line that increments `_parent.counter` whenever the condition is satisfied.

```
on (release) {
    nextFrame ();
    eval("_root."+_parent.arrayname+"selection") = "";
    _parent.counter = 0;
    for (var i = 1; i<=eval("_root."+_parent.arrayname+"count");
➡ i++) {
```

```
if (eval("_parent.choice"+i)._currentframe == 2) {
        addValue = eval("_parent.choice"+i+".option");
        eval("_root."+_parent.arrayname+"selection") +=
    ➥ addValue+", ";
        _parent.counter++;
        }
    }
}
```

5. Now that the counter is set up, we're ready to write a script that checks whether or not a new item can be selected. To do this, everything currently inside the on(release) statement must be encased in an if action. Add the if statement's opening line right below the on(release) { line and add its closing bracket immediately above the closing bracket for the on command.

```
on (release) {
    if () {
        nextFrame ();
        eval("_root."+_parent.arrayname+"selection") = "";
        _parent.counter = 0;
        for (var i = 1; i<=eval("_root."+_parent.arrayname+
    ➥ "Count"); i++) {
                if (eval("_parent.choice"+i)._currentframe == 2) {
                        addValue = eval("_parent.choice"+
                    ➥ i+".option");
                        eval("_root."+_parent.arrayname+
                    ➥ "selection")+= addValue+", ";
                _parent.counter++;
                }
        }
    }
}
```

```
Object Actions
 Object Actions                                                          ? ▶
+ - Object Actions                                                       ▼ ▲
on (release) {
    if () {
        nextFrame ();
        eval("_root."+_parent.arrayname+"selection") = "";
        _parent.counter = 0;
        for (var i = 1; i<=eval("_root."+_parent.arrayname+"Count"); i++) {
            if (eval("_parent.choice"+i)._currentframe == 2) {
                addValue = eval("_parent.choice"+i+".option");
                eval("_root."+_parent.arrayname+"selection") += addvalue+", ";
                _parent.counter++;
            }
        }
    }
}
Line 2 of 15, Col 6                                                      ⊕
```

6. Now we need to set up the condition. All requests to turn a box off should always be accepted, as well as any request to turn a box on if it's under the limit. In other words, the box should be turned on if the _currentframe equals 2 or the counter is less

than the limit, (as you might remember from the previous chapter, the || operator means 'or'.) The final version of the button actions should look like this:

```
on (release) {
    if (_currentframe == 2 ||
    ➡ _parent.counter<eval("_root."+_parent.arrayname+"Limit")) {
        nextFrame ();
        eval("_root."+_parent.arrayname+"selection") = "";
        _parent.counter = 0;
        for (var i = 1; i<=eval("_root."+_parent.arrayname+
        ➡ "Count"); i++) {
            if (eval("_parent.choice"+i)._currentframe == 2) {
                addValue = eval("_parent.choice"+
                ➡ i+".option");
                eval("_root."+_parent.arrayname+
                ➡ "selection") += addValue+", ";
                _parent.counter++;
            }
        }
    }
}
```

Now that you've got a working check box menu going, our hypothetical client has changed its mind (can you believe even the hypothetical clients can't resist making changes??). Two free items was way too generous. Instead, you need to be able to pick only one item. This really eliminates the usefulness of the check boxes here since they are really designed for multiple selections. Luckily there's a similarly formatted item that will do just the trick: the radio button. With this type of menu you can only select one item, but if one is already selected when you click, it immediately gets deselected and your new choice is activated. Lucky for us, you'll see that there is very little change from the check boxes, allowing us to re-purpose this last exercise pretty quickly.

Radio buttons

Radio buttons are an interface element that allow you to select one item from a predefined list. In terms of final result, they are very similar to a combo box, however in practice, they are set up like check boxes. A radio button is just a check box with a limit of one possible selected item.

Adapting the check box example to the radio button

We'll build one now, or rather, adapt the check box code we just made to create radio buttons. The source for this example is radiobuttons.fla on the CD.

1. Since the setup of radio buttons is so similar to that of check boxes, I'd suggest saving a new copy of your check box file, and making the necessary cosmetic changes to create a series of radio buttons:

2. Then all you need to do is change the code in the button inside the `choice1` movie clip. Right now it should be a very big script filled with `if` statements; go ahead and delete everything inside the `on(release)` command (just make sure you are in the right file and not deleting the only copy of all the work you just did in the last section!).

```
on (release) {
}
```

3. Because we're dealing with radio buttons that only allow a single selection, we need to turn off whatever is turned on, and then turn on the radio button that is selected. Instead of figuring out what is on and switching it off, all we need to do is make a `for` loop that tells all of the radio buttons to go to frame 1. The construction of the `for` loop is the same as others we've done. And inside we need to add a line telling the particular choice movie clip to go to frame 1.

```
on (release) {
    for (var i = 1; i<=eval("_root."+_parent.arrayname+"count");
➡ i++) {
    eval("_parent.choice"+i).gotoAndStop(1);
    }
}
```

4. Then use a `gotoAndStop(2)` to turn the current radio button on.

```
on (release) {
    for (var i = 1; i<=eval("_root."+_parent.arrayname+"count");
➡ i++) {
    eval("_parent.choice"+i).gotoAndStop(1);
    }
    gotoAndStop (2);
}
```

5. All that's left to do then is to set the `extraSelection` variable (the variable out on the root that holds the selected data) to the value of the local option variable (the current menu item's name). Here's the code:

```
on (release) {
    for (var i = 1; i<=eval("_root."+_parent.arrayname+"count");
➡ i++){
    eval("_parent.choice"+i).gotoAndStop(1);
    }
    gotoAndStop (2);
    eval("_root."+_parent.arrayname+"Selection") = option;
}
```

And with that final example, we've covered all the key form elements, so we'll move on to preprocessing and validation. With Flash 5's strong abilities in substring methods, there is no reason to tax your server, making it do the error checking for you. In the next section we'll cover how to make the client computer do the work.

Form checking and parsing

When you're storing large amounts of data in a database as it comes in from a web form, it's extremely important that the data is consistent. Form checking allows you to go through all of your variables and make sure they contain specific characters; in fact, that they contain characters at all and haven't been left blank, and are otherwise formatted correctly. Having this correction take place in Flash saves a call to your database, which saves your server resources, and saves your user the time it would take for the server to respond.

Since you can only send text to your database or middleware application, form checking is an exercise in parsing. So, what's parsing?

Parsing

Parsing text means breaking down a string into smaller pieces and analyzing those pieces instead of just looking at the whole. With there being so many string operators available in Flash 5, parsing (and constructing strings) is a skill that can be used extensively in Flash for efficiently coding and reading multiple pieces of information in a single variable. For instance, a game like *Simon* (if you remember, the player has to copy a random sequence of flashing colors) works by adding a new number to a string each turn and then waiting for the user to parse through the string by clicking the appropriate buttons. Once you're comfortable with variable parsing, you'll find there are many interesting applications for it.

One that I commonly used in Flash 4 was to name instances of movie clips in a way that had meaning. The movie clip would parse its own name and assign part of the name to variables. For instance I might have a movie clip with an instance name of A50. In the first frame of the movie clip I would parse the second and third characters, assigning it to a variable. This could then be used in the movie clip's script to alter its actions. If a goto command referenced this variable, sending the movie clip to frame 50, then I've been able to customize the script to a limited degree. This is essentially a rudimentary version of what smart clips and clip events can do in Flash 5.

In this section, though, we're primarily concerned with the applications of parsing that allows us to check for data formatting errors. In order to do that, we first have to be familiar with the string operations that can be used to perform the check.

First, the most basic are the equality operators, == and !=. Notice that these are the same as the numeric operators. Unlike in Flash 4, these operators are flexible, recognizing what they are trying to compare. When used alone, these operators are commonly used to check for the empty string "", in other words, making sure the field has any value. Flash 5 is case sensitive, so these operators are extremely useful for checking for absolute matches. These operators are at their most powerful used in conjunction with string methods. The methods of the string object can be loosely grouped into three areas: properties, substrings, and formatting.

String property methods

These are the property methods:

- **length**, which you probably remember using in the previous chapter. length reports back the total number of characters in a variable including spaces and newline (hard return) characters. This is particularly useful for setting the condition when parsing through a variable one character at a time using a loop. Otherwise it can be used to check variables that have a common number of characters, like zip codes and phone numbers.

- **scroll**, which we worked with in the scrolling text example earlier in the chapter. It's useful in cases where you are more concerned with the space that text takes up rather than the number of characters.

- **Maxscroll**, which we used to detect when an input box has gone over its allotted space.

Substring methods

These are the real powerhouses of text checking, and Flash 5 has several methods to choose from. Substrings allow you to take part of a string and deal with just that part. These four methods do essentially the same thing, the differences between them are subtle but well worth exploring.

- **slice** as you saw in chapter 2, copies and returns a slice of the string.

- **substr**, returns a string that begins at a specified starting index for the number of characters you specify.

- **substring**, returns the string between two specified points.

- **charAt** returns a single character at an index you provide.

They allow you to specify where to begin reading and either how far to read, or on what character to stop. For the most part we'll be using substr. Also lumped into this section are the methods to search for a substring within a string:

- **indexOf** reports back the index of where the substring begins for the first time.

- **lastIndex** reports back the index of where the substring begins for the last time.

There are several other string methods, but they are not really applicable to checking data so we're not going to be looking at them here.

String formatting methods

The most general of the string commands is the string method itself. Its purpose is to turn its arguments into strings. For instance trace(1+1) would result in 2; however if you wrote trace (string(1) + 1) the result would be 11. There are only a few uses of this operation that I've found, the first is to force numbers into strings as we've just seen. The other practical use is to take code and allow you to apply string methods to it. After introducing the case methods, we'll cover a practical example of this.

There are two case conversion methods, both of which are new to the current version of Flash:

- toLowerCase

- toUpperCase

Just as you would expect, these methods take single or mixed case strings and return them, converting all characters to the specified case. All strings are case-sensitive, so 'Flash' wouldn't be equal to 'flash' even though to us they are made up of the same letters. If you use the equality operators or the indexOf method you may not want to restrict the matching to exact case matches. To take case-sensitivity out of play, you can deal with the strings converted to only one case.

Let's say you have a variable called val, which is equal to the string "Flash" and you want to search for 'f's within the text. Since you most likely don't want to permanently change case just to do your error checking, it would be nice to run indexOf on the expression val.toLowerCase. You can't append another method on the end of the expression, but you can convert it to a string, then run indexOf on the string like this:

```
string(val.toLowerCase()).indexOf("f")
```

Now that we have our arsenal of string checking scripting elements, let's look at some practical examples of checking strings. We'll begin by checking an email address field, and then look at an extension of error-checking, password protection.

Verifying an email address field

Email addresses have a standardized form, so we can run a more accurate validity check on this variable than simply making sure it contains a value at all. We'll check for one and only one @ character, and make sure that there aren't any characters that cannot be included in an email address, such as spaces and special characters.

Since checking one field is a long way from checking a whole form, let's create this as a custom function to go inside some larger form checking script. This function needs to return true if the value of the text field email conforms to the rules above. Otherwise, the function should return false. The source for this example is email parse.fla on the CD.

1. In a new Flash file, create a single line input text field with the variable name address, this is where users will enter their email address. Also add a button to the right of this field for them to request verification:

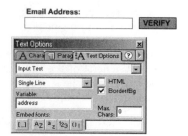

2. Underneath this, create a single line dynamic text box with the variable name `result`. This will tell the user if their email address has been accepted:

Email Address:

VERIFY

Text Options

A Chara | Parag | A Text Options | ? | ▶

Dynamic Text

Single Line ▾ ☐ HTML
☐ Border/Bg
Variable:
result
☐ Selectable
Embed fonts:
[..] Az az 123 0 1

Now for the verification script. Let's start out by checking for the @ symbol.

3. Let's add another layer to the main timeline to contain our ActionScript. In frame 1 we'll define the function `checkAddress`, which should take the argument `email` (the supplied email address).

```
function checkAddress (email) {
}
```

To set up an `if` statement that searches for the symbol appropriately, we need to clearly define where the @ can and can't be. The username part of an email address must be at least one character and the shortest domain name must be at least one character with at least three more characters after that (for the dot and the top level domain). So, our code will check:

- That the `indexof` for @ is greater than zero and less than the length of the address minus four. (Remember: `indexOf` starts counting from zero.)

- That there is only one @ in the address, the value for `indexOf` and `lastIndexOf` must be the same.

Valid @ placements:	**Invalid @ placements:**
	@XXX.XX
X@X.XX	XXXXXX@X
XXXXX@XXXX.XXX	XXXX@X.X
	XXXX@XX

4. The `if` statement for this check should look something like the following (I've set some local variables in the beginning to make the code a bit more legible):

```
function checkAddress (email) {
    var atFirst = email.indexOf("@");
    var atLast = email.lastIndexOf("@");
    var L = email.length;
    if (atFirst != atLast || atFirst<1 || atFirst>(L-4)) {
➥ return false;
    }
}
```

5. We also need to check for the last dot. It needs to be either the third, forth or fifth character from the end, to accommodate .com, .uk or one of the new TLDs like .coop. If it's outside that area, return false:

```
function checkAddress (email) {
    var atFirst = email.indexOf("@");
    var atLast = email.lastIndexOf("@");
    var L = email.length;
    if (atFirst != atLast || atFirst<1 || atFirst>(L-4)) {
    ➡ return false;
    }
var lastDot = email.lastIndexOf(".");
    if (L-lastDot<3 || L-lastDot>5) {
    return false;
    }
}
```

6. To find out whether the address contains any special characters could take quite a while if we checked for each one individually. Instead, we'll make a string that contains all of the characters that we want to check for, and then create a loop that parses through the special character variable character by character, testing it against the email string. We'll use the fact that indexOf returns a value of −1 when the character isn't found in the string for verification. We'll also need to escape some of the characters we're searching for using the backslash: \\, \", \', \r and \n, because these characters can't be entered in ActionScripting unless escaped this way.

If any of the tests return a non-negative number then the script should stop and return false. Since this is the last criterion we're checking for, we will need to add a statement that returns true at the end to say the check was completed without finding an error. Since return commands break out of functions, the return true command will never be reached if a return false command is issued first. This is the final completed code:

```
function checkAddress (email) {
    var atFirst = email.indexOf("@");
    var atLast = email.lastIndexOf("@");
    var L = email.length;
    if (atFirst != atLast || atFirst<1 || atFirst>(L-4)) {
    ➡ return false;
    }
    var specialChar = " ~!#$%^&*()_+|=-`[]{};:<>,?/\\\"'r\n";
    for (i=0; i<specialChar.length; i++) {
        if (email.indexOf(specialChar.substr(i, 1))>=0) {
        ➡ return false;
        }
    }
    return true;
}
```

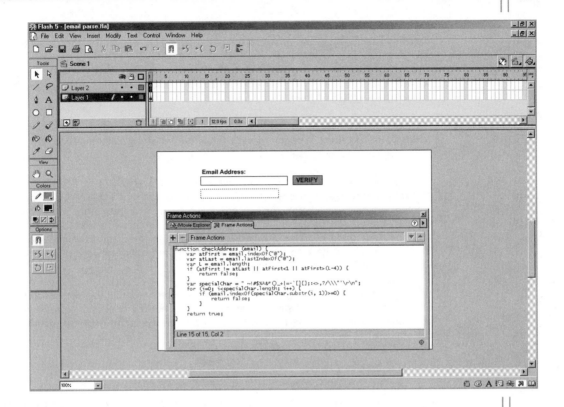

We also need to add some code to the button:

```
on (release) {
    if (checkAddress(address)) {
        result = "passed";
    } else {
        result = "failed";
    }
}
```

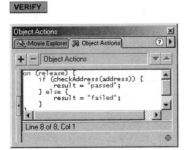

This code will check whether the inputted address meets the requirements that we specified previously in the `checkAddress` function and will display the result to the user in the `result` field.

7. Now test your movie! Try omitting the required @ or dot, placing them incorrectly or including special characters.

This sort of error checking can be done in many ways, depending on the data that needs to be checked. Experiment with the different string commands to see which ones give you the best result.

The great advantage that custom form elements have over plain text fields is the fact that they preprocess the user's response. If you need to check a different type of form element, such as a check box, the procedure is quite a bit simpler. Since you've already dictated the possible answers, all you need to do is to check to make sure that the appropriate number of items checked is acceptable. In the case of the check box we built earlier, all you have to do is a simple numeric equality test against the selected variable inside the check box movie.

General forms aren't the only use of these sorts of commands; in the next section we'll look at two very important strings that need to be checked: user and login. As well as any parsing issues that arise here, we'll be faced with the larger issues of security and the ability of someone to pry into your SWF.

Front end password protection

An extension of form validation is user validation. Password protection can be useful for protecting your work from prying eyes, or for authenticating a user in a web-based application. Before you decide to incorporate this into a Flash project there are several things you need to know.

SWF is an open source file format. While this provides many benefits to the development community, there are some drawbacks. One of these is the fact that SWFs can be de-compiled and all of the scripting read. Since this is the case, storing passwords or any other sensitive information in Flash isn't a good idea.

For a secure user login, Flash must only be a front end. You should have a server-side application that verifies login data and returns a session code. Anything less could be a potential target for an easy hack. Keep in mind, though, that even if you use a secure login, any information or graphics in the SWF itself are still vulnerable. The secure login is only to guard against sensitive data on the server being downloaded to a hacked SWF.

That said, there are uses for having a Flash-based password system. If you're just interested in mild security, then this is a perfectly viable solution. This sort of password protection keeps honest people honest.

There are, however, a few steps you should take to make sure that your password screen can't be circumvented. A common error I've seen is that people will have a good password checker and that when the password is correctly entered, it only advances the movie to the next frame. This isn't a great idea because it's easy to skip to the next frame by right-clicking and using the contextual menu. Disabling the menu doesn't prevent this. Since the menu is set in the HTML, if you view the page source and then directly access the SWF file, that protection disappears. To correct this problem, create a frame that loops to your password screen. Then make your log in script jump past that frame after a successful login.

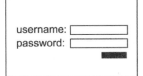

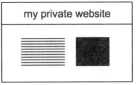

Frame 1: password screen   Frame 2: redirect to frame 1   Frame 3: content

The only way to get to the content is to enter the correct user and password information. If you try to bypass the menu using the forward or play context menu items, you will be brought back to frame 1.

I've heard of people that have used a server-side script to authenticate the user and then send back a variable like `loggedIn=1`. Keep in mind that this also is not completely foolproof, because users can feed in variables through the URL to a SWF file. No matter how you set up password protection in your Flash movie, my advice is to look at the open source software available and to try to think of all the possible ways someone might try to get around your password setup.

One of the best ways is to have nothing in the file that does the login. The user information is submitted to a server-side authentication script and then that script redirects the browser to the page that actually contains the SWF with the secure data. What someone can't find, they can't hack.

Summary

We've certainly covered a lot in the past two chapters. In the midst of recreating traditional web interface elements, we've covered:

- Simple actions
- Looping
- Clip events
- Text parsing
- Form checking
- Masking
- Accessing and setting movie clip properties
- Movie clip duplication

Your arsenal of customizable, dynamic interface elements should now include:

- Dialog boxes
- Persistent effect buttons
- Scrollers
- Combo boxes
- Check boxes
- Radio buttons
- Preloaders

In the next chapter, we'll continue with these principles but we'll begin to break away from conventional elements and start showing Flash for what it can really do. While some of these elements are fairly traditional, you'll see that looking at the same ideas in a new way will create Flash effects that simply couldn't be done any other way on the web.

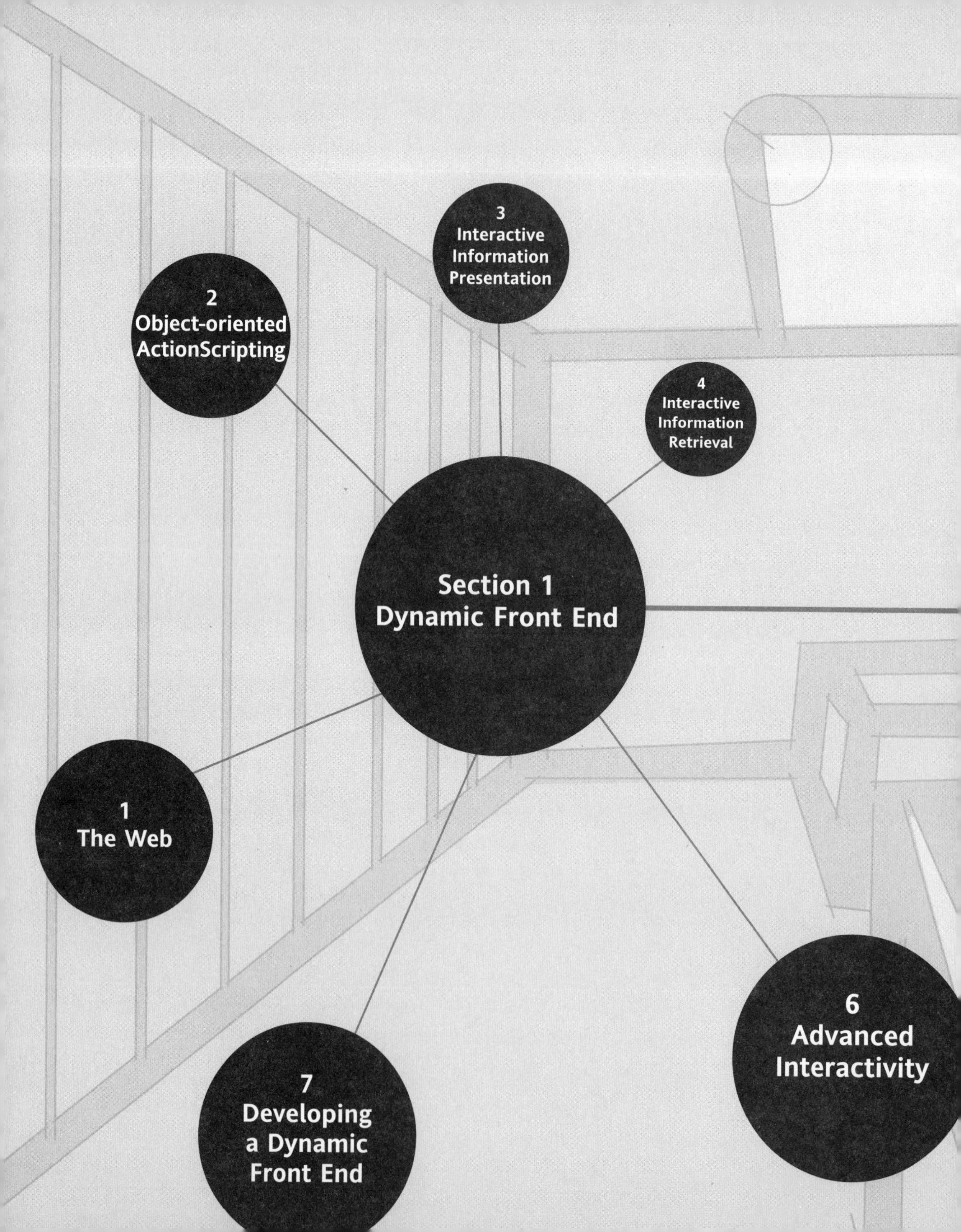

3
Interactive
Information
Presentation

2
Object-oriented
ActionScripting

4
Interactive
Information
Retrieval

Section 1
Dynamic Front End

1
The Web

6
Advanced
Interactivity

7
Developing
a Dynamic
Front End

Chapter 5
Event-driven
Effects

In this chapter we're going to depart from pure web analogs like form elements, and start really working with Flash's strengths. We'll be creating the kind of elements that transform a static site into a dynamic and interactive one, the sort of elements that you can use to create rich interfaces and games. Some places in this chapter are a bit technical – it seems that in Flash, the more complex the script, the more interesting the effect.

Many of the examples we'll work with here are in the context of game development, although they can all be used within an interface as well. This is because I feel that's it's simply more fun to learn while you make games than it is to learn while you make isolated interface elements: I hope that by the end of the chapter you agree!

We'll be dealing with a fair bit of math in several sections, but I've tried to present alternatives for those who insist math is a torture practice. Basic algebra and a few broad points in geometry is all that you need in order to grasp the more complex topics in this chapter. I've always been told that programming involves a lot of math. I can't say that I've found it to be true, though if you happen to like math, there are lots of interesting things you can do.

In this chapter, we'll walk through the following exercises:

- Mouse trails

- Turning the mouse trails script into airplane controls

- Two examples of dragging an object in a non-rectangular shape

- Collision detection

We'll start this chapter off by dealing with the mouse, because it's really the most common focus of web interactivity. Unless your user is going to be filling in data, or playing a game, you are most likely to be gearing site interactivity around the mouse. We'll start with cursor effects like mouse trails, and then see how the same scripting concepts can be used to create the controls of a game. Following that, we'll work on constraining the dragging area of an object in shapes other than rectangles. This can be good for an interface or a game, and it's a handy script to have in your arsenal.

As an extension of the non-rectangular dragging example, we'll go into depth on collision detection. Up to this point, the chapter is all about finding out where the mouse is, but as you'll see in this example, collision detection can be with the mouse or any other object on the stage. The example for this technique will be driving a small dot-shaped movie clip around the stage. As it moves over a shape, Flash will run a script. As you might guess, this has many applications for game creation.

This chapter will be a bit faster paced than the last one, assuming that you are becoming more familiar with Flash's operation as you go through the chapters. As we continue building on previous examples, I still encourage you to revisit previous sections if you're unclear on any of the techniques that I take for granted in this chapter.

Cursor effects

The most common form of Flash interactivity involves the mouse. Whether it's for a game or a website, adding effects to the cursor can complete or enhance the impact of your project. Mouse effects usually fall into two categories: moving objects in response to the mouse, or changing the appearance of the mouse. We'll work with both of these effects. Once we've covered the basics, we'll build a mouse trail engine, and then controls for an airplane, combining the two features to give a more immersive game environment.

The simplest cursor-based effect is the startDrag command, which allows you to see an object moving in response to your mouse. In both examples we're going to build on this concept to create a delayed drag. The built-in drag function always moves its target object at a one-to-one ratio compared to the cursor movement. In many cases though, having the dragged object respond a little sluggishly will help the realism of the movement.

The key to a delayed drag is to not move in a one-to-one ratio with the mouse. The object that is being dragged should only move some fraction of the way to where the mouse is. This way, it will take several frames to catch up, even after you stop the mouse.

Let's say we have an object moving halfway to the cursor every frame. If it starts out 100 pixels from the cursor and the cursor doesn't move, then in the second frame it will be 50 pixels away then 25, 12.5, 6.25, etc, so it looks like it's decelerating as it approaches its target. Although this movement will never actually theoretically hit zero, it will appear to. Flash can still only render the motion in terms of the screen pixels, so once the difference becomes too small, a computer monitor can't show the difference.

This is a representation of a line moving towards
its target at half distance increments

Before we begin the practical examples, let's build a simple delayed drag object that we can bring into both.

Creating a delayed drag object

We'll create a simple object that can be dragged around the screen, controlling the movement using the onClipEvent handler that came with Flash 5. We'll use the enterFrame parameter to update the location of the movie clip every frame. Be sure not to use the mouseMove trigger since the object would stop whenever the mouse stopped (Note: clip events can only take place on movie clip objects, so make sure the drag movie clip is selected before you add the following code). The source for this example is delayedDrag.fla on the CD.

1. Open a new document in Flash and change the frame rate to something like 20 (the faster the frame rate, the smoother the effect will appear.) Draw any shape you want on the stage, make it into a movie clip and give it an instance name drag.

2. Still in the main scene, select the `drag` movie clip object, and we'll add the following `onClipEvent` action in its Object Actions panel:

```
onClipEvent (enterFrame) {
}
```

We'll set the `_x` and `_y` properties of the movie clip inside the clip event, first defining some variables to simplify the script later on. These variables will find the x and y positions of the mouse coordinates, so we can use the `_xmouse` and `_ymouse` properties.

The mouse coordinate properties work like any other movie clip property; they report their values based on the movie clip specified. In the case of movie clips, the pivot point of the movie clip is used for the (0,0) point, and the scale and rotation of the movie clip is taken into consideration when reporting the value. On the main timeline, the registration point is considered the upper left-hand corner (also 0,0).

Let's say that you have a movie clip whose registration point is at (0,0) for the main stage. The mouse position reported by the root of this movie clip would be the same. If we rotated the movie clip 180 degrees and scaled it down to 50 percent, the movie clip would report back a value twice as large as the root, but it would also be negative. This is because when you move the mouse to the right on the root, according to the orientation of the movie clip, you've just moved left.

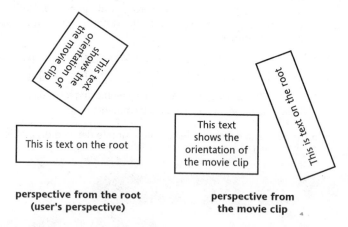

perspective from the root   **perspective from**
(user's perspective)   **the movie clip**

3. Since we're planning to move the `drag` movie clip on the main stage, we need to get the mouse coordinates of the `_root`. Set the two target variables like this:

```
onClipEvent (enterFrame) {
     //The x position of the mouse
     xTarget = _root._xmouse;
     //The y position of the mouse
     yTarget = _root._ymouse;
}
```

4. We'll also set a `fraction` variable that will determine how much of the difference to the target the object should move. The value of this variable can either be expressed as a traditional fraction (1/10) or as a decimal value (.1)

```
onClipEvent (enterFrame) {
          xTarget = _root._xmouse;
          yTarget = _root._ymouse;
     //This value will determine what fraction of the gap to
     //cover every time the script is called
     fraction = .1;
}
```

To make the drag movie move only part way to the mouse, we need to first find out how far the movie clip is away from its target, the mouse, and multiply that amount by whatever fraction of the distance it should cover, in our case the `fraction` variable with the value .1.

5. To do this, we will take the `Target` variables and subtract the current `drag` movie clip position from it, then multiply that value by the `fraction` variable. That equation gives us the amount the clip needs to move, so all we need to do is add it on to the current position of the `drag` movie clip. The code for each axis must be separated like in the following code:

```
onClipEvent (enterFrame) {
          xTarget = _root._xmouse;
          yTarget = _root._ymouse;
          fraction = .1;
     //these two lines determine the gap between the current
     //location of drag and the target.  fraction is then used
     // to determine how much of the gap to cover.
     _y += (yTarget-_y)*fraction;
     _x += (xTarget-_x)*fraction;
}
```

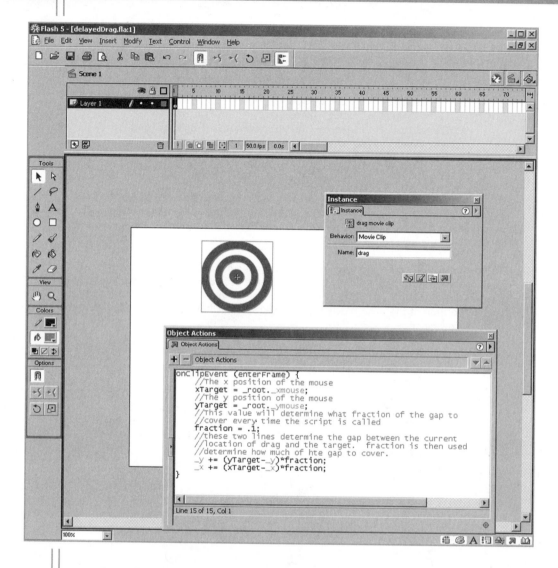

6. If you test this, you should now have a movie clip that moves 1/5 of the distance to the mouse every frame. To speed this process up, or slow it down, change the value of the fraction variable.

With a few modifications, you can turn this simple delayed drag effect into a full-blown mouse trailer. Mouse trailers are a series of movie clips following each other. They're fun to play with, but a lot of people think they're pretty pointless because they add little to the overall project. While I normally agree with that assessment, there are some sites around where mouse trailers have been an integral and interesting part of the user experience. I'd suggest using them sparingly, but don't be afraid to experiment with them in new and creative ways.

Mouse trailer

A mouse trailer is really just the delayed drag prototype, where each successive trail targets the coordinates of the movie clip before it. The purpose of this example is to show you how to create a mouse trail dynamically, by duplicating the first member of the trail using a `for` loop and the `duplicateMovieClip` command. You'll see how this avoids having to set up each individual element. The source for this example is `mouse trailer.fla` on the CD. After that, I'll outline a few techniques you can try to make the effect more exciting.

Creating a mouse trail

1. Let's start by making the script that will replicate the drag movie clip. To start, place a shape on the stage, and make it into a movie clip with the instance name `drag0`. We'll name the duplicate movie clips `drag1`, `drag2` etc. as we make them, so that they all conform to the same naming convention.

2. In frame 1 of the main timeline, set a variable called `copies` to whatever number you want; I've set mine to ten. This will determine how many items will be trailed. Keep in mind though, the more you add, the more processing power it will take to render all of their positions:

```
// total number of mouse trail items
copies = 10;
```

3. Next, underneath the `copies` variable, we'll script the `for` loop that duplicates `drag0` based on the variable we just set. Since we already have `drag0`, the index should start at 1, and the condition inside the loop should be set so that the index variable is less than the value of copies. So, the loop will stop when we have nine copies, numbered 1 to 9 inclusive, and ten movie clip instances in all (accounting for `drag0`). After each loop, the index variable should be incremented by one. We'll begin by declaring an index variable, `i`, inside the `for` loop that will keep track of the number of times the loop runs, so that we can stop it when we've made all nine copies:

```
copies = 10;
// loop creating mouse trail items
for (var i = 1; i<copies; i++) {
}
```

4. Inside the loop, we need to add a `duplicateMovieClip` command that copies `drag0` and names the new copy `dragX` (X being whatever the value of the index is.) We'll also set the depth of the new movie clip to the same number as its name, using the index variable:

```
copies = 10;
for (var i = 1; i<copies; i++) {
    // Duplicates the original item
    duplicateMovieClip ("drag0", "drag"+i, i);
}
```

5. It's going to be useful later on in the code, when each drag movie clip targets the movie clip with the next lowest number, to be able to identify which movie clip is which, without resorting to parsing the identifying number back out of the _name property each time we need it. So we'll add a line that sets a variable called `num` inside the new movie clip equal to this identifying number.

To identify the new movie clip as where you want to set the variable, you'll have to concatenate the string `drag` with the value of the current index variable (much like we did when naming the movie clip), and then `eval` it so it's an object. Just like setting a variable inside any other object, we just need to write `.num` after the object. This variable should also be set to the value of the index:

```
copies = 10;
for (var i = 1; i<copies; i++) {
    duplicateMovieClip ("drag0", "drag"+i, i);
    // Sets a variable in the MC for easy access to its own
number
    // so that it can determine what the previous movie clip is
    // without checking a substring of the _name property.
    eval("drag"+i).num = i;
}
```

6. If you were to test the system now, it would work correctly, but you won't be able to see your new duplicated objects. This is because they've been placed on top of each other, and are all following the same object at the same speed. To correct this, we need to take another look at the clip event for `drag0`. Right now, it's always setting the `yTarget` and `xTarget` to the mouse coordinates. We still need that to happen for `drag0`. The rest of the trailers, however, should target the coordinates of the preceding drag movie. When you select `drag0`, the following code should already be there:

```
onClipEvent (enterFrame) {
            xTarget = _root._xmouse;
            yTarget = _root._ymouse;
            fraction = .1;
    _y += (yTarget-_y)*fraction;
    _x += (xTarget-_x)*fraction;
}
```

7. Since we're going to have a lot of movie clips trailing (each moving a fraction of the way to the next, which is only moving a fraction of the way to its next target....) the effect will have the appearance of slowing down unless you increase the fraction variable. So let's bump it up to .2.

8. Now, to start making the movie clips follow each other instead of the mouse, go into the actions frame of the onClipEvent and put the target variables (but not the fraction variable) inside an if statement.

```
onClipEvent (enterFrame) {
    if () {
                        xTarget = _root._xmouse;
                        yTarget = _root._ymouse;
    }
            fraction = .2;
    _y += (yTarget-_y)*fraction;
    _x += (xTarget-_x)*fraction;
}
```

9. The if statement will check whether or not num has been defined using the logical NOT operator (!). You've seen it used already as part of the inequality operator, !=. Logical NOT is a way of doing the opposite of what the code would do, such as equal being turned into inequality. In if statements, true or 1 will cause the condition to be fulfilled and false will 0 prevent that. By putting a NOT in front of a value in an if statement, it reverses it from true to false or vice versa. In our case, the condition will be !num. If a variable has any value, it's considered true, and if equal to 0 or undefined it's considered false. By putting the NOT operator in front of it, we are in essence saying: if num is undefined, do the following. Since num has been set in all of the instances except drag0 this is an easy way to tell it apart. The beginning of the conditional statement should be:

```
onClipEvent (enterFrame) {
    if (!num) {
        xTarget = _root._xmouse;
        yTarget = _root._ymouse;
    }
    fraction = .2;
    _y += (yTarget-_y)*fraction;
    _x += (xTarget-_x)*fraction;
}
```

10. After the if statement, we need to add an else that will set the x and y properties for the rest of the trailing movie clips. Unlike the first one that needs to target the mouse, the target variables need to find out where the movie clip with the next number lower is. For instance, in drag5, this script needs to determine the x and y positions in drag4. To get the previous number, we just need to take the value of num, and subtract 1 from it. After that, concatenate that number with drag, and you have the new target. To make the concatenated name an object, just remember to

construct the name in an `eval` command. When it's complete, the whole clip event should look like the code below.

```
onClipEvent (enterFrame) {
    if (!num) {
        xTarget = _root._xmouse;
        yTarget = _root._ymouse;
    } else {
        // The x position of the previous MC
        xTarget = eval("_root.drag"+(num-1))._x;
        // The y position of the previous MC
        yTarget = eval("_root.drag"+(num-1))._y;
    }
    fraction = .2;
    _y += (yTarget-_y)*fraction;
    _x += (xTarget-_x)*fraction;
}
```

Test your movie now, and you will see all the trailing duplicate objects:

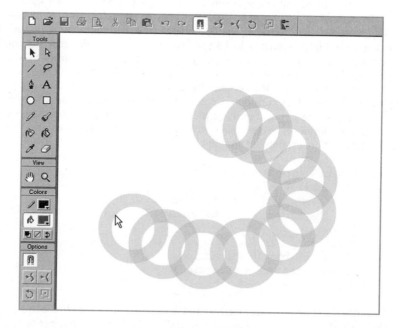

Now that you have the basic mouse trailer established, you might want to try some of the following modifications to make the effect more interesting.

Finishing touches: embellishing your mouse trailer

Modifying the properties of the duplicate clips

To make each trail seem a bit different, you might want to try changing some of the properties of the duplicated movie clips as they are produced. For instance, to have each element's alpha fall off a bit more towards zero, you could add a statement inside the `for` loop in frame 1 of the main timeline that sets the alpha of the new movie clip to `100-(100*i/copies)`. The formula inside the parentheses makes a percentage by multiplying 100 against the ratio of the current index value divided by copies (the limit for the index variable). Since the movie clips with the lowest numbers are the ones that should have the highest alpha settings, we then need to subtract that value from 100. The code should be placed like the following:

```
copies = 10;
for (var i = 1; i<copies; i++) {
    duplicateMovieClip ("drag0", "drag"+i, i);
    eval("drag"+i).num = i;
    eval("drag"+i)._alpha = 100-(100*i/copies);
}
```

Another common change is to draw the shape in the `drag` movie clip off the pivot, and then rotate each progressive movie clip. In this case it would be 360 divided by the value of `copies` multiplied by the index variable. Any of the editable properties can be changed to make an effect like this. The code would go in the exact same place as the alpha settings, and look like this:

```
eval("drag"+i)._rotation = 360/copies*i;
```

Different elements in different frames

Up to this point we've just used the same shape for all the parts of the trail, but you can also try having each segment as a piece of a larger picture or effect. This will give the appearance of a whole object when the cursor is still and it will fly apart when the cursor is moved. To do this, place each part of the picture in a different frame and send the movie clip to the appropriate frame based on the index variable in the for loop. To see a simple version of this, take a look at the mouse trailer example (`mouse trailer options.fla`) on the CD.

Animating the objects

Animating a moving object for the mouse trailer can give the effect of a complex secondary motion when the cursor is moved. Play around with several different motions for different effects, and try using scripting inside the object. For instance, you could use the `atan2()` method of the Math object to cause each element to point at the one before it, and finally to point at the cursor. Arctangent (`atan2`) takes a y coordinate and an x coordinate, and reports back the angle that something at (0,0) would need to be at to point at that (x,y) coordinate. Unfortunately, all trigonometry deals with angles in radians, not degrees, so you'd also need to write a line of code to convert radians to degrees (a full circle is 360 expressed in degrees, and 2π expressed in radians). This example is included on the CD in `mouse trailer trig.fla`.

```
onClipEvent (enterFrame) {
    if (!num) {
        xTarget = _root._xmouse;
        yTarget = _root._ymouse;
    } else {
        xTarget = eval("_root.drag"+(num-1))._x;
        yTarget = eval("_root.drag"+(num-1))._y;
    }
    //atan2 takes a y value and an x value, and reports back
    //the angle it would take something at (0,0) to point at it.
    atanVal = Math.atan2((yTarget-_y), (xTarget-_x));
    //The angle is in radians instead of degrees, so this
    //equation will convert it to degrees
    this._rotation = (atanVal*360)/(2*Math.PI);
    fraction = .2;
    _y += (yTarget-_y)*fraction;
    _x += (xTarget-_x)*fraction;
}
```

Align to another object

Just as each of the duplicated movie clips targets the preceding movie clip to find its own target, there is nothing to say that the first target has to be the cursor. If you want the effect of a mouse trail, but want the system to control where it moves, animate a movie clip moving along a motion guide, and make that the first target.

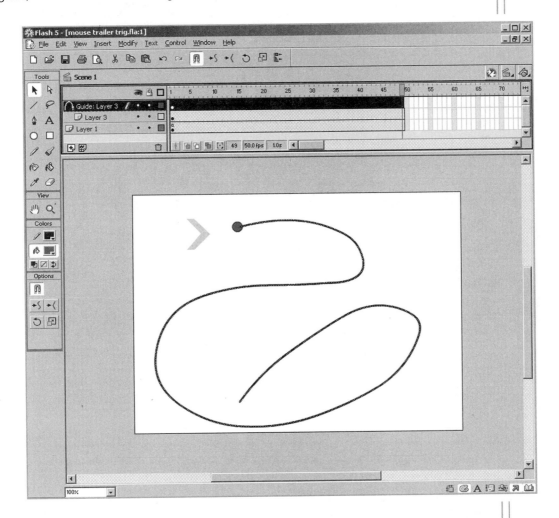

Practical applications for delayed dragging

> *A delayed drag can have the object move in a controlled way, in keeping with the reality of a game. Flash's built-in drag action can cause a visible jump if the user moves their cursor faster than Flash can render it. You can also usefully employ a delayed drag object for, say, a user's avatar to prevent such visible jumps.*

Using Flash's drag operation can cause objects to jump if the mouse moves too fast

Using a delayed drag forces the object to move shorter distances allowing it to interact with objects in its path

 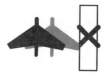

Creating smooth airplane controls

In this example, we'll make a plane for an aerial view scrolling game and give it the appearance of banking for the turns as it moves to reach its target position.

You can either create your own animation of a plane banking, which we'll walk through next, or use the one I've created in this example's source file. To use the one I have already created, drag a copy of the airplane shape movie clip from the library in airplane.fla onto the stage in your own movie.

To create a simple plane yourself, you just need to create two parts: a symbol containing the wings and body, and a symbol of a tail fin. You should make a tween going from the extreme left turn, to a set of keyframes in the middle representing the top down view of the plane, and then continuing on to the extreme right turn. If you want something that looks more realistic and you have access to one of the 3D to vector tools (like Vecta3D), you might try modeling a simple plane, then animating it to make the left turn to right turn movie clip.

If you decide to use the animation from the CD, you may still want to browse this next section, just to familiarize yourself with why the animation is set up in this particular way.

Creating the airplane shape

1. Start by opening a new file in Flash. For the first component, let's draw the wing and body of the plane on the main timeline. Since the wing is a symmetric shape, I find it easier to draw half of it, then just make a copy for the other half. Because it's just a simple drawing of a plane, I've just made mine of straight lines. Though you can do it any way you feel comfortable, I'll quickly cover the way I find easiest to do this sort of drawing.

2. To begin the wing shape, draw a rectangle on the stage like this.

3. To refine the shape, use the selection arrow and grab onto a corner of the rectangle. You can then deform the shape into a wing shape:

4. Once you have a wing shape that you're happy with, select it, copy it, and paste it onto the stage. You'll then want to use the Flip Horizontal command in the Modify>Transform menu. Now drag the new shape so that it matches up with your first wing:

5. With a pretty good wing in place, we just need to add a line to act as the airplane body. Do this by drawing a vertical line next to the wing, and then moving it to the center of the wing shape. To get a thick enough body for the airplane, you may need to increase the weight of your line via the Stroke panel. It's probably best to make the body of the plane away from the wings, because if you draw it directly in place and then try to adjust it, you'll find that the line has been segmented.

6. Now do any tweaks to the graphic that you want such as scaling the shape, or trimming down the line.

Creating the tween

7. Once you are happy with the airplane on your stage, make it a movie clip called main airplane movie. Since the point of this airplane is to have a range of animations that make it look like it's turning, let's go into the movie clip and do the first part of the tweening.

8. Inside the movie clip, you should now just have one frame with the same raw airplane shapes from before. Rename Layer 1 as plane. To make some room for the animation, add a keyframe in frame 30. In frame 30, select the airplane movie clip and use the Scale tool to squash it horizontally a little bit to make it look like it's turning. Enhance the effect by rotating the squashed shape a few degrees clockwise. For my airplane, I changed the x scale to 66 percent and the rotation to 5.5 degrees:

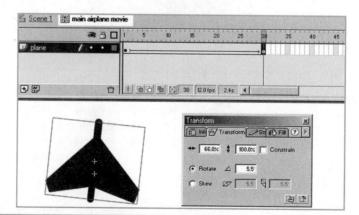

9. Once you're done, go back to frame 1 and create a motion tween.

> *Motion tweening takes the contents of two keyframes and, provided they each contain the same symbol, will transition the symbol from one position, or property to the position or property in the second keyframe. Keep in mind though that in a single layer only one object can be tweened at any one time, so make sure you don't have anything else other than the symbol in the two keyframes.*

If you shuttle through the frames you should now have a smooth tween of the airplane turning to the right. Since we're also going to need to make the plane turn left, let's make some room for that animation.

10. Instead of adding more frames, let's grab frame 1 in the timeline and move it to frame 15. This should leave a blank keyframe in frame 1 and the animation should now go from frame 15 to frame 30.

11. We need the airplane to do just the reverse of the right turn, so select frame 30 in the timeline, right-click on it and select Copy Frames. Back in frame 1, select the frame in the timeline, right-click and select Paste Frames. This will put the airplane in frame 1 in the right turn position.

12. To make the left turn position, simply go into the Transform panel and change the rotation value to −5.5 (or whatever rotation you chose).

13. Now make frame 1 motion tween to frame 15 just like you did before.

You should now have the full range of motion of the airplane. When an airplane turns though, there is one other characteristic that needs to change – its tail fin. As you turn, you should be able to see more of its profile.

Don't forget the tail fin!

14. To make the tail fin, we'll first create a new layer called tail. Insert a keyframe in frame 15 of the new layer, draw in a short straight line coming out of the back of the plane and make it into a movie clip symbol called tail fin:

Now we just need to go through the process for adjusting the tail in frame 30 and reversing it for frame 1.

15. Make a keyframe in frame 30 and adjust the tail to the position and rotation you want. I turned mine 45 degrees, then moved it so that the joint of the tail and the body aligned correctly:

16. In frame 15, set the motion tween. Then select frame 30, copy the frame and paste it into frame 1. From here, just change the sign on the rotation and move as needed. Be sure not to do a flip horizontal here, as it will mess up the tween.

17. Finally, set up the tween from frame 1 to frame 15, and then you're all set:

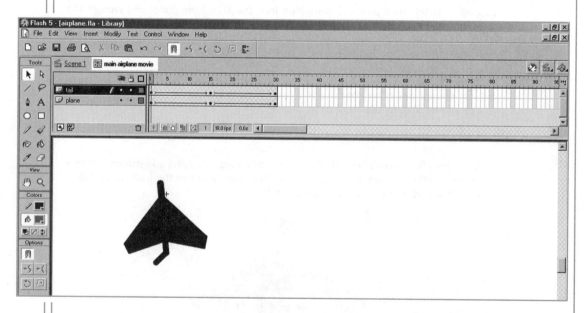

Scripting the controls

Once you have the airplane turn animation ready, we then need to script the side-to-side control of the airplane as well as its turns. This movement is going to be very similar to the delayed drag object described earlier in this section with one exception. While it will still move a fraction of the distance between itself and the cursor, if that value is higher than a certain amount, the movement amount will be limited. This in essence imposes a speed limit on the object. The speed limit can be controlled by a variable, thereby allowing you to change the difficulty of a game.

For the plane example, we are just going to be controlling the x position of the plane. As in many games, the main character's avatar is locked in place vertically, while the rest of the game scrolls towards it.

The commands for controlling the airplane are going to be very similar to the ones for the delayed drag script.

1. In the main scene, select the main airplane movie clip object, and add an `onClipEvent (enterFrame)` object action to hold all of the movement scripts:

```
onClipEvent (enterFrame) {
}
```

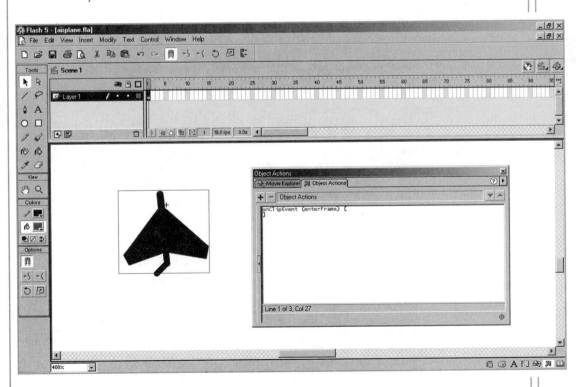

2. Let's set some of the variables inside the onClipEvent. Like we did in the previous examples, we'll use an xTarget, and a fraction variable. For this example, we won't need a yTarget variable since the y position never changes.

```
onClipEvent (enterFrame) {
    // the x position of the mouse
    xTarget = _root._xmouse;
    // the ratio of how much of the gap to close
    // between current and target loactions
    fraction = .1;
}
```

3. We'll also need a speedLimit variable, which we'll set equal to 20 for now. speedLimit, as its name implies, will set the maximum distance the airplane can move per frame (expressed in pixels). We'll use this later in the script to check the movements of the airplane so that it can't jump too far at one time:

```
onClipEvent (enterFrame) {
    xTarget = _root._xmouse;
    fraction = .1;
    // maximum number of pixels that can be moved in one hop
    speedLimit = 20;
}
```

4. The last variable is xspeed. We'll use xspeed to find the difference between the airplane's current position and its target position, and then multiply that by the fraction variable. You may recognize this line from the previous example as the one used to move the dragged object. Since we have one more step to go through before moving the airplane, we need it as a variable:

```
onClipEvent (enterFrame) {
    xTarget = _root._xmouse;
    fraction = .1;
    speedLimit = 20;
    // determines the gap, which is speed (how many pixels do
    // you have to move to get to where you need to be in this
    // slice of time
    xspeed = (xTarget-_x)*fraction;
}
```

5. Now that we have the variables set up, we need to check the value of xspeed to make sure it's not too high. Add an if statement that checks to see whether xspeed is greater than speedLimit, and if so sets xspeed equal to the speedLimit:

```
onClipEvent (enterFrame) {
xTarget = _root._xmouse;
fraction = .1;
speedLimit = 20;
xspeed = (xTarget-_x)*fraction;
```

```
      // checking to see if the speed is outside the limits.
      // when the plane is moving to the left, speed is negative.
      // if outside, set speed to nearest limit.
      if (xspeed>=speedLimit) {
            xspeed = speedLimit;
      }
}
```

6. Then use an `else if` statement to make sure `xspeed` is not less than negative `xspeed`. If it is, then set `xspeed` equal to negative `speedLimit`. Because of a limitation in just a few steps, it's going to be best if the speed is never actually equal to negative `speedLimit`. So, let's add a small amount such as `.01` onto the corrected value:

```
onClipEvent (enterFrame) {
      xTarget = _root._xmouse;
      fraction = .1;
      speedLimit = 20;
      xspeed = (xTarget-_x)*fraction;
      if (xspeed>=speedLimit) {
            xspeed = speedLimit;
      } else if (xspeed<=-speedLimit) {
            xspeed = -speedLimit + .01;
      }
}
```

7. Now that we've adjusted `xspeed` to fall within the limits, we need to add it on to the current `_x` position. If you test at this point, the plane should use the correct delay, however the plane will just loop through its animation:

```
onClipEvent (enterFrame) {
      xTarget = _root._xmouse;
      fraction = .1;
      speedLimit = 20;
      xspeed = (xTarget-_x)*fraction;
      if (xspeed>=speedLimit) {
            xspeed = speedLimit;
      } else if (xspeed<=-speedLimit) {
            xspeed = -speedLimit + .01;
      }
      // move according to adjusted speed
      _x += xspeed;
}
```

8. Next, we need to control the animation of the plane turning by sending the current movie clip to a frame number based on the `xspeed` variable in relation to the speed limit extremes. The `xspeed` and `speedLimit` have to be corrected to all positive numbers since we can't send the plane animation to a negative number. That way, if we're at the negative `speedLimit`, the movie will go to frame 1, and if at `speedLimit`, the movie will go to the last frame, which we can find by using the `_totalframes` property. Any other value for `xspeed` will send the animation to the

appropriate frame in the middle. Let's start by making the ratio of where xspeed is along the spectrum from negative speedLimit to positive speedLimit. To do this, we need to keep in mind that the spectrum is twice the size of the speedLimit variable, to account for negative to zero and zero to positive. Also, keep in mind that xspeed starts from zero, which is now the middle. The value must be corrected by adding the value of speedLimit on to it. Negative xspeed values then will reduce it back towards 0 and positive xspeed values will move it towards 1.

```
onClipEvent (enterFrame) {
    xTarget = _root._xmouse;
    fraction = .1;
    speedLimit = 20;
    xspeed = (xTarget-_x)*fraction;
    if (xspeed>=speedLimit) {
        xspeed = speedLimit;
    } else if (xspeed<=-speedLimit) {
        xspeed = -speedLimit + .01;
    }
    _x += xspeed;
    // this presents the whole spectrum of speeds from -speedLimit
    // to +speedLimit as a range of positive values. It then finds
    // where xspeed is along this scale, adjusting it as well for
    // the new range.
    speedLimitRatio = (xspeed+speedLimit)/(2*speedLimit);
}
```

9. With the ratio in place now, we need to do something with it. We need to tell this movie clip to go to and stop at the percentage of _totalframes. To do this, we'll multiply the two values, so we need to make sure we don't end up with a decimal value. There are several ways of converting numbers to integers, depending on which way they should round, but in this case we're going to want to round up, no matter how small the amount over the whole number is. To do this, we use a method of the Math object, ceil. We want to round up the numbers so that if the value is less than 1, the movie will always at least be sent to frame 1. Since sending xspeed to negative speedLimit would have resulted in trying to go to frame 0, which doesn't exist, we had to make it so the system could never equal negative speedLimit.

```
onClipEvent (enterFrame) {
    xTarget = _root._xmouse;
    fraction = .1;
    speedLimit = 20;
    xspeed = (xTarget-_x)*fraction;
    if (xspeed>=speedLimit) {
        xspeed = speedLimit;
    } else if (xspeed<=-speedLimit) {
        xspeed = -speedLimit + .01;
    }
    _x += xspeed;
    speedLimitRatio = (xspeed+speedLimit)/(2*speedLimit);
```

```
// this sends the plane animation inside this movieclip to the
// appropriate frame, making sure that the value is an integer.

this.gotoAndStop(Math.ceil(this._totalframes*SpeedLimitRatio));
}
```

So altogether, your code looks like this:

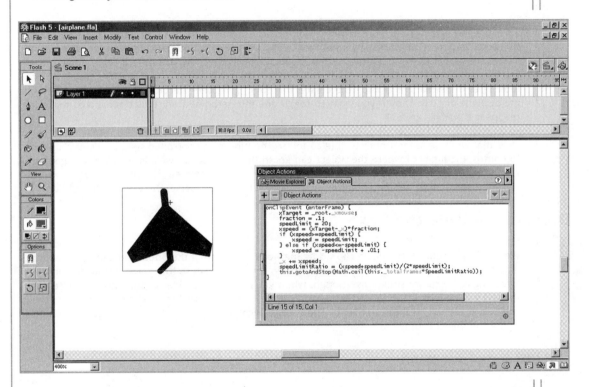

Now test your movie!

To make this effect a bit more realistic, you could use `Mouse.hide()` in frame 1 of the main timeline. The `Mouse` object has two methods: `hide` and `show`. As you might imagine, these control the visible aspect of the operating system's cursor. No matter how you have it set though, once the cursor leaves the area of the Flash movie, the cursor will become visible. Now, instead of it looking as if the plane is chasing the cursor, the effect gives the illusion that you are controlling the airplane directly. Should you want to toggle the mouse on and off, the command to make it reappear is `Mouse.show()`.

Now that we have several objects able to follow the mouse at controlled speeds, it's also useful to control the limits of where the object can go. In the next section we'll look at ways of getting around Flash's limitation of only defining a rectangular dragging area. The next section is where we'll get into a bit of geometry, but if you're completely math averse, there is another option!

Dragging outside the box

We briefly introduced the movie clip's drag methods earlier on in the book. You can use them to drag any movie clip around the stage, and you can limit this effect so that you can only drag inside a rectangle. There are situations, though, when you'd like to be able to drag inside a different shape. Here we'll look at two strategies for creating this effect. The first uses a movie clip and the collision detection method, `hitTest`. The second technique uses mathematic functions to limit where the object is dragged.

hitTest-based dragging

The first example, using the movie clip's `hitTest` method, is best for projects where the shape that you want to confine the drag inside is very complex or irregular. It's also good for people who don't want to deal with mathematic equations, which is what we'll be doing in the next example.

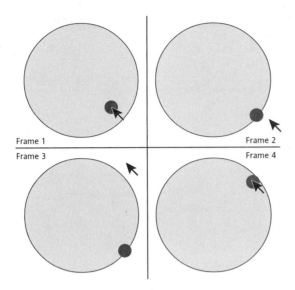

Frame 1

Frame 2

Frame 3

Frame 4

The button only follows the cursor when it is inside the circle

In this project we're going to make a movie clip that the user can drag within a circle when they click on it (Frame 1, above). When the cursor leaves the circle, the button will stop following it (Frames 2 and 3), but as long as the mouse is still down when the cursor reenters the circle, the button will snap back to the mouse (Frame 4).

Dragging a movie clip inside an irregular shape

The general premise of this example is to use basic collision detection to determine when to move your 'dragged' object. While pressing the object, it will keep up with the mouse position as long as the mouse collides with a background movie clip, which acts as the draggable area. If you drag out of the area, the object will follow the cursor to the boundary and stop, only to snap back to the mouse if you re-enter the area without having release the mouse button. The source for this example, nonrectdrag.fla, can be found on the CD.

1. To begin, draw a circle on the stage, make sure it is filled with a color, and convert it into a movie clip called circle. So that we can target it with the hitTest script later, let's give the circle the instance name circle too. Back on the main stage, create a small circular button named dot, encase it in a movie clip named dot MC, and give it the instance name dot. We need to have the button in the movie clip so that we can use the functionality of button, while also being able to access properties (like and x and y positions of the object.) Move the dot movie clip so that it's in the center of the circle.

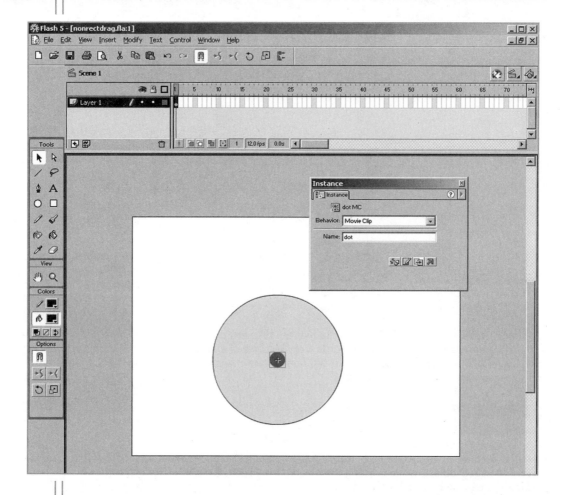

Let's go ahead and add the necessary scripting on the button inside the movie clip, dot.

2.   Pull up the Actions panel and select the button.

In an on(press) action, we want to start our drag operation. Since we can't use Flash's drag operations to drag only within a circle, and we need the script to update the position of this movie clip every time the mouse moves, we'll need to set up a script that constantly updates the position when the button is pressed. Does this remind you of the slider example in Chapter 3, where we needed to make doSlide() perform when the mouse was pressed on the handle? Exactly as in that example, we'll need to add a dummy movie clip in frame 2 that will run the location updating, and just have the button move us between frame 1 and frame 2, effectively turning the script on and off.

3.   So, in an on(press) action on the button, add a gotoAndStop action telling the current timeline to go to frame 2:

```
on (press) {
        gotoAndStop (2);
    }
```

The user might let go of the button when they're still inside the circle, or when they are outside, in which case the cursor is no longer on the button. Because of this, we need to use both the release and the releaseOutside event handlers. When this triggers, the script needs to reset the movie clip to its original state using gotoAndStop(1). Since the loop, which we'll make next, will exist only in frame 2, it will turn the drag off. Your button's ActionScript should look like this:

```
on (press) {
        gotoAndStop (2);
}
    on (release, releaseOutside) {
            gotoAndStop (1);
    }
```

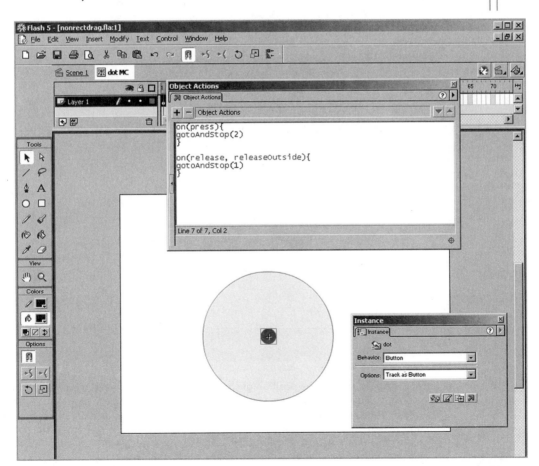

4. Since the button will be sending us to frame 2, we need to make a place for the script. Add a frame to the dot movie clip timeline. The button is now in both frames, which we need so that the button can still register the release. Since we only need to add the script in frame 2, add another layer, and create a blank keyframe in frame 2. This is where we'll house the script, so you might want to call the layer scripts. Put a stop action in frame 1 of this new layer so that the movie clip doesn't continuously loop once we render the movie.

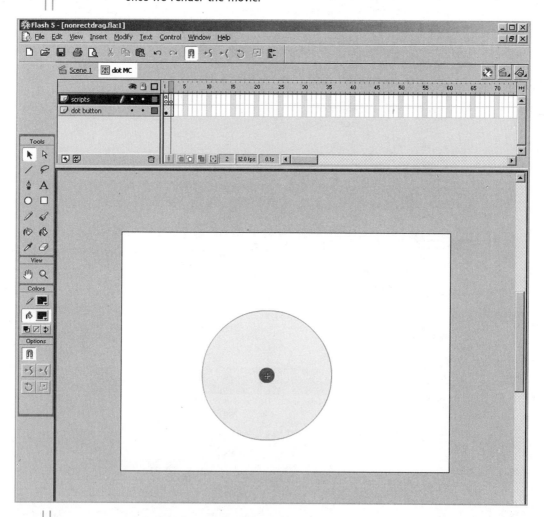

5. The script to update the position of the movie clip should be executed every time the mouse is moved. The only way to achieve this is to use a movie clip's onClipEvent, and in order to use this, we need to create a dummy movie clip as we did in the slider and persistent effect buttons in Chapter 3. Create any shape in frame 2 of the new layer, and make it into a movie clip called dummy MC. Now go inside your new symbol, delete the shape and return to the dot timeline.

6.   Bring up the Actions panel and select the dummy movie clip. Add an onClipEvent, using mouseMove as the trigger.

```
onClipEvent (mouseMove) {
}
```

The script we're going to use will determine if the mouse is over the guide shape (circle, out on the main timeline), and if so, move the dot movie clip to the position of the mouse. As the logic suggests, we'll need to use an if statement to determine the collision status of the mouse in relationship to the circle. Inside the if statement we'll set a condition that uses the collision detection method of the movie clip object, called hitTest. Collision detection will be covered in greater detail in the next section, but for this example we'll be using one small technique of collision detection, checking a single coordinate against the shape of a movie clip.

hitTest can be called as the method of a movie clip, and takes a specified target as a parameter, so we can pass it the circle movie clip. Either _root.circle or _parent._parent.circle, will work, because the scripting inside onClipEvents is considered to be part of the selected movie clip's timeline.

7.   So all you have to do is add hitTest to the end of your target:

```
onClipEvent (mouseMove) {
     if (_root.circle.hitTest()) {
     }
}
```

We need to put the x and y coordinates of the mouse inside the parentheses, separated by a comma, and finally add true at the end. Having true there just makes sure that it uses the shape of the target movie clip as it appears to us on the stage. As we discussed in the mouse trail example, it's very important that you get the mouse properties from the right timeline, since each timeline reports the mouse position in terms of its own pivot point.

For instance, if we took this._xmouse, as long as we're dragging the object it would report back zero since we're dragging dot at its pivot. In terms of circle, which is sitting out on the root, performing a hitTest with coordinates (0,0) would fail because (0,0) is the upper left corner of the stage, and nowhere near the circle movie clip.

8.   To feed hitTest appropriate data, since circle is on the _root, we can use _root._xmouse and _root._ymouse:

```
onClipEvent (mouseMove) {
     if (_root.circe.hitTest()) {
     }
}
```

9. Finally, we need to add some code inside the `if` statement that moves the button movie clip to the mouse. To do this, we'll set the x and y positions of the dummy movie clip's parent object (the button movie clip dot MC) equal to the mouse coordinates in the same timeline we used for the collision detection. So, altogether, the final script you need looks like this:

```
onClipEvent (mouseMove) {
    if (_root.circle.hitTest(_root._xmouse, _root._ymouse, true))
{
        _parent._x = _root._xmouse;
        _parent._y = _root._ymouse;
    }
}
```

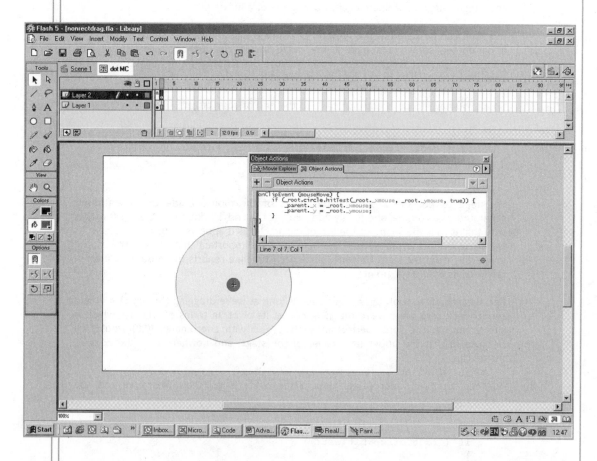

Go ahead and test here. The dot should drag with the mouse while in the circle and stop at the edge where the mouse leaves it. It's a bit clunky, but if you hate math and you're dealing with complex shapes, it will get the job done. While this technique is relatively simple, it has one large drawback. When you move the mouse outside of the circle, it stops moving completely. However, when you're using the Flash drag operations to constrain a drag to a rectangle, the dragged object still tries to stay as close as possible to the cursor even when it's outside the rectangle. The easiest way to create this effect on a non-rectangular shape is to use a mathematical equation. When the cursor is on the wrong side of the equation, instead of doing nothing, it sets the position of the shape to a position along the equation.

Equation-based dragging

Before we begin the mechanics of how to set this up in Flash, I want to do a little refresher from high school math. When I talk about equations, I'm actually talking about functions like f(x) and f(y). For the purposes of this example, a function is a graphed shape that for any horizontal position only has one vertical position or a shape that for any vertical point only has one horizontal point. Said a bit more plainly, they can't loop back on themselves. An 's' shape for instance can't be a function.

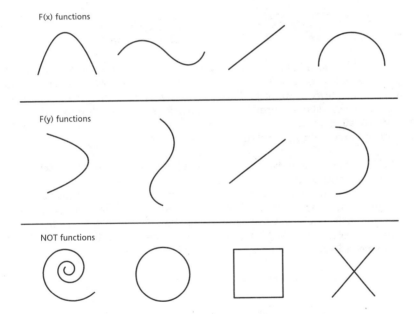

The simplest function is a line. The general equation for a line is y=mx+b, where m equals the slope of the line and b shifts the line up or down depending on the number. For example, y=1x + 0 makes a 45 degree line that passes through the (0,0) point. Y=1x+10 is also a 45 degree line, however it does not pass through (0,0), but instead goes through (0,10).

In this example, we're going to make a trapezoid, which is built out of four lines, two horizontal ones, and two diagonal ones. This will come in handy if you ever need to drag something in perspective.

Flash 5 Dynamic Content Studio

Think of this trapezoid as a square table that you are looking across.

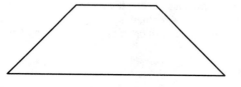 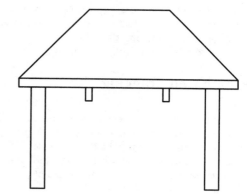

This is a trapezoid with sides at 45 degrees and negative 45 degrees. On the right is the same trapezoid visualized as a tabletop.

Dragging a movie clip mathematically

In this exercise, we'll define a boundary for up, down, left, and right for where you can drag your chosen object. The vertical boundaries for the left and right though won't be simple coordinates but an equation that allows us to make diagonal lines or curves. When the mouse is inside the defined area, the object will drag normally. When outside though, the dragged object will lock to the boundary's equation, moving along the boundary to stay as close as possible to the cursor. The source for this exercise is nonrectdragmath.fla on the CD.

1. We'll use the previous example, to save us building everything from scratch, so save a new copy of the hitTest drag exercise. In this new copy, delete the circle movie clip, then go into the button movie clip and bring up the Actions panel to edit the script on the dummy movie clip in frame 2 (since we deleted the shape in the dummy movie clip, it should now appear as a white dot). Go ahead and delete the contents of the onClipEvent. (We'll still be using if logic, but this time we'll need two statements.) You should now have:

```
onClipEvent (mouseMove) {
}
```

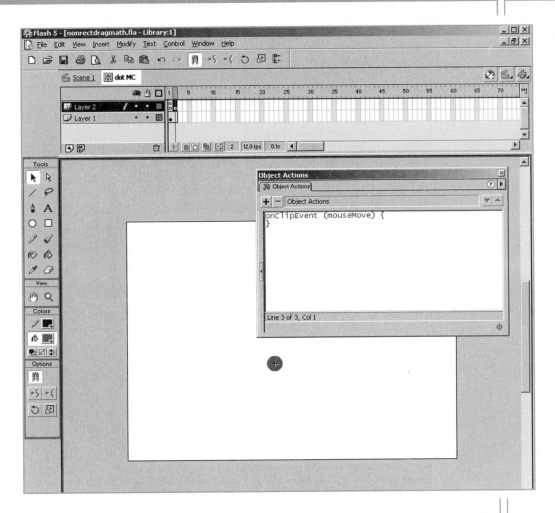

2. Let's start by making the boundaries by defining the upper drag limit. To do this we'll use an if statement to check the vertical position of the cursor and see if it's out of range. If we want to make the object stop dragging above the y coordinate 100, we'd need to call the y position of the mouse and see if it is less than 100. Checking for a number under 100 ensures that the statements inside the if statement run when the mouse is above 100, since up in Flash is towards negative infinity. Inside the if statement, when the mouse is out of bounds, we just need to set the y position of the object to the limit, 100.

```
onClipEvent (mouseMove) {
    if (_root._ymouse<100) {
        //if above the upper limit
        _parent._y = 100;
    }
}
```

3. To set the lower limit, which we'll set to 300 for now, we need to do a similar process. However, since we can know that the mouse can't simultaneously be above and below the limit, we can use an else if. That way we only need to check if it's below the lower limit if we know it's not above the upper limit.

```
onClipEvent (mouseMove) {
    if (_root._ymouse<100) {
        _parent._y = 100;
    } else if (_root._ymouse>300) {
        //if below the lower limit
        _parent._y = 300;
    }
}
```

4. If you were to test now, dot would jump from one limit to another as you moved your mouse up and down the stage. We effectively eliminated the cases where the mouse falls outside the bounds, so all that's left is inside them. To cause it to move with the mouse while in between the limits, we just need to add an else case that updates the y position of the dot movie clip to the y position of the mouse on the root.

```
onClipEvent (mouseMove) {
    if (_root._ymouse<100) {
        _parent._y = 100;
    } else if (_root._ymouse>300) {
        _parent._y = 300;
    } else {
        //otherwise drag the movie
        _parent._y = _root._ymouse;
    }
}
```

5. In a linear function, once you know either x or y, you can figure out what the other is equal to. Now that we have the y position set by the above script, we can use it to determine the x limits of the dragged object. Based on whether the x position of the mouse is greater or less than each of the limits, we can determine how to place the x position of the dot movie clip. We'll set these limits in two variables, one equal to the left x limit, xlimitl, and the other equal to the right x limit, xlimitr. The value of each variable is the equation of the left and right lines respectively, both solved for x. Since the variables will be reset each time the mouse moves, we are in essence taking a snapshot for this one particular y position, creating static left and right boundaries which we can plug into an if statement almost exactly like the one we just made.

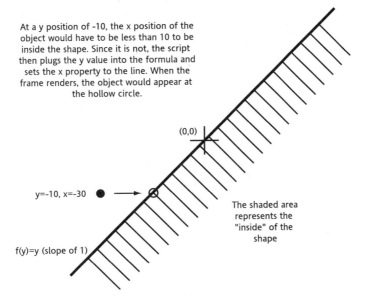

At a y position of -10, the x position of the object would have to be less than 10 to be inside the shape. Since it is not, the script then plugs the y value into the formula and sets the x property to the line. When the frame renders, the object would appear at the hollow circle.

(0,0)

y=-10, x=-30

f(y)=y (slope of 1)

The shaded area represents the "inside" of the shape

The generic linear equation, $y = mx+b$, for x instead of y, is $x = (y-b)/m$. (b is an offset amount to slide the line up or down, m is the slope of the line) To simplify the process, let's make this trapezoid out of lines with slopes of −1 and 1 (this means a line with a 45 degree slope). The diagram on the next page shows what the draggable area will be in dark gray. As you can see, lines normally go through the (0,0) point, which would place half of the draggable area off the stage. To correct that we need to adjust the 'b' or offset value to compensate, and push the shape into the center of the stage.

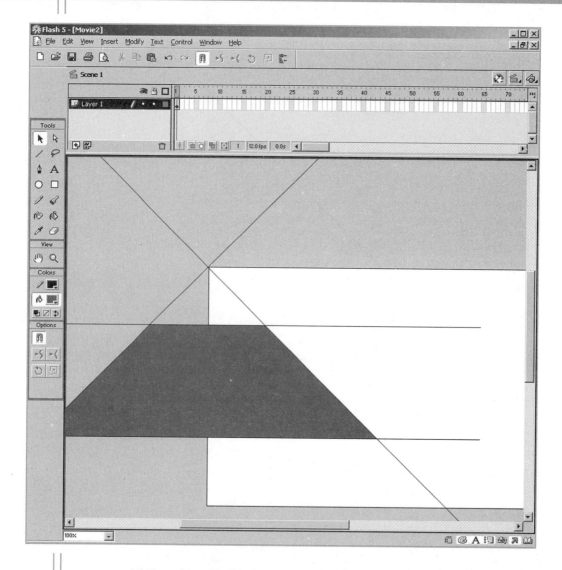

We'll need to make 'b' a large positive number for the left line so that it is moved down enough so that it will act as a barrier on the stage (giving the line the appearance of moving to the right). The 'b' for the right line needs to be a large negative number to move it up enough to allow there to be some open space (also giving the appearance of moving the line to the right).

6.   These variables should look something like the following, although you can adjust the slope and offset to change the shape of the trapezoid.

```
onClipEvent (mouseMove) {
     if (_root._ymouse<100) {
          _parent._y = 100;
     } else if (_root._ymouse>300) {
          _parent._y = 300;
     } else {
          _parent._y = _root._ymouse;
     }
     //determine the horizontal limits
     //at this particular y value
     xlimitl = 300-_parent._y;
     xlimitr = _parent._y+200;
}
```

Figuring out the equations for those two lines is the most math intensive this example will get. From here on out, the script just checks the x position of the mouse against the limits just like it did with the y position but using the variables instead of static values. The code for the whole script looks like this:

```
onClipEvent (mouseMove) {
     if (_root._ymouse<100) {
          _parent._y = 100;
     } else if (_root._ymouse>300) {
          _parent._y = 300;
     } else {
          _parent._y = _root._ymouse;
     }
     xlimitl = 300-_parent._y;
     xlimitr = _parent._y+200;
     if (_root._xmouse<xlimitl) {
          //if to the left of the left limit
          _parent._x = xlimitl;
     } else if (_root._xmouse>xlimitr) {
          //if to the right of the right limit
          _parent._x = xlimitr;
     } else {
          //otherwise drag the movie
          _parent._x = _root._xmouse;
     }
}
```

You can use any equations you want to create this effect. But don't be limited to this technique. Every shape that you might want to drag inside will have a slightly different method. For instance, if you wanted to make a draggable area in the shape of a circle, instead of looking above and below curves, you would use the x and y position of the cursor in relation to the center of the circle, then use Pythagorus's Theorem to determine the actual distance from the center point. If it's less than the radius of the circle, then allow the drag, otherwise set the position of the movie clip to a proportion of the x and y distances whose hypotenuse equals the radius of the circle.

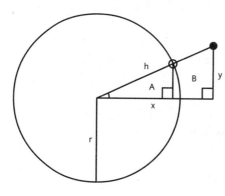

Pythagoras' Theorem in terms of the hypotenuse (h), and the x and y positions:

$$h^2 = x^2 + y^2$$

Solved for the hypotenuse:

$$h = \sqrt{x^2 + y^2}$$

If r >= h then it is inside the circle, otherwise the object needs to be aligned to the circle.

To do this, we need to turn the large triangle B into the small triangle A. The triangles have proportional sides, so multiplying x and y by the ratio (r/h) will give you the right coordinates.

Detecting collisions

Collision detection is one of the most important features for game developers. It allows the system to recognize if two objects have collided. The applications of collision detection are numerous, from movement, like we used in the last example, to firing weapons in games like asteroids. Outside games, you'll use collision detection in sites with drag-and-drop interfaces.

In Flash 5, there are several ways of doing collision detection. The most basic form is, again, the button. When you mouse over a button, it detects the mouse's position in relation to the hit area. While this only works with the mouse, it's often a quick way to create the effect.

Another form is **drop targeting**. Accessing the _droptarget of a dragged object will report back the name and path of whatever movie clip is highest at the cursor point (even if lock to cursor isn't set). Unlike the next method, you don't need to know ahead of time what to check for, _droptarget tells you what it has collided with. To use drop targeting though, a movie clip must be dragged, and must call the _droptarget property of that movie clip. Keep in mind though that the path that drop targeting responds with is written in a Flash 4 style, using slashes so that it is backwards compatible. With the many new features of Flash 5, I have a feeling that the usefulness of _droptarget will be much less than in the previous version.

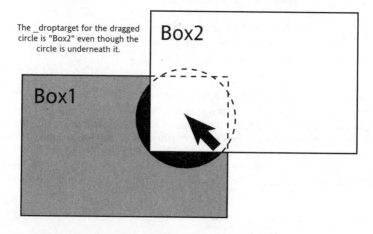

The _droptarget for the dragged circle is "Box2" even though the circle is underneath it.

The other way is using the `hitTest` method, used in the non-rectangular dragging example. `hitTest` works either between a movie clip and a point, or between two movie clips. While the first works pretty flawlessly, the second still leaves a lot to be desired. When using the movie clip/point technique, the point is compared to the exact shape of the movie clip, however when you try to compare two movie clips, it compares only the **bounding box** of each.

The bounding box

A bounding box is a box like the one you see in Flash surrounding a symbol when it's selected. Try drawing a diagonal line in Flash and making it into a symbol. Notice how much area is covered by the square compared to how little area the line takes up.

Bounding boxes for different shapes

Because of the severe limitation of movie clip to movie clip collision detection, I doubt that I'd use it except in the most limited of ways. The movie clip/point `hitTest` however is quite handy for small objects like projectiles in games. The next example in this section will cover movie clip to point collision detection. After that, I'll discuss how to script movie clip to movie clip collision detection. The difference in coding is extremely minor.

Movie clip to point collision, using arrow keys

In this example, since we've already used the mouse with the `hitTest` method, we're going to make an object that is controlled by the arrow keys. If the center of the object that is being moved around the screen collides with a shape on the stage, it will report that back through a dynamic text field. The source for this example is `collision.fla` on the CD.

1.   To begin, open a new Flash file, rename Layer 1 as shape and use the paintbrush to draw a large irregular shape. Select it and make it into a movie clip called big shape with an instance name of shape. Also, add a dynamic text field on the stage and give it the variable name hit. For the last element, add a layer called dot. In this layer, draw a very small circle on the stage and make it a button called dot. Select the button and make it a movie clip called dot MC with an instance name dot.

Now that we have all of the pieces created, let's think through how the example is going to work. As you press the arrow keys, the dot will move in the specified direction. Once it has moved it needs to see if it's colliding with the shape. Either way, it needs to report back something to the hit text field. Since this check has to happen every time the dot is moved in any direction, this is a good opportunity to make a function that each of the button actions can call. For the sake of simplicity, let's add this function in the root of the movie; we'll do this by adding it as a frame action to frame 1.

2. We'll define the function in frame 1 of the main timeline. Let's give the function the name myDetect and not assign it any arguments since checking to see if dot has collided with shape doesn't require any variable data.

```
function myDetect () {
}
```

Inside the function, we need to set up an if statement to check if the center point of dot is touching the shape on the stage. Much like we did in the hitTest drag example, we need to first specify the name of the movie clip we want to test against, which is _root.shape, then attach a hitTest method that checks the x and y coordinates of the dot movie clip.

There is a third parameter of hitTest that we only briefly touched upon in the previous section. After the x and y coordinates, you can either type true or false, which flags whether to check the actual shape or only the bounding box. If it's left unspecified, it assumes that you want to check the bounding box (false). As we go through this example, feel free to change the value of this flag to see the difference in the area covered by the bounding box versus a shape.

3. Let's add this to our code:

```
function myDetect () {
    if (shape.hitTest(dot._x, dot._y, true)) {
    }
}
```

4. Inside the if statement, set the value of the variable hit to the string "collision". Then add an else to set the variable hit back to the string "no collision" when they are no longer colliding:

```
function myDetect () {
    if (shape.hitTest(dot._x, dot._y, true)) {
        hit = "collision";
    } else {
        hit = "no collision";
    }
}
```

That's all there is for the function. Before we leave this frame though, let's set a variable that will determine how far the dot moves every time you use one of the buttons.

5. Set a variable named `travel` equal to 5 for right now. Make sure you add this line outside the function. Frame 1's script should look like this:

```
function myDetect () {
    if (shape.hitTest(dot._x, dot._y, true)) {
        hit = "collision";
    } else {
        hit = "no collision";
    }
}
travel=5
```

All that's left to program is the button inside dot.

6. Go into the dot movie clip, bring up the Actions panel and select the button. We're going to need four on statements, one for each of the arrow keys. The trigger for each is keypress, and then <Up>, <Down>, <Right>, or <Left>. Inside these on statements we need to move dot, and then call the myDetect function.

   If you're using Normal mode for editing your ActionScript, you'll need to use the eval command from the actions menu for this next part. The eval command allows you to write a line of advanced code without switching modes (the eval in the Normal mode action is different from the eval command that you would use to evaluate and a variable or object).

7. To move the dot movie clip, we need to move the object to its current position plus or minus the value of travel, depending on the direction of movement. To do this, use the += and -= operators to add or subtract the value on the right from the variable's value. After that, the myDetect() function needs to be called to check for the collision. Since the function isn't in this timeline, but on the root, the expression should look like this: _root.myDetect(). When you're all done, the whole button code should look like this:

```
on (keyPress "<Up>") {
 _y -= _root.travel;
 _root.myDetect();
}
on (keyPress "<Down>") {
 _y += _root.travel;
 _root.myDetect();
}
on (keyPress "<Left>") {
 _x -= _root.travel;
 _root.myDetect();
}
on (keyPress "<Right>") {
```

continues overleaf

```
    _x += _root.travel;
    _root.myDetect();
}
```

When you test it, you should be able to move the dot around, and when the center of the dot is over the shape, the text field should change its message. If you try changing the `hitTest` flag to `false` inside `myDetect`, you should then notice the effect of the bounding area. We'll be using movie clip to point collision detection in the game chapter, when we're working with projectiles.

Movie clip to movie clip collision

While I don't find this part nearly as useful as the last, to be fair, I should say that using bounding boxes was pretty much how collision detection was done in Flash 4, but it was a much more complicated process than it is now. I would recommend this only for movie clips that overall have a very rectangular shape. The code however is extremely similar to the code in the previous example. In this case you just substitute the coordinates and flag for the target of the second movie clip. An example of this code would look like the following:

```
movieclip1.hitTest(_root.path.movieclip2)
```

As before, `hitTest` will respond with a `true` or `false` value.

One last note on bounding boxes: in the slider example, we were able to rotate it, and it still functioned because inside the movie clip the system was still dealing with horizontal movement. Bounding boxes don't work quite the same way. No matter how deep a symbol and no matter how the symbols are rotated, the bounding box is drawn in relation to the root of the movie. As an example, imagine you had two squares bouncing into each other in a movie clip. Using the movie clip to movie clip collision detection, if you rotated the main movie clip 45 degrees on the main stage, Flash would then treat the squares like diamonds and draw larger bounding boxes around them, and potentially throwing off the scripting.

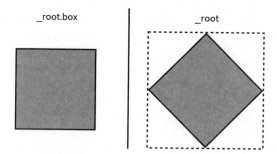

Even if the bounding box is tight against the shape inside
a symbol, if the instance is rotated, the bounding box forms
around the rotated shape.

ummary

We have covered several interactive mouse effects in this chapter, starting with a basic delayed drag object. We developed that delayed drag into a mouse trail, and saw how to enhance it by changing the alpha settings and rotation of the movie clip instances. Then we expanded on this to create our airplane application, with the help of some motion tweening, and were used some script to control the speed of the plane.

Then we worked through two different methods for dragging a movie clip inside an irregular shape: by using `hitTest` and mathematically defining the drag area.

Finally, we created a collision detection movie, again using the `hitTest` method, but this time with keyboard control.

So far we've moved things left, right, up and down; in the next chapter we'll start working with the third dimension. Just hook up your holographic monitors and you'll be all set. What? No 3D monitor? It's just as well; Flash's manipulation of depth is pretty rudimentary anyway, amounting to not much more than being able to flip between windows in your operating system. Just remember that there's always a stacking order, and two things can't occupy the same depth at once. Still it's good to be able to work with depth in Flash, however rudimentary it is, so that, amongst other things, is what we'll do.

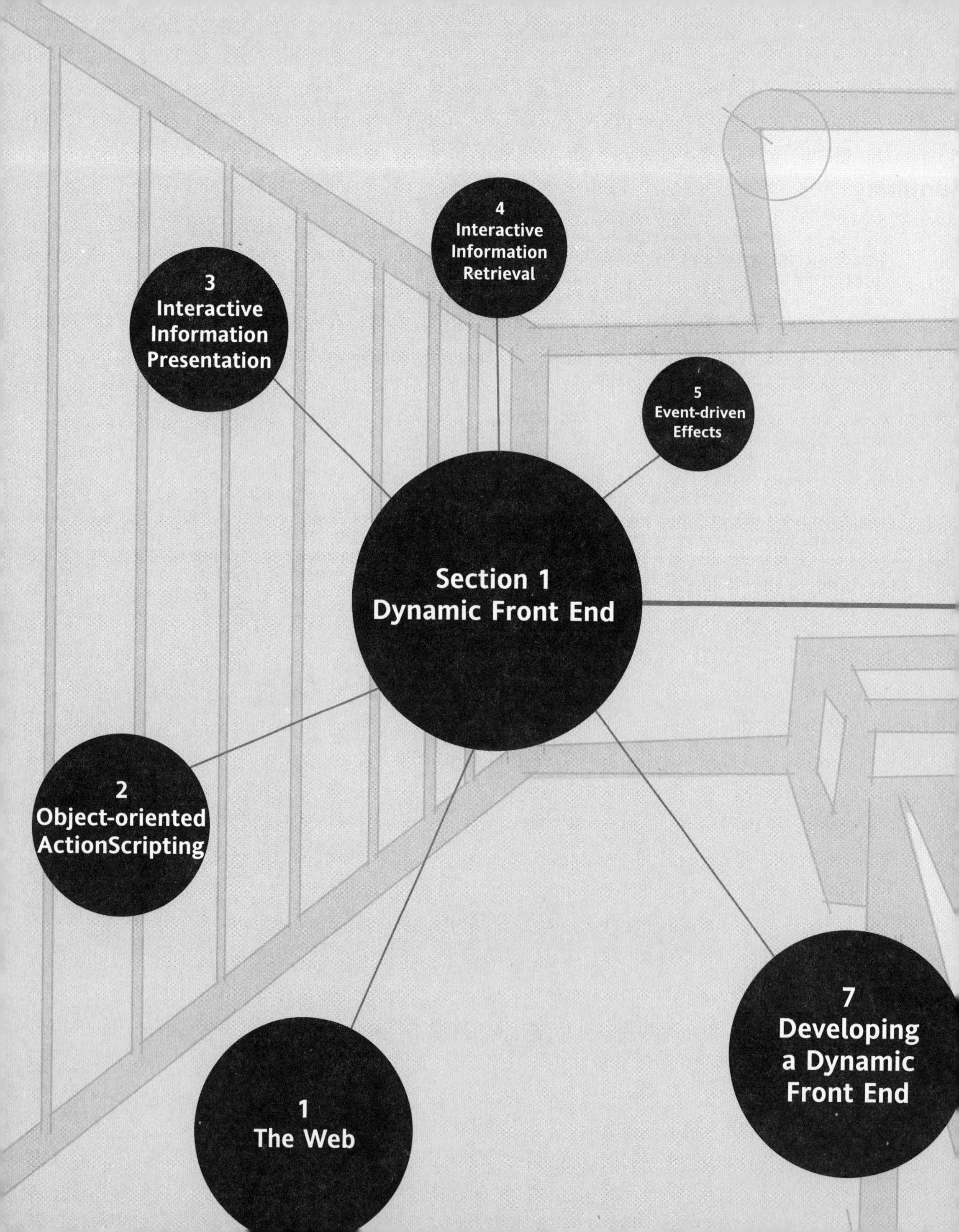

3
Interactive
Information
Presentation

4
Interactive
Information
Retrieval

5
Event-driven
Effects

Section 1
Dynamic Front End

2
Object-oriented
ActionScripting

7
Developing
a Dynamic
Front End

1
The Web

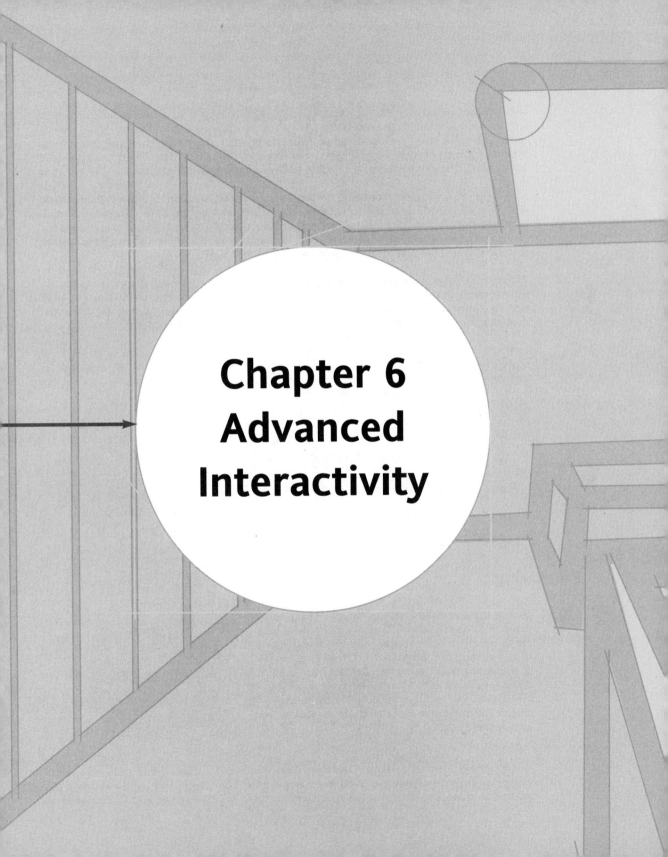

Chapter 6
Advanced
Interactivity

Now that we've used the x and y coordinate plane quite a bit, both for movement and detection, let's work our way out in the z-axis. Flash 5 has a limited ability to stack movie clips in a changing order, and this is what you'll need to use to create effects with a perspective view, and change the stacking order of your visual elements – you wouldn't want a large close object moving behind a small distant object, for example, it would totally ruin the illusion of distance.

So once we've investgated z-ordering, we'll change gears and focus on data manipulation. We'll work with shuffling first, creating a virtual deck of cards and then shuffling it. Unlike the other examples, this script doesn't use any properties of the objects on the stage, but uses instead the very powerful `array` object. Since we're going to want to actually use the deck, we'll add a script that does some quick parsing and reports the card to the stage.

After that we'll explore two more Flash objects, `sound` and `color`. Although these objects interact with elements on the stage, they do it very differently to any of the other property changes we've worked with so far. We'll use the slider from chapter 3 (or from the example on the CD) in the examples that work with these two objects: a color picker and a volume control.

Finally we'll wrap up the chapter with another mini-app. This one is the panorama effect. We'll create the appearance of an infinite ribbon of pictures, which will give the illusion the user is spinning a full 360 degrees in a virtual environment.

In this chapter, we'll cover:

- Restacking movie clips using z-ordering

- Shuffling

- Two ways to set a movie clip's color

- Volume and pan controls for sounds

- A Spinning panorama effect

Z-ordering

'Z-ordering' is really just a fancy name for changing the depth of an object. Since Flash uses x and y coordinates for its two dimensions, people started calling depth 'z-ordering', the z-axis being the third dimension. In Flash 4, z-ordering was somewhat difficult. You had to duplicate a movie clip at a new depth and then remove the original one; and if you specified a depth that was already filled, the new clip would erase whatever was already there.

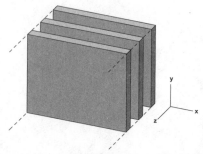

Things are much better in Flash 5. Now we have a movie clip method that deals with depth swapping for you: `swapDepths`. We'll begin the worked examples in this section by using this method to move an object that the user clicks to the top. This example could be adapted to create something like a jigsaw puzzle. In fact, any perspective-based game would benefit from easy transitions between depths.

If you want a preview of our next exercise, go to your computer, open four folders and click between them. See how the window comes to the front when you click it. We're going to do the same with movie clips.

Swapping the depths of movie clips

In this example, we'll make four movies. When you select one by clicking on it, it will move to the top of the stacking order and you'll be able to drag it around the stage. The source for this example is swapdepth.fla on the CD.

1. The first thing we need is a draggable button, like the ones we have used in previous examples. Create a large button on the stage, and call it button. It doesn't need to be fancy, you can just draw a square and turn it into a button. Put a dynamic text field just large enough to hold one character on top of the button (not inside it). Make the field non-selectable, and give it the variable name letter. The select both the field and the button, and turn them into a movie clip called letter MC. Give the new clip the instance name A.

    Most of the scripting we'll use in this example is will go on the button, but we need to add one small script to the movie clip itself first.

2. Bring up the actions panel and select the movie clip. We'll use the onClipEvent(load) action to set the value of the letter variable. This won't affect the depth script we are going to write next, but it will make the effect easier to see. Set the variable letter equal to its own _name property inside the onClipEvent, so that when we create new copies of this block in a moment, we'll be able to change the label through the the instance name.

    ```
    onClipEvent (load) {
        letter = this._name;
    }
    ```

3. Now copy the whole movie clip and paste it several times, changing each instance name to the next letter in the alphabet.

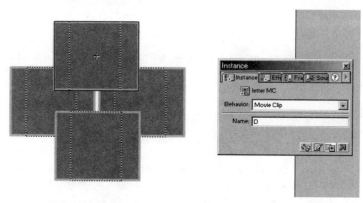

Now We're ready to create the depth swapping script.

4. Go into one of the movie clips on the stage. It doesn't matter which, since any changes we make inside the movie clip will show up in all its instances. Pull up the actions panel and select the button. The movie clip will go to the top depth when it's pressed, and start being dragged by the mouse, so we'll put the script inside an `on(press)` event.

```
on (press) {
}
```

Of course, we need to know what the new depth should be before we can set it. The `swapDepths` method gives us two options: either we can trade the movie clip's current depth with another movie clip, by referencing its target (which also moves the other movie clip to the first movie clip's original depth), or we can simply state a new depth as an integer. The interesting thing here is that if we specify a depth and it is turns out that it has already been taken, the contents of that depth go to the first movie clip's original depth, instead of destroying it.

Since we just need the movie clip to move to the top, we can just make a variable that all of the buttons can access. When it needs to swap depths, it increments the variable by one, then performs the `swapDepths` command. Since we haven't defined the variable previously, when we first increment it, it will be treated as a zero value and get incremented to one. If you're wondering why we can start with 1 since we already have several movie clips on the stage with a stacking order, this is because depth is something that can only be accessed by scripting. Anything you do in the Flash editing environment is below depth 1 (you also can't move things back down to that depth once it's been programmatically assigned a depth).

5. This variable needs to be accessed by all of the movie clips, so it should be placed on the _root. The first line in the `on(press)` command should be set to `_root.depth++`. After it's been incremented, we just need to swap the depth and drag it. Since we're swapping the depth of the current movie clip, we don't need a target. I've noticed though that the color-coding in the actions panel for this one method doesn't turn on unless it has a target. So if you want to, feel free to attach `this` at the beginning.

The code should look like this:

```
on (press) {
    _root.depth++;
    this.swapDepths(_root.depth);
}
```

Since we also want the movie clip to drag, add in a line telling it to do just that. If you want to add the optional parameters to the drag line go ahead, though they aren't really needed for this example.

```
on (press) {
    _root.depth++;
    this.swapDepths(_root.depth);
    startDrag (this);
}
```

6. All that's left is to add an `on(release)` command with a `stopDrag` in it to stop dragging the movie clip. The full code should look like the following:

```
on (press) {
    _root.depth++;
    this.swapDepths(_root.depth);
    startDrag (this);
}
on (release) {
    stopDrag ();
}
```

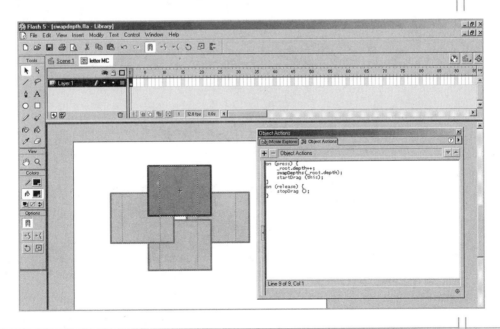

If you test at this point, you should be able to change the stacking order by pressing on the movie clips.

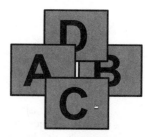

Try dragging the buttons around to see the overlapping of several buttons.

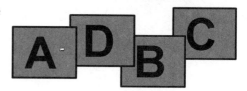

Games relying on perspectives such as shooting galleries or a 3D pong could use a property like the y position to determine depth. As long as the depths are updating constantly, even if depths collide, the difference in depths that the two movie clips would be so small that they would most likely not effect the overall z-ordering of the scene.

Shuffling a pack of cards

Shuffling virtual objects is jus the same as shuffling real ones, taking information and randomizing its order. Shuffling most often comes in handy for games like concentration or any card game, though it can be used anytime you need data in a random, non-repeating order. In this example, we'll be building a deck of cards in an **array**, and using some of the basic array commands to deal it out.

It would be pretty impractical to hard code a name like `Ace of Spades` and then write a script to parse that. Instead we'll reduce the card to a number. Since there are four suits, we can assign each a number from 1 to 4. Likewise since there are 13 members of each suit, we can give each member of the suit a number from 1 to 13. If you represented spades using the number 1, then the card code we'd generate for the ace of spades would be `11` and the king of spades, `113`. At this point it's a very easy thing to parse the first character as the suit, then parse what's left as the card value.

1 of spades

Building a deck of cards is a simple matter of iterative loops. We'll be using nested loops to make all the values of one suit before advancing to the next suit. Then we'll put the card randomly in the array using a `while` loop, that keeps checking random slots in the array until it finds one that is empty. The card is then assigned to the slot.

Scripting the deck and the shuffle

There's likely to be more than one event that triggers a shuffle – the beginning of a game, or when the deck is empty, for example, so we'll write the shuffle script in a function, and call it Shuffle.

1. Create a new movie and select frame 1 and bring up the actions panel. Let's add the function definition line, calling it shuffle.

```
function shuffle () {
}
```

2. The first step of the function should be to create a new array to hold our cards. Initializing the array first will make sure that if there was already a partially used card array, it will be destroyed before we begin. Having remnants still in the array would cause major problems in the script later. To create an array object, follow the same procedure as for assigning a variable. The value of the variable, call it card, needs to be the array constructing script, new Array(52). Even though it's optional, I've included the length of the array since we know how many cards must make up a deck. One thing to mention about arrays is that they count from 0. The 52 slots in the array we just created are numbered 0 through 51.

```
function shuffle () {
      //creates the array object
      card = new Array(52);
}
```

3. Next, we need to create the for loop that will iterate through the suits. Since there are four suits, each starting at 1, the index variable which we'll call suitIndex should be initialized at 1. The condition checks whether suitIndex is less than or equal to 4, and the index variable increments after each loop. The code for this statement should look like this:

```
function shuffle () {
      card = new Array(52);
      // loop 1: making each suit
      for (suitIndex=1; suitIndex<=4; suitIndex++) {
      }
}
```

4. We need to nest another loop inside this one. This nested loop will go through each card value (ace to king). Since it's inside the suit loop, this loop will be repeated for each of the four times the suit loop cycles. This loop should be set up like the previous one, but it must have a different index variable. Go ahead and name this one rankIndex, and make its condition less than or equal to 13, the number of possible values.

The code to this point should look like the following:

```
function shuffle () {
    card = new Array(52);
    for (suitIndex=1; suitIndex<=4; suitIndex++) {
        // loop 2: making each card for a particular suit
        for (var rankIndex = 1; rankIndex<=13; rankIndex++) {
        }
    }
}
```

5. The actual work of the script will go on inside this loop. To make the order of the cards random, we'll be adding the card into a random slot in the array – of course, as we keep looping through, creating cards, there will be a better and better chance that the random slot that is picked will already be full. To get around this, we'll pick a slot at random and first check to see if anything is in it. If it is, then we need to pick a new slot and try again. To do this, let's set a variable like randslot equal to random(52). (Placing the random value in a variable allows us to remember the value. It's not much help finding an empty slot if we've lost what the random number was that we just used.) As you might remember, arrays and random start counting at 0, so we're checking random numbers from 0 to 51:

```
function shuffle () {
    card = new Array(52);
    for (suitIndex=1; suitIndex<=4; suitIndex++) {
        for (var rankIndex = 1; rankIndex<=13; rankIndex++) {
            // pick a slot
            var randslot = random(52);
        }
    }
}
```

6. Now that we have the random number, we need to see if that slot is filled. Since we'll have to keep checking until a suitable slot is found, let's make this the condition of a while loop. The while loop is preferable here since we don't need to progressively increment a value. Much like the if statement, while continues as long as the condition doesn't return a null or 0 value. Since we're looking for an array slot that has an undefined value, we can just use value of the potential array slot as the condition. The loop will continue until an undefined slot comes along. A value in an array is found by naming the array and then calling for a slot within brackets. The syntax of this condition is:

```
function shuffle () {
    card = new Array(52);
    for (suitIndex=1; suitIndex<=4; suitIndex++) {
        for (var rankIndex = 1; rankIndex<=13; rankIndex++) {
            var randslot = random(52);
            while (card[randslot]) {
            }
        }
    }
}
```

While the loop continues, we need to reassign the value of randslot so the condition of the loop can try new slots. Once again, assign the value of randslot to random(52) and then close the while loop:

```
function shuffle () {
    card = new Array(52);
    for (suitIndex=1; suitIndex<=4; suitIndex++) {
        for (var rankIndex = 1; rankIndex<=13; rankIndex++) {
            var randslot = random(52);
            // if that slot's taken, keep picking
            while (card[randslot]) {
                var randslot = random(52);
            }
        }
    }
}
```

Once the loop breaks by finding an empty slot, we must fill that slot with the code for the suit and value. Luckily, we can use the index variables for the code, suitIndex for the suit and rankIndex for the value. Since both of these variables are numbers, we need to use the string function to make sure the variables are treated as strings and concatenated, not added as numbers.

7. So, if you put this all together, the entire function in frame 1 looks like the following:

```
function shuffle () {
    card = new Array(52);
    for (suitIndex=1; suitIndex<=4; suitIndex++) {
        for (var rankIndex = 1; rankIndex<=13; rankIndex++) {
            var randslot = random(52);
            while (card[randslot]) {
                var randslot = random(52);
            }
            // we have an open slot, put the card in it
            card[randslot] =
String(suitIndex)+String(rankIndex);
        }
    }
}
```

Once the function is called, you'll have a deck of cards ready to be used. Now we need to add a line to run the shuffle function, and a key to decipher the suits. Card values will be returned to us as "11" all the way to "413". The first number will always be the suit though, so let's make a way to convert that to text. As we've just seen, arrays are indexed by numbers. So, a good way to do this is to create a new array, like suit and set suit[1] to spades, suit[2] to hearts, suit[3] to diamonds and suit[4] to clubs. That way, the index will associate with the card's suit value. Arrays do count from 0, but in this case suit[0] is simply undefined.

```
function shuffle () {
    card = new Array(52);
    for (suitIndex=1; suitIndex<=4; suitIndex++) {
        for (var rankIndex = 1; rankIndex<=13; rankIndex++) {
            var randslot = random(52);
            while (card[randslot]) {
                var randslot = random(52);
            }
            // we have an open slot, put the card in it
            card[randslot] =
String(suitIndex)+String(rankIndex);
        }
    }
}
// make the shuffle function run
shuffle();
// an array containing a key to the suit names
suit = new Array();
suit[1] = "spades";
suit[2] = "hearts";
suit[3] = "diamonds";
suit[4] = "clubs";
```

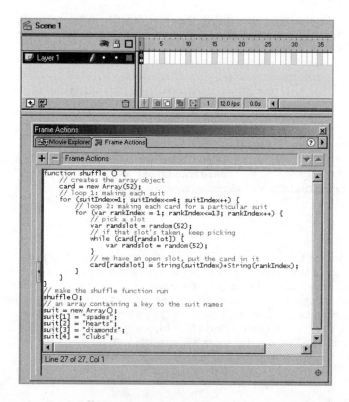

Dealing a card

We now just need to create a button that deals the cards. This button can really do anything you want, but for now, let's make one that deals out one card, parses the suit and displays a description of the card in a text field.

1. To do this put a dynamic text field on the stage with the variable name dealt. Also add two buttons, one to deal the next card, and one to re-shuffle the deck:

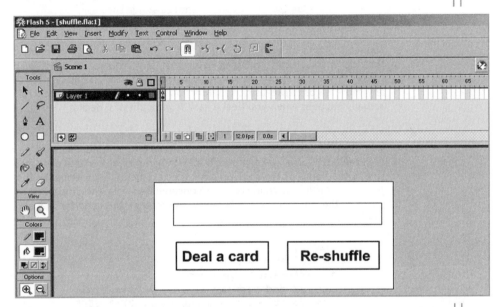

We'll use an on(release) event on the Deal a card button, and deal cards by **popping** an element off the array. Popping is an array command that says "To take the last element of an array, return its value, then remove that element from the array". This sort of process is know as a **destructive action** since by calling it, you're altering the array. Before we pop a card off the array, we need to make sure there is a card left in the deck. To do that, we'll set up an if statement to check the length property of the card array and see if it (card.length) is greater than zero. If it is, then the card will be popped and a description reported in the dynamic text box dealt. When there are no cards left in the array, we'll set the dealt variable to the string please shuffle again.

2. So, first add the on (release) command and test the length property of card followed by the else statement:

```
on (release) {
    // if the deck isn't empty
    if (card.length>0) {
    } else {
        // otherwise tell the user to shuffle again
        dealt = "please shuffle again";
    }
}
```

3. Add a variable named `popcard` and set it equal to the expression `card.pop()`:

```
on (release) {
    if (card.length>0) {
        // remove the next card from the deck
        popcard = card.pop();
    } else {
        dealt = "please shuffle again";
}
```

Since popping is a destructive action, when you need to use the returned value more than once, you need to assign it to a variable, as you've just done. By popping each element of the array off, we will eventually be left with an empty array that can't deal any more cards. I like using this function here because it's a good match for what actually happens when you deal a card from a physical deck.

4. To make a more human readable card description for the `dealt` variable to display, we'll need to concatenate the value of the card with its suit. Since we set a key earlier, with the `suit` array, we can plug the first character of the card code into the array to return the name of the suit. Let's set the text field `dealt` equal to the substring of `popcard` starting at character one concatenated with the string `of` and finally the name of the suit from the `suit` array. Altogether, the code for that should look like the following:

```
on (release) {
    if (card.length>0) {
        popcard = card.pop();
        // and display it in the text field
        dealt = popcard.substr(1, 2)+" of "
        ➥ +suit[popcard.charAt(0)];
    } else {
        dealt = "please shuffle again";
    }
}
```

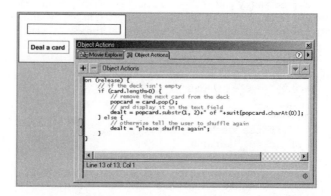

5.   We simply use the `shuffle` function behind the Re-shuffle button, :

```
on (release) {
    // reshuffle
    shuffle();
}
```

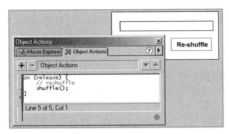

6.   Now test your movie!

12 of hearts

Deal a card   ### Re-shuffle

To make the description of the cards better, you could also make a key that turns the value of the cards from just numbers, to the numbers and the face card names. However, if you wanted to make a visual representation of a card, I'd recommend creating a generic card movie clip, and using the two parts of code to tell parts of the movie clip to go to different frames.

Shuffling isn't only for a deck of playing cards. This is a script that randomizes content but doesn't allow the same element to be recalled unless you reshuffle. You could use something very similar for a Flash jukebox, where you want the songs to play randomly, but you don't want to use a simple random function since that would keep calling in the same song. Or you could use it for Flash ad banner rotations.

Now that we've been introduced to arrays, let's look at some of Flash's other objects. First we'll look at color, and then sound. Flash has several primitive object types, all introduced in Flash 5. We've actually been dealing with objects all along – everything we've been doing with movie clips makes use of the movie clip object; we hid the mouse using the mouse object, and did our parsing using the string object. For these next two sections though we'll be dealing not only with the color and sound objects but also a **generic object**, which is an interesting way of organizing multiple pieces of information to handle one object.

Colors in Flash

Colors in Flash are based on a combination of the three primary colors of light: red, green and blue, otherwise known as **RGB**. Depending on how much of each is used, you can produce a wide array of colors at any brightness. Each color can have a value of zero to 255, zero meaning the color is not used, and 255 meaning that the color is being used to its maximum.

Zero to 255 might seem like an arbitrary range, but like many computer systems, it's based on the hexadecimal system (base 16 numbers). Each of the primary colors can be expressed as a two digit hexadecimal number. When all of the primary colors are together they form a string of six hexadecimal values. You might recognize this from HTML. If you've ever expressed a color like white as #FFFFFF you've used a hexadecimal based color system. Since we don't have characters to represent numbers higher than 9, we use the letters A through F to represent them. #FFFFFF is actually just saying in base 10 that red, green and blue should all be 255. In Flash, instead of using the hash sign (#), you type 0xFFFFFF.

Before you can set any movie clip's color in Flash though, you have to initialize a variable that will link to the color attributes of a movie clip. The color methods in Flash 5 don't actually reference the movie clip itself, but instead, work with the variable containing the color object. So, when you use one of the color methods on the variable/object, it immediately updates the movie's color attributes. To set this type of variable, you would set up the name as always, but the value of the variable should be a new color object constructor. To do this, the code should look something like:

```
colorVar = new Color(_root.targetMovieclip)
```

This variable can be placed anywhere, just as long as the path to the movie clip is correct. It's best to either set the variable inside the target movie clip for organizational purposes, or (as I like to do) put it wherever my script is that is setting the color. This way, all of my script that works together is grouped together. So, anytime you needed to change the color of the target movie clip, you would run the color changing methods as methods of the variable/object colorVar.

The color object

There are four methods to Flash's color object, two that set color, setRGB and setTransform, and two that return the information set previously, getRGB and getTransform. We're going to be setting colors in the following examples, but before we begin, there are a few things you should know about these methods.

setRGB

According to the Flash documentation, setRGB takes a hexadecimal, like 0xFFFFFF, as its argument. The only problem with this method is that it requires a number data type. If you directly type a value into your script, the system accepts it as a number, but I haven't found a way of constructing a variable in the hexadecimal form that Flash will recognize as a number when used in this method. To convert a number out of base 10 in effect converts the data type to a string.

However, there is an un-documented way to use this method. If you just type in a base 10 number, the color will change, because the method accepts decimal values. You just need to convert the hexadecimal value back to base 10 as one number. The formula is:

$$((R * 65536) + (G * 256) + B) \quad -OR- \quad ((R * 16^4) + (G * 16^2) + (B * 16^0)$$

So for white, FFFFFF, or 255, 255, 255, the value would be 16777215. For those of you that just want it to work, use the first formula using base 10 values for each of the colors (0-255) and plug the resulting number into the setRGB method. It will work every time. For those that want to know exactly why this works, here's the fuller explanation.

For me, when I started learning about colors on the Web, I though of a value like FFFFFF as three different values concatenated together. In reality that isn't so. Red isn't FF concatenated with 00 and 00; it's FF0000 + 0 + 0. This may seem like a minor point, but when you convert from base 16 to base 10, it makes a huge difference. The maximum red value, expressed in base 10 is 255, but to add those place values to show red's real value means multiplying by 65536. As you can see, unless you know your multiplication tables up to 65536, in base 10 it's not quite as simple as adding four zeros.

To convert your three color values into one number, we just need to add in the equivalent of the appropriate base 16 place values to each of the color values. Blue exists in the first two place values of base 16 so it doesn't need to have anything added to it. Green exists in the next two place values, so we need to multiply it by 256 (hexadecimal 100 in base 10 is 256). Red, as we mentioned before exists in the fifth and sixth place values, so we need to multiply 65536 by the red value (hexadecimal 10000 in base 10 is 65536).

setTransform

The setTransform method allows you to set the percentages and offsets of red, green, blue, and alpha (transparency). The percentage and offset of an object change its color by running the two values through an equation. Offset will do just that, it takes a value for a color, like 255 red and offsets that by an amount. If the offset is at –255 all red is eliminated in the picture.

Let's say you have an object in your movie that has a red box in it and a purple one. If we use the Effect panel in advanced mode to set a percentage of 0 and an offset of 0 for blue, nothing will happen to the red box, but the purple box will turn red. This is because the panel takes all of the current values of blue in the object and multiplies them by 0%, and then will add 0 onto them. Since red does not have any blue in it, the color is left alone. The purple, though, which is made up of red and blue, has its blue value reduced to zero, leaving it only with a red property.

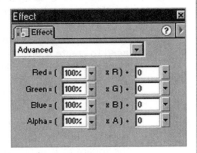

If this is unclear, try experimenting with this panel keeping in mind the equation offset plus the percentage of the current color value. You can create some really neat effects using this panel.

We'll use both of these color-changing methods in the following example applications. First, we'll create a mini-application that dynamically changes the color of a movie clip according to the user's selection. Applications of this sort of effect can range from an online coloring book to setting preferred colors on a customizable site. You might use it for a multi-user application like a chat engine, for example, enabling each user to set a personal color so that their messages and actions are recognizable to other users on the system.

Setting color with RGB

For this example we're going to use the documented form of the setRGB method, by using hexadecimal values as you would in HTML. The source for this example is colorbuttons.fla on the CD.

While this technique is pretty simple, it can't be made dynamic without the use of the formula mentioned above using base 10 numbers. The other alternative is to use the code in the next example, which uses the setTransform method.

1. To start this example, let's create a simple shape, like a square. Since you can only change the color property of movie clips, let's make the square into a movie clip called target and give it an instance name square.

2. As I said before, to modify the color of a movie clip, we need to create a color object for this movie clip. Since a color object is placed in a variable, it gets some of the properties of a variable. As with all global variables, it can be placed in any timeline. It's then up to you to provide the correct path back to your target movie clip. We only need to create it once, so let's make it a frame action in frame 1 of the main timeline. The code should look like this:

```
squareColor = new Color(square)
```

3. Now we are ready to start making buttons that will change the color of the square. Let's set up buttons that will change the square to true red, true green or true blue. (A true color is one where the primary is set to its maximum and the other two colors are set to zero.) To do this, make a simple button on the stage called color button and copy two more instances of it onto the stage.

4. Use the Effect panel in Tint mode to change their tints to true red, true green and true blue respectively.

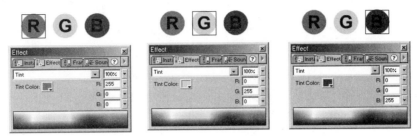

5. On each button we'll add an on(release) command, put the setRGB method inside it and pass in the relevant hexadecimal value as an argument. For red, the code is 0xFF0000, for green, it's 0x00FF00, and for blue it's 0x0000FF. This is the script you should use for your red button, for example:

```
on (release) {
squareColor.setRGB(0xFF0000);
}
```

6. Go ahead and add the appropriate code to each button, and test the movie. You'll notice that the square first appears with exactly the same coloring that you gave it when you drew it. If you click on the buttons though, it changes to the color of that button, and remains that color until you click another button. With just this method, there is no way of resetting the original color properties of the object. Also, with this technique, any transparency that you set in the original movie clip will be maintained when you convert the color.

Now that we've gotten our feet wet in a color object, it's time to meet the object object. No, that wasn't a typo. There is a **generic object** type that we'll need in the next exercise. Think of a generic object as a container that can hold whatever data you want.

In the next example, we'll look at the setTransform method, which duplicates the functionality of the Advanced section of the Effect panel. That panel has 8 fields, and all of them are optional when using this method. Therefore Flash needs a better way to deal with the data than something like setTransform(255,,,,55,100,20,99) where you would have to remember the order of the arguments, and where you would have to remember to put all of the commas in for the settings you didn't want to affect. Instead of that nightmare, we will just make a generic object holding a variable for each of the settings you want changed. Any variable that isn't defined in the object is assumed to be one that the script is opting not to supply.

Let's go ahead into the next exercise now and see this in practice.

A dynamic color picker: using transform

In this example, we only want to set the object to a single color, instead of tweaking what's already there. We'll set the movie clip to a 0% color value, to delete all color values, and then use the offsets to build the color back up. When the value is set at 0%, the offset of 0 to 255 is just the base 10 expression of the hexadecimal system we were working with before. Since we'll be setting a base 10 number, it's a very easy thing to set dynamically. The source for this example is `colorpicker.fla` on the CD.

1. We'll need a setup fairly similar to the one we've just made for the dynamic color picker, so go ahead and save a new copy of the `setRGB` example, calling it `colorPicker` this time. We'll be using three sliders instead of buttons for this example, so go ahead and delete the three buttons; you should be left with the square and the code that sets the color object.

2. Now we need to add the sliders. If you coded the slider as it was laid out in Chapter 3, you should be able to copy it from that example file (or just borrow one from the example on the CD). Make sure to copy it from the stage instead of dragging it from the library. The version on the stage has the `doSlide` function already defined on it. Paste a copy of the slider into this new file below the square:

In the slider example, we used a custom function in an `onClipEvent` to set properties. This example will show why that was so important. We'll need three sliders, one for each color. Since each needs to be setting something different, the code that does the setting must be tied only to the instance, otherwise you'd have to create completely different symbols every time you wanted to have more than one slider on the stage.

3. Let's make this first slider control the red color. Right now your slider should be reporting a number from zero to one to a function called `doSlide`. We need to set a variable from inside this function to the `_root` called `red`. The value of `red` needs to be an integer from 0 to 255 so it can be applied as an offset to the `color` object later. We'll multiply the ratio by the upper limit, 255, to get the correct proportional value, and then use the `Math.round` function to change it to its closest integer.

That line should end up looking like this:

```
_root.red = Math.round(ratio * 255);
```

Since we also need to set the color of the square, let's reference a function that we'll create later. The reason for creating a function is that all three of the sliders will be doing the same thing at this point, so it's better to have the code in only one place in case you should decide that the code needs to be changed later.

4. Let's call the function setColor and assume it's placed in the root. The final scripting for the onClipEvent for the red slider should be:

```
onClipEvent (load) {
function doSlide (ratio) {
_root.red = Math.round(ratio*255);
_root.setColor();
}
}
```

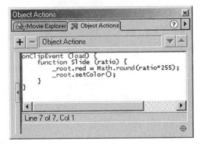

5. Now you need to copy the slider and paste it onto the stage twice, one as the green slider and the other as the blue slider. At this point, you should also add some labels on the stage to identify the sliders.

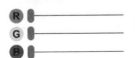

6. Also, change the instance names of the sliders to something like `sliderRed`, `sliderGreen` and `sliderBlue`. Then go through the green and blue sliders to change the variable name to the appropriate color. All that's left is to write the `setColor` method.

7. Since the `setColor` custom function is going to be looked for in the _root, let's write it in frame 1 of the main timeline under the color object definition. Name the function `setColor` and leave the attributes field blank. The function will reference the three variables as needed:

```
//defines the color object
squareColor = new Color(square);
//takes the data from the variables
//set by the slider and changes the
//color of the target.
function setColor () {
}
```

8. Now for the `setTranform` method. Since `setTransform` can set the percentage and offset for four properties, it needs the data organized in a **generic object**. For this sort of purpose, think of a generic object as folder for several variables. We can then just pass this one folder of variables to the `setTransform` method, and it can find the values of the variables it needs inside, provided we have named them correctly. We first need to create the object, which we can do just like we did with the `color` object, this time with `new Object`. Let's give this `new Object` the name `squarec`:

```
squareColor = new Color(square);
function setColor () {
    squarec = new Object();
}
```

Then simply make each property of the color that we want to change into a variable held inside the `squarec` object. Any property that we don't want to change we can just ignore; we aren't working with transparency, so we can leave that out of this function.

There are two values for each color, a percentage (the `a` value) and an offset (the `b` value). The `a` and `b` values for each color (and transparency) each have a different variable name. They are: `ra`, `rb`, `ga`, `gb`, `ba`, `bb`, `aa`, and `ab`. These are set names that you have to use with the `setTransform` method. Any other variable names will be ignored. We can specify each color property by setting any of these variables in our generic object, `squarec`. For example, `squarec.ra` will set a percentage of the red property of the generic object `squarec`.

9. Since we want to change the color to a target color instead of modifying the default color, we need to set all of the percentages to 0, in effect turning the object black. We can then use the offsets to create the specified color. To determine the offsets, use each of the variables we set in the slider. Keep in mind though that if the slider hasn't been used yet, the value is undefined and therefore zero.

```
squareColor = new Color(square);
function setColor () {
    squarec = new Object();
    squarec.ra = 0;
    squarec.ga = 0;
    squarec.ba = 0;
    squarec.rb = red;
    squarec.gb = green;
    squarec.bb = blue;
}
```

10. Finally, we set the color of the square by using the setTransform method on the color object using squarec as its argument. This will allow all of the variables in the generic object to be read and used in setting the color. This is the code for the entire function:

```
squareColor = new Color(square);
function setColor () {
    squarec = new Object();
    squarec.ra = 0;
    squarec.ga = 0;
    squarec.ba = 0;
    squarec.rb = red;
    squarec.gb = green;
    squarec.bb = blue;
    squarecolor.setTransform(squarec);
}
```

11. When you test this movie, the original colors of the square movie clip will show through. Once you move any of the sliders, the whole object will become a single color based on the position of the slider. If you want the object to start at black, you can add a line after your function definition that calls the function. This will use the pre-initialized values of the color variables and set the movie clip to black:

```
squareColor = new Color(square);
function setColor () {
    squarec = new Object();
    squarec.ra = 0;
    squarec.ga = 0;
    squarec.ba = 0;
    squarec.rb = red;
    squarec.gb = green;
    squarec.bb = blue;
    squarecolor.setTransform(squarec);
}
//runs setColor() once to make the target black
setColor();
```

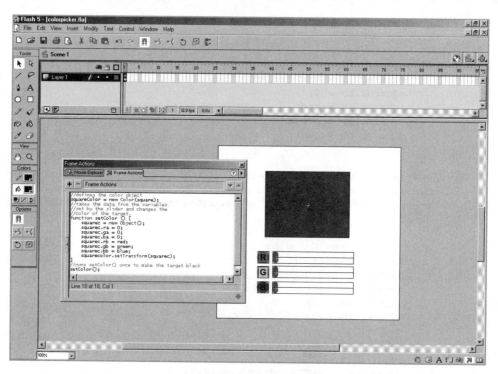

Should you ever want a reset button that reasserts the original colors of the movie clip, create an action that sets all of the a values to 100 (percentages) and all of the b values to 0 (offsets).

If you want to work with transparency, you can adjust it just as you did any of the other colors. Just add another slider, and the appropriate variables in the setColor function.

Color picker
Included in the source file for this example is a second version of the color picker. If you look in Scene 2, you'll see a color picker that looks like what you would find in most graphics software packages. It works on the same general principal as the three bar slider, but allows for a better graphic representation. If you're interested in creating this sort of color picker, there are comments in the code that talk about its construction. The hardest part in that example is understanding how the colors are set up mathematically. After that, you're back at more or less the same general function.

Going along the top of the main box you can see red, yellow, green, cyan, blue, purple and red again. As we've talked about before, there are three primary colors of light: red, green and blue.

The other colors in the list are combinations of two primary colors. So, if we started subdividing the box into columns, we could put a divider at the middle of each of the secondary colors.

Cyan for instance is full green and full blue. As you move to the right, green will trail off, while blue will be unchanged. Green will continue to decrease until you achieve pure blue. Green will do the same thing to the left of yellow, trailing off until it reaches 0 at pure red. Between yellow and cyan though green will always be at full strength. As you can see, each primary color is dominant for one third of the area, and is the lesser of two colors in a third of the area, and absent for the final third. By setting up boundaries, you can determine what the value of the color should be based on the x position of the color selector.

Going along the bottom of the color area, there is only one color, mid gray, which is 128, 128, 128. All of the colors in the middle of the area are just tending towards the full color or towards this gray in a linear fashion. For instance the color at the extreme left edge of the area, but exactly in the middle vertically, would be halfway between 255,0,0 and 128,128,128. This value would be 192, 64, 64.

After that, the slider on the right side of the color area is simple. Here you are doing the same as moving between the full color and the gray, but here, the color you chose on the left is in the middle and going up tends to pure white and going down tends to pure black.

Feel free to browse the color picker on the CD to look at the math and the boundaries I've set up to do the color selection.

As we touched on earlier, there are several advanced objects in Flash 5 that allow us to customize our environment in many ways. Another one of these objects is the sound object. Though sounds and colors are extremely different, even using different sense, programming them in Flash is extraordinarily similar.

Sounds, like colors, are controlled by defining an object and using methods on that object to control the desired feature. The sound object comes with setVolume and setPan methods that roughly correspond to the setRGB method of the color object. There's also a setTransform method, among others, which uses different variable names, but otherwise works like its color counterpart.

ound volume and balance controls

Just like on a stereo, you can set the volume and balance (or pan) of sounds. Flash allows you to control sounds either universally or timeline by timeline. With this effect, you can give your user control over sound controls in a website. In more complex applications, you could create a mixer that lowers and raises the volume of particular looping sounds to effect the overall music. In games, you can increase realism by using the _x property of any object to set the pan of its sound effects.

In the color example, setRGB was complex because of its number base. There are no such complications in this scheme. setVolume is a 0 to 100 scale (higher numbers amplify the sound past its default though at the expense of sound quality). setPan is a −100 to 100 scale. SetTransform uses a more complex system that allows you to set a volume for the left and right channel for both the left and the right speaker. By default, the left channel only plays in the left speaker and the right channel only the right, but using `setTransform` you can have any combination up to and including both channels playing at full volume out of both speakers or the left channel playing out of the right speaker and vice versa.

In the example for this section we'll create a volume slider and a pan slider. The source for the example is `sound.fla` on the CD. Although this example will use two different sliders, you could also make a handle that is draggable within a square and use the `_x` position for volume and the `_y` position for the pan. I call this a two dimensional slider. If you're interested in this technique, you can look at the example on the CD, `sound2.fla`.

The sound sliders

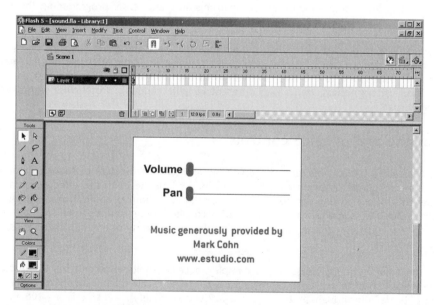

1. Once again, copy two sliders from previous examples onto the stage. Also find a sound loop and import it into the current file or use the MP3 available on the CD. Select frame 1 of the main timeline and use the Sound panel to add the sound as an event with many loops.

2. We need to create a sound object that will allow scripting to control this sound. Let's create a sound object called soundObj in frame 1 of the main timeline. The code for adding a sound object is:

```
soundObj= new Sound()
```

Sound can have a movie clip path as its argument if you only need to control a specific timeline's sounds. If you don't specify an argument, the sound object controls all sounds in the entire movie.

3. Let's now take a look at the scripting in each of the sliders. In the volume slider, we need to change the custom function to run the setVolume command on the soundObj using the ratio to determine a value of 0 to 100.

```
onClipEvent (load) {
    //set the volume
    function doSlide (ratio) {
        _root.soundObj.setVolume(Math.round(ratio*100));
    }
}
```

4. Also in the onClipEvent (but outside the function), we need to make sure that the position of the handle is correct for the default volume setting when you render the movie. Since the volume starts at 100, we need to move the _x position of the handle movie clip to the _length of the line movie clip. The code for that should look like the following:

```
onClipEvent (load) {
    //set the initial position of the handle
    handle._x = line._width;
    function doSlide (ratio) {
        _root.soundObj.setVolume(Math.round(ratio*100));
    }
}
```

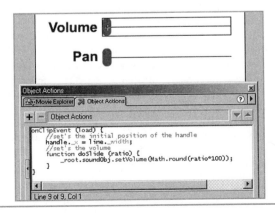

5. We need to add very similar script to the balance/pan slider. In this case we use the `setPan` method, and to make a range from –100 to 100 we'll need to multiply `ratio` by 200 and then subtract 100 to center it back on 0. Since the pan defaults to 0, we will want to move the handle of the slider to the center of the slider when the movie is first rendered. To do that, the `_x` of the handle should be set to half the `_width` of line:

```
onClipEvent (load) {
            handle._x = (.5*line._width);
    //set the pan
    function doSlide (ratio) {
            _root.soundObj.setPan(Math.round(ratio*200)-100);
    }
}
```

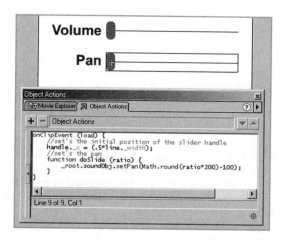

When you test this movie, the sound should start out at a normal volume and centered in both speakers. You can then use the sliders to lower the volume or move the sound to one speaker or another. This same effect can be made using the `setTransform` method for sounds, but I think for this sort of use, the `setVolume` and `setPan` are much easier to use.

We've covered a lot of effects in this chapter. To wrap up, we're going to do a panorama. While not precisely using any particular element we've worked on before, many of the techniques we've learned along the way will be very useful. We'll work with movie clip duplication, repositioning a movie clip, clip events, working with mouse position data, masking to create this mini-app.

This effect takes one image, duplicates it, placing the duplicates end to end in a long ribbon, and then allows you to move your mouse controlling the direction and speed the ribbon moves. Panorama effects can be used to create side-scrolling interfaces, a simulation of a virtual environment, or whatever else you can imagine.

The general feel of this example will most likely remind you of the slider exercise and airplane controls exercise. Keep these two in mind as we go through the example seeing how we repurpose both code and skills to create a completely new effect.

Creating a panorama effect

In this example we'll be creating a landscape that will scroll across the screen as if it were on a never-ending conveyer belt. As you might have already guessed this is going to be an illusion, but I'm happy to say, a pretty convincing one. What's actually happening is that there is a movie clip containing several copies of the same landscape. As you move the mouse to one side of the screen, the panorama will start to move. Once the central copy of the landscape moves off to the side, one of the copies will appear on the screen. If the whole movie clip moves too far in one direction it will then be moved back a precise amount so that the central landscape is now exactly where the copy of the landscape was. Since any landmarks in the panorama have essentially kept the same position, the user does not know anything has happened. The diagram below should help makes things a bit clearer.

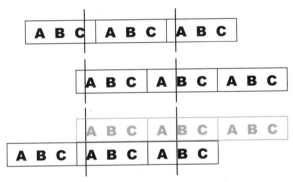

As the panorma moves in one direction, the system will move the
movieclip back exactly one width of a panel when it moves too far.
This way as you can see in the third line, all of the elements of the
panels line up perfectly and there is no visible disturbance.

Building the landscape
You can either use the landscape from the source file for this example or create your own. Feel free to use either a vector object or a bitmap. The landscape can be whatever you want; however it should have compatible seams. Seams are the edges where the image is going to wrap. Anything split at the right edge of your image should be completed on the left edge. Keep in mind that you will want the panorama to be much wider than it is tall so you have a true sense of turning around in a circle.

1. Once you've got your landscape ready, select it and turn it into a movie clip called panorama image. Since we're going to create duplicates of this strip of landscape later, let's give this movie clip the instance name `strip1`.

2. Once all of the duplicates are made (we'll use the `duplicateMovieClip` method), one of the scripts is going to move all of them according to the mouse position. To make it so we only have to move one object, let's encase the `strip1` movie clip in

another movie clip called main panorama MC and give it the instance name panorama. This way, when we duplicate strip1, the copies will also be inside panorama.

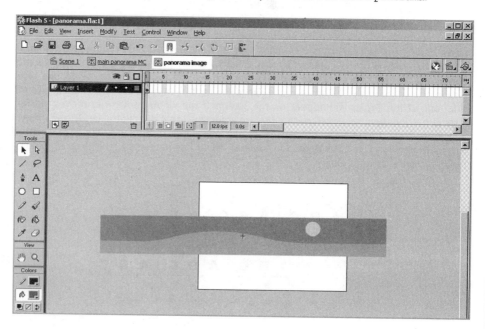

Scripting the panorama

The scripting for this effect will be broken up into two parts, the initialization and the interactivity. The initialization will do the duplication dynamically based on the width of the landscape and the area it's being shown in. It will also set several key variables that will be used in the interactivity section. The two phases of the scripting will each be broken up into their own onClipEvents attached to panorama. Since initialization only happens once, we'll use an onClipEvent(load) event. The interactivity, however, needs to happen constantly so we'll use onClipEvent(EnterFrame) for that.

1. Let's start with the the onClipEvent(load) script, which we'll put in the main stage. First we'll set up some variables. We'll need the width of the landscape, which we can get by taking the _width property of strip1. We'll also need the left and right bounds of the panorama, which will essentially be the left and right edges of the 'field of vision'. You can set these variables as numbers, or, as I often like to do, by creating a vertical line for each side and turning each into a movie clip, and giving them the instance names rightLimit and leftLimit respectively. I can then use their _x values. The advantage to doing it this way is that I never need to change the value; I just have to line up the movie clips with the new graphic elements, instead of finding the numeric value and coming back to the script. Since I don't generally want two lines visible in the final product, I add onClipEvent(load) actions to them to change their visibility (_visible) to 0 at render.

Your code so far should look like this:

```
onClipEvent (load) {
        widthStrip = _width;
        rightLimit = _root.rightMarkerPanorama._x;
        leftLimit = _root.leftMarkerPanorama._x;
}
```

2. After the limits are established, we can use these values to figure out the width of the panorama area and the center point of the panorama's screen. The center is important to know so that we can move the panorama to start from the middle automatically. It will also be used later in the interactivity phase. To this point the code should look like the following:

```
onClipEvent (load) {
        widthStrip = strip1._width;
        rightLimit = _root.rightMarkerPanorama._x;
        leftLimit = _root.leftMarkerPanorama._x;
        widthscreen = rightLimit-leftLimit;
        center=(.5 * widthScreen) + leftLimit
        _x = center
}
```

3. The last variable to be initialized is the number of duplicates needed. The duplicates are necessary on both sides of the main landscape so that as it moves one direction or other the user will never see an edge. The duplication script we are going to write next will always add a duplicate movie clip to both the left and the right of strip1. The number of times the duplication script needs to run is 1 plus the number of times the landscape fits inside the panorama screen, divided by 2 (since each pass of the duplication script creates two duplicates). This guarantees at least one pass of the duplication script but will then only create as many extra copies as needed, which will reduce the amount that Flash has to process later. The code for this variable is:

```
onClipEvent (load) {
    //records the width of the image
    widthStrip = _width;
    //records where the right edge of the panorama is
    rightLimit = _root.rightMarkerPanorama._x;
    //records where the left edge of the panorama is
    leftLimit = _root.leftMarkerPanorama._x;
    //calculates distance from edge to edge
    widthscreen = rightLimit-leftLimit;
    //calculates the center point between the edges
    center = (.5*widthScreen)+leftLimit;
    //centers the movie
    _x = center;
    //determines how many duplication passes are needed
    duplicatesNeeded = (widthScreen/(2*widthStrip))+1;
}
```

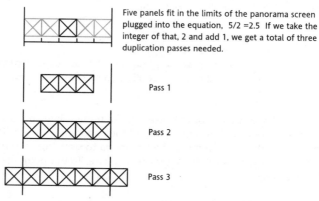

Five panels fit in the limits of the panorama screen plugged into the equation, 5/2 =2.5 If we take the integer of that, 2 and add 1, we get a total of three duplication passes needed.

Pass 1

Pass 2

Pass 3

4. As you might have guessed, when I mentioned the number of times that a script needs to run, it was signaling a `for` loop. The last variable that we just set up will be used as the condition for the loop. The setup for the loop should be pretty typical, the index variable set at 1, the condition being less than or equal to the number of duplicates needed and having the index incremented at the end of each loop:

```
onClipEvent (load) {
    widthStrip = _width;
    rightLimit = _root.rightMarkerPanorama._x;
    leftLimit = _root.leftMarkerPanorama._x;
    widthscreen = rightLimit-leftLimit;
    center = (.5*widthScreen)+leftLimit;
    _x = center;
    duplicatesNeeded = (widthScreen/(2*widthStrip))+1;
    //loop that does the duplication
    for (var i = 1; i<=duplicatesNeeded; i++) {
    }
}
```

5. Inside the loop, however, the code will look a little different than in previous examples. Normally I concatenate the index variable onto the new movie clip name and also use it as the new depth. In this case I can't do that since we'll be duplicating two objects for each pass. So the first thing we have to do inside the `for` loop if is set up two variables, one for both the left and right duplications; let's call them `dupR` and `dupL`. So we can give all of the copies unique depth and names, let's set `dupR` to two times `i` and `dupL` to two times `i` plus 1:

```
onClipEvent (load) {
    widthStrip = _width;
    rightLimit = _root.rightMarkerPanorama._x;
    leftLimit = _root.leftMarkerPanorama._x;
    widthscreen = rightLimit-leftLimit;
    center = (.5*widthScreen)+leftLimit;
    _x = center;
```

```
        duplicatesNeeded = (widthScreen/(2*widthStrip))+1;
        for (var i = 1; i<=duplicatesNeeded; i++) {
                //each pass creates a duplicate on the right and left
                dupR = 2*i;
                dupL = (2*i)+1;
        }
}
```

6. We then need to use the `duplicateMovieClip` method on each, concatenating the `dup` variable onto its name as well as using it for the depth. In addition to duplicating each movie clip, we need to set its `_x` position. The right movie clip should be placed at `i` times the width of the landscape. The left movie clip should be positioned at negative `i` times the width of the landscape. The reason for doing this is that `strip1` is centered on the 0,0 coordinated, so when you position the center of the new movie clip, you only need to account for half of `strip1`'s width and half of the new movie clip's width.

The code for all of the initialization should look like the following:

```
onClipEvent (load) {
        widthStrip = _width;
        rightLimit = _root.rightMarkerPanorama._x;
        leftLimit = _root.leftMarkerPanorama._x;
        widthscreen = rightLimit-leftLimit;
        center = (.5*widthScreen)+leftLimit;
        _x = center;
        duplicatesNeeded = (widthScreen/(2*widthStrip))+1;
        for (var i = 1; i<=duplicatesNeeded; i++) {
                dupR = 2*i;
                dupL = (2*i)+1;
                duplicateMovieClip (strip1, "strip"+dupR, dupR);
                setProperty ("strip"+dupR, _x, i*widthstrip);
                duplicateMovieClip (strip1, "strip"+dupL, dupL);
                setProperty ("strip"+dupL, _x, i*-widthstrip);
        }
}
```

Somewhat amazingly, the code for actually moving panorama around, which we'll put inside an `onClipEvent(enterFrame)` event, is quite a bit shorter than the initialization code. This process will involve moving the panorama based on the position of the cursor and then correcting its position at certain points to keep the loop effect functioning. When you look to the left, you see more of whatever is to the left of you. When trying to simulate this in Flash, it's not your head that moves, but instead the scene. This means that if you look left (move your mouse left), the scene must move to the right to reveal more on the left side.

7. We'll use the center of the panorama screen as looking forward, and the further the mouse is off that center point, the faster the scene will go by. To set this motion, the `_x` of the panorama should equal its current value minus (to reverse the direction) the x position of the mouse in terms of the `_root`. This is going to set the motion going

very fast once you move off center, so you will most likely want to multiply the amount added onto the current _x by some small number like 1. This will decrease the sensitivity of the mouse and allow a more realistic motion. You should experiment with this number until it suits your purposes.

```
onClipEvent (enterFrame) {
    //moves the strip as a function of distance from the center
    _x += (center-_root._xmouse)*.1;
}
```

8. Finally, we'll check to see if the _x of panorama has moved off the center point by more than half the width of strip1 in either direction. If so, then the panorama is moved back towards center by the full width of strip1. By moving in whole units of strip1's width, the user can't see that anything has changed. Altogether, the code looks like this:

```
onClipEvent (enterFrame) {
            _x += (center-_root._xmouse)*.1;
    //if the strip has traveled too far, it jumps back
    if (_x>center+(widthStrip/2)) {
            _x -= widthStrip;
    } else if (_x<center-(widthStrip/2)) {
            _x += widthStrip;
    }
}
```

Before testing this movie, you may want to add a mask on the main stage that only allows the panorama to show through between the left and right limits. If you allow the panorama to show through, the illusion would be ruined since the user would see the edges approach the limits and then jump back. If the user can only see the area inside the limits, then all you see is looping scenery.

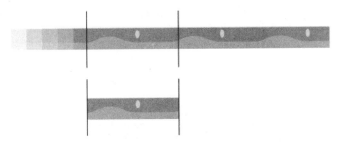

Some other effects you might want to try with this are adding a button over the panorama area that sets a variable to 1 on rollover and to 0 on release. That way you can set the contents of the onClipEvent(enterFrame) statement inside an if statement that only runs the command when the variable equals 1. I highly recommend this technique if you're planning on making the panorama part of a larger application. That way, the panorama won't be spinning the whole time. This can then be made more sophisticated by setting an else statement that tells the panorama to move at a fixed rate when the cursor is outside its area.

Lastly, you may want to try a cursor effect when over the panorama. You can use Mouse.hide with the button on roll over. You can then start dragging a movie clip that looks like a double-headed arrow to show your user the interactive options available to them. If you reference back to the airplane example in the previous chapter, you could modify the script that sets the airplane animation to a particular frame based on its distance from the cursor to a script that tells the dragged movie clip to go to a particular frame based on its distance from the center point of the panorama. This would allow you to make cursors that looked like arrows indicating in which direction and how fast you are moving.

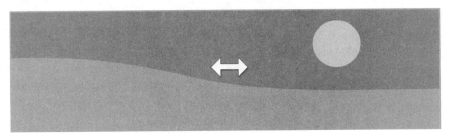

Summary

Using little more than these scripting techniques you're ready to start making some engrossing applications and games. Think about the features we've covered in the past couple of chapters not as single exercises to be used independently, but as tools to create more complex elements.

For instance, let's briefly sketch out a game combining several of the exercises from the chapters. The airplane controls example with the panorama could allow not only the airplane to move but have scenery to move along with it. This would take care of the background and controls.

Also you could make obstacles using the `hitTest` method. If you chose to make the perspective of the game so that you are looking from behind the airplane instead of from above it, the `swapDepths` command would be handy for controlling the stacking of all of the obstacles to keep them in the correct relationship to each other.

In perspective games, one issue you'll quickly run into is that as things move off into the distance they need to have the appearance of slowing down. This is because off in the distance things look smaller, so moving an object a uniform amount would appear to cross more area with the smaller scale. In this chapter we have a great example of deceleration. You could repurpose the delayed drag object into some sort of projectile weapon like a cannon or gun. When the gun is fired you would simple assign the target x and y coordinates to where the gun shot should go and then let the delayed drag script do the rest.

If you wanted to add a sound to the airplane, the pan exercise would be a wonderful addition allowing the engine noises to move from speaker to speaker as you move the plane.

In that outline of a game, we've used all but two of the major features we covered in the past two chapters, shuffling and color change. Color change could easily be worked in to change the color of the plane depending on health fuel or some sort of other status. I personally wouldn't shoehorn shuffling into this sort of game, but of all the examples in this chapter, to me this one is the most overtly game oriented. Card games are an excellent use of shuffling, but are also good game projects to work on if you want to really practice your conditional logic due to their generally rigid rules.

With all of this talk of games, it's time to introduce the next chapter. We're going to build a whole application instead of just working on fragments. Continuing my theory that it's more fun to learn by making games, we're going to look at creating an Asteroids clone. We'll use some of the principles learned in this chapter, but for the most part, we'll cover some other effects such as motion, trajectory, and the key object among many other things. For those of you who skipped the equation-based dragging exercise, guess what! A little more math. Don't worry, not much, and we'll take it slowly.

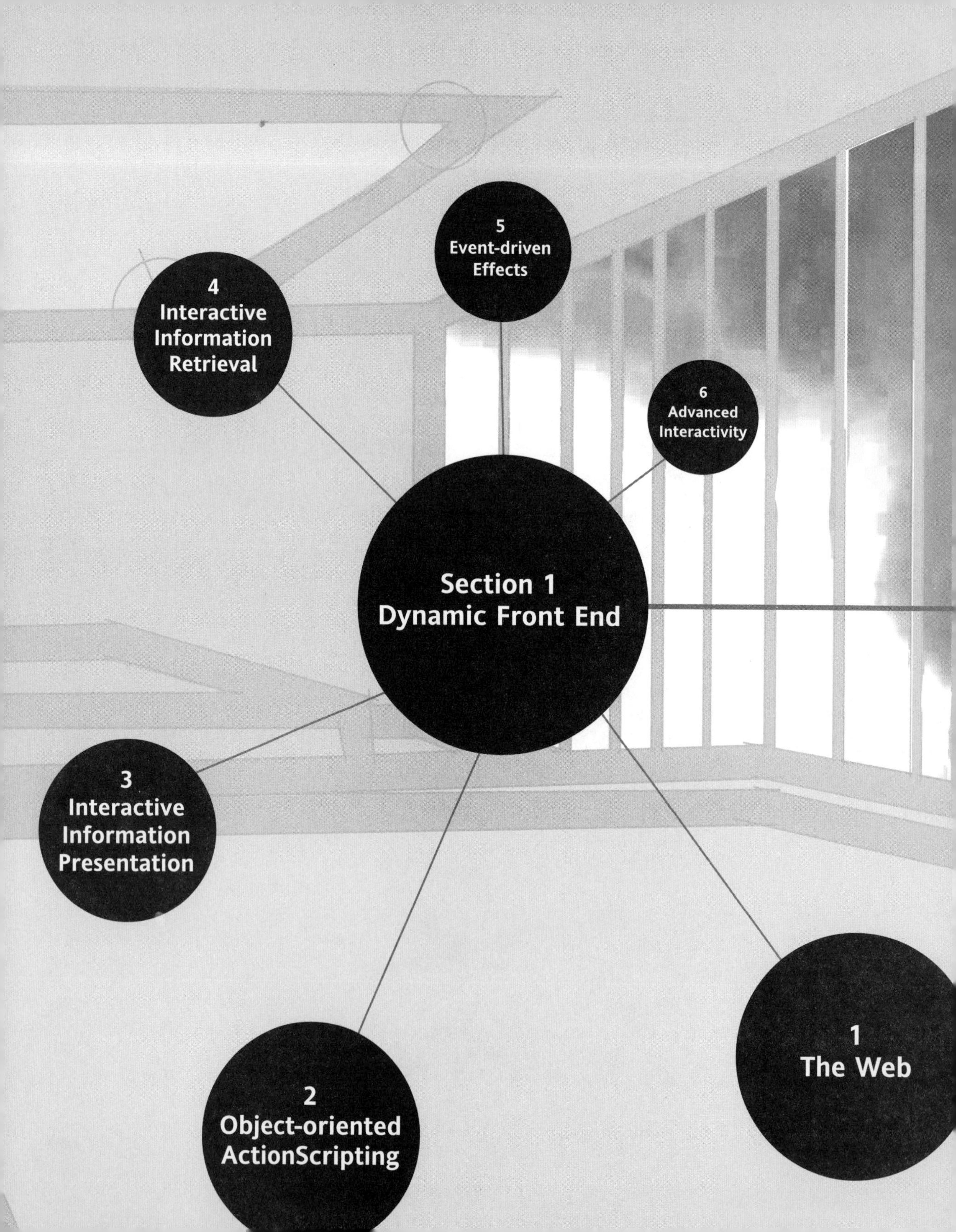

Section 1
Dynamic Front End

5
Event-driven
Effects

4
Interactive
Information
Retrieval

6
Advanced
Interactivity

3
Interactive
Information
Presentation

2
Object-oriented
ActionScripting

1
The Web

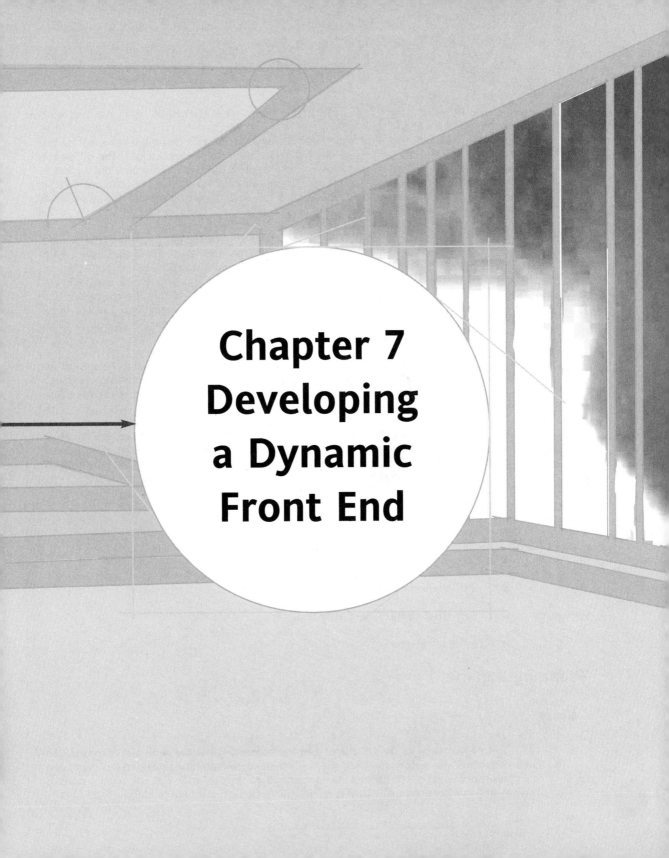

Chapter 7
Developing
a Dynamic
Front End

In this chapter, we're going to put many of the things we've learned so far to use, and walk through the creation of a full game. The game we'll construct here is Space Mines, a clone of the arcade classic Asteroids first produced in the '70s by Atari. We'll be creating a game, but by the end you'll be able to lift sections of the engine for use in other applications. The difference between a game and an engine is that an engine is a set of controls and reactions but a game is the engine placed in a context. For instance, there's nothing to say that the code couldn't be reused with different graphics and turned into a top-down view of a person playing paintball against computer-controlled people.

The context is just the wrapping of the game engine in relevant pictures, story and sounds. Normally, a game engine isn't much fun to play. Think of a game you know and replace each graphic element with a square. The game would still work, but it would be boring. Now think of all of the things that the square could be changed into. For each idea, you have a new game, but you've used the same engine. Throughout the chapter, keep in mind that the engine and the game's story can be separated, but if you already have a theme developed, then it makes sense to develop the two concurrently. In fact, generally work with a story, context, theme or situation, and then come up with game play that fits these predefined elements.

Often a game engine can be turned into many games with only slight scripting changes. When you're dealing with a client, keep in mind that a game engine is inherently more valuable than a game, but all games contain an engine. When you're negotiating with a prospective client, be sure to cover ownership and usage terms of the underlying game structure.

Games can vary drastically in the style of play, the types of enemies, goals, and general structure of the game. Before we begin constructing a specific game, it would be best to start off with some discussion of general arcade game parts and concepts. After that, we'll get into the nitty gritty of the specific game we'll be building, Space Mines.

So in this chapter, we'll:

- Look at the story line of the game

- Cover some basic topics of game design and structure

- Build the components of the game, piece-by-piece

- Program the controls and behaviors

- Put it all together!

Planning a game

Story

The key to any game is its story. Think of it as the framework that the game play is constructed upon. How much of a story you need will really depend on individual situations, the depth and complexity of the game, but I always like to create more story than the user will actually need to play it. Having a developed story is very useful, but is also just plain fun to make.

The story of a game must make sense, and it should entertain, but it will also help in creating a consistent game. By creating the universe where the game takes place, you're in a better position to decide how things need to happen in that framework. Also, even if you never hint at the story in the game itself, a story can be a powerful tool when pitching a game. Instead of pitching a game solely on its functionality and design, using a story will make the game seem better thought out and more entertaining (and with a story the game *is* generally better thought out and more entertaining).

Layout

Once you have your story, you need to consider the layout; you need to settle on the layout of the game before you can begin work on the contols or the scripting details. Games generally fall into one of three categories, depending on how things move, and how the player views the scene. Most games can be classified as scrolling, stationary or perspective gaming.

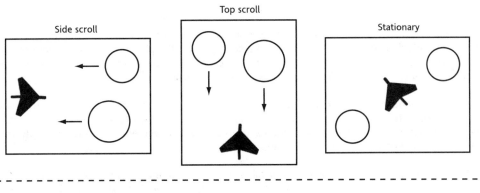

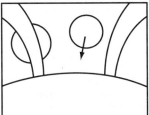

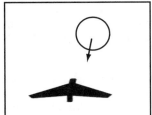

First Person Perspective   Third Person Perspective

Scrolling games have a character fixed in one dimension (or with limited movement) and are generally set up so that the player is looking down on them. Movement is achieved by scrolling the scenery towards the player – can be oriented in any direction.

Stationary games are like their scrolling counterparts, just without the scrolling. Instead of a stationary character and a moving scene, the scene is fixed and your character does all of the moving. These are generally much easier to process, since moving a small object is a lot simpler moving a whole scene. These are usually be top-down or side view.

Perspective games are often more visually interesting games, and are among the most challenging. A first person perspective game gives you the illusion of 'being there' by giving you an eye-line view, while a third person view has the view behind, and often slightly above your character. Perspective games are generally 3D or in the case of Flash, fake 3D.

It's this fake 3D that causes the complexity. Flash has no built in 3D support, so perspective must be managed by programmatically scaling objects, and using `swapDepths` to maintain z-ordering (as you'll remember from chapter 5). Third person view games, generally link depth and the y axis as linked. Making the scaling and depth of a distant object a function of its y position will work nicely for objects that are coming from a horizon line positioned higher than your character. For first person games, where the horizon is at eye level, you have to use a variable that controls depth. If an object is coming towards you at a constant rate from the horizon, incrementing a variable after every frame that the object exists will let you track the depth reasonably well tracking of the depth.

Characters

Once you've thought about how the game will be laid out, it's time to start putting things on the screen. For arcade games, you'll usually need a character for the player, and one or more enemy characters. How your character, or avatar, moves depend on your controls and on any environmental conditions you're creating, like wind, collision, gravity, and so on.

Enemy movements have to be controlled by the same environmental effects as well, but they also have to take in to account some sort of general control scheme, so that the system can move them. The system's control can be anything from random movement to complex scripts that attempt to simulate intelligent behavior and strategy.

Making an omniscient enemy is generally fairly easy – the script just accesses the location of movie clips and moves towards or away from them as needed. The same would be true for targeting. The problem if you are too accurate, though, is that the enemy would be insurpassable, and it's pretty important that the player has some kind of chance. If the game is to be interesting you can give your enemy weaknesses by adding and subtracting random amounts to the actual coordinates.

For instance, if you're throwing something at the enemy, the enemy can extrapolate exactly where the object is going to hit. But if you take those coordinates and offset them by a random amount, the computer can still work from hard values. Essentially the computer thinks it knows exactly where the object will land, it may just be off by a bit.

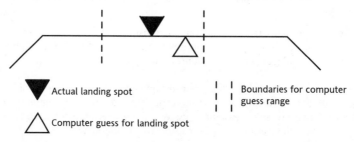

Actual landing spot

Boundaries for computer
guess range

Computer guess for landing spot

I like using randomization because it seems to replicate human actions pretty well! If I see something being thrown at me, I know generally where it's going to land within a range, but the exact spot I guess may be off by quite a bit. From level to level in the game, it's certainly possible to let the computer pick from a progressively smaller and smaller range of possible points or to allow the script to re-guess a certain time based on the level, where each re-guess is within the smaller range of possible points. This is also a good analog of human thinking: as a ball leaves someone's hand I have very little idea where the ball will land,but as I watch it moving I get a better idea. My guess will become more and more accurate until I see it land.

Randomly moving enemies are much easier to script in general, since they move to a random location at certain intervals, or are initialized with a certain random direction and simply keep moving for as long as they are present.

The enemy style you choose will largely depend on the story of the game. If a character is an intelligent creature, it needs to act that way, but if it's inanimate or not sentient, it needs to act in very predictable ways.

Controls

The next step in the planning process should be the controls of your avatar. I put this after the controls of the enemy, since often the most challenging scripting elements are there. It's probably best to plan out a viable enemy control, before spending the time planning the easier controls.

To create controls you need to keep in mind that the user can only use the keyboard, mouse movement and left mouse button in Flash. The other big limitation, which may seem a bit obvious, is that the user only has two hands. At absolute maximum, I have no more than a few commands for a hand on the keyboard and then only one for the mouse button and a general action for mouse movement. No matter how good a game idea is, it won't be successful unless the user can use the controls comfortably and with little confusion.

In keyboard games, it's generally the user operates the arrow keys with the right hand and, if needed, use their left hand to hit the spacebar and whatever other keys they need to use. It's always a good idea to keep the controls pretty simple. Although the player will be using their right hand to control four separate arrow buttons, these tend to be conceptually linked commands, so the keys are laid out well for intuitive use. Hitting the space bar, the biggest key on the keyboard, with the other hand is easy, but remember that any other keys you choose are sitting in a field of similar keys. A fast paced arcade game can get way too hard if you're hunting for the right key at the wrong time.

I personally like assigning secondary action to the T key when I'm using the space bar since if I put my thumb on the center of the space bar and relax my hand, my index finger naturally falls on the T key. As you're designing your own games, remember that comfort is a big part of the equation. So if the player has to use always using one of your predefined keys to repeatedly issue commands, the keys are placed too close together or too far apart, people might find your game rather awkward.

One last note about the key selection: not everyone has the same keyboard. While it would be fine to use the Y key instead of the T key on a regular keyboard, it wouldn't be too good for players using an ergonomic keyboard because the Y is on the right half of the split. Remember that the player will be using their right hand to operate the arrow keys and even arrow keys can also be placed irregularly. For example, on laptops they might be placed in a row, or in a bad location compared to a track pad if you're using mouse control.

Game play and levels

Assuming that we have all of the characters thought out, their rules for movement and a story to set them to, it's time to let the game begin. All interactions should happen be consistent with the story behind the game, and most importantly, it should exciting and fun because this is what distinguishes one game from another. (If this section were formulaic at all, we would have a lot of the same game.)

We won't really address game play as a general concept: often the one concept that does cross most game styles is leveling. This provides a short-term goal for the game as well as a way of making the game increasingly difficult in a controlled and predictable way.

It's also the best way of letting the user know how far they've reached in the game. By providing a metric of how far the player has advanced, he or she will often try again so that they can get to a higher level. If you don't provide this sort of information, the player may think that there's no other goal to the game and stop playing.

This concept of getting people to return, or to choose to remain at a site, is known by the rather unfortunate word **sticky**. Creating ways of drawing users back to a site or an application is an important feature for any Flash project. The more people that come back, the more people that are likely to buy your product, see your ads, or experience the message of your site, whatever the underlying goal is. Heck, if the goal is just to make a fun game or compelling design, that'll do too.

In some games, the idea of a goal is completely illusory. The system will go to higher and higher levels until the player loses. In this sort of game it's just a contest to see how high a score has been reached or how many levels have been passed before inevitably losing.

In other games, levels are a progression towards a real goal with a real ending. In these games too the same sort of incrementing should occur, but after a certain amount of levels have passed, an end sequence will play. Either model is perfectly valid, it all depends on your own preference and any dictates from the game idea itself. A tournament style game will obviously necessitate an end at some point.

The purpose of the game can also help determine the structure. One of the most common uses of games in Flash is to serve as entertainment while you're waiting for a larger download to finish. In this case you may want to structure the game with infinite levels since the focus for a preloader game isn't really the game, but instead keeping the player occupied for as long as it takes to load the rest of the project. If so, you won't want the user to have finished the game before the load process is finished, giving the game an ending would also increase file size. Since there's a larger download that we must consider, creating a lean game is more important than one that has a great end animation. The chances are as well that, once the project has loaded in, the player would abandon the game and might never see the end.

I'd like to add a note if you use Flash for interface and presentation work. As someone who has done that, if your interest is really in making games, preloader games are a great way to get your company to allow you to do just that. If you ever run up against a large download time, suggest creating a preloader game to fill what is essentially dead air time. Keeping a user engaged during a time when they might otherwise be considering not waiting for your download is very valuable. Failing that, try making holiday games to send around the office. They're fun to make and may help your cause later on. Also submitting games to the many Flash resource web sites is another great avenue.

Space Mines: planning the game

Now that we've covered some of the general game concepts, let's put them into practice. We'll go through the same planning steps as above but this time focusing on the project at hand, making an asteroids clone. For this game, that means:

- Story
- Perspective
- Ship and its controls
- Mine and its controls
- Levels

After the planning is done, we'll move into construction and then scripting. The source file for the game is `spacemines.fla` on the CD.

The story

During the third expansion wave of earth, colonists encounter a new civilization more advanced than our own. Their prime advantage is the efficiency of their plasma energy systems and weapons. Due to many misunderstandings, tensions mounted until war broke out.

You are the pilot of a new breed of spaceship assigned to clear out the limited self-replicating mines laid in Earth space. Your ship, the latest in plasma-based energy drives, which was only acquired after capturing an enemy mine intact, is equipped with a main thruster and two quarter power retro-thrusters.

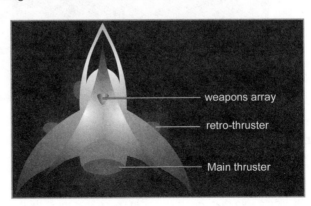

As well as propulsion, you have tactical and defensive systems. The plasma cannon linked directly to your main drive is capable of shooting eight short-range plasma shots before needing to recharge. One plasma shot should be sufficient to deal with any mine you encounter. If you don't have time to turn your ship to shoot a nearby mine, you can activate your defensive shields with emitters located on the nose and wing tips.

As you test the new ship successfully, you'll be assigned to more and more densely packed areas. On the way to your next area, your shields will recharge slightly. Due to high-speed transit between mine areas, the drain on the main thruster must be kept minimal. The shields will only be recharged by 15% so be careful. Importantly, since this is a new technology, we only have four of these ships standing between earth and a full blockade. Finally, in compliance with the Government Motivation Act of 2105, you have been authorized to receive a commission of 150 credits per mine destroyed and a variable bonus based on your speed in completing the mission. Good luck.

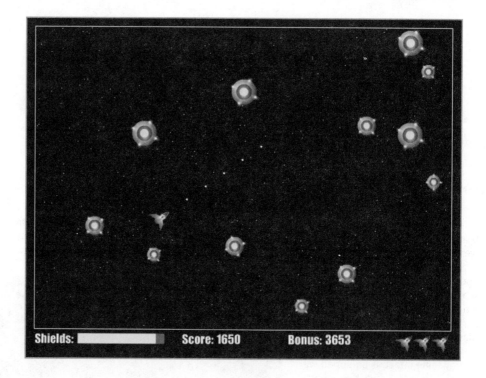

Perspective

This game will be a top-down stationary view game. The ship will be able to move freely within the screen and will wrap to the other side if it attempts to go off screen. There's nothing about having a ship that shoots mines in space that must tie it to a top down view. Conveniently, it also happens to be the easiest to script, as well as giving the user a view of all the mines at once.

Controls

In the Space Mines game the movement is going to be entirely on the keyboard. The player will use one hand on the arrow keys to control rotation and thrust. They'll use the other hand on the T key for shields and the space bar to fire the cannon. As I said in the general controls section, I find that I can comfortably use the T key and the SPACE BAR with one hand. If you disagree, feel free to pick another. Sometimes choosing keys that are related to the command name can be useful, such as S for shields.

Enemies

The enemy in this game is an inanimate mine, which just moves according to its initial inertia. When the mine spawns at the beginning of the level it will start off screen with a randomly set movement value. Once it's moving, it just needs to continue moving, and check to see whether it has run into the ship.

If it collides with the ship, the ship's shields or a plasma shot, it is destroyed. If it grows above a certain size, it self replicates and spawns two smaller mines. In this case, the script that determines when it's hit lives inside the plasma shot. As this picture shows, a single mine at the beginning of a level can subdivide once. Both of the new, smaller mines can subdivide once. Once the smallest of the mines has been destroyed, they simply disappear.

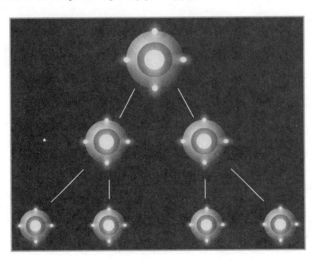

Game levels

Each level in Space Mines is completed once the player has destroyed all of the mines on the screen. Winning a level will play through a screen showing the next level number, then increment a variable in the root, and finally trigger a script that starts the new skill level by duplicating the appropriate new number of mines, which is determined by the level variable, and also replacing the ship at the center of the stage. At the end of the level a bonus based on how fast you completed the level is awarded, and the shields are partially recharged.

Space Mines: building the game

Now we're ready to begin the actual construction. We'll start off by setting up the FLA, then build the visual elements of the game. From there we'll start the task of scripting all of the components, then polishing the final presentation of the game.

Setting up the FLA

While the FLA for a game is really no different than any other application, there are a few settings that could affect how well a game functions. We'll be setting dimensions, background color and frame rate in this section.

Game speed can really make a difference to the difficulty of a game, as well as its general effect. While Flash generally defaults animations to 12 frames per second (fps), I like to make games in the 25-30 fps range. It provides smoother motion and helps dramatically with collision detection since both player and enemy can cover smaller spaces between frames. The smaller the amount moved, the less likely that you've jumped over a target without colliding with it.

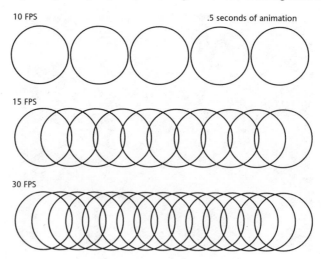

One warning against using higher frame rates is that if you use a lot of frame-by-frame traditional animation, the overall file size will increase. Having 30 frames of animation versus 12 for one second of animation is simply a lot more data that must be stored in the SWF. In our game, though, there will be almost no animation other than what's performed by the scripting during the game play. Since this sort of motion is executed during the playing of the movie, and isn't a matter of keyframes, changing the rate of the movie won't affect file size, but will only affect how frequently the scripts are executed.

1. Let's set the fps to 30 in the Movie Properties window (Modify > Movie). Also, let's change the background color to black so it looks like we're in space. I rather arbitrarily picked 540 by 430 as the dimensions of the game. These can be whatever you want but always make sure that the dimensions suit your game. A top-down scrolling game generally needs a taller screen and a side scrolling game needs a wider screen.

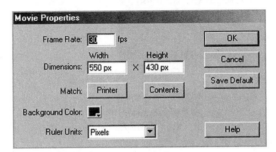

While we're dealing with the more administrative elements of the game setup, I just want to remind you about Flash's coordinate system. This game will be using a fair amount of math, so as we deal with concepts in Flash that may also be familiar to you from your math classes, I'd like to cover any disparity between the two here, before we get started.

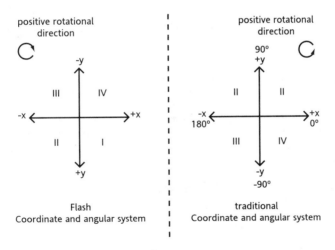

You'll notice the figure above shows both Flash's coordinate system and the traditional Cartesian coordinate system. As we've discussed, Flash's system is an upside down version of the traditional. This diagram makes it seem that rotation is also backwards, but really it isn't. Since Flash's system is upside down, if you imagined it flipped back over it would be going in the same direction as the traditional system.

The big difference, though, is that for the traditional system 0 degrees points straight out to the right and then to increment degrees, it moves around the origin in a counter-clockwise circle. Flash's rotation works generally the same way, but 0 degrees doesn't 'point' in any direction. It's more a matter of orientation. When you make something into a symbol, that orientation is 0 degrees. If you use the Rotation tool or scripting to change the rotation to 10 degrees, that means that it's 10 degrees clockwise of the initial orientation. The reason for discussing this here is that we'll be using trigonometry later on to control the motion of the ship. Trigonometry is tied to the orientation of the traditional angular system. So, to have the trig work well with the ship, for instance, we need to artificially align it to what we thought of as 0 degrees in our math classes.

Lastly, trigonometry doesn't use degrees; instead it uses a unit called **radians**. A full circle, which is 360 degrees expressed in radians, is 2 Pi. Whenever we use trigonometric functions, we'll have to convert the angles from degrees to radians. To do that we divide the rotation value (expressed in degrees) by 360 to create an angle expressed as a ratio of a full circle, then multiply that ratio by 2 Pi. Once we've done this, all of our math will be completely compatible between the two systems.

```
angle = ((ship._rotation)/360)*2*Math.PI;
```

Don't worry, as we have need of these math principles, we'll talk about them again in their specific context. I just wanted to make sure that these differences weren't lost within the instructions for doing the actual scripting. Aside from the Space Mine games, you'll want to keep these things in mind whenever you are dealing with math in Flash generally.

Building the graphics

We now have a movie all primed for us to start building the graphical elements of the game. In this section you can either create your own graphics or use the ones in the source file for this chapter. As you'll see later, the choices you make when designing your characters will affect the game play. In this game I've chosen to have fun with the design and I've used a fair number of gradients that go to transparent to create glow effects. While these can be pretty, transparency can really slow down a game.

To get an idea of the size of the graphics, have a look back at the screenshot at the end of the story section above. A lot of the screenshots in this chapter are enlarged to show graphical details of the various components of the game. You can adjust your view of the stage using the menu at the bottom left of the editing area, or in the View menu.

Creating the ship

1. On the stage in the main timeline rename Layer 1 as ship, then go ahead and draw a space ship. I made mine around 30 x 30 pixels.

    As you design the ship, think about its actions. For this game, there will be lots of rapid turning and moving to get out of the way of nearby mines. Because of the problems we saw in Chapter 5 for objects and their bounding boxes, movie clip-to-movie clip hitTest isn't really an option. Instead, we'll have to rely on point-to-movie clip detection. As we'll see in the collision detection script section, while better than comparing bounding boxes this method is less than perfect since it allows some overlapping before the collision will be detected. We'll get around this a bit when it comes to actually scripting the collision detection, but the more flared out parts there are, the greater chance there will be of an overlap without detecting a collision. So, the ship can really look however you want it to, but it's still a good idea to keep the shape compact for a better result when testing for collision. Also, a ship that is disproportionately long would appear very awkward when pivoting in place.

2. After you've drawn a basic ship, make it into a movie clip called ship. It will be very important when we rotate the ship that it remains centered on the pivot inside the movie clip. The pivot in this case is acting like the center of gravity for the ship. Also, make sure that the ship has its nose pointing to the right. This will allow for that artificial alignment to the traditional angular system we talked about earlier.

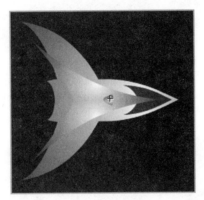

3. We'll add secondary movie clips inside the ship movie clip for the thrusters. These secondary effects aren't absolutely necessary, but they can enhance the experience of the game. Add a layer to your ship movie clip called main engine. Create an image for the main thruster and make it into a movie clip called green glowing element and give it an instance name thrust.

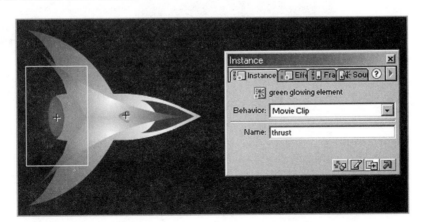

4. Now add a layer called retro thrusters. Create your retro thrusters as you see here and turn them into a movie clip called retro thrusters with an instance name of `retro`.

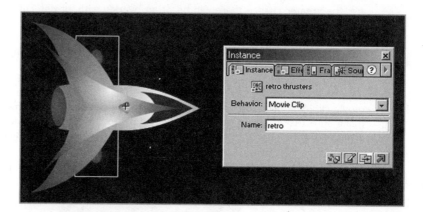

Also, instead of actually using an animation or firing thrusters, I've set their Alpha to 30% by default (using the Effects panel). I then use scripting to change the Alpha to 100% when the thruster is in use and by scripting back to 30% when no longer in use.

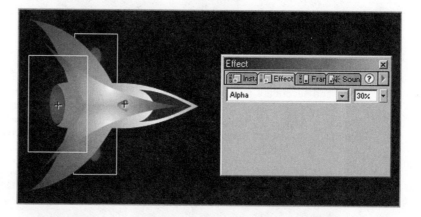

5. At this point you'll also want to create the shield, so add a new layer to your ship movie clip called shield. Create a shield similar to mine and make it into a movie clip called shield with an instance name `shield`.

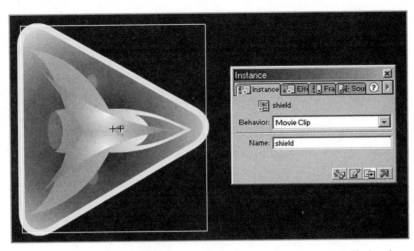

We want to turn the shield on and off and make sure that while it's off, the shape of the shield doesn't figure into the collision detection we'll be setting later. To do this, we'll need to give the movie clip two frames.

6. Go inside the shield movie clip and add a blank keyframe in frame 2. Put a stop action in frame 1.

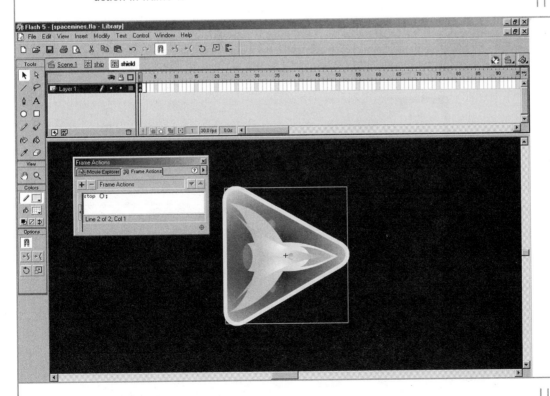

By using a two-frame movie clip instead of adjusting visibility or transparency, the shield is simply not there while off, and doesn't affect the dimensions of the movie clip. This is important for running the collision detection script. If your shields don't hug your ship, and are totally transparent, the collision detection would be set off too early.

For an example of this, if you had super-powerful shields that could extend around a ship five times your size, as in this image here, that large shape would register a collision with a mine even if the shields were set to transparent or invisible. When the shields are down, the mines should only be able to hit the shape of the ship.

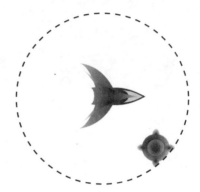

7. Now that we have a ship, we need to give it an instance name so that all of the other game elements can interact with it. Go back out onto the main stage, and give the ship movie clip the instance name `ship`.

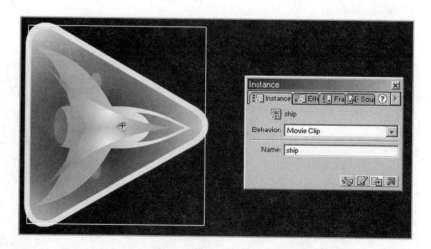

Creating the mines

Now that we're back out on the main stage, let's make the next main visual element, the mine. It's not much of a villain, but it's still the enemy in the game. It should be a fairly simple object. If you make one that's too complex, the system will begin to chug as you hit higher levels. As you can see if you play the game as I've made it, I had some fun with some rotating lights with glows on them. Once you get to level 8 or so, the game starts to slow down. If I were producing them for anything other than a tutorial, I would probably change the mine to be a little less processor-intensive. Now that I've said to not go overboard, I would still encourage you to strike a balance between plain and complex since you're going to be looking at a lot of them. The mine will actually be one of the key artistic elements of the game.

1. Add another layer to the main timeline called mine and create your mine.

2. Once you've drawn one on the stage, make it into a movie clip called mine and give it an instance name mine.

The way we'll be making so many mines during the game is to use the duplicateMovieClip at the beginning of each level. This mine is going to be the template by which all other mines are created. Since it needs to be there as the stock copy of a mine, it can't ever be used during the game (it would otherwise get destroyed). Since it's just going to work behind the scenes, we need to move it off the side of the stage so the player never sees it.

With a ship, an enemy mine, and the weapon that we're about to create, you can be sure we'll need an explosion animation. The mine is always going to be the thing that does the exploding whether it hits the ship, or is hit by a plasma shot, so it's best to put the animation in there.

The mine explosion

1. Go back into the mine movie clip and add a new layer called explosion. Add a keyframe at frame 5. In frames 2 through 5, make an animation of an explosion. I chose to do a stylized explosion, which is a shape tween of a small circle with a radial gradient going from transparent in the middle to bright green on the edge, going to a larger version of the same in frame 5.

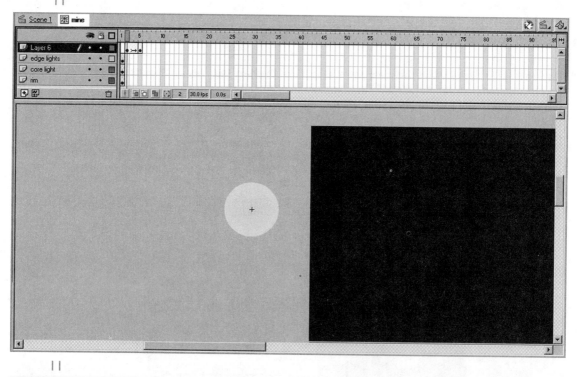

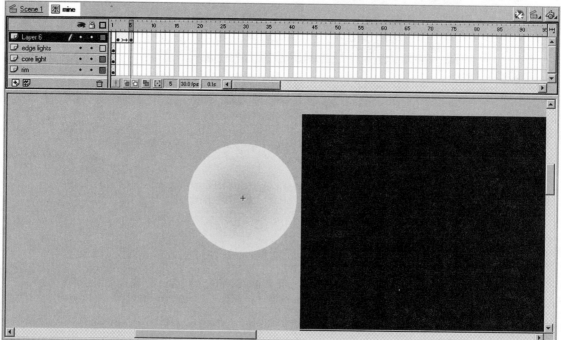

2. Add a blank keyframe in frame 6 because we want the explosion to disappear leaving a blank screen.

3. In frame 1, we need to add a `stop` action so the mine doesn't instantly explode. Also, since the mines are going to be duplicates of a stock mine movie, let's go ahead and add the code that removes the mine movie clip once it has exploded. To do that, add the this action to frame 6:

```
removeMovieClip (this);
```

The plasma shot

Well since we've gone to the trouble of making an explosion, I guess we just have to make something violent to force the mine to blow up. That way we can see the nifty explosion animation.

1. Back out on the main stage, create a new layer called shot. The third element we need to make is the weapon shot that the ship will fire at the mines. This step will be the hardest artistic task in the whole project. Brace yourself. You need to draw... a dot, and a pretty small dot at that. When we start running collision detection using the shot, we're going to compare its coordinates to the movie clip of the mine. Since it's a point to movie clip comparison, the smaller you make the shot, the more accurate the appearance will be when it's fired at the mine.

2. Make the dot into a movie clip called plasma burst and give it the name shot. Making it into a new symbol means that the dot should be centered on the pivot of the movie clip. It needs to remain that way so that the collision detection will work properly. Much like the mines, shots will be duplicated as needed, using this movie clip as a template. So, you'll need to move it off the stage as well:

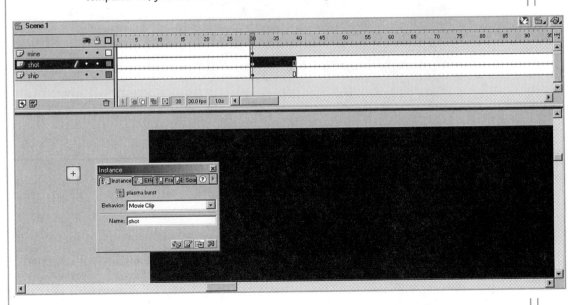

The interface

This is the last major visual element necessary for the game to function. During the game, the player needs to be able to see certain pieces of information (shield level, points, bonus, and lives). While some of that may just seem like a convenience to the user, the shield and life segments will actually figure into the function of the game. We aren't going to script the interface yet, but we'll get it set up for the scripting in the next section.

The interface always needs to be on a higher level than the game elements. It would be bad, for instance, if the mine covered the score. As we've been talking about duplicating movie clips for the mines and the shots, we need to remember they'll be placed in depths higher than anything we can put in the FLA itself. Therefore, we'll have to also raise the interface above everything else.

As long as we are doing that, we should make a mat to act like a mask and hide everything outside the game area. We can then put the interface elements on top of that. The purpose for the mat is to act like a mask without being a mask layer - it will be a movie clip and will have a depth property. When a wrap occurs, you'll only see the ship pass off one side and immediately come in the other side without a visible jump. This will also cover over the templates that we placed off the side of the stage.

1. To begin, let's create a new layer on the main stage called mat. To make a mat, draw a rectangle that's much larger than the stage and then make a cutout in it so that the game can show through it. To make the cutout, you can just draw another rectangle on the large one, 550 pixels wide by 400 tall, select the fill inside it, then delete the fill.

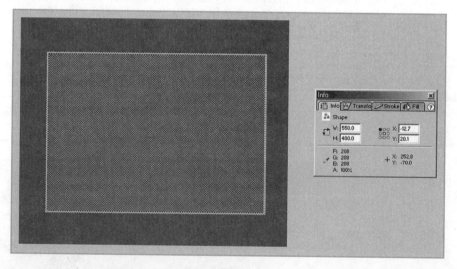

2. Our original file is 550 pixels wide by 430 pixels tall. We have now made the game area take up all but the bottom 30 pixels of the screen. This is where we'll put all of the information the user needs to see. The cutout will go right along the boundaries so that the bottom 30 pixels of the stage would be covered.

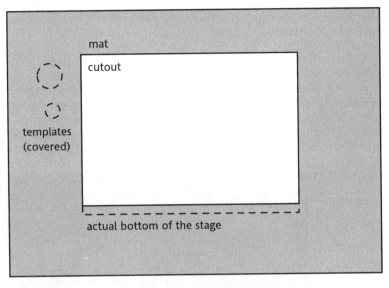

2. Once you've made the mat, select it and make it into a movie clip called mat with an instance name of `interface`. Inside `interface`, we'll be building all of the informational items to give the user feedback. Once inside the mat, you may want to add a stroke to the inside of the cutout so the user can see where the edge of the game screen is.

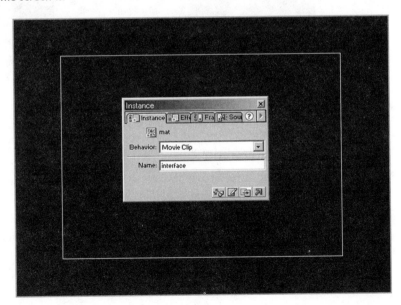

From here we can start adding the interface elements. We'll be making a thermometer bar like we did in the preloader section of Chapter 5 to represent remaining shields. The score and bonus will just be dynamic text fields just like the ones we've used in several previous examples.

Lastly, the lives will be displayed as a movie clip where each frame has one less ship. Let's add a new layer to hold our interface elements.

Shields

1. Think of the shields as a feature running off a rechargeable battery. Before you use your shields it's a good idea to know how much more power you have left. We'll make a bar to display this charge. To make the shield bar draw a rectangle where you want to place it (in the 30 pixel overlap of the mat and the stage) and then make it into a movie clip called active shield bar with an instance name shield.

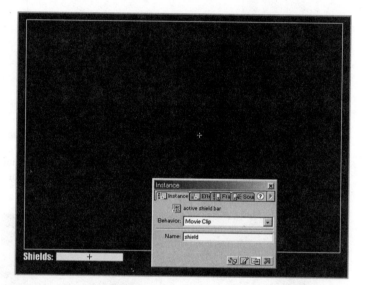

2. Inside shield, we'll need both the bar that moves and a background to show the full range of the bar. To make the background you need to copy the rectangle and paste it in place in a new layer. In the lower layer, change the color of the bar to something darker to show a contrast between the empty area and the filled area.

3. Now add a keyframe at frame 200 on both layers. This will give you a beginning and ending point for the tween that you're about to create.

4. In frame 200 of the upper layer squash the rectangle horizontally to one side of the bar so that it's nothing more than a thin line that looks like less than one percent. Now set up a shape tween in frame 1. You now have a functional thermometer bar:

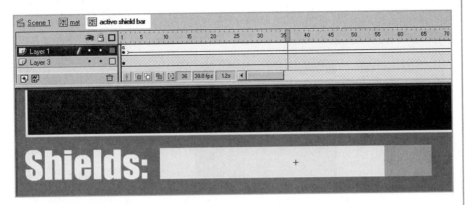

5. In the first keyframe, be sure to add a stop action so that the thermometer does not play on its own. Also, at the end of the animation, add one more frame and make the frame in the upper layer a blank keyframe. This way, when you run completely out of shields, the shield bar will be completely gone.

Score and Bonus

The score is just a dynamic text box, with a label next to it. Back out in the interface movie clip, add these two elements next to the shield bar. The dynamic text box should have the variable name of score and be set non-selectable and single line. The label should just be a static textbox with Score: in it. The bonus textbox is set up in the exact same way as the score with both a dynamic textbox and a static text label.

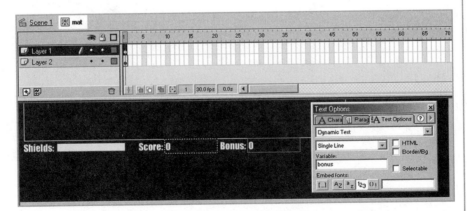

Lives

1. The last element of interface is the lives. To create a ship icon to represent each life, go to the ship symbol in the library and edit it. Select everything but the shield and copy it. Now go back to the interface and paste it. Go ahead and make this into a graphic symbol called life ship, then scale and position it however you want so that it fits down in the area with the rest of the interface.

2. Once you have the ship positioned, select it and make it into a movie clip called lives. Give this movie clip an instance name `ships`.

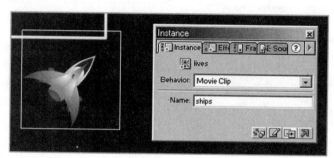

3. Inside `ships`, let's copy and paste the life ship graphic symbol twice so we have a total of three ship icons. Space them evenly. Once they're in place, add a new frame and make it a keyframe. In the new keyframe, delete one ship. Repeat this process with frame 2, so that in frame 3 there is only now one ship. Add two more frames and make each a blank keyframe. The first blank frame is for when you're playing when with your last ship. The second blank frame will eventually hold the script ending the game. In frame 1, be sure to add a `stop` action so the animation doesn't play straight through.

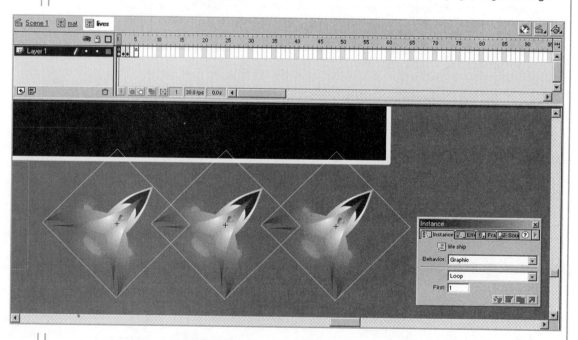

4. Let's add one bit of code to the `interface` movie clip. We've been talking about template movie clips that will be duplicated to form the mines and shots in the game. Since these are going to be put in a depth higher than the interface, we need to add code to the interface to move it up higher than the other objects. To do that, go out to the main stage, select the `interface` movie clip, then bring up the Actions panel. We need to add an `onClipEvent (load)` command to hold the script to swap the depth of itself to something very high like 9000000:

```
onClipEvent (load) {
    this.swapDepths(9000000);
}
```

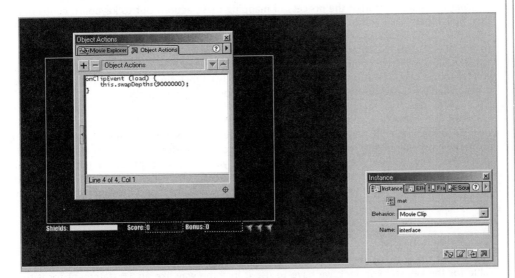

We're done with the interface for now, so let's move it out of our way for the moment. Its job, which is partially to block out things that are off the stage, is going to get in the way as we're trying to script the template movie clips. So, for now, turn this layer's visibility off by clicking the visibility dot (the one under the eyeball). The dot should turn to an x and the interface should disappear, revealing the movie clips that are offstage.

Now that we have all of the visual elements of the game play developed, it's time to bring them to life with scripting. With all of the interdependency between game elements, it's going to be extremely useful that there is now a visual reference for each element. We've also now been introduced to all of the elements so it should be easier to see how they function together. In the scripting section, we'll be covering:

- Ship movement

- Mine movement

- Shields

- Firing

- Events (new level, death, and game over)

Scripting the game

Ship movement

Our ship moves in two conceptually different ways: it can rotate and it can thrust. Within each movement there are two actions: you can rotate left and right and you can move forwards and backwards. We'll go through the process of mapping these actions out to keyboard controls, and then make them take action on the stage.

To actually control the rotation and thrust, we'll need to write scripts for the arrow buttons to interact with. While we could set up buttons to run the actions, they have one major problem. If you try to use two keys at once, the last one pressed will block the other from registering the key press. When we try to do two things at once, this would be problematic.

We need to be able to accelerate, turn, fire and eventually raise shields all at once. To allow this, we'll be using Flash 5's new `Key` object. The `Key` object has four methods and a number of properties associated with it. These properties are constants associated with the key code value of different keys, so `Key.LEFT`, for example, allows you to write script for the left arrow key on the keyboard. We can set any key using the `Key` object's properties and pass it to one of the methods as an argument. To find out if the left arrow key has been pressed, for example, we would write:

```
if (Key.isDown(Key.LEFT))
```

Notice that the `isDown` method is used in a conditional expression since it returns a Boolean value for the key state. In fact, we have to use it in some way like an `if` statement for it to do something.

An actual button with a key press event works much like typing in a word processor. If you hold down a key, it will trigger once, pause and then quickly keep repeating until you let go of the button. While you're holding down that key, if you press another it will stop the first key and use the new key. So using the key triggers the scripts to run as often as the key would send to a word processor.

The `isDown` method doesn't work this way. The simple act of holding down the key does nothing. Instead, it's when a script checks to see whether a particular key is down that this method returns a true value. Because it's checking whether or not a key is pressed instead of performing commands based on the event of the key sending data to the computer, you can check if multiple keys are being pressed. It's now just a matter of making sure that there's a script checking the state of the controlling keys.

Rotation

To rotate the ship, we'll be linking the right and left arrow keys to scripts that set the `_rotation` properties of the ship. As we've done in many of the examples in the last chapters, we'll be placing most of the code for the ship in `OnClipEvents`. Since the scripts need to check the state of the game control keys, we'll use the `enterFrame` event so that the check happens constantly. As for where to put it, these commands are specific to the ship and only need to happen when it's on the screen, so the best place for this script is attached to the ship movie clip itself.

1. On the main stage, select the ship and open the Actions panel. Let's start by adding the onClipEvent(enterFrame):

```
onClipEvent (enterFrame) {
}
```

We'll create an if statement inside that to check for the position of the left arrow key. We do this by referring to the Key.LEFT key position, using the isDown property of the Key object:

```
onClipEvent (enterFrame) {
    // turn Counter Clockwise
    if (Key.isDown(Key.LEFT)) {
    }
}
```

2. Changing the rotation then is easy; we're just going to decrement it by some value:

```
onClipEvent (enterFrame) {
    if (Key.isDown(Key.LEFT)) {
        this._rotation -= 9;
    }
}
```

As you can see, I decremented by 9 just because it gave me the rotation speed I wanted. I do recommend choosing a value that divides 180 evenly. If you used a number like 7, which doesn't, you won't be able to face in an exactly opposite direction. This may not sound like such a horrible fate, but it will be awkward when you try to stop yourself by turning around and firing your thruster. You wouldn't be able to completely cancel out the thrust and come to a full stop.

To turn clockwise, the code would be the same but tied to the right arrow key, and this time you would *add* 9 degrees onto the current rotation. Altogether, then, here's the code for both the left and right buttons:

```
onClipEvent (enterFrame) {
    // turn Counter Clockwise
    if (Key.isDown(Key.LEFT)) {
        this._rotation -= 9;
    }
    // turn Clockwise
    if (Key.isDown(Key.RIGHT)) {
        this._rotation += 9;
    }
}
```

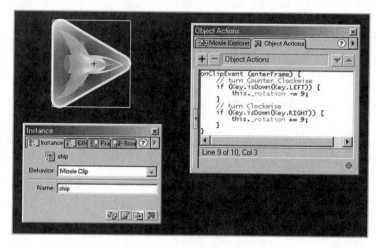

If you test your movie now, your ship should be able to spin in place. To actually get somewhere, let's add some thrust.

Thrust

Thrust is the most math we'll be doing in this game. We need to use the ship's heading (rotation) and move a certain amount in that direction. Unfortunately we can't say move 10 pixels in the direction the ship is facing. To move an object in Flash, we have to set both its _x and _y properties, essentially breaking a diagonal line into its two constituent directions, horizontal and vertical. These three distances, the diagonal, the x and the y, make up a right triangle.

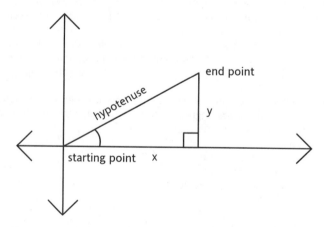

Because of the high frame rate of this movie, the amount we would move at one time has to be very small. For this game, let's make the distance 0.5 pixels. Keep in mind as well that this ship is in space, and once the ship thrusts 0.5 pixels, inertia is going to keep carrying it at that speed. So, that small value will also add up quickly as you hold down the thrust button.

At this point we know the angle of the ship (_rotation) and how far we need to go (.5), we just need to know what the values are when broken up into x and y. The only way to do this is to use trigonometry. If you're about to close the book in mortal terror, don't worry, this foray into trig will be brief, and once we've set it up once in a function, all of the trig will be done there. If you really don't want to have a refresher course, you may just want to use the code and accept the fact that it works.

The script that we're about to build to move the ship is going to be very similar to the one we use to move the plasma shot. If you think about it, the shot will move in a direction based on the rotation of the ship but will move a longer distance than the ship (since it needs to go much faster than the ship).

When we have situations with similar code, it's a good idea to make a single function to do the job for both. In this case we'll make a function that takes the rotation of the ship, finds the component x any y movement values and reports them back. Since we'll be using the function for both the ship and the shots, we'll need the function to be able to take different travel distances and then report back to different movie clips. To do this, we need to supply the function with two pieces of information:

- Which movie clip is using the function?

- How much do you want to accelerate the ship?

With those two pieces of information as arguments of the function, we should be able to figure out the rest. Since the function will be accessible to many movie clips, let's write the function in an accessible location. For general functions, I like to define them in frame 1 of the main timeline. This way, they are immediately defined and always available to be used.

Scripting the findDist function

1. Since we're going to doing the trig in a function on the _root, let's add a new layer to the main timeline called Actions/Events. Select frame 1 of the main timeline and open the Actions panel. Create a new function called findDist. The purpose of findDist will be to take the angle of the ship and a distance to travel, and supply an x movement increment and a y movement increment back to the movie clip that called the function. Let's call these arguments MC for the movie clip that will be specified and radius for the distance that the object should travel. The function definition should look like this:

```
function findDist (MC, radius) {
}
```

2. To find the distance for the x and y components, we'll take the angle of the ships rotation and apply the sine and cosine math methods. As I said in the general setup section, trig requires that angles be specified in radians. Let's do the conversion just like we discussed earlier. We make a ratio of the ships angle in degrees and divide it by the total number of degrees in a circle. This creates a ratio that we can use then to multiply by the total number of radians in a circle.

The script is like this:

```
function findDist (MC, radius) {
        //convert to radians
        angle = ((ship._rotation)/360)*2*Math.PI;
}
```

Since we're going to do a little trigonometry now, let's review some of the general principals. For a right triangle the three sides have specific names for use in trigonometry. The **Hypotenuse** is the side opposite the right angle. The 'adjacent' side is the other side that makes up the angle theta (the angle that we figured out above). The last side is the 'opposite' side, which is aptly named since it's the side opposite of the angle that's in question. For us that angle, theta, is the rotation of the ship. The x distance then is the adjacent side and the y distance is the opposite side. We know the length of the hypotenuse since it's the amount to be traveled supplied as one of the arguments when the function is called.

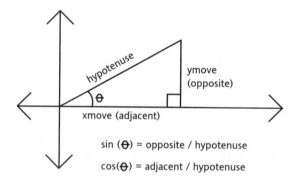

$$\sin (\theta) = opposite / hypotenuse$$

$$\cos(\theta) = adjacent / hypotenuse$$

The sine of an angle is equal to the ratio of the opposite side to the hypotenuse. Since we know what the hypotenuse is, we can multiply it by the sin value. What we're left with then is the y distance value (the opposite side). Cosine has much the same effect, but is a ratio of the adjacent side to the hypotenuse. Once again if we cancel out the hypotenuse from that ratio, we're left with another of the missing sides, this time the x distance.

By specifying a movie clip object to function, we can use the variable MC in its place. We could call properties, variables or methods of the movie clip by using the variable, just as if we were specifying the movie clip directly. So, we can increment the value of the variables xmove and ymove the movie clip by the value of the sides we just derived. The code for the findDist function should look like this:

```
function findDist (MC, radius) {
        angle = ((ship._rotation)/360)*2*Math.PI;
        //report back x and y components to the movie clip
        MC.xmove += radius*Math.cos(angle);
        MC.ymove += radius*Math.sin(angle);
}
```

Acceleration

1. Now that we have a function defined, we need to use it. Back in the `onclipEvent(enterFrame)` on the ship movie clip, we need to write code that will trigger the function to run. Exactly like we did with the rotation commands, we'll use `Key.isDown()` in an `if` statement to issue the command. Inside the `if` statement, we need to call the function. To tell the function to return the values to the current movie clip, we just need to use the `this` command. The `radius` argument, let's set at .5, though you should feel free to change this value to whatever you want.

    ```
    onClipEvent (enterFrame) {
        if (Key.isDown(Key.LEFT)) {
            this._rotation -= 9;
        }
        if (Key.isDown(Key.RIGHT)) {
            this._rotation += 9;
        }
        // thrust
        if (Key.isDown(Key.UP)) {
            _root.findDist(this, .5);
        }
    }
    ```

2. When we made the ship's graphics I mentioned that I created the thruster as a movie clip and then manually adjusted its Alpha. Our script now needs to change the Alpha to 100 when the key is down, and change back to 30 when the key is not pressed.

    ```
    onClipEvent (enterFrame) {
        if (Key.isDown(Key.LEFT)) {
            this._rotation -= 9;
        }
        if (Key.isDown(Key.RIGHT)) {
            this._rotation += 9;
        }
        if (Key.isDown(Key.UP)) {
            _root.findDist(this, .5);
            // show thruster as opaque
            thrust._alpha = 100;
        } else {
            // dim thruster to 30% opaque
            thrust._alpha = 30;
        }
    }
    ```

3. We'll also want to make another command that works for the retro-thruster. This uses the down arrow key, and since the retro thrusters should be less powerful than the main engine we'll need to change the script slightly. Though we still need to call the `findDist` function, the radius should be negative to make the ship go backwards, and

closer to zero, so that it accelerates backwards slower. Also note the same commands to change the _alpha properties of the thruster movie clips.

```
onClipEvent (enterFrame) {
    if (Key.isDown(Key.LEFT)) {
        this._rotation -= 9;
    }
    if (Key.isDown(Key.RIGHT)) {
        this._rotation += 9;
    }
    if (Key.isDown(Key.UP)) {
        _root.findDist(this, .5);
        thrust._alpha = 100;
    } else {
        thrust._alpha = 30;
    }
    // half powered retrothrust
    if (Key.isDown(Key.DOWN)) {
        _root.findDist(this, -.25);
        retro._alpha = 100;
    } else {
        retro._alpha = 30;
    }
}
```

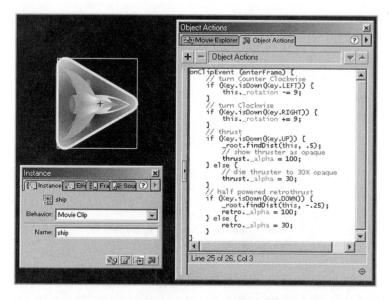

If you tested the movie now, not much more would happen than after you put the rotation script in. Only the thrusters would change intensity when you used the right keys. This is because our function has just returned some variable values. It hasn't actually moved anything. Unlike with the rotation, movements won't be as discreet an operation. With movement, we need to consider inertia, and also a speed limit. In the next part, we'll actually get the lead out and move this bucket of pixels.

Coding the ship's movement

Now that the `findDist` function, living in the root, has supplied the ship with incremented `xmove` and `ymove` variables, we need to write a script that actually uses them to move the ship, within the ship's clip event. Right now, the code here should look like this:

```
onClipEvent (enterFrame) {
    if (Key.isDown(Key.LEFT)) {
        this._rotation -= 9;
    }
    if (Key.isDown(Key.RIGHT)) {
        this._rotation += 9;
    }
    if (Key.isDown(Key.UP)) {
        _root.findDist(this, .5);
        thrust._alpha = 100;
    } else {
        thrust._alpha = 30;
    }
    if (Key.isDown(Key.DOWN)) {
        _root.findDist(this, -.25);
        retro._alpha = 100;
    } else {
        retro._alpha = 30;
    }
    // We'll put the movement script here
}
```

Since the code is starting to get a bit long, let's assume that the ActionScript we add here is where the comment is. When we're done with the code segment, we'll view it in the full context.

1. We'll begin by using an `if` statement to make sure that at least one of the two variables `xmove` and `ymove` has a value; if both of them equal 0, then there's no need to run the code as the ship won't be going anywhere anyway. We'll use the `!=` operator for each variable and the logical OR, `||` so that the `if` statement will pass if either is a non-zero number:

    ```
    if (xmove != 0 || ymove != 0) {
    }
    ```

2. Now that we know that ship is ready to move, we just need to take the `xmove` and `ymove` variables and add them onto the current x and y positions of the ship:

    ```
    if (xmove != 0 || ymove != 0) {
        _x += xmove;
        _y += ymove;
    }
    ```

If you test now, your ship will move, although there will be two problems. Firstly your ship will go flying off the screen, and secondly, as long as you keep pressing the thrust keys, the ship is going to keep accelerating. We'll take care of wrapping the ship to the other side of the screen in a moment, but first let's talk about putting a speed limit on the ship.

As the ship accelerates, it will move by skipping larger and larger areas. If there's a mine sitting in one of those gaps, your ship will have managed to fly right through a mine without being damaged. I mentioned this same problem in the chapter 5 in the context of the airplane controls. We're going to need a similar solution here, but as you'll see the execution is slightly different.

3. Let's start by defining the `speedLimit` variable equal to 15. You can really use any value depending on your preferences, but I found that 15 is a good rate to allow you to go fast without skipping any collisions.

```
if (xmove != 0 || ymove != 0) {
        _x += xmove;
        _y += ymove;
        speedLimit = 15;
}
```

4. The speed limit is the distance that the ship can go in one hop. Given the value of `xmove` and `ymove`, which was set by all of the times `findDist` was called, we need to find how far the ship will be from its current position. Now we're facing the opposite problem to the one that we faced in the thrust section. We have an `x` distance and a `y` distance, but we need the hypotenuse. Luckily, going this direction is much easier. According to Pythagorean's Theorem, the hypotenuse equals the square root of the sum of the square of the other two sides. Or:

```
if (xmove != 0 || ymove != 0) {
        _x += xmove;
        _y += ymove;
        speedLimit = 15;
        hypotenuse = Math.sqrt((xmove*xmove)+(ymove*ymove));
}
```

While the Flash 5 math object has a `pow` method that raises a number to an exponent, there is a small bug in it that if you ask it for zero squared, it reports back that it is not a number. Since this would break our script, it is easier to just do the longhand multiplication.

Once we have a value for the hypotenuse, we need to check it against the `speedLimit`. If it is less than or equal to `speedLimit`, then we can leave it as is. Otherwise, we need to shrink the `xmove` and `ymove` values proportionally so that `hypotenuse` fits within the `speedLimit`.

What we are really doing is shrinking the whole right triangle to the point where the hypotenuse equals `speedLimit`. To determine how much to shrink the move variables, we need to set up a ratio of a side of the smaller triangle (the one based on `speedLimit`) to the corresponding side of the larger triangle (the one based on `hypotenuse`). Since the only side we know the value of for both of the triangles is the hypotenuse, we need to set up a ratio between the two values. This ratio can then be used to figure out the new move variables by multiplying it with the current move variables.

To do this we simply multiply `xmove` and `ymove` by the ratio of `speedLimit` divided by `hypotenuse`. Once the variables are corrected to the `speedLimit`, the new values can be added onto the current `_x` and `_y` values. Altogether then, the code you're adding inside the `onClipEvent`, after the code we've already placed there, should look like this:

```
if (xmove != 0 || ymove != 0) {
        _x += xmove;
        _y += ymove;
        speedLimit = 15;
        hypotenuse = Math.sqrt((xmove*xmove)+(ymove*ymove));
        if (hypotenuse>speedLimit) {
                xmove *= speedLimit/hypotenuse;
                ymove *= speedLimit/hypotenuse;
        }
    }
}
```

5. If you test the movie now, you should be able to fully control your ship. As it is, though, you can still send the ship right of the screen, never to be seen again. Since that would be a pretty short game, we need to write a script to make the ship wrap to the opposite side of the screen to the one it has disappeared off. Since the plasma shot and the mines are also going to have to wrap as well, we'll make this another function in frame 1 of the `_root`.

6. Before we go back to frame 1 of the main timeline, go ahead and add a line of code to reference the function at the end of the `onClipEvent`, just before the closing bracket. This function will determine if the ship, in this case, needs to be wrapped and if so, will change the appropriate coordinate value. The complete code in the `onClipEvent` (for now) should look like this:

```
onClipEvent (enterFrame) {
    if (Key.isDown(Key.LEFT)) {
            this._rotation -= 9;
    }
    if (Key.isDown(Key.RIGHT)) {
            this._rotation += 9;
    }
    if (Key.isDown(Key.UP)) {
            _root.findDist(this, .5);
            thrust._alpha = 100;
    } else {
```

continues overleaf

```
                    thrust._alpha = 30;
        }
        if (Key.isDown(Key.DOWN)) {
                _root.findDist(this, -.25);
                retro._alpha = 100;
        } else {
                retro._alpha = 30;
        }
        // Movement
        if (xmove != 0 || ymove != 0) {
                _x += xmove;
                _y += ymove;
                speedLimit = 15;
                hypotenuse = Math.sqrt((xmove*xmove)+(ymove*ymove));
                if (hypotenuse>speedLimit) {
                        xmove *= speedLimit/hypotenuse;
                        ymove *= speedLimit/hypotenuse;
                }
                _root.wrap(this);
        }
}
```

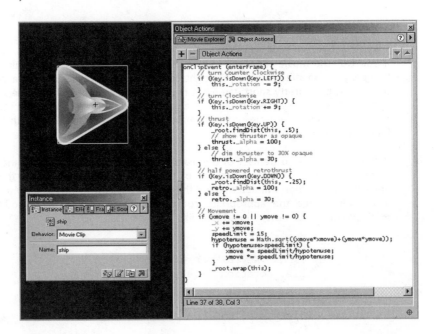

Wrapping across the screen

Now let's write the wrap function. When we wrote the line calling this function, we supplied it with a movie clip object just like we did in the findDist function. Since the function can be used on many objects, we'll use this to move the object by proxy. In the function definition, we need to add an argument that represents this movie clip. Let's name that MC like we did before.

```
function wrap (MC) {
}
```

The logic of the function is broken up into two parts, one that checks the _x position and one that checks the _y position of the ship and compares it to the dimensions of the game play area. These must be done independently in case the object should move into a corner requiring us to wrap the object along both the x and the y axis.

To determine if the object needs to wrap, we need to have some boundaries. Since the screen dimensions are 550 by 430, and we put the interface in the bottom 30 pixels of the stage, that would give a left boundary of zero, a right boundary of 550, a top boundary of 0 and a bottom boundary of 400.

The game would look pretty awkward if only the center of the ship passed the boundary (half of the ship still sticking out) and we wrapped to the other side, so we need to make sure that the whole object is past the boundary. To do that, we just need to check for the boundary plus (or minus depending on the direction) half the height or width of the object. Once we've determined that an object needs to wrap, it must be moved past the opposite boundary once again by half its height or width.

Since the place that we will be moving the ship to is another location that would make the object wrap back to the first boundary, we need to check which direction the object is moving. If it is moving back in towards the middle of the screen, don't move it. If it is trying to keep moving off screen wrap it. The diagram below shows the general logic of it. Keep in mind though that these ship icons represent the direction the ship is moving. The actual rotation means little since you could hold down the thrust button until you are going pretty fast then rotate the ship, giving it the appearance of going backwards.

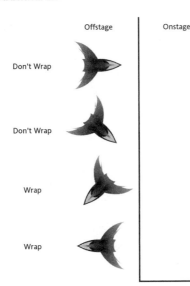

Offstage   Onstage

Don't Wrap

Don't Wrap

Wrap

Wrap

To find the direction the object is moving, we use its xmove and ymove values. The code for the wrap function is as follows:

```
function findDist (MC, radius) {
    angle = ((ship._rotation)/360)*2*Math.PI;
    MC.xmove += radius*Math.cos(angle);
    MC.ymove += radius*Math.sin(angle);
}

function wrap (MC) {
    if (MC._y<(-MC._height/2) && MC.ymove<0) {
        //if past upper boundary, wrap to the bottom
        MC._y = 400+MC._height/2;
    } else if (MC._y>(400+MC._height/2) && MC.ymove>0) {
        //if past lower boundary, wrap to the top
        MC._y = -MC._height/2;
    }
    if (MC._x<(-MC._width/2) && MC.xmove<0) {
        //if past left boundary, wrap to the right
        MC._x = 550+MC._width/2;
    } else if (MC._x>(550+MC._width/2) && MC.xmove>0) {
        //if past right boundary, wrap to the left
        MC._x = -MC._width/2;
    }
}
```

If you test now, the ship should move around just like it will in the final game. Try testing all of the boundaries to make sure each works and delivers you to where you expect. Before we start scripting the mine movement, let's first set up the shield control. After all, if there are live mines floating around the screen I'd sure like to defend my ship.

Setting shield controls

Shield control is largely a function of having a variable set correctly. If the shields are on, then you are safe, if not, you aren't. All that's left then is determining if you have enough energy to actually have the shields on.

Before we begin the code to activate the shields, there are a few things we need to set up. The shield bar in the interface needs a line of code and there are a few variables that need to be initialized in the ship.

1. Go into the `interface` movie clip, which is out on the main stage. Then go into the shield bar tween we set up. In the last frame, we need to set a variable telling the movie that the shields are out of power. Select the blank keyframe at the end of the movie clip and add the following line through the actions panel:

   ```
   _root.shieldSAvail = 0;
   ```

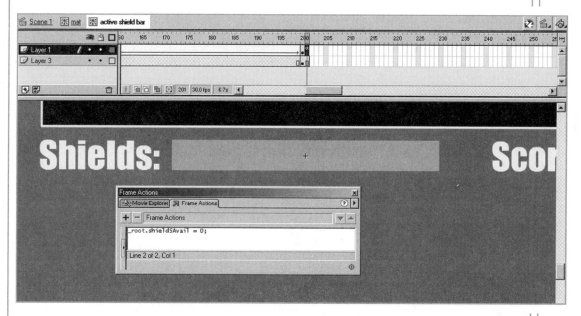

2. After you've done that, go back out to the main stage and select the ship. The rest of this script will live there.

3. Unlike the other ship controls, the shields won't be exclusively controlled by the user. There are times that it will be good for the system to turn the shields on automatically. For instance, at the beginning of a new level or after you've respawned from having lost a life, it's good to have the shields on for a short period just in case a mine should be where you first appear, your ship is not instantly destroyed. To start this, let's

initialize a variable in an onClipEvent (load) every time the ship loads. This variable will be the number of frames that the free shields stay on.

```
onClipEvent (load) {
    // this sets the shields into free mode for 50 frames
    safety = 50;
}
```

When the ship loads, it has either been destroyed or you are starting a level. Either way, you should have some shields. If it is a new ship, its shields will be full. If you are starting a new level your shields have been recharged 15 percent. We need to make sure that the variable indicating shield availability is set to 1, meaning it is available.

```
onClipEvent (load) {
    safety = 50;
    //whenever the ship loads, at least some shields
    //will always be available
    _root.shieldSAvail = 1;
}
```

As long as we are initializing things in the ship, let's also set the rotation of the ship to –90. This way when the ship appears it will be pointing straight up, not to the right. All the ship's actions together should look like below.

```
onClipEvent (load) {
    safety = 50;
    _root.shieldSAvail = 1;
    //turn the ship so it starts pointing up
    _rotation = -90
}
onClipEvent (enterFrame) {
    if (Key.isDown(Key.LEFT)) {
        this._rotation -= 9;
    }
    if (Key.isDown(Key.RIGHT)) {
        this._rotation += 9;
    }
    if (Key.isDown(Key.UP)) {
        _root.findDist(this, .5);
        thrust._alpha = 100;
    } else {
        thrust._alpha = 30;
    }
    if (Key.isDown(Key.DOWN)) {
        _root.findDist(this, -.25);
        retro._alpha = 100;
    } else {
        retro._alpha = 30;
    }
```

```
            if (xmove != 0 || ymove != 0) {
                _x += xmove;
                _y += ymove;
                speedLimit = 15;
                hypotenuse = Math.sqrt((xmove*xmove)+(ymove*ymove));
                if (hypotenuse>speedLimit) {
                        xmove *= speedLimit/hypotenuse;
                        ymove *= speedLimit/hypotenuse;
                }
                _root.wrap(this);
        }
// Place shield code here
}
```

We'll be adding the rest of the code where the comment is at the bottom of the
enterFrame clip event block.

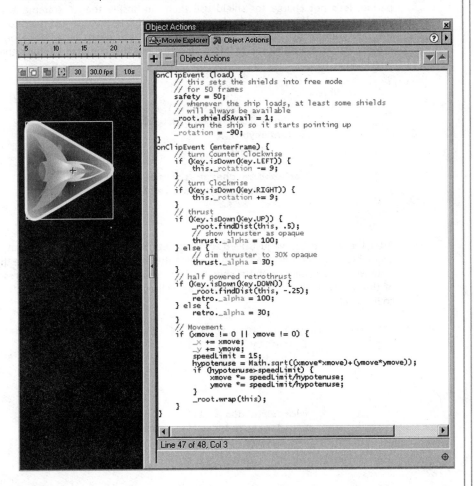

Instead of checking just for the key state of the control, we also have to check to see if the safety period is in effect. Lastly, we also have to check if the shields are available. This really only applies to using the button though. The logic for this condition is if safety is greater than zero or the key is being pressed while the shields are available to do the next part of the script.

Checking to see if a letter key is selected is slightly different from checking a special key such as the arrow keys. In this case, you have to supply the key code. The key code for T is 84. A full listing of key codes is available in the Flash manuals. (Key codes are the same as the ASCII code for the uppercase letter of the key)

```
// Shields
if (safety>0 || (Key.isDown(84) && _root.shieldsAvail == 1)) {
}
```

Since the user can't pick whether or not to turn the shields on or off during the safety period, let's not charge for shield use then. So, inside the if statement, let's add another one checking to see if safety is in effect. If it is, then we just need to decrease the safety count by 1, and if it's not, the shield bar needs to advance one frame, moving it one frame closer to the frame holding the command setting the shields unavailable.

```
// Shields
if (safety>0 || (Key.isDown(84) && _root.shieldsAvail == 1)) {
        // check for "free" shield use variable
        if (safety>0) {
                safety--;
        } else {
        //otherwise charge for the shield use
                _root.interface.shield.nextFrame();
        }
}
```

After the nested if, we just need to actually turn the shields on. To do that, let's set a variable shieldOn on the root to 1 which the mines can use to determine the shield state when they collide with the ship. Also we need to turn on the visual representation of the mines so that we can see them as well as changing the shape that the mines collides with.

```
if (safety>0 || (Key.isDown(84) && _root.shieldsAvail == 1)) {
        if (safety>0) {
                safety--;
        } else {
                _root.interface.shield.nextFrame();
        }
        _root.shieldOn = 1;
        shield.gotoAndStop(1);
}
```

4. To make the shield look like it is made of energy, let's add an effect to make it flicker slightly. Since the alpha of a symbol is on a 100 point scale, fluctuating between 80 and 100 would give this appearance. To do this, set the _alpha of the shield to a random value between 0 and 20, then add that onto a base value of 80. I originally tried it without the flicker, but the effect was pretty boring.

```
if (safety>0 || (Key.isDown(84) && _root.shieldsAvail == 1)) {
        if (safety>0) {
                safety—;
        } else {
                _root.interface.shield.nextFrame();
        }
        _root.shieldOn = 1;
        shield.gotoAndStop(1);
        shield._alpha = random(20)+80;
}
```

Finally, we need an else case. This will trigger if we are out of the safety period, no key is being pressed, or it is being pressed and the shields are just empty. In the else statement, we need to turn the shield off both visually and programmatically. So far the ship's code should look like this:

```
onClipEvent (load) {
    safety = 50;
    _root.shieldSAvail = 1;
    _rotation = -90;
}
onClipEvent (enterFrame) {
    if (Key.isDown(Key.LEFT)) {
            this._rotation -= 9;
    }
    if (Key.isDown(Key.RIGHT)) {
            this._rotation += 9;
    }
    if (Key.isDown(Key.UP)) {
            _root.findDist(this, .5);
            thrust._alpha = 100;
    } else {
            thrust._alpha = 30;
    }
    if (Key.isDown(Key.DOWN)) {
            _root.findDist(this, -.25);
            retro._alpha = 100;
    } else {
            retro._alpha = 30;
    }
    if (xmove != 0 || ymove != 0) {
            _x += xmove;
            _y += ymove;
            speedLimit = 15;
```

continues overleaf

```
                        hypotenuse = Math.sqrt((xmove*xmove)+(ymove*ymove));
                        if (hypotenuse>speedLimit) {
                                xmove *= speedLimit/hypotenuse;
                                ymove *= speedLimit/hypotenuse;
                        }
                        _root.wrap(this);
                }
        if (safety>0 || (Key.isDown(84) && _root.shieldsAvail == 1))
        {
                if (safety>0) {
                        safety—;
                } else {
                        _root.interface.shield.nextFrame();
                }
                _root.shieldOn = 1;
                shield.gotoAndStop(1);
                shield._alpha = random(20)+80;
        } else {
                shield.gotoAndStop(2);
                _root.shieldOn = 0;
        }
```

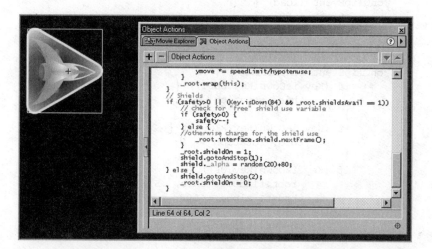

You can now test your movie to see the shields operate. When it opens, the shields should be on for a couple of seconds and then turn off. At that point using the shield buttons should turn them on, and if you use them too much they should fail as the shield bar in the interface runs out.

Now that we have a proper defense, let's start making some enemies!

Moving the mines

The mines in this game are pretty simple in that they don't steer. Once they are created, they are assigned a velocity and a direction, and keep moving. While they are moving though, they will need to wrap just like the ship. After we've finished getting them to move, we'll start on the actual game interaction, where the mine collides with the ship.

1. Out on the main stage, select the mine and open the actions panel. The mine has two things it needs to do right now, initialize, then constantly run the scripts that move it. This means we need to use two onClipEvents, one with a load event to initialize and the other with an enterFrame event to constantly move the mine.

```
onClipEvent (load) {
}
onClipEvent (enterFrame) {
}
```

2. Let's start with the initialization since we'll be using the variables set here to move the mine. Setting random movement is a much easier thing than setting movement based on an object's orientation like we did with the ship. In this case, we can just set the mine's xmove and ymove variable once, based on a random value generated by the math objects random method. These variables are separate from the xmove and ymove variables in the ship's movie clip. In the wrap function we just wrote, we check the object's xmove and ymove variable. In order for the wrap function to work for the mine, these values need to be used for the movement.

    There are a few cases however that we'd like to avoid. For instance we don't want the mine to be initialized with both an xmove and a ymove of 0, leaving the mine dead in space and potentially out of sight. If we set each of the variables equal to random(5), which means the value could be from 0 to 4, there is a possibility that both could be set to zero and we'd have just that case. To correct that, we can set each to random(5) + 2 so that there is a minimum movement of 2 in either axis.

```
onClipEvent (load) {
    //set a random movement, with at least a 2,2 movement
    xmove = random(5)+2;
    ymove = random(5)+2;
}
onClipEvent (enterFrame) {
}
```

3. At this point the value is always going to be positive, and to create movement in any direction, we need to create an equal chance of the ymove and/or xmove value being negative. If you look at the if statements below the variable assignment, you'll see that there is a 50% chance of each variable being made negative.

```
onClipEvent (load) {
    xmove = random(5)+2;
    ymove = random(5)+2;
    //then possible invert one or both
    //directions to account for all directions
    if (random(2) == 1) {
        xmove *= -1;
    }
```

continues overleaf

```
if (random(2) == 1) {
        ymove *= -1;
    }
}
onClipEvent (enterFrame) {
}
```

As we discussed when making the mine, it is a template that is never actually used. It's just going to be the stock that other mines are created from. To keep the mine from moving out onto the stage, we need to block the template's initialization, but we need to do it in a way that allows the copies to work: using the _name property and checking to see if it is mine. If it's not, then the initialization can take place. Any duplicated mine must be given a unique name anyway, so looking at the name is a fairly easy way to do this check. The _name property does not actually return a string though, so you have to use the string command to check for the inequality. The code for this looks like:

```
onClipEvent (load) {
    //if this movie clip is not the template
    if (String(_name) != "mine") {
        xmove = random(5)+2;
        ymove = random(5)+2;
        if (random(2) == 1) {
            xmove *= -1;
        }
        if (random(2) == 1) {
            ymove *= -1;
        }
    }
}
onClipEvent (enterFrame) {
}
```

4. After the initialization in the onClipEvent(load) command, we need to make a script that uses the xmove and ymove variables to keep the mine moving. We'll do this in the onClipEvent(enterFrame). Unlike the way we used these variables in the ship, the mine's speed is constant, so there is no need to have a speed limit. In essence the speed limit is the range of possible values in the random() script. When we move the mine though we should make sure it is still in tact. Our explosion animation starts in frame 2, so let's just make sure that we are still in frame 1.

```
onClipEvent (load) {
    if (String(_name) != "mine") {
        xmove = random(5)+2;
        ymove = random(5)+2;
        if (random(2) == 1) {
            xmove *= -1;
        }
        if (random(2) == 1) {
            ymove *= -1;
        }
    }
```

```
    }
onClipEvent (enterFrame) {
    if (_currentframe == 1) {
        //move the mine
        _x += xmove;
        _y += ymove;
    }
}
```

5. Also, we are going to want to make sure that the mines wrap along the same boundaries as the ship. To do that, we just need to add a line calling the `wrap()` function. Altogether, then, the code in the onCipEvents for the mine that's currently of the side of the stage should look like this:

```
onClipEvent (load) {
    if (String(_name) != "mine") {
        xmove = random(5)+2;
        ymove = random(5)+2;
        if (random(2) == 1) {
            xmove *= -1;
        }
        if (random(2) == 1) {
            ymove *= -1;
        }
    }
}
onClipEvent (enterFrame) {
    if (_currentframe == 1) {
        _x += xmove;
        _y += ymove;
        _root.wrap(this);
    }
}
```

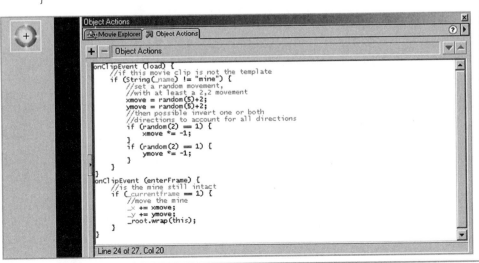

If you were to test the movie right now, the mine would not move because the only mine in the movie has the name `mine`. For the moment, so you can see the effect of the mine moving, copy `mine` and paste it on the stage a couple times. Be sure to copy the one we just programmed since the point is to test the scripts. Copying the symbol from the library won't have the instance-specific code on it.

Give these copies new instance names like `mine1`, `mine2`, etc. Testing the movie now should let you see how the mines work. What you've just done manually is something that we'll build a script to do later when we build the level scripts. The script we'll build later will work in much the same way, giving the new copies names in the same format. Since we are going to add more scripting to the mine template later, go ahead and delete the copies so that there is no confusion later on.

Detecting collisions

To do their jobs, mines have to be able to hurt nearby ships. While in real life two mines that collide would hurt each other, in this game that would be far too convenient for the player. In our future universe, the aliens have figured out a way to keep such mishaps from happening. Whether it's through some sort of phasing from normal space or if it's just a matter of not exploding, the humans just aren't sure. But either way, one thing is for certain, they will hurt your ship.

So, the collision detection in the mine only needs to detect a collision with the ship. We'll add this script in the mine's code in the `onClipEvent(enterFrame)`. Right now that should look like:

```
onClipEvent (load) {
    if (String(_name) != "mine") {
        xmove = random(5)+2;
        ymove = random(5)+2;
        if (random(2) == 1) {
            xmove *= -1;
        }
        if (random(2) == 1) {
            ymove *= -1;
        }
    }
}
onClipEvent (enterFrame) {
    if (_currentframe == 1) {
                    _x += xmove;
        _y += ymove;
        _root.wrap(this);
        // collision detection goes here
    }
}
```

1. The collision detection script will be placed where the collision detection comment is located in the code block above.

   Since we are doing point to movie clip collision detection, it's best to check both the mine's point against the ship movie clip, and the ship's point against the mine movieclip. While this is not a substitute for real collision detection, it does allow us to have a better chance of catching a collision detection. It's also helpful since we have three sizes of mines. Generally when you do point to movie clip `hitTest()`, the smaller movieclip is the point. With three sizes, the mine may be bigger, smaller or the same size as the ship.

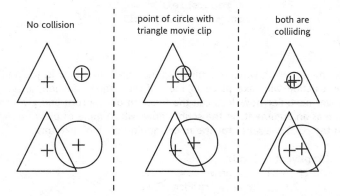

No collision   point of circle with triangle movie clip   both are colliiding

2. To do the collision detection, checking both movie clips against each other, we need to set up an `if` statement with the two conditions separated by a logical OR. In both cases, the movie clip that is having its shape used it the movie clip that the method is attached to. Also, both of the movie clips must be in the same timeline for this script to work as written. That way, their locations are based of the same (0,0) point.

```
if (this.hitTest(_root.ship._x, _root.ship._y) ||
➥ _root.ship.hitTest(_x, _y)) {
}
```

Notice here that we aren't blocking the template from colliding. This is because the mine is not moving and is sitting off the edge of the stage. To make sure that it never interacts with the ship, make sure that it is sitting far enough off the stage that the ship won't collide with it just before it wraps to the other side of the stage.

3. Now we have set up a collision detection statement, we need to figure out if the ship's shields are up or down. Rather conveniently, we set up a variable in the last section to make this process very easy. If the variable in the root called `ShieldOn` is 0, then the shields are down, but if it's set to 1, the shields are up and you are safe.

```
if (this.hitTest(_root.ship._x, _root.ship._y) ||
➥ _root.ship.hitTest(_x, _y)) {
    //if the shields are off, you die
    if (_root.shieldOn == 0) {
    }
}
```

Later when we cover the events section (death, new level, and game over), there will be a frame label called kill for when your ship is destroyed which will remove the ship, but will allow the mines to keep moving around.

4. Let's go ahead and add the code sending the root to the frame kill, if the shields were down.

```
if (this.hitTest(_root.ship._x, _root.ship._y) ||
➥_root.ship.hitTest(_x, _y)) {
        if (_root.shieldOn == 0) {
        _root.gotoAndPlay("kill");
    }
}
```

5. No matter what, when the mine hits the ship, it has done its job and is destroyed. That destruction will take place in the self-replication function, minesplit, which we'll cover next. For now, let's call the function on the root and give it the current movie clip as an argument, so the script knows which mine to blow up. Altogether the code in the onClipEvent for the mine should now look like this:

```
onClipEvent (load) {
    if (String(_name) != "mine") {
        xmove = random(5)+2;
        ymove = random(5)+2;
        if (random(2) == 1) {
            xmove *= -1;
        }
        if (random(2) == 1) {
            ymove *= -1;
        }
    }
}
onClipEvent (enterFrame) {
    if (_currentframe == 1) {
        _x += xmove;
        _y += ymove;
        _root.wrap(this);
        if (this.hitTest(_root.ship._x, _root.ship._y) ||
➥_root.ship.hitTest(_x, _y)) {
            if (_root.shieldOn == 0) {
                _root.gotoAndPlay("kill");
            }
            //regardless, destroy the mine
            _root.minesplit(this);
        }
    }
}
```

Mine self-replication

When a mine is destroyed, if it is above a certain size, it's able to self-replicate. That is, it will divide into two smaller mines. The script we are going to build will have three levels of mines: large and medium mines, which can replicate; and small mines, which are fully destroyed when hit. To entirely destroy a large mine the user will have to hit 7 mines (one large, two medium and four small).

Mine self-replication or destruction won't only be caused by running into a mine with your ship. You'll also be able to shoot the mines later. The process to destroy the mine though is the same. Because of this, let's make a function calls `minesplit` in frame 1 of the root right under the `wrap` function.

1. Let's add this function, which we'll call `minesplit`, under the `wrap` function in frame 1 of the main timeline. It will need to take one argument, which is the mine movie clip that needs to be destroyed. As we've done in the previous functions, let's call this `MC` inside the function.

```
function minesplit (MC) {
}
```

2. The first part of the function is concerned with making two copies of the mine, provided that the scale of the original mine is at least 75. Since the scale of the mine is always proportional, we only need to check against the scale of one axis. After the new mines have been made, they need to become smaller:

```
function minesplit (MC) {
    if (MC._Yscale>=75) {
    }
}
```

Since this function needs to create more than one mine, this process of duplication and shrinking is inside an iterative loop. By having the condition be that `i` (which started as 1) is less than three, the loop will run twice. If you want the mine to spawn a different number of mines, you could just change the number.

```
function minesplit (MC) {
    if (MC._Yscale>=75) {
        //if the mine is big enough, replicate it twice
        for (var i = 1; i<3; i++) {
        }
    }
}
```

You could also set a variable equal to a random number and use that as the limit of the loop. That way it would always be unpredictable number of mines produced.

In the loop, we need to create a new mine duplicated based on `MC` otherwise know as the mine that is being destroyed. Then we need to reduce the size of the new mine to 75% of its original size. If `MC` was full size, that will make the new mine have scale properties at 75. If `MC` was medium size, the new mine's scale will be about 56. The smallest mines would not have made it past the `if` statement, so would not replicate.

In previous examples where we have duplicated a movie clip, we've constructed the name using a string and the index variable. Here though that would create a lot of mines called `mine1` and `mine2`. Since each mine must have a unique name, we'll use a variable called `mineCount` which only will get reset at the beginning of a level. That way, during a single level, there will never be a conflicting name. For now the first time it runs, `mineCount` will be undefined and changed to 1. That will work for now, but eventually when we have a script setting up each level, `mineCount` would have already been incremented by having created the levels original mines.

3. We'll be setting the scale properties of the new mine by using the `with` command. This is a handy command to use when you need to set multiple properties of a movie clip other than the current one. It's especially helpful when the name of the target movie clip is constructed using the `eval` command since those are a bit harder to understand when you are trying to read several of them in a block of code.

```
function minesplit (MC) {
    if (MC._Yscale>=75) {
        for (var i = 1; i<3; i++) {
            mineCount++;
            duplicateMovieClip (MC, "mine"+mineCount,
            ➥ mineCount+1000000);
            with (eval("mine"+mineCount)) {
                //and make it 25% smaller
                _yscale *= .75;
                _xscale *= .75;
            }
        }
    }
}
```

If you are curious as to why the depth for the duplicate movieclips is so high, this is to account for the script we'll be using in the next section. The plasma shots and the mines are both on the stage and when they are duplicated, they must have unique depths. Adding a very large number to the `mineCount` variable effectively puts them in different ranges. I suppose I should point out that the game would break if someone fires over 1,000,000 plasma shots in a single game. If someone actually does, I think having a broken Flash game is going to be one of their smaller problems.

If you were to test now by copying some mines out on the stage and giving them new instance names, the effect won't quite work. Shooting the mines will just cause more and more to appear without getting rid of the old ones.

4. Now that we've replicated the mine, we need to get rid of the first as well as taking care of some administrative things like adding onto the player's score and checking for the end of the level. Let's start by giving the player some points. When we set up the interface, we made a dynamic textbox called `score`. We need to take that value and add 150 points on it.

```
function minesplit (MC) {
    if (MC._Yscale>=75) {
        for (var i = 1; i<3; i++) {
            mineCount++;
            duplicateMovieClip (MC, "mine"+mineCount,
            ➥ mineCount+1000000);
```

```
                       with (eval("mine"+mineCount)) {
                               _yscale *= .75;
                               _xscale *= .75;
                       }
               }
       }
       //award points
       _root.interface.score += 150;
       }
```

5. After that we need to get rid of the original mine. To do that, we are going to send it to its explosion animation and then change its name, which will take it out of contention for collision with a plasma shot (which we'll be coding next). Once the mine is in frame 2, the enterFrame actions won't be called because of the check we put in the if statement.

```
function minesplit (MC) {
    if (MC._Yscale>=75) {
        for (var i = 1; i<3; i++) {
            mineCount++;
            duplicateMovieClip (MC, "mine"+mineCount,
            ➥ mineCount+1000000);
            with (eval("mine"+mineCount)) {
                //and make it 25% smaller
                _yscale *= .75;
                _xscale *= .75;
            }
        }
    }
    _root.interface.score += 150;
    //tell the mine to go to its explosion
    MC.gotoAndPlay(2);
    //and change its name so a shot can't collide with it again
    MC._name += "destroyed"
}
```

6. After a mine has been destroyed, we need to check if there are any left. If there aren't any left, the level is over. To find out if all of the mines have been destroyed, let's increment a variable called destroyed. When that variable equals mineCount, which is an accurate representation of how many mines have been created in the level, then all of the mines are gone. Much like we did for the case when the ship is destroyed, we need to send the main timeline to a frame that will handle the end of a level. Let's call this frame newLevel We'll assign the actual frame label later. The final code for minesplit should be:

```
function minesplit (MC) {
    if (MC._Yscale>=75) {
        for (var i = 1; i<3; i++) {
            mineCount++;
            duplicateMovieClip (MC, "mine"+mineCount,
```

continues overleaf

```
                              ➡ mineCount+1000000);
                              with (eval("mine"+mineCount)) {
                                      _yscale *= .75;
                                      _xscale *= .75;
                              }
                      }
              }
              _root.interface.score += 150;
              MC.gotoAndPlay(2);
              MC._name += "destroyed"
              //increment the destroyed variable
              destroyed++;
              //if you've destroyed all of the mines, end the level
               if (destroyed == mineCount) {
                      gotoAndPlay ("newLevel");
              }
      }
```

Now that the mine is being sent to the explosion animation, we also need to add a script there to actually remove the movie clip when it's finished exploding. I find that play and stop commands can get overridden at times when there is a lot going on. Most likely this is caused by some strange timing issue. Luckily there is an easy way around it.

7. Go into the mine movie clip and go to frame 2, the beginning of the explosion. Select the keyframe and open the actions panel. By adding a play command here, the animation won't stall. Then, in the last frame, select the keyframe and add a line of code in the actions panel that says the following:

```
removeMovieClip (this);
```

This will permanently remove the mine from the movie. If you manually create some mines, you should be able to run into them with your shields on, and they should explode and replicate. There should no longer be an issue of creating way too many mines. For now, go ahead and leave the manually created mines on the stage. We'll use them to test the plasma shot that we'll create next.

minesplit was our last function, so let's take a look at all of the code in frame 1. Your frame 1 should have these same three functions.

```
function findDist (MC, radius) {
      angle = ((ship._rotation)/360)*2*Math.PI;
      MC.xmove += radius*Math.cos(angle);
      MC.ymove += radius*Math.sin(angle);
}
function wrap (MC) {
      if (MC._y<(-MC._height/2) && MC.ymove<0) {
              MC._y = 400+MC._height/2;
      } else if (MC._y>(400+MC._height/2) && MC.ymove>0) {
              MC._y = -MC._height/2;
      }
      if (MC._x<(-MC._width/2) && MC.xmove<0) {
```

```
                    MC._x = 550+MC._width/2;
            } else if (MC._x>(550+MC._width/2) && MC.xmove>0) {
                    MC._x = -MC._width/2;
            }
    }
    function minesplit (MC) {
            if (MC._Yscale>=75) {
                    for (var i = 1; i<3; i++) {
                            mineCount++;
                            duplicateMovieClip (MC, "mine"+mineCount,
                            ➥ mineCount+1000000);
                            with (eval("mine"+mineCount)) {
                                    _yscale *= .75;
                                    _xscale *= .75;
                            }
                    }
            }
            _root.interface.score += 150;
            MC.gotoAndPlay(2);
            MC._name += "destroyed"
            destroyed++;
            if (destroyed == mineCount) {
                    gotoAndPlay ("newLevel");
            }
    }
```

Weapon controls

Now that we have replicating mines, shields just aren't enough. We need to go on the offensive. To do that, let's script our plasma shot controls. The controls for firing the shot go into the ship's `onClipEvent(enterFrame)` just like the rest of the controls.

To make the gun fire, we'll be copying the shot template movie clip, placing it at the ship's coordinates, and giving it a direction to move in, with a set speed which is then added onto the ship's current inertia.

After that, the shot is going to take over, and control itself by way of an `onClipEvent(enterFrame)`. It will keep moving itself in the same direction, but will also limit how long the shot will exist. If we didn't program in a death time for the shot, it would just keep going and going, wrapping back the other side of the screen.

While moving around, the shot will also be detecting for collisions with the mines. This means that in every frame, the shot has to check its position against each mine. Any projectile that is going to be testing for collision detection with a potentially large number of objects could easily make a game chug. For that reason, there needs to be some limits on the number of shots on the stage at one time. As a new shot is duplicated, a variable on the _root called `liveshots` will be incremented. Then, whenever the system receives a command to fire, it can compare against the number of active shots.

When the shot goes away, the `liveshots` variable can then be decremented, opening a slot for a new shot to be fired.

Lastly, at 30 FPS, the shots would come out very close together if you were to hold down the space bar. So, we'll also create an artificial delay that starts a count at about 3, right after a shot has been successfully fired. No matter what the state of `liveshots`, another shot won't be able to be fired until the timer is 0 or less.

The operation of the shot may seem very complex, but we'll be able to simplify it greatly by using the three functions we've already created. Let's get started by adding the keyboard control for firing the shot. Right now, the code on the ship looks like this. We'll be adding the firing controls where the firing comment is at the bottom of the clip event code.

```
onClipEvent (load) {
    safety = 50;
    _root.shieldSAvail = 1;
    _rotation = -90;
}
onClipEvent (enterFrame) {
    if (Key.isDown(Key.LEFT)) {
        this._rotation -= 9;
    }
    if (Key.isDown(Key.RIGHT)) {
        this._rotation += 9;
    }
```

```
if (Key.isDown(Key.UP)) {
        _root.findDist(this, .5);
        thrust._alpha = 100;
} else {
        thrust._alpha = 30;
}
if (Key.isDown(Key.DOWN)) {
        _root.findDist(this, -.25);
        retro._alpha = 100;
} else {
        retro._alpha = 30;
}
if (xmove != 0 || ymove != 0) {
        _x += xmove;
        _y += ymove;
        speedLimit = 15;
        hypotenuse = Math.sqrt((xmove*xmove)+(ymove*ymove));
        if (hypotenuse>speedLimit) {
                xmove *= speedLimit/hypotenuse;
                ymove *= speedLimit/hypotenuse;
        }
        _root.wrap(this);
}
if (safety>0 || (Key.isDown(84) && _root.shieldsAvail == 1))
{
        if (safety>0) {
                safety--;
        } else {
                _root.interface.shield.nextFrame();
        }
        _root.shieldOn = 1;
        shield.gotoAndStop(1);
        shield._alpha = random(20)+80;
} else {
        shield.gotoAndStop(2);
        _root.shieldOn = 0;
}
// Add firing code here
}
```

1. Since we are using the space bar for the control of the firing, the code for the `if` statement should look like the following:

```
if (Key.isDown(Key.SPACE)) {
}
```

Inside of that, we need to do a check against `liveshots` and `shottimer`. Neither of these have been initialized but that's ok. When the game starts, you haven't fired anything, so both of these values should be 0 anyway. `shottimer` will be set after we successfully fire a shot. It will then count back towards 0 each frame. To be able to fire again, the shottimer must be less than 1.

2. Before firing though, we also need to check that there aren't too many shots already on the stage. When a shot is successfully fired, liveshots will be incremented. You can choose whatever limit you want; I decided to go for 6. The smaller the number, the more challenging the game will be since you won't be able to fire again until the live shots die off.

```
if (Key.isDown(Key.SPACE)) {
    if (shottimer<1 && _root.liveshots<6) {
    }
}
```

3. Outside of the if statement (the key check if statement that is), we need to add the command that decrements shotTimer. Having it outside the keyboard control code means that no matter what, shotTimer will be decremented. If it were places as an else of the nested if, shotTimer would only decrement when the space bar was being pressed, which could result in an unwanted delay the next time the space bar is pressed.

```
if (Key.isDown(Key.SPACE)) {
    if (shottimer<1 && _root.liveshots<6) {
    }
}
shottimer--;
```

4. Inside the if statements are the actual actions creating the shot. First, liveshots, which is on the root, is incremented. A variable called shotcount, which lives in the ship movie clip is also incremented. This variable serves the same purpose as the mineCount variable in that it provides a running tally of shots so that the new shot can be duplicated to a unique level.

```
if (Key.isDown(Key.SPACE)) {
    if (shottimer<1 && _root.liveshots<6) {
        _root.liveshots++;
        shotcount++;
    }
}
shottimer--;
```

5. After this the shot is duplicated out on the root, being given a unique depth and name using shotcount. Once it's duplicated, shottimer is set to prevent the next shot from happening too soon.

```
if (Key.isDown(Key.SPACE)) {
    if (shottimer<1 && _root.liveshots<6) {
        _root.liveshots++;
        shotcount++;
        duplicateMovieClip (_root.shot, "shot"+shotcount,
```

```
➥shotcount);
                shotTimer = 3;
        }
    }
}
shottimer- -;
}
```

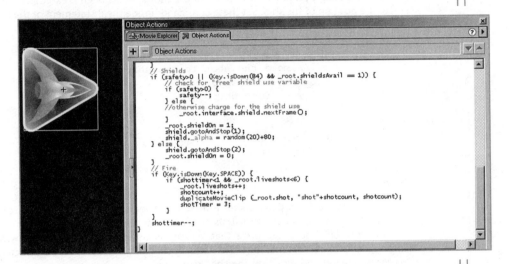

That's all there is for inside the control script. The shot will initialize itself and control its own movement. If you were to test now, nothing would appear to happen. In reality the shot would be created but it would just be sitting offstage directly over the shot template. To make the shot function, let's take a look at the template movie clip itself.

6. Select the shot movie clip which should be offstage near the mine template. Bring up the actions panel. The shot is going to have to initialize its position then move itself based on that initialization every frame. The setup is going to be similar to the mine's script. We'll use an `onClipEvent(load)` for the initialization and an `onClipEvent(enterFrame)` for the movement.

```
onClipEvent (load) {
}
onClipEvent (enterFrame) {
}
```

7. In both statements, we need to make sure that the code only executes if it's not the template. We can do that the same way we did for the mine.

```
onClipEvent (load) {
    // if this isn't the template
    if (String(_name) != "shot") {
    }
}
```

continues overleaf

```
onClipEvent (enterFrame) {
    // if this isn't the template
    if (String(_name) != "shot") {
    }
}
```

8. The first thing that needs to happen to the shot after its been created is to move itself to the position of the ship. Set these commands inside the if statement of the load event.

```
onClipEvent (load) {
    if (String(_name) != "shot") {
        // move the shot to the ship
        _x = _root.ship._x;
        _y = _root.ship._y;
    }
}
onClipEvent (enterFrame) {
    if (String(_name) != "shot") {
    }
}
```

The movement for a plasma shot is a cross between the movement styles of the ship and of the mines. Like the thrust, its direction is determined by the rotation of the ship, but more like the mine, once that velocity is set, it will continue that way until it impacts a mine or times out. The velocity of the shot will also be affected by the current speed and direction the ship is moving.

9. To determine the direction, let's use the findDist function out on the root. We only need to supply it with the this object and a radius. The radius can be whatever you want, but I've found that 10 is a pretty good value. The findDist function will then set an xmove and ymove value in the shot, but that is not going to be quite enough. Since the ship can be moving while shooting, we need to add on the xmove and ymove of the ship to simulate the inertia that should already be in the shot.

```
onClipEvent (load) {
    if (String(_name) != "shot") {
        _x = _root.ship._x;
        _y = _root.ship._y;
        // determine the move variables of the shot
        _root.findDist(this, 10);
        // offset by the ship's intertia
        xmove += _root.ship.xmove;
        ymove += _root.ship.ymove;
    }
}
onClipEvent (enterFrame) {
    if (String(_name) != "shot") {
    }
}
```

10. The last part of the initialization is to set a variable determining how long the shot will live. This timer will work a lot like `shottimer`, where we will set it to a value and each time a frame passes, it will reduce the value by 1. In this case, once `life` reaches zero, even if it hasn't hit a mine, it will be removed. Let's make the lifespan of the shot start at 25 frames.

```
onClipEvent (load) {
    if (String(_name) != "shot") {
        _x = _root.ship._x;
        _y = _root.ship._y;
        _root.findDist(this, 10);
        xmove += _root.ship.xmove;
        ymove += _root.ship.ymove;
        // how many frames this shot will last
        life = 25;
    }
}
onClipEvent (enterFrame) {
    if (String(_name) != "shot") {
    }
}
```

11. Let's add the script to decrement the life variable and remove the shot if necessary. Inside the `if` statement of the `enterFrame` event, we need to add the decrement command, then add an `if` statement to see if life equals 0 yet. If it does we need to lower the `liveshots` variable so that another shot can be fired, then remove the movie clip just like we did at the end of the mine explosion.

```
onClipEvent (load) {
    if (String(_name) != "shot") {
        _x = _root.ship._x;
        _y = _root.ship._y;
        _root.findDist(this, 10);
        xmove += _root.ship.xmove;
        ymove += _root.ship.ymove;
        life = 25;
    }
}
onClipEvent (enterFrame) {
        if (String(_name) != "shot") {
        // count down life
        life--;
        // get rid of the shot if it is too old
        if (life == 0) {
                _root.liveshots--;
                removeMovieClip (this);
        }
    }
}
```

12. Now we need to move the shot. With the initial velocity set, the movement is just like the mine movement with wrapping. We need to add the xmove value to the x position and the ymove value to the y position. After that, we call the wrap function on the root and provide it with the this object so that it can wrap the shot.

```
onClipEvent (load) {
    if (String(_name) != "shot") {
        _x = _root.ship._x;
        _y = _root.ship._y;
        _root.findDist(this, 10);
        xmove += _root.ship.xmove;
        ymove += _root.ship.ymove;
        life = 25;
    }
}
onClipEvent (enterFrame) {
    if (String(_name) != "shot") {
        life—;
        if (life == 0) {
            _root.liveshots—;
            removeMovieClip (this);
        }
        // otherwise move
        _x += xmove;
        _y += ymove;
        _root.wrap(this);
    }
}
```

13. While the plasma shot is flying through space it needs to interact with its environment. Every time it moves, it needs to see if it's colliding with any of the mines. We'll need to create a loop to do the checking for us. In this loop, we can use the variable _root.mineCount as the condition since it is the number of targets that have been created since the start of the level. Inside the loop, we need to check the collision status of a mine who's name is the concatenation of the string "mine" and the index number. The coordinates of the shot are then plugged into the hitTest method being called on that mine. The code should look like this:

```
onClipEvent (load) {
    if (String(_name) != "shot") {
        _x = _root.ship._x;
        _y = _root.ship._y;
        _root.findDist(this, 10);
        xmove += _root.ship.xmove;
        ymove += _root.ship.ymove;
        life = 25;
    }
}
onClipEvent (enterFrame) {
    if (String(_name) != "shot") {
```

```
              life—;
              if (life == 0) {
                      _root.liveshots—;
                      removeMovieClip (this);
              }
              _x += xmove;
              _y += ymove;
              _root.wrap(this);
              // and check for collisions
              for (i=1; i<=_root.mineCount; i++) {
                      if (eval("_root.mine"+i).hitTest(_x, _y)) {
                      }
              }
      }
}
```

14. Inside the if statement checking for collisions, we need to enter the last bits of code here, which would lower liveshots and then run the mineSplit function out on the root, and finally remove itself.

```
onClipEvent (load) {
      if (String(_name) != "shot") {
              _x = _root.ship._x;
              _y = _root.ship._y;
              _root.findDist(this, 10);
              xmove += _root.ship.xmove;
              ymove += _root.ship.ymove;
              life = 25;
      }
}
onClipEvent (enterFrame) {
      if (String(_name) != "shot") {
              life—;
              if (life == 0) {
                      _root.liveshots—;
                      removeMovieClip (this);
              }
              _x += xmove;
              _y += ymove;
              _root.wrap(this);
              for (i=1; i<=_root.mineCount; i++) {
                      if (eval("_root.mine"+i).hitTest(_x, _y)) {
                              // if collison, destroy the mine
                              _root.minesplit(eval("_root.mine"+i));
                              // and get rid of the shot
                              _root.liveshots—;
                              removeMovieClip (this);
                      }
              }
      }
}
```

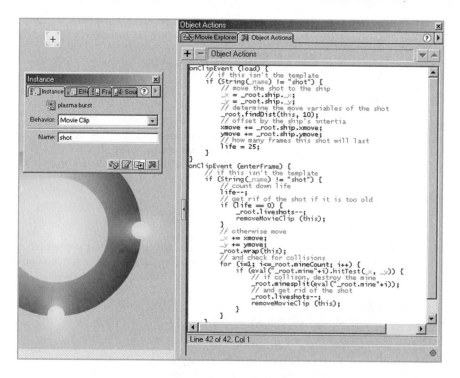

If you test now, with the manually created mines, you have a pretty functional game. You can now fly around, raise shields, shoot and destroy mines. Once you are done testing, delete the manually created mines (leaving the template!). We are ready now to move on to the events of the game.

Putting it all together

Main timeline structure

In the game up till now, we have only stayed in frame 1 on the main timeline. For the three major events, new level, death and game over, it's actually much better to add frames to the timeline in order to take advantage of some interesting features.

1.   Let's organize the main timeline into an approximation of what we'll want the final game to be like. Let's start by arranging certain elements on different layers. The ship, shot, mine and mat should all be on different layers. After that, let's add several regular frames after frame 1 on the main timeline.

2.   Now let's add some frame labels to the Actions/Events layer. We'll be using these later in scripting, but having names will allow us to easily refer to these frames. The frames should be named according to the following chart:

Frame 1	init	initialization frame
Frame 10	menu	main menu
Frame 20	instructions	instruction screen
Frame 30	gameplay	where the regular gameplay takes place
Frame 40	Kill	beginning of the lose a life sequence
Frame 50	newLevel	beginning of the level script
Frame 60	gameOver	beginning of the game over sequence

3. Let's move the keyframes of the ship, mine and shot to the gameplay frame. The mat needs to only exist in the init frame, so let's keep it where it is but add a blank keyframe in frame 9 to block it. After the interface has swapped its depth, it's not really attached to a frame anymore, so Flash can get confused if we ever go back to a frame that has it which would break its functionality. Therefore, it's better just to have it in frame 1. This is also a handy way to keep the interface from covering over your template symbols while you are still trying to work with them.

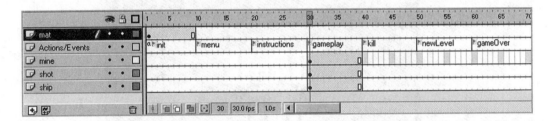

If we use a blank keyframe to stop the ship from existing in certain frames as well, when we go back to a frame where it does exist, it will default back to its original position and settings and run the OnClipEvent (load) again. This will be a very handy tool when resetting the stop between deaths and levels. So, let's make it so that the ship and shot only exist in the gameplay frame by adding a blank keyframe at the end of the gameplay section.

4. The mines must exist from the gameplay frame through the end of the timeline so that when the new level scripts run, the template mine is present to be duplicated.

Finally, let's add new layer called text/menus, that we will use for instructions and information for the user. Also add approximately 50 frames after Kill, newLevel and gameOver. This will be the time that the user spends looking at whatever message each of the three sequences has to display, such as in this picture:

init

The initialization should hold the mat as mentioned before, but it's also a good place to put the functions that we've had in frame 1 all along. Once a function has been defined, it can be called anywhere in that timeline. Also, if you want to, you can add a star field in the background to make it seem as if you are in space. You can either make a static one, or use the script included in the source FLA which builds a star field automatically. If you add a star field, make sure that it exists across all of the frames of the movie.

menu

The main menu is the screen where the user can choose either to play the game or read the instructions. This is also a good place for credits, links, etc. Since you can either get here when you first start the movie, or after your game has ended, we need to set the variables to initialize a game.

```
// stop at the menu
stop ();
// initialize the variables for a new game
_root.interface.bonus = 0;
_root.interface.shields.gotoAndStop(1);
_root.interface.ships.gotoAndStop(1);
level = 0;
```

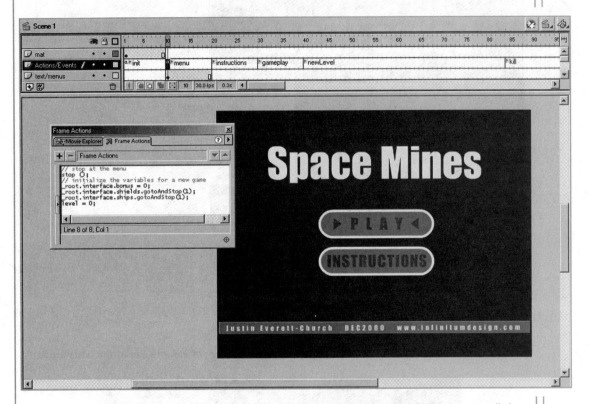

When the game is over, we still want the score to appear at the bottom of the screen until they begin a new game. The button to play the game will actually erase the score, just before it sends the timeline to play at the newLevel frame.

```
on (release) {
    //initialize the score here so you can
    //see your old score until the next game
    interface.score = 0;
    //start the game
    gotoAndPlay ("newLevel");
}
```

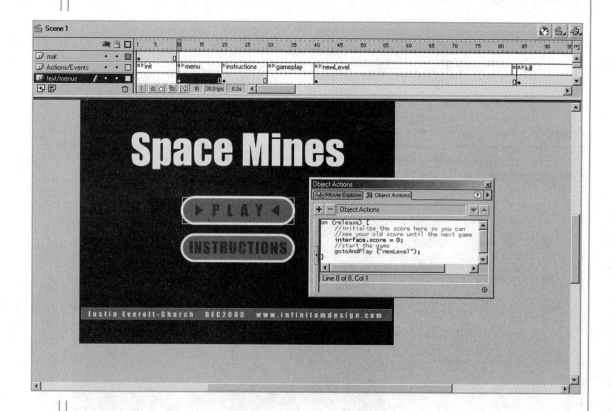

instructions

The instructions button in the main menu should just send the timeline to the instructions frame.

Here there should be instructions telling the player what the game controls are, the object of the game, and any other pertinent information. Also showing enemies and your own ship would be a good idea at this point so that there is no possible confusion when the game begins.

gameplay

All of the time when you are in control of the ship will take place here. By leaving the frame for the end of a level or when you lose a ship, the ship will respawn in the middle of the screen and reinitialize. Add a `stop` action to the gameplay frame.

newLevel

Whenever you begin a new level, it's helpful to the player to tell them exactly what level they are entering. To do that, let's make a dynamic text field on the stage called `level` that will automatically read the `level` variable that has already been defined.

Since we are displaying the `level` variable, we need to increment it the moment it is displayed. To do that, add a line of code to the newLevel keyframe incrementing `level`. This is also why we initialized the level to 0. Since the play game button starts us here, it will then bump up to 1 and start the game.

```
//increment the level
level++;
```

Once we've played through the newLevel sequence, we are also going to want to run some actions right before the game play resumes. These actions will add the bonus to the score, boost the shields, reset level specific variables like `bonus`, `mineCount` and `destroyed` then create the new mines.

The `mineCount` variable should be set to the value of the `level` variable because, once we create there new mines, there will be as many as the value of `level`. The destroyed variable also needs to be reset, but this one should be 0. This way the variable can build back up as you obliterate mines.

```
// initialize the new level's variables
mineCount = level;
destroyed = 0;
```

We also need to make good on our promise to partially regenerate the shields. To do it, we need to create a loop that runs 30 times (30 is 15% of 200, which is the number of frames in the shield bar tween) The reason for recharging the shield via a loop is the fact that if we tried to set it to its `_currentFrame` minus 30 when the shield level was only at frame 10, the shields would not get recharged at all since it can't go to frame –20. Scrolling back the shield energy animation frame by frame though allows us to avoid that problem.

```
mineCount = level;
destroyed = 0;
// move the shield thermometer bar back 30 frames
// if you tried _currentframe - 30 and were at
// less than frame 30, nothing would happen, hence
// a loop, one frame at a time.
for (var i = 1; i<=30; i++) {
    _root.interface.shield.prevFrame();
}
```

Next we need to award the end of level bonus, then set the bonus to its new value which is a function of the level number.

```
mineCount = level;
destroyed = 0;
for (var i = 1; i<=30; i++) {
    _root.interface.shield.prevFrame();
}
// award the level bonus
_root.interface.score += Number(_root.interface.bonus);
// set up new bonus amount for next level
_root.interface.bonus = 500*level;
```

The last thing to do before going back to the gameplay frame is to create new mines. After its been created, we need to set the initial position of the mine. If we do nothing, it will start from the template's position off stage. If we keep it at its same x position but randomized its y position, the mines would all appear to start from the sides of the screen. Mines that are heading towards the stage would come in from the left. Mines heading away from the stage would instantly wrap to the right side of the stage and come in from that side.

```
mineCount = level;
destroyed = 0;
for (var i = 1; i<=30; i++) {
    _root.interface.shield.prevFrame();
}
_root.interface.score += Number(_root.interface.bonus);
_root.interface.bonus = 500*level;
// create the mines for the level and place them randomly
for (var i = 1; i<=level; i++) {
    duplicateMovieClip ("mine", "mine"+i, i+1000000);
    eval("_root.mine"+i)._y = random(400);
}
// start playing again
gotoAndStop ("gameplay");
```

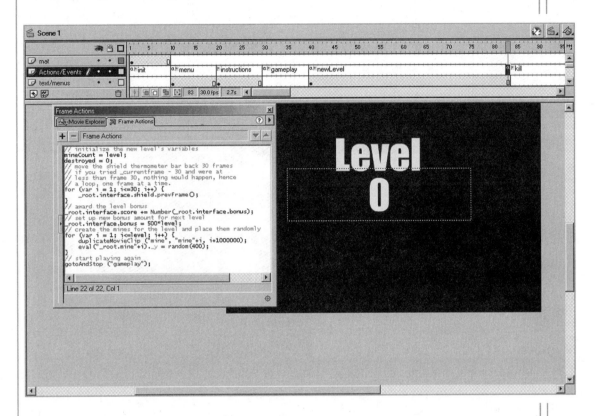

Before moving onto the next section, there is one other control we need to set. In order for the bonus to work properly, it needs to get reduced as long as your ship is on the stage since it's a time-based bonus. To add this functionality, go back to the gameplay frame, select the ship and open the actions panel. In there, there should be both of the onClipEvents. We need to add this code to the enterFrame event. Right below the shottimer−; line, add the following code to make the bonus go down as long as it is still above 0.

```
if (_root.interface.bonus>0) {
    _root.interface.bonus−;
}
```

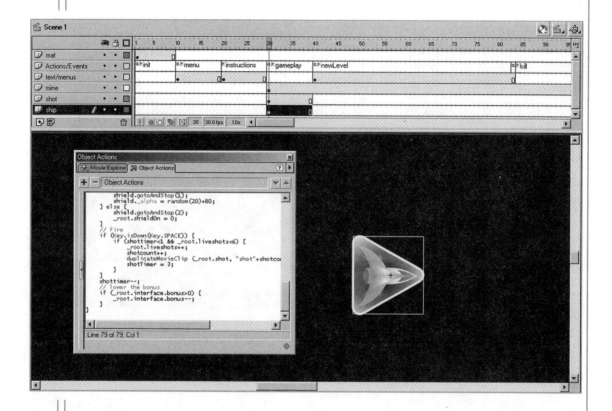

kill

If a mine should hit you while your shields are down, you will lose a life. When we set up the collision detection scripts for the mines, you may recall that we set up a goto script going to kill when the ship is destroyed. When the ship is destroyed, all that needs to happen is sending the interface.ships movieclip to the next frame to indicate a life has been lost and sending the shield bar back to frame 1 since bringing out a new ship, would mean that the ship would have fully charged shields

1.   Since it is possible to run into the last mine on a level which would cause you to lose a life and win the level simultaneously, we need to add an extra line checking if mineCount and destroyed are equal. If they are, you can send the timeline to the newLevel frame since you've already deducted the life. So here are the actions for the kill frame:

```
//lose a ship in the interface
_root.interface.ships.nextFrame();
//full shields for a new ship
_root.interface.shield.gotoAndStop(1);
//just in case you die destroying the last mine,
```

```
//you still lose a life but you also go onto the
//next level
if (destroyed == mineCount) {
    startLevel();
};
```

2. While the sequence is playing, you may want to add a message on the screen like ready or some sort of countdown to indicate when they will be sent back to the game.

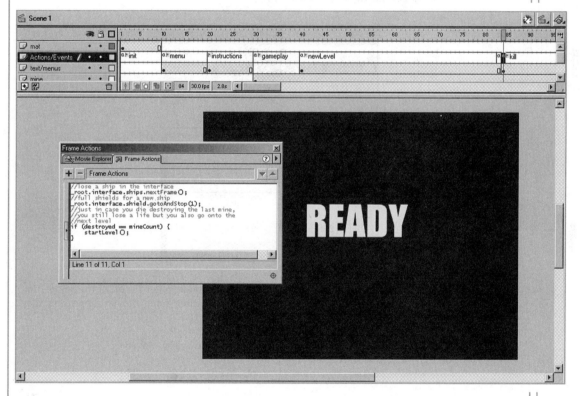

3. At the end of the kill sequence, the timeline just has to be sent back to the gamePlay frame. Add a keyframe in the last frame of the kill section with the following actions:

```
//go back to playing the game with your new ship
gotoAndStop ("gameplay");
```

Also keep in mind that since you are going to be sent back to the same level, it is crucial that the mines are not disturbed during this process.

gameOver

The game ends when you run out of lives, so let's go back to the ships movieclip in interface, to add a frame action when you run out of lives. Whenever the animation gets to this point, we just need to send the _root's timeline to play at the gameOver frame. So, let's add the following command to the second blank keyframe we added in the ships movie when we first made it.

```
_root.gotoAndPlay("gameover");
```

1. In the first frame of the gameOver sequence, we need to get rid of all the mines. To do that, we just need to iterate through the possible mine movie clips using the mineCount variable as the limit of the condition.

```
//remove the rest of the mines since the game is over
for (i=1; i<=mineCount; i++) {
    removeMovieClip (eval("_root.mine"+i));
}
```

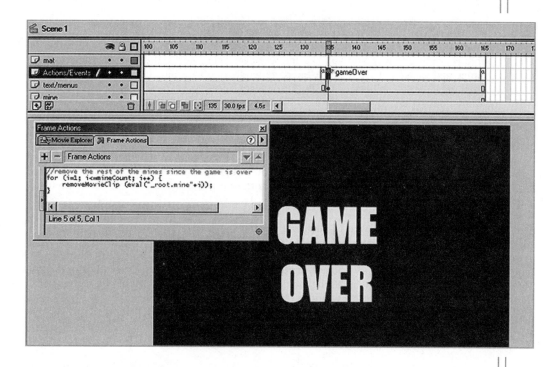

In the last frame of the sequence showing the Game Over message, the timeline should then be sent back to the main menu where the process starts again:

```
gotoAndStop("menu");
```

Playing the game

All that's left to do now is to test your game and play it. Wow, isn't it fun. Well, if you don't think so, there are two things to keep in mind. First, you've just developed this game. It holds no surprises for you. Also, through all of the testing, you've probably played this enough for several lifetimes. If it's a bit stale to you, check with some friends and watch them play. If it's fun to them, then it's probably OK. If it's still fun for you, all the better!

Once you start asking people to play your game you get into a very important part of any game's life, QA (Quality Assurance). In QA, you need to be checking for several things.

- Do the people playing it understand the game without your verbally having to explain your intentions?

If your players get confused and need to be prompted by you, users that don't have you over their shoulder will obviously get confused.

- Does anything undesirable happen during the game?

At first I planned to write 'unexpected' but it was not accurate. As long as your game functions in a reproducible way, and you like the way everything works, there is no problem. I've several times had things not work as expected, generally due to a bug, but the overall effect is better than my intention so I leave it in. Bugs can every once in a while actually become features. If you game doesn't function, then try as I might, I probably can't see that as a very useful feature.

- Do people enjoy playing it?

This is pretty self-explanatory. A game is meant to entertain, if it doesn't then you need to consider making some changes. Generally you would have gotten a sense of whether or not it was fun as you were developing it, so if you've gotten to this point you should not to be too worried here.

- Do people want to play it again after they've played it once?

Repeat visits to a game or a site is often referred to as 'stickiness'. A game that you play through once but want to go back and play again is considered a sticky game. Elements that help this are different levels, differing goals, or multiple paths. Once again, this should be thought of more in the planning stages, but every one is different and verifying the games repeat appeal is certainly worth the effort.

- Does the game function on all platforms/browsers?

This is generally the heart of the technical aspect in QA—functionality. Generally you need to test many browser types, browser versions, and plugin versions. Another major consideration for the functionality is the processor in the computer. Flash is an incredibly processor intensive operation and the speed of the computer will greatly affect gameplay. It's generally a good idea to decide what the minimum requirements are for the game and test on a machine that barely meets them. After that, try and test the program on the most powerful machine you can. The disparity between the two should be minimal if the game is correctly tuned to the minimum requirements. That said, as a developer I try to push the minimum requirements as high as I can since that allows me to do more interesting things in the development process.

Modifying the game

As with any of the examples in this book, this is just a starting point intended to set you going in the right direction. One key to successful development is using effects in new ways or combining more than one effect to create a completely new one. For instance, you may want to add new features to the game such as gravity wells, indestructible mines, and homing mines.

A gravity well could be made by checking your position in relation ship to the well and altering the trajectory of the ship towards the well. Indestructible mines could be made either by giving it a name outside the system that the bullet checks for, or change its reaction to being such as changing the trajectory of the mine. A homing mine could simply be done by modifying the mouse trailer script so that the mine is always slowly moving towards the ship.

As I mentioned at the beginning of the chapter, the theme of the game can also easily be changed to make a new game. Let's say that instead of a space game you wanted to make a demolition derby. Overall the game is very similar. You would need new graphics, but you would be able to use the majority of the scripts you've already created. As an example, in a derby, your car can only travel for the most part in the direction that the car is facing. By altering what is done with the xmove and ymove variables after they are returned to the car by findDist, this change would be pretty simple.

One last quick mention is the geometry and trigonometry used in this game. If you have a mortal fear of math, and you've made it to this point, you're a great sport. For that, I'll let you in on a little secret. Though math was by far the best way of doing this game, there are always many ways of doing any task in Flash. If you'd rather not deal with the rotation and the radius to create the findDist function, you could always set up a movie clip with just a line in it going through the pivot. Then just make sure it always rotates with the ship and when you need xmove, just find the width of the movie clip and when you need ymove similarly, use its height. This was a lot more useful in Flash 4 when there was no built in trig, but for those that simply don't want to use trig, this just shows that there are other options. In the image below you can see how having a line rotated along with the ship essentially makes the hypotenuse of the right triangle we were working with earlier. The height and width then are the equivalent of the two sides.

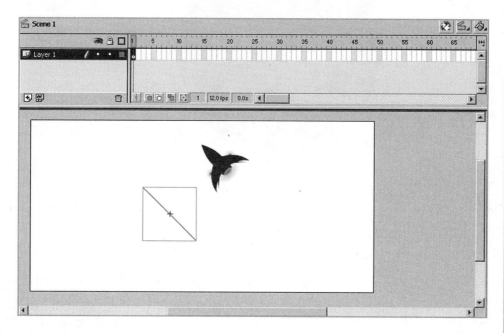

Summary

Now that you have the basics down, from here on out is the best part, making your own games. Once you are done, there are plenty of places to publish your games on the Web. As you get started in this area, posting to Flash resource sites is a great way of getting feedback as well as serving to get your name out there.

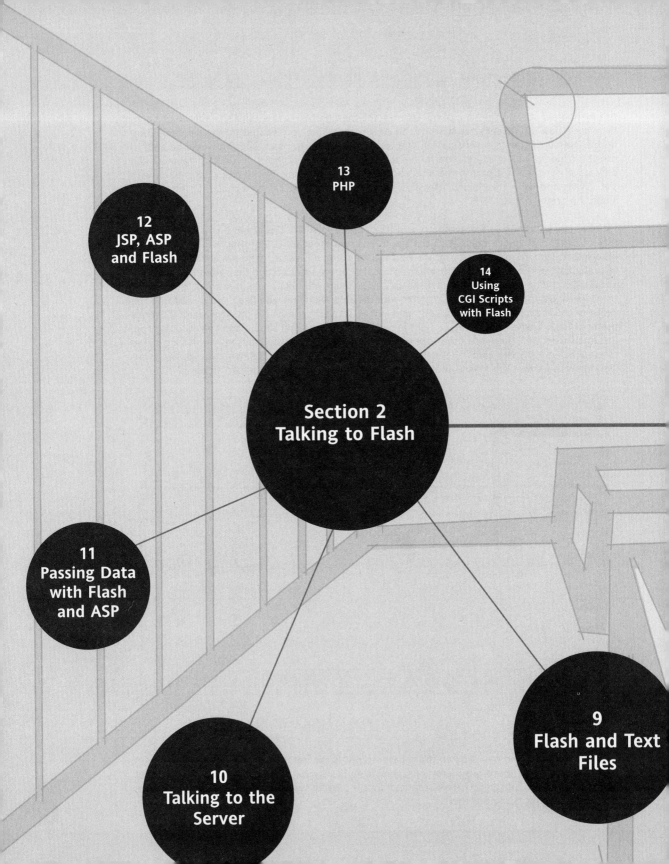

Chapter 8
Flash and
JavaScript
Integration

You've probably already seen some JavaScript; it's all over the Internet, so the chances are you've already seen some of what it can do. JavaScript is most commonly used as a client-side scripting language, meaning that the scripts are executed within the web browser and not on the server. It can be used for many purposes, including setting and retrieving cookies, manipulating form data, cascading style sheets and dynamically enhancing the HTML elements of a web page. JavaScript can also be used to interact with an embedded Flash movie on a web page.

If you're already using JavaScript in your Flash development, this chapter should help confirm the things you already know, and hopefully give you some new ideas for using JavaScript with Flash. If you haven't, however, this is a great place to begin.

We'll cover the very basics: using the `fscommand`, and embedding JavaScript in your HTML default template (Program Files\Macromedia\Flash 5\Html\Default.html). Then we'll move on to look at some of the Flash methods that you can use through JavaScript, and follow this with an example that uses JavaScript's Flash-specific Tell Target. We'll finish the worked examples with a relatively complex script that uses JavaScript and Flash together to create a Flash clock.

As you might already know, there are plenty of similarities between JavaScript and ActionScript, and you might have heard it said that first-time Flashers who already use JavaScript in their web pages find the new ActionScript environment very accessible. Of course, the same is true in reverse, and because of all the ActionScripting you've looked at so far it makes sense to approach JavaScript from this angle. Therefore, we'll begin this chapter by looking at what the two languages have in common. Recognizing the similarities between the two languages should give you the confidence to further your experiments. So, to begin this chapter, we'll have a quick look at those similarities.

Comparing JavaScript and ActionScript

Flash 5's ActionScript is modeled on the same scripting standard as JavaScript, called ECMAScript. The similarities between the two are, as a result, fairly far reaching.

Variables

You've already been using ActionScript variables fairly extensively in earlier chapters. As you already know, variables store data by using data types, and in ActionScript there are three: number, string and Boolean. JavaScript uses these three data types, and another two, **Null** and **Undefined**:

Data Type	Values	Examples
Number	Numerical	`-23; 57; 2.34;-7.69;`
String	Single or Multi-Character	`"Hello World"; "a";`
Boolean	One-bit (true or false)	`true; false;`
Null	Zero or none	`null;`
Undefined	No declared value	`undefined`

Many programming languages require that you declare your variables explicitly before you use them, for example, C++ requires that you explicitly declare whether the number you're intending to store in the variable is of `int` or `double` data type. Neither JavaScript nor ActionScript need you to explicitly declare variables, they just do it themselves according to the value that you've stored in the variable, and this makes for easy coding. If you declared six JavaScript values like this:

```
value1 = 23, value2 = 23.99, value3 = "hello";
value4 = false, value5 = null, value6 = undefined;
```

JavaScript would dynamically interpret value1 and value2 as number types, value3 as a string type, value4 as a Boolean type, value5 as a null type, and an undefined variable in value6.

OOP

JavaScript and ActionScript are both object-oriented languages, in that they can use abstract data types known as **objects** to access data and carry out tasks. Both languages use **dot syntax** for this purpose. For example, JavaScript has a window object that has an open method. To use this function to open a new browser window, you might pass in some parameters for the window like this:

```
open("index2.html", "new", "width=500, height=200");
```

User-defined functions

JavaScript and ActionScript both use functions similarly, and require functions to be declared in the same way. Suppose you wanted to create a function that adds two numbers together in Flash, and use the trace action to send the result to an output window. You'd probably want to declare it in the first frame of the timeline, so that it's accessible throughout the movie, using this syntax:

```
function sumOf(num1, num2) {
    trace(num1+num2);
}
```

You could then evoke sumOf from anywhere on the main timeline like this:

```
sumOf(num1, num2);
```

So if you used:

```
sumOf(5, 6);
```

You'd get an output box with the number 11 in it. You could also evoke the function from another timeline, by using _root:

```
_root.sumOf(5,6);
```

In JavaScript, functions are usually declared at the top of an HTML page, before the <body> tag. You could write the sumOf function in JavaScript, using the alert method of JavaScript's window object (an instance of the window object is automatically created for each browser window open, and you do not have to explicitly name it in order to use its methods and properties). The alert method displays a pop up box with a message and an OK button.

Your code would look like this:

```
function sumOf(num1, num2) {
    alert(num1+num2);
}
```

You could also call that function from anywhere else in the HTML document simply by using sumOf(1,2) (followed by a semi-colon if called on its own line), and you'd get a pop up a box with the value 3 in it. You could also call this function from a link, like this:

```
<a href="javascript:sumOf(1,2)">
    Click here for the sum of 1 and 2
</a>
```

Comments

Comments are the same in JavaScript and ActionScript. Comments enable you to annotate your algorithms with plain English so you don't have to spend time decoding it every time you look at it. Single-line comments in both ActionScript and JavaScript are preceded by two forward slashes (//) and multi-line comments are enclosed between a forward slash followed by an asterisk (/*), and an asterisk followed by a forward slash (*/). Here's some commented ActionScript code:

```
/*
helloWorld.fla
by Joe Flash
10/23/2000
*/

//Function traces "hello" to the output window
function helloWorld() {
    trace("Hello World!");
}

//Say hello to the world
helloWorld ();
```

Writing comments is a very important part of programming. It not only makes it easier for you to remember what you were trying to do with pieces of code, but if you ever release the code to the public (or ask someone to evaluate it), it makes it much easier for them to figure out what's going on in the code. Also, for programmers using advanced algorithms in their code, coming back to it months later, they may not realize the way they got things done months before. Use them liberally – you'll be glad that you did later on.

Those are some of the similarities between ActionScript and JavaScript, and I hope that knowing about them will help make your progress through this chapter a little easier! Let's move onto the first aspect of Flash and JavaScript programming: the fscommand.

The fscommand action

Flash uses the `fscommand` action to send a command or some data to the external application hosting the movie, a projector or a web browser, and to communicate with other client-side scripting languages.

Some of the older Flash players don't work with the `fscommand`. You can find a list of these in Macromedia's Flash Player Browser Support Matrix at:

www.macromedia.com/support/flash/ts/documents/browser_support_matrix.htm

This is the syntax for the `fscommand`:

```
fscommand("command", "arguments");
```

You name the `fscommand` using the `command` parameter, which is important if you want to use more than one. You can include any variables that you want to send to the script as arguments (although these are optional), such as data the user has entered into the movie, or an error message you want to display with JavaScript.

We'll begin by implementing the `fscommand` in a simple example. We'll make a Flash movie that stores three message strings inside three buttons, using a variable, and send them to a JavaScript function that will display them in a browser alert.

Passing strings with fscommand

1. Fire up Flash, and create 3 simple buttons on your main stage. Put static text labels on them: Button 1, Button 2, and Button 3.

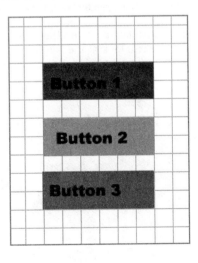

We'll store a message in a variable inside each button, and use the fscommand to send them to the HTML page for JavaScript processing.

2. Inside button 1, set a variable called strMsg with the value You clicked the 1st button.

3. Add an fscommand, call it popUp, and pass it the strMsg variable as an argument, as shown in the following screenshot:

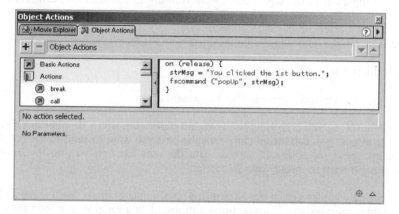

4. Do the same thing to the other two buttons, changing the message text to You clicked the 2nd button and You clicked the 3rd button according to the button, and save your movie as fscommand.fla.

5. Go into the Publish Settings for the movie, and make sure that both the Flash and HTML formats are selected. Flash includes an HTML template, that contains the code required to detect the fscommand. This is different from the default HTML template that we looked at earlier in this chapter and does not need editing. Select the HTML tab, and select Flash with FSCommand from the Template drop-down list, and then select Publish.

Now we need to write some JavaScript into the HTML page to display the messages we stored in the variables. Take a look at the JavaScript contained in the <HEAD> section of the document – it's well commented, using the same // as ActionScript uses to make sure that comments aren't executed.

> *Note: You'll see a difference between Internet Explorer and Netscape - at the bottom of the code you'll see that the JavaScript checks the browser being used and writes a few lines of VBScript for Internet Explorer browsers. This will be written into the document as the page is loaded. The reason for this is that the Flash plug-in fires an* fscommand *to an IE browser through a technology called ActiveX which VBScript communicates with.*

This is the section of the code that performs the `fscommand`:

```
function FSCommand_DoFSCommand (command, args) {
   var fsCommandObj =
 ➤ InternetExplorer ? fsCommand : document.fsCommand;
   //
   // Place your code here...
```

We'll check the name of the `fscommand` being sent, by checking the value of the `command` variable, and then taking the value of the `args` variable and displaying it in the `alert` pop up message box.

6. Find the comment line, `//Place your code here...` and add the following code below it:

```
//check name of command
if(command == "popUp") {
    //Display the variable passed in the argument in a window
    //alert box and send args variable to a browser alert
    alert (args);
}
```

7. Now save your HTML page and open it in your preferred browser.

Clicking any of the buttons in your Flash movie should display an alert telling you which button you clicked. If you have any problems getting it to work, make sure that you are using a JavaScript enabled browser and then thoroughly check the syntax and spelling of your code.

Now let's suppose you wanted to send more than one `fscommand` from your Flash movie.

Sending more than one fscommand

We'll nest two `fscommand` actions inside the HTML page and use JavaScript to perform a different task depending on the command sent from the movie. We'll use nesting to make Button 2 send its message to the status bar of the browser instead of a browser alert.

1. Open up `fsCommand.fla` and select Button 2, and go into its Object Actions window. Change the name of the `fscommand` from `popUp` to `status` in the Object Actions window. Your code for Button 2 should now look like this:

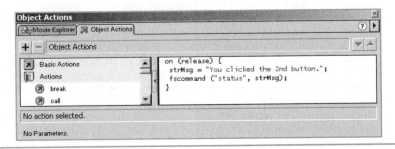

2. Now go into the Publish Settings window and uncheck the HTML box on the Formats tab so that you don't overwrite the existing JavaScript function, and Publish the movie. Now we need to change the HTML page and tell JavaScript to look out for a command called status. So, open your HTML page in a text editor again and add a couple more lines to your previous bit of code, so that it reads as follows:

```
//check name of command
if (command == "popUp") {
   window.alert(args);
} else {
   //if it's not popup then it must be status,
   //so display args variable in the status bar
   window.status = args;
}
```

This code is fairly intuitive, using an if...else loop to check the name of the fscommand for a condition, and where it's not applicable (when the fscommand is called status) to move on to execute the else instruction.

3. Now save your HTML page and open it again in your preferred browser and click each of the buttons in turn. When you click on Button 2, the message is displayed in the status bar, whereas the other buttons still display their messages in a browser alert.

So, that's the fscommand. You can adapt it to work with any piece of JavaScript that you want.

One of the advantages of using the fscommand is that Flash provides a JavaScript enabled HTML page for you, so you don't have to worry about any JavaScript coding beyond the functionality you want to add yourself. Using JavaScript with your Flash movie in any other way, as we're going to do next, requires that you prepare the HTML page yourself. So before we go any further, we'll look at a few JavaScript essentials.

Embedding your movie in an HTML page

It's probably not news to you that Internet Explorer and Netscape read Flash movies and JavaScript differently. Internet Explorer displays a Flash movie by reading the HTML parameters contained in the <OBJECT> tag, and JavaScript uses the ID parameter of this tag to reference the movie.

Netscape displays a Flash movie by reading the HTML parameters contained in the <EMBED> tag. JavaScript uses the NAME parameter of this tag to reference the movie. Netscape also uses an additional <EMBED> parameter, SWLIVECONNECT, which starts Java, which is in turn necessary for the fscommand to work. The value of this parameter should be set to TRUE whenever you need Java to start with the Flash player (not 1, which can often be substituted for TRUE). However, you should be careful about using it unless it's strictly necessary, because it does slow down your movies.

When you publish your Flash movie using the Default HTML template, these parameters are not included. So, to ensure you can use Flash and JavaScript together, you'll need to either change the Default HTML template, or get into the habit of adding these parameters after publishing.

We'll change the template now to make the following examples easier and quicker to code, so, go to the Flash 5 directory on your machine then open the HTML subfolder. Now open the Default.html file in a text editor such as Notepad, find the <OBJECT> tag and add this parameter, which replaces the ID parameter with the name of the movie:

```
ID=$TI
```

So that the <OBJECT> tag now looks like this:

```
<OBJECT classid="clsid:D27CDB6E-AE6D-11cf-96B8-444553540000"
codebase="http://download.macromedia.com/pub/shockwave/cabs/flash
➥ swflash.cab#version=5,0,0,0"
WIDTH=$WI HEIGHT=$HE ID=$TI>
```

Now find the <EMBED> tag and add:

```
NAME=$TI SWLIVECONNECT=TRUE
```

So that the tag now looks like this:

```
<EMBED $PE WIDTH=$WI HEIGHT=$HE NAME=$TI SWLIVECONNECT=TRUE
➥ TYPE="application/x-shockwave-flash"

PLUGINSPAGE="http://www.macromedia.com/shockwave/download/index.cg
➥ i?P1_Prod_Version=ShockwaveFlash"></EMBED>
</OBJECT>
```

This sets the NAME parameter of the <EMBED> tag to the name of the movie, and the SWLIVECONNECT parameter to TRUE.

Check that your template looks like this one, and then save it:

The examples used from here on in will assume that you have altered your default template. If you haven't, and some people prefer not to, just make sure you add in these changes manually when you go to put some JavaScript in the HTML pages.

JavaScript scripting

Before we start writing JavaScript, let's take a look at a simple example script incorporating all the essentials:

```
<SCRIPT LANGUAGE='JavaScript'>
<!— hide from old browsers
function test() {
    alert("test")
}

// stop hiding —>
</SCRIPT>
```

The first line is the `<SCRIPT>` tag that tells the browser which scripting language is being used, and the tag is closed off at the bottom of the script: `</SCRIPT>`.

The second line is simply to prevent older browsers that don't understand JavaScript from getting confused. The comment code simply hides the JavaScript from browsers that can't deal with it. Again this is closed off at the bottom of the code (commented out with a JavaScript comment).

Then we declared a new function and called it test, `function test ()`. The parentheses following the function's name are to hold any parameters that we may want to pass to the function, and braces are always placed around the code that the function performs.

So, inside this function we put the `window` object's `alert` method, passing the string we want the alert box to display as a message, `test`.

The main rule about scripting is to close each tag or parenthesis that you open – if you open a script tag (`<SCRIPT>`) you always need a closing tag (`</SCRIPT>`.) If you open a brace, then somewhere later on you need to close it. The same also goes for brackets and quotes.

And that's it, now we're ready to get back to using JavaScript and Flash together. We'll start by using `getURL` to pass parameters to JavaScript.

getURL

The `getURL` action can be used for several different functions. It can be used to open a browser window at a specified URL, it can be used to pass variables to a script for processing (more on scripting in the following chapters), or it can be used to call a JavaScript function in the same page as the movie. I actually find the `getURL` method simpler than using the `fscommand`, but it certainly helps to know both so that you can make up your own mind.

Although you can use getURL to open a specified URL in a new browser window directly from your Flash movie, it doesn't allow you to size the window, or to control any of the many elements of the browser window that JavaScript can control. So, we'll write a simple piece of JavaScript that you can call from your Flash movie to display a specified URL in an exact-sized pop-up window.

Using getURL with JavaScript

1. Begin a new movie and create four buttons similar to those shown in the screenshot below. Name your buttons Page1, Page2, Page3 and Page4.

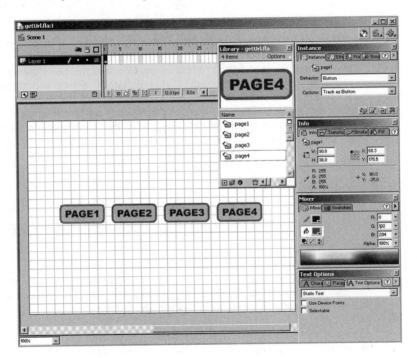

2. Add getURL actions into the on(release) event of each of the buttons, the first one behind Button 1 like this:

```
getURL ("JavaScript: popUp('page1.html')");
```

The parameter we've passed here specifies a JavaScript popUp function that we'll build into the HTML page next, and the page that will be opened (we'll build four of these little HTML pages later as well). Add the same action to the other three buttons, changing the page number to the number of the button it sits behind (page2.html for Button 2 and so on).

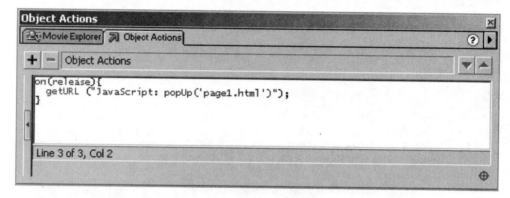

3. Save your movie as getURL.fla, and publish it using the default settings, Flash and HTML.

4. Open the getUrl.html page in a text editor. Notice at this point there is no JavaScript on the page as we used the default HTML template. The NAME and ID parameters will be set to the name of the movie, getURL, if you changed the template earlier – if you didn't, change the HTML page manually now. Then go to the end of the </TITLE> line and hit RETURN a couple of times so you've got some space to work. Now we're ready to start scripting. First add in the <SCRIPT> tag and the <!– shields up! tag.

```
<SCRIPT LANGUAGE='JavaScript'>
<!– shields up!
```

We need to create a new function called popUp next, with a parameter called page (in which we'll store the URL of the web page you want to be displayed later on):

```
function popUp(page) {
```

We'll also define a variable, win2, using the var command. We'll use JavaScript's open function to open the URL contained in page in a new browser window, called winname, and set all controllable elements of the window to false:

```
var win2=window.open(page, "winname","width=70,height=120,toolbar=0,
➥ location=0,directories=0,status=0,menubar=0,scrollbars=0,
➥ resizable=0,copyhistory=0");
```

If you wanted to display any of these elements, you would simply need to set their values to 1 (True).

Finally, we'll also set the focus to the newly opened window, using the win2.focus() command. This ensures that it appears above any other windows on the desktop:

```
    win2.focus();
    }
```

Then finish off the script by using // down shields! –> and then closing the <SCRIPT> tag.

The completed code will look like this:

```
<HTML>
<HEAD>
<TITLE>getUrl</TITLE>
   <SCRIPT LANGUAGE='JavaScript'>
<!- shields up!

//define popup function and accept the URL argument
//in a parameter called page
function popUp(page) {

//define win2 as a new window and open the specified URL value
//in a sized window named winname.
//All controllable elements of the window are set to false
var win2=window.open(page,"winname","width=70,height=120,toolbar=0,
➥ location=0,directories=0,status=0,menubar=0,scrollbars=0,resizable=
➥0,copyhistory=0");

//bring the newly opened window into focus(front of the screen)
win2.focus();
}
// down shields! -->
</SCRIPT>
...
```

Note that we haven't included the whole HTML page, because there's a lot of automatically generated code in there, but you can find this working example, called getUrl.html, on the CD if you want to see it in its entirety.

Save the changes you made to getUrl.html. Now all we need are four new HTML pages that will be displayed in the pop-up window.

5. Open your text editor and create four very basic HTML pages in the same location as your getUrl.fla movie, saving them as page1.html, page2.html etc. and changing the text enclosed by the <BODY> tag to match that of the filename:

```
<HTML>
   <HEAD>
   </HEAD>
   <BODY>

        Page1

   </BODY>
</HTML>
```

Now you're ready to test the movie, so open getUrl.html page in your preferred browser and click one of the buttons.

The associated HTML page will be displayed in a sized pop-up window that has no status bar, location, menu bar or scroll bars:

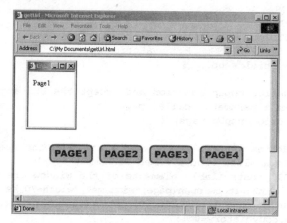

You can experiment with the different window elements you can control by changing the popUp function – try changing the window size, and displaying the status bar or scroll bars.

It's a neat little script, as far as it goes, but wouldn't it be nice to display the pop-up window in the centre of the screen regardless of screen resolution? To do this, we'll just add a few lines of code to the popUp function.

6. Go back into the getURL.html page, and define a new variable intScrWidth. We'll store a calculation in the variable that halves the screen width (window.screen.width/2) and takes from that the sum of half the new window width (remember we set it as 70 earlier) plus 10 pixels (to account for the window borders). We'll use the resulting coordinate to left align the new window:

```
var intScrWidth = (window.screen.width/2) - (35 + 10)
```

Note the use of dots to reference the properties of an object: .screen is a property of the window and .width is a property of the screen.

We'll also define another variable, intScrHeight that does the same thing with the height of the screen but adding 40 pixels to the halved window height to account for the title bar and window borders. This sum will give us a coordinate for top-aligning the new window:

```
var intScrHeight = (window.screen.height/2) - (60 + 40)
```

We'll use these two variables as the co-ordinate parameters in the window.open function, to position the new window based on the screen width and height:

```
var win2=window.open(page,"winname","width=70,height=120,toolbar=0,
➥ location=0,directories=0,status=0,menubar=0,scrollbars=0,resizable
➥ =0,copyhistory=0,left=" + intScrWidth + ",top=" + intScrHeight
➥ + ",screenX=" + intScrWidth + ",screenY=" + intScrHeight)
```

Put it all together and your script should look like this:

```
<SCRIPT LANGUAGE='JavaScript'>
<!- shields up!

function popUp(page) {
    var intScrWidth = (window.screen.width/2) - (35 + 10);
    var intScrHeight = (window.screen.height/2) - (60 + 40);
    var win2=window.open(page,"winname","width=70,height=120,
        ➥toolbar=0,location=0,directories=0,status=0,menubar=0,
        ➥scrollbars=0,resizable=0,copyhistory=0,left=" +
        ➥intScrWidth + ",top=" + intScrHeight ➥ + ",screenX=" +
        ➥intScrWidth + ",screenY=" + intScrHeight);

    win2.focus();
}

// down shields! ->
</SCRIPT>
```

7. Save the page and open it again in your web browser. This time, when you click a button the relevant page is opened in a centered pop-up window. If you have any problems running this, look hard for typos. There's a working copy of the HTML document on the CD called getUrlPositioned.html, which you can experiment with as well.

So far in this chapter you've used two of Flash's actions that you can use to call and pass variables to JavaScript from your Flash movie, and you can use either of them to use any JavaScript you write or find. The story doesn't end there, however. You can also call some of Flash's own methods and use them from within your JavaScript. We'll look at these next.

Using Flash-specific methods from JavaScript

You've already met a number of the methods that come with Flash. They are specific to the Flash player, and can be used with client-side scripting languages, like JavaScript (as we'll be doing here), VBScript, or JScript. These methods send calls or pass parameters to a Flash movie. Many of the functions available in Flash's ActionScript can be used as methods too – for example Play, GotoFrame, and Zoom. You can find a complete listing of the Flash methods you can use with JavaScript and their correct syntax on the Macromedia site – the URL is at the end of the chapter.

Before you can execute a Flash method with JavaScript, you have to identify the movie within the HTML page – this is where the ID and NAME parameters of the <OBJECT> and <EMBED> tags come in. For example, if the value of your ID and NAME parameters is myMovie then you could reference the myMovie object with the following code

```
var FlashMovie = window.document.myMovie;
```

Notice we are referencing the document property of the window (which relates to the web page) and the myMovie property of the document (which relates to the embedded Flash movie).

The variable FlashMovie can then be used whenever you want to reference your movie through a method in JavaScript.

> *Many of Flash's methods won't work until the movie has fully loaded. The best way to prevent any errors is to test that the movie has fully loaded before executing your JavaScript function, which you can do using Flash's* PercentLoaded *method.*

The PercentLoaded method

The PercentLoaded method returns a value between 0 and 100 that indicates the actual percentage of the movie that has loaded. This is the syntax:

```
var FlashMovie=window.document.mymovie;

//check that the value returned by the PercentLoaded method
//is 100
if(FlashMovie.PercentLoaded() == 100)  {

    //execute some code
}
```

We'll use this and some other Flash methods next, but first we need a movie to control.

Controlling a movie from JavaScript using Flash methods

1. Create a simple movie, like the one opposite, sized at 300 x 200 pixels. Put the number of the frame on the corresponding ball image on each frame from 1 to 10 (1 on frame 1, 2 on frame 2, etc.), and set your frame rate to 4 fps so the numbers don't change too quickly. Save the movie as flashMethods.fla. If you'd rather just use mine, pull it off the CD and move onto the next section.

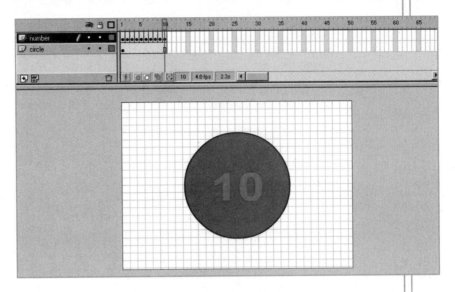

2. Before you publish the movie, go into the Publish Settings window, accept the default formats, Flash and HTML, go to the HTML tab and check the Paused At Start, and Loop check boxes. Then hit Publish.

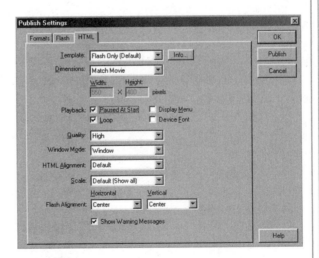

3. Now we're ready to start scripting, so go to where you saved your movie and open the flashMethods.html page in a text editor. If the ID and NAME parameters of the <OBJECT> and <EMBED> tags are not set to flashMethods then do this now (they should be if you changed your default template earlier).

We checked the Paused At Start box to True because I want to show you how to use the Play method. If you were to open flashMethods.html page in your web browser, you'll find that the movie doesn't play but pauses on the first frame. The `Play` method, which we'll look at here, simply tells the movie to start playing. We'll use it here to create a `Play` function in JavaScript that is executed by the user clicking a `Play` link on the page.

4.   We are going to add some JavaScript into the head section of the document, underneath the title tags as we did earlier. First we'll declare a new function:

```
function playFlashMovie() {
```

Then we identify the movie and assign it to a `FlashMovie` variable:

```
var FlashMovie=window.document.flashMethods;
```

We'll use an `if...else` loop to check whether the `PercentLoaded` method has returned `100`, and if so, execute the `Play` method:

```
if (FlashMovie.PercentLoaded() == 100) {
    FlashMovie.Play();
} else {
```

If the movie hasn't yet loaded, we'll set a timeout of 10 milliseconds before this function is executed again:

```
        setTimeout("playFlashMovie()",10)
    }
```

Then finish off the functions by closing the braces, the shield, and the script:

```
}
// down shields! -->
</SCRIPT>
```

All together, the code looks like this:

```
<SCRIPT LANGUAGE='JavaScript'>
<!- shields up!

function playFlashMovie() {
    var FlashMovie=window.document.flashMethods;

    if (FlashMovie.PercentLoaded() == 100) {
        FlashMovie.Play();
    } else {
        setTimeout("playFlashMovie()",10)
    }
}
// down shields! -->
</SCRIPT>
```

5. Finally we'll add the link to the page that calls the `playFlashMovie` function. Type the following code below your `</OBJECT>` tag and above your `</BODY>` tag:

```
<P><A HREF="JavaScript: playFlashMovie();">PLAY</A>
```

What we're doing here is telling the browser that clicking the link should call the JavaScript function `playFlashMovie`.

Your HTML code should look like this:

```
<HTML>
<HEAD>
<TITLE>flashMethods</TITLE>
<SCRIPT LANGUAGE='JavaScript'>
<!-- shields up!
function playFlashMovie() {

var FlashMovie=window.document.flashMethods;

if(FlashMovie.PercentLoaded() == 100) {
FlashMovie.Play();
} else {
setTimeout("playFlashMovie()",10)
}
}
// down shields! -->
</SCRIPT>
</HEAD>
<BODY bgcolor="#FFFFFF">
<!-- URL's used in the movie-->
<!-- text used in the movie-->
<!--1 2 3 4 5 6 7 8 9 10 --><OBJECT classid="clsid:D27CDB6E-AE6D-11cf-96B8-444553540000"
 codebase="http://download.macromedia.com/pub/shockwave/cabs/flash/swflash.cab#version=5,0,0,0"
 WIDTH=300 HEIGHT=200 ID=flashMethods>
 <PARAM NAME=movie VALUE="flashMethods.swf"> <PARAM NAME=play VALUE=false> <PARAM NAME=menu
VALUE=false> <PARAM NAME=quality VALUE=high> <PARAM NAME=bgcolor VALUE=#FFFFFF>
<EMBED src="flashMethods.swf" play=false menu=false quality=high bgcolor=#FFFFFF  WIDTH=300
HEIGHT=200 NAME=flashMethods SWLIVECONNECT=TRUE
 TYPE="application/x-shockwave-flash"
PLUGINSPAGE="http://www.macromedia.com/shockwave/download/index.cgi?P1_Prod_Version=ShockwaveFlash">
</EMBED>
</OBJECT>
<P><A HREF="JavaScript: playFlashMovie();">PLAY</A>
</BODY>
</HTML>
```

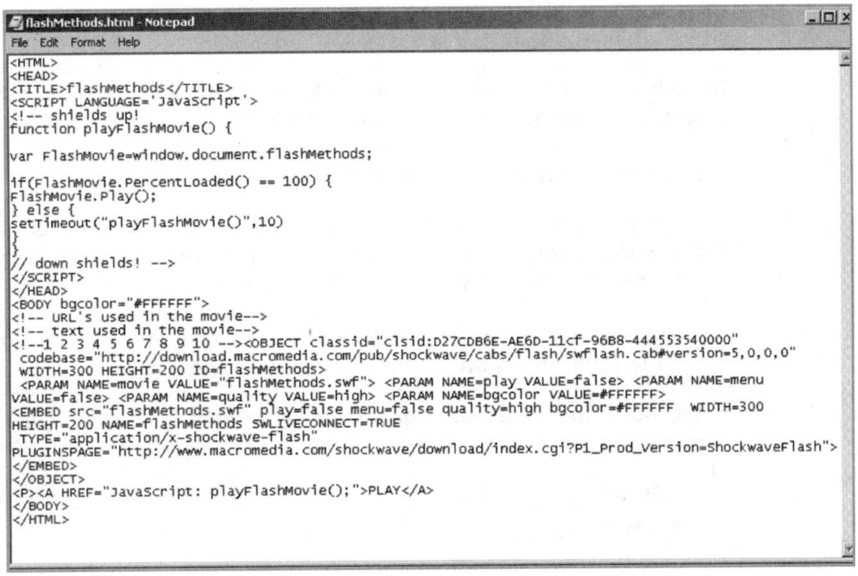

6. Save the changes and you're ready to test your movie, so open the HTML page in your web browser. Click the PLAY link, and the JavaScript function plays the movie.

We'll use the `StopPlay` method to stop the movie playing.

7. Open the `flashMethods.html` file in your text editor and add a new `stopFlashMovie` function to your script, as shown in this excerpt:

```
<SCRIPT LANGUAGE='JavaScript'>
<!— shields up!

function playFlashMovie() {
   var FlashMovie = window.document.flashMethods;

   if (FlashMovie.PercentLoaded() == 100) {
      FlashMovie.Play();
   } else {
      setTimeout("playFlashMovie()",10)
```

continues overleaf

```
        }
    }
    function stopFlashMovie() {
        var FlashMovie=window.document.flashMethods;
        FlashMovie.StopPlay();
    }
    // down shields! ->
</SCRIPT>
```

The stopFlashMovie function is much simpler than the playFlashMovie function. All we did was identify the movie, as with the previous function, and execute the StopPlay method.

8. To finish the code, add another link to flashMethods.html that calls the stopFlashMovie function below the PLAY link:

    ```
    <P><A HREF="JavaScript: stopFlashMovie();">STOP</A>
    ```

9. Save your flashMethods.html file and open it in your web browser. You can find a working copy on the CD called PlayStopFlashMethods.html, use this to check for syntax errors if your own code isn't working properly.

    Let's add one last method to this page before moving on. We'll now use the Rewind method to return the movie to the first frame on the timeline.

10. Again, open the flashMethods.html file in your text editor and add another function, rewindFlashMovie:

    ```
    <SCRIPT LANGUAGE='JavaScript'>
    <!- shields up!

    function playFlashMovie() {
        var FlashMovie=window.document.flashMethods;

        if (FlashMovie.PercentLoaded() == 100) {
            FlashMovie.Play();
        } else {
            setTimeout("playFlashMovie()",10)
        }
    }

    function stopFlashMovie() {
        var FlashMovie = window.document.flashMethods;
        FlashMovie.StopPlay();
    }

    function rewindFlashMovie() {
        var FlashMovie = window.document.flashMethods;
        FlashMovie.Rewind();
    }
    ```

```
// down shields! —>
</SCRIPT>
```

11. Type one final link to the page to call the `rewindFlashMovie()` function, underneath the STOP link:

    ```
    <P><A HREF="JavaScript: rewindFlashMovie();">REWIND</A>
    ```

12. Save your `flashMethods.html` page and test it in your web browser. You can add as many functions as you like to this code – try using some from the appendix and see what you can make happen.

TellTarget methods

So far we've looked at a few of the standard Flash methods you can use to control the main timeline of your movie from outside the SWF itself. You can also use **TellTarget methods**, identifiable by the prefix 'T', such as TSetProperty, TGotoFrame and TStopPlay that you can use with Flash. These methods are used to control movie clips sitting on your main movie's timeline.

TellTarget methods have to have the name of the movie clip passed to them, as you might expect. This is the syntax:

```
var FlashMovie=window.document.mymovie;
FlashMovie.TPlay("/MovieClip");
```

Let's put some of these TellTarget methods into action.

Using TellTarget methods

We need a new Flash movie clip to control with the TellTarget methods so we'll build a very simple animation here:

1. Open Flash and insert a new **movie clip symbol** and call it myClip. For the purpose of this tutorial we'll stick to a really simple animation, so on frame 1 draw a square in the centre of your stage, convert it to a graphic symbol, and call it square.

2. Create a keyframe on frame 20, and set the rotation of the square symbol to 180°. Then create a motion tween from frame 1 to frame 20, and your myClip symbol should look something like this:

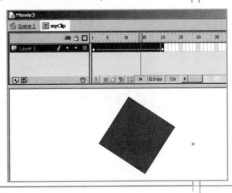

3. Now click the Scene 1 tab to return to the main timeline, and drag an instance of the myClip movie symbol from the library onto the center of your main stage. On the Instance panel, name your movie clip instance myClip.

4. We'll add a simple animation to the main timeline of the movie just so we can distinguish between this and the myClip movie. Add a new layer, and on this layer draw a red circle on the bottom right hand side of your movie. You should have something like this:

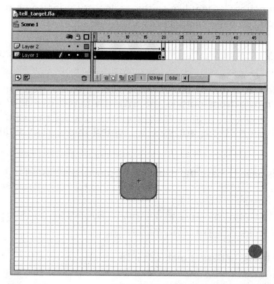

5. Now add a keyframe to select frame 15 on both layers, and on frame 15 of layer 2, select the red circle and drag it across to the bottom left side of the movie. (You might need to lock layer 1.) Insert a shape tween on layer 2. When you test your movie the square should rotate in the center of the screen, and the red circle run from right to left, repeating continuously.

6. Save your movie as tell_target.fla and publish it. Now we have a very simple animation to begin working with.

7. Open up tell_target.html in a text editor, and check that ID and NAME have changed to tell_target (and change them if they haven't).

Create a new function called stopFlashMovieClip, assign the movie to a variable, and execute the TStopPlay method, (passing the name of the movie clip we want to stop). Prefix the name of the movie clip with the '/' character, so that it maps the path from the main timeline of the movie. Your script should go into the <HEAD> section of the document:

```
<SCRIPT LANGUAGE='JavaScript'>
<!- shields up!
```

```
//function to stop movie clip
function stopFlashMovieClip(){

    //define movie
    var FlashMovie=window.document.tell_target;

    //execute the TStopPlay method
    FlashMovie.TStopPlay("/myClip");
}
// down shields! ->
</SCRIPT>
```

8. Create a link on the page to call the `stopFlashMovieClip` function below the `</OBJECT>` tag and above the `</BODY>` tag of your document:

```
<P><A HREF="JavaScript:;" OnClick="stopFlashMovieClip();">STOP</A>
```

And your HTML page should look like this:

9. Save your `tell_target.html` page and open the page in your browser. Clicking the STOP link will make the `myClip` symbol (the green square) stop, while the main movie (the red circle) continues to play. If you have problems getting it to work, check that you called the instance of the movie clip `myClip`.

That brings us to the end of the quick Flash method tutorials. If you'd like to experiment some more, you can use the JavaScript appendix to create some more elaborate examples before we move onto the final tutorial.

We'll conclude this chapter with another tutorial that introduces a new method, and some more extensive JavaScript code. We'll create a real time working Flash clock that uses a JavaScript function to send the current time into your Flash movie every second. After completing this tutorial, you will be able to add the clock to any Flash movie you create.

Creating a JavaScript and Flash clock

1. Begin, as ever, by creating the Flash movie. Simply draw a dynamic, single line text field on your main stage and give it the variable name `clock`.

2. Add a `getURL` action to frame 1, with the URL `Javascript: startclock()`. This will start the JavaScript clock function that we'll create next. Save the movie as `clock.fla`, and then publish it.

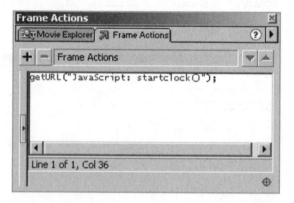

3. Open the `clock.html` page in your text editor, and we'll add some JavaScript into the `<HEAD>` section of the document.

    First define two variables `timerID` and `timerRunning`, which we'll use to control the timer. Both variables will be set when the code is executed.

    ```
    var timerID = null;
    var timerRunning = false;
    ```

    Now we'll create a `stopclock` function that stops the timer from running, allowing the current time to be displayed. We've already seen the `setTimeout` method earlier in this chapter, but notice here we use the `clearTimeout` method to stop it from running:

    ```
    function stopclock (){
        if (timerRunning)
        clearTimeout (timerID);
        timerRunning = false;
    }
    ```

This function displays the current time:

```
function showtime () {
```

We then need to define the Flash movie...

```
    var FlashMovie = window.document.clock;
```

...and the variable to be used further on in the loop to check if the movie has loaded:

```
    var FlashIsLoaded = false;
```

This is how we get the current date from the system clock:

```
    var now = new Date();
```

We will then parse the hours, minutes and seconds from the date:

```
    var hours = now.getHours();

    var minutes = now.getMinutes();

    var seconds = now.getSeconds();
```

The getHours, getMinutes and getSeconds methods simply return the hours, minutes and seconds values (respectively) from a date/time variable.

The following piece of code defines the timeValue variable, converts the time to the 12 hour clock, and formats the 'hours' part of the time.

```
    var timeValue = "" + ((hours >12) ? hours -12 :hours);
    if (timeValue == "0") timeValue = 12;
```

Let's look at that one step at a time. First we reset the variable timeValue by assigning it a null string ("").

We then evaluate whether the hours variable is greater than 12. If it is, we assign the value of the hours variable -12 to timeValue.

If the value of timeValue is now 0, we set it to 12 to format the hour portion of the time correctly.

In the same way, we format the minutes and seconds, and combine them with the timeValue:

```
    timeValue += ((minutes < 10) ? ":0" : ":") + minutes;

    timeValue += ((seconds < 10) ? ":0" : ":") + seconds;
```

Notice how we use `timeValue +=` in these cases; this is because we are appending the values of `minutes` and `seconds` to the value already stored in the `timeValue` variable.

We then check if the time is am or pm, and combine this with the time value:

```
timeValue += (hours >= 12) ? " pm" : " am";
```

We'll use a `while` loop to check whether the movie has loaded, before executing the next piece of code (the exclamation mark, `!`, means 'not'):

```
if (!FlashIsLoaded) {
    while (!FlashIsLoaded) {
        if (FlashMovie.PercentLoaded() == 100) {
```

When `PercentLoaded` returns 100, we then execute the `SetVariable` method to send the value of the `timevalue` variable into our Flash variable named `clock`:

```
FlashMovie.SetVariable("clock", timeValue);
```

We then set a timer that will call the `showtime` function again after 1 second. This gives the impression of a clock ticking away with every passing second.

```
timerID = setTimeout("showtime()",1000);
timerRunning = true;
```

To break the loop, we set the `FlashIsLoaded` variable to `true`:

```
FlashIsLoaded = true;
```

This function will be called from our Flash movie to stop the timer and show the current time:

```
function startclock() {
    stopclock();
    showtime();
}
```

Put it all together, and your code should look like this:

```
<HTML>
<HEAD>
<TITLE>clock</TITLE>
<SCRIPT LANGUAGE='JavaScript'>
<!— shields up!

var timerID = null;
var timerRunning = false;
```

```
function stopclock () {
   if (timerRunning)
      clearTimeout(timerID);
   timerRunning = false;
}

function showtime () {
   var FlashMovie = window.document.clock;
   var FlashIsLoaded = false;
   var now = new Date();
   var hours = now.getHours();
   var minutes = now.getMinutes();
   var seconds = now.getSeconds()
   var timeValue = "" + ((hours >12) ? hours -12 :hours)

   if (timeValue == "0")
      timeValue = 12;
   timeValue += ((minutes < 10) ? ":0" : ":") + minutes
   timeValue += ((seconds < 10) ? ":0" : ":") + seconds
   timeValue += (hours >= 12) ? " pm" : " am"

   if (!FlashIsLoaded) {
      while (!FlashIsLoaded) {
         if (FlashMovie.PercentLoaded() == 100) {
            FlashMovie.SetVariable("clock", timeValue);
            timerID = setTimeout("showtime()", 100);
            timerRunning = true;
            FlashIsLoaded = true;
         }
      }
   }
}

function startclock() {
   stopclock();
   showtime();
}

// down shields! -->
</SCRIPT>
```

4. Save your clock.html page and open it in your web browser – et voila! a working clock in Flash!

Summary

So, in this chapter we have looked at how JavaScript functions can be called and passed parameters from your Flash movie by using the `fscommand` and by using `getURL`. We have also looked at the use of Flash methods to control your movie and set variables and properties.

With this knowledge and a little imagination, you can create some pretty advanced applications. You can even borrow many of the free JavaScripts you can find on the Internet and find ways to integrate their functionality into your Flash movies and web sites – have fun!

You can find a helpful tech note on the JavaScript Flash specific methods at Macromedia called Macromedia Flash – Scripting with Flash 5: Flash Methods. I recommend that you experiment with these once you have a good grasp of the fundamentals. It's located at http://www.macromedia.com/support/flash/publishexport/scriptingwithflash/scriptingwithflash_03.html

One final note: A good place to follow this chapter up and compound your JavaScript knowledge (without downing any cash) is Netscape's JavaScript Developer Central at: http://developer.netscape.com/tech/javascript/index.html.

Chapter 9
Flash and
Text Files

As you're probably only too aware, many web sites use Flash for visual effects only. Visual effects and interactivity are great; but make your Flash dynamic, and you've got a really powerful site. Making Flash dynamic can be as simple as updating your movies using a text file – with little or no modification to the original Flash movie. This method of creating Flash movies not only saves time, but also makes Flash practical and functional.

For example, suppose you have a medium size site with, say, twenty Flash movies and a lot of embedded text. If you needed to update any of the text in the movies before Flash 4, you would have had to go into each file to make your changes and then re-export the file. Using a text file to read the text into the movie, you only have to change the text in the text file to update every applicable Flash file.

So not only is your life easier, your client's life is easier too, because they can update the textual content of their movies without your help. And, of course, using a text file to update your movie is just one small step away from using external script files to update your movies, giving you even more practical functionality, especially if you want your sites to interact with databases.

In this chapter we'll begin by bringing variables from a text file into your movie, loading them both into the movie itself, and also into a movie clip within the movie. Then we'll begin making the movie more interactive with the variables as they come in – developing a dynamic button list from text field variables on the fly, and a movie that allows users to scroll through larger pieces of text.

We'll develop all of these examples modularly, so that they can be copied from one file to another to aid development time and effort, so to conclude the chapter we'll wind the applications we'll have developed into one slightly bigger project.

So, let's begin by investigating how exactly you load variables into Flash from text files, and where they can be loaded to.

Loading variables into Flash

You may already be familiar with HTML forms, which are nothing more than a few elements in an HTML file that allow users to send data back to the server through the browser. When you use an HTML form, information is sent from the form to a server-side script or program in an environment variable called a **query string**. The query string format stipulates that the variable names and their respective values are placed in pairs using an equal to (=) sign, with the pairs being separated from each other using the ampersand (&) symbol. Any spaces within the values of variables should also be replaced with a plus (+) sign.

Not quite sure what I mean? Well here's an example. Let's say that our variable names are *name*, *email*, *address* and *telephone_no*, and that their respective values are *nik*, *nik@nuthing.com*, *new york* and *2124566789*. Our query string will then look like this:

name=nik&email=nik@nuthing.com&address=new+york&telephone_no=2124566789

Flash uses the same method to read variables and their values from a text file, so if Flash is to be able to read the variables, the information in the text file must be in this **query string** format.

GET and POST

To load variables into your movie, you use `loadVariables` or `loadVariablesNum`; we'll be using both to load information from text files located on a web server or on a local hard disk. So what's the difference? We'll it's pretty straightforward:

`loadVariablesNum`   loads variables into a specified level of a movie, which is indicated by a numeral (hence `Num`),

`loadVariables`   loads variables into a movie clip in your flash movie.

Both methods take three parameters, the URL of the file to be loaded into the Flash movie (this can be a full web address or it can be relative), the instance of the movie clip into which the movie should be loaded, or the level at which it should be loaded, and an optional parameter that allows you to send variables back to the script. There are three options for this parameter:

- Do not send any variables

- Send variables using `GET`

- Send variables using `POST`

The `GET` methods sends information to the script in the form of a query string while the `POST` method sends it via a buffer. The `POST` method is preferred if you are sending a lot of information to the script. The script should know which method you are using because the methods to access the data sent is different in each case. The default method used is `GET`.

```
loadVariables (url ,instance  , [variables]);

loadVariablesNum (url ,level , [variables]);
```

A reminder about levels

As you might remember from earlier chapters, Flash can store information and movies in different hierarchical layers called **levels**, in which movies and data are stacked up, one on top of the other inside the Flash plug-in, kind of like a pile of sheets of paper. This is important because while movie clips and scripts can access variables occupying the same level as they are in, any movie or script in a different level has to refer first to the level in order to access the variable.

A variable will overwrite the value of any other variable that has the same name in a specific level or target.

If you loaded a variable called `data` into level 2, a movie clip in level 2 could then access this variable's data by declaring a new variable, say, `newdata`, and then assigning the value of the `data` variable to it, like this:

```
newData = data;
```

A movie clip or a script in level 4 could access the same variable, but would have to first specify the level at which that data is stored in. In this case our `data` variable is in the second level, written as `level2`. Note that if we have already declared the variable before, we do not need the `var`.

```
newData = _level2.data;
```

Similarly, we can load information into the **root** of the movie, allowing other movie clips to access to access the information by referring to the initial movie clip that holds the information. So, if a `data` variable was in a movie clip instance called `movie1` (in the root level), a movie clip in another level could access the information like this:

```
anotherdata = _root.movie1.data;
```

The variables option allows you to send variables from the current level to server scripts, using `POST`, as well as to receive them using `GET`. For this chapter, we'll just be loading variables in using `GET`. Once the variables are loaded into Flash, we can then begin to use them to set flags, update information, carry out calculations and much more.

Using text tile variables inside Flash

We'll load two text files into a movie, one into the root level and the other into a movie clip, using `loadVariables`. We'll also reference these variables from other levels and targets, so that we explore the full set possibilities of `loadVariables`.

1.   We'll create the two text files first. The first text file, `myText.txt`, will be loaded into the root level of the movie (into the main timeline). We'll put three variables in this text file using the query string format we looked at earlier, called `myText` (to hold a paragraph of introductory text), `name` and `tel_no`. So, open Notepad and type in this query string, and save it as `myText.txt`:

    ```
    myText=lots of text here to go be loaded into a instance or
    ➥ level.&name=nik khilnani&tel_no=212 345 2671
    ```

    Now create the second text file called `email.txt`, putting just one variable, `email`, into it, that stores an email address:

    ```
    email=nik@nuthing.com
    ```

2.   It would definitely be good if our Flash movie played smoothly, and without skipping, so we should make sure everything is downloaded in the user's web browser. We'll add some script to the text files to allow us to check this. If we didn't, there's a chance that the movie would start without all the variables having loaded, which really is courting disaster.

    All we do to preload the files is add an extra variable to the end of the list of variables in every text file, and then use this variable as a flag in order to detect the presence of a complete text file. We'll call this variable `done`, and set it to `1`. The variables in a text file are automatically parsed in the order that they appear, and are immediately available for use in the Flash Player once they're loaded. Placing a variable at the end of the list, allows you to check that all the variables have been loaded correctly, since done will not equal 1 until Flash reaches the end of the file.

3. So, add &done=1 to the end of the list of variables in each text file making sure that there are no spaces (that is trailing spaces) after the code at the end of the variables list in the text file. myText now looks like this:

```
myText=lots of text here to go be loaded into a instance or
➡ level.&name=nik khilnani&tel_no=212 345 2671&done=1
```

email.txt looks like this:

```
email=nik@nuthing.com&done=1
```

4. Now we need a movie to load these text files into, so fire up Flash and create a new movie called variables.fla. We'll need two scenes in this movie clip (just choose scene from the insert menu.) Call the first scene front, which we'll use to make sure that the entire movie and all of its related information has been loaded. The second scene should be called content, and this is where we'll have the functioning movie elements. So, name the two scenes, and add a new layer called actions to both to help keep things organized. Also add a text layer, and a buttons layer in the front scene.

5. We need to load the first text file, myText.txt, into the root level of the movie (0) so that we can access the information it holds. We'll load this into the first frame of the front scene. Since we are loading the file into level 0, and not a instance, we use the loadVariablesNum method:

```
loadVariablesNum ("myText.txt", 0);
```

Put some text into the text layer, so that user's have something to look at while the movie loads.

6. To help organize our code, we'll divide the load process into sections using frame labels in the front scene. Frame 1 contains the code to load the text file. Frames 2 to 7 will be the loop or wait section and frame 8 will be done loading variables section. So, add keyframes and frame labels at frames 2 and 8, wait and done loading variables respectively

7. We'll check the value of done within the Flash movie. If the variable contains the value we gave it in the text file (1), then we know that the variables that come before it in the text file must have also been loaded. So we'll add some code into frame 7, to allow the movie some time to get all the variables loaded before we check the value of the done variable using a conditional statement.

When everything is loaded, we send the movie to the frame labeled done loading variables, in frame 8, otherwise we send the movie back to the second frame labeled wait:

```
if (_root.done == "1") {
          gotoAndStop ("done loading variables");
} else {
          gotoAndPlay ("wait");
}
```

That deals with the text file, but what about the movie itself? Flash 5's getBytesLoaded and getBytesTotal actions allow us to find out the total file size of the movie and the current number of bytes loaded by the browser. We'll pop these actions into another conditional statement that contains code to be executed only if the movie clip is completely loaded:

```
If( getBytesLoaded () == getBytesTotal ()) {
    // Code placed here executed only if all the bytes are loaded
    }
```

These two separate if conditions can be combined to incorporate both loading conditions; if our done loading variable is loaded (_root.done == "1") and if the entire movie is loaded (getBytesLoaded() == getBytesTotal()), then we can use one nice little step to finish the process of loading the text file and movie. Here's the final code that we need to have in frame 7, go ahead and add it:

```
if ((_root.done == "1") && (getBytesLoaded() == getBytesTotal()))
{
    gotoAndStop ("done loading variables");
} else {
    gotoAndPlay ("wait");
}
```

8. Place a stop action in the done loading variables frame, and add a button in the buttons layer at the same frame, so that the user can send the Flash movie to the next part of the movie when he is ready. (If your file is 400kb in size and the user is on a 56k modem, he might have gone to get a soda.) My button is just a purple rectangle with the text continue. Add some simple ActionScript to the button to make the movie start playing from the first frame of the content scene:

```
on (release) {
          gotoAndPlay ("content", 1);
}
```

Your timeline should now look something like this:

Frame 7 contains the condition to check if the text file has been loaded. If not then it makes the movie loop between frames 5 and 7.

Frame 1 with the code to load the first text file.

Frame 8 contains a stop command. I've placed a button at this frame in the buttons layer to go to the next scene.

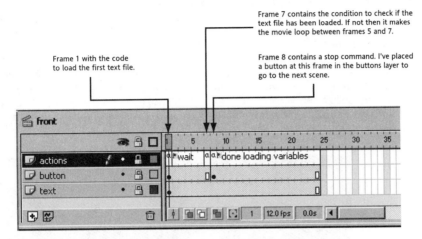

The front scene of my stage looks like this:

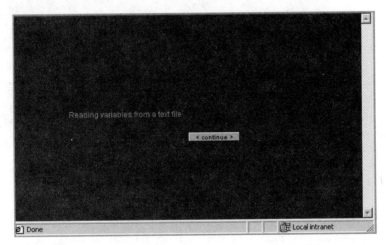

9. So, now we've made sure that the whole movie `variables.fla` and the text file `myText.txt` has been loaded, we're ready to move on to the content scene.

First we need to add three more layers to the actions layer already there. You'll need:

- text, to hold the text elements

- email MC to hold the movie clip `emailMC` into which we'll load the second text file

- background, to contain any background symbols you might want to embellish your movie with.

10. We'll use three dynamic text boxes on the text layer to take the variables loaded into the root level. Make the first a multiline dynamic text box with the variable name _root.myText, so that it will reference the myText variable. Make two more single line with the variable references _root.name and _root.tel_no, and add static labels to them.

11. We'll use another dynamic text box to demonstrate content being pulled into variables from different places within the movie. So, add another dynamic single line text box to reference a new variable root.all. We'll assign the email variable that gets loaded into the emailMC movie clip into this variable as well, and append to it the name and tel_no variables from the myText.txt file.

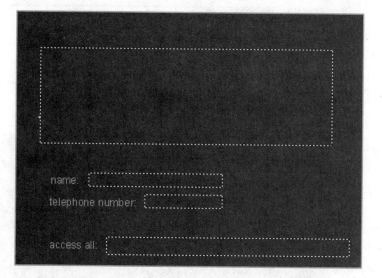

12. Now we're ready to create the emailMC movie clip on the email MC layer. First insert a new movie clip symbol and name it emailMC, F8+CTRL is the shortcut. Give it the instance name emailMC as well, and position it on the stage.

13. We'll load the email.txt text file containing the variable email into this new emailMC movie clip, so we can reference the variable email as if it were defined within the movie clip itself, (as a local variable). So add another dynamic text box inside the new movie clip that references the variable email.

14. Now that we have all the symbols ready, all we need to do is load email.txt into the emailMC movie clip. (Notice that since we are loading the content into an instance and not a level - indicated by a numeral - the code is not loadVariablesNum but loadVariables.)

Put this code into frame 1 of the actions layer of the content scene:

```
loadVariables ("email.txt", "_root.emailMC");
```

Your movie should now look something like this, with the text boxes and the emailMC movie clip. I've also added a background to mine. Make sure you adjust the size of your text boxes depending on the values the variables hold.

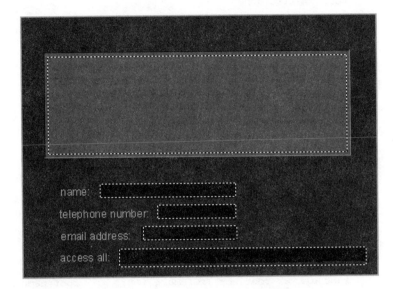

Check the structure of the content scene using the Movie Explorer. It should look like this:

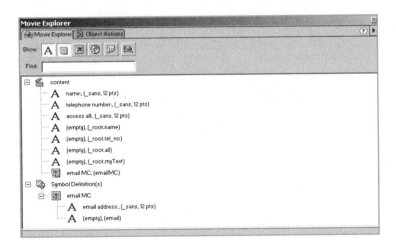

15. We need to make sure the text files have been loaded into the Flash movie, so we'll check the done variable just as we did in the front scene but with a couple of differences. We loaded email.txt into the emailMC movie clip; so we need to specify that the variable to be checked is inside the movie clip, and not the done variable in myText.txt that we loaded into the root level earlier. We'll specify the variable we want to check like this:

_root.emailMC.done

Put the preloading condition code into frame 3 of the actions layer, and loop back to the second frame until the second text file is loaded:

```
if (_root.emailMC.done <> 1) {
    gotoAndPlay (2);
}
```

We could leave it there, but we won't, we'll append the _root.name and root.tel_no variables, as well, like this:

```
_root.all = _root.emailMC.email add " " add  _root.name add " "
➡ add _root.tel_no;
```

So, putting all the code together, this is what you should put into frame 3:

```
if (_root.emailMC.done <> 1) {
            gotoAndPlay (2);
            } else {
_root.all = _root.emailMC.email + " " +  _root.name add " " +
➡ _root.tel_no;
}
```

Which translates as:

*if (the variable done in the movie clip emailMC is not equal to 1)
loop back to frame 2 start again. Else concatenate the variables
name and tel_no from the main timeline*

16. Finish off by putting a stop action in any frame you like after frame 3, and test the movie. Here's what mine looks like:

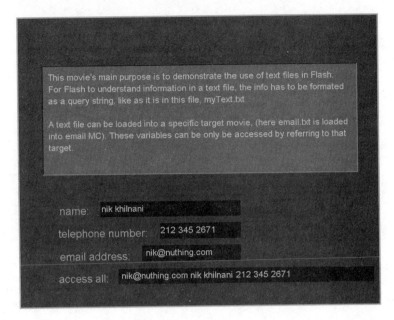

To change any of the values of the variables you've used in this movie, simply update the text files. Using `loadVariables` allows you to update Flash movies quickly and easily,

We've loaded variables into different levels and targets to help organize the information, and to prevent having to use more than one variable for one value, because the value of each variable within the text files remains constant throughout. Using the `all` variable, for instance, we were able to amalgamate other variable values into a new variable, without having to type them all out again.

We also used more than one variable with the same name, the `done` variable, which is fine so long as each variable is in a different level or different instance. If we had placed all the variables in the root level we would have needed a lot of different variable names for essentially the same things, like `done1`, `done2` and `done3`. You can work around this by setting the `done` variable to 0 before you load another text file, but it can get confusing, especially when you're creating a complex movie that uses a lot of variables. Once you've worked with variables enough, you'll soon find a method that you're comfortable with.

Combining text file variables with Flash effects

Loading variables in from a text file as we just have done is all well and good, but there'll be times when you'll want to do more exciting things with your variables once they're in the movie.

In the next example we'll create a dynamic list of buttons in real-time, using the variables in the text file to customize the buttons.

We'll use be using `duplicateMovieClip`, which you've seen being used in previous chapters. It enables us to duplicate and reuse any movie clip instance in a situation where we need multiple copies of a movie clip with similar properties. This allows us to keep the file size of a Flash movie small – which is extremely important today, because an awful lot of users are still using 56k modems. This example creates and names each new movie clip, assuming i is a variable within a loop that increments as the loop creates buttons:

```
button.duplicateMovieClip ("button"+ i, 1);
```

> *The number denoting depth in fact denotes the order in which the duplicated instances are placed in relation to one another; an instance with higher depth is above one with lower depth, rather like the layers concept. Keep in mind, though, that depth has nothing to do with levels, and that a movie duplicated to depth 2 will not replace the movies in, or put the movies into, level 2.*

We'll be duplicating instances of movie clips that access variables from a particular level in the next example – we'll create a dynamic list of buttons that access variables from the root level, and then manipulate them locally in order to create a customized dynamic menu system.

We'll also use the setProperty action and the getProperty functions, which you've been using extensively in earlier chapters.

> *All you need to remember is that while the properties you access with getProperty begin with an underscore, have no spaces, and are lowercase, those you use with setProperty start with capital letters and can have spaces. For example, the vertical position parameter is called Y position in setProperty, but _y in getProperty.*

Creating a button list from a text file dynamically

Let's begin. We'll create a dynamic list of buttons with a mouse over effect. We'll make the button increase in size and intensity when the user moves the mouse over it, creating a kind of magnifying effect. It'll look something like this:

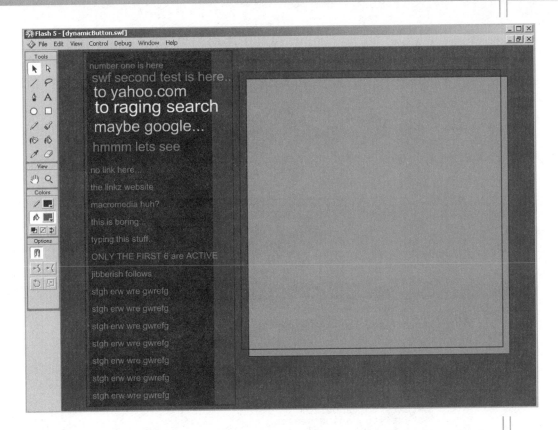

The buttons can be used to open up a new URL, or load a Flash movie, and you can customize the display text, the button links, the number of buttons, and the URLs they point to just by modifying the text file. Try out the version on the CD called `dynamicButton.fla` if you like.

1.   So, create a text file containing a variable `total` that contains all the buttons and their text (`btext1`, `btext2` and so on), button links (`link1`, `link2` and so on) and flag variables (`swf1`, `swf2` and so on) for each button.

> *The flag variables are Boolean variables, that contain either a* `true` *or false value, and when no value is defined, default to false.*

We'll use the `done=1` variable as we did before, to ensure that the text file has loaded, using the preloading code that was discussed earlier.

So, put together a text file with some variables and call it `dynamicButton.txt`:

```
total=20&btext1=number one is here
                    &btext2=swf second test is here..
                    &btext3=to yahoo.com
                    &btext4=to raging search
                    &btext5=maybe google...
                    &btext6=another one
                    &btext7=no link here...
                    &btext8=the linkz website
                    &btext9=and another
                    &btext10=and another
                    &btext11=and another
                    &btext12=yet more
                    &btext13=jibberish follows

        ...

&link1=test_1.swf&link2=test_2.swf&link3=http://www.yahoo.com&link
➥  =http://www.raging.com&link5=http://www.google.com&link6=blank
➥  &swf1=true&swf2=true&swf3=false&done=1
```

Mine looks something like this:

2.   To try to make things a consistent, we'll follow the same format of the first example. We'll call the first scene front, and use it to preload the Flash movie and the related

text files. Then we'll load the content into the second scene content. Hopefully, at this stage you will be able to create the first (front) scene by yourself. Remember to load the `dynamicButton.txt` file into the front scene, and make sure the movie has been downloaded. When you're ready, let's start making the content scene.

3. This scene will contain one movie clip, main. It's in this movie clip that we'll place the code that does the duplication to create our list of buttons dynamically. Put the main movie clip in a dedicated layer, I called mine content, and put any background graphics you might want to add into another layer, mine's bg. Since the content scene only holds one movie clip, main movie clip, place a `stop` action in frame 1 of the actions layer.

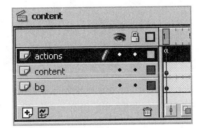

The essence of this movie is the list of buttons that will be created dynamically, by duplicating and reusing one button according to the information in the `dynamicButton.txt` file.

The list of buttons needs to be dynamic, so we need to be able to duplicate the button that we create. As Flash doesn't allow you to create multiple instances of buttons, we'll enclose the button inside a movie clip, dynamicButtonMC and duplicate this movie clip to create the list. We'll do all of this inside the main movie clip. So let's do that now:

4. In the main movie clip, create another movie clip called dynamicButtonMC. Now place a dynamic text box with the variable name `text` in the dynamicButtonMC movie clip, making sure that you include all font outlines (in the Text Options panel) so that the entire font is embedded, and write text on it for now.

5. Now place an instance of the dynamicButtonMC movie clip towards the top left corner of the stage in the main movie clip, giving it the instance name of `DynamicButtonMC`. Why put it there? Well, because we want our menu to have a format that is familiar to our users, we'll make the list look like a standard vertical menu bar.

6. Place the main movie clip towards the top left hand corner of the stage, and give it the instance name `main`. The main movie clip will perform the duplication. We'll duplicate the `dynamicButtonMC` instance, and arranging the duplicate instances vertically. Having the original in the top left corner just makes life a little easier for us to build our menu.

Check the Movie Explorer panel, and you should see something like this:

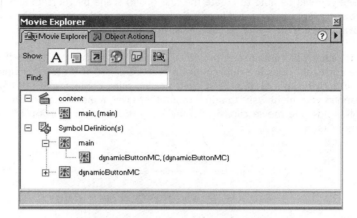

So now we're ready to actually create the dynamic buttons, so we need to write some code for the main movie clip. Let's try to figure out how we're going to accomplish this before we begin coding.

The first thing we need to do is create a loop that will duplicate dynamicButtonMC, but how many copies of the dynamicbuttonMC movie clip do we need to make? Well, if you remember, we actually used the text file to specify the total number of buttons that we wanted to have created, (by assigning the total variable in the text file the value of 20), so the next step is to actually go about creating the copies of the dynamicbuttonMC, each inside its own movie clip.

We'll use a loop to create the dynamicButtonMC, using the index variable i to keep count of the number of buttons created and assigning each one to the root _root.i. We'll also use this index number to give each new dynamicButtonMC a name, so that we can refer to it easily later on, and we'll also use it to assign a new depth to each new button, since the most recent button would otherwise replace the previous one. The loop without the duplication code, then, will look like this:

```
_root.i = 1;
while (_root.i<=_root.total) {
// duplication code goes here
dynamicButtonMC.duplicateMovieClip "dynamicButtonMC" + _root.i,
_root.i);
// more code comes here
// increment the counter
    _root.i = _root.i+1;
}
```

We don't want the buttons to be created one on top of the other, so we'll adjust the vertical (y-axis) position of each button as we go, using the vertical position of the original dynamicButtonMC instance movie clip as a reference point. (If we didn't adjust each button according to the previous button, we'd need to find the exact x and y-axis coordinates each and every time we wanted to move the button menu position. So doing this also makes any future modifications to button positioning far easier.) We'll use some script that looks like this:

```
setProperty ("dynamicButtonMC" + _root.i, _y, getProperty
➡ ("dynamicButtonMC", _y)+Number((getProperty ("dynamicButtonMC",
➡ height)*root.i)));
```

We'll add another step that gives the button movie clips a cool mouse over effect, by making the buttons brighter when our mouse is over the button. To do this we will fade the button out in its natural state, and brighten the button back to 100% alpha when the mouse is over the button. So for the natural state, give the new movie clips an alpha of 50%, or fade it by 50%.

```
setProperty ("dynamicButtonMC",_root.i, _alpha, 50);
```

Now we need to uniquely identify each button by its index number. Using this information as a reference we can find the index numbers of buttons directly above and below the current button. Storing the index number of a button within the button enables us to organize functionality that will improve the **scalability** of our project. By scalable, I mean that we can alter the total number of buttons without having to make adjustments to the existing code in the movie. We do this by setting a variable contained in the duplicated dynamicButtonMC movie clip to the counter or index value:

```
set ("dynamicButtonMC" + _root.i + ".n", _root.i);
```

So, let's put all this code together, to get something that looks like this:

```
_root.i = 1;
    while (_root.i<=_root.total) {
    dynamicButtonMC.duplicateMovieClip ("dynamicButtonMC" +
    ➡ _root.i, _root.i);
    setProperty ("dynamicButtonMC" + _root.i, _y, getProperty
    ➡ ("dynamicButtonMC",_y)+Number((getProperty
    ➡ ("dynamicButtonMC", height)*root.i)));
    setProperty ("dynamicButtonMC" + _root.i, _alpha, 50);
    set ("dynamicButtonMC" + _root.i + ".n", _root.i);
    ➡ _root.i = _root.i+1;
}
```

Finally we'll make the default clip invisible, because it's just a dummy being used to create the new clips. Changing its visibility property by using the setProperty action easily does this:

```
setProperty ("dynamicButtonMC", _visible, false);
```

7. So, put all this code together, and add it to frame 1 of the `main` movie clip. Then add a `stop` action in a keyframe at frame 2 so that we don't loop the `main` movie clip.

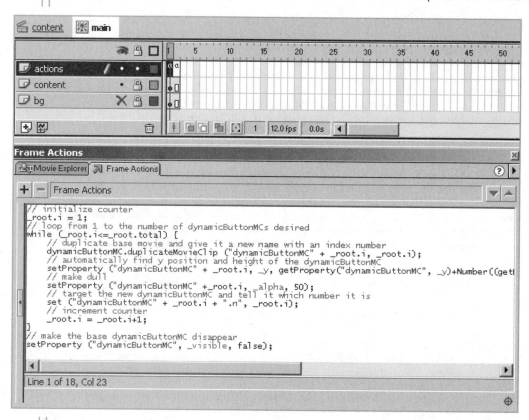

```
// initialize counter
_root.i = 1;
// loop from 1 to the number of dynamicButtonMCs desired
while (_root.i<=_root.total) {
    // duplicate base movie and give it a new name with an index number
    dynamicButtonMC.duplicateMovieClip ("dynamicButtonMC" + _root.i, _root.i);
    // automatically find y position and height of the dynamicButtonMC
    setProperty ("dynamicButtonMC" + _root.i, _y, getProperty("dynamicButtonMC", _y)+Number((getl
    // make dull
    setProperty ("dynamicButtonMC" +_root.i, _alpha, 50);
    // target the new dynamicButtonMC and tell it which number it is
    set ("dynamicButtonMC" + _root.i + ".n", _root.i);
    // increment counter
    _root.i = _root.i+1;
}
// make the base dynamicButtonMC disappear
setProperty ("dynamicButtonMC", _visible, false);
```

Line 1 of 18, Col 23

8. Now go back to the `dynamicButtonMC` and have it access the information from the text file.

Since we assigned the index `i` to the variable `n` we can use this value to obtain the text (`btextX`), link (`linkX`) and flag (`swfX`) variables from the text file for the current duplicated copy of `dynamicButtonMC`. We just concatenate the index number to each variable's name, and use the `eval` function to obtain the data stored. In this manner we can modify the properties of the button by changing only the code in this movie clip, and don't need to touch any other code. So, here's the code you need in the first frame in the actions layer of the `dynamicButtonMC`:

```
text = eval("_root.btext" + n);
link = eval("_rooot.link" + n);
swf = eval("_root.swf" + n);
```

9. Now we can finally create the real button. Create a new layer in the dynamicButtonMC movie clip to hold the button, and create an empty button (a rectangle shape in the hit keyframe only) over the dynamic text box we created earlier. Making the button empty will allow us to see the text in the lower layer. (In Flash, empty buttons have a translucent blue color.)

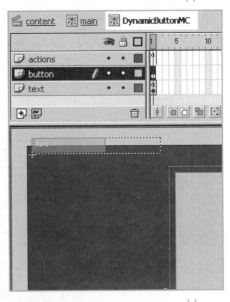

10. We need to check whether the swf variable for a button is true or not when it is clicked, so that we can open a URL in a new window or load a Flash movie if appropriate. All we need to do that is a simple conditional statement; something like this code behind the button should do the trick:

```
on (release) {
    // if swf flag is true load movie else open the url
    if (swf == "true") {
        loadMovie (link, 2);
    } else {
        getURL (link, "_blank");
    }
}
```

Now we need to create the cool mouse over effect. The ActionScript for this is divided into two parts, one for when the mouse is over the button, and another for when the mouse rolls off the button. Our code will manipulate the containing movie clip and the visible properties of the other movie clips to create a cool mouse over. We set this effect up earlier when we set the alpha of the duplicate movie clips.

We want this rollover code to increase the alpha setting of the current movie to 100 so that it looks like a mouse over, and increase its own size and that of the other movie clips, so that the mouse over effect is made more pronounced.

To create a steady transition between the sizes of the current movie clip and the others, we'll increase the size of the current movie clip (i.e. the movie clip with index number n) by 200%, that is ones immediately above and below ($n+1$ and $n-1$) by 180%, and the clips one above and below those clips ($n+2$ and $n-2$) by 150%.

We'll also increase the alpha setting of the current movie clip to 100%. To make sure that the other movie clips are duller in comparison, and that we get a nice transition between the selected clip and its neighbors, we set the alpha values of the clips immediately above and below the current clip to 85%. We don't need to worry about altering the alpha values for any of the other clips, since the transition in alpha value from 85% to 50% between adjacent clips is barely noticable.

It works like this:

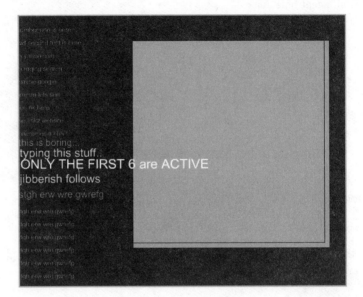

11. We can do this using the `setProperty` action. We'll use the `_parent.button` notation to refer to the button movie clips created in the parent movie clip `main`, which contains the current movie clip instance `dynamicButtonMC`.

So add this code to the new button symbol in the `dynamicButtonMC`, before the `on (release)` code we just added:

```
on (rollOver) {
    setProperty ("", _alpha, 100);
    setProperty ("", _xscale, 200);
    setProperty ("", _yscale, 200);
    setProperty ("_parent.dynamicButtonMC " + (n - 1), _alpha, 85);
    setProperty ("_parent.dynamicButtonMC " + (n - 1), _xscale, 180);
    setProperty ("_parent.dynamicButtonMC " + (n - 1), _yscale, 180);
    setProperty ("_parent.dynamicButtonMC " + (n + 1), _alpha, 85);
    setProperty ("_parent.dynamicButtonMC " + (n + 1), _xscale, 180);
    setProperty ("_parent.dynamicButtonMC " + (n + 1), _yscale, 180);
    setProperty ("_parent.dynamicButtonMC " + (n - 2), _xscale, 150);
    setProperty ("_parent.dynamicButtonMC " + (n - 2), _yscale, 150);
    setProperty ("_parent.dynamicButtonMC " + (n + 2), _xscale, 150);
    setProperty ("_parent.dynamicButtonMC " + (n + 2), _yscale, 150);
}
```

12. All the rollout code does is reset the properties of the current movie clip and the other movie clips, so add this code after the on(rollover) and before the on(release) events:

```
on (releaseOutside, rollOut) {
    setProperty ("", _alpha, 50);
    setProperty ("", _xscale, 100);
    setProperty ("", _yscale, 100);
    setProperty ("_parent.dynamicButtonMC " + (n - 1), _alpha, 50);
    setProperty ("_parent.dynamicButtonMC " + (n - 1), _xscale, 100);
    setProperty ("_parent.dynamicButtonMC " + (n - 1), _yscale, 100);
    setProperty ("_parent.dynamicButtonMC " + (n + 1), _alpha, 50);
    setProperty ("_parent.dynamicButtonMC " + (n + 1), _xscale, 100);
    setProperty ("_parent.dynamicButtonMC " + (n + 1), _yscale, 100);
    setProperty ("_parent.dynamicButtonMC " + (n - 2), _xscale, 100);
    setProperty ("_parent.dynamicButtonMC " + (n - 2), _yscale, 100);
    setProperty ("_parent.dynamicButtonMC " + (n + 2), _xscale, 100);
    setProperty ("_parent.dynamicButtonMC " + (n + 2), _yscale, 100);
}
```

Now check your Movie Explorer one last time; you should have this:

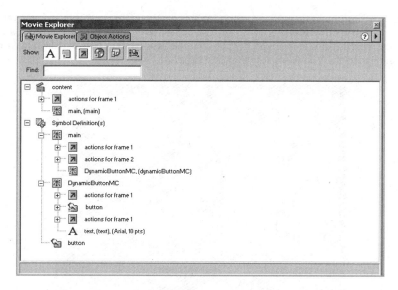

That's it – test your movie. You'll see how the setProperty action and the getProperty function to create special effects over the buttons that are being created dynamically from the text file using the duplicateMovieClip method.

That's one way to make the text that you're loading in from the text file a bit more dynamic and interactive. It's a nice effect that you can build on, and work more smoothly with some more scripting – but, of course, you'd only really use this when you're loading a text list into the movie.

There'll be times when you want to load quite a bit of text into your movie from outside, and one of the best ways to treat a bigger quantity of text in a movie is to scroll though it. We'll build an example that does this next.

There are a great many ways to do this, but before you begin, make sure you really do need to: are you making your text field a variable because you'll want to change it later on? If not, don't bother making a variable at all, just use a standard text block, you can format that block all you want. (If you need the content of the text field to be a variable, though, don't enter the contents into the value section of the Actions panel. Simply declare a variable, assign the content to it and refer to it using a dynamic text box.)

So, let's have Flash read the variable information from a text file. Remember that if the text box is going to be placed in a movie clip that will be masked, then the font has to be embedded in order for the text to be visible.

Scrolling through loaded text

Most web sites display text of some sort. To make it really functional, users usually need to be able to control text boxes using buttons and scrollbars. The next example that we'll build (dynamicTextScrolling.fla) will demonstrate just how to do this.

The only extra Flash methods we'll be using for this example are, as you might have anticipated, those designed to modify the properties of text boxes, both of which you've done a little work with already; scroll and maxscroll. Our example will contain two buttons and a draggable scrollbar, similar to the Window's scrollbar interface.

Sure, Flash enables us to create text boxes. But, most of the time the size of the text box is limited, and when we're dealing with text it's often the case that we actually want more than one line of text to be displayed. In this case we want to display more text than actually fits in the text box. Not to worry, Flash can help us out here, by allowing us to use a property called .scroll, which is a property given to text boxes by which we can control the text displayed in the top line of a text box. For example, if our text uses twenty lines and our text box is limited to, say, just six lines, using the .scroll property we can choose to have the text box display text beginning from any line we choose by setting the text box's .scroll property.

So if you're ready, then let's begin.

Scrolling through a large text file variable

1. Create a front scene, as you did for the last examples (or simply use that one from those examples) and load in a text file containing some dummy text assigned to a variable called text. The second scene is where we'll put the elements responsible for the function of the movie.

2. So, in the content scene, create a new movie clip symbol, called content, living on its own dedicated layer. This is where we'll create the scrollbar and the text box.

3. Now we need to create the scroll bar on its own layer, scroll bar, inside the content movie clip.

   First you need to make the line for the scroll bar itself. Use a graphic or a simple vector line, it's up to you.

   Then you need a scroller movie clip, which the user will control by pressing a button. Use any graphic you like, but make sure it's in the absolute center of the scroller movie clip. Drag an instance onto the stage and give it the instance name scroller.

   You also need an empty button that defines where the user can drag scroller, so create an empty rectangular button, call it Detect Mouse Down, and position it over the scroller and the scroll bar. You should have something that looks a bit like this:

4. Now we need the dynamic text box to load the text into. Put this on another layer, text, (still inside the content symbol). Make the dynamic text box multiline, with Word Wrap enabled. Assign the text box to the value of the text variable that we've already loaded (in the first preloading scene) into the root level, _root.text.

5. Put your content movie clip on the scroll bar layer in frame 1. Your stage should look something like this (I also placed a background graphic in a separate layer in the content scene):

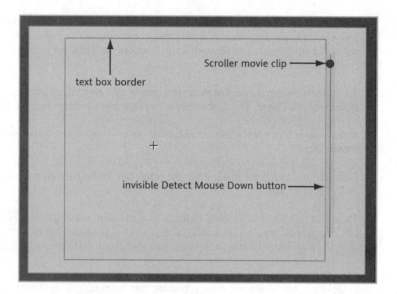

Then add a stop action to the first frame of the content scene; this scene only needs one frame with a stop action in it to prevent looping, because all of the symbols responsible for the scrolling will be placed in the content movie clip.

6. Now we need to add the actions to the Detect Mouse Down button that will allow users to drag the scroller instance. We'll use the startDrag action together with the stopDrag action.

By specifying bounding/constraint rectangle values, we can restrict the area in which the scroller can be dragged – in this case, to the vertical line inside the area we set using Detect Mouse Down button. In order to do this, we need to know the exact position of the scroller, and we can use the Info panel to find this out:

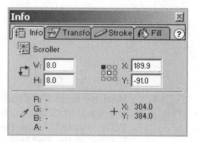

Whenever the mouse is released, scroller should stop moving, otherwise it'll move every time the mouse does, and that's really not what we want at all. So, let's add the code to the Detect Mouse Down button to help us get what we *do* want:

```
on (press) {
    startDrag ("scroller", false, 194, -91, 194, 89);
}
on (release, releaseOutside) {
    stopDrag ();
}
```

Let's just check through what we've done so far: we have on the stage a *scroller*, and a Detect Mouse Down button that drags scroller using the ActionScript code in the button's events. We've also created a text box with Multiline and Word wrap properties enabled.

Good. Now we need the movie to detect when the scroller is moved and adjust the position of the text accordingly. To do this, the content movie clip, which contains the scroll bar symbols, should loop so that our movie clip is continuously checking to see if scroller has been moved.

We'll do this by modifying the top line displayed in the text box, using the scroll property of the text variable. We'll need to calculate this move relative to the total number of lines in the text box and the total height available to drag the scroller.

We can find the total number of lines in the text box is by using the maxscroll property of the text box. Then we employ simple ratios and proportions to convert the position of the scrollbar to the number of the line to be displayed at the top of the text box.

7. So, first make the content movie clip two frames long, (Flash requires at least two frames to make a movie loop), and then give the instance on the main stage the name content. Next we'll write the script we need inside the onClipEvent of the content movie clip.

We'll need to use an integer value, (no decimals), because we can't have any half lines in the text box. We'll have to add or subtract numbers from the getProperty function according to scroller's y-position (which we found out from the clip's Info panel, here it's –91).

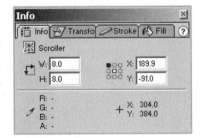

So, if the y-position is –91, we'll just add 91 to it to bring the value up to 0, (just to make calculations easier).

Then we'll assign the total vertical distance we allow the scroller instance to be dragged to a variable, ht. We'll use the constrain values that we've already set in the startDrag code in the Detect Mouse Down **button**, and use the int method for the _root.text.scroll assignment statement, to prevent any real numbers being assigned.

Altogether then, this is the script that should go onto the onClipEvent of the content instance of the content movie clip on the main stage – you might find that it takes a couple of passes to check for errors before you finally get it working:

```
onClipEvent (enterFrame) {
    ht = 180;
    pos = Number(getProperty("scroller", _y))+91;
    _root.text.scroll = int(_root.text.maxscroll*pos/ht);
}
```

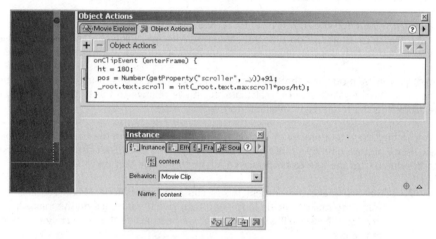

8.   We're nearly finished; but the scrollbar just doesn't look right without arrow buttons at either end of the scrollbar for the users to click to scroll the text. Let's make those now: create a button with an arrow or similar graphic on it, call it scroll button, copy it, and put one at either end of the scrollbar:

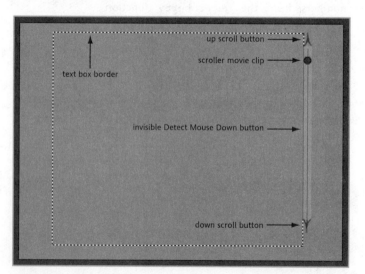

Now we need to add the code to the buttons that will change the scroll property of the text box when pressed. Remember that the movie positions the text according to the position of the `scroller`? The arrow buttons will need to adjust the position of the `scroller` whenever they are pressed. Again, we need to use ratio and proportion, only this time we go in the opposite direction. This code should be executed after the scroll property of the text field has been adjusted, since only then can we adjust the position of the `scroller` in relation to the scroll property of the text box.

```
_root.text.scroll = _root.text.scroll-8;
setProperty ("scroller", _y,
int(_root.text.scroll*ht/(_root.text.maxscroll))-91);
```

9. So let's add the code for the up and down scroll buttons. The only difference between them is whether they go forward a line of text or backward. This is the code I used for the up scroll button:

```
on (press, keyPress "<PageUp>") {
        _root.text.scroll = _root.text.scroll-8;
        setProperty ("scroller", _y,
    ➥ int(_root.text.scroll*ht/(_root.text.maxscroll))-91);
}
```

This code for the downward pointing button:

```
on (press, keyPress "<PageDown>") {
        _root.text.scroll = Number(_root.text.scroll)+8;
        setProperty ("scroller", _y,
    ➥ int(_root.text.scroll*ht/(_root.text.maxscroll))-91);
}
```

Finally, check the structure of your Flash file:

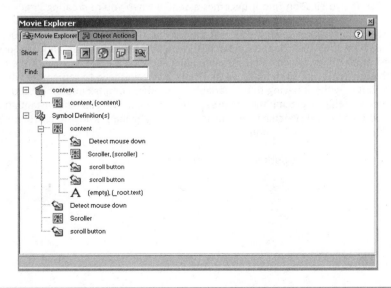

And test your movie. You can find my version on the CD if you have any problems and want to refer back to it.

There we have it. You can change the graphics for the scrollbar and text in the text file to whatever you please. Don't panic if you don't get this working the first time you try it; keep going, check back over the text, and check it against the FLA I've provided. Once you have it in full working order, you'll find the technique is one you can use time and time again in Flash. Scrollable text and graphics are absolutely necessary on a dynamic web site, because you're always limited by available screen real estate.

Although this technique leads really nicely into scrolling through a graphic or a movie clip that's too big for the screen, you've actually covered that technique in Chapter 6, so I won't go through it again here. I have included a working example on the CD though, for you to work with; it'll also make the final example, where we'll put everything together, a bit more interesting!

Putting the pieces together: modular development

One thing you might have noticed as you've been building the examples is that we've put all the important components in each example inside a single movie clip. We did this to make each little movie clip modular, making it easy to reuse the clip in other Flash movies without much modification; it's good practice that'll save you time and effort in the long run.

We'll put some of these components together in the final example (`allTogether.fla`). All we need to do is copy the single movie clips of the other Flash examples and paste them into a single, dedicated layer. Since these clips were developed to be modular, copy and pasting is pretty simple. If we had created the effects covered in the earlier examples in any other way, reusing them here would require more modification.

Modular programming not only makes for better reusability, but it also helps keep the content of your Flash projects organized. While this may not seem fundamental in the small examples we've covered so far, you'll soon find it becomes essential when you're creating larger Flash projects.

Many Flash movies have several different scenes that the user can browse through. The method we've used through the chapter so far has involved creating scenes and background graphics, amongst other things, which can become tedious and increase the file size of the movie. Another thing to consider is that sometimes we may want a certain scene to remember where it was when the user left it, without having to use variables and other complex implementation in order to do so. We can do this by placing the scene's content into a movie clip, and instantiating it in its own layer, and then simply switching the movie clip off by making it invisible, when it's not needed, through the `setProperty` action.

So, how will we go about putting it all together?

Putting everything together

1. Create a new movie in Flash, and place each of the content holding movie clips from the previous two examples into their own individual layers, renaming them to something like `main1`, `main2`, and `main3`. Obviously, we need to ensure that none of our variable names are synonyms, so do a check to see if any variable names clash. If so, replace that variable name with a new one. You can also use the `content` clip from scrolling graphic example on the CD as well, if you like.

2. The first scene should be, as usual, the preloading scene, which makes sure that the movie and the related text files are loaded. We don't want all the main movie clips to be visible at the same time, so we need to decide which one is visible first. Let's use `main1`. We need some code that will make the movie clip instances `main2` and `main3` invisible. We can do this using two simple `setProperty` statements, as shown in the next code fragment:

    ```
    setProperty ("_root.main2", _visible, false);
    setProperty ("_root.main3", _visible, false);
    ```

    As movie clips are visible by default, `main1` will be visible.

3. Now all you need to do is create a menu that allows your site visitors to switch between those main movie clips. Create three buttons in another layer, and let each button make one of the main movie clips visible, and the other clips invisible. And that's it.

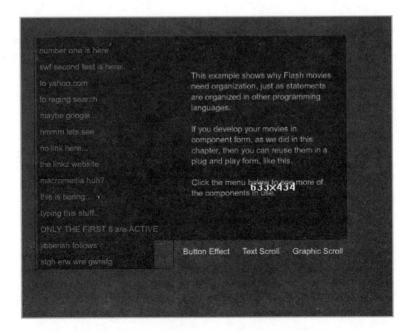

While this is fine for a small movie, in a larger movie writing the necessary code to handle all the visibility switching could prove to be very time consuming and cause a lot of confusion, not to mention increasing the file size and repeating code unnecessarily. But there is a way around this. How? By using **functions**... of course!

4.   All we need to do is create a movie clip called subroutine in its own layer, and write a function that will make the right movie clip visible, and the others invisible. We'll use a function called change, and use a numbering system to send instructions to the function: the number 2, for example, will make main2 visible and main1 and main3 invisible.

The simplest method is to create a loop with a variable, say i, which would cycle through the number 1 through 3. We would compare the value of i to the number sent to the function. If i is equal to the number sent, we make that movie (that is, maini) visible, otherwise we make it invisible. I've described one way of doing this, you might find a different method. Here is the code I wrote:

```
function change (which) {
    var i = 1;
    while (i<=3) {
        if (i == which) {
            setProperty ("_root.main" && i, _visible, true);
        } else {
            setProperty ("_root.main" && i, _visible, false);
        }
        i = i+1;
    }
}
```

In our example we only have one function. In bigger projects, though, you will probably have more, so you should remember to give your functions descriptive and easily identifiable names.

5.   Now put the code in each of the buttons that calls the function and sends it an instruction, making one movie clip visible. This code would make the movie clip main2 visible:

```
on (release) {
    _root.myFunction.change(2);
}
```

It's that simple.

o, what have we covered?

We've covered a lot in this chapter; importing text file variables into Flash, and working with them in a number of ways once they are there. We built up these examples in the organized, modular approach that is really necessary if you are to create dynamic Flash content for interactive and functional web sites that can be easily maintained.

Although we did a lot of work, this chapter alone could only scratch the surface of what you can do; if you experiment with lots more examples, and make your own up, you'll really get to grips with what can be done using Flash and text files together. I hope that playing with this code will help you really understand Flash programming, and help you create more effective Flash movies. Remember, there's more to Flash than visual effects!

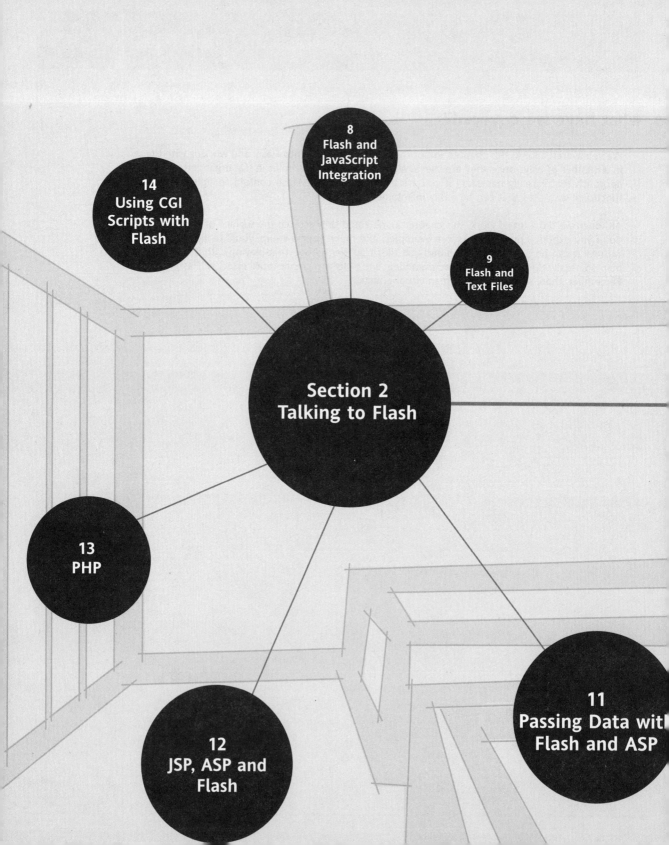

8
Flash and
JavaScript
Integration

14
Using CGI
Scripts with
Flash

9
Flash and
Text Files

Section 2
Talking to Flash

13
PHP

11
Passing Data with
Flash and ASP

12
JSP, ASP and
Flash

Chapter 10
Talking to
the Server

In previous chapters, you've investigated the ins and outs of ActionScript very thoroughly. You've created some impressive Flash interactivity, using ActionScript and JavaScript, learned how to manipulate variables within your Flash movies using ActionScript, and how to update your Flash movies from information that's being held in a text file.

In the rest of the book, you'll learn how to send variables to the server for processing, how to generate information for the browser specifically intended for the user who asked for it, how to use databases for your web sites, how to generate graphics dynamically...there's a lot to cover! You'll find a myriad of examples that use server-side processing to create truly dynamic Flash applications, opening up a host of new ideas that you can integrate into Flash-based sites. This is where it all gets really exciting!

Before we begin down this path, though, there are a few things that we need to take care of by way of preparation, and that's what this chapter is about:

- The server and the client

- Why Flash developers use server-side scripts

- Installing a server on your desktop computer

- Sending and receiving variables using Flash and server-side scripts (`getURL`, `loadVariables`, `GET`, and `POST`)

- Ensuring that Flash can use the variables you're sending to your movies

We'll create a couple of examples, to make things more interesting, but essentially this chapter is intended to prepare the ground for all those that follow.

The server and the client

There are two places that you can put the code that responds to a user: on the *client*, where it's executed by the user's web browser, or on the *server*.

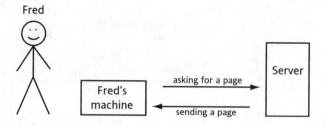

You've already been creating Flash applications that respond to the user – ActionScripting and JavaScript are both very good examples of client-side scripting, allowing you to respond to users in a rich interactive way. You've also been using text files to load in information to your Flash application, which means that you can change the textual content of your Flash movie without actually having to go into Flash again to do so.

Publishing all of the work you've done so far on the web does, of course, require that you use a server: your server serves up the scripts.

That's just the beginning of what your server can do for you though. This chapter is where we start really using the server: truly powerful web applications use the server as a processing tool. Server-side technologies take your web applications to a, quite literally, *deeper* level. It makes your applications dynamic.

Harnessing the power of the server

'What's so good about server-side processing?' you might be wondering; or even 'what exactly to do you mean by dynamic?' Well, server-side processing means you can do pretty much anything and everything on the web, all the way from creating an online guestbook that your users can browse and submit their comments to, to fully functional and secure e-commerce applications. With a little server-side help, you can let your site visitors:

- Contribute to your site online: chat boards, guestbooks, submit online ratings etc.

- Access up to the minute (or even second) data and information

- Send email from your site

- Send you feedback

- Buy goods or services

- And much more

You, as the web developer, on the other hand can:

- Collect, organize and analyze the information that the user submits

- Generate up to the second information and graphics

- Automatically generate email

- Receive site feedback

- Moderate online discussions

- Implement personalization

- And so on and so on...

Even then, we're only scratching the surface of the power that using server-side code can bring you. By using and understanding server-side code effectively, you really can unleash the power of fully-fledged web applications. And the good news is, it isn't even that hard. Really! As you'll see.

Processing on the server versus processing on the client

The good thing about client-side scripting, which you've already been using in the form of JavaScript and ActionScript, is that it adds a lot of client-side functionality, making some great visual and audio effects possible – just by using the visiting web browser's own resources.

When you're using a server simply to serve up pages, all it does is send out your HTML, your SWF, and perhaps the information in your text file. Nothing is executed until it reaches the browser – the server doesn't actually do anything to the content it's sending.

As you may already have found when you're using JavaScript, you can run into trouble because you have to rely on the client's machine having JavaScript capabilities.

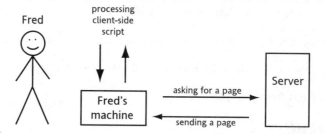

While you can work around that possibility, you simply can't do anything about the fact that client-side script can't access files on the server, or directories, or databases. You can't go loading databases up to the client's machine, (and even if you could, it would mean certain death to the network, not to mention the confidentiality of your database records).

Neither can you generate information dynamically, in response to the user's decisions. In short, extensive though the work has been that you've done so far, it isn't dynamic in the way that truly powerful web applications are. It doesn't *use* the server.

To use the server, you need some server-side code. Then you can communicate with data sources on the server, send email, track site visitors' behavior, incorporate personalization, develop online commerce, and much, much more.

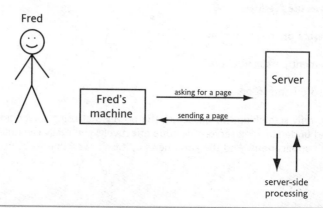

Because server-side programming uses your server's resources to parse the information you're generating dynamically, it can slow down your web site (especially during periods of high traffic). This is simply a price that has to be paid for the functionality server-side processing gives you. And, of course, there are plenty of things you can do to optimize performance, both on the server itself, and within your code.

Of course, you don't have to worry about the client browser nearly as much either – as long as your server can run the processes that you want doing, and can serve up the appropriate web pages, then you're fine.

Why do Flash programmers want to use server-side programming?

Flash programmers want to use server-side programming because they want dynamic web sites with real power; they want to implement the kind of functionality that we've just looked at. In terms of your web site, this means real-time information, and generating the visual effects that users want when they want them – and *that* means accessing, adding to, taking from, or manipulating a data source. And of course, one of the great things about using Flash is that you can update your movies without even having to refresh the page.

If you still need convincing, check out some of these sites that have been built using server-side code:

www.rocketsnail.com/games/penguins	A real-time online chat system with Flash animation.
www.shockfusion.com	A message board built with PHP
www.tedbaker.co.uk	An online Flash store
www.football.com/games/index.shtml (click Trivia Playoff)	A trivia game that tracks the results of the answers in a database, and calculates the top scores
www.flashkit.com/guestbook/index.shtml	A guest book that users can sign with a personalized message. (The great thing about this example is that it's free for anybody to download, and uses a CGI script to help you set it up and learn how to get it working. More about downloading and using CGI in the CGI chapter.)

But of course, what you need first is a server.

Installing a web server

One of the first things you need to do is install a web server. If you're working through this book on a desktop PC running a version of the Microsoft Windows operating system, this is very straightforward, and we'll run through what you need to do here. If you're using Windows 9x, you can use Personal Web Server (PWS), while if you have a Windows 2000 machine, you can use Internet Information Server (IIS).

Installing and testing your server

Personal Web Server allows you to run a web server that can handle a small intranet or web site. It also allows you to test applications on your PC without being connected to an external network server or the Internet, and it's a good test bed for the examples we'll be looking at here. IIS is simply a more powerful server. (There are, of course, lots of other differences between the two – check out www.Microsoft.com to get more information.)

1. So, before you do anything else, close down any applications still running. Then insert your Windows CD, locate PWS or IIS and start the installation.

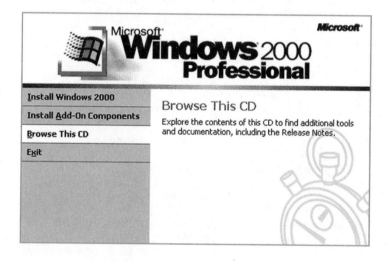

Or, you can go to the Control Panel, and select Add/Remove Programs, and browse through the add-ons available:

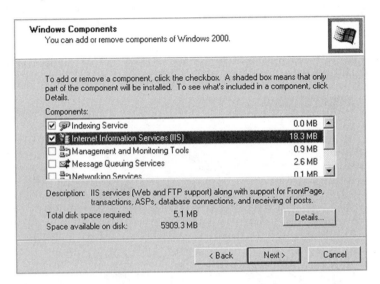

2. If you're installing PWS on Windows, select the **Typical** installation:

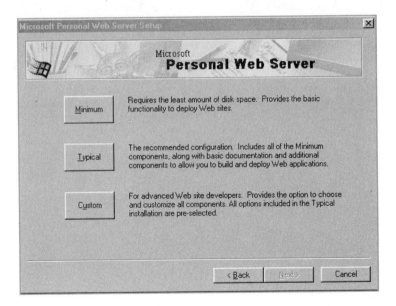

3.   You'll get a dialogue showing you where the installation will be made – accept the default.

4.   When the installation is completed, reboot your computer and you're all set to go. You should find that an icon has been dropped into the tray at the bottom right hand of your screen [icon].

Double click on it to get the Personal Web Manager up, and you should have a screen that looks like this:

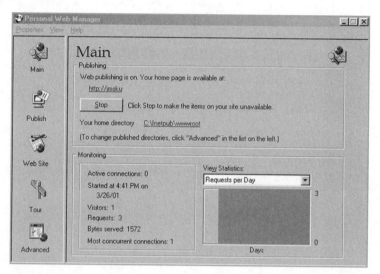

First make sure the server is running. Then notice the HTTP address of your web page (mine here is HTTP://jmsku) and your home directory – it's probably set up to C:\Inetpub\wwwroot like mine. This is where you need to put the web pages that you want to publish.

5.   Finally, check your C:\ directory, and you should find some new files have been put there during installation. They'll look like this:

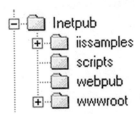

The wwwroot folder is where you'll put the pages that you want to test through the browser. Let's test it now.

6.   We'll create a simple HTML test page to check that everything is working as it should (although you can just as easily copy a Flash movie that you already have published into the directory; if you do, make sure you copy the SWF and the HTML page across). This is the HTML test page, just type it into notepad or another text editor, and save it as firstpage.html inside wwwroot:

```
<HTML>
<BODY>
        hello World Wide Web
</BODY>
</HTML>
```

7.   Now for the moment of truth: fire up your browser, and type in the URL for your server. There are three ways you can access the server: though your computer's network name, by using http://localhost, or http://127.0.0.1.

Try them out:

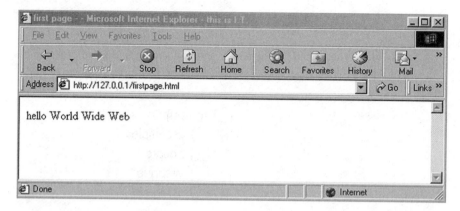

8. When you're creating a number of applications, you'll be using folders within the wwwroot directory to separate them. You can either access these through the URL (`http://jmsku/test/MyNewPage.html`, for example) or by changing the home directory within Personal Web Manager.

    You should start organizing your folders right from day one, so let's do that now. Create a new directory in wwwroot, and call it test and put your test page inside.

    Now call it through your browser, by adding its directory location to the URL like this: http://127.0.0.1/test/firstpage.html

9. Now we'll use the server to call the new directory instead. Double click on the Personal Web Manager icon on your desktop, and go into the Advanced window:

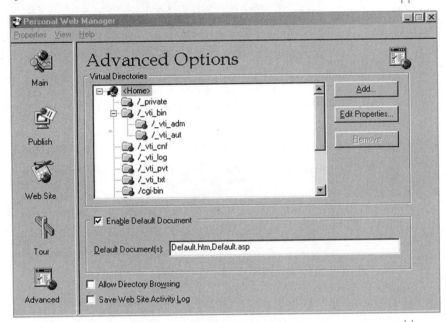

Select Edit Properties, and then browse to the test directory through the Edit Directory window.

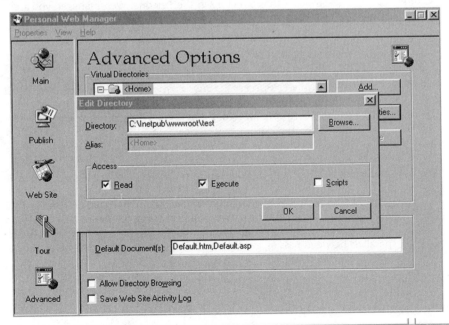

> *Notice the three check boxes at the bottom of the Edit Directory window. Make sure you check Execute here - it's not important for the sake of the examples we're creating now, but it will be later on when we'll create a simple ASP script.*

Now try calling up `firstpage.html` again through your browser, but this time leaving the URL as you first used it, before you created the test directory (`http://127.0.0.1/firstpage.html`):

It still works. Even though the page isn't in wwwroot and you haven't pointed your URL to it's specific location, your server has found the page for you.

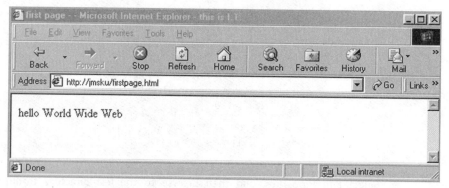

In fact, if you try pointing the browser through the test directory as well, now that you've set that directory in the Personal Web manager, you'll either get a HTTP error 404 page not found error, or your browser will try and correct the URL for you, by taking test out again.

> *When you're using Personal Web Manager to point to the correct web directory, always make sure you set it correctly for each subsequent application directory you create. Leaving it pointing to one directory when you're trying to test another one can be a frustrating experience!*

And that's all there is to it. Now you're set to get Flash talking to server-side scripts.

We'll be reviewing passing variables in the rest of this chapter, because this is going to be the principle way you'll be using server-side processing for the rest of this section of the book. We'll begin by looking at how HTML passes variables, because, as you might expect, there are plenty of parallels between passing variables in HTML and in Flash, and you might well be already familiar with the HTML approach.

Using the GET and POST methods

There are two methods of sending variables within web pages, GET and POST. You might well already be familiar with the way HTML handles user input. If you created an HTML form, for example, you would use a set of `<form>` tags to enclose the input fields that carry the variables to the server. This HTML page that allows a visitor to submit their email address to an ASP page, getinfo.asp, sitting on the root directory of a website:

```
<HTML>
<BODY>
        <form name="submitmail" method="get" action="getinfo.asp">
        Your Email Address:
        <input type="text" name="emailadd">
        <input type="submit" name="Submit" value="Submit">
        </form>
</BODY>
</HTML>
```

The HTML creates an input box with the variable name emailadd. When the user clicks on the submit button, their email address is sent to an ASP page on the server (getinfo.asp), where, if we'd created the ASP page, we'd do something with it. If you try this out, you'll get something looking like this:

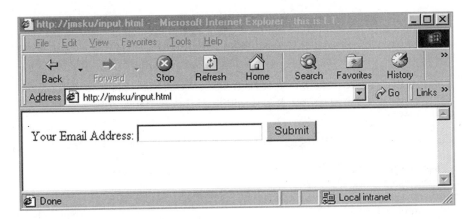

It's not very functional, of course, because there isn't a getinfo.asp page on the server. If we were to construct an ASP page for this example, though, we would have it receive the variable of the same name, emailadd. The value of this variable will be the email address that the user types into the text box (for example *visitor@yourwebsite.com*):

What you do with the email address once it has been submitted is up to you: you could have it sent to the site's webmaster, or add it to a database of other addresses that you use to send out a newsletter, or you could send an email back to the user thanking them.

The work is being done by `method="get"` inside the `<form>` tag; it sends the variables by appending the variable name and value to the URL of the script. So visiting the URL:

http://www.yourserver.com/getinfo.asp?emailadd=visitor@yourwebsite.com

Would have same affect as sending the variable using the form in a web page.

Notice the '?' after the address of the ASP script, followed by the variable name, an equals sign, and the variable value – this part of the URL is called the **query string**. If additional variables were to be sent, the script would add an ampersand character (`&`) and the variable name and value as before. So an appended script might look like this:

http://www.yourserver.com/getinfo.asp?emailadd=visitor@yourwebsite.com&yourname=myname

Sending variables using the `GET` method is useful because you can see which variables are being sent to the script, which makes your pages easier to debug. On the downside, URLs are limited to 8192 characters, so it's really only suitable for fairly short forms. Moreover, because the `GET` method appends the URL, users can bookmark the resulting page, which isn't always a good thing.

Using POST in HTML

Sending variables using the `POST` method passes the variables in the header of the HTTP request. This means that they are invisible to the user, and as there is almost no limit to the number of variables you can send, you'll find this method is better when you want to send long strings to your script.

So what does this all have to do with your Flash movies? Well, Flash can send variables to server-side scripts in exactly the same way as you can do with HTML based forms; using `getURL` and `loadVariables`.

Parallels Between HTML Web Page Forms and Objects in your Flash Movie

Web Page Forms	**Flash movie**
Form object name (`name="a name"`)	Variable name
Form object value (`value="a value"`)	Variable value
Hidden form object	Any variable set within Flash movie
(`<input type="hidden" value="a value">`)	
Text box (`<input type="text">`)	Single Line Input Text box
Multiline text box (`<textarea>`)	Multiline Input Text box
Submit button (`<input type="submit">`)	Button object
Form action (`<form action="anASPScript.asp">`)	getURL or loadVariables action

So now let's start talking about Flash more specifically.

Sending variables into Flash using getURL and loadVariables

The `getURL` command allows you to load a document into either a new window or to a specific frame – just as you've used it in previous chapters. It also allows you to send variables stored in your Flash movie to the URL you are loading, using the `GET` or `POST` methods.

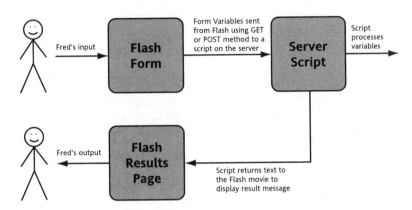

You've already been using the `getURL` action. It's usually used with a button to load a document, just as it is in an HTML form. Let's build a quick example that uses `getURL` to send a search variable to Yahoo!'s search engine, which will process it and send users to a new window showing the results of the search.

Using getURL to search Yahoo!

1. In your movie you need a button and an input box. The input box needs the variable `p` (the variable name that *Yahoo*'s search script needs):

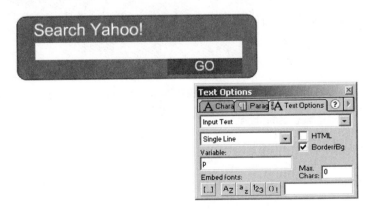

Then all you need is the button that sends the search variable to Yahoo!

2.   Add the button and set a getURL action with GET:

```
on (release, keyPress "<Enter>") {
    getURL ("http://search.yahoo.com/bin/search", "_blank", "GET");
}
```

This will send the search variable to Yahoo!'s script at:

http://search.yahoo.com/bin/search

3.   Publish it to the test directory and try it out. You'll see that the page that opens when you click on the Search button is exactly the same as if you typed your search query into Yahoo's own homepage (www.yahoo.com). Notice the resulting URL of this page – with the variable name and value appended to the URL. Depending on what variable name you gave your input box, it'll look something like this:

http://search.yahoo.com/bin/search?p=flash

So that's how getURL works. Simple really. There will be times when it's just not practical to send your variables appended to a URL; when you're doing password validation, for example. We'll build one more quick example that does password validation using the POST method next. We'll check two variables entered by a user into a Flash movie against a hidden ASP page.

Using the POST method for a simple password

We'll check the two variables against a password and user name set in an ASP page. The POST method is good for this because, as you may remember, it hides the variable values and prevents the protected page from being bookmarked.

> *Please note that this is not a secure way to create password protection for a site, it just hides the variables from immediate view.*

1.   So, create two input text boxes with variable names Username and Password. Then create a button that will submit the details using a getURL action pointing to a page called hidden.asp using POST.

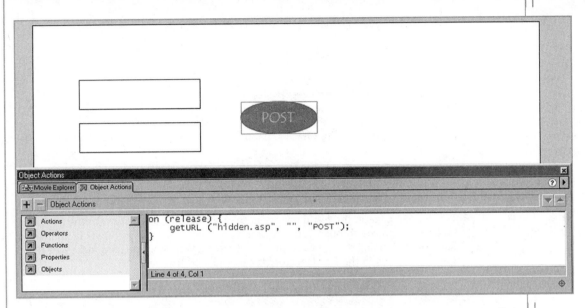

2.   Export the SWF to the test directory in the wwwroot directory of your server. I called mine password.swf

3.   Now we need to create the ASP code that will check the password and username.

Although the code we're using here is ASP, and this might be the first time that you've used ASP, you'll find that it's quite readable. The code starts off by declaring the language that it's written in (VBScript) inside the ASP tags (<% and %>).

```
<%@ LANGUAGE="VBScript" %>
```

Then comes the ASP code itself, also enclosed in the tags.

```
<%@ LANGUAGE="VBScript" %>
<%
'set the required username and password in an If else statement
If Request.Form("username")="user1" and
➡ Request.Form("password")="acceptme" Then
                response.write "Logon Accepted!"
      'and tell users what's happened if they can't get in
      Else
                response.write "Access Denied!"
      End If
%>
```

We're using an If...Then...Else loop to check the variable values names being passed in from Flash; if the value of username is user1, and the value of password is acceptme, then the user will be sent the message 'Logon Accepted'.

Here's all the code together. Open Notepad and type it in, and save it as `hidden.asp`:

```
<%@ LANGUAGE="VBScript" %>
<%
'set the required username and password in an If else statement
If Request.Form("username")="user1" and
➥ Request.Form("password")="acceptme" Then
                    response.write "Logon Accepted!"
        'and tell users what's happened if they can't get in
        Else
                    response.write "Access Denied!"
End If
%>
```

4. Put the ASP page in the test directory in the root of your directory with the SWF file and test the movie through your browser. (http://localhost/password.swf) (If you have any trouble running this, go back into your Personal Web Manager, and make sure that the Execute box in the Edit Directory is checked, and try again.)

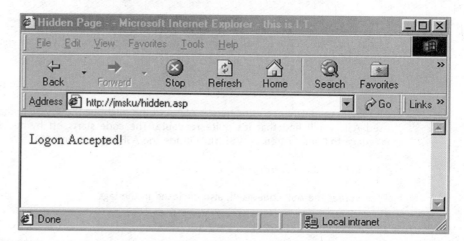

If you enter a username and password that the ASP page is expecting, you'll get a success message – otherwise, access is denied. You'll also get the Access Denied! message if you browse straight to the ASP page, bypassing the SWF form, because the ASP page will simply contain empty strings instead of variable values.

Variables you don't want to send to the server

When you're developing real world applications, chances are that your movie will contain a number of variables, for various actions within the movie, that you don't actually want Flash to send to your script.

Flash doesn't allow you to select which variables to send – it just sends all the variables within the timeline. Although your script will simply ignore any unused variables that you send, it's not a very good idea to send an extremely long string of unnecessary variables: that's just a waste of processing power.

You can work around this by manually building an expression that builds a URL mimicking the way variables are sent using the GET method. Suppose you only wanted to send the first two of these three variables:

> Variable `logon`, **value** User Name
> Variable `password`, **value** myPassword
> Variable `frameNumber`, **value** 50

Left to its own devices, the GET method would send the information built into a URL like this:
www.yourserver.com/myscript.asp?logon=User%20Name&password=myPassword&frameNumber=50

Flash would automatically send all the variables. You could create your own `getURL` action that sends only the variables you're interested in, like this:

http://www.yourserver.com/myscript.asp?logon="+ logon +"&password=" +password

All you're doing is imitating the URL that the `getURL` action would build itself, using the GET command, but without the `frameNumber` variable. The getURL action that you had built would call a URL like this:

www.yourserver.com/myscript?logon=User%20Name&password=myPassword

Of course, this technique won't work if you have to send variables using the POST method. In that scenario you would either have to amend your script to detect variables sent using GET, or simply ignore all but the required variables.

Sending and receiving variables using loadVariables

Using the `getURL` method to send variables to a script is all well and good if you're happy for your user to leave your Flash movie in order to see the results of the scripted page (either in the same window, a frame, or new window).

If you don't want your site visitors leaving your movie to go to a new page, you need the `loadVariables` action, which allows you to send variables to a script and bring the results of the script back into the Flash movie dynamically – no new windows involved.

You used `loadVariables` to bring text in from a text file to update your Flash movie in earlier chapters. It works just the same with scripts, the script simply processes some of the information you've asked it to process and then returns the results back to the movie. It's easy enough to ensure that the script returns text in a format that Flash understands, and can insert into a dynamic text box, or even values that can be manipulated within the Flash movie. Because you've worked with `loadVariables` a lot already in the book, we won't put it into practice again here. What we will do, though, is talk about making the variables that come into a Flash movie from outside useful to Flash.

Making HTML output useful for Flash

The one thing you have to be really careful about, when you're creating a server-side script to use with the `loadVariables` command, is the output that the script creates. You have to make sure that the first line of the script's output contains the ampersand, variable name and an equals sign (`&variablename=`) so that Flash will know that it needs to load the information that follows. (You can, of course, load more than one variable at a time from a script. Flash can load a number of variables at the same time.)

You will also need to remember that if your script does not output the information in URL Encoded format you're likely to have problems with the layout, or displaying special characters in your Flash movie – and it's easy enough to make sure that the script will URL Encode that format for you. In ASP you simply use:

```
response.write Server.URLEncode
```

You'll find plenty more information about making sure your script variables are Flash-friendly in the following chapters. As long as you remember to URL Encode everything, and that Flash will only recognize HTML when you're loading information into a dynamic text box set to read HTML, then you'll be fine.

Summary

Well, now you're ready to begin creating server-side scripts to work with Flash. You have a server up and running, and you know the basic mechanisms. I hope you're confident with the `getURL` and `loadVariable` actions, and using the `GET` and `POST` methods – when to use them and how they work. It only takes a bit more work before you're creating database-driven content, pulling content from other sources (like news or weather sites), creating online chat interfaces, bulletin boards...the list is endless!

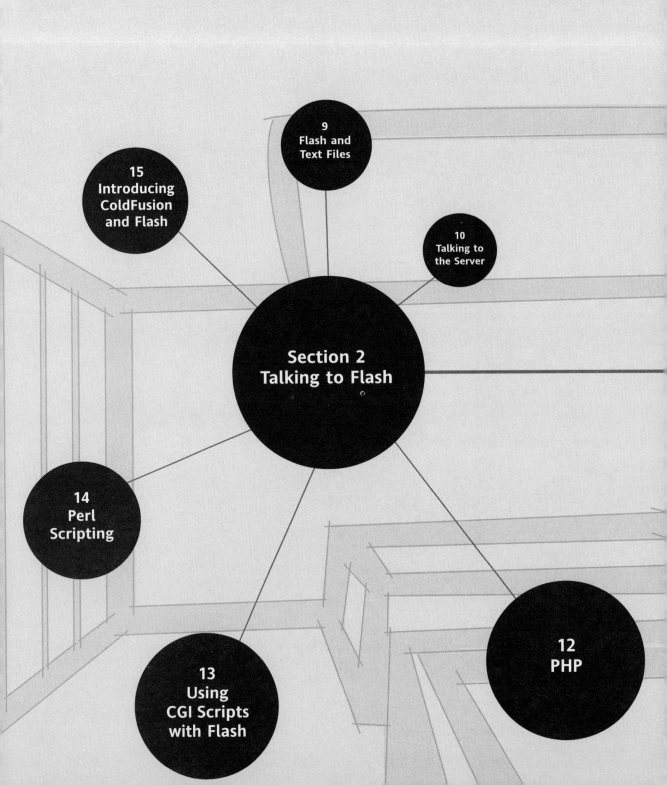

9
Flash and
Text Files

15
Introducing
ColdFusion
and Flash

10
Talking to
the Server

Section 2
Talking to Flash

14
Perl
Scripting

13
Using
CGI Scripts
with Flash

12
PHP

Chapter 11
Passing Data with Flash and ASP

What is ASP?

ASP is an acronym for Active Server Pages. These are web pages that can process scripts on a server before returning the values to the web page to be viewed. They can call functions written in VBScript (the Visual Basic scripting language) or Jscript, Microsoft's version of JavaScript. So, if you're building or running a web site, ASP enables you to carry out some very useful tasks, such as track a user's journey through your web site, gather information about the user, and even change the way your site looks each time a given user returns. These things are accomplished using ASP objects. ASP objects are components that are installed on the server to handle tasks associated with ASP. The beauty of ASP lies in the fact that it stores the site information in a database and simply calls the required information each time a user visits your site. This enables you to write code once and display the results on many pages, change the website attributes (font color, size, page layout), and even update a page without ever even touching the actual page itself. Who wouldn't want quicker web page turnover and less web site maintenance?

Active Server Pages can have a mix of scripts and HTML on the same page. The ASP code is contained within delimiters (`<%` and `%>`), and is processed by the server; meanwhile, the rest of the page (for example, HTML, JavaScript, and Flash) is processed by the browser. Active Server Pages end with the `.asp` extension.

The uses for ASP are endless, as you will see in the examples given in this chapter.

For more information on ASP, check out http://msdn.microsoft.com/.

What you will learn in this chapter

Communication and interactivity are the keys to what we will accomplish. The examples you'll build as you work through the chapter will show you how to pass, store, and retrieve variables between Flash, ASP, and a database. You'll learn how to use ASP in your web pages (with a little JavaScript thrown in), and ActionScript in Flash. The range of projects discussed will show you how Flash and ASP can enhance any web page and make it truly interactive, and will hopefully give you some insight into scripting for the web, and show you how to use some of the tools in Flash that you may not be familiar with. I chose the examples for this book because all of the projects create tools that anyone could use on a daily basis.

We'll be using ASP to:

- Show the current date in Flash, using ASP's `Date()` function

- Make a visitor counter for your web site

- Construct a search using Flash with ASP

- Construct a login and password section for your web site

What you need

ASP can be written in any text editor – trusty old Notepad will do just fine, although many people prefer to use an editor such as Macromedia Dreamweaver, Microsoft Interdev or Allaire Homesite instead. These editors are not strictly necessary, but they can drastically reduce your development time, and they also make server-side editing much easier by providing you with features such as color-coding.

You will also need a server on which to process your ASP – you could use Microsoft Personal Web Server for your PC running Windows as the OS, or a Microsoft NT Server such as IIS (flip back to the previous chapter if you've not yet installed these). The projects you will make need to be saved in the root directory of your web server (this is usually C:\Inetpub\wwwroot) and, unlike HTML files, ASP files must be opened in an 'active' browser window – which simply means that you need to enter a web address to access your files (for example http://localhost/myfile.asp or http://127.0.0.1/myfile.asp loop back to the local machine's server).

The examples you will make will show how to pass, store and retrieve variables between Flash, ASP, and, in some examples, a very simple database. For these examples we will use Microsoft Access but if you have a Microsoft SQL Server handy, the code is the same.

Using ASP's date function to pass the current date to Flash

Sometimes, it's the smallest things we do as developers/designers that help enrich our sites the most. At times, something as simple as adding the current date to a page can really add to a site's appeal. In VBScript (which is what we are going to be using to write the ASP code) we can implement such a feature by using the date function, which is simply date(). Passing data between ASP and Flash can be very simple. Not long ago, Flash-based web sites were mostly just to look at. But, intertwining server-side technology with multimedia such as Flash has opened a lot of new doors to the capabilities for the Web. We can force variables into a Flash movie by adding the ? character plus the variables to the source path of the Flash movie in our HTML Object and Embed tags. The <Object></Object> tags are an Internet Explorer specific tag to call the plug in that displays our Flash movie. The <Embed></Embed> tags are the Netscape equivalent. The question mark acts as a delimiter when used to pass variables, so by adding this to the end of the Flash movie's path, we can force a variable into Flash, for example:

```
<param name="movie"
➥value="your_movie.swf?variable_name=variable_value">
```

This is a pretty limited function, in that you can't do much more than send an established variable, but used thoughtfully, it can be very useful.

1. Create a new folder in the wwwroot directory of your web server and call it Date.

2.   Open a new movie in Flash and create a dynamic textbox with the variable name `date`. Give it a ***border*** and then add some static text to the left of the textbox that reads: The date is.

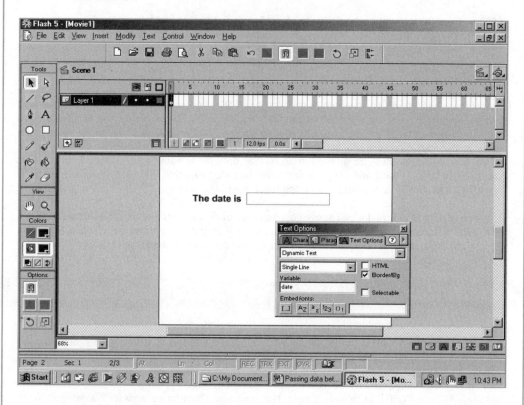

3.   Save your work to your new Date folder as date.fla and then publish it in the default formats, SWF and HTML.

Now we need to create the ASP page.

4.   Open the HTML version of your movie, and save it as an ASP file, in this case `date.asp`.

So, now you have your `date.asp` file, we can now insert the `date` variable.

5.   Find the `<Param name=Movie value="date.swf">` line, and add the ? delimiter and the ASP code for the date, `date=<%=date%>`, which will then give you:

```
<PARAM NAME=movie VALUE="date.swf?date=<%=date%>">
```

Then modify the `<Embed>` tag you'll find it's kind of similar:

```
<EMBED src="date.swf?date=<%=date%>"
```

This is how the complete code should look:

```
<HTML>
<HEAD>
<TITLE>date</TITLE>
</HEAD>
<BODY bgcolor="#FFFFFF">
<!- URL's used in the movie->
<!- text used in the movie->
<OBJECT classid="clsid:D27CDB6E-AE6D-11cf-96B8-444553540000"
➡codebase="http://download.macromedia.com/pub/shockwave/cabs/flas
➡h/swflash.cab#version=5,0,0,0" WIDTH=550 HEIGHT=400 ID=date>
<PARAM NAME=movie VALUE="date.swf?date=<%=date%>"> <PARAM
➡NAME=quality VALUE=high> <PARAM NAME=bgcolor VALUE=#FFFFFF>
➡<EMBED src="date.swf?date=<%=date%>" quality=high
➡bgcolor=#FFFFFF  WIDTH=550 HEIGHT=400 NAME=date
➡SWLIVECONNECT=TRUE
➡TYPE="application/x-shockwave-flash"
➡PLUGINSPAGE="http://www.macromedia.com/shockwave/download/index.
➡cgi?P1_Prod_Version=ShockwaveFlash"></EMBED>
</OBJECT>
</BODY>
</HTML>
```

ASP passes the date variable to Flash using the date() function. The delimiters <% and %> let the server know that this code should be processed on the server (don't forget to include the = symbol).

6. Now open the page in your browser, all being well, you should get something like this:

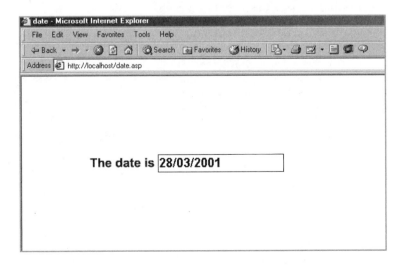

Pretty good. So, now you've seen how to get variables into Flash from ASP, let's move on to something a little more interesting...

The visitor counter

Nothing boosts your ego quite like seeing the amount of traffic your web site is generating, and a visitor counter is a great tool to get some indication as to just how many people have visited your site. There are many different ways of going about building a visitor counter, for instance, you could use application level variables (variables defined in a global.asa file that have site wide range) or a text file using the File System Object which is a built-in component of ASP. However, the counter we'll build here will use a simple database that will be updated each time someone visits your page. The counter will work like this:

- A user comes to your site

- When the server is loading the page, it reads your ASP code and opens the connection to the database that stores the visitor count

- The ASP page then reads in a variable from the database that describes how many visitors your site has had, adds one to it, and then sends the modified number of visitors back to the database, where it is kept until the next user connects to the database.

And that's how our simple counter will work.

Creating your database

Although we're not going to be discussing databases in depth here - you can find full database discussion in chapter 22 – we will be setting one up.

1. Start by creating a new directory called projects in the wwwroot folder of your server – this is where you'll need to save your database to, so start up Microsoft Access, and in the subsequent dialog, choose to create a new database using a Blank Access Database, then click OK.

Note that if you put your database in the root of your server it could be downloaded by a user if they were able to figure out the database name. An alternative would be to put the database in the cgi-bin directory of your web server.

2. You will then be asked to select where you want your new database to be kept. Navigate to your wwwroot and select the projects folder that you just created. Name your database flash-asp and then click Create.

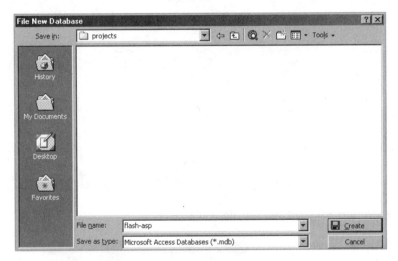

3. In the next window, double-click on Create table in Design view, and this will let you create your first table in the database.

4. You will then be presented with a table that has three columns (Field Name, Data Type and Description). In the first row of the table name the field visitorCount, and assign a Data Type of Number (this is easily done using the drop-down combo box that appears when you click on this column). On the General tab of the Field Properties frame at the bottom of the window, ensure that the field size is set to Long Integer and set the default value to 0.

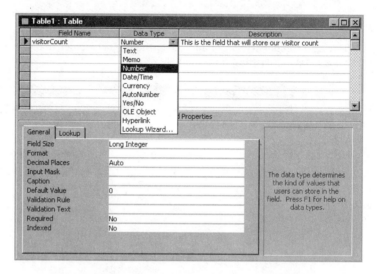

5. Now go ahead and save this table, calling it counter.

6. You will then be asked if you want to create a primary key, click No and close the counter table.

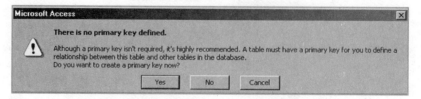

7. Back at the flash-asp Database window, you should now see your new counter database beneath all of the Create... options:

Double-click on the counter table to open it, and type 0 (zero) into the visitorCount field. Another line should appear below the first:

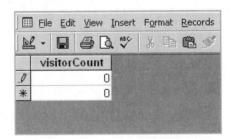

That's the database finished, you can now save it and close Access.

OK, so now we've created our database, we need to enable our ASP page to access it, and to do this we need to be able to connect our ASP page to the database. We'll do this using what is called a DSN connection.

Setting the DSN

The Data Source Name (DSN) refers to the connection between your ASP page and the database.

1. To set up the DSN, click on My Computer and then open up the Control Panel, and then click ODBC Data Sources (32 bit).

> ***Windows 2000 users, things are slightly different on your operating system, so you'll need to go to the*** Start ***menu, select*** Settings > Control Panel > Administrative Tools, ***and then select*** Data Sources (ODBC).

2.   Now select the System DSN tab and then click the Add... button.

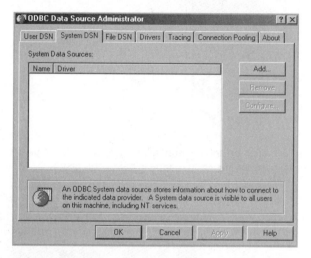

3.   Select the Microsoft Access Driver and then click Finish.

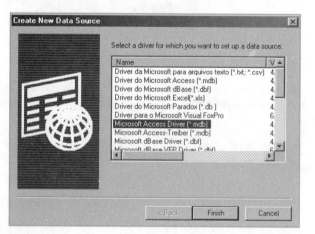

4.   The ODBC Microsoft Access Setup dialog will then be displayed. In this dialog, name your data source projects and type flash-asp projects as the description.

5. Now, in the Database frame, click the Select... button and then use the tree view to browse to the database that you've just created in Access.

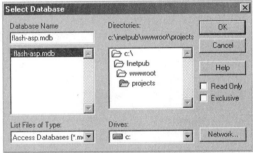

6. Once you've found your database, select it and then click OK. The dialog will then show the database to which we wish to connect, and the connection path:

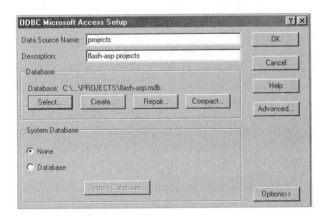

Click OK again, which will take you back to the ODBC Data Source Administrator dialog, click OK here as well.

You've now established a DSN connection to the projects database, and this DSN will be used by the projects in this chapter.

So, now we've got the database table and done the groundwork for the connection that we'll be using for our visitor counter.

Creating the Flash movie

1.   Open a new movie in Flash and rename the default layer as text. Create a dynamic textbox 450 pixels long and set its *variable* name to counter. I know that the box is empty, but trust me, it'll all work out.

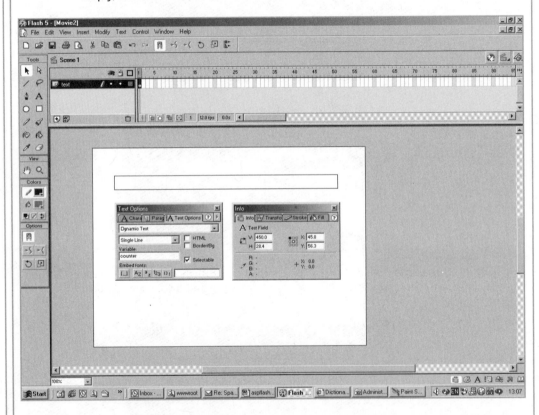

2.   Now go ahead and add a new layer, and name it actions. Add the following ActionScript to frame 1 of the actions layer:

```
loadVariables ("count.asp", "");
```

3.   Create a new folder called Counter inside the projects folder that we created earlier, and then save the file that we've been working on in this new folder, calling it counter.fla. Publish your movie in the default SWF and HTML formats. Now close Flash and open the editor of your choice.

The ASP code

1. Create a new page in your editor and save it as `count.asp` in the Counter directory. This page does not need any HTML at all because it will be called from the Flash movie and will do all of its work on the server. It will send its results to be displayed in the Flash movie that is already in the browser. It will be used as a processing page to open the counter table in the projects database and get the current visitor count.

   Now we are going to create the database connection in ASP – we'll build up the code as we go. Throughout the code, you'll notice that I've inserted comments to explain what's going on; it's worth noting that doing this is seen as good practice in whichever language you are working in. I've separated my comments from the actual code that I want to be compiled by inserting a ' '' ' character between the code and my comments. This works because ASP knows that when it compiles code and comes across the ' '' ' character, the information following it is actually just a comment, and simply ignores it.

2. First of all, we put in our opening ASP delimiter tag, `<%`, to tell the server to process the code inside them, and then we need to declare `option explicit`. What does `option explicit` do? Well, it tells the page that we must declare all of the variables that we are going to use on the ASP page. This means that before we use a variable we must declare it using `Dim SomeVariableName`, e.g. `Dim strText`. If we use a variable name that is undeclared, or if we spell a variable name wrong, then we will get an error message on the ASP page saying that the variable has not been declared, and on which line of the code the error occurred. Using `option explicit` as we are here is not essential, but it is a very good programming habit to get into early on, especially as it makes debugging code so much easier.

   ```
   <% option explicit
   ```

3. OK, so once we've done that, we need to declare all of the variables that will be used in this script:

   ```
   dim oConn            'this is the connection variable
   dim oRs              'this is the recordset variable
   dim IntCount         'this is the counter variable
   dim strSql           'this is the database query variable
   ```

   You may be wondering what `oConn`, `oRs`, `IntCount`, and `strSql` stand for. The name `oConn` is a reference to the Connection object that we use to create the connection to the database, `oRs` is the reference to the Recordset object, `IntCount` tells us that the value passed is an integer and `strSql` is our string Sql statement. These names, used to reference the objects, strings, and other variables we use, are not necessary but are good programming practice. It may be easy to remember what everything is now but the next time you need to update your code, your memory might not be so sharp – and if anyone else needs to update your code, they will be able to see what is going on.

   Are you scared yet? Well, take a deep breath and prepare for some coding.

Are you scared yet? Well, take a deep breath and prepare for some coding.

4. First, we'll create what's called the **connection object**. This allows us to use the DSN that we created earlier as the path to our Access database. By default in ASP, this is called an ADODB connection:

```
Set oConn = Server.CreateObject("ADODB.Connection")
```

5. We then open the connection object with the Data Source Name (DSN):

```
oConn.open "dsn=projects"
```

6. Next, we do the same for the recordset. The recordset is our data source. It could be a text file, Excel spreadsheet, SQL database, or an Access database as in this example:

```
Set oRs = Server.CreateObject("ADODB.Recordset")
```

7. Here we give strSql its value, and tell it to select everything out of the table that we called counter:

```
StrSql = "Select * From counter"
```

And then open the recordset for reading and editing

```
oRs.open strSql,oConn,1,3
```

1 and 3 refer to the cursor types used in this recordset.

8. Now we use IntCount, which is the counter variable that we declared back at the beginning. In this case, we need to make IntCount equal to the number in the field called visitorCount, plus 1; we add 1 here to account for the current user loading the page:

```
IntCount = oRs("visitorCount") + 1
```

9. Once we have added one to the count, we update the recordset using oRs.Update, preparing it for when the next user loads the page:

```
oRs("visitorCount") = intCount
oRs.Update
```

10. Now we need to make ASP write the results of the count in a way that Flash can understand. The ampersand (&) is a delimiter, which is used to add things together, thereby allowing us to create a sentence made up of plain text English (some text for the counter in this case) and some ASP logic (in this case to carry variables to Flash):

```
Response.Write ("counter=This page has had " & IntCount & "
➥visitors.")
```

11. Once we've done that, the only thing left to do is close the database connection and insert the closing ASP `%>` delimiter:

```
    Set oConn = nothing
    Set oRs = nothing
%>
```

So, your complete code should look something like this:

```
<%option explicit
    dim oConn
    dim oRs
    dim IntCount
    dim strSql

    'create the database connection
    Set oConn = Server.CreateObject("ADODB.Connection")

    '"projects" is the Data Source Name
    oConn.Open "dsn=projects"

    'open the recordset
    Set oRs = Server.CreateObject("ADODB.Recordset")

    'This is the database query
    strSql = "Select * from counter"
    oRs.Open strSql,oConn,1,3

    'IntCount is our counter variable
    IntCount  = oRs("visitorCount") + 1
    oRs("visitorCount") = intCount
    oRs.Update

    Response.Write ("counter=This page has had " & IntCount & "
    ➥visitors.")
    Set oConn = nothing
    Set oRs = nothing

%>
```

12. Now save your work and open this page in an active browser window. All being well, you should see something like this:

This page has had 1 visitors

If you don't see this, check any errors you might see in its place.

> *Having problems? If you've received an error, don't worry. First, check the syntax of your code. Second, make sure that you have the database in the* projects *folder in the root of your web server. Third, make sure you are testing this application in an 'active' browser and that count.asp has been saved in the proper directory. Remember, ASP is processed on the server and cannot be called from the hard drive like an HTML page.*

13.   Now, while you still have active browser window open, type in the address of your counter.html page, you should see a page that looks like this:

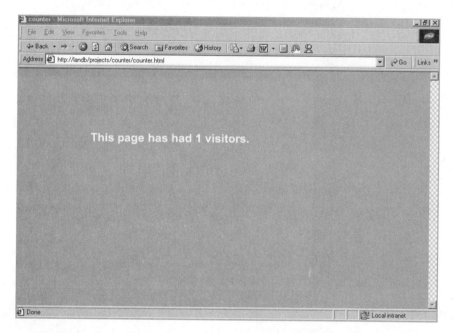

Now you see your visitor counter in all its glory. Just waiting to count your daily visitors. Good work! OK, next we'll move on to building another useful tool.

Creating a search engine

One of the most common web applications is the search engine. The search engine executes a massive task when the user asks it to find information. It carries out this task so efficiently, that many users take it for granted, indeed, most of the time the hardest decision that the user has to make when searching for information is whether to look for the information they want on the entire Web or whether to restrict their search to the web site that they're visiting. The search engine does the rest. Your site may offer specialized or categorized information, or have pages of links for users to look through in order to find the information they need. A search engine can free up those crowded pages and help you guide the user to their destination more efficiently. The search engine that we'll develop here will use a Flash front end, an ASP page to process the information, and our handy Access database, to store the information. OK, first let's create another database table.

The database table

1. Open your flash-asp database in Access.

2. In the next window, double-click Create table in Design view.

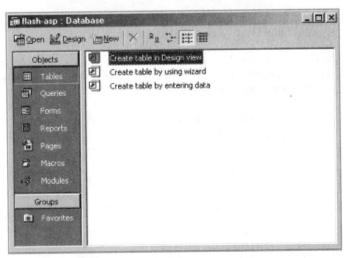

3. Hopefully you'll see a table appear. In the first row of the table, enter firstname into the Field Name column, and set the Data Type to be Text. In the second row, enter lastname in the Field Name column, and set the Data Type to Text as well:

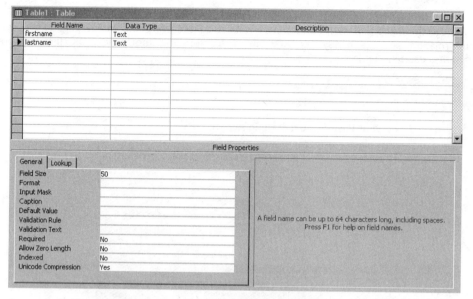

4.   These are the only fields we need, so save this table, naming it search:

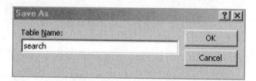

Again, we don't need a primary key for this exercise.

5.   Okay, now for some fun (like this isn't fun!). Double-click your search table, open it and then populate your search table with some names so that you have something to search. Try to add at least ten rows of first and last names to the table:

OK, now save your work and close Access.

The Flash front end

All we really need for our Flash front end is a basic user interface.

Submitting the search

1. First of all, create a new folder called search within the projects directory.

2. Open a new movie in Flash and rename the default layer as input.

3. Now create an input textbox on this layer with a variable name name. Also make sure that the Border/Bg checkbox is checked.

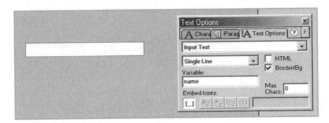

4. Now, create a new layer, and call it button. On this layer insert a keyframe in frame 1 and create a generic button on stage called button.

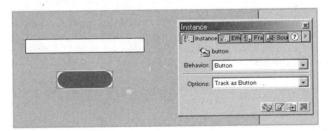

5. Open up the Library and right-click on the button symbol, in the subsequent context menu choose Duplicate. Name the duplicate button submit. Now right-click on the submit button icon in the Library, and from the context menu that appears, select Edit.

6. Add a label to the submit button with the caption: Submit.

7. Next, go back to the main screen and select your generic button. In the instance panel, click the Swap Symbol button and switch the generic button with the submit button. This will make it much easier to position our new button. Now save your work in the search folder as search.fla.

8. Now make a new layer and name it actions. Label frame 1 of this layer as submit and add the following frame action:

```
stop();
```

9. Now add the following code to your submit button:

```
on (release) {
    mode = "search";
    loadVariables ("process.asp", "", "POST");
    gotoAndPlay ("searching");
    name = ""
}
```

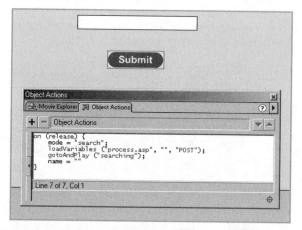

So what does this code do? Well, first we have set a variable called mode equal to search. When the button is released, it will send the variables we have defined to process.asp to be processed. Then onto the frame labeled searching and last, we set the variable name equal to nothing.

10. Add a new layer called text. This is where we will tell the user what to do:

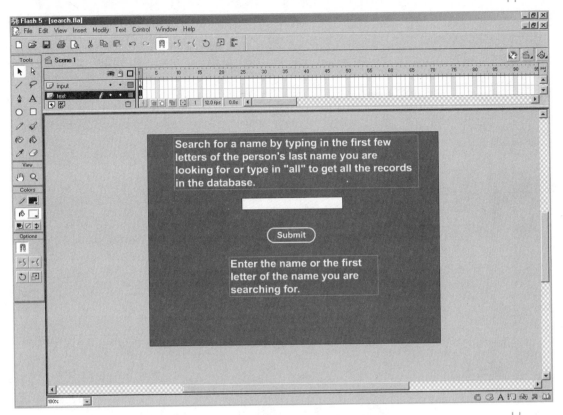

11. Save your work again and add a new keyframe to the second frame of the actions layer. Label this frame searching. In this frame we need to add some ActionScript that will display the results of the search if there are any:

```
if (results != "") {
   gotoAndStop("results")
}
```

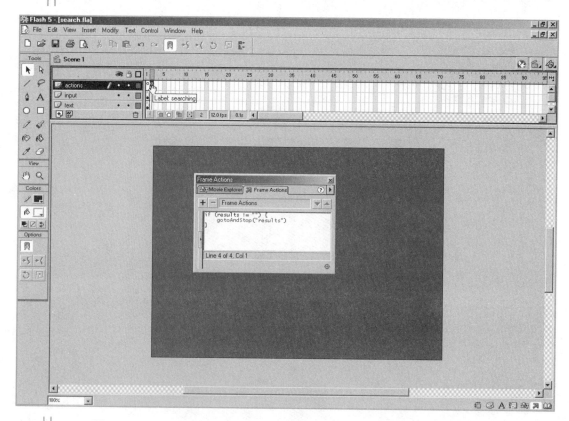

12. Add a new layer and name it searchMovie. In frame 2 of this layer, add some static text to the screen that reads Searching. Then convert the text to a graphic symbol called searchMovie.

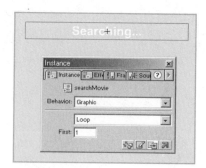

13. Now, go to frame 7 and add a keyframe on the searchMovie layer. Select the searchMovie symbol on stage and in the Effect panel, set the alpha value to 0.

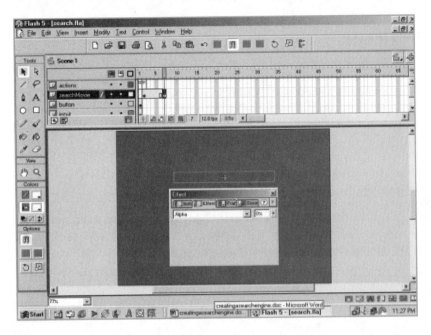

14. Create a motion tween between frame 2 and frame 7.

15. Add a keyframe to frame 7 of the actions layer and then add the following code:

```
gotoAndPlay("searching");
```

So now, after the user enters a name to check for in the database, the searchMovie clip will play over and over until we get some results back from the ASP page. If nothing is returned from the database, the user will receive a 'not found' message and can go back to the start and try again. If the user enters information into the search and there is a value to return, the user will be taken to the 'results' screen we will make shortly to see, well, the results.

Displaying the results

1. Now, on frame 8 of the button layer, add a new keyframe, open your Library, duplicate the generic button that we created earlier, and name it back. Then go to the edit screen and add a back label to your new button.

2. Now go back to frame 8 in the main timeline, swap the current button symbol for the new back button, and add the following code to it:

```
on (release) {
    gotoAndPlay ("submit");
}
```

This code will enable the user to go back to the beginning and start a new search.

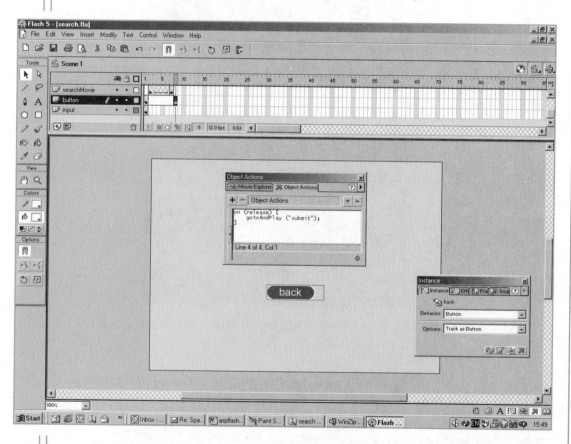

3. Now add a blank keyframe to frame 2 of the button layer. This will stop the Submit button being seen while the Searching animation is playing.

4. Add one more keyframe to the actions layer at frame 8 and label it results. Add a stop action to this frame.

5. Make a new layer named results and add a keyframe to this layer at frame 8. Above the back button, create a dynamic textbox with the variable name results. Check the Border/Bg check box to make a border for our results.

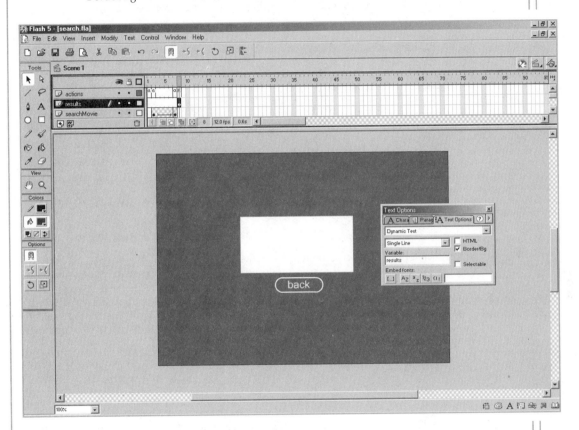

6. Above the results textbox, add the following text: Here are the results of your query. Click the back button to search again..

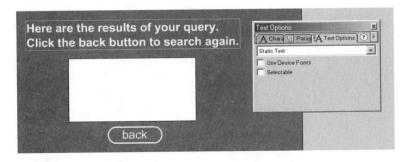

Now we have a screen to display the results of the search and the back button to let the user search again. The last thing we need to do is add scroll buttons to let the user scroll through the results once they are returned to the screen.

7. Add one last layer called scroll and put a keyframe in frame 8 of this layer. To the right of the results field, create an arrow shape pointing upwards and convert it into a button called scrollUp. Add the following code to the scrollUp button:

```
on (release) {
    results.scroll = results.scroll-1;
}
```

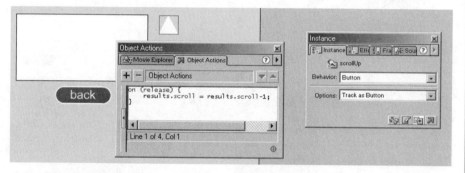

This will let the user scroll up in increments of one character. The scroll property is a built-in feature of Flash that can be used to scroll text up or down inside a textbox.

8. Now bring up your Library and duplicate this symbol. Name the duplicate scrollDown. Now drag this symbol underneath the other scroll button. From the toolbar, select Modify > Transform > Flip Vertical to turn the new button upside down. Now add the following code to this button:

```
on (release) {
    results.scroll = results.scroll+1;
}
```

This will move the scroll down one character each time the button is pressed. Our user will now be able to scroll up or down through the results of their search.

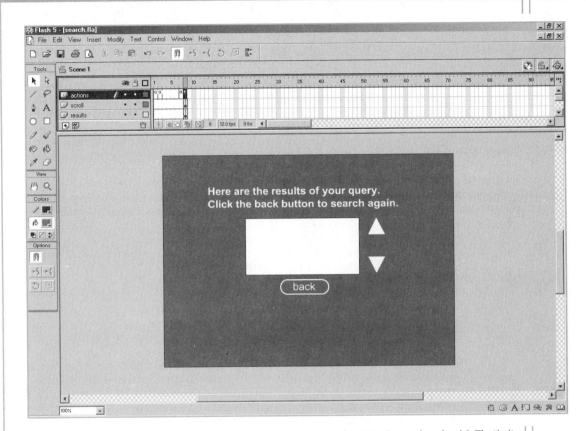

Save your work and publish it in the default formats SWF and HTML. Pretty handy eh? That's it for the Flash side of our search application, now it's time to open our text editor and get into some ASP coding.

The ASP script

1. Let's start by creating a new file in the search folder named process.asp. The first thing we need to add is our opening <% delimiter and declaration of option explicit. Next, we declare our variables that will be used and their values that were sent from the Flash movie.

```
<%
option explicit
dim oConn
dim oRs
dim strSql
dim strSearch
dim results
dim mode
```

```
mode = request("mode")
strSearch = Request("name")
```

The variable oConn represents our connection object, and oRs represents the recordset object, strSql represents the SQL statement and strSearch is the variable name that we are sending from Flash. The connection object (oConn), creates the connection to the database and oRs creates the object that will carry our data to and from the database. StrSql represents the Sql command that tells the recordset(oRs), what we want to do. results is the variable that we sent back to Flash and mode is equal to the variable mode that we send to the ASP page from the Flash movie. This variable is not absolutely necessary, but is used here as a security precaution so that the database information is not released to the page until it is called. We could preload all of the information from the database before we call it to the Flash movie, but then anyone that looked at process.asp in their browser would be able to see all of the database contents written to the page waiting to be sent to the Flash movie.

2.   OK. Next we need to use an if...then statement. This will compare the mode variable against what is sent from the movie and only allow the code to run if the conditions are right.

```
if mode = "search" then
```

In other words, if the variable called mode = search then our code will run.

3.   Now we will create an instance of our connection object and open the connection to the database using oConn.Open, which is the path to the database, with this code.

```
set oConn = Server.CreateObject("ADODB.Connection")
   oConn.Open "DSN=projects"
```

4.   Remember that our Data Source Name (DSN) is the one we created earlier and is called projects. Next, we need to create an instance of the recordset object using the code below. This object (as we described earlier), will carry our info to the database.

```
set oRs = Server.CreateObject("ADODB.Recordset")
```

5.   Now we have another if...then statement that compares the name of that variable we sent from the Flash movie. This statement says something to the effect of 'If the variable is all or the variable is equal to nothing, meaning that the user submitted an empty textbox, then all the records are returned from the database table search':

```
if strSearch = "all" or strSearch = "" then
    strSql = "Select * From search"
   else
    strSql = "Select * From search where lastname Like '" &
   ➥strSearch & "%'"
   end if
```

The else statement says to Select all the entries from the search table where the last name is Like (thereby making a comparison to) our name variable. The % delimiter is a wildcard character that tells the SQL statement to find similar matches to our name variable.

> **Note: If you are using Microsoft Access 97, the wildcard delimiter is the asterisk character *.**

Next, we open the recordset using oRs.Open, the SQL statement (strSQL), and the database connection (oConn):

```
oRs.Open strSql,oConn
```

Now we have another if...then statement to determine the variable we send back to Flash. If we get to the end of the recordset without finding a match (oRs.EOF, where EOF is an acronym for End Of File), we use:

```
if oRs.EOF then
    Response.Write "results=Sorry, but there was no match" & _
            ➥vbCr & "for your query. Click the back" & _
            ➥vbCr & "button to try again."
```

This is our error message that will appear in the textbox named results.

In all other cases, we must have found values in the database that match the users query, and we write this back using Response.Write "results=". This is a little different in that we will be putting the whole variable to be sent back in two pieces. We'll write out the results to the ASP page using the results variable, equal to the first and last names from the database. Then to break to the next line for the textbox in Flash, we use the command vbCr, which is a Visual Basic command for a carriage return, and we then continue looping through the recordset adding the new results to the results variable. Then we write out the second part of the values that we are sending back to Flash with the second Response.Write statement. The last part of this script block is to close our if statement using end if.

```
else
    Response.Write "results="
do while not oRs.EOF
    results = results & oRs("firstname") & " " & oRs("lastname")
    ➥& vbCr
    oRs.MoveNext
Loop
    Response.Write(results)
end if
```

As a result, If we submit a query, we get something like this:

Results=Brandon Ellis

6. Lastly, we have to close our first if...then statement with another end if and set our connection object and recordset object equal to nothing.

```
end if

Set oRs = nothing
Set oConn = nothing
%>
```

Here is the complete code:

```
<%
option explicit
dim oConn
dim oRs
dim strSql
dim strSearch
dim results
dim mode

mode = request("mode")
strSearch = Request("name")

if mode = "search" then

      set oConn = Server.CreateObject("ADODB.Connection")
      oConn.Open "DSN=projects"

      set oRs = Server.CreateObject("ADODB.Recordset")

      if strSearch = "all" or strSearch = "" then
            strSql = "Select * From search"
      else
            strSql = "Select * From search where lastname Like '"
            ➥& strSearch & "%'"
      end if

      oRs.Open strSql,oConn

      if oRs.EOF then
Response.Write "results=Sorry, but there was no match" & _
            ➥vbCr & "for your query. Click the back" & _
            ➥vbCr & "button to try again."
      else
            Response.Write "results="
      do while not oRs.EOF
            results = results & oRs("firstname") & " " &
```

```
            ➥oRs("lastname") & vbCr
            oRs.MoveNext
      Loop
            Response.Write(results)
      end if

   end if

   Set oRs = nothing
   Set oConn = nothing
   %>
```

7. Save your work and open `process.asp` in an active browser to check for any errors. If everything is right, you should just see a blank screen. If not, look at your error and make the necessary corrections and try again. Once you see a blank page, open `search.html` in an active browser and try it out. If the searchMovie clip plays for a long time and nothing else happens, check your ASP page again for errors. When everything is working properly, try out your new search application. This application can be easily changed to return all kinds of information, or the ASP code could be used to write formatted HTML blocks to the page from the database. Experiment with it. Good Luck!

Login and password

Have you ever wanted to post something on your site that only certain people can see? How about wanting to control exactly who is viewing your web site? This example will show how to build a login and password application for your site. Users will be able to log in to your site, or just the parts that you, as the designer/developer want them to have access to. Users will also be able to register to your site and we will use some ASP/SQL and ActionScript validation, together with some self-written backend ASP security to keep the crackers out. What we will need to do this is a new table in the flash-asp database, Flash, and our text editor of choice. If you're ready, then let's go!

1. First, let's create the new table in the flash-asp database.

2. Open the flash-asp database in Access and double-click on the Create table in Design view option.

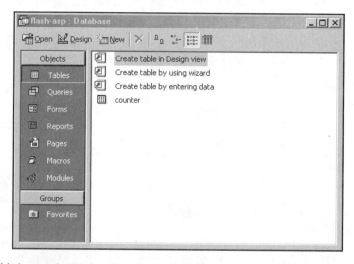

That will bring up the Design view that we will use to add our fields. Our first field will be an identification field (id) that will let us see how many registered users there are, for this field we'll set the Data Type to AutoNumber. The second field is the login name (login) and the third field will be password (set the Data Type for both of these fields to be Text). We'll also put in a date field (with its Data Type set to Date/Time); so that we can see how often people are registering at your site.

3. Click on the id field name, then the key icon in the toolbar to set this as our primary key.

> *A primary key is an index that uniquely identifies the column or columns whose values uniquely identify a row of data in the table.*

You may notice that we are not doing any validation against duplicate entries here, but we will take care of that in the ASP page.

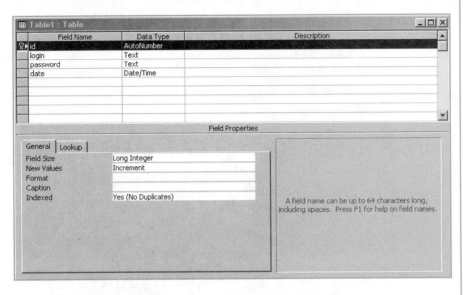

4. Now save the table as login

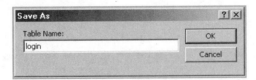

5. Close the Design view and double-click on the login table icon in the flash-asp database window.

Enter a login name into the login field and one in the password field.

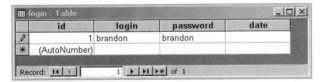

Save and close Access and open up Flash. We are now going to build the interface for logging in.

The Flash interface
1. In a new Flash movie, add 5 layers (for a total of 6). Name them: login, password, buttons, text, register, and actions. Label frame 1 in the actions layer as login.

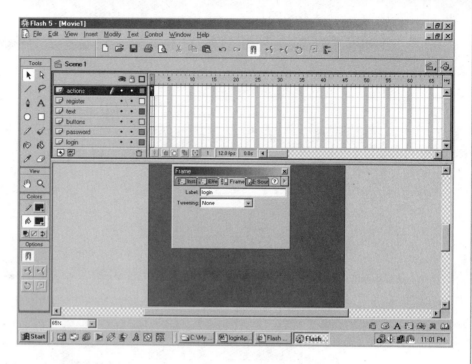

2. Add the following code to the first frame of the actions layer:

```
if (go == "true") {
    gotoAndStop ("welcome");
}
if (go == "false") {
    gotoAndStop ("error");
}
if (duplicate == "true") {
    gotoAndStop ("submit");
}
```

This ActionScript will form the basis of our main loop. It checks the state of two variables, go and duplicate – which will be defined by the ASP, and sends the user to the desired frame.

3. In the login layer, create an input textbox on the stage and give it a variable name login.

4. Now select the password layer and underneath the login textbox create another input textbox. This time give it a variable name of password, and change the type of textbox from Single Line to Password.

This means that instead of displaying the characters that are entered, Flash will display asterisks preventing anybody else from seeing what is being typed.

5. Now would be a good time to save your project. Create a new folder in your projects directory and call it LoginAndPassword. Save your movie as login.fla within this directory.

6. Now we are going to label the two input boxes we just created. Make two static text fields in the text layer above each of the input boxes, and label them appropriately – Login and Password.

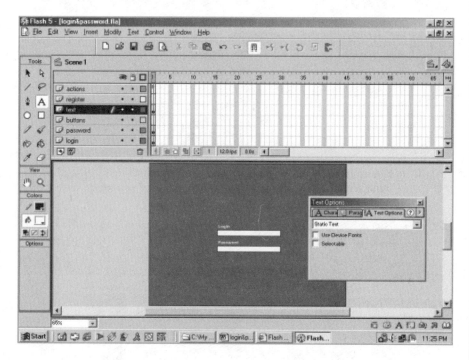

Now let's make a generic button that we can copy to make all of the buttons we'll need here.

7. On the buttons layer, create a button and name it button. Now, bring up your Library, right-click on the button and select Duplicate.

Do not use the copy command to make a copy of the button. It has to be duplicated to have its own properties.

8. Name this button enter, right-click on your new button symbol in the library and select edit. Add the text Enter to a new layer in the button symbol. When you are happy with your button, go back to the main stage, select the original button and then in the Instance panel, use the Swap Symbol button to switch to the enter button. This will place the enter button exactly where you want it. Easy!

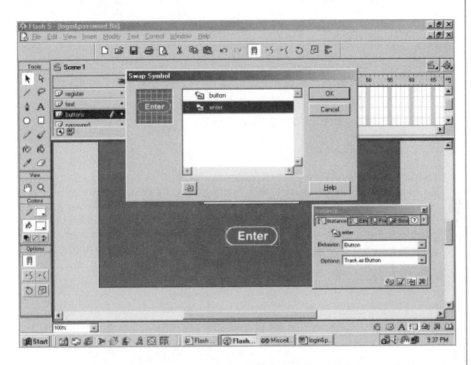

Since we are making buttons, let's make one more for this frame. When all those site visitors come and want to register, they need to know where to go.

9. Underneath the enter button, add some text that reads something like: Need to register? Click here! Make this into a button called register. It's also a good idea to add a filled rectangle over the text in the Hit state of the button, this will make it easier to select. We'll then use this button to take users to the registration screen, which we will make in a bit.

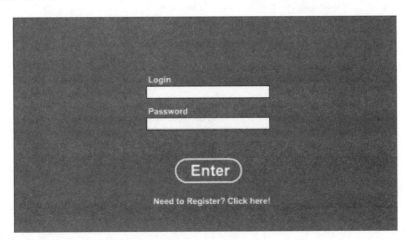

10. Now let's use a little ActionScript. First, select the enter button and add the following code to it:

```
on (release) {
    mode = "login";
    go = "";
    duplicate = "";
    loadVariables ("post.asp", "", "POST");
    login = "";
    password = "";
}
```

What we are doing here is first setting the variable mode equal to login (don't worry, I'll explain that one in a moment). We then set two other variables, go and duplicate, to be blank strings. Next, the script tells Flash to send the variables in the movie to the ASP page to be processed (we will be creating post.asp in the next section). Finally, we are resetting the variables login and password back to nothing. That way, no one else can see the data that was entered.

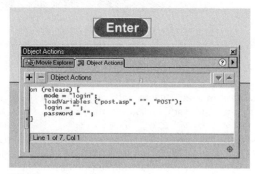

11. Now give the following code to the register button:

```
on (release) {
    gotoAndStop ("submit");
}
```

When a user wants to register, this will take them to the registration (submit) screen, which we'll make shortly.

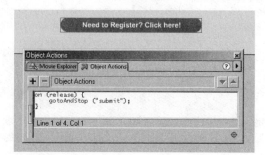

Well that was easy enough. Let's move on to frame 2.

12. In frame 2 of the actions layer, add this code:

```
gotoAndPlay ("login");
```

This code just loops back to frame 1 to carry on checking the state of the go and duplicate variables.

13. Now add another frame to each of the text, buttons, login, and password layers. These frames will not change yet. In fact, this is another good place to save your work, so go ahead and save. Well, that's been pretty easy. A little ActionScripting does a lot of work. So, what's next? On to the third frame...

14. Add a keyframe to frame 3 of the actions layer and label it error. Insert a keyframe in frame 3 of the text layer. First, delete the login and password text from the screen (in frame 3 only). Place a static text error message on the screen that reads:

Sorry, but we were unable to find a matching username and password. Click the back button to try again.

Back button? What back button?

15. Add a keyframe to the buttons layer and open the Library. Make another duplicate (not a copy) of the button symbol and name this one back. Edit the symbol by adding the label back to the button the same way you added the text to the enter button. When you are happy with your work, go back to the main stage, open the Instance panel again and swap the enter button for the back button. Remember to leave the register button alone. This is what you should have:

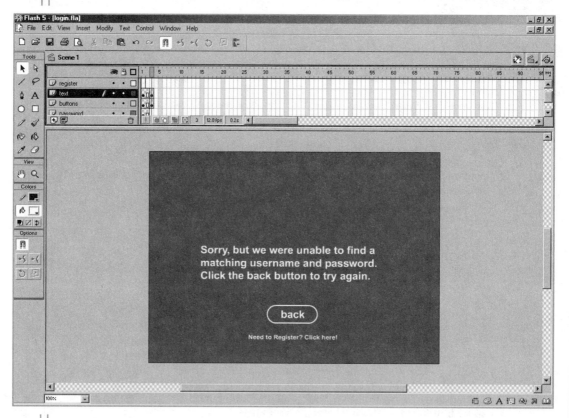

16. Open the actions panel for the new back button and add the following code:

```
on (release) {
    go = "";
    login = "";
    password = "";
    getURL ("javascript:document.reload");
    gotoAndPlay ("login");
}
```

What we are doing here is clearing all of our variables so that the user can go back to the beginning and try again. We are also using this JavaScript function to clear the variables from the user's Internet cache.

Now it's on to the next frame (frame 4).

17. First go to the actions layer, add a keyframe at frame 4 and label it submit. Add a keyframe to the text layer and delete the text that was used on the previous screen. Next is the buttons layer; add a keyframe here too. Let's make one more button. Once more, make a duplicate of the generic button, name it submit, and swap it with the back button as we did earlier. You can delete the register button in this frame. OK, now we have to do something tricky.

18. Add a new keyframe to frame 4 of the login and password layers. Well, that wasn't too tricky, but did you notice that Flash added frames for the input boxes in frame 3? Select frame 3 of the login layer and insert a blank keyframe. Do the same for the password layer. That will take out the input boxes that were added to the third frame. Now back in frame 4, bring up the Text Options panel for the login input box, and change the name to newLogin. Do the same for the password input, by changing the name to newPassword. Now we need to add a message to tell the user if they have chosen a login name that is already taken. Place a dynamic textbox on the stage and give it a variable name dupe. In the actions layer, add the following code:

```
if(duplicate == "true"){
    dupe = "Sorry, but someone already has that login name. Please
    ➡choose another."
}
```

Now, if a user enters a login name that is taken, the ASP page will return true or false to the movie. Until the variable duplicate is true, the text will never be seen. Pretty good! Now is a good time to save your work. This is what you should have:

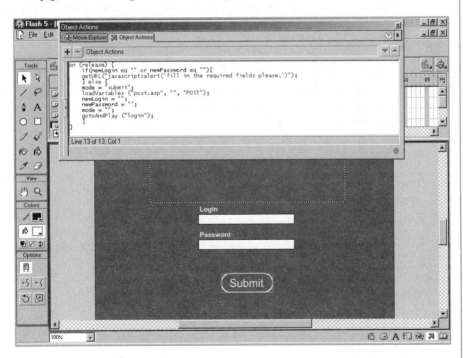

19. You may also want to add the static text labels saying login and password that we had before. The easiest way to do this is to copy them from the first frame, and paste them in place in this one.

20. Bring up the Object Actions window for the submit button and delete the actions from the window. Add the following code to the empty Object Actions window of the submit button:

```
on (release) {
    if (newLogin == undefined || newPassword == undefined) {
      getURL ("javascript:alert('fill in the required fields
      ➥please.')");
    } else {
      mode = "submit";
      go = "";
      duplicate = "";
      loadVariables ("post.asp", "", "POST");
      newLogin = "";
      newPassword = "";
      mode = "";
      gotoAndPlay ("login");
    }
}
```

First we have some ActionScript form validation. Here we check that both fields (newLogin and newPassword), have values. If either field has been left blank, we use the getURL command to alert the user to fill in both fields. Once the fields pass the validation, we go on to submitting the variables. By making mode = submit, we tell the ASP page to only run the code for the submit actions.

We then set all the recent variables equal to nothing as a security measure, so that no one else could come onto the user's computer later, and see the variables that the user had used.

Save your work here and get ready to finish up the .fla file.

21. Label frame 5 of the actions layer welcome. Add a keyframe at frame 5 of the register layer. Add a dynamic textbox to the screen with the variable name return.

22. In frame 5 of the text layer, add a keyframe and get the Text tool ready again. This time we're going to add some static text. Nothing fancy, just our welcome. Add the text: Welcome, to the textbox. Leave the textbox to the left of the return textbox, just like we have it here:

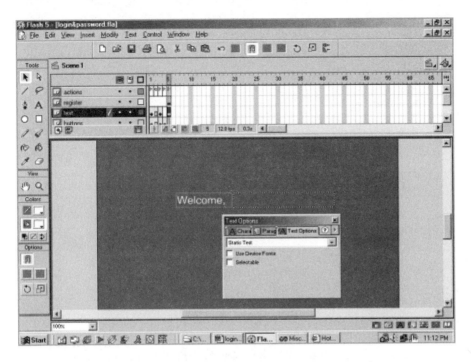

Remember way back in the first frame where we added the code:

```
if go == "true"
    gotoAndStop("welcome")
if go == "false"
    gotoAndStop("error")
```

This is where we finally get to deal with it. If go equals true, then the user is taken to the welcome screen and we will return the login name to the return textbox. Save your work and export the movie to the LoginAndPassword directory on your server. Close Flash and take a breather, go make yourself a coffee, because that's it for the Flash side of this project. Well done!

So, now that you've had a bit of a break, open the text editor of your choice and get ready to write some ASP code!

The ASP script:

Now we need to construct the post.asp file that we referred to in the ActionScript of our Flash movie.

1. To start our ASP code for this section, the first thing we need is our first <% delimiter, which tells the server to process the information between the <% and %> delimiters.

2. Next we declare `option explicit` which helps us to debug our code and will raise any errors when the page is displayed in the browser. Now we declare the variables that are used in the ASP:

```
'here are our variables
dim oConn
dim oRs
dim strSql
dim strLogin
dim strPassword
dim strNewLogin
dim strNewPassword
dim login
dim mode
```

3. Since we've declared our variables, we can give them their values:

```
strNewLogin = Request("newlogin")
strNewPassword = Request("newpassword")
strLogin = Request("login")
strPassword = Request("password")
mode = Request("mode")  'mode will either be login or submit
```

The `Request` variables are what we are sending from Flash to the ASP page. The string (`strNewLogin` etc.) variables will relay the information to the database and back to Flash.

4. Here we create and open the database connection. `oConn` is our connection object used to create the connection:

```
Set oConn = Server.CreateObject("ADODB.Connection")
```

5. Now we open the connection to the database using the DSN that we created earlier:

```
oConn.Open "DSN=projects"
```

6. We do the same thing to create the recordset object.

```
Set oRs = Server.CreateObject("ADODB.Recordset")
```

7. Next, we will be using the modes (`login`, `submit`), to determine what we want the ASP to do for us.

```
if mode = "submit" then
    strSql = "Select * From login Where login='"& strNewLogin &
    ➥"'"
     oRs.Open strSql,oConn,1,3
     if oRs.EOF then
            oRs.AddNew 'add a new record
```

```
            oRs("login") = strNewLogin 'new login name
            oRs("password") = strNewPassword 'new password
            oRs("date") = Date()
            oRs.Update 'update the recordset
            response.Write "duplicate=false"
    else
            response.Write "duplicate=true"
    end if
end if
```

First of all, the if statement that checks to see if the mode is equal to submit. If it is, then we go to the next line to define our SQL statement and open the connection to the recordset. Let's take a closer look at the SQL statement to see what's going on:

```
strSql = "Select * From login Where login='"& strNewLogin & "'"
```

Our base statement is Select * From Login. This will open all the fields in the login table. How does it know to look at all the fields in the login table? The asterisk (*) is a wildcard for SQL statements that means to look at all fields. By adding Where, we are refining our query to only look in the field specified. The one we are specifying is login. OK, what we have so far is the SQL statement:

```
"Select * From login where login"
```

Where login what? Where a value in the login field is equal to strNewLogin.

```
"Select * From login where login='" & strNewLogin & "'"
```

If you are wondering about the quotations and the ampersands, they are helping to append the strNewLogin variable to the SQL statement. The single quotes are holding the new string (strNewLogin), the double quotes are nesting the value of the new string, and the ampersands hold everything together.

Alright, now that we understand what the SQL is doing, let's go down another line to:

```
oRs.Open strSql,oConn,1,3
```

This is a lot easier to explain. First we open our recordset (strSql), open the oConnection object (oConn) and set our recordset cursor types

> *For more information on the different types of cursors available check out "Beginning ASP Databases" written by John Kaufman and published by Wrox Press.*

Now that we have our open Recordset we will use another if statement to guide the actions of ASP.

```
if oRs.EOF then
    oRs.AddNew 'add a new record
    oRs("login") = strNewLogin 'new login name
    oRs("password") = strNewPassword 'new password
    oRs("date") = Date()
    oRs.Update 'update the recordset
    response.Write "duplicate=false"
else
    response.Write "duplicate=true"
end if
```

In this code fragment if oRs.EOF then means that if our SQL query goes through the recordset to the end of the file (EOF), without finding a match to strNewLogin, go to the next line (oRs.AddNew) with which we are going to add a new record to the login table. We are only adding three columns here strNewLogin, strNewPassword, and Date. The field login (oRs("login")) is equal to strNewLogin and the field called password (oRs("password")) is equal to strNewPassword. Once we have inserted these values into the login table, we use the update command (oRs.Update) to add them to the proper fields. Now we use the Response.Write command in ASP to communicate to the movie that the values have been added and that there were no duplicate entries. Way back at if oRs.EOF and if a record had been found before the end of the file, the ASP script would have been instructed to skip the script block about adding the new records and gone to the else part of the if statement. It would then and sent back duplicate=true using Response.Write to tell the movie that a duplicate has been found and to show the duplicate message on the "submit" screen.

Now onto the next if statement:

```
if mode = "login"
    strSql = "Select * From login Where login='"& strLogin & "' "
    ➡& _
     " And password= '" & strPassword & "';"
    oRs.Open strSql,oConn,1,3
            if oRs.EOF then
                    Response.Write ("go=false")
            else
                    Response.Write ("return="&oRs("Login") &
                    ➡"&go=true")
            end if
    end if
```

This is pretty similar to the submit script block since we are looking at our recordset and checking to see if there is a matching login and password record. Here's the same code with a few comments. First, the ASP checks to see if the mode is equal to login:

```
'if the mode is login then
    if mode = "login"
        strSql = "Select * From login Where login='"& strLogin & "'
        ➡" & _
                " And password= '" & strPassword & "';"
```

```
oRs.Open strSql,oConn,1,3
        if oRs.EOF
        'the go variable sent back to the movie is false
        Response.Write ("go=false")
else
        'we found it
        Response.Write ("return="&oRs("Login") & "&go=true")
    end if
end if
```

If so, we move onto the next line. Here we define the SQL statement for the checking of the user's login name and password:

```
strSql = "Select * From login Where login='"& strLogin & "' " &
_
    " And password= '" & strPassword & "';"
```

This is almost the same statement as we use for checking "submits", except that we are also checking the password field as well. Notice that we are still using the quotations and ampersands to build our SQL statement. We open the recordset as before (oRs.open), and use oRs.EOF to cycle through the table searching for a matching login and password. If we do not find the matches, we tell the movie that the login was not valid using Response.Write "go=false". This sets the variable go equal to false and tells the movie to take the user to the error screen. If we do find a matching login and password, we go to the else statement and set the variable go equal to true and the variable return equal to the login name found in the database:

```
Response.Write ("return="&oRs("Login") & "&go=true")
```

This tells the movie to go to the "welcome" screen and display the greeting to the user.

Finally, we close the connection and the recordset, and add the closing delimiter %> to the ASP page:

```
set oRs = nothing
    set oConn = nothing
%>
```

Here is the complete ASP code:

```
<%
    'helps us debug our code
    Option Explicit
      'here are our variables
    dim oConn
    dim oRs
    dim strSql
    dim strLogin
    dim strPassword
    dim strNewLogin
    dim strNewPassword
```

```
dim login
dim mode

'our string variables equal our form variables
strNewLogin = Request("newlogin")
strNewPassword = Request("newpassword")
strLogin = Request("login")
strPassword = Request("password")
mode = Request("mode") 'mode will either be login or submit

'create the database connection
Set oConn = Server.CreateObject("ADODB.Connection")
'open the database
oConn.Open "DSN=projects"

'open the recordset
Set oRs = Server.CreateObject("ADODB.Recordset")

        'if the mode is submit
        if mode = "submit" then
                strSql = "Select * From login Where login='"&
                ➥strNewLogin & "'"
                oRs.Open strSql,oConn,1,3
                if oRs.EOF then
                        oRs.AddNew 'add a new record
                        oRs("login") = strNewLogin 'new login
                        ➥name
                        oRs("password") = strNewPassword 'new
                        ➥password
                        oRs("date") = Date()
                        oRs.Update 'update the recordset
                        response.Write "duplicate=false"
                else
                        response.Write "duplicate=true"
                end if
        end if

        'if the mode is login then
        if mode = "login" then
                strSql = "Select * From login Where login='"&
                ➥strLogin & "' " & _
                                " And password= '" &
                                ➥strPassword & "';"
                oRs.Open strSql,oConn,1,3
                        if oRs.EOF then
                        'the go variable sent back to the movie
                        ➥is false
                        Response.Write ("go=false")
                        else
                                'we found it
```

```
                                    Response.Write
                                    ➡ ("return="&oRs("Login") &
                                    ➡ "&go=true")
                        end if
            end if

        'clean up and close
        set oRs = nothing
        set oConn = nothing
    %>
```

Save your work and test out the ASP page, by opening this page in an active browser. If you added your code with no syntax errors and saved your files to the correct directories, you should be looking at a blank screen. If you are looking at an error message, go back and correct any errors you may have.

All that is left to do now is try it out. Open login.html in your active browser and click the Enter button. You will be taken to the error screen. Now go back and enter the login name and password that you put into the database and try again. If you are not taken to the welcome screen, check post.asp for any errors that may have occurred.

If, however, you were taken to the welcome screen, then congratulations! You now have a functioning login and password application for your website. Good work!

I hope that you have learned from these real world examples. Hopefully you have a broader understanding of server-side programming and what it has to offer you as a web designer or developer. Like I was saying in the beginning, communication and interactivity are the keys to successful websites. Now, a head start on the knowledge you need to hold the user's attention and keep them coming back for more.

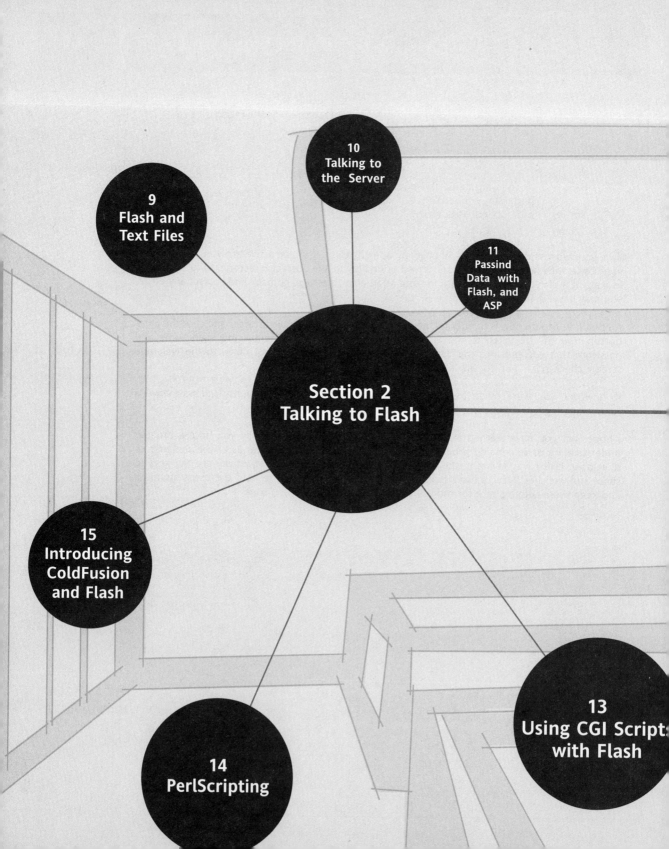

9
Flash and
Text Files

10
Talking to
the Server

11
Passind
Data with
Flash, and
ASP

Section 2
Talking to Flash

15
Introducing
ColdFusion
and Flash

14
PerlScripting

13
Using CGI Scripts
with Flash

Chapter 12
PHP

The main advantage of PHP is that it's an Open Source project. This means that, like Perl, it is available for almost every web server/operating system combination. However, PHP does not suffer from the performance disadvantages of Perl, making it ideal for small, medium and large web sites. The large community of developers using and improving PHP ensures its continuing success as one of the most popular and efficient server-side scripting technologies in existence.

So, what are we going to be discussing in this chapter?

- **What is PHP?** - An outline of the history of PHP, how it came to be, and where to find out more information.

- **Installing PHP** - We'll discuss the merits of some of the PHP installation options available to you.

- **PHP basics** - Here we will cover the basics of the PHP language such as variables, data types, variable functions, operators and statements. We will create a basic PHP skeleton script that we can use later in the chapter to build the rest of our scripts. We will then investigate the basic commands and constructs available to us in PHP.

- **More PHP** - Once the basics are out of the way, we will look at a few of the more advanced capabilities of PHP that are essential for creating functional, efficient, scalable scripts such as arrays, GET and POST methods, and sending email from PHP.

- **Flash integration** - In order to use PHP with Flash we need to know which ActionScript commands exist in Flash to allow us to integrate the two by means of variables.

- **Sample application** - Knowing how to integrate Flash with PHP isn't much use without a practical example to get your teeth into. So, to help illustrate matters, we'll build up a user feedback form using Flash 5 and PHP.

What is PHP?

In 1994, a guy called Rasmus Lerdorf created a bunch of Perl scripts to allow him to see who was looking at his resume. Inevitably, people began to ask where they could get the scripts, so that they could use them on their own sites. So, being a nice chap, Rasmus released them as a package called Personal Home Page tools. This was the first incarnation of PHP.

Around mid 1995, as the Internet became more widely available, Rasmus developed a scripting engine, and added scripts for processing HTML forms, which he called Form Interpreter. This was collectively known as PHP/FI or PHP2. However, this time, PHP stood for: PHP Hypertext Preprocessor ...just to confuse everyone!

People were soon using the tools that Rasmus had made for things he had not even thought about. It was at this point that the development changed from one man, to a whole group of developers who were responsible for the project and its organization. This was the beginning of the third incarnation of PHP, or PHP3, as it's more commonly known. The developers improved the scripting engine, and changed the syntax of the language so that it was more like a cross between C/C++ and Perl, lending itself to Object Oriented Programming techniques. An API

(Application Programming Interface) was also added to allow third party developers to extend PHP by writing their own modules for it. Unfortunately, PHP3 was beginning to show signs of old age. Some of the code had been carried over from the original PHP, and for today's applications, it wasn't as efficient as it could be. So, to rectify this situation, enter...

PHP4, the current incarnation of the PHP scripting engine. It has been completely rewritten from the ground up to provide a much more efficient engine, and to bring about new features that PHP developers had been crying out for. The API was extended and improved, allowing for more efficient interaction between third party modules and PHP, and the OOP capabilities were extended greatly to allow developers to really take advantage of OOP techniques.

To find out more about PHP, have a look at these websites:

www.zend.com - Zend is the scripting engine behind PHP4, and this site is an invaluable resource for any PHP programmer. Here you will find downloads for the PHP scripting engine as well as discussion forums, downloads, tutorials and open source movies to download.

www.php.net - The old home of the PHP scripting engine before version 4. This site is still a useful resource for PHP programmers.

www.phpbuilder.com - Another great site for PHP programmers. This site includes a lively discussion board with experts on hand to answer any problems that you may have with PHP. There are also articles on various PHP related issues as well as open source code to download and learn from.

Installing PHP

In the following section we will be discussing the installation and configuration of the PHP interpreter on a Windows 9x/NT system running IIS and PWS. This follows on from the IIS installation instructions provided in the *Talking to the Server* chapter, and so you need to have followed these instructions before continuing with the rest of this section.

If you are using a third party to host your site, then it is extremely unlikely that you will have to install the PHP interpreter yourself, and as such, you can safely skip the rest of this section.

Also worth noting is that installation instructions for other operating systems and/or servers can be found in the PHP documentation, both at www.php.net and on the CD that came with this book in the /php_chapter/install directory.

Getting the installation files

The first thing we need to do is to get hold of the PHP installation files for Windows 9x/NT. You will find the latest version that was available at the time of writing in the /php_chapter/install directory on the CD that came with this book.

Please note that as PHP is being updated all the time, this is likely not the latest version of the PHP interpreter and was included for convenience. To get hold of the latest Windows installation executable, check out the downloads section of www.php.net.

An alternative version of the installation executable can be found at http://php.weblogs.com. This is an installation package built by John Lim, which includes a lot of the common libraries that are not included with the official installation executable for Windows. However, for the rest of this section we will be concentrating on the official installer provided at www.php.net.

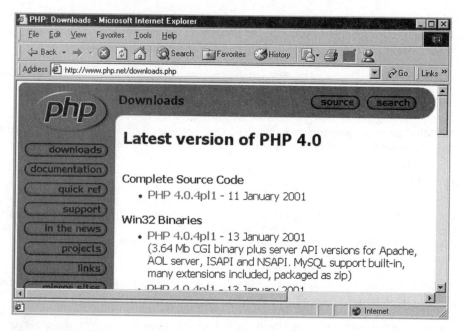

Running the installer

Before installing the PHP interpreter, it is recommended (and in some instances, necessary) to halt your IIS/PWS server to allow the configuration of certain aspects of these programs. Refer to the relevant documentation for more information on this.

Once you've obtained the installer (either from the CD, or from the Web), all you need to do is simply double-click on the executable file. This file will be named in the following manner php *[ver]*-installer.exe, with *[ver]* being replaced by the version number of your distribution.

Once you've done that, you'll be presented with an installation wizard, which will guide you through the installation process. Just select the option(s) appropriate to your situation, hitting the Next button on each screen to progress.

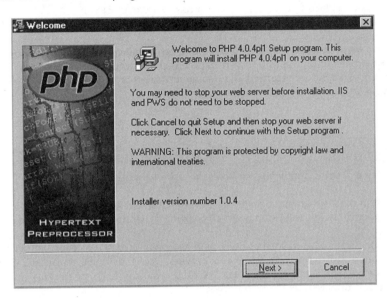

Configuring PHP

Configuring PHP used to be a cumbersome task involving the manual editing of configuration files using a text editor. Thankfully, the Windows binary installer performs much of this configuration for us, meaning that we only need to manually delve into the configuration files if we want to optimize our installation. Such optimization is not covered in this chapter, and should you wish to undertake such a task, refer to the PHP manual for more information.

PHP basics

Since PHP scripts are basically just ASCII text files, you can use any editor that can save plain text files, such as Notepad, Emacs and so on. However, there are some good freeware PHP editors around which offer features such as syntax highlighting, and auto-completion. One of the better ones is PHPEd, written by Soysal. You can install PHPEd from the setup file on the CD, or download the latest version from www.soysal.com/phped.

Now that we know what PHP is, we can start to create our first PHP pages.

Normally, PHP code is embedded within an HTML file to produce dynamic web pages. Since we're only interested in how we can use PHP, we will dispense with the HTML code in the scripts we create.

So, a simple PHP script looks like this:

```php
<?php
  echo("Wow! I really like this PHP stuff!");
?>
```

Let's take this script apart. `<?php` and `?>` are the opening and closing PHP tags (respectively). This tells the PHP processor on the web server that the code between these two tags is PHP code and should be processed before returning the document to the browser. All your scripts will need to contain these tags, with your code between them.

The only PHP statement in the script above is `echo ("Wow! I really like this PHP stuff!");`

The PHP `echo` function takes a string, and outputs it to the client. This can be either a literal string as shown above, a string containing variables, or just a variable itself.

Note that, as in the C programming language, every statement MUST be followed by a semi-colon (`;`). Failure to include this will result in an error being generated by the PHP processor.

Type this code in, and save this file as `test.php` and upload/copy it to your web server. Navigate to the uploaded PHP script with your web browser. You should see an output similar to the screenshot below. This script simply writes "Wow! I really like this PHP stuff!" to the client and this is displayed by the web browser.

> Note: If you're using IIS, you may find that you have trouble displaying the test.php file. If you are, first make sure that you have a copy of the file in your webroot (usually `C:\Inetpub\wwwroot\`) and then try using the URL: http://127.0.0.1/test.php.

To fully understand what happens when a PHP script is executed, let's have a look at the source of the page as the browser sees it. You'll notice that all of the PHP code has disappeared, leaving just the text that we put in the call to the `echo` function.

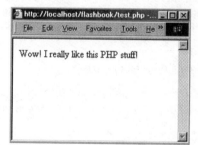
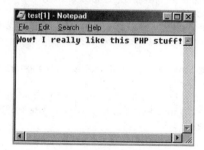

Variables

As with most other languages, PHP allows you to store information in variables. In PHP, much like Perl, a variable name must start with the $ symbol. PHP is a weakly typed language, which means that we do not need to state the type of data a variable will hold before we use it. It also means that we can easily change the type of a variable to suit particular uses.

In other languages such as C/C++ you have to specifically set aside memory for each variable before it can be used. This technique is knows as **declaration**. In PHP, it is not necessary to explicitly declare variables before they are used, as this is done automatically when you first assign values to them – a process known as **initialization**.

An example of a variable being **initialized** and used can be seen below.

```php
<?php
  // Store book title and display it
  $booktitle = "Flash 5 Dynamic Content Studio";
  echo($booktitle);
?>
```

As you've probably guessed already, all this code does is print Flash 5 Dynamic Content Studio in the browser window when we run the script. Let's take a closer look at what's happening here...

Notice the PHP tags at the start and end of the script. As we've already discovered, all lines that appear between these tags are sent to the PHP processor for execution (off with their heads!).

Following the opening tag is a PHP comment. Comments are sections of your script code that are completely ignored by the PHP processor, and they are mainly used to annotate the script to help you, or other programmers to understand what the code is doing, without actually having to read the whole script. Single line comments in PHP can either begin with a double slash (//) or the (#) symbol , as these characters tell the computer that the rest of the line is to be ignored. Multi-line comments can be created by using the /* and */ character sequences.

The next line is an example of variable **initialization**:

```php
$booktitle = "Flash 5 Dynamic Content Studio";
```

This line tells PHP to store the string, Flash 5 Dynamic Content Studio, in a variable called $booktitle. If the variable already exists, then the new string overwrites the value that it contained prior to the execution of this code, and if it doesn't exist, then it is created.

Next we have a call to the echo function, which we've already met. However, instead of being passed the actual string to print (called a string literal), we use the variable name $booktitle to pass the content of the variable to the echo function.

Data types

PHP has three basic data types:

- **Integers** – used to store whole numbers (not fractions) within a range of approximately -2,000,000,000 to +2,000,000,000. For example, 5.

- **Doubles** (also known as float or real numbers) – used to represent numbers that have a decimal value or an exponential part, for example 2.765 or even 2.0.

- **Strings** – used to represent non-numerical values, for instance: "I am a non-numerical value" or even "2".

As we've already discovered, PHP is a weakly typed language. The type of a given variable can be changed by re-assignment, or can be adapted by the way in which it's used. For example, let's look at the following code...

```php
<?php
  $first = "1";
  $second = "2";
  $result = $first + $second;
  echo("The result was: $result");
?>
```

Here, we are initializing two variables $first, and $second with string values. Then, we add the two variables together, store them in a third variable $result, and the echo function then outputs the value of this variable.

In general, the process of adding two strings together is known as **concatenation**, and results in the two strings being joined. With this in mind, it would be perfectly reasonable to assume that the value assigned to the $result variable would be 12 as a result of the concatenation of the two string variables.

However, since + in PHP is a mathematical operator (designed to work with numbers), what actually happens is that the values contained in the string variables are first translated into the appropriate number types, and then mathematically added together. This means that the value in $result is not "12" (as a string), but 3 (an integer). The values and types of the $first and $second variables have not been altered, as they were only translated for the purposes of the addition.

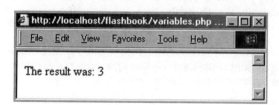

If we actually wanted to link (concatenate) the two strings together, we would have to use PHP's concatenation operator ".". So, if we'd changed the code to:

```
$result = $first . $second;
```

...then $result would have been assigned the string "12" as expected.

Specifying data types

As we've just seen, PHP will automatically translate the data type of a variable for the purposes of a particular operation, whilst leaving the original data type intact. It is possible to override the data type of a particular value using a method known as **type casting**.

```php
<?php
    $a = 7.332;                        // $a is a double
    echo "A is a double. Value: " . $a . "\n";
    $a = (int) $a;                     // $a is an integer (7)
    echo "A is an integer. Value: " . $a . "\n";
    $a = (double) $a;                       // $a is a double (7)
    echo "A is a double. Value: " . $a . "\n";
    $a = (string) $a;                       // $a is a string ("7")
    echo "A is a string. Value: " . $a . "\n";
?>
```

It's worth paying special attention to what happens between lines one and three. Originally $a was of type double and held the value 7.332. Then, we converted it to an integer using type casting, after which it held the value of 7. Then, we converted it back to a double, again using type casting, and it held a value of 7. So, what happened to the extra .332? When the variable was converted from a double to an integer on line two, the fractional part of the number was discarded, because an integer can only hold whole numbers. When we converted it back to a double, the fractional part could not just be put back on again since no record of it was kept.

Variable functions

PHP has a number of useful functions for dealing with variables. Some of them are detailed here:

gettype()

gettype() determines the type of a given variable. It returns one of the following strings:

- "integer"

- "double"

- "string"

- "array"

- "object"

- "class"

- "unknown type"

The first three data types should be familiar to you. We will discuss arrays later in this chapter. Objects and classes are elements of OOP and are beyond the scope of this book. An example of using gettype() is presented below.

```php
<?php
    $input = 15;
    echo "The type of the input variable is: " . gettype($input);
?>
```

settype()

Having already met gettype, it is fairly obvious what the settype function does. It's used as another way of expressly specifying the type of a particular value. Using (with the exception of the last two) the same values as the return values of gettype() you can specify which type a variable should be. settype() is used in the following manner:

```php
<?php
    $age = 7.5;
    echo "Age: " . $age . " Type: " . gettype($age) . "\n";
    settype($age, "integer");
    echo "Age: " . $age . " Type: " . gettype($age) . "\n";
?>
```

isset(), unset() and empty()

The isset() function is used to tell whether a specific variable exists. If the variable has been initialized, the isset() function returns true, otherwise it returns false.

The unset() function is used to destroy a given variable.

The empty() function is the opposite of the isset() function. It returns true if the variable does not exist, or if it has a value of zero or an empty string.

Take the following code for example:

```php
$name = "Steve Webster";
if (isset($name))
{
    echo("Hello $name");
}
```

Because we have initialized $name, we know that the variable exists, so the above script will print: "Hello Steve Webster".

However, if we were to then destroy the variable by using unset() as follows...

```php
$name = "Steve Webster";
unset($name);
if (isset($name))
{
    echo("Hello $name");
}
```

...then nothing will be printed by the echo function because isset will find that the variable does not exist.

is...() functions

These functions are used to determine the type of a given variable. If the variable is of the appropriate type, then the function returns true, otherwise it returns false.

```
is_int()      is used to determine if a given variable is an integer.
is_double()   is used to determine if a given variable is a double.
is_string()   is used to determine if a given variable is a string.
```

Other functions include is_object() and is_array().

Operators

An **operator** is used to determine a value based on an operation on one or more values. A value that is used in an operation is known as an **operand**. Addition is one of the simplest operations. In the expression 5 + 7, 5 and 7 are operands, and the '+' is the operator. In this section we will look at the most commonly used operators:

Arithmetic operators

Operator	Meaning	Example	Result
+	Addition	6 + 2	6 + 2 = 8
–	Subtraction	6 – 2	6 – 2 = 4
/	Division	6 / 2	6 / 2 = 3
*	Multiplication	6 * 2	6 * 2 = 12

Negation operator

The minus sign "–" can also be used with a single operand to negate the number (make a positive number, negative, and a negative number positive).

```php
<?php
    $num1 = 57;          // 57
    $num2 = - $num1;     // -57
    $num3 = - $num2;     // 57
    echo $num1 . " " . $num2 . " " . $num3;
?>
```

Assignment operator

As we've already seen, the assignment operator, "=", is used to assign a particular value to a variable.

Concatenation operator

We've already seen the string concatenation operator earlier in the chapter. It is used to join two or more strings together.

```php
<?php
    $string1 = "Hello";
    $string2 = ", world!";
    $string3 = $string1 . $string2;
    echo $string3;
?>
```

Comparison operators

Operator	Meaning	Example	Evaluates to true if:
==	is equal to	$a == $b	$a is equal to $b
!=	is not equal to	$a != $b	$a is not equal to $b
<	is less than	$a < $b	$a is less than $b
>	is greater than	$a > $b	$a is greater than $b
<=	is less then or equal to	$a <= $b	$a is less than or equal to $b
>=	is greater than or equal to	$a >= $b	$a is greater than or equal to $b

Logical operators

Operator	Meaning	Example	Evaluates to true if:
&&	AND	$a && $b	$a and $b evaluate to true
||	OR	$a || $b	$a or $b evaluate to true
and	AND	$a and $b	$a and $b evaluate to true
or	OR	$a or $b	$a or $b evaluate to true
xor	Exclusive OR	$a xor $b	$a or $b evaluate to true, but not both
!	NOT	! $a	$a evaluates to false

Compound operators

Operator	Example	Equivalent to
++	$a++	$a = $a + 1
- -	$a- -	$a = $a - 1
+=	$a += $b	$a = $a + $b
-=	$a -= $b	$a = $a - $b
/=	$a /= $b	$a = $a / $b
*=	$a *= $a	$a = $a * $b
.=	$a .= $b	$a = $a . $b

Operator precedence

Operator precedence in PHP follows the same rules as real world mathematics (BODMAS). Where two operators have equal precedence, the rules of associative mathematics are used (left-to-right). As with real world mathematics, parentheses (rounded brackets) can be used to force the precedence of a particular expression.

```
$a = 4 + 6 / 2 - 7;        // $a = 4 + (6 / 2) - 7 = 4 + 3 - 7 = 0
$b = (4 + 6) / 2 - 7;      // $b = (10 / 2) - 7 = 5 - 7 = -2
$c = (4 + 6) / (2 - 7);    // $c = 10 / (-5) = -2
```

Statements

A script is basically made up of three basic constructs: **sequence**, **selection** and **iteration**.

- **Sequence** - Do this, then do that.

- **Selection** - Do this, or do that.

- **Iteration** - Do this a number of times.

Sequence is fairly simple, and we've already used it in some of the examples in this chapter. It basically refers to performing a series of statements one after another.

We have met an example of selection already, but it hasn't really been explained. The main selection statement in PHP is the if statement. We'll explore this further in this section.

Iteration is something we haven't covered yet, but by the end of this section you will be an iteration expert!

Selection

There are basically two types of selection statements available in PHP: if and switch. Both of these are explained in detail in this section.

If... statements

The if statement allows the execution of specific lines of code based on a set of conditions. If the condition is true, a specific line of code is executed. An example of an if statement is shown below:

```
if ($name == "Steve Webster");
{
    echo("You are the author of this chapter!");
}
```

Here we see the if statement followed by the condition in parentheses. The most commonly used operators for an if statement are those listed in the *Comparison operators* and *Logical operators* sections above.

The second and fourth lines of code contain opening and closing braces respectively. This signifies the scope of the command to be executed, subject to the conditions listed in the `if` statement.

The third line is just a simple `echo` command to output a string. Note that this line will only be executed if the value held in the `$name` variable is equal to "Steve Webster".

The condition inside the parentheses is interpreted as a **Boolean** value (which can only be either `true` or `false`) and, if it evaluates to `true`, the statement within the braces is executed.

On it's own, the standard `if` statement is a powerful tool for the programmer. There are, however, more complex, and (arguably) more useful forms of the `if` statement.

The `if` statement will also allow you to test for multiple conditions using the logical operators discussed earlier.

```
if ($name == "Steve Webster" && $age == 21)
{
    echo "You are the author of this chapter AND 21!";
}
```

if..else.. statements

This is an extension of the standard `if` statement, and allows you to not only specify what code to execute if a given condition is met, but also to include code to be executed if the condition is not met. An example of an `if..else` statement is shown below:

```
$name = "Steve Webster";
if ($name == "Steve Webster")
{
    echo("You are the author of this chapter!");
}
else
{
    echo("You are not the author of this chapter!");
}
```

The first four lines are simply copied over from the previous example, and should look familiar.

Then you see the `else` keyword. This tells PHP that the next block of code (a block is a group of one or more statements contained within braces) is to be executed if the condition specified in the `if` statement is not met.

Try changing the value of the `$name` variable to see the different outputs.

if..elseif..else.. statements

This variation on the standard `if` statement allows you to specify alternative conditions if the condition in the `if` statement is not met. Again, an example is presented below:

```
if ($name == "Steve Webster")
{
```

```
        echo("You ARE the author of this chapter!");
}
elseif ($age == 21)
{
        echo("You are NOT the author of this chapter, but ARE 21");
}
else
{
        echo("You are NEITHER the author of this chapter NOR 21!");
}
```

If you look at the three echo statements on lines three, seven and eleven, in conjunction with the conditional statements on lines one and five, it should be almost self-explanatory as to how the if..elseif..else.. statement works.

Basically, if the condition in the if statement is not met, then the condition in the elseif statement is evaluated. If this is true then the proceeding block of code is executed. If the condition in the elseif statement is also not met, then the block of code following the else statement is executed.

It is perfectly valid to have many elseif parts to an if statement, but you can only have one else section for every if statement. You can also have an if statement within any of the blocks of another if statement. This is known as **nesting**.

Switch statements
The switch statement is useful for testing a single expression against a number of different values. While this can be done with if statements, it quite often leads to multiple nested if statements, which, at the best of times, are hard to follow.

Consider the nested if statements below:

```
<?php
  $language = "PHP";

  if ($language == "PHP")
  {
      echo("Good choice. PHP is cool!");
  }
  else
  {
      if ($language == "Perl")
      {
          echo("Not bad. You might want to learn PHP though!");
      }
      else
      {
          if ($language == "ASP")
          {
              echo("ASP...Well, it's your choice I suppose!");
          }
```
continues overleaf

```
            else
            {
                echo("You're not using PHP, Perl or ASP!");
            }
        }
    }
?>
```

Note that the style of indentation used here is not mandatory. Should you feel like it, you could enter the whole of the above code on just one line, and it would still work. However, it is a good idea to lay your code out in a manner similar to the above, as it allows easy visualization of nested statements, and the overall structure of your code.

In this fragment of code, we are comparing the value in the $language variable to a series of three string values. With what you've learned about if statements so far you should be able to follow this code without too much of a problem. However, consider what would happen if we had to compare a variable or expression against twenty values... it starts getting complicated.

Enter the almighty switch statement. The following code would perform the same operation as the multiple if statements above.

```
<?php
$language = "PHP";
switch($language)
{
    case "PHP":
        echo("Good choice. PHP is cool!");
        break;

    case "Perl":
        echo("Not bad. You might want to learn PHP though!");
        break;

    case "ASP":
        echo("ASP...Well, it's your choice I suppose!");
        break;

    default:
        echo("You're not using PHP, Perl or ASP!");
        break;
}
?>
```

The variable or expression to be tested is placed between parentheses after the switch keyword. Then for each value that you want to compare the variable/expression against you have a case keyword followed by the value and a colon, ":".

You then list the statements you wish to be executed if the variable/expression matches that particular value, followed by a break keyword. The break keyword stops the execution of the switch statement, and is generally used once you've found a match for the variable being tested.

If the break keyword isn't encountered, then all statements will be executed until the end of the switch statement. This includes those statements that are contained within other case blocks.

The default section of the switch statement is much like the else section of an if statement. If no matching case has been found for the variable/expression given, then the statements in the default section are executed. It is perfectly valid to not include a default section in a switch statement, in which case if no matching case has been found for the variable/expression given, then no statements are executed, and execution passes out of the switch statement and onto the next line of code.

It is worth noting that a switch statement can only test for equality. That is, it can only test to see if the given variable/expression is exactly equal (==) to the values in the case statements. If you tried to test for a range of values in a case statement it would generate an error:

```php
switch($age)
{
    // WRONG! Will not work!
    case <15:
        echo("Good choice. PHP is cool!");
        break;

    // CORRECT! Will work!
    case 21:
        echo("Good choice. PHP is cool!");
        break;
}
```

Also, unlike many other languages, PHP will let you use variables in case conditions. The following is a perfectly valid fragment of code:

```php
$age = 10;
$a = 2;
$b = 7;
$c = 10;

switch($age)
{
    // $age == 2? FALSE
    case $a:
        echo("You can use a computer at 2? Genius!");
        break;

    // $age == 7? FALSE
    case $b:
        echo("7 yrs old and learning to program? Gifted!");
        break;

    // $age == 10? TRUE
    case $c:
```

continues overleaf

```
        echo("You're 10, the same age as me when I started!");
        break;
}
```

Iteration

Iteration (or **looping**) is a means by which we can execute a block of one or more PHP statements, repeating them a specific number of times, or until a condition is met, before moving on to the next line of code. Imagine that we had to output all of the numbers from one to ten. The following code would do this:

```
echo("1\n");
echo("2\n");
echo("3\n");
echo("4\n");
echo("5\n");
echo("6\n");
echo("7\n");
echo("8\n");
echo("9\n");
echo("10\n");
```

However, this isn't very efficient, and typing this out would get really tedious if we had to print all the numbers from one to a hundred. In situations like this, looping is the programmer's best friend. PHP offers 3 different looping statements, just as in Flash 5: while, do..while and for – each of which we'll discuss in turn.

while loops

Let's look at an example of a while loop:

```
$count = 1;

while ($count <= 10)
{
    echo($count . "\n");
    $count++;
}
```

On line one we initialize the $count variable. This should be old hat to you by now, so I won't dwell on this anymore.

Following that, we have the whole while loop. Firstly, we have the while keyword followed by a condition in parentheses while ($count <= 10). We then have the block of code to be executed if the condition evaluates to true. As discussed earlier in the *Operators* section, the ++ operator that is applied to the $count variable in the above example simply adds 1 to the variable. We need to do this in the loop as otherwise the value of $count will never change from that assigned in the first line of this script, and therefore we will be stuck in the while loop forever!

Also worthy of note is that in this situation the $count variable is often referred to as the **loop control variable**.

You may have guessed by now that this loop gives exactly the same output as the ten earlier statements. I think you'll agree that it's much more efficient.

To summarize, when PHP encounters a while loop, the following process happens:

1. The condition between the parentheses is evaluated.

2. If the condition evaluates to true then we execute the block of statements. We then need to test the condition again, so go back to step 1.

3. If the condition evaluates to false, then the loop is broken, and the next statement outside the while loop is executed.

A while loop is known as a "zero or more times" loop because the condition is evaluated before the first iteration of the loop (or at the start).

do..while loops

A do..while loop is really just a variation of the while loop, except that they are known as "one or more times" loops. This is because the condition for the loop is evaluated at the end of an iteration, therefore resulting in the loop always being executed at least once.

An equivalent to the above piece of code implemented with a do..while loop would look something like this:

```php
$count = 1;

do
{
    echo($count . "\n");
    $count++;
}
while ($count <= 10);
```

There are a couple of things to note about a do..while loop. Firstly, you'll see that the while(condition) section has been moved to the bottom of the loop, and, in its place, the do keyword has been inserted. Note that a semi-colon has been appended to the former. This is required, and PHP will show an error if it is omitted.

We can see how the do..while loop differs from the while loop if we examine the order in which operations are performed:

1. The block of statements attached to the loop are executed

2. The condition between the parentheses is evaluated. If it's true, then go back to step 1.

3. If the condition evaluates to false, then the loop is broken, and the next statement outside the do..while loop is executed.

for loops

for loops are generally used when you know how many times a given loop needs to be executed. The syntax of a for loop is slightly more complex than that of the while and do..while loops:

```
for(initialize; condition; control)
{
    statement(s)
}
```

The for loop takes three expressions inside its parentheses, separated by a semi-colon. The first expression, initialize, is used to initialize the loop control variable. The second expression, condition, is used to specify the condition, which if true will continue the loop. The final section, labeled here as control, is used to manipulate the loop control variable. Often this is just a simple increment or decrement expression.

So, now you know what a for loop is, let's take a look at a real one:

```
for($count = 1; $count <= 10; $count++)
{
    echo($count);
}
```

Yes, you've guessed it! This does exactly the same as the two preceding examples. If you look closely at the examples you'll see that all we've done is move all the statements referring to the loop control variable within the for loop. If we look at the steps of what happens when PHP encounters a for loop, however, we can pick out some fundamental differences:

1. The initialise section of the for loop is executed.

2. The condition section of the for loop is evaluated. If true, go to step 3, else go to step 6.

3. The statements within the block attached to the loop are executed.

4. The control section of the for loop is executed.

5. Go back to step 2.

6. If the condition evaluates as false then the loop is broken and the next statement outside the for loop is executed.

Premature exit from PHP script

Sometimes it may be desirable to halt the execution of a PHP script at a certain point in the code. This may be because some information passed to the PHP script via or GET or POST (see the GET & POST methods section) was either missing, or does not have the expected value. On the other hand, it may just be that it is the most elegant way of exiting from your script when you've finished doing what you wanted to do.

For these and similar situations, PHP has provided the exit command. Put simply, if PHP encounters and executes an exit command, script execution is stopped immediately, and any code that remains will be left unexecuted.

An example of the exit command can be seen below:

```
echo("This line is executed");

exit;

echo("This line is never executed");
```

Congratulations! You now know most of the basics of the PHP language. We have learnt about the basic data types, and constructs that are available to you as a PHP programmer, and have laid the foundation for the next section.

More PHP

Arrays

The easiest way to think of an array is as a list of variables all referenced by the same name. In order to access the individual variables (or elements) in an array we use what is known as array **index notation**.

In PHP, the simplest array consists of a series of elements with indices starting from zero, and incrementing sequentially to subsequent elements. Let's look at an example of such an array. Suppose that we wanted to create an array to hold 10 names. The structure might look something like this:

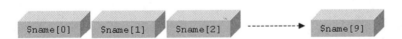

Here we have ten array elements, with each element being represented by a box with the name of the array, and the appropriate element index contained in square brackets. This is how individual elements of an array are referenced in PHP, as well as in Flash.

Creating arrays

Now that we know what an array is, we need to know how to create one. PHP provides a number of different methods for creating an array, and we'll discuss the most common here.

With arrays in PHP, as with variables, you do not need to declare them before you can use them. Instead, an array is created when a value is first assigned to it.

The simplest way of creating an array is to assign values to the array in the following manner:

```
$name[] = "Steve Webster";
$name[] = "Joe Bloggs";
$name[] = "John Doe";
```

This creates an array called $name which has three elements. Since we didn't explicitly state the element indices when assigning the values to the array, they are automatically placed at positions 0, 1, and 2 in the array. The same thing could have been achieved with the following code:

```
$name[0] = "Steve Webster";
$name[1] = "Joe Bloggs";
$name[2] = "John Doe";
```

The difference here is that we're explicitly stating the element indices when assigning the values to the array. Note that in PHP, unlike in C, you can have elements in the array holding different data types. This is because of the weak data type system that PHP has. So the following is perfectly valid (although it probably doesn't make much sense):

```
$name[0] = "Steve Webster";      // A string
$name[1] = 15;                   // An integer
$name[2] = -24.17;               // A double
```

It's good programming practice to assign array elements sequentially (at sequential indices), as this makes looping through an array much easier. However, there are times when we might want to put elements at non-sequential indices. These are known in other languages as **sparse arrays**, and are commonly used in the writing of spreadsheet programs.

```
$name[77] = "John Doe";
$name[0]  = "Steve Webster";
$name[34] = "Joe Bloggs";
```

The above is perfectly valid, but it's worth paying special attention to what happens to subsequent simple array assignments. In this case, the highest array index is 77. Now if we add another element using the simple array assignment method like so:

```
$name[] = "Jane Doe";                    // Assigned to $name[78]
```

The new element is entered into the array at an index one higher than the current highest array index, in this case 78.

Arrays can also be created (initialized) using the array() construct. To use this construct, we simply pass it the values that we want to assign to our new array, and store the returned value in a variable. For example, the following code will create an array identical to the one we first encountered in this section:

```
$name = array("Steve Webster", "Joe Bloggs", "John Doe");
```

So far, we've only created arrays with integers as indices. However, you can also have an element whose index is a string value. For example, we could create the following array:

```
$book["Title"] = "Flash 5 Dynamic Content Studio";
$book["Publisher"] = "friends of ED";
$book["Subject"] = "Web Design";
$book["Rating"] = 10;
```

We could then output the publisher of this book as follows:

```
echo($book["Publisher"]);          // Would print "friends of ED";
```

Looping through a sequential array

So far, you may be thinking that you could do without arrays, and just use individual variables to store the values that you need. However, the real power of an array becomes apparent when we use it in conjunction with looping.

Imagine that your script had to store and print four names to the browser window. Using individual variables this could be accomplished with the following code:

```
$name1 = "Steve Webster";
$name2 = "Joe Bloggs";
$name3 = "John Doe";
$name4 = "Jane Doe";

echo($name1);
echo($name2);
echo($name3);
echo($name4);
```

This may not be too bad for just four names, but imagine what would happen if we had to store and print 100 names...you'd have to have one echo statement for every name that had to be printed. If we use an array in conjunction with a for loop then this task can be made much simpler:

```
$name = array("Steve Webster", "Joe Bloggs", "John Doe", "Jane Doe");

for ($index = 0; $index < count($name); $index++)
{
    echo($name[$index]);
}
```

The first line creates a sequentially indexed array with our four names in it. We then introduce a for loop using a variable called $index as the loop control variable. Probably the most interesting part of this loop is the $index < count($name) section. The count() function returns the number of elements in the array (in this case four), and that value is checked against the value of $index every time we go through the loop.

Note that count() returns the number of elements in the array, not the highest index of the array. If we go back to this example:

```
$name[77] = "John Doe";
$name[0]  = "Steve Webster";
$name[34] = "Joe Bloggs";
```

Then count($name) would return the number of elements in the array (3) and not the highest index of the array (77).

Looping through a non-sequential array

As we've discovered, we need to treat non-sequentially indexed arrays in a special way. A non-sequential array can be one whose integer indices don't form a sequence, or an array whose elements are indexed though a string value (as seen previously). Luckily for us, PHP provides facilities for working with these types of array.

An array, whether sequential or non-sequential, has a built-in pointer. This pointer keeps track of the current array element. When an array is first created, the pointer will point to the first element in an array. We can read the value of this array element by using the current() function, and the element's index with the key() function.

We can illustrate the use of these functions if we return to our previous example:

```
$name[77] = "John Doe";
$name[0]  = "Steve Webster";
$name[34] = "Joe Bloggs";

$currentvalue = current($name);
$currentindex = key($name);

echo("$currentindex: $currentvalue");
```

Because the array has just been created, the pointer is pointing to the first element in the array. So, this code will print 77: John Doe. This may be a little unexpected, but this was the first element in the array (regardless of its index), because it was the first to be assigned to the array.

Note though that neither current() nor key() will change (advance) the internal pointer. For that job we need to enlist the help of the each() and list() functions. An example of a loop that will print out all of the values in our non-sequential $name array would be this:

```
reset($name);
while (list($key, $value) = each($name))
{
    echo("$key: $value<br>\n");
}
```

The reset() function returns the internal array pointer to the first element of the array. We may not need to do this (the array may have just been created) but it's worth using anyway, so that we definitely know where the pointer is!

The each() function is then passed an array. It then returns the key and value of the current element, and moves on to the next array element. When the last element of an array is reached, it returns false. Because this function returns two values, it has to return them as an array, which is where the list() function comes into play.

The list() function basically breaks apart the return value of the each() function (an array), and stores them in two variables ($key and $value).

The \n at the end of the string passed to the echo statement is used to insert a carriage return (or new line) at the end of the output line. This is required because we want each key/value pair on its own line. This is known as an **escape character**. You'll probably recognize <br>...it's the HTML line break tag that causes a new line to be displayed in the browser.

The output would look like this:

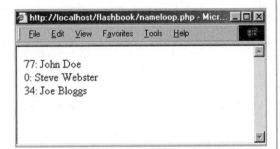

This same loop would work for our string indexed array:

```php
$book["Title"] = "Flash 5 Dynamic Content Studio";
$book["Publisher"] = "friends of ED";
$book["Subject"] = "Web Design";
$book["Rating"] = 10;

reset($book);
while (list($key, $value) = each($book))
{
    echo("$key: $value<br>\n");
}
```

For which the output would look like this:

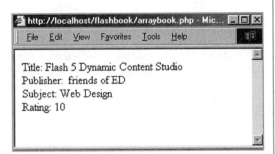

There are many more advanced techniques that you can use with arrays but they are beyond the scope of this book.

GET & POST methods

You should recognize GET and POST as the methods of submitting the contents of an HTML form to some kind of script. Take a look at the following HTML page:

```html
<html>
<form action="process.php" method="POST">
<pre>
Name: <input type="text" name="name">
Age:  <input type="text" name="age">
</pre>
<input type="submit"> <input type="reset">
</form>
</html>
```

With the GET method, the data is passed as an appendage to the URL. This can cause problems if you're trying to pass a large amount of data, as there are limits to the amount of information you can send this way – although that limit is determined by the web browsers involved. The POST method sends the data using input streams, and is the preferred method of passing data to scripts.

This page is a simple form designed to obtain a user's name and age. When we use such a form with a PHP script, in this case process.php, the PHP engine will automatically take the name attribute of each form element, and create a variable by that name. The value of that variable is set to the value attribute of the corresponding form element.

So for example, this is what the HTML code above might look like with the values filled in:

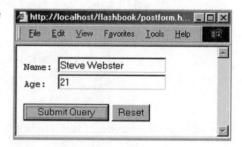

When this form is submitted, we would have two automatically created variables in our PHP script called $name and $age with the values *"Steve Webster"* and *"21"* respectively.

```php
<?php
    echo("Hello $name. Your age is $age!");
?>
```

Using this PHP script with the above form and input would give us the following output:

Hello Steve Webster. Your age is 21!

If PHP's track_vars feature is turned on (via the track_vars configuration item in the PHP.INI file) then variables submitted via the POST or GET methods will also be found in the global associative arrays $HTTP_POST_VARS and $HTTP_GET_VARS as appropriate. With PHP versions v4.0.3 onwards, the track_vars feature is **always** turned on!

So, we could change the previous code to the following:

```php
<?php
    echo("Hello " . $HTTP_POST_VARS["name"] . ". ");
    echo("Your age is " . $HTTP_POST_VARS["age"] . "!");
?>
```

This may seem a bit like a backward step from the previous code, but imagine what would happen if, for some reason, we needed to process all of the variables sent from the HTML form. How would we know which variables were sent? Using these associative arrays (string indexed) we can loop through all the values (using methods we've already covered in the Arrays section) and process them.

Whether you use GET or POST is pretty much down to choice, though there are a few drawbacks if you choose GET:

- You are limited by the browser on how much data can be sent. This is because all data passed using GET is appended to the URL of the processing script. A typical limit for this kind of information is 1024 bytes.

- If the exact same URL appears in the browser's cache, then the browser, thinking it's saving the visitor time, may display the cached output for the script. This could cause problems if you change your script, or your script is designed to give a different output each time.

The POST method overcomes both of these drawbacks, so it may be **preferable** to keep all your form posting methods to POST.

Sending email from PHP

This is probably one of the most useful aspects of PHP. The power to send emails from PHP is all wrapped up in one function, mail(). This function depends upon the local mail delivery system (on the server), which should be available, but it is possible on certain servers for this method to be disabled. This can by verified by running the following script and looking for the `mail` entry on the output.

```php
<?php
  phpinfo();
?>
```

The syntax of the `mail()` function is this:

```
mail (to_address(es), email_subject, message_body[,
extra_headers]);
```

to_address	Email address for the recipient of the email. If more than one recipient is required, then they must be separated by a comma.
email_subject	The subject of the email.
message_body	The main body of the email.
extra_headers	This is optional. Here you can supply any additional email headers you wish to include. An example might be: `"From: you@your.com"`

The following example will send an email to a single recipient:

```
mail("me@myaddress", "This is the subject", "This is the message");
```

Obviously, that is a very simple email, but you can also send multi-line messages with the `mail()` function:

```
mail("me@myaddress, you@youraddress", "Feedback",
"Hello,

Thank you for your interest in our company. We are a small
business specialising in web development using Macromedia Flash
technology.

For more information visit our web site at http://www.anything.com
or telephone 04512 1232453.

Regards,

Joe Bloggs
CEO Anything.com", "From: Joe@anything.com");
```

You'll notice here that we've used the `extra_headers` portion of the `mail()` function to set the `From:` address for the email. We're also sending the mail out to two email addresses.

Although not used here, the `mail()` function returns `true` or `false` depending on whether it was possible to send the email using the local mail system. There are more advanced ways of sending email from PHP, but they are beyond the scope of this book.

Flash integration

Now that we know what PHP is, and how to use it, we need to look at the methods we can use to integrate it into our Flash movies. First we'll review how to load variables into your Flash movies from a text file, before discussing how to send and receive variables from our PHP scripts.

Loading variables from a text file

Recall from the *Flash and Text Files* chapter that it's possible to load variables into your Flash movie from a simple text file using the loadVariables ActionScript action. Let's just take a little time to review the technique here.

The syntax for the loadVariables action looks like this:

```
loadVariables (url, location [, variables])
```

url
:   This is the URL of the text file or script where the variables are located. It can be specified relative to the HTML/SWF file, or as an absolute path.
    Note: The host for the URL must be in the same subdomain as the movie when accessed using a web browser. Basically, this means that your movie, and the text file (or script) must be hosted in the same domain in order for the loadVariables action to work. This is a security feature built into Flash, and more information can be found at:
    www.macromedia.com/support/flash/technotes/

location
:   A level, or target within your Flash movie to receive the variables.

variables
:   This is an optional argument that allows you to send variables from your Flash movie to a server-side script for processing in addition to loading the variables output from the script.

The text at the specified URL must be URL encoded (or to give it its proper name application/x-www-urlformencoded). As mentioned before, the text file or script must be on the same domain as the movie, or the loadVariables action will not work. You can load as many variables as you like from the URL, but they must be in the following format:

```
&var1name=var1value&var2name=var2value&var3name=var3value
```

The variables are split into name/value pairs, with each pair separated by an ampersand (&). So, for example, if we were to load variables holding information on this book into a Flash movie, the text file variables.txt would look like this:

```
&Title=Flash 5 Dynamic Content Studio&Publisher=friends of ED
Subject=Web Design&Rating=10
```

So, in Flash we would need a button that will load these variables when clicked. The ActionScript for such a button would look something like:

```
on (release) {
   loadVariables ("variables.txt", "");
}
```

In this instance, we're loading the variables from the file called `variables.txt` into the current timeline or movie clip.

One important thing to remember about the `loadVariables` action is that it doesn't wait until the variables have been loaded before the script carries on. When the `loadVariables` action is executed, an HTTP GET request is issued. This is basically just asking the server "Can I please have this file?", but it can take a while for the server to respond, so your variables may not appear instantly.

Once the server has fetched the requested file, your variables will be available in your Flash movie. We can then use these variables as we would any other ActionScript variables. In the above example we were loading variables that contained information about this book. If we had some dynamic text boxes on the stage named `Title`, `Publisher`, `Subject`, and `Rating`, then the loaded values would then appear in these text boxes.

loadVariables and PHP

From the point of view of your Flash movie, it doesn't know whether it's loading its variables from a text file, or from a server-side script like PHP. This is because the script is processed on the server before it is passed to the Flash movie. All we need to do is to format the output of our PHP scripts to be the same as that of a text file containing variables.

Taking the previous example, we could ask our PHP script to output exactly the same information as is contained in the `variables.txt` text file:

```php
<?php
$book["Title"] = "Flash 5 Dynamic Content Studio";
$book["Publisher"] = "friends of ED";
$book["Subject"] = "Web Design";
$book["Rating"] = 10;

reset($book);
while (list($key, $value) = each($book))
{
    $value = urlencode($value);
    echo("&$key=$value");
}
?>
```

This is the same script as we constructed in the *Arrays* section, except for that fact that we've adapted the output to fit in line with the required format. The `urlencode()` function performs URL encoding on the string.

If we ran the script directly, the output would look like this:

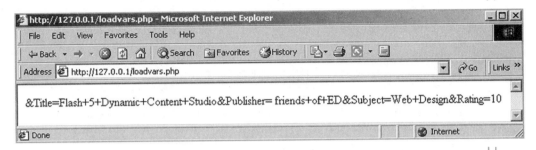

So we can now use PHP scripts to load variables into a Flash movie. This on its own is useful but the real power comes when we look at how we can take variables from a Flash movie and pass them to the PHP script so that they can be used to give a desired output.

Passing variables between Flash and PHP

Let's take another look at the Flash loadVariables action:

```
loadVariables (url, location[, variables])
```

Using the loadVariables action we can send variables using either the GET or the POST methods, just as you can with an HTML form. If we set the variables argument to either GET or POST, the loadVariables action will send all variables that exist on the timeline, identified by the location argument, to the script specified by the url argument. It will then perform its normal duties of fetching the output of the script back into the Flash movie as variables.

Given that we know that all variables passed to a PHP script using GET or POST are automatically converted into PHP variables, we can use the information passed from the Flash movie in our scripts.

Have a look at this Flash movie:

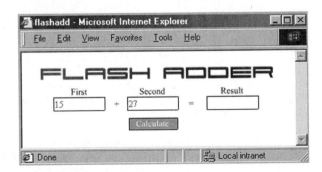

It's just a simple movie that contains three dynamic text boxes (which are given the variable names First, Second and Result), and a button. We will use it to call a PHP script, pass our variables to it, let PHP perform the calculation, receive the result from the PHP script, and display it in our movie.

Let's look at what the ActionScript might look like for the Calculate button

```
on (release) {
    loadVariables ("flashadd.php", "", "POST");
}
```

Here we can see that we're loading variables from the flashadd.php script, but we're also sending variables to the script that is. the values entered in the two text boxes.

If we now look at the flashadd.php script, we can see how this all ties together:

```
<?php
$Result = $First + $Second;
echo("&Result=$Result");
?>
```

So, the script just takes the $First and $Second variables passed from the Flash movie, calculates their sum, and then outputs the result in a format that can be loaded back into our Flash movie. Because we've got a text box called Result on the timeline already, the result will automatically be displayed here:

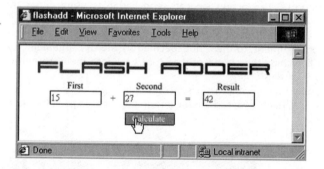

Sample application

In this section, we'll build up a web site feedback application to gather comments/suggestions from our visitors, and send them (via email), to a designated address. The application will consist of two parts: a PHP script, and a Flash movie.

Although we'll be building this application up piece by piece in this section, you can find the completed FLA and PHP script on the CD that came with this book. You may find it beneficial to walk through the whole of this tutorial with these items open on your computer, before attempting to construct your own from scratch.

The Flash movie

We're going to split the movie up into four basic sections, as seen on the timeline below:

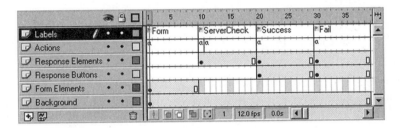

We'll dissect and discuss each of these four sections (Form, ServerCheck, Success, and Fail) in just a minute. For now, create and label the frames and layers as best you can, and we'll talk about adding the finishing touches to each layer as we walk through discussing each section. Copy any resources you need to build the example from the `flashmailer.fla` file (on the CD).

Form

This is the feedback entry screen. The dynamic text fields here are given the variable names *name*, *email*, *subject*, and *comments* from top to bottom. Although you can add as many items to this feedback form as you like, it's important that these names are all entered in lowercase letters.

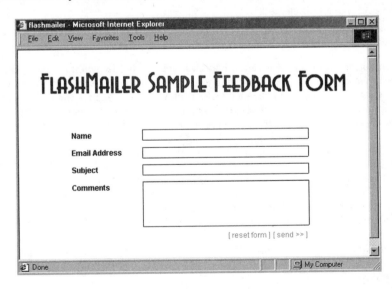

Remember, PHP is case-sensitive and will treat *name* and *Name* as completely different entities!

The reset form and send >> items are actually text buttons that will take on similar roles to the Reset and Submit buttons of an HTML form. The ActionScript for the reset form button is as follows:

```
on (release) {
    name = "";
    email = "";
    subject = "";
    comments = "";
}
```

Essentially, all that this code does is clear each of the form elements that we have on the main stage. If you add more form elements to the feedback form then you should add them to this button code so that they also get cleared when the reset form button is pressed.

Here's the ActionScript for the send>> button:

```
on (release) {
    result = "";
    loadVariables ("flashmailer.php", "", "POST");
    gotoAndPlay ("ServerCheck");
}
```

The code for the send button is the most important part of the whole movie, as this is where the PHP script will be invoked.

First, the `result` variable is cleared:

```
result = "";
```

This is an important step, as we'll rely on this variable to tell us whether the email was sent successfully. If we didn't clear this variable, and our feedback form was used twice by the same visitor on the same visit, we could have a bit of a problem. You see, once the visitor had sent one successful email, the movie would report that any subsequent emails were also sent successfully, even if they weren't. Clearing this variable here avoids this problem.

Next, the `flashmailer.php` script is invoked by the `loadVariables` action:

```
loadVariables ("flashmailer.php", "", "POST");
```

You can see by the makeup of the action here that we're sending all variables from the current timeline (denoted by the second parameter) to the script using the POST method.

Lastly, we tell Flash to go to the frame labeled `ServerCheck`, and then continue playing:

```
gotoAndPlay ("ServerCheck");
```

This is where we'll check that the email has been sent successfully.

ServerCheck

We use the ServerCheck section to verify whether the PHP script has completed its operation, and if so, whether or not the operation was successful. This section consists of a two-frame loop to check the value of the result variable, and then go to the appropriate frame according to its value.

Take a look at the ActionScript for frame 10 of the Actions layer:

```
if (result == "okay") {
    gotoAndPlay  ("Success");
} else if (result == "fail") {
    gotoAndPlay ("Fail");
}
```

In this part, we compare the result variable against the possible return values of the PHP script. Because we cleared the value of result before we invoked the PHP script, we know that if this variable holds a value, then the PHP script has finished its work.

If the script succeeded in sending the email, then result == "okay" will be true, our movie will go to the Success frame, and then continue playing.

If the script has failed for some reason, then result == "fail" will be true, our movie will go to the Fail frame, and will again, continue playing.

Here's the ActionScript for the following frame, frame 11:

```
gotoAndPlay("ServerCheck");
```

If the result variable didn't match either of the values in the previous frame, then the movie will move on to this frame. As this means that the result variable hasn't been sent from the PHP script yet, we know that the script is still doing its business. Therefore, we'll want to keep returning to the previous frame (labeled ServerCheck) until a value has been returned.

There is a visual element to this section that informs the user that the email is being sent, and asks them to wait. Screenshots are not shown here for reasons of space, so your best bet is to refer to the FLA included on the CD with this book.

Success

The only thing the Success section has to do in terms of ActionScripting is to stop the movie from going any further, so that we don't run on to the Fail section. There is also a [<< back button to take the visitor back to the Form section. This has the following ActionScript assigned to it:

```
on (release) {
    result= "";
    gotoAndPlay("Form");
}
```

Other than that, this is a purely visual frame to let the visitor know that everything was sent okay. You should probably include a thank you message, indicate whether they will receive a response back from you, and if so, how long this is likely to take... visitors like to know this!

Fail

We use the Fail section to tell the user that something has gone wrong during the sending process, for example:

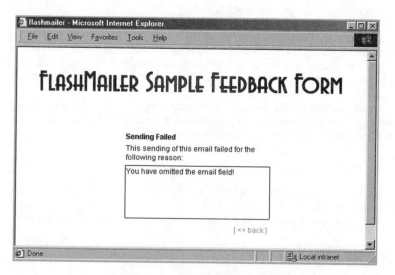

The main element of the Fail section is the multiline text box that'll hold the error message returned from the PHP script. Since this error message is returned in the errormessage variable (as you'll see later), we can have Flash automatically insert the error message in this text box by giving it the same name.

The only ActionScript assigned to this frame (frame 30) is a `stop` action, which is used to prevent the movie from carrying on.

As with the `Success` section, there is also a << back button to take the visitor back to the Form section. The code for this button is exactly the same as the other one, so we won't list it here.

The PHP script

In this section we'll build the PHP script up in stages. You can find a complete code listing at the end of this section, as well as on the CD.

The beginning

```
<?PHP
```

All we've got here is the opening PHP tag that is required in all your scripts...it's an easy part to forget though!

The variables

In this part, we initialize the variable to hold the email address of the recipient of the feedback emails:

```
$Recipient = "you@yourdomain.com";
```

It's perfectly valid to include multiple email addresses in here, the only stipulation being that they must be separated by a comma.

Next, we create an array to hold the names of all the fields that must be filled out before the email will be sent:

```
$Required = array ("name", "email", "subject", "comments");
```

This will stop visitors sending blank feedback forms, or those with essential items not filled out. Here we've listed all the form elements present in our Flash movie, but you can change this as you see fit.

> *Note that the letter case of the form element names must exactly match that entered in your Flash movie.*

Since ALL variables are sent from the active timeline in Flash, we may want to exclude some of them from our feedback email. These may be any control variables that we've used, or indeed, returned variables, from previous executions of this script by the same user on the same visit. For example, if the user tried to send the form with any of the form elements in the $Required array left blank, then we wouldn't want to include the previous errormessage or result variables in the email that will be sent. Thus, we add them to the $Ignore array so that they can be excluded later (the junk variable will be explained later).

```
$Ignored = array ("result","errormessage","junk");
```

Checking the data

Now that we've defined which items should either be required or ignored, we can check the data for these items, and act accordingly.

In this next part we loop through each element in the $Required array, and check to see if it appears in either the $HTTP_POST_VARS or $HTTP_GET_VARS arrays using the empty function (all of which were covered in the earlier *Arrays* section in this chapter).

```
while (list($Key, $Value) = each($Required))
{
    if ((empty($HTTP_POST_VARS[$Value])) &&
        (empty($HTTP_GET_VARS[$Value])))
```

If the element is not found in either of these arrays, then an error message is reported back to Flash. The result variable is set to false to ensure that the Flash movie knows that an error occurred, and the errormessage variable is set to the appropriate error message.

```
    {

        $ErrorMsg = urlencode("The $Value field is required!");
        print "&result=fail&errormessage=" . $ErrorMsg . "&junk=1";

        exit;
    }
}
```

The junk variable is appended to the returned values because some free web space providers add their own code (usually to display banners) to the end off all server-side script output. This is fine if the output is going to be processed as HTML by a web browser, but is undesirable when we're using it for Flash (and can even cause errors). The junk variable is never actually used in our Flash movie, but is added for this purpose.

Next we unset each element of $HTTP_POST_VARS and $HTTP_GET_VARS that appears as in the $Ignored array. This is done so that they're not sent in the email message that will be constructed in the next section.

```
while (list($Key, $Value) = each($Ignored))
{
  unset($HTTP_POST_VARS[$Value]);
  unset($HTTP_GET_VARS[$Value]);
}
```

Building the email

We now need to build up the main body of the email message. We're going to add a small message to the beginning of the email to inform the recipient that this is a feedback email. You can add as much as you like here, but for now, let's keep it nice and simple:

```
$MailMsg = "Hello. The following info has been submitted\n\n";
```

Next we need to process all information that was passed to the script using the GET method. First of all we reset the $HTTP_GET_VARS array, just in case we've been playing with it before (which we haven't, but it's always best to be safe). Then we loop through the array using the list and each functions, and append each key/value pair to the message body using the compound concatenation operator, .=.

```
reset($HTTP_GET_VARS);

while (list($Key, $Value) = each($HTTP_GET_VARS))
{
    $MailMsg .= $Key . ": " . $Value . "\n";
}
```

We now do exactly the same operation, but this time on the $HTTP_GET_VARS array, in order to process all information that was passed to the script using the POST method.

```
reset($HTTP_POST_VARS);

while (list($Key, $Value) = each($HTTP_POST_VARS))
{
    $MailMsg .= $Key . ": " . $Value . "\n";
}
```

By processing both GET and POST information, we ensure that the information is sent regardless of which method was used.

Sending the email

Sending email with PHP is, as we've discovered, about as simple as it gets.

```
$success = mail($Recipient, "Visitor Feedback", $MailMsg);
```

Using the mail function, we send the email to the address designated in the $Recipient variable. We set the subject of the email to something appropriate, and use the message we've just built-up in our $MailMsg variable as the body of the email.

Since the `mail` function returns `true` or `false` depending on whether it was possible to send the email using the local mail system, we can store this in a variable, called `$success`, and use it later to report back to Flash on the success of the operation.

Reporting back

The final thing we need to do is to tell Flash whether the operation was a success or not. Here we check the value returned by the `mail` function, and either output the success message if it's `true`, or an error message if it's `false`. All output is in the format required by Flash, so that the values are available as variables within the Flash movie. Again, the `junk` variable is appended to ensure the integrity of the output.

```php
if($success == true)
{
    print "&result=okay&junk=1";
}
else
{

    $ErrorMsg = urlencode("The mail() function failed.");
    print "&result=fail&errormessage=" . $ErrorMsg . "&junk=1";
}
```

Lastly, we add the closing PHP tag to signify the end of our script.

```php
?>
```

Save the file, and call it `flashmailer.php`.

The whole script

The script we've just built up is presented here in full for your convenience:

```php
<?PHP

$Recipient = "you@yourdomain.com";

$Required = array ("name", "email", "subject", "comments");

$Ignored = array ("result","errormessage","junk");

    while (list($Key, $Value) = each($Required))
    {

    if ((empty($HTTP_POST_VARS[$Value])) &&
        (empty($HTTP_GET_VARS[$Value])))
    {

        $ErrorMsg = urlencode("The $Value field is required!");
```

```php
                print "&result=fail&errormessage=" . $ErrorMsg . "&junk=1";

                exit;
        }
}

    while (list($Key, $Value) = each($Ignored))
    {
            unset($HTTP_POST_VARS[$Value]);
            unset($HTTP_GET_VARS[$Value]);
}

    $MailMsg = "Hello. The following info has been submitted\n\n";

reset($HTTP_GET_VARS);

while (list($Key, $Value) = each($HTTP_GET_VARS))
{

    $MailMsg .= $Key . ": " . $Value . "\n";
}

    reset($HTTP_POST_VARS);

while (list($Key, $Value) = each($HTTP_POST_VARS))
{

    $MailMsg .= $Key . ": " . $Value . "\n";
}

$success = mail($Recipient, "Visitor Feedback", $MailMsg);

if($success == true)
{

    print "&result=okay&junk=1";
}
else
{

    $ErrorMsg = urlencode("The mail() function failed.");
    print "&result=fail&errormessage=" . $ErrorMsg . "&junk=1";
}

    ?>
```

Summary

So, let's just look at what we've done in this chapter. Well, we've discussed what the PHP language is, and how it compares to other server-side scripting languages. We've covered all the main aspects of the PHP language to such an extent that you should now be able to write your own basic PHP scripts. We've also looked at the ActionScript commands available within Flash, and the techniques necessary to integrate PHP and Flash movies.

To conclude, we created a user feedback system for a web site using just PHP and Flash. This is just a basic user feedback system, and there is a lot of potential to add features to it if you feel you want to. Here are some of the things that are really missing, which you should be able to implement after reading this chapter:

- **A timeout facility** – this could be used to give the user an error message if no response is received from the PHP script within a given amount of time. This would have to be implemented purely in Flash, but would definitely be a useful addition to this project.

- **Autoresponder** – it would be nice if, in addition to sending all the information submitted by the user to the webmaster, you could also send an email to the user thanking them for taking the time to fill out the form.

Further reading

If this chapter has given you a thirst for PHP, then there's no real substitute for a good book on the subject. Here are a couple of good ones:

Beginning PHP4, published by Wrox Press, ISBN 1-861003-73-0
Authors: Wrox author team.

Professional PHP Programming, published by Wrox Press, ISBN: 1-861002-96-3
Authors: Jesus Castegnetto et al.

11
Passing Data
with Flash
and ASP

10
Talking to
the Server

12
PHP

Section 2
Talking to Flash

9
Flash and
Text Files

14
Perl Scripting

15
Introducing
ColdFusion
and Flash

Chapter 13
Using CGI Scripts with Flash

In this chapter we're going to look at one of the most common ways of using server-side scripts – the **CGI** (**Common Gateway Interface**) format. You've probably heard of CGI scripts; there are plenty of them about on the Internet, and you may well have wondered what they really are. Well, in this chapter you'll find out.

A word of warning before we begin

Everything so far in this book (and everything after this chapter and the next, for that matter) has been geared towards testing on your local Windows machine. Perl and CGI are where things become, well, a little more open source. Although you can do many of the things we'll talk about here on Windows, (setting up Perl to run on your machine, and running programs from the console, as we'll do in the next chapter), using a Unix based server is the better option at the moment, because there can be some incompatibility issues between IIS and the current version of Perl. So we'll be looking not only at Perl and CGI, but also uploading scripts to a remote host, working with an Apache server, and so on. If you have access to a remote site, then you'd be well advised to get ready to start using that here.

If you're absolutely Windows centric, then you can download and install Apache, which we'll cover here too. Be warned, though, configuration can get a bit complex, and isn't for those with a nervous disposition. Think carefully about the approach that suits you before you begin, and how much of this coverage you need. That said: welcome! I hope you learn what you came here to learn. We'll discuss:

- What CGI actually is

- Uploading your scripts to a remote server: Linux and Windows

- Perl CGI scripting essentials

- Sending email from Flash using CGI

- Creating an online straw poll with Flash and Perl CGI

Be prepared for a great journey!

Overview of CGI

CGI, like the other scripting languages that you've already been using, makes dynamic communication with the users possible by updating your Flash on the fly.

There are a lot of designers out there who feel that CGI scripting is 'over their heads'; but it's totally untrue! There are many online help resources, and I really recommend that you have a look at some of them – if you don't take advantage of the community, not to mention the capabilities of your web server, then you may be coming up short. Where CGI really gives you some extra help is through the massive CGI community on the net; all sorts of sites that will give you all the scripts that you could wish for, absolutely free. Some of them will even help you learn Perl as well:

Hot Scripts	http://www.hotscripts.com
CGI Resources	http://www.cgi-resources.com

Matt's Script Archive http://www.worldwidemart.com/scripts

Talk about speeding up development time!

All you need to know to use CGI scripts effectively is the essentially basic skills of downloading the scripts from web sites, uploading correctly, and setting them up. Once you can do that, you're well on your way to creating visually appealing and functional web sites, and in turn, satisfying your clients' ever growing needs. Flash is growing at such an enormous rate that it won't be long before you start seeing e-commerce web sites created entirely with the application.

What is CGI?

CGI is a specification that allows web programmers to develop programs that can be executed on the web server, in order to generate web content on the fly. It isn't a programming language itself – it's actually an interface that allows programs or scripts to be run over the Internet, expanding functionality of web sites over and above what either HTML or Flash can provide to developers. You can write CGI scripts in a lot of programming languages, but here we're going to be using Perl. A majority of users won't know (or want to) a lot about CGI, so quite a few scripts are available for you to download from web sites.

To use a CGI script with Flash, you simply use the `loadVariables` or the `getURL` actions inside the Flash file, to send the information to the script on the web server. We'll be using this approach in some worked examples later – so you see, you've already got the skills you need to get CGI scripts working with your Flash movies.

What's CGI programmed in?

Perl (**P**ractical **E**xtraction and **R**eporting **L**anguage) is the most common choice for programming a CGI script. One very good reason for choosing Perl is its powerful text manipulation capabilities, in particular the 'regular' expression which can test a string to see if it matches a pattern, replace or substitute some string pattern inside a text string, and extract substring based on certain text pattern.

In very simple terms, Perl was originally developed to deal with, format, and manipulate multiple text fields. It's also used to write CGI scripts, and by Unix and Linux system administrators to perform various tasks such as maintaining web site statistics. Some of the most advanced web site statistic software is written in Perl. Other languages used to write CGI Scripts are (in descending order of popularity) C/C++, Visual Basic, AppleScript, UNIX Shell, and Tcl.

So let's go on to see how we can implement CGI scripts and Flash together to create some interesting and fun web pages!!

Hang on: what's all this I've been hearing about security?

Ah yes, that thorny question of security. Because CGI scripts allow web site visitors to interact with the web server, there is a risk involved unless the script you're using is 100% secure. To handle this situation, you must make sure that your scripts meet all of the security regulations, so that they don't crash the system itself by allowing in unwanted visitors.

The principle security issues with CGI are:

- Potentially they can, intentionally or unintentionally, leak information about the site host system. This makes it possible for hackers to break into the server, if they were actively looking for it.

- When a remote user input script does a form or searching feature, the server may be vulnerable to attacks, because it can be tricked into executing commands.

Sometimes a CGI script still has enough privileges to mail out the system password file, or examine network information maps (if they were looking for it). Even if your Unix server runs in a chroot directory (a directory that is locked and only accessible to the user who owns it), the general form of a command from the prompt is still:

```
chroot directory command
```

Where *directory* is the new root directory and *command* is the command to run under that directory. Here's an example that could be run from a prompt:

```
chroot /www httpd
```

This would make /www the new directory, and anything not under /www will not be accessible. A buggy CGI script can leak sufficient system information to compromise the host.

The best way to prevent any problems occurring with your server is to make sure that all scripts are downloaded from reputable web sites, such as the ones listed above. You can get hold of some good information here: http://www.w3.org/Security/Faq/wwwsf1.html#Q5

What do I need to write CGI scripts?

All you need to create CGI scripts is Perl installed on the server, somewhere to execute them, and something to edit the file with. Since Perl scripts are simply plain ASCII text files, an application as basic as Notepad is fine for making the changes you need to the script.

If you know how to telnet to the Unix web server, you can use a command called whereis to find out the paths to your Perl and sendmail installations. Telnet is a telecommunications program included with Windows that allows you to connect to a remote location computer, and unlike an FTP program won't allow you to transfer files from one computer to another. Type in whereis perl and whereis sendmail to display the correct paths. If whereis gives you an error message, simply try which instead on a Unix based server. Note that Perl 4 scripts will work with a path to a Perl 5 location but the reverse may not always be true. Contacting the server provider is perhaps the best way to determine the answer to which of the locations to use in the scripts.

Of course, you also need a cgi-bin to run a CGI script on a Unix based server.

The cgi-bin

Where did the name cgi-bin come from? Original NCSA (the National Center for Supercomputing Applications) web servers housed two directories, the cgi-src and the cgi-bin:

- The cgi-src contained the source code for the CGI programs that were run on the server

- The cgi-bin contained the compiled executables of the source code, which were called binaries (where the bin term came from)

Today, web servers don't usually have a cgi-src directory, but the 'default' location for the executable CGI programs remains the cgi-bin.

The cgi-bin located on the web server is designed to allow the files to be executed, so the web server knows that any file that is retrieved from the cgi-bin should be executed and the results outputted to the client. Should an HTML file find its way into the directory, the server will try to run it as a program, instead of just sending it as a file to be viewed by the browser.

Unfortunately, there is more to the cgi-bin than creating the directory and changing the authority on the files that will be housed there – it depends on a setting in the configuration file for the web server where various options are set, called the httpd.conf file. Quite often site owners can't simply create the cgi-bin directory by themselves – it's a directory that has to be set up by a system administrator. It's also important to note that if you simply put the files there it doesn't make them executable, the 'executor' must have specific rights to the file. It's becoming more commonplace for servers to recognize .cgi and .pl scripts from anywhere, because the first line is the path to the perl program to execute the script against.

Uploading CGI scripts

Web servers are usually based on one of two operating systems; Unix/Linux or Windows NT, so check with the hosting company to find out which Operating System the server you're dealing with is on. Uploading CGI scripts isn't so very different from transferring your web page files, but, as you'll see, has one or two important distinctions.

We'll deal with uploading to a Unix/Linux host first, because most remote hosting companies are Unix/Linux, and then we'll look at loading up to a Windows host after that, (so you can skip the section that doesn't apply to you, if you'd rather).

Uploading your CGI scripts to a remote Linux/Unix host

When you're working with a Linux/Unix host you have to set two things: the **transfer type**, and the **script permissions**. You don't need to do this for Windows-based systems; Win32 platforms don't have the same mechanisms for setting permissions on files as UNIX does. For files on FAT partitions (which means all files in Windows 95), you don't have to set permissions explicitly on a file. All files are available to all users.

Transfer types

Firstly, there are two modes of uploading files to the server:

ASCII   You transfer .cgi, .pl, .cfg (configuration files), or .txt files in ASCII mode, simply because they are just text files.

Binary   You need to transfer any files like images, Flash files, audio, or video in Binary mode in order for them to work properly

The server will not be able to execute scripts that you've uploaded in Binary mode. If you do accidentally upload in Binary mode, simply delete the server file and send up a fresh copy from your computer.

So what do you use to upload your files? I'm using CuteFTP for this example, because it's by far the most popular FTP program, has the highest rating, and is quite easy for new users to get used to fairly quickly. There are other programs available that are similar. Simply check out a shareware site such as CNET's download.com site for other FTP applications.

Using CuteFTP version 4.2.3 to change the transfer type

If you're using the CuteFTP FTP program (available at http://www.cuteftp.com) then changing the transfer type is quite simple. Choose the Transfer option from the menu bar, then the Transfer type option. This enables you to select the ASCII option from the menu, which will allow files you send to the server to be straight ASCII or text files.

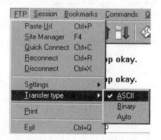

Setting script permissions

When you load up a CGI script to your Linux/Unix host, you also have to change the permissions of the file in order for it to be executable. This is one aspect that a majority of users have problems with, simply because it can be a bit confusing until you do it a couple of times. There are quite a few permissions you need to set: **User Types**, **File Permissions**, **Directory Permissions** and **Permission Values**.

User Types

There are three different ways of dealing with CGI scripts:

User   Defined as the 'owner' of the script (whoever logged in and uploaded it to the server)

Group — Defined as users who are part of the owner's group (not really used on the web server)

Other — Everyone else (in other words, the world)

These are abbreviated to **U**, **G**, and **O**.

To set the permission for a directory or file, you have to first specify the values for all three user types.

File permissions

All files have permissions associated with them in order to determine what can be done with the file and who has the authority to do it. Once again, there are three possibilities for each:

Read — Simply reads the file

Write — Can modify or delete the file

EXecute — Can execute (run) the file

The owner of the script (whoever uploaded it) can adjust the permissions of the files for each type using FTP or Telnet. The properties of these values are abbreviated as **R**, **W** and **X**.

Directory permissions

Permissions used with directories work a little differently:

Read — View the directory contents

Write — Create or delete files

EXecute — Access to the directory

> *You need to be aware that it is in fact possible for somebody with write permission to a directory to delete a file in that directory, even if they don't have write permission to that actual file*

Permission values

Each of the different permissions has a numeric value associated with it.

Read = 4

Write = 2

EXecute = 1

When assigning the permissions you simply add together the values for the ones you wish to allow, using 0 if you don't want to enable any of the options.

To set the permission for a directory or file, you have to specify the values for User, Group, and Other, in that order. These values correspond to Read, Write, and Execute.

You can change the permissions of a script thought the `telnet` `chmod` (CHange MODe) command, or an FTP program such as CuteFTP. This is how you'd change the permissions to 755:

User: RWX = 4 + 2 + 1 = 7

Group: R-X = 4 + 0 + 1 = 5

Other: R-X = 4 + 0 + 1 = 5

This sets the script so that the user can read, run, and modify that file while the rest of the world can only read and execute it.

Here are some examples of the most commonly used settings:

- 755 – (drwxr-xr-x) - Directories containing CGI file
  Gives directory permissions for users to read, write, execute. Both the Group and Others can read and write from the directory, but can't execute anything.

- 777 – (drwxrwxrwx) – Directories not containing CGI files
  Gives directory permission to users, group, and other to all read, write and execute.

- 755 – (-rwxr-xr-x) – CGI files
  Gives file permissions to users to read, write and execute. The group and others can read and write from the file, but can't execute them.

- 666 – (-rw-rw-rw-) – Log files
  All three groups are able to read and write from these files.

- 777 – (-rwxrwxrwx) – HTML files
  All three groups have read, write and execute access to these files.

Changing File Attributes with CuteFTP 4.23

Changing the file or directory permission using an FTP program such as CuteFTP is really quite simple. Once you've uploaded the script to the server using ASCII format, just go to Commands on the menu bar at the top, choose File Actions from the menu, and then the CHMOD option from the resulting menu.

You can also change set permissions by right-clicking the file you want to change and choosing the CHMOD option or from the same menu (shown right). This box allows the user to change all the necessary permissions quickly and easily.

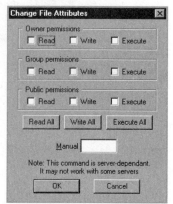

It really is easy to set up CGI scripts, and to see how they work. If you're all set we can begin putting together a couple of Flash 5 files that use CGI. If, on the other hand, you need to set up a Windows system, read on.

Setting up your Windows machine to run Perl CGI scripts

If you want to work with a Windows system, the best thing to do is set up the Apache Web Server for Windows (http://www.apache.org). Select C:\Apache for your installation folder.

Then collect the Active Perl intel build from the CD, to install Perl at C:\Perl, or go to: http://www.activestate.com/Products/ActivePerl/index.html

When installation has finished, open Notepad, and go to the file C:\Apache\conf\httpd.conf. Find the line ServerName, uncomment it and change to the loop-back address that targets your own machine:

```
ServerName 127.0.0.1
```

(not #ServerName 127.0.0.1)

Apache runs by selecting Start Apache from the start menu. Start it (you'll get a console window which you can minimize), then start your web browser, and enter http://127.0.0.1 (you don't have to be on the Internet, it works fine offline). If you get a message that says Go offline, press cancel.

You should see the Apache's help. If not, try putting any HTML document named index.html in the directory C:\Apache\htdocs\ to check that everything is OK.

Note that whenever CGI Scripts are to be run, Apache must be loaded and working. If Apache's window opens and closes very fast, it hasn't been loaded. Check the frequently asked questions (FAQ) if this happens.

Now you're ready. Whatever CGI script you put in directory C:\Apache\cgi-bin, can be run by loading up the address in your browser http://127.0.0.1/cgi-bin/*script.cgi* (or whatever the name of your script is).

> To run CGI scripts in Windows, you must change the first line to:#!C:\Perl\bin\perl.exe *(directed to wherever your Perl interpreter lives)*.
>
> When you upload them afterwards to a Unix server, change it to: #!/usr/local/bin/perl *(or the location of Perl on the server)*.

Working with CGI scripts

Although you'll be taking a closer look in the next chapter at how Perl works, this chapter is more concerned with helping you get going using CGI scripts than teaching you about Perl's syntax and capabilities (which isn't to say that these aren't a good thing to know about – on the contrary, it's the logical next step if want to be able to use CGI confidently and effectively, which is why the next chapter will introduce you to Perl).

The very first line of all Perl scripts is called shebang and is a user-defined option that is going to be the path to your host's Perl language installation, preceded by the characters "#!". Two common examples are:

```
#!/usr/bin/perl
#!/usr/local/bin/perl
```

Comments

The # character is Perl's comment character, and is used the same way that // and /* (open) */ (closing) are used in Flash 5 ActionScript. Lines that begin with a # aren't executed by the interpreter.

You can use the # character after a script statement, and then add comments about the statement and how it works inside the script. For example, you could see the following statement in a script:

```
$maxdisplay = 25;        # Maximum of threads to display
```

This is an option in the script that can be set by the user, and if you were coming across it for the first time, you'd be able to adjust it accordingly.

Variables

Once you open up a CGI file in an editor, the first thing that you're likely to see is a series of variables defined at the top of the script. All these begin with a $. Variables are assigned here so that people who download scripts can make the necessary changes without needing to read and edit the entire script while still having it work correctly.

The values could be as simple as the user email address for the form to be sent to, changing the color of the background of a HTML table, or perhaps setting the values that enable or disable particular options (like 1, 0, y, or n).

```
$YourEmail = 'sryder@webryder.com';.
$color{'titlebg'} = "\#0066ff";
$enable_notification = 1;
```

System information may be required in other script variables. One of the most common is to set the sendmail program on a Unix server. This program is used to send any input information from your site to you or the users by email. Later in the chapter, we'll see a very basic example for an email form, which will use the sendmail program to send the details to your email account, and some options for setting up the required programs in a Windows environment. These are a couple of common examples of the location (be sure to check with hosting company):

```
/usr/sbin/sendmail
/usr/lib/sendmail
```

System paths

Quite often a script will ask you for the system (also called absolute and direct) path as a user defined variable, which is the location of the site from the server's point of view, (*not* the URL of the site from the Internet). If the system administrator had allowed the site access to a CGI-bin, they should also tell you the system path, which is required for many scripts. Two common examples of a system path are:

```
/usr/local/etc/usersites/'your unique web site identifier'/
/home/httpd/www/cgi-bin
```

Occasionally the script will require the actual URL of the web site, with or without the exact location of the CGI-bin or the script itself. It is quite straightforward, simply something that looks like:

```
http://www.yourdomainname.com/cgi-bin/
```

All of this may seem a little overwhelming at first, but, once you've done it a couple of times, should become easier with the future scripts.

So, now we've looked at the principles of changing CGI scripts to work for your site, and have seen how you upload them to the server, so we're ready to begin working with CGI scripts and Flash.

Sending email from Flash using CGI

This first example will use a CGI script to enable the Flash 5 file to send an email form from the web site to the specified user. If you're using a Unix server, you can just go ahead and begin. If you're on Windows, though, there's one more thing you need to do. Unix comes with a Sendmail function that Windows hasn't got, so you'll need to collect one from somewhere else.

Sendmail for Windows
There are various programs to set up the sendmail equivalent for Windows, including:

http://www.indigostar.com/

This is a command line program for sending email messages over the Internet and is a Windows version of the popular Unix Sendmail program. It allows easy migration of Perl Scripts from Unix to Windows, since it uses the same interface as the Unix Sendmail. There is lots of documentation online for the set up, and a free trial download is available.

http://www.ntsendmail.com/

Ntsendmail is a UNIX Sendmail replacement for Windows NT and is released under a public license. Designed to enable scripts created for UNIX to run correctly in a Windows environment. All of the set up information is online and the free software is available to download from the site.

So, now you have everything you need, let's begin working with a CGI script.

1. To start configuring the CGI script, open it up your text editor – you can find it on the CD called `mail.cgi`. The first thing you need to do is modify the shebang for your system. If you're working on a Linux setup, use this:

    ```
    #!/usr/bin/perl                        #Unix shebang
    ```

    On a Windows system, you might have something like this:

    ```
    #!C:\perl\bin\perl.exe                 #Windows shebang (adjust
                                           #depending on where Perl is
                                           #installed)
    ```

2. Next you'll need to configure the location of `MAIL` for to the correct Perl email program on your server your system; I've highlighted the line you'll need to modify. It's usually `/usr/lib/sendmail` in a Unix environment, but you should check with your web host.

    You then import the module CGI

    ```
    use CGI;
    ```

    and create an instance of it that is assigned to the $query variable.

    ```
    $query = new CGI;

    for ($query->param) { $in{$_} = $query->param($_); }

    unless(open(MAIL,"|/usr/lib/sendmail -t")) {
        print "Content-type: text/html\n\n";
        print "Unable to open sendmail binary.";
        exit;
    }
    ```

    The `print` commands will get their values from four variables that we'll set up in Flash: `mail_to`, `mail_subject`, `mail_from` and `mail_message`. This code will create the email from the variables and send it.

    ```
    print MAIL "To: $in{mail_to}\n";            #Defined Flash var
    print MAIL "Subject: $in{mail_subject}\n";  #User assigned value
    print MAIL "From: $in{mail_from}\n\n";      #User assigned value
    print MAIL $in{mail_message};               #User assigned value
    close(MAIL);
    ```

The final line of the script is the location command, that tells the browser which URL it will go to after the script has been executed.

```
print "Location: http://www.webryder.com\n\n"; #change URL
```

Simply change the `Location` in the last print command to the location you want to go to once the user submits the form. If you don't I will be getting a lot of hits from your email that is sent to you (not necessarily a bad thing)!!

3. Upload the script up to the `cgi-bin` directory in ASCII form, and change the authority to 755. (You might need to flick back a few pages to remind yourself how to do that).

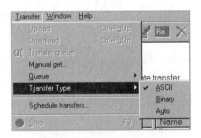

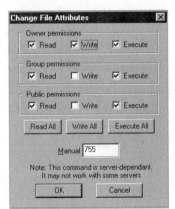

That's all there is to the CGI file. Now we'll create the Flash movie that will send the variable values to the CGI script once the user has inputted the information.

4. Fire up Flash and create a layer for each input text field, one for the text that the user will see, one for actions, and one for a submit button that we'll use to send the variables to the CGI script.

5. We'll begin with the values that the user will input, the `mail_subject`, `mail_from` and `mail_message` variables. These will be inputted through text input fields with the appropriate variable names, and then sent from Flash to the script.

    So add three input text fields, one for each of these variables, and give them the appropriate variable names: `mail_subject`, `mail_from` and `mail_message`. Make the `mail_message` a multiline field, and check Border/Bg on all three. Specify a maximum number of characters for these fields and a font style if you want to.

6. Add the Submit button that we'll use to process the script, send the variables to the CGI script, and redirect the user to the location defined in the CGI script.

7. For this example, simply put the objects in the first scene of the movie, and place a `stop` action in the very first frame. This will make the movie stop and wait for user input. Of course, if you want to make it more animated you can do so easily enough.

8. Now set your email address in the `mail_to` variable in the first frame of the Actions layer (make sure this is your own email address or I will be getting a lot of your emails!)

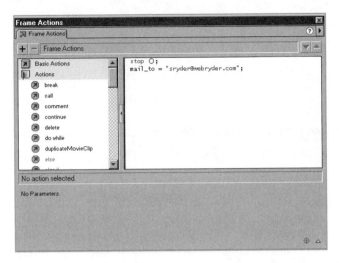

9. As we're only using four variables in the Flash file, we'll just send them all at once, rather than defining the necessary ones. The Submit button is simply a button assigned the necessary actions to send out the variables. The variables contained in the file are then sent to the designated CGI script using the getURL command using POST in the on(release) event of the button:

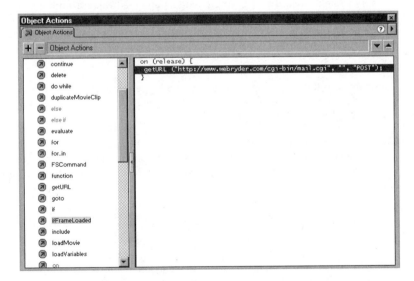

We're sending the variables using the POST method so that the values are sent into the script, and are parsed in the script itself. The script in turn processes it, sends off the email, and takes the user's browser to the URL you defined earlier. As you know, the GET command appends the variables to the end of the URL, and so it's better used for scripts that submit search criteria, or something of that nature.

10. That's it – publish your Flash movie, load the HTML file and the SWF up to the server, and try it out.

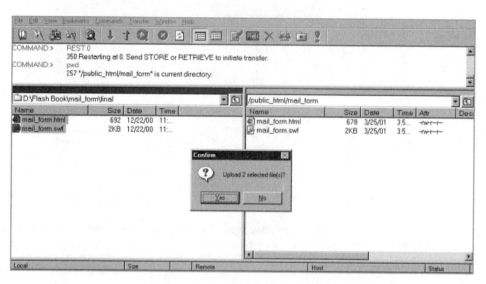

This is a very straightforward script, simply sending an email value from the input text variable. It would be a good idea to implement some error checking; as it is, the email address isn't checked for validity, or even an @ symbol. There are plenty of ways you could do some error checking, like setting up a script that loops through the characters of the `email` variable looking for the @ symbol.

You'd probably use this very simple movie inside a bigger Flash movie, and by getting the Submit button to take users to another keyframe in the movie once the variables have been sent, and continuing from there. You can experiment as much as you like!

So now you've seen a very simple CGI script at work, let's move on to a more complex example. The next application we'll build is an online poll. Although it's a bit more involved, it would make an interesting addition to a web site; in fact you can find this kind of thing on quite a few web sites currently.

Creating an online straw poll with CGI and Flash

This online poll instantly updates to show the current result each time the user enters their response. I created this poll for a television show that you might recognize. I hope that building this example will help clarify the CGI theories we discussed earlier.

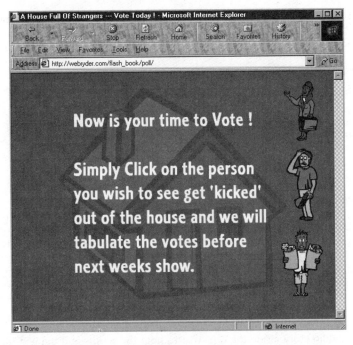

The poll collects voters' opinions, and displays the running total of votes.

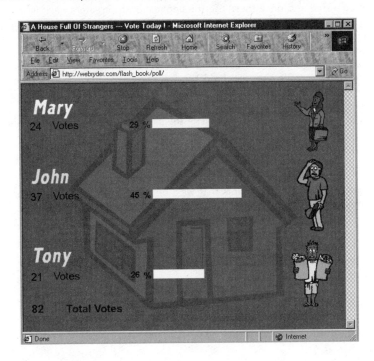

There are two scripts required to create this poll: `read.pl` and `write.pl`. The former reads from a text file that contains a set of variables on a server, and the other script writes back to the very same file on the host server.

> The following scripts were created by Jeroen C. Kessels, http://www.kessels.com, an Internet Engineer located in Amsterdam. He was kind enough to allow me to use the code for this example. If you would like you can reach him at jeroen@kessels.com.

Setting up your system

We'll be using these two scripts to read and write the variables to and from Flash using a text file called `variables.txt`. We'll assign this text file to a `$Filename` variable in both Perl scripts, because they'll both be using it – one will read from it, and the other write to it. This variable will also be defined in the Flash file, so that the script knows the name of the text file the variables are being read from and written to. In other words the Perl scripts are acting as the intermediary between the text file on the server and the Flash file by writing results and reading them from the text file, according to the request sent by the Flash file.

We'll create a new directory inside the `cgi-bin` to hold the scripts and the text file, which we'll call data. In order to do this, all we need to do is use our FTP program to connect to the server, navigate to the `cgi-bin` and once there use the application to create a new directory.

Finally, we need to know the absolute location of the directory where the files are going to be stored, because we'll need it to set a `$Database` variable. This variable is used to define the system path that we had talked about before. It is the absolute location to the directory that will house the scripts and text file that will hold the variables, you may need to check with your hosting company for the absolute path to this directory. This directory should be outside the document-tree of your web server, and have proper read/write permissions so that `read.pl` can read/write files in it. This setting must be exactly the same in both the `read.pl` and `write.pl` scripts.

The Perl scripts

Now we can start working with the scripts that we'll be using, and modify them for your system setup. You can find both of them on the CD, in the directory for this example in this chapter. First open up `read.pl` in a text editor – Notepad is fine.

read.pl

First we'll work with the source for the `read.pl` script, which we'll use to hold the variables that we'll collect from Flash file.

Microsoft users: use forward-slashes '/' instead of back-slashes '\'.

1. The first thing you need to do is configure the script to work with your system set up. First set up the shebang:

```
#!/usr/bin/perl                #Unix users
```

Or

```
#!C:\perl\bin\perl.exe         #Windows users, depending where Perl is
                               #installed
```

Then define the $Database variable:

```
$Database = '/home/httpd/www/cgi-bin/data';        #set to your
                                                   #system
```

Change this into the data directory – the directory on the hard disk of your web server that will hold the text file, and the Perl scripts. It must be an absolute path, you can't use constructions like '..' or '$USER', or an entire URL.

2. That's the end of the configuration; now for initialization. You don't need to change any of this, I'll just walk you through what's going on. The default filename is the process-id sent from Flash, which in this case will be defined as variables inside the Flash file without the .txt extension that will be added later in the script:

```
use Config;
$Filename = "$$";
```

Next the script sends the standard HTTP header, making sure the output is not cached in the user's browser:

```
print "Content-type: text/html\n";
print "Expires: Thu, 01 Dec 1994 16:00:00 GMT\n";
print "Cache-Control: no-cache, must-revalidate\n";
print "Pragma: no-cache\n";
print "\n";
```

Next the script gets the filename from the parameters that we define above (variables for this example). If there are special characters in the filename, like '/' and '\', they are translated into spaces, and '..' is removed all together. This is done in order to create some security against hackers. The script also checks to see if an actual value is assigned to the variable, if not it will exit the script totally and if so will simply continue on.

```
if ($ENV{'REQUEST_METHOD'} eq 'POST') {
    binmode(STDIN);
    read(STDIN,$in,$ENV{'CONTENT_LENGTH'});
  } else {
    $in = $ENV{'QUERY_STRING'};
  }
```

```
@args = split(/[&;]/,$in);
foreach $i (0 .. $#args) {
  $args[$i] =~ s/\+/ /g;
  ($key, $val) = split(/=/,$args[$i],2);
  $key =~ s/%([A-Fa-f0-9]{2})/pack("c",hex($1))/ge;
  $val =~ s/%([A-Fa-f0-9]{2})/pack("c",hex($1))/ge;
  $val =~ s/[^a-zA-Z0-9]//g;
  if (($key eq 'filename') && ($val ne '')) {
    if ($val =~ /^([\w]+)$/) { $Filename = $1; }
    }
  }
if ($Filename eq '') {
  print "state=no_filename_specified";
  exit 0;
  }
```

The file is opened and then locked – if the file can't be opened then we exit. This is done in order to prevent multiple people accessing the file at the same time, hopefully cutting down on any possible errors that may occur.

```
$fn = $Database . $Filename . ".txt";
if (!open(FILE,"<$fn")) {
  print "state=cannot_open_file";
  exit 0;
  }
if ($Config{'d_flock'} eq "define") { flock(FILE,2); }
binmode(FILE);
```

The script takes the contents of the file and prints it into Flash

```
print "state=done&";
print <FILE>;
```

And finally, closes and unlocks the file on the disk.

```
if ($Config{'d_flock'} eq "define") { flock(FILE,8); }
close(FILE);
```

Save and close the file. With relatively little work at all, we've used a CGI file provided by someone else, and modified it to suit our system. Not bad! Now we'll do the same with write.pl.

write.pl

1. Open up the write.pl Perl script in your text editor. This script will write the Flash file variables out to the variables.txt file on the host server for storage:

2. First configure the shebang:

```
#!/usr/bin/perl              #Unix users
```

or

```
#!C:\perl\bin\perl.exe        #Windows users, change according to
                              Perl installation
```

Then change the path to the directory on the web server that holds the data. (Remember that it has to be an absolute path, no constructions like '..' or '$USER', or URLs; and that the directory should be outside the document-tree of your webserver, with the proper read/write permissions.) This setting must be exactly the same in both the read.pl and write.pl scripts.

Windows-NT users: use forward-slashes "/", not back-slashes "\"

```
$Database = '/home/httpd/www/cgi-bin/data';
```

3. That's the end of the configuration, now let's look at the initialization. This also looks a lot like the read.pl script. The default filename is the process-id sent from Flash, which once again, as before, will be defined as variables inside of the Flash file and sent out to the script:

```
use Config;
$Filename = "$$";
```

The following print statements send out the standard HTTP header, while making sure that the output is not cashed in the user's browser.

```
print "Content-type: text/html\n";
print "Expires: Thu, 01 Dec 1994 16:00:00 GMT\n";
print "Cache-Control: no-cache, must-revalidate\n";
print "Pragma: no-cache\n";
print "\n";
```

Just like the read.pl script, we want to get the filename from the parameters, again translating special characters in the filename like '/' and '\' into spaces and removing '..' altogether to give us some security against hackers.

```
if ($ENV{'REQUEST_METHOD'} eq 'POST') {
    binmode(STDIN);
    read(STDIN,$in,$ENV{'CONTENT_LENGTH'});
  } else {
    $in = $ENV{'QUERY_STRING'};
    }
@args = split(/[&;]/,$in);
$Output = '';
foreach $i (0 .. $#args) {
  $Argument = $args[$i];
  $Argument =~ s/\+/ /g;
  ($key, $val) = split(/=/,$Argument,2);
  $key =~ s/%([A-Fa-f0-9]{2})/pack("c",hex($1))/ge;
```

```
$val =~ s/%([A-Fa-f0-9]{2})/pack("c",hex($1))/ge;
$val =~ s/[^a-zA-Z0-9]//g;
if (($key eq 'filename') && ($val ne '')) {
  if ($val =~ /^([\w]+)$/) { $Filename = $1; }
  }
if (($key ne '') && ($key ne 'filename') && ($key ne 'state'))
{
    if ($Output ne "") { $Output .= "&"; }
    $Output .= $args[$i];
    }
  }
```

Once again we want to open and lock the file, and if the file cannot be opened then we exit.

```
$fn = $Database . $Filename . ".txt";
if (!open(FILE,">$fn")) {
  print "state=cannot_open_file";
  exit 0;
  }
if ($Config{'d_flock'} eq "define") { flock(FILE,2); }
binmode(FILE);
```

Finally we come to the only difference between the two files; writing the output string to the file (variables.txt) on the server directory we created in order to update the file (variables.txt).

print FILE $Output;

The file is closed and locked

```
if ($Config{'d_flock'} eq "define ") { flock(FILE,8); }
close(FILE);
```

And the the filename returned back to Flash.

print "filename=$Filename&state=done";

That's all we need to do with the files. Once you have modified the two scripts, just upload them to the cgi-bin (into the data directory for this example) on your server and give them the authority 755, to allow them to have the permission to run correctly.

Now we'll put a simple text file into this location that will read and write the appropriate variables from the Flash movie.

The Text File
We'll create a simple text file that holds the five variables that will be read into the Flash movie:

answer1   To track the first option in the poll

`answer2`	To track the second option in the poll
`answer3`	To track the third option in the poll
`total`	To track the total number of votes that have been placed
`status`	To allow us to check that all the text variables have been loaded from the text file before the movie goes any further

1. So open up a new text file, and set the following variables:

   `status=1&total=0&answer1=0&answer2=0&answer3=0`

   Save the file as `variables.txt`.

2. Now upload it to the server, giving it the '755' permission and putting it in the same data directory in the `cgi-bin` as `write.pl` and the `read.pl` script files.

The Flash movie

We can now create the Flash movie. In the full version there's an intro scene, called opening scene that tells the users the name of the television show and how "You Can Vote Now!" with some simple text effects. This scene doesn't really do anything though, it just finishes running and automatically moves onto the second scene, the main scene. This is where we begin to do some interesting things! We'll just work on the main scene here, as it's where the work of the movie is done.

The main scene

1. Set your scene up to look like this:

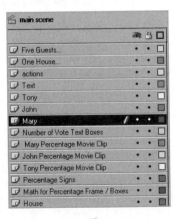

2. The first thing we should do is create two variables to begin reading the data from the text file on the actions layer. First set a `status` variable to `0`, (remember we assigned status the value `1` in the text file? We'll just set up a loop that holds the movie up until the value of status changes to `1` in a minute.)

```
status = "0";
```

We'll use this variable to ensure that all the variables have been loaded in from the incoming script before the movie continues, (preventing Flash from resetting the variables, which it would do if we allowed it to move on before they have been fully loaded, and then send back false settings to the text file.)

Then set a `filename` variable, with the value `variables`, to tell Flash to load in the variables. Remember the `$Filename = "$$"` statement at the top of `read.pl` that you saw earlier? When the text file is read, the `filename` variable will be set to `variables`, (the `.txt` part of the filename is added by the script), and the effect of calling the Perl file using the `getURL` action that we'll add next, is that Flash will load in the variables held in the text file..

```
status = "0";
filename = "variables";
```

3. Then we need to pull in the variables using the `read.pl` script we modified earlier, using a `loadVariables` action and the `GET` method. (You don't need to worry about the level at the moment, because the variables all lie in the same layer of this movie clip.)

```
status = "0";
filename = "variables";
getURL ("wwww.your server/cgi_bin/data/read.pl", "", "GET");
```

(Remember to change *your server* to the name of your web server)

So we've loaded in the variables from the text file and read all of the variables and their corresponding values from that file into Flash. Now we can begin working with them.

4. We'll set up the loop that checks the value of the `status` variable at frame 5, sending the movie back to frame 2 until the value has been retrieved from the `variables.txt` file, when it will change to 1.

```
if (status==0){
gotoAndPlay (2);
}
```

Once the file is sure that all variables are loaded, it's safe for the movie to continue.

5. Now we need three option buttons, (representing the three individuals), for the users to choose between. Put each of these on a separate layer, add some text to tell users what they should do, and jump forward to any frame you like after frame 5. I'm using frame 107.

Frame 107

1. With all options (buttons representing individuals) and text in place, the file is just waiting for the user to pick the individual they want to vote out of the house. First we'll put a keyframe in the Actions layer and increment the value of the total variable, because we now have one more viewer then we had previously. Then add a stop action, to stop the movie advancing until we're ready:

```
total++
stop()
```

We'll use the total variable to figure out the percentage of votes that each person has later on in the movie, and to represent the percentage graphically using a percentage bar.

2. Now assign the actions to the buttons that will respond to the user's selection. We'll use the variables answer1, answer2, and answer3 that we brought into the movie from the text file to record the user's vote.

Assign the following actions to the button representing Mary, to record when the user selects Mary, and progress the movie:

```
on(release){
answer1++;
nextFrame()
}
```

Then do the same for the button representing John:

```
on(release){
answer2++;
nextFrame()
}
```

And finally, do the same for the button representing Tony:

```
on(release){
answer3++;
nextFrame()
}
```

By moving users to the next frame after they have made their selection, the user can only choose one of the options, and can't 'pad' their choice without 'refreshing' and doing it again.

So once users have made their choices, we need to process their results and show how the poll stands. We'll do this in frame 108.

Frame 108
We'll have each of the names of the contestants in this frame, and the total number of votes for each person so far, and the percentage of the total vote that each member has received.

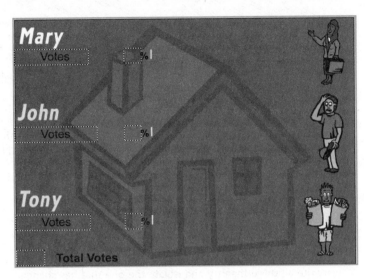

1. Let's begin with the three dynamic text boxes that show the value of each of the variables that represent the number of votes for each contestant.

   Create three dynamic text boxes to display those values, giving them the right variable names (answer2 for John, for example). Make sure you deselect the Selectable option so that users can't highlight and copy the values. Add a static text box to each dynamic text box to tell users what they're looking at.

2. The Total Votes field works pretty much the same way. Create a dynamic text box with the variable total, and label it with a static text field to the side Total Votes.

3. Now we'll deal with the percentage bar that shows the percentages graphically. Let's start a movie clip that represents the percentages. Create a new symbol, I called mine Percentage Bar Movie Clip, and give it 100 frames, one for each percent.

4. Put a symbol, Bar for Percentage in the first frame, and resize it into a small rectangle by changing the horizontal aspect of it (but not the vertical). This frame also contains a stop action to keep it from playing through once it's placed on the stage of the movie.

   Put the full size version of the same box on frame 100, making sure that both boxes are left aligned and in the center of the stage. Now all you need to do it is set a motion tween between the two keyframes (at 1 and 100).

5. Put three copies of the Percentage Bar Movie Clip, each on their own appropriately labeled layer and with an appropriate instance name at frame 108, (or the next frame after the button is clicked). I called mine option1, option2 and option3.

The instance names allow each individual movie to communicate with the others, and with the appropriate variables; so `option1` will correspond with `answer1` (Mary), `option2` with `answer2` (John), and `option3` for `answer3` (Tony).

6. We can put most of the actions we need into a keyframe on the Actions layer, in frame 108. Before we tie the percentage bar graphical elements to the results, though, we should write the new values back to the variables held in the text file. Define the filename variable as `variables` again, this time in readiness to send the variables out to the `variables.txt` file on the server. Then you need to use the `loadVariables` action, this time to POST the variables back to `write.pl` in the cgi-bin on the server. We need to send the four variables that are still in use at this point in the script, `total`, which will have been updated, and `answer1`, `answer2`, and `answer3`, one of which will have been updated.

```
filename = "variables";
loadVariablesNum ("www.your server.com/cgi-bin/data", 0, "POST");
```

Although only one of the answer variables will have changed, it's just quicker to overwrite all three than try and isolate the one that has changed and send that back. They are now in the text file and are ready to be used by the next user wanting to vote someone out of the house.

7. Now let's do the math that calculates the percentage of votes that each person has had allotted, and use that number on the Percentage Bar Movie Clip. We'll need to round that number off to the closest integer (this will make it easier to use with the instances of the Percentage Bar Movie Clips later), which we can do by using the `round` method of the `Math` object at the same time. The easiest way is to do this is to make the calculation and assign it to a new variable. Mary's percentage will be kept in the `option1percent` variable:

```
option1percent = Math.round(Number(answer1)/Number(total)*100);
```

This takes the numeric value of `answer1`, divides it by the value of the total, multiples it all by 100, and then takes that number and rounds it to the closest integer. Do the same for the other two instances, and the code you have so far in frame 107 should look like this:

```
filename = "variables";
loadVariablesNum ("www.your server.com/cgi-bin/data",0, "POST");
option1percent = Math.round(Number(answer1)/Number(total)*100);
option2percent = Math.round(Number(answer2)/Number(total)*100);
option3percent = Math.round(Number(answer3)/Number(total)*100);
```

Then we need to tell the three instances of the Percentage Bar Movie Clip which frame to go to in each individual movie, using a `gotoAndStop` action and passing it the value of the `option1percent` variables. (One of the reasons we rounded off the number is because frame numbers are Integers.) So, again for Mary, your code should look like this:

```
option1.gotoAndStop(option1percent);
```

Add a `stop` action to the script, and altogether, your code in frame 107 should look like this:

```
filename = "variables";
loadVariablesNum ("www.your server.com/cgi-bin/data",0, "POST");
option1percent = Math.round(Number(answer1)/Number(total)*100);
option2percent = Math.round(Number(answer2)/Number(total)*100);
option3percent = Math.round(Number(answer3)/Number(total)*100);
option1.gotoAndStop(option1percent);
option2.gotoAndStop(option2percent);
option3.gotoAndStop(option3percent);
stop()
```

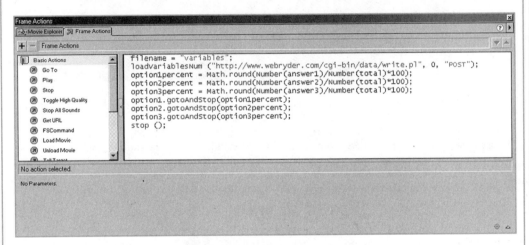

8. To finish off, we'll put the percentage values that we have created into dynamic text boxes so that the user can see the percentage of votes for each of the individuals. We'll do this the same way we displayed the number of votes for each individual, using three non-selectable dynamic text boxes, and assigning each of the option percentage numbers to them. The user can then see the results both numerically and visually:

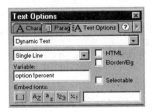

9. Finally, load everything up to the server, and test the movie.

Note that if two or more users view the Flash file within approximately ten seconds of one another, one answer will overwrite another one. The variables are pulled into the file as the first action of the main scene, then the characters are introduced, instructions, and finally the vote is cast. This entire process takes approximately ten seconds to do, and if there were another user to view the file within that amount of time, they would actually pull in the same variable values as the other user. When one casts their vote the value would take, but when the other one casts their vote it would overwrite the other's vote because it sends out all the values from that user again.

One way to work around this would be to have the values of the variables read in to the file later on, the vote happen quite quickly after doing so, and thereby cutting down on the amount of time that the values are required to be held within the Flash file.

Summary

I hope this chapter will help you to bring your own creative ideas to life and give you the necessary skills to continue growing with the Flash application for years to come. There certainly could be lots of ideas generated from the chapter itself, as connecting Flash with CGI scripts can be a powerful feature for any web site. In the chapter we covered in-depth aspects of interaction between Flash and CGI, while at the same time keeping the files visually appealing to the users thereby perhaps generating more interest in the site's overall function.

If you have any questions or comments, please feel free to contact me at: friendsofed@webryder.com and visit: http://www.webryder.com to learn more about me!

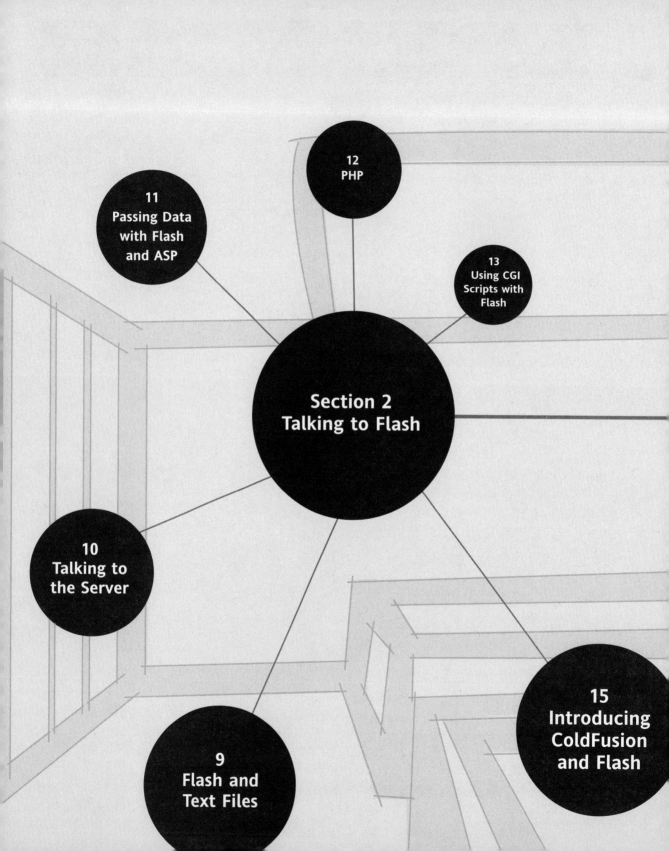

12
PHP

11
Passing Data
with Flash
and ASP

13
Using CGI
Scripts with
Flash

Section 2
Talking to Flash

10
Talking to
the Server

15
Introducing
ColdFusion
and Flash

9
Flash and
Text Files

Chapter 14
Perl Scripting

You've already been working with CGI scripts programmed in Perl; this chapter aims to take you that one step further and start you writing your own Perl scripts from scratch. We'll be investigating the Perl language itself, and look at some of the things that make it such a powerful server-side scripting language.

Perl is different from CGI. While Perl is a scripting language, CGI (Common Gateway Interface) is a protocol. CGI describes the process that allows a client or an external program to interact with a web server, and allows information to be passed back and forth. And, of course, the majority of CGI programs are written in Perl, which explains Perl's popularity.

Perl is what's known as·a general-purpose programming language – which means it can do just about anything most other programming languages can do. In fact a great deal of Perl's functionality was borrowed from other programming languages.

If you're new to programming, you can produce simple Perl scripts without much difficulty. If you're familiar with any other programming languages, and if you've been working through this book progressively, then you'll find much of Perl syntax pretty similar to the syntax you've already been using.

In this chapter, we cover the Perl basics:

- How Perl deals with data, formatting, testing, and assigning it to variables.

- Dealing with external files; reading from, writing to and appending text files.

- Subroutines; making sure all the variables you need are returned to the script, some script security, and searching files.

- Integrating Perl and Flash in a game scoring application, using a Perl script that you'll be able to write from scratch.

As you've already been working with Perl, I'll assume that you're all set up to load scripts to and from your server, which you'll need for the Perl and Flash integration. I'd also recommend that you install Perl on your local Windows machine as well though, because many of the concepts and syntax in the first half of this chapter can just as easily be run in your command prompt window. ActivePerl is the latest Perl binary distribution from Active State and replaces what was previously distributed as Perl for Win32. The latest release of ActivePerl and other professional tools for Perl developers are available from the ActiveState web site at www.ActiveState.com . You can load from the CD, or go to this URL.

http://www.activestate.com/Products/ActivePerl/Download.html

Remember: To run CGI scripts in Windows, you must change the first line of the script to: `#!C:\Perl\bin\perl.exe` (directed at where you have your Perl interpreter). If you're uploading them to a Unix server later, though, change to: `#!/usr/local/bin/perl` (or the location of Perl on the server).

Introducing Perl

The very first line of all Perl scripts is called shebang. It's the path to the Perl interpreter. It begins with '#!', which you'll recognize because you've already been using it. Depending on setup you're working with, the shebang in your scripts might look like this:

```
#!/usr/bin/perl
#!/usr/local/bin/perl
```

Or, if you're testing on Windows, like this:

```
#!C:\Perl\bin\perl.exe
```

This is the very simple Perl script that we'll be running next:

```
#!/usr/bin/perl
print "This is my first Perl script\n";
```

On your system you may need to specify a different path such as #!/usr/local/bin/perl or #!C:\Perl\bin\perl.exe.

Running your first Perl script

We'll begin by running some very simple Perl scripts from the command line, so that you can see what happens, and then talk through it.

1. Open up your text editor and type the code (ensuring that the first line of the code points to your perl interpreter, you might need to change this to suit your machine set up). Create a new directory for example test on the C drive, and save the file inside as first.pl:

```
#!/usr/bin/perl
print "This is my first Perl script\n";
```

2. Bring up your command prompt. You can do this from the Start menu by selecting Run and typing in command. You should get the prompt looking something like this:

```
C:\>_
```

It's pointing to the directory on your machine that is currently active, so in this example, the root directory C:\. We need to change the directory to the one in which you saved your first.pl file.

You do this by using the CD (change directory) command and specifying the directory path. I saved my first.pl script to the test folder on my machine, so I would type:

```
CD C:\test
```

The command prompt now displays the prompt:

```
C:\TEST\>_
```

3.   This tells you that you have changed the active directory successfully. Now all you need to do is type in the instruction, like this:

```
perl first.pl
```

Perl will run the script you saved as first.pl, and you should see this on your screen:

This is my first Perl script.

And that's how Perl scripts are executed. If you have problems getting this to work, go back and make sure that your installation is where you think it is, and try re-booting again.

Although you ran this example locally, you could just as easily have uploaded it to the cgi-bin of your web server, and then run it through your browser, by pointing your web browser at the path to the script.

There are a lot of really good Perl resources on the web that will help get you up and running with your installation if you're having any trouble. Try Robert's Perl Tutorial, at **www.netcat.co.uk/rob/perl/win32perltut.html** if you're having trouble.

So, we executed and tested a Perl script, but what exactly is going on there? Well, you specified the path of the Perl installation in the first line of first.pl, using the #! sign. You'd use the hash symbol by itself if you wanted to comment out pieces of the script, or to add in descriptions of what the script is doing.

The second line, as you probably guessed, tells Perl to print the string 'This is my first Perl script'. As you can see the string we are asking Perl to print is enclosed in a set of double quotation marks, although Perl will also accept a string enclosed in single quotation marks.

Finally, we used a semicolon to end the statement. You'll be very used to using a semicolon to end a statement of line of code by now, and Perl is no different.

We also used the \n sign after the word script in the code. This is a string escape character that sends a Newline command. We'll look at the way Perl understands certain characters next.

erl basics

There are plenty of other string escape characters you can use in Perl:

\n	Newline
\t	Tab
\r	Carriage Return
\b	Backspace
\u	Change next character to uppercase
\l	Change next character to lowercase
\\	A literal backslash character
\'	Quotation within a string enclosed in single quotation marks
\"	Quotation within in a string enclosed in double quotation marks

So if you put this in your file:

```
print "\uMonday\nTuesday";
```

The output would be:

Monday
Tuesday

Or you might use:

```
print "ABC\tDEF";
```

To give the output:

ABC   DEF

Or you could use:

```
print "\"I really like PERL\" he said.\n\"Not as much as I do\" I
➥replied.";
```

To give you:

"I really like PERL" he said.
"Not as much as I do" I replied.

Try them out if you like. The quotes in the last statement make the script itself a bit unintelligible, so you could use another method enclosing strings in quotation marks, the q and qq operators like so:

```
print q('Perl's really cool ');
print qq("I really like Perl" he said.);
```

You can use any non-alpha or non-numeric character as a delimiter to enclose the string for both of these operators. You could use '~' instead for exactly the same effect:

```
print q~'PERL's really cool'~;
print qq /"I really like PERL" he said./ ;
```

All the statements we have looked at so far use data that is set or hard-coded into the script. This kind of data cannot change, and is known as a constant. Data that can be assigned at runtime and can be changed within the script is known as a variable (which will be very familiar to you by now.)

Perl variables

To assign data to a variable, you need to prefix your variable name with the $ character. The variable name can contain alpha and numeric characters, or the underscore character, '_'.

In Perl, variable names are case-sensitive, so you'll have to be consistent when you're writing your scripts, or things won't work quite as expected. Other than that, assigning data to a variable in Perl couldn't be easier:

```
$customer_name = "Joe Bloggs";
$customer_age = 26;
```

Notice that the $customer_age assignment, 26, was not enclosed in quotation marks. This is because we want to treat it as a numeric data type, (otherwise known as an integer), and not as a string.

Let's modify the first.pl script so we can see the assignment working. Open the script in a text editor and change it so that it reads like the following (again, you may need to use a different path to me, just keep the path that worked for you the first time if this is the case):

```
#!/usr/bin/perl
$line = "This is my first Perl script\n";
print $line;
```

Now run the script, just as you did before, and you'll get exactly the same output as last time. Not terribly exciting, it's true, but it does make the point!

So, now you can assign data to variables, which allows you to get some interesting stuff done. Let's take a look at some of the things you can do with variables next.

Operators

We've already used one of Perl's operators, the **assignment operator,** '=', used to assign data to a variable. An operator is used to control or manipulate variables and expressions.

An **expression** is simply a value. It can be a straightforward assignment such as:

```
$today = "Wednesday";
```

Where Wednesday is the expression assigned to the variable named $today.
Or a more complex evaluation such as:

```
$total_value = 10 * (5*2);
```

Where the expression 10 * (5*2) is assigned to the variable called $total_value. Try it out if you like, using print $total_value as before.

The second evaluation uses themultiplication operator, the * character. (5*2) is 10, and 10 * 10 is 100. So, hopefully your result is 100.

These are Perl's arithmetic operators and their syntax:

+	Addition operator	10 + 10	Adds 10 and 10 to give 20
-	Subtraction operator	6 − 1	Takes 1 from 6 to give 5
*	Multiplication operator	4 * 5	Multiplies 4 by 5 to give 20
/	Division operator	12 / 6	Divides 12 by 6 to give 2
%	Modulus operator	24 % 5	Divides 24 by 5 and returns remainder, 4
**	Exponentiation operator	8 ** 2	8 raised to the 2nd power = 64

The arithmetic operators can be used with constants or variables, so the following code:

```
$price = 10.99;
$post_packing = 2.50;
$total =  $price + $post_packing;
```

Would give the $total variable the following value:

```
$total = 10.99 + 2.50;
```

The Perl shortcuts for incrementing and decrementing probably look pretty familiar to you:

```
$count = 1;
$count++;
```

This will give you a value of 2 for the $count variable.
The decrement works exactly the same way:

```
$count = 10;
$count−;
```

String operators

Strings and string variables can also be controlled and manipulated with operators. You've already seen the assignment operator, which assigns a value to a variable, but there are plenty of others.

Concatenation

The concatenation operator,' . ',is used to join two strings together. This code, for example:

```
$a = "PERL IS ";
$b = "REALLY COOL";

$c = $a . $b;
```

Will give the variable $c the string value **PERL IS REALLY COOL**. Put it into your Perl file and try it if you like, using `Print $c` to print new value on the screen.

Repetition

Another useful operator is the repetition operator x, which as you might have guessed, repeats strings or characters. This script, for example:

```
$ten_stars = "*" x 10;
```

Would assign the value `'**********'` to the variable named $ten_stars.

So, now you know how to assign values to variables, format and manipulate the data in Perl. Next we should look at how you can control the flow of your script, and how you can test and evaluate the data.

Controlling the flow of a script

Very few programs or scripts execute every line of code from top to bottom. Most of the time you are going to need to test your data to determine what should be done with it; telling the program which lines of data to execute depending on the outcome. Perl's testing conditions use constructs that you'll be familiar with by now.

The `if` statement allows you to test for conditions and determine which script should be executed accordingly:

```
if (expression) {
#statement/s go here
}
```

Whatever you have enclosed in the braces will be executed only when the expression returns true.

Just as in ActionScript, the if statement can be accompanied by an else statement which will execute if the expression being tested returns false. Try it out using this code, if you like:

```perl
#!/usr/bin/perl
$age = 26;

if ($age < 20) {
   print "You are a teenager!";
}
else {
print "You are an adult!";
}
```

As you'd probably expect, you should get the text:

You are an adult!

The < character that we used to test whether $age is less than 20 is known as a relational, or comparative, operator. There are two different categories of relational operators you can use:

Numeric relational operators   used for testing numbers
Alphanumeric relational operators   used for testing strings.

These are the Numeric relational operators:

Operator	Example	
==	$a == $b	Returns true if $a equals $b
>	$a > $b	Returns true if $a is greater than $b
<	$a < $b	Returns true if $a is less than $b
>=	$a >= $b	Returns true if $a is greater than or equal to $b
<=	$a <= $b	Returns true if $a is less than or equal to $b
!=	$a != $b	Returns true if $a does not equal $b

And these are the Alphanumeric relational operators:

Operator	Example	
eq	$a eq $b	Returns true if $a equals $b
gt	$a gt $b	Returns true if $a is greater than $b
lt	$a lt $b	Returns true if $a is less than $b
ge	$a ge $b	Returns true if $a is greater than or equal to $b
le	$a le $b	Returns true if $a is less than or equal to $b
ne	$a ne $b	Returns true if $a does not equal $b

What does Perl see as true and false? When testing data, in most cases what's true and false is quite obvious. For example if you were testing whether the number 10 is greater than the number 5, this is obviously true. Sometimes though, a true and false value may not be so apparent.

Perl sees each of the following values as being `false`:

- The number 0

- An empty string, " ", or a zero string, "0",

- An undefined variable

To Perl, anything else is `true`, which is rather handy; you can use it to test that a variable has been populated before using it, like this:

```
if   ($customer_name){
     #statement/s go here
}
```

The statement(s) enclosed in braces will be executed only if the variable `$customer_name` had been populated a value. Try it out if you like:

```
#!/usr/bin/perl
if   ($customer_name){
     print "no customer yet";
}

$customer_name="Fred";

if   ($customer_name){
     print $customer_name;
}
```

The line "no customer yet" never gets printed.

Testing for more than one condition

Often you'll need to test for more than one condition before executing some code. You can use one of the logical operators to do so, the and operator, '&&' or the or operator, '||' for this sort of testing. This next print statement, for example, will only be executed if both comparisons are true:

```
if (($a > 10) && ($b == 1 )){
print "both true";
}
```

If you wanted the statement to be executed as long as at least one of the statements is true, you'd use the or operator:

```
if (($a > 10) || ($b == 1 )){
print "at least one is true";
}
```

You can also write either of these operators literally, using and instead of &&, and or instead of ||.

These are the more basic elements of controlling the flow of your script, but there will be times when you need a more complex evaluation to take place. Then you'll need loops, so we'll look at those next.

Looping

There are different ways of looping in Perl. We'll look at the most common of these here, beginning with the while loop. The while loop executes for as long as the expression being tested returns true.

While loops
Take a look at this example:

```
$x = 0;
while ($x < 10) {
   print "The value of x is now $x\n";
   $x++;
}
```

Pretty familiar stuff by now. If you test it, you'll get this:

The value of x is now 0
The value of x is now 1
The value of x is now 2
The value of x is now 3
The value of x is now 4
The value of x is now 5
The value of x is now 6
The value of x is now 7
The value of x is now 8
The value of x is now 9

Notice that it is the value of the variable $x that is printed, rather than $x itself.

Perl always searches strings enclosed in double quotation marks for variable names, replacing any it finds with the variable's value. Strings enclosed in single quotation marks, on the other hand, are simply printed as is.

So, if you modify the code to look like this and test it again:

```
$x = 0;
while ($x < 10) {
   print 'The value of x is now $x ';
   $x++;
}
```

You'll get this instead:

The value of x is now $x The value of x is now $x The value of x is now $x The value of x is now $x The value of x is now $x The value of x is now $x The value of x is now $x The value of x is now $x
The value of x is now $x The value of x is now $x

Not quite the same at all!

For loops

The `for` loop looks a little bit more complicated, but once you know the correct syntax it's easy enough. This loop does exactly the same thing as the first `while` loop did:

```
for ($x = 0 ; $x < 10 ; $x++){
print "The value of x is now $x\n";
}
```

The `for` loop takes three arguments, each separated by a semicolon. First the loop is initialized, and then the expression that has been set tested (it is tested after each iteration of the loop), and then the modifier, or control statement is carried out at the end of each loop, its value changing as it iterates.

Working with external files

So far all of our Perl scripting has only dealt with internal statements and the data that we have used is confined to the script itself. Perl, however, is probably used most of the time for writing to files, and reading from files. And this is what's most interesting to us as Flash developers, of course. (Remember the CGI file that you used in the previous chapter to keep track of the number of votes that each member in the house had received?)

In order to open a file in Perl, you have to specify three arguments:

- The file handle (the name you want to refer to the file by)

- The mode you wish to open the file by (read, overwrite or append)

- The path and file name (the server path, not the www. address)

The three most common file modes are shown in the listing below. I'm using `MYFILE` as the file handle, and `textfile.txt` as the filename.

File Open Mode	Read	Write	Append
open(MYFILE, "<textfile.txt");	Y	N	N
open(MYFILE, ">textfile.txt");	N	Y	N
open(MYFILE, ">>textfile.txt");	N	Y	Y

When you open a file in append mode, anything you write to the file will be added at the bottom; if you use write mode, however, the existing content of the file will be overwritten.

Read is the default file open mode, so you don't need to explicitly specify it:

```
open(MYFILE, "textfile.txt");
```

If a file cannot be opened, Perl performs something called 'die', and quite literally the file opening statement dies. You can use this by specifying another statement that Perl should execute when it happens, for example:

```
open(MYFILE, "textfile.txt") || die "cannot open textfile.txt";
```

If the file wasn't found or couldn't be opened, a die message would be printed stating `cannot open textfile.txt`.

Printing to an open file is easy, you simply use the print statement and the file handle followed by the value or values you wish to print, like this:

```
print MYFILE "Customer Name: $customer_name";
```

Reading from a file isn't difficult either; you can just assign everything to a variable. If you had a single line text file, for example, or wanted to read the first line of some data (everything up to a newline character), you'd simply use some code like this:

```
open(MYFILE, "textfile.txt") || die "cannot open textfile.txt";
$line = <MYFILE>;
```

The `$line` variable now contains everything Perl found before it reached a newline character or the end of the data.

Reading from and writing to a text file

Let's begin with a quick example that reads everything from a text file. First we'll write the Perl file:

1. The easiest way to do this is to use a `while` loop:

```
open(MYFILE, "textfile.txt") || die "cannot open textfile.txt";
while (<MYFILE>){
  print $_;
}
```

Because we don't specify a variable for the file input, Perl automatically assigns the line of input to its default variable `$_`.

2. Now create a short text file, put some text inside it, and save it to the same directory as the Perl file `textfile.txt`.

3. Run the Perl file and see the text being read out into the console. Simple!

Now let's try writing to `textfile.txt`. Remember that writing to a file overwrites anything else that's already in there.

4.   Amend the text in `textfile.txt` so that it looks like this:

```
open(MYFILE,">textfile.txt") || die "cannot open
textfile.txt";for ($x = 0 ; $x < 10 ; $x++){
print MYFILE "The value of x is now $x";
}
 close MYFILE;
```

Then open up `textfile.txt` and see the changes.

5.   Finally, to amend the file rather than overwrite it, simply add in one more >
symbol, like this:

```
open(MYFILE,">>textfile.txt") || die "cannot open textfile.txt";
for ($x = 0 ; $x < 10 ; $x++){
print MYFILE "The value of x is now $x";
}
close MYFILE;
```

There is a lot more that Perl can do with files, and I encourage you to look further for more information if it's sparked your interest. It really is a strong language, with a thriving online community. You should however now be able to accomplish the basics of reading and writing data to and from files.

Perl and CGI

You've already been using CGI files in the previous chapter. Perl is most commonly used to act as a CGI (Common Gateway Interface) between a web page and the web server. This enables Perl to accept variables that are posted from an HTML form or a Flash file.

Working with incoming data

When the data is sent to your Perl script, you need to decode all of the data and strip out the variable names and their values so they can be used in your script. The code snippet here (surrounded in comments, which is how I like to separate out longer scripts) strips out any variable names and values available, and assigns them to a variable called $contents{$name}:

```
####################################################################
####
#check variables sent use post
if ($ENV{'REQUEST_METHOD'} eq 'POST')
{
    #read posted variables into $buffer
    read(STDIN, $buffer, $ENV{'CONTENT_LENGTH'});
    #variables will be received in a name1=value1&name2=value2
    format
    #split buffer by '&' to split variable names and values and
    store
```

```
#these in the @pairs array
@pairs = split(/&/, $buffer);
#split each element of the array by '=' format the values and
#store in the $contents{$name} = $value variable
foreach $pair (@pairs)
{
        ($name, $value) = split(/=/, $pair);
        $value =~ tr/+/ /;
        $value =~ s/%([a-fA-F0-9][a-fA-F0-9])/pack("C",
        hex($1))/eg;
        $contents{$name} = $value;

}
}
######################################################################
####
```

If you posted a variable called name with the value Dan, to this script, you access it using $contents('name'), and get Perl to print the string Dan. You'd use this code at the top of your scripts to ensure that your variables are initialized before you try to use them.

Suppose you had posted name, age and email variables to a script with this code in it. You could simply access the variables like this:

```
$contents{'name'}

$contents{'age'}

$contents{'email'}
```

Simple really. Once you've got hold of the variable values, you could work with the methods we looked at earlier to test, format or manipulate these variables. You could even store them in a file.

Sending data out from the script

To send data back to the browser or to a Flash movie from your Perl script, you simply use the print function. The only thing you need to beware of is making sure you output a content type before printing.

If you want your data to go to an HTML page, you need to use this line of code:

```
print "Content-type: text/html\n\n ";
```

If you're sending your data to a Flash file, then you need to use this:

```
print "Content-type: text/plain\n\n ";
```

Before we finish this introduction to Perl, and start using Flash and Perl together, there's one more really useful structure we should look at: subroutines.

Subroutines

Subroutines are defined chunks of code or functions that you can define and then call from anywhere in your script. You can pass variables to a subroutine to process, and you can have the subroutine return variables based on the processing it performs.

For the purpose of this chapter we're going to keep it simple – we're just going to look at how subroutines are defined and how subroutines are called. I've put some useful subroutines at the end if this section so that you can incorporate them into your own scripts.

OK, let's begin. Take a look at this script:

```
sub my_first_sub {
print "This is my first Subroutine!";
}
```

All subroutines are defined with the word `sub`, and all the statements that make up a subroutine must be enclosed within braces like in the example above.

To call a subroutine you simply use the ampersand symbol, '`&`', followed by the subroutine name. So to call the sub in the example above you would simply use the following:

```
&my_first_sub;
```

Writing a simple subroutine

Subroutines can be called in any order from anywhere in your script.

1. Try this code snippet in a Perl file (you could call it call it `subroutine.pl`) to see how it works:

```
&one;
&two;
&three;
sub one {
print "Subroutine One!\n";
}
sub two {
print "Subroutine Two!\n";
}
sub three {
print "Subroutine Three!\n";
}
```

2. Test it, and you should get this:

Subroutine One!
Subroutine Two!
Subroutine Three!

3. Now try amending the script, so that it looks like this:

```
&one;
&three;
&two;
sub one {
print "Subroutine One!\n";
}
sub two {
print "Subroutine Two!\n";
}
sub three {
print "Subroutine Three!\n";
}
```

4. Test it, and you'll get this on your screen instead:

Subroutine One!
Subroutine Three!
Subroutine Two!

So as you can see, subroutines are a great way to organize chunks of repeatable code – and they're very easy to use.

Some useful subroutines

Below are a few useful subroutines that you can incorporate into your own Perl scripts. These subroutines are quite basic, but I hope you'll find a use for them.

Form checking

You can use the not_complete subroutine to check that all variables you need have been posted to your script from a form. If, for example, you had asked your user to enter their name, email and address, you could check that they had submitted all the information using the unless keyword together with the not_complete subroutine:

```
&not_complete unless $contents('name'};
&not_complete unless $contents{'age'};
&not_complete unless $contents{'email'};

print "Content-type: text/html\n\n ";
print "All variables received.";
exit;
```

continues overleaf

```
sub not_complete {
    print "Content-type: text/html\n\n ";
    print "Sorry you must complete Name, Age and Email - please
try again.";
    exit;
}
```

The first three lines of the script check whether the required variables have a value, and if they don't, call the subroutine not_complete, which prints an error message back to the web browser and exits the script. As you can see, a subroutine can be called from anywhere in the script. As long as all three variables have been initialized, the script prints All variables received and then exits.

This is a very basic form of validation. You could modify it for far more advanced error checking.

Script security

This subroutine allows you to validate the domain calling your Perl script, to prevent malicious people from doing things that they shouldn't. It uses a subroutine called valid_page, and checks against a list of domains that we've defined within the script as being acceptable, exiting where the calling domain isn't one of those we've previously defined:

```
#define Domains allowed access to script and store in the
#@okaydomains array
@okaydomains = ( "http://technomedia.org",
"http://www.technomedia.org",         "http://technomedia.co.uk",
"http://www.technomedia.co.uk");

#calling valid_page subroutine
&valid_page;
print "Content-type: text/html\n\n ";
print "Valid page!.";
exit;

#subroutine that checks domain calling script against the list of
#OK domains we defied earlier
sub valid_page
  {
#if no domains have been assigned to @okaydomains return to main
#script
  if (@okaydomains == 0) {return;}
   $DOMAIN_OK=0;
   #assign http referer to the $RF variable and format
     $RF=$ENV{'HTTP_REFERER'};
   $RF=~tr/A-Z/a-z/;
     #check http referer against each entry in the @okaydomains
array
   foreach $ts (@okaydomains)
     {
       if ($RF =~ /$ts/)
         { $DOMAIN_OK=1; }#a valid domain called this script
```

```
        }
        if ( $DOMAIN_OK == 0)#an inavlid domain called this script -
                        #print error
          { print "Content-type: text/html\n\n Security Violation!";
           exit;
          }
      }
```

The script begins by defining the domains that we are going to allow access to the script, which are separated by commas. We call the subroutine valid_page, which checks the script calling domain against the list of valid domains. When no match is found, we print the text 'Security Violation!' back to the web browser and exit the script. If the domain is valid the script prints the text Valid page! and then exits.

Searching a file
The following subroutine will search a file for a specified value or search string and return any line where the search value is found:

```
#define the file to be searched
$file = 'http://www.technomedia.co.uk/myfile.txt';

#define the string you want to search for
$search = $contents{'search_string'};

#call subroutine
&search_for;

sub search_for {

#open the file specified in $file and assign it the filehandle of
#INFO
open(INFO, $file);
#read file contents into an array of data called @lines
@lines = <INFO>;
close (INFO);#close the file

chop $search;
$x=0;
#print output type for text and HTML files
print "Content-type: text/html\n\n ";
print"\n";
for ($i = 0; $i < $#lines; ++$i) #loop though the lines
{
$_ = @lines[$i];
$L=$i+1;
        if (/$search/)
          {
            #print the line number
            print ("Your Text has been found at line $L");
            print"\n";
```

continues overleaf

```
                         print"\n";
                          #print the content of the line
                         print @lines[$i];
                         print"\n";
                          $x++
                        }
          }

          if ($x==0) {
          print "Your search text was not found!";
          }
          exit;
          }
```

Once the file to search is loaded into the script, and the string you want to search for has been defined, we call the search_for subroutine, which strips any whitespace from the search string and searches each line of the file for the search string.

If the search string is found, the script prints the line number and line of data in which your search string was found to the web browser. When the string is not found, it prints Your search text was not found! to the web browser.

These routines are quite basic and should be adaptable to your own needs, but hopefully you have learned enough in this chapter to create your own reusable subroutines by now! Although we've only just begun looking at Perl, I hope you've learnt enough in this chapter so far to begin thinking up some of your own basic applications and use an HTML or a Flash interface to interact with a Perl script and files on the web server.

So, having got this far, let's start using Flash and Perl together, building the Perl files from scratch this time.

Integrating Flash and Perl: a game score program

In this section of the chapter we'll build a generic high score program that you can use with any Flash game you create.

The main elements of this tutorial are the Flash interface, the Perl script and a text file you will use to store the names and high scores of the players.

For the purpose of this tutorial I'm going to keep my score table simple by limiting the number of high scores saved to three. You can of course adapt the examples and techniques you learn in the tutorial to create a high score table that stores 10 of the highest scores or even 100.

Before we jump straight in and start coding I'll just explain how it will work. We'll create a Flash application that loads up a text file containing some fictional high scores into Flash variables.

We then check to see if the player's current score beats any of the high scores (which we'll ask users to enter into a text box, for the purposes of the example). If the player has a score that's higher than the three we've loaded into the application, then we'll replace the lower score with their score, asking them to input their name, and replacing the relevant score variable in Flash.

We then POST the high score variables to our Perl script which writes the scores to our text file and posts a congratulations response back into the Flash movie. Simple really!

Creating the high scores program

The first thing the high score program does is load the existing high scores from a text file so let's start there. We'll create a text file to hold the scores, and add in some fictitious ones to begin.

1. Open your text editor, type the following code and save the file as `score.txt`:

    ```
    NAME1=DAN&HIGHSCORE1=150&NAME2=FRED&HIGHSCORE2=100&NAME3=BOB&HIGHS
    ➡CORE3=50
    ```

2. Now open Flash and create a new movie, called `score.fla` in the same directory as `score.txt` file. We need to create the text fields that will display the top three names and scores, so on frame 1, draw six dynamic text fields with the following variable names in this arrangement, and label the layer they're on - I called mine `highscores`:

    ```
    NAME1                    HIGHSCORE1
    NAME2                    HIGHSCORE2
    NAME3                    HIGHSCORE3
    ```

3. We'll load the text file into frame 1 of a new actions layer. Before we do, though, we should clear all the variable fields, to make sure that there aren't any values hanging around in the system that will distort the scoring.

    ```
    NAME1 = "";
    NAME2 = "";
    NAME3 = "";
    HIGHSCORE1 = "";
    HIGHSCORE2 = "";
    HIGHSCORE3 = "";
    loadVariablesNum ("score.txt", 0);
    ```

4. Then we need an `if` loop to hold the movie steady until all the variables have loaded. So add a new layer, labels, then add a label frame 5 of the layer Loaded, and add the `if` loop to frame 2 of the actions layer:

    ```
    If (HIGHSCORE3!="") {
    GotoAndPlay ("Loaded");
    }
    ```

    Complete the loop by sending the movie back to frame 3 from frame 2 until the variable contains a value:

    ```
    GotoAndPlay (2);
    ```

    And stop the movie at frame 5

    ```
    stop ();
    ```

The next thing we want to do is check if the player's score beats any of the previous high scores. When you put this high score program to use, the player's score will come from the game. For the purpose of this tutorial, though, we'll just simulate a game score that you can enter into a text field (so you can win every time if you want to!). Because we're simulating the arrival of the score into the movie, by having a user enter a score, we'll also have to have a button that progresses the movie once the score has been entered.

5.   Begin by adding a single line input text field for you to enter a score into at frame 5 of the gameScore layer, giving it the variable name score. Add a button to progress the movie once the score has been entered, and use it to send the movie to a label (that we'll add next) at frame 10 called Check:

```
on (release) {
    gotoAndPlay ("Check");
}
```

So now add the check label at frame 10 of the labels layer.

We'll compare the scores, and if the inputted score is greater than the HIGHSCORE3 variable, we'll get the new winner to enter their name so that we can replace them on the scoreboard. If they're score is less than the HIGHSCORE3 variable, we'll send them to a TryAgain frame.

6.   Label frame 15 of the labels layer TryAgain, and add the dynamic text field to frame 15 of the gameScore layer, giving it the variable name response. Your movie should now look something like this (give or take a few keyframes and labels):

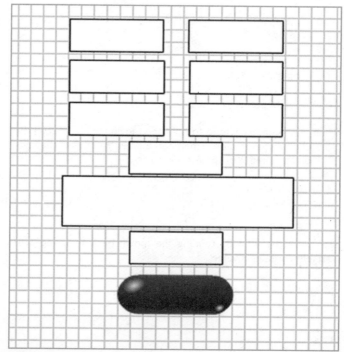

7. On the TryAgain frame we're going to use the response field to display a message telling the player that they didn't beat any of the high scores and to try again. On frame 15 of the actions layer enter the following ActionScript:

```
response = "you didn't beat a high score this time - please try
➡again!";
```

8. Now add keyframes at frame 20 across all the layers, and label the keyframe at frame 20 of the labels layer Input. On the Input frame we're going to use the response field to display a message telling the player that they beat one of the high scores, and asking them to input their name. So add the following ActionScript to frame 20 of the actions layer:

```
response = "Congratulations - please enter your name into the high
➡score table";
```

Now we need to evaluate the score to see if it has beaten any of the high scores. Because the HIGHSCORE3 variable will contain the lowest of the high scores we will use this for our evaluation.

9. We'll do this check in Frame 10 of the actions layer, so add this script there:

```
if (Number(score)<=Number (HIGHSCORE3)) {
    gotoAndStop ("TryAgain");
} else {
    gotoAndStop ("Input");
}
```

Save your movie and test it by entering a game score then clicking the button.

If you enter a game score value greater than the HIGHSCORE3 variable you will see the Input frame and response or else you will see the TryAgain frame and response.

10. Now we need the player to be able to enter his/her name, and click on a button to take them to another frame and continue the movie.

11. Begin by adding a new layer and calling it input. Add an input text field with the variable playerName at frame 20 of the input layer. (Position this text field below the others to keep it separate) and add another instance of the button you used at frame 5 as well to allow users to submit their name.

We'll send the players to a new frame label when they click the button, which we'll call send, so add this on(release) event:

```
on (release) {
gotoAndStop ("send");
}
```

Then you need to add the send label to frame 25 of the labels layer.

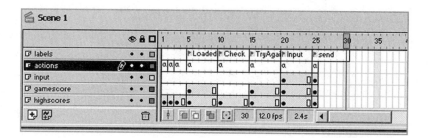

Now we need to reorder the scoreboard with the new game score and player name, and POST the variables of the high score table to a Perl script (which we'll write in a minute).

12.   We'll work down the high score table, checking if the value of the new game score against each of the high scores, juggling the old scores around the new one when we need to, and inserting the new game score in the relevant place. We'll do this at frame 25 of the actions layer:

```
if   (Number(score)>Number(highscore1)) {
highscore3 = highscore2;
name3 = name2;
highscore2 = highscore1;
name2 = name1;
highscore1 = score;
name1 = playerName;
} else if (Number(score)>Number(highscore2)) {
highscore3 = highscore2;
name3 = name2;
highscore2 = score;
name2 = playerName;
} else if (Number(score)>Number(highscore3)) {
highscore3 = score;
name3 = playerName;
}
```

Save and test your movie - you can add yourself into the table as many times as you like!

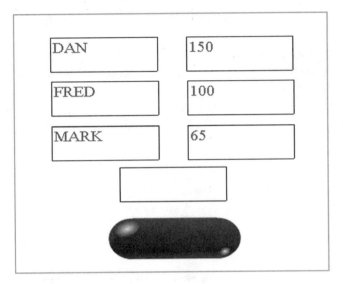

13. Now we want to tell the player to wait through the response text fields, while we POST the variables back to the Perl script (which we'll call `score.pl`). So add that instruction to the actions in frame 25:

```
if (Number(score)>Number(highscore1)) {
    highscore3 = highscore2;
    name3 = name2;
    highscore2 = highscore1;
    name2 = name1;
    highscore1 = score;
    name1 = playerName;
} else if (Number(score)>Number(highscore2)) {
    highscore3 = highscore2;
    name3 = name2;
    highscore2 = score;
    name2 = playerName;
} else if (Number(score)>Number(highscore3)) {
    highscore3 = score;
    name3 = playerName;
}
response = "please wait whilst we update your score..";
```

14. Now all we need to do is call the Perl scripts using a loadVariables action:

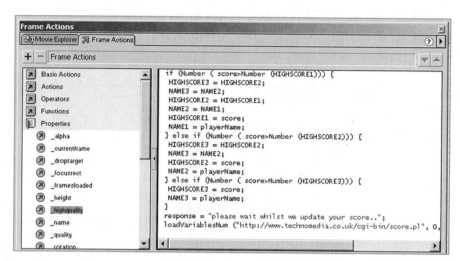

Amend the URL to suit your own setup, save your movie and hit Shift+F12 to publish with the default settings.

The Perl script

We're now ready to write our Perl script, so open a text editor like Notepad and we'll work through the script:

1. Begin by defining the path to Perl, and set the variable $file with the path to the score.txt file (amend both of these to suit your set up):

```
#! /usr/bin/perl # ammend according to your set up
$file ="/home/httpd/vhtdocs/technomedia/score/score.txt";
```

2. Next we decode the variables that were posted to the script and split the variable names and values into a variable array. This allows us to access any variable from the Flash movie using $contents{'varname'} (where varname is the variable name used in the Flash movie).

```
###############################################################

if ($ENV{'REQUEST_METHOD'} eq 'POST')
{
    read(STDIN, $buffer, $ENV{'CONTENT_LENGTH'.});
    @pairs = split(/&/, $buffer);
    foreach $pair (@pairs)
    {
        ($name, $value) = split(/=/, $pair);
        $value =~ tr/+/ /;
        $value =~ s/%([a-fA-F0-9][a-fA-F0-9])/pack("C",
➥hex($1))/eg;
```

```
                    $contents{$name} = $value;

        }
}
################################################################
```

3. Next we set the content type of the output to plain text – Flash requires this format
    when receiving variables:

    ```
    print "Content-type: text/plain\n\n";
    ```

    Then check that all three names and scores have been received, using
    &not_complete:

    ```
    &not_complete unless $contents{'name1'};
    &not_complete unless $contents{'score1'};
    &not_complete unless $contents{'name2'};
    &not_complete unless $contents{'score2'};
    &not_complete unless $contents{'name3'};
    &not_complete unless $contents{'score3'};
    ```

4. Once we know that all the variables are present, we can write them into the
    score.txt file. We'll open the score file with the handle OUTPUT. The file name and
    location are replaced by the $file variable which we defined earlier in the script:

    ```
    open(OUTPUT, ">$file");
    print OUTPUT "NAME1=$contents{'inputname1'}&";
    print OUTPUT "HIGHSCORE1=$contents{'inputscore1'}&";
    print OUTPUT "NAME2=$contents{'inputname2'}&";
    print OUTPUT "HIGHSCORE2=$contents{'inputscore2'}&";
    print OUTPUT "NAME3=$contents{'inputname3'}&";
    print OUTPUT "HIGHSCORE3=$contents{'inputscore3'}";
    ```

    Notice the > character prefixing the $file variable – this tells Perl to overwrite the
    existing file contents. If we were to use >> instead, we would just append anything to
    the end of the file.

5. Finally, we close the file and post a success message back into the response field of
    our Flash movie and exit the script:

    ```
    close (OUTPUT);
    print "Content-type: text/plain\n\n";
    print "&response=well done $contents{'playerName'} your score has
    ➦been recorded";
    exit;
    ```

If all the variables are not present, we call the sub routine called not_complete, which will send an error message back into the response field in our Flash movie, and exit the script:

```
sub not_complete
{
print "Content-type: text/plain\n\n";
print "&response=sorry $contents{'playerName'} an error has
➥occured - your score cannot be recorded.";
exit;
}
```

Notice that we customized the success and error message by using $contents{'playerName'}, which contains the name of the player passed from the Flash movie.

That's it - save your script as score.pl.

Here is the complete Perl script, with comments:

```
#! /usr/bin/perl

# this is the score file that will be written to and read by the
#flash file
$file ="/home/httpd/vhtdocs/technomedia/score/score.txt";

#split out all the posted variables and values
#############################################################

if ($ENV{'REQUEST_METHOD'} eq 'POST')
{
    read(STDIN, $buffer, $ENV{'CONTENT_LENGTH'});
    @pairs = split(/&/, $buffer);
    foreach $pair (@pairs)
    {
        ($name, $value) = split(/=/, $pair);
        $value =~ tr/+/ /;
        $value =~ s/%([a-fA-F0-9][a-fA-F0-9])/pack("C",
➥hex($1))/eg;
        $contents{$name} = $value;


    }
}
#############################################################

#############################################################
# Has to output a Content-type
print "Content-type: text/plain\n\n";

# Check to see if all required variables were received
&not_complete unless $contents{'name1'};
&not_complete unless $contents{'score1'};
```

```
&not_complete unless $contents{'name2'};
&not_complete unless $contents{'score2'};
&not_complete unless $contents{'name3'};
&not_complete unless $contents{'score3'};

#if all variables present - save to score file
open(OUTPUT, ">$file");
print OUTPUT "NAME1=$contents{'inputname1'}&";
print OUTPUT "HIGHSCORE1=$contents{'inputscore1'}&";
print OUTPUT "NAME2=$contents{'inputname2'}&";
print OUTPUT "HIGHSCORE2=$contents{'inputscore2'}&";
print OUTPUT "NAME3=$contents{'inputname3'}&";
print OUTPUT "HIGHSCORE3=$contents{'inputscore3'}";
close (OUTPUT);
print "Content-type: text/plain\n\n";
print "&response=well done $contents{'playerName'
➥} your score has been recorded";
exit;

#do this if variables failed to be posted
sub not_complete
{
print "Content-type: text/plain\n\n";
print "&response=sorry $contents{'playerName'} an error has
➥occured - your score cannot be recorded.";
exit;
}
```

Right, now we're ready to load the files up to the web server.

6. I'm going to create a new folder called score. This is where I'll be posting the Flash movie, the HTML page and the score.txt file. You can do the same and create a separate folder, or you can upload the files to the root directory of your web server.

7. Load the score.pl file into your cgi-bin. Wherever you choose to load your files, make surethat you reference them correctly in the Flash movie and the Perl script. Upload the four files with the following settings:

```
score.swf    777
score.txt    777
score.htm    777
score.pl     755
```

Now run and test your movie from your browser. To make this work in a real game situation, all you need to do is hook up the Flash movie with the game that generates the results, and send those into the text field dynamically, rather than asking users to input their game score.

Conclusion

In this chapter we have shown you enough of Perl to see that it isn't too difficult to create your own Perl scripts and applications or modify/use elements of the many free Perl scripts you can find on the Internet.

Taking Flash further by integrating your movies with Perl allows for dynamic content and the ability to store and receive external data from within your Flash movies. This should give you the scope for some pretty powerful applications – your imagination is the only limit. For Perl information, scripts and further tutorials, take a look these websites:

www.perl.com

www.cpan.org

www.freeperlcode.com

www.worldwidemart.com/scripts

Commercial support for ActivePerl is available through the PerlClinic at www.ActiveState.com . Peer support recources for ActivePearl issues can also be found at the ActiveState Web site under support at www.ActiveState.com/support/.

The ActiveState Repository has a large collection of modules and extensions in binary packages that are easy to install and use. To view and install these packages, use the Perl package manager (PPM) which is included with Active Perl.

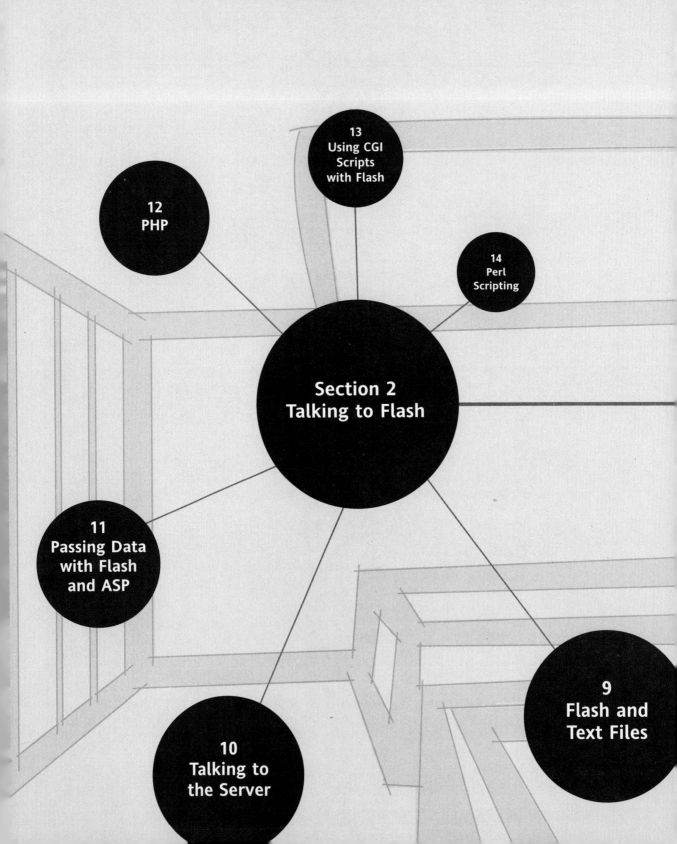

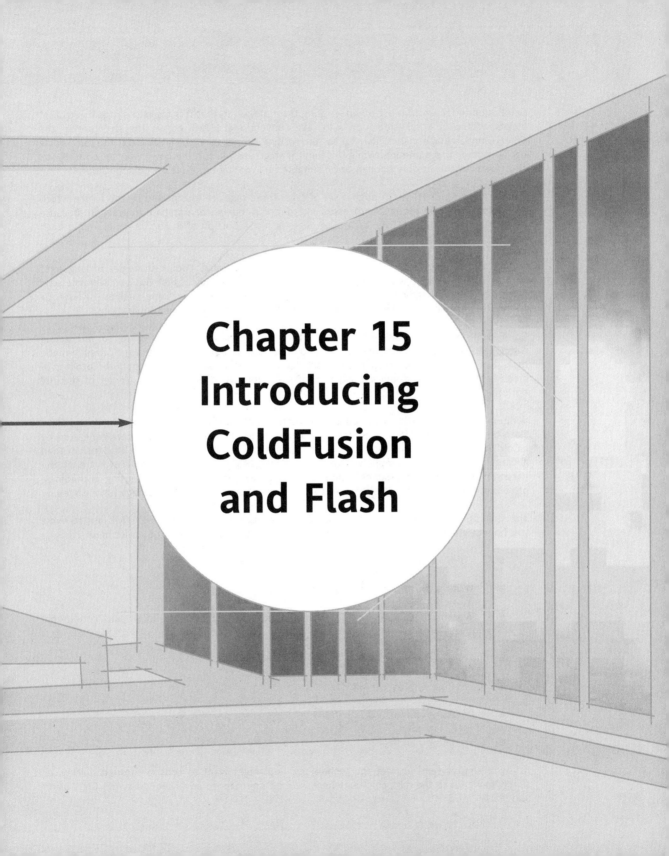

Chapter 15
Introducing
ColdFusion
and Flash

ColdFusion differs from most other scripting technologies in that it is tag-based; this means that scripts written in ColdFusion look a lot like conventional HTML pages. The structure of the ColdFusion language means it's easy to start writing scripts very quickly without the need for a background in programming. While this familiar structure will suit the newcomer to scripting, it's also powerful and flexible enough to be suitable for creating large-scale web applications.

ColdFusion extends HTML through a set of tags. These tags are interpreted by the server, which then carries out the required processes, like decision-making or database interaction. Because ColdFusion tags extend HTML, the entire page, or just a portion of it, can be generated at each request.

For the experienced programmer used to the more 'traditional' coding strategies of languages such as C++ or Visual Basic, ColdFusion can seem a little unwieldy at first. But perseverance pays off and there are already widely used programming methodologies available, such as the Fusebox system (see fusebox.org), which can help you to design highly structured applications.

ColdFusion's main strengths (in my opinion) lie in the simple interface it provides for interacting with Open Database Connectivity (ODBC) and other data sources, and in the range of ready-made tools it offers the web developer. There are, for instance, special tags to simplify the process of creating forms (such as built-in validation of user input), and a comprehensive set of security options.

Some of these features become redundant when you're using ColdFusion as the back end for a Flash-based site, since Flash doesn't accept data in HTML format. Getting the data generated by a ColdFusion script into the format required by Flash can, as we'll see later, be a little trickier than it would be with, for example, Active Server Pages (ASP). But provided you're aware of the necessary tricks and techniques, ColdFusion is an excellent choice of scripting technology, providing a versatile and reliable means to create client-server Flash applications for the Web.

The main purpose of this chapter is to introduce you to the basics of writing CFML, and to show you how to integrate your ColdFusion templates with Flash. We'll cover the basics here:

- ColdFusion: Server, Studio and CFML

- Writing your first ColdFusion template

- Working with ColdFusion variables, conditional statements, loops and conditional loops

- ColdFusion functions

- Working with user input

- Database connectivity

- ColdFusion and Flash

If you're already familiar with the technology, you might want to browse through quickly, or simply move on to the next chapter, where we'll be doing more advanced work with ColdFusion and Flash.

ColdFusion Server and ColdFusion Studio

ColdFusion comes in two parts: ColdFusion Server and ColdFusion Studio. ColdFusion Server is the application server software that you install on your web server, which we'll do in a minute. ColdFusion Studio is separate piece of software that helps you to write your ColdFusion code.

If you've ever used Allaire's HomeSite web authoring software, you'll instantly see the similarities between HomeSite and ColdFusion Studio – the interface is almost identical. ColdFusion Studio is (at the simplest level) a text editor, allowing you to create and save documents. Although you can write your ColdFusion code in any text editor, ColdFusion Studio is designed specifically for the task, being a full IDE (Integrated Development Environment). It provides syntax highlighting, debugging tools, remote file access, a range of wizards, and integration with external source-control technologies (to aid team development).

Whether or not you choose to use ColdFusion Studio is entirely up to you; certainly the scripts we'll be using in this chapter can be written in any text editor. However, for serious application development, using ColdFusion Studio is probably a good idea. You can find a time-limited evaluation version of this software on the CD, or at Allaire (http://www.allaire.com). ColdFusion is included under license from Allaire Corporation. Copyright 1995-2000, Allaire Corporation. All rights reserved.

How does ColdFusion work?

A ColdFusion document is called a **template**. This is just another word for a web page that contains some CFML (Cold Fusion Markup Language) script. ColdFusion templates have the file extension .cfm, which tells the web server that the page needs to be pre-processed by the ColdFusion Server software before it is sent to the user (in contrast with a normal HTML file that doesn't require any pre-processing).

You need to store your ColdFusion templates in the same directory on the server as all your other Internet content. While ordinary HTML files are simply delivered to the client's browser, the web server passes ColdFusion templates to the ColdFusion Server, which interprets any CFML script in the file. The output from the script is then slotted back into the page ready for the web server to send it off to the client's browser. Since only the output from the script is returned to the client, the browser doesn't need to be able to understand CFML itself. All the browser sees is HTML, so ColdFusion-generated pages are completely browser-independent.

Where do I get it?

Well, from the CD, but you should also know that ColdFusion comes in several editions (with different levels of functionality) and is available in versions for Windows, Linux, Solaris and HP-UX servers. A free version, ColdFusion Express is, at the time of writing, available for download from the Allaire site (allaire.com). Many web hosts now also offer ColdFusion as part of an overall hosting package.

Installing ColdFusion

Once you've got your software, installation is relatively simple. First make sure you have some suitable web server software (such as Microsoft's free Personal Web Server or IIS) installed. Then just follow the instructions provided to install ColdFusion, choosing Personal Web Server or IIS in the options as your web server. Once it's installed, you will need to reboot. Two icons will then appear in your system tray. One of these has the right-click option to open ColdFusion Administrator; you can use this to finish configuring the server (extensive instructions are provided as part of the installation), and it will be ready for use. Files with the extension .cfm will now be automatically processed by ColdFusion when you use them in your web site.

So what is CFML?

CFML is a tag-based language, using '<'and '>' to enclose script elements. If you already know how to write enough HTML to construct a simple web page then it will all look very familiar, because CFML uses tags enclosed in angle brackets in exactly the same way as HTML.

It's easy to spot a ColdFusion tag because they always begin with 'CF', like <CFOUTPUT>, <CFQUERY> and <CFSET>, for example. There are currently around sixty ColdFusion tags (comprehensive documentation is available at the Allaire site). The good news is that you only need to know about half a dozen of these to be able to construct a wide range of templates. It's like guitar chords; people have gone a long way without needing to use most of them, the key is in learning to use just a few of them well. You can also write your own ColdFusion tags, and there are a large number of ready-made custom tags available for downloaded from Allaire and other sites.

Writing a ColdFusion template

There's nothing like jumping in at the deep end, so let's get swimming. We'll start with a simple HTML web page, and then add some ColdFusion tags to it.

1. Open up your text editor, type in this HTML and save the document into a directory on your web server with the filename simple.html

    ```
    <HTML>
        <BODY>
            This is a simple HTML document.
        </BODY>
    </HTML>
    ```

2. Open it in your web browser (through its web address, not locally), and you should get:

    This is a simple HTML document.

3. Nothing new there of course. Now let's introduce a CFML tag, `<CFOUTPUT>`.

```
<HTML>
    <BODY>
        <CFOUTPUT>
            This is a simple ColdFusion template.
        </CFOUTPUT>
    </BODY>
</HTML>
```

4. Save this document as `simple.cfm` to the same directory as your HTML document, and test it again through the browser. You should get this:

This is a simple ColdFusion template.

The role of `<CFOUTPUT>` is, as its name suggests, to display output from a script. So all we're done here is tell the server to write some plain text into the document. You can see that there is also a closing `</CFOUTPUT>` tag, just as there would be if this were plain HTML.

5. Between the `<CFOUTPUT>` tags, you can insert anything you'd like to appear in your page. You can use `<CFOUPUT>` tags as many times in a page as you wish (although they shouldn't generally be nested). So, for example, you could add another one to your code like this:

```
<HTML>
    <BODY>
        <CFOUTPUT>
            This is a simple ColdFusion template.
        </CFOUTPUT>
        <BR>
        <CFOUTPUT>
            This is a second line of text.
        </CFOUTPUT>
    </BODY>
<HTML>
```

I've just shown this as an example. In practice you should use as few `<CFOUTPUT>` tags as you can, since their excessive use can make the page slow to process.

So far we haven't achieved anything we couldn't have managed without ColdFusion. So let's introduce some more tags to get things moving along.

Variables and <CFSET>

`<CFSET>` is the ColdFusion tag that sets variables. You set the variable inside the tag; for example, you might have a line that reads:

```
<CFSET speed = 30>
```

This stores the number 30 in a variable `speed`. This kind of statement is usually called an **assignment statement** because it assigns a value to a variable.

Working with ColdFusion variables

1. If you stored the variable in a script, you could use `<CFOUTPUT>` to display its value:

```
<HTML>
    <BODY>
        <CFSET speed = 30>
        <CFOUTPUT>
         The speed is #speed#
        </CFOUTPUT>
    </BODY>
</HTML>
```

As you might expect, the script will give you output:

The speed is 30

Notice the symbols around the variable name between the `<CFOUTPUT>` tags. These are used to enclose a variable name to retrieve the value. The server finds the symbols between `<CFOUTPUT>` tags, goes to look up the variable, and inserts its value (in this case 30).

> *You only need to enclose a variable in # symbols when you write it out to the browser with `<CFOUTPUT>`. If you need to output a # symbol within a set of `<CFOUTPUT>` tags, you should replace it with a double #. For example, if you wanted to output the HTML color value, #FF0000, you would have to prefix it with another hash symbol: ##FF0000.*

2. You can manipulate the value that a variable holds, (and if you couldn't, they'd be called **constants**.) You can add, subtract, take the square root, or do any number of other things with our variables. Have a look at this script:

```
<HTML>
    <BODY>
        <CFSET speed = 30>
        <CFSET increase = 20>
        <CFOUTPUT>
            The speed is #speed#<BR>
        </CFOUTPUT>
```

```
        <CFSET speed = speed + increase>
        <CFOUTPUT>
            After an increase of #increase#,the speed is now #speed#
        </CFOUTPUT>
    </BODY>
</HTML>
```

The output in the browser is:

The speed is 30
After an increase of 20, the speed is now 50

The line `<CFSET speed = speed + increase>` is doing the work. It translates as 'set speed to be equal to the sum of the values of speed and increase', so the new value of speed after this line is processed is 50.

The addition symbol is an **operator**, in that it performs an operation, in this case addition, on our two values and produces a result.

ColdFusion supports a whole range of operators, most of which will be familiar if you have ever used a programming language such as JavaScript or VBScript. Here are a few more examples of operators in action:

`<CFSET a = b * c>`   Set a to equal b multiplied by c

`<CFSET a = b / a>`   Set a to be equal to b divided by a

`<CFSET a = b ^ c>`   Set a to be equal to b raised to the power c

Operators aren't just for manipulating numbers. Some can be used with pieces of text (strings).

3. Try this script:
```
<HTML>
    <BODY>
        <CFSET String1 = "I do not like ">
        <CFSET String2 = "Green Eggs and Ham">
        <CFSET String3 = String1 & String2>
        <CFOUTPUT>#String3#</CFOUTPUT>
    </BODY>
</HTML>
```

Here we use CFSET to set values for String1 and String2. I've done something slightly different here, and placed the `<CFOUTPUT>` tags on the same line as the output, #String3#, which works just as well.

> *Note that when you assign a text string (rather than a number) to a variable, it's always enclosed in double quotes. If you don't use the quotes the script will produce an error.*

Take a look at the line where we set String3 to be String1 & String2. The ampersand symbol & concatenates the strings together in the order in which the strings are listed. I put a space after like in the first <CFSET> tag to ensure that there is a space between like and Green.

4. You can join strings directly without assigning them to variables. This version of the previous script uses the strings directly.

```
<HTML>
    <BODY>
        <CFSET String3 = "I do not like " & "Green Eggs and Ham">
        <CFOUTPUT>#String3#</CFOUTPUT>
    </BODY>
</HTML>
```

As well as joining strings to other strings, you can also combine text with numbers. ColdFusion will convert numbers into their string equivalents automatically.

5. Here's an example:

```
<HTML>
    <BODY>
        <CFSET wrongAge = 2+1>
        <CFSET rightAge = 2&1>
        <CFSET OutputText = "You're not "& wrongAge &",you're " &
            ➥rightAge>
        <CFOUTPUT>
        #OutputText#
        </CFOUTPUT>
    </BODY>
</HTML>
```

The value of wrongAge is converted automatically to a string and joined with some explanatory text in the output, but in order to get the age right in rightAge we added the numbers as if they were strings. That can be pretty useful.

> *If you try to combine a string with a number using the + operator instead of &, ColdFusion will assume that you mean 'add' and not 'join' and give you an error unless the string contains something that can be understood as a number. This uncertainty means that it isn't good practice to use the + operator with strings.*

Conditional statements, loops and conditional loops

Conditional statements in ColdFusion work just as they do in Flash. You already use these sorts of statements in everyday language. For example, *"If it's raining I'll wear a coat"* and *"If it's the weekend I'll be at home, but if it's a weekday I'll be at work"* are both examples of conditional statements. Here's a very simple ColdFusion conditional statement:

```
<HTML>
    <BODY>
        <CFSET MyNumber = 100>
        <CFIF MyNumber IS 100>
            The number is 100
        </CFIF>
    </BODY>
</HTML>
```

Note the new tags, `<CFIF>` and `</CFIF>`. The script checks to see whether `MyNumber` equals 100. If it does, it goes on to carry out whatever tasks are enclosed between the `<CFIF>` and `</CFIF>` tags. In this case, that means printing some text, which HTML will take care of in this example. If the condition is not met (that is if `MyNumber` doesn't equal 100), then whatever is enclosed in the `<CFIF>` block will be ignored. Try this for yourself by changing the value of `MyNumber` to something else.

Notice that we use `IS` and not `=` to compare the value of `MyNumber`, because ColdFusion uses '=' to assign values to a variable.

These are some of the most common symbols used for comparison (called **comparison operators**):

Comparison Operator	Description	Example
IS EQ EQUAL	Returns True if the values are the same. Disregards case in strings.	`<CFIF MyNumber IS 100>`
IS NOT NEQ NOT EQUAL	Returns True if the two values are not the same, disregarding case.	`<CFIF MyNumber IS NOT 100>`
CONTAINS	Returns True if the first string contains the second string.	`<CFIF MyText CONTAINS "monkey">`
DOES NOT CONTAIN	The opposite of CONTAINS.	`<CFIF MyText DOES NOT CONTAIN "monkey">`
GREATER THAN GT	Returns True if the numeric value on the left is greater than the value on the right.	`<CFIF MyNumber GT 100>`

LESS THAN LT	The opposite of GREATER THAN.	`<CFIF MyNumber LT 100>`
GREATER THAN OR EQUAL TO GE GTE	Returns True if the numeric value on the left is greater than or equal to the value on the right.	`<CFIF MyNumber GE 100>`
LESS THAN OR EQUAL TO LE LTE	Returns True if the numeric value on the left is less than or equal to the value on the right.	`<CFIF MyNumber LE 100>`

Working with conditional statements

1. Suppose we wanted to test whether a number was less than, equal to, or greater than 100. We could just use three different <CFIF> blocks to check for these three conditions:

```
<HTML>
    <BODY>
       <CFSET MyNumber = 100>
       <CFIF MyNumber IS 100>
          <CFOUTPUT>The number is 100</CFOUTPUT>
       </CFIF>
       <CFIF MyNumber LESS THAN 100>
          <CFOUTPUT>The number is less than 100</CFOUTPUT>
       </CFIF>
       <CFIF MyNumber GREATER THAN 100>
          <CFOUTPUT>The number is more than 100</CFOUTPUT>
       </CFIF>
    </BODY>
</HTML>
```

2. Try it and see. There's a more efficient way to test for more than one condition. Here's a replacement script. The <CFIF> ... </CFIF> tags can be extended using <CFELSEIF> and <CFELSE>:

```
<HTML>
    <BODY>
        <CFSET MyNumber = 100>
        <CFIF MyNumber IS 100>
           <CFOUTPUT>The number is 100</CFOUTPUT>
        <CFELSEIF MyNumber LESS THAN 100>
           <CFOUTPUT>The number is less than 100</CFOUTPUT>
        <CFELSE>
           <CFOUTPUT>The number is more than 100</CFOUTPUT>
```

```
        </CFIF>
    </BODY>
</HTML>
```

The script is pretty readable, it translates as *'If the number is 100, display a message. Else if it is less than 100, display a different message. Else display a different message'*

Note that `<CFELSEIF>` can be used as many times as you wish within a `<CFIF>` block. This allows you to test for many conditions within a single `<CFIF>`. `<CFELSE>` is then used to catch all remaining cases.

3. You can also test for more than one condition at the same time, and there is usually more than one way to do this. The first is to use Boolean operators. These are just things like AND and OR which do exactly what they look like they ought to do:

```
<HTML>
    <BODY>
        <CFSET FirstNumber = 100>
        <CFSET SecondNumber = 200>
        <CFIF FirstNumber IS 100 AND SecondNumber IS 100>
            <CFOUTPUT>Both numbers are 100</CFOUTPUT>
        <CFELSEIF FirstNumber IS 100 OR SecondNumber IS 100>
            <CFOUTPUT>At least one of the numbers is 100</CFOUTPUT>
        <CFELSE>
            <CFOUTPUT>Neither of the numbers is 100</CFOUTPUT>
        </CFIF>
    </BODY>
</HTML>
```

Here we first test to see whether the first AND second numbers are both 100, and display the message to say so if they are. If not, we test to see whether either the first OR the second number is 100, and display a different message if so. Finally we use `<CFELSE>` to catch all the exceptions (where neither value is 100).

4. Another way to write this script is to use nested `<CFIF>` blocks. Here's how the same result could be achieved using nested `<CFIF>` blocks.

```
<HTML>
    <BODY>
        <CFSET FirstNumber = 100>
        <CFSET SecondNumber = 200>
        <CFIF FirstNumber IS 100 AND SecondNumber IS 100>
            <CFOUTPUT>Both numbers are 100</CFOUTPUT>
        <CFELSE>
            <CFIF FirstNumber IS 100 OR SecondNumber IS 100>
                <CFOUTPUT>At least one of the numbers is 100</CFOUTPUT>
            <CFELSE>
                <CFOUTPUT>Neither of the numbers is 100</CFOUTPUT>
            </CFIF>
        </CFIF>
```

continues overleaf

```
    </BODY>
</HTML>
```

This script behaves in exactly the same way as the previous example. But this time, there are two <CFIF> blocks, one inside another. The second block is only executed if both numbers are not 100.

> <CFIF> *blocks, particularly when you nest them, form the basis of all decision-making in ColdFusion.*

Working with loops

Loops, as you've already seen in previous chapters, are pieces of script that repeat an action, so you don't have to write the same piece of script over and over again. The tag used in ColdFusion to perform loops is <CFLOOP>.

1. Try this <CFLOOP> and see what happens:

```
<HTML>
    <BODY>
        <CFLOOP INDEX="LoopVariable" FROM="1" TO="20">
            This is loop number <CFOUTPUT>#LoopVariable#</CFOUTPUT><BR>
        </CFLOOP>
    </BODY>
</HTML>
```

You have to specify three parameters for <CFLOOP>; the loop counter variable, INDEX, which stores the position of the loop, and FROM and TO, the boundaries of the loop. In this case LoopVariable runs FROM "1" TO "20".

<CFLOOP> counts up in steps of 1 by default. We used <CFOUTPUT> to display the loopVariable's value, so you can watch its ascent.

2. Using another parameter, STEP, we can change the <CFLOOP> default behavior:

```
<HTML>
    <BODY>
        <CFLOOP INDEX="LoopVariable" FROM="100" TO="200" STEP="20">
        The value of LoopVariable is
        <CFOUTPUT>#LoopVariable#</CFOUTPUT><BR>
        </CFLOOP>
    </BODY>
</HTML>
```

Here the loop starts at 100 and increases by steps of 20 until it reaches 200. So the output looks like this:

```
The value of LoopVariable is 100
The value of LoopVariable is 120
The value of LoopVariable is 140
The value of LoopVariable is 160
The value of LoopVariable is 180
The value of LoopVariable is 200
```

3. If STEP has a negative value, the loop decreases by this value. As you'd expect, using a negative value for STEP, means that FROM must be smaller than TO. For example:

```
<HTML>
    <BODY>
        <CFLOOP INDEX="LoopVariable" FROM="1000" TO="0" STEP="-100">
            The value of LoopVariable is
            <CFOUTPUT>#LoopVariable#</CFOUTPUT><BR>
        </CFLOOP>
    </BODY>
</HTML>
```

In this case the output will look like this:

```
The value of LoopVariable is 1000
The value of LoopVariable is 900
The value of LoopVariable is 800
The value of LoopVariable is 700
The value of LoopVariable is 600
The value of LoopVariable is 500
The value of LoopVariable is 400
The value of LoopVariable is 300
The value of LoopVariable is 200
The value of LoopVariable is 100
The value of LoopVariable is 0
```

4. Let's put all the tags we've used so far together into one script:

```
<HTML>
    <BODY>
        <CFSET MyNumber = 6>
        <CFLOOP INDEX="LoopVariable" FROM="1" TO="10">
            <CFIF MyNumber GT LoopVariable>
                <CFOUTPUT>
                    #MyNumber# is greater than #LoopVariable#
                </CFOUTPUT><BR>
            <CFELSEIF MyNumber IS LoopVariable>
                <CFOUTPUT>#MyNumber# equals
#LoopVariable#</CFOUTPUT><BR>
```

continues overleaf

```
            <CFELSE>
                <CFOUTPUT>
                    #MyNumber# is less than #LoopVariable#
                </CFOUTPUT><BR>
            </CFIF>
        </CFLOOP>
    </BODY>
</HTML>
```

Your output from this script is:

```
6 is greater than 1
6 is greater than 2
6 is greater than 3
6 is greater than 4
6 is greater than 5
6 equals 6
6 is less than 7
6 is less than 8
6 is less than 9
6 is less than 10
```

Not thrilling, it's true, but it does show how easy it is use a loop to carry out a repeated action.

5.   `<CFLOOP>` blocks can be nested too. Here's an example that performs a useful task, constructing a simple HTML table and filling in values:

```
<HTML>
    <BODY>
        <CFSET SidesPerDice = 6>
        Possible combinations of two dice rolls:<BR>
            <TABLE BORDER="1">
                <CFLOOP INDEX="OuterLoop" FROM="1" TO="#SidesPerDice#">
                    <CFLOOP INDEX="InnerLoop" FROM="1" TO="#OuterLoop#">
                        <TR>
                            <TD><CFOUTPUT>#OuterLoop#</CFOUTPUT></TD>
                            <TD><CFOUTPUT>#InnerLoop#</CFOUTPUT></TD>
                        </TR>
                    </CFLOOP>
                </CFLOOP>
            </TABLE>
    </BODY>
</HTML>
```

So, as you've seen, not only can you nest two loops, but you can also use variables for the TO and FROM parameters in a loop. Using variables like this changes the range of the inner loop depending on the current value of the OuterLoop variable. As a result, you can calculate every possible combination of two dice throws, ignoring the order in which the dice land.

Working with conditional loops

A conditional loop works without a specified number until a specified condition is met.

1. Here's a conditional loop to try out:

```
<HTML>
  <BODY>
    <CFSET MyNumber = 6>
      <CFLOOP CONDITION="MyNumber LT 10">
        <CFOUTPUT>My number is #MyNumber#</CFOUTPUT><BR>
        <CFSET MyNumber = MyNumber + 1>
      </CFLOOP>
  </BODY>
</HTML>
```

In this case the loop will continue provided that the value of MyNumber is less than (LT) 10. Each time the loop goes round it adds 1 to MyNumber, so this is what you should see:

My number is 6
My number is 7
My number is 8
My number is 9

Notice that nothing is displayed when MyNumber equals 10. This is because the condition is checked at the start of each loop. When the value is 9, the condition is still true, so the value is displayed. Then we add one to the value to make it 10. The loop starts again, but because the condition is now false (MyNumber is _not_ less than 10), the loop ends, and nothing is displayed. Of course we can get round this by using LE (Less than or equal to) instead of LT if that's what we want to do.

Using <CFBREAK>

You can make the code inside a <CFLOOP> block 'break out' of the loop before the loop conditions are met. The <CFBREAK> tag forces the code to exit the loop whenever you wish.

2. Here's a simple example that breaks the conditional loop before its condition is met:

```
<HTML>
    <BODY>
        <CFLOOP INDEX="LoopVariable" FROM="1" TO="10">
        The value of LoopVariable is
            <CFOUTPUT>#LoopVariable#</CFOUTPUT><BR>
            <CFIF LoopVariable is 5>
                        <CFBREAK>
                </CFIF>
        </CFLOOP>
    </BODY>
</HTML>
```

When you run this script, you see that although LoopVariable runs from 1 to 10, the conditional statement inside it tests to see if the value of LoopVariable is 5, and calls <CFBREAK> when it is, ending the loop prematurely.

Hopefully by now you've got a good understanding of how CFML, the language of ColdFusion, can be used to display data, set and manipulate variables, test for different conditions, and perform repeated actions. At this point you'd be well advised to take your shoes off, pour yourself whatever cold or hot liquid you deserve and gloat about how clever you are. You're about halfway there.

Functions in ColdFusion

Functions are the toolbox of any language. They're built-in routines that do any little jobs you'd rather avoid, or get information that you aren't able or willing to get for yourself. There are lots and lots of functions available and, as with tags, there are some you'll use a lot and some you'll probably never use. The best approach is probably to spend a little time browsing through

Allaire's ColdFusion function reference, make a note of the useful ones, and look up the rest when you need them.

When you use a function, you usually pass it one or more **inputs**: numbers, strings, or something else. All functions produce an **output**. My calculator has a square-root key. When I enter 7 (my input) and press the square-root function key, the screen shows the output (2.645...and about 20 more digits). It just so happens that I know how to calculate a square root using a pen and paper, but as long as there's a supply of AA batteries I don't have to. Sometimes a function has no inputs. When I press the date button on my watch, it tells what day of the month and what month it is. Functions with no input are relatively rare, but there are a few.

Working with functions

1. Here are some examples of functions in ColdFusion, tidily packaged into one script for convenience:

    ```
    <HTML>
        <BODY>
            <CFSET Num1 = 100>
            <CFSET Num2 = 200>
            <CFSET String1 = "This is a string">
            <CFSET Result1 = Sqr(Num1)>
            <CFOUTPUT>The square root of #Num1# is #Result1#</CFOUTPUT>
            <BR>
            <CFSET Result2 = Len(String1)>
            <CFOUTPUT>The length of "#String1#" is #Result2#</CFOUTPUT>
            <BR>
            <CFSET Result3 = Len("Mice like Rice")>
            <CFOUTPUT>The length of "Mice like Rice" is
    ➥#Result3#</CFOUTPUT>
            <BR>
            <CFSET Result4 = Max(Num1, Num2)>
            <CFOUTPUT>
            The maximum of #Num1# and #Num2# is #Result4#
            </CFOUTPUT>
        </BODY>
    </HTML>
    ```

    This is the output you should get:

    The square root of 100 is 10
    The length of "This is a string" is 16
    The length of "Mice like Rice" is 14
    The maximum of 100 and 200 is 200

    There are three functions being used here: Sqr, Len and Max. Notice that a pair of parentheses always follows a function. The inputs for the function go inside the parentheses, and where there is more than one input, they are separated by commas. If there is no input, we still use the parentheses but leave them empty, that is `()`. To get the output from a function, we just assign it to a variable. Let's look at each of the examples we used in the script:

`Sqr()`	Square-root function. Calculates the square root of the input (`Num1`).	`<CFSET Result1 = Sqr(Num1)>`
`Max()`	Takes two inputs. As the name suggests, determines which number is the larger and then returns that number as its output.	`<CFSET Result4 = Max(Num1,Num2)>`
`Len()`	Len is short for '*length*'. Takes a string input and outputs the length of the string (the number of characters in the string).	`<CFSET Result3 = Len("Mice like Rice")>` `<CFSET Result2 = Len(String1)>`

Although mathematical functions are good for illustrating how functions work, you'll probably use string functions much more often. After all, we're designing websites here, not spreadsheets. We've already looked at `Len`, and there's a good selection of the most commonly used string functions at the back of the book. We'll look at another string function next, but for the sake of space and good progress we won't iterate through them all here.

We'll look at one more string function before we move on, the `Find` function, which looks like this:

`Find(substring, string, [ start ])`

The `Find` function requires two inputs, and can take a third optional input, (shown in square brackets). It's used to search a *string* for a specific piece of text (*substring*) starting from position *start*, and returns the position as a number.

2. Try this small script:

```
<HTML>
    <BODY>
        <CFSET Position = Find("elf", "Shelf")>
            <CFOUTPUT>#Position# </CFOUTPUT>
    </BODY>
</HTML>
```

This searches for the string `elf` within the string `Shelf` and sets the variable `Position` to equal the position of the first character. The result is 3.

Sometimes the function won't be able to find the substring inside the string being searched. In this case, it returns 0 (zero), which indicates, '*not found*' (the same as false).

3. Try another example:

```
<HTML>
    <BODY>
        <CFSET Position = Find("health", "Shelf")>
            <CFOUTPUT>#Position# </CFOUTPUT>
    </BODY>
</HTML>
```

The value of Position is 0, because the string Shelf doesn't contain the string health.

You'll see that I didn't specify a third input (that is, I didn't give a value for *start*) in those two examples. Since I didn't specify a starting position, the function automatically assumed that I wanted to search the whole string from the first character.

Date and time functions

There is a set of handy functions in ColdFusion that allow you to retrieve information about the current date and time (well, the date and time wherever your web server happens to be; mine is probably five time zones away). Let's look at a few of the more important ones.

Now

The Now function is very simple in that it has no parameters. It returns a value for the current date and time. This value is in a special format called a **date time object**.

4. The output isn't terribly reader friendly unless you make it so. Try this for example:

```
<HTML>
    <BODY>
        <CFSET Time=NOW( )>
        <CFOUTPUT> #TIME# </CFOUTPUT>
    </BODY>
</HYML>
```

It'll give you an output that looks something like this:

{ts '2001-03-05 13:44:03'}

While this is readable as 1:44 PM on March 5th, 2000, it isn't really in a form suitable to display. Fortunately there are other functions that allow you to display the date and time however you want it.

DateFormat

DateFormat takes a valid date time object (such as that returned by the Now function) and outputs a readable date in whatever format you specify:

DateFormat (*date* [,*mask*])

The *mask* parameter is an optional string that you can use to provide formatting information. This mask would generate the output *5 March 20001*, for example:

```
DateFormat("{ts '2001-03-05 13:44:03'}", "d mmmm yyyy")
```
There are special masking codes to specify how the day, month and year should be given. Here's a list of the masking codes for DateFormat:

Mask	Description	Output Examples
d	Day of month (digits with no leading zero)	1, 13, 24
dd	Day of month (with leading zero if necessary)	01, 07, 14
ddd	Day of week (3 letter abbreviation for name)	Mon, Wed, Sat
dddd	Day of week (full name)	Monday, Wednesday, Saturday
m	Month (digits with no leading zero)	1, 5, 9
mm	Month (digits with leading zero if necessary)	02, 09, 11
mmm	Month (3 letter abbreviation for name)	Jan, Jul, October
mmmm	Month (full name)	February, May, July
y	Year (last 2 digits no leading zero)	97, 0, 2
yy	Year (last 2 digits with leading zero if necessary)	99, 01, 05
yyyy	Year (full 4 digits)	1998, 2000, 2003

These are a couple of examples showing different values for mask along with the corresponding output from the DateFormat function:

Mask Output	TimeFormat
dd-mm-yy	05-03-01
dddd dd mmmm yyyy	Monday 05 March 2001
ddd mmm d yyyy	Mon Mar 5 2001

TimeFormat

This is a very similar function to DateFormat. It takes a date time object and outputs a readable time, again in the format you specify:

```
TimeFormat (time [, mask ])
```

The masks that you can use follow the same syntax as for the date:

Mask	Description	Examples
h	Hours (no leading zero, 12 hour clock)	1, 6, 10
hh	Hours (leading zero, 12 hour clock)	01, 07, 12
H	Hours (no leading zero, 24 hour clock)	1, 5, 11
HH	Hours (leading zero, 24 hour clock)	02, 07, 23
m	Minutes (no leading zero)	1, 5, 9
mm	Minutes (leading zero)	02, 09, 11
s	Seconds (no leading zero)	6, 8, 47
ss	Seconds (leading zero)	03, 09, 57
t	Time Marker (single letter)	A or P
tt	Time Marker (multiple letter)	AM or PM

Let's use DateFormat and TimeFormat together in a script:

5. This script uses DateFormat and TimeFormat in an HTML page, assigning variables to hold the parameters for the functions.

```
<HTML>
    <BODY>
        <CFSET DateMask="dddd dd mmmm yyyy">
        <CFSET TimeMask="h:mm tt">
        <CFSET CurrentDateAndTime=Now()>
            <CFOUTPUT>
```

continues overleaf

```
                              Date: #DateFormat(CurrentDateAndTime, DateMask)#
                              <BR>
                              Time: #TimeFormat(CurrentDateAndTime, TimeMask)#
                              </CFOUTPUT>
              </BODY>
       </HTML>
```

You should get something in this format:

Date: Monday 05 March 2001
Time: 1:53 PM

6. We could have nested the Now function directly inside the DateFormat and
    TimeFormat functions like this:

```
<HTML>
    <BODY>
      <CFSET DateMask="dddd dd mmmm yyyy">
      <CFSET TimeMask="h:mm tt">
          <CFOUTPUT>#DateFormat(Now(), DateMask)#</CFOUTPUT>
          <CFOUTPUT>#TimeFormat(Now(), TimeMask)#</CFOUTPUT>
    </BODY>
</HTML>
```

The Now function is evaluated first because it is the innermost function. Its value is
returned and then passed directly as a parameter to the DateFormat function. Doing
things this way reduces the number of variables you need to use, but it's not as easy
to read. It is also slightly less efficient, because you end up having to use the Now
function twice (once with DateFormat and once with TimeFormat). Programmers
like to think of themselves as efficient people and so frown on such waste (meanwhile
filling their fifth plastic cup of the day from the office water-cooler).

There are other date and time functions which will, (among other things), tell you how many days
there are in a given month, what the date will be a given number of days from now and even
whether a particular date is in a leap year. It's probably best just to research these as you need them.

Dealing with user input

No server-side scripting system is complete without a means to process user input. When a user
enters some information into an HTML form or into input fields in a Flash movie you need to be
able to accept this information and process it.

Working with the user's data

1. You've met a basic HTML form before in the book; this time we'll create one that sends
    information to a ColdFusion template:

```
<HTML>
    <BODY>
        <FORM ACTION="form_submit.cfm" METHOD="GET">
            Enter Your Name:
            <INPUT TYPE="text" NAME="username">
            <INPUT TYPE="submit" VALUE="SEND">
        </FORM>
    </BODY>
</HTML>
```

2. Save it as `form_enter.html` (you can find a sample of this on the CD with the same name.) This script creates a simple form containing a single text-entry field with the name `username`, along with a submit button which will send the contents of the form to the script `form_submit.cfm`. The GET method is used to send the information, which means that the user's data will be sent as part of the URL. In other words, if you open the page in your browser, enter your name and click on Send, you will see that it tries to open a URL that looks something like this:

http://pipeyserver/form_submit.cfm?username=Bob+Lettuce

Your server name will be different, and your name certainly won't be Bob Lettuce, but you can see how the form packages the form input into the URL and sends it to `form_submit.cfm` – which doesn't actually exist yet, so you get a page not found error. Let's go on and put together the other file so we can process this data.

3. The ColdFusion template `form_submit.cfm` will receive the information coded in the URL as one or more variables (only one in this case). Having already learned how variables work in ColdFusion, you'll be pleased to hear that the data submitted though the form behaves very much like the ordinary variables we've already seen. The only difference is that variables sent from a form using the GET method should appear in the ColdFusion template as `URL.Variablename`. The variable name is prefixed with URL to indicate that the variable was passed using the page URL.

This is the script, called `form_submit.cfm`, which we'll use to process the variable returned from `form_enter.html`:

```
<HTML>
    <BODY>
        Your name is<BR>
        <CFOUTPUT>#URL.username#</CFOUTPUT>
    </BODY>
</HTML>
```

4. Test it. If you view the source of the HTML page, you'll see that data returned from the form appears in the page as the variable `URL.username`. All we've done is output the value of the variable to the browser. Of course, in the real world you'd probably want to do something useful with the data: perhaps store it in a database or check it against a list of authorized user names. In any event, `URL.username` is a variable just like those we've already seen, and it can be treated in just the same way.

If you know a little about HTML forms you'll know that there are in fact two ways of submitting data from a form. The one we've just seen is GET (where the data is sent in the URL). The other is POST, which uses a different method to pass the data to the target script, and it doesn't encode it into the URL.

Forms using POST are constructed in just the same way, except that the METHOD parameter of the <FORM> tag has the value POST instead of GET:

5. Modify form_enter.html so it looks like this, and save it as form_enter2.html:

```
<HTML>
   <BODY>
      <FORM ACTION="form_submit_post.cfm" METHOD="POST">
         Enter Your Name:
         <INPUT TYPE="text" NAME="username">
         <INPUT TYPE="submit" VALUE="SEND">
      </FORM>
   </BODY>
</HTML>
```

Processing data sent via POST works in much the same way it does with GET, except that instead of using URL.Variablename, we have to preface the variable name with Form instead: Form.Variablename.

6. So the script form_submit_post.cfm, used to process the data, looks like this:

```
<HTML>
   <BODY>
      Your name is<BR>
      <CFOUTPUT>#Form.username#</CFOUTPUT>
   </BODY>
</HTML>
```

There's one more other thing we need to consider. What happens if the variable we are expecting doesn't arrive? This could happen if a user opened form_submit.cfm or form_submit_post.cfm directly in their browser, for example. Unfortunately an error occurs, because the variables URL.username or Form.username haven't been sent any values yet.

Luckily there's a simple function that comes to our rescue, called IsDefined. IsDefined simply checks to see if a particular variable has been defined anywhere in the application. In this case we can use it to check to see if any data in the form or variables has been passed to the script. By using a conditional statement we can make our script a little more bullet proof.

7. Here's the slightly safer version of form_submit.cfm:

```
<HTML>
```

```
<BODY>
  <CFIF IsDdefined ("URL.username")>
      Your name is<BR>
      CFOUTPUT>#URL.username#</CFOUTPUT>
  <CFELSE>
      <CFOUTPUT>No name entered!</CFOUTPUT>
  </CFIF>
</BODY>
</HTML>
```

All this does is to check to see if URL.username exists. If it does, the value is displayed; if not, we now have an error message (and not an error!). Notice that URL.username is enclosed in quotes. The input to the function IsDefined is a string expression containing the name of the variable whose existence we're testing for. Without the quotes, the IsDefined function would try to look at the *value* of URL.username, which may not be defined!

8. Of course what we might want to do is to create the variable if it doesn't already exist. Here's how we could do that:

```
<HTML>
  <BODY>
    <CFIF NOT IsDefined("URL.username")>
        <CFSET URL.username="Mr/Ms NoName">
    </CFIF>
    Your name is<BR>
    <CFOUTPUT>#URL.username#</CFOUTPUT>
  </BODY>
</HTML>
```

You'll notice that here I've checked to see if URL.username is *not* defined. If it isn't defined, it gets created using <CFSET>. It might seem strange that we can create URL.username within the script, since it's supposed to have originated from a form, but you might find it useful for those occasions when you want to supply default information when information which has not been supplied by the user.

Using <CFPARAM>

It just so happens that you could achieve the same result in an even tidier way by using the <CFPARAM> tag. This tag automatically tests for a named variable and then creates the variable with a default value if it doesn't already exist. The script you wrote earlier could then be rewritten like this:

```
<HTML>
  <BODY>
      <CFPARAM NAME="URL.username" DEFAULT="Mr/Ms NoName">
      Your name is<br>
      <CFOUTPUT>#URL.username#</CFOUTPUT>
  </BODY>
</HTML>
```

Using <CFLOCATION>

Sometimes you'll want to make certain that the user is directed to another page, whenever they do or don't enter text into the form. For instance, suppose a user asks for the page searchresults.cfm, which expects to receive search parameters in the URL (because it's part of a search engine). It would be nice to just redirect the user to another page, say search.cfm where they can type in their search string. To do this you use the <CFLOCATION> tag, which redirects the user to another page. Here's a script to illustrate this:

```
<HTML>
    <BODY>
      <CFIF NOT IsDefined("URL.searchString")>
        <CFLOCATION url="search.cfm">
      </CFIF>
      <!-- Code to do search goes here -->
    </BODY>
</HTML>
```

You can see that the <CFLOCATION> tag has a url parameter that specifies the page to which the user should be taken. So now if the user accidentally opens this page (searchresults.cfm) in their browser, they will be automatically be transferred to search.cfm if the text field named searchString wasn't filled in.

As you can see, it doesn't take much work to make your scripts idiot-proof, one way or another.

ColdFusion and databases

No coverage of a scripting language would be complete without reference to database connectivity. Fortunately, ColdFusion makes accessing databases surprisingly simple. There is a ColdFusion tag which does almost all the work of querying a database. Its name is <CFQUERY>. Here's an example of <CFQUERY> at work:

```
<CFQUERY NAME="Departments" DATASOURCE="cfsnippets">
SELECT * FROM Departments
</CFQUERY>
```

The two parameters of <CFQUERY> are NAME and DATASOURCE.

NAME is the name we choose to give our query. This will be used when we extract the results from the query.

DATASOURCE is the name of an ODBC (or other) data source connected to our database. In this case I've used cfsnippets. This is one of the example data sources that are set up when you installed ColdFusion. ODBC data sources can be configured through ColdFusion Administrator, or through the Windows Control Panel (on the Windows platform).

You can create new data sources as required in Windows Control Panel by using the ODBC (32-bit) applet. A data source is just a means by which Windows makes a database available for use by ColdFusion, ASP or any other database-enabled language that uses ODBC. ODBC data sources can be configured for a range of different database types, and provide information about all the necessary drivers and login details. But I'm not going to cover the setting up and configuring of data sources here; there are numerous books and online resources that deal with this area. Suffice it to say for now that cfsnippets is a data source, which gives us access to a specific database file in a form ColdFusion can use.

Between the opening and closing <CFQUERY> tags is the query, written in the commonest database language, SQL (Structured Query Language). Again, I'm not going to teach SQL here because it's a subject in itself. The query in the example simply says, 'Select all records in the table Departments'.

Once you've defined a query, you can process the results. To actually read the values from the returned data, we would normally use a special version of <CFOUTPUT>. This has the additional QUERY parameter, which tells <CFOUTPUT> to step through each record from the query. Let's try it out.

Querying ColdFusion's cfsnippets database

1. Here's a full ColdFusion template that queries the cfsnippets database using <CFQUERY>, and displays the output with <CFOUTPUT>:

    ```
    <HTML>
       <BODY>
          <CFQUERY NAME="Departments" DATASOURCE="cfsnippets">
             SELECT * FROM Departments
          </CFQUERY>
          <CFOUTPUT QUERY="Departments">
           #Dept_ID# - #Dept_Name#<br>
          </CFOUTPUT>
       </BODY>
    </HTML>
    ```

    Dept_Name and Dept_ID are the name of fields in the Departments table. <CFOUTPUT>, since it has been associated with the query Departments, will loop through all the records returned. For each record, it displays the values of Dept_ID and Dept_Name. Notice how within the <CFOUTPUT> loop, the field names behave just like variables.

2. Save and test the page; this is what you should get:

    BIOL – Biology
    CHEM – Chemistry
    ECON – Economics
    MATH – Mathematics

    So, there were four records in the table, and the department ID and name is displayed for each. And that's essentially all there is to pulling records from a database.

3. `<CFOUTPUT>` isn't the only way to work through a set of records from a query. If we want to go through the results without necessarily displaying anything, we can use `<CFLOOP>`, again with a `QUERY` parameter. Try this example:

```
<HTML>
    <BODY>
        <CFQUERY NAME="Departments" DATASOURCE="cfsnippets">
            SELECT * FROM Departments
        </CFQUERY>
        <CFLOOP QUERY="Departments">
            <CFOUTPUT>
            #Dept_ID# - #Dept_Name#
            </CFOUTPUT><br>
        </CFLOOP>
    </BODY>
</HTML>
```

This produces the same output as the earlier query, which used `<CFOUTPUT>`. Although I use `<CFOUTPUT>` here to display the records, you could carry out any other action, such as modifying each record, within the loop.

4. Of course, selecting data from a database isn't the only task you might want to perform. `<CFQUERY>` can execute queries to insert or change data as well. Here's one that will insert a new record into the `Departments` table:

```
<HTML>
    <BODY>
        <CFQUERY NAME="AddDepartment" DATASOURCE="cfsnippets">
            INSERT INTO Departments (Dept_ID, Dept_Name)
            VALUES ('ARCH', 'Archeology')
        </CFQUERY>
    Record Added.
    </BODY>
</HTML>
```

With this query, no records are returned, so we don't use a `<CFOUTPUT>` tag to display any results; there's just a bit of text at the end to give the document some visible content.

5. Similarly, we can modify existing data using an `UPDATE` query:

```
<HTML>
    <BODY>
        <CFQUERY NAME="ChangeDepartment" DATASOURCE="cfsnippets">
        UPDATE Departments
        SET Dept_Name='Archways'
        WHERE Dept_ID='ARCH'
        </CFQUERY>
        Record Changed.
    </BODY>
</HTML>
```

6. Finally, here's an example that deletes the new record from the table:

```
<HTML>
    <BODY>
        <CFQUERY NAME="ChangeDepartment" DATASOURCE="cfsnippets">
            DELETE FROM Departments
            WHERE Dept_ID='ARCH'
        </CFQUERY>
        Record(s) Deleted.
    </BODY>
</HTML>
```

So by using suitable SQL queries and commands, you can accomplish any of the routine tasks of interacting with a database - selecting and displaying records, adding new records or modifying existing ones. You should note that what I've provided here is really only a short introduction to a very large subject. If you're interested in working with databases in ColdFusion, I would encourage you to look for more information about SQL and ColdFusion database access.

Generating ColdFusion output for Flash

Having reached this point in the chapter, you should have learned enough of the basic syntax and structure of CFML to be able to write simple ColdFusion templates (or at least read one without getting too confused). That's nice, but of course it's just the first step. Now we have to get ColdFusion to interact with Flash.

As you'll be well aware by now, Flash expects variable values to be provided in a very strict form from any server-side technology, and while it's not strictly necessary to URL-encode the data you send to Flash, it can help to avoid problems if you do so, and so it's generally good practice.

Fortunately, there's a function in ColdFusion that does all the encoding on the server side for you. This is the URLEncodedFormat function, a string function that will convert any data we feed into it into URL-encoded data so that Flash can read it. It's a bit like television. The TV station encodes the signal, your TV set decodes it, and so you don't have to know how to translate those electromagnetic signals yourself (and anyway, you'd need a TV set even if you knew how).

There's another problem though: ColdFusion templates tend to generate a lot of surplus white space (blank lines) in their output. View the source of any of the examples you've already tried in this chapter from the browser and you'll see that the HTML generated is pretty spaced-out. This is because every line with a CFML tag is rendered in the HTML as a blank line. The larger the ColdFusion template, the more blank lines and spaces get generated along the way.

While a web browser will ignore white space, it can upset Flash quite badly, because it can break up the URL-encoded output and often render the information meaningless to Flash. Luckily there is an easy way to work around this problem, because CFML contains a special tag to remove all unwanted space:

```
<CFSETTING ENABLECFOUTPUTONLY="Yes">
```

What this setting does (as its name suggests) is get the server to ignore all output except things that appear between `<CFOUTPUT>` tags. By using this tag, we can exert much better control over the formatting of the output. The setting can be turned off again later in the page should you wish to output further HTML (something you probably wouldn't do if you're writing the script to work with Flash).

Generating output for Flash

1. To see these two important elements in action, here's a simple script to output some data suitable for Flash:

    ```
    <CFSETTING ENABLECFOUTPUTONLY="Yes">
    <CFSET FlashVariable="This is a test">
    <CFOUTPUT>&MyVariable=#URLEncodedFormat(FlashVariable)#&
        ➡</CFOUTPUT>
    ```

    It's a simple little script. Notice the absence of any HTML tags. These aren't used because the output is for Flash; this isn't an HTML document. In the first line, we set the server so that it only outputs things inside `<CFOUTPUT>` tags. In the second line, we set a variable to store a piece of text. In the third line, we use `<CFOUTPUT>` to output the variable name and the URL-encoded value. The only output displayed in the browser is the output generated between the `<CFOUTPUT>` tags.

    You might have noticed the extra ampersands (&) at the beginning and end of the output. These look a little unconventional, but are a good idea because they act as terminators for the output. I make a point of adding an extra & to the end of all the templates I write, because this prevents any further output (blank lines or spaces) from being interpreted as part of the last variable.

2. Even though we're not outputting properly formed HTML (with `<html>` and `<body>` tags), you can still examine the result of the script in a browser. This allows you to test and debug your script separately from your Flash movie, which is a great help. Here's the output of the script:

    &MyVariable=This%20is%20a%20test&

    Flash can understand that perfectly.

    Note that we returned a different variable name in the output to the one we actually set in the ColdFusion template. We used the variable `FlashVariable` in the ColdFusion template, but set the output variable name as `MyVariable`, which would be the name of the variable we would use in Flash (if we were to send the variable to Flash, of course). Whether you use the same names (often a good idea) or different names for ColdFusion and Flash variables is entirely up to you. The two sets of variables are distinct and separate.

    Usually you'll want to send several items of data to Flash, and not just one variable. (I recently wrote a Flash movie that generates graphs of financial statistics. The script I ended up writing returned over seven hundred variables and values to my Flash movie.) All your script has to do to return multiple variables is to separate them with the ampersand (&) symbol.

3. Here's a script that generates ten variables using a loop:

```
<CFSETTING ENABLECFOUTPUTONLY="Yes">
<CFLOOP INDEX="LoopCount" FROM="1" TO="10">
<CFSET NextVariable="This is value " & LoopCount>
<CFOUTPUT>&Variable#LoopCount#=#URLEncodedFormat(NextVariable)
➡#&</CFOUTPUT>
</CFLOOP>
<CFOUTPUT>VariableCount=10&</CFOUTPUT>
```

This script simply loops ten times, and outputs ten variables, generating the variable names as well as the values from the loop variable LoopCount. Notice the & symbol just before the closing </CFOUTPUT> tag. This separates each of the variable/value pairs.

At the end of the script I added another variable, VariableCount, because you usually need to tell Flash how many variables to expect when you're returning a lot of them; it makes things easier when writing the ActionScript in Flash.

The output this little script will give you looks like this (word-wrapping due to the limitations of paper only - in reality this is all one line):

&Variable1=This%20is%20value%201&Variable2=This%20is%20value%202&Variab
➡le3=This%20is%20value%203&Variable4=This%20is%20value%204&Variable5=T
➡his%20is%20value%205&Variable6=This%20is%20value%206&Variable7=This%
➡20is%20value%207&Variable8=This%20is%20value%208&Variable9=This%20is%
➡20value%209&Variable10=This%20is%20value%2010&VariableCount=10&

You can see all the variables and their URL-encoded values here. You'll also notice that there are no extra white space, no spaces at all, and no carriage returns.

So now we're ready to begin integrating a ColdFusion template with a Flash movie.

A simple example: Flash and ColdFusion integration

We're going to construct a very basic Flash movie for this example.

1. Create a new movie, call it getvars.fla, and add two dynamic text fields with the variable names TestVariable1 and TestVariable2. I also turned on the border and background and selected the [...] font option to ensure that all characters are available. After all, we don't know what might be in the text returned from the ColdFusion template. Add a button.

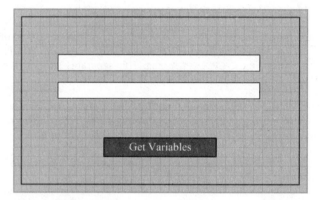

2. The movie will load some variables from a ColdFusion template, flashvars.cfm, into the root when the button is pressed, so first add a stop action to frame 1 on a new Actions layer to make sure they don't load automatically. Then pick a frame a bit further on, label it GetData, and add the following script to it:

```
Result = "";
loadVariables ("flashvars.cfm", _root, "POST");
```

We've assigned the variable Result an empty string so that we can use it to test for data returned from the script on the server.

3. Two frames on from the GetData frame, create a loop to wait for data to be returned from the server. We'll make the last variable in the ColdFusion template 'Result=OK', so you can use that:

```
if (Result == "OK") {
   gotoAndStop (1);
   } else {
   prevFrame ();
   play ();
}
```

This is what you should have so far (if you've labeled the layer holding the text fields and button Graphics and Text of course):

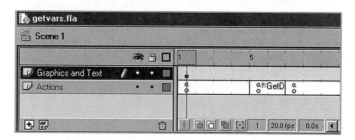

4. Add some ActionScript to the button to tell the movie to go to the frame GetData:

    ```
    on (release) {
    gotoAndPlay ("GetData");
    }
    ```

    Well, that's the Flash movie finished. Doesn't get much simpler than that. Save and publish the movie along with an HTML file into a directory on your web server, and we're ready to make the ColdFusion template, flashvars.cfm.

5. Since this is only a demonstration of the technique for retrieving data from a ColdFusion template using Flash, the template isn't complicated. All it does is return values for the variables (the two text-field variables and the extra check variable Result). Here's what it looks like:

    ```
    <CFSETTING ENABLECFOUTPUTONLY="Yes">
    <CFSET Variable1="This is a test variable">
    <CFSET Variable2="This is another test variable">
    <CFOUTPUT>&TestVariable1=#URLEncodedFormat(Variable1)#&TestVaria
    ➥ble2=#URLEncodedFormat(Variable2)#&Result=OK&</CFOUTPUT>
    ```

    All we've done is set some variables and returned them in URL-encoded format. Notice that the returned variable names are the same as the variables in the Flash movie TestVariable1 and TestVariable2. The extra 'Result=OK' sets the value of the Result variable in the Flash movie, and stops the loop.

6. Test the ColdFusion template page in the browser, to make sure there aren't any spaces or errors, and this is what you should get (again, without the word-wrap):

    &TestVariable1=This%20is%20a%20test%20variable&TestVariable2=This%20is%20a
    ➥nother%20test%20vriable&Result=OK&

7. Make sure the `flashvars.cfm` template is in the same directory as the Flash movie and its HTML file on your web server, open the Flash page in your browser, and click the button. You should see something like this:

Success! We've created a Flash movie that requests variables from a ColdFusion template on the server, and then displays the values.

Of course, what we've achieved is only one-way communication. It would be nice to be able to send information to the server as well. So let's do that now.

We'll change the movie's first dynamic text field into an input field, so that it accepts data and sends it to the ColdFusion template, and from there back into Flash.

8. Create a copy of the `getvars.fla` movie, giving it a new name such as `getvars2.fla`. Select the first dynamic text field (`TestVariable1`) and make it an input text field instead.

The value, since it has the same name as a text field, will appear in `TestVariable2`. Surprisingly perhaps, that's all we need to do to the Flash movie. We've already got the line:

```
loadVariables ("flashvars.cfm", _root, "POST");
```

The `loadVariables` action sends any variables from our movie using the POST method (just like an HTML form), and these will be available to the ColdFusion template. All we've done is to make one of the text fields editable, allowing us to enter our own text.

9. Save and export the movie with an HTML page, just as you did with `getvars.fla`.

10. Now we just need to modify the `flashvars.cfm` template to read the value of the text field. Here's the modified template:

```
<CFSETTING ENABLECFOUTPUTONLY="Yes">
<CFSET Variable2="You typed: " & Form.TestVariable1>
<CFOUTPUT>&TestVariable2=#URLEncodedFormat(Variable2)#Result=OK&</
    ➥CFOUTPUT>
```

As you can see, this template just retrieves the value of `TestVariable1`, which was posted from Flash, and then feeds it back to the Flash movie as part of `TestVariable2`. Here's the result:

It's not the most exciting example, but it does illustrate the techniques you can use to send data from Flash to ColdFusion and back again. With a little more work you could recreate any HTML form in Flash. Text fields are the most simple interface components because Flash provided them for you. But it isn't difficult to create Flash versions of many other interface elements such as check boxes or radio buttons, and to send the values of these components as variables.

So far in this chapter, you've learned the essential components of a ColdFusion template, and learned to integrate ColdFusion with Flash movies. Being able to send information to a ColdFusion template opens up a range of possibilities. You could for instance create a guestbook in Flash, and use a ColdFusion template to store visitors' comments in a database or a text file. You could add a high score table to a game or even create a chat-room environment. Let's look at how you might go about doing some of these things next.

Using Flash, ColdFusion and a database

We're going to be building a fairly simple application that takes two pieces of input from the user, sends them into a ColdFusion template and displays them in a new browser window. This exercise is only one step away from posting the variables to a database, so, not being one to miss an opportunity, I'll show you how to modify the example slightly to do exactly that. We'll create a very simple Access database, connect to it using ColdFusion's Server Administrator, and then send variables into it from Flash. The great thing about this example is that although it is so simple; it'll show you everything you need to know to start working with databases, Flash and ColdFusion –understanding how it all works is just a short step to making your applications truly sophisticated.

Sending Flash variables into the browser

The first thing we'll do is create a very simple Flash file, that will take data from users and send them to a new browser window, via ColdFusion.

1. So make a simple Flash movie, with a Text, Buttons, and Actions layer. Put two input text boxes with borders on the Text layer, with the variable names `firstname`, and `lastname`, and put a `Stop` action on the first frame of the Actions layer.

2. We'll POST the variables from the user into a ColdFusion template called `geturl.cfm`, and open up a new window so that we can display the template. These actions behind the go button will do it:

    ```
    on (release, keyPress "<Enter>") {
      getURL ("geturl.cfm", "_blank", "POST");
    }
    ```

    The `_blank` property opens up a new browser window to display the template, and of course the POST property sends the variables in a separate HTTP header, (you'll usually use this for long strings of variables).

3. Once this is set up, publish your movie to the folder you'll be keeping your test files in as `getURL.swf`. This will be where you need to save your ColdFusion templates as well.

    > *As your application grows in size and complexity, it is a good idea to organize your files in a logical directory structure. Although it might be tempting just to dump everything in one folder, you'll soon end up with a really confusing mess of files if you're not careful.*

4. Now we need to write the `geturl.cfm` template. All we need is the `<CFOUTPUT>` tag that will display the content delivered by the Flash movie, so type it into your text editor, and save it to the same directory as your Flash movie:

    ```
    <!--- this template will display the variables entered into the
    input boxes of our flash movie --->
    <CFOUTPUT>
        Hello #FORM.firstname# #FORM.lastname#
    </CFOUTPUT>
    ```

I used ColdFusion's comment tags here, which will be stripped out when the template is passed to the ColdFusion server (unlike HTML comments, which look very similar: `<!--- --->`). Although they aren't strictly necessary here, (it's not hard to see what's going on), I wanted to introduce you to them as soon as possible. Comments are great for keeping track of your code as you build your templates up; commenting your code is something you should get into doing as soon as possible.

Now you should have the `getURL.swf` and `geturl.cfm` files in the same directory.

5. And that's all you need to do for now, so fire up your browser, open `geturl.swf`, and try it out. If you enter a name and press the go button, a new browser window should open and you will something like this:

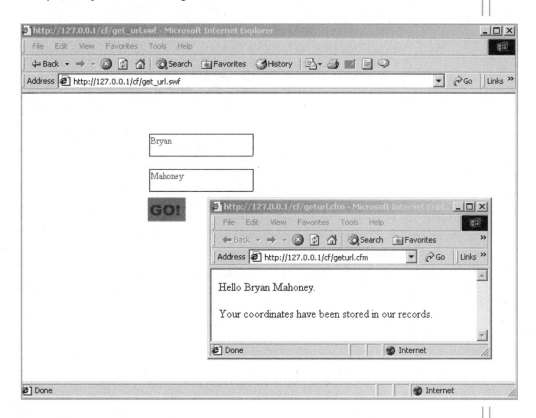

If you have any trouble getting this going, check your web server settings, and make sure that you have set up execute privileges on it.

And there you have it: displaying Flash variables in a ColdFusion template. Not difficult! Of course, you're not really going to be able to get a very powerful application going like this; what you really need to be able to do is store your information in a database. So next we'll do exactly that – get ColdFusion to save these records to a database.

Updating an Access database from ColdFusion

Although we'll build a very simple database here, you'll need more sophisticated databases for your more complex ColdFusion applications. I'd suggest that you investigate SQL server, or MySQL when you get to that stage, and there's a much more detailed look at databases later on in the book. For now, though, I'll just walk you though building a simple MS Access database to use in the next few examples, and then we'll connect to it using the ColdFusion Administrator.

1. Open Microsoft Access, create a blank Access database, call it `flash.mdb`, and save it to the same folder as your Flash and ColdFusion files. For testing purposes, we are going to keep the database in this folder. For live applications, though, you should keep your databases in a more secure location.

2. Once you have created and saved you database, you'll be asked to select how you'd like to design your database. Select the first option, Create table in design view and set up the following fields in your new table (just type the field names into the Field Name column, and select the data types from the drop down lists that appear when you click in the relevant field in the Data Type column):

   ID   AutoNumber. Set it as your primary key (click on the little gold key)
   firstname   Text, with a Field Size of 50, with Allow Zero Length set to Yes
   lastname   Text with a Field Size of 50 again, allowing zero length strings

3. Finally, save your table, calling it names. And that's all there is to the database – I told you it was simple!

   When you've finished, your screen should look like this:

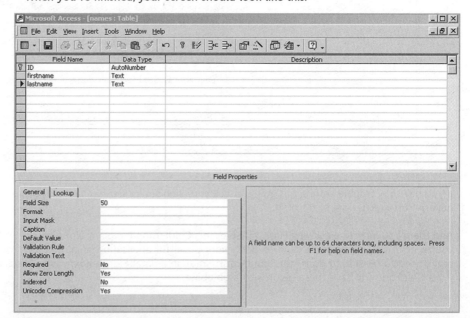

Next we need to create a Data Source Name so that we can access the database. You could just do this in Windows, but I think that as we're using ColdFusion, we really ought to use the ColdFusion Administrator.

The ColdFusion Administrator

4. Open up your ColdFusion Administrator, by going to the click Start menu, selecting ColdFusion Server 4.5 and then ColdFusion Administrator. You'll need to enter the password that you specified on installation.

5. From the main menu to your left, select ODBC under the heading data sources. This should bring up the following screen:

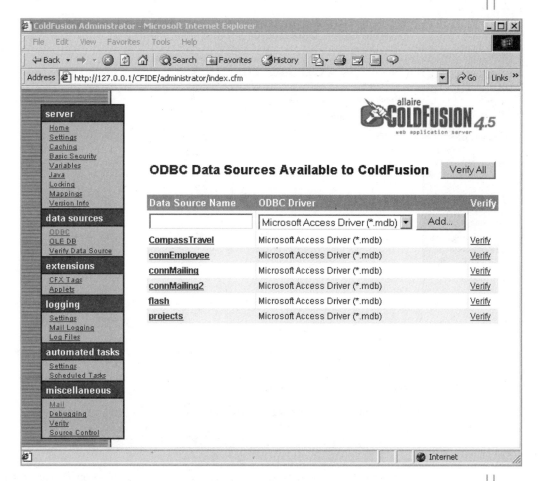

6. Enter the name for your data source in the Data Source Name box – I used flash. Select Microsoft Access Driver as your ODBC Driver and click on Add.

7. In the next screen that comes up, click on the browse server button next to the Database File field. Browse to your flash.mdb database and click on OK.

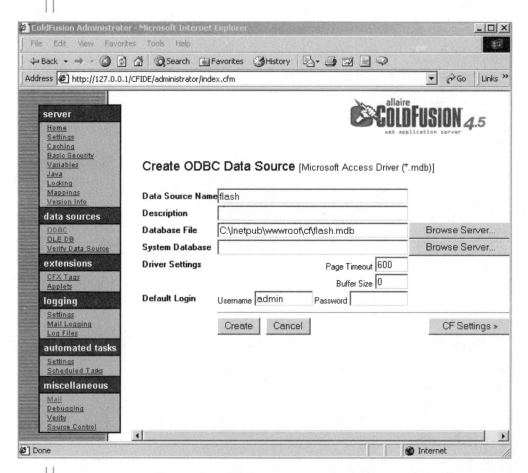

8. Finally click the create button, and you'll be brought back to the window we began in, only with time with flash in the Data Source Name list.

> Note: Make sure that the database is closed before you try and assign the data source name

So now we have our data source, the flash.mdb file and its connection set up, we can go ahead and use it from our ColdFusion templates. We'll begin by modifying the ColdFusion template we made earlier to send the user's details into the database.

Sending the user's info to the database

9. Open up the `geturl.cfm` template. We'll use the `<CFINSERT>` statement to send the data into the database, so make these additions to your code:

```
<!--- we need output tags to display the info properly --->
<CFINSERT DATASOURCE="flash" TABLENAME="names" DBTYPE="ODBC">
<CFOUTPUT>
            Hello #FORM.firstname# #FORM.lastname#.<BR><BR>
            Your coordinates have been stored in our records.
</CFOUTPUT>
```

There should be something a bit familiar about this; we called two of the fields in the database `firstname` and `lastname`, just as we called the Flash variables `firstname` and `lastname` variables in the `get_url.fla` movie.

> *The variable names that you use in your Flash movie have to match the column names in your database, in order for the `<CFINSERT>` statement to work properly.*

We can use the `<CFINSERT>` statement in ColdFusion because we added the auto-number field ID to the database. The ID field automatically increments each time the `geturl.cfm` template is accessed. The first time this template is used to insert data into the `names` table of our database, an ID number will be assigned to that record (usually this will be the number 1); the next time that the `geturl.cfm` template is accessed, the next row of data will be assigned the ID value of 2, and so on.

That's all you need to do to the ColdFusion file; in fact, we've done everything necessary for this example to work. The `on (release)` event we used for the go button is fine as it is:

```
on (release, keyPress "<Enter>") {
    getURL ("geturl.cfm", "_blank", "POST");
}
```

10. So, finally, export the movie to the directory on your server that holds the database and the ColdFusion template, browse to it and test it.

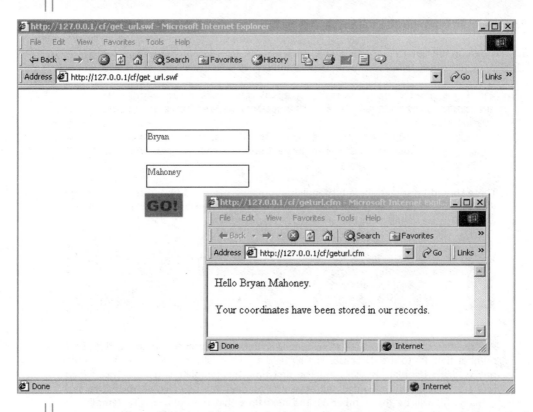

If you fill in input boxes and press the go button, you'll see the window popping up and letting you know that your details have been entered into the database. This time, though, if you open up the names table of your database, you'll see the first name and last name you entered into the Flash movie have been inserted into it.

Did we need to use the getURL command to load those variables into the database? Well, no, we could just as easily have used the loadVariables command. In fact, let's try that quickly, and see what happens.

Using loadVariables instead of getURL

11. Go back into geturl.fla and modify the script in the go button so that it looks like this:

```
on (release, keyPress "<Enter>") {
    loadVariablesNum ("geturl.cfm", 0, "POST");
            name = firstname+" "+lastname;
    gotoAndStop (5);
}
```

12. Then all we need is a dynamic text box on frame 5 with the variable name `name`. Export the movie and test it.

This time you won't get any new windows popping up, but the name you entered appears in Flash instead, as you might expect. The variables are still being sent to the database, but this time your user doesn't have any visual clues to tell them that this is what's being done with their input. Open the database and check.

> *If you get any errors, when you're testing this, make sure that your database is closed.*

So, those are the two ways that we can get Flash variables into our Access database using ColdFusion. Of course, those weren't the most exciting examples in the world, but there are plenty of things that you might want to create with this kind of functionality. Like a Contact Us page that sends an email, for example....

Creating a Contact Us Flash form with ColdFusion

Many web sites feature some sort of 'contact us' Flash form that mails the information that has been entered into it to the administrator. ColdFusion is the perfect tool for this, you can email the contents of a form to the administrator, send a personalized auto-response to the individual who filled out the form, and store the information entered into the form in a database for safekeeping. All very quickly and easily, as you'll see.

The form we'll create will be pretty simple, being just for the purposes of example. Of course you can embellish it as much as you like, but it's always a good idea to start simple, so that you only have to concentrate your debugging efforts on the database and form connectivity and functionality. Once you've got it working, though, apply your Flash skills to the form all you like, you could add animations, drop-down menus, radio buttons... the list is endless

Begin by carefully planning the structure of your application; plan the fields you want to include, and the variable names you'll need, and make sure that the variable names you'll be assigning to the Flash input boxes match the column names you'll be using in your database. When you're designing an application that will work with a database, you should always begin designing from the bottom up, and sort out your database needs first.

The 'Contact Us' application

We'll collect four pieces of information from our users: their first and last names, their email addresses, and their comments. We need one additional field in the database keep track of the records we collect; we'll use this as the primary key. And that's it: the planning for this application isn't particularly extensive!

Database field	Flash variable
firstname	firstname
lastname	lastname
email	email
comments	comments
Contact_id	

We'll begin by making and exporting the SWF file, then we'll set up the database, and finally create a ColdFusion file to 'glue' the database and Flash form together, and send an email to the administrator containing the user's comments.

The Flash front end

1. Let's start by making the Flash movie. I set mine to 400 x 400 and set up three layers: Text, Buttons, and Actions layers. You need a `stop` action on the first frame of the Actions layer, and the four input text fields on the Text layer (it's a good idea to keep borders around them as well):

firstname	Single Line
lastname	Single Line
email	Single Line
comments	Multiline with Word Wrap

2. You also need a Submit button on the Buttons layer. We'll use this button to submit the users input to the ColdFusion template we'll build later, `contact_us.cfm`, using a `loadVariables` action. Then we'll assign their first and last names to a `thankyou` variable, and send the users to a later thank you frame later on in the movie, where we'll thank the user for having submitted their comments.

```
on (release) {
    loadVariablesNum ("contact_us.cfm", 0, "POST");
    thankyou = "Thank you " + firstname + " " + lastname + newline +
➥   "Your comments have been received.";
    gotoAndPlay ("thank you");
}
```

3. All we need now is the thank you frame, (I put mine at frame 5 of the movie), a dynamic text box with the variable name `thankyou` at the same frame, and a `stop` action.

Altogether you should have something like this:

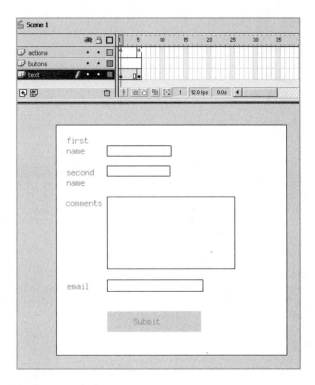

4. Before you export the movie, just make sure that everything is working as you expect it to. The debugger should pop up telling you that Flash can't locate the file, but everything else should work just as we intended; as long as it does, export the file as contact_us.swf.

Setting up the database

We'll save the information we're collecting from the user in another table of the Flash database we created earlier.

5. So create a new table using the same field names as the ones you used in Flash. You should also add one extra AutoNumber field, called contact_id, and make it the primary key. Call the table contacts and save it into the same directory folder as contact_us.swf.

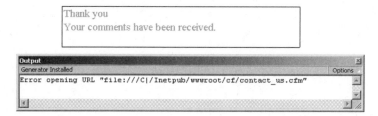

Now all we need is the contact_us.cfm template.

The ColdFusion template

We'll send everything that the user has entered into the form inside the email, using ColdFusion's <CFMAIL> tag. You'll find this tag particularly useful if you want to moderate feedback before displaying it on your site, for an online guestbook for example.

Using the <CFMAIL> tag

The thing to remember about the <CFMAIL> tag is that you need to provide a valid SMTP mail server inside it, or supply one by default through the ColdFusion Administrator. You also have to be connected to the Internet for the template to send out the message – unsurprising, perhaps, but I though it worth mentioning just in case!

6. We'll set up the mail server though the ColdFusion Administrator, so go into the Administrator, select Mail from the left hand bar, and you should come to this screen:

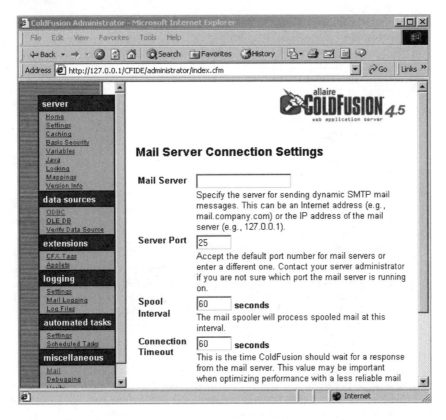

Fill in your mail server address, click Apply and then verify the connection to make sure that everything is OK.

ColdFusion connected to your server. Verification completed
without error.

Go Back

Now we're ready to write the template. The template will throw back errors if it's expecting a variable and doesn't receive it. We can make sure that this doesn't happen by assigning default values to each of the variables, so that if one of the variables doesn't get a value from the Flash form, it can just use the default instead. The <CFPARAM> tag is ideal for the task, allowing us to assign a default value to each variable.

If variables of the same name are passed to the template, the default value will just be overwritten by the new value being passed. When no variables are passed, however, the default values can be used instead, preventing errors – simple really. So the <CFPARAM> tag is a very good way of cutting down potential errors in an application.

7. So let's begin. Open up your text editor, and set up the default values in the first few lines of the `contact_us.cfm` template:

```
<!--- template to process a contact form from flash --->
<!--- set default values --->
<CFPARAM NAME="firstname" DEFAULT="none">
<CFPARAM NAME="lastname" DEFAULT="none">
<CFPARAM NAME="email" DEFAULT="noone@nothing.com">
<CFPARAM NAME="comments" DEFAULT="none">
```

Then insert the Flash variables into the `contacts` table in the database, using the `<CFINSERT>` statement:

```
<!--- use insert statement to save info from Flash form --->
<CFINSERT DATASOURCE="flash" TABLENAME="contacts" DBTYPE="ODBC">
```

> *Notice that we don't actually have to tell the template which value goes where, because the names of the fields in the database are exactly the same as the variable names being sent from the Flash form. This is one of the first things that you should check if you get any errors when you're testing the examples in this chapter.*

Next we need to specify the email address that the email will be sent to, who it's from, the subject of the email, and the server sending the email. All of this information goes onside the first `<CFMAIL>` tag (make sure you exchange your email address for you@youremail.com, and your mail server for `mail.yourserver.com`)

```
<CFMAIL TO="you@youremail.com" FROM="#email#" SUBJECT="Contact Us
➡ Form" SERVER="mail.yourserver.com">
```

> *Note that the email will only be sent if the FROM address specified is what ColdFusion interprets as a valid email address, so when you're implementing this on a live web application, you should carry out some error checking before the address gets this far.*

The content of the message, (the variables from the Flash form), just goes between the first <CFMAIL> tag and the second. You don't need to use <CFOUTPUT> tags (or rather, you can't use them) between the <CFMAIL> tags.

So altogether your template should look like this:

```
<!--- template to process a contact form from Flash --->
<!--- set default values --->
<CFPARAM NAME="firstname" DEFAULT="none">
<CFPARAM NAME="lastname" DEFAULT="none">
<CFPARAM NAME="email" DEFAULT="noone@nothing.com">
<CFPARAM NAME="comments" DEFAULT="none">

<!--- use insert statement to save info from Flash form --->
<CFINSERT DATASOURCE="flash" TABLENAME="contacts" DBTYPE="ODBC">
<CFMAIL TO="you@youremail.com" FROM="#email#" SUBJECT="Contact Us
   Form" SERVER="mail.yourserver.com">
   A contact us form has been filled out:

   Here are the results:

   First Name: #firstname#
   Last Name: #lastname#
   Email: #email#
   Comments: #comments#
</CFMAIL>
```

> *The text that appears between the <CFMAIL> tags includes white space, so you can't use HTML formatting (line breaks, fonts, etc.), unless you specify in the tag that you want to send an HTML email – and if you do that, then you have to format the entire message with HTML tags.*

8. Save the file as contact_us.cfm. You'll be able to point your browser straight at this page without getting any errors, because of the default values we set up at the beginning – in fact, if you do point the form straight from the browser, you'll receive an email from the system containing the default information. Not a very interesting read, but at least you know that everything's working OK.

9. Now all the pieces are ready, and hopefully all saved in the same place on your server, so go ahead and test contact_us.swf. Once you've submitted the form, you should get the final screen like this:

> Thank you Bryan Mahoney
> Your comments have been received.

Check the contacts table of your database to see the details you submitted and, fairly soon, depending on your mail server, you should receive the email notification at the address you specified in the <CFMAIL> tag.

That was a fairly simple example, though I hope effective, example of some of the things ColdFusion can let you do really simply. You've sent information from Flash into a database and into and email using ColdFusion as the go-between.

Summary

In this chapter you've built some simple but extremely functional applications, and seen how ColdFusion can make that development process so much easier. You built only a couple of applications, but I hope it should provide all the basics that you need to start building more and more complex and dynamic Flash movies. Don't forget to use the resources at www.allaire.com , and the language reference that is installed when you install ColdFusion. Good luck!

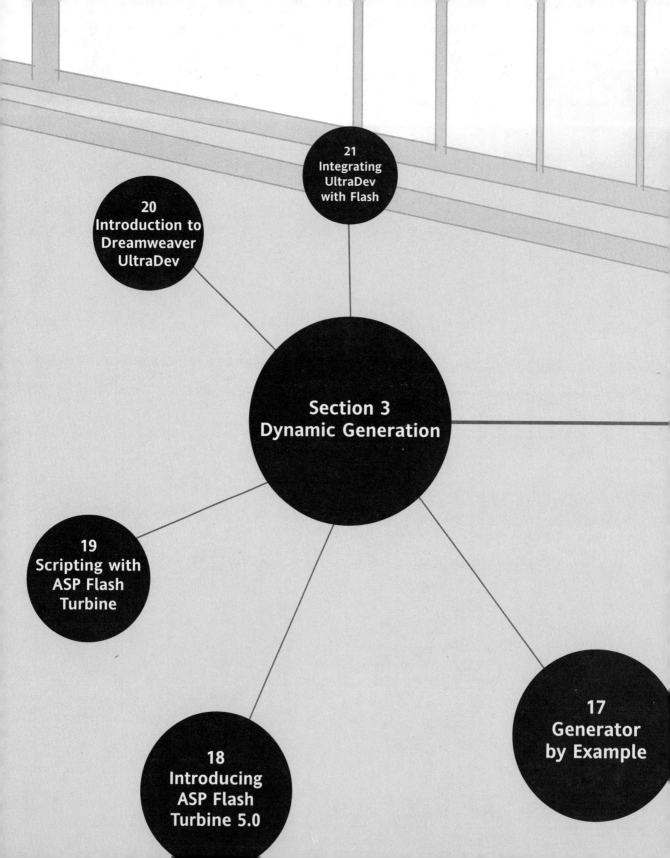

Chapter 16
Introducing
Macromedia
Generator

This chapter is intended to give you a general introduction to Macromedia Generator; what it is, what it does, and how it works. We'll look at the benefits and limitations of Generator's different modes, **authoring**, **online**, and **offline**, and the different packages available to you. We'll also look at some of the aspects of Generator best suited to creating dynamic Flash/Generator content: objects, variables, and data sources.

The chapter that follows this, *Generator by Example*, puts Generator to work, building an example application that incorporates almost all of what you'll see in this chapter. Let's deal with the fundamental questions first: '*What is Generator?*' and '*Doesn't it cost too much?*'

What is Generator?

This question is asked time and again; everybody has heard of Generator, but few people actually know what it is or what it does.

Adding to the mystery is the fact that nobody has really *seen* Generator. They may have seen Generator output, but strangely, Generator itself has no user interface of its own. The closest thing would be a couple of Generator windows/panels that show up in the Flash authoring environment when the authoring extensions are installed. A Flash designer who may be thinking about exploring this 'Generator' thing they've heard about, can't just open-up Generator and start playing with menu options to see what they do, because there simply is nothing *to* open-up, there *is* no menu bar. As many Flash developers tend to concentrate on the graphical front end, a software product that they can't see is pretty hard to make much sense of, so it's hardly surprising that Generator is perceived as a little mysterious.

So what is it? The generic answer is that Generator is a dynamic graphical content delivery solution that works through Flash. What that means is that Generator feeds various types of content (textual, graphic, or audio for example) into a Flash template, and assembles a file in any of the formats that Flash can export plus a few (client-side and server-side image maps, text, debugging logs) at run-time.

> *Run-time is defined as the point in time when the template is accessed and processed. Run-time can happen at various times and be triggered by various events according to the mode you're using; by users accessing a web site template and server, for example, or when you're publishing files directly from Flash using the Generator authoring extensions. A Generator template, or SWT, is very similar to a SWF, in that it's authored the same way in Flash, but contains placeholders where Generator content will be pulled in.*

Isn't Generator too expensive?

This is another frequent question, to which the answer should be a qualified no. There are different Generator packages available, each with a different market and pricing.

Generator Authoring Extensions are absolutely free, and have huge benefits for developers, mostly by way of time saving. This is a tool that everybody should have, and Macromedia seems to agree, because the authoring extensions ship with Flash 5.

The **Enterprise Edition** of Generator uses a pricing model that is in line with large-scale implementations and starts in the four figure range for a single CPU. As most applications on this scale utilize numerous CPUs this can quickly add up to a substantial sum. However, with this price tag comes a whole set of among other things, extremely advanced caching capabilities and an administration servlet, all absolute essentials for large-scale applications. If someone needs the features that come with the Enterprise Edition, they're unlikely to be unable to afford it; it's just part of the large investment that enterprise-level hardware and software development entails.

The **Developer Edition** falls between the other two in terms of both price and features, and is in the three-figure range. It satisfies most of the needs of smaller scale projects, and has a fairly robust set of features. You can find a trial version of the Developer Edition on the accompanying CD.

How does it work?

Generating dynamic content begins with the Flash authoring environment. The developer creates templates, in Flash, with placeholders for the content that Generator will fill in. These placeholders can be Generator objects, which are bitmaps, sounds, charts, tickers, lists, etc., or they can be Generator variables, which will be replaced by values. The variables can be used for a number of things ranging from strings of text, to parameter values, frame labels or instance names. The information that Generator uses to populate and create the content is stored in data sources - more on these later.

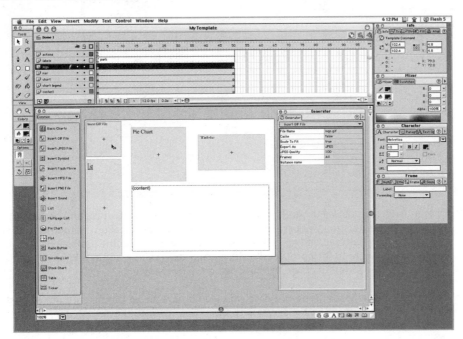

Once completed, the template can be used in one of three modes: **authoring**, **offline** or **online**.

Authoring mode

Authoring mode can be used without having any of the server components (which comprise the Enterprise and Developer Editions) installed. You simply use Flash together with the Generator authoring extensions that come with Flash 5, to develop and produce a template, from which you create your output. In this mode, Generator is essentially just a development tool that allows you to test a template without having to run it through the server component in order to see the final output. Essentially, it creates a preview of what the template would generate had it been run through the server, but as this preview file is a real and fully functional SWF (or any other format that you choose), it can be used as is.

For example, you might create a template that graphically represents some statistical data in a pie chart. Let's say, for example, that this data will ultimately be coming in from a database recording the results of a live online survey. You may not have access to the live data while you're building the template and laying it out; the Generator server components may not even be installed yet. It couldn't matter less, authoring mode still allows you to create and preview templates.

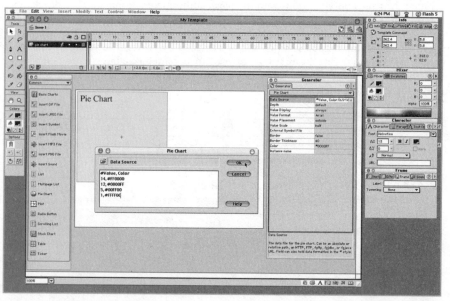

In fact, even if the live data and server components were available, it would still be much more efficient to do the production work solely in authoring mode using local test data. This is because there's only one step between editing and previewing the content that the template will generate (provided your template is set up properly with a valid data source and the Publish Settings in Flash include the Generator Template format). Just do a Test Movie.

In order to test the template using live data, you would have to go through a number of steps: publish the template, place it on the server with the proper path to the data source, and then hit the template through a web browser. This can get pretty time consuming, especially if you're wrapped-up in tweaking layout and display issues. Authoring mode's one-step preview allows you to generate your content immediately. Here's the output from our previous example:

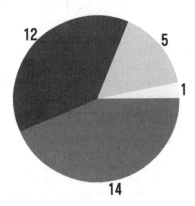

When you're working with data that won't change, though, and you don't need the server components, what was previously a testing and previewing step now becomes the final step in the production process; you simply use Generator in authoring mode as a production tool and save yourself what could have been hours drawing the pie chart in Flash.

So, authoring mode is basically just a first step – creating the template – towards using Generator in its more powerful offline and online modes. But because authoring mode gives you a final product, it eliminates dependence on server components, allowing you to use it alone as an incredibly useful tool.

On its own terms, authoring mode is beneficial in a number of ways. It is a tremendous time saver. Anything that can be done with Generator can could also be done manually – charts, lists, tickers, etc. can all be built from scratch in Flash, but it takes quite a bit of time, whereas Generator authoring mode does it, literally, in an instant. It also allows you to edit content quickly and easily without modifying the FLA, since the content editing can be done in the data sources. In this mode, Generator is essentially just a development mode, and the data sources are most often plain text files.

Another quick and simple way to pass data to the template in authoring mode is to use the Parameters fields on the Generator tab of Flash's Publish Settings (see the Generator Publish Settings section for more information). This is a great way of testing the template's output without having to create a separate data source. Just remember to clear the fields before exporting the final template so that test data isn't being sent as well, because that would cause you problems when you want to pull data in from other data sources. You can create complex 3D charts, infinite scrolling tickers and other graphically rich content, incredibly easily; just let Generator handle all the calculations, drawing and animation. You don't even have to layout the cash for the server components. We'll take a closer look at these examples later.

The limitations of authoring mode are mainly the result of not having access to the server components. For example, it may be very easy to update Flash content by making changes to a plain text Generator data source rather than editing an FLA, but the Flash application still needs to be opened in order to publish a final output file in authoring mode. So authoring mode is not as dynamic as the other Generator modes.

Offline mode

Working in offline mode involves using Generator to process a template and create a final output file on the server. That file can then be accessed by any appropriate client application.

So, while you still use Flash to create the template, in offline mode, Generator processes the template on the server, and Flash is no longer needed once the template has been created.

Offline Generator is invoked from a command line, like the MS-DOS prompt or a UNIX/LINUX shell, or can be run from a batch file or CGI script. Offline mode is commonly used to schedule generation to take place whenever content needs to be updated: weekly, daily, hourly, every ten minutes, or whatever is warranted. You can use an additional application like Windows Task Scheduler, or Cron, to run specified programs or commands at given times or intervals.

The basic `generate` command looks like this:

```
generate -swf MyMovie.swf MyTemplate.swt
```

It simply means: *'generate this file type (`swf`), named this (`MyMovie.swf`), from this template (`MyTemplate.swt`).'*

You can create a lot of file types using offline mode: SWF, GIF, JPG, PNG, QuickTime, text, server-side and client-side image maps, and both Windows and Macintosh projectors. Log files can also be generated in offline mode, to different levels of detail. You simply specify a level from 1 to 3. If you wanted a verbose log file, detailing all errors, warnings, and data sources, you'd use a command line like this:

```
generate -swf MyMovie.swf -log MyLog.txt -debug 3 MyTemplate.swt
```

You can use the standard output instead of having Generator write to a file. This is often necessary when you're working with CGI scripts, and is achieved with a hyphen in place of the file name, like this:

```
generate -swf - MyTemplate.swt
```

You can send variables to the template by using the parameter option `-param` in the command line, like this:

```
generate -jpg MyBitmap.jpg MyTemplate.swt -param MyVar MyValue
```

Make sure you surround the entire value with quotes when spaces are included in the value:

```
generate -jpg MyBitmap.jpg MyTemplate.swt -param MyVar "This is
my string!"
```

You can create many files from the same template and place them in different directories on your web server simultaneously, and all with a single command.

For example:

```
generate -swf C:\MyRoot\MyMovie.swf
         -gif C:\MyRoot\MyNonFlash\MyImages\MyBitmap.gif
         -xwin32 C:\MyRoot\MyDownloads\MyProjector.exe
         -xmacppc C:\MyRoot\MyDownloads\MyProjector.hqx
         C:\MyRoot\MyTemplates\MyTemplate.swt
```

This single command would process the template and create a SWF in the root, a GIF in the image directory of the non-Flash site, and a Windows and a Macintosh projector in the downloads directory. As you can see, complete file paths can be specified for any files, including the template. This allows freedom of organization within any directory structure. In fact, even the generate command can be specified with a complete file path. However, for simplicity's sake it is recommended that the command be run from the Generator directory, or that the path to the Generator directory be included in the system path.

The command line syntax is completely standard, and, since Flash is out of the picture at this point, anybody can update the site, they don't even need to know Flash.

This mode is useful for sites that don't require real-time content updates. For example, if a company's home page changes its features daily, it would only require offline mode to run once a day, and could be scheduled to run every day at midnight. If the company issues a big press release and wants the site updated immediately, rather than waiting until the automatic update at midnight, then they just call anyone who can run the command or batch file and it's done. Simple. That person need never have opened Flash, an image editor, or QuickTime, but they can still create the SWFs, GIFs, JPGs, PNGs, and QuickTime movies.

The benefit of offline mode over online mode is that it reduces the load on the server. If offline mode runs once a day, the generated file can be served out to each of the 10,000 users who access the site on a given day. In online mode, that would mean 10,000 instances of Generator that get run in one day, and it would all be wasted processor cycles since the content doesn't change.

However, offline mode would not be the right choice for something like an e-commerce application, such as a shopping cart and order tracking system, since that requires real-time data. Say a user places an order online at an e-commerce site that is using offline mode. Should the user place their order and then immediately check their account status page, the order wouldn't show up on the page, because offline Generator hasn't been run since the order was placed a few seconds ago. This is a job for online mode.

Offline mode can simulate online generation by placing a CGI script in the mix. Users access the script, which in turn triggers offline Generator to create a final output file. This file is then served to the client. CGI scripts are also an easy way to remotely invoke offline generation from anywhere with Internet access. However, this is just a simulation, and is slower and not nearly as powerful as the real online mode.

Online mode

Online mode places the template right inside the live client-to-server path. The client accesses the template, which is usually embedded in an HTML page or within another movie/template, and that triggers Generator to create the specified content on the fly and send it directly out to the client browser.

Unlike offline mode, online mode Generator is not invoked through a command line. Since online Generator is an extension of the web server, a request for a SWT template file is what triggers it. In other words, when a user hits a web page, be it an HTML document or a Flash file, with a SWT embedded in it, the web server knows to process the template and serve out the resulting content rather than serving out the SWT file as is.

The specification of the file type to serve out is set using the reserved type variable appended to the URL of the template. The syntax is standard:

```
MyTemplate.swt?type=gif
```

This template's URL replaces the URL of the file that is being generated. In other words, if a GIF is being generated, as it is in this example, then the URL would go into the appropriate HTML image tags, like so:

```
<IMG SRC="MyTemplate.swt?type=gif">
```

The template URL would not go in the Object/Embed tags, since GIFs are supported natively by HTML and don't need to be embedded as Flash movies and other media do. So wherever the URL of the media type being generated goes is where the template URL with that file type specification goes. GIFs, JPGs and PNGs go into IMG tags, Flash movies go into Object/Embed tags, and QuickTime movies in Embed tags.

Online mode can generate SWFs, GIFs, JPGs, PNGs and QuickTime movies. Image maps are not generated in online mode since they require integration into an HTML page or server-side CGI script, and cannot be fed directly to the client the way the aforementioned file types can. Standalone projector files are another output file type not supported by online mode since they cannot be served directly to the client either.

SWF is the default file type and therefore does not need a type specified in the URL, though specifying it does no harm. Either of the following URLs in the Object/Embed tags would generate a SWF in online mode:

```
MyTemplate.swt
```

```
MyTemplate.swt?type=swf
```

Just as variables can be sent to the template in offline mode via the command line, variables can be passed to the template in online mode by appending them to the URL in the same manner as the file type specification, such as:

```
MyTemplate.swt?MyVar1=MyValue1&MyVar2=MyValue2
```

These variables, as well as the file type specifications, can either be hard-coded into the HTML containing the templates, or they can be appended to a template URL entered directly into a browser. Note that to include values with spaces or special characters, standard URL-encoding must be used.

Online mode is the choice for serving out real-time data. Online financial applications, e-commerce, real-time stock charts, live sports scores; these are all great uses of online Generator.

Take a look at USABancShares (www.usabancshares.com/broadband) for example. The 100% Flash user interface was co-developed by Braincraft and USABancShares.com in-house developers, and uses Generator's online mode to generate real-time Flash data for clients, so transactions can be made just as easily as at an ATM. It's also much faster than HTML online banks, because the entire page doesn't have to be loaded for every new set of content. Instead, a simple Flash loadMovie action is used to load the new content in tiny movies, while the rest of the interface stays put. You could say that online Generator has revolutionized online banking the same way online banking has revolutionized personal finance!

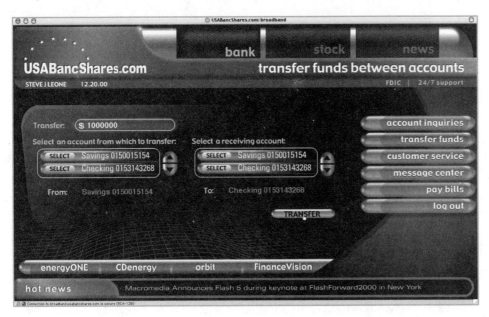

While we're talking about online financial applications and e-commerce applications, we should address the question of security. So, can usernames/passwords, credit card numbers and other sensitive information be safely sent using Flash and Generator? Absolutely. Think about the process and the elements involved, and it soon becomes obvious that it can be just as secure as, say Amazon.com's HTML-based site. Flash is just the front-end interface that can live on a secure server. Generator is just a server extension that takes the data and builds Flash files according to the templates. Transmission of the files to the client is fully encrypted just as any other file served out from a secure server. The data source can live on the secure server or it can be retrieved from an outside source. In the latter case, the transmission of data to the template can be encrypted as well. Go to https://broadband.usabancshares.com and the browser will indicate that it is a secure site. View the certificate. Be at ease.

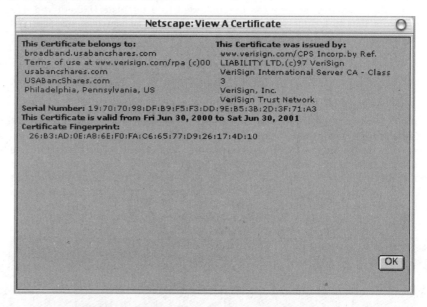

You can use online mode to customize and personalize everything from content, to the user interface, to advertisements. With a single template, any number of clients can be served; each with individually branded interfaces that can be further customized and saved for their next visit. On each subsequent visit, while the interface would remain exactly how they had personalized it, the content would be fresh. One template, countless 'skins', and unique content for each and every visitor - that's the power of online Generator.

Limitations to Generator's online mode aren't many in number, and really only come into play according to the edition you're using.

So, now you know about Generator modes, we should look at what options are available to you.

Generator authoring extensions

The Generator authoring extensions are a free set of what are called **Generator Objects**, that add onto the functionality of Flash, giving you a powerful set of tools to help you create things like charts, tickers, scrolling lists, etc. easily. Along with the objects, the ability to use Generator variables is another added benefit of the authoring extensions. As we've already seen, these extensions are essentially used to author Generator templates, but because previewing/testing them creates real files, they are essentially being used to author Generator content.

The authoring extensions can be installed on any Windows or Macintosh system running Flash 4 or 5. The authoring extensions ship with Flash 5 (though require a distinct installation), and the free extensions for Flash 4 can be downloaded from Macromedia's site at www.Macromedia.com/generator.

To verify that the authoring extensions are installed, choose Window > Generator Objects from the Flash menu. If the palette of objects appears, the extensions are there.

Included with the authoring extensions are the Generator SDK (**S**oftware **D**evelopers **K**it) and API (**A**pplication **P**rogramming **I**nterface) that allow you to extend Generator's functionality by creating custom objects. For example, Java developers can create their own objects that will display data in any number of ways. We'll look more closely at Generator's own objects later.

Any Flash developer who wants to can author or use an extension; and although many people don't use them, they are available and immensely helpful. Just as with most high-end software applications, there are numerous built-in tools, shortcuts, and extensions that many users never take the time to learn (and waste precious development time because they don't.) The Generator authoring extensions are just such a tool, and I can't encourage you enough to start working with them!

The key benefits of using authoring extensions include development timesaving, quick and easy updating, and of course, learning the template creating tools that you would have to use should you decide to work with the more robust Developer and Enterprise Editions.

The limitations of the authoring extensions are pretty much inline with those of authoring mode since they go hand in hand. No server components are available with the authoring extensions alone, so you can't use offline or online modes, only the authoring mode. Limitations of the objects themselves are somewhat negated by the inclusion of the SDK/API since this opens them up for modification or creation from scratch.

Generator 2 Developer Edition

While the authoring extensions offer huge benefits to developers at no cost, the Developer Edition extends those offerings by adding the server components that really let Generator flex its muscle. It allows you to set up a site and just walk away, leaving Generator to handle the updates, and users to dictate the dynamic content they receive.

In addition to everything in authoring mode, Developer Edition supports both offline and online modes. For offline generation, it can be installed on Windows, Sun Solaris and Red Hat Linux. For online generation, which functions as an extension of a web server, Internet Information Server, Personal Web Server, iPlanet Web Server, Apache HTTP Server and Netscape Enterprise Server are all supported. See Macromedia's documentation for the latest specific version and configuration requirements.

While a detailed discussion is unwarranted here, it is worth mentioning that you can change the default configuration of the Developer Edition by editing the generator.properties file. This text file lives in the properties directory within the Generator directory, and gives you control over a limited number of administrative settings (see the documentation for more details). Note that once the properties file has been edited, Generator must be restarted for the changes to take effect.

Developer Edition will fulfill the needs of most projects, since it is capable of both offline and online generation. How many sites truly need to handle more than a couple of requests per second in online mode? Very few, and Developer Edition can handle the rest. Most will really only need offline mode, and with the ability to easily automate content generation, and schedule it to run as often as necessary, most bases are covered.

Developer Edition has some limitations in terms of scalability and performance. Developer Edition is single-threaded, so it can only handle one request at a time. It is not able to take advantage of multiple processors either. The other major feature that is lacking in Developer Edition is caching, which aids performance immensely, especially under heavy server loads. These features are included in the Enterprise Edition.

Again, most projects will need nothing more than the Developer Edition, but for those that need to handle high-traffic real-time content generation, it simply won't do. That's a job for Enterprise Edition.

Generator 2 Enterprise Edition

In addition to all of the features of Developer Edition, Enterprise Edition adds all the things necessary to allow a web site to serve out ultra-fast, real-time, rich content to multitudes of simultaneous users.

There are two main features of Enterprise Edition that make it so powerful. The first is that it is **multi-threaded**, so can handle several requests simultaneously. It is also able to take advantage of multiple processors, so it is highly scalable. If the site starts getting too much traffic and users have to wait, or are denied access altogether, simply add more CPUs and Generator Enterprise Edition can support them.

The other main feature that really boosts performance is **caching**. Similar to the way that web browsers cache files locally so they can be accessed faster than if they had to be downloaded again, Generator takes the idea further and employs it on different levels. Generator caching works in a number of inter-related ways to achieve significant performance boosts.

First, it allows content that doesn't change in real-time to be generated once and cached for a specified period of time on the server. After that specified time expires, the next time the template is hit, a new file is created and cached. Although this sounds very much like what happens with the automation and scheduling of Generator in offline mode, the performance is better with caching because the file is stored in memory (or a disk cache) and can be served out faster. In offline mode the server's file system has to be accessed every time that file is served out. Think of how much faster data stored in RAM can be accessed compared to data stored on the hard drive. This is one of the key ways that Generator caches content on the server.

Another advantage of caching is that it reduces load on the server since the content isn't generated every time the template is hit, it's served directly from the cache.

The caches break down into the **request cache**, the **media cache** and the **font cache**. These all live in memory. There is also a **file cache** that lives on disk.

The request cache stores the entire output of previously processed templates in whatever file format has been specified. So if a template is processed and its output is cached, the content is then served from the cache and the template is not processed again until the cache expires.

The media cache stores media such as bitmaps that are used in templates, in memory, thus reducing the time required to access them when processing the template.

The file cache stores the same media files in a disk cache, and so is slower than the media cache but still faster than having to retrieve them from the file system.

The font cache also lives in memory, and greatly speeds up content generation.

In addition to these, there is a global cache setting that controls all the caches. The settings for each of the caches, as well as the default configuration settings, can all be set in Enterprise Edition's web-based administration servlet. Being web-based, the servlet allows remote administration, and since use of the servlet does not require Generator to be restarted, changes can be made in real-time. Note that all settings in the servlet can also be changed in the `generator.properties` file, though this method does require that Generator be restarted. The user interface for the servlet is in Flash:

The caching properties for a site can be set in all sorts of combinations, and with some fine-tuning, a Generator Enterprise Edition-driven site can run at peak efficiency. Cache properties include the maximum size of each cache, whether the cache dumps the oldest files as new files come in, how long files are kept in the cache, whether to override individual file settings and simply cache everything, whether to check for newer versions of files before using the cached ones, etc.

Cache parameters can also be set in the Generator panel of the Flash authoring environment. Any object requiring media that can be cached will have this parameter. Although this parameter appears and can be edited with the authoring extensions and the Developer Edition, it is only functional with the Enterprise Edition, since that's the only version with the caching feature.

Some cache parameters can also be set in the template URL; the parameters for the request and media caches as well as the expiration of each. URL cache settings will override those set in the Generator panel, and are in turn overridden by the settings in the administration servlet. The syntax of the URL would be:

```
MyBitmap.jpg?gmc=true&gme=3600

MyTemplate.swt?grc=true&gre=300
```

This would cache `MyBitmap.jpg`, used with the Insert JPEG object, in the media cache for one hour (3600 seconds), and the `MyTemplate.swt` in the request cache for 5 minutes.

The administration servlet also creates transaction reports, (including the statistics of the types of files requested, file sizes and response times) as well as a 90-day report, broken down into three 30-day reports, and including peak and average requests, how many consecutive days the server has been running, and the average response time.

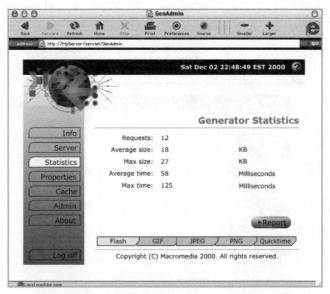

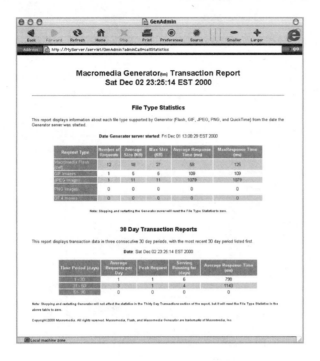

As the Developer Edition is capable of so much, the market for the Enterprise Edition is really limited to large-scale applications receiving lots of traffic like e-commerce sites, online financial applications and sites that use dynamic branding, marketing or content personalization. The USABancShares site we looked at earlier uses the Enterprise Edition. The Amazon.coms, Citibanks and Yahoo!s of the world are the types of clients that would require Enterprise Edition.

As Enterprise Edition is the big daddy of them all, its limitations are pretty much the limitations of Generator and Flash themselves. However, limitations such as those of the default Generator objects don't really count because to the inclusion of the SDK and open API. In the Generator objects section we'll look at how you might extend Generator's capabilities with these tools.

So far we've talked about the basic idea of Generator as a tool, its various modes of operation, the different packages available, and what they do. Now let's get into the nitty-gritty of how Generator actually builds dynamic content. At the heart of it all is the template. Within the template, and associated with it, are three types of items that make the content dynamic – **Generator variables**, **Generator objects** and **data sources**. Remember that since these are elements of templates, which are essential to all content generation, these three items are all applicable and necessary in all three modes of operation.

Generating dynamic content

Before discussing the three main elements that make up the template, we should talk about the template settings that are specified under the Generator tab of Flash's Publish Settings;

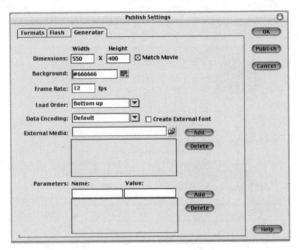

Generator's Publish Settings

The Generator Publish Settings enable you to control many things, and where these settings overlap those in the Movie Properties, or in the Flash Publish Settings, Generator's Publish Settings take precedence.

The Dimensions, Background Color and Frame Rate are the same settings as are found in the Movie Properties window. However, the Background Color setting in the Generator panel offers an extra field in addition to the color picker. In this field, color values can be entered as hexadecimal values, such as #FF9900 or 0xFF9900, or as web-safe color names such as orange.

> *Note that when entering a hex value the swatch color will change dynamically to match what is entered, but when entering a color name the swatch will not update – so, there may actually be two different colors represented. In this case the name will take precedence, however in order to avoid confusion it is recommended that color names be avoided in favor of hex values or the use of the color picker.*

Load Order is the same setting as is found in the Flash Publish Settings, and again the Generator settings will override the Flash settings.

Data Encoding specifies what type of encoding was used when creating the data source or sources used in the template. Generator can read several types of data encoding. The types of data encoding accepted are ASCII, UTF8, SJIS, EUC_JP and MacRoman. There is also a Default setting that uses whatever encoding method is the default of the system that the template lives on.

The Create External Font checkbox does just that. It creates external font files that can be cached (with the Enterprise Edition) to aid in the performance of processing templates.

External Media specifies the location of one or more templates that contain symbols to be used in the current template. The libraries of the specified templates are made accessible to the current template as if they were native. If there are any duplicate symbol names, the external media symbols will overwrite those that already exist in the current library. If duplicate symbol names exist among multiple external media files, the symbols in the file added earliest to the list will take precedence. The idea is similar to Flash's shared libraries, but is actually easier to use since there is no need to set and refer to a Linkage Identifier. This Identifier must be specified for shared libraries since part of the optimization of SWF files includes removing unused library items, and without it the symbol might not be exported with the SWF. Templates on the other hand, are never downloaded, so file size is not an issue and they do not need to be optimized in this way. The entire library is included in the SWT and symbols are referred to directly by their name in the library. This can be very useful since a template can exist solely as a repository for all symbols, and any other template can have access to that library as if it were native simply by including that template as an external media file.

The Parameters fields are just another way to pass variables to the template, which is great for testing purposes, because you don't have to create an external data source.

> *Remember to remove these variable entries after testing so they don't cause conflicts with the real data when the template is processed.*

Generator variables

We'll work with Generator variables in more detail in the next chapter, so we'll just look at what they are and what they can do here.

By now you'll be familiar with the idea that a variable is a container that gets filled in with a value. Generator variables are different only in that they are always string values (so unlike Flash ActionScript variables, they are not typed as numeric or Boolean.) However, numeric values such as those passed as color values, and Boolean True/False values can be passed through Generator variables as strings (since these values are represented in the code by textual strings anyway) into Flash, and will be correctly interpreted by Flash in the end.

These variables are reserved for use by Generator, and therefore require a special syntax to identify them as such. Curly brackets denote Generator variables, like so:

```
{MyGenVariable}
```

Generator variables are quite versatile, and can be used in a number of places; for example, they can be used to populate text fields. From blocks of textual content to text in buttons, as the figure below shows, this is a simple but very effective use of Generator variables, and is a great way to separate textual content from Flash and allow it to be updated without having to edit the FLA.

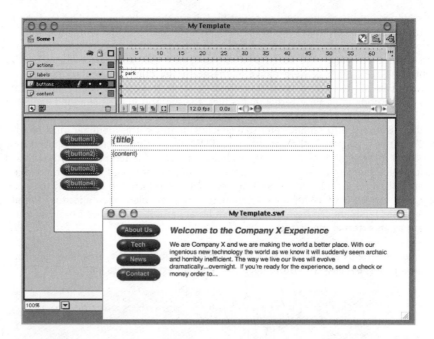

Variables can be used to fill in values for parameter settings in the Generator panel. Any parameter field can take a Generator variable. This allows a huge amount of flexibility since things like the data source and instance names of Generator objects can be dynamically assigned from outside of Flash. For example, if a chart needs to display a different set of data depending upon a given set of circumstances, only one chart object needs to be used as long as the data source parameter is a Generator variable. Then that single chart object can display data from any number of data sources, with the appropriate one being sent to the template via the variable. The figure opposite shows the data source being chosen with the variable {ChartToDisplay}.

Generator variables can also be used inside ActionScript. Any action's parameter field that takes a text string can take a Generator variable. So, if you think about it, an entire movie's functionality can be dynamically dictated by an outside data source. Loop counts, `loadMovie` commands, properties, `goto` commands, and so on can all be sent parameters and arguments from outside of Flash.

Say, for example, you're using Flash alone to build a complex automobile engine simulator that takes into account all the different things that affect engine performance: air density, air temperature, fuel quality, etc. In the simulator, these values can be changed through dynamic text fields, and the engine performance can be gauged accordingly. A pretty interesting application.

If you added Generator to the mix, and used Generator variables in the ActionScript for all the variables that determine engine performance, the data source could supply real-time values based on geographic location. Therefore, things like altitude, current weather conditions, quality of fuel available in the area, and so on could all be used to model real-world, real-time engine performance. This turns an application that started out fairly interestingly, into something pretty amazing, and far more useful.

> *One thing you should remember when you're using Generator variables with ActionScript is that they are treated as strings, and therefore, unlike ActionScript variables, they need to be enclosed in double quotes. So an ActionScript variable would be used like this:*
>
> ```
> gotoAndStop ( FrameLabelVar );
> ```
>
> *However, a Generator variable would require this syntax:*
>
> ```
> gotoAndStop ("{FrameLabelVar}");
> ```

You can also use Generator variables in the Flash environment in both the frame label and instance name fields. These do not need to be enclosed in double quotes.

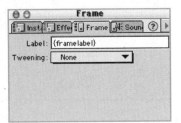
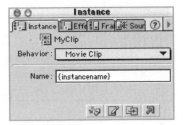

While there are many other ways to get outside variables into Flash, most of which are outlined in this book, using Generator variables is one of the easiest and most effective methods, because of their tight integration with Flash.

You can also dynamically modify Flash graphic symbols and movie clip instances through Generator variables. You don't actually have to use variables, but using the commands we'll look at next without Generator variables essentially strips them of their usefulness. While you can get some of the same results for movie clip instances by using a combination of ActionScript and Generator variables, only these commands will produce the desired results with graphic symbols.

To access these commands, open the Generator panel and select the symbol instance on the stage that is to be modified. Note that these commands work on symbol instances otherwise unrelated to Generator – not on Generator objects.

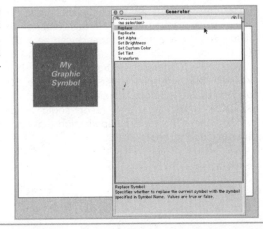

Again, these will be covered in more detail in the next chapter, but let's briefly go over them. Remember that any of the parameter fields can take Generator variables.

The Replace command does exactly what you'd expect; it simply replaces an instance of a symbol with another symbol. You might use it when there is only an occasional need for a different symbol, and a default symbol is used for the rest of the time. In this case, the parameters can be set with Generator variables so that an outside data source can tell Generator whether or not to replace the default symbol, and if so, what symbol to replace it with. The Replace command is a typical example of the fact that, without a Generator variable to specify the symbol to be replaced, there isn't much value in the command, since it's not dynamic.

The Replicate command is a bit more complex. It reproduces the symbol instance for each row of the data source, using the data in that row. The final output is essentially a movie clip, where each instance is populated with the supplied data and laid sequentially end-to-end. You can then loop through the instances. Or, by putting a `stop` action and a button with a `play` action into the original instance, you can let the user go manually to the next instance. The Replicate command requires its own data source, but column names are not essential, only those variables used in the original symbol instance are needed.

Alpha, Brightness and Tint can also be set for instances using the Generator Panel.

The Set Custom Color command differs from the Set Tint command in that it makes changes to the instance's color(s) based on its current color settings. It applies relative values rather than absolute values the way Set Tint does. Basically, Set Tint is used to apply a single solid color to the entire instance while Set Custom Color works on multiple colors and changes them relative to their current values.

Transform allows manipulation of X and Y scale, X and Y offset, and rotation.

Note that these commands can only be applied one at a time to any particular instance. So, in order to apply multiple commands to an instance, you have to nest the instance into as many movie clips as there are commands, and then apply one command to each movie clip instance. So for example, to apply a Transform and a Set Tint command to a symbol instance, you would have to nest the symbol inside a movie clip and then apply the Set Tint command directly to the symbol and the Transform command to its parent movie clip (or vice versa).

Generator objects

While Generator variables are extremely versatile and powerful, they don't necessarily aid in the areas of creating graphically rich content elements. Generator objects address this by using standard textual data to arrange, animate, and create visually rich content that would otherwise require lots of valuable time to create by hand.

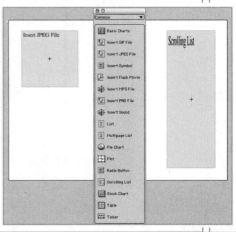

Detailed examples of using the default Generator objects are given in the next chapter so I won't provide in-depth examples or coverage of the various parameter settings of each object here.

Generator objects can be broken down into two basic types, those that insert media and those that dynamically build content elements.

The Insert media objects

The Insert media objects are all very similar. They insert the specified type of media into the placeholder whether it is a bitmap image, a sound, a library symbol or a Flash movie. The objects include:

> Insert GIF File
> Insert JPEG File
> Insert Symbol
> Insert Flash Movie
> Insert MP3 File
> Insert PNG File
> Insert Sound

In place of a data source specification, these objects require a file name (or symbol name as applicable) to be specified.

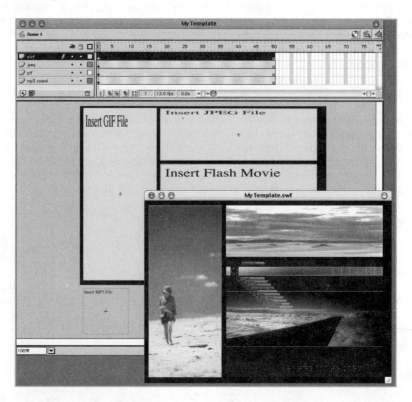

Since they are in fact objects, they all have Instance name parameters so they can be targeted. All but the sound objects also have a Scale To Fit parameter, to scale the content to the size of the object placeholder on the stage.

Bitmaps have Export As (format) and JPEG Quality settings. The two Export As options are JPEG and Lossless. Select JPEG to have Flash use that compression method on the image no matter what the original image format is. A JPEG Quality setting of 100 retains the original compression of a JPEG, and since no re-compression is required, the performance of the Insert JPEG object is greatly enhanced. Lower settings mean lower image quality, but also smaller file size. Selecting JPEG for the Insert GIF or Insert PNG objects will recompress the image as a JPEG. The Lossless option can be chosen for GIFs and PNGs to retain their original image quality without recompressing them as JPEGs. Lossless can also be chosen for JPEGs, but this is not recommended since it has far inferior results compared to exporting as a JPEG with quality set to 100.

The other parameters are specific to the type of media being inserted, such as Loop Count for the Insert Sound object, or the Frames setting that deals with animated GIFs in the Insert GIF object.

As mentioned earlier in the Enterprise Edition section, any of the Insert media objects that pull in external media – as opposed to those pulling in symbols from the library – will have a Cache parameter. Remember that even though the setting is there and a parameter can be specified, it will only have an effect with the Enterprise Edition running in online mode, since this is the only combination that uses the caching feature.

The other default objects are the ones that add a lot of value in terms of presenting visually rich representations of data. They are also the ones that save the most development time when compared to creating the same output by hand.

Objects that dynamically build content

All of these objects require their own data sources, and have certain columns that may be required or optional depending upon the object and the type of data it needs. These objects also all have Instance name parameters to allow them to be targeted.

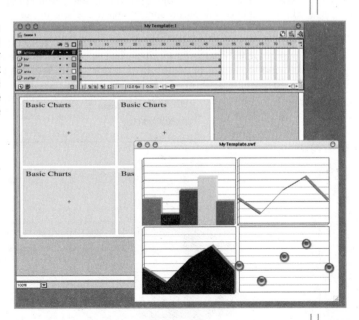

Going down the list of these objects, the first is the Basic Charts object. This is actually like several objects in one, in that it can create eight different types of charts: bar charts, line charts, area charts, scatter charts as well as stacked versions of each. There are well over two dozen parameters that can be set for these charts that control just about every possible aspect of how the charts will be displayed once the template is processed. These parameters are actually quite good fun to play with, and that is really the best way to learn them. They are very straightforward and the Generator panel gives explanations of what each one does. So get in there, play around and the benefits of Generator will soon become apparent.

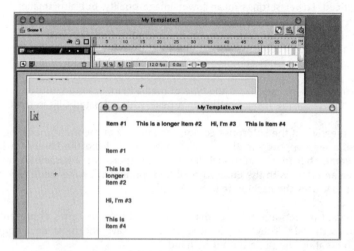

Next up is the List object. This just creates a simple list, either vertical or horizontal, using the symbol(s) specified in the data source. It's great for creating menus or just for automatically spacing items. The List object, as well as the Scrolling List and Ticker objects (which we'll discuss in a moment), will automatically adjust the spacing of its elements depending upon how much content is in them. For example, if you were to create a vertical menu using a single movie clip with a Generator variable inside for the button text, the object would automatically space the items evenly whether the button text is one line or twenty lines. Using Generator this way can amend the height or width of the text in a text field dynamically.

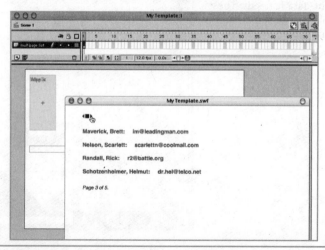

The Multipage List object generates a series of pages containing subsections of the entire list. It provides Next, Previous, and Home buttons that allow users to page through the information. Default buttons are included with the object, but parameters allow developers to specify their own symbols for each of the buttons as well. There are also some variables associated with this object that allow access to specific information about any particular instance of the object. These variables give the total number of pages in the list (numPages), the total number of items in the list (numItems) and the page in the list that the user is currently on (currentPage). These can be used to display useful reference information like 'Page 3 of 5.'

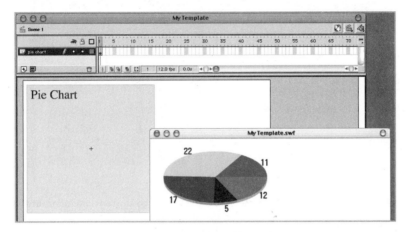

The next one is the Pie Chart object. This object has similar counterparts in Microsoft Excel and other data processing applications that create a pie chart from the user's data. The reason pie chart utilities are found in these applications is because pie charts are an excellent visual representation of statistics/data. Isn't Flash perfect for giving great visual representations? Yes, but without the Pie Chart Generator object, creating a pie chart in Flash can be a real headache. Fortunately, the objects are given to you in the authoring mode, so you don't have to, and, of course, you can drive it with dynamic data.

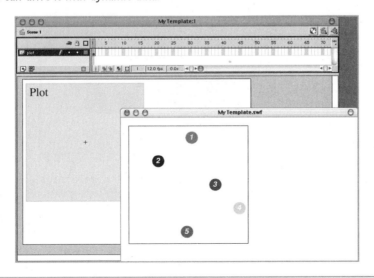

The Plot object allows developers to dynamically place symbols at specific coordinates on the stage. The symbols can be scaled, rotated, and targeted individually as well. Consider this object used with Generator variables filling in the parameters. Existing data sources could be tapped to display the progress of contestants in an around-the-world yacht race, the planets orbiting the sun, whatever, and all in Flash.

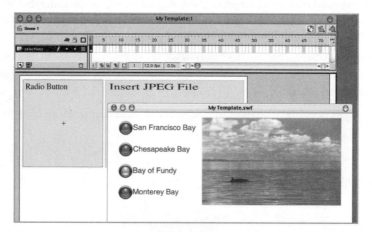

The Radio Button object creates a simple vertical set of radio buttons. Included in the object is a variable that holds the value of the selected button. The default variable name is radioVar, but a parameter setting allows the assignment of any variable name. This can be used to pass that value to the back-end or to some Flash ActionScript.

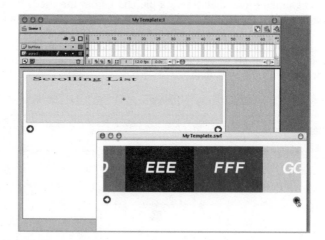

The Scrolling List object essentially generates a movie clip with a tween that moves a list vertically or horizontally from one end to the other. While this is an effective means of scrolling through content, the fact that the movement is timeline-based opens up interesting possibilities such as variable-speed scrolling that uses different buttons with different scripts to either scroll normally one frame at a time, or at high-speed by only hitting every third frame or so.

Programming/scripting movement based on sending the playhead to specific frames rather than doing it by continually resetting X or Y coordinates is often easier for some developers to understand, especially since the scroll limits are automatically created by the tween.

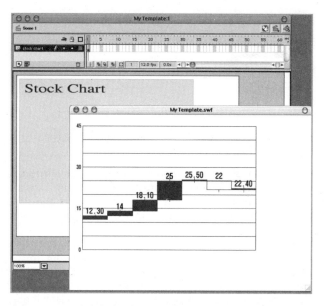

Stock charts have become essential viewing on the web nowadays, and Generator gives us a Stock Chart object that has over thirty parameter settings, and can be customized to look exactly as desired.

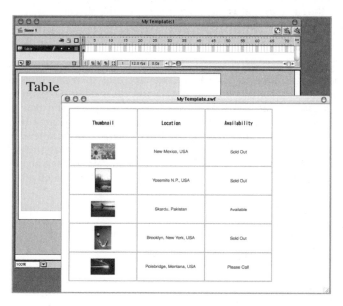

The Table object takes the movie clip(s) specified in the data source and generates a spreadsheet-like table of columns and rows. It's very basic, but very useful if you're dealing with data that needs this type of layout, especially large amounts of it.

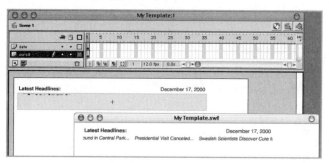

Finally we come to the Ticker object, which creates a vertical or horizontal, infinitely scrolling ticker. Similar to the Scrolling List object, this creates a movie clip with a tween of the ticker content that plays in a continuous loop. This is a very handy object and since it is also timeline-based, some interesting effects can be achieved with some very basic scripting.

Enterprising Java developers can extend Generator's capabilities by building customized objects to suit their needs. All you need to create your own Java objects ships with Generator: the Generator SDK and the open API, as well as the source code for three objects, ship with Generator. Custom objects can be added to the Generator Objects window and then be accessed just as the default objects are. The objects window to the right shows several custom objects installed and ready to use. See the *More Information and Resources* section at the end of the chapter to find out where to get some really useful custom objects, such as the ones pictured to the right, as well as more information on the SDK and open API.

Data sources

Data sources are, well, sources of data that Generator uses to create dynamic content. The type of data contained in these data sources is determined by the object(s) being created, what data is being used in the template, and how it's being used. Again, this is a vague definition, but remember that every single thing Generator creates requires a data source, so there's a proportional level of diversity and complexity in data sources. Everything we've looked at so far – objects, variables, and parameters – are all dependent upon data sources, and the formatting and contents of the data vary depending upon how it is to be used.

The sources of this data come in many forms:

- Comma-delimited text files, both external and native

- Database queries

- Java classes

- CGI scripts (or other web applications)

- Variables passed directly to the template

Comma-delimited text files

Comma-delimited text files are one of the most common data sources Generator developers use. They are incredibly simple, incredibly versatile, and require no additional knowledge to create. All you need is a text editor like SimpleText or Notepad, and a few simple rules.

There are two types, or formats, of comma-delimited text files that Generator uses. They can both be thought of as having columns and rows like a spreadsheet or database table. Columns are separated by commas, and rows are separated by line breaks.

The first is the name/value format. This format of data source contains variable name/value pairs where there is a single variable name and a single variable value per row of the data source. There are only two columns: Name and Value.

```
Name, Value
stringVar, "This is a string of text."
numberVar, "10"
colorVar, "#FFCC00"
```

The first row of a name/value data source must be:

```
Name, Value
```

Subsequent rows are then made up of the variable name in the first column, a comma to delineate the end of the data in that column, the value assigned to the variable in the second column, and if there is another row of data to follow, a line break to mark the end of the row.

The second type is the column name/value format. In the column name/value format, the first row declares the variable names and subsequent rows contain corresponding variable values. This is the format used when there are multiple sets of values for the same set of variables, just like many of the objects we discussed earlier.

```
stringVar, colorVar, linkVar
"Macromedia", "#0000FF", "http://www.macromedia.com"
"Braincraft", "#FF9900", "http://www.braincraft.com"
"Flash Bank", "#000000", "http://www.usabancshares.com"
```

This is the format generally returned by SQL database queries.

Database queries

JDBC/ODBC databases are directly accessible with Generator. Any SQL query that returns a SQL database table – a format that Generator can accept – may be used. The data source specified in the template would look similar to this:

```
fgjdbc:///?driver=sun.jdbc.odbc.JdbcOdbcDriver&url=jdbc:odbc:MyDat
➥ aSourceName&userid=MyID&password=MyPassword&query=SELECT%20*%20
➥ FROM%20MyTableName;
```

The `fgjdbc:///` tells Generator to process what follows it as a JDBC/ODBC database call. The `driver` and `url` are specified, with `MyDataSourceName` being the name of the data source to be queried. The `userid` and `password` variables are required in the string even if no values are passed with them. Finally, `query` is the URL-encoded SQL query. Note that the semicolon at the end of the string is what is terminating the SQL statement within the data source specification, and is not required by the data source specification itself.

Java classes

Custom Java classes are also valid Generator data sources. With the Java class installed in the `classes` directory of the `Generator` folder, the template's data source would be similar to this:

```
fgjava:///MyJavaClassName?MyArgument1=MyValue1&MyArgument2=MyValue2
```

The `fgjava:///` tells Generator that it is dealing with a Java data source. Then comes the name of the Java class and any arguments that will get passed to it.

Scripting languages

A data source file might also be a CGI script, or an ASP, PHP, ColdFusion script that returns text variables and values. In this case the script file itself is not the actual data source. The data source specified in the template is the script file, but it is not directly read in as data. Generator accesses the script file, which in turn feeds text variables and values back to Generator.

Variables passed directly to the template

Variables can be passed directly to the template in a few ways. They can be appended to the URL as we saw earlier with the online mode, they can be passed via the command line as discussed with offline mode, and they can also be passed using the Parameters fields in the Generator panel of Flash's Publish Settings, as we saw in the authoring mode.

Data sources can be retrieved from the web using HTTP, from an FTP server, or from a local drive. The data source specification in the template can be relative or absolute. Absolute URLs would use the appropriate prefix to tell Generator how to retrieve the data source, similar to the way the `fgjdbc:///` and `fgjava://` prefixes do. (Absolute prefixes include `HTTP://`, `FTP://`, `FGFTP://`, and `FILE:///`.) These are all standard except for `FGFTP://`, which is specific to Generator. `FGFTP://` tells Generator to send an FTP request using authentication, as opposed to the standard `FTP://`, which will only work for truly anonymous FTP access. The `FGFTP://` URL would look similar to this:

```
fgftp://MyUserName|MyPassword@MyFTPHostName:PortNumber/MyDirectory
➦ /MySubDirectory/MyFile
```

There are two ways that data sources can be tied to the template: as a Generator environment variable, or as a Generator object/command data source.

Environment variables allow data sources to be assigned to an entire timeline. They are assigned using the **Generator environment variable** button at the top right of the stage window.

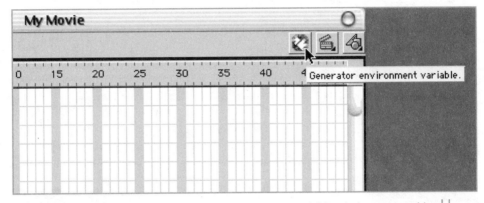

Note that this button appears and opens the Generator environment variable window on graphic symbol and button timelines. However it has no effect on these timelines since they are not true timelines/environments. It only works for the main timeline or the timelines of movie clips.

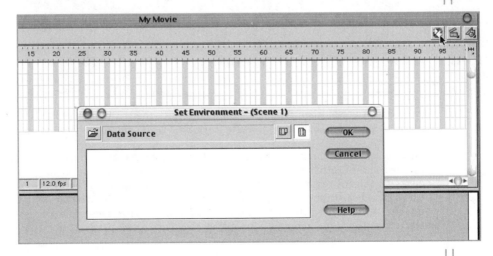

The two buttons at the top right of the Generator environment variable window are to specify the format of the data source, either name/value or column name/value. Be sure to set this correctly or Generator will read the data incorrectly, which could potentially cause hours of frustrating debugging.

The environment data source setting accepts any of the previously discussed data source specifications as well as one more: native data sources. These can be input directly into the environment variable window, thus storing them inside the template itself. A hash symbol (#) is the prefix that tells Generator to treat what follows as native data. The following screenshot shows a native data source entered into the environment variable window:

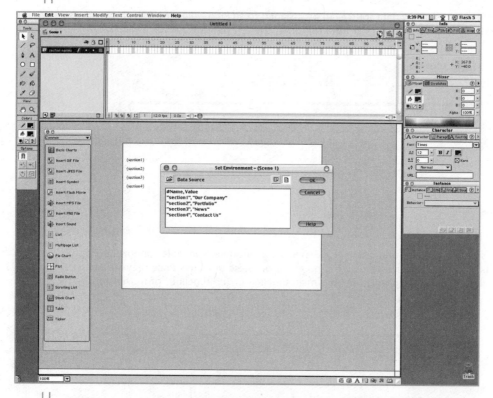

Native data is useful when developing templates since there is no need to create or maintain an outside data source. There is no need to leave the Flash authoring environment.

Generator object/command data sources are tied to objects rather than timelines. As previously discussed in the Objects section, the data source is specified in the Generator Panel. Generator objects/commands can also use native data sources. The button to the right of the data source field will spawn a window where native data can be entered, prefixed by the # symbol. Notice that there are no data source format buttons in this window. Since these data sources are specific to objects/commands, the required format is already known and preset.

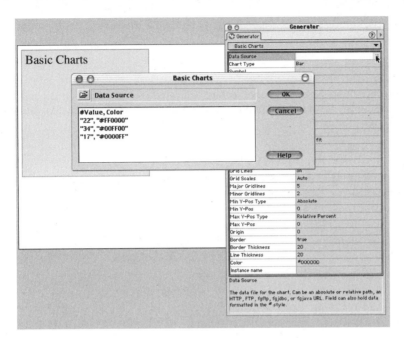

Generator is also able to read external data sources in a number of different types of encoding. This is very useful when working with data that has been output from a different operating system or different language. For more detailed information see the Generator Publish Settings section.

Conclusion

Macromedia Generator is, as this chapter has shown, an extremely robust, extensible and scalable solution for creating dynamic content. It has numerous uses that provide benefits to everyone from the developer to the client to the user. With some of these benefits coming at zero cost, developers owe it to themselves to give Generator a try. Read on, as the next chapter details real-world examples of Generator in use.

More Information and Resources

More information and Resources about Macromedia Generator can be found online at one of the following sites.

www.macromedia.com/generator

This is the official source with product information, purchasing, free trial downloads, tech notes, training information, developer community links, and more.

www.markme.com/

Outside of Macromedia's own site, this is the definitive place to go for Generator resources. Created and maintained by Mike Chambers, this site is a hub to all things Generator: custom

Generator objects, tutorials, white papers, articles, SDK/API information, newsgroups, forums, daily tips and more.

www.gendev.net

The Generator Developers Network is another site dedicated to Generator and dynamic content. Packed full of resources, forums, tools and more, this is another excellent place for Gen-heads to learn and exchange information.

www.macromedia.com/exchange/flash

This is the Flash Exchange, a place for developers to share extensions such as Generator objects, Flash Smart Clips, etc.

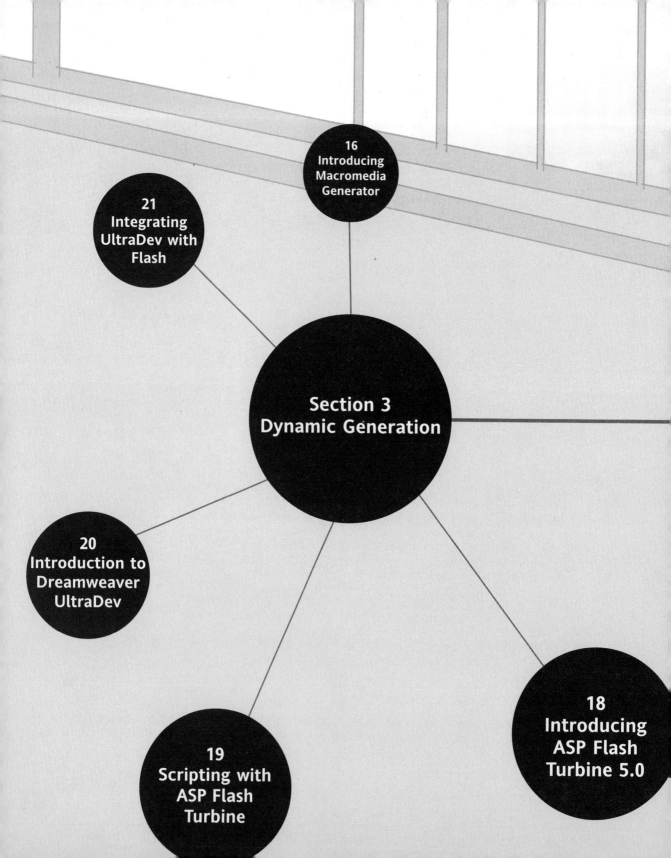

16
Introducing
Macromedia
Generator

21
Integrating
UltraDev with
Flash

Section 3
Dynamic Generation

20
Introduction to
Dreamweaver
UltraDev

19
Scripting with
ASP Flash
Turbine

18
Introducing
ASP Flash
Turbine 5.0

Chapter 17
Generator
by Example

Macromedia has been kind enough to produce a suite of products designed to enable users of one specific application to make a transition to another with a minimal learning curve. As is often the case, while the product specifics may be easy to pick up, the background experience required to use a product to its full potential is often lacking. Such is the case with Macromedia Generator.

Generator 2 was originally released as a late accompaniment to Flash 4 that enabled content to be dynamically created on the server-side and then pushed out to the user in various formats. Since the vast majority of Flash developers were crossovers from the design community, the potential for user specific customization, as well as that of e-commerce and e-business was not acknowledged by the developer community as a whole for quite some time.

As a crossover myself, I was given the incredible opportunity to be part of a team that helped to change how Generator was viewed by the Internet industry at a time when the product was just taking hold. The opportunity that became available to me, allowed me to become involved in the development of USABancShares.com, an online bank as well as stock and news resource built entirely in Flash.

Taking advantage of Flash's ability to pull in content via loaded movies, our team used Generator to push secure banking information to user machines in small packets that were then loaded into a pre-loaded shell. By taking advantage of these two products we were able to create an extremely graphically rich user interface that was faster, more user friendly, and more easily updateable than any bank online at the time. While not currently incorporated, these same technologies would allow future versions to be customizable on a user-to-user basis. Imagine being able to customize everything about your bank, from what content you receive, to the manner in which you see it, the color of your graphics, the style of your graphics, even your entire layout... with Generator, this is possible.

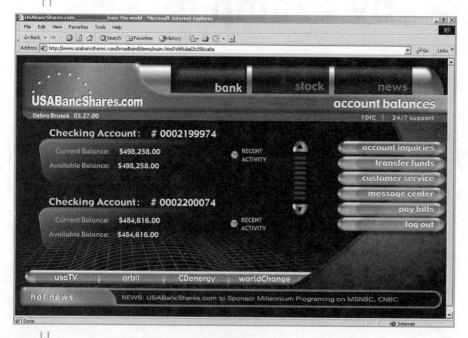

At the same time as we were producing the bank site, Tiffany.com (http://tiffany.com/), released a Flash version of their site that pushed out dynamic imagery using Generator. This was another big push for Generator as a product, partly due to Tiffany's worldwide recognition. The music artist Maxwell, was also taking advantage of Generator during his 1999 world tour to 'push out' tour and concert information to fans whilst on the road.

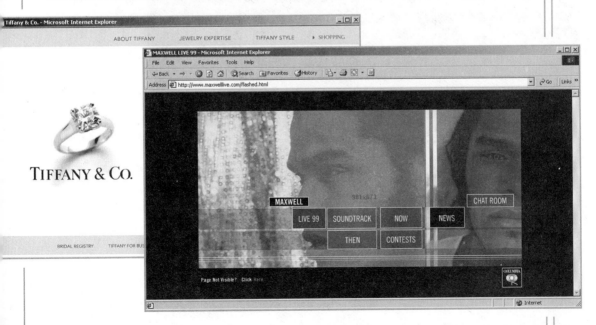

Since then, the Generator bandwagon has picked up incredible speed. Companies such as the Nexus Group are using Generator SWTs to produce broadcast production ready `.mov` and `.avi` files for television. Another, more recent example would be SPACE.com (http://space.com/spacearcade) who have used Generator as a production tool for their SpaceArcade section.

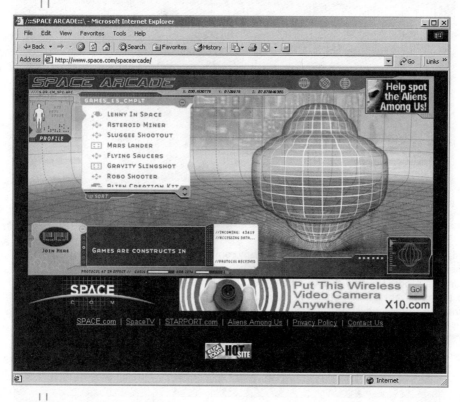

© 2001 SPACE.com., Inc

Rydex Funds (www.rydexfunds.com/) is also using Generator's dynamic charts to display time sensitive market information.

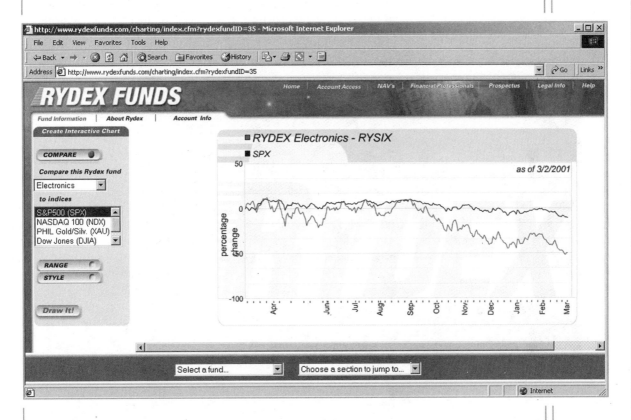

© 2001 Rydex Funds, Rockville, Md.

Similarly, content from Flash sites is being pushed out in GIF and JPEG format through Generator and sent out to PalmOS devices, this same content is also being pushed out in Flash 4 onto WinCE devices. Another example of how Generator is being used, is how web development companies such as Braincraft and Oven Digital are using Generator as a production tool to help expedite development cycles. So, as you can see, interest in Generator is growing very quickly indeed.

With market penetration of the Flash plug-in well over the 90th percentile, and more and more Flash sites popping up every day, Generator is the obvious choice for adding personalized content and customization features to complex, media-rich sites. With Generator's capabilities, we are no longer strictly delivering preset information based content, but allowing users to decide what content they want, how they want it, and even allowing them to add, edit, and share content. Generator is enabling us to build true online applications that work for the user.

That said, it's obvious what a powerful and versatile tool Generator is, and should be equally as obvious that I could in no way expect to cover every aspect of its real world usage in only one chapter. So, in lieu of giving you a little information about a lot of things, I will instead attempt to provide you with an in-depth perspective on Generator as it is used in a production environment. In doing so, we will examine the process of determining what aspects of a site benefit from Generator's use, how Generator can be used to speed up the production process, and how best to implement Generator so it is most easily updateable. Along the way we will walk through examples of creating both Online and Offline content, as well as show how Generator can benefit developers solely in the production environment.

My goal is to introduce Generator to those of you not using it, and for those amongst you who are, maybe give some insight into a more efficient and broader use of the product. So, without further ado, let's get crackin'!

Generator components

Before we move onto the examples, I'd like to reiterate, and possibly clarify, some of the major points about Generator from the previous chapter.

Generator variables

Customizing content and pulling in server data via Generator requires the use of Generator variables. Generator variables distinguish themselves from other variables by being enclosed in curly brackets like this:

This is a Generator variable: This is a Flash variable:

```
{variable}                                    _root.variable
```

Most often, these variables are used to pull in text from a data source, and can be written directly on the stage.

However, these curly bracketed variables can also be used in the data source fields of the various Generator objects or even the Environment data source fields, as well as within ActionScript as string literals.

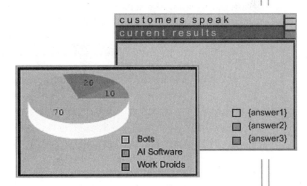

The dynamic nature of these various options is quite obvious, and can allow for certain scripts and objects to have multiple uses, and content depending on the user and/or the location within the web site or application.

For example, I was recently involved in building a training demo for Macromedia that required a fully implemented Generator-based portal as an example of Generator's full capabilities. One of the components of this portal was a "my weather" section that would display the weekly weather forecast for a user-specific zip code.

Since our team was already implementing the whole project in Flash, it made sense to display the weather forecast as animated icons, similar to the ones used on TV. In our movie library we had a set of weather-related icons, and on the stage for each day of the week we had a Generator Insert Symbol object, with a variable symbol name specified. Using Online mode, based on the variables supplied, the appropriate icon would then be called from the library and the weather report would be displayed.

As a production tool, these same variables can be modified to change the look of a site quickly, edit text, or switch calls to the server throughout an entire Flash site by only changing one instance of it. I have found this last point to be extremely useful in beta testing and production.

It is a rare occurrence to be working on a site or application, and be constructing it on the actual server it is to be deployed upon. At the same time, it is quite common for all of a particular Generator project's variables to be retrieved from a single ASP file, PHP file, or other data source on a server. In lieu of having all of your server calls written out in full, pointing to a testing sever (for example: http://201.141.775.48/data.asp), and then editing all of those instances when the site is to be launched, the process can be expedited by employing variables in all those calls and declaring their value in a single data source (e.g. {serveraddress}). In the example below, we are determining the server's location by attaching the {serveraddress} variable to the end of our movie value string within the HTML page:

A not so well documented fact is that data source fields can accept multiple sources delimited by semicolons. In the screenshot below, we are in fact using a Generator variable as a data source, as well as a Java class, and a text file:

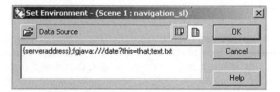

So, as you can see, Generator variables are pretty versatile things, and you'll soon come to realize just how useful they can be. Now let's take a look at what else Generator has to offer us...

Generator objects

Generator objects allow us to insert various types of media as well as pre-programmed widgets (which could otherwise be quite time consuming to script out using ActionScript). From a Flash production standpoint, these objects can become our best friends.

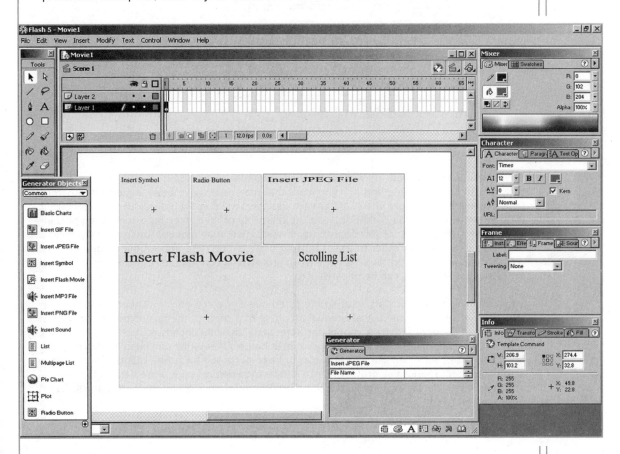

Being able to insert Generator objects can be a huge asset when dealing with client supplied media. It always seems to be that clients have a million grandiose ideas about how their sites should be implemented, and are constantly making design changes, but they never seem to hold up their end of the deal by delivering the content that we (the people who are building the site) need on time. It's often the case that the design has been approved, the copywriter has delivered, and then we're left waiting for the client to make up their mind, and supply us with the approved marketing images. Once the approved images do finally arrive, they have to be incorporated into the development. This would normally require popping open the FLA, finding all instances of the images and replacing each one. However, using the Generator authoring templates, this operation now only requires changing the names of the images in your directory or in a TXT file, and then simply re-exporting or publishing the FLA. If you know your client is fickle in terms of their requirements (for example, they may have already given you several replacement images for placement in the same location), you can store all of these images in a directory and just continue to change the value of the variable in your data source.

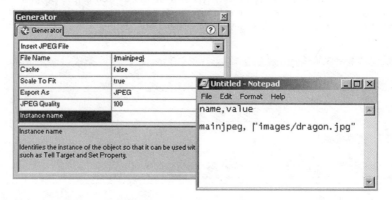

With Flash 5 ActionScript now at a true programming level, Flash developers are finding themselves conceptualizing and building ideas that may never have been implemented before. Often, during the discovery phase of a project, designers will approach developers and producers with questions concerning bandwidth, and the feasibility of ideas they have considered pitching to the client. Often, we as developers are in a position that requires us to actually build a prototype of the idea in order to give a truly accurate answer, and not put our company or the designer in an awkward position. As such, when prototyping concepts for a client, the benefits of the Generator templates can be unparalleled.

When building these concepts, with a little forethought, we can construct them in such a way that when it is time for the actual production phase of a project, the prototype can be used as a final asset as opposed to a model for something that still needs to be built. Using the Generator templates here not only cuts down man hours by requiring one build instead of many, but it also allows for proof of concept pieces to be re-purposed for future clients with a minimal amount of work. These same prototypes can also be modified for sales presentations to potential clients. In other words, this one asset can be used on numerous occasions in as many different places as you need.

A simple example

Let's say our client wants a full-blown Flash/Generator site that provides periodically updated content with some customization. At the same time, one of the design requirements is a Flash version of one of their newest marketing pieces, and it needs to be embedded in the design of our development. Let's also say that the marketing group on the client side is very particular, and requires that they build the advertising piece. In lieu of waiting for them to provide the piece, we simply consult all parties involved, and agree on the width, height, and perhaps file size of the movie that is to be supplied by the marketing group. With this information in hand, we can then go ahead and design our project, accounting for the movie by including an Insert Flash Movie object (which will eventually contain the movie). The result of this is that we don't have to worry about where and how to implement the movie when we receive it, it's all accounted for. This method also enables the client to change the inserted movie without much effort.

Think of this concept in terms of HTML frames. Sites using HTML frames often do so to keep the static elements of a site from refreshing as a user navigates through the site. Elements such as navigation controls are locked in place while the content is refreshed each time a user makes a selection. In Flash, a shell movie could be built with all the navigation controls present, and an Insert Flash Movie object could be placed where all content is to appear. When a user hits the site, the object loads the default movie and navigation. From there, each time a user clicks a new navigation button, a variable is passed to the server and the Insert Flash Movie object is updated with a new Flash movie while the navigation stays present. Clients would be free to swap movies on the server, or change the content at will.

While we will not be covering them within this chapter, it should be noted that many third party developers are extending the capabilities of Generator by creating their own custom objects using the Generator SDK (Software Development Kit). Macromedia is in full support of this, and offers many of these custom objects via the Flash exchange:

www.macromedia.com/exchange/flash/

There are also many third party sites that make these available, as well as provide SDK resources and help forums. Some examples of such sites are provided below:

www.markme.com
www.flashlite.net
www.were-here.com

Posting and receiving

As long as Generator receives content in the comma-delimited format, it's not too picky about where the content originates, in fact, Generator data source fields can accept HTTP, FTP, or file calls.

When dealing with vast amounts of potential data, especially data that changes frequently, it's a good idea to use an intermediary technology between the database and Generator. Consider a database that contains all the NASDAQ stock listings for a particular day. Our web site, which uses this database, has a Generator List object that lists the top 10 highest priced stocks. We could have Generator make an HTTP call to an application (CGI, ASP, PHP, ColdFusion, Tango etc.) that evaluates all the stocks based on that criteria, and then outputs the top 10 in a format acceptable to Generator.

We could also use customized Java classes, which can also be targeted in the data source fields in the same manner as HTTP, FTP, and file calls. Depending on the circumstances of a particular project, using Java classes may be a more viable option because classes are pre-compiled executables, meaning that the server doesn't have to parse each line of code, which often results in quicker retrieval of data.

This is not to say that Generator cannot make a direct query to a database. Generator can use any JBDC/ODBC-compliant database as a data source. Re-applying the example above, we could have Generator make a direct SQL call to the server and retrieve all the NASDAQ listings for a particular day. However, it should be noted that issues can arise in relation to the formatting of the data when using a direct query. Things like special characters, and spacing in database tables can make the data un-interpretable by Generator, so it's often the case that using a technology in the middle is a better way to go.

Lastly, Generator can accept variables attached to a URL string. Attaching variables and their values at the end of a URL string comes in handy when testing applications during production. If we had a variable called `color` and another called `car`, we could add these variables to the path in our browser window, hit refresh and view the outcome. The URL string would look something like this:

www.oursite.com/template_file.swt?color=red&car=ferrari

Macromedia have published some white papers, which are available on their web site at www.macromedia.com/support/generator/, as well as information included in the previous chapter and the Generator manual, for all of the methods to retrieve data in a manner acceptable to Generator. Using these various methods can enable Generator compatibility with a much broader range of databases.

The posting of variables to a database can be triggered through a frame action or button action in your Flash movie and can be accomplished in two ways. The first and most recommended method for enterprise level solutions is using the `loadVariables` action in Flash ActionScript. `loadVariables` assembles sets of variables based on a specified target and posts them to the server or file specified. Upon receiving the post, the server then returns information that can be used to perform client-side logic. The server can also store these variables in a database to be called upon at a later date, as may be the case with passwords, preferences, or user IDs.

Within the `loadVariables` action, leaving the location parameter blank, will post the variables for the entire timeline you are writing the `loadVariables` action within, while specifying a target or level will post only variables specific to that segment of your application or site. The `url` parameter for the post command should be set to target the data source or another file specified by the server administrator or engineer. This field will also accept Generator text variables.

```
loadVariables ("{serveraddress}"," clip_sl", "POST");
```

The second method of posting to a database, as mentioned previously, is by attaching variables to URL strings via the `getURL` or `loadMovie` actions. The `getURL` action is not recommended for fully-customized, robust applications because of the immense number of variables you may be tracking at any given time, and because it will trigger your browser to refresh. However, this can be quite handy when you are loading an entirely new SWF or when opening a separate browser window. When using these methods we should follow the same format we used to change parameters via a browser window.

www.oursite.com/template_file.swt?height=44&width=127

Format versatility

SWTs can deliver formats other than Flash files. With some forethought, you can design your applications and sites in a manner where the content would be acceptable pushed out as a PNG, JPG, QuickTime movie or GIF.

This feature is coming more and more into play as the proliferation of handheld devices seems to grow exponentially. While WinCE devices now support Flash 4 running on Pocket Internet Explorer, Palm devices still have a much greater market share. The same content can be pushed to both these devices in two different formats.

As an example, consider a portal based around financial services. Most likely this portal would offer some form of personal stock tracking as well as charts associated with your portfolio. On synchronization, or when accessing the portal via the wireless web, you would retrieve either a dynamic Generator chart and ticker, or a static GIF of the corresponding information depending upon the device you use.

Enabling content to be user format specific is actually much simpler than it sounds. The key is establishing the type of device a user owns. To do this, Macromedia has provided a Pocket PC Flash Developer kit, which is freely available on their web site:

www.macromedia.com/software/flash/download/deployment_kit/

Within this kit is a section containing ActionScript that will determine the processor speed of the end users device, and whether or not that device supports Flash. From these two values, developers can make general assumptions of the type of device the user is on, and set variables accordingly. From there it's just a matter of appending the format type to the end of the URL string of the content to be loaded:

www.mysite.com/template.swt?type=gif
www.mysite.com/template.swt?type=jpeg
www.mysite.com/template.swt?type=swf

Generator example projects

So you've got a general idea of how Generator works, and a basic understanding of the concepts behind Generator, but are you ready to start building Generator based sites and applications? Probably not. We're going to need some practice first. As discussed in the previous chapter Generator has three modes: Online, Offline and as an authoring tool. This next section will walk you through building out a Generator-based home page starting with using Generator in a production capacity and working through both Offline and Online modes. Tighten your seatbelts folks; we're going in.

Before we proceed, I should point out that we are going to make some general assumptions here. Assumption number one is that you or someone you work with has installed the 30 day Generator Developer Edition trial included on the CD accompanying this book (the instructions for doing so are included within that trial). If this has not been done, please take the time to do this before moving forward. Second, we are going to assume that you are working in a Windows environment. Windows, I believe, should be the server platform most of the readers of this book are familiar with. That said, onward and upward.

Generator build-out in production mode

It makes the most sense to start a demonstration of Generator in production mode, because in a real world situation that's where, you would be starting. To begin, we're going to need Flash 5 with the Generator Authoring Extensions installed. Once you've got that part settled, pop-open the demo included in the DEMO folder on the CD accompanying this book.

Create a new folder of your own (name it as you see fit). This is going to be the folder that contains all your test files. Copy logo.gif from the DEMO folder into the folder you just created. Note that throughout this example, we'll be building various files, and for your convenience, we have included copies of each of these files on the CD.

Our client for this example is IKRON Industries, a fictional company that deals in robotic supplies and Artificial Intelligence software. IKRON is new to the Web, and while we were able to easily sell them on using Flash to build their site, our efforts to get them to use Generator were in vain. IKRON has proved to be a troublesome client and has changed the design so many times that we are now at a point where we are building the site as individual items are approved. So far, this client has only signed off the look of the navigation bar, and we're wary that there are going to be many edits to follow. As a result, we decide to use Generator as a production tool to ease the burden of having to change the various graphical elements and content of the navigation bar every time the client changes its mind.

First off, open the final demo.swf in the Flash player and look at it sans functionality, as though it was merely a composite (comp). When beginning the production process on a site, the primary step is brainstorming methods of building it.

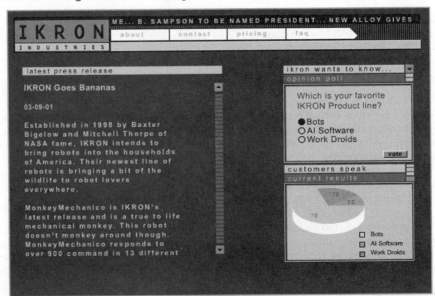

With HTML sites, developers view comps, and try to determine how to implement them in tables, and frames. When looking at a potential Flash/Generator project we want to view comps, and determine areas in which Generator objects and variables would serve to accomplish the site's intended goals, as well as where its use could streamline the production process.

During this process, Flash asset creation can begin, so other resources are not waiting in limbo. This is a prime opportunity for non-Flash designers or developers to brush-up on their Flash drawing skills, as well as educate each other in techniques for optimization without feeling as though they are holding up the process. This also affords designers more control over the implementation of their design.

Looking at the demo, there are some obvious pieces of the navigation bar that stand out as potential Generator objects. For example, all of the text could be implemented via Generator variables. The news ticker at the top is a definite Generator candidate. The logo could be an inserted GIF or JPEG. What else is there? Well, the top navigation is comprised of buttons that are all of the same likeness and all appear to have similar rollover states. This area could all be created from a single movie clip using the Generator List object. The radio button poll could be built using the radio button object.

As an entire site is eventually built-up, more and more uses for Generator will arise. Insert Symbol objects will start to come into play, perhaps the use of the Table object will be justified. Use of the Brightness, Alpha, Custom Color and Tint commands may be implemented later, to allow users to customize their experience. If internal or external advertising is added, we may want to make use of the Insert Flash Movie object. Keeping all of this in mind, let's break the example into segments and walk through their creation.

1. Open a new FLA and then select Modify > Movie. The Movie Properties panel should then pop-up. Set the background color to the value #333333. Set the width of the movie to 585 pixels, the height to 400 pixels, and then click OK.

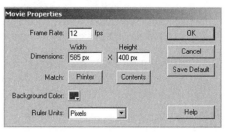

These numbers are completely arbitrary, but for the sake of this walk-through it would be best for your file to resemble the demo.fla file as closely as possible.

2. Now select File > Publish Settings. In the subsequent Publish Settings panel you'll notice that the first tab is labeled Formats, and that it lists the numerous types of file format that Flash can export. Make sure that the checkboxes next to Flash, Generator, and HTML are checked, and then click OK. If Generator is left unselected, your files won't display generated content. This is easily overlooked, so it's a good idea to always double check.

3. Next, select Window > Generator Objects. A panel should pop-up that displays all of the Generator objects supplied by Macromedia:

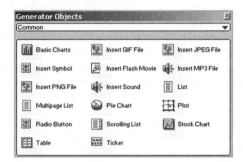

4. Now let's start being creative. To begin with, we'll build the header that contains the navigation. During production it's better to maintain the autonomy of each self-functioning unit by creating each within its own movie clip in the FLA. There are two reasons for this. First, coordinate (0,0) on the main timeline is in the top left corner of the stage. Within movie clips, coordinate (0,0) lies at the crosshair in the center of the stage. Since a project is seldom done by an individual, but rather teams, if movie clips are created separately in individual files and done so within the main timeline, developers using these assets within the final piece often lose all settings related to location. Secondly, teams swapping files and using one another's assets are often modifying these assets so that they work within a separately created environment. Assets are much more portable and developer friendly when they are kept out of the main timeline.

To start building the header, create a new movie clip called header_sl. Adding the suffix _sl, (my initials) is a recommended naming convention which developers that I work with have established to ensure that Flash does not leave out assets when multiple pieces of a project are combined for a final build. If more than one symbol have the same name, Flash will automatically assume that the one native to the file you are working on is the correct version and not import the other. You can imagine the problems that this could cause on large projects with multiple files. If each developer adds his or her initials to the symbols in their files, it keeps this from happening, and makes the production process that much faster. Obviously, feel free to change _sl to your own initials.

5. Within the header_sl movie clip we wanted to add the background graphic into the first frame of the timeline. You can either create your own graphic, or copy headerBgAssets_sl from the Library of demo.fla. Label this layer as background:

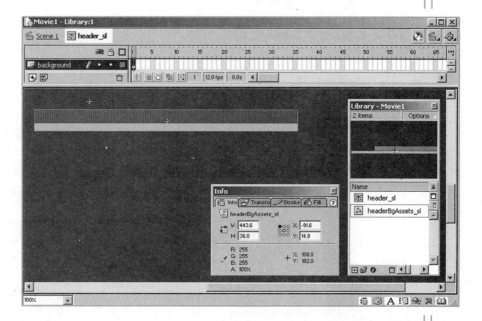

6. After creating or importing the Flash assets to display the background image in the header, we will add the logo by using the Insert GIF File object. A point to note here is that using the Insert GIF File object for a logo is usually unnecessary. Most company logos seldom change with any frequency, and as such, the logo is probably much better suited to be part of the background images. However, this is an opportunity to demonstrate the quirks of the various insert media objects at little cost to file size or outcome of the final demo.

7. Lock the layer labeled background, and create a new layer in the header_sl movie clip, and label it logo.

8. From the Generator Objects panel, locate the Insert GIF File object, drag and drop an instance of it to a point within the movie clip that is approximately where the logo should be. A transparent gray square will appear that says Insert GIF File. This is the Insert GIF File object.

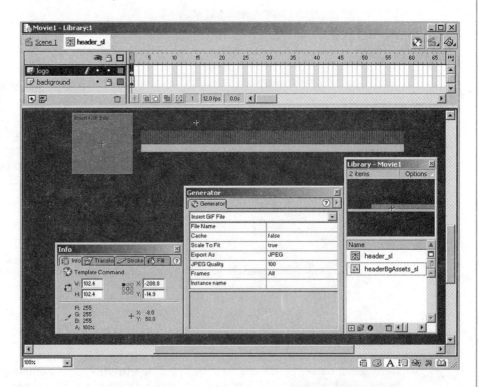

9. Upon adding the Insert GIF File object, a Generator panel should have popped-open, showing a set of options. These options are parameters for how to display the GIF we are going to insert.

File Name is the parameter we are most concerned with here, and we have two options on regarding what to enter in this field. The first option would be to put a direct path to the image we want to use, logo.gif. Now, while this would function perfectly OK, it still means that if we ever wanted to update this logo, we'd have to open the FLA to make any changes. Instead, we are going to go with what is our second option, and fill this field with a Generator curly bracket variable, {logo}.

Cache allows us to set caching on or off for our object, assuming we are running Generator Enterprise Edition with caching activated on our server. This setting can be over-ridden by setting caching within HTML parameters or in the Enterprise Edition Administration Servlet. Since we are not implementing the Enterprise Edition in this example, we'll not concern ourselves with this parameter.

Scale To Fit is the next parameter that concerns us. This parameter only accepts true or false. Setting this to true causes the image that is to be loaded to scale to fit the width and height of the transparent gray box. Aspect ratio is not maintained, so unless you have managed to set the width and height of your object to the same aspect ratio as your image, your image will appear distorted. false maintains the GIF's original size. For this demo we want to make sure it's set to false.

Export As specifies the format of the output of the generated image. Possible values are JPEG (compresses the image), and Lossless (which attempts to maintain as much of the original quality of the image as possible). Set this parameter to JPEG.

Directly below this field is the parameter for JPEG Quality. It is here that we set the compression quality of our exported JPEG via a number representing a percentage. For now, leave this at 100.

Frames is a parameter associated with animated GIF files. We are able to choose to see every frame of the animated GIF or to select a single frame. I've found that this parameter often does not work the way it is supposed to, and as a result, animated GIFs tend to act unpredictably. I personally would advise against using animated GIFs with the Insert GIF File object, but for now, just set this parameter to All.

Since we used a Generator variable to define our File Name parameter, we need to define the data source that specifies the value for that variable. We do so by clicking on the Set Environment icon on the top right corner of your FLA file

The Set Environment window should appear. You'll see that it contains a text field, and immediately to the right of the text field are two icons that resemble sheets of paper. The icon on the left is for **Column Name/Value** data sources. The one to the right is for **Name/Value** formatted data sources. Column/Name Value data sources are necessary for Generator objects whose variables can contain more than one value (such as the Plot object). Name/ Value data sources are for those objects whose variables only have one value. Since our variable is to only have one value (logo.jpg) make sure that the Name/Value format is selected.

Name/Value Format:	**Column Name /Value Format:**
name, value	var1, var2, var3
var1, value1	value1a, value2a, value3a
var2, value2	value1b, value2b, value3b

The following Generator Objects require a Column Name/Value formatted data source:

- Basic Charts, Pie Charts and Stock Charts

- Lists, MultiPage Lists and Scrolling Lists

- Tickers

- Plot

- Radio Button

- Table

We'll define our data source in what is currently the blank text field. Since we are dealing with the header portion of the movie, let's name our data source `header.txt`. Type the name `header.txt`, and then click OK.

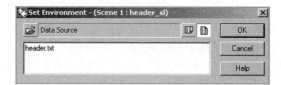

For this demo, all our data sources will be in the same directory. However, this is seldom the case when working on large projects. You should make it a habit when specifying data sources in different directories to always use relative paths. Absolute paths created when working locally are bound to be different when the site is actually hosted on a live web server. To keep from having to retrace your steps and re-write all your data source paths, make all your paths relative.

Relative: `.../header.txt` (one level up from the directory we are calling from)

Absolute: `open_projectz:book:demo:header.txt` (direct local path)

10. Drag the `header_sl` movie clip from the Library onto the first frame of the main timeline and place it so it is aligned towards the top left of the stage. Label this layer header. Doesn't look like much, does it?

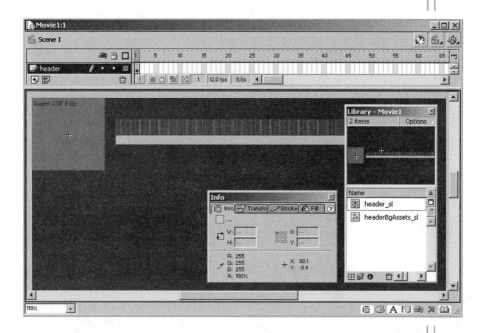

This is a good point to mention one of Generator's few caveats, which is that until you publish your movie, you have no way of truly knowing what your output will look like. When working with sites and applications that require perfect alignment, you often find yourself spending a lot of time publishing your movie, viewing it, going back to the FLA, "pixel pushing" then publishing again, and again, until you get it right. You should also always make sure that you preview your changes within a browser. You'll notice minute changes in alignment between the Flash Player and your browser, and since the majority of your audience will most likely be viewing your site in a browser, use that as your final reference. There should be no discrepancies in alignment within Flash movies between different types of browsers.

1.   Our next step is to create the data source, header.txt. We do this by opening any program that supports the TXT file format (Word, Simple Text, Notepad, etc.) and setting up Name and Value columns. In their respective columns, we put:

   1.   The name of the variable, in this case logo.

   2.   The file that we want this value to represent, in this case, logo.gif.

Make sure that all of your values are listed in quotes, as spaces and special characters can cause Generator to misunderstand the file if these things exist outside of quotation. Save this file (in the folder you created earlier) as header.txt and return to your FLA.

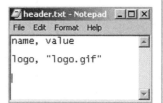

Before going any further, we will need to test this movie to make sure our inserted GIF is aligned correctly and that everything we have done so far is working. Save your FLA as myDemo.fla in the new folder that you created earlier. Now select File > Publish Preview > Flash. You could also have selected File > Export Movie. However, this option would only export the SWF. While such a SWF would work just fine, I want to point out that selecting Publish Preview > Flash generates not only a SWF, but also a SWT and an HTML file as well (remember these were the options we selected in the Publish Settings at the beginning of this example?).

2. Drag the newly generated HTML file into your favorite browser and check it out. Chances are that the alignment of logo.gif is way off. As mentioned earlier, one of the flaws of Generator is its inability to display your object values in any way without testing your movie. Go back into your FLA and "pixel push" until it is lined up correctly:

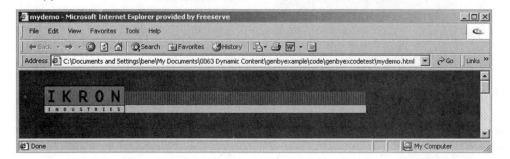

3. The next thing that we're going to do is add the news ticker. The way the Ticker object works is that it references a movie clip with a variable written in the specified font, color and size. From this movie clip it replicates that variable as many times as there are values in your text file. So, before we do anything else, we need to define a text variable that is formatted with the correct font, color, and size for our ticker within a movie clip.

Create a new movie clip called ticker_sl. Label the first layer of this movie clip as text. In the first frame of the text layer, write {text} in the font of your choice (the example uses Arial point size 9). Placement of this text should be located at coordinate $(0,0)$, that is, in the top left corner of the bottom right quadrant of the stage. The item spacing of clips that are called into Generator originates from coordinate $(0,0)$, so unless you require some form of offset it's best to line things up relative to this coordinate.

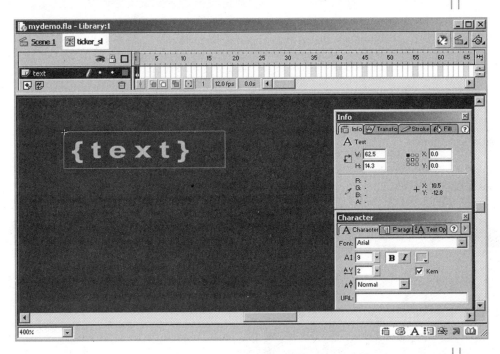

Another concern that we must address is the fact that we have a variable whose values have yet to be determined. These values may very well extend the limits of the text field in which our variable is typed. To ensure that there is enough room to encompass any value we care to choose, we need to extend our text field as far out as we feel the maximum value will need. To do this, highlight the variable so that it is editable. You'll notice that a small circle appears attached to the top right border of the outline. Click on this circle and drag the text field out by an appropriate amount of space, and then release. You'll notice that the circle has now become a square. This square signifies that this field now has a fixed width. Any text that reaches beyond this point will wrap to the next line.

Do not use the scale tool to set the fixed width of your text field. This will only cause the content to scale in the direction you pushed or pulled the field.

4. Since the ticker is contained within the header portion of our file, we are going to add the Ticker object to the header_sl movie clip. Go to this clip, add a new layer, and label it ticker. Drag an instance of the Ticker object from the Generator Objects panel to the appropriate place on the stage and then drop it into position. A translucent gray box labeled Ticker should appear. Click on the Ticker object so that the Generator panel parameters are now specific to the Ticker object.

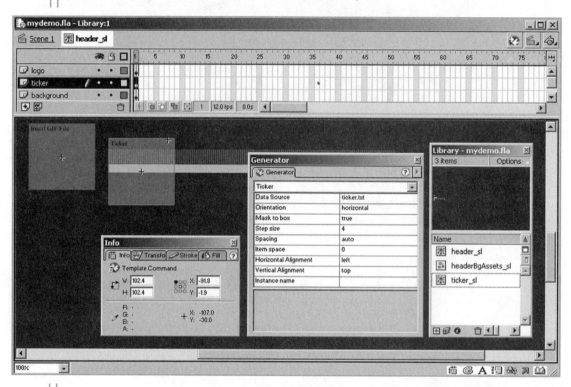

The first parameter here is for the Data Source. You'll remember that when we used the Insert GIF File object, we specified the data source within the Generator Environment window. For the Ticker object we specify it directly within the parameters. Type ticker.txt into this field. This will be the name of the text file we'll create later.

The second parameter is Orientation. This determines the direction in which our ticker is to scroll (horizontal or vertical). Select horizontal.

The next parameter is Mask to box. With the Ticker object (as well as the list objects), you have the option of masking your content to a predefined area. That area is the width and height of the Ticker object itself (the gray translucent box labeled Ticker). Set this to true. A setting of false would cause your content to scroll across the entire movie.

Now, knowing that we are masking the content of the ticker to the width and height of the object, you may have realized that the Ticker object you have on the stage in the header_sl movie clip is not even close to the height and width of the ticker in the demo. Position the object at a point on the stage relative to the demo and use the scale tool to adjust it so it resembles the height and width of the ticker in the demo.

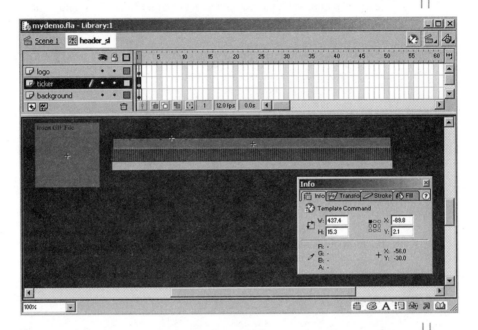

Step size is the next parameter we need to specify. This is the number of pixels per frame that the ticker will move in the direction you specified. While one pixel per second would obviously be the smoothest motion, it would also be extremely slow. Throughout testing you will most likely be adjusting this number, but for now, let's set it to 4.

The Spacing parameter should be set to auto. This sets the spacing between each item to just as much as each item needs. If we had set it to fixed, it would set the spacing of each item to the number specified in the following parameter, Item space. We can also use Item space to subtract or add pixels to the area given to our items if the Spacing parameter is set to auto.

Set the Horizontal Alignment to left and the Vertical Alignment to top. These setting are in relation to the x and y values of your Ticker object. For example, with our current settings, you could actually scale the ticker object vertically so it covered the entire stage, and the values moving across would still be exactly where you wanted them to be. Conversely, if we changed the Vertical Alignment to bottom, the values would move across the bottom of the stage. Obviously, these settings are dependent upon where you place your ticker, and how you want your information displayed.

5. Our last step is to create the data source associated with this ticker. Open up a new file in your favorite text editor, and set up a **Column Name/Value** data source with two columns, clip and text. clip will specify the Library name of the movie clip that contains our text variable. text is derived from the actual name of that variable {text}. Had we chosen to use a Generator variable called {content} in the movie clip ticker_sl, then our columns would be titled clip and content.

Below clip and text we need to specify values, which in this case will be ticker_sl, and the associated text. Since tickers can have as much or as little text as you desire, specifying a new set of values below the original set will add that text to the ticker. Since all our headlines are formatted in the same manner, we can just repeat the value ticker_sl and modify the associated text each time. Fill in your text file as in the example below, and then save this file as ticker.txt.

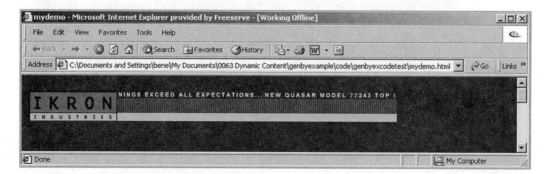

6. Publish your movie, and view it in a browser to ensure it is lined up properly. Make adjustments if necessary.

7. It is now time to create our navigation. Our goal is to enable the developer to add, remove, and change the order or the name of each button in our menu without having to make edits to the FLA. To do this, we are going to use the List object.

Our first step is to create a default button. This button will be the template for any and all buttons within the navigation. Pull the button_sl button into your library from the demo.fla file. You'll notice that on the second layer of the button, we have placed the variable {nav}. This will be the variable for the text labels that will appear on all the buttons. Make sure that this variable resides in the over, hit and down states. Feel free to change the size or color of the variable between the various states to enhance the effect.

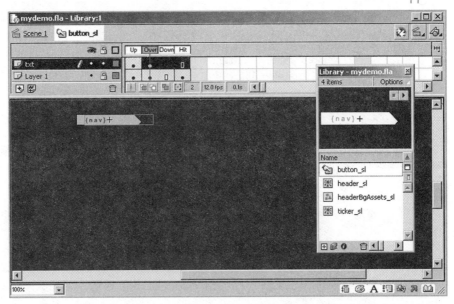

Generator objects, such as the List object, that work by replicating a defined template cannot replicate a button symbol. Our template for our navigation must reside within a movie clip, as such we need to place button_sl within a parent movie clip so that Generator can work with it. Create a new movie clip called navigation_sl. Label the first layer of this movie clip as button. Drag button_sl from the Library and place it in the first frame of the button layer. Make sure to align the top left corner of button_sl to point (0,0) on the stage:

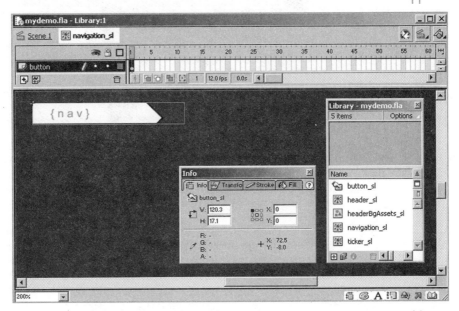

8. Next, return to the header_sl movie clip. Add another new layer, and label it navigation. Now drag an instance of the List object from the Generator Objects panel onto the stage. The List object builds a list from top to bottom or left to right. Since we are making a horizontal list, place the translucent gray box as close as you can to where you think the button on the extreme left will be located:

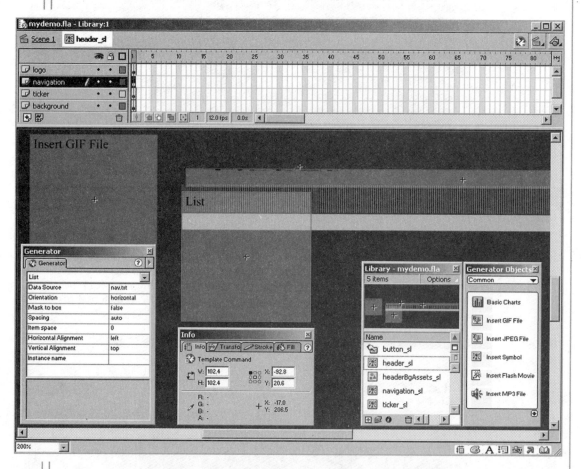

Click on the List object so its parameters appear in the Generator panel. Once again, we see that the first parameter is Data Source, which in this case we need to set to nav.txt. Again, this is going to be the name of our text file data source. Like the Ticker object, we want to set the Orientation parameter to horizontal.

Now, unlike the ticker, we want to set the Mask to box parameter to false, since our buttons are not moving, and we don't wish to hide any portion of them. Had we set this parameter to true, we would've had to make sure that the translucent gray box of the List object was wide enough and tall enough to show all of the buttons. Since we don't want to add an extra step to this process, we'll leave the setting as false. This way, the height and width of the box are irrelevant and as long as the top left corner of the List object is in the correct location, our buttons will be too.

The Spacing parameter should be set to auto. This is navigation and does not require any additional space between elements, Item space should remain set to 0 for now. We are going to come back to this, but I want to demonstrate something first.

Make sure that Horizontal Alignment and Vertical Alignment read left, and top respectively.

9. With all that settled, once again we need to create the data source. Now, since the Ticker object uses multiple values for the same variable, we want to use a **Column Name/Value** data source again. So, create a new TXT file called nav.txt, in a Column Name/Value format that contains the columns clip and nav. The clip column will be used to denote the name of the movie clip containing our default button. Looking back at our movie Library, we see that the movie clip called navigation_sl. nav is the name of the Generator text variable within button_sl of the navigation_sl movie clip. We have to specify values for this variable to suit our application. Fill out the two columns as shown in the following screenshot. Again, just as we did with the Ticker object, we will specify multiple values for these two column headers. Each set of values will start with navigation_sl and end with the title of the button:

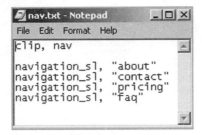

10. Now publish your movie and view it in a browser:

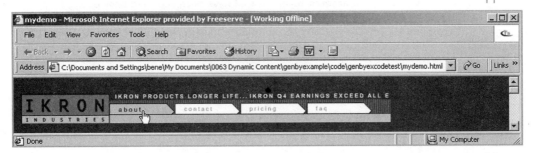

Assuming everything so far has been implemented correctly, you'll notice that while all your navigation buttons appear with the correct text, they do look a little awkward on account of their rather angular right side. In order to address this awkwardness, the buttons in the demonstration file on the CD are actually overlapped slightly, whilst the version we've built here has gaps in between each item. Earlier, when I was talking about the Item space parameter for the List object, I suggested that there was a complication with it, and that I wanted to get back to it, after I'd given you a demonstration. Well, this is precisely that point. You see, by making a slight modification to the Item space parameter, we can overlap the buttons just enough to avoid this untidiness on the right-hand side of each button. Let's have a look at how we can do this...

11.   Return to the header_sl movie clip, and click on the List object. In the Generator panel, you'll notice that the parameter setting in the Item space field is set to 0. To introduce the button overlap that we were just talking about, we need to subtract a certain number of pixels from the spacing of each item. Using a negative number as the value for this parameter will cause the buttons to begin to overlap. Set the value to –20, re-publish your movie, and then view it in a browser. The buttons should now overlap, giving a much tidier appearance.

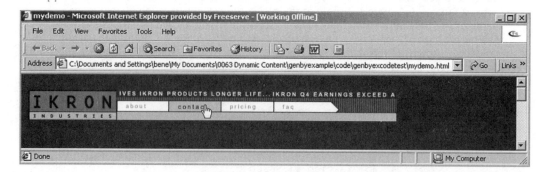

12.   Re-open the nav.txt file. Notice that the order of entries in the nav column is directly related to the order of the buttons in your published SWF. To experiment a little, see what happens if you change the order of the entries in this column, you could even try adding or deleting rows from the text file. Re-publish your FLA, and see what affect your changes have had. Notice how the buttons always line up correctly, and adjust to account for items that have been removed or added.

So far, we have focused on Generator variables being used within the Generator object parameters, and as variable text items. Now let's see how they work within ActionScript.

13.   Return to your FLA, and go to the main timeline (or root). You should have a layer labeled header, which contains a keyframe with the header_sl movie clip. Add two new layers above the header layer and name them labels and actions. Add a layer below the header and label it content. Extend the timeline out to 100 frames. In the labels layer, put blank keyframes at frames 15, 25, 35 and 45. Label these frames with the same titles as the buttons in your navigation, which are the same titles as in the nav column in your nav.txt file.

14.   In frames 1, 15, 25, 35 and 45 of the actions layer, add blank keyframes with a stop action in each. These should line up with the keyframes in the labels layer.

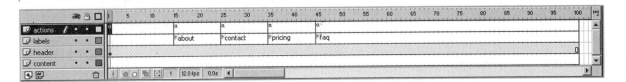

15. Now, in the content layer, add keyframes to frames 15, 25, 35, and 45. In each individual frame, add a static text field displaying the name of the label somewhere on the stage. These are going to be used as references to ensure that your code works when you test your file.

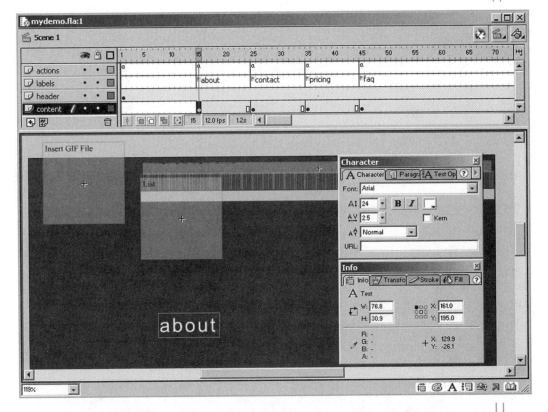

16. OK, the next thing you need to do is go into the navigation_sl movie clip, and click on your default button. Make sure the Object Actions window is open, and then add the following code to the button:

```
on (release, releaseOutside) {
    _root.gotoAndStop("{nav}");
}
```

You'll notice, that this code contains the Generator variable, {nav}. This is the same variable that we used to label our buttons, and is consequently the same variable we used for the labels in the main timeline. You'll also notice that this Generator variable is enclosed in quotes. Because this variable is returning a string value, we must enclose it in quotes, otherwise, it will be returned as a local Flash variable. On publishing, Generator will go through the nav.txt file, and will replicate navigation_sl as many times as there are rows in our data source. At the same time, Generator will replace any Generator variables with the values we have specified. Essentially what Generator interprets is this:

Button 1

```
on (release, releaseOutside) {
    _root.gotoAndStop("about");
}
```

Button 2

```
on (release, releaseOutside) {
    _root.gotoAndStop("contact");
}
```

etc., etc., etc...

17. Publish your FLA and open it in a browser. Clicking on the buttons in the navigation should cause your movie to jump to the appropriate spot in the timeline. You'll know it's working if the text you wrote out in the middle of the screen matches the text on the button you clicked.

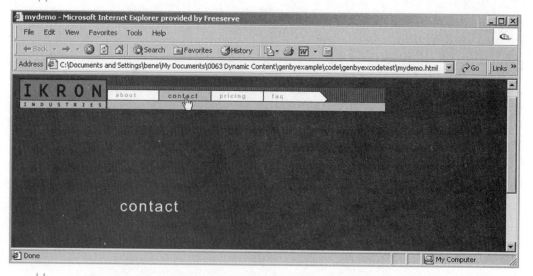

18. From this example, it could be assumed that whatever variable you use to name your navigation buttons must be the same value as the labels within the timeline in order for Generator to publish your file correctly. Well, in actual fact, that is not the case. What if we wanted to link our buttons to other external web pages not contained within this movie? This is just a matter of adding a new variable column to our data source.

Open `nav.txt`. On the first line where it currently reads:

```
clip, nav
```

Add a third column and change your data source to read:

```
clip, nav, url
```

We have just added a new variable column called `url`. Add a third item to each row in `nav.txt`. Make this item a URL, any URL, as in the following example:

```
clip, nav, url

navigation_sl, "about", "http://www.friendsofed.com"
navigation_sl, "contact", "http://www.macromedia.com"
navigation_sl, "pricing", "http://www.space.com"
navigation_sl, "faq", "http://www.usabancshares.com"
```

Anything written within this column will replace the {url} Generator variable within the movie clip navigation_sl. But, we don't have a Generator variable called {url} in the movie clip navigation_sl. Well, let's fix that!

19. Go to the navigation_sl movie clip and select your default button. The code for this button should appear in the Object Actions window. Modify this code so it reads as shown here:

```
on (release, releaseOutside) {
    getURL ("{url}", "_blank");
}
```

We have just replaced the {nav} variable with the {url} variable.

20. Now, publish your movie and open it up in a browser window. The text on the buttons should still be as it was, but clicking on them should bring up a new window linking to the URL you specified in your data source.

Feel free to leave your `nav.txt` file as js, or revert to the previous version. The same applies to the code within navigation_sl.

We have now finished creating the header, and so ends our introduction to the production aspect of Generator. After going through these steps, it becomes quite clear how Generator can expedite workflow by making updates to graphics, text, and links a snap. Once you've established the foundation for your file, a client can call at any time with changes to the elements and it only requires an update to a text file and republishing your FLA. Oh, and don't forget, this didn't cost you a dime more than it would have, had you built the whole thing without the Generator Authoring Extensions!

Speaking of money, IKRON has just notified you that you are going to have to add a "home" button between the pricing and faq buttons. Tell them it'll take a few hours, take two minutes to edit the data source, republish your FLA and then go to lunch. They'll be none the wiser.

Continuation of build-out in Offline mode

As discussed in the previous chapter, Offline Generator is invoked either from the Windows command line, a UNIX command line in a shell, through an MS-DOS batch file, or Perl script. The major difference between Offline and Online, is that Offline Generator is triggered by the administrator, whereas in Online mode, Generator is triggered by the client browser. It is also possible to mimic Online Generator using Offline Generator by using a CGI script. This can be extremely handy when using web based administration tools, but in general is not recommended for true Online Generator functionality.

OK, your client at IKRON, likes the look of the header, and loves the motion and feel that Flash provides, but is in a dilemma. You see, part of the functionality he thinks the site is supposed to offer, is that the home page should be updated as often as need be, in order to display the most current press release. He's starting to worry about agreeing to use Flash on the site, mainly because he couldn't find his way around an FLA if you paid him, and he doesn't want to have to call your office every time this information needs to be updated. You've mentioned Generator, but every time the word comes up, the client gets all flustered, and starts mumbling something about $30,000. Set his mind at ease. The muscle needed to provide the kind of easy updating that the client wants can be found in our low cost buddy, Generator Developer Edition running in Offline mode.

We're going to implement the press release on the home page, and enable it to be updated with ease, but first we have to build it in the production environment. The press release calls for the use of the Scrolling List Object. This handy little object, which is an embellishment of the List object we used to create the navigation, dynamically adds enough frames to a list to scroll to the end of the list.

1. First we are going to create the buttons that scroll the list. Scrolling is not an innate function within the Scrolling List object, and so we must do a little ActionScripting to get it going. Create a new button called scrollBut_sl. Give the button up, down and hit states. Again, you are welcome to copy scrollBut_sl from the Library of demo.fla.

2. Next we are going to create the default template for the text to be scrolled. Create a new movie clip called pressTxt_sl. Label the first layer of this movie clip as text. Within this movie clip we are going to put some Generator variables that will be replaced with the values of our press release. These values are {title}, {date}, and {txt}. In the text layer, create a static text field, and in the first line type {title}, hit RETURN, type {date}, hit RETURN, then type {txt}, and then hit RETURN again. There is a reason why we are including all of these items within the same text field, and it's that when these variables are replaced with values, these values can be any size. So, say the {title} of a press release on a particular date was, "IKRON Industries first to market with

New Metal Alloy, lighter than Aluminum, stronger than Steel". Most likely, this title will wrap to encompass two, possibly three lines of text. Since all of these items are within the same text field, they will follow the attributes given to them no matter how many lines each value takes up. This means that even if the {title} ended up taking up 10 lines, {date} would still appear one line below. If these variables had each been in their own text fields, the 10 line {title} would end up overlapping both {date} and {txt}.

Another thing that we want to be sure of is that the text field in question has a fixed width. If it does not, the text will continue to push to the right and our scrolling list will not display all our text. Using demo.swf as a reference, click on the text field until its background turns white, and the text is editable. Just as we did with the ticker variable earlier, you'll notice that there is a small circle in the top right corner of your textbox. Click and drag this circle until the width of your text field is comparable to the width of the text in demo.swf. When it looks about right, release. When you release, you'll see that the now familiar circle in the top right corner has become a square. This signifies that your text field has a fixed width, and any dynamic content will wrap at that width.

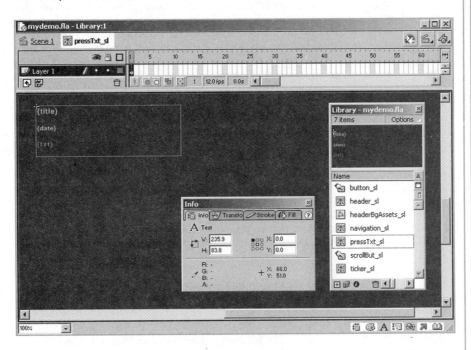

3. We need to set a data source for this movie clip and will do so in the Set Environment window. Click the icon in the top right corner – hopefully, we're at a point now where you already knew what to do. In the field provided type, pressRelease.txt. Make sure that the **Name/Value** icon is also depressed.

Before going further, let's also create this data source:

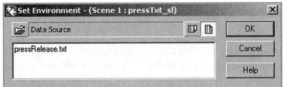

4. Pop-open that text editor again, and set up **Name/Value** columns. For now, populate these columns with mock data based on the variables we used in the pressTxt_sl movie clip. See the example below for a reference (or just use the copy of pressRelease.txt from the CD)

```
name, value

title, "IKRON Goes Bananas"
date, "03-09-01"
txt, "Established in 1998 by Baxter Bigelow and Mitchell Thorpe
➡of NASA fame, IKRON intends to bring robots into the households
➡of America. Their newest line of robots is bringing a bit of
➡the wildlife to robot lovers everywhere. \r\n\r\nMonkeyMechanico
➡is IKRON's latest release and is a true to life mechanical
➡monkey. This robot doesn't monkey around though. MonkeyMechanico
➡responds to over 900 command in 13 different languages and is
➡fully equipped to work as a security guard, a house keeper or
➡even an accountant. \r\n\r\nUnlike IKRON's  past robots,
➡MonkeyMechanico does not have the intimidating feel that cold
➡steel and gears often present robot owners. MonkeyMechanico's
➡entire robotic shell has been lined with a space age polymer
➡plastic that looks like fur and lasts a lifetime."
```

If you took the time to examine the text for the variable txt you may have noticed some unusual syntax: \r\n\r\n. This syntax, or: \r\n specifically, is how a carriage return is implemented in Generator data sources. A regular carriage return will cause any text below it to not appear in the outputted SWF. There are a few instances in Generator data sources (such as when trying to implement quotation marks ("")), question marks (?) and curly braces ({}) where special syntax such as \r\n is required.

Special characters for use within Generator data sources:

\r\n	A carriage return ("First line of text. \r\nSecond line of text").
\	Treats the following character as an escaped character.
\\	Literal backslash "\" (This is a backslash \\).
\"	Quotation mark (\"These are quoted,\" I said).
{{	Curly brace ({{var1}} is a Generator variable).

5. Save this file as pressRelease.txt.

So, we've got buttons, we've got a default text template...where's the scrolling list? Cool your jets there speedy, one step at a time...

Creating the scrolling list

1. Create a new movie clip and call it press_sl. This clip is where all your pieces will be put together into one working unit.

2. Label the first layer as scrolling list. From the Generator Objects Panel, drag the Scrolling List object onto the stage in this layer.

3. Add a new layer and label it scrollbar_sl. Drag scrollBar_sl from demo.fla into the first frame of this layer.

4. Create a third layer called header. Copy the pressHeader_sl movie clip from the demo.fla library, into this layer.

5. Lastly, create a final layer called buttons. For now, leave this layer blank.

6. Arrange the pressHeader_sl movie clip in the header layer so that it lines up at coordinate (0,0) on the stage. Below this, line the Scrolling List object in the scrolling list layer to coordinate (0, 25). Both items should be aligned left to coordinate (0,0) with a vertical separation of 25 pixels. Scale the scrolling list object so it's width is nearly equal to that of the pressHeader_sl. This way, when used as a mask it will reveal the appropriate amount of text. To the right of the Scrolling List object, line up the scrollBar_sl movie clip so that it looks visually appealing. Use demo.swf as a reference:

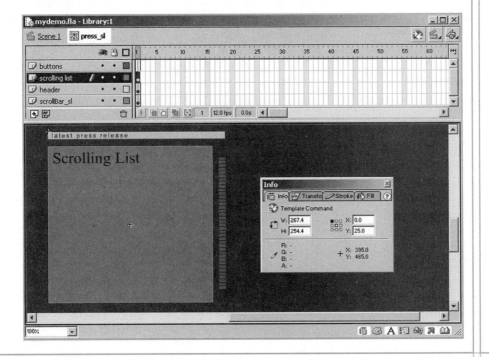

7. Click on the Scrolling List object so that the Generator panel shows the parameters for that object. The first field, as usual, specifies the data source. In this field, set it to scrolling.txt. Set Orientation to vertical and Mask to box to true. Set the Step size to 20. Again, Spacing will be set to auto, Item space should be set to 0 and we want to align the values to left and top.

The last parameter in this panel is Instance name. This parameter has been available to us in every object so far, but we have neglected to fill it in... until now that is. Instance name enables us to give a name to a Generator object so that we can target it just like a movie clip. Since our buttons are going to eventually have to target this object to enable scrolling, we'll want to give this object a name. Enter scrollList_sl into this field.

8. There's one more step before we can move on to making buttons that scroll the object. We need to create the data source for this scrolling list. Hit that text editor one more time, and create a **Column Name/Value** data source with one column. Since we are not setting any variables here, only determining the movie clip that holds the variable template for our press releases, this all we need to specify. Type clip as the column header of the data source. Below this, specify the template movie clip, pressTxt_sl. Like this:

```
clip

pressTxt_sl
```

Keep in mind, that we could have specified multiple clip values within this data source. If we had typed something like the following, our scrolling list would contain all these clips spaced out evenly in the order they appear in the data source:

```
clip

pressTxt_sl
pressTxt2_sl
pressTxt3_sl
```

9. Save this file as scrolling.txt.

10. Now we can finally create the buttons that scroll the list. Yes, we've already created the buttons, but in order to have them scroll the Scrolling List object, we need to put these buttons into an individual movie clip and provide the appropriate code. So, create a new movie clip called scrollButtonMovie_sl. Label the first layer of this movie clip, button.

11. Drag two copies of scrollBut_sl into the first frame of the button layer. Rotate one button so we end up with one button pointing up, and the other pointing down. Place the up facing button at coordinate (0,0) on the stage.

12. Add the following code to the Object Actions window for this button:

```
on (press) {
    _root.scrolling = "up";
}
on (release, dragOut) {
    _root.scrolling = "off";
}
```

You'll notice here, that we are using a new variable called `scrolling` (`_root.scrolling`). Since this is our "up" button, we set the scrolling variable equal to `up` when it is depressed. On release, we set it to `off`. Scrolling is the variable we will be tracking when we create the `enterFrame` loop that scrolls our press release.

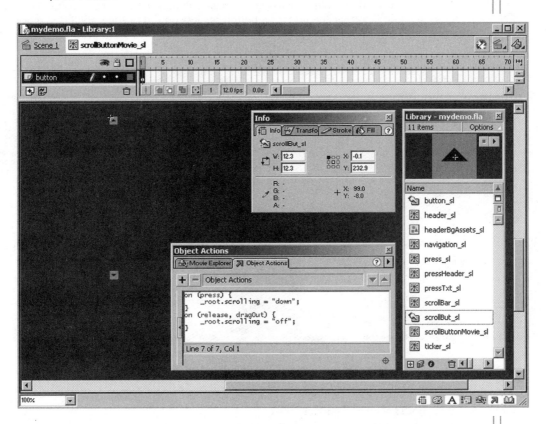

13. Position the down facing button so that it lines up vertically with the up facing button. Move the down facing button towards the bottom of the screen so that the distance between the two buttons is roughly equivalent to the height of our Scrolling List object. Use `demo.swf` as a reference.

Add the following code to the Object Actions window for the down button:

```
on (press) {
    _root.scrolling = "down";
}
on (release, dragOut) {
    _root.scrolling = "off";
}
```

You'll notice that this code is almost identical to the "up" code, except that we are setting the scrolling variable to equal down instead of up.

14. Now, return to the parent movie clip press_sl. Remember earlier when we added a buttons layer to this movie clip, but chose to leave it blank? Well, now we're going to fill it. Drag the scrollButtonMovie_sl movie clip into the first frame of this layer, and position it so that the up facing button sits just on top of the scrollBar_sl movie clip and the down facing button sits just below it. Feel free to return to scrollButtonMovie_sl to make spacing adjustments.

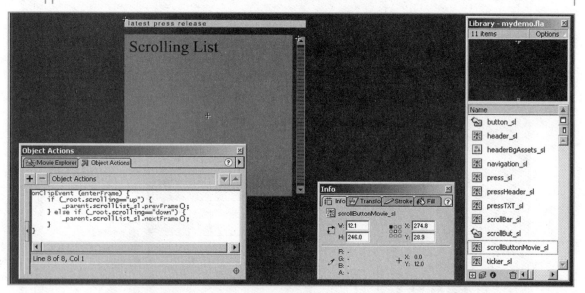

15. To finish setting up our scrolling, we need to add an onClipEvent action to our scrollButtonMovie_sl movie clip:

```
onClipEvent (enterFrame) {
    if (_root.scrolling=="up") {
        _parent.scrollList_sl.prevFrame();
    } else if (_root.scrolling=="down") {
        _parent.scrollList_sl.nextFrame();
    }
}
```

The Scrolling List object works by creating a frame animation in the downward direction based on the amount of text we have and the size of our scrolling list mask. So, sending the scrollList_sl movie clip to the nextFrame over and over, creates a downward scroll, while sending it to the prevFrame animates it in the opposite direction. The code is constantly checking the variable _root.scrolling to see which direction, if any, we wish the text to scroll.

You will notice I used a relative path (_parent) to target scrollList_sl. Since the movie clip scrollButtonMovie_sl lies inside of the parent movie clip scrollList_sl this will work just fine. There is, however, another reason for doing so. When working with teams on a project, you may often swap files, and may be working on an individual piece of the whole. When working this way, you have no idea how many levels down your piece may reside in the final build. Using relative paths as shown here, ensures that your code will work no matter where it is placed in the final project.

16. Now go back to the main scene, insert another layer, and label it as scrolling list. Dragan instance of the press_sl movie clip into the first frame of this layer (positioning it in approximately the same place as you would find it in demo.fla), and then insert a blank keyframe on frame 15:

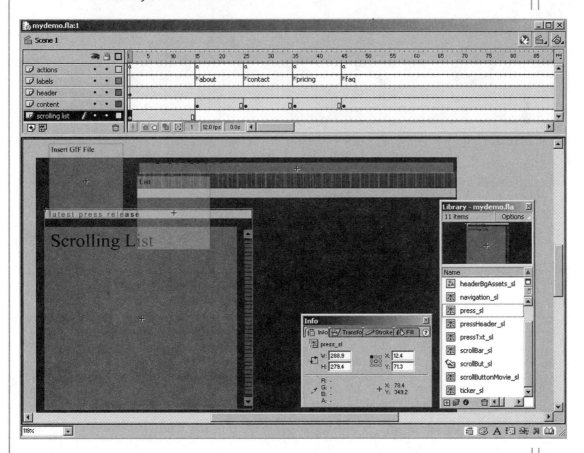

17. Publish the FLA, and view it in a browser to make sure everything was completed correctly. If you didn't choose to use the mock text I provided you with, you may find that your version is not scrolling. This may be because your text doesn't need to be scrolled and is fully visible. Before going back and retracing your steps, try adding additional text to the `pressRelease.txt` variable `txt`. Republish the FLA, and try it out again in the browser. Assuming everything is working as it should, let's now see how our client could update this press release with relative ease using Generator in Offline mode.

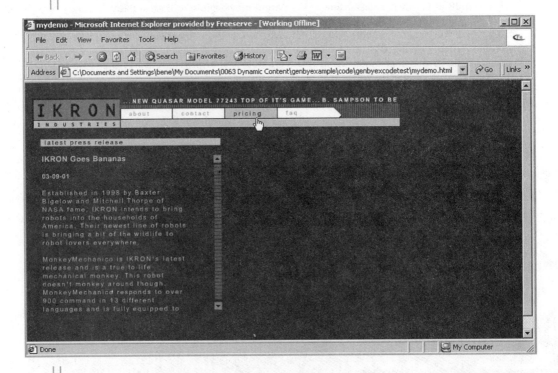

We want to place all the appropriate text, SWT, and SWF files created from the FLA we've been working on into the web root of the web server running Generator. We should always make sure when transferring the data source (TXT) files via FTP, that the transfer mode is set to BINARY and not TEXT. Certain FTP clients have a tendency to corrupt files from various operating systems during TEXT. mode transfers.

Whenever Generator is invoked Offline, all the appropriate values for all the Generator variables will be pulled from the text files into the SWT template, and a new SWF file will be generated to replace the old one. This is the file that the end user's machine will be requesting. The simplest way to invoke Generator in Offline mode is via the command line. Our client over at IKRON could simply modify the `pressRelease.txt` file with the latest information, and save it to the server. Then an administrator, or even the client himself, could invoke Generator to create the new SWF via the Windows command line using the following syntax:

```
generate -swf c:\inetpub\wwwroot\ikron.swf ikron.swt
```

Et voila! A new SWF with the newest information has just been generated in the web root.

Using the command line you can also pass variables to your template as you invoke Generator. Obviously, we wouldn't want to pass the entire content of a press release. However, seeing as humans are prone to error, maybe we accidentally forgot to change the date before we processed the template. Not to worry, we just pop up the command prompt again and pass the variable with the generate command like this:

```
Command Prompt                                                        _ □ ×
Microsoft Windows 2000 [Version 5.00.2195]
(C) Copyright 1985-1999 Microsoft Corp.

C:\>generate -swf c:\inetpub\wwwroot\ikron.swf ikron.swt -param date "3-04-01"
```

Problem solved.

As easy as this may be, some clients just aren't happy with anything even remotely manual. What if the client at IKRON wanted this process to be automated? Well, we could invoke Generator at timed intervals through a batch process. This way, new files would be generated hourly, daily, weekly, monthly... whatever, regardless of whether or not there was any new content. There are many ways to achieve this, but one of the simpler methods is by creating a batch file, and then using Windows Scheduler to automate the batch process.

A batch file (.bat) is simply a file that contains a sequence of commands, in this case the commands are the same ones that we used when invoking Generator from the Windows command line (generate -swf c:\inetpub\wwwroot\ikron.swf ikron.swt). So, using a text editor such as Notepad, create such a file, and call it ikron.bat, and then save this file to a memorable location on your computer.

Now, open up the Windows Scheduler. You will be walked through a step-by-step process that simply asks what program you want to schedule to run (for this example, ikron.bat) and how often you want this to take place. That's it, couldn't be easier...

Now only the text files need to be updated by the client, everything else is automated. Keep in mind, that this example referenced `pressRelase.txt`, but any changes made to `ticker.txt`, `nav.txt` or any others would also be updated when the new SWF was produced.

Batch processes can also be triggered via the web, by a CGI script. This can come in handy when creating web based administration tools. For example, the clients at IKRON would not have to edit data source text files, and save them on the server. Instead, they could fill out a web based form, click Submit, and pass those values to a CGI based intermediate technology, e.g. ASP/JSP etc. The variables are put into a format acceptable by Generator, and then passed to the server. At the same time a command is sent to invoke Generator to churn out some new files.

Continuation of build-out in Online mode

So, our client is pleased as punch that he doesn't have to contact anyone when he wants to update the site, and is becoming more and more of a Generator fanatic by the minute. He decides to add some personalization to his site, and wants customers to vote on their favorite IKRON product line. He feels customers are more likely to vote, if they can see how their opinion affects the total result. The best approach, in his mind, is to depict this in a pie chart. It's time to take this baby Online.

Now, as discussed in the previous chapter, Online Generator doesn't necessarily mean using Generator Enterprise Edition. Developer Edition can also run in Online mode, and is quite capable of handling something of this nature. Keep in mind that this is IKRON we're dealing with, not Yahoo. The amount of users that will actually be invoking Generator at the same time during any given period will fall well into Developer Edition's capabilities. That said, let's start building.

Since this portion of our example is going to be triggering Generator in Online mode, we'll need to have a database table set up. A table contains information that is stored in the database. A database can contain one or more tables of related information. Each table is divided into columns or fields. Our table will contain three columns that will specify the values ID, `Choices` and `Color` for our pie chart.

ID	Choices	Color
1	9	CCCC99
2	5	999999
3	11	92ABDA
(AutoNumber)	0	

Record: 4 of 4

ID is directly related to the user selection. In this demo, we are going to be giving the user a choice of three answers to a particular question. Whichever choice the user makes will fall into ID category one, two, or three. These values will always remain the same.

`Color` will also be a constant value, and simply specifies the output color of that portion of our pie chart.

Choices will not be constant. These values will be updated every time a user places a vote. You'll notice that we have already supplied some numbers within this column. This was done so when the chart first loads, it actually has some values to start with.

We will not be walking through the steps of creating the database table within this demo. I say this because we haven't yet covered databases in this book, and in a real world production environment this will most likely not be the job of the Flash developer/programmer. Included in the demo folder on the accompanying CD, you will see a file called Leohub.mdb (*created by Ryan Provost, contact@aboutryan.com*). This is a Microsoft Access database file, and should be compatible with most web servers running the Windows platform. Check with your system administrator to make sure that you don't need to download any additional drivers for this to work.

1. OK, within this file, we have created the database table shown above. Upload this file to your web root. You may have noticed two other files in the demo folder with an .asp extension, vote.asp and tally.asp. Place these files in your web root as well. We'll be discussing these later.

2. Let's start by creating the poll question. Create a new movie clip, and label it voteContent_sl. First we'll want to add a nice looking backdrop to this section of the site, so label the first layer bg, and then copy voteBg_sl from the library of demo.fla, into the library of the movie you are working on. Place voteBg_sl in the first frame of the bg layer. Align it to coordinate (0,0).

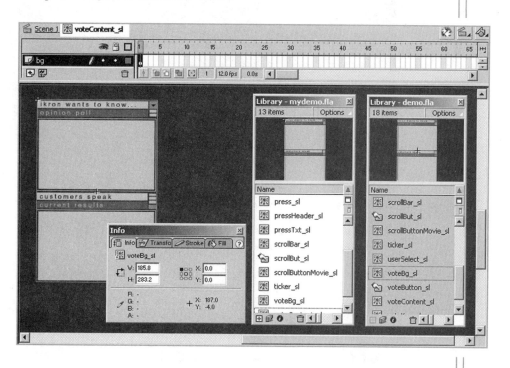

3.   Now we want to add the poll question variable. Add a new layer, and label it question. Keeping within the borders defined by your background image, type {question} into the top left area of the topmost box. Now, since {question} is a variable whose value is yet to be determined, and may change often, we want to ensure that the text that replaces this variable doesn't run outside of the visual borders we have defined for it with our background image. Just as we did with the scrolling list variables, we want to give this text a fixed width. So, highlight the text so it is editable, and so the top right corner has a circle attached to it. Click on the circle, and stretch the text field so it ends just inside the rightmost limits of our bounding area. Release, and our circle should be replaced by a square indicating that this variable now has a fixed width:

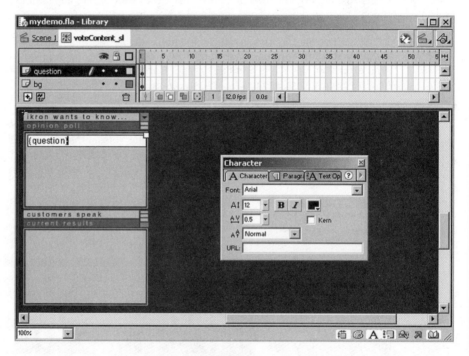

4.   We now want to give this variable a data source. If I've done my job correctly, you're already moving your mouse towards the Set Environment icon in the top right corner of the screen. Click on this icon, and the now familiar window should appear. Make sure that the **Name/Value** format icon is selected, and type question.txt into the field provided. By now this should be second nature. Click OK.

5.   Before we move on to creating the data source for this variable, we must consider our users. If users are voting in a poll, and are able to view their results via a pie chart, we'll probably want to give them a key to the values displayed within the pie chart. Since these values will also be variables with a Name/Value formatted data source, and located within the same movie clip, it only makes sense to use the same data source as our {question} variable used. So, let's create our key. Create a new layer and label it key. From the demo.fla library, drag the voteKey_sl movie clip into the first frame of this layer. Notice that this movie clip is simply three color-coded squares. You could have easily created these yourself. However, the color values for the pie chart in this demo are defined within our database file (leohub.mdb). Since we will not be editing this file in this demo, I want to make sure all the color values match up in our final output. Move the voteKey_sl clip so that it is within the bottom-right corner of the lower box. Keep in mind that we are going to add text variable labels to these color blocks, so make sure there is enough space to the right of each block to allow for these. Let's add these variables now.

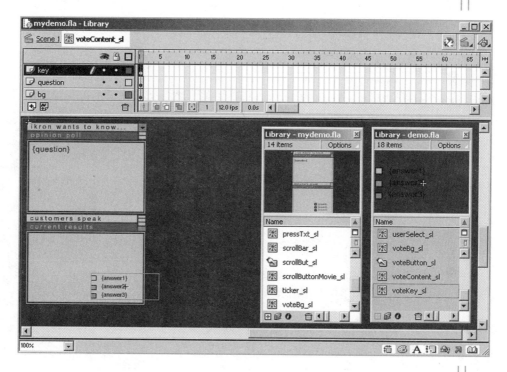

6. Now let's create the data source, question.txt. In your text editor, create a new file (called, none other than question.txt). Set up a two-column **Name/Value** layout. Name number one should be question, and its value should be: Which is your favorite IKRON Product line? Be sure to enclose this value within quotations. Fill out the rest of your data source as per the example below, and then save your file:

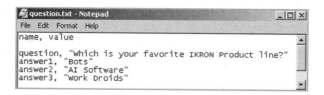

7.   Before we publish, we need to put the voteContent_sl movie clip into the main timeline. Go to the main timeline of your file, and add a new layer called poll. Place the voteContent_sl movie clip in the first frame of the poll layer and give it the instance name of votecontent_sl. Move the voteContent_sl movie clip to the right side of the stage, and align it so that the top border is aligned with the top border of our press release section.

8.   Publish this file, and view it in a browser window. It should look something like this:

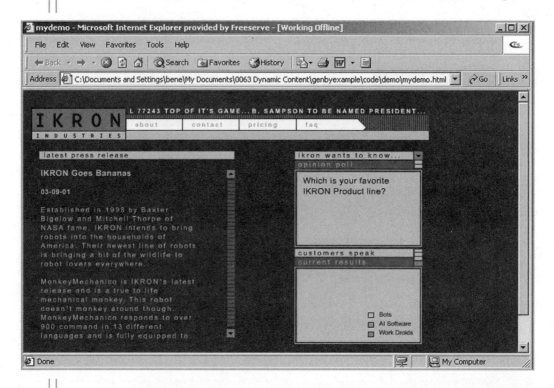

9.   Next we are going to add the choices the user has to select from. As mentioned in the beginning of this section, Generator comes equipped with the Radio Button object, which is designed specifically for purposes such as this. Within voteContent_sl, add a new layer called radio button. Find the Radio Button object on the Generator Objects panel, and drag an instance of it into the first frame of the radio button layer. Again, we should be looking at an all too familiar gray translucent box. Unlike other objects, the Radio Button doesn't allow for any masking features, so we need not concern ourselves with the height and width of this gray box. We do however need to concern ourselves with placement. User choices for the Radio Button object are listed vertically starting from the top left, so we need to place our object so that the top left corner is located where we want our choices to begin. Move the translucent box so it aligns vertically with the {question} variable, and is low enough within the boundaries of the topmost box so that the value for the {question} variable will not overlap:

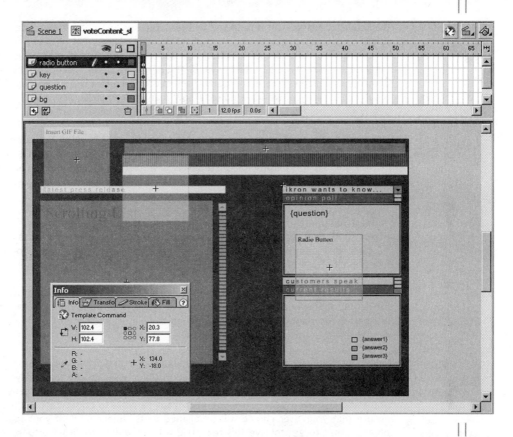

10. Click on the Radio Button object so that the Generator panel shows the parameters for this object. As usual, our first parameter is for the data source. Set this parameter to radio.txt, don't worry; we'll create this data source later. Our next two fields are ones we haven't come across before in this demo. On Symbol and Off Symbol are parameters that allow us to define a library symbol to be our default radio button states. Leaving these two parameters blank will cause our radio buttons to be default buttons provided by Macromedia, and for this demo, we will do just that.

Our next parameter, Text Symbol, enables us to define a movie clip as the default template for all of our text values. Type, userSelect_sl in this field we will create this movie clip later. This is followed by the `Line spacing` parameter. `Line spacing` refers to the distance between each potential user choice. This is measured in pixels, so in order for this to look aesthetically appealing, we should make this spacing of fairly decent size. Type 50 into this field. The next parameter, `Selected by Default`, determines which choice is the default selection. Since this is a Generator object, and is subject to change, we have no idea how many potential choices could be available at any given point in time. Therefore, it's best to set this parameter to 1.

Once again, our next parameter is one we have yet to encounter. `Selected Button Variable` allows us to set a variable name for the item the user selects, so that we can track it. Set this parameter to radioVar. This way, if a user were to choose answer number 2, then radioVar would equal 2. If he/she selected choice 1, radioVar would equal 1, and so on.

The last parameter for this object is `Instance Name`. We've seen this field in every object so far, but to reiterate, this parameter gives us the ability to name our objects so that they can be targeted just like a movie clip. We're going to need that functionality for this object, so type radioButton into this field.

11. Now that our parameters are established, let's create our text template movie clip. This movie clip is the one we defined within the Text Symbol parameter. Looking back at our parameter panel, we see that we named this clip userSelect_sl. Create a new movie clip, and name it as such.

12. Label the first layer of this movie clip as text. In the first frame type {text} in black. Unlike other text variables, the Radio Button object specifically requires you to use a variable named {text}. Any other variable used here will result in our generated text not being displayed. Make sure you align your variable to coordinate (0,0). This will ensure that your user choice will be aligned to the placement of your Radio Button object. Don't forget to give this text field a fixed width. You'll have to guess on the exact width to set the text field, but the goal is to have the text not extend past the borders of the background image in the voteContent_sl movie clip. View the last SWF you exported in your browser, and use it as a guide:

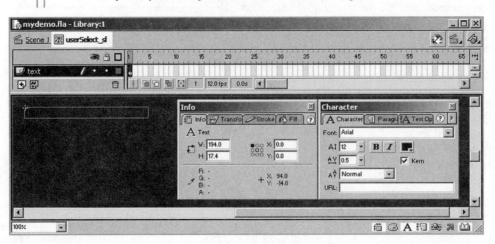

13. We need not specify a data source for this text variable because we have already established one within the Radio Button object's Data Source parameter. Remember that we typed radio.txt into this field? Let's create that file now.

In your text editor, open a new file, and save it as radio.txt. Set up a **Column Name/Value** data source with one column labeled text. Below this, insert the following values:

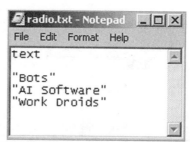

14. Save this file. Publish your movie, and view it from within a browser. It should look something like the next illustration. Notice how choice one, Bots, is the default selection, just as we specified using the Radio Button object parameters:

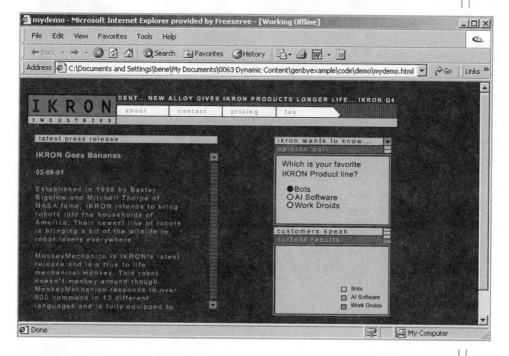

15. You may have realized, that while we have our poll question, and the various answers for the user to select from, we are lacking a Submit button to let the user actually make their vote count. Let's create that now.

Copy voteButton_sl from the demo.fla library. In the voteContent_sl movie clip create a new layer, and label it vote button. Put voteButton_sl in the first frame of this layer, and align it in the bottom right corner of the uppermost background box.

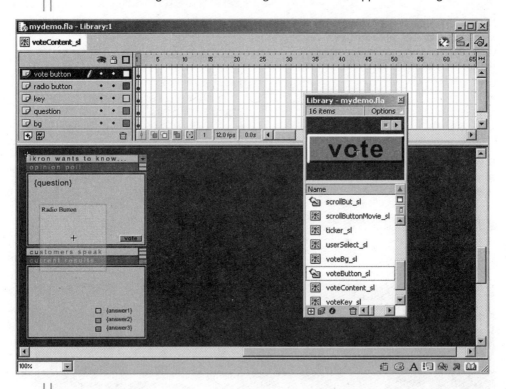

16.   We need to add actions to this button in order for our customer votes to be passed to the server. Click on voteButton_sl, and bring up its Object Actions window. Add the following code to the window:

```
on (release) {
    _root.userChoice = radioButton.radioVar;
    loadVariablesNum ("http://yourWebServer/vote.asp", 0);
    loadMovie ("chart.swt", "_root.voteContent_sl.chart");
}
```

There are a couple of things I should point out about this syntax. First, you'll notice that we created a new variable called _root.userChoice, which has the value radioButton.radioVar. Remember that radioVar was the variable we chose to determine which choice the user had selected. You may be wondering why we didn't just use this variable directly. The reason is because of the way the Radio Button object works. When a user makes a selection, the variable radioVar changes to that selection, but does not pass this information anywhere. You could say that it sort of holds onto this information until it is requested. By setting a new variable, in this case _root.userChoice, with the value radioButton.radioVar we are requesting that information. You'll also notice that we request that information by following the path to radioVar. Meaning, we first go through the radioButton object to get to radioVar. Realize, that this would not be possible had we not filled in the Instance Name parameter with the value radioButton.

The next line of code loads our variables to the server. Be sure to replace the line yourWebserver with your own server address.

17. You'll notice that we are not loading these directly to the server, but using an intermediate technology as mentioned earlier. In this case, our intermediate technology is in the form of an ASP file called vote.asp. We'll touch on this more later, but let's take a brief look at how this works.

```
<%
' Set request variable
userChoice = Request("userChoice")

' Define path and type of database
cst = "Driver={Microsoft Access Driver (*.mdb)};DBQ=" &
➡server.mappath("/leohub.mdb")

' Initiate database connection
set DBConn = server.createobject("adodb.connection")

' Open database
DBConn.Open cst

' Create string to determine number of votes
strCount = "SELECT ID, Choices FROM Vote WHERE ID = " &
➡CLng(userChoice)

' Declare statement to extract the vote count from the database
csCount = DBConn.Execute (strCount)

' Variable holder for incremented tally
varCount = csCount("Choices") + 1

' Update database with new value
DBConn.Execute "UPDATE Vote SET Choices = " & varCount & " WHERE
➡ID = " & CLng(userChoice)

' Close database to free system resources
SET csCount = Nothing
DBConn.Close
%>
```

ASP code provided courtesy of Ryan Provost (contact@aboutryan.com)

vote.asp receives the variable userChoice from our Flash movie. vote.asp then opens a connection to our database, leohub.mdb. Depending on which choice the user selected (1, 2 or 3), the ASP file adds one vote (+1) to that row in the Choices column within the database table, and then closes the connection to our database. Does that make sense? I hope so.

The last line of code in our voteButton_sl button tells our Flash movie to load a new movie called chart.swf into a target called chart. You may have thought the previous sentence contained a typo because the code clearly says that we are loading chart.swt. This is not a typo. Chart.swt is a generator template. Meaning that when we call this file, we are not loading this file into our movie, but triggering Generator to use this template in conjunction with our database values to create an output with all the newest values. By default, Generator generates a SWF, so we are actually then loading the movie chart.swf.

18. Before we create the chart movie, let's create the target that it is to load into. In the voteContent_sl movie clip, add a new layer above the bg layer and label it chart. Create a new movie clip called chart_sl. Within this movie, we need not add any graphical elements because they will only be replaced by our loaded movie. However, we do want to add some actions to the first frame. Label the first layer actions, and in the first frame add the following frame action:

```
loadMovie ("chart.swt", "_root.voteContent_sl.chart_sl");
```

You should recognize this code as being similar to the code we included in our button, voteButton_sl. We are including it here, to ensure that when a user first hits this page the most recent voting data is loaded, and the chart appears on the screen. Otherwise, the user will not see the pie chart until he or she places their vote.

19. Return to voteContent_sl, and drag the chart_sl movie clip into the first frame of the chart layer, give it the instance name of chart_sl. Since we did not include any graphical elements within this clip, it appears on the stage as a small hollow circle. This circle is coordinate (0,0) within the chart_sl movie clip. This means that any value loaded into this clip will be aligned to this point from its (0,0) position. Remember this, because it will come up in the next section. Publish this movie.

Creating the chart movie

We now need to create the chart movie. Since this movie is to be loaded into our base movie, it will absorb all of the values of that base movie. As a result, we do not need to concern ourselves with any of the movie property settings. We do, however, need to make sure we are publishing this movie as a Generator template.

Right OK, now this is a point to note, up until now, if you've been a little confused by the text in this chapter, perhaps regarding the placement of objects in your FLA, I've suggested that you look back at demo.fla for hints. Well, with regards to incorporating this Pie Chart object, I want to offer you a word of warning. You see, the Pie Chart object in demo.fla is actually only there for illustration purposes, it's local, which is not what we're aiming for. So why is it there? Well, remember back to the start of the chapter, where I suggested that you have a look at the finished project, and that you could do this by opening up a single SWF file? Well, that's the reason. You see, in our case, to actually recreate a dynamic Pie Chart object would require us having files all over the place, and at that point in the chapter, it seemed more apt to supply you with a single file from which you could get a good idea as to what we would be doing in this chapter. Now that's settled, let's move on...

1. Let's get started. Open a new movie and call it `chart.fla`. Select File > Publish Settings. On the Formats tab of the panel that pops up, make sure that both the Flash and Generator templates are selected. Click OK. Now we will create our chart.

2. Hopefully, you'll remember how I told you that this movie will be aligned in our base movie relative to coordinate `(0,0)` when it is loaded. You may also recollect that earlier in the chapter we discussed that, within movie clips, coordinate `(0,0)` is located in the center of the stage at the crosshairs, but within the main time line, coordinate `(0,0)` is located in the top left corner of the stage. This is important, because we are going to build the `chart` object within the main timeline of `chart.fla`.

3. Rename the first layer of the main timeline of `chart.fla` as chart. Drag an instance of the Pie Chart Generator object onto the stage. You should see a familiar translucent gray box. This is our Pie Chart object. The size of this object is directly related to the width and height of the pie chart that will be displayed. Scale this object so that, when the pie chart is created, it will fit into the space provided in our base FLA file, use `demo.swf` as a reference.

4. Now, since coordinate `(0,0)` is in the top left corner of our stage, we want to position our Pie Chart object so its top left corner aligns to coordinate `(0,0)`. Once we've done this, we can go about setting the parameters for this object.

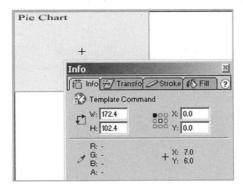

Click on the Pie Chart object so that its parameters appear within the Generator panel. Again, Data Source is our first parameter. In this field, type `tally.asp`. In the past, this field has always contained a TXT file, so you may be wondering why we are now specifying an `.asp` file. If you remember back when we were passing the variables to the server through our vote button, we were using an `.asp` file called `vote.asp`, as our intermediary to open a connection to the database, add one vote to the appropriate database column, and then close the connection. Well, with `tally.asp` we are using the same method to open a connection to the database, and retrieve those database values in a method readable to Generator. Here, have a look at the following code:

```
<%
' Define path and type of database
cst = "Driver={Microsoft Access Driver (*.mdb)};DBQ=" &
➥server.mappath("/leohub.mdb")

' Initiate database connection
set DBConn = server.createobject("adodb.connection")

' Open database
DBConn.Open cst

' Create string to determine number of votes
strCount = "SELECT ID, Choices, Color FROM Vote"

' Declare statement to extract the vote count from the database
SET csCount = DBConn.Execute (strCount)

Response.ContentType = "text/plain"

' Begin header for generator output
Response.Write "value, color" & vbCrlf

' Loop through all choices
DO UNTIL csCount.EOF
Response.Write csCount("Choices") & ", " & csCount("Color") &
➥vbCrlf
csCount.MoveNext
Loop

' Close database to free system resources
SET csCount = Nothing
DBConn.Close
%>
```

You'll notice that this code handles a few things. First, it opens the database connection to leohub.mdb:

```
' Initiate database connection
set DBConn = server.createobject("adodb.connection")

' Open database
DBConn.Open cst
```

Next, it extracts the value from the database table.

```
' Declare statement to extract the vote count from the database
SET csCount = DBConn.Execute (strCount)

Response.ContentType = "text/plain"
```

Lastly, it sets the data up in a **Column Name/Value** format, and loops through it to get all the vote values as well as Color and Choices values. It then closes the connection.

```
' Begin header for generator output
Response.Write "value, color" & vbCrlf

' Loop through all choices
DO UNTIL csCount.EOF
Response.Write csCount("Choices") & ", " & csCount("Color") &
➡vbCrlf
csCount.MoveNext
Loop

' Close database to free system resources
SET csCount = Nothing
DBConn.Close
%>
```

The information that gets passed back to our SWT template, chart.swt, ends up looking something like this:

```
value, color

70, "#cccc99"
20, "#999999"
10, "#92abda"
```

Our SWF file, chart.swf, is then generated from this data.

The next parameter for our Pie Chart object is Depth. This parameter allows us to give our pie chart some dimension, to make it look as though it has some weight. The larger the number, the heavier our chart will appear. Set this field to 300.

Have a look at the following pie charts, their depth's are set to zero, 100, and 300 respectively.

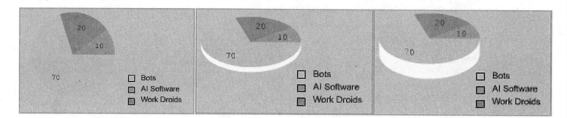

The `Value Display` parameter enables us to specify whether or not our pie chart should display the graphically represented data in a numerical format as well. We have three options here: `always`, `never`, and `rollover`. Set this parameter to `always`.

The following three parameters give us control over how these numerical values are displayed.

`Value Format` enables us to define the system font for our numerical values. Since we've been using the Arial font throughout this example, set this parameter to `Arial`.

`Value Placement` determines where our numerical values appear. A setting of `auto` is the default, but is usually not the most visually appealing. `Inside` results in our values being displayed inside the pie chart, whereas `outside` will result in the variables appearing outside the borders of the chart. Set this parameter to `inside`.

The last display parameter is `Value Scale`. This determines the size of our numerical values. There are default settings available that are self-explanatory, but this field also allows for numeric settings. Since our chart is relatively small, and we have specified that the numeric values are to be within the borders of this chart, let's set this value to .25 (a quarter) of the default size.

The `External Symbol File` parameter allows us to specify an external movie clip that Generator will use to enhance the look of the value display. For this demo, we are going to leave this blank.

The next three parameters deal with borders. `Border` refers to the outline of the actual Generator object, meaning that if we set `Border` to `on`, our chart would display within a box the size of the translucent gray box that represents the Pie Chart object in our FLA. In most cases this is not desirable, so we will leave this blank along with the parameters that specify the `Thickness` and `Color` of our border.

As usual, our last parameter is `Instance Name`. Since we will not need to target our pie chart for any reason, we will leave this parameter blank as well.

5.   Right, so we have our question, we have our user choices, and we have our chart. We're all set to give this movie a try. Well, almost... in order to make sure that our Pie Chart object has all the data it needs to display the pie chart, we need to copy some

of our files across to the webroot. So, copy `mydemo.html`, `mydemo.swt`, and `mydemo.swf` from your local folder, into your webroot. OK, we're ready, go ahead, and publish `chart.fla`, which should produce `chart.swf` and `chart.swt`. Copy `chart.swt` to your web server. Also copy the latest SWF and SWT files from our base movie, `question.txt`, and `radio.txt` to the server. Open a browser window, and type in the address of your web server being sure to add the name of the HTML file associated with your base SWF (for example: http://201.141.236.78/demo.html).

All being well, your output should look like this:

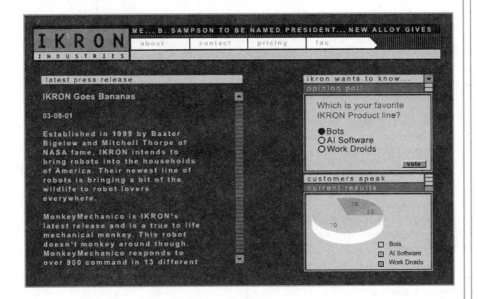

Place a few different votes, and watch as the chart updates to reflect the recent changes. Keep in mind, that while we are using Generator in an Online capacity, we are only doing so for the chart. Any changes made to any of the text files associated with our base SWF will still have to be processed offline from the command line or through a batch process. So if we want to change the question we are asking, {question}, or add another choice, {text}, we still have to update the associated text files, and then invoke Generator through one of the previously mentioned Offline methods.

Bringing it all to a close...

So our client, IKRON, is satisfied, and it looks as though the rest of the project is going to continue on rather smoothly. We stayed within the budget, and we were actually able to cover the cost of Generator Developer Edition because of the time we saved using Generator as a production tool. There is real time graphical information displayed with Generator in Online mode at little or no bandwidth cost to the end user. Lastly, once the project is done, there won't need to be any form of site maintenance on your end, because you have put the client in control through Generator in Offline mode. IKRON is ecstatic, and swears to name their first new robot after you. Life is good.

Obviously, this demo was only a small subset of what an entire site could potentially be. We weren't able to cover the quirks of every individual Generator object, and with the current flux of third party developers creating them; we may never be able to. However, the objects we did cover should be a strong introduction to the ones to follow. Keep in mind too, that Generator does come with a manual, and that the online community is more than helpful.

As I stated in the beginning of this chapter, my goal was to introduce, and expand your knowledge of Generator as a tool, as well as open your mind to potential applications both present, and future. As we learned about each object, and walked through each stage of the demo construction, I looked to give examples as well as tips from a real world production viewpoint.

There are a few key points that I would like to touch (or re-touch) on here. Using Generator as a production tool is 100% free if you own Flash 5. It only requires the Generator Authoring Extensions that are included with the program. Once you start using these extensions during the production process, you'll never understand how you were able to work without them. Macromedia thought long and hard when constructing these extensions, and there seems to be one for just about any scenario you can imagine. If you run into a situation where you can't find the object you need, check out the third party developer sites, or the Macromedia Exchange. You'll almost certainly find custom objects that have been built by developers who ran into the same issues you have, and decided to extend Generator's capabilities to suit their needs. If you use one of these third party objects, be sure to send a thank you email to the creators. These guys put a lot of time and effort into these things, and offer them to you at little or no cost. If you still cannot find what you are looking for, try creating an object yourself, or requesting your extension from Macromedia. The Generator SDK is available, and Macromedia love getting feedback from developers.

Offline and Online Generator do not require Enterprise Edition. Chances are that, if your company cannot afford the cost of Enterprise Edition, you probably don't need it. Developer Edition is suited to handle most of our needs. Enterprise level clients such as banks, portals, high-traffic shopping sites, and online brokers are the target audience for Enterprise Edition, and it's well within their budgets to afford to use it. Macromedia provides an excellent FAQ which will help you decide which product best suits your needs. It can be found at:

www.macromedia.com/software/generator/productinfo/faq/

Do not be intimidated by Generator because it is a server-side technology. As designers and front-end developers, we often find ourselves fearing the unknown realm of the server world. There's a reason Generator shares an interface with Flash. Macromedia designed Generator with the front-end developer in mind.

Do not assume that templating a site, or piece of a site, means that Generator is moving us towards applications and sites that will all look identical. What Generator enables us to do is quite the opposite. It allows us to template pieces (or individual application engines) so that the process of re-facing and re-purposing sites is much easier, and can be done dynamically. Generator is actually extending our possibilities, allowing one site to have multiple looks, functionality, and output formats to reach the broadest audience.

Lastly, don't use Generator just for the sake of it. This book highlights the multitude of ways to pull dynamic content into Flash, and there are benefits and caveats to each. Think about all the possibilities before coming to a final decision on which technology to use. Ask yourself questions like:

"How much will this cost?"
"How often will my content be updated?"
"Are there inherent benefits to handling the processing on the server side?"

Generator is a groundbreaking tool that is still only in gestation. As the product matures along with the other technologies it shares information with, we will see much more robust applications that have true functionality, personalization, and customization.

Hopefully, if you were already familiar with Generator, I was able to illuminate a more forward looking implementation of its potential...and for those of you just getting into the product, I hope I was able to put it into a perspective that was both informative, and easily understood.

Grace in battle,

The sites mentioned within this chapter can be found at the following URLs:

www.braincraft.com

www.macromedia.com

www.mcom8.com

www.oven.com

www.rydexfunds.com

www.tiffany.com

www.usabancshares.com/broadband/demo/main.html

www.SPACE.com

www.maxwellive.com **was developed by Iframe** (www.Iframe.com).

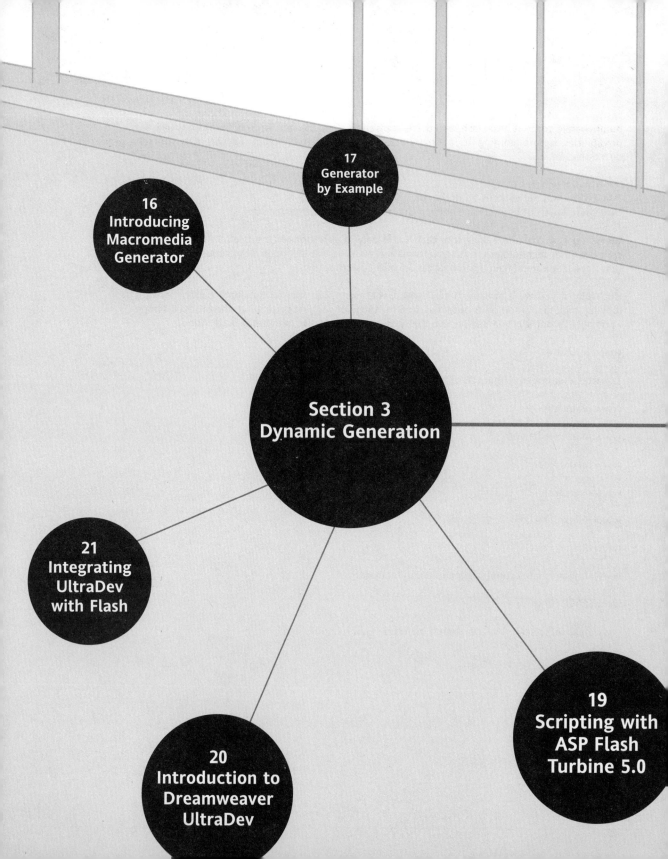

Chapter 18
Introducing ASP
Flash Turbine 5.0

Flash technology is pretty near ubiquitous – a huge number of sites are using Flash in one way or another, dominant web browsers are shipping with the Flash plug-in, and Flash players are being ported to devices like PDAs, internet mobile phones and set top boxes; all this on top of the 300+ million Flash capable computers on the planet. Flash technology, with its lightweight yet powerful multimedia capabilities, is being used to present information in compelling and impressive sites.

While Flash's anti-aliased text, image and sound capabilities make it an excellent presentation technology, generating your Flash content dynamically can prove time consuming. Although Flash's built-in `loadVariables` command and XML content integration features allow you to integrate information retrieved from a server, this information is strictly textual; Flash alone can't create more sophisticated effects like images and charts. For these effects, you usually have to work in the Flash authoring environment and individually export SWF files. Clearly, crafting large numbers of Flash movies is a tedious, labor-intensive process; but of course you already know that, it's why you're reading this book.

Flash Turbine is a range of dynamic Flash engines designed to help separate presentation and content. It gives you all the advantages of the Flash technology, together with the ability to produce dynamic, frequently changing content. We'll focus mainly on **ASP Flash Turbine** here, which gives you a simple yet powerful interface for generating Flash dynamically from inside an ASP script. (PHP Flash Turbine presents roughly the same features for the PHP scripting platform.)

In this chapter we'll look at:

- The presentation versus content divide in Flash

- What Flash Turbine can do to help

- Installing ASP Flash Turbine

- Flash templates

- Working with Turbine objects, commands, and drivers

- Generating dynamic content: Turbine variables, and dynamic text, images, sound and movie clips

- Structured content access: introducing DataSets (a group of variables in tabular form)

In the next chapter, we'll work with the ASP Flash Turbine scripting interface, and begin using Turbine with ASP scripts. We'll also cover database interaction and develop an integrated application, which should give you a broad overview of the key elements of creating a real-life dynamic Flash application using Flash Turbine.

Let's start by clarifying exactly why Flash Turbine exists.

The dynamic Flash challenge: presentation vs. content

To many developers, a site done in Flash is worth many done in HTML. The ease of use and graphical appeal of Flash is unmatched. Where many of us get stuck, though, is at the question

"*How am I going to integrate data into Flash from an external source?*" The answer to this question is also the key to a frighteningly successful web site.

By borrowing some useful concepts from traditional software engineering, we can divide a software application, like a web site, into two layers:

- **Presentation**: everything related to the look of the application, for example the page design and layout, the navigation.

- **Content**: the pure information available on the site, for example product lists, names, descriptions, and prices.

In a perfect world, and software engineer's dreams, there would be a clear separation between presentation and content, so that we can change one without affecting the other. You could update the look of a site and display the existing content in new way, for example, or insert new content and have it displayed like the existing content.

Unfortunately, back in the real world this isn't an easy goal to achieve, particularly when using Flash technology where these two layers are tightly connected. When updating a Flash movie, for example, to change only minor content requires you to go into the Flash authoring environment right in the middle of the movie's presentation layer.

At this point a software engineer would tell you that separation of presentation and content is a good thing because it makes your applications and web sites much more updateable, in terms of presentation and content layers. Imagine that there was some way in which you could separate these, and edit the appearance using a Flash editor, and have content spearated, for example. Well... this is exactly what we can do with Flash Turbine!

Flash Turbine

The Flash Turbine range includes three tools: ASP Flash Turbine, PHP Flash Turbine and Direct Flash Turbine. They have all been designed to be as inter-compatible as possible – for example the Flash template commands are fully compatible across the three products. The distinctive points about each tool are:

- **ASP Flash Turbine**: running inside Active Server Pages, presents a powerful scripting interface to manipulate content inclusion in Flash templates. The tight integration with the ASP scripting platform allows easy access to many data sources. For example by using the powerful ADO universal database access functionality, content from a large variety of database systems can be included in generated Flash movies.

  ASP Flash Turbine works with Microsoft Internet Information Server (IIS) versions 4 and 5 (Windows 2000). To allow for the best possible integration with the ASP environment it's implemented as a COM component (also known as ActiveX server component). You're not restricted to using the VBScript language with ASP Flash Turbine, you can use any scripting language supported by the ASP environment: JavaScript, Perl, and others.

- **PHP Flash Turbine**: generates template-based dynamic Flash from inside PHP scripts. Like ASP Flash Turbine, this tool allows easy content integration with any data source accessible to the scripting platform.

  PHP Flash Turbine is implemented as a dynamic PHP 4 module, running over the PHP engine on Windows and Linux (Intel), on any web server supported by the PHP engine. After installation, the PHP Flash Turbine object is available as a PHP object in a very similar way to ASP Flash Turbine – in fact most of the scripting commands are identical within the two products.

- **Direct Flash Turbine:** a template oriented dynamic Flash processor; it works by processing commands defined inside a Flash template file when such a file is requested from the web server. Direct Flash Turbine will process all the content inclusion commands defined inside the file and will generate a Flash movie in response.

  The Direct Flash Turbine works with IIS versions 4 and 5 (Windows 2000) and with Apache running on Linux (Intel). Because performance is a major issue for server components, both the Windows and Linux versions of Direct Turbine are implemented as server extensions, tightly integrated with the respective web servers – the fastest implementation for web server components.

All the products share a common core - the Flash Turbine dynamic engine, responsible for the Flash/content blending. As a result, all three products are entirely compatible in the Flash template commands. ASP Flash Turbine, for example, can seamlessly use a template file created for Direct Flash Turbine.

A future tool under development is ColdFusion Flash Turbine, targeting this widely used web-scripting platform.

Since ASP Flash Turbine is the most popular and widely used product, these chapters will mainly focus on ASP Flash Turbine product. However, the sections on the Template commands in this first chapter are fully compatible with all products.

What can you do with Flash Turbine?

Flash Turbine works with the web server to supply content to a Flash template each time a movie is requested by a web browser. Presentation is separated from content using templates (usually files with the .swt extension). These templates do a fresh content blend to include text, image content, database query results, or the results of other web scripts, each time they are requested by the server.

By now you're possibly tired of all this presentation and content talk, so let's move on to firmer ground. Here are some of the most important things you can do with ASP Flash Turbine 5.0:

- Drag-and-drop editing of template Turbine objects

- Generate tables and lists with text or image content

- Generate charts based on external sources like text files or database queries, create and customize chart types

- Read XML documents and use the information in DataSets (data tables used inside Turbine)

- Use content from your local disk, remote HTTP locations, or database queries

- Use image files with JPEG, PNG, or BMP formats and others through the conversion interface

- Include streaming MP3 sound

- Use dynamic variables, as well as freely aligned and wrapping text

- Draw shapes, text, images, and place movie clips by using the built-in Draw Script language

- Generate Flash movies to local files allowing for batch automation

- Widget automation: add scroll bars or draggable window bars to any Turbine object

- Cache generated movies, to improve web server scalability and performance

The web browser, Turbine, and dynamic content: how it all works

ASP Flash Turbine works by processing Flash templates when an HTTP request is made to the web server by a web browser. When an ASP script is requested, the ASP Flash Turbine COM object is created. The ASP script tells the object which Flash template file to use, and the content is accessed and included inside the template. Finally, the resulting Flash movie is sent over the wire to be played in the web browser. These interactions look something like this:

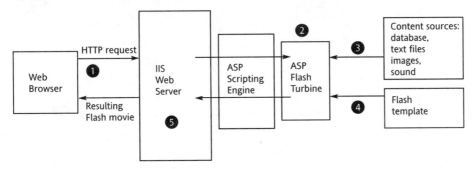

❶ The web browser requests the ASP script URL.

❷ The web server runs the ASP script, which creates a Flash Turbine object.

❸ The ASP script and/or Turbine accesses databases, text files, images files, etc.

❹ The content is integrated with the Flash template producing a Flash movie.

❺ The generated Flash movie is then sent to the web browser in response to the initial request.

This binding of the content and presentation is performed just before the user sees the Flash movie, so they always see the latest available content. While this approach will have an impact on your web server performance, it does ensure that you are always sending fresh content to the user, and makes editing your content a much faster and easier process.

For content that changes less frequently, Flash Turbine offers caching capabilities designed to alleviate the web server load and improve overall performance and response times. By caching a generated Flash movie for some period of time, you can significantly reduce the resources spent on accessing content or databases. For example, a daily online news site could have its pages cached for 24 hours, since the content will not change during that time. We'll look at caching in more detail in the next chapter.

Flash Turbine works by performing internal operations in the Open-SWF Flash format, which Macromedia made a publicly available open file specification. So, now you have a good idea of what ASP Flash Turbine is, let's install it.

Installing ASP Flash Turbine

A free evaluation version of the most recent ASP Flash Turbine can be downloaded from the CD or alternatively from: www.blue-pac.com/aspturbine.

You can install the ASP Flash Turbine on a computer with a web server by simply executing the `ASPTurbine50.exe` file.

aspturbine50...

Follow the simple set up instructions, and when you have finished installing ASP Turbine, check the new directory. It should look something like this:

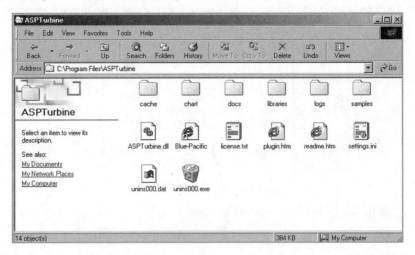

It's a good idea to test the samples included with it on your web server, so that you can see them running. All you need to do is web-share the disk directory that runs ASP scripts, in this case you should web-share the Turbine installation directory.

Web-sharing your disk directory

Windows 2000 and IIS

1. Go into your Internet Services Manager.

2. Select your web server in the left pane, then right-click on Default Web Site in the right pane. Choose New > Virtual Directory and you will be presented with the Virtual Directory Creation Wizard.

3. Click Next and enter an alias for the new virtual Directory (e.g. Turbine). Then browse to the location of the ASPTurbine directory that you previously installed.

4. Finally, check the boxes for the following access permissions: Read, Run scripts and Browse.

Make sure that the Cache ISAPI setting is enabled, because there is a known error in Internet Explorer that can occur if Cache ISAPI is disabled (your movie may not load).

Windows 95/98 and PWS

1. Go into Personal Web Manager and click on Advanced.

2. Click on Add, browse to the location of the ASPTurbine directory that you previously installed and insert an Alias name (e.g. Turbine). Make sure that the Read and Scripts Access boxes are checked.

3. Return to the Main window and ensure that Allow Directory Browsing is also checked.

Check the docs/install.htm page inside your Turbine installation for more information if you need it.

Testing the installation

1. To test your installation, open your web browser and enter a URL with the following format:

   http://servername/alias/readme.htm

   For example

   http://localhost/Turbine/readme.htm

2.   You should get the following HTML page:

3.   Scroll to the bottom of this page and click on Samples.

4.   Click on the Hello World sample, enter your name and click Submit. You should see a screen saying Hello to you and welcoming you to Turbine.

This means you have correctly installed ASP Flash Turbine! Test out the other samples as you require them.

Using Flash templates

When you're using Flash Turbine, think of a Flash movie as a form or a template that allows text, images, charts and sounds (and much more) to be included. You create a Flash template that includes some place-holders for these text or images, then craft the ASP script that will access the information you want included, and then integrate it with the Flash template. This way, the content is kept separate from the presentation. Take for example an online store – when the price of a product changes, you can simply modify the associated database entry, rather than the whole Flash movie.

Some content can simply be included in your Flash templates using simple commands. Other actions have to be performed by your ASP code, like specifying the template file, generating the movie to the web browser, or loading content from a database. The basic unit of content in Turbine is a variable. You can define Turbine variables from your ASP code, and load them from files or a database. If you're using lots of variables, like tables or lists of data, you can simplify things by using a DataSet instead.

Turbine also enables text, images and DataSets to be loaded through HTTP requests. You can include a text generated by a script running on another web server in your generated movie, for example. We'll see more on variables and DataSets shortly. Let's start by looking at how you create a template.

Creating Flash Turbine templates

Flash Turbine uses templates to define the look of the Flash movie to be generated. Flash templates are really just normal Flash movies, saved in a slightly expanded format. In fact, since these files are really just augmented Flash movies, they can be played with the regular Flash player.

Building a Flash template is exactly the same as creating a normal Flash movie. The only difference is that when you're exporting the movie, you need to specify that you want to export a .SWT file. To do this, choose File > Export Movie, and select Generator Template (*.swt) in the Save as type field of the Export Movie dialog. You can skip this exporting process after saving for the first time; simply hit CTRL+ENTER and the Flash template will be exported.

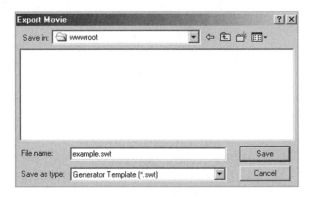

One thing you'll notice about Flash template files is that they're usually larger than the same movie exported to normal Flash SWF format. This is because Flash template files carry complete font and glyph information for all the text fonts used in the movie, while regular Flash movies only include the font and glyph information needed for the exact text included in the movie. Because the size of the generated movies does matter (the user could be waiting for the movie to arrive over a 14kbps line!), Flash Turbine performs heavy optimization before sending the movies. Actually, this optimization step sometimes creates Flash movies smaller than the ones generated from Flash.

Turbine objects and commands

Since dynamic content must be inserted in the middle of a Flash movie, the Flash Turbine design team figured that the best way to do this would be to allow the user to place the content insertion commands in the exact position of the movie where they are needed. For example, the command to insert an image in a particular frame of the Flash movie should be entered at the exact location where the image should appear, as this provides the best interaction with the rest of the movie during development.

There are two ways of making Turbine work at the Flash template level – Turbine objects and Turbine commands.

Turbine objects

Turbine objects are the easiest way of using the capabilities of Flash Turbine. Turbine objects are available from the `Turbine Objects.fla` library, installed by the Turbine installation program in your Flash library directory (C:\ASPTurbine\libraries by default). This library can be accessed in the Flash player by opening Window > Common Libraries – there you'll find a Turbine Objects entry. Turbine objects are made available from a library window similar to this one:

Using the Turbine objects is as easy as drag-and-drop: just drag the desired object icon from the Turbine library window and place it in the necessary frame and location. You can specify the visual transformations applied to the object by manipulating the respective icons with the usual Flash tools. For example, to specify the size of a Turbine chart, simply use the Scale tool to resize the respective Turbine object icon; to make an image transparent, just change the alpha channel settings of the corresponding Turbine object.

So, to create a movie frame with two charts and an image, simply drag, place, and resize the respective Turbine object icons in the necessary locations:

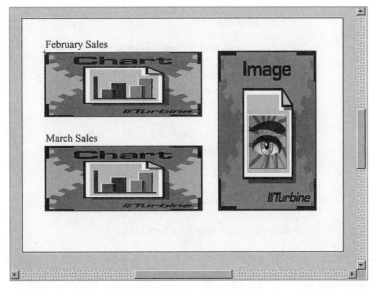

To set the parameters for each one of these icons, you need to open the Clip Parameters panel. Then, once you select a Turbine object icon, the correspondent parameters will appear (together with a help text below). For example, the image object will display:

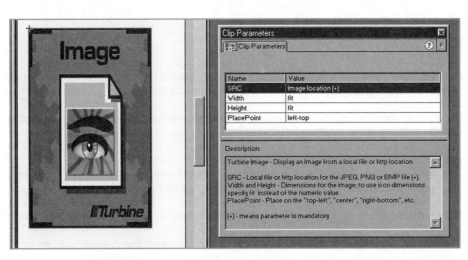

You can set the object's behavior by double-clicking the relevant parameter. For example, to specify which image to include, simply enter the respective location in the SRC parameter field.

Flash Turbine includes a variety of objects. The ones you're likely to use are:

AutoImage	Automatically displays a table of images
AutoMovieClip	Displays a movie clip table
Chart	Renders data charts
Draw File	Includes a Draw Script command file
GenerateHTMLFirst	Generates an initial HTML page with the Flash plug-in that will load the generated Flash movie
Image	Inserts an image
List	Creates a text list
Sound	Includes an MP3 sound file
Table	Displays a text table
TextFile	Displays the contents of a text file

For ease of use, Turbine objects are implemented as Flash smart clips, so they're available as libraries. However, a Turbine object is interpreted by the Flash Turbine engine and used to generate content, unlike ordinary smart clips, which are included in the generated movie. Turbine icon shapes, for example, will not be sent to the browser, which saves bandwidth.

We'll explore most of these objects in the following sections. First, let's see a simple example.

A Hello World Example

We'll start by looking at a simple example of using ASP Turbine to create dynamic Flash movies. The source for this example can be found in the `helloworld` directory of the Turbine examples.

1. Open the Flash editor and create a new movie. Put the following text on the stage:

    Hello {name}

2. Save the movie as a Flash template by selecting Export Movie from the File menu. In the Save as type box select the Generator Template (.swt) export format, and enter a filename - let's use the name `helloworld.swt`. Save the file into the `wwwroot` directory on your web server. An options dialog will then appear - just click OK.

    That's all there is to the Flash template, it just asks for some dynamic content, so let's create a simple ASP script that will inject content into our template.

3. Using a text editor, create an ASP file named `helloworld.asp` and save it in the same place as your `.swt` file. Enter the following ASP script code:

```
<%
Set Turbine=Server.CreateObject("Turbine.ASP")
Turbine.Template = "helloworld.swt"
Turbine.Variable("{name}") = "World"
Turbine.GenerateFlash
%>
```

In the first line we find the command to create the ASP Flash Turbine object. The second line tells the Turbine object which Flash Template file to use. After that comes the magical command that gives the Turbine variable name the text value `World`. The final command makes Turbine generate the movie and to send it back to the browser that made the request.

4. Request `helloworld.asp` with a web browser, and you should get the generated Flash movie:

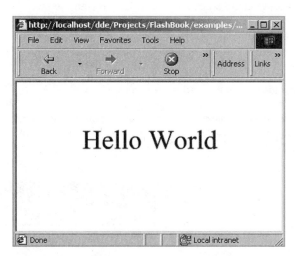

So, we defined the Flash movie using a Flash Template (`helloworld.swt`), and injected the content of that movie (`World`) from an ASP script.

"Big deal!" I can hear you say. Well, yes, just defining the `name` variable with the text `World` isn't that great, but with ASP scripting you can grab content from a wide range of data repositories. That includes any sort of database, LDAP directories, e-mail servers, and just about any other data source you can access from ASP scripts. It's this combination of easy data access and easy Flash media integration that makes Flash Turbine a useful tool.

That's just one way to use objects; you can also use Turbine commands for all of the features that objects make available (and a few more).

Turbine commands

Turbine commands can be placed in input text fields or frame labels. They are very similar to HTML tags, and like them, use a format tag:

```
<Command parameter="stuff" size=100 alpha="50%">
```

Both the command and parameter names are case insensitive. The Command is the action to perform, while the parameters specify the behavior of the action. Text parameters, like file names, have to be enclosed in double quotes, since they might contain spaces or other evil characters that could disturb the command parsing.

Also note that while Turbine objects we've seen depend on Flash 5, the Turbine commands can also be used with Flash 4.

Like HTML tags, each Turbine command supports a specific set of parameters. For example, to include an image we could place an input text field with the tag:

```
<Image src="picture.jpg">
```

The image will be put exactly where you put the input text field with the command.

Turbine commands can be entered in two types of places:

- **Input text fields**: you can position the command exactly on stage, and in the right frame, to define where the content will be placed. To insert a Turbine command in an input text field, select the Text tool ⒜ and make sure the Input Text type is selected in   the   Text   Options   panel:

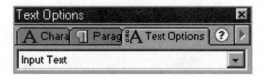

Clicking on the stage will create the input text field to hold a Turbine command:

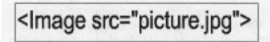

Turbine commands can also be placed in dynamic text fields, but we'll be using them in input text fields for now.

- **Frame Labels**: if you don't need to place the command exactly on the stage, if you're loading variables from a file for example, then you can put your Turbine command in a frame label, by using the Label field of the frame panel:

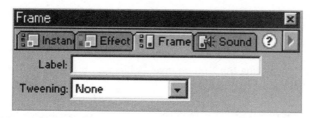

Turbine drivers

Turbine drivers allow you to perform user interface automation with the Turbine objects. This can be achieved by using the Turbine drivers library, also available from the Common Libraries menu:

The driver library includes a set of common user interface elements:

- Vertical scroll bars

- Horizontal scroll bars

- Window managers (drag bars, minimize buttons, etc)

- Tickers

Let's use it in a quick example.

Using Turbine drivers

Suppose we have a large vertical image, and would like to display it in a scrolling window, controlled by a vertical scroll bar. The image I have used in this example is a skyscraper (you can find the file `skyscraper.jpg` on the CD).

1. Start by placing the Turbine Image object on the stage and fill in the appropriate clip parameters:

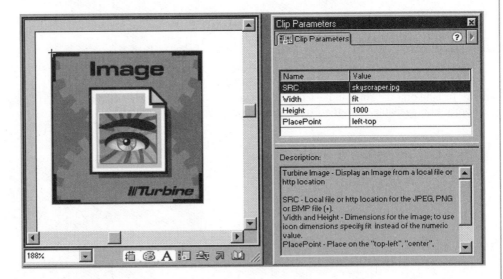

2. Then drag a vertical scroll bar from the Library-Turbine Drivers window to near one of the corners of the image icon. By placing and aligning the driver with the image object you are attaching the driver to that specific object, so that the driver will later control the image object. For the Turbine driver and object to engage in this association, they must be within a 30 pixels distance of each other. In this example we're using the included Mach Vertical Scroll Bar Turbine driver:

Once generated and seen on the web browser, the scroll bar is perfectly integrated with the nearby Turbine object and fully controls it.

We can also combine multiple drivers. Suppose we'd like the image to be dragged around, minimized and closed – we just need to place the respective drivers near one of the corners of the Turbine object icon.

3. To accomplish this, we drag the Window Bar – Horizontal Turbine driver from the library and place it under the Turbine icon, like this:

4. Export your movie as sky.swt.

5. The ASP file (sky.asp) for this example is pretty straightforward:

```
<%
Set Turbine=Server.CreateObject("Turbine.ASP")
Turbine.Template = "sky.swt"
Turbine.GenerateFlash
%>
```

Et voilà: once generated by Flash Turbine, we'll get a nice draggable, scrolling skyscraper image:

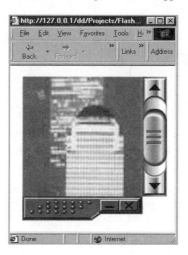

The Turbine objects and drivers are working together in complete synthesis, so they can be minimized, closed, and freely moved around. (The sources for this quick example are in the `skyscraper` directory of the Turbine examples on the CD.)

Turbine drivers are simple smart clips that conform to certain characteristics of the Turbine objects. You can modify the appearance of the existing drivers to fit in with the other elements of your overall movie design, and create reusable, customized user interface widgets.

Error reporting

Errors... you can't live with them, you can't live without them. ASP Flash Turbine can generate two types of errors:

- **ASP scripting errors**: for example, not finding the desired Flash template. These errors are reported as normal ASP errors, with the error line and short description, for example:

  Turbine.ASP.4 error '80020009'
  Could not find Flash Template
  //dd/aspturbine/samples/charts/charts.asp, line 12

- **Flash template errors**: these errors are usually related to a template processing error, for example not finding a text file. Since these errors aren't show-stoppers, they are displayed in the generated movie, in the same frame where they occurred:

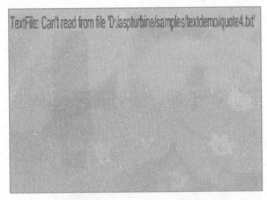

TextFile: Can't read from file 'D:\aspturbine\samples\textdemo\quote4.txt'

To avoid errors appearing in the final generated movies, template error output can be disabled either on a per-movie basis or for the whole server, by changing the setting in the `settings.ini` file.

Flash Turbine can also log error messages to a log file, in the `error.log` file of the `logs` directory. This combination of error reporting methods was designed to shorten the development time, by allowing faster and more precise access to the errors.

Using content from local files or URL locations

All of the template commands that use external content (the `Image` command, for example, or the `TextFile` command) can use files on either the local disk or an HTTP URL completely transparently. In case of a remote HTTP request, Turbine will seamlessly fetch the content before using it. For example there's nothing stopping you from using the output of another ASP script in the generated movie. Such a remote script could output text, or a set of Turbine variables, or an image.

Both in local file paths or HTTP URLs, either absolute or relative locations can be freely used. This allows content to be fetched from other web servers or application servers. It also provides a chance for back-end load balancing mechanisms to be implemented, if necessary. Because too much freedom can cause security problems, it's possible to restrict the accessed location, both for local file or remote URLs.

Using dynamic content

Now that you've met Flash Turbine and seen how it works, let's examine it in a little more detail. In the rest of this chapter we're going to look at using:

- Turbine variables

- Dynamic text

- Dynamic images

- Sound

- Movie clips

Turbine variables

Turbine variables work just like Flash variables; you can use variables in your Flash template, just as you would in any Flash movie, assign it a value once and it can be used anywhere.

Turbine variables, as you might remember from the first example we used, are always enclosed in braces. For example:

```
{greeting}
{planet}
{address}
```

Turbine variables can be used, or referenced from within text blocks. You might have a text block like this in your Flash template:

```
Name: {customerName}
Address: {customerAddress}
```

Turbine variables can also be from within ActionScript. Take the `getURL` command for example:

```
getURL ("http://host/{productPage}")
```

This will also work in template commands, which is how we'll use it later on. The following command, for example, loads an image based on the value of the `{imageLocation}` variable:

```
<Image src="{imageLocation}">
```

You should keep in mind the following rules when using Turbine variables:

- Variable names, as we've seen, are case insensitive; the variables `{name}`, `{Name}`, and `{NAME}` all refer to the same variable and value.

- Variable names must be enclosed in braces {}.

- Variable names can have a maximum of 55 characters.

- You can use any letter, number, and the _ , : , ~, and $ characters to name your variables.

- Turbine variable values can have up to 32000 characters.

Turbine variables can be used in:

- All Flash Turbine template commands

- Text blocks

- Input text fields

- Smart clip parameters

- ActionScript commands and variables

- URLs, targets, frame labels, etc.

Defining Turbine variables

Turbine variables are global variables, and can be defined in several ways. For example, they can be defined from within ASP scripts by using the following syntax:

```
Turbine.Variable("{someVariable}") = "some value"
```

or:

```
Turbine.Var ("{someVariable}") = "some value"
```

Using these ASP script commands would allow you to call the variable someVariable from anywhere within the Flash template, regardless, for example, of movie clip levels.

Another way to define variables is from inside the Flash template itself, by placing a Turbine command with the following syntax:

```
<SetVar name="someVariable" value="some value" >
```

This will also give the variable named someVariable the text value some value. Even if it doesn't look terribly useful, this can be the best way to define some values that won't change often – for example server names to be used in URLs and similar rarely-changing stuff.

Loading Turbine variables from a file

Sometimes it's useful to store variables in a text file, so that they can be redefined without changes to the Flash template or the ASP script. You do this by storing the variable attribution in a text file with the following format:

```
{variable1} = some value1
{variable2} = some value2
{variable3} = some value3
```

On each line of a Turbine variable file you can store a variable attribution. All the text after the equals sign (excluding preceding and trailing spaces) will be assigned to each variable.

We'll call these variable definition files **variable files**. Variable files can be loaded by using a Turbine object:

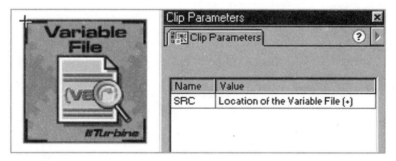

Or they can be loaded by inserting the following command in a frame label or input text field:

```
<VarFile src="varfile_location" >
```

The varfile_location parameter can be any absolute or a relative path to the location of the ASP script.

As we've seen previously, local variable files or remote HTTP URL variable files can also be used transparently, making it possible to receive the output of other ASP scripts, with variable definitions.

Built-in Turbine variables

Flash Turbine includes some useful built-in variables that are commonly used, such as the actual date and time, random number generation, and movie parameters manipulation. These built-in variables are always properly defined, and can be used anywhere that variables can be referenced. While a few of these variables are also available at the client as ActionScript commands, the advantage of these built-in Turbine variables is that they're available at the server, when the movie is generated – this makes it easier to include random banners, for example, by using the random number variables. We'll look at a few of these variables here. The complete reference can be found in the ASP Flash Turbine manual. (www.blue-pac.com/products/aspturbine/docs/manual.htm)

Time variables

Quite often you'll want to include the current time in a Flash movie. You can do this by using some of the time related variables. The following table shows some of the built-in variables available:

Variable	Description	Format
{Time.Year}	Current year in four digits	yyyy (e.g. 1999)
{Time.Year2}	Current year in two digits	yy (e.g. 99)
{Time.Month}	Current month in one or two digits(1 – 12)	m or mm (e.g. 2)
{Time.Month0}	Current month in two digits (01 – 12)	always mm, (e.g. 02)
{Time.MonthName}	Full name of month	January, February, etc.
{Time.WeekDay}	Day of the week in one digit	(1 - 7)
{Time.WeekDayName}	Full name of the day of the week	Sunday, Monday, etc.
{Time.Day}	Day of the month (1 – 31)	d or dd (e.g. 4)
{Time.Hour}	Hour (0 – 23)	h or hh (e.g. 8)
{Time.HourAmPm}	Hour (00 – 11)	hh left-pads with 0 (e.g. 08)
{Time.AmPm}	Am or Pm symbol, depending on actual time	tt (eg. Am)
{Time.Minute}	Current minute	(0 – 59) m or mm (e.g. 7)
{Time.Second}	Current second (0 – 59)	s or ss (e.g. 57)

For example, the text Today is {Time.Day} / {Time.Month} / {Time.Year} would display: Today is 12/06/2000 on 12 June 2000.

Random variables

Random behavior in Flash is often used to show the user different information on each visit to generate more diversity, for example, when displaying advertising information.

Some of the available variables are:

Variable	Description
{Random.NewN}	Generates a new random number. The number has N digits up to a maximum of 6 digits.
{Random.NewColor} {Random.NewColorAlpha}	Generates a new random color in HTML style with the format RRGGBB or AARRGGBB

The Random variable might be used like this, for example:

```
<Image src="ad{Random.New1}.jpg" >
```

If we had images named ad0.jpg, ad1.jpg, ..., ad9.jpg in the same directory as the Flash template, this line would randomly select and include one of these images.

Movie variables

This variable group allows some characteristics of the movie to be used and changed. While the built-in variables you've seen so far have been read-only, these variables allow properties of the movie to be set by assigning them values. Here are the most significant ones:

Variable	Description
{Movie.Width}	The width, in pixels, of the Flash template. You can change the width of the generated movie by using this variable.
{Movie.Height}	The height, in pixels, of the Flash template. You can also change the height of the generated movie by using this variable.
{Movie.Color}	This is the background color of the movie. You can use it to change the generated background color.
{Movie.FrameRate}	The template's frame rate in frames per second. This can also be changed.
{Movie.NumFrames}	Total number of frames for the template (and generated movie).
{Movie.Script}	The complete path to the script being executed.
{Movie.Query}	The query string used to call this script.
{Movie.Location}	The path and query used to request this script – very useful for self-referencing scripts.

As an example of the movie variable family, to have a self-referencing `getUrl` ActionScript command we would simply use:

```
getUrl ("{Movie.Location}")
```

This might be useful, for example, for refresh buttons.

Dynamic text

Now let's see how we can use dynamic text in Flash movies. There are two ways of including dynamic text: by using Turbine variables, or by loading text from an external file.

Say we want to make the following piece of text dynamic:

Welcome {name}, there are {numUsers} users currently online
Please check today's promotion: {promoText}

We just need to define the `name`, `numUsers`, and `promoText` Turbine variables. For example, we can define them in the ASP script with:

```
Turbine.Variable("{name}") = "James"
Turbine.Variable("{numUsers}") = 56
Turbine.Variable("{promoText}") = "New silver sunglasses!"
```

These Turbine variables would be replaced in the above text with the values defined in the ASP script:

Welcome James, there are 56 users currently online
Please check today's promotion: New silver sunglasses!

Sometimes we may need to use new-line characters or tabs. These characters can be included using the following escape characters:

\t   Tab character, which corresponds to four spaces

\n   New line

Text alignment and wrapping

All dynamic text will use the alignment settings of the text block inside Flash where we've defined it, but we can also define the alignment from inside the text, by using these escape characters:

\l   Left align the following text

\c   Center the following text

\r   Right align the following text

\j   Justify the following text

We can also control how the text behaves in respect to the text box limits – some applications rely on having the text bounded by the left and right margins of the text block. Text wrapping can be controlled in a similar way to the alignment, with the following escape characters:

- \w The usual Flash editor text wrapping style; for example, words will break only at word boundaries

- \x As above, but don't break long words bigger than the text area

- \a Wrap text per character

- \o No wrap at all, text just goes on until a line feed.

Since the text will use the settings of the text block where it will appear we can simply define the alignment in the Flash editor. Here's an example of the wrapping mode differences:

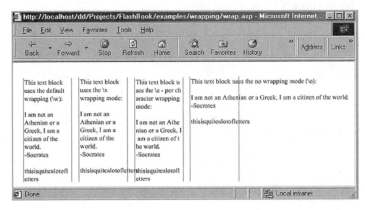

Note the differences between the various text wrapping types. If you want to take a closer look at this example, the source can be found in the `wrapping` directory of the Turbine examples on the CD.

Including text from files

Text can be included from files by using the Text File object:

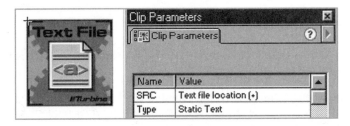

You can also include text using a command:

```
<TextFile src="text_location" >
```

The parameter text_location is the path to a text file, whether it be an absolute path or a path relative to the location of the ASP script file. For example, to include text from a text file in the same directory as the script, and assuming that the text file is named description.txt we would use:

```
<TextFile src="description.txt" >
```

Or, we could use an absolute path:

```
<TextFile src="D:\website\text\description.txt" >
```

We could use the text files we'd normally use for HTML server-side includes in this manner. These files are usually common for a large set of pages, for example company contacts. In fact, it's good for any textual information that can change and needs to be edited frequently.

Including text from URLs

Flash Turbine also allows text files to be included from an HTTP location, by simply using the respective URL:

```
<TextFile src="http://www.domain.com/atext.txt" >
```

Since it's a normal HTTP URL, there's nothing stopping us from using the output of an ASP, Perl, or any other CGI application. For example suppose stock.asp generates stock market information. All we need to do to use such information is:

```
<TextFile src="http://www.domain.com/stock.asp" >
```

The only way to access URLs on another machine is by using an absolute, well-formed URL. However, we can use special relative URLs to access locations on the same machine. This is done by using the following general format:

```
<TextFile src="http://relative_location" >
```

The term relative_location is the path to the URL resource relative to the current ASP script. This location must always start with ./ or ../. For example, to get the result of the stock.asp ASP script, if it runs on that same web server and same directory as the calling ASP script, we would simply do:

```
<TextFile src="http://./stock.asp" >
```

This lets Flash Turbine know it's a relative HTTP request. Note that an HTTP request will be made, not a direct local file access.

One last point: when you're using HTTP requested content in your movies, make sure you have fast access between your Turbine web server and the web server requesting the content. Delays will of course negatively impact the web user experience.

As we've seen, URLs can be used in all the Flash template commands where external files are used. This feature, along with a proper use of the movie caching features, can create very powerful Flash applications.

Dynamic images

The ability to dynamically include images is most useful for situations like product catalogs, where you need to display images of the available products. Flash Turbine allows images in the following native formats to be used:

- JPEG format: good for photographs and non uniform images

- PNG format: good for images with lots of uniform color areas

- BMP format: excellent for uniform color images

We can include an image by entering the following text in an input text field:

```
<Image src="image_location" >
```

`image_location` is the image path relative to the location of the ASP. For example, to include a JPEG image from a file in the same directory as the ASP script, we would insert:

```
<Image src="product.jpg" >
```

We can use all sorts of absolute or relative paths. For example, `../../images/productlogo.jpg` will load the image from the specified path relative to the ASP script.

Images can also be loaded from HTTP URL requests, for example:

```
<Image src="http://www.domain.com/product.jpg" >
```

By default the image is positioned at the top left corner of the input text field.

The `Image` command is actually capable of more powerful things than simply including an image. Just for the record, here is the full Image command syntax with all the possible parameters:

```
<Image src=location
       x=n
       y=n
       width=n
       height=n
       angle=n
       alpha=n
       placepoint= left | right | center | top | bottom >
```

The meaning of each of these parameters is fairly obvious. You don't have to specify all of these parameters, as they'll automatically assume their respective default values. For example if you don't insert width/height values, the image's original width/height will be used instead; if you don't specify an angle value, 0 degrees will be assumed; a default alpha value of 100% will be assumed, and so on... Right, but what's that weird placepoint parameter? An image is positioned by its top left corner by default, but you can specify any of the other corners, or the center position, of the movie using this parameter.

So, to include the `logo.png` image in the generated Flash movie we would use:

```
<Image src="logo.png">
```

And to place the `logo.png` image with a size of 120x90 pixels:

```
<Image src="logo.png" width="120" height="90" >
```

Even if placed several times, an image definition is only included once in the generated Flash movie. This keeps file sizes to a minimum, no matter how many times you include the same image.

Choosing the best image file format

All of the common JPEG formats are supported, including interlaced/progressive encoding. PNG images must have been saved with the standard encoding format (not the Interlaced/Progressive format). If an encoding format other than standard is used, the image will not be included and an error will be displayed in the generated movie. Alpha channel PNG images are fully supported. 24 bit and palletized BMPs are also supported.

Including large PNG files may delay the response time, as they need to be fully decompressed, then processed and compressed in a Flash format suitable to be sent to the client. If you're not using alpha channel, then the same file in BMP format is much more quickly processed, and will occupy exactly the same size in the generated Flash movie.

According to the makers of the Flash Turbine range, GIF format files are not supported for two main reasons:

- PNG format is now universally supported, and has better compression levels (besides supporting alpha and 24 bit images, which are not available in the GIF format).

- The UNISYS/Compuserve patent over GIF usage. Software patents such as these appear to be dead weights in terms of Internet technology advance.

But image use in Turbine is not limited to these native formats, since Turbine includes an image conversion interface. Basically, it allows for the use of an external conversion program, to handle unsupported (non-native) formats. If you need to include PCX format images, just configure Turbine with the conversion software (for example PCX to BMP) and Turbine will include the converted image. Together with the Turbine caching capabilities, this allows you to use just about any graphic format, provided you obtain the apprrpriate conversion program.

For example the `convert.exe` utility from the ImageMagick suite of tools www.simplesystems.org ➥/ImageMagick/ includes conversion from just about any graphic format known to mankind. (Please note that any conversion from GIF format requires obtaining a license from UNISYS, due to the existing patent over the format.)

Using sound

Flash Turbine supports the inclusion of MP3 sound using the Turbine Sound object:

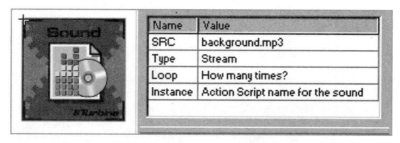

Name	Value
SRC	background.mp3
Type	Stream
Loop	How many times?
Instance	Action Script name for the sound

There's also a command:

```
<Sound src="sound_location" type="sound_type" >
```

Sounds can be of three types: `start`, `event`, or `stream`. An instance name for the generated sound can be defined so that it can be used from ActionScript code at the client, allowing for interactive fade-in/fade-out, panning and volume changes.

Placing movie clips

The ability to place movie clips dynamically can be very useful. Weather map movies use them, for example, to place a cloud on a region with rain, or a sun symbol where it is sunny. Movie clips can be placed with the `MovieClip` command, which needs to be placed in an input text field:

```
<MovieClip symbol="movie_clip_name" >
```

Actually, this is the minimum format of the command. There are more parameters available to control movie clip placing:

```
<MovieClip symbol=movie_clip_name
           instance=name
           x=n
           y=n
           scalex=n
           scaley=n
           angle=n
           alpha=n>
```

The `symbol` parameter is the actual name of the movie clip in the library; `instance` is the instance name of the created movie clip; `x` and `y` are the pixel coordinates relative to the input text field; `scalex` and `scaley` are the horizontal and vertical scaling ratios to apply, with 1.0 being the original movie clip size.

For example, we can substitute the input text field where the command was issued with an instance of the `logo_movieclip` symbol:

```
<MovieClip symbol="logo_movieclip">
```

You could place an instance of the `logo_movieclip` named `main` with 50% transparency:

```
<MovieClip symbol="logo_movieclip" instance="main" alpha="50%" >
```

> *One very important thing to note about dynamic movie clip placing is that the movie clips can only be placed after they've been defined in the movie. This means that you must place the movie clips in a frame of the Flash movie before the frame where you're issuing this command (or in the same frame). We suggest you have a separate layer where you place invisible instances of all the movie clips you'll be using later. Typically, a good place to do this is in the (pre-)loading screen of the Flash movie – you can place them in the first frame with an alpha of 0 (invisible) or a scaling of 0 (so small it can't be seen).*

Structured content access

We've seen how you can use Turbine variables and include text or images dynamically in order to separate presentation from content in Flash. There are more sophisticated things we can do with dynamic content, but for that to happen we need to be able to deal with data in more powerful ways.

Suppose for example that we need to display a table containing text. We could define a large number of variables, and call them `cell00`, `cell01`, `cell02`, and so on, but that could potentially turn into a nightmare!

To handle this sort of more structured content, we'll start by introducing the DataSet concept, and will then see some Turbine template commands that use it, like the `List`, `Table`, and `MovieClip List` commands. Let's start by talking about DataSets.

What are DataSets?

A **DataSet** is a group of variables that are defined and used as a table.

For example, suppose we had an online store and needed to list the products in stock, together with the characteristics, price, etc. Naturally, this information assumes a tabular format, for example:

	A	B	C	D	E	F	G	H	I
1	ProductID	Name	Color	Price	Quantity	Size	Weight	Arrival	MadeIn
2	145	Blue Ball	blue	1.5	7	10cm	2	10/10	Brazil
3	287	Red Car	red	2.1	1	2cm	1.5	10/09	India
4	378	Blue Mozilla	blue	2.3	0	120cm	4	11/10	Kenia
5	621	Gray Box	gray	21.1	56	70cm	5	12/11	USA
6	987	Square Ball	white	11.5	1	88cm	2	10/10	Peru
7	1119	Slick Toy	green	2.5	1000	51cm	2.1	1/19	Egypt
8	5321	Glue Gun	black	6.4	90	40cm	4	2/31	UK
9	6361	Brown Bag	brown	9.5	3	60cm	8.4	8/09	France

This is the kind of structured information we can get from database queries or spreadsheets. To be able to use structured information in Flash Turbine we need to load it. ASP Flash Turbine supports three ways to load DataSets:

- Loading from a file or URL

- Manual loading from an ASP script

- Loading from an ADO recordset, from a database query

Therefore a DataSet is something of a table, complete with column names and cells, holding and grouping information for use in Turbine template objects and commands.

Loading DataSets from a file or URL

To load DataSets from a file or URL location we employ the DataSet File Turbine object:

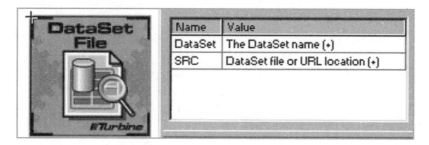

Name	Value
DataSet	The DataSet name (+)
SRC	DataSet file or URL location (+)

or the corresponding command:

```
<DataSetFile dataset="data_set_name" src="data_set_location" >
```

The `data_set_location` parameter is an absolute or relative path to the file. The `data_set_name` parameter is the name that the DataSet can be referenced by, and is used in the Flash template.

DataSet File objects and commands can be placed anywhere in the Flash template. That's because they are loaded in a pre-process passing of the Turbine engine, so that the loaded content is available to any command.

As with other commands that access external files, you can also specify a URL. For example:

```
<DataSetFile dataset="ProductDataSet"
    src="http://www.domain.com/customers.php" >
```

So, what's the format of this file? DataSet files are simply comma separated format files, with a special first line that indicates the column names to be used in the DataSet, while the following lines hold the comma separated values that constitute the sequence of cells and rows in the table. The general format for a DataSet file is:

<Column1,	Column2,	...	Column#>
Row1Column1,	Row1Column2,	...	Row1Column#
Row2Column1,	Row2Column2,	...	Row2Column#
...	...	...	...
Row#Column1,	Row#Column2,	...	Row#Column#

As you can see, commas delimit the values of each cell, and each row must be specified on a separate line. Each of these cell values can have any characters, except new line characters. Also, if the cell value can have commas, you need to enclose it in double-quote characters. An example of a DataSet is:

```
<ProductID, Name, Color, Price, Quantity, Size, Weight, Arrival,
MadeIn>
145, "Blue Ball", "blue", 1.50, 7, "10cm", 2, "10/10", "Brazil"
287, "Red Car", "red", 2.10, 1, "2cm", 1.5, "10/09", "India"
378, "Blue Mozilla", "blue", 2.30, 0, "120cm", 4, "11/10", "Kenya"
621, "Gray Box", "gray", 21.1, 56, "70cm", 5, "12/11", "USA"
987, "Square Ball", "white", 11.50, 1, "88cm", 2, "10/10", "Peru"
1119, "Slick Toy", "green", 2.50, 1000, "51cm", 2.1, "1/19", "Egypt"
5321, "Glue Gun", "black", 6.40, 90, "40cm", 4, "2/31", "UK"
6361, "Brown Bag", "brown", 9.50, 3, "60cm", 8.4, "8/09", "France"
```

We'll be using this file (`product_dataset.txt`) in an example shortly.

Each of the values in a DataSet can also be accessed in the normal Turbine variable syntax, with this special variable naming syntax:

```
{DataSetName$ColumnName.LineNumber}
```

Row numbers start at 1, so the first row is LineNumber 1, next is LineNumber 2, and so on as expected. For example, to use the name of the product in the first row of a DataSet called ProductDataSet we could use:

```
{ProductDataSet$Name.1}
```

Or the price of the second product (on the second row) would be:

```
{ProductDataSet$Price.2}
```

Building DataSets from an ASP script

DataSets can be created from inside ASP scripts in three basic ways.

The first is by using the Turbine object's LoadDataSetFile function, which can be used to load the DataSet from a file. The format for this call is:

```
Turbine.LoadDataSetFile dataset_filename, data_set_name
```

If it fails (for example because it can't find the DataSet file) this command can launch an exception that will cause an ASP script error. However, the exception can be caught in the usual way – for example in VBScript with the OnError command.

We can also manually load the DataSet from an ASP script by using a Turbine function that defines the header, and then using another function (multiple times) that will define each row.

Possibly the most powerful way to create DataSets from ASP scripting is by using an ASP Flash Turbine function that converts an ADO recordset holding the results of a database query directly into a Turbine DataSet, queried for example from an Oracle, SQL Server or Access database. This allows very simple integration between structured content coming from a database and Flash presentation capabilities.

Since these functions are more closely related to ASP scripting, we'll cover them in the next chapter, together with all the scripting functionalities that ASP Flash Turbine offers.

Phew! After all this DataSet creation theory, let's see it working.

The List object and command

The List template object and command displays a DataSet column as a text list. This can be accomplished by inserting either an object:

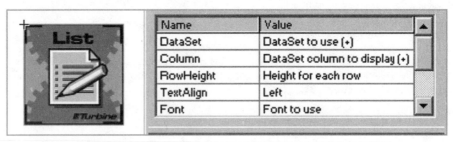

or a Turbine command in an input text field with the following format:

```
<List dataset="data_set_name" column="column_name" >
```

The parameters can be used to specify which DataSet and column to use, alignment, etc. If you use the object, some settings need to be explicitly specified, like which font to use. On the other hand, if you use the command, the text settings of the input text field where the command was issued will automatically be used as defaults, the width (for wrapping purposes), color, font and font size to use will be the same as the respective input text field.

The generated List object is placed inside a synthetic movie clip, so that you can manipulate it from ActionScript (on the client). The instance name of this movie clip is the variable name of the input text field where the command was issued.

List command example

Let's work through an example using the List command with the ProductDataSet we've seen above, by loading it from a file.

1.   Create a new Flash movie and insert an input text field with the following text:

```
<List dataset="ProductDataSet" column="Name" >
```

This will display a list of the contents the of Name column of the ProductDataSet. We then need to export this Flash movie to a Flash template file (.swt) – let's call it list.swt (wow, that's creativity!).

2.   Now we need to load the DataSet file, and as we've already seen, one way to do so from an ASP script is by using the LoadDataSetFile function from the ASP Flash Turbine object. So that would give us the following script, list.asp:

```
<%
Set Turbine=Server.CreateObject("Turbine.ASP")
Turbine.Template = "list.swt"
Turbine.LoadDataSetFile "product_dataset.txt", "ProductDataSet"
Turbine.GenerateFlash
%>
```

The first line creates the scripting Turbine object, the second line loads the list.swt template that we've previously created, and then on line three we load the DataSet file product_dataset.txt, which is located in the same directory as the ASP script. The last line tells the Turbine object to generate the Flash movie and send it over to the web client.

You can find the source for this example in the list directory of the Turbine examples on the CD.

If you request list.asp with a web browser you'll get the contents of the Name column of the DataSet displayed by the List command:

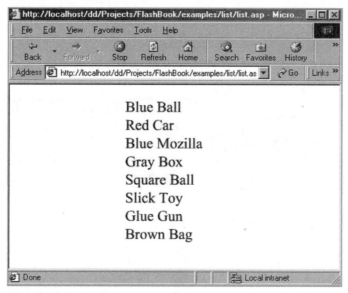

The Table object and command

In a similar fashion, the Table object and the Table command display the complete contents of a DataSet:

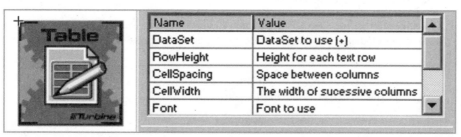

or:

```
<Table dataset="data_set_name" >
```

Like the List command, the Table command's generated text will be displayed with the font, font height, font color, and alignment of the input text field where the command was issued, while with the object you'll have to specify these settings.

Also common to these template commands is the fact that the generated object is placed inside a synthetic movie clip, so that we can manipulate it with ActionScript (on the client). The instance name of this movie clip is the variable name of the input text field where the command was issued.

Table Object example

Let's see an example using the Table object.

1. On a blank Flash movie, drag the Turbine Table object from the Turbine object library window and set the clip parameters as below, then export it as a Flash template named `table.swt`:

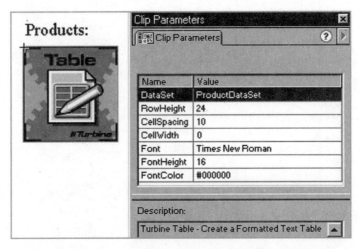

So we're creating a table driven by a DataSet named `ProductDataSet` with a RowHeight of 24 pixels, etc.

2. The ASP script, `table.asp`, is quite simple, and is similar to the List example – while we're loading a different Flash template, everything else is the same:

```
<%
Set Turbine=Server.CreateObject("Turbine.ASP")
Turbine.Template = "table.swt"
```

```
Turbine.LoadDataSetFile "product_dataset.txt", "ProductDataSet"
Turbine.GenerateFlash
%>
```

And here are the results you'll see displayed if you request `table.asp` in a web browser:

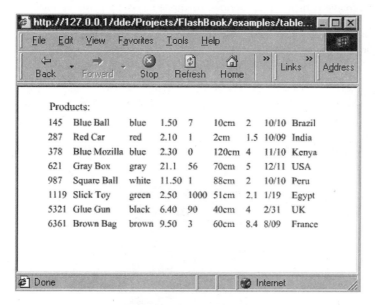

The Table command, by the way, is a great way of visualizing your DataSets. For example, use it for debugging purposes, to check if you're getting the correct information into your DataSet.

The source for this example is available in the `table` directory of the Turbine examples on the CD.

Dynamic movie clip lists

Movie clip lists are great for creating menus and all kinds of link lists. Turbine automates this task with the MovieClip List object:

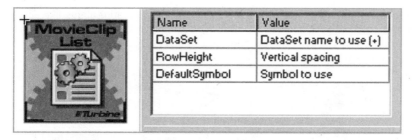

This places movie clips and defines ActionScript variables (which are visible as dynamic or input text fields) according to the specified DataSet. For example, a DataSet with the columns `title`

and `url` will define such named variables in each created movie clip instance. The name of the movie clip is specified by the DefaultSymbol parameter.

For example, to create a link list or link menu we simply create a movie clip with a dynamic text field named `title` and a button which will jump to the location contained in the `url` ActionScript variable (which will be defined by the `MovieClip List` command). We'll see how this is done in the next chapter.

By using a DataSet similar to this one:

```
<title, url>
"Anne's Bazaar", "http://abazaar2001.com"
"Paul's Bazaar", "http://pbazaar2001.com"
...
```

And then placing the MovieClip List Turbine object on the stage, we'd achieve something like:

If we want this list to have a scroll bar, we'd only need to drag one from the Turbine driver library window near to a corner of the Turbine object, and there we'd have it – a scrolling link list.

You can find this sample in the `moviecliplist` directory of the Turbine samples on the CD.

The AutoMovieClip object

AutoMovieClip is a really powerful way of automatically generating items like spots on maps, grids, menus, combo-boxes, and all sorts of widgets. Simply put, the AutoMovieClip object places movie clips driven by values in the columns of a DataSet – each row of the DataSet originates a placement of a movie clip.

Name	Value
DataSet	DataSet name to use (+)
DefaultSymbol	-
DX	Default horizontal move
DY	Default vertical move

The only required parameter is the DataSet entry: all the others can be left untouched. This object works by creating movie clips driven by each line of the DataSet. The driving DataSet can have the following columns, whose values will influence the placement and properties of those movie clips:

```
<_symbol,_instance,_x,_y,_scalex,_scaley,_angle,_alpha,...>
```

These columns have the behavior expected from their names (which are the names of the Movie Clip command described above), and will be applied to each generated movie clip. The movie clip placement requires that they be defined in the Flash movie prior to the placement of the AutoMovieClip object, just as in the MovieClip command – both depend on the Movie Clip Palette concept.

Let's overview how can we place movie clip symbols over a map – suppose we place this object in a Flash template, over an image of a map:

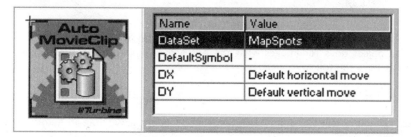

Name	Value
DataSet	MapSpots
DefaultSymbol	-
DX	Default horizontal move
DY	Default vertical move

Then, in some location, for example a file or a database table, we store the MapSpots DataSet; This DataSet contains the type and coordinate location where the symbol should be placed, for example:

```
<_symbol, _x, _y>
"hotel_movieclip", 20, 50
"park_movieclip", 45, 80
"beach_movieclip", 110, 50
```

The AutoMovieClip object, driven by such DataSet, would display three movie clips over the map in the locations specified by the _x and _y of the DataSet.

Automatic images – AutoImage

The AutoImage object places images driven by values from a DataSet – each row of the DataSet originates the placement of an image. The driving DataSet needs to have some specially named columns with information like the width, height, alpha channel value, scaling, etc.

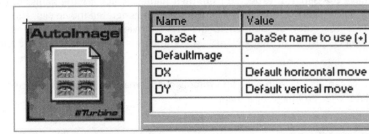

These parameters have meanings similar to what we've seen in the AutoMovieClip object – the AutoImage object does for images what the AutoMovieClip does for movie clips. The driving DataSet can have the following headers:

```
<_src, _x,_y,_width,_height, _angle, _alpha, _place_point>
```

Let's see how this object could draw an image mosaic. Suppose we drag an AutoImage object and then define the DataSet parameter to be CorporateLogos:

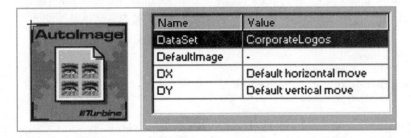

Then we create the CorporateLogos DataSet with the contents:

```
<_src, _x, _y>
"logo1.png", 0, 0
"logo2.png", 100, 0
"logo3.png", 0, 100
"logo4.png", 100, 100
```

This would display a four-image mosaic, with the images placed in the positions specified by the _x and _y columns. Like the AutoMovieClip object, the AutoImage object is also available as a regular command.

Drawing charts with the chart object

Flash Turbine includes Chart display functionalities based on DataSet content. We can specify which DataSet column will provide the numerical values for the bars, which column will provide the horizontal axis labels, and the minimum and maximum values for the vertical axis. Some of the chart types supported are:

Line3d

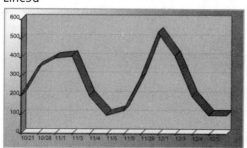

LineMarker

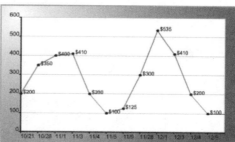

Triangle3d

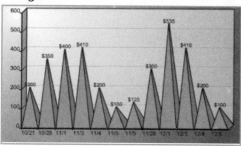

Area

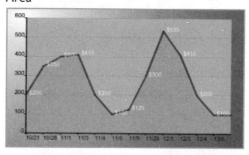

Area3d

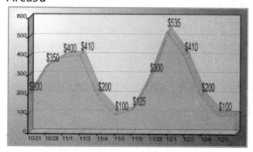

Column3d

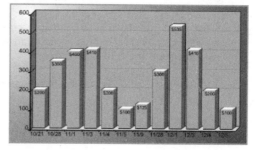

CoolColumn

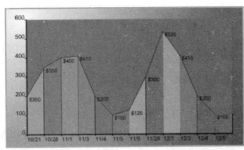

Plain

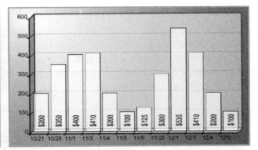

Glass

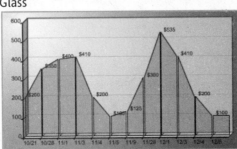

Stick

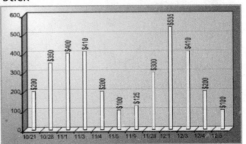

Scatter

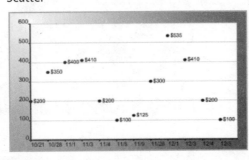

Besides the included chart types, custom chart types can be created and used. Flash Turbine includes a modular, plug-in-like chart type system, based on the Draw Script language which we'll introduce in the next chapter.

You can find a complete chart example in the samples included with the ASP Flash Turbine installation.

Summary

In this chapter, we've seen some of the ways in which ASP Flash Turbine can help with handling dynamic content using the Flash technology. ASP Flash Turbine is an ASP scripting component that works from within ASP scripts to integrate dynamically accessed content with Flash movie templates. This component processes a set of template commands, and provides a scripting interface that can be used from inside the ASP scripting environment, in any of the supported languages.

Flash Turbine includes data type support for variables and structured, tabular variable sets named DataSets. Several objects and commands are available in Flash templates to permit a precise integration of the content, while the ASP scripting interface presents several scripting commands, mostly used for loading content into the templates. Flash Turbine provides support for text, image, and sound inclusion, and for a range of DataSet driven commands – the `List`, `Table`, `MovieClip List`, `AutoMovieClip`, and `AutoImage` commands. Flash Turbine also supports Chart graphics rendered from DataSet provided content.

In the next chapter, we'll go on to look at how to put all we've learnt here into practice.

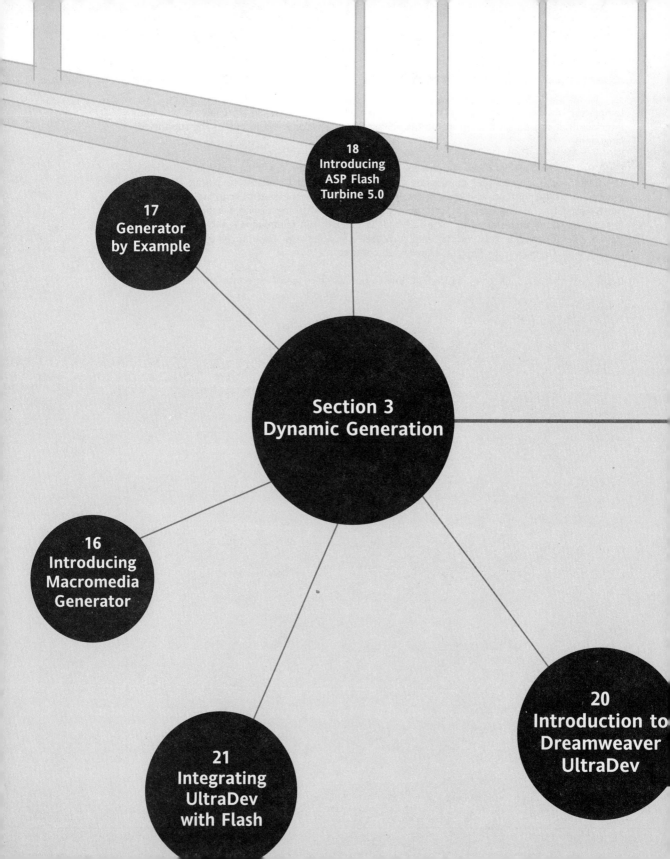

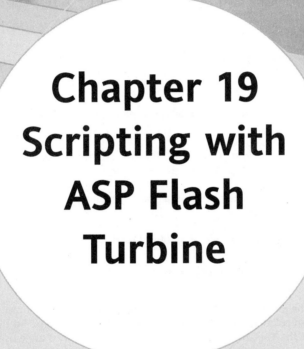

Chapter 19
Scripting with
ASP Flash
Turbine

The previous chapter described how the placement of Flash Turbine objects and commands in the Flash template allows a precise definition of how external content will be integrated. We've also briefly seen some ASP scripting commands that allowed us to define variables, load DataSets, and a few more.

So why is a scripting interface needed when we can already include content by using the template commands? This is precisely what we'll see in this chapter. A short answer is that the ASP Flash Turbine scripting interface gives us much more powerful data access capabilities – notably making database access very simple. And the advantage of using the ASP scripting engine is that it allows advanced logic to be easily programmed. With ASP Flash Turbine and ASP scripting, complex web sites with content display and updating can be implemented in Flash media.

In this chapter we'll describe:

- The scripting interface, and what can be done with it

- ASP database access

- How to build a simple database to be used with ASP Flash Turbine, and displayed in Flash

- The Draw Script language, which allows arbitrary shapes, text, and movie clip drawing (for dynamic maps, graphs, games, etc.)

- Caching capabilities, which really are mandatory to handle the zillions of hits your site is about to receive

- An integrated example of all this at work

Creating the ASP Flash Turbine object

As we saw in the previous chapter, we can use all the scripting functionality available in ASP Flash Turbine by manipulating a COM component named `Turbine.asp`. So that's easy enough – we need to create the `Turbine` object so that we can use it. This is done using:

```
Set Turbine = Server.CreateObject("Turbine.asp")
```

From this instruction onwards we can use the `Turbine` object to manipulate the Flash movie to be served. This object will be the interface we'll employ to use a Flash template, define variables, load DataSets, and finally generate the assembled Flash movie.

A quick note about performance – Turbine is implemented as a "page scope multi-threaded component". These kinds of components can give the best possible performance for page-based components. While it's a regular COM component, the ASP Turbine component works directly with the ASP scripting engine to make some page interactions easier.

From now on we'll assume the ASP Flash Turbine object we created with the above command is named Turbine.

Loading the Flash template

A Flash template is loaded by assigning its filename to the `Template` property of the ASP `Turbine` object. It can be specified in an absolute path or a path relative to the current ASP script. For example:

```
Turbine.Template= "template.swt"
```

Here's an example of the powerful things the scripting interface can do. Suppose we want to use different templates, depending on whether today is a workday or not: on a workday we want to use the `open.swt` Flash template, at weekends we display `closed.swt` instead. This could be as simple as:

```
<%
Set Turbine = Server.CreateObject("Turbine.asp")

if weekday(now) = 7 or weekday(now) = 1 then
   Turbine.Template = "closed.swt"
else
   Turbine.Template = "open.swt"
end if

Turbine.GenerateFlash
%>
```

The first line creates the `Turbine` object, then we check if today is a Saturday or Sunday. If it is, we set `Turbine.template = "closed.swt"` to use that template. Otherwise, it must be Monday to Friday, so we'll set `Turbine.Template= "open.swt"` to use the `open.swt` template. Then we might want to do some work on the template, for instance defining variables, and after that the `Turbine.GenerateFlash` command will push the assembled movie to the web browser.

You can study the simple source for this example in the `template` directory of the Turbine examples on the CD.

Hello World becomes interactive

The Hello World example we saw in the previous chapter was not terribly interesting – even if part of the text came from outside the Flash template, well it just displayed Hello World. Let's expand that example to make it display a name submitted from an HTML form.

1. Create the following HTML page, and call it `helloworld2.htm`:

```
<HTML>
<BODY>

<FORM action="helloworld2.asp" method="GET">
```

```
Enter your Name:
<INPUT type="TEXT" name="name">
<BR>
<INPUT type="SUBMIT">

</FORM>

</BODY>
</HTML>
```

2. This HTML form will be submitted to the `helloworld2.asp` script. This ASP script is virtually the same as our primitive `helloworld.asp` from the previous chapter, except for one small difference:

```
<%
Set Turbine = Server.CreateObject("Turbine.ASP")

Turbine.Template = "helloworld.swt"

Turbine.Variable("{name}") = Request("name')

Turbine.GenerateFlash
%>
```

Notice how we define the Turbine variable name with the value of the name parameter that was submitted from the HTML form. This name parameter holds whatever we've entered in the HTML form.

When you enter a name into the form in `helloworld2.htm` and click Submit Query, you should see something like this:

By taking advantage of the ASP script environment, we've been able to interact with the web browser and integrate the results inside a Flash movie.

The script and template for this example are available in the `helloworld2` directory of the Turbine examples on the CD.

Loading Turbine variables and DataSets

As we've previously seen, variables can be loaded from inside ASP scripting by using the `Variable` (or simply `Var`) property:

```
Turbine.Variable("{name}") = Request("name")
```

In the same manner, variables can be loaded from files by using the `LoadVariableFile` command:

```
Turbine.LoadVariableFile variable_filename
```

The format for this file is described in the "Loading Variables From a File" section in the previous chapter.

DataSets can be loaded either from a file:

```
Turbine.LoadDataSetFile dataset_filename, data_set_name
```

Or created directly (some call it 'manually') in the script, by using the next two commands: one to define the columns of the DataSet, the other to add consecutive rows:

```
Turbine.MakeDataSet "dataset_name", "columns"
Turbine.AddDataSetRow "row"
```

The `MakeDataSet` command accepts two parameters: `dataset_name` is a string with the name that can later be used to access the DataSet, while `columns` is a string holding the names of the DataSet columns, delimited by commas.

Then we need to define the rows of the DataSet, and to do so we use the `AddDataSetRow` command that accepts the comma-separated values for each of the columns in that row.

In practice, suppose we want to create a DataSet like this:

```
<Caption,        URL>
Main Page,       /www/
Monthly          /zx1561/
Content,
Free Content,    /www/free21
Premium          /www/premium5
Content,         6
```

We'd start by defining the columns (Caption and URL). Suppose we name the DataSet "Navigation":

```
Turbine.MakeDataSet "Navigation", 'Caption, URL'
```

Then, to fill the DataSet rows we'd use:

```
Turbine.AddDataSetRow "Main Page, /www/"
Turbine.AddDataSetRow "Monthly Content, /zx1561/"
Turbine.AddDataSetRow "Free Content, /www/free21"
Turbine.AddDataSetRow "Premium Content, /www/premium56'
```

Auto-magically generating the HTML plug-in page

All the examples we've seen so far display the generated movie in a full browser window. Sometimes, however, it's preferable to display the generated movie inside the Flash plug-in running in the middle of an HTML page. To do so, it's usually necessary to have an HTML page that requests the Flash movie. For example, the following HTML page includes the Flash plug-in tags:

```
<OBJECT classid="clsid:D27CDB6E-AE6D-11cf-96B8-444553540000"
        ➡WIDTH="90%" HEIGHT="90%">

  <PARAM NAME=movie VALUE="movie.asp">
  <EMBED src="movie.asp"  WIDTH=550 HEIGHT=400
        ➡TYPE="application/x-shockwave-flash" ></EMBED>

</OBJECT>
```

Note, however, that this can present a problem. For example, if you're receiving a submission from an HTML form, you need to arrange the query string properly to include the Flash plug-in movie loading parameters ("movie.asp", in the HTML above). To do so you'd need another ASP script, and this means more complexity and effort.

ASP Flash Turbine features the GenerateHTMLFirst scripting command that takes care of this for you:

```
Turbine.GenerateHTMLFirst "html_plugin_page"
```

This command has the effect of sending to the browser an HTML page with the necessary Flash plug-in HTML code, arranged so as to automatically load the movie generated by that ASP script. What this means is that the ASP script will actually be invoked twice:

- The first time by the original request. GenerateHTMLFirst will generate an HTML page, which will request this same URL again (but this second time expecting a Flash movie). In this case, script execution will stop right after the GenerateHTMLFirst command.

- The second time, the ASP script will be invoked by the Flash plug-in inside the previously generated HTML page. This time it will generate the expected Flash movie.

The ASP script will be requested with the same query string from the original request. The magic part is that you don't have to worry about these mechanics, simply place the GenerateHTMLFirst command in your script.

The command accepts one parameter, which is the HTML page that will be sent on the first request. If you leave this parameter empty, a default HTML page named plugin.htm, located in the Turbine installation directory, will be used instead.

Generating the HTML plug-in page example

So it seems that to add this capability to our Hello World example all we need to do is add a single line.

Modify the previous Hello World ASP file as follows:

```
<%
Set Turbine = Server.CreateObject("Turbine.asp")
Turbine.Template = "helloworld.swt"
Turbine.GenerateHTMLFirst ""
Turbine.Variable("{name}") = Request("name')
Turbine.GenerateFlash
%>
```

This will display the generated Flash movie inside an HTML page. Note there's an HTML link at the bottom of the page – it's the generated HTML page holding the generated Flash movie in the center:

You can check the full example in the `helloworld3` directory of the Turbine examples on the CD.

Generating the Flash movie

The last step in a usual ASP script using ASP Flash Turbine, after defining the template and loading the content, is to actually send something to the web user. Nothing more simple than placing the `GenerateFlash` command:

```
Turbine.GenerateFlash
```

This will have the effect of assembling all the content into the Flash template and creating an optimized Flash movie to send to the web browser.

Not all scripts need to generate Flash media, you can choose, for example, to send an HTML page instead. This can be done in the usual ASP script manner – just don't call the `Turbine.GenerateFlash` command.

Generating to local files – batch automation!

ASP Flash Turbine can also save the generated movies locally, on the web server disk, by means of the `GenerateToFile` command:

```
Turbine.GenerateToFile output_filename
```

Generating to local files can be useful for many things. You can choose to pre-generate your site's Flash movies on a periodic basis (although the cache functionality can be more simple to use for this, as we'll see below). Or, you can use it for classic batch automation tasks, for example generating a quantity of Flash movies for use in a CD-ROM project. Since you can easily access many data sources, notably databases, this can make a lot of sense in some projects.

Batch automation example

Let's see an example that creates a quantity of files – we'll create Flash movie files featuring different text (actually a different number) in each one.

Create the following ASP script and call it `generate.asp`:

```
<%
Set Turbine=Server.CreateObject("Turbine.asp")
Turbine.Template= "amovie.swt"

for MovieNumber = 1 to 30

    Turbine.Variable("{string}") =
            "This is the text for movie " & MovieNumber
```

```
        Turbine.GenerateToFile("output/movie" & MovieNumber & ".swf")

    next

    %>
```

What we're doing here is generating the dynamic Flash movies to local files in the output directory, relative to the ASP script location. Much of the work is done inside the `for` loop, starting on the third line. We define the `String Turbine` variable as "This is the text for movie 1", "This is the Text for movie 2", and so on, 30 times. And each of these movies will be generated to the files `movie1.swf`, `movie2.swf`, and so on.

Once we're finished, we inform the user:

```
Done! Movies were generated to the
        <a href="output/">output/ directory</a>
```

The Flash movies produced are based on the `amovie.swt` Flash template, which simply displays two rotating animations of the text we've defined in the `string Turbine` variable. If we were to open `movie1.swf`, this is one of the frames we'd see:

Imagine how useful this capability can be if you need to create a CD with 279 products retrieved from a database...

The complete source for this sample is available in the `cdrom` directory of the examples on the CD.

The typical skeleton for a Turbine ASP script

As we've seen in the previous examples, most ASP scripts have a similar structure. That means we could create a skeleton script – one that can be used when starting an ASP script that uses Turbine. So, you can start with something like this:

```
<%
' create the Turbine object:
Set Turbine = Server.CreateObject("Turbine.asp")

' specify the Flash template:
Turbine.Template = "template.swt"

' generate an HTML plug-in page:
Turbine.GenerateHTMLFirst ""

' ... fetch content to include in the movie ...

' finally generate the Flash movie:
Turbine.GenerateFlash
%>
```

The first line creates the ASP Flash Turbine component, after which the next line defines which template to use. The third line makes the generated movie appear inside an HTML page with the plug-in – this might not be desirable, for example if the movie is being loaded in a loadMovie, or if you require a full browser movie.

The next stage usually features the necessary code to access content, define variables, load DataSets and just about anything possible from ASP scripting.

Finally the movie is generated and sent to the web browser, to create a happy web user!

Using database content with Flash Turbine

In the previous chapter we saw some Turbine commands, either template or scripting commands, that used files from the local disk or accessed by an HTTP request.

If text can be stored and used from plain files, variables, and DataSets too, then who needs databases? Databases are necessary for a number of reasons:

- If you have lots of information: text files can be OK for 20 products, but what about 200 products? And 2000 products?

- Do you need to query or search your data? Plain text files are difficult to search in a meaningful manner. With databases and a language named SQL it's a trivial thing!

- Does the information need to be accessed or edited by multiple users? With text files it will be a mess. Databases can do a good job of synchronizing multiple simultaneous data modifications.

- Performance and scalability demands that larger sites be split between several machines. Text files will not handle this easily. However, many databases include transparent built-in load-balancing mechanisms.

- Databases are also a great way to help separate content from presentation, since you can only store information there – databases are pure content stores.

Clearly, there's a level of complexity of the content used in a site, beyond which a database is absolutely necessary. We'll spend the rest of this section describing how database content can be used inside Turbine.

Using ADO from ASP scripts

The easiest way to access databases from inside ASP scripts is by using the Microsoft ADO interface. ADO stands for **Active Data Objects**, and it works with a database interface layer named **ODBC – Open DataBase Connectivity**. The idea behind ODBC is to decouple applications from the database they use, so that one can easily change database engine, and all the code will seamlessly carry on working. ADO and ODBC allow access to a large number of database engines: SQL Server, Oracle, Sybase, Informix, Access, dBase, FoxPro, and many others (you can even use MS Excel files as databases!).

An important thing about the current database engines is that they follow a theoretical model – the relational model – and are thus called **relational databases**. This name arises from their internal data organization, which is based upon tables (similar to DataSets we've seen previously) and relations between tables. Relations are important to model relationships between specific data. For example, a table with product categories will be related to the product table, since every product has a category – the product category Fruit is related to the products Apple, Orange, Kiwi, etc. The ability to model relationships between sets of data is very helpful when trying to model real life information.

Let's study what's needed to use databases with ASP Flash Turbine, by creating an Access database. All the principles we'll see also work (unchanged) with larger scale database engines, such as Oracle or SQL Server, due to the ODBC abstraction layer. We'll use Access because it's a database that most people are familiar with. However, please keep in mind that Access is not designed to handle large volumes of simultaneous requests – for that you'll need to get a more powerful database engine.

Creating a database

To explore database interaction with Flash Turbine, let's create a database of products that will include information similar to the ProductDataSet we saw in the previous chapter, in the DataSets section. (You can find this database file with the table filled in, in the database folder of the Turbine examples directory on the CD.)

1. Start Microsoft Access (we'll use the Access 2000 version), and select Blank Access database. You'll be asked about the location and name of the database file – name it `Product.mdb` and save it in the wwwroot folder of your server.

2. The next step is to create the table that will hold the product information we're interested in. Select Create table in Design view.

3. Design view will allow us to specify the **fields** to use in the table. Fields are similar to (but more powerful than) the DataSet columns we've seen previously. These fields have a name and a data type that we need to define. Enter the following fields:

Notice that the fields have the same names as the `ProductDataSet` we used in the last chapter. The data types for the various fields are Number where we have quantities, Currency where we have money quantities (in the Price field), and Text in the other fields.

4. Save the table definition by pressing CTRL + S, name the table Product, and there we have a new table waiting to be filled with all sorts of products! You'll be prompted to create a primary key for the table – this is not necessary for this exercise – just answer no.

5. To insert values into the table simply double-click on the icon named Product and a data entry dialog will appear. After entering the values, we'll see this:

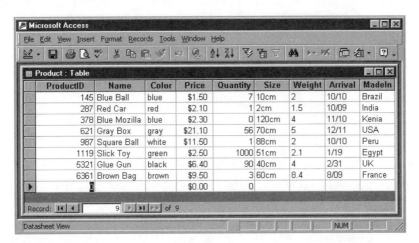

We now have a database with a table full of products to be used in Flash movies, but how do we access it?

Accessing the database

Database tables can be queried by using a language named **SQL – Structured Query Language**. For our purposes we'll only use simple SQL commands, but this language is capable of very powerful things like comprehensive textual data searches, complex "data joins" between tables, flexible sorting and grouping, and much more.

Before we can access our database from ASP scripts we need to be able to connect to it, and the easiest way to do this is by creating a **DSN – Data Source Name**. As we've seen, a DSN is a system-wide name that applications can use to access a database. A DSN is related to the ODBC database-independent layer, to allow database access independent of the actual database engine. The idea is that if we decided to move our products database, for example to Oracle, we need only create a DSN with the same name pointing to the Oracle database – by magic all our code will keep on working because it's using the DSN, and not directly going to the database engine.

1. Remember, in order to create a DSN, open the Windows Control Panel and then ODBC Data Sources (or Administrative Tools > Data Sources (ODBC) in Windows 2000). Select the System DSN tab, click the Add button, choose Microsoft Access Driver (*.mdb) and click Finish. Type Product_DSN in the Data Source Name field:

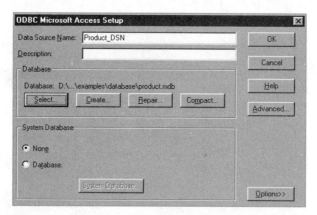

2. Then click the Select button to specify the location of the Product.mdb database we created above. After clicking OK, we'll see the Product_DSN entry that we just created in the System DSN data sources list:

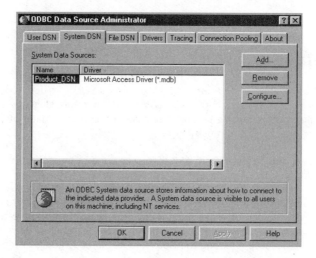

We now have a database in place with content that we are about to use dynamically in Flash.

Query and integrate

To access the content in this database from ASP scripts, so that we can include it in dynamic Flash movies, we can use a small piece of code similar to this one:

```
<%
Set Conn = Server.CreateObject("ADODB.Connection")
Conn.Open "DSN=Product_DSN"

SQLQuery = "Select * from Product"
Set RS = Conn.Execute(SQLQuery)
```

```
        ProductID = RS("ProductID")
        Name = RS("Name")
        Color = RS("Color")
        %>
```

This is standard code to open a database connection by using a DSN, and to perform a query to a database table – let's review it step by step.

It all starts by creating an `ADODB.Connection` object named `Conn`. We use this on line two to open a connection to our database by opening the DSN we created above – named `Product_DSN`:

```
        Conn.Open "DSN=Product_DSN"
```

We now have a database connection, which we use in the next two lines to perform the following SQL query:

```
        Select * from Product
```

This SQL command simply means select **all** the fields (denoted by the `*`) from the `Product` table.

Next the `Conn.Execute` command will get us a `Recordset` object that we can use to manipulate the query results. Finally, we access the contents of this Recordset – the individual fields, which can be accessed by a simple syntax:

```
        RS("field_name")
```

So we access the `ProductID`, `Name` and `Color` fields, and assign them to variables. Notice that we've only accessed the first row returned by the query. To be able to get more rows, we would need to browse through the Recordset, by doing as many `RS.MoveNext`'s as needed to fetch the available rows.

Inserting the results into a Flash template

Let's expand the above code to define Turbine variables so that the results of the query can be inserted into a Flash template.

1. Start by crafting a simple template like this one (graphical beautification is possible and actually strongly suggested!):

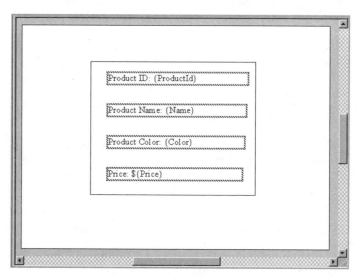

We have four text blocks that reference the `ProductID`, `Name`, `Color`, and `Price` Turbine variables. This template will be named `query.swt`.

2. Then we take the previous two ASP scripts and perform some minor plastic surgery on them. The result is:

```
<%
Set Conn = Server.CreateObject("ADODB.Connection")
Conn.Open "DSN=Product_DSN"

SQLQuery = "Select * from Product"
Set RS = Conn.Execute(SQLQuery)

Set Turbine = Server.CreateObject("Turbine.asp")

Turbine.Template = "query.swt"

Turbine.GenerateHTMLFirst ("")

Turbine.Variable("{ProductID}") = RS("ProductID")
Turbine.Variable("{Name}") = RS("Name")
Turbine.Variable("{Color}") = RS("Color")
Turbine.Variable("{Price}") = RS("Price")

Turbine.GenerateFlash
%>
```

The top lines of the script open the database connection, and perform the SQL query, the bottom lines are the usual Turbine skeleton – all we do is define the Turbine variables to have the contents of the row fetched by the query. *Et voilà*, we obtain a Flash movie with database content:

The complete source for this example is located in the `database_vars` directory of the Turbine samples on the CD.

Converting database tables to Turbine DataSets

Have you noticed how database tables and DataSets are quite alike? Both organize and store information in a tabular manner, ordered by columns. ASP Flash Turbine can convert between query results stored in a database recordset and a Turbine DataSet. This is performed by the `LoadDataSetRS` command:

```
Turbine.LoadDataSetRS recordset, data_set_name
```

The first parameter, `recordset`, is a normal ADO recordset with the contents of a query, while the `data_set_name` parameter is the name of the DataSet to be defined. Each of the columns returned by the query will create a similar column in the DataSet. All the rows returned by the query will be available in the new DataSet, thus effectively making the results of the query available to Turbine Flash template commands.

Since the recordset is the result of the SQL query, we can sort the resulting rows in any way, group them by fields, anything that's possible from SQL. The column and row order in the generated DataSet will be identical to that of the original recordset – you can fully manipulate this in the SQL query that originated the recordset.

Once we have a Turbine DataSet, it can be used in all the Flash template objects and commands we've seen in the previous chapter – Lists, Tables, Movie Clip Lists, AutoMovieClips, Charts, etc. How about a text table?

Displaying text tables

Let's see an example of Flash displaying a DataSet created from an ADO recordset. We'll use the
`LoadDataSetRS` command to create a DataSet to be used by the Table template command to
display a text table.

1. Start by inserting a Turbine Table object in a new Flash template, together with a title,
    Products:, and a humble rectangular border:

2. Make the object use ProductDataSet, as defined in the first parameter, and
    define the RowHeight as 24 pixels, Cellspacing as 10, and Cellwidth as 0. Save this
    Flash template as `table.swt`.

3. By recycling our ASP scripts, we can obtain a script that uses elements from the
    previous examples plus the `LoadDataSetRS` command, which will load and define the
    DataSet named ProductDataSet, needed by the Table object:

```
<%
Set Conn = Server.CreateObject("ADODB.Connection")
Conn.Open "DSN=Product_DSN"

SQLQuery = "Select * from Product"
Set RS = Conn.Execute(SQLQuery)

Set Turbine=Server.CreateObject("Turbine.asp")
Turbine.Template= "table.swt"
```

```
Turbine.GenerateHTMLFirst("")
Turbine.LoadDataSetRS RS, "ProductDataSet"
Turbine.GenerateFlash
%>
```

It's really as simple as that. The recordset is assimilated into a Turbine DataSet, and will then be available to be used in any template object or command that accepts DataSets. And we get a nice text table, directly from our database:

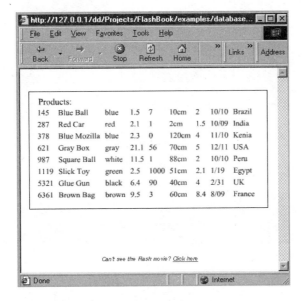

The source for this example can be found in the `database_table` directory on the CD.

Automating the table

Now let's do some user interface automation. Suppose the design company asked you to make changes to the previous Flash template - the area of the generated table should be reduced to half of its vertical space, because they need to place a rectangular advertisement in the bottom half of the screen. This is a problem because tables with many rows will have trouble fitting into the remaining area. This calls for a vertical scroll bar on the table!

First of all stretch the Table object icon using the scale tool, to define the new area of the generated table that will be scrolled by the Turbine driver. Then, choose the Glass Class scroll bar, from the Turbine driver library and place it at the top right corner of the Table object icon:

2.   After adding the rectangular area for the advert, save the new Flash template. The web browser will then show us a fully functional scrolling list of products that will work for any number of products:

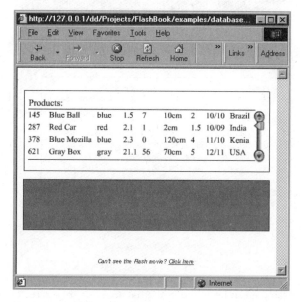

Not too pretty, but you get the point.

The source for this example can be found in the `database_table2` directory on the CD.

Advanced features

In this section we'll introduce two important features, the Draw Script language and movie caching.

The Draw Script language

Draw Script is a simple language that can be used to draw shapes, text, images, and movie clips inside Flash movies. The advantage of using this language over drawing in the Flash editor is the ability to use it in a dynamic manner. A good example is drawing a route on a map depending on user choices, or dynamic parameters.

You can use Draw Script by placing the Draw command in an input text field somewhere in your Flash template:

```
<Draw>
    draw_script_commands()
</Draw>
```

The various draw_script_commands can be any of the ones we'll see in the next section. For example, to draw an X shape we would do:

```
<Draw>
    Line(0,0,  100,100)
    Line(0,100,  100,0)
</Draw>
```

This example would draw an X shape like this:

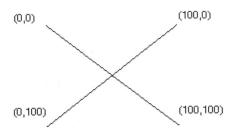

All the points used in these commands are in pixel units, relative to the top left corner of the input text field where the command was issued. The Draw Script commands can be on distinct lines, or on the same line. Comment lines can be introduced by starting the line with a hash sign (#this is a comment).

Within Draw Script commands, you can freely use Turbine variables. For example, it's perfectly possible to have:

```
<Draw>
    Line({x1},{y1},  {x2},{y2})
</Draw>
```

If we define the variables x1, y1, x2, and y2, this command will draw a line between the two points. You can even define groups of Draw Script commands into a single Turbine variable. For example, define the Turbine variable DrawCommands as Line(0,0,100,100) Line(0,100,100,0), and then place:

```
<Draw>
    {DrawCommands}
</Draw>
```

Draw Script commands can also be loaded from a file. This is accomplished by the `DrawFile` template command (the `DrawFile` Turbine object is also available in the Turbine Object library):

```
<DrawFile src="draw_script_file_location">
```

The parameter `src="draw_script_file_location"` is the relative or absolute path, or an HTTP URL to a file with Draw Script commands. But just what are these commands?

Drawing shapes

These commands let us draw lines and polygons. The line width and color can be specified, as well as the fill color. These are the most important commands with examples of usage:

Command	Examples	Visual Results
Line(x1,y1,x2,y2)	Line(0,0,100,100)	
MoveTo(x,y) and LineTo(x,y)	MoveTo(0,50) LineTo(100,50)	
LineStyle(width,color)	LineStyle(9,#FF0000) Line(0,100,100,0)	
Triangle (x1,y1,x2,y2,x3,y3)	Triangle (0,50,100,100,100,0)	
Rectangle(x1,y1,x2,y2)	Rectangle(0,0,100,100)	
FillColorLeft(color)	FillColorLeft(#FF0000) Rectangle(0,0,100,100)	

Colors can be specified in the usual manner, with or without the alpha channel component: #RRGGBB or #AARRGGBB. For example #FF0000 is pure red (no transparency) while #80FF0000 is semi-transparent red.

Placing text

Text can be drawn with the same freedom as shapes:

Command	Examples	Visual Results
Text("str",x,y,scalex, scaley rotation,alpha)	Text("Amsterdam", 50,50,1,1,30)	Amsterdam

(only the first 3 parameters are mandatory)

TextFont(size,"font_face")	TextFont(40,"Arial") Text("North", 50,50)	North

TextColor(color)	TextColor(#FF0000) Text("South",50,50)	South

One limitation that applies is that you can only use fonts defined (used at least once) in the movie.

Placing images and movie clips

The ability to draw images and movie clips dynamically can also be extremely useful:

Command	Examples	Visual Results
Image("image_filename", x,y,width, height,angle, alpha, "center-point")	Image("logo.png", 0,0)	///Turbine

(only the first 3 parameters are mandatory)

MovieClip("name","instance_ name",x,y,scalex, scaley,angle,alpha)	MovieClip("water_ drop", "drop1",50, 0)	

(only the first 4 parameters are mandatory)

The rules for the Image and Movie Clip template commands that we've seen in the previous chapter also apply to these Draw Script commands.

Caching movies

Our friend, the software engineer, just appeared with an uneasy question: Is it really a good idea to generate dynamic movies on each and every web request?

The point is that the data access operations involved in generating a Flash movie can impose heavy loads on database servers or other back-office servers, so the more dynamic movies a site holds, the more load the machinery will have to take (this is also an issue for normal CGI scripts, of course).

Even worse, while the generated movies sometimes include content that might be unique to each request, at other times content will be identical for most consecutive requests. Typical examples of this are online news sites, which update their content only a few times per day or week.

As we mentioned in the previous chapters, ASP Flash Turbine includes movie-caching functionality, fully tunable from inside ASP scripts. By caching a generated movie for a certain period of time, all the requests for the movie during this period will receive the cached version of the original generated movie, thus avoiding any data access – it's simply served from the disk cache. After the caching period terminates, the subsequent movies will be generated as usual. For example, suppose you want to cache a generated movie for 24 hours; the first request after that 24-hour period expires will generate a fresh movie that will be cached for another 24 hour period, and so on.

Generated movie caching is done by calling a scripting command – the `Cache` command:

```
Turbine.Cache "expires"
```

The `expires` parameter specifies how long the generated movie should be stored in the cache. During this period, all the requested movies will be served straight from this cache, avoiding any content inclusion or database access that the ASP script might do. This period can be specified in three different ways:

- The end date of the caching period, specified in a format like YYYYMMDDHHMMSS – where the YYYY stands for the year, MM the month, DD the day and so on till seconds. For example, 20011225000000 the movie will be cached until December 25, 2001 at 00:00:00.

- A time interval counting from the moment the command is called – for example, cache the movie for the next six hours. Typically, this is the simplest way to reduce load on sites that don't change frequently. This interval is specified by the ++ syntax. For example: ++0100 means cache for one minute from serve time.

- A subset of a date – for example, cache until the current hour, 59 minutes and 59 seconds. This would generate one movie per hour.

If a valid movie is found in the cache, it will be served. ASP script processing will stop right there, thus avoiding extra generation effort. However if the movie is not in the cache, or has expired, the movie will be generated as usual and added to the cache, so that next time it will be directly served from there.

Usually you will want to use the Cache command in the following sequence:

```
<%
'...
'  ... cache for 30 minutes
Turbine.Cache "++3000"

'  ... else do the heavy content access work

Turbine.GenerateFlash

%>
```

> *If the movie is cached, script execution will stop at the Turbine.Cache command. When this doesn't happen, execution will continue with any data access being performed. Later, when the movie is generated (by Turbine.GenerateFlash), the resulting movie will be quietly added to the cache to be available for the next requests.*

The movie cache is located inside the `cache` directory inside the Turbine installation directory. All the cached movies are stored there in normal `.swf` format.

An integrated example: TNN, Turbine Network News

This section will discuss the issues behind the implementation of a real world dynamic content Flash situation. We'll cover a news web site displaying news articles with summaries, pictures, and sound.

We chose this illustration because it contains all the necessary techniques for many other common types of web sites, for example live discussion forums, e-commerce and web stores, or personalized portals. Our news articles will also be sorted into different categories, as most modern-day web site applications can be modeled by using some sort of hierarchical organization of categories and items. All of the techniques that you'll see discussed here are applicable for those sites as well.

Because it's always a good idea to give a site an identity, this featured web application will be called TNN – the Turbine Network News!

Structuring the TNN site

Thinking about the structure of our news site, we'll have the following areas:

- A front page movie with the major article headlines – the articles will be listed in the order of their publication date, and will display links to each article, as well as to the various news sections of the site.

- Various news categories – for example Internet, Technology, Sports, etc. These will be dynamic sections, stored in a database, and each article will belong to one of these sections.

- An article area displaying the attributes of the article – a title, a summary, the body of the article, an image associated with the article and an MP3 sound clip (for example an interview or commentary).

In this section we'll work through the creation of this web application, and you can find its full source code in the tnn directory of the Turbine samples on the CD if you want to follow the discussion with a source review.

Now, as advised by our friend the software engineer, we'll start with data definition – which data do we need to store?

Data Design: Articles and Sections

Let's first consider what we need in order to store this information. For instructional purposes, we'll use a common MS Access database – of course, more serious users would have to use some other hi-volume database, since Access wasn't really made for such adventures.

We'll design a database with two tables – Section and Article – the two main data entities we have here. After some crafting in Access we have two tables with defined fields:

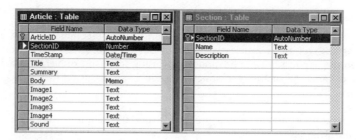

These two tables will store the relevant information relating to the articles and the existing sections. The Article table stores the article's title, summary, and text body. The ImageLocation field stores the local file system path to an image related to the article, and the SoundLocation field stores the path to an MP3 sound file to be included. Another important field is the TimeStamp column, which will be used for ordering the Article lists so that the most recent ones are displayed first. Since each article must belong to a section, the `Article` table has a field named `SectionID`, which will be the foreign key (a link between tables) of the `Section` table — it means the article will belong to that section.

The `Section` table keeps the `SectionId` identification, as well as the name and description of the news sections.

So that we have some content to get us started, we'll fill in a few article sections:

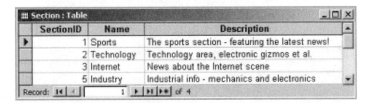

And some articles:

TimeStamp	Title	Summary	Body	ImageLocation
10/10/00	Bears Beat Lakers	The Rome Bears defeat the Paris La	Quid pro quo non sequitur. Dum spir	images/image2.jp
10/12/00	Olympic Games as an	The Olympic Games are considered	Mihi cura futuri; veritas vos liberabit,	images/image3.jp
10/14/00	New Space Technolog	A great new space technolgy will pe	Non compos mentis sui generis mer	images/image1.jp
10/20/00	Yahoo changes Desigr	The Yahoo portal has decided to eve	Terras irradient, nil sine magno labor	images/image1.jp
10/21/00	Flash player on 300 Mi	The Macromedia Flash player is nov	Facio liberos - non sibi, sed suis. Cr	images/image2.jp
10/22/00	DSL Permits Slower B	A communications expert speaks or	Scientia sol mentis, sapientia et doc	images/image4.jp
10/25/00	Electrical Turbine Prod	Statistics reveal that more electrical	Mihi cura futuri; veritas vos liberabit,	images/image3.jp

The Front Page movie

The next step is to create the Flash template for the front page movie (frontmovie.swt), which will consist of two interactive areas: an article list and a section list. When it's finished, it'll look something like this:

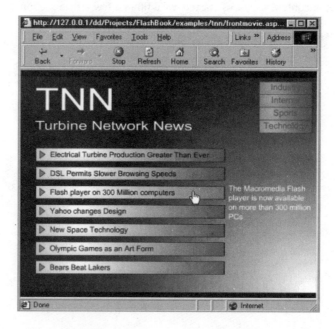

These two areas represent the two different routes for navigating the site. The article list on the left displays the most recent news articles and will allow users to jump directly to the selected article, where they'll be able to see the full text, image, and sound. Alternatively, clicking on one of the sections listed at the top right will take users to a list of the most recent articles belonging to that particular section.

So from this we can see that we'll need to create a couple of dynamic link lists. This looks like a job for the Turbine MovieClip List Object! We'll first design the two movie clips, which will each hold a button to do the actual jump.

Creating the dynamic article list

1.   Open up Flash, create a new movie clip and name it ArticleMovie. Rename Layer 1 of the movie clip as text & button and add a stop action to frame 1. On the stage, create a long rectangular shape similar to this:

2.   Convert the shape into a button named CellButton.

I have also created a triangular arrow on another layer (tri) for effect, although it is not essential to the movie.

3.   We'll be using the button as a way to jump into the actual article, by means of some simple ActionScript, so add this to the button:

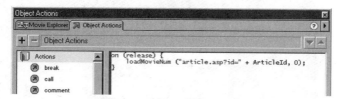

When the user presses the button, the `loadMovieNum` command will be executed, and will request `article.asp`, with the query string parameter id set to the ActionScript variable `ArticleId` (more about this later on).

4.   In order to display the article title over the button we'll create a dynamic text field and give it the variable name `Title`:

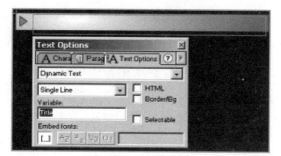

Not only will this button show the article title, but also a summary of the article when the mouse cursor rolls over it! To achieve this let's add another layer to the ArticleMovie movie clip called summary and create a second frame on its timeline with a dynamic text field to hold the summary text – this dynamic text field will have the variable name `Summary`. Don't forget to also add frames to the other two layers to bring them level with summary:

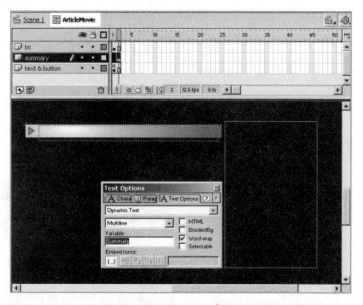

The dynamic text box outlined on the right side will be used to display the article summary, when the mouse rolls over the button. When this happens movie execution will jump to frame 2, until the mouse leaves the button hit area. To do this we add the following ActionScript to the button, after the code we previously inserted:

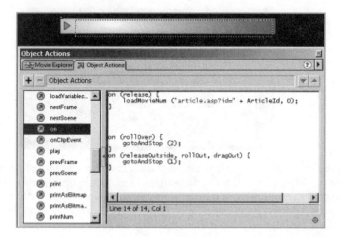

Note that we use gotoAndStop at frame 2 when the mouse enters the button hit area (the rollOver event), and gotoAndStop back to frame 1 when the mouse leaves (on the releaseOutside, rollOut or dragOut events – all the sneaky ways the mouse could escape!). Since the Summary text field is displayed only in frame 2, it will effectively appear when the mouse moves over the button, and disappear when it leaves the button area.

Now that we've created our ArticleMovie movie clip, let's go back to the main stage. Rename Layer 1 as article list. To generate a list of buttons where each one has the Title and Summary text fields and the ArticleId variable defined with information from a DataSet, we'll use the MovieClip List Turbine object. Let's place it on the template (please note the stylish TNN background design, slick minimalism at its best!):

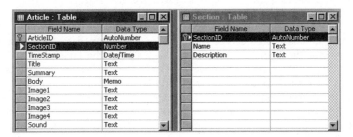

The MovieClip List object will generate a list of instances of the movie clip we've created above filled with information from the database, by means of the FrontArticleDataSet DataSet. Note that the DefaultSymbol field of the MovieClip List object above is set to ArticleMovie, the name of our movie clip.

For the script to access the database we need a DSN – let's call it News_DSN and define it so that it points to our Access database (a DSN can be defined as previously described in the "Accessing the Database" section).

Let's start with the frontmovie.asp script:

```asp
<%
' make sure the movie is not cached by the browser:
Response.Expires=-1

' create the Turbine object:
Set Turbine=Server.CreateObject("Turbine.asp")

' use Flash template frontmovie.swt:
Turbine.Template = "frontmovie.swt"

' open the database connection:
Set Conn = Server.CreateObject("ADODB.Connection")
Conn.Open "DSN=News_DSN"

' query for the 7 most recent articles:
SQLQuery = "Select top 7 ArticleId, Title, Summary from Article
➡order by TimeStamp desc"
Set RS = Conn.Execute(SQLQuery)

' create the FrontArticleDataSet DataSet with the queryresults:
Turbine.LoadDataSetRS RS, "FrontArticleDataSet"
```

```
' finally generate the Flash movie:
Turbine.GenerateFlash
%>
```

The above script will first set the page's `Response.Expires` to -1: this will have the effect of stopping the client browser from caching this movie. We then proceed to create an ASP Turbine object and define which Flash template to use – `frontmovie.swt`.

Next we set up a database connection through the `News_DSN` data source. A query is then performed, asking for the 7 most recent articles – we'll get the latest articles because of the `order by TimeStamp desc` clause, and we'll get only 7 because of the `top 7` term. This query is performed and the results are then pumped inside Turbine with the `Turbine.LoadDataSetRS` command that loads them into the `FrontArticleDataSet` DataSet. This way we'll have a DataSet ready to be used in the MovieClip List object – this DataSet will feature the column fields fetched by the query: `ArticleId`, `Title` and `Summary`. The MovieClip List object will define an instance of the `ArticleMovie` movie clip for each DataSet row, causing each of these synthesized movie clips to have the `ArticleId`, `Title` and `Summary` ActionScript variables defined with the contents of the respective DataSet columns for that row.

Creating the dynamic section list

Now all we need to do to complete the front page is create the list of the article sections in the top right corner.

1. Almost exactly as above, we'll create a new movie clip and call it SectionMovie.

    This movie clip will consist of a small button that will display the section headings and will jump to the relevant section when clicked.

2. Rename Layer 1 of your movie clip as button.

3. Drag an instance of our CellButton from the library and make, it about one third of the original length by using the Scale tool.

4. The ActionScript for this button's release event is:

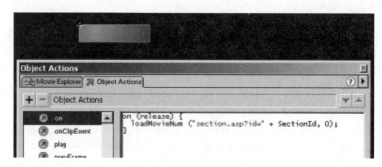

5. We want to display the section name on top of the button, so add a new layer to the movie clip and call it text. On this layer, add a single line dynamic text field over the button with the variable name Name:

6. Now go back to the main stage and insert another layer named section list. On this layer place another MovieClip List object on the stage, this time top right. In the clip parameter panel, we need to specify the DataSet as SectionDataSet and we're using SectionMovie as the DefaultSymbol, we've also set the RowHeight to 24 this time to bring the rows closer together:

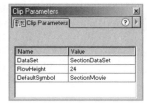

7. Let's go back into our frontmovie.asp script. We need to add the code required to obtain the list of the available sections, which are themselves dynamically obtained from a query to the Section table:

```
<%
' make sure the movie is not cached by the browser:
Response.Expires=-1

' create the Turbine object:
Set Turbine=Server.CreateObject("Turbine.asp")

' use Flash template frontmovie.swt:
Turbine.Template = "frontmovie.swt"

' open the database connection:
Set Conn = Server.CreateObject("ADODB.Connection")
Conn.Open "DSN=News_DSN"

' query for the 7 most recent articles:
SQLQuery = "Select top 7 ArticleId, Title, Summary from Article
➥order by TimeStamp desc"
Set RS = Conn.Execute(SQLQuery)

' create the FrontArticleDataSet DataSet with the query result:
Turbine.LoadDataSetRS RS, "FrontArticleDataSet"

' query for the article sections:
SQLQuery = "Select SectionId, Name from Section order by Name
asc"
```

```
Set RS = Conn.Execute(SQLQuery)

' create the SectionDataSet DataSet with the query result:
Turbine.LoadDataSetRS RS, "SectionDataSet"

' finally generate the Flash movie:
Turbine.GenerateFlash
%>
```

Similar to the article query above we query for the available sections, and then define the results as the `SectionDataSet` DataSet, using the `Turbine.LoadDataSetRS` command. The created `SectionDataSet` DataSet will have two columns: `SectionId` and `Name`, and these will be defined as ActionScript variables inside each instance of SectionMovie synthesized by the MovieClip List object.

8.   Drag instances of ArticleMovie and SectionMovie onto the main stage, and then either set their alpha to 0, or just drag them off-stage so they won't be seen when the page is viewed.

9.   Save your changes to `frontmovie.asp`. By requesting this file through a web browser we'll obtain a working Flash movie, dynamically fed from the database that we defined:

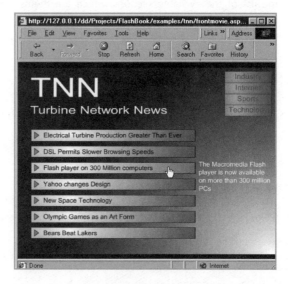

On the left we have the output of the MovieClip List object – a list of movie clips (instances of the ArticleMovie movie clip) filled with information from the `FrontArticleDataSet` DataSet, straight from our `Article` database table. When the mouse rolls over the generated buttons, a summary tool-tip is displayed to the right of the button.

In the top right corner we have another MovieClip List object, with the available section list, retrieved from the `Section` database table. When the user clicks on the section list, we'll jump (by using the `loadMovieNum` command as we've seen above) to the `section.asp` script, which will generate the articles in the selected section. We'll create the section articles area next.

The section articles

This area of the site will present the user with a list of the latest articles in a chosen section. As before we'll use the MovieClip List object, but now we need to do a query that retrieves the most recent articles *from the current section*.

1. We will create a new ASP script called `section.asp`, which is very similar to `frontmovie.asp`, it's just a matter of referencing a new template `section.swt` and changing the database query slightly, by adding the `SectionId` constraint:

```
<%
' make sure the movie is not cached by the browser:
Response.Expires=-1

' create the Turbine object:
Set Turbine=Server.CreateObject("Turbine.asp")

' use Flash template section.swt:
Turbine.Template = "section.swt"

' the id query string parameter has the section id to display:
SectionId = Request("id")

' open the database connection:
Set Conn = Server.CreateObject("ADODB.Connection")
Conn.Open "DSN=News_DSN"

' load the section name and description:
SQLQuery = "Select Name, Description from Section where SectionId
➥= " & SectionId
Set RS = Conn.Execute(SQLQuery)

' define Turbine variables from the query fields:
Turbine.Variable("{SectionName}") = RS("Name")
Turbine.Variable("{SectionDescription}") = RS("Description")

' query the 7 most recent news for this section:
SQLQuery = "Select top 7 ArticleId, Title, Summary from Article
➥where SectionId = " & SectionId & " order by TimeStamp desc"
Set RS = Conn.Execute(SQLQuery)

' create the SectionArticleDataSet Data Set with the query
' result:
Turbine.LoadDataSetRS RS, "SectionArticleDataSet"

' finally generate the Flash movie:
```

```
Turbine.GenerateFlash
%>
```

If you look back at the `loadMovieNum` ActionScript command we placed on the button in the SectionMovie movie clip, you will see that it performs an HTTP request with a query string of the form:

```
section.asp?id=
```

The `id` query string parameter carries the id of the section to display, which we accessed in our ASP script with the following code:

```
SectionId = Request("id")
```

And we then use the `SectionId` VBScript variable to restrict the query to get us only the Section table rows whose `SectionId` column is equal to the number passed in the id query string parameter – this is expressed by:

```
"Select ... where SectionId = " & SectionId
```

Two database queries are performed, the first to define two Turbine variables with the name and description of the section (SectionName and SectionDescription) and a second one that defines the `SectionArticleDataSet` DataSet with the 7 latest articles on the current section.

Let's save this script as `section.asp` and we're ready to define the `section.swt` Flash template, which will have yet another MovieClip List object!

2. Create a new file called `section`, and rename Layer 1 as article list. If you're using the same minimalist backdrop as us, you'll also want to copy that over into this movie. You can also add some static text for the 'TNN – Turbine Network News' tagline, and a border separating the titles from the main content.

3. We'll be using the ArticleMovie movie clip for the list of movie clip elements to be generated, exactly as on the previous `frontmovie.swt` Flash template. To do this, just open up the Library from the original `frontmovie` file and drag the ArticleMovie clip out of there and onto the stage of `section`. Hide it off-stage as you did before.

4. We'll also by adding some Turbine variables. Using the text tool, add the text {SectionName} News and {SectionDescription} to the stage as shown:

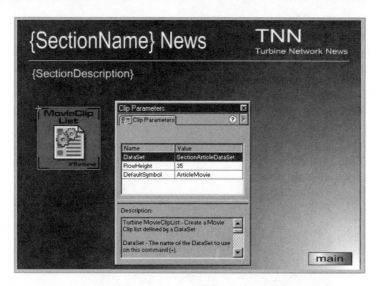

The SectionName and SectionDescription Turbine variables will be substituted by the values defined in the previous ASP script.

5.   You'll also no doubt have noticed that there's a MovieClip List object in the middle of the screen. Drag this out of the Common Library and give it the parameters shown.

6.   We've also added a main button to take the user back to the main screen. This is just a movie clip with a button inside it that contains the following code:

```
on (release) {
loadMovieNum("frontmovie.asp", 0);
}
```

7.   Finally, just save the file, and export it as section.swt.

Now, if the user clicked on the Internet section button on the front page, they'd reach this movie:

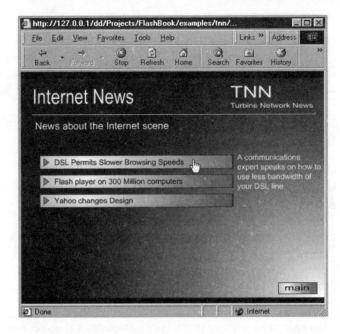

When at last the user clicks on one of the generated article link buttons, we jump to the article display area, constructed from the `article.asp` script and `article.swt` Flash template, which we'll look at next.

The article

This is the movie where the actual article body text will be displayed to the user, together with an image and sound clip, if available.

1. Let's start by defining the text areas we want to display – the title, the summary, and the body text. Rename Layer 1 of your movie as text. On this layer we will place the Turbine variables `ArticleTitle`, and `ArticleSummary`, which are long static text fields, and `ArticleBody` which is a multiline dynamic text field that covers the whole of the rectangle in the screen shot:

2. These variables will be defined from a database query that retrieves information for the specified article – this is of course performed in the article.asp script, which is again similar to the other ASP scripts:

```
<%
' make sure the movie is not cached by the browser:
Response.Expires=-1

' create the Turbine object:
Set Turbine=Server.CreateObject("Turbine.asp")

' use Flash template article.swt:
Turbine.Template = "article.swt"

' the id query string parameter has the article id to display:
ArticleId = Request("id")

' open the database connection:
Set Conn = Server.CreateObject("ADODB.Connection")
Conn.Open "DSN=News_DSN"

' query for the desired article:
SQLQuery = "Select * from Article where ArticleId=" & ArticleId
Set RS = Conn.Execute(SQLQuery)

' define Turbine variables from the query fields:
Turbine.Variable("{ArticleTitle}") = RS("Title")
Turbine.Variable("{ArticleSummary}") = RS("Summary")
Turbine.Variable("{ArticleBody}") = RS("Body")

' finally generate the Flash movie:
```

```
Turbine.GenerateFlash
%>
```

The `id` query string parameter holds the article id for the specific article to be displayed, and we use it to restrict the database query:

```
"Select ... where ArticleId=" & ArticleId
```

Here the `ArticleId` VBScript variable holds the content of the `id` query string parameter. We then define the `ArticleTitle`, `ArticleSummary` and `ArticleBody` Turbine variables to the values of the Title, Summary and Body fields of the query fetched from the Article database table.

3. Each article will also have an attached image and sound clip, so create a new layer called image & sound.

4. The ImageLocation table column specifies the location of each image – the actual image is stored in the web server file system. Let's place an Image Turbine object on the Flash template to the right of the article body area, and specify the SRC for the image to be the Turbine variable {ImageLocation}, which we'll need to define in the ASP script. The Image Turbine object is defined as:

5. The articles will also have an MP3 sound clip - in a similar manner we place a Sound Turbine object on the Flash template, and define the {SoundLocation} Turbine variable on the ASP script to be after the contents of the SoundLocation column fetched from the Article database table:

It doesn't matter where on the stage this is placed, as it represents a sound and therefore won't be seen in the final movie.

6. Now we need to add the code to define the ImageLocation and SoundLocation Turbine variables, ending up with the following ASP script:

```
<%
' make sure the movie is not cached by the browser:
Response.Expires=-1

' create the Turbine object:
Set Turbine=Server.CreateObject("Turbine.asp")

' use Flash template section.swt:
Turbine.Template = "article.swt"
' the id query string parameter has the article id to display:
ArticleId = Request("id")

' open the database connection:
Set Conn = Server.CreateObject("ADODB.Connection")
Conn.Open "DSN=News_DSN"

' query for the desired article:
SQLQuery = "Select * from Article where ArticleId=" & ArticleId
Set RS = Conn.Execute(SQLQuery)

' define Turbine variables from the query fields:
Turbine.Variable("{ArticleTitle}") = RS("Title")
Turbine.Variable("{ArticleSummary}") = RS("Summary")
Turbine.Variable("{ArticleBody}") = RS("Body")

Turbine.Variable("{ImageLocation}") = RS("ImageLocation")
Turbine.Variable("{SoundLocation}") = RS("SoundLocation")

' finally generate the Flash movie:
Turbine.GenerateFlash
%>
```

Here we've defined the ImageLocation and SoundLocation Turbine variables to have the contents of the respective Article database fields.

Now after putting it all together and exporting the SWT, we should be able to run the file. When we access the initial frontmovie.asp through the browser, and select an article, we obtain the complete generated movie:

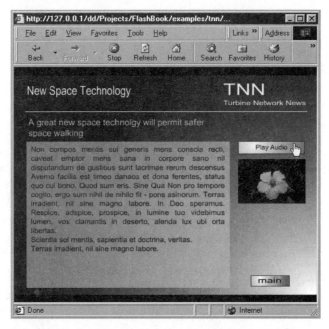

I've also added the same main button from the section file to the bottom right corner, and also a play audio button. Clicking the play audio button will play the MP3 sound file with the ActionScript play command, causing the generated sound to be played by the Flash plug-in. Remember to add a stop action to the first frame of the movie, otherwise the sound will play forever!

Caching for performance

News articles are excellent for caching purposes because the article is composed once, generated from the database, added to the cache, and no more database transactions need to be performed after that since all subsequent requests can be served straight from the movie cache. Of course if the movie includes other items, for example personalized menus, this might not apply directly; however even in those situations it might be possible to separate navigation from the actual content, and keep it in another movie, loaded into some other timeline level.

Cache support can be used by placing the Turbine.Cache scripting command into the ASP Script like this:

```
<%
'... create the Turbine object, specify the Flash template to use ...

Turbine.Cache "++120000"

'... do the database content access and generate the movie ...
%>
```

This scripting command would have the effect of caching the generated movie for 12 hours from the moment it's served.

Expanding TNN

This example could be augmented in many directions, for example:

- By making the article body text scrollable, to allow for any text size

- Adding a scrolling ticker with clickable links – this can be done by using the MovieClip List object together with the Ticker driver, included in the Turbine Driver library

- Allowing for the display of multiple images, maybe a separate template with panning and zoom controls

- Adding an area with links to related articles

- Actually adding some compelling animation would also be great – after all this is the brave new Flash world, not HTML!

The principles that we've seen here allow many similar applications to be deployed, harnessing the power of dynamic content over Flash media.

Summary

Carrying on from the previous chapter, which concentrated on the Turbine template commands, this chapter covered the scripting interface, describing the most important commands available in the ASP Flash Turbine component.

We've seen that:

- Scripting commands are available for variable definition, DataSet loading, automatic HTML plug-in page generation, caching, and more

- The scripting interface of ASP Flash Turbine permits simple integration with content from any data source available from the ASP engine. We've discussed how important databases can be for more complex sites with large data collections, reviewed the creation of a simple database, and explored the mechanics of integrating query results into a Flash template

- The Draw Script language allows dynamic drawing in Flash movies. We've seen some of the possible commands and effects

- The movie caching possibilities can help to produce more scalable and better performing dynamic Flash web sites. How many millions of hits can a nice site like yours take?

- We can integrate Flash media and database supplied content – the TNN example includes some of the principles involved in creating anything ranging from the smallest online newspaper to a gigantic e-commerce site, making them dynamic and cute too!

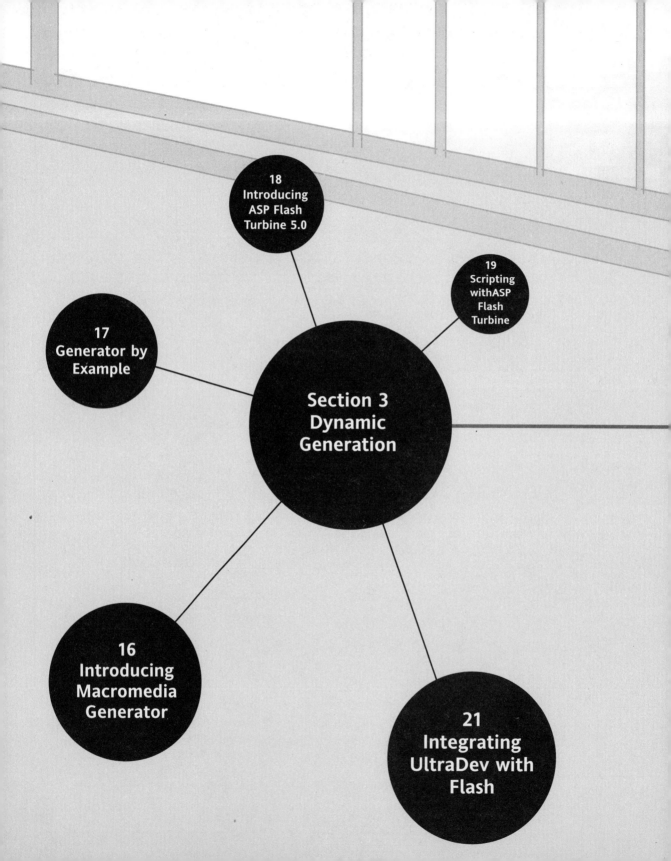

18
Introducing
ASP Flash
Turbine 5.0

19
Scripting
withASP
Flash
Turbine

17
Generator by
Example

Section 3
Dynamic
Generation

16
Introducing
Macromedia
Generator

21
Integrating
UltraDev with
Flash

Chapter 20
Introduction to Dreamweaver UltraDev

Dreamweaver UltraDev is Macromedia's solution for creating data-driven applications. The latest version is the recently released UltraDev 4, so called to bring it in line with Fireworks and Dreamweaver, both currently in their 4th version. Dreamweaver UltraDev adds server-side functionality to the Dreamweaver product, allowing you to connect to databases easily, and generating the necessary JSP, ASP, or CFML code for you. It's powerful stuff!

There are many really powerful web applications on the net today. Among my favorite sites that have been built with UltraDev, is the Snap-On site (www.snapon.com). Snap-On is an international manufacturer of tools and diagnostic equipment. The site developers say that using UltraDev has improved their productivity, while leaving them with complete control over their code.

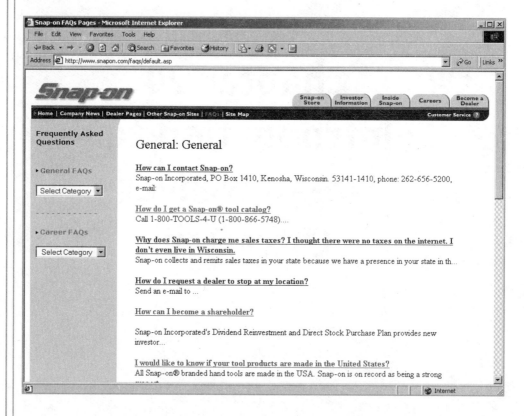

Using UltraDev really does make web application development easy, and in this chapter I'm going to try and show you how. We'll talk though the principles application development, look at how UltraDev manages things for you, and develop a small UltraDev application (although, not from scratch; I've provided a database and some basic pages for you on the CD).

I've made certain assumptions as I've written this chapter: that you've had little or no exposure to UltraDev, that you have a passing familiarity with data-driven web design terminology, and that you're are keen to start creating data-driven sites. So if that describes you, you're in the right place!

By the time you have finished working with this chapter, I hope that you will be armed with enough knowledge of the product to begin creating your own web applications with this extremely powerful tool. You'll certainly be ready to start working with Flash and UltraDev together, which is what we'll do in the next chapter.

So, without further ado, let's get started.

What do you mean by "web application"?

For the purposes of our discussions in this chapter, a web application is simply a collection of pages, sources of data, and other resources that interact in conjunction with a web server. Broadly speaking, it is made up of three things: **linked pages**, **web servers**, and **databases**. Let's look at each of these in turn:

Linked pages
Some of the data displayed on the pages of a web application is likely to be coming in from an external source, so it's thought of as 'dynamic' in that it changes as the source data changes. The data that is going to be added to the web page dynamically is entered onto the web pages in the form of links to the data source (usually a database), when the application itself is built. A link to a piece of data can be used in as many pages as you like within an application.

Web servers
A web server does two things: it serves pages to remote computers that have requested them, and it carries out server-side processing.

UltraDev uses scripting languages for its dynamic data retrieval. Once a page has been requested, the web server processes any scripting language code contained within it, and then sends the page back to the browser in browser readable form (most often HTML). As you'll see later on, a dynamic UltraDev page looks very different to the page the browser gets.

Databases
A database is, of course, a data store. There are a number of databases that you can use with UltraDev, all the way from a simple Access database, to a huge SQL Server enterprise database that can serve thousands of transactions per day. We'll talk about the way you can connect to a database, and request information from it later in the chapter. This won't, however, be a detailed look at databases per se, for that you'll have to check out the database chapters. You will be surprised at how easy UltraDev makes establishing connections with databases, and to add, display, and modify the data within them.

And that's all you need to know about the basic framework of a powerful web application to begin working with UltraDev.

The Dreamweaver UltraDev environment

UltraDev has been built firmly on the foundations of Dreamweaver, so we'll begin our investigation with a look at Dreamweaver's interface and design creation process.

Dreamweaver is what's known as an editor or a **generator**. It allows you to design your site visually. HTML is generated each time you drag and drop a page element onto the workspace, and is kept out of sight unless you choose to view it in a separate window, where you can also manually modify it.

There are three main features in Dreamweaver that make site creation a quick and easy process: visual editing, an extremely clean design interface, and Roundtrip HTML.

Visual editing

It's pretty hard to visualize your design if you're looking at a page of HTML. However, Dreamweaver enables you to create a page to your liking by manipulating objects via a graphical interface. Dreamweaver will then automatically generate the necessary HTML code for you. This also makes any future alterations to the page much easier.

Clean design interface

You are fully in control of Dreamweaver's interface; you can simply "hide" the interface tools that you're not using. To design a page in Dreamweaver you simply switch between views, the visual editor, the text editor, and the floating palettes.

Roundtrip HTML

There are other HTML editors that generate HTML in the background while you work in the visual editor, but all too often, such editors won't accept changes you make to the HTML itself. Dreamweaver, however, will leave well alone any hand coding you do, allowing you to move between code and design views confidently.

Dreamweaver UltraDev incorporates the Dreamweaver interface, and adds server-side functionality to it, allowing you to do both your server-side coding and your designing at the same time.

It is also extremely configurable. The user interface may seem daunting at first, but once you're a used to it, you'll come to appreciate it. The design workspace consists of a main window, in which you design your project, and a set of floating toolbars allowing you to insert Dreamweaver objects, such as forms and tables. You'll also see a menu bar across the top of this workspace with a massive group of design options.

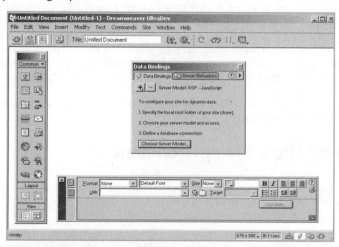

The Objects toolbar

The key to the UltraDev environment is its drag-and-drop functionality. The objects available to you are grouped into palettes, according to the functions they perform. There are eight object palettes by default, and you can supplement these with downloadable extensions.

Let's look at the palette groups available to you. Launch the Objects toolbar, by going to Window>Objects, and select the Common palette from the drop-down list at the top of the toolbar.

Common palette

The Common palette contains sixteen of the most commonly used web page objects, such as tables, layers and email links. You can select these objects using the links on the main menu bar at the top of the workspace, but using the common palette is that little bit quicker. The common palette also allows you to insert items from other Macromedia programs, such as Generator and Flash, as well as SSI (Server Side Includes).

Characters palette

The Characters palette is essentially a group of timesaving buttons that make entering text onto the web page a little quicker. Previous versions of Dreamweaver required users to use keyboard shortcuts to add special characters (such as Yen, Pound, Euro or Copyright symbols) to the page. Now all we have to do is simply click the button on the palette and the character pops up on the page. The Characters palette comes with twelve custom symbols and an Insert Other Character button, which brings up a character map, enabling you to add more shortcut buttons to the palette for extra characters.

Forms palette

The Form**s** palette includes everything you need to insert a Form into a web page, such as text fields, checkboxes, and hidden fields. There are a total of ten available objects.

Frames palette

Anyone who has created frames in raw HTML will appreciate how mind-numbingly tedious it can be. If you use frames in your pages, UltraDev is probably worth the investment for the Frames palette alone. The eight frame objects allow you to specify where your frame should be.

Head palette

The Head palette deals with the unseen content of the web page, and is generally used by search engines to categorize sites. Inserting head content into your web pages is helpful if you want them to be indexed by the engines in order to enable your pages to be listed on the web.

You use the head content of your web site to provide information about your site, its purpose and intended market. For example, if I was in the unlikely position of developing a website for the actor, Arnold Schwarzeneger, I could add keywords such as 'Muscleman' 'Actor', and 'Terminator'. I could also enter a brief description of the site such as 'A definitive biography of the film career of Arnold Schwarzeneger'. Among the objects are Insert Keywords and Insert Meta.

A <meta> tag is a head element that records information about the current page, such as the character encoding, author, copyright, or keywords. These tags can also be used to provide information to the server, such as page expiry date, refresh interval, and the PICS rating for the page. The Platform for Internet Content Selection (www.w3.org/PICS) provides a method for assigning ratings, such as movie ratings, to web pages.

Invisibles palette

The purpose of the Invisibles palette is to make it quicker for you to add in the, well, invisible, but important nonetheless elements of a page; anchors or comments, for example.

A named anchor allows you to link to a specific place in a document. If you've ever read a web document with a link on it that simply sent you further down the same page when you clicked on it, then you've already seen a named anchor in action.

There is also an Insert Script object that allows you to insert a script without switching over to code view. Clicking on it brings you to a window that allows you to specify what sort of script you want to write, VBScript or JavaScript (1.0, 1.1 or 1.2), and then you simply enter your script straight into the content box.

Insert Comment is used to insert comments that are invisible to the browser in an area on the page in either design or code view. The syntax for these comments appears like this:

```
<!--comment text in here -->.
```

Live palette

This palette can be used to add live elements to the page. Live elements are intelligent server behaviors that help speed up the development process. By providing us with objects like Insert Record Update Form, the live palette can significantly reduce the amount of time spent on development.

Special palette

This palette makes adding multimedia elements (such as Applets and plug-ins) to your page quick and easy.

The Properties window

A web page is full of objects and text, and in the course of designing, you're bound to want to change the attributes of various objects on the page. This is where the Properties window comes into play. To launch the Properties window, go to the Window menu and choose Properties.

To use it, simply place an object or enter text onto the page and highlight the content. The Properties window will then enable you to modify any of the attributes.

In this way, the Properties window works in unison with the Objects toolbar, and indeed, the program as a whole. The UltraDev interface is always anticipating your next move, changing according to the tools you are using; which can be a little unnerving at first, but once you're used to it, you'll find it invaluable.

The Launcher

Activated by choosing Window>Launcher, the Launcher's objects can open up the other windows used by UltraDev, including the HTML Source window that allows you to view and modify the HTML code generated by UltraDev. Among the other options on this toolbar are the Data Bindings, Server Behaviors and Site windows, which we'll be working with later on in the chapter.

The Preferences window

To access the Preferences window, go to the Edit menu and choose Preferences. You'll see that there are a lot of preferences that you can set. For example, although UltraDev does have its own HTML editor, which can be accessed via the Launcher, you can opt to use an external editor or graphics editor instead. You can change anything from text color to file extensions through this window.

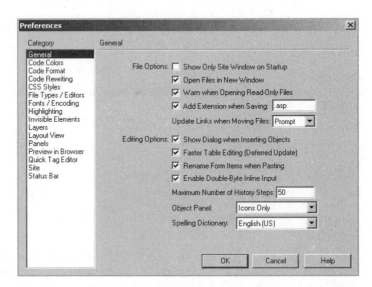

We have briefly covered the interface and tools that you can use to design your web pages using UltraDev, although it has so many features that it's impossible to cover them in just a chapter or two, so I really recommend that you investigate further.

The next thing we should discuss is the technologies available for your use within your projects.

Scripting languages, servers, and databases according to UltraDev

UltraDev currently has support for three scripting languages:

Scripting Language	Servers
CFML	Any web server with ColdFusion 4.0 installed
JSP	IBM Websphere, Allaire Jrun 2.3.3, and any other web server that supports the JSP 1.0 specification
ASP	PWS, IIS or Chilisoft

If you've been working your way through this book from one end to the other, you'll have already worked with all three of these scripting languages. However, for the purposes of this chapter, there are a few things worth noting about each of them.

CFML has good support for database connectivity, as well as good support for HTML editors, because the editors can separate the CFML tags from HTML without interfering with them. CFML can be run on all the major servers, as long as ColdFusion 4.0 or greater is installed, including Windows 9x, NT, 2000, Linux and Unix platforms.

JSP, on the other hand, is a much more widely used technology than ColdFusion, although many people find JSP syntax rather frustrating at first.

Microsoft's ASP is without doubt the most widely supported active content scripting language around today, and fits into HTML pages nicely. Because of its wide user base, you'll find that there are plenty of cheap, if not free, components that you can plug-in to help you carry out certain tasks – uploading files, or sending emails, for example.

Fortunately, like most things, scripting languages are all documented extensively on the Internet. Here are some links may be of use to you when you're deciding which technologies to settle on:

www.deja.com	Search for Macromedia UltraDev in the deja.com discussion forums, where the UltraDev community meet to discuss and solve their UltraDev related issues.
www.15seconds.com	Excellent ASP support: articles, tutorials and components.
www.allaire.com	Good articles and information on CFML scripting language.

| http://sun.java.com | Sun Microsystems provides the latest specs of the APIs and a whole host of other information. |
| http://msdn.microsoft.com | The homepage of the Microsoft Developer Network. |

A word about databases

The number of hits and transactions that you expect your web site to have to deal with will determine the size and power of the database you'll need to use. For a small site, a desktop database system like Microsoft Access or Lotus Approach should be sufficient. If a larger site is in production, then an enterprise scale database like Microsoft SQL Server or Oracle 8I should be considered

In this chapter, as in the rest of the book, we're going to assume that you're using a Windows platform. This immediately suggests an appropriate database: Access. It isn't altogether unrealistic to plump for a database and server model from such considerations; when you're developing application for real, you'll often find that the server you'll have to use will be prescribed rather than a free choice.

Site management UltraDev style

Site management is an extremely important area of web site design. You simply can't spend too much time planning your web site, before you even get near to the workspace and begin creating pages. Think of site management as the process of organizing files; ensuring that they won't be overwritten, and that the corresponding file and folder structures remain intact.

Most web sites are a combination of HTML and image files. It's not uncommon for someone to design a web page on their hard drive, limit their site management process to two folders (one holding all the HTML files, and the other folder containing all the images) and then load the whole lot up to an external server. The pages may look beautiful on the local machine, but unless you're really careful, links will start breaking as soon as you get as far as uploading to an external web server.

Fortunately, UltraDev makes the whole process a great deal easier. The entire site on the local machine lives in one root folder, and every single file lives somewhere inside the root folder or subfolders within the root folder. So, you might still only have two folders, one for HTML pages and the other for images, but they'd be inside subfolders in the root folder. As a result, uploading to a web server wouldn't destroy a single link.

With UltraDev, all the work involved in this process is taken care of. Should you need to change the name of a file or folder, you simply go into what's known as the Site window and rename it there, and UltraDev updates all the necessary links to the newly renamed file or folder.

> *Bearing this in mind, it is important to mention, (although it might seem a bit obvious), that UltraDev cannot take care of files outside of its root folder. Everything must be structured in a way that the root folder is pivotal to the whole site.*

Inside the Site window

You can access the Site window in UltraDev by going to the Window menu and choosing Site Files. The default setting within UltraDev is to have the Local Folder in the right-hand pane and the Remote Site in the left-hand pane.

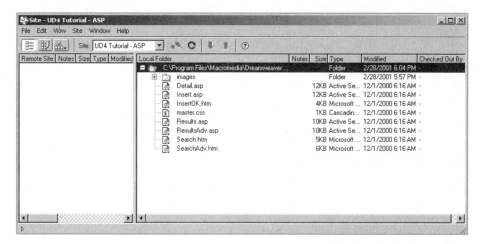

There are some useful options that relate to working with remote sites through FTP within the Site FTP area of the Preferences window. You can also find options that help you work with an external site located behind a firewall. This window essentially has everything you need to configure an externally hosted site.

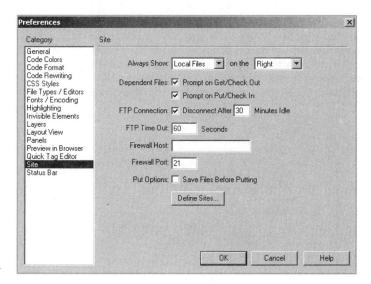

Go back to the Site window, and look at the toolbar at the top. This contains several important options.

Working from the left, let's take a look at the buttons on this toolbar and their functions:

Site Files	Shows all the files in your site.
Application Server	Connects you to the application server-side of your site window.
Site Map	Prepares a site map that visually represents all the linked pages in the site oriented around the default home page. (See figure below)
Connect to remote host	Enables you to connect disconnect from a remote site.
Refresh	In UltraDev, files can be created within the site window or the workspace window. If sites are created outside of the site window while this window is open, hitting refresh will recreate the site within the site window.
Get File(s)	Gets files from the remote site; highlight them in the Remote Folder and click.
Put File(s)	Puts files into the remote folder: highlight one or more files in the Local Site pane and click.

UltraDev's Site Map window (Window > Site Map) provides a visual representation of the navigation of your site. This window is an excellent tool for examining the structure of your site; you might even use it to demonstrate the results of your hard work to a client or design team. You can change the links in the site from inside the site map. Notice that all the files are coming from the index.html file in this example, which is the home page of the site.

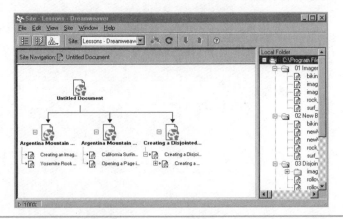

Working with the Site window

Working with the Site window to update a remote web server is, thankfully, extremely intuitive. As long as you have a very clear idea of the shape of your site, and have thought carefully about site management, you can realize your ideas extremely easily by using UltraDev.

Later on in this chapter we'll be working with an example site, and once you've populated it locally with enough files, you'll want to upload it to the remote server. To do all this, all you need to do is go to the Site menu and choose Synchronize.

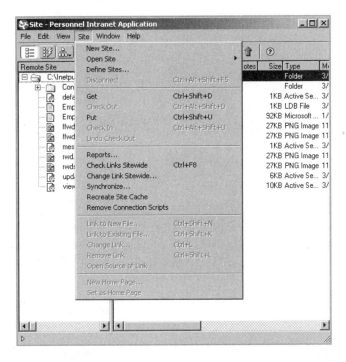

Once you've chosen the Synchronize option, a little option box comes up asking you to specify the level of synchronization you want.

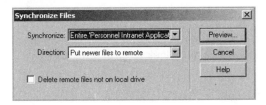

There are a number of options available to you:

Synchronize field	Direction field	Result
Entire Site	Put newer files to remote	Takes all files from the local site and puts them in the remote folder. This option will have the effect of overwriting any older versions of files on the remote site with newer ones from the local site.
Entire Site	Get newer files from remote	Replaces older versions of files on the local site with the newer versions from the remote site.
Entire Site	Get and Put newer files	Updates both the local and remote sites with newer versions of any files.
Selected Local, Files Only	Put Newer Files to Remote	Place selected files from the local site in the remote site. This option will have the effect of overwriting any older versions of files on the remote site with newer ones from the local site.
Selected Local Files Only	Get Newer Files from Remote	Replaces older versions of selected files on the local site with the newer versions from the Remote Site.
Selected Local Files Only	Get and Put Newer Files	Updates both the local and remote sites with newer versions of the selected files.
Delete Remote Files not on Local Drive		Deletes any files from the remote web site that do not exist on the local site on synchronization.

Both the site window and the site map will really help you develop your site. If you're intending to develop web applications as part for a team, there are two more features of UltraDev that you should know about, so we'll take a quick look at them next.

Design notes

Design Notes are available both in the site and design windows, under the File menu. They do pretty much what you might imagine, allowing you and your co-developers to add comments about the progress of particular site file throughout the development process.

You can alter the status of the file in the development process using design notes, for example labeling them draft or beta, and provide comments through the dialogue box provided about the progress of each file.

Visual Source Safe integration and WebDAV
This feature allows you to access version control of your site files from within the Site window. **WebDAV** (Web Distributed Authoring Protocol) is a protocol supported by IIS5 and Apache Web Server. It controls the versioning of team development applications. You can connect to Visual Source Safe databases or servers, which support the WebDAV protocol.

Visual Source Safe (VSS) is a database that controls versioning and helps team development run smoothly. Clients who wish to attach to a VSS database using the WebDAV protocol must have Microsoft's Visual Source Safe Client 6 installed.

Now, I think it is fair to say that we have covered the theory essentials behind developing data-driven sites with UltraDev, so we're ready to start constructing a web application using UltraDev.

We will define a site on a web server, and develop a database for the web application. We will also, of course, design the required UltraDev pages and connect to the database.

Developing an employee records intranet application

It's about time we actually started doing something useful with UltraDev, so let's build an intranet application using the tools and techniques UltraDev has to offer.

We'll build a simple company intranet application. Our fictitious company has set up an Intranet service in their offices, and wants the staff in the personnel department to be able to view and update the company's employee database using their browsers. The personnel staff need to be able to view the data, add records to it, and run searches.

In order to build this application, we will have to:

- Configure the web server so that it can host the active content pages that we will create in UltraDev.

- Define the site inside UltraDev, and connect it to the web server.

- Connect the Access database to the pages that we built within UltraDev, so that we can view and update the contents of the tables.

Technology choices

Before we go on any further, I should point out that for this section I will be using ASP 2.0 with VBScript as the scripting language, and the database will be Microsoft Access. For my web server I will be using Personal Web Server, which comes free with Windows 95, 98 and 98 ME and 2000. I'll just spend a minute or two discussing why I have chosen this model.

I have chosen ASP 2.0 because it's supported in UltraDev, and of course, UltraDev generates ASP code. As a result, the active content that we'll be using in our dynamic pages will be generated by UltraDev, and executed by the web server at run time, on the fly.

I have chosen Access as it an extremely versatile desktop Database application. The ODBC drivers for the database are widely available, and for the purpose of this small application, it is ideal for our needs.

I have included the Access database that we shall be using on the CD accompanying this. For information on databases in general and how they can be linked in with Flash projects, you'll find the databases chapters of this book to be a good source of information.

To help you gain specific knowledge of Access, help is available via the Access homepage at:

www.microsoft.com/office/access/

IIS is the standard choice for hosting web applications on the Internet due to its superiority over Personal Web Server (PWS). PWS is a cut down version of IIS, and is very easy to use and configure for small sites with up to 5 concurrent connections. We'll walk through configuring PWS and then IIS, so if you're using IIS, you can just skip the next couple of pages.

Configuring your PWS server

As I am using a PWS / Windows 98 solution, this is the method I am using to configure both my local and remote site folders. If you are using a different web server you may wish to skip this section or simply use it as a pointer.

You can find out the status of your installation of PWS by holding your mouse over the icon it dropped onto your toolbar when you first installed it (there's an installation walk though in the *Talking to the Server* chapter, so flick back to there if you need that). If all is well, the ToolTip should say Personal Web Server is running.

Double-click the PWS icon, to bring up the Personal Web Manager. This is an extremely basic version of the Microsoft Management Console (MMC) that ships with IIS. We will use this window to configure our remote site for use with UltraDev.

You can use the Personal Web Manager to monitor your web server. You can see how many users have accessed your site, how many concurrent connections you have had, and take advantage of the host of other monitoring options that are available.

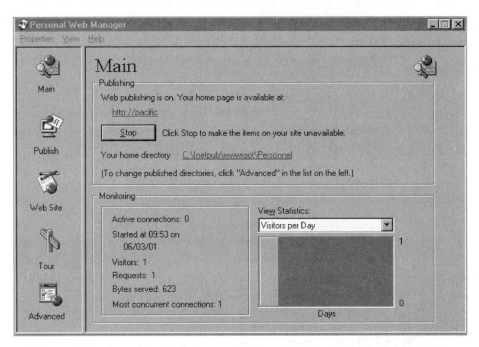

The image above shows the Main window of my Personal Web Manager. From this you can see that my local web site is called http://pacific; this is because pacific is the name of my machine, and my homepage is configured to run on http://pacific. (You can use http://localhost or even http://127.0.0.1 to access the server on any machine, as well as the computer's network name).

We'll create a remote web site folder on our web server, in Personal Web Manager, to host our UltraDev web application. It is in this folder that the ASP code in our active content pages will be turned into a browser-friendly web page at runtime.

Creating a remote folder

To create a remote folder to host the web site on the server, note that the default PWS location for remote folders is within C:\Inetpub\wwwroot. It is in this location we will create a folder to host our server-side web application.

We'll create a folder in the C:\Inetpub\wwwroot folder on our hard drive, and name it Personnel. It should be noted that if PWS is installed on another hard drive or different partition with a different drive letter than C: then you must substitute C: for the letter of the required drive.

Once our Personnel folder has been created in the correct location, all we have to do is point our web server towards it.

1. Go back into Personal Web Manager and click the Stop button to stop the web server, so that we can change the location of the default web site and homepage to

suit our needs for this project. When PWS has been stopped, we can move into the Advanced window to begin configuring PWS to host our remote site.

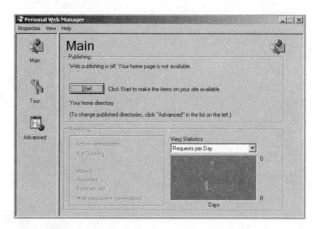

You'll find all the options available for configuring a web site inside the advanced view of PWS. There are the virtual directories, a list of options regarding the default homepage name, and a list of other security related checkboxes.

All you need to do is change the title of the default document, and then browse to the Personnel folder on your hard drive to show PWS the location of the remote folder.

2.   So, we do in fact want to set our default document to be default.asp (which is an ASP page you'll find on the CD). It is very similar to Index.html in web design, in the sense that a web server always considers this file to be the first page in a site. Of course, because we'll be using ASP, we need to use the .asp extension throughout the site. Change your Default Document to default.asp (if it isn't already), and ensure that the Enable Default Document checkbox is checked, as we want this to confirm that this will be our default document.

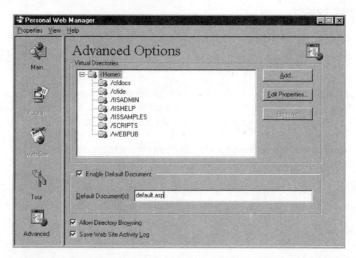

3. Now that your Default Document is set as `default.asp`, let's set our remote folder within PWS. Browse to the Personnel folder that we set up within Windows Explorer earlier. In the Advanced view of Personal Web Manager, highlight the <Home> virtual directory within the Virtual Directories field. Click the Edit Properties button and then click the Browse button.

4. Navigate to C:\Inetpub\wwwroot\Personnel and click OK. You'll see that the Directory: field is set to C:\Inetpub\wwwroot\Personnel.

5. For the purpose of setting up a simple application on PWS, we'll leave the Read, Execute and Scripts checkboxes checked. Click OK again and you are back in the advanced view again. All that remains in our PWS set up is to check that it was successful.

6. Go back into the Main view and click on the Start button to restart PWS. When the server restarts we will see that Your home directory is configured to C:\Inetpub\wwwroot\Personnel. Now close the PWS manager – you've finished configuring your web server for your remote site!

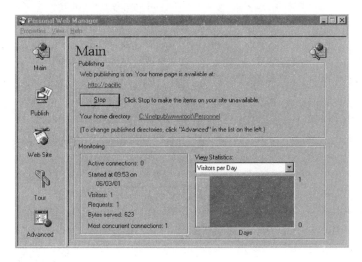

Working with IIS

Although I am working with PWS in these chapters, you might prefer to work with IIS (Internet Information Services), so I'll talk about its configuration here. First, though, it would be a good idea to talk about the differences and similarities between PWS and IIS. We will look briefly at the installation and configuration of IIS within the focus of our project.

Why not use IIS?

Before writing these chapters on UltraDev, I thought about using IIS as the preferred web server for the UltraDev web applications. Given that IIS is the standard web server for the Windows 2000 and NT platforms, I thought, why not simply stick to the standard of using this server and leave

PWS as an optional web server for the readers of this chapter? I decided that to only use IIS as the web server for our applications would discriminate against certain readers and actually bar them from using UltraDev on their local machines for the following reasons:

- **IIS only works on NT Server and 2000**: For users of Windows NT Workstation, 95 and 98, there is no option of using IIS as a web server on the local machine, as the operating systems cannot support the technology. It would not be fair to assume that every reader has an operating system capable of running IIS. So, for that reason I decided to stick with PWS as it runs on all of the operating systems we have mentioned here (Windows 95, 98, NT Workstation and 2000 Professional).

- **IIS is a 'bigger' technology than PWS**: PWS is a basic version of IIS. I feel IIS has a host of extremely powerful and versatile options that may distract us from the UltraDev learning process, and as a result, we could end up talking about IIS all day and never move on to UltraDev. PWS on the other hand, is great for the simple process of hosting a local or small Intranet site and processing the active content on our pages. But make no mistake; if I were considering having one of my sites on the Internet for general use - I would only consider using IIS or some other industrial strength web server as the backbone for my site, PWS will simply not cut the mustard!

IIS has, of course, many advantages over PWS; it has many of them being great enterprise-level advantages, some of which include:

- Index Server: indexes a site, and can be used as the basis for searching the content.

- SMTP (Simple Mail Transport Protocol) Service: meaning that IIS can be used as an email server.

- NNTP (Network News Transfer Protocol) Service: hosts private newsgroups with IIS.

- Security: IIS has powerful industry standard security settings, and administrative tools that make it easy to control its security features.

However, PWS does have some great advantages for local/small Intranet development, precisely because PWS is the 'little brother' of IIS, and the two programs are built from the same technology. These advantages include:

- Simple Administration.

- Statistics: PWS Manager can provide you with some simple but valuable statistics on the level of traffic on your site.

What you do need to bear in mind is this: PWS has a five concurrent connection limit. If your project is going to require more than five users to be connected to your site at once, then it is time to upgrade to IIS.

Now that I have put to you some of my reasons for using PWS over IIS, we'll look at how you configure IIS for UltraDev.

Configuring your IIS server

1. If you installed IIS earlier, you can access it by going to Start>Settings>Control Panel>Administrative Tools and choosing Internet Services Manager.

2. You should now be in the IIS Management Console window. Click on your machine name in the left-hand pane.

3. You'll see up to three icons appear in the right-hand pane (Default FTP, Default Web Site, Default SMTP Virtual Server). Check that the State of the Default Web Site is Running in the right-hand pane. If it isn't, right-click on the Default Web Site icon and select Start. (If IIS isn't running, we won't be able to see any of our active content in a browser; which is akin to working blind!).

4. To finalize configuration, right-click the Default Web Site icon and select Properties. Now we're ready to configure the IP address and default directory.

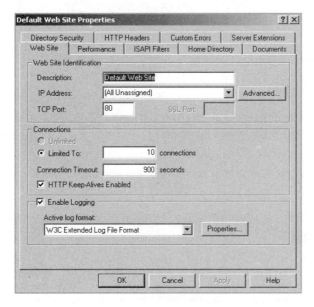

5. On the Web Site tab of the Default Web Site Properties window, ensure that the IP Address is (All Unassigned).

6. Now switch to the Home Directory tab. In mine the home directory is C:\Inetpub\wwwroot\UD Webs.

IIS will process and host your pages in this folder. You can have your home directory put anywhere on your hard drive.

IIS, PWS and UltraDev

One of the subtle differences between using IIS and PWS with UltraDev, is that IIS considers a site hosted on a local machine to be a local site, whereas PWS considers the site to be in a remote folder.

So that's all there is to it. You've installed and configured IIS, and now you're ready to start working with UltraDev.

Defining the employee application UltraDev site

We'll create the local site next. This is where, in a production environment, all the pages would be kept before they are sent off to the web server for processing. We will look in detail at the process, which should help illustrate some of what UltraDev has to offer.

Creating a local folder

UltraDev requires a root folder to hold all the elements of the web application. This is as good a time as any to create a folder on our hard drive to host your local web application.

It's not too important where the local folder is kept on your hard drive, as long it's not in the folder structure of your web server folders i.e. C:\Inetpub\. I have a folder on my hard drive called UD Web Sites for all my local web site files. I keep them in this folder as it makes administering local sites a little easier. In these days of ever-expanding hard drive sizes, it is not a good idea to have local sites scattered all over your file structure, as they may become rather difficult to find!

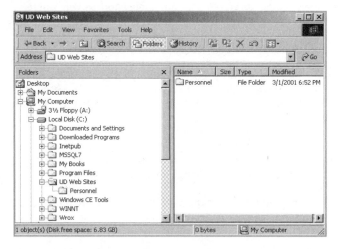

1. Create the local site folder using Windows Explorer, and call it Personnel, to keep everything in line with the naming conventions we assumed earlier by calling our remote folder Personnel.

   With the local root folder safely created on our hard drive, let's press on and define our site within UltraDev.

2. Fire-up UltraDev, and go into the Site window. Choose Site>New Site. This will bring up the Site Definition dialog that we will need in order to define our site. This is the area where we can set all of the required preferences for both our local and remote sites.

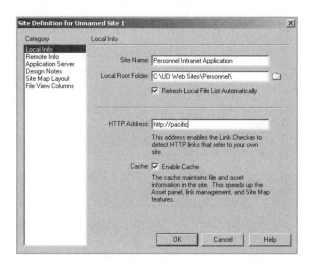

There are six possible categories that we can use to define an UltraDev site. We only need worry about three right now: Local Info, which is used to set all the local attributes for our web application, Web Server Info, which is used to set or modify our web server folder preferences, and Application Server, where we set the attributes relating to our scripting language model and live data server model.

3.   At this point we should inspect all of the attributes we have set here in the Local Info category window. In the Site Name section, I entered Personnel Intranet Application (the Site Name that you choose is entirely up to you). The name is only used to help you browse between the sites that you have within UltraDev. You can view every site that you have defined within the UltraDev Site window by selecting them from the Site drop-down list on the toolbar.

4.   I browsed to the locally defined folder on my hard drive area that will be the Local Root Folder. This is where the local site lives. To browse, click the yellow folder to the right of the text box, which brings up a Windows Explorer type window.

5.   Finally, leave the Refresh Local File List Automatically option checked. This means that when files are created or deleted or renamed in an external program, like Windows Explorer, the UltraDev file list will be updated automatically.

These are the only options you need to set to define a site locally within UltraDev. In the other options I have given the HTTP Address as http://pacific. This is the name of my local machine. When I launch this link within a browser on my local machine, it will display the default homepage of any site defined on the machine, this will be shown later. You might also like to Enable Cache, as this will speed up the browsing process.

6.   Now that you've defined the local site, let's move on to the next category, Remote Info. This is where we need to define the web server location of our remote site.

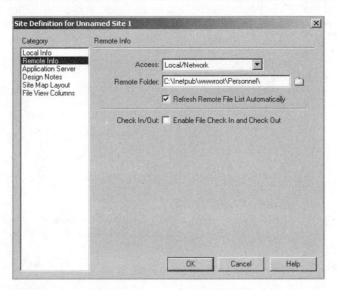

7. The first option you have is the Access field. Choose Local/Network if your remote folder resides on your local machine. The other options are:

- None which should be chosen where there is no active content on the site's pages, and a web server is therefore not needed.

- FTP, which is normally used when the site is uploaded to an external web host, for example, an ISP. The party responsible for the FTP host will normally provide the requisite FTP information.

8. Browse to the location of the remote folder on the web server through the Remote Folder field that you defined earlier. I also left the default option to Refresh Remote File List Automatically checked.

9. Now we need to set the attributes inside the Application Server category. Define the Server Model as ASP 2.0 because we will be using ASP in this example.

10. The URL Prefix that I used was http://localhost. You can use http://localhost as long as the Live Data and web servers both reside on the same machine as UltraDev.

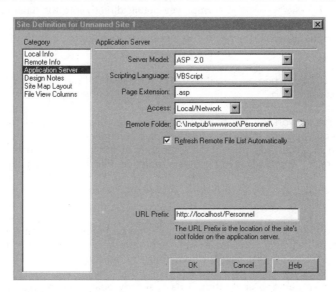

Now you're site is fully defined, so click OK, and check the Enable Cache checkbox, as this will greatly speed up the performance.

Once you've created the cache, you should see a link appear to the Personnel folder that you set up on your hard drive earlier in the Local Folder. In the Remote Site, there should be a link to the Personnel folder that we created on the web server. All is well!

Now we've successfully defined the UltraDev site, all we have to do is get some files into the Local Folder, and begin working with pages.

12. There are some files on the CD for you to use, so go into the CD, and copy the contents of the UltraDev folder into your Local Folder C:\UD Web Sites\Personnel. This populates the Local Folder with some partly completed ASP files that we can work with to get a feel for how UltraDev works.

13. When the files are copied across, go back into UltraDev. The files should now be visible in the Local Folder pane of UltraDev's Site window. If they are not, hit the Refresh button and they should then appear.

The Local Folder should now contain three ASP files, four image files and an Access Database. I have provided a small description into the background and purpose of each file:

`default.asp`	Homepage of Personnel Intranet Application. This partly completed file acts as a menu to link to the other pages in the application.
`view.asp`	This partly-completed file is where the contents of the database can be viewed `update.asp` A partly completed form page where the user of the application can enter new employee details directly into the database.
`Employee_Details.mdb`	A completed Access database in which the employee details are kept.
`ffwd.png, ffwdend.png, rwd.png, rwdsta.png`	Image files for the use of navigation buttons in `view.asp`

Now we can start work on the pages within our site. Once the site is completed locally and uploaded to our web site, it will be a functioning web application with full database connectivity. While simple in layout and presentation, the aim of this application is to show you just how powerful UltraDev is, providing you with the tools required to build web applications rapidly.

The default.asp page

The first page in the site is `default.asp`. It should be noted that when a web server with ASP hosting capabilities first receives a web application, it will look for the existence of a `default.asp` file as the first page, or home page to index by.

In the context of our web application, I have already built some of `default.asp` in order to demonstrate how to turn text on a web page into a hyperlink to other pages within the site. In our application, `default.asp` will act as a welcome page to the user and provide them with a link to the other pages in the site.

Creating a hyperlink

1. To begin working with our default.asp file, open up the Site window, go to the Local Folder window and double-click on the default.asp file to launch it into the UltraDev workspace:

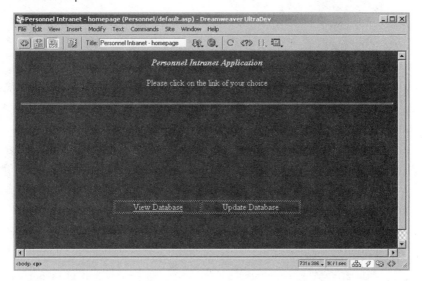

The file in the workspace window has a heading that tells the user to click on the link of their choice of the two options beneath (View Database or Update Database). Notice that the View Database option is a link and the Update Database one is not. Let's start by looking at the View Database link.

2. To do this, highlight the text with your mouse. Then go to the Window menu and choose Properties. The properties of the highlighted text will then be displayed in the Properties window:

Within the properties of the highlighted text, look at the Link, it is pointing to a file called view.asp. We know that view.asp is the ASP page in which the database can be viewed.

We also want the Update Database text on our web page to point towards the ASP page update.asp. Let's see how we would accomplish this.

3. In the workspace, highlight the text Update Database. Within the Properties window, click on the little browse folder to the right of the Link field. Once the browsing window is active, select the update.asp file, then click OK. Once this is done, the Update Database text will become linked to the update.asp file within our site.

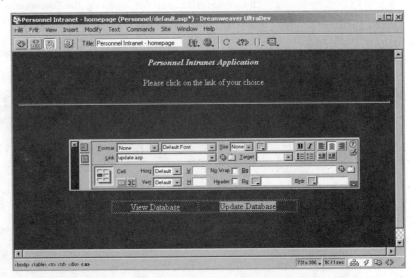

From the image, we can see that the text is now updated to link to the correct update.asp file. That's how easy it is to create a link between two pages within UltraDev. This completes our default.asp page, and gives our welcome page a navigation system that works.

ASP database connectivity

At the heart of our web application is our database. Outside of default.asp, the other pages in the application involve active content and database interaction. Before we press ahead and complete the other pages, we should look at the components and behaviors related to our database and application pages that we should utilize.

Our web application involves page-to-database and database-to-page data flow. While our database is simple, in the terms that it has only one table, the processes involved in connecting it to a web page would be exactly the same if we were connecting a web page to an enterprise level multi-table database.

Before we start work on our data-driven web pages, we have to lay the groundwork for setting up a database connection that we can use within UltraDev. To do this we have to create a connection that can be used by anyone who works on the machine. The connection will not be site specific so we can use it on other sites, but it will be specific to the desired database that we want to use. It will also have to be specific to the database application and version we are using.

We'll make this connection from Windows, and then access it from outside UltraDev, so that we could, if we wanted, use it with another development tool later on.

The technology we will be using to create a connection to our database is known as ODBC. This stands for Open DataBase Connectivity and will be the basis of our web page/database connection. Think of ODBC as being an agent between a web application and a database that exists because a web application cannot interact with a database directly. (Databases are examined in their own right in later chapters, so we're not going to examine database theory here.)

Connecting to the database

1. To create a DSN (Data Source Name) for the connection, go into the Control Panel and double-click on the Data Sources (ODBC) icon. This will bring up the ODBC Data Source Administrator window where we will create the connection to our database. Note that if you're using Windows 2000, the data sources will be in the Administrative Tools section.

> *A DSN is simply defines a connection to a database that can be used by many different web applications. The DSN holds details on the type of database and its path on our system. Once created, a DSN can be reused countless times.*

2. Once you're inside the ODBC Data Source Administrator, click on the System DSN tab. It is imperative that we create a System DSN, otherwise the DSN will not be accessible to all users.

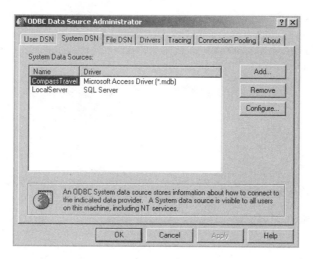

3.   We want to create a new DSN, so click the Add... button. Select a Microsoft Access driver (.mdb) driver, and then click Finish.

> *If you do not have the correct driver installed on your system for the type of database you are using, contact the vendor of your database solution, to check the availability of drivers.*

The ODBC Microsoft Access Setup window will come up. This is where we can connect the DSN to the Employee_Details database.

4.   Call the DSN Employee, and put anything descriptive you like in the Description field.

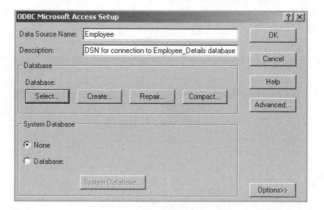

5.   Then click Select and browse to the location of the Employee_Details.mdb Access database with the .mdb extension on your hard drive. It should be in the root folder of the web application – the root folder of my application is inside the C:\UD Web Sites\Personnel folder.

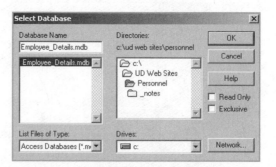

6.   Once you have selected the database, click OK (notice the path to the database is visible in the ODBC Microsoft Access Setup window).

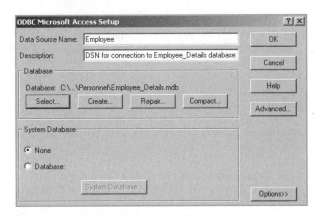

7. Now click OK again, and you'll find yourself back in the ODBC Data Source Administrator window. You'll see that the Employee DSN has been added to the list of system data sources. Click OK to exit and finish.

What we've done by setting up this DSN is made the data in the Employee_Details database available to any program that knows how to use ODBC, so that other programs can access the information stored in the database without having to actually open the database. Pretty cool huh?

Now we've created the database connection, we can begin work on the ASP pages in the site, and look at the appropriate technologies that we will be using in the UltraDev workspace to add active content to our web application.

How does UltraDev provide active content?

We'll look at some of the techniques that we will be using to get active content into our pages. Then we will complete the update.asp and view.asp pages, upload our site to the server and preview it.

Go back into UltraDev and then into update.asp, by launching it from the Site window. When the page is up on screen, go to the Window menu and select Data Bindings. In this window you can see that there are two tabs, one for Data Bindings and one for Server Behaviors. These tabs provide you with an alternative to hand coding, and allow you to place active content onto your web pages.

Server behaviors are components that you insert into page elements to make them active. In the server behaviors section, there are number of things you can accomplish relating to the manipulation of data from and to a database. We will be using server behaviors for certain ASP functions.

Data bindings are about binding of data to ASP components, such as Request and Session variables and recordsets.

Now that we got that out of the way, lets continue with our site development.

The update.asp file

The update.asp file in our application will look after the data that the user inputs into the database. The purpose of this form is to update our database with new employee data. The form will take the required data from the user and place it into the respective fields in the database. The form itself cannot populate the required fields with data, so another medium, in this case ASP, has to come into play.

Dreamweaver, the predecessor to UltraDev, allowed forms to be designed within its interface. However, when the form was submitted to a database or other store, an external component such as a CGI script was necessary, or the developer would have to intervene and code some ASP by hand in order to enable the front end to interact with a back end data source. UltraDev eliminates the need for this, as the program's own data bindings and server behaviors can handle the workload seamlessly.

Creating forms in UltraDev

Now we can tie the update.asp file into our web application and get it functioning with the rest of our site. With the update.asp page open, we can see the partially completed form that will act as the vehicle for our users to update our database.

You'll see that there are two fields missing in the form, the Sex field and the Department field. We'll create these two appropriate fields. We'll start with the Sex field – which holds, you guessed it, the sex of the employee that the user is entering into the Employee_Details database.

The previous fields are all text fields, which are of course important for entries that are likely to be different each time. However, in this field there will be only be two possible entries, male or female. So we'll used a list box for this type of data entry.

1. Click on the blank cell to the right of the cell labeled Sex. With this cell active, click on the Window menu and choose Objects. When the Objects toolbar comes up, choose Forms from the drop-down box. From the Forms toolbar, click on the Insert List/Menu button and this field will appear in the selected cell.

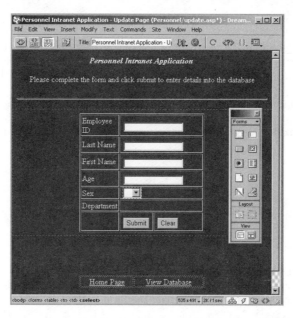

2. Once the appropriate list/menu field has been inserted into the form, you can configure it to be used with the form. In order to edit the attributes of any element within the form we need to work with its properties. To change the properties of our list box, highlight it, and press CTRL+F3 or go to the Window menu and choose Properties. When the properties of the form are active, we can get to work on configuring it.

3. In the Properties window, change the List/Menu field to a name that will identify the object. I have named this field SexField. In the Type field, I have changed the setting from Menu to List.

4. Using the List Values button enter M and F for both the item label and value respectively, as is shown below. Confirm this setting by clicking OK.

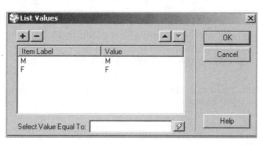

Now we will set the bottom field of the form to accept Department values.

5.   We will need a text field to accept the value entered by the user, so click on the cell to the right of the cell labeled Department, launch the Objects toolbar and select the icon labeled Insert Text Field.

6.   Once the required text field is on the page, we can configure it, again though the Properties window, so click on the TextField name and change it to Department. The textbox has now been given a meaningful name to make it easier to work with.

Save your changes to update.asp.

Now that the fields have been attributed with the correct field types and suitable names, we can set all the fields in the form to bind to their respective fields within the database. To do this, we bind the form to the DSN that we created earlier.

7.   In the UltraDev workspace, go to the Modify menu and choose Connections. Within the Connections window choose New and then specify a DSN connection. This will bring up a window from which we can select the DSN that we created earlier.

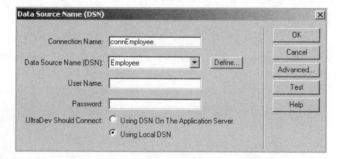

8.   Change the Connection Name to connEmployee to match the System DSN name we made earlier. Note that the correct naming convention is to place the term conn before a connection and not a DSN.

9.   Click on the Test button to complete the connection, which brings up a prompt that, with any luck, notifies you that the connection between the page and the database has been successful. Now that the connection has been made successfully click OK, then Done to confirm the ADO connection. That's it, save your work.

Congratulations you have just connected your ASP page to a database!

Binding to the database

The next step is to bind the fields of our form to the database fields. You do this by selecting Insert Record from the Server Behaviors.

1. While you're in the update.asp file, launch Server Behaviors to connect to the database and insert the records into the appropriate database fields. Click on the + symbol within Server Behaviors, select Insert Record from the drop-down menu.

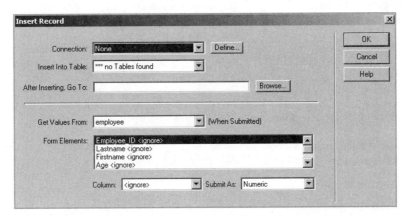

2. In the first section of the window, select the correct DSN Connection (connEmployee) and the table that you're going to be updating (Employee). We also need to set a page for the application to redirect to after a record has been inserted. I have chosen to go back to the default.asp page, although a page that thanks the user for inserting a record could also be entered.

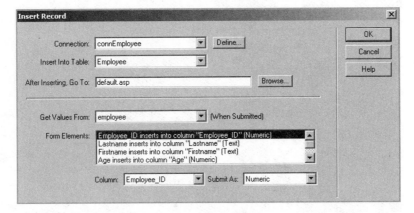

The second section in the Insert Record window contains a list of the Form Elements, some of which we created earlier. The first form element, Employee ID is the text input box on the UltraDev form into which we'll enter the new employees' Employee ID into.

3. With this highlighted, go to the Column dropdown list and choose Employee_ID, as that is the database column that we will want the data to be entered into. In the Submit As drop-down list choose Numeric, as that is the appropriate data type that will populate the Employee_ID column. Now highlight the second form element, Last Name, and select the corresponding database column Lastname and the data type Text.

4. Continue this process for each of the form elements in turn, using the following information as a guide:

Form Element Name	Database Column	Access Data Type
Employee ID	Employee_ID	Numeric
Last name	Lastname	Text
First name	Firstname	Text
Age	Age	Numeric
SexField	Sex	Text
Department	Department	Text

5. Once you've done that, click OK, and save your work.

We've just built a page that will allow the users of our application to insert records directly into our database - pretty cool, huh? We'll upload and preview our work after completing the final page, view.asp.

The view.asp page

The aim of view.asp is to present the users of our application with a page to view the contents of our database. If you open the view.asp file from the Site window, you'll see the framework the page will be based upon.

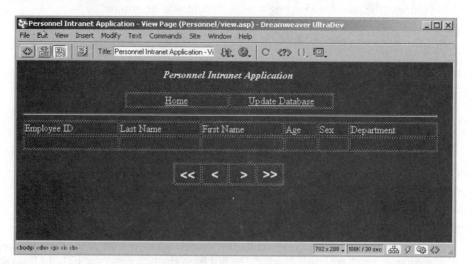

At the top of the page, there are two links to the other pages within the application. Below these are a set of column headings that should look familiar; the columns in the database table that we're going to display. Finally, underneath this is a set of four symbols. These will act as a navigation system for the user to page through the database (backwards or forwards) through one screen at a time or between the start and finish of the records in the database. With this in mind, let's start working on this page.

Display the data

The first thing we have to do in this page is get the column headings to display the contents of the database. To do this we have to bind the rows in our database to the view.asp page.

We'll use an UltraDev Data Binding called a **recordset**. A recordset is a collection of records returned from a database query. We will query the database in order to return a group of records based on certain criteria.

1. Open up the Data Bindings window (Window > Data Bindings), click on the + button and choose Recordset(Query). This opens the Recordset creating window, within which we can structure our recordset query to return the results we would like.

2. There are four fields in the window that concern us. First, the Name field – this is wha we will call our recordset. Call yours rsEmployee. (Recordsets are prefixed with 'rs', by convention). The second field is the Connection field, which is where UltraDev wants you to specify a DSN in order to query the database. We will use connEmployee. Table is the field in which we specify the database table that we want to use. The Columns field is where we tell UltraDev which columns to select and display from the database, and in this case, we will be displaying All in this particular query.

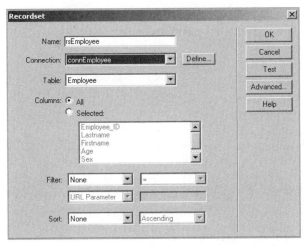

3. Now that you have the recordset in place, click on the Test button to display all the fields in our query. The recordset displays all the data in the database!

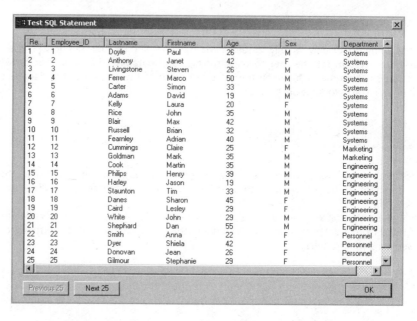

4. When you're finished, click on OK, and then on OK again, to close the Recordset window, then save your work.

5. In order to bind the results of our query to our web page, you need to have the Data Binding window open (Window > Data Bindings.) You'll see the recordset that we created in this window. Click on the + sign next to the Recordset (rsEmployee) text to bring up all the fields in the query that are to be displayed on the page.

6. All we have to do here is simply click on the destination of each piece of active content and then insert it into the correct table cell.

7. Highlight the cell below Employee ID on the page, then go into the Data Bindings window and click on the Insert button, or drag-and-drop the individual data bindings onto the page. This will insert the dynamic data into the required table cell.

8. Repeat these steps for the remaining cells in the table window by inserting Lastname, Firstname, Age, Department and Sex into the corresponding cells to complete the process.

Once you've finished, your page should look something like this - a row of active content placeholders, with braces indicating where there is active content that will be displayed.

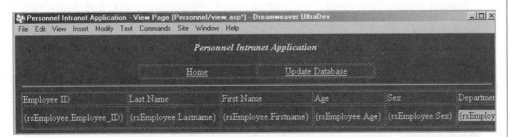

If we left the page like this, it would only display the first record in our recordset when it was tested, so the next stage is to make the records in our recordset repeat all the way through our page. To do this we need to insert a server behavior known as a **repeat region**, which will make the page display all the records in the query.

9. Go to the second row of our table, where the active content placeholder should read {rsEmployee.Employee_ID}, place the mouse cursor at the very left hand side of the cell, until the mouse arrow turns into a pointer. Then click to highlight the entire row. With the entire row highlighted, open up the Server Behaviors window. Click on the + symbol and select Repeat Region. We want to display ten records at a time, so accept the default option, click OK and save your work.

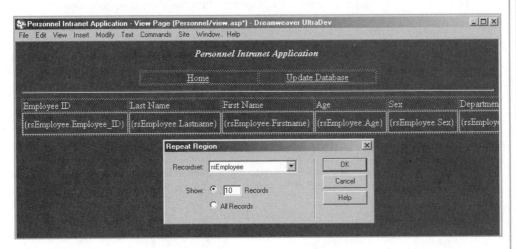

10. Let's test the recordset and repeat region on the page, using Live Data Preview to see what the active content on our page will look like (without having to upload the page to a server.) Go to the View menu and choose Live. The live data preview should return something like this:

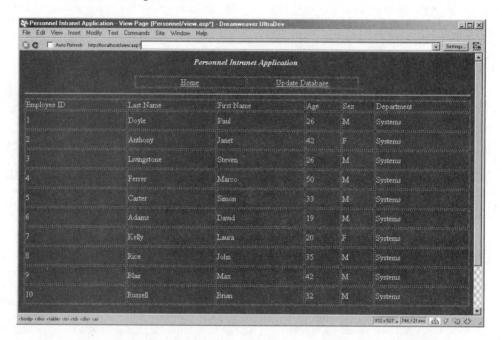

11. To close the Live Data window, just go back into the View menu and uncheck Live Data. Live Data is a great demonstration of how powerful and fast UltraDev is at producing database driven web applications!

Navigating through the data

We should configure the navigation system to allow us to page through the recordsets. This is something that UltraDev's **Server Behaviors** can do for you.

We will attach a group of server behaviors to the buttons to help us navigate through the recordsets. Then we'll attach server behaviors to allow us to hide the buttons when they are no longer required i.e. if we can go no further forward or backward through the recordset.

These are our navigation buttons and their actions:

Symbol	Button Name	Button Action
<	rwd.png	Move back to previous records
<<	rwdsta.pnd	Go back to start of records

>   `ffwd.png`   Move on to next records

>>   `ffwdend.png`   Go on to end of records.

1. Let's start with `rwdsta.png`. Highlight the image (<<) and go to the Server Behaviors window. Click on the + button and from the drop-down menu, choose Move to Record, then Move to First Record. The Move To First Record server behavior window will come up with the selected image name and the relevant recordset name:

2. Click OK to accept the image and recordset as the behavior defined, and the setting will be applied to the image at runtime. Now apply the following behaviors to the other images:

Button	Server Behavior
`rwdsta.png`	Move to First Record
`rwd.png`	Move to Previous Record
`ffwd.png`	Move to Next Record
`ffwdend.png`	Move to Last record

Now we'll complete this page by adding the finishing touches to our recordset navigation system. The things we need to take into account are:

- There are thirty five records in the database.

- We should only display appropriate navigation images: if someone loads the `view.asp` page for the first time, they don't need to see the Move to First Record or the Move to Previous Record buttons. Nor do they need to see the Move to Next Record and Move to Last Record buttons if they are at the end of the recordset.

We need a way of hiding these buttons from the user when they are not required. Fortunately, UltraDev has just the thing for our requirements, a Hide Region Server Behavior that we can use when we require the navigational buttons to disappear.

Let's will start with `rwdsta.png`, and set a circumstance for when this behavior should be hidden.

3. Highlight `rwdsta.png` and click on the + sign in the Server Behavior window. Go to Show Region, choose Show Region If Not First Record from the drop-down list, and you'll see the following window:

4. This is where we choose the applicable recordset. Opt for the rsEmployee recordset. We want `rwdsta.png` to show only if the first record in the recordset is not being displayed. The complete set of Show Region behaviors we want to apply to our navigation buttons are as follows:

Button Name	Show Region Behavior
rwdsta.png	Show if Not First Record
rwd.png	Show if Not First Record
ffwd.png	Show if Not Last Record
ffwdend.png	Show if Not Last Record

5. Once you've attached all the right behaviors to the `view.asp` page, the Server Behavior window should look like this:

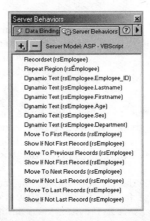

> Note: Just as you can add both Server Behaviors and Data Bindings through the inspector window, you can delete them there too. UltraDev generated the ASP that will run on the web server and generate the active content display at the click of the click of the + button. It is just as easily removed by clicking on the - button.
>
> To remove a binding such as a recordset in the Data Bindings window, we have to remove the root object of the recordset.

6. Save your work, and prepare to upload the site to your web server and see the web application in action!

Let's just take a moment to contemplate what we have done here, with these easy steps.

We created a recordset to display the contents from a database. Then we created a navigation system for the web page, to help users page through the contents of our database, rather than confronting them with the entire database on one page.

Pretty smart, when you consider that we did all of this without any hand-coding!

Uploading the site

Now that all the work has been completed on the site, we should upload it to the server. This is of course done in the Site window.

You can see all the completed files in the Local Folder in the Site window. All you have to do to get them across to the Remote Site folder is Synchronize, and the site will be loaded across to the web server.

1.   Go to Site > Synchronize and bring the option window up. We want to synchronize the entire site and Put newer files to remote.

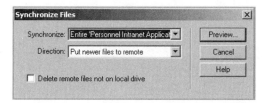

2.   Click Preview... and a window will come up with a list of all the files that have to be uploaded. Leave all the files checked, and then click OK to start the upload.

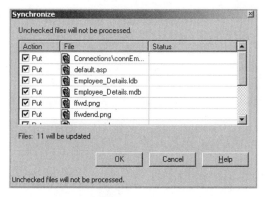

3.   Once the process is finished, UltraDev will give you the option to save a synchronization log or close the window along with a listing of all the files successfully

uploaded. We won't be saving a synchronization log at this time, however this log can report all the synchronization activity that has been executed by UltraDev.

So now you've finished. Look over your work in a web browser, and try adding some entries to the database in update.asp. Try viewing the whole recordset in view.asp. Just call up http://localhost/default.asp into the browser address bar, and our default.asp file will be displayed.

And there it is. We have covered the UltraDev environment, and built a web application, learned how to configure our web server, connect to a database, and display the dynamic data using UltraDev.

Hopefully this chapter has given you a taste for UltraDev. The next chapter will build on what you learned here, and bring Flash into the equation. There are many advantages to using UltraDev with Flash to create data driven movies, and we'll be looking at those next.

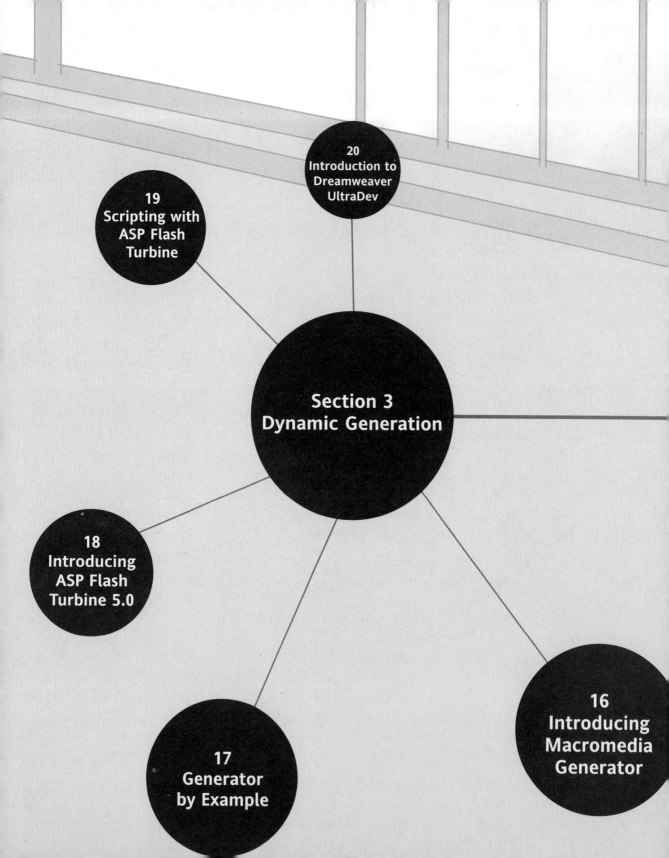

Chapter 21
Integrating
UltraDev with
Flash

In the previous chapter we began developing web applications with UltraDev. In this chapter we'll take this a step forward, and use UltraDev and Flash together. As you'll see, using UltraDev this way will speed up your application development time considerably - in fact, you won't actually need to do any hand-coding at all.

We'll build a subscription application that takes information from the user though a Flash interface and adds it to an Access database, integrating the Flash front-end with our application in the UltraDev environment. If you thought the previous chapter took on a slightly theoretical approach, then I promise you that this is where the theory ends!

UltraDev, and more recently Flash, can be extended by downloading extensions from the Macromedia Exchange. We will take advantage of the Exchange here, downloading, installing and using an extension, the JavaScript Integration Kit (JIK). We'll use this extension to add some validation code to the subscription application quickly and easily.

We won't be building the Flash interface from scratch; it's a basic interface that you'd have no trouble putting together yourself, but I've provided it in a state of almost completion so that you don't have to spend more time than necessary fiddling around inside Flash. We'll also use a very simple database in the application, that's also on the CD - again, it's not complicated, but building a database isn't the focus of this chapter, so I've just provided it for you.

Before we begin, though, I should tackle another question: *"why use UltraDev and Flash together at all?"* There are some very good reasons for working with this partnership, which we'll look at first.

A case for using Flash with UltraDev

When we began developing this book, there were some decidedly raised eyebrows at the prospect of putting Flash and UltraDev together. Admittedly, they might at first appear to make strange partners, having different target audiences, and very different objectives. But then, it wasn't so very long ago that the idea of Flash designers actually getting their hands dirty with any scripting outside ActionScript was a relatively novel one.

Once you've seen the extensibility and rapid development processes that UltraDev brings you, I hope you'll begin to appreciate how well it supports Flash's own design capabilities. Among some of the many advantages of using the two programs together are:

Common User Interface
Given that UltraDev and Flash are both made by Macromedia, it'll come as no surprise that the look and feel of their interfaces are not so very different. Although the content of those interfaces is completely distinct, because of what the programs do, they do share floating pallets and drag-and-drop usability. So if you're coming to UltraDev from a Flash background, as you'll probably already have found, the interface is considerably more accessible to you than if you'd never worked with Flash at all.

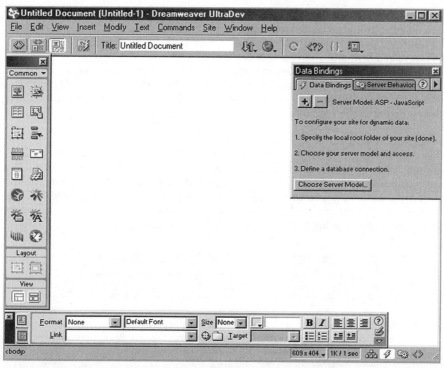

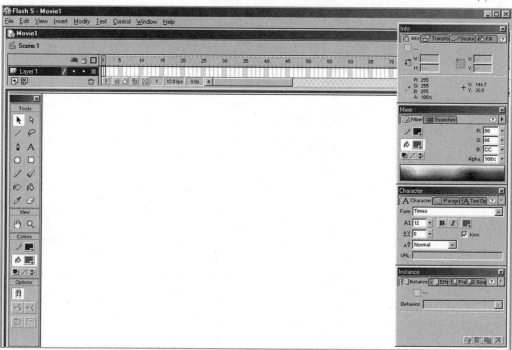

Designers coming from either background - Flash or UltraDev - don't have to learn a completely new user interface for each respective program.

Enhances your Flash site management

We've already seen how well UltraDev manages your site in the previous chapter. Using UltraDev as the basis for your Flash web application gives you access to its powerful site manageability features. As you'll see, UltraDev has built-in Flash content handling capabilities; you can integrate your Flash content at the click of a button.

Less Hand-Coding

Whether your site model is ASP, JSP, or CFML, UltraDev will generate the necessary script in the background when an active content element is put onto the page. Add to that UltraDev's Roundtrip authoring, (you can still go into the code and modify your code by hand, and UltraDev won't modify those changes to suit its own idea of what your code should look like, even if it doesn't understand programming logic) and you've got a very useful partnership set up for you. (You access the code by going to the Window menu and choosing HTML Source.)

```
mailing - Code Inspector                                              ×
 <> Code Inspector                                                 ?  ►
 ⏶ ◉.  C  <?>  {}. ▦.
</script>                                                              ▲
</head>
<body bgcolor="#FFFFFF" onLoad="FDK_AddEmailValidation('udform:
'http://www.macromedia.com/shockwave/download/?P1_Prod_Version=
<object classid="clsid:D27CDB6E-AE6D-11cf-96B8-444553540000" cc
   <param name=movie value="mailing.swf">
   <param name=quality value=high>
   <embed src="mailing.swf" quality=high pluginspage="http://www
   </embed>
</object>
<form name="udform1" method="post" action="<%=MM_editAction%>"
   <input type="hidden" name="udfield1">
   <input type="hidden" name="udfield2">
   <input type="hidden" name="udfield3">
   <input type="hidden" name="udfield4">
   <input type="hidden" name="udfield5">
   <input type="hidden" name="udfield6">
   <input type="hidden" name="udfield7">
   <input type="hidden" name="udfield8">
   <input type="hidden" name="udfield9">
   <input type="hidden" name="udfield10">
   <input type="hidden" name="MM_insert" value="true">
</form>
</body>
</html>                                                               ▼
◄                                                                ►
```

Those are just some of the advantages of using UltraDev to build your dynamic Flash sites. Let's crack on with defining a project that we can use to show how the two applications can work extremely well together. We'll begin by installing the extensions that we'll be using in the application.

Extensions: slashing your development time

There are many **extensions** available for both Flash and Dreamweaver UltraDev, which help you speed up the process of web applications development. UltraDev and Flash are designed to be extensible, in that users who are proficient in JavaScript can go in and write their own objects, behaviors, commands, and property inspectors.

There is a strong community of users who build extensions and make them available on the Macromedia Exchange sites for others to download. The massive collection of extensions available for download ranges from design timesaving programs, through to e-commerce development extensions. You will also find discussion forums on the Exchange site for each extension.

UltraDev comes with an **Extension Manager**, which enables you to add or remove extensions as you work. It comes with a handy link that'll take you directly to the Macromedia Exchange site, where you can search for, and learn about, more extensions.

The Extension Manager opens automatically when you double-click on a Macromedia Extension Package for installation. You can also access the Extension Manger by going to the Commands menu in the design window, and choosing Manage Extensions.

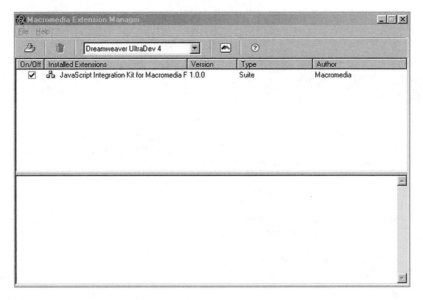

Extensions and the Extension Manager are available from the UltraDev and Flash Exchange sites, (you do have to download the manager for Flash 5; although Dreamweaver UltraDev 4 comes with it ready installed):

www.macromedia.com/exchange/ultradev
www.macromedia.com/exchange/flash

In this application we'll be using the JavaScript Integration Kit extension.

The JavaScript Integration Kit extension

The JIK is a Dreamweaver extension for Flash 5. It provides a suite of behaviors that you can use to implement certain functionalities within your web page. You might remember that we used server behaviors in the previous chapter.

A behavior, generally speaking, provides the code that allows you to perform certain actions. If you look at the Behaviors window (by going to the Window menu and choosing Behaviors) you can see a list of the behaviors available in the workspace:

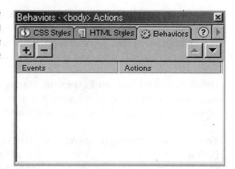

The JIK allows you to perform server validation in response to certain user actions, like the user clicking a submit button, for example. We'll be using it in an example application later on, so let's download and install it now.

Installing the JIK

1. First you need to download the extension from the CD or the Macromedia Dreamweaver Exchange. This URL has some good background information and a small tutorial on the implementations of the JIK.

    www.macromedia.com/support/flash/programs/form_validations_tut/

    In order to download files from the exchange, you first have to become a member; the instructions are on the Macromedia Exchange site and are very straightforward.

2. Once you have located the JIK, put it somewhere on your hard drive, and we're ready to install it. It looks like this:

    The JIK is known as MX100630_mmJIK.mxp. The file extension .mxp stands for Macromedia Extension Package. Before you install it, I'd recommend that you ensure that *no programs are running on your machine*. Although closing everything first isn't always essential, it's easier on your system, and it helps avoid complications. When you're ready, double click the icon.

3. The installer will bring up an Extension Disclaimer form, which you should read and Accept (if you agree with the terms and conditions, of course), and the installation will continue.

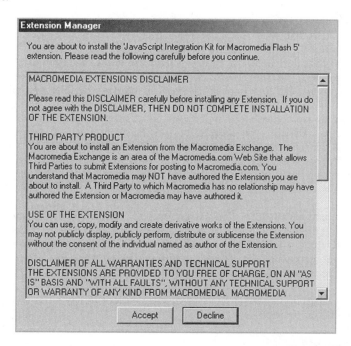

Once the package is installed on your system, and the installer should bring up the following message:

4. Click OK to accept the installation and you're done. You can see the JIK present in the Extension Manager. Have a read over the details that Macromedia have provided about the Extension, and then close the Extension Manager.

Now the JIK is installed, we're all set to create the subscription application with Flash and UltraDev.

A web subscription application with Flash and UltraDev

While I can talk forever about the advantages of using Flash and UltraDev in unison, actually working with a practical example is probably far more useful, and will help demonstrate what the main advantages are.

Project outline

Let's suppose that we have been recruited to work on a project to help a company construct a web application that will allow its users to subscribe to its mailing list.

The company has decided to use an Access Database as the data store for the data it receives from its new customers. The company owners are very excited by the excellent Flash user interfaces they have seen around, and they want to have a Flash interface for their data-driven site.

However, they are concerned that some of their customer base may not have the appropriate Flash plug-in, and won't be able to see the Flash interface. So, we'll construct a site that automatically installs the Flash plug-in (where the client browser allows it), provides a link for the user to download the required plug-in for their browser (for users who are a bit wary of automatic installations), and with an HTML version, for users who don't want the plug-in on their machines, or are, for whatever reason, unable to get it installed.

We'll construct a Flash form that allows users to fill in their details and submit them to the company. We'll make some validity checks on the data that the customer enters into the form before submitting it to the database. (The company might get a bit upset if their database gets filled up with junk data.) Finally, we'll send a thank you message to the user after the data has been sent, to let them know that the operation has been successful.

With this background information in mind, let's consider the methods and tools that we need to prototype our application.

Form requirements

Our Flash form will be fairly simple, containing the following input field variables that will hold user's details, and a submit button:

firstname	User's first name.
lastname	User's last name
street	The first line of the users address
city	The second line of the users address
state	The third line of the users address
postcode/zipcode	The fourth line of the users address
email	Holds the users email address
telephone	The user's phone number
password	The user's password
confirmpassword	Password confirmation field

Scripting language

In the previous chapter we used Active Server Pages to provide the dynamic content of our Intranet Application. We will also use ASP for this application, as UltraDev can generate the required ASP on the fly.

Web server requirements

For ease of use, I will be using Microsoft's Personal Web Server (PWS) as the remote server that will host our remote site. PWS has full support for ASP and is extremely easy to use and configure, later on in this chapter we will look briefly at configuring a remote site for use within this project.

Access database

The database for this chapter can be found on the CD. It has all the fields that are present in our data entry form, except the password confirmation field, and looks something like this:

firstname	Text
lastname	Text
street	Text
city	Text
state	Text
postcode/zipcode	Text
email	Text (Primary Key)
telephone	Number
password	Text

Data validation

We'll check the user's data for validity once he or she has entered it into the form, before it's transferred into the database, and supply error messages so that user knows what to do if there are errors. Once the data passes the tests set by our rules of validation, it will be entered into the database.

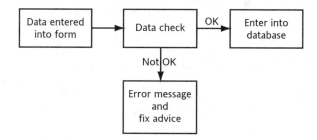

So how do we validate the data within the Flash data input form? Ideally, we want to stick to the rapid development standards of UltraDev and use a tool that will make the process of validating our forms easy. Well, remember that JIK we just downloaded?

We can set all our rules for the validation of our data-entry form using the JIK extension that we installed earlier. This kit has three main functions:

- It allows you to design a customized, interactive movie player for your web page

- Provides powerful JavaScript features that you can incorporate in your Flash movies; creating image rollovers, opening a new browser window, and sending cookies from your Flash movies to a user's computer, for example. You can also select an item in an HTML list or menu, or add an item to it.

- Provides advanced form validation behaviors that enable you to verify data entered in Flash forms.

This third function is the one we will be using in our application to validate our form data.

JavaScript is a client-side scripting solution, so it runs on the client rather than the web server. One of the best things about this is that it frees up web server resources. In the case of the JIK, the data validation of the user's input will be carried out on the user's machine, so the web server will only come into action when the form data is passed from the client to the server. While this works well enough for the purposes of example here, many browsers in the real world don't handle JavaScript adequately, or indeed, at all. If you wanted to expand this application for Internet scale use, you could create a script to run the data validation routine on the server-side.

This disadvantage of server-side validation is, of course, using up server resources to execute the script, which will impact the performance of the server and possibly the bandwidth of such an application (if it was on a corporate Intranet, for example). As we want to keep the transactions on our server to a minimum it is generally a good idea to keep the process of data validation on the browser.

Project design: laying the groundwork for the web application

Now that we have the background to the project, we should lay the groundwork for the web application by setting up both a local and remote site for our work. In the previous chapter we looked at the Site Management features of UltraDev and Personal Web Server (PWS) to define the sites for our Intranet Application, we will use this model again in this application.

Setting up the Site Management

Before starting any work within PWS or UltraDev, it is good practice to create two folders; one on the local site, and the other the remote site folder. Synchronization will transfer them from the local folder into the remote folder.

Creating the local folder

1. Let's start by creating a local folder. Its location on the hard drive is not too important, as long as it is easy to find. I called mine Mailing List, and saved it in my UD Web Sites directory.

   ```
   C:\UD Web Sites\Mailing List
   ```

   The Mailing List folder is where I will store all the files that I will create within the Mailing List Application.

2. Once you've created the local folder, you can copy across the two files on the CD for upload. You can locate them under this chapter on the CD – they are `mailing.fla` and a `Mailing List Subscriptions.mdb` database. These are the files we'll work with.

Creating a Remote Folder

3. As I am using PWS, if you will remember from the previous chapter, all remote folders have to go into the \Inetpub\wwwroot folder for the web server to access and process the files within the folder. Again, I called mine Mailing List

   `C:\Inetpub\wwwroot\Mailing List`

   It is good practice to give your local and remote folders the same name like; it helps avoid confusion later on.

Now that we have created our folders within Windows, let's start defining our site in UltraDev.

Site Definition

We will define our Mailing List Application in the same way as we did for the Personnel Intranet Application in the previous chapter, so I will keep the instructions brief. Refer to the previous chapter if you need your memory refreshing!

4. You define the site within the Site window, so open it and go to the Site menu and choose New Site. This will bring up the window Site Definition for Unnamed Site 1.

5. Starting with the Local Info window, I have named my site Mailing List Application, you can call your site whatever you like. The Local Root Folder will be the one we created earlier in C:\UD Web Sites\Mailing List\. Check both the Refresh Local File List Automatically box and the Enable Cache box, and then insert your own HTTP Address.

6. Within the Remote Info window, I have chosen the Server Access to be Local/Network, as we are working with a web server within our local machine. The Remote Folder is of course, the folder we created in C:\Inetpub\wwwroot\Mailing List\. I have checked the box Refresh Remote File List Automatically to ease the site management process.

7. Within the Application Server window, I have chosen ASP 2.0 as our Server Model, with VBScript as our Scripting Language. The URL Prefix should remain at http://localhost/ so mine at this point is http://localhost/Mailing List.

   With all these options set, click on OK and now we have our site defined. If you go into the Site window you'll see the two files that you copied from the CD sitting in the local folder.

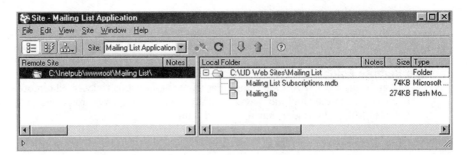

`Mailing.fla` is a partially completed Flash movie that we'll complete later, and `Mailing List Subscriptions.mdb` is a blank database that will be the data store for our subscription details.

Configuring the web server

Before we start configuring the files within the application, we need to get the web server to tie in with the remote folder (in this case, Personal Web Server).

1. To configure PWS to work with the remote folder, first of all double-click on the PWS tray icon on the Windows system tray, or access your server though the Control Panel.

   The Personal Web Manager window should spring to life.

2. If PWS is running, click on the Stop button to stop the server and then go to the Advanced icon. Click on Edit Properties to the right of the screen. With the Edit Directory window open, browse to the location of the remote folder on your hard drive. (If you've set it up like mine, then the remote folder is in C:\Inetpub\wwwroot\Mailing List\.) Click on OK to complete the configuration of our folder.

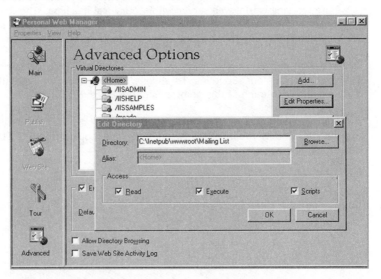

3. Rename your default document to `mailing.asp`, go back to the Main window and click on Start to restart PWS, and your window should look like this:

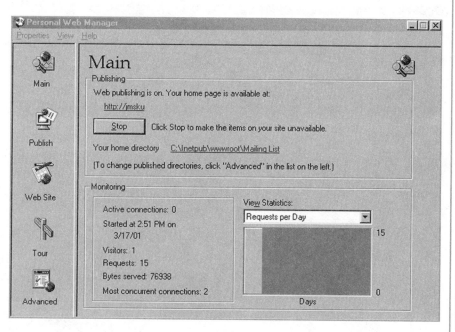

That's all there is to configuring the web server, so close the Personal Web Manager window and re-enter the UltraDev Site window. The next thing we'll do is complete the Flash form and enable it to work with the JIK.

Configuring the Flash form to work with the JIK

In this section we will look at configuring our Flash movie for use with our application. The movie I have designed is extremely simple – its purpose is to show you how UltraDev and Flash interact. We'll first complete this very basic form, and then set it up to work with the JIK

1. In the Site window, double-click on `Mailing.Fla`, and the Flash movie will open up.

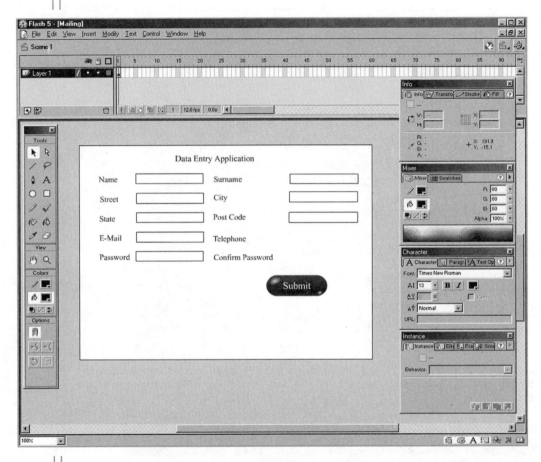

The movie already has several input fields that correspond to the fields in the database, and a Submit button. As the form is nearly finished, all you need to fill in are the Telephone and Confirm Password text fields.

2. To complete the form, create the following input boxes.

Variable Name	Input Type	Line Type	Border/bg
telephone	Input	Single Line	Yes
confirmpassword	Input	Password	Yes

Once you've set these, your form should look like this:

Now that we have a finished Flash form, we can start preparing it for use with the JIK.

Configuring the form for use with the JIK

The Submit button on the form will initialize the JIK to validate the data in the Flash form. We will add some actions to our Flash form to launch the JIK, and to display an error message that will tell the user why the form couldn't be submitted if there are any problems. We will start configuring the form to load the fields of our Flash movie into UltraDev.

To load the form data into the JIK, which will be located in our UltraDev site, we'll use an `on` `(press)` action behind the Submit button, and some JavaScript. The code will add all the fields of the Flash form into the fields of the UltraDev file that we will create later on in this chapter. The code is on the CD in the file called `js.txt`. You can just copy and paste the JavaScript from there if you'd rather not type it in yourself.

3. With the `Mailing.Fla` file open, add an `on(press)` and a `getURL` action to the Submit button:

   Add the following JavaScript to the `getURL` action (either type it out, or copy and paste it from the `js.txt` file on the CD).

```
"javascript:FDK_setFormText('UDform1','UDfield1','" add firstname add
➡ "');FDK_setFormText('UDform1','UDfield2','" add lastname add
➡"');FDK_setFormText('UDform1','UDfield3','" add street add
➡"');FDK_setFormText('UDform1','UDfield4','" add city add
➡"');FDK_setFormText('UDform1','UDfield5','" add state add
➡"');FDK_setFormText('UDform1','UDfield6','" add postcode add
➡"');FDK_setFormText('UDform1','UDfield7','" add email add
➡"');FDK_setFormText('UDform1','UDfield8','" add telephone add
➡"');FDK_setFormText('UDform1','UDfield9','" add password add
➡"');FDK_setFormText('UDform1','UDfield10', '" add confirmpassword add
➡"');"
```

Once you've done that, add a `getURL` action inside the `on (release)` event of the Submit button, and enter the following code (or copy and paste it from `js.txt`):

```
"javascript:FDK_Validate('UDform1',false,true,'Sorry, the Form
Could Not Be Submitted\\n\\n');"
```

This will generate an error for the user if there is a problem with submitting the form. UltraDev will handle the posting of the variables into the database, as we shall see later, so that's all you need to do for now. Your Object Actions window should look like this:

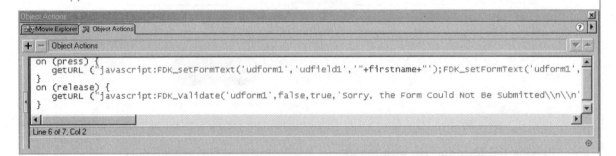

Sometimes people get a bit stuck on whether they should or shouldn't send the variables from the Flash movie; just make sure that you're not sending either set of variables. The beauty of using UltraDev with Flash is that it eliminates the need to use any load variables command: UltraDev will take care of this once the Flash movie is nested into our ASP page.

4. Now that the proper actions have been inserted into our movie, close the Object Actions window, and save `Mailing.Fla`. The only thing left to do is to export the movie so that it can be used within the code we'll create within UltraDev. We won't be able to embed the FLA file into the ASP file we'll be creating next until we have exported it in SWF format.

5. Go to File and choose Export Movie. I called my new SWF file `mailing.swf`. Once this is saved in the C:\UD Web Sites\Mailing List folder, accept the default options that come up in the Export Flash Player window by choosing OK. We have now created a SWF file that we can use within `mailing.asp`, the ASP page we'll create next.

6. To confirm that we have successfully exported the `mailing.swf` into our UltraDev site, have a look in the Site window, and you should now have three files:

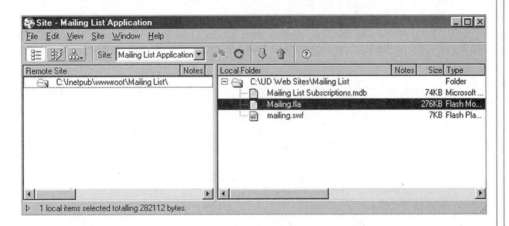

Now the SWF is ready, we can create the ASP page we need to use it in UltraDev.

Creating the ASP page

You need to be in the Site window of UltraDev, with Mailing List Application as the active site. We'll create an ASP file that we can export our Flash movie into. Once we have embedded the exported Flash movie into it, we can begin the process of setting our validation rules and create the ASP code required to insert the data on our form into our database.

1. With the Site window open, go to the File menu and choose New File, this will bring up a file called `untitled.asp`.

> *Remember, when we defined our site earlier, we made the default file extension .asp, so when we create any new files, unless we change the file extension, all new files will be called *.asp.*

2. We are going to call the new file `mailing.asp` (because that's the name we set inside PWS for the site's default document), so adjust the name accordingly.

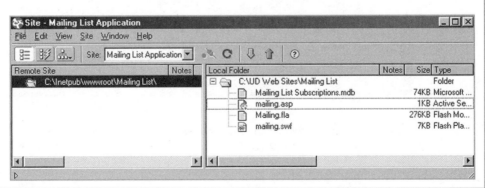

Importing our Flash Movie into our ASP File

3.   From the Site window, double-click on `mailing.asp` to open it. This ASP page will act as the loading page for our SWF file. You can begin the file import by going to the Common Objects panel, and clicking on the insert Flash button.

Now select the `mailing.swf` file and click OK. If the file has been successfully inserted, you should be presented with this type of screen:

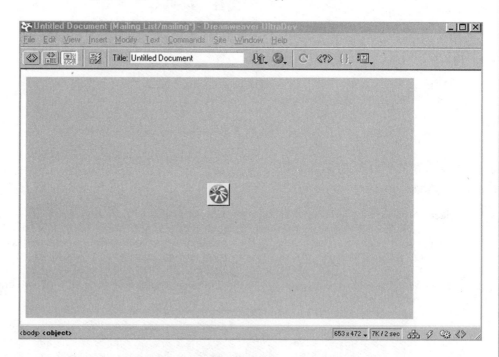

The large gray area within the UltraDev workspace is your embedded Flash form.

5.   Right-click on the embedded form and select Properties. When the Properties window pops up, expand it using the arrow on the lower right hand corner, and enter mailing in both the ID and title fields. This helps for scripting purposes.

6.   Close the Properties window and save your work.

Setting Up the Form and Hidden Fields

Now that we have the SWF file in our page, we have to make UltraDev aware of the fields within the form. To do this, we have to insert a form and hidden fields. The form and hidden fields will be invisible at runtime, but for scripting purposes, the hidden form fields will correspond with the Flash form fields and this will allow the JavaScript in the Actions we set earlier in the Flash form to load.

7. To insert a form, select Forms from the Object panel, and click on the form icon (or go to the Insert menu and choose Form.).

The form will show up in the shape of two parallel horizontal lines, if you cannot see the lines go to the View menu and ensure that Invisible Elements is checked.

8. Now go to the Window menu and choose Properties. The Property inspector will appear.

Change the Form Name to UDform1:

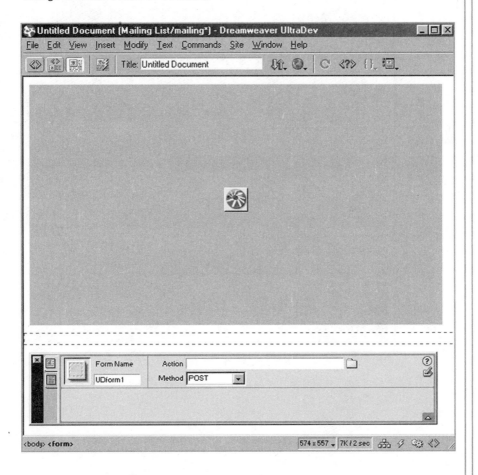

9. To insert the hidden fields, simply choose hidden field 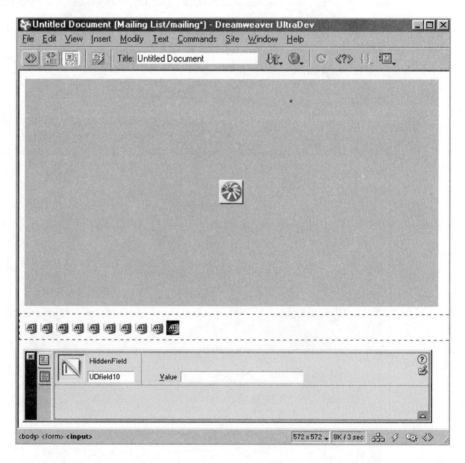 from the Form panel, (or go to the Insert menu again and choose Form Object then Hidden Field.)

Once the field is in the form (it will appear as a small blue square icon) change the name of the hidden field to UDfield1:

10. Carry on entering hidden fields inside the form, incrementing the number on the name of each one, (UDfield2, and so on) until you reach UDfield10. (If UltraDev pops up a window asking you if you want to create another form while you're doing this – just select no.) When you've finished, you should have a SWF file, and a form with ten hidden fields inside on your ASP page.

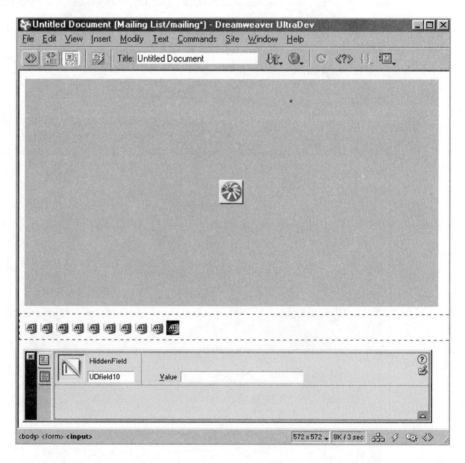

Setting Up the Form Data Validation

Now that we have our form and hidden fields in place, we will start putting our data validation in place, with the help of the JavaScript Integration Kit. Many people get into all sorts of trouble with the data validation features of the JIK, simply because they assign the validation behaviors to the wrong area of the page. Take care using the JIK and it will serve you well!

The first thing we have to do to set up validation is configure our form for advanced form validations:

11. Select the Form object within the page (by clicking on one of the red horizontal lines), and go to the Window menu and choose Behaviors. Click on the + sign inside the Behaviors window, and select Advanced Validate Form behavior.

12. The window that pops up allows us to send a message to let the user know about any problems caused as soon as the form opens, or to let the form go through without flagging any errors.

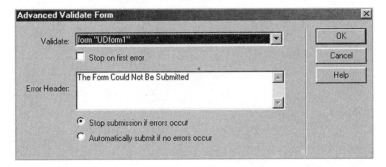

We'll flag up any errors that occur, so check the Stop on first error box, and select the Stop submission if errors occur radio button. Click OK to save the changes and close the window.

> *If you have any problems getting at the appropriate behaviors within the inspector, it might be because the incorrect page element is selected - go back, make sure that you have the form selected by clicking on one of the red dashes that represent the box, and try again.*

13. The next stage in setting up form validation is to set the FDK_setFormText option. This has the effect of passing the fields in our Flash form into our ASP file. Go to the Commands menu and select Browser Scripts for Flash. When the window comes up, check the FDK_setFormText option, click Apply then OK.

Now we can set up validations for each of the fields that we wish to query. We'll check that the email field contains a valid email address (that it holds an @ symbol and a dot symbol.) We'll also make the password field at least five characters long, and check that the entry in the password check field is the same as the original password field entry. All advanced form validations go into the <BODY> tag of the document and are onLoad events.

14. To set validation on the forms elements, select the <BODY> tag <body> from the status bar at the bottom of our page. Then go to the Window menu and choose Behaviors.

Make sure the email address that the user enters contains a @ and a dot.

- Click the + symbol and from Advanced Form Validations,

- Choose E-mail Validation,

- Leave the message as it is, and leave Value checked as it is Required.

- For Named Field, select hidden "UDfield7" in form "UDform1", and click OK

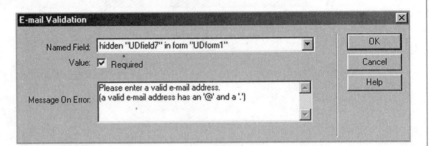

15. Set the password minimum length to five characters:

- Add the Entry Length Validation behavior

- Set the Named Field to be hidden "UDfield9" in form "UDform1",

- Enter 5 in the field Range: From

- Click OK.

16. Finally, to ensure that the Confirm Password field is the same as our original Password field, set a Like Entry Validation behavior on the field.

- The Source Field is hidden "UDfield9" in form "UDform1"

- The Target Field is hidden "UDfield10" in form "UDform1"

- Check the boxes that require data in the field to Clear on Error and Case Sensitive.

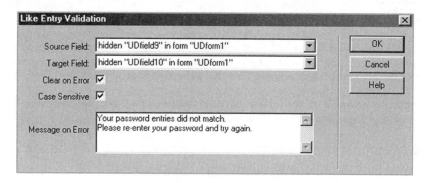

The Behaviors window should now look like this:

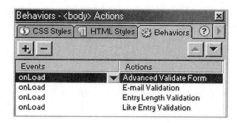

17. Once you have saved your work, you can preview it in a browser by going to File > Preview in Browser. Have a go at filling in the fields and getting different error messages. (If you have problems calling it up using the preview, try synchronizing the relevant files to the remote folder, and test it that way, using http://localHost or your machine's network name.)

If you get any runtime errors when viewing mailing.asp in the browser, it may be that mailing.swf hasn't been properly identified within the UltraDev Property inspector window. Make sure that the ID tab is set to mailing within the properties of mailing.swf.

If that still doesn't fix it, go back and check the JavaScript you added to Mailing.Fla. If you opened JS.txt in a program other than Notepad, it might have added some peculiar characters to the script. Try opening js.txt with notepad, and copying and pasting again; or simply type the code directly into the URL box

So hopefully you've got that going. We have not quite finished yet though, because all that valid data isn't actually going anywhere when users click Submit. In the next section we will look at using UltraDev to insert our Flash form data into our database.

Submitting the form data to a database and thanking the user

Now it is time to use the power of UltraDev to insert our data into our Access database. After we have completed this task we will have created a Flash form that is validated with client-side JavaScript and uses ASP and UltraDev with database connectivity. Not a bad conclusion if you consider the amount of development time this project has taken!

First, though, we need to set up the page to reassure the user that something has actually happened, and their data is being dealt with. Just a simple ASP page will do.

Entering the data into the database

After users have put data into our form, and got past the validation rules we set, there is not a lot to tell them that the form data is actually going anywhere. Without any onscreen response to the user pressing the Submit button they're left a bit blind. We need to create a page that will inform the user that the data that they have successfully entered into our form has been entered into our database. We just need a simple page with a message on it thanking the user for their input.

Creating the acknowledgment page

1. With the UltraDev Site window open go to the File menu and choose New File. The Site window will enter a new file for us to name accordingly. I have called my acknowledgement page, thanks.asp.

2. Once the page has been renamed, hit the return key to confirm the name. Now double-click on thanks.asp to open it up.

3. Once thanks.asp has been opened, type a message on the page that the user will see on successful entry to our database.

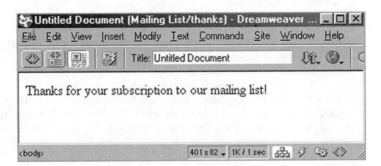

You can, of course, be as elaborate as you wish. When you've finished, save and close the page. Now that we have created a page for the users' reference, we can connect the form to the database.

Creating the system DSN

In the previous chapter we discussed how to use UltraDev to connect to a database using System DSNs. We will create a System DSN again here.

4. To begin, enter Windows Control Panel and open Data Sources (ODBC). (If you're using Windows 2000, go inside Administrative Tools, to find it). In here we can see the available DSNs that we have. Go into the System DSN tab and click Add.

5. Again, this step varies a little between '98 and 2000. In 2000, from the driver list, highlight Microsoft Access Driver and click Finish. This takes you to the ODBC Microsoft Access Setup window where you have to enter a name and description for the DSN, and then select the database. Call your DSN connMailing, (remember that it is good naming convention to name DSNs with the prefix conn), enter a description of the connection, and click on select to get to the Mailing List Subscription database that is the local site folder. This will be something like: C:\UD Web Sites\Mailing List\Mailing List Subscriptions.mdb.

   When you've set everything, click OK to finish.

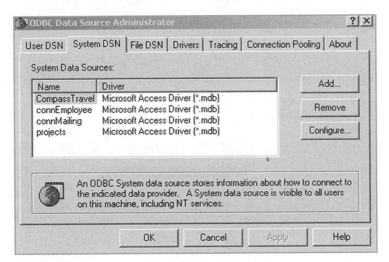

6. Now close down Control Panel, go back into the familiar territory of the UltraDev Site window, and open up Mailing.asp where we will configure the page to connect and insert records into the database.

Connecting to the database in mailing.asp

There are two things we need to do here: connect mailing.asp to the database using the DSN we created earlier, and send data from the form to the database – we'll use UltraDev's Server Behaviors to do that.

As you saw in the previous chapter, Server Behaviors create ASP code on the fly, which will be processed by the web server at runtime, and load the variables from the form into the relevant tables of the database.

7. To connect to the database from mailing.asp go to the Modify menu and choose connections. There will be a list of any previously created connections within the window, but as UltraDev has not yet been introduced to the connMailing DSN, the

one we want isn't there yet. Click on New, and select Data Source Name (DSN), and the Define Connection window will come up. This is where we configure the connection to work with the DSN we just created in the Windows Control Panel.

8. Name the connection connMailing, as this is consistent with the name of our DSN, and select the connMailing DSN from the DSN drop-down list. Then click on the test button to ensure that the connection between UltraDev and the DSN is OK.

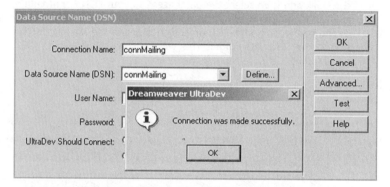

If you get the success message, click OK and you're ready to finalize the setting. Click Done, and you're finished.

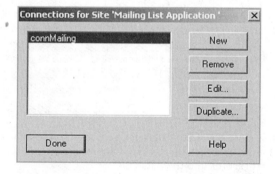

If you didn't receive a success message, go back and verify that you have successfully created a connection, and try again.

9. If everything appears to be working OK, go ahead and insert an Insert Record Server Behavior: choose Server Behaviors from the Window menu, click on the + sign inside the Server Behavior window and choose Insert Record. The Insert Record window will pop up.

In this window you can specify your connection, choose a database table, and associate the form fields and database columns. You can also specify a page to redirect users to once the records have been successfully entered into the database. We'll direct the user to our page with the thank you message, so in the Go To URL field, browse to the `thanks.asp` file.

Then choose the connMailing connection as the DSN to connect to the database. We will be inserting into the only available table, the customers table. The database will get the values from the form UDform1, which is the form on our `Mailing.asp` page, containing the hidden fields.

Using the Form Elements window, we can specify the form fields and their corresponding database columns. Use this table to do that:

UDfield1 (corresponds to Flash variable `firstname`)	firstname
UDfield2 (corresponds to Flash variable `lastname`)	lastname
UDfield3 (corresponds to Flash variable `street`)	street
UDfield4 (corresponds to Flash variable `city`)	city
UDfield5 (corresponds to Flash form `state`)	state
UDfield6 (corresponds to Flash form `postcode`)	postcode
UDfield7 (corresponds to Flash form `email`)	email
UDfield8 (corresponds to Flash form `telephone`)	telephone
UDfield9 (corresponds to Flash form `password`)	password
UDfield10 (corresponds to Flash variable `confirmpassword`	**<Ignore>**

UDfield1 should contain the value of the Flash field for `firstname`, and its value will be inserted into the firstname database column, and so on. Ignore UDfield10 when you reach it, because it corresponds to the Confirm Password field, which is not entered into any database column, as it would simply duplicate the values given in the password field.

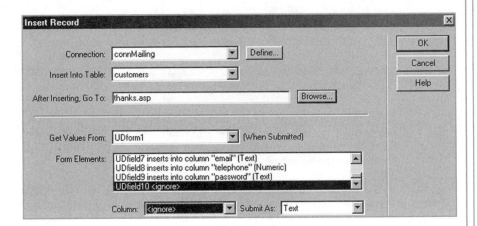

When you've finished, click on OK, save your work, and then shut down `Mailing.asp`.

All that's left to do now is to synchronize to the web application, and view your work in a browser.

Uploading the site to the web server

So now we're ready to view the application in a web browser. As you might expect, ASP pages can't be previewed in a browser unless they have been uploaded to a web server that can process the server-side code and generate the dynamic data. So, next we'll load the pages up to the server.

1. Go back into the Site window, and then into the Site menu and choose Synchronize. We want to synchronize the Entire 'Mailing List Application' Site, putting all the newer files into our remote folder.

2. Click preview to go into the preview window, letting you select which files you want to be put across:

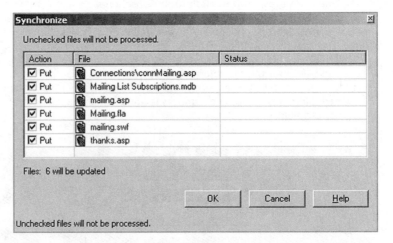

To let the entire site go across, just click OK and synchronization will begin. Once it has finished, preview your work in a browser, and then enter some details into the form. Try putting in several entries with different email addresses, and check the database to see what happens.

And that's all there is to it. You have created a fully functioning web application that allows you to enter details into an Access database from inside a Flash form, using JavaScript data validation.

To finish off this application, we'll use the JIK with UltraDev to make sure that the web application users have the correct plug-in to view our Flash form.

Detecting the Flash plug-in
As you'll be only too aware, a user without the plug-in isn't going to be able to view your Flash front end. The JIK allows you to check this. You can check whether the browser has the correct

plug-in installed, and even whether it's the correct version of the player. You can also decide whether you'd like to try to auto-install the plug-in when users don't have it, or to automatically redirect them to a URL to download the plug-in. Some users may not want a Flash player installed on their systems – amazing but true – and it's a good idea to send them to the URL of an HTML version instead.

The JavaScript Integration Kit has a **Flash Dispatcher** behavior, which makes the process of detecting plug-ins and redirecting users, based on pre-determined rules, both easy and seamless.

Workflow of Flash form display

So what do we want to happen when users load up the Flash form in their browser?

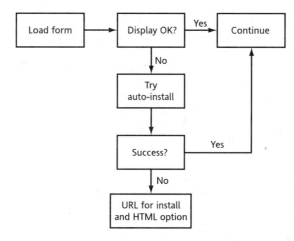

When a user's browser opens up the Flash movie containing our form, the browser will check that the correct plug-in is present. If it's not, and the browser cannot automatically install the required plug-in, then we will redirect the browser to a URL, which will allow users to select the HTML version or download the plug-in.

So, let's fire up the UltraDev Site window and begin working with the Flash Dispatcher behavior.

Detecting the Flash plug-in using the Flash Dispatcher

We won't actually create the HTML version of the form, but just a blank dummy version, to demonstrate the Flash Dispatcher behavior in action. We'll redirect users who don't want the Flash plug-in or can't for some reason get it, there instead.

Creating a dummy HTML page

1. Go into the UltraDev Site window in view, go to the File menu and select New File. A new file will appear in your Local Folder by the name of untitled.asp. Rename this file as mailing.html.

Although your new file is called `mailing.html`, if you look at the file Type column, you'll see that UltraDev still believes this file to be an ASP page! This is because we configured our site's default page extension to be `.asp`.

You can rectify that situation by hitting the Refresh button within the Site window and, UltraDev will recognize the file as an HTML page.

We won't do anything with the HTML page in this exercise - we just need to have one in order to use the Flash Dispatcher behavior.

Detecting the Flash plug-in with the Flash Dispatcher

To use the JIK to make sure that users have the correct version of the Flash player is installed, we have to do two things:

- Create an entry page for the user to browse to; we'll call it `detection.html`

- Attach the Macromedia Flash Dispatcher Behavior to the page. This will redirect or download the user according to the rules that we set in this page.

We'll create the entry page first, to act as the placeholder for the dispatcher behavior. We could place the behavior on every page, but by creating an entry page we only have to check for the existence of a Flash player on the user's machine once. So let's begin:

2. In the site window, create a new page called `detection.html`.

3. Open up the page and bring the Behavior inspector up (Window > Behaviors). Click on the + sign and select Macromedia Flash Dispatcher Behavior.

   The Flash Dispatcher behavior inspector will open.

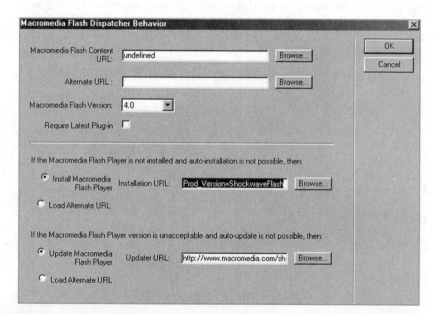

There are effectively three sections in this window. The first section allows you to set the pages that host the Flash and HTML content respectively, and respond to the users circumstances. It has four options:

Macromedia Flash Content URL	Enter the pages with Flash content here
Alternate URL	Set an alternative URL for HTML page here
Macromedia Flash Version	Set the version of your Flash movie here
Version Requires Latest Plug-in	Specify whether the page requires the very latest plug-in to view the content here

The second section is where you specify how to respond to a browser without the Flash player version, and without auto-installation enabled.

Install Macromedia Flash Player	The default URL for the downloadable version of the Flash player is http://www.macromedia.com/shockwave/ ➥ download/?P1_Prod_Version= ➥ ShockwaveFlash
Load Alternate URL	If the user does not have or want Flash player, load the HTML page

The third and final section is concerned with updating the user's Flash player plug-in version.

Update Flash Player	URL where the user can be sent automatically to download an update Flash Player. By default: http://www.macromedia.com/shockwave/ ➥ download/?P1_Prod_Version= ➥ ShockwaveFlash
Load Alternate	If user fails to choose the required version or if the update fails, send the user to the HTML page that we defined.

4. Inside this window, you should browse to the page that holds our Flash content, `mailing.asp`, and set the HTML version of the page - we'll use the blank HTML page, `Mailing.html`, which we created earlier (as this would normally be the HTML equivalent of the Flash page we have created) as the Alternate URL.

I have also specified the Macromedia Flash Version as 5.0, as this is the version I used to export the Flash movie.

I think it is best practice to load the HTML page if the user does not have the Flash player installed and if the auto-installation fails. If the user really doesn't want Flash, it makes the best sense to simply take them to a HTML version of our page.

I selected to take users to the HTML version of the page when their player version is different to mine; it might encourage them to upgrade their player so that they can view our Flash page.

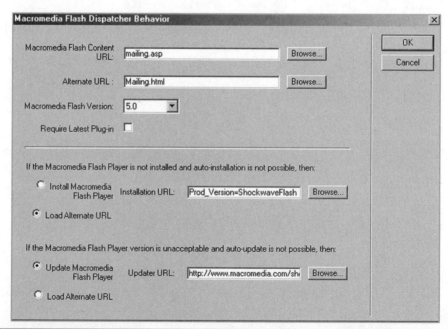

Once you have selected all your preferences in the Behaviors window, click OK and the Macromedia Flash Dispatcher Behavior is present in the Behaviors window:

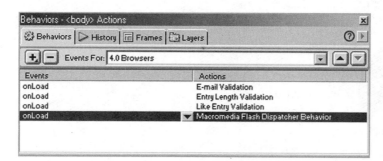

Notice that the Macromedia Flash Dispatcher Behavior has an onLoad event, as the detection and redirection of browsers must be executed before loading any Flash pages.

5.   Close the Behavior window and then save and close your work. If you check the site window you'll see that you have mysteriously acquired two new files. The first, Dispatcher.js, holds the JavaScript that will carry out the detection and redirection process, and the second detectFlash.swf, is a Flash movie that has been nested in the site by the Flash Dispatcher, to execute Flash Player detection.

6.   For the final time we can now synchronize our site, to do this go to the Site menu and choose Synchronize. Once synchronization is complete, view your work in a browser and check out the fruits of your labor!

Conclusion

In this chapter on UltraDev, we looked at the many features of UltraDev and how it interacts with Flash. As I mentioned at the beginning, Flash and UltraDev are not the most obviously compatible design tools, and many people would automatically look at hand coding or using Macromedia Generator for their Dynamic Flash. I think, though, that the program's intuitive user interface and excellent site management features make it an extremely valuable addition to any developer's toolkit.

The UltraDev community is also a great resource for extending and learning all about UltraDev. These are some of the sources of valuable information when you're developing with UltraDev:

www.deja.com	A great resource for Usenet groups devoted to UltraDev, Flash and other Macromedia products.
www.macromedia.com/ ➡ software/ultradev/	The official Macromedia UltraDev site, for news examples, technotes, tutorials and links to the Macromedia Exchange for UltraDev.
www.UltraDevextensions.com	An exhaustive link of tutorials and extensions provided by third parties relating to UltraDev.

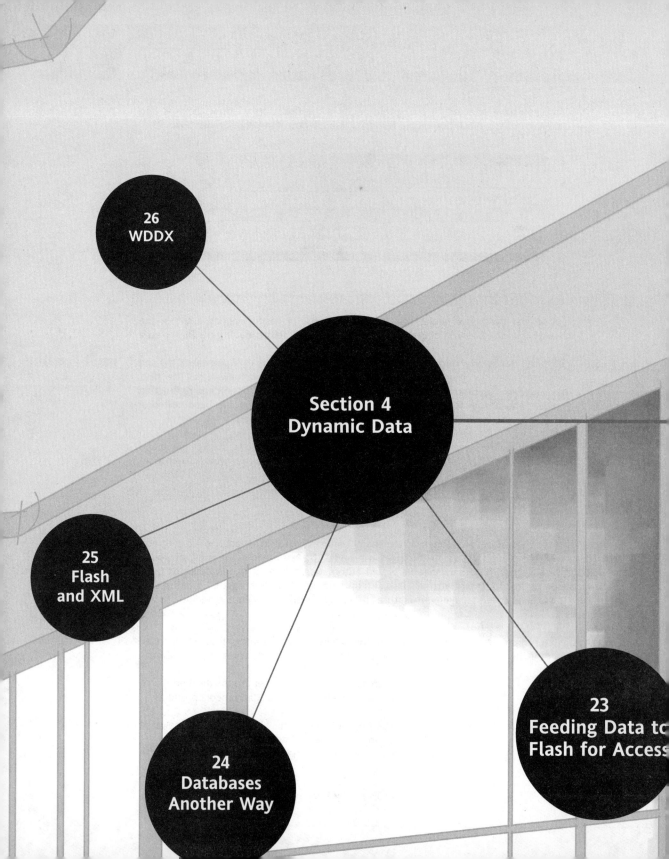

26
WDDX

Section 4
Dynamic Data

25
Flash
and XML

23
Feeding Data to
Flash for Access

24
Databases
Another Way

Chapter 22
Introducing
Databases

I put off working with databases for much longer than I should have done; I thought it would take me far too long to learn how to create one, and even longer to learn how to connect it to my web site, and so I spent hours sending and retrieving information to text files on my server instead. Well, I put my hands up, I was wrong. The truth is that making a database for your web site is not hard. I'm hoping to dispel the myth that databases are only for computer programmers and large companies over the course of this chapter and the next.

So, in this chapter, we'll cover the essentials:

- The benefits of using a database

- What a database is, and how it organizes data

- The types of database that are available, and their relative strengths and weaknesses

- The main database programs that are available to you, to help you decide which one best suits your needs

- Microsoft Access 2000, which is an ideal entry-level database solution

- Creating a database from scratch

I hope that by the time you've finished this chapter, you'll be able to visualize what a database is, how it works, and how it can benefit you – after all, it would be a great waste to create a database for your site without realizing its full potential.

What a database can do for you

Once I made the progression from a text file to a database the only thing I regretted was not doing so sooner. If you do decide to adopt the database approach, it does not mean that you have to stop using text files - you simply need to look at your development in detail and then decide whether you need to use a text file, flat-file database or relational database. More on those later, first, let's talk about why you might want to even entertain the idea of learning about databases – after all, you're a designer, right?

Improve your Flash knowledge
No, really! I have found that my knowledge of Flash has greatly improved since I started connecting to databases; I think that it helped give me a greater understanding of how Flash works, and how it can interact with other elements. So, when the time comes to start using the other backend features of Flash, you will hopefully already have a solid grounding in the principles involved.

Earning potential: reaping the rewards of your hard work
Being able to integrate Flash with a database will really come in useful here. When I'm employing Flash designers I am always willing to offer a higher salary to the person who is familiar with databases, and for certain developments I would not employ a Flash designer unless they had database experience.

As more and more people start to learn Flash, you will find greater competition when applying for jobs and contracts, and so being able to use the backend and database capabilities of Flash will give you the added edge that will help you to secure your position.

Enhance your capabilities

Once you have mastered the basics of databases and are able to create simple databases, you will greatly increase your development capabilities. I've found that having just a little database knowledge has opened a number of new doors for me. It's not just a case of learning about a database; it's also to do with understanding the entire concept. Being able to create stunning sites using Flash *and* connect to a backend database will enable you to create anything from a simple mailing list to a shopping cart.

And, of course, the best thing about learning about databases now is that you're already half way there – you've already started working with scripting languages like ASP and CGI (in earlier chapters), which you need to connect Flash to the database.

Connecting a Flash web site to a database

When you have made your database, you will need to connect it to your web site so that it can be accessed from the Internet, after all I expect this is one of the main reasons that you are learning about databases in the first place.

You can't connect your web site directly to your database, instead you need to use a scripting language such as ASP, CGI or PHP to act as a bridge between Flash and your database. The "bridging" script is required between Flash and the database because Flash alone does not possess the ability to talk to a database.

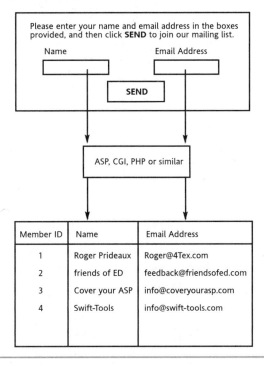

So now we've done the groundwork, let's start talking databases.

What is a database?

This is a question that I have been asked, and have asked many times; and it could be answered: *"A **database** is a collection of information or **data** that is specifically **related** and **organized** for easy **access** and **management**".*

Unfortunately, that explanation doesn't tell you much about the functionality of a database, nor does it enable you to visualize what a database is or what it can do for you.

At this point I would usually revert to paper and a pencil to illustrate and describe a database to you. However, what with the lack of my presence (some would say this a good thing!), I will endeavor to simply describe and illustrate a database throughout this chapter. Once you've finished the chapter, I hope to have furnished you with a complete answer to the question *"what is a database?"* and that you will then feel more capable of moving on to the next of chapter and actually understand how to incorporate databases into your Flash projects. So just what is a database?

I expect that you, like me, have an address book. If you have, then I have some good news for you...perhaps unwittingly you have actually already created a type of database:

	Name	Address	Telephone
	Roger Prideaux	14 New street, Truro	01782 224555

P

Data

Data is basically **information**; think of the names and telephone numbers in your address book; each name, number, and address is a form of data.

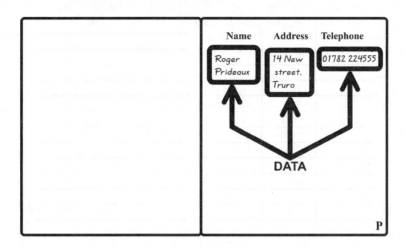

Organizing data

My address book, like many others, has the details of my contacts arranged alphabetically, according to their surname. This is fine until I want to find someone's details and I have forgotten their surname. Then I have to flick through my address book, page by page, looking for their first name in order to find the information (data) that I need.

Now, if I had my address book set up on a computerized database, I could locate someone's details, as long as I could remember something about them. My database would enable me to organize, sort or search my data using a number of different criteria. So, I could search the database for a first name, or any of their other details that I could remember. This act of searching a database for data based upon some form of criteria is referred to in database terminology as a **query**.

The database

So, you've got a whole lot of data that you want to organize, and you've decided that a computerized database is the best way for you to store and retrieve it. Now, from what I've said so far about databases in comparison to a simple address book, you're probably wondering how these programs seem to be so good at enabling us to (amongst other things) find the data that we want, quickly, and effectively. To explain this, we first have to appreciate that a database can only work effectively if the data within it is well organized, and then we need to be able to picture how the data is organized and stored within the database.

Tables

If your address book is anything like mine, then your personal numbers are probably intermingled with work numbers and you've probably even got a few numbers for taxi firms, and pizza takeaways in there too. So, in order to set-up an effective database to act as our address book; we'll have to organize our contact details. To do this we'll start by splitting our contact details into say, three categories, e.g. Personal (for friends' details), Company (for work contacts), and Miscellaneous (for the taxi and pizza numbers).

So, we've split our data into three categories. Now let's organize one of them, the personal contacts category. We'll put all the personal contacts together in one place. To do this we draw up a **table**, made up (as most tables are) of rows and columns.

What's the most obvious way to organize our personal contacts into a personal contacts table? What data do we have about each contact? Well, we've got each contact's name, postal address, and telephone number, so we'll assign one row for each contact's data, and enter the details in the columns along the row. We'll have a column for our contact names, a column for their postal addresses, and a column for their phone numbers — a bit like this:

Name	Postal Address	Telephone
Billy Bob Brewski	1184 Minesanothercoldone Ave Beersville, Somestate	090 2075 4817
Josh Mills	Apt 8b, Water St, Oshawa, Ontario	048 7319 5367

Doesn't look that much different to what you'd expect to find in an address book, really. To be honest there isn't a lot of difference either. But note that we have already started to organize our data (the data is now sorted alphabetically, as it was in the address book, and within each table, the data is of the same type), and that's a step towards being able to find information more quickly and easily.

I've already mentioned how we can divide our original data into **tables** (and our address book example had three of them). In fact, the term **table** is the term used in database circles to describe exactly the sort of thing that we've been talking about here; places for storing collections of related data. There are two more terms that you need to become familiar with: **records** and **fields**; but don't worry, you've actually already been learning about these without knowing it.

Notice in the last sentence, that I said "collections of related data". It's a bit ambiguous isn't it? I mean, you know what I'm saying more or less, the data's related, sure, but we also know that the data in the table is actually inter-related in different ways. The data in the table is related in that it pertains to contacts that have been categorized as personal contacts, but we also know that the data on each row of the table is related too, in that all the data on a specific row refers to the same contact. And that's where records and fields come in, they help us describe to others what's going on in our database table.

Records

My table now has a row for each of my contacts, and a row like this, which contains data for the same contact, is called a **record**. A record is a unit of related data columns (in this case they're all related by the Name column). So, for example you could now refer to the second row in the table as being the Josh Mills record. Fancy another example? Well, let's look at another table, for instance the Company table that we could have created for the work-related contacts in our address book (note how, according to how we contact our acquaintances, we may have different types of information for contacts that belong to different categories):

Company Name	Email	URL
4Tex Group	contact@4tex.com	http://4tex.com
friends of ED	feedback@friendsofed.com	http://www.friendsofed.com
Cover your ASP	info@coveryourasp.com	http://www.coveryourasp.com
Swift - Tools	info@swift-tools.com	http://www.swift-tools.com
Macromedia	europe@macromedia.com	http://www.macromedia

This is the friends of ED record of the Company table.

As you can see, the table has a total of five records each containing Company Name, Email and URL columns. OK, now hopefully that has given you some idea of what a record is...now, what are fields?

Fields

Just a few seconds ago, when I was talking about records, I said that each record had certain information associated with it, and that this information was stored in columns. Well, just to confuse you, these columns are in fact referred to in database circles as **fields**, obscure I know, but there you have it. A field is a subset of a record, containing one piece of data that is related to the record in which it exists.

Company Name	Email	URL
4Tex Group	contact@4tex.com	http://4tex.com
friends of ED	feedback@friendsofed.com	http://www.friendsofed.com
Cover your ASP	info@coveryourasp.com	http://www.coveryourasp.com
Swift - Tools	info@swift-tools.com	http://www.swift-tools.com
Macromedia	europe@macromedia.com	http://www.macromedia

This is the URL field for the records in the Company table.

I guess that at this point you're following what I've said about fields and records etc., but you're probably wondering why we're talking about it at all: is it just a case of terminology for terminology's sake? Well, you'll be pleased to hear, there is a reason for it.

The main reason that we wanted to use a database to store our address book was so that we could find contact details more easily if we had forgotten certain important details. Well, by implementing a database program as our address book (or any information resource for that matter), there are many operations (including searching) that we are then capable of performing on our data. For example, we can append, join, sort, display, manipulate, and transform our data (in fact, if you can think of something that seems like a sensible thing that you'd want to do with data, you can probably get a database to do it for you). We could make some new tables, by taking a row from one table and making it into a column for our new table. As such, by the time we've done all these things to our original table, what are the chances of our final tables looking the same as when we started? Is it still reasonable to call the row that we turned into a column "a row"? By referring to things as tables, records, or fields, or whatever is actually appropriate, we ensure that no matter what sort of changes we make to our data, it'll retain the same identity throughout.

You can think of how a database organizes data as being a little like how we would organize data in a filing cabinet. This schematic may help consolidate some of what we've discussed so far:

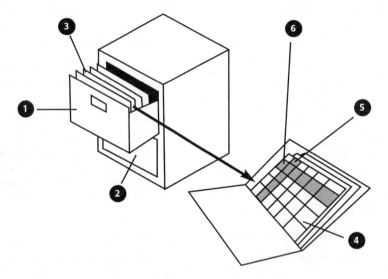

1. The filing cabinet drawer would be the actual database program itself. In this drawer we would be able to store a number of separate files (each of which would be our databases)

2. Ah, but what if I had another drawer in my filing cabinet? Well, that would simply be analogous to another database program, capable of holding even more databases.

3. Each individual file in the drawer would be a database, for example our address book database.

4. Each file in the drawer would contain some sheets of paper. Each sheet of paper would be a database TABLE. So for our example address book database, we would have three sheets of paper, one for the Company table, one for the Personal table and one for the Miscellaneous table.

5. Each row on our table sheets would represent the RECORDS of our address book database.

6. Each individual column in our table would contain one specific piece of information for each of the records in the table. These columns would be the FIELDS of the tables within our address book database.

Relational or flat-file?

A database is often referred to as a **DBMS**, which is an acronym for DataBase Management System. A DBMS can either be a **flat-file** DBMS or a **Relational** DBMS, which is abbreviated to **RDBMS.**

The difference between a flat-file database and a relational database goes something like this...

A flat-file DBMS

A flat-file database is simply a database that contains only one table, with all fields and records being contained within that table. For example, imagine having a database with just our personal numbers in, it would only have one table, and this one table would contain all of the fields and records. A lot of the time a flat-file database is adequate for online purposes and it would therefore not be necessary to create a relational database.

A relational DBMS

A relational database contains **multiple tables**, which contain data that is **related**. That is, if the data in one table is altered, the data in another related table would also change accordingly. I used to find it hard to understand what was meant when people talked about relationships between tables in a database; so to give you some idea of what's meant, here's an example of a relationship that might exist between two tables:

The Flash Fitness gym (yes that is the most original name I could think of) has three different levels of membership, $75 per year, $100 per year and $125 per year.

A table for the member information might look like this:

Member Information Table

Member ID	First Name	Last Name	Address	Town	Phone Number	Membership Cost
1	Roger	Prideaux	14 New Street	Truro	01782 224555	$125
2	Al	Oakley	18 Essex Road	Bodmin	01225 958 231	$125
3	Elly	Long	22 Duck Street	St Austell	01344 848 992	$75
4	Sophie	Edwards	13 Regal Street	Olton	01443 231 881	$100
5	Eleanor	Baylis	44 Fields View	Olton	01443 828 291	$100

This looks fine doesn't it? All the data is clearly displayed in one table. But what happens if Flash Fitness decides to increase the cost of membership? You've guessed it, I would have to change the membership cost for every member. This may not seem like a big task, but just to check, I asked at my local gym how many members they have in their database, and I was surprised to hear that they actually have over 7000 registered members. Imagine the time it would take to change the membership cost for 7000 members!

This is where a relational database can help us a great deal. What we do is create a new field called Membership Rate in place of the Membership Cost field. Next we create a new table, which we'll call the membership cost table, and use this table to relate Membership Rate to Membership Cost. Then we create a relationship between the Membership Rate fields of the two tables. Not too sure as to what I mean? Have a look at the following diagram to see if it makes matters a little more clear:

Member Information Table

Member ID	First Name	Last Name	Address	Town	Phone Number	Membership Rate
1	Roger	Prideaux	14 New Street	Truro	01782 224555	3
2	Al	Oakley	18 Essex Road	Bodmin	01225 958 231	3
3	Elly	Long	22 Duck Street	St Austell	01344 848 992	1
4	Sophie	Edwards	13 Regal Street	Olton	01443 231 881	2
5	Eleanor	Baylis	44 Fields View	Olton	01443 828 291	2

Membership Rate	Membership Cost
1	$75
2	$100
3	$125

The beauty of creating our tables in this manner, and then setting up such a relationship between these tables is that if the gym were to increase its membership cost, and we wanted to update our member information table with these changes, we would only need to update the three records in the membership cost table, and the 7000 member's records would then automatically reflect the changes.

In order to implement a relationship (such as the one I've just described) within an RDBMS, each table within the database must have what is called a **primary key**, and if we want to relate a table to the other tables in the database, we'll also need to use something called a **foreign key**. Keys? Huh? What's this guy talking about?

Primary keys

A **primary key** is a field of data within a table that can be used to uniquely identify a record within that table. So for example, in the member information table, the primary key would be the Member ID field. You can use the primary key to locate a specific record. For example, if a member telephones the gym to find out their membership cost, all the operator has to do is ask them their Member ID, and then query the database to find the record with that Member ID. Hey presto, the correct customer details are displayed.

You could argue that Phone Number, Address, or even Name could be used as primary keys, but then of course you'd run into difficulties if there was more that one member with the same address, or a couple of members who use the same phone. Or even, I know it's unlikely, but more than one member with the same name (then again, 7000 members, and I don't live in a big town – it could happen). If we'd used these fields as the primary keys, then we would end up looking at the wrong data for the caller's enquiry. Of course, we are just talking about a simple gym membership, but there would be big security implications if you were dealing with a database holding more sensitive information.

A **foreign key** is a field in one table that points to the primary key in another table (this links in with the idea of creating relationships between tables). An example of a foreign key in our example would be Membership Rate in the member information table, which points to the primary key of the membership cost table, which also happens to be the Membership Rate field. Not sure what I mean? Have a look at the following schematic bearing in mind what the definition of primary and foreign keys are, and you won't go far wrong:

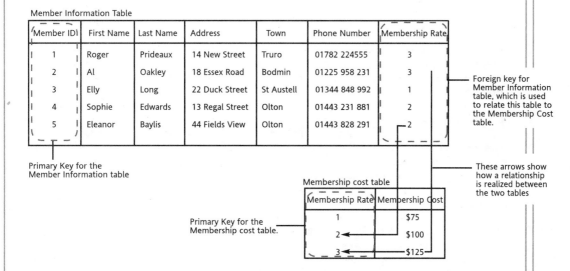

Member Information Table

Member ID	First Name	Last Name	Address	Town	Phone Number	Membership Rate
1	Roger	Prideaux	14 New Street	Truro	01782 224555	3
2	Al	Oakley	18 Essex Road	Bodmin	01225 958 231	3
3	Elly	Long	22 Duck Street	St Austell	01344 848 992	1
4	Sophie	Edwards	13 Regal Street	Olton	01443 231 881	2
5	Eleanor	Baylis	44 Fields View	Olton	01443 828 291	2

Foreign key for Member Information table, which is used to relate this table to the Membership Cost table.

Primary Key for the Member Information table

These arrows show how a relationship is realized between the two tables

Membership cost table

Membership Rate	Membership Cost
1	$75
2	$100
3	$125

Primary Key for the Membership cost table.

About data duplication

Before you develop a database you need to plan around any reusable or changeable data. This is important, because it will help you avoid data duplication. Storing the same piece of data in different locations in a database can cause you all sorts of problems.

Firstly, if we duplicate data, we need more storage space (remember the aim is to keep the database as small and efficient as possible). Second, and perhaps more importantly, imagine that we had the same data stored in a few different places, for instance, say we had the same phone number held in a few different tables. What would happen if the contact's phone number changed? We'd have to search through every table in the database to ensure that every instance of the phone number in all of the tables was updated with the new number, and that could involve a lot more work than simply updating the phone number in just one instance. And even then, who's to say we could be sure that all instances of the phone number had been updated? If we had accidentally missed one, we'd have incorrect data stored within our database, and how much use is that?

So, a lot of thought needs to go into designing a database. I always prefer to draw my database table structure with a pencil and paper, and then think about which fields contain data that could be reused by a number of records, or that is likely to change. This stage of database design where we try to reduce the amount of duplicated data is referred to as **normalization**.

Queries

Remember back the address book example we talked about earlier, when I said about looking for someone's phone number in the address book? Well, what we were actually describing was what's known as submitting a **query**. A query is a request made by the user, to be supplied with (usually specific) information from the database.

So in our earlier example, the user was, well, "us" I guess, our database was the address book, and our query would've been something like: "What's the phone number for Josh Mills?" To find out the answer to this, we would have flicked through our address book until we found the correct page and then we would have read the entry. In much the same way, a user can query a database, which is capable of holding far greater volumes of information, and let the database program carry out the task of finding the requested information.

Going back to our address book example again, when we searched for the phone number of our contact, we would have automatically come across all the other information that we had about them too; their full name and their address (it's all written on the same page, we have no choice but to find all that information as well as their phone number). Well, there doesn't seem to be a problem with that, after all, it could be quite helpful to see that information as well.

In a database, however, you might actually have far more information associated with a given record than we would need to know at any one time. For example, imagine we had a database with sales figures for a large company stored on it, and we wanted to find out the sales figures of a specific product for last week. If we had no way of specifying the precise information that we wanted to find out, our query would return all of the sales figures, and we could easily find ourselves deluged with irrelevant information.

What we need to be able to do is select specific data from our database relevant to our query; and that is exactly what makes computerized databases so useful. Databases allow us to manipulate data to suit our needs. We can use detailed queries to choose specific data that we want to have displayed from within your database.

For example, let's look back at the Flash Fitness gym. Suppose the gym was having a special promotion, and to inform all of their members of the special offer, they were going to give each member a quick phone call (7000 phone calls is a lot of phone calls, but this is just to illustrate a point). What information would the telephonist need in order to call each member? Well, full name, Phone Number and Member ID should just about do it (I included Member ID just in case the member asks for supplementary information regarding their account), and with a computerized database, it would be possible to submit a query such that only the Member ID, First Name, Last Name and Phone Number fields were displayed:

Member ID	First Name	Last Name	Phone Number
1	Roger	Prideaux	01782 224555
2	Al	Oakley	01225 958 231
3	Elly	Long	01344 848 992
4	Sophie	Edwards	01443 231 881
5	Eleanor	Baylis	01443 828 291

Imagine how much more manageable this amount of information is, compared to the situation where (as in our paper address book) we would have returned all of the information in each record. In short, queries are extremely useful for finding the specific information that you want.

So how do you submit a query? Well, you can't just ask the database for the information in natural language, you have to use what's known as a **query language**. Many query languages are actually designed to approximate to the English language; for example, the basic structure of a query may look something like this:

SELECT PHONE_NUMBER FROM MEMBERS WHERE MEMBER_ID=3

It's not totally incomprehensible, is it? We can see that a query of this form could be used to retrieve the telephone number of the record in the Members table, which has a Member ID value of 3, which in our Flash Fitness example, would correspond to the telephone number of Elly Long.

The subject of query languages is actually quite complex, so we won't go any further into it here. In the next chapter, though, I'll show you how to retrieve information from an Access database using queries via Flash and an intermediary scripting language, which is far more appropriate to the scope of this book.

Forms

OK, now we know roughly how our database organizes our data, and we've now got some idea of how we can ask our database to retrieve the data that we want to see displayed. Now, how does the database actually display the data? Well, the database uses an object called a **form**. A form is simply a graphical screen display, a window if you like, which looks, well, like a form. You've probably seen this type of screen display before; they look similar to the type of page that you might have used in an online bookstore, or for registering for a web site. Forms enable the information returned from records as the result of a query to be displayed in a clear, concise manner. Using a form you can modify or add a record, and typically, a standard form displays one record at a time.

Here's an example of a form for the member information table. It tells us that we are viewing record number 1 of 5 in the record details at the bottom of the form, and displays all of the fields within the record:

Should I use a flat-file or relational database?

Every time a database is implemented, it is set up to meet the specific requirements of the task at hand. As such it is not always necessary to use a relational database, as in some instances a flat-file DBMS will suffice. Microsoft Access is a RDBMS but this does not mean that it cannot be used to make a flat-file database.

For instance, if I was going to make a simple mailing list for a web site where the only fields required were Name and email address, there would be no need to produce a relational database. So when do we decide to use a RDBMS? Once you have become more familiar with using databases, you will instinctively have an idea as to which kind of database you should be using, but for now, you will need to use the issues raised by the design/normalization process to help you decide. It is quite important that you decide whether you need to use a FFDBMS or RDBMS before you start to create the database as changes later on will prove tedious and may sometimes prove impractical. The simplest way to decide is to look at the information that the database will store and see if it is subject to change (normalization). If it is, then you just need to decide if it's possible and/or necessary to split the information up into separate tables that relate to one another.

Database options: which database should I use?

There are a lot of database programs available on the market, and I could talk for hours about each program and manufacturer. I think you will be pleased to know that I won't though, I'll just give you a brief overview of the more commonly used database options.

Microsoft Access 2000

Microsoft Access 2000 is an **RDBMS**, and I recommend using this program to make your first online database. Access 2000 was developed to be web-oriented, and features web-enabled information sharing, allowing you to host a database within your browser.

A handy new feature of Access 2000 is that you can 'down-rev' your Access 2000 database so that you can share your files with users that have earlier versions of Access.
One of the features that makes Microsoft Access such a viable option is its impressive scalability. An Access 2000 database can even be scaled up to a SQL Server database, which is great should your database needs grow.

Microsoft Access 2000 in plain English

This is a great database program for your first online/offline database, and is ideal for a small database like a scoreboard or members list. If the size of your database starts to increase a great deal, or you wish to enable a large number of users to access the data at the same time, you can convert your Access 2000 database to Microsoft SQL Server, which is a simple process.

As you will learn later in this chapter, Microsoft Access 2000 is very user-friendly; the scalability alone makes this my top recommendation, as it allows you to create a very simple database that can grow with your needs.

Basic system requirements

To run Microsoft Access 2000 you will require a PC with a 75 MHz processor or higher running Windows 95 or later. Go to www.microsoft.com/office/access/ to find out more.

Microsoft SQL Server

Microsoft SQL Server is a **RDBMS** better suited to applications that require a large database. You can scale your developments up to 32 CPU's and 64 GB – which should give you an idea of the scale of this database. It offers support for rich XML, which means that you can now access your data without the need for complex coding and can manipulate your data in XML using Transaction SQL (T-SQL). To give you an idea of this program's capabilities, companies such as Ask Jeeves, (www.ask.com), Barnes and Noble (www.bn.com), and Dell (www.dell.com) have all used Microsoft SQL Server 2000 for their web developments.

Microsoft SQL Server in plain English

Microsoft SQL Server is really only a sensible option if you intend to have a very large database, or if you need to be able to have a large number of simultaneous users. For example, I use this program when I am creating web-based training courses. I do this, not because I intend to have a large database, but because I want a large number of users to be able to access the data at the same time with speed and efficiency. Bear in mind though, that administering a Microsoft SQL Server database is not an easy task if you are an inexperienced user. Microsoft SQL Server 2000 has improved XML features and capabilities, which are proving very popular and are sure to prove useful with the addition of XML support in Flash 5.

Basic system requirements

To run Microsoft SQL 7 you will need a PC with a 166 MHz processor or higher, running Microsoft Windows NT Server 4.0 or Microsoft Windows NT 4.0 Enterprise Edition with Service Pack 4 or Windows 2000 server. Try www.microsoft.com/sql/ for more information.

MySQL

MySQL is also an **RDBMS**. What sets MySQL apart from other RDBMS is that it is open source software, which means that if you feel inclined to do so, you can study and modify the source code to suit your needs. This also means that MySQL is free, subject to certain restrictions.

MySQL is suitable for a wide range of applications, large or small. For example, I was surprised to find out that Yahoo (www.yahoo.com) use MySQL; by contrast, I also know people who use MySQL to create very small databases, which goes to show that MySQL is accessible to everyone.

"There's no such thing as a free lunch" is an expression that comes to mind in the case of MySQL, as the price you pay for a free program is absence of structured support and some rather confusing documentation.

MySQL in plain English

MySQL is very widely used throughout the Flash community and is becoming ever more popular, especially as MySQL supports all types of servers including operating systems based on Windows, Linux, UNIX and OS2. I personally prefer to use Microsoft Access 2000 and Microsoft SQL Server because of their relative ease of use, the support offered and their compatibility. However, I do recommend visiting MySQL.com (www.mysql.com) to find out more, as MySQL is a free and viable alternative to the Microsoft options, if of course you are willing to sacrifice clear documentation and structured support. We'll be working with MySQL (with PHP) later on in the book.

Database applications in action

Let's conclude this section by looking at the sorts of applications that you're already likely to have used, which will be using a database.

Mailing lists

How many times have you visited a web site and been asked to join their newsletter or mailing list? Well if you were to enter your name and email address, your details would be entered into their mailing list database.

This type of database is probably one of the simplest that you could create, needing only three fields: Member ID number, member Name and member Email Address. As it only contains one table, this is a flat-file database; there would be no need to try to create a relational database, as the data is so simple that it could even be written to a text file.

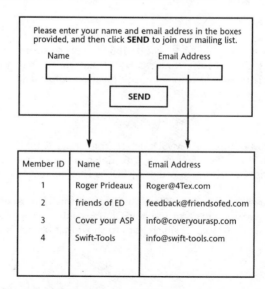

Game scoreboards

So, you've just finished making a fantastic game for your site and you would like to build a scoreboard.

If you only wanted to display the names of users who have completed the game you could use a simple method, which is fairly similar to the mailing list database. However, if you want to display the scores in a specific order such as by high/low score, then this is where matters get a little tricky. To do this, you need to be able to sort your score data into ascending/descending order to suit. The methods I have seen for doing this include sorting the scores using the scripting language you use to connect to the database, although I have to say that my favorite method is to create some custom Flash coding to sort and display the scores.

Dynamic site creation

Dynamic site creation is when a site dynamically displays the information that the user requires, and that information only. In other words, it doesn't load unnecessary information. This method is used a great deal in HTML/ASP (and HTML/PHP, HTML/JSP or XML) based sites and is now starting to become more popular with Flash developers.

A good way to visualize this in use is to imagine that you are creating a web site for a car sales company, which we will call "Flash Cars" (my naming system may be a little predictable). OK, on our site, we want to display a list of cars that are currently for sale, and we want it to be that each car on the list can be clicked on, to display the car's full details such as manufacturer, model, description, price, and a picture of the car. Everyday, cars are being sold and new cars are arriving, and it would not be practical to update the site everyday to accommodate the changing stock and it would also create a very large site if all of the information and pictures were contained within one Flash file.

How do we get around this? We enter all of these details into a database that is connected to Flash, so we can dynamically load only the details relevant to the car that the user is interested in. Also imagine the time it would take without using a database, to create and manage a Flash site like this for a car sales company that had over 1000 cars in stock.

Here's an example of how the tables for such a database might look:

Vehicle Information table

VehicleID	Manufacturer	Model	Description	PriceID	Picture/SWF location
1	Peugot	306 Meridian	Air con, leather trimmed	1	flashcar_images/peugot/Peu106Mer.swf
2	Ford	Puma 1.7 LX	Metallic paint, CD Player	9	flashcar_images/ford/FordPuma.swf
3	Suzuki	Swift 1.0 GLS	Engine immobilizer	4	flashcar_images/suzuki/SuzSwift.swf
4	Ford	Ka Now	Power Steering, drivers airbag	4	flashcar_images/ford/FordKaNow.swf
5	Volkswagen	Golf 1.9 TDI GT	ESP climate control	7	flashcar_images/vw/VWGolf.swf

Relationship created between tables using PriceID as a foreign key in the Vehicle table, and PriceID as the primary key in the Price table

Vehicle Cost Table

PriceID	Price
1	£4,999.00
2	£5,499.00
3	£5,999.00
4	£6,499.00
5	£6,999.00
6	£7,499.00
7	£7,999.00
8	£8,499.00
9	£8,999.00
10	£9,499.00

Notice how the information is displayed in different tables, a Vehicle Information table and Vehicle Cost table. Using multiple tables like this avoids duplication of stored data, and also helps to make updating faster and simpler. This would prove very useful if the car sales company decided to have a short sale and wanted to temporarily reduce the cost of all of the vehicles by 5%. With the tables arranged in this way, the database administrator would only need to reduce the cost of the figures in the vehicle cost table, which is much quicker than having to reduce the cost of 1000+ vehicle records.

Each vehicle model has a picture that has been converted into a Flash file (SWF), and the location of each SWF is detailed so that when this data is loaded into Flash as a variable, a loadMovie action will occur to load the relevant SWF.

Online stores

I frequently use Flash to create online shops with shopping carts. This requires good planning and a well-developed database. Many designers choose to use third party software, because at first glance it looks like the simplest option, but I suspect that once you have mastered the basics you will be keen to develop your own online Flash shop.

So how would you go about planning a database for, say, an online shop for a company that sold T-shirts? Well, one of the first decisions you would have to make would be whether you want to store the T-shirt details in the same table as the T-shirt price. This may seem like a trivial consideration but I want to reiterate this point again, as not considering this now could cause a great deal of extra work in the future, and might even render the database unsuitable for the purpose for which it was originally intended.

OK, let's put the T-shirt details and price in the same table; can you spot what could cause a problem?

TS-ID	T-shirt Logo	T-Shirt Description	T-shirt Price
1	4Tex Group	A short-sleeved cotton T-shirt with logo on the front and back	£15.00
2	friends of ED	A short-sleeved cotton T-shirt with logo on the front and back	£15.00
3	Swift-Tools	A short-sleeved cotton T-shirt with logo on the front	£10.00
4	Cover your ASP	A short-sleeved cotton T-shirt with logo on the front	£10.00

On the face of it, this may appear to be fine. Think about the price for a moment. Now imagine that after a few months of trading you have 3000 different T-shirts for sale, and then your T-shirt manufacturer increases their prices by 10%. Of course, you would then have to raise your prices by 10%, but that would mean that you would have to increase the price of 3000 T-shirts by 10%, one-by-one, a task that I for one wouldn't relish.

How could you design your database tables to avoid such a scenario? Well, a good method would be to store the data in three related tables like this:

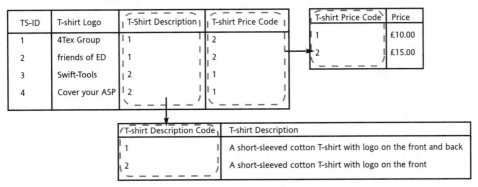

As the T-shirt Price table shows, there are two different prices for T-shirts, so if, as in our example, you had to increase all prices by 10%, you would only have to change two records rather than

3000, which I think you'll agree is a more efficient way of updating your records to keep up with market trends.

You'll notice that I have emphasized this point more than once in this chapter, and there is good reason for this; it is one of the fundamental features of a relational database. Understanding this concept is key to being able to visualize the full capabilities of a RDBMS.

That's it for database theory. We've covered everything you need to know in order to begin working with databases in about half a chapter, so in the next half, we'll start putting it all into practice. I'll show you how simple it is to create a flat-file or relational database using Microsoft Access 2000. Before we do, though, let's just consolidate what we've done so far.

Summarizing database theory

A database is a collection of related information, or data, organized for easy access and management.

A database contains a table or tables.

A table is a collection of records sharing a common theme or topic.

A record is an individual row of fields.

A field is a column of data that can be sorted into the same group.

A flat-file database contains only one table, whereas a relational database can contain multiple tables.

In order to implement relationships between tables, as would be found in a RDBMS, each table in a relational database must have a primary key, which is a piece of unique data to each record, which is used to link all the data together, thus creating the desired relationships.

You can also define supplementary relationships between tables using foreign keys.

You use a query to select the data that you want to display from the database.

You can use a form to display records in an easily viewable manner, and to modify or add a record. Standard forms display one record at a time.

Introducing Microsoft Access 2000

I am going to walk you through the process of creating your first Microsoft Access database step-by-step, assuming no previous knowledge of Microsoft Access at all – so if you've worked through every proceeding chapter in order, I will inevitably cover some things that you've already done.

By the time you've finished you'll be able to make a basic flat-file or relational database that would work perfectly well for an online database. We'll cover:

- Getting to know Access 2000

- Creating a flat-file database using the database wizard, and creating a form

- Turning a flat-file database into a relational database

To illustrate the different ways in which you can carry out tasks in Microsoft Access, we'll build a database application for storing and retrieving contact details, the sort of information you'd find in an address book.

Creating a flat-file database to hold address book details

To save confusion, if you have Access 2000 open please save anything you may be working on and close the program so that we can make a fresh start.

1. Open Access 2000 by going to Start>Programs>Microsoft Access. A dialog will appear, and we want to create a blank database, so select Blank Access database and click OK.

2. The File New Database dialog box will appear, decide where you are going to save your database (I made a new folder called Access 2000), name your database Contacts DB and click the Create button.

3. You should then see the Access 2000 workspace, as shown below. Let's take a look at the basic features.

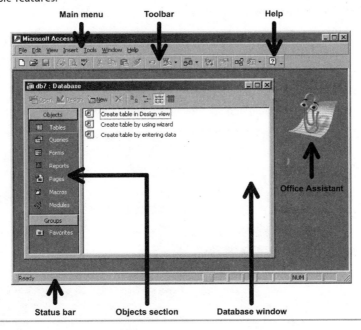

Main menu   Toolbar   Help

Office Assistant

Status bar   Objects section   Database window

- As with any program, it is important that you save your work regularly, so get into the habit of clicking the Save icon (which depicts a 3.5" floppy disk)

- The Toolbar provides quick access to virtually all the functions/commands that you will need. It automatically changes to accommodate different functions you will need at various stages throughout your database development. It is easily customizable, and many advanced users customize it to suit their own purposes.

- The Office Assistant is probably familiar to you already, although some people find him hugely irritating – and if you're one of these right-click and select Hide. (He can be useful when you're looking for help.)

- Help. Access 2000 help is very comprehensive, and if you don't already have all of the help features installed, I strongly recommend it as a must-have addition. When you select Help, the Office Assistant appears in his one and only really useful role, whereby he enables you to search for help on a given subject by simply typing-in your question.

- The Status bar is pretty handy too. It's worth keeping your eye on for information about your current activities within Access.

- The Database window holds all the information about the database you are working on.

- The Objects section is where you can add the different elements that make a database. You can add tables, queries, forms etc, and you are able to create these elements manually or by using the Wizards, this is a good example of when the Toolbar can prove to be very useful.

Let's get back to creating the Contacts. DB database...

4. The next thing we need to do is create a contacts table to hold all of our address book data. Make sure that you have Tables selected in the objects section. Access 2000 has wizards that help create most of your database, and these can help you pull your database together in a matter of minutes. We'll use one here, so in the database window, double-click on the Create table by using wizard option. The Table Wizard dialog box should appear, looking something like this:

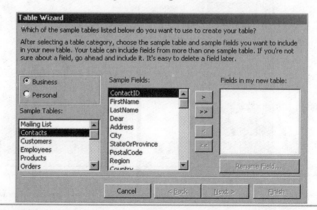

5. We are then given the choice between a business or a personal table, the difference between them being the sample fields included. Select Business, the sample Contacts table, and then add the fields ContactID, FirstName, LastName, Address, City and HomePhone. We can add a field to the table from the Sample Fields by either double-clicking on them, or by clicking the field name and then clicking the single right arrow. The fields we have selected will appear in the Fields in my new table box. We can remove the field the same way – either by double-clicking on it, or selecting the field in the right-hand pane, and then clicking the left arrow button.

The thing about pre-prepared fields is, of course, that they're not always the ones we want, so we'll rename some of them. Change the name of the City field in the Fields in my new table box, by clicking the City field and then selecting the Rename Field button at the bottom right-hand corner of the dialog box. The Rename field dialog box will appear, enabling you to rename the field. Rename the field as Town and click OK. Rename HomePhone to Phone Number the same way.

The Table Wizard dialog box should now look like this:

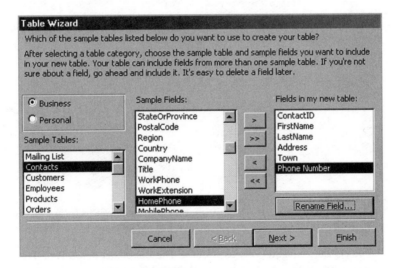

Click Finish, and the Access 2000 table wizard will create our first table and open a new window.

6. When the table wizard creates a table it makes a couple of choices for us. One of these decisions is the view in which the table opens up – look for the following icon to the left of the toolbar, by default it is on the database toolbar.

The table is currently in **Datasheet View**, and if you click on the black arrow to the right of the icon you'll see that we can also view it in what's referred to as **Design View**. This view enables us to inspect and modify the attributes of fields and relationships within the table. Once you have made a few databases and have become more familiar with database design you will be able to create tables in design view rather than using the table wizard.

The displayed icon is perhaps a little confusing because it displays the icon for the view that we haven't selected - so if we had selected Design View from the menu, we would see this icon ▦ ▾ on the toolbar, which if clicked, would take us to Datasheet view.

7.   If you're not already there, go to Design View, and you'll then be able to see the Contacts DB database in Design View, and it should look something like this:

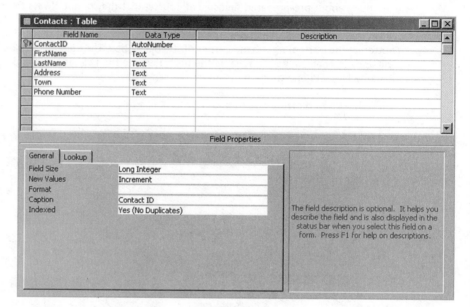

The main features of Design View that are of benefit to us are its capabilities to add a description for a field and to change the Data Type.

8.   Click the ContactID row to select it. The ContactID field's Data Type is AutoNumber, which means that every time a new record is added to the table it is automatically given a number. If you click in the Data Type row, a dropdown menu will appear allowing to choose your preferred data type from Text, Memo, Number, Date/Time, Currency, AutoNumber, Yes/No, OLE Object, Hyperlink and Lookup Wizard.

Apart from the ContactID field, which has an AutoNumber data type, we will leave all the other fields as Text (as the telephone number has no function it does not matter that we shall leave it as Text).

Click on the Phone Number row and then look at the General tab, notice that there is an Input Mask, which helps with data input. In the example below, the Input Mask is for a US telephone number which kind of gets in the way if you are working (or developing an application for use) in another country.

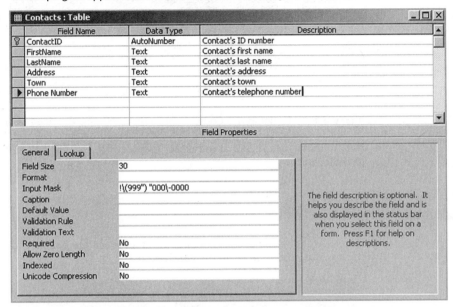

There is a really easy way around this: delete the entire Input mask text for the Phone Number field. It is also a good idea to add a description for each field, it may not seem like much now, but when you start to use Access 2000 frequently, you will be glad that you got into the habit of doing it, as Access displays such information on the status bar.

9. To enter data into the Contacts table we need to get back to the Datasheet View, so click on the Datasheet View icon. If you have not saved since you made the changes, you will see a pop-up message asking you if you want to save the table. Just click on Yes and you will be back in Datasheet View.

If you want to change the width of a field, position your mouse pointer between two fields and the pointer will change to a ⟷. This will enable you to drag the border of the selected field to the desired width. In the example below, the mouse pointer has been positioned between the Last Name and Address fields. A useful tip is that double-clicking on this area will automatically adjust the width to the correct length of the field.

10. Enter the following data in the Contacts table. You can use the up, down, left and right arrows to move the cursor around the table.

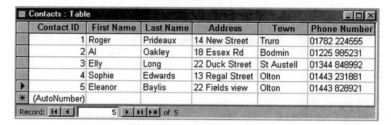

And that's a flat-file database. Couldn't be easier. Viewing this data is fine in this format, but of course as you get more data, it's going to become less suitable. Forms are used to display one record at a time for easy viewing, so we'll look at how to use one of those next.

Creating a form

1. Select Forms from the Objects section. In the database window double-click on Create form by using wizard to bring up the Form Wizard:

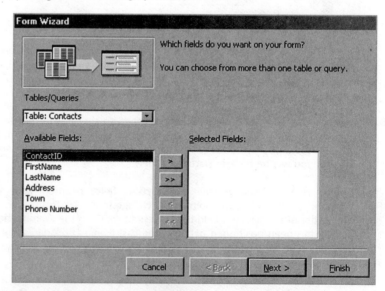

Assuming the only fields in the form that we want to see are FirstName, LastName, and Phone Number, double-click on each of these fields – although you could of course select them one at a time and press the single arrow to send them into the Selected Fields pane (are these actions becoming familiar?)

When you're done, with FirstName, LastName, and Phone Number displayed in the Selected Fields window, click Next to move on to the next step.

2. This window allows you to select different looks for your form, but for now we can stick with the standard Columnar look. Click Next to get to the window that allows you to choose a style for your form.

3. Sumi painting? Perhaps not – I went for that old reliable, Standard. Make your selection and Finish, and that's it. If you made the same selections as I did, your completed form should look like this:

Take a minute to become familiar with the Contacts form, use the back and forward arrows to move through the records from record 1 to 5, and save when you're finished.

So that was a flat-file database and form. Go and make a coffee and prepare yourself for working on your relationships...

Creating a relational database

Now we will create a simple relational database so that we can see the relationship between data in a database. We'll use the Flash Fitness gym example we talked about earlier in the chapter. The Flash Fitness gym database will have two tables: a Membership Info table and a Membership Rate table. Rather than create the database from scratch, we'll modify the Contacts DB database, which will give us a chance to check out some of the other features of Access 2000.

1. Let's start by closing Access 2000. Now reopen Access 2000, and you should see a Microsoft Access dialog box. Select Open an existing file, click on Contacts DB and then OK. Access 2000 will then open the (by now) familiar database window.

2. First we're going to create a table that holds the various gym membership prices. As a quick reminder, we are going to make two separate tables, one will hold the Member Information and the other will hold the Membership Rate (cost). This is because many people will have the same membership rate and if the price was increased in the future, only the price in the membership rate table will be changed and each record that links to this table will access the new rate. Double-click on Create table by using wizard as before.

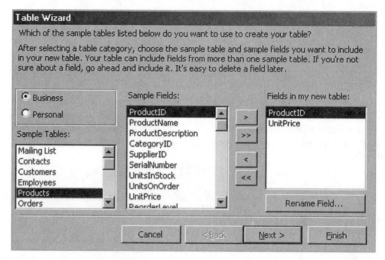

3. Choose the Business category, to display a different set of sample tables, and select Products. Add ProductID, UnitPrice to the Fields in my new table and select Finish. You should get a Products table like this:

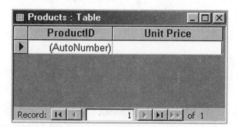

4. Next, we need to give the fields more appropriate names, so rename the ProductID column by right-clicking, selecting Rename column and calling it RateID. In the name of experimentation (who says databases aren't exciting?) double-click on the Unit Price field by double clicking on the Unit Price text and rename it Membership Cost. Alternatively, you could also switch to Design View and rename the columns there.

    The Products table should now look like this:

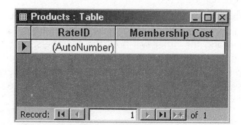

    Close the Products table, and click Yes in the subsequent dialog box to save the changes.

5. Now we'll rename the tables. The Database window should now look something like this:

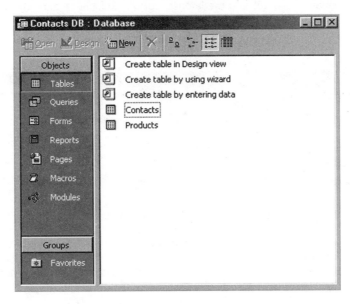

Right-click on the Contacts table and select Rename from the menu, calling it Membership Info. Rename the Products table as Membership Rate

6. Now we'll modify the new Membership Info table.

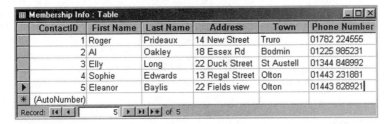

Open up the table by double-clicking on it. Now rename the Contact ID field as MemberID. Then right-click on the Phone Number field heading and select Insert Column from the menu. A new column will then be inserted into the Membership Info table. Click on the Field1 heading to select the entire column, as shown below:

MemberID	First Name	Last Name	Address	Town	Field1	Phone Number
1	Roger	Prideaux	14 New Street	Truro		01782 224555
2	Al	Oakley	18 Essex Rd	Bodmin		01225 985231
3	Elly	Long	22 Duck Street	St Austell		01344 848992
4	Sophie	Edwards	13 Regal Street	Olton		01443 231881
5	Eleanor	Baylis	22 Fields view	Olton		01443 828921
*	(AutoNumber)					

Record: 1 of 5

Now click and drag the whole of the Field1 column to the right of the Phone Number column and release the mouse button. Rename the newly positioned Field1 as Membership Rate.

The Membership Info table should now look like this:

	MemberID	First Name	Last Name	Address	Town	Phone Number	Membership Rate
	1	Roger	Prideaux	14 New Street	Truro	01782 224555	
	2	Al	Oakley	18 Essex Rd	Bodmin	01225 985231	
	3	Elly	Long	22 Duck Street	St Austell	01344 848992	
	4	Sophie	Edwards	13 Regal Street	Olton	01443 231881	
▶	5	Eleanor	Baylis	22 Fields view	Olton	01443 828921	
*	(AutoNumber)						

Record: I◀ ◀ | 5 | ▶ ▶I ▶* of 5

7. Let's say that there are three different membership rates for the Flash Fitness gym, rate 1 at $75, rate 2 at $100 and rate 3 at $125. As the rates are numbers, we need to ensure that the Membership Rate field is configured to handle numbers, so click on the Design View icon to change the data type of the Membership Rate field to Number. Similarly, change the data type properties of the Membership Cost and RateID fields (in the Membership Rate table) to Number.

8. Now we need to go back to the Membership Info table to make a few modifications. First add a description to the Membership Rate field. At the bottom of the General tab you will see an Indexed option. Clicking on this will display a drop-down menu, which we need to set to Yes (Duplicates OK). This tells Access that it is OK for two members to have the same Membership Rate. A point to note here is that if you set duplicates to No it means that no two records can hold the same information, as would be the case in the MemberID field, as no two members can have the same Member ID.

On the General tab there is also a Default Value option. We don't actually want a default value membership rate, because each member has a personal rate, so delete the 0 in this box. Those are all the changes that we need to make.

Note that the primary key has been automatically set by Access on the table using the key icon 🔑 , on the MemberID field. Your table should look like the one opposite. Save the changes, and close it.

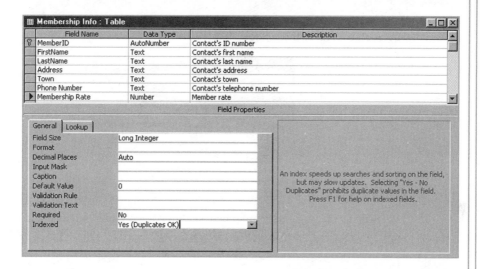

9. Now we need to add some details to the Membership Rate table, so open it up and enter the following information to the table, so that it looks like this one:

10. Next we need to enter the Membership Rate number for each member into the Membership Info table, and to do that we need to know what everyone pays. Let's say that Roger and Al each pay $125 so their Membership Rate is 3. Elly pays $75 so her Membership Rate is 1. Sophie and Eleanor each pay $100 so their Membership Rate is 2.

   Enter these figures into the Membership Rate table, so that it looks like this:

	MemberID	First Name	Last Name	Address	Town	Phone Number	Membership Rate
	1	Roger	Prideaux	14 New Street	Truro	01782 224555	3
	2	Al	Oakley	18 Essex Rd	Bodmin	01225 985231	3
	3	Elly	Long	22 Duck Street	St Austell	01344 848992	1
	4	Sophie	Edwards	13 Regal Street	Olton	01443 231881	2
	5	Eleanor	Baylis	22 Fields view	Olton	01443 828921	2
*	(AutoNumber)						

Record: 5 of 5

11. Close both tables and make sure you save them.

   Now, here comes the fun part! We are about to create a relationship between the Membership Info table and the Membership Rate table.

12. On the toolbar you have a Relationships button. Click this button to bring up the Relationships window. Now press and hold SHIFT, and then select both the

Membership Info table and the Membership Rate table, then click Add, which brings up another view of the window.

13. We want to create a relationship between the Membership Rate field and the RateID field. To do this, click on the Membership Rate field, drag it onto the Rate ID field, and then release the mouse.

An Edit Relationships window will appear:

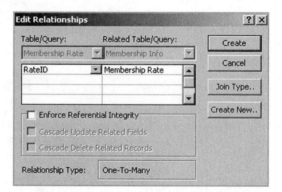

14. Click Join Type, which will bring up the Join Properties window. Select the first option, Only include rows where the joined fields from both tables are equal and press OK. You'll be brought back to the Edit Relationships window. Click Create and you will see a visual representation of the relationship between the two tables.

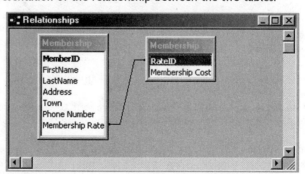

15. Now close the window, and select Yes to save the changes when you're prompted to do so. All that's left to do now is look at the results.

16. Open the Membership Rate table, and see if you notice anything new:

To the left of the RateID column, 3 little plus symbols have appeared. If you click on these, you'll see the relationship between the two tables is displayed, which should look a bit like this:

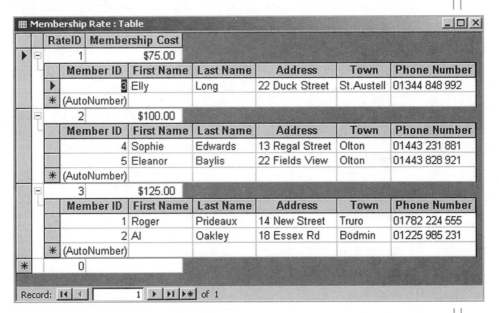

That's how to set up the relationship between the RateID field, in the Membership Rate table, and the information in the Membership Info table. The beauty of this method is that if the gym were to increase its membership cost, we would only need to update the three records in the membership table, and the members' records would automatically be linked to the new charges.

Conclusion

We've covered a lot in this chapter: the fundamental concepts in database design, creating a flat-file database, and then turning it into a relational database. I hope that now you are more comfortable with the subject of databases, and that you are more familiar with Microsoft Access 2000.

Creating the relational database in this chapter will help you to visualize how the database is working in the background when you are using it with Flash. When we connect to the database using ASP in the next chapter, the relationship will not be created by Access, but by the ASP script, it is however important that you understand the concept of how the relationship works. If you are in anyway unsure, I suggest having another look through this chapter, using Access' own built-in help feature, and, of course, checking out the wealth of free information available on the net (try www.ask.com).

It would have taken an entire book to teach you all the features of Access 2000. If you would like a more in-depth knowledge of Access 2000, you might like to look at *Beginning Access 2000 VBA* published by *Wrox Press* (ISBN 1-861001-76-2), or check out some of the other available titles. If you decide to purchase an Access 2000 book from an online book company I recommend trying to get to a local book store to have a quick flick through first; I say this as I have noticed in the past that a great deal of database books cover offline databases in detail but greatly lack online databases and connections.

Before you move onto the next chapter, it would be a good idea to make a few simple flat-file databases to become even more familiar with Access 2000. When you have done this, try converting some of your flat-file databases into relational databases as well as creating a couple of relational databases from scratch.

What you have learned in this chapter can also help you to manage your offline data/information more efficiently; maybe you could practice by creating a database to catalogue your CD, video, DVD or book collection.

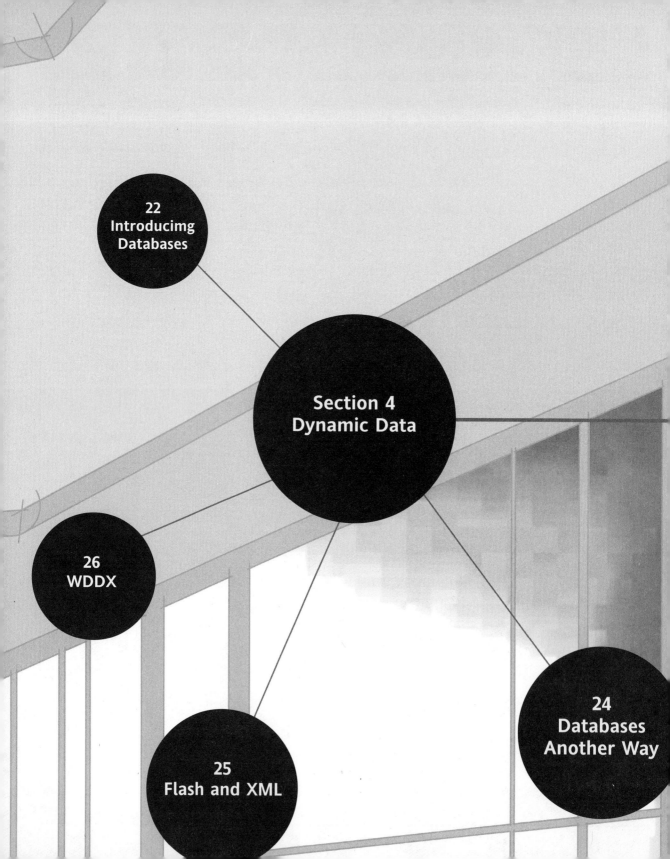

22
Introducimg
Databases

Section 4
Dynamic Data

26
WDDX

25
Flash and XML

24
Databases
Another Way

Chapter 23
Flash, Access
and ASP

In this chapter we'll create an online database for a T-shirt company called 4Tex Flash T-shirts. The site will enable users to search for a T-shirt in the database, and if a matching T-shirt is found, display the relevant details.

To achieve our aim, we'll create Flash T-shirts using an MS Access 2000 database, and a SWF for the front end. ASP will be used to connect the Flash front end database. So, we'll look at:

- Designing a relational database with a difference.

- Retrieving data from the database using Flash.

- Creating an ASP file that will connect Flash to the database.

- Seeing your online database in action.

Creating a relational database differently

In the last chapter we created two database tables, and then created the relationship between them. This time around, we'll create a database that contains two tables with related fields, but which are in fact related by an ASP file – we won't be using Access 2000 to create the relationship.

Creating the database

Let's begin by creating the database, working through the same steps as we did in the last chapter, but this time we'll do so at a bit more of a pace. If you feel you need more information, simply flick back a few pages to the relevant sections in the previous chapter.

> *A tip: Whatever else you do, always remember to save your work frequently using the save icon:* 💾.

OK, for this database we are going to create two tables. The first is going to hold information about the T-shirts that we have for sale, so we'll call this table... wait for it.... Tshirts, and in it we'll add the following fields:

TSID	We'll use this as an identification number for each T-shirt.
Name	Go on, have a guess...
Description	What it looks like.
Tsize	Size.
PriceID	We've seen this before.

The second table will be called Price, and will only contain two fields: PriceID and Price. The PriceID field in the Price table will relate directly to the PriceID field in the Tshirts table. So, let's set this all up:

1. Open Access 2000, select Create a new database using a Blank Access database, and then click OK.

2. Decide where you're going to save your database (I saved mine in My Documents\T Shirt DB), name your database T-shirt DB, and click Create.

3. You should now have the Database window open. Double-click on the Create table by using wizard option to open the Table Wizard so that we can create the T-shirt table. You should now see the Table Wizard, select Business and choose Products as your sample table. Add ProductID, ProductName, ProductDescription, ProductName again (which will appear as ProductName1), and ProductID again too (which will appear as ProductID1).

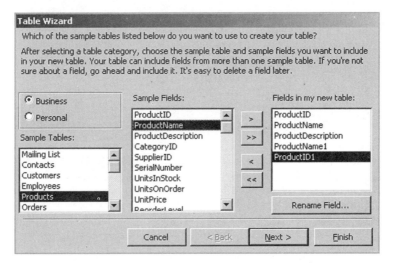

4. Now rename the fields to the following:

ProductID	TSID
ProductName	Name
ProductDescription	Description
ProductName1	TSize
ProductID	PriceID

And then click Next.

> *I learned something important when I created this database and connected it to Flash using ASP. I had originally named the TSize field as Size, which seemed fine to me, and I had never named a field Size before. It turns out that Size is a reserved word in ASP and this caused a problem... well, you learn something new everyday...*

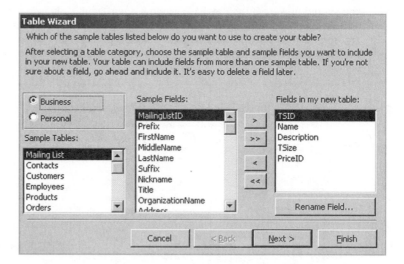

5. In the next window, you'll be asked what you want to call your table. Give the table the name Tshirts, and then click Finish

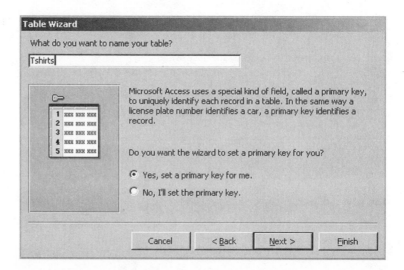

6. You will now see the Tshirts table in datasheet view as shown below, save and then close the table.

7. Now we'll build the Price table, so double-click on Create table by using wizard to open the Table Wizard again.

8. Once again, select the Products sample Business table, and then add the ProductID, and UnitPrice fields. Now rename ProductID to PriceID, and the UnitPrice field to Price. Click Next, rename the table as Price and then click Finish.

9. All being well, you should then see the Price table in datasheet view as shown here:

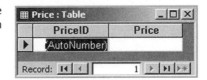

10. Now we'll enter the relevant data into the Price table.

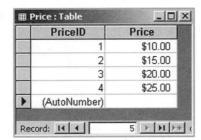

Notice that as you enter the data, you don't need to enter anything into the PriceID field. This is because it's the primary key for the table, and has been automatically set to AutoNumber. All we have to do is simply enter the numeric digit for the Price field, and it will be automatically converted to currency when we press ENTER, or move to the next field.

Close and save the Price table.

11. Enter the following data into the Tshirts table, and then click Save.

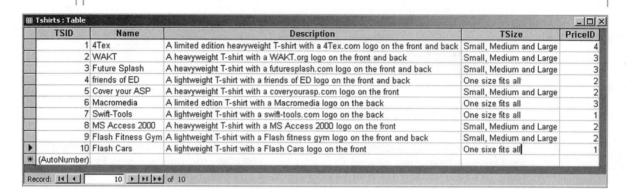

	TSID	Name	Description	TSize	PriceID
	1	4Tex	A limited edition heavyweight T-shirt with a 4Tex.com logo on the front and back	Small, Medium and Large	4
	2	WAKT	A heavyweight T-shirt with a WAKT.org logo on the front and back	Small, Medium and Large	3
	3	Future Splash	A heavyweight T-shirt with a futuresplash.com logo on the front and back	Small, Medium and Large	3
	4	friends of ED	A lightweight T-shirt with a friends of ED logo on the front and back	One size fits all	2
	5	Cover your ASP	A heavyweight T-shirt with a coveryourasp.com logo on the front	Small, Medium and Large	2
	6	Macromedia	A limited edtion T-shirt with a Macromedia logo on the back	One size fits all	3
	7	Swift-Tools	A lightweight T-shirt with a swift-tools.com logo on the back	One size fits all	1
	8	MS Access 2000	A heavyweight T-shirt with a MS Access 2000 logo on the front	Small, Medium and Large	2
	9	Flash Fitness Gym	A lightweight T-shirt with a Flash fitness gym logo on the front and back	Small, Medium and Large	2
▶	10	Flash Cars	A lightweight T-shirt with a Flash Cars logo on the front	One sixe fits all	1
*	(AutoNumber)				

Record: 10 of 10

12. Making sure both of the tables are saved and closed, click the Relationship icon on the toolbar.

You should then see the Relationships window appear, as shown below. If the Show Table window doesn't appear, simply right-click, and select Show Table from the menu. Click on the Tables tab.

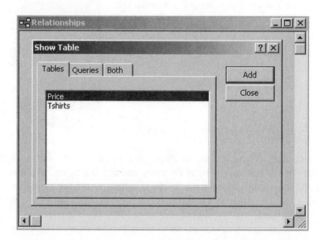

13. Select Price, and whilst holding SHIFT on your keyboard, select Tshirts, which will select both of the tables. Click Add, and then click Close.

14. Within the Relationships window you should now see a Price box containing all the fields in the Price table and a Tshirts box containing all the fields from the Tshirts table.

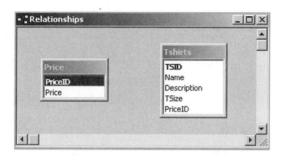

15. Click on the PriceID field in the Tshirts box, and drag it onto the PriceID field in the Price box, and then release the mouse. The Edit Relationships window should appear:

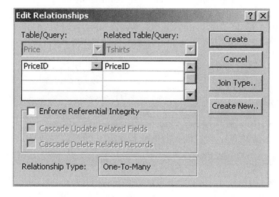

16. Click on Join Type, and the Join Properties window should then appear. Select option 1, to make sure that a relationship is created between the PriceID field in the Tshirts table and the PriceID field in the Price table only when the data in both fields are equal. Click OK to apply your changes.

17. So now let's finally create the relationship. Click Create in the Edit Relationships window. You should now be able to actually see the relationship between the PriceID fields in the Tshirts and Price tables.

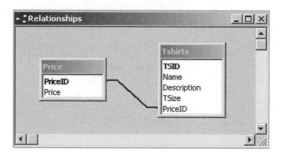

Close the Relationships window, and make sure you click Yes to save your changes.

18. So now, we have a fully functional, relational database just like the one shown in the next screenshot, with the PriceID field of the Price table relating to the T-shirt with the same ID in the Tshirts table. Make sure you save all of your hard work, and then close Access 2000, as we're not going to need it for the rest of the chapter.

Price : Table

PriceID	Price
1	$10.00

TSID	Name	Description	TSize
7	Swift-Tools	A lightweight T-shirt with a swift-tools.com logo on the back	One size fits all
10	Flash Cars	A lightweight T-shirt with a Flash Cars logo on the front	One sixe fits all
(AutoNumber)			

PriceID	Price
2	$15.00

TSID	Name	Description	TSize
4	friends of ED	A lightweight T-shirt with a friends of ED logo on the front and back	One size fits all
5	Cover your ASP	A heavyweight T-shirt with a coveryourasp.com logo on the front	Small, Medium and Large
8	MS Access 2000	A heavyweight T-shirt with a MS Access 2000 logo on the front	Small, Medium and Large
9	Flash Fitness Gym	A lightweight T-shirt with a Flash fitness gym logo on the front and back	Small, Medium and Large
(AutoNumber)			

PriceID	Price
3	$20.00

TSID	Name	Description	TSize
2	WAKT	A heavyweight T-shirt with a WAKT.org logo on the front and back	Small, Medium and Large
3	Future Splash	A heavyweight T-shirt with a futuresplash.com logo on the front and back	Small, Medium and Large
6	Macromedia	A limited edtion T-shirt with a Macromedia logo on the back	One size fits all
(AutoNumber)			

PriceID	Price
4	$25.00

TSID	Name	Description	TSize
1	4Tex	A limited edition heavyweight T-shirt with a 4Tex.com logo on the front and back	Small, Medium and Large
(AutoNumber)			
(AutoNumber)			

Record: 5 of 5

Retrieving data from your database using Flash

And now finally, we can open Flash and have some fun. It's not that databases aren't interesting, but you know what I mean...

Here's what we are going to achieve in this section of the chapter:

From the user's point of view, the SWF will appear, presenting all the names of the T-shirts that we have for sale. The user can select one, and view all the information that we hold about it in the database. So, we'll need to:

- Create a SWF that will load all of the T-shirt names into Flash from our Access database.

- Add a search feature.

OK, let's get started.

Building a Flash front end

1. Open a new Flash movie, and set the movie properties to 600 by 400 pixels with a frame rate of 24 frames per second (or some other frame rate if you feel you have preference).

2. We'd better make this example a little presentable, and it's a good idea to 'block' a functional Flash project before working on the aesthetics, so create a really basic background just to give us a good foundation to work from. Name the first layer Background, and add a basic background to frame 1, as I have done in my example below (no laughing – remember I did say "basic"!)

To keep things nice and tidy, I've converted all the graphics on the Background layer to a graphic symbol called Background, I've also locked the layer so I won't be able to move anything on the stage by mistake.

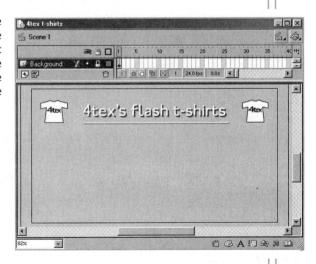

3.   We'll use a preloader (in time honored Flash tradition) to ensure that the entire movie has loaded before anyone tries to connect to the database. So, create a new layer, call it Preloader, insert a blank keyframe at frame 50, and give this keyframe the label end. When we've finished, we'll place this keyframe in the last frame of the movie. Now, we want our background to persist for the duration of the movie, so extend the timeline for this layer out to frame 50 too.

4.   Insert a keyframe in frame 1 of the Preloader layer, and add the following ActionScript to it:

```
ifFrameLoaded ("end") {
    gotoAndPlay (4);
}
```

5.   Now, in frame 3 of the Preloader layer, insert a blank keyframe with the following ActionScript in it:

```
gotoAndPlay (1);
```

Your movie should be looking like this:

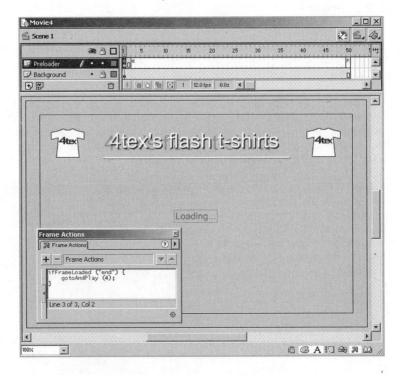

So, what did we just do?

Well, the keyframe in frame 1 checks to see if the frame label, end, has loaded yet, if it has, the movie will go to frame 4 and play. If not, the movie will continue to play until it gets to frame 3. At frame 3, the movie will go back to frame 1, play again, and this loop will continue until the end frame label has loaded. Of course, it's a good idea if the user knows what's going on, so put some text in frame 1 of the Preloader layer letting them know that the movie is loading. I used the old favorite of entering the word Loading..., at least it's informative. Lock this layer before you move on, to avoid moving the wrong things about on the stage, and we've now created a basic preloader.

6. Now that we know the movie has loaded, we need to load all the names of the T-shirts that we have in stock. So create a new layer, and call it Load stock list, and then insert a blank keyframe in frame 4. We'll use a loadVariables action to activate the ASP script (we'll call it GetList.asp) that will load the list into Flash. Open the Frame Actions window for the keyframe in frame 4 of the Load stock list layer, and then add the following ActionScript to it:

```
loadVariablesNum ("GetList.asp", 0, "GET");
```

7. When we write the ASP script, we'll add in a piece of code to check whether the list has been successfully compiled or not. The code will output the variable ListMatch=Yes when the list has been successfully compiled, when it hasn't been compiled the variable will simply be output as ListMatch=No.

    We'll use Flash's if action to look for the variable ListMatch, so let's add some ActionScripting to a keyframe in frame 5 of the Load stock list layer to do this.

    The code that we need to add starts by looking for a match to the ListMatch variable, and checks that it does contain something, or in other words (as the code prefers to put it), that it "does not equal nothing", which is abbreviated to: "". If it does, which it must, then processing continues.

```
if (ListMatch != "") {
```

The variable might have come from the ASP script as ListMatch=No, in which case we need the code to stop right there, so we send it out of the loop to stop at frame 8:

```
    if (ListMatch == "No") {
        gotoAndStop (8);
```

Ideally, however, the ASP script will send the variable ListMatch=Yes, in which case, processing should continue at frame 9:

```
    } else if (ListMatch == "Yes") {
        gotoAndStop (9);
    }
}
```

So, altogether we have something that looks like this:

```
if (ListMatch != "") {
    if (ListMatch == "No") {
        gotoAndStop (8);
    } else if (ListMatch == "Yes") {
        gotoAndStop (9);
    }
}
```

8. We need to loop the `if` action in the previous step until the variable `ListMatch` equals "Yes" or "No", so create a new keyframe in frame 7 of the Load stock list layer, and enter the following code to tell the movie to go to and play from frame 5:

```
gotoAndPlay (5);
```

This loop will continue until `ListMatch` equals something!!

9. Your timeline should now be looking something like this:

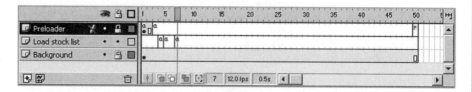

10. It wouldn't be good for business if visitors thought that the site was broken, and left while everything was loading, so we'll add in some visuals to let them know that information is being loaded from the database.

    Create a new layer, and name it List graphics. Insert a blank keyframe at frame 5, and enter some text to let the user know what's happening - something to the point like: Loading data from database... Inserting another blank keyframe at frame 7 of the same layer will make the text flash, which has the added advantage that you also know that this section of the movie is looping correctly whilst the data is being retrieved.

11. Back in step 7, we used an `if` action to test if the variable `ListMatch` had the value No, and if it did, we added code so that the movie would go to frame 8 and stop. This result would be returned when it hasn't been possible to collect the information from the database, and would realistically only occur if we were to connect to a blank database. Just in case something odd like that should happen, we'll code around it. Put a keyframe in frame 8 of the List graphics layer, and enter a text message for the user to inform them of the situation – something like: Unfortunately it has not been possible to retrieve any data from our database should do the trick.

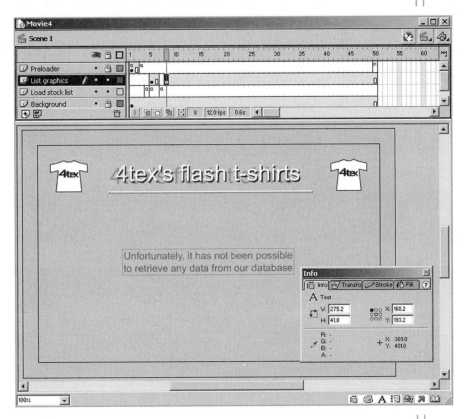

12. We also created an `if` action that would send the movie to frame 9 when the `ListMatch` variable had the value `Yes`. This is the frame where we'll display a list of all the T-shirts that we have in stock.

The `GetList.asp` file is going to output two variables. The first will be a variable named `List`, containing a complete list of all the T-shirts we have in stock, and the second variable is, of course, the `ListMatch` variable.

Insert a blank keyframe at frame 9 of the List graphics layer, and create a dynamic, single line text field for the `List` variable by setting the variable name to `List`. You might also want to add a text heading above the text field to explain it to the user; the text I entered was: Here is a list of the T-shirts that we currently have in stock.

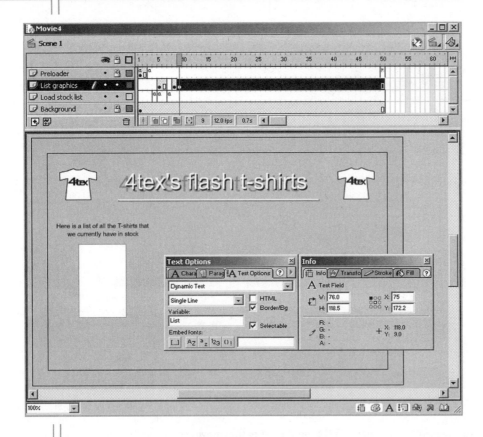

Well, we've now completed creating the area of the movie that will list the T-shirts that we have in stock, and our next step is to begin creating the area of the movie that will allow the user to display full details of a chosen T-shirt.

We're going to create a text field called SearchDB so that the user can enter the name of the T-shirt that they would like to find out more about. We'll also provide a more info button that the user will need to click to send the SearchDB variable to the ASP script.

13. Create a new layer called Search, and on frame 9 of this layer insert a blank keyframe. In this new keyframe create an input text, single line text field for the SearchDB variable to be entered into, calling the variable SearchDB.

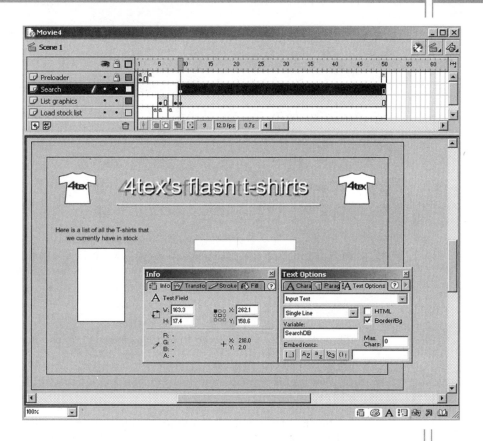

14. Now we need to add a button so that we can send the input text variable, SearchDB, to the ASP file. The ASP file that we're going to send the input text variable to is called GetShirtInfo.asp

Staying with the Search layer at frame 9, make a simple button, and add the following code to it:

```
on (release) {
    gotoAndPlay (10);
}
```

Again, I added a text heading above the text field to explain its purpose to the user: 'Enter a name from our stock list on the left and click 'More info'.'

15. Insert a blank keyframe in frame 10 of the Search layer. This is the keyframe where we will load the T-shirt name that we want to search for, into the GetShirtInfo.asp script. This is another job for loadVariables.

Add the following ActionScript to the keyframe that we've just added:

```
loadVariablesNum ("GetShirtInfo.asp", 0, "GET");
```

16. Insert a blank keyframe in frame 11 of the Search layer, and enter the following code into the frame (this code is based on a similar principle to the code we developed earlier in step 7):

```
if (Match != "") {
    if (Match == "No") {
        gotoAndStop (14);
    } else if (Match == "Yes") {
        gotoAndStop (15);
    }
}
```

17. We need to loop the `if` command we've just introduced until the variable `Match` equals `Yes` or `No`. So, insert a blank keyframe on the Search layer at frame 13, and add the following code:

```
gotoAndPlay (11);
```

This code tells the movie to go to and play frame 11, a loop that will continue until `Match` equals `Yes` or `No`.

18. OK, now we need some more visuals to let the user know what's going on while the information is being collected.

Create a new layer, and name it Search graphics. In frame 10 insert a new keyframe, and enter some text to let the user know what is happening, something like "Loading T-shirt details from database...". In the same layer, insert a blank keyframe at frame 13, this will make the text flash, and will also help you to know that this area is looping correctly whilst retrieving data from the database.

Your timeline should now look very similar to the one below:

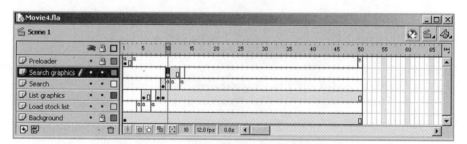

19. In step 16 we implemented an `if` action so that if the `Match` variable equaled `No`, the movie would go to frame 14 and stop, meaning that the user has entered a name of a T-shirt that doesn't exist in the database. We need to let the user know that their search was unsuccessful, so to do this, insert a blank keyframe in frame 14 of the Search graphics layer, and enter the following text: Sorry there was no match for. Bear with me on this one, as we'll make it such that the final output will complete the sentence with the user's choice.

Next create a single line input, dynamic text field for the `SearchDB` variable to be re-entered into, calling it, `SearchDB`.

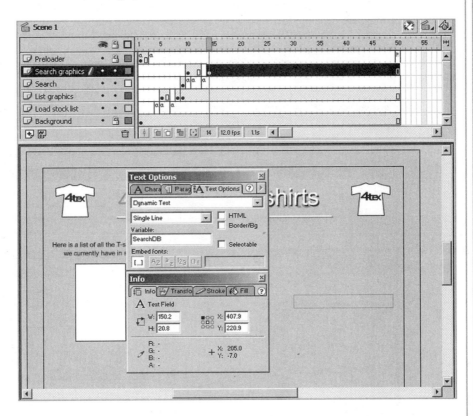

20. If the user has just had an unsuccessful match after searching our database, it would be a good idea to give them the option to search the database again, we must therefore create a Search again button.

In frame 14 of the Search graphics, add a Search again button with the following code:

```
on (release) {
    Match = "";
    SearchDB = "";
    gotoAndStop (9);
}
```

The expression Match = "" resets the Match variable by setting its value to "" (sets the value to nothing/blank), and SearchDB = "" does the same for the SearchDB variable. Finally, the movie is sent to frame 9 so that another search can be carried out.

21. In step 16 we used an if action to make sure that if the variable Match had the value Yes, the movie would go to and stop at frame 15. If the variable Match equals Yes, then we know that the search was successful, and we can then display the results.

In frame 15 of the Search graphics layer, insert a blank keyframe. In this frame you need to enter a text field for each of the database fields Name, Description and Size using the following details. Add a single line dynamic text field with the variable name name, a multiline dynamic text field with the variable name description, and a single line dynamic text field with the variable name size. On the text box labeled description, make sure that you also choose Word wrap from the Text Options tab, so that the full description will be displayed when the description is longer than one line. Also check the Border/Bg check box. Your stage should now look something like this:

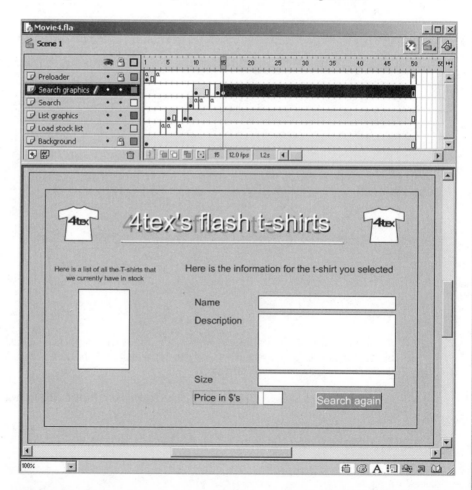

22. Now we need to display the price of each T-shirt to the user. When we view the price within the Access 2000 database it appears as $10, $15 etc, but this is only a visual formatting element of Access, and it will unfortunately output the price as 10, 15 etc, so we need to add a '$' (or whichever currency that you are using) to the price before we display it to the user.

To do this, we need to insert a blank keyframe in frame 15 of the Search layer, and then add the following code:

```
Pricepound = "$" add Price;
```

Pricepound is a literal string, and "$" add Price; is an expression.

23. We now need to add a Pricepound text field to our page, so in frame 15 of the Search graphics layer, add a single line dynamic text field with a variable name of Pricepound

24. We now need to add the Search again button to keyframe 15 of the Search graphics layer. You can simply copy the Search again button from frame 14 of the Search graphics layer, which we created back in step 18 – the code on the button doesn't need to be changed.

25. We've almost finished creating our Flash file, so all we need to do now is move the end frame in the preloader layer to frame 15 and delete all the frames after frame 15 on every layer.

Your stage and timeline should now look similar to the example on the next page:

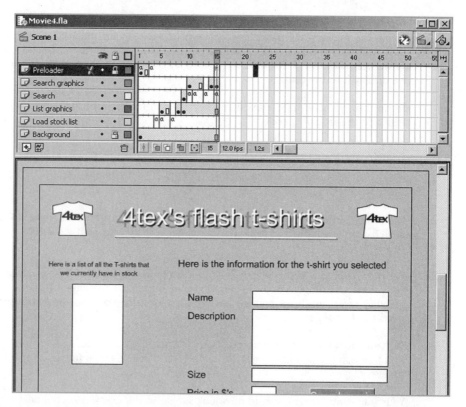

Well, now that you've now made your Flash file, and are about to start looking into learning a little bit about ASP, save your work, and export it as `Tshirt.swf` for use later in the chapter.

Creating an ASP file that will connect Flash to the database

In the final section of this chapter we are going to create the ASP scripts that we will need to connect Flash to the Access 2000 database that we created earlier in this chapter.

We're going to create two ASP scripts so that we can simplify the process. We'll be using the first script to load the names of all of the T-shirts into Flash, and we'll use the second script to search the database for a particular record. We'll progress through each script step-by-step, and I'll explain as we go.

Many people think that ASP is a language, well actually it's not. ASP is a collection of six objects, and to use these objects you must use a scripting language, the most common being VBScript (Visual Basic script) and coming in at a close second is JavaScript. There are other third party languages such as PerlScript, but these are very rarely used within ASP. It would therefore be correct to say "I write ASP applications" and not "I write in ASP"

I've previously used VBScript for all of my ASP scripts, but as Flash 5 is now so tightly interwoven with JavaScript, I have a special treat for you. I enlisted the help of a colleague of mine called James Shaw, who is a JavaScript/ASP expert. James runs www.coveryourasp.com, and we have worked together on our different specialist areas of Flash and ASP, to create two JavaScript ASP scripts, which will hopefully become more familiar as you get to grips with the JavaScript capabilities of Flash. That's not the end of the treats, as James has also added a special DSN-less connection line of code to the script, so that you don't need to worry about configuring ODBC data sources etc., which can prove a little tricky to configure on your server.

Please note, it wouldn't be possible to teach you how to code the ASP scripts within one chapter, so if you want to learn ASP in more detail (which I strongly suggest), check out the ASP chapter in this book. I recommend visiting www.coveryourasp.com, as James covers JavaScript ASP in great detail, and will have book recommendations there.

Here are the main points that we are going to cover in this section:

- The ASP script we use to retrieve a complete list of the T-shirts within our database

- The ASP script we use to search our database for an exact match

The ASP script we'll use to retrieve a complete list of the T-shirts within our database

We'll begin by walking through GetList.asp, which is a script that retrieves a complete list of all the T-shirts that we have in the T-shirt database. Let's take a look at the code in a little detail to get an idea as to what it does and how it does it. We start by setting the language of the ASP script as JavaScript:

```
<%@ Language=JavaScript %>
```

We then buffer the data sent to client, and ensure that we get fresh content from the database every time it is searched:

```
<%Response.Buffer=true;
Response.Expires=0;
%>
```

Then we add some code that gives us access to the ADO (database) constants:

```
<!--METADATA NAME="Microsoft ActiveX Data Objects 2.5 Library"
➥TYPE="TypeLib" UUID="{00000205-0000-0010-8000-00AA006D2EA4}"-->
```

In the next step we create a connection object:

```
<%var oConn = Server.CreateObject( 'ADODB.Connection' );
```

We then open the connection to the database (if you have server access, and need the latest free database drivers you can get them from www.microsoft.com/data/download.htm):

```
oConn.Open( 'Provider=Microsoft.Jet.OLEDB.4.0; Data Source=' +
➡ Server.MapPath ( 'T-shirt DB.mdb' ) );
```

OK, the next thing we need to do is create a recordset object:

```
var oRS = Server.CreateObject( 'ADODB.Recordset' );
```

We then use a SQL statement to select the Name field from the Tshirts table, and then order/sort the results according to Name:

```
var sSQL = 'SELECT Name FROM Tshirts ORDER BY Name';
```

The next line of code searches for records that match our request:

```
oRS.Open ( sSQL, oConn, adOpenForwardOnly, adLockReadOnly );
```

And we then check to see if we have any results.

```
if ( !oRS.EOF )
{
```

Once all of the names have been retrieved from the Tshirts table, we need to join them all together to create a string, and we do this by using the & Flash command:

```
var sSep = '&';
Response.Write ( 'List=' );
```

We then make sure that we loop until there are no more results to add to the string:

```
while ( !oRS.EOF )
{
```

There's only one field in the recordset, so we use a numerical offset, which is quicker than oRS (Name), note that 0 denotes the first field. When the string is outputted to Flash, we want to display each name on a separate line, so we use the \r JavaScript command (which is &0D in Flash), which enters a carriage return between each name in the string, thus putting each result on a separate line within the same text field.

```
Response.Write ( Server.URLEncode ( oRS ( 0 ) + '\r' ) );
```

We then move on to the next record:

```
oRS.moveNext ( );
}
Response.Write ( sSep + 'ListMatch=Yes' );
}
else
{
```

When no records are found, we send the variable ListMatch=No to Flash:

```
Response.Write ( 'ListMatch=No');
}%>
```

And that's it. Let's have a look at that code all together, in one piece so to speak:

```
<%@ Language=JavaScript %>

<%
Response.Buffer=true;        // always buffer data sent to client
Response.Expires=0;          // always get fresh content from
                             //database

// the line below gives us access to the ADO (database) constants
%>

<!—METADATA NAME="Microsoft ActiveX Data Objects 2.5 Library"
➥TYPE="TypeLib" UUID="{00000205-0000-0010-8000-00AA006D2EA4}"—>

<%
    // create a connection object
    var oConn = Server.CreateObject ( 'ADODB.Connection' );

    // open the connection to the database
    // you can get the latest free database drivers from
    // http://www.microsoft.com/data/download.htm
    oConn.Open ( 'Provider=Microsoft.Jet.OLEDB.4.0; Data Source='
    ➥+ Server.MapPath ( 'T-shirt DB.mdb' ) );

    // create a recordset object
    var oRS = Server.CreateObject ( 'ADODB.Recordset' );

    // make up the SQL statement
    var sSQL = 'SELECT Name FROM Tshirts ORDER BY Name';

    // search for records that match
    oRS.Open ( sSQL, oConn, adOpenForwardOnly, adLockReadOnly );

    // did we get any results?
    if ( !oRS.EOF )
    {
            var sSep = '&';        // flash parameter separator

            // output list of names, separated by cr
            // (\r in JavaScript, &0D in Flash)
            Response.Write ( 'List=' );

            // loop until no more
```

continues overleaf

```
                      while ( !oRS.EOF )
                      {
                              // only one field in recordset, so I'll use a
                              //numeric offset - it's
                              // quicker than oRS ( 'Name' ).  Note 0 ==
                              //first field
                              Response.Write ( Server.URLEncode ( oRS ( 0 )
                              ➡+ '\r' ) );

                              // move to next record
                              oRS.moveNext ( );
                      }

                      Response.Write ( sSep + 'ListMatch=Yes' );
              }
              else
              {

                      // no records found
                      Response.Write ( 'ListMatch=No' );
              }
      %>
```

Add this code to Notepad, and save it as `Getlist.asp`, or when we come to use this file, simply use the version from the CD accompanying this book.

The ASP script we'll use to search our database for an exact match

We'll use the `GetShirtInfo.asp` script to search our T-shirt database for an exact match. This code breaks down easily too. We start just as we did with the earlier code, by setting the language of the ASP script to JavaScript, buffering the data that is sent to the client, and making sure we get fresh content from the database at each subsequent search:

```
<%@ Language=JavaScript %>
<%
Response.Buffer=true;
Response.Expires=0;
%>
```

Then we access the ADO (database) constants, create a connection object, and open the connection to the database:

```
<!—METADATA NAME="Microsoft ActiveX Data Objects 2.5 Library"
TYPE="TypeLib" UUID="{00000205-0000-0010-8000-00AA006D2EA4}"—>
<%
var oConn = Server.CreateObject( 'ADODB.Connection' );
oConn.Open( 'Provider=Microsoft.Jet.OLEDB.4.0; Data Source=' +
➡ Server.MapPath ( 'T-shirt DB.mdb' ) );
```

Then we create a recordset object:

```
var oRS = Server.CreateObject ( 'ADODB.Recordset' );
```

And now we search for the variable of the SeachDB that we entered in Flash:

```
var sShirt = '' + Request.QueryString ( 'SearchDB' );
```

Then we use a SQL statement to select the TSID, Name, Description, Tsize, and Price fields from our T-Shirt database. If you look carefully on the second line of code you can see where the relationship is created between the PriceID field in the Tshirts table, and the PriceID field in the Price table:

```
var sSQL = 'SELECT TSID,Name,Description,TSize,Price ';
sSQL += 'FROM Tshirts INNER JOIN Price ON Tshirts.PriceID =
➥ Price.PriceID ';
sSQL += 'WHERE Name = \'' + sShirt + '\'';
```

The next step is to search for records that match the SearchDB variable, and then check for results, bringing the separate variables into Flash separated by the all-important & character:

```
oRS.Open ( sSQL, oConn, adOpenForwardOnly, adLockReadOnly );
if ( !oRS.EOF )
    {
        var sSep = '&';
```

Next, we'll use the Server.URLEncode command to URL encode the output to Flash so that we don't have any problems, for example, SPACE becomes +, / becomes %2F, = becomes %3D. This allows us to have special characters such as & in the output string:

```
Response.Write ( 'TSID=' + Server.URLEncode ( oRS ( 'TSID' ) ) + sSep );
Response.Write ( 'Name=' + Server.URLEncode ( oRS ( 'Name' ) ) + sSep );
Response.Write ( 'Description=' + Server.URLEncode ( oRS
➥ ( 'Description' ) ) + sSep );
Response.Write ( 'Size=' + Server.URLEncode ( oRS ( 'TSize' ) ) + sSep );
Response.Write ( 'Price=' + Server.URLEncode ( oRS ( 'Price' ) ) + sSep );
```

Then we use the if command to wait for the Flash movie to display the results:

```
Response.Write ( 'Match=Yes' );
}
else
{
```

And where no matches are found, we tell Flash's if command to let the user know that their search has been unsuccessful.

```
Response.Write ( 'Match=No' );
}
%>
```

Putting it all together, and we should have something like this:

```
<%@ Language=JavaScript %>

<%
Response.Buffer=true;        // always buffer data sent to client
Response.Expires=0;          // always get fresh content from
                             //database

// the line below gives us access to the ADO (database) constants
%>

<!—METADATA NAME="Microsoft ActiveX Data Objects 2.5 Library"
TYPE="TypeLib" UUID="{00000205-0000-0010-8000-00AA006D2EA4}"—>

<%
    // create a connection object
    var oConn = Server.CreateObject( 'ADODB.Connection' );

    // open the connection to the database
    // you can get the latest free database drivers from
    // http://www.microsoft.com/data/download.htm
    oConn.Open( 'Provider=Microsoft.Jet.OLEDB.4.0; Data Source='
    ➤ + Server.MapPath ( 'T-shirt DB.mdb' ) );

    // create a recordset object
    var oRS = Server.CreateObject( 'ADODB.Recordset' );

    // what do we need to search for?
    var sShirt = '' + Request.QueryString ( 'SearchDB' );

    // make up the SQL statement
    var sSQL = 'SELECT TSID,Name,Description,TSize,Price ';
    sSQL += 'FROM Tshirts INNER JOIN Price ON Tshirts.PriceID =
    ➤ Price.PriceID ';
    sSQL += 'WHERE Name = \'' + sShirt + '\'';

    // search for records that match
    oRS.Open ( sSQL, oConn, adOpenForwardOnly, adLockReadOnly );

    // did we get any results?
    if ( !oRS.EOF )
    {
        var sSep = '&';        // flash parameter separator

        // output fields to Flash
        // Server.URLEncode turns problem characters to URL-
        //safe equivalents
        // e.g. space becomes +, / becomes %2F, = becomes %3D
```

```
                    // this allows us to have special characters like &
                    //in the output stream
                    Response.Write ( 'TSID=' + Server.URLEncode ( oRS (
                 ➡ 'TSID' ) ) + sSep );
                    Response.Write ( 'Name=' + Server.URLEncode ( oRS (
                 ➡ 'Name' ) ) + sSep );
                    Response.Write ( 'Description=' + Server.URLEncode (
                 ➡ oRS ( 'Description' ) ) + sSep );
                    Response.Write ( 'Size=' + Server.URLEncode ( oRS (
                 ➡ 'TSize' ) ) + sSep );
                    Response.Write ( 'Price=' + Server.URLEncode ( oRS (
                 ➡ 'Price' ) ) + sSep );
                    Response.Write ( 'Match=Yes' );
            }
            else
            {
                    // no records found
                    Response.Write ( 'Match=No' );
            }
        %>
```

Enter the code into Notepad, and save it as GetShirtInfo.asp, or, again, use the copy from the CD.

You should now have the following files:

- An MS Access 2000 database file: T-shirt DB.mdb

- A Flash file: Tshirt.swf

- Two ASP files: GetList.asp and GetShirtInfo.asp

All you need to do to test your newfound powers is to embed the Tshirt.swf in a HTML page, and then upload the files to your web server – good luck.

Conclusion

Now that you're familiar with Access 2000, have a go at making a few different databases that relate to you, or your company. Start by creating a couple of simple flat-file databases from scratch, and when you feel comfortable, design a relational database. When designing a relational database, I always start with a pencil and a piece of paper, this may sound rather old fashioned, but reverting back to the basics is a process I carry out even when creating a simple database. I do this because it helps me to visualize the structure of the database that I'm designing, and I often find that when you see it on paper, you can spot and eliminate possible errors more easily.

There are many ways that your database knowledge can benefit your Flash sites. For example, online shopping/carts are becoming more and more popular on a daily basis, and I feel this is an area that many Flash designers shy away from as it's always portrayed as a complicated process. Well it's time to put on your brightest clothes and get to work, because by tweaking the knowledge you've gained in the last two chapters, you'll be able to create a fully functioning, database-driven online shop. Not only can you have your cake and eat it, but now you can sell it too!

There are so many different uses for a database-driven Flash site; I think I could fill an entire book! Well, we haven't got space for that, so here are just a few ideas...

- A good learning project is to create a simple address book/contacts database, as we saw in the "*Introducing Databases*" chapter. Try creating a flat-file database with 3 fields: `userID`, `name` and `email address`. You could then add more fields, and start to get relational.

- Ever thought of making an online game? Well now you can store, retrieve, and sort all the scores in a database. Have a look at the Flash gaming example towards the end of this book for a bit more of an idea as to how you could do this.

- Do you need to develop a site with a great deal of content? Well, rather than create a large Flash file, you could store all of the content in a database, and only load the text that is required. This principle of dynamic site creation can dramatically reduce the time it takes to load a site, and also makes updating and adding more content easier to manage. It would also be a relatively simple process to add a search facility to search and display the content from the database.

- I often use a relational database to create Flash sites in different languages, a process which requires a fair bit of planning, but can save a great deal of development time, and also makes adding support for an extra language quite simple.

I would recommend using ASP to connect your Flash site to the database. As I mentioned earlier in this chapter, ASP uses either VBScript or JavaScript, and my top choice is JavaScript. I strongly suggest going out and getting yourself a good JavaScript book and reading it obsessively, as it will not only help you to make great ASP scripts, but it will also benefit your Flash ActionScripting tremendously. Check out "*Beginning JavaScript*" published by Wrox Press, ISBN 1861004060.

Well, that brings me to the end of my database adventures, and my parting advice to you is to get your hands dirty, play with the code, play with Access 2000, and make yourself familiar with the way everything works. Set your goals, and don't give up until you achieve them!!

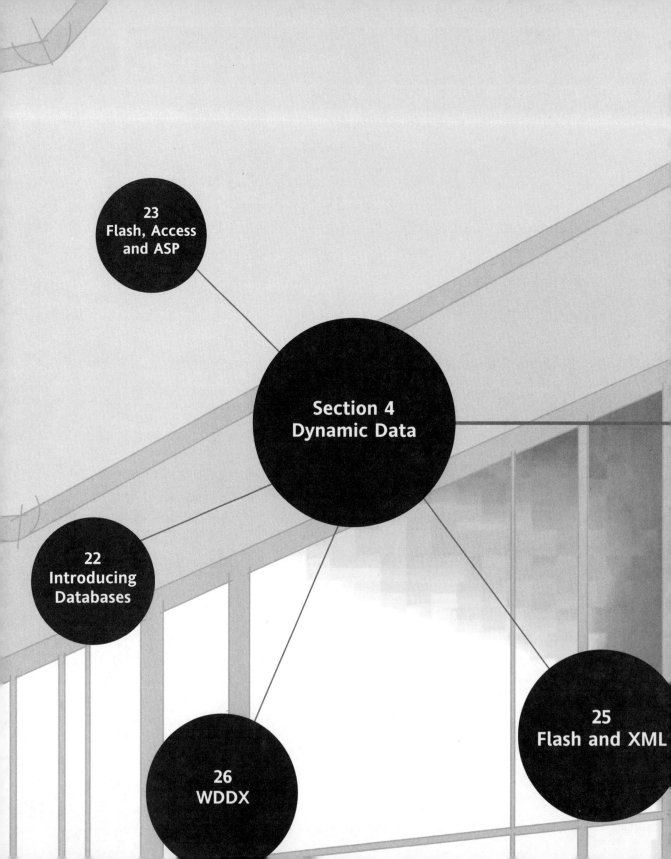

Chapter 24
Databases
Another Way

Although we've just spent two chapters working with the Access database, there are, of course, other less Microsoft-centric options for your database work and connectivity. In this chapter we'll look at one of those options: MySQL.

We'll begin with an outline of the history of MySQL, how it came to be, and where you can go for more information, and then we'll move onto installing and configuring it for IIS/PWS. We'll cover the installation of the pre-compiled binary version of MySQL from an automated installer, and discuss the basic configuration options that you'll need to know to get you up and running.

We'll also look at the operations necessary to run and maintain MySQL, starting and stopping the MySQL server, and working with the MySQL Monitor program that we will use in the following section to test our MySQL commands.

Then we'll cover the most commonly used elements of the MySQL language. We will discuss the creation and deletion of databases and tables with MySQL, including a discussion of the data types available in MySQL. We will also cover the various commands available for manipulating your databases.

Having got the database sorted out, we'll need some middle-ware scripting to access it from the Web, so we'll discuss the functions available to you within PHP to connect to and query your database.

Knowing how to integrate Flash with MySQL isn't much use without a practical example to get your teeth into, so we'll round up the chapter with a sample application. Here we will build up a simple guestbook application using Flash 5, PHP and MySQL.

What is MySQL?

MySQL was developed in 1996 by a Swedish consultancy named TcX. They required a relational database system that was affordable, flexible, fast and could handle large amounts of data. Although there were other Database Management Systems available at that time, none of them quite suited their needs – so they made their own!

I am a huge fan of MySQL, which is a hugely popular database solution both within and outside the Internet world. Here are just some of the features that have helped make MySQL as successful as it is today:

Open Source
A key feature of MySQL is that it is provided Open Source. This means that not only do you get a whiz-bang Relational Database Management System (RDBMS) product, but also get the source code for it. If there's a feature you'd like to see added to MySQL then there's no reason why you couldn't add it yourself by modifying the source code.

MySQL is licensed with the GNU General Public License. More information can be found at www.gnu.org.

Cost
While many vendors are charging astronomical prices for their RDBMS products, MySQL is free for personal, non-profit use on a non Windows OS, and extremely cheap otherwise. At the time

of writing, a standard MySQL license costs $200 [USD], which is a steal compared to other RDBMS products.

The Windows version of MySQL is free to use for 30 days from the date of first installation, after which point you are required to purchase a license. This condition applies even if you're just using it to play around with and learn MySQL. This is because in order to develop the Windows version of MySQL the developers are required to purchase a commercial compiler such as those offered by Microsoft and Borland. This is in contrast to developing on a Unix or Linux based system where suitable compilers are available free of charge.

Support
In the beginning, MySQL was used mainly by Universities and non-profit organisations. This is because, until recently, the business world was reluctant to put their trust into products that were being given away for free, and were concerned as to the level of support that would be provided for them.

Over the past few years the rise of Linux (an Open Source operating system) has instilled a confidence among businesses for Open Source products in the workplace. Indeed, the majority of the Internet is housed and served from computers running Linux. This has led to a drastically increased user base for MySQL, ensuring its continued support and development.

MySQL is often confused as being a form of Structured Query Language (SQL), which was developed by IBM. SQL is a query language that was primarily developed for fetching and sending information to/from databases. MySQL *uses*, and in some cases *expands* on, SQL to perform operations and manipulate its databases.

Just as a piece of trivia, SQL is pronounced 'sequel' while MySQL is pronounced 'my ess que ell'. This is obviously not set in stone and pronunciation is as much a case on interpretation as anything else, but at least you'll know how it was intended to be pronounced.

nstalling, configuring and running MySQL

If you are using a third party for your web site hosting then the installation and configuration of MySQL on your server will likely have been done for you. Therefore you should be pretty safe in skipping the remainder of these next two sections and moving on to the **MySQL Language** section. Otherwise, on with the show!

Before we can start using MySQL we first need to install and configure it on our system. The instructions given assume that you're using the pre-compiled Win32 binary version of MySQL. The latest version at the time of writing is supplied on the CD that came with this book in the \mysql\installs directory. Alternatively, you can download the necessary files direct from the MySQL website at www.mysql.com.

Installation

The installation files for MySQL come packaged in a ZIP file so the first thing we'll need to do is to unzip them to a temporary directory. For this your can use a tool like WinZip, (a trial version of which is available from www.winzip.com).

Once we've unzipped the files you'll need to locate and run the `setup.exe` file. This will start an install wizard that will guide you through the rest of the installation procedure.

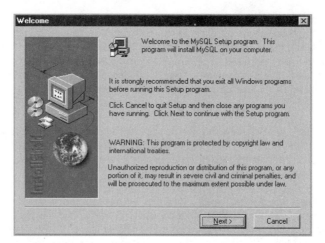

During the install process you will be asked where on your system you would like MySQL installed. It's a good idea to install it to the default `c:\mysql\` directory suggested for the sake of compatibility with other software.

Installation instructions for other operating systems and platforms can be found in the online MySQL documentation at www.mysql.com.

Once the wizard has completed its task and MySQL has been installed, it's time to find out how to control the MySQL daemon from within Windows.

Daemon control

The MySQL daemon –we'll call it `mysqld` from here on in – can be thought of as a listening device. It is a program whose job is to sit around and listen for client requests for our MySQL server. When such a request is received, `mysqld` will fetch the required information and return a response to the calling client.

So, the first thing we need to do is to start `mysqld`. Firstly, you will need to navigate to your chosen installation directory for MySQL. You should see a directory structure similar to the one shown below:

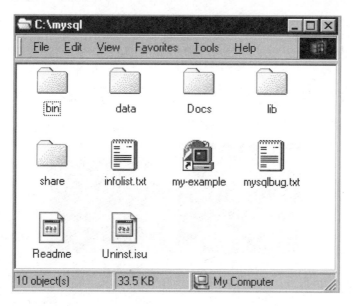

Open the bin directory and locate and double-click on the mysqld.exe file to launch the MySQL daemon. mysqld runs as a background process and there will be no outwardly visible sign that it's running. The easiest way to ensure that mysqld is running is to check the Windows Task Manager by pressing CTRL-ALT-DEL on your keyboard – you should see an entry labelled mysqld. Alternatively, you can use the MySQL Monitor program, which will be covered in the next section.

To stop mysqld gracefully you will need to open up an MS-DOS Command Prompt and navigate to your MySQL directory. Next, type the following, followed by the ENTER key.

```
bin\mysqladmin shutdown
```

Use the Task Manager again to confirm that mysqld has indeed been shut down.

Note that you could have used the Windows Task Manager to kill the process but this can have some unpredictable results. At best, mysqld will be shut down and you will keep all of your data intact – at worst, you could scramble your databases and lose all of your data! In short: Graceful = Good!

Windows NT and 2000

On Windows NT and 2000 machines you should install mysqld as a service as follows. Navigate to your mysql\bin directory by entering cd \mysql\bin at the command line prompt. Then you can enter the following to launch the MySQL daemon:

```
mysqld-nt --install
```

You can now start and stop mysqld as follows:

```
NET START mysql
```

```
NET STOP mysql
```

Note that in this case you can't use any other options for mysqld! You can remove the service as follows:

```
mysqld-nt --remove
```

So, launch the MySQL daemon:

MySQL Monitor

Although it has a fairly grand name, the MySQL Monitor is little more than a console interface to MySQL. It does, however, allow you to perform almost all MySQL related tasks, including the creation and manipulation of databases, tables and data.

To start the MySQL Monitor you will again need to open an MS-DOS Command Prompt and navigate to the MySQL directory. Then, type the following, followed by the ENTER key.

```
bin\mysql
```

If the MySQL Monitor can connect to the MySQL daemon then you will see something like the following output.

If the mysqld program isn't running when you attempt to start the MySQL monitor then you will see something like the following output.

```
C:\mysql>bin\mysql
ERROR 2003: Can't connect to MySQL server on 'localhost' (10061)
```

If you get this output then mysqld is not running on the local machine. Please return to the previous section on starting the MySQL daemon and try again.

To escape from the MySQL Monitor simply type exit followed by the ENTER key. You will be returned to the command prompt.

We will be using the MySQL Monitor in the next section to familiarise ourselves with the MySQL language.

None shall pass: MySQL security

MySQL has a strict set of security features. You can restrict who can access your databases, where they can access from, which databases they can access, what they can do with the databases and much more. This is an extremely important feature to get to grips with if you're going to be letting the general public loose on your servers.

However, such configuration has been known to fill whole books even bigger than this one. For this reason we will not be discussing the security features of MySQL in this chapter and you should either refer to the MySQL manual or some of the books in the **Further Reading** section at the end of this chapter.

Database theory

Before we get stuck in using MySQL, it would be a good idea to cover a little ground on database theory. I give you advance warning that this section is going to seem incredibly dry – unfortunately database theory isn't all that riveting!

Let's look at a simple hierarchical model of MySQL before we discuss each part in detail.

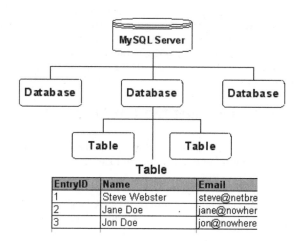

Here we can see that a single installation of MySQL can have many *databases*, and that each database can have a number of *tables*. Each *table* contains specific data, which may or may not be related to the other *tables* in the *database*. The *tables* are made up of a number of *columns* and *rows*, much like a spreadsheet. The point at which a *column* and *row* meet is called a *field*.

Each record in the table is stored in its own *row*, and each *column* has a name and a type of data that can be stored in it. A given *field* contains data designated by the *column* for that *row* or record in the *table*.

As mentioned previously, the tables in our database(s) can contain data that is related or completely separate from the other tables in the database. There is a concept known as *relationships* or *joins* that can be used with related data in MySQL but that is beyond the scope of this chapter.

The MySQL language

In this section we will discuss the use of Structured Query Language to create/manipulate our databases. We will take a look at the most common SQL commands and discuss how they will work with MySQL. This is divided into sub-sections to deal with the different classes of SQL and/or MySQL commands.

As mentioned previously, MySQL uses the SQL language to manipulate and perform operations on its databases. However, MySQL expands upon the SQL language, introducing new commands not present in SQL. Because this chapter is specifically focused on MySQL rather than SQL itself, I use the terms 'SQL command' and 'MySQL command' interchangeably in this section. Having said that, where a command is introduced that is not part of the SQL language it has been noted.

Since we have covered the installation of MySQL on a Windows 9x/NT system, the rest of this section will assume that you've started the MySQL daemon and that you're using the MySQL monitor to enter the examples presented.

For those of you who are using a third party to host your website, and therefore haven't installed MySQL on your system, it is worth running through this section anyway to familiarise yourself with the SQL commands. The next section in this chapter will cover the functions available within PHP to enable you to create/manipulate your MySQL database(s). However, it's a really good idea to install MySQL on your system and follow along with the examples in this section – you can always uninstall it when you're done.

Creating databases and tables using the CREATE command

These commands are used to build and destroy both whole databases and tables in MySQL. These commands are extremely powerful and important and can be destructive so we will have to use caution when invoking them.

The CREATE command is the main building tool of the SQL language and we will use it in MySQL to create our databases and tables. The syntax for creating databases is one of the simplest you'll come across:

```
CREATE DATABASE databasename;
```

...where *databasename* is the name of the database to create.

Note that the semicolon at the end of the whole command is necessary to tell MySQL that you've finished entering the command and it can commence execution. This is so that you can enter long SQL commands legibly using multiple lines. The usefulness of this feature will become apparent later in this chapter.

Creating a database and tables

1. We'll create a database here that we'll use for the remainder of this chapter. Type the following command into the MySQL Monitor:

```
CREATE DATABASE flash5dcs;
```

Now, before we can do anything else to our database we will need to select it as the active database. For this we will require the USE command. The syntax of the USE command is shown below.

```
USE databasename;
```

2. So to select our database we will need to enter the following command into the MySQL Monitor:

```
USE flash5dcs;
```

This is a common step to miss out when you're learning MySQL and can be the root cause of some frustrating problems when trying to manipulate your newly created database. Everyone makes this mistake at least once at some point so you'll be in good company when you do.

Remember, each MySQL command ends with a semi-colon.

Creating tables

Now that we have created our database, we should add some tables. Again we will do this using the CREATE command, but in a slightly different way. The basic syntax for creating a table is more complex than for creating a database, because we need to define a name and datatype for all columns in our table.

Before we delve into this command it is worth mentioning what we mean by the word 'datatype' in this context. In MySQL, a **datatype** is the type of information that a given column can hold – whether it's a string ("Hello"), a number (174) or something else such as a date or time. You cannot store a string in a column that has been designated to hold a number and vice versa.

This is in contrast to the variables in both Flash and PHP, for which you do not have to specify a datatype, and the datatype can be changed throughout your script to suit your particular needs.

We'll discuss some of the datatypes available in MySQL a little further on in this section but for now let's get back to creating tables...

The basic syntax for the CREATE TABLE command is:

        CREATE TABLE tablename (column_definition);

Where *tablename* is the name of the table to create and *column_definition* is in the following syntax:

        column_name type [NOT NULL | NULL] [DEFAULT def_val]
                    [AUTO_INCREMENT] [PRIMARY KEY]

Where *column_name* is the name of the column to create and *type* is a MySQL data type (discussed below) for that column.

Note that you will need to include one *column_definition* entry for each column that you require in your table, with each one being separated by a comma.

The directives after the datatype are an important part of MySQL and are tabulated below. Note that the fact that these directives are shown in square brackets indicates that they are optional, though the square brackets do not form part of the SQL command.

NOT NULL | NULL	Indicates whether the column has to be filled in for each row (NOT NULL) or whether it is permitted to not supply a value for this column (NULL). If not explicitly defined then NULL is assumed.
DEFAULT def_val	Used if the column contains particular value (def_val) not expressly filled out for a given row.
AUTO_INCREMENT	Gives each row's data for that column a unique value. It will assign a data particular row as one more than the highest value for that column.
PRIMARY KEY	Designates a particular column as the primary key for that table. Making a key in a table aids in searching/sorting the contents but it can only be performed on a column whose data is assured of containing a unique value. It is good practice to ensure that each table has a PRIMARY KEY column.

Now you're probably wondering which datatypes you have at your disposal in MySQL. Below are some of the most frequently used; a complete list can be found in the MySQL documentation, which is installed with MySQL in the Docs directory within the MySQL directory:

Data	Type Description
INTEGER	Numerical value to hold an integer (non fractional) value. Range: -2,147,483,648 > 2,147,483,647
VARCHAR (n)	A variable length character field [string] of at most n characters. The maximum length of a varchar field is 255 characters.
CHAR (*n*)	A character type [string] of exactly n characters. The maximum length of a char field is 255 characters.
TEXT	A type to hold textual data with a maximum length of 65535 characters.
MEDIUMTEXT	A type to hold textual data with a maximum length of 16,777,215 characters.
DATETIME	A type used to store date/time information in the format 'YYYY-MM-DD HH:MM:SS'
TIMESTAMP	If not explicitly assigned a value in an INSERT or UPDATE command, or if it is set to NULL or NOW(), TIMESTAMP fields will be set to the current time. This is a handy feature and means that we can use it as a simple 'last updated' counter without having to worry about explicitly assigning it a value.

1. We'll create some tables in our database, so go ahead and type this command into the MySQL Monitor:

```
CREATE TABLE guestbook (
EntryID INTEGER AUTO_INCREMENT PRIMARY KEY,
Name VARCHAR(25),
Email VARCHAR(50),
URL VARCHAR(255),
Comments TEXT,
Posted DATETIME);
```

We'll be using this one later in the chapter to build our Flash based PHP/MySQL guestbook so it's worth taking special note of the structure of the above snippet of code. Ensure that you understand what we're doing here before moving on, re-reading the last section if necessary.

To ensure that we've created the table, type the following into the MySQL monitor:

```
SHOW TABLES;
```

This will produce a list of all the tables in the current database. The output should look like this:

If you want to see what columns exist in your table then type the following into the MySQL Monitor:

```
DESCRIBE guestbook;
```

Removing databases and tables: the DROP command

While we're on the subject of creating databases and tables in MySQL, it is worth mentioning the commands used to destroy or delete them too.

The DROP command can be thought of as the bulldozer of the MySQL world. Its job is to destroy databases and tables that we no longer want. Generally, you'll only want to do this when a database or table is not required anymore, for example if you've radically updated your site, and it is no longer used.

> *Be very, very careful when you're using the DROP command; you'll see that there's no warning or confirmation request given, the data and structure of the database/table is just sent straight to join the great data bin in the sky.*

The syntax for that DROP command is pretty much the same for removing both databases and tables from MySQL.

```
DROP DATABASE databasename;
DROP TABLE tablename1 [,tablename2, ... , tablenamen];
```

It may seem fairly obvious, but it's worth noting that dropping a database will also drop all the tables inside that database. Also, it is worth repeating that once the drop command is issued there's no going back - your data is toast! Well, that's not actually totally correct - it is possible to salvage your data from the MySQL log files but it's not a pleasant experience!!! Check out the MySQL documentation for more information.

There are several other forms of the DROP command that are used to remove indices and functions from our databases, but we're not going to be using them here. Refer to the MySQL documentation for more information.

So, if you wanted to drop the table we just created in the last section, you'd issue the following MySQL command:

```
DROP TABLE guestbook;
```

Try it out if you like, and type it into the MySQL Monitor - just ensure that you go back and re-create the table before moving on to the next section, because we'll use it with some of the other MySQL commands next.

Note that you can drop more than one table at a time by supplying the name of the tables one after the other separated by a comma. So, if we also had a table called users that we wanted to remove along with the guestbook table, we could do something like the following:

```
DROP TABLE guesbook, users;
```

Unfortunately (or fortunately if you don't enjoy mass destruction) you can only drop one database at a time.

Manipulating your databases and tables

In this section we'll cover all the commands that you'll need to know to manipulate your databases. By manipulate, I mean we will discuss how to add, remove and update data to/from/in our tables.

INSERT

The INSERT command is used to populate the rows in our tables with data. Each successful INSERT command will create a new row in the table. The syntax of the INSERT command is:

```
INSERT [LOW_PRIORITY | DELAYED] [IGNORE]
INTO tablename [(columns)] VALUES (values);
```

where

tablename is the name of the table into which you want to insert the data
columns is an optional list of columns in the table

values is a comma separated list of data to be inserted into the table

The LOW_PRIORITY option can be used to wait until no other client is reading the table before inserting the new row. This will cause the client to wait for completion of the statement before carrying on. If you don't want to wait then you can use the DELAYED option, which will perform a similar operation as LOW_PRIORITY but will return control immediately back to the client.

The IGNORE option is used to ignore errors when trying to insert a new row into a table where our new row may have the same value as another on a unique column. In this case the INSERT statement is ignored instead of generating a database error and no new row is added to the table.

A simple statement to insert data into our guestbook table could be:

```
INSERT INTO guestbook VALUES (NULL, 'Steve Webster',
'Steve@netbreed.co.uk', 'http://www.netbreed.co.uk',
    'This is my comment', NOW());
```

Note that we set the first column EntryID for this row to NULL so that it will assign its own value. This will happen because of the AUTO_INCREMENT we added to the column definition when we created the table.

The values section of this statement contains all the data that we want to make up a new row of our guestbook table. Note that the values are specified in the SAME ORDER as the columns were declared earlier in this chapter. If you do not include the *columns* section of the INSERT command then you must specify the data in this order to ensure that the data is put in the correct column for the row. The final command, NOW() is an internal MySQL function used for fetching the current system time and date and we're using it here to insert that information into our row as the value for the Posted column. MySQL has many internal functions, some of which you will encounter during the remainder of this chapter. For a complete list please refer to the MySQL manual.

The optional *columns* section is used when you either only want to fill in some of the fields for the new row of a table, or when you want to provide the data in a particular order in the *values* section. It is often worth doing this anyway just to make sure that you're adding the data to the columns that you think you are. So, if we rewrite the previous statement but this time with the *columns* section included, we would have:

```
INSERT INTO guestbook  (Name, Email, URL, Comments, Posted)
VALUES ('Steve Webster', 'Steve@netbreed.co.uk',
'http://www.netbreed.co.uk',
'This is my comment', NOW());
```

Note that because we have specified which columns we want to fill out for this row in the *columns* section, we can exclude the EntryID column from the *values* section. This is because it is designated as an AUTO_INCREMENT column and the value for it in our new row will be set automatically to 1 higher than the current highest value for that column.

Working within the database

1. Go ahead and use this technique to add 7 more rows to the table we created earlier. This will give us some data to work with in the later sections of this chapter. Don't forget to change the details such as name etc. for each row or they'll all be the same!

   REPLACE
   The REPLACE command is specific to MySQL (i.e. it is not part of the SQL language). Its syntax is almost identical to that of the INSERT command and it performs a similar task. However, as you might expect, if another row exists with the same value in a column that has been designated as a unique index, then the new record replaces the old one. If no such row exists then the new row will be added to the table as if an INSERT command were executed.

   The general syntax is:

   ```
   REPLACE [LOW_PRIORITY | DELAYED] [IGNORE]
   INTO tablename [(columns)] VALUES (values);
   ```

   The options work the same way as those for the INSERT command.

2. Change some data using the REPLACE command

   UPDATE
   The UPDATE command is used to change the values of one or more columns in an existing row or rows. The general syntax is:

   ```
   UPDATE [LOW_PRIORITY] tablename SET colname=value,...
       [WHERE condition] [LIMIT #];
   ```

   In this command:

   tablename is the name of the table to be updated
   colname is the name of a column in that table
   value is the new value for that column
   condition is the criteria that a row has to match in order to be updated
   # is the maximum number of rows to be affected by this statement.

   Note that you can have multiple colname=value expressions to update more than one column at a time. Simply separate each expression with a comma. If we omit the WHERE block, all the rows in the given table will be updated.

   A simple example of the UPDATE command would be like this:

   ```
   UPDATE guestbook SET Name='Joe Bloggs', Email=''
       WHERE EntryID=1;
   ```

This statement will update the Name and Email of the guestbook table entry whose EntryID is 1.

3. Go ahead and update some of the data for the rows in your tables using the UPDATE command.

DELETE

The DELETE command is used to remove one or more rows from a given table. Like the UPDATE command, this can be limited to rows that match a particular criteria using a WHERE block within the statement. You can limit the number of affected rows by the use of the LIMIT block, also described previously.

The general syntax for the DELETE command is:

```
DELETE [LOW_PRIORITY] FROM tablename
[WHERE condition] [LIMIT #];
```

> *If you omit both the* WHERE *and* LIMIT *clauses,* **all rows** *in the given table will be removed - no warning will be given and your data will be long gone!*

If you wanted to remove all entries from the guestbook, say those entered longer than two weeks ago, we would use the following statement:

```
DELETE FROM guestbook
WHERE Posted < DATE_SUB(NOW(), INTERVAL 14 DAY);
```

This statement will remove all rows from our guestbook table whose Posted datestamp is more than two weeks old using DATE_SUB(), another internal MySQL function, and is used to subtract a certain amount of time from a given date. You should refer to the MySQL manual for a full description of this and other MySQL internal functions.

You might want to perform this type of pruning regularly on your guestbook, although you might want to change the amount of time to six months or so unless you're site is really busy!

```
DELETE FROM guestbook
WHERE Posted < DATE_SUB(NOW(), INTERVAL 6 MONTH);
```

5. Let's remove the last row of our table using the DELETE command. Hint: use WHERE EntryID = 8 (so long as you added eight rows of data in the earlier section of course).

Searching your databases and tables

Once you've got your data into your database you'll want to be able to get it out again or search it for certain criteria.

SELECT

The SELECT command is part of the SQL language and you can use it to retrieve rows or columns of data in your web applications from your MySQL database. It is an extremely powerful command, and because of this has a fairly complex syntax. The most commonly used aspects of the syntax are shown below:

```
SELECT expression FROM tablename
    [WHERE condition]
    [GROUP BY colname]
    [LIMIT #];
```

Note that the options **must** appear in the order shown above. (This is not the complete syntax of the SELECT command, for which you should refer to the MySQL manual.) The expression statement can be either a list of columns whose information you want returned or an asterisk (in which case all columns are returned) if a particular row matches any given criteria.

Searching our guestbook database

1. Return all the columns for all the rows in our guestbook table with the following statement:

    ```
    SELECT * FROM guestbook;
    ```

    All the information that you've entered so far into the table will be displayed in the MySQL Monitor when you enter this command – though it may look a little strange due to the 80 character width limit of the MS-DOS Command Prompt.

2. You can return all the columns from the first 5 entries in our guestbook, by using the LIMIT block:

    ```
    SELECT * FROM guestbook LIMIT 5;
    ```

3. You can specify that you just want the EntryID and Name columns of these first 5 entries by expanding the statement like so:

    ```
    SELECT EntryID, Name FROM guestbook LIMIT 5;
    ```

    You should see output similar to the following (although your names will depend on what you've entered into the database in the previous section):

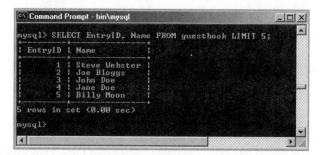

Of course, if you only have 3 rows in your table then you will only be returned that amount. You can't get what isn't there!

We can use the WHERE clause to limit the data returned to rows that match a certain criteria, much like we did with the DELETE and UPDATE commands. For example, if we wanted to list the Name and Email addresses from all entries that have been posted in the past week, we could use the following statement:

```
SELECT Name, Email FROM guestbook
WHERE Posted > DATE_SUB(NOW(), INTERVAL 7 DAY);
```

Given that you're likely following the whole of this chapter over the course of a single or a few days, you probably won't have any entries over 7 days old and so all of your entries will be listed with the above statement.

4. For something a bit more useful you may want to try the following statement. This will return the Name and Email addresses of everyone whose email address comes from a .co.uk domain.

```
SELECT Name, Email FROM guestbook
WHERE Email LIKE '%.co.uk';
```

Here we've introduced a new option for the WHERE block - the LIKE operator. This is a pattern matching function, which will return true if the column specified matches the expression given. You can include **wildcard** characters in the expression - a '%' character in the expression will match one or more characters, whereas a '_' will only match a single character.

5. You can, of course, specify more than one condition in the WHERE clause with the use of the logical AND, OR and NOT operators. For example, to return the Name and Email information for all guestbook entries whose email address ends in .co.uk **and** that has been posted in the last week, we could use the following statement:

```
SELECT Name, Email FROM guestbook
WHERE Email LIKE '%.co.uk' AND
Posted > DATE_SUB(NOW(), INTERVAL 7 DAY);
```

The last part of the SELECT command we must discuss is the ORDER BY block. This allows you to order the data returned by a given column, either ascending (ASC) or descending (DESC).

6. Let's return the EntryID and Name information of the first 5 entries in our table, and order the data returned alphabetically on the Name column, using the following statement:

```
SELECT EntryID, Name FROM guestbook
ORDER BY Name LIMIT 5;
```

Note that we've had to put the ORDER BY block before the LIMIT block in order to comply with the SELECT command syntax. Based on the output given previously, the output would look like:

Integrating MySQL with PHP

Now that we know the main point of the MySQL language, it is time to learn how we can use PHP scripts to access our MySQL databases. We need to do this because Flash cannot access the MySQL databases itself so we have to use PHP as a kind of gopher – fetching the information for us at our command.

PHP has many built-in functions for accessing MySQL databases and we will be discussing these in this section.

At the time of writing, there are 33 MySQL related functions built into PHP, many of which will perform similar or more obscure tasks to the MySQL/SQL commands mentioned earlier. Covering all of these functions here would take a great many pages so we'll just discuss the most commonly used ones. You should check the PHP documentation for more information: www.php.net.

Before continuing with this chapter, please ensure that you have installed PHP as detailed in the PHP chapter.

Connecting to the MySQL server

The first thing we need to do in any PHP script that we want to interact with MySQL is to connect to the MySQL server. We need to do this because, unlike the MySQL Monitor, your PHP scripts will not have access to MySQL unless they specifically ask for it. The syntax for this function is:

```
mysql_connect([hostname] [, username] [, password]);
```

The *hostname* is the name of the host running your MySQL server. If the MySQL server and the web server (IIS/PWS) are running on the same machine then this can be set to "localhost". This is the default value if *hostname* is not specified.

The *username* is the name of the user allowed to connect to the MySQL server. We're not going to go into the thorny issue of security here, so users connecting through localhost will be permitted access. The *password* is the password assigned to that particular user.

The function will return a positive integer referencing the connection, called the link identifier, if successful, or false otherwise. The link identifier will be used in future calls to MySQL related PHP functions.

Using PHP with MySQL

1. Type this script into your text editor, save it as connect.php, and copy it to your web server root directory.

```php
<?php
    $link = mysql_connect("localhost");
    echo "Link ID is " . $link;
?>
```

Load up your web browser and enter your web address: http://localhost/connect.php. You should see output similar to the following:

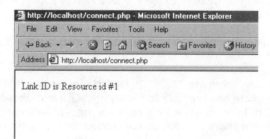

So what does it mean? The 1 (or any other positive integer) in the output indicates that the connection to the MySQL server was successful. The following output would indicate a failure:

Link ID is

You may also get a plethora of error messages in with this output. These are automatically generated by PHP and can be suppressed by placing an @ character before the function call, which we'll do next.

3. The value returned by mysql_connect() is false if our script failed to connect to the MySQL server, so we can test this value within our script to intelligently handle such errors. We'll use a bad host name so that you can see what's happening. Make the following changes to the script, rename it connectbad.php, load it up and refresh your browser:

```php
<?php
    $link = @mysql_connect("notarealhost");

    if ($link == false) {echo "Failed to connect to MySQL server";
    exit;
    }

echo "Link ID is " . $link;
    ?>
```

The hostname argument of the mysql_connect() function is wrong, so you'll produce an error. We used the error suppressing symbol before the call to the mysql_connect() function in order to have complete control of how the error is reported on screen:

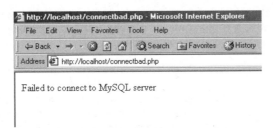

If we omitted the error suppressing symbol, we would get the full error message similar to this:

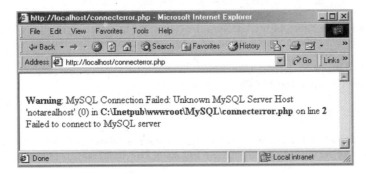

Disconnecting from the MySQL server

The PHP engine automatically disconnects from the MySQL server upon exiting the PHP script. However, it is good programming practice to explicitly disconnect using the mysql_close() function when you are finished using the server. You do that using this syntax:

```
mysql_close(link_id);
```

1. Edit the script we've written to explicitly close the connection to the MySQL server, and rename it close.php. Altogether, your script should look like this:

```php
<?php
    $link = @mysql_connect("localhost");
    if ($link == false) {
    echo "Failed to connect to MySQL server";
    exit;
    }
echo "Link ID is " . $link;
mysql_close($link);
?>
```

Note that we've changed the hostname parameter of the mysql_connect() function back to localhost so that we can test proper execution.

While creating and terminating connections to the MySQL server is no doubt useful, even essential, it is by no means riveting stuff. Moving on, we'll look at how you can perform various operations on our data.

Selecting a database

Just as with the MySQL monitor, before we can do anything in MySQL we need to select the database that we want to use. The easiest way of doing this with PHP is to use the mysql_select_db() function, (there is another way that we'll look at later in the section.) The syntax for this function is:

```
mysql_select_db(db_name [, link_id]);
```

The db_name is the name of the database that we want to select. link_id is the link identifier for our connection but is optional in this function. If it is omitted then the last opened link is used.

This function returns true if the operation was successful, or false otherwise. Note that this function is akin to using this MySQL command:

```
USE db_name;
```

So, if we were to want to connect to our flash5dcs database that we created earlier in the MySQL language section, we could use the following PHP script (selectdb.php):

```php
<?php
    $link = @mysql_connect("localhost");

    if ($link == false) {
      echo "Failed to connect to MySQL server!";
      exit;
    }

    if (mysql_select_db("flash5dcs") == false) {
      echo "Error selecting database flash5dcs!";
      exit;
    }

    echo "Database flash5dcs selected!";

    mysql_close($link);
?>
```

We have included another error checking block here to handle errors selecting the desired database. We are aborting the execution of the rest of the script if such an error occurs because the rest of the script would likely depend on the database being selected successfully.

Creating a MySQL database through PHP

You can set up your MySQL databases using a PHP script, as opposed to going into the MySQL Monitor. This is especially useful when you don't have access to the MySQL Monitor, for example if you're using a third party to host your website. The PHP mysql_create_db() function allows you to do this. It looks like this:

```php
mysql_create_db(db_name [, link_id]);
```

The db_name is the name of the database you want to create. Again, the link_id is the link identifier for the connection to the MySQL server and is optional. The function returns true if the database was created successfully, and false otherwise. This is akin to this MySQL command:

```sql
CREATE DATABASE db_name;
```

Since we've already created the database we're going to use in the sample application later on, we'll just create a sample one here that can be deleted later. Let's call this script createdb.php.

```php
<?php
    $link = @mysql_connect("localhost");

    if ($link == false) {
    echo "Failed to connect to MySQL server!";
    exit;
}

    if (mysql_create_db("sampledb") == false) {
```

```
        echo "Error creating database sampledb!";
        exit;
        }

    echo "Database sampledb created!" ;

    mysql_close($link);
?>
```

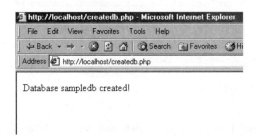

You can use the MySQL monitor to view your new database by using the SHOW DATABASES command.

Dropping a database

You can also drop databases through PHP. Like its MySQL command counterpart, the mysql_drop_db() function gives no warnings that you're about to lose all your data in the specified database. The syntax looks like this:

```
mysql_drop_db(db_name, [, link_id]);
```

The db_name is the name of the database that you want to drop. This function returns true if the database was successfully dropped, and false otherwise. So, let's drop the database we just created:

To drop the sampledb database, use this script (we'll call it dropdb.php):

```
<?php
    $link = @mysql_connect("localhost");

    if ($link == false) {
    echo "Failed to connect to MySQL server!";
    exit;
    }

    if (mysql_drop_db("sampledb") == false) {
    echo "Error dropping database sampledb!";
    exit;
    }
```

```
        echo "Database sampledb dropped!";

        mysql_close($link);
    ?>
```

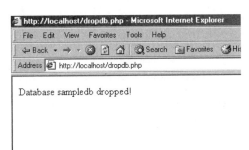

Executing MySQL queries with PHP

OK, now that we know how to select, create and drop MySQL databases using the built-in PHP functions, we need to know how to query databases. This will let us perform the kind of operations we've seen previously with the CREATE/DROP TABLE, INSERT, REPLACE, UPDATE, DELETE and SELECT MySQL commands.

This is mainly the job of one function, mysql_query(), but for some operations we'll need to employ a few others as well. The general syntax for this function is:

```
        mysql_query(query_string [, link_id]);
```

The *query_string* should be a string containing a valid MySQL query made up of the MySQL statements we met earlier in this chapter. According to the PHP manual the *query_*string should not end with a semi-colon as we did when we entered commands into the MySQL Monitor. This function will return different values depending on which type of query you execute.

We'll look at each of the different types of query you can use next, and investigate the use of this function in each particular case.

Data Definition: CREATE, DROP
The mysql_query() function can be used to replace the mysql_create_db()   and mysql_drop_db() functions discussed previously by using the raw MySQL commands to perform the operation.

In the case of Data Definition Language (DDL) statements, the mysql_query() function returns either true or false depending upon the success of the operation. Data Definition Language statements are basically those MySQL/SQL commands that create or remove databases and tables.

1.   For example, we could have used this function to create the guestbook table like so. Go ahead and create this script (querycreate.php), use it, and see what happens:

```php
<?php
  $link = @mysql_connect("localhost");
    if ($link == false) {
    echo "Failed to connect to MySQL server!";
    exit;
}
    if (mysql_select_db("flash5dcs") == false) {
    echo "Error selecting database flash5dcs!";
    exit;
}
    $query = "CREATE TABLE guestbook (
    EntryID INTEGER AUTO_INCREMENT PRIMARY KEY,
    Name VARCHAR(25),
    Email VARCHAR(50),
    URL VARCHAR(255),
    Comments TEXT,
    Posted DATETIME)";

    if (mysql_query($query) == false) {
    echo "Error creating table guestbook!";
    } else {
    echo "Successfully created table guestbook";
    }

  mysql_close($link);
?>
```

Note that because we have already created this table using the MySQL monitor back near the beginning of this chapter, you will receive an error:

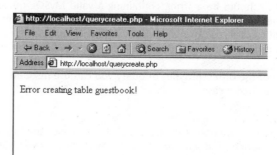

2. To get around this we'll need to run the next script first to drop the table. This is querydrop.php:

```php
<?php
  $link = @mysql_connect("localhost");
    if ($link == false) {
    echo "Failed to connect to MySQL server!";
    exit;
```

```
        }
        if (mysql_select_db("flash5dcs") == false) {
        echo("Error selecting database flash5dcs!");
        exit;
        }
        if (mysql_query("DROP TABLE guestbook") == false) {
        echo "Error dropping table guestbook!";
        } else {
        echo "Table guestbook dropped";
        }

    mysql_close($link);
?>
```

Data manipulation: INSERT, REPLACE, UPDATE, DELETE

With Data Manipulation Language (DML) statements, the return value of the mysql_query() function is true on success or false if the query could not be executed. We can find out the number of rows affected by these statements by calling the mysql_affected_rows() function. MySQL/SQL commands that belong in the Data Manipulation Language group are those, cunningly enough, which we use to manipulate our data.

1. So, insert some more data into the guestbook table using the following script, queryinsert.php:

```
<?php
    // Set up data
    $Name = "Steve Webster";
    $Email = "Steve@netbreed.co.uk";
    $URL = "http://www.netbreed.co.uk";
    $Comments = "This is my comment!";

    // Connect to MySQL and test
    $link = @mysql_connect("localhost");

      if ($link == false) {
      echo "Failed to connect to MySQL server!";
      exit;
      }

    // Select out flash5dcs database
      if (mysql_select_db("flash5dcs") == false) {
      echo("Error selecting database flash5dcs!");
      exit;
      }

    // Build query
    $query = "INSERT INTO guestbook VALUES(NULL,";
    $query .= "'" . $Name . "',";
    $query .= "'" . $Email . "',";
    $query .= "'" . $URL . "',";
```

```
    $query .= "'" . $Comments . "', NOW())";

// Execute query and test
  if (mysql_query($query) == false) {
  echo "Error executing query!";
  } else {
  $rows = mysql_affected_rows();
  echo $rows . " rows(s) affected!";
  }

// Disconnect from MySQL
  mysql_close($link);
?>
```

2. We'll be reusing some of the code in this script later when we come to build our Flash guestbook. For now, just run the script a few more times with different details for Name, Email, URL and Comments as this will give us some content to work with when we move on to the SELECT queries from PHP. You can go and check the data you've entered using the MySQL monitor.

Data manipulation: SELECT

Although it is part of the Data Manipulation Language (DML) family of MySQL commands, running the SELECT query from PHP deserves special attention. This is because the results of the query are not displayed directly on screen (as they were in the MySQL Monitor) but are instead stashed away in a resultset. The mysql_query() function returns the result identifier for this resultset when executing a SELECT query.

In order to fetch the results from this resultset we need to use the mysql_fetch_array() function. What this function does is to fetch the next row of the resultset and return it as an associative array – moving to the next row afterwards. If no more rows are available this function returns false. If you're not familiar with associative arrays then it may be worth trekking back to the PHP chapter for a refresher. The general syntax for this function is:

```
mysql_fetch_array(result_id [, result_type]);
```

The result_id is the result identifier returned by mysql_query(). The result_type is an optional argument that allows you to specify the type of array that is returned and can have the following values:

MYSQL_NUM	The array returned will have numeric indices only. This is useful if you either don't know or don't want to rely on the column names for the table.
MYSQL_ASSOC	The array returned will have associative indices only. Individual values can be accessed using the column name as the array index.
MYSQL_BOTH	The array will have both numeric and associative indices. This allows you to access the individual values using either the column name or a number. This is the default value if the result_type argument is omitted.

Once we are finished with the results we could use `mysql_free_result()` to free up the memory associated with the resultset. This is the syntax:

```
mysql_free_result(result_id);
```

This is generally only used if you think your script is using too much memory when running. If this is not used all result sets are freed once the script ends.

1. So, let's use a simple script (we'll call it `queryselect.php`) that displays the contents of the `guestbook` table, using the `mysql_query()` and `mysql_fetch_array()` functions in tandem:

```php
<?php
    $link = @mysql_connect("localhost");
    if ($link == false) {
        echo "Failed to connect to MySQL server!";
        exit;
    }
    if (mysql_select_db("flash5dcs") == false) {
        echo(""Error selecting database flash5dcs!");
        exit;
    }

    $query = "SELECT * FROM guestbook";
    $result = mysql_query($query);
    if ($result == false) {
        echo "Error executing query!";
        } else {
            echo "Query successful!\n\n";
            while ($row = mysql_fetch_array($result)) {
            echo "EntryID: " . $row["EntryID"] . "\n";
            echo "Name: " . $row["Name"] . "\n";
            echo "Email: " . $row["Email"] . "\n";
            echo "URL: " . $row["URL"] . "\n";
            echo "Comments: " . $row["Comments"] . "\n";
            echo "Posted: " . $row["Posted"] . "\n";
            echo "——————————\n\n";
            }
        }

    mysql_close($link);
?>
```

This script will display all the details of every entry in your `guestbook` table. Again, we'll reuse some of this code to build our sample guestbook application.

Using PHP and MYSQL summary
We've covered all of the necessary (for our purposes) PHP functions that allow us to access and manipulate our MySQL databases. We're able to establish and close connections to the MySQL server, add/remove databases and tables, and manipulate our data using standard SQL queries. It

is now time to put all of this into practice and build our sample application. But first, take a well-deserved breather!!!

Sample application: guestbook

In this section we are going to be building a Flash based guestbook that'll run off of a MySQL backend using PHP scripts as middleware. That is, we'll build the user interface for our guestbook in Flash, store the information entered in a MySQL database, and use PHP scripts to communicate between the two.

We'll be working on the PHP scripts first but to give you a teaser of where we're headed this is what we'll be building!

The main design points such as how to create the 3D bevel effect and buttons etc. will not be covered in this example, because we're purely concerned with the technical aspects that actually do the work. However, you'll find that the example FLA included on the CD has the design – feel free to pick it apart as much as you want to!

The scripts
The first thing we need to do is to build the scripts to interact with the guestbook table that we created earlier. When building this script we'll have to keep in the kind of output that the Flash movie will expect.

The setup script

For the sake of completeness you'll find below a slight modification of the script we developed earlier to create the flash5dcs database and guestbook table. With the exception of comments added to the script, all the notable points about this code have, at some point or another, been discussed earlier in the chapter. For this reason the script is presented without in-depth discussion. We'll call this script setup.php.

```php
<?php
// setup.php
// Attempt connection to MySQL server
$link = @mysql_connect("localhost");
        if ($link == false) {
        echo "Failed to connect to MySQL server!";
        exit;
        }

// Attempt to create DB
mysql_create_db("flash5dcs");
        // Attempt to select newly created DB
        if (mysql_select_db("flash5dcs") == false) {
        echo "Error creating database flash5dcs!\n";
        echo "Error: " . mysql_error($link);
        exit;
        }

// Construct query for building our table
$query = "CREATE TABLE guestbook (
        EntryID INTEGER AUTO_INCREMENT PRIMARY KEY,
        Name VARCHAR(25), Email VARCHAR(50),
        URL VARCHAR(255), Comments TEXT,
        Posted DATETIME)";

        // Execute query and test
        if (mysql_query($query) == false) {
        echo "Error creating table guestbook!\n";
        echo "Error: " . mysql_error($link);
        } else {
        echo "Successfully created table guestbook";
        }

// Close link to MySQL server
mysql_close($link);
?>
```

You will need to run this script once in your browser to set up the database and table for the guest book:

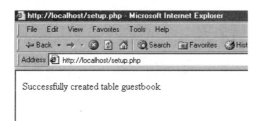

Note that this script is intended to run directly from your web browser so no special formatting of the script output is necessary. Note too that if you're using a third party to host your site you'll likely already have a database set up for you. In this case you won't need the line in this script that creates the database, and you'll need to change the name of the database we're trying to select (shown in **bold**) to the name of the database created for you.

Reading the guestbook through PHP

This is the first of the two scripts that we'll be building that'll actually interface between the MySQL server and our Flash movie. This first script will fetch all of the information in our `guestbook` table and return it in a format that Flash can read and understand. We'll build it up piece-by-piece - altogether, the script will make one file called `readbook.php`

1. We'll begin the script by connecting to the MySQL server and select the database. If an error occurs we need to relay that back to Flash so that our movie can handle it intelligently.

    ```php
    <?php
        / Attempt connection to MySQL server
        $link = @mysql_connect("localhost");
        if ($link == false) {
                echo "&result=Fail&errormsg=";
                echo urlencode("Failed to connect to MySQL server!");
                echo "&";
                exit;
        }
    ```

2. Next, we need to select our database that contains the `guestbook` table. Again, if an error occurs we need to relay that back to Flash in the standard format. Also remember if you're using a third party to host your site that you may need to change the name of the database (shown in **bold**) appropriately. Add this to the script:

    ```php
    // Attempt to select our DB
    if (mysql_select_db("flash5dcs") == false) {
    echo "&result=Fail&errormsg=";
    echo urlencode("Error selecting database!\n");
    echo urlencode("Error: " . mysql_error($link));
    echo "&";
    exit;
    }
    ```

3. Now it is time to build and execute the MySQL query that'll return all the data in the `guestbook` table into a resultset.

    ```php
    // Build and execute query
    $query = "SELECT * FROM guestbook";
    $result = @mysql_query($query);
    ```

You can see from this that we're using the SELECT command to get all the data for all the rows of our guestbook. If you had an absolutely huge guestbook you might want to limit the number of rows loaded into the Flash movie using the LIMIT block. However, since we're starting from scratch here I'll leave you to make that decision as and when it becomes necessary!

4. Moving on, we now need to fetch the guestbook entries from the resultset and send them on back to our Flash movie. We'll use a while loop for this but first we need to set up some variables that will be essential to this loop:

```
$count = 0;
$output = "";
```

We'll use these two variables to keep count of the number of records we've fetched and to build the output that will be sent to Flash respectively.

Now we come to the loop proper. As in the previous example we will use a while loop to fetch each row of the resultset and build the necessary output to be sent back to Flash.

```
while ($row = mysql_fetch_array($result)) {
```

The first thing we need to do inside this loop is to remove the backslashes automatically added by PHP to any special characters that there might be in our data. If we had an undetermined or great number of columns in our database we could use another while loop for this but for the 5 data columns that we're interested in we may as well do it manually.

```
$Name = stripslashes($row['Name']);
$Email = stripslashes($row['Email']);
$URL = stripslashes($row['URL']);
$Comments = stripslashes($row['Comments']);
$Posted = stripslashes($row['Posted']);
```

The stripslashes() function is built into PHP. It takes a string as its argument and returns that string without the slashes in it. For more information on this function please refer to the PHP manual.

Now that we have the data for the current row (minus the slashes) stashed in our five variables we can add these to the output string. The way we're going to be returning our data to flash looks something like:

```
&name1=value&email1=value.....$name7=value...
```

We'll formulate the variable names by appending the record number to the column names and we'll URL encode the value for each variable using the urlencode() function.

```
$output .= "&name" . $count . "=" . urlencode($Name);
```

```
$output .= "&email" . $count . "=" . urlencode($Email);
$output .= "&url" . $count . "=" . urlencode($URL);
$output .= "&comments" . $count . "=" . urlencode($Comments);
$output .= "&date" . $count . "=" . urlencode($Posted);
```

The last thing we need to do in our loop is to increment the $count variable to keep track of how many entries we've fetched from our guestbook so far.

```
$count++;
}
```

5. Finally, our script needs to actually send all this data back to Flash. In addition to the guestbook data we'll also need to let Flash know how many guestbook entries in total we've returned and that the operation was a success.

```
echo $output . "&records=" . $count . "&result=Okay&";
?>
```

That's it! Well, that's it for the readbook.php script anyway. Here's the completed script:

```
<?php
    // readbook.php

    // Attempt connection to MySQL server
    $link = @mysql_connect("localhost");

    if ($link == false) {
        echo "&result=Fail&errormsg=";
        echo urlencode("Failed to connect to MySQL server!");
        echo "&";
        exit;
    }

    // Attempt to select our DB
    if (mysql_select_db("flash5dcs") == false) {
        echo "&result=Fail&errormsg=";
        echo urlencode("Error selecting database!\n");
        echo urlencode("Error: " . mysql_error($link));
        echo "&";
        exit;
    }

    // Build and execute query
    $query = "SELECT * FROM guestbook";
    $result = @mysql_query($query);

    $count = 0;
    $output = "";
```

```
        while ($row = mysql_fetch_array($result)) {

                $Name = stripslashes($row['Name']);
                $Email = stripslashes($row['Email']);
                $URL = stripslashes($row['URL']);
                $Comments = stripslashes($row['Comments']);
                $Posted = stripslashes($row['Posted']);

                $output .= "&name" . $count . "=" . urlencode($Name);
                $output .= "&email" . $count . "=" .
                ➥urlencode($Email);
                $output .= "&url" . $count . "=" . urlencode($URL);
                $output .= "&comments" . $count . "=" .
                ➥urlencode($Comments);
                $output .= "&date" . $count . "=" .
                ➥urlencode($Posted);
                $count++;
        }

        echo $output . "&records=" . $count . "&result=Okay&";
    ?>
```

Signing the guestbook

It's all very well being able to read the guestbook but it's not much of a guestbook if your visitors can't sign it! Obviously the job of this next script, signbook.php script will be to take the user input entered into the Flash movie and store that in our guestbook table.

1. For the most part this script is identical to readbook.php, only differing when we come to the query part. So, the first section of the script will be the same:

```php
<?php
    // Attempt connection to MySQL server
    $link = @mysql_connect("localhost");
            if ($link == false) {
                    echo "&result=Fail&errormsg=";
                    echo urlencode("Failed to connect to MySQL
                    ➥server!");
                    echo "&";
                    exit;
            }
    // Attempt to select our DB
            if (mysql_select_db("flash5dcs") == false) {
                    echo "&result=Fail&errormsg=";
                    echo urlencode("Error selecting database!\n");
                    echo urlencode("Error: " .
                    ➥mysql_error($link));
                    echo "&";
                    exit;
             }
```

(Again if you're using a third party to host your site you may need to change the database name (shown in **bold**) accordingly.)

2.   Since PHP automatically adds slashes to any special characters in the data that it receives through GET or POST methods we don't need to do anything to the data before storing it into the guestbook table. We just construct the MySQL query like so:

```
$query = "INSERT INTO guestbook VALUES(NULL,";
$query .= "'" . $enter_name . "',";
$query .= "'" . $enter_email . "',";
$query .= "'" . $enter_url . "',";
$query .= "'" . $enter_comments . "',";
$query .= "NOW());";
```

Take special note of the names of the variables we're inserting into the query string as we'll need to make sure that we use the same variables names when we come to construct the section of the Flash movie where the users can sign the guestbook.

3.   All that's left to do now is to execute the query and report to Flash that the operation was successful. Note that we're trusting a little that the MySQL query will be successful but because we're controlling the data that goes into it from the Flash movie we can be pretty confident that the query will succeed. If you're so inclined you can implement the techniques covered earlier in the chapter to test the success of the query and act accordingly.

```
    mysql_query($query);
    echo "&result=Okay&";
?>
```

All done! Again, the full script is presented below for your convenience!

```
<?php
    // signbook.php

    // Attempt connection to MySQL server
    $link = @mysql_connect("localhost");

    if ($link == false) {
        echo "&result=Fail&errormsg=";
        echo urlencode("Failed to connect to MySQL server!");
        echo "&";
        exit;
    }

    // Attempt to select our DB
    if (mysql_select_db("flash5dcs") == false) {
        echo "&result=Fail&errormsg=";
        echo urlencode("Error selecting database!\n");
    echo urlencode("Error: " . mysql_error($link));
```

```
echo "&";
exit;
   }

  $query = "INSERT INTO guestbook VALUES(NULL,";
  $query .= "'" . $enter_name . "',";
  $query .= "'" . $enter_email . "',";
  $query .= "'" . $enter_url . "',";
  $query .= "'" . $enter_comments . "',";
  $query .= "NOW());";

  mysql_query($query);
  echo "&result=Okay&";
?>
```

The Flash movie front end

It's now time to build the Flash movie that will be the user interface of our guestbook. As mentioned previously, this project will be presented without any regard for design issues. Indeed, many of the screenshots will have all design elements removed from them to allow us to concentrate on the technical aspects of the project.

Building the FLA

First things first, let's take a look at the timeline for the movie we'll be creating:

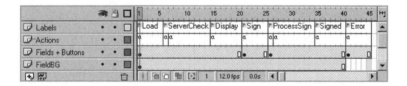

This shows the major sections of the movie we'll be creating. We'll go through each section in turn discussing the keyframes on the various layers in each.

Create and name the layers and labels shown above in your Flash movie. Also, as we go through, build up your own interpretation of the screenshots presented.

The Load section

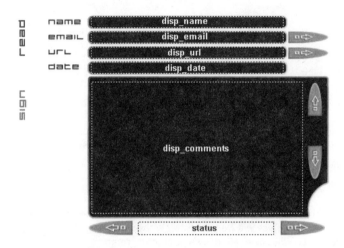

As its name suggests, the FieldBG layer simply contains the background for the guestbook fields. This layer is common throughout all but the last section of the movie.

This Load section of the movie will be responsible for calling the readbook.php script as well as setting up some variables. We'll start by adding the necessary ActionScript to frame 1

1.   The ActionScript in frame 1 of the Actions layer is:

```
result = "";
status = "Loading...";
loadVariables ("readbook.php", this, "POST");
gotoAndPlay ("ServerCheck");
```

Note that although we aren't using any variables from our Flash movie in the readbook.php script we're using the POST method to send them anyway. This helps to ensure that the results of the PHP script aren't just loaded from the cache.

2.   All the buttons and dynamic text fields are on the Fields + Buttons layer. The variable names for each of the dynamic fields are shown in the center of each field in the above diagram. The buttons to the right of the disp_email and disp_url fields will be used to launch the default email app with a new email addressed to the address shown, and to launch the URL shown in a new browser window respectively. The code behind the email button should be:

```
on (release) {
    if (_root.disp_email != "") {
    getURL ("mailto:" add _root.disp_email);
    }
}
```

The code behind the URL button should look like this:

```
on (release) {
   if (_root.disp_url != "") {
   getURL (_root.disp_url, "_blank");

}
```

3.   The buttons either side of the status field will be used to navigate forwards and backwards through the entries in our guestbook. It will take the variable for the current entry and copy its values into the display fields. This is what the code behind the back pointing arrow should look like:

```
on (release) {
   count--;
   if (Number(count) < 0) {
   count = Number(records) - 1;
   }
   disp_name = this["name" add count];
   disp_email = this["email" add count];
   disp_url = this["url" add count];
   disp_date = this["date" add count];
   disp_comments = this["comments" add count];
   status = "Entry " add (count+1) add " of " add
   ➡Number(records);
}
```

The code behind the forward button is very similar:

```
on (release) {
   count++;
   if (Number(count)>=Number(records)) {
   count = 0;
   }
   disp_name = this["name" add count];
   disp_email = this["email" add count];
   disp_url = this["url" add count];
   disp_date = this["date" add count];
   disp_comments = this["comments" add count];
   status = "Entry " add (count+1) add " of " add
   ➡Number(records);
}
```

4.   The two buttons to the right of the disp_comments field will be used to scroll the disp_comments field when the comments of a given entry are too big to be displayed. The ActionScript for these buttons uses the scroll property of Flash dynamic text boxes, so for the scroll up button looks like this:

```
on (release) {
    disp_comments.scroll = disp_comments.scroll - 1;
}
```

The scroll down button code should look like this:

```
on (release) {
    disp_comments.scroll = disp_comments.scroll + 1;
}
```

5. The final thing to do in this section of the movie is code the read and sign buttons at the top left of the stage. These allow the user to switch between the two functions of the guestbook, by sending the movie to later frame labels. Add this code to the read button:

```
on (release) {
    gotoAndPlay ("Load");
}
```

The code behind the sign button is, as you've probably guessed, very similar:

```
on (release) {
    gotoAndPlay ("Sign");
}
```

The ServerCheck section

This section simply loops the movie until a response is received from the PHP script, so all the work is done in the Actions layer. Once a response is received then the movie is sent to a particular frame depending on whether the operation within the PHP script was a success or not (according to the result variable returned from the PHP script).

1. The frame 6 ActionScript checks the result variable, sending the movie to the other frames depending on what the variable holds:

```
if (result == "Okay") {
    gotoAndPlay ("Display");
} else if (result == "Fail") {
    gotoAndPlay ("Error");
}
```

Frame 7 simply loops the movie until the result variable has loaded:

```
gotoAndPlay ("ServerCheck");
```

The Display section

The only addition we need to make to the Display section that differs from the previous two is some ActionScript in frame 15. This code stops the movie at its current location and sets up a count variable that we'll use to keep track of which guestbook entry is currently being viewed. It then tests the records variable, which is returned by the readbook.php script, to see if the guestbook is empty or not. If the guestbook is empty all display fields are blanked and the status field is updated to inform the user that there are no entries in the guestbook.

If, on the other hand, the guestbook has at least one entry, the display fields are set to the relevant values of the first entry. The status field is updated to show the users position within the guestbook.

1.   Altogether, the code for frame 15 looks like this:

```
// Stop Movie
   stop ();
// Set up some variables
count = 0;

if (Number(records) == 0) {
   disp_name = "";
   disp_email = "";
   disp_url = "";
   disp_date = "";
   disp_comments = "";
   status = "No entries in guestbook";
   } else {
// Display first record (0) returned
   disp_name = this["name" add count];
   disp_email = this["email" add count];
   disp_url = this["url" add count];
   disp_date = this["date" add count];
   disp_comments = this["comments" add count];
   status = "Entry " add (count+1) add " of " add
   ➥Number(records);
}
```

The Sign section
This section allows the user to enter their details in the fields provided, and submit them to the guestbook.

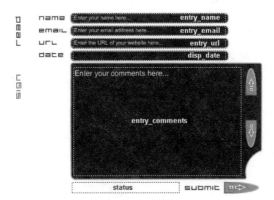

1. You will need to change four of the dynamic text fields originally set up, to input text fields and rename their variables as shown above. These input fields' variable names are required by our `signbook.php` script. You will need to remove the two buttons either side of the status field. You may also wish to add instructions to the user to enter their name, email address, URL and comments as shown above.

2. Now we need to add a new button, submit, *to the right of the* status *field.*

3. The ActionScript code in frame 21 performs the task of fetching and formatting the current date and placing it in the `disp_date` field. Note that although we do this in the Flash movie the PHP scripts takes no regard of it whatsoever, instead using the NOW() MySQL internal function to fetch the current date/time information. This code will also set the status field to invite the user to enter their details, and stops the movie.

```
daysOfWeek = new Array("Sunday", "Monday", "Tuesday",
    ➥"Wednesday", "Thursday", "Friday", "Saturday");
monthsOfYear = new Array("Jan", "Feb", "Mar", "Apr",
    ➥"May", "Jun", "Jul", "Aug", "Sep", "Oct", "Nov", "Dec");
now = new Date();
// Form date string like : Sunday 7 Jan, 2001
disp_date = daysOfWeek[now.getDay()] add " " add
    ➥now.getDate() add " " add monthsOfYear[now.getMonth()]
    ➥add ", " add (now.getYear() + 1900);

status = "Please enter your details...";

stop ();
```

4. Now for the submit button. This performs the task of taking the user's data and submitting it to the `signbook.php` script.

```
on (release) {
    if (enter_name != "" && enter_comments != "") {
        result = "";
        loadVariables ("signbook.php", this, "POST");
        status = "Processing entry. Please wait...";
        gotoAndPlay ("ProcessSign");
    } else {
        status = "You have omitted a required element";
    }
}
```

You can see that we also perform some rudimentary error checking on the data entered so that they at least have to enter something in the `enter_name` and `enter_comments` fields before the movie will allow submission of the data. We could have performed this error checking from within the PHP script and retuned an error if there was a problem. However, checking *before* sending the data reduces the unnecessary load on the server.

The ProcessSign section

1. This section acts much like the ServerCheck section, in that it waits for confirmation from the script before allowing the movie to proceed. In frame 26 the ActionScript looks like this:

```
if (result == "Okay") {
    status = "Details successfully stored in guestbook";
    gotoAndPlay ("Signed");
} else if (result == "Fail") {
    gotoAndPlay ("Error");
}
```

Frame 27 just loops back until the movie breaks the loop by getting a result:

```
gotoAndPlay("ProcessSign");
```

This script just hangs around until the result variable is received and then acts accordingly depending on its value.

The Signed section

This section is just used to give the user confirmation that their guestbook entry was successful. The ActionScript in frame 35 just stops the movie at the current location:

```
stop();
```

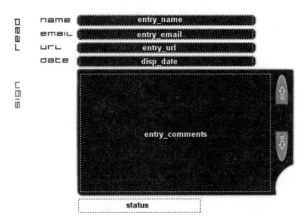

The Error section

Finally, we come to the section where all errors are reported. Frame 41 contains some static text, a dynamic text box for the display of the error message, and a button to return to the guestbook.

Click here to return to guestbook

2. Add the `errormsg` dynamic text box, named so that it will automatically contain the error messages returned by either of the PHP scripts. Then add the Click here to return to guestbook button and add the code that will return the user to the loading interface:

```
on (release) {
    gotoAndPlay ("Load");
}
```

3. Finally, add a stop action to frame 41:

```
stop();
```

4. Test the movie!

Summary

Well, that's it then! We've covered some massive ground in the space of this chapter and it's a lot to take in at once. You may well benefit from going back and reading the chapter over again now that you know where you're heading and why you're heading there.

We've looked at the installation and configuration of the MySQL server and how to start and stop the mysqld daemon. We've played around with the MySQL monitor and covered all the necessary MySQL commands to give ourselves a good base from which to move on and expand our knowledge. We've covered all of the important MySQL related functions that are available to us as PHP programmers and learned how to use them in sample scripts.

Then we put it all together and developed a useful and usable application for any web site - a MySQL/PHP backed Flash guestbook. We got all the basics in, but of course, there are a lot of features you could add to it. Here are some of the things that you could add; you should be able to implement them all now you've read this chapter:

- **A timeout facility**: to give the user an error message if no response is received from the PHP scripts within a given amount of time. You could implement it purely in Flash.

- **Post moderation**: sometimes it's a good idea to have entries held until a moderator has confirmed that they are OK. You could do this by changing the database to hold entries until they're verified or have them emailed to the moderator for approval and manual entry.

- **Email linkup**. It would be nice if we could give the users the opportunity to email others who have signed the guestbook; you could use the Flash emailer we built in the PHP chapter.

Further reading

If this chapter has given you a thirst for PHP and MySQL then there's no real substitute for a good book on the subject.

Beginning PHP4
Publisher: Wrox Press
Authors: Wankyu Choi, Allan Kent, Chris Lea, Ganesh Prasad, Chris Ullman
ISBN: 1-861003-73-0

Useful websites

www.friendsofed.com
Friends of ED are the publishers of this book and so their site is a must visit. A community where designers come together, the message boards are open to all to post questions and opinions on this and other friends of ED books. You can also download all of the source code and movies used in this book and find out about other friends of ED titles.

www.mysql.com
This is the home of MySQL. Here you can download the latest versions of MySQL, read the online documentation and you'll find many links to MySQL related websites. This is an invaluable resource for any MySQL developer.

www.flashkit.com
This site is an unmissable resource for any Flash designer/developer. With tons of open source movies and tutorials and a discussion forum with over 100,000 members and 25+ topics, it's the definitive site for anyone who uses Flash. With a specific section for Scripting & Backend this is a site not to be missed!

25
Flash and XML

Section 4
Dynamic Data

24
Databases
Another Way

23
Flash, Access
and ASP

22
Introducing
Databases

Chapter 25
Flash and XML

This chapter is intended to provide you with the knowledge and resources you'll need to immediately begin working with XML in Flash 5. For this reason, only those aspects of XML handling which are relevant to Flash's XML capabilities have been addressed. The sections of this chapter are ordered as progressively more sophisticated discussions of XML's application within the Flash environment. If you're already familiar with XML you might want to skip ahead to the discussion of the XML object methods. If you'd like an introduction to, or to refresh your knowledge of, XML start here!

Macromedia's introduction of XML handling capabilities to the Flash 5 player and authoring environment marks a dramatic evolution in the nature of Flash technology. Flash is renowned as the most powerful visual medium on the Web, and it now has the potential of becoming among its most versatile. Taken in line with the adaptation of ActionScript to an ECMA compliant scripting language, as well as the introduction of persistent TCP sockets, the presence of XML processing opens the door to a tremendous variety of potential applications for Flash design and programming. Flash has truly become a web programming medium.

XML makes data comprehensible

Information is only significant to the degree that it can be defined and interpreted in relation to other information. Suppose you had a single piece of data that described the height of something, say the Empire State building. That piece of data - the height - is completely meaningless unless you also know what it applies to - the Empire State Building. Without that, it's merely a number - a number that could signify virtually anything. This is where XML comes into the picture; it gives us a coherent and flexible framework within which data can be represented alongside its properties, definitions, meanings, and relationships. It allows us to represent a piece of data within the context of the rest of the data - and it is this behind the linguistic or cybernetic terminology frequently applied to XML. XML is said to provide a medium that can possess semantic properties, establish grammatical rules and relationships, and to yield new 'languages' for expressing various forms of information.

So what do people mean when applying these attributes to XML? A well thought out and implemented XML document does more than simply aggregate data elements - it provides a higher order of data representation altogether. You can design an XML document that conveys semantic and semiotic qualities, that implements an interpretation of the internal structure and meaning. Semiotics is about the signs and symbols used in conveying information and meaning - in this case, words. When looking at "the walls of my house" example later on, you'll find that it's these qualities that enable you to read through the XML structure and interpret its meaning without relying on a legend or any further translation. You'll be able to understand the meaning of the example intuitively, because it uses vocabulary that you're familiar with — the hierarchical relationships of walls, rooms, and houses. When this principle is extended to more sophisticated representations of data, for example, market data deriving from a securities exchange, the potential to convey this data using grammatical and semantic rules becomes invaluable. This isn't to say that all XML structures are inherently effective in their self-description. Poorly designed XML documents will convey information poorly. If an XML structure is assembled arbitrarily, or without regard for the contextual nature of the data it conveys, little advantage is provided simply by the fact that this data is borne within an XML document.

We're going to investigate some of the key features of XML, by:

- Comparing XML and HTML - both of which are markup specifications

- Discussing the 'self describing' nature of XML documents

- Looking at the ways in which XML can be compared to human languages

- Discussing some of the implementations of XML documents

What is XML (Extensible Markup Language)?

XML is simply a means of representing data, and the relationships between the elements of data, within a document according to a few basic rules - rules that enable an XML document to be interpreted by all sorts of applications and processes. As we work through the examples presented in this chapter you'll see that XML provides a very intuitive way of constructing and representing information. Don't let the vernacular which surrounds XML intimidate you – you're probably familiar with its key tenets already. If you've ever written an outline for a book report, or even a complicated grocery list, you've structured information in a way that is very similar to that used within XML documents.

XML takes the form of a markup specification, like HTML, and structurally, it looks very much like the familiar HTML document. This is, however, a misleading likeness - for while XML *describes* data using a set of tags that you, the developer, designate, HTML uses a set of pre-defined tags within a pre-defined structure to *present* the data in the document in a browser (in heading one style, for example, italics, in a table, and so on). So while HTML documents assign these elements predefined methods of presentation and interactivity, the tags in an XML document define and represent the data itself, and the structure of that data. An XML document doesn't usually take care of the presentation of this data or structure, but uses complementing technologies such as XSL (Extensible Style Language), HTML or, and this is, of course, why it's in this book, Flash, for presentation.

So, in short, XML allows you make up your own tags to suit the data that you're working with. This, for example, is one line of an XML document that describes the kitchen wall in my house:

```
<kitchen>paint over drywall</kitchen>
```

You'll notice that XML looks very much like HTML - or indeed ColdFusion - in that it follows the certain basic conventions of markup languages wherein tag values are framed between < and > characters, and that these tags are incorporated either in pairs (<kitchen></kitchen>) or as a single tag with a trailing forward slash which closes the tag (<TAG />)

XML tags are *self-describing*, in that their names and internal relationships model not only the individual pieces of data, but also the relationships between that data. The tag names themselves are significant because they provide the subordinate tags that they enclose, as well as the value of these tags, with a meaningful association.

So, for example, here's that line of XML in a complete, if very small, XML document that describes the walls in my house:

```
<?xml version="1.0" encoding="iso-8859-1" ?>
    <the_walls_of_my_house>
        <floor value="1">
            <rooms>
                <den>artificial wood panelling</den>
                <kitchen>paint over drywall</kitchen>
                <dining_room>fine velvet wallpaper</dining_room>
                <foyer>wall to wall mirrors</foyer>
            </rooms>
        </floor>
    </the_walls_of_my_house>
```

Let's go through that line by line. The `<?xml version="1.0" encoding="iso-8859-1" ?>` at the beginning of the document is called the XML declaration. In this example, it's doing two things: it announces that the document should be interpreted under the XML specification version 1.0 (in fact this is the only version available at this point in time), and it attaches an attribute to the whole document - the encoding attribute. All this does is specify the encoding standard that should be used to process the text found between the subsequent tags of the document. The encoding attribute doesn't have to be included within the XML declaration (`<?xml version="1.0">` would suffice), but is useful for specifying how various character sets should be handled and for facilitating the translation of documents into various languages.

There is a similar use of attributes associated with the `floor` tag. The expression `value="1"` signifies that the value attribute of the floor element is equivalent to one. Within the context of this example we can assume that these are the rooms of the first floor. The rooms themselves are the den, the kitchen, the dining room, and the foyer. Each of these rooms, on the first floor, has its own value appropriate to describing `the_walls_of_my_house` - the den has artificial wood panelling, the kitchen walls are paint over drywall, the dining room has fine velvet wallpaper, and the foyer has wall-to-wall mirrors.

This structure assumes nothing about the intended application that will use the data marked up in XML - which is another key distinction between XML and HTML. The "walls of my house" XML document could feasibly be interpreted by any XML-aware application, be it a web browser, a COM component, or CGI script. Because the role of XML in web design has been one of the most highly promoted applications for this specification it's easy to become confused as to its broader potential and the fundamental significance of XML concerning the representation and communication of information.

The DTD

Although the DTD isn't strictly applicable to Flash with XML, it's an important concept to XML itself, so we'll take a brief look at it here. An XML document is made up of elements, which are named and ordered according to the kind of information held within the document. These elements, and the methods that will be used to process them within the overall XML structure, can be made to conform to a standardized representation, by using a **Document Type Definition** (**DTD**).

A DTD could be said to define the grammatical structure of a document. The DTD assists in declaring the hierarchy of elements within a document, whether an element contains subordinated child elements, how many instances of these elements are expected or allowed, as well as the attributes of the element. It can also pass processing instructions to a 'validating' XML parser that assists in further refining how various aspects of the XML document should be handled.

What is a parser?

An XML parser processes each line of an XML document looking for the occurrence of open markup tags and translates, or 'maps', the contents of these to one of several potential structural models. The most common of these models is the Document Object Model (DOM). Flash 5's XML parser is a DOM-type parser. This is why we can approach the handling of XML documents using methods which are typical to those you may have encountered when processing HTML documents using JavaScript or other DOM-aware languages. In fact web browsers utilize DOM-aware parsers to process HTML documents. These are similar to XML parsers except that they're not quite as strict when recognizing well-formed documents and are dedicated to HTML standards rather than the broader XML specification.

One characteristic of DOM parsers which is relevant to the use of XML within Flash applications is that DOM parsers must receive the entirety of a document before they begin parsing it. This impacts the potential size of documents that can be parsed as well as the behavior of Flash 5's 'XML sockets' feature.

Because DOM parsers render a complete mapping of an XML document, including the parent, child, sibling, value, and name properties of each node, they can absorb the available memory of an application rather quickly. While this isn't a tremendous concern within the desktop environment, it can be problematic for plug-ins. It's advisable that you pre-process large XML documents before they are transmitted to a Flash application. This simply involves breaking the document down into multiple smaller elements. You could either do this by hand, or by developing a server side routine which reads the document and separates it into discrete blocks according to certain rules.

A Simple DTD

The following is a very simple DTD for 'the walls of my house' example:

```
<?xml version="1.0"?>
<!DOCTYPE the_walls_of_my_house [
```

The 'root node' of the XML document is given primacy as the DOCTYPE :

```
<!ELEMENT the_walls_of_my_house (floor)>
```

Logically this is the first element declared along with its child node:

```
<!ELEMENT floor (rooms)>
```

Then this 'child node' is declared as an element along with its own child node:

```
<!ELEMENT rooms (den,kitchen,dining_room,foyer)>
```

Continuing in this manner "rooms" is recognized, and its child nodes declared in parenthesis.

```
<!ELEMENT den (#PCDATA)>
```

These subordinate 'child nodes' do not have further child nodes, but do contain data which is the text nested within these nodes:

```
<!ELEMENT kitchen (#PCDATA)>

<!ELEMENT dining_room (#PCDATA)>
```

This is recognized as Parsed Character Data (PCDATA):

```
<!ELEMENT foyer   (#PCDATA)>
]>
<the_walls_of_my_house>
    <floor value="1">
          <rooms>

                  <den>artificial wood panelling</den>
                  <kitchen>paint over drywall</kitchen>
                  <dining_room>fine velvet wallpaper</dining_room>
                  <foyer>wall to wall mirrors</foyer>
          </rooms>
      </floor>
</the_walls_of_my_house>
```

What you'll notice is that each of the element declarations above (!ELEMENT) mirrors a node within 'the walls of my house' example. The node named in parenthesis next to the element declaration is a 'child node' of the declared element (e.g. floor within <!ELEMENT the_walls_of_my_house (floor)>), which means that this node is subordinated to the declared element within the hierarchy of this XML document. The term PCDATA (#PCDATA) refers to parsed character data. This signifies that the declared element contains further data that should be rendered by the parser. The construction and implementation of DTDs is beyond the scope of this chapter - because Flash 5's XML parser doesn't read DTDs natively. If you're interested in learning more about DTDs, there's a wealth of good resources available online.

Flash 5's XML parser is *non-validating*, and as such doesn't read DTDs natively. This isn't a flaw in the parser - many XML parsers are non-validating - it's simply necessary to keep the size of the Flash plug-in to a minimum. The reason that I've brought DTDs into this discussion is to demonstrate how XML documents can be designed to conform to commonly agreed upon standards of representation. This enables XML documents to be designed for a specific type of information and for the resulting structure to be interpreted uniformly across a variety of applications.

Extensibility

Another significant attribute of XML documents is their extensibility - hence the acronym Extensible Markup Language (XML). Extensibility simply means that the document can be revised to incorporate additional elements, and even entire constellations of new elements whenever required. For instance, we could extend 'the walls of my house' example to include the internal lighting of each of the rooms described. This is a very simple, yet significant, principle.

As an example let's assume that the previous document was a bit more sophisticated and recognized the presence of a walls element subordinated to each of the child nodes of rooms.

```
<the_walls_of_my_house>
    <floor value="1">
        <rooms>
            <den>
                <walls>artificial wood paneling</walls>
            </den>
etc...
```

This structure could then be extended simply by creating additional child elements for each of the declared rooms.

We'll demonstrate this by incorporating a node that describes the interior lighting of each of these rooms:

```
<the_walls_of_my_house>
    <floor value="1">
        <rooms>
            <den>
                <walls>artificial wood paneling</walls>
                <lighting>floor lamps</lighting>
            </den>
            <kitchen>
                <walls>paint over drywall</walls>
                <lighting>recessed lights</lighting>
            </kitchen>
            <dining_room>
                <walls>fine velvet wallpaper</walls>
                <lighting>chandelier</lighting>
            </dining_room>
            <foyer>
                <walls>wall to wall mirrors</walls>
                <lighting>illuminated disco ball</lighting>
            </foyer>
        </rooms>
    </floor>
</the_walls_of_my_house>
```

This flexibility highlights an advantage of XML over traditional database tables. XML documents can be extended without corrupting the overall structure of the document, nor affecting an application's ability to read this document. Additional information can be incorporated into an XML document which is specific to only a subsection of the document. For example, if we were to add a `furniture` node to the `dining room` node element we wouldn't be required to also add a `furniture` node to each of the other rooms. Unlike a database table, XML elements can contain sub-elements, which are unique to each aspect of the data structure. This also enables an XML document to be extended without requiring that the applications that read this document be modified. In other words, an application that's responsible for extracting information from the XML document may not need to be rewritten to accommodate an extension to that document - if this extension has been adapted properly within the overall XML structure.

One set of data, many uses

Let's say that the walls of my house document was going to be submitted to my interior designer Mr. Frank, to guide him in suggesting furniture and potential home renovations which suited my peculiar tastes. He might store the document in his own computer and also forward the XML document to two different parties - one a building contractor and another a lighting and furnishings showroom. Again, the document being used is slightly different from the example in the beginning of this chapter because the description of the walls is incorporated within a specific `walls` node and not simply assigned to the child nodes of `rooms`.

Each party utilizing this document will treat the information it contains differently. For example, the showroom is solely concerned with the values present within the `walls` and `lighting` nodes. Mr. Frank needs this information as well, but will also look at how these elements contribute to the ambiance of the house in relation to their situation within adjoining rooms and passages. The contractor isn't particularly concerned with how my house is decorated, but needs to know its general layout to plan any renovations. The processes that these parties use in integrating this information may differ significantly. Mr. Frank will likely store the document en bloc within a client database, the showroom will simply extract the 'inventory' of my house and store this under my name within an account database, and the contractor might reduce the entire document to a description of the floor plan of the first floor, print this out, and file it as a physical document.

Now if this document were further extended to suit the contractor, by providing dimensions for each of the rooms, neither Mr. Frank nor the furniture showroom would need to revise their account handling procedures.

```
<the_walls_of_my_house>
    <floor value="1">
        <rooms>
            <den>

                    <length>20</length>  – this information can be
                    further clarified by utilizing a node "attribute" such
                    as  <length unit="feet">.
                    <width>15</width>
                    <walls>artificial wood paneling</walls>
                    <lighting>floor lamps</lighting>
            </den>
```

So, XML can be used to provide a common representation of information, which can then be implemented across many diverse applications and processes - it might even be used as a medium for communicating among these processes.

For example, a technique known as **serialization** allows you to abstract, among other things, programming structures - conditional statements, arrays, loops and so on - from a variety of programming languages into a common representation of these structures which may than be translated by a foreign programming language. That is, a programming routine written in Perl may be serialized and subsequently translated, or *deserialized*, by a TCL application. What's so great about this is that it allows applications to be developed across a variety of programming environments, bringing down the cost and complexity of making everything conform to the same basic tools and technologies.

The same concept applies if you're developing applications that rely on distributed processes, a number of diverse computing objects that all play their own part towards processing and rendering some information. Object models such as these are at the core of technologies like ActiveX, COM, and CORBA. While it might seem a bit audacious to suggest that Flash could play a role in similarly sophisticated computing architectures, simply being able to use XML in the Flash programming environment really does have enormous potential to greatly extend the range of Flash applications. Being able to read and write XML documentation gives you a mechanism for communicating complex data structures to a great variety of applications. The fact that this data may come from a Flash based application rather than any other application isn't what's important - what's important is that Flash can now access and make use of this wealth of data representation - it is the medium of communication. As long as there is a way of establishing a connection with an XML aware application, through HTTP, a TCP socket, or even through an FSCOMMAND transaction with an external JavaScript function, the potential is there.

To summarize, because XML is self describing, extensible, possesses grammatical attributes, and can be structured and defined to suit a specific set of data, it becomes a medium which is appropriate for a tremendous variety of applications. When an XML structure is adopted uniformly by multiple developers, within a given industry or category of software products, it can serve as the basis of a standard for data representation. This standard can then serve as a common method of conveying information across multiple, disparate processes. A single document structure can be employed within a diversity of applications and can be exploited to render multiple distinct combinations and interactions among the data it conveys. Many software developers anticipate that the representation of program intelligence using XML will become a fundamental aspect of future software platforms, and that XML will facilitate a dramatic shift in the way that software is developed, upgraded, and deployed.

What is XML being used for now?

Data storage

An obvious, and very popular, application for XML is in data storage and retrieval. By embedding information into a document structure, which itself describes the data it conveys, there's far less to do when you're actually trying to interpret and use this information. For instance, you could simply bring the sample XML document we've been using directly into a Flash movie, and present it to users within a set of text fields that reflect the native hierarchy of the document. For a simple presentation such as this no further query or processing routines would be necessary beyond assigning these text field appropriate variable names. Because the elements of the XML document are descriptive they can often be incorporated directly into the presentation of information to the user. This is how XML representation comes to be in many ways superior to traditional database tables, because it can represent nested hierarchies of data, and their internal relationships, far more effectively than a table structure.

Let's look at how this information might be represented:

XML to text fields

Very simple - by assigning variable names to text fields within the Text Options panel you can develop an interface for presenting and manipulating information derived from an XML document.

The walls of my house
    Floor : 1

Room: den	**Wall Covering:** artificial wood panelling
Room: kitchen	**Wall Covering:** paint over drywall
Room: dining room	**Wall Covering:** fine velvet wallpaper
Room: foyer	**Wall Covering:** wall to wall mirrors

XML to a database table

```
<the_walls_of_my_house>
    <floor value="1">
        <rooms>
            <den>artificial wood panelling</den>
            <kitchen>paint over drywall</kitchen>
            <dining_room>fine velvet wallpaper</dining_room>
            <foyer>wall to wall mirrors</foyer>
        </rooms>
    </floor>
</the_walls_of_my_house>
```

might be reflected in a database table as :

TABLE: the walls of my house

floor	rooms	value
1	den	artificial wood panelling
1	kitchen	paint over drywall
1	dining_room	fine velvet wallpaper
1	foyer	wall to wall mirrors

If our XML sample were more sophisticated, the translation of this structure to a single database table might become inefficient. Suppose we wanted to implement an XML document to convey the "interior design of my house". Each room might be described not only according to its walls, but also its floor covering, interior lighting, furnishings, size, and so forth. Beyond this, certain rooms would possess aspects that were different from the other rooms, such as an adjoining bathroom or closet. In these situations you would need to create an original database table for each room.

This isn't to imply that XML is incompatible with object and relational databases; quite the opposite. There are good number of commercial, and even open source, database systems which make use of XML as either a native or complementary medium for storing and representing data. XML can actually be used to mirror the schema of a database and convey sophisticated composite views of the internal data structure. Traditional object and relational databases usually possess a performance advantage over a database which stores XML documents in a pre-parsed form - such as a flat file database which stores XML documents under an indexed directory system. High performance XML databases often resemble object oriented databases where the XML document is parsed and translated into one or multiple data "object" data representations. These are then restructured as an original XML representation in response to the criteria of specific queries and views. XML has proven quite useful in adapting legacy database systems to web platforms because the extensible nature of an XML document can be exploited to combine the output of multiple queries into a single representation.

Data serialization

Data serialization can be applied in a variety of situations where structured information is communicated among divergent databases and processes. This concept has become especially popular as a means for transacting programming and object oriented data structures with databases. The WDDX example below demonstrates the serialization of an array structure and its variables. You could just as easily design a WDDX packet to carry a database table containing account information or a mailing list. This document could be sent to, and received from, a WDDX enabled database. WDDX has been developed by the Allaire corporation, and is supported by their ColdFusion server and development environment.

```
<?xml version="1.0" ?>
- <wddxPacket version="1.0">
  <header />
- <data>
- <array length="3">
- <struct>
- <var name="a">
- <array length="4">
  <number>1</number>
  <number>2</number>
  <number>3</number>
  <number>4</number>
  </array>
  </var>
- <var name="b">
  <string>this is object 0</string>
  </var>
- <var name="c">
  <dateTime>1999-12-23T0:0:0-4:0</dateTime>
  </var>
  </struct>
  </data>
  </wddxPacket>
```

When this is translated into a programming language the resulting expressions might be represented as such:

```
Array[a][0] = 1
Array[a][1] = 2
Array[a][2] = 3
Array[a][3] = 4
Array[b] = "this is object 0"
Array[c] = "1999-12-23T0:0:0-4:0"
```

WDDX is also very useful for representing the fields of a database table in a way which describes the intended structure of the table. This is an especially powerful concept when applied to object databases. Because the semantics and structure of an XML document are often synonymous, either aspect can be analyzed to reveal information about the other. That is, by looking at the ordination and hierarchy of information within the document you can make certain assumptions about the significance of its grammatical attributes. Conversely by reviewing the same document's grammatical aspects, you should be better informed regarding the context of the information it conveys, and the role of individual elements of this data.

Document publishing and conversion

As we saw at the beginning of this chapter, XML is fundamentally a markup specification. It actually derives from another, somewhat more esoteric, specification called **SGML** (Standard Generalized Markup Language). SGML was designed specifically as a document encoding format. While XML doesn't possess innate formatting semantics, an XML document can easily be designed to represent document elements in such a way that they can be interpreted by format literate languages such as XSL (Extensible Style Language), and CSS (Cascading Style Sheets). XML can also facilitate the translation of documents into various alternative formats and standards. These include HTML, SGML, PDF, PostScript files, and even common word processor formats such as MS Word and WordPerfect. The translation of an XML document into an alternative format relies on an intervening process or application which converts the text found within given elements of the XML document to a format specific encoding of that text. In this way XML serves simply as a means of conveying the text of a document along with basic formatting criteria.

The following XML document –

```
<?xml version="1.0" ?>
  <Document name="MyDoc">
    <Header position="center">This Document was Originally
Written in XML</Header>
      <body>
        <text_block position="center">
While this XML structure is not very elaborate, it does
accommodate the basic requirement for presenting a document
through various formats.  It is assumed that the final layout of
this document will be governed by an environment and/or language
more adept at formatting and pagination such as Macromedia's
Flash5, XSL, CSS, or even HTML.
        </text_block>
```

```
            <text_block position="center">
    You might wonder why XML would be used in this situation if it
    doesn't offer sophisticated formatting and layout capabilities -
    why not originate the document in a format more appropriate to
    document publishing ?  This is because while these other
    languages are very good at controlling the layout of a document,
    they are too restrictive with regards to where and how the
    document can be presented. With XML you can write the document
    once and present it in any environment which can read and
    translate XML.
            </text_block>
        </body>
    </Document>
```

Could be presented as..

This document was originally written in XML

While this XML structure is not very elaborate, it does accommodate the basic requirement for presenting a document through various formats. It's assumed that the final layout of this document will be governed by an environment and/or language more adept at formatting and pagination such as Macromedia's Flash5, XSL, CSS, or even HTML.

You might wonder why XML would be used in this situation if it doesn't offer sophisticated formatting and layout capabilities - why not originate the document in a format more appropriate to document publishing? This is because while these other languages are very good at controlling the layout of a document, they are too restrictive with regards to where and how the document can be presented. With XML you can write the document once and present it in any environment which can read and translate XML.

Distributed processes

The role of XML in communicating among distributed and decentralized computing processes has been alluded to in the previous section. Below is an example of the SOAP protocol (Standard Object Access Protocol), which demonstrates this concept. SOAP is intended to provide a common representation for structured information within a distributed processing environment as well as among discrete computing objects within a common architecture.

The following demonstrates a SOAP message that carries stock trading information:

```
<SOAP-ENV:Envelope xmlns:SOAP-
ENV="http://schemas.xmlsoap.org/soap/envelope/"
    SOAP-
ENV:encodingStyle="http://schemas.xmlsoap.org/soap/encoding/"/>
    <SOAP-ENV:Body>
        <m:GetLastTradePriceDetailed xmlns:m="Some-URI">
            <Symbol>DEF</Symbol>
            <Company>DEF Corp</Company>
            <Price>34.1</Price>
```

continues overleaf

```
        </m:GetLastTradePriceDetailed>
     </SOAP-ENV:Body>
  </SOAP-ENV:Envelope>
```

The relevant information within this document is highlighted. This is a response to a request for the current trading price of DEF Corp., which is apparently $34.10. The elements surrounding this information (e.g. `<SOAP-ENV:Body>`) express the attributes and structure of the SOAP message. Because these have been standardized, any application which recognizes the SOAP protocol can potentially understand this message. These applications may be developed in different programming languages, use different operating systems, and be communicated using different networking protocols. Because the fundamental representation of the information they use has been encoded to XML, none of these factors are a problem.

Below you'll find a hypothetical Flash implementation of this principle, which should bring the concept into more familiar terrain.

```
<FLOAP-Object:Envelope Instance_Name="_root.XMLapp.xmlArray" />
   <FLOAP-Object:Body> ~ the body of the FLOAD message
      <message:loadArray:_root.XMLapp.xmlArray
xmlns:m="AS_Functions">

<!—the message tells Flash to apply the loadArray function to
_root.XMLapp.xmlArray. This is recognized under the general
category of ActionScript functions>

            <Instance>_root.XMLapp</Instance>
            <Object>xmlArray</Object>
            <Function>loadArray</Function>
             <Argument>XMLDoc.xml</Argument>

      </m:message:load:_root.XMLapp.xmlArray>
   </FLOAP-Object:Body>
</FLOAP-Object:Envelope>
```

Here an ActionScript function, `loadArray`, is told to load the document `XMLDoc.xml` into the array `_root.XMLapp.xmlArray` . The message element `message:loadArray:_root` ➥ `.XMLapp.xmlArray` indicates that the `loadArray` function is to be applied to the array instance within `_root.XMLapp`. The document to be loaded is specified within the `Argument` element because it is the argument to the function `loadArray` (eg `loadArray("XMLDoc.xml")`).

Messaging

Distributed processing is predicated on the ability to pass structured information between systems and processes. This transmission of information is basically a message from one process to another. If the content of this message is presented to a person, rather than an application or component of an application, it can be regarded as a form of messaging much like email or instant messaging (eg. ICQ, or AIM). The use of XML in this situation is very similar. It's the manner in which these messages are interpreted and presented to the user which differs.

This is a simple XML messaging document:

```
<?xml version="1.0" ?>
<message to="NASA_CommandCentral" from="Neil_Armstrong">
    <subject>Landing Successful !!</subject>
    <body>
this is one small step for man..one giant leap for mankind
    </body>
</message>
```

The interpretation of this document should be obvious. When it's processed, the to and from attributes of the message element will be used to route the document or, within a groupchat context, declare the sender, and intended recipient. The text within the subject and body elements can be assigned to fields within the messaging client to present the subject of the message in relation to its content. Later in this chapter, there's an example of a simple chat application which demonstrates this.

XML standards

XML is being used in applications ranging from Artificial Intelligence to Musical Notation. Suffice to say that most of these exploit XML for one, or more, of the general aptitudes we've described. If you're interested in determining whether there is an XML standard emerging for a specific application go to www.oasis-open.org/cover/xml.html#applications. This page is maintained by the OASIS organization (Organization for the Advancement of Structured Information Standards), an industry consortia supporting the standardization of structured information processes across various industries and working groups.

Recap of XML introduction

In the brief introduction to XML, we saw that:

- XML is a markup specification

- XML is written in a manner very similar to that of HTML

- The significant distinction between XML and HTML is that XML tags can be named anything you like.

- XML documents are *self describing*, which means that their structure and constituent elements are significant to the kind of information they are used to convey

- XML structures possess attributes similar to those of human languages

    - Grammar

    - Semantics

    - Pragmatic Interpretation ~ they can be read by people

- XML documents can be employed in a diversity of applications and may render different combinations and interactions of data from the same document

  - Data Storage

  - Data Serialization

  - Publishing and Document Conversion

  - Distributed Processes

  - Messaging

XML in depth: How is an XML document structured?

In this section we'll be working with the simple XML document inside Flash using Flash's debugging tool to see what's happening inside the code. We'll use the XML document that we've already been looking at, "the walls of my house":

```
<?xml version="1.0" encoding="iso-8859-1" ?>
    <the_walls_of_my_house>
        <floor value="1">
            <rooms>
                <den>artificial wood panelling</den>
                <kitchen>paint over drywall</kitchen>
                <dining_room>fine velvet wallpaper</dining_room>
                <foyer>wall to wall mirrors</foyer>
            </rooms>
        </floor>
    </the_walls_of_my_house>
```

Before delving into the internal structure of this example, we should introduce a few terms relevant to the XML Document Object Model (DOM). You may be familiar with the DOM, as it applies to web pages and the browser environment. XML relies upon the same fundamental elements (i.e. objects, methods, and properties), and refines these to enable a detailed mapping of the constituent parts of an XML document. The XML Document Object Model is a uniform way of describing the structure of an XML document through a hierarchical representation of its elements and properties. It also defines the methods used in processing XML documents. The DOM is the basis of Flash5 ActionScript's XML handling methodology.

Where the generic term "markup tag" is appropriate in describing how XML elements are written, it tells us nothing about their role or significance within the document. For this reason XML tags are described as demarcating **nodes,** and these nodes are defined according to a variety of significant properties and relationships. The topology of these attributes within the context of an XML document is referred to as the **DOM Node Tree Model**. The term *node tree* derives from the fact that the hierarchical structure of an XML document, when represented graphically, resembles a tree - with the trunk representing the root node of the document, and its child elements forming the branches.

A node is more than a tag that divides information; it actually encompasses the information that is nested between its beginning and end points. The node shown below, which begins with `<rooms>` below encompasses the child node `<den>` as well as the value of the `<den>` node `artificial wood paneling`. This is why the value of `<den>` can be retrieved by addressing its position relative to the `rooms` node.

```
<floor value="1">
    <rooms>
    <den> artificial wood panelling</den>
</room>
```

The node `<floor>` above has one child `<rooms>` which itself has one child `<den>`. In this example `<rooms>` is both a child node of `<floor>` and parent node of `<den>`. The parent/child hierarchy only extends to the immediate parents or children of a node. For example the node `<den>` is the child of `<rooms>` but not recognized as the child node of `<floor>`. While this may be a bit confusing at first, just remember that parents can have only one generation of children, and children one generation of parents - XML doesn't extend this model of the family to grandparents or grandchildren ;-)

You'll often hear the terms *node* and *element* used interchangeably when an XML document is being described. Elements are actually a type of node; as are data nodes, document nodes, processing instructions, and comments. These will be dealt with later in the chapter. All you need to remember at this point is that each aspect of an XML document falls under one of these node types, and each has specific characteristics according to the XML DOM. This greatly facilitates the handling of an XML document because you can separate certain types of nodes from others through the fundamental XML handling methods provided by Flash 5.

Now let's look at how Flash 5's XML parser renders a generic XML object in accordance with the DOM. We'll simply instantiate an XML object without actually loading an XML document into it and look at the resulting structure in Flash's debugger - this can be found by choosing Debug > List Variables from the command bar.

By instantiating the XML object like this: `foo = new XML`, and choosing Control > Test Movie or Control > Debug Movie, the following will appear in the debugger.

Here's an annotated portion of our original example:

```
Variable _level0.foo = [object #1] {
    nodeType:1,
    nextSibling:null,
    previousSibling:null,
    parentNode:null,
    firstChild:null,
    lastChild:null,
    childNodes:[object #2] [],
    attributes:[object #3] {},
    nodeName:null,
    nodeValue:null,
    xmlDecl:undefined,
```

continues overleaf

```
            docTypeDecl:undefined,
            status:0
    }
```

You'll notice the basic parent and child node assignments discussed earlier along with several new child types (`firstChild`, `lastChild`, `previousSibling`, and `nextSibling`). These identify the relative order of child nodes - again, these are referred to as node *properties*. Also notice that `childNodes` is recognized as an array (`childNodes:[object #2] []` represents an array primitive). When you request the child nodes of a parent node these children are indexed within an array. This makes it relatively easy to iterate through and locate child nodes as they're each assigned a numerical key from "0" through to the index value of the last child. These properties are currently null because we haven't loaded a document into the XML object yet.

The nature of the `firstChild`, `lastChild`, `previousSibling` and `nextSibling` node properties should be self-evident.

```
    <rooms>
        <den>artificial wood panelling</den>
        <kitchen>paint over drywall</kitchen>
        <dining_room>fine velvet wallpaper</dining_room>
        <foyer>wall to wall mirrors</foyer>
    </rooms>
```

The `firstChild` property is assigned to the first child node of the parent element. In the walls of my house example the `firstChild` property of `<rooms>` is assigned to the node `<den>`. Similarly the `lastChild` property is assigned to the node named `<foyer>`. The `previousSibling` of `<foyer>` is the node named `<dining_room>` while the `nextSibling` of `<den>` is the node `<kitchen>`. `PreviousSibling` and `nextSibling` relationships provide an ability to *walk* through an element's child nodes in much the same way that that the `childNodes` array does. By requesting the `nextSibling` of the `nextSibling` of the `firstChild` you would arrive at the `<dining_rooms>` node. This would often be accomplished within the context of a loop construct, though it can also be achieved by explicitly addressing the node. As we move into our discussion of Flash5's XML object we'll show you how to address the DOM's node tree model explicitly as well as through conditional and iterative (looping) statements.

The other important properties apparent within the debugger read-out deal with the characteristics and values assigned to individual nodes. Actually, node values are formally recognized as data nodes, but these must always be nested within a properly formed node element.

```
        nodeType:1,
        attributes:[object #3] {},
        nodeName:null,
        nodeValue:null,
```

For the time being we're going to focus on the node types that are immediately useful to XML handling within Flash 5. Several of the node types presented, such as entity references, aren't applicable to XML handling within Flash due to the fact that Flash's XML parser cannot interpret Document Type Definitions (DTDs). These are used to test XML documents for compliance against a predefined structure as well as to inform the processor of how to treat certain sections of the received document.

The usefulness of comparing XML nodes against their nodeType properties derives from the fact that they provide a way of screening nodes that are encountered when processing an XML document. Much of the data you'll extract from an XML document will be retrieved by iterating through an array of child nodes and extracting these according to name and/or nodeType. For instance, a nodeType of 1 is an element, and can be expected to have a nodeName property and potentially attributes. A nodeType of 3 is a text, or data, node and is associated with the nodeValue property; this is usually the value you wish to extract for presentation to the user or for incorporation into an external process.

This is probably an appropriate point to introduce a few concrete examples.

We'll be working with a section of the 'walls of my house' XML document which is formatted as such:

```
<?xml version="1.0"?>
    <the_walls_of_my_house>
        <floor value="1">
            <rooms>
                <den>artificial wood panelling</den>
                <kitchen>paint over drywall</kitchen>
                <dining_room>fine velvet wallpaper</dining_room>
                <foyer>wall to wall mirrors</foyer>
            </rooms>
        </floor>
    </the_walls_of_my_house>
```

We'll also be using a simple ActionScript routine which filters the above XML and renders a few node properties of the root node of the document. This code will provide you with a simple algorithm for extracting XML data for incorporation into your Flash Movies.

The Flash 5 XML object:

The Flash 5 XML object is native to the new object-oriented implementation of ActionScript. As with other objects, the XML object gives you access to several pre-defined methods and properties for processing and writing XML documents

- **new XML** – The XML object constructor. This instantiates an original XML object along with its attendant properties and methods. This is expressed as foo = new XML;. The new XML constructor can also be written as new XML(source) where source is a either a previously loaded XML document, an XML document generated within the Flash environment during runtime, or a previously instantiated XML object.

- **load** – loads the named XML document into the object instance created by new XML. This is expressed as foo.load("yourXMLdoc.xml");. The load method will accept document assignments as simple file names (eg XMLfile.xml), URL assignments (that is http://yourDomain/XMLfile.xml), and variables (e.g. *bar = "XMLfile.xml" ; foo.load(bar);*) .

■ **onLoad** – We'll be implementing `onLoad` as an event handler which triggers its assigned function once the XML file named by the `load` method has been successfully loaded into the base XML object. This is expressed as `foo.onLoad = anyFunction;`. The default implementation of `onLoad`, which isn't used in the following example, simply returns a Boolean value of true or false within a variable assigned as it's argument. This is expressed as `foo.onLoad(success);` with the `success` variable carrying a true or false value depending on the status of the `load` method. This method would be employed within the context of a conditional statement (eg. `if (success ) {…} );` .

■ **length** – `length` is an array property which returns the highest index value of the array plus one (that is `length = index + 1`). Array indices begin with "0", so an index value of 3 actually means that there are four values in the array (eg. 0,1,2,3). Therefore the length of the array is actually four.

■ **xmlDecl** – This is the XML declaration property and is expressed as `foo.xmlDecl` . `xmlDecl` and returns `<?xml version="1.0"?>`

■ **nodeName** – The `nodeName` property returns the name of the target node - `nodeName` returns *null* if no node name is available or the targeted node is not a type 1 `nodeType`. The `nodeName` property is expressed as `foo.nodeName` .

■ **nodeType** – The `nodeType` property returns a value appropriate the various node types discussed previously. If the target node doesn't return a valid node type the value is "undefined". The node types we'll be concerned with in the following example are type 1 (ELEMENT) and type 3 (TEXT) nodes. The syntax for `nodeType` is `foo.nodeType` .

■ **childNodes** – `childnodes` is formally recognized as a 'collection' of XML object references which represent each of the child nodes of the targeted parent node. This collection of XML object references is passed as an array to the base object - this is why you can determine the node properties of an array index even though the array isn't an XML object. The syntax used is `foo.childNodes`. `childnodes` can also be employed similarly to an array by appending an index at the end as such `foo.childNodes[index]`. For most practical purposes the `childNodes` collection can be treated as a property which generates an array of child nodes.

The code

The following code simply extracts the `nodeName` of the `RootNode` of this document, along with its `nodeType` and the number of elements within the root's `childNode` array.

```
function screen () {

  trace("This is the XML declaration: "+foo.xmlDecl);
  bar = foo.childNodes ;

  // pass the childNodes of foo into the array "bar"

  trace("bar.length= "+bar.length);
```

```
for (x=0; x < bar.length; ++x) {

// iterate through the "bar" array until the variable "x" is equal
// to one less than the highest index value of  "bar"

   if( ( bar[x].nodeName != null) & ( bar[x].nodeType = 1) ) {

// establish a simple filter on the properties of foo's child nodes
// - these must be Elements and have a name

   trace("bar["+x+"].nodeType= "+bar[x].nodeType)
   trace("bar["+x+"].nodeName= "+bar[x].nodeName)
   }
 }
}

bar = new Array ;

// instantiate a new array and new XML object

foo = new XML ;
foo.onLoad = screen ;

// load "wall0house.xml" into foo and when loaded launch the function
// "screen"

foo.load("wall0house.xml");
```

This produces the following reading of the trace statements placed within the above code:

```
This is the XML declaration: <?xml version="1.0"?>
bar.length= 4
bar[2].nodeType= 1
bar[2].nodeName= the_walls_of_my_house
```

The length (bar.length) property of the XML object returns the number of stations in the childNode array. You'll notice that this value is 4 while the index value of the walls of my house node is 2. The reason for this is that Flash 5's parser is non-validating, and as such needs to treat regions of whitespace beyond the opening tag of a node as significant. Validating parsers recognize what is known as "parsed character data" (PCDATA) declarations which tell them where to apply parser processing. Without the availability of this distinction, Flash 5's parser must attempt to parse all data found within the root node - remember, a node isn't simply a tag, it's the data which is found between the opening and closing tags of an element.

Let's look at this same routine without the filter applied. I've simply commented-out the conditional statement and its closing brace

```
//   if( ( bar[x].nodeName != null) & ( bar[x].nodeType = 1) ) {

    trace("bar["+x+"].nodeType= "+bar[x].nodeType)
    trace("bar["+x+"].nodeName= "+bar[x].nodeName)

// }
```

This is the new trace reading:

```
This is the XML declaration: <?xml version="1.0"?>
bar.length= 4
bar[0].nodeType=
bar[0].nodeName=
bar[1].nodeType= 3
bar[1].nodeName= null
bar[2].nodeType= 1
bar[2].nodeName= the_walls_of_my_house
bar[3].nodeType= 3
bar[3].nodeName= null
```

As you can see, without the node properties filter we're picking up all sorts of errata including two ghost nodes which are registering as type 3 (text) nodeTypes. These are actually caused by regions of whitespace delimited by new line and line feed expressions. Don't worry, we'll be investigating ways of addressing this issue, and in the latter half of this chapter introduce a new object type that eliminates the problem almost entirely.

The use of identifying node properties can also be employed to step through the DOM structure adaptively. That is, they can direct the processing of the XML document in response to the characteristics of nodes encountered while the node tree is being analyzed. This enables XML handling to be generalized so that nodes don't have to be addressed explicitly and the same routine can therefore be used to process any XML document, or document sub-section. Many examples of Flash 5 XML processing that I've come across so far rely on algorithms which search the node tree for certain key words. These are correlated with node names present within a predefined XML structure. While this method is effective if the XML document is already defined, and isn't going to be altered by user input or server side processing, it's not very flexible and breaks down if the document is ever extended.

Another practice you may come across is to treat the processing of the XML document as a two stage effort in which string handling methods are first applied to the document structure in order to remove 'whitespace' and concatenate the markup tags into a string. The resulting document is then parsed using the methods available through the XML object. I strongly advise against this latter method. Flash 5's string handling routines are very slow and will result in a breach of Flash's time-lapse threshold (approximately 15 seconds of continuous processing) if the subject document is more then a dozen elements or so.

Our next example will apply the concept of adaptive processing to determine all valid node names within the walls_of_my_house document. This is based on the same code which has been used previously; the significant difference being that we're analyzing any nested groups of node elements where they arise.

One new node property has been introduced:

- **haschildNodes** – a method which return a Boolean true or false depending on whether the base XML Element has child Nodes. This is expressed as foo.haschildNodes;.

The code :

```
function screen () {

  bar = foo.childNodes ;

  trace("bar.length= "+bar.length);
  trace("Begin Node~~~~~~~~~~o");
  trace("COUNT= "+count);

  for (x=0; x < bar.length; ++x) {

  if (( bar[x].nodeName != null) && ( bar[x].nodeType = 1)) {
      trace("bar["+x+"].nodeType= "+bar[x].nodeType)
      trace("bar["+x+"].nodeName= "+bar[x].nodeName)

  // if node Element "bar[x]" has child nodes proceed to the nested
  //conditional loop "while (z < loo.length) {.."

  if ( bar[x].hasChildNodes ) {
      var z = 0 ;
      loo = new Array ;
      loo = bar[x].childNodes ;

  // load the child  nodes of "bar[x]" into the "loo" array

      while( z < loo.length) {

  // index through the "loo" array until the last station of the array
  // throughout this process test the nodes referenced by "loo" to
  // determine if they have valid node names - if so, what are they?

  if (loo[z].nodeName != null) {
  trace("bar_child["+z+"].nodeName= "+loo[z].nodeName)
      }
      ++z}
```

continues overleaf

```
// the following statements reassign "foo" to the "bar[x]" node
// element and then call the "screen" function with foo as both the
// subject and referent. This is what is known as a recursive
// operation.

   foo = bar[x]
   foo = screen() ;   }

   }

++count}


   }

   // "count" simply counts the number of times the "screen" function is
   // called through recursion.

count = 0 ;
bar = new Array ;
foo = new XML ;
foo.onLoad = screen ;
foo.load("housewalls.xml");
```

The trace reading for this example is:

```
bar.length= 4
Begin Node~~~~~~~~~~o
```

The first cycle of this routine has identified the root node "the walls of my house", bar[2], and its child node floor , bar_child[1].nodeName .

```
COUNT= 0
bar[2].nodeType= 1
bar[2].nodeName= the_walls_of_my_house
bar_child[1].nodeName= floor
bar.length= 3
Begin Node~~~~~~~~~~o
```

The function screen is then re-initiated to analyze floor. This reveals that the sole childNode of floor is rooms.

```
COUNT= 2
bar[1].nodeType= 1
bar[1].nodeName= floor
bar_child[1].nodeName= rooms
bar.length= 3
Begin Node~~~~~~~~~~o
```

When rooms is subject to the screen function it's revealed that it has four child nodes.

```
COUNT= 3
bar[1].nodeType= 1
bar[1].nodeName= rooms
bar_child[1].nodeName= den
bar_child[3].nodeName= kitchen
bar_child[5].nodeName= dining_room
bar_child[7].nodeName= foyer
bar.length= 9
Begin Node~~~~~~~~~~o
```

The recursion is aborted at den because there are no further type 1 child nodes present.

```
COUNT= 4
bar[1].nodeType= 1
bar[1].nodeName= den
bar.length= 1
Begin Node~~~~~~~~~~o
COUNT= 5
```

Recursion is a technique in which the internal elements of the original subject of a function call (*foo = screen*) become the reference points of that same function call over successive cycles. This occurs when *foo = bar[x]; foo = screen();* are encountered. The benefit in this technique is that a hierarchical, tree like, data structure such as XML can be broken down through recursion to produce successively more acute views of the XML data while retaining the context of that data - its parent and sibling nodes. The trace reading above demonstrates this on a simple document like 'the walls of my house'.

By extending the screen function slightly we can increase the scope of data captured through recursion to reveal the value of all nodes in this document, including the data nodes. The second conditional statement simply needs to be modified to direct child nodes – which themselves possess child nodes - through their own screen function cycle. This isn't a perfect solution though, as you'll see in the trace reading.

I'm not sure how to simplify the subsequent section without breaking the code! Perhaps we should say something to the effect of "Why don't you load this into a Flash movie, along with the sample XML doc, and test these scripts as you read through the following discussion."

```
function screen () {

    trace(" ");
    bar = foo.childNodes ;

    //trace("bar.length= "+bar.length);
    //trace("Begin Node~~~~~~~~~~o");
    //trace("COUNT= "+count);

    for (x=0; x < bar.length; ++x) {
```

```
            if (( bar[x].nodeName != null) && ( bar[x].nodeType = 1)) {
                //trace("bar["+x+"].nodeType= "+bar[x].nodeType)
                trace("ParentNode="+bar[x].parentNode.nodeName)
                trace("nodeName= "+bar[x].nodeName)


            if( bar[x].hasChildNodes ) {
                var z = 0 ;
                loo = new Array ;
                loo = bar[x].childNodes ;
                while( z < loo.length) {
            if (loo[z].nodeName != null) {
             trace(" ");
             trace("ParentNode="+loo[z].parentNode.nodeName)
             trace("childNode["+z+"]= "+loo[z].nodeName)
                if(loo[z].hasChildNodes) {foo = loo[z];foo=screen()} ;
            }
                ++z}

            //foo = bar[x]
            //foo = screen() ;
            }

                } else { trace("nodeName= "+bar[x].parentNode.nodeName);
                trace("nodeValue= "+bar[x].nodeValue) }
        ++count }

            }
```

The trace read out is:

```
ParentNode=null
nodeName= the_walls_of_my_house

ParentNode=the_walls_of_my_house
childNode[1]= floor

nodeName= floor
nodeValue=

ParentNode=floor
nodeName= rooms

ParentNode=rooms
childNode[1]= den

nodeName= den
nodeValue= artificial wood panelling

ParentNode=rooms
childNode[3]= kitchen
```

```
nodeName= kitchen
nodeValue= paint over drywall

ParentNode=rooms
childNode[5]= dining_room

nodeName= dining_room
nodeValue= fine velvet wallpaper

ParentNode=rooms
childNode[7]= foyer

nodeName= foyer
nodeValue= wall to wall mirrors
```

The trace reading actually continues by returning to the kitchen node and completing one more cycle of each subsequent node. This produces a redundant index of each of the child nodes, and node values, beginning with kitchen. Using a more sophisticated screen function would enable us to either abort further cycles past the last child node, or by establishing a lock on the number of cycles based on the number of child nodes to the root node. Such a control, within the context of the above example, would be largely cosmetic though, as the additional information rendered doesn't distort the accuracy or usability of the read-out.

The following example provides a method for refining the output of the screen function by mapping this output to an array. This will enable you to process any received XML document once and from that point forward treat the XML document structure, and its constituent properties and values, as a simple set of array objects.

There are no new XML properties or methods employed in this example. Notice though that a new array object has been instantiated prior to loading the XML doc (xml_array = new Array ;).

```
function screen () {

  trace(" .");
  bar = foo.childNodes ;
  parno = foo.nodeName ;
```

foo is assigned as the subject of the screen function throughout each cycle of recursion. We've assigned the parno variable to the nodeName of foo so as to establish an associative key which will hold the child nodes of foo as indices within a multidimensional array.

```
  xml_array[parno] = new Array ;

  for (x=0; x < bar.length; ++x) {

      if ( bar[x].nodeValue != null ){
      xml_array[bar[x].parentNode.nodeName][x]= bar[x].nodeValue ;
  }
```

The statement above screens the child nodes of foo for a valid nodeValue. If one exists it is assigned to the index value (x) of a multidimensional array which itself is associated with the parent node of bar[x] .

```
if (( bar[x].nodeName != null) && ( bar[x].nodeType = 1)) {

    trace("ParentNode="+bar[x].parentNode.nodeName)
    trace("nodeName= "+bar[x].nodeName)
```

xml_array[count] will assign index values to the child nodes of foo based upon the number of iterations of the count variable.

```
xml_array[count] = bar[x].nodeName
xml_array[parno][x] = bar[x].nodeName;
```

xml_array[parno][x] is a multidimensional array which indexes the child nodes of foo under their appropriate parent nodes.

```
barno = bar[x].nodeName ;
xml_array[barno] = new Array ;
```

The barno variable holds the current node name of child node bar[x]. This variable is then employed to establish an original key under the name of that child node.

```
if( bar[x].hasChildNodes ) {
    var z = 0 ;
    loo = new Array ;
    loo = bar[x].childNodes ;
```

If the bar[x] child node itself has child nodes generate a new array under loo and assign the node collection of bar[x] to that array.

```
while( z < loo.length) {
    if (loo[z].nodeName != null) {
    trace(" ") ;
    trace("ParentNode1="+loo[z].parentNode.nodeName)
    trace("childNode1["+z+"]= "+loo[z].nodeName)
    xml_array[barno][z] = loo[z].nodeName
```

Assign the node name of child node z to a multidimensional array associated with the barno key - barno is the parent node of the loo[z] child node , barno is itself the child node foo.

```
if ( loo[z].hasChildNodes ) {  ++count ;
xml_array[count] = loo[z].nodeName ;
foo = loo[z] ; foo=screen()
}
```

The above statement simply tests the loo[z] child node to determine whether this itself has child nodes, and if so, increments the count variable to reflect an additional cycle of the screen function. The node name of the `loo[z]` child node is then assigned as a value of `xml_array` under the new index value `count`. The `screen` function is then called with `loo[z]` as both the subject and reference of the `screen` function.

```
    }
          ++z}

    }

  } else { trace("nodeName= "+bar[x].parentNode.nodeName);
          trace("nodeValue= "+bar[x].nodeValue);
          xml_array[barno][bar[x].parentNode.nodeName+"Value"] =
          ➡ bar[x].nodeValue
    }
```

`xml_array[barno][bar[x].parentNode.nodeName+"Value"]` generates a subordinate key value which is named for the node name of the parent node of `bar[x]`. The word `Value` is attached to this key value in order to provide a convenient way of addressing the array when you're looking for the various node values (see the debugger read-out for an example).

```
  ++count }

  }

  count = 0 ;
  xml_array = new Array ;
  bar = new Array ;
  foo = new XML ;
  foo.onLoad = screen ;
  foo.load("housewalls.xml");
```

Before we analyze the debugger read-out we should be familiar with how it represents data structures.

The Flash 5 debugger presents both the addresses and constituent elements of an array structure as a set of nested properties and values.

```
  Variable _level0.myArray = [object #1] [
    myArray_key:[object #2] [
        0:"index value 0"
        1:"index value 1"
        2:"index value 2"
    ]
  ]
```

The above reflects an instance of a multidimensional array named `myArray` on the root level of the movie (`_level0.myArray`). This is recognized as the first object instance encountered by the debugger (`[object #1]`). MyArray is also shown to possess a subordinate array called `myArray_key`, this has three values which are assigned to the indices of `myArray_key` (index value 0 through 2). The syntax used to determine the value of the third index of `myArray_key` would be `myArray[myArray_key][2]` which would return `"index value 2"`.

So now let's apply this to the debugger read-out from the example.

```
Variable _level0.xml_array = [object #3] [
    null:[object #4] [
```

This is the XML declaration element of "the walls of my house", and as such has no node name; hence the null value. Fortunately the root node has also been caught by `xml_array[count]` where `count` equals 2 below.

```
        1:"\n    ",
        2:"the_walls_of_my_house"
    ],
```

End of `xml_array[null]`

```
        2:"the_walls_of_my_house",
```

Here 'the walls of my house' root node is recognized under index 2 of the `xml_array` array.

```
        the_walls_of_my_house:[object #5] [
```

The node name of this element is established as the associative key of a multidimensional array which will contain the child nodes of the element (`xml_array[the_walls_of_my_house]` ➡ `[childNode index ]`).

```
            1:"floor",
```

The floor node is the only child of the root node.

```
            floorValue:"\n        "
        ],
```

end of `xml_array[the_walls_of_my_house]`

```
            3:"floor",
            floor:[object #6] [
```

`floor` is then established as an associative key of another multidimensional array which contains its child node.

```
                0:"\n            ",
```

Aha ! Another ghost node - we'll address how to avoid these within the next section.

```
        1:"rooms"
```

rooms is the child node of floor and would be addressed as xml_array[floor][1]

```
        ],
```

This is the end of xml_array[floor].

```
        4:"rooms",
        rooms:[object #7]  [  ~
```

rooms is then established as an array which contains the following child nodes:

```
        1:"den",
```

den is the first child node of rooms.

```
        denValue:"artificial wood panelling",
```

denValue is an array variable which contains the nodeValue of den.

```
        3:"kitchen",
        kitchenValue:"paint over drywall",
        5:"dining_room",
        dining_roomValue:"fine velvet wallpaper",
        7:"foyer",
        foyerValue:"wall to wall mirrors"
    ],
```

This is the end of xml_array[rooms].

Indexes 5 through 11 provide direct access the child nodes of rooms. These can be addressed either through their index values (e.g. xml_array[5] = den) or by naming them as keys to the xml_array array (e.g. xml_array[den][0] = "artificial wood paneling").

```
        5:"den",
        den:[object #8]  [
            0:"artificial wood paneling"
    ],
        7:"kitchen",
        kitchen:[object #9]  [
        0:"paint over drywall"
    ],
        9:"dining_room",
        dining_room:[object #10]  [
        0:"fine velvet wallpaper"
    ],
        11:"foyer",
        foyer:[object #11]  [
        0:"wall to wall mirrors"
```

```
        ],
            14:"kitchen",
```

Indexes 14 through 18 are redundant. They appear because the proper control mechanism has not been applied to the screen function. Again, this will be addressed in the next section.

```
            16:"dining_room",
            18:"foyer"
        ]
```

This is the end of xml_array.

Perhaps the first thing you'll notice about the debugger read-out is that the xml_array index values are often not in a consistent, incremental sequence. This is caused by the whitespace (ghost node) problem discussed earlier. The parser is recognizing regions of whitespace delimited by new line and line feed expressions as child node elements. While these can be often be filtered out using node property criteria, this method alone won't catch all of them. Those ghost nodes which are caught, are simply passed to the else contingency at the end of the conditional statement:

```
if (( bar[x].nodeName != null) && ( bar[x].nodeType = 1)) {.
```

The count variable is still incremented in this situation thus the xml_array index value is incremented as well. Also, if you look at the representation of the floor array you'll notice that the first index - 0, equals \n. What has happened here is that the expression \n is being recognized as a valid node name.

```
        floor:[object #6] [
            0:"\n            ",
            1:"rooms"
        ],
```

Within a more sophisticated process, these can often be filtered by first assigning the node property to a variable (e.g. *moo = xmlnode.nodeName*) and then imposing a conditional filter which checks the typeof operator (eg. *if (typeof(moo) != "undefined") {...}*). This technique will be demonstrated during our discussion of the FlaXimaL object at the end of the chapter. It's important that you first understand the idiosyncrasies that will arise in processing XML documents, how these manifest, and how they will affect the information rendered using Flash 5's core XML properties and methods. With this knowledge, you'll be better able to adapt custom techniques for utilizing XML in a variety of situations.

The following is a simple demonstration of how the array structure, which has been rendered by the screen function, can be employed to present XML data, as well as pass it to a Flash movie - this will also provide a method for properly sequencing array indices. Let's say we simply want to determine the node value of the child nodes of rooms, but we don't yet know the names of the rooms or how many there are. We'll develop a routine which walks the child nodes of rooms and displays node name and node value pairs. This would obviously be run after the XML document has been loaded and processed by the screen function.

```
        val = 0;
        nv = 0;
        node = "rooms"          // The node variable holds the name of the
                                // associative array element
```

```
        roo = xml_array[node].length

        // roo holds the length of the array in order to control the
        // following  conditional loop.

        node_values = new Array    // The node_values array will hold the
                                   // extracted node values.
        while (val <= roo ) {
          if (xml_array[node][val] != null) {

        // Provides a simple filter to determine that only valid nodes are
        // being passed along.
             child = xml_array[node][val] ;

        // The child variable holds the name of each valid child node

          trace("parentNode = "+ node);
          trace("childNode = "+xml_array[node][val]);
          trace("nodeValue = "+xml_array[child][0]);

        // Because we know that these child nodes have also been
        // assigned as associative array elements, we can now call
        // them directly to determine their value.

          node_values[nv] = xml_array[child][0] ;

        // The node values presented by xml_array[child][0] are
        // loaded into the node_values array under the index value
        // provided by  the "nv" variable.

          ++nv
          trace(" ");
          }
        ++val}
```

The resulting trace reading produces:

parentNode = rooms
childNode = den
nodeValue = artificial wood panelling

parentNode = rooms
childNode = kitchen
nodeValue = paint over drywall

parentNode = rooms
childNode = dining_room
nodeValue = fine velvet wallpaper

parentNode = rooms

childNode = foyer
nodeValue = wall to wall mirrors

along with a new array :

```
Variable _level0.node_values = [object #81] [
    0:"artificial wood paneling",
    1:"paint over drywall",
    2:"fine velvet wallpaper",
    3:"wall to wall mirrors"
  ]
```

Conveniently this routine provides us with a way of ordering the array indices properly, and could be employed to re-order any set of indices within this example. The resulting array (node_values) contains all node values within the rooms node element. By distinguishing, in this example, between the loop control variable (val) and the array indices variable (nv) we can selectively increment array indices based on conditions encountered within the loop construct. The nv variable is only incremented if the condition if (xml_array[node][val] != null) { is met, while the val variable increments regardless of the success or failure of this condition. This is how we get a proper sequencing of the node_values indices. These can now be deployed wherever you like within your Flash movie. Of course, this array needn't be generated specifically for the above routine. The same technique can be used to extend or replace values within an existing array anywhere within the movie.

Before proceeding to the next section we should review the concepts we've encountered so far:

- The structure of an XML document derives from the Document Object Model (DOM)

- An XML document is comprised of various types of nodes:

    - Elements

    - Data nodes

    - Comments

    - Processing instructions

- A node is not simply an isolated markup tag, but the entire body of data found between the beginning and end points of the tags which delimit that node.

- Nodes possess parent and child relationships which extend only one generation.

- Nodes possess a variety of node properties which can be employed to extract information about the node and the data which it comprises:

    - Node Type

    - Node name

- Node value

- Parent nodes

- Child nodes

- First child nodes

- Last child nodes

- Siblings

- An array of child nodes represents a 'collection' of XML object references

Flash 5's XML objects, properties and methods:

The following objects, properties, and methods have been used in our previous examples:

- **new XML** – The XML Object Constructor instantiates an original XML object along with its attendant properties and methods. This is expressed as *foo = new XML;*

- **load** – loads the named XML document into the object instance created by new XML. This is expressed as *foo.load("yourXMLdoc.xml");*. The load method will accept document assignments as simple file names (XMLfile.xml), URL assignments (http://yourDomain/XMLfile.xml), and variables (*bar = "XMLfile.xml" ; foo.load(bar);*).

- **onLoad** – We'll be implementing onLoad as an event handler which triggers its assigned function once the XML file named by the load method has been successfully loaded into the base XML object. This is expressed as *foo.onLoad = anyFunction;*. The default implementation of onLoad, which isn't used in the following example, simply returns a Boolean value of true or false within a variable assigned as its argument. This is expressed as *foo.onLoad(success);* with the success variable carrying a true or false value depending on the status of the load method. This method would be employed within the context of a conditional statement (*if (success) {...});*.

- **length** – length is an array property which returns the highest index value of the array plus one (ie. length = index + 1). Array indices begin with 0, so an index value of 3 actually means that there are four values in the array (eg. 0,1,2,3). Therefore the length of the array is four.

- **xmlDecl** – This is the XML Declaration property and is expressed as *foo.xmlDecl*. xmlDecl returns <?xml version="1.0"?>.

- **nodeName** – The nodeName property returns the name of the target node - nodeName returns *null* if no node name is available or the targeted node is not a type 1 nodeType. The nodeName property is expressed as *foo.nodeName*.

- **nodeType** – The `nodeType` property returns a value appropriate the various node types discussed previously. If the target node doesn't return a valid node type the value is 'undefined'. The node types we'll be concerned with in the following example are type 1 (ELEMENT) and type 3 (TEXT) nodes. The syntax for `nodeType` is `foo.nodeType`.

- **childNodes** – `childNodes` is formally recognized as a collection of XML object references which represent each of the child nodes of the targeted parent node. This collection of XML object references is passed as an array to the base object - this is why you can determine the node properties of an array index even though the array is not an XML object. The syntax used is `foo.childNodes`. `childNodes` can also be employed similarly to an array by appending an index at the end as such `foo.childNodes[index]`. For most practical purposes the `childNodes` collection can be treated as a property which generates an array of child nodes.

- **parentNode** – returns the parent node of the target node. A `parentNode` is recognized as the parent of each of its child nodes. The syntax used is `foo.parentNode`.

- **haschildNodes** – a method which simply return a Boolean true or false depending on whether the base XML Element has child nodes. This is expressed as `foo.haschildNodes;`.

The following section will provide examples of Flash 5's XML document writing methods in the form of a simple flat file XML database. This example will introduce the following new objects, methods, and properties.

- **firstChild** – returns the first child node of the subject parent node. The syntax for `firstChild` is `foo.firstChild`. It is important to remember that the first child node of a node element is always recognized in relation to its immediate parent element, and that this relationship only extends for one generation. Also, when an XML document is presented as a string (a concatenated series of tags) the `firstChild` property can be used to retrieve the node value of an element. This method is often more effective than using the `nodeValue` property when XML objects are presented as strings.

```
<?xml version="1.0"?>
  <the_walls_of_my_house>
     <floor value="1">
        <rooms>
            <den>artificial wood panelling</den>
```

The `firstChild` node of `<the_walls_of_my_house>` is `<floor>`; the `firstChild` node of `<floor>` is `<rooms>`.

- **lastChild** – returns the last child node of the subject parent node. This is expressed as `foo.lastChild`.

The `lastChild` property is basically the inverse of the `firstChild` property, though it's not effective in extracting node values from XML objects in string form.

- **nextSibling** – returns the next child node within a set of child nodes. The nextSibling relationship is determined relative to another childNode of comparable status within the DOM hierarchy. The order of nextSibling nodes begins with the nextSibling of the firstChild node through to the lastChild node. The syntax for calling the nextSibling property is *foo.nextSibling*.

```
<xml_document>
  <root_node>
      <firstChild_node_of_root/>
      <nextSibling_node/>
      <nextSibling_node/>
      <lastChild_node/>
  </root_node>
```

The lastChild node above could also be recognized as the nextSibling of the nextSibling of the nextSibling of the firstChild node (xmlObj.firstChild.nextSibling. nextSibling.nextSibling).

- **previousSibling** – The previousSibling node is numbered similarly to the nextSibling node, but in inverse order.

```
<xml_document>
  <root_node>
      <firstChild_node />
      <previousSibling_node/>
      <previousSibling_node/>
      <lastChild_node/>
  </root_node>
```

Beginning with the lastChild node of the root node each previousSibling ascends the node tree up to, and including, the firstChild node.

The firstChild and lastChild node properties provide an ability to address child nodes in a more acute manner than is available through the use of long-form node attribution. For instance targeting the previousSibling node of the lastChild node above as *foo.lastChild. previousSibling* is simpler that attempting to call this node with the statement *foo.firstChild.nextSibling.nextSibling*.

Methods and properties for writing XML from Flash:

ActionScript can be used to write XML documents in string form, and also as XML objects. The creation of an XML document through ActionScript utilizes addressing conventions which are similar to those used in XML data extraction with a few significant differences. Because the XML document being created doesn't yet exist as a DOM structure, the use of relative node positions, such as nextSibling nodes, tend not be effective. The flat-file XML database example we'll be reviewing will cover nearly all of the XML writing methods available and should help to demonstrate how these are employed.

The methods and properties used in this example are as follows:

appendChild – This method attaches a new child node to the subject parent node and is expressed as *foo.appendChild(node)*. The node value declaration is most effective when *node* reflects either an existing XML object, an object property such the childNode of another XML object, or is written as a compound statement which instantiates a new XML object within the node argument.

For example:

```
foo.appendChild((new XML()).createElement("element_name"))
```

createElement – The constructor method used in generating new XML node elements. The createElement method is expressed as *foo.createElement(name)* where *name* is the name of the element to be generated.

The *foo* argument should reflect an existing XML object. Also createElement should be used in conjunction with appendChild as below. This is because the base XML object primitive is actually being appended with a new child node element relative to the XML declaration.

For example, the following statements will generate a new XML element named NODE:

```
xmlObj = new XML();
xmlObj.xmlDecl = "<?xml version=\"1.0\" ?>";
xmlObj.appendChild((new XML).createElement("NODE"));
trace(xmlObj);
```

This produces : `<?xml version="1.0" ?><NODE/>`

createTextNode – This is a constructor method used in creating new text nodes (aka. Data nodes). The createTextNode method works similarly to the createElement constructor method by appending a new data node to the subject node element.

```
xmlObj = new XML();
xmlObj.xmlDecl = "<?xml version=\"1.0\" ?>";
xmlObj.appendChild((new XML).createElement("NODE"));

data_node="hello world";
xmlObj.firstChild.appendChild((new
XML).createTextNode(data_node));

trace(xmlObj);
```

This produces: `<?xml version="1.0" ?><NODE>hello world</NODE>`

You'll notice that createTextNode is being appended to the firstChild node of xmlObj (<NODE>). If firstChild were not utilized, hello world would be appended to the XML declaration, and thus create a poorly formed document.

There are a few other methods available for writing XML documents with ActionScript which aren't incorporated in the following example. These are...

cloneNode(Boolean) – This method is used to replicate the DOM structure of the target XML object, or node element, and is expressed as xmlObj.cloneNode(Boolean). The Boolean value can be either true or false and specifies whether the target object or node is to be cloned or not. The purpose of the Boolean argument is to enable the clone node method to be switched either on or off selectively in response to rules applied to the XML document writing process. Boolean values can also be express as either 0, false, or 1, true, and as such may be manipulated by incrementing or de-incrementing a variable in the Boolean argument position.

```
xmlObj = new XML();
xmlObj.xmlDecl = "<?xml version=\"1.0\" ?>";
xmlObj.appendChild((new XML).createElement("NODE"));

data_node="hello world";
xmlObj.firstChild.appendChild((new
XML).createTextNode(data_node));

clone=xmlObj.cloneNode(true);
xmlObj.appendChild(clone);
trace(xmlObj);
```

This produces: <?xml version="1.0" ?><NODE>hello world</NODE><NODE>hello world</NODE>

If the statement clone=xmlObj.cloneNode(true); were modified to clone=xmlObj.firstChild.firstChild.cloneNode(true); the output of this routine would produce <?xml version="1.0" ?><NODE>hello world</NODE>hello world .

This is because the data node "hello world" is actually the first child node of the <NODE> element. In this way, cloneNode enables you to either copy an entire XML document structure or to isolate elements of that structure using the document node tree model.

removeNode – The removeNode method erases the targeted node element.

```
xmlObj = new XML();
xmlObj.xmlDecl = "<?xml version=\"1.0\" ?>";
xmlObj.appendChild((new XML).createElement("NODE"));

data_node="hello world";
xmlObj.firstChild.appendChild((new
XML).createTextNode(data_node));

clone=xmlObj.cloneNode(true);
xmlObj.appendChild(clone);
trace(xmlObj);

xmlObj.lastChild.removeNode();
trace(xmlObj);
```

This action changes the previous output `<?xml version="1.0" ?><NODE>hello world</NODE><NODE>hello world</NODE>` to the following by removing the `lastChild` node, `<?xml version="1.0" ?><NODE>hello world</NODE>`

A simple flat file XML database for Flash 5

The following is a very simple set of scripts which implement a 'flat file' XML database. This example creates a user registry through which the visitors, or the membership, of a site can log personal information and comments. These entries can be retrieved by the user and modified as well. The CGI aspect reads XML documents generated within a Flash movie and writes these to two separate files. One file is recorded under the name of the user while the other is a compilation of all user submissions compiled into a well-formed XML document. The various processes involved have been purposefully separated into discrete units so that it will be easier to understand what is going on. This also provides a better ability for you to implement these features selectively.

The Perl Scripts – the source files can be found on the accompanying CD.
My comments are in italics and should **not** be included in the code you post to your server.

xmlDB.pl

```
# ! "write the path to your perl interpreter here"

use CGI qw(:standard);
use CGI::Carp qw(fatalsToBrowser);

$EXCLUSIVE = 2;
$UNLOCK    = 8;
$key=time();
$entry = param(file);
```

This parameter determines the name of the XML file generated by this script

```
$database= $entry ;
$returnto="add.html";
```

This is the response page:

```
$record = param(entry);
```

The entry parameter holds the XML document which is sent from the Flash movie

```
&AddRecord($database,$returnto,$record); ~ calls the AddRecord subroutine

sub AddRecord{
  $database=$_[0];
      $returnto=$_[1];
      $record  =$_[2];

      open (DB,">$database") or die "Error: $!\n";
```

Opens the file named above for writing. The > operator signifies that any contents of the file should be overwritten by new information.

```
#flock DB, $EXCLUSIVE;      # Lock the file so nobody else uses it.
```

If your system supports file locking, you can uncomment this line:

```
seek DB, 0, 2;
print DB "$record\n";
```

Writes the XML document to the file:

```
#flock DB, $UNLOCK;
close(DB);
```

Closes the file

```
print "status=submission+accomplished !!";
```

Send a status confirmation back to your Flash movie:

```
return;
}
```

The database entry generated when a file is created, or modified, by this script will appear as such:

```
<user><name>neilsbohr</name><user_data><age>42</age><occupation>ph
ysicist</occupation><interests>billiards</interests><notes>atoms
are like billiard
balls</notes><email>nb@atoms.org</email></user_data></user>
```

This XML document is being written within the Flash movie and output as a string. When it's written to the file it is actually one long concatenation of tags.

Under standard formatting this information would appear as below:

```
<user>
  <name>neilsbohr</name>
     <user_data><age>42</age>
         <occupation>physicist</occupation>
         <interests>billiards</interests>
         <notes>atoms are like billiard balls</notes>
         <email>nb@atoms.org</email>
     </user_data>
  </user>
```

masterXMLdb.pl

The masterXMLdb script is identical to xmlDB with the exception that the line

```
open (DB,">$database") or die "Error: $!\n";
```

has been modified to

```
open (DB,">>$database") or die "Error: $!\n";
```

The difference here is that rather than replacing the contents of the file we're simply appending it with new entries. This script generates the administrator's master document and provides the following XML structure:

```
<?xml version="1.0"?>\n
  <user>
      <name>marco polo</name>
      <user_data>
          <age>36</age>
          <occupation>ship's pilot</occupation>
          <interests>finding japan!!</interests>
          <notes>where might I find japan ??</notes>
          <email>marco@polo.com</email>
      </user_data>
  </user>
  <user>
      <name>neils bohr</name>
      <user_data>
          <age>42</age>
          <occupation>physicist</occupation>
          <interests>billiards</interests>
          <notes>atoms are like billiard balls</notes>
          <email>nb@atoms.org</email>
      </user_data>
  </user>
  <user>
      <name>nickola tesla</name>
      <user_data>
          <age>50</age>
          <occupation>inventor/eccentric</occupation>
          <interests>everything</interests>
          <notes>no, I did not explode Tunguska !</notes>
          <email>nickola@energy.com</email>
      </user_data>
  </user>
  <user>
      <name>madam curie</name>
      <user_data>
          <age>36</age>
          <occupation>physicist</occupation>
```

```
            <interests>radioactivity</interests>
            <notes>I think I'll call it radium</notes>
            <email>curie@nukeme.com</email>
        </user_data>
    </user>
```

Again, this information will be formatted as a continuous string of tags. The above is simply to show you how the XML representation which is generated is structured.

The corresponding Flash application will be presented on a frame-by-frame basis. I've broken this down so that each aspect of the process is discrete.

Frame 1:

```
        #include "XDB.as"
        stop();
```

The XDB.as file is basically the same routine we're using to generate arrays from extracted XML data earlier in the chapter. The primary modification occurs in line 15 where the statement:

```
        xml_array[bar[x].nodeName+"value"] = bar[x].firstChild.nodeValue;
```

is added to enable this process to extract the text values nested within the <user_data> element. The other addition is the statement state="complete"; at the end of the routine. This is used to signal that the extraction and mapping processes are complete. XDB is used when XML files are loaded from the server and need to be presented to the user. The arrays derived from this script are translated into variables underlying each field of the user interface.

Frame 2:

```
        db = new XML();

        db.appendChild((new XML()).createElement("user"));
        db.firstChild.appendChild((new XML()).createElement("name"));
        db.firstChild.firstChild.appendChild((new
        ➥ XML()).createTextNode(firstname+" "+lastname));
        db.firstChild.appendChild((new XML()).createElement("user_data"));
        db.firstChild.lastChild.appendChild((new
        XML()).createElement("age"));
        db.firstChild.lastChild.appendChild((new
        ➥ XML()).createElement("occupation"));
        db.firstChild.lastChild.appendChild((new
        ➥ XML()).createElement("interests"));
        db.firstChild.lastChild.appendChild((new
        XML()).createElement("notes"));
        db.firstChild.lastChild.appendChild((new
        XML()).createElement("email"));
        dbArr= new Array;
        dbArr= db.firstChild.lastChild.childNodes;
```

```
x=0
while(x<=dbArr.length) {
dbVal = dbArr[x].nodeName.toLowerCase();
dbArr[x].appendChild((new XML()).createTextNode(eval(dbVal)));
++x}

entry = db.toString();
id = firstname+lastname
file = id+".xml";
loadVariablesNum ("http://localhost/generator/masterXMLdb.pl",
0,"GET");
loadVariablesNum ("http://localhost/generator/xmlDB.pl", 0,
"GET");
```

This is the routine that writes the XML entry to the database. The first section generates the structure of the document by creating the "user" root node element, the "name" element, the "user_data" element, and each of the child nodes of "user_data". You'll see that after the "name" node is created (db.firstChild.appendChild((new XML()).createElement("name"));), it's immediately followed by a statement which assigns the field entries for the user's name as its node values.

The other text nodes aren't assigned in this way because they require their parent nodes to be recognized as siblings of each other and are better handled through the while operation which follows.

The XML produced by this section would appear as below prior to the introduction of text values:

```
<user>
  <name>mel torme</name>
    <user_data>
        <age/>
        <occupation/>
        <interests/>
        <notes/>
        <email/>
    <user_data>
</user>
```

Once this skeleton has been established, the various data nodes of these elements can be introduced.

```
dbArr= new Array;
dbArr= db.firstChild.lastChild.childNodes;
```

These statements instantiate a new array to capture the child nodes of <user_data>. The values of this array are then extracted to provide a key (dbVal), which can be used to assign entry values to their corresponding node elements. This is facilitated by the fact that the variables underlying the user's entry fields are identical to the names used for the node names of the elements we've generated - the text node of the email element is matched with the "email" field in the UI. The loop below simply extracts the names of these elements in series and uses these names as a variable in the subsequent statement (`.createTextNode(eval(dbVal))`).

```
x=0
while(x<=dbArr.length) {
dbVal = dbArr[x].nodeName.toLowerCase();
dbArr[x].appendChild((new XML()).createTextNode(eval(dbVal)));
++x}
```

If you remember, an array of the child nodes of an XML object is actually a collection of *references* to the child nodes of that object. This is why the base XML object db is affected by the above statements. By appending text elements to the object references provided by `dbArr[ 0 - n ]` we're also appending these elements to the child node of the base element to which they refer.

After this has been accomplished, the db XML object is converted to a string and passed to the Perl scripts as their `entry` parameter. The `id` variable is generated by simply concatenating the user's first and last names. If you wanted to add a layer of security to this, you could include a password entry within the UI and hash this value into the id variable. The Perl script's `file` parameter is simply the `id` variable prepended to an XML file suffix - `.xml`.

These variables are all then sent to the Perl scripts as a URL-encoded string using GET.

```
entry = db.toString();
id = firstname+lastname
file = id+".xml";
loadVariablesNum ("http://localhost/generator/masterXMLdb.pl",
➡ 0,"GET");
loadVariablesNum ("http://localhost/generator/xmlDB.pl", 0,
➡ "GET");
```

Frame 3:
This frame is left blank to accommodate the frame loop in frame 4.

Frame 4:

```
if (typeof(status) == "undefined") {
  gotoAndPlay(3);
  } else { gotoAndPlay(5) }
```

To accommodate the latency inherent in the transmission and processing of the XML document we're using a simple frame loop which waits until the status variable is assigned a value - until it is, the `typeof` operator will be "undefined". The Perl scripts will return "`status=submission+accomplished !!`" which signals that the user and master documents have been updated. This information is then passed to frame 5.

Frame 5:

```
notes=" STATUS = "+status;

stop();
```

Here the status of the user's entry is reflected in the `notes` text field. After this is accomplished the frame sequence stops and the user can choose to either retrieve and modify their entry, submit another entry, or proceed through the rest of the site.

Frame 6:

```
lname=""
fname=""
stop();
```

When a user chooses to retrieve their information they're presented with two fields asking for their first and last names. By pressing ENTER these values are concatenated and stored under the variable `getfile`. Frame 7 is then loaded.

```
on (keyPress "<Enter>") {
  getfile = fname+lname;
  gotoAndPlay (7);
}
```

Frame 7:
Here the `getfile` variable is appended to the URL of the directory used to hold user's files. `getfile` itself is appended with the `.xml` suffix. This information is held within the variable `file_local`.

```
_root.file_local = "http://localhost/generator/"+getfile+".xml";

count = 0 ;
xml_array = new Array ;
bar = new Array ;
foo = new XML ;
foo.onLoad = screen ;
foo.load(file_local);
```

The above routine calls the `screen` function and instantiates several new objects - `xml_array`, `bar`, and `foo`. Screen is the function which had been loaded in the first frame by the statement `#include "XDB.as"`. This is the same routine we'd been using during our discussion of mapping XML documents to array structures. The XML document that has been loaded will be rendered into the following set of arrays.

```
xml_array = [object #47] [
  null:[object #48] [
      0:"user"
  ],
  uservalue:null,
  0:"user",
  user:[object #49] [
      0:"name",
      namevalue:"aNew User",
      1:"user_data"
  ],
```

```
            1:"name",
            name:[object #50] [
                0:"aNew User"
            ],
            3:"age",
            user_data:[object #51] [
                0:"age",
                1:"occupation",
                2:"interests",
                3:"notes",
                4:"email"
            ],
            agevalue:"100",
            age:[object #52] [],
            occupationvalue:"Astronaut",
            4:"occupation",
            occupation:[object #53] [],
            interestsvalue:"distant planets",
            5:"interests",
            interests:[object #54] [],
            notesvalue:"hello, I am a new user",
            6:"notes",
            notes:[object #55] [],
            emailvalue:"moony@themoon.com",
            7:"email",
            email:[object #56] []
        ]
```

Frame 8:

Frame 8 is left blank to accommodate the loop established in Frame 9

Frame 9:

```
        if(typeof(state)=="undefined"){
        gotoAndPlay(8);
        }
```

The state variable is returned by the screen function at the summation of its processing. Until this has been loaded the playhead is told to continually repeat frame 8.

Frame 10:

The set of arrays produced by the screen function are then translated to the variables which underlie the user interface. Voila!

```
        firstname=fname
        lastname=lname
        email= xml_array["emailvalue"];
        notes= xml_array["notesvalue"];
        interests= xml_array["interestsvalue"];
        age= xml_array["agevalue"];
```

continues overleaf

```
occupation= xml_array["occupationvalue"];
//stop();
```

The user can now modify their entry and resubmit it if they choose.

XML UI configuration

XML documents can also be used to configure Flash movies, influencing their presentation and functionality. By representing the various parameters involved in establishing the orientation of objects on stage, and the values of variables and properties employed within the underlying code of the movie, an XML 'template' can facilitate both the customization and extensibility of a Flash based application. The following example of a customizable user interface demonstrates this principle. This will utilize the same XMLDB Perl scripts we'd used previously, but rather than capturing user information these will be employed to store the coordinates of UI components on-stage. Because the XML documents we're employing are rendered within Flash there's no need to revise our Perl scripts.

This example doesn't introduce any new methods or properties, though it does incorporate the flaximaL XML handling object discussed at the end of this chapter.

A user interacts with the customizable UI by entering the name of the desired configuration within the 'load' field. If they don't wish to load an existing interface they can simply press the load button and proceed to the workspace screen. If the user wishes to save their current UI configuration they can do so by pressing log off which will present an entry field next to a button stating save environment as. The environment name typed within this field can then be used to call this environment during subsequent sessions.

The object instances incorporated within this example are:

- **The interface elements** – recognized as movie instances a,b,c,d,e,f

- **A Load button** – this loads the desired UI configuration by name

- **A Log-Off button** – this takes the user to a prompt where they can save the current UI configuration

- **A 'save environment as..' button** – the user is provided a field wherein they can name the current environment and save their configuration.

- **The Brain object** – monitors the loading of XML configuration templates and activates the process which configures the user's UI.

- **The Transmitter object** – this is a movie instance which collects the XML template and file parameters from a UI mapping function. The transmitter then sends these along to the server.

The order of events is:

1. Launch the customUI SWF
2. Enter the name of the UI environment into the field provided
3. Press Load
4. Reconfigure the UI elements as desired
5. Press the Log Off button
6. Enter a name for the new UI configuration
7. Press the Save Environment As.. button

_Level0-Frame 1:

The code within this frame captures the original position of each UI element within the user interface and loads a set of functions specific to interpreting, as well as writing, the XML template used to orient the UI. The role of each element is highlighted in the comments below:

```
#include "flaxObject.as"

// You'll need to place the flaxObject.as file in the same folder
// as customUI.swf

// Capture the original position of each UI element.

initAX=_root.a._x;
initAY=_root.a._y;
initBX=_root.b._x;
initBY=_root.b._y;
initCX=_root.c._x;
initCY=_root.c._y;
initDX=_root.d._x;
initDY=_root.d._y;
initEX=_root.e._x;
initEY=_root.e._y;
initFX=_root.f._x;
initFY=_root.f._y;
```

_root.cui is the variable associated with a text field on-screen and provides the user with information regarding the current status of loading or transmitting their configuration.

```
// Orient these elements based on an object's received coordinates .
// These are encoded within the XML template.

function orient(){

// UI.UIconf_parentof is an array associated with the UI object
// instantiated by the flaXiMaL object.

  L=_root.UI.UIconf_parentof.length;
  for(o=0;o < L ;o++){
      var obj=_root.UI.UIconf_parentof[o];
```

```
      eval(obj).xp=_root.UI.xco[o];
      eval(obj).yp=_root.UI.yco[o];
      eval(obj).gotoAndPlay(2);
  }
}
```

The two functions below are specific to the flaximaL object, which is discussed later in the chapter.

```
function loaded(){
  _root.cui="loaded";
  foo.generate() ;
}

function config(env){
  foo = new flaximal("UI");
  foo.flaximal_obj.onLoad=loaded;
  foo.load(env);
}
```

mapUI generates a new XML template based on the position of UI elements on stage. It does this by creating an XML node under the name of each specific object along with two child nodes which record the x and y positions of the object. These coordinates are recorded by the UI elements themselves as .xco and .yco properties.

```
function mapUI(){
  _root.cui="MAP";
  ConPar=new XML();
  ConPar.xmlDecl="<?xml version=\"1.0\"?>";
  ConPar.appendChild((new XML()).createElement("UIconf"));
  CPnode=new Array();

// read through the array of objects on _level0

  for(x in _level0){

// if the object is not a UI element , ignore it.

  if(_level0[x].xco != undefined && (x=='a' || x=='b' || x=='c' ||
➡ x=='d' || x=='e' || x=='f')){
    trace(x);

// create an original node with the name of the UI object.

      ConPar.firstChild.appendChild((new XML()).createElement(x));
  }


  }
// load the Cpnode array with the XML nodes representing
// each UI element.
```

```
CPnode=ConPar.firstChild.childNodes

for(y=0;y<CPnode.length;y++){
```

// iterate through these and generate xco and yco nodes to record
// their respective coordinates.

```
CPnode[y].appendChild((new XML()).createElement('xco'));
CPnode[y].appendChild((new XML()).createElement('yco'));
CPNN=CPnode[y].nodeName
CPnode[y].firstChild.appendChild((new
➡ XML()).createTextNode(_level0[CPNN].xco));
CPnode[y].lastChild.appendChild((new
➡ XML()).createTextNode(_level0[CPNN].yco));

}
```

// pass the resulting template to the 'transmit' object so that it
// can be relayed to the server.

```
_root.transmit.entry=ConPar.toString()
_root.transmit.id = _root.enviro
_root.transmit.file = _root.transmit.id+".xml";
_root.transmit.gotoAndPlay(2);

}

stop();
```

The brain object – this is a simple looping movie instance which monitors the UI object instantiated by flaXiMaL and activates the orient function above once the XML template has been successfully mapped.

_root.brain Frame 1 :

// if there are childnodes apparent within the received configuration
// template , active the 'orient' function.

```
if (_root.UI.UIconf_parentof.length>0){
    _root.cui="orient";
    _root.orient();
    _root.gotoAndStop(2);
}
```

Frame 2

```
gotoAndPlay(1);
```

_Level0-Frame 2:

If an environment name has been provided this configuration has been established and the user can re-design the environment by dragging the various UI elements into a new configuration. The Log Off button is apparent at the bottom of the screen to close their session.

Log Off

Log Off simply takes you to frame 3where you can enter a name for the new UI configuration.

```
on(release){
  //mapUI();
  gotoAndStop(3);
}
```

_Level0-Frame 3 :

Frame 3 presents the Save Environment As button and configuration name entry field. The Transmit object is also present off-screen to capture the XML template and file parameters to be delivered to the XMLDB Perl script.

Save As Environment

This button activates the map function which was loaded in Frame 1, clears the base UI object from memory, and resets the UI elements to the perimeters of the workspace. The user is then taken back to Frame 1 so that they can load a new environment.

```
on(release){
  _root.mapUI();
  delete _root.UI;
  _root.enviro="";

_root.a._x=initAX;
_root.a._y=initAY;
_root.b._x=initBX;
_root.b._y=initBY;
_root.c._x=initCX;
_root.c._y=initCY;
_root.d._x=initDX;
_root.d._y=initDY;
_root.e._x=initEX;
_root.e._y=initEY;
_root.f._x=initFX;
_root.f._y=initFY;


gotoAndStop(1);
}
```

The Transmit object

Transmit serves to isolate the XML template and file parameters being sent to the server. Because `loadVariables` will send all public variables within the movie instance it's a good idea to employ a transmitter of this sort. Otherwise you're passing a lot of garbage to the server and can inadvertently corrupt the processing of the script.

Frame 1 : `stop()`
Frame 2 : change the URL below to the location of your script

```
loadVariablesNum ("http://localhost/generator/xmlDB.pl", 0,
"GET");
root.cui="transmitted";
gotoAndStop(1);
```

XML Driven chat

Flash 5 possesses the ability to establish persistent TCP socket connections. These exploit a form of 'streaming' sockets which utilize 'null bytes' (that is. 0x00) delimiters to define the completion of XML message packets. That is, the end of the XML document is immediately followed by a null terminator, which signals that the packet has ended. Persistent socket connections differ from HTTP socket connects in that the connection between the client and server is maintained indefinitely, whereas HTTP style connections are transactional. The Flash 5 TCP socket protocol requires the receiver of these packets, whether a server or peer application, to recognize and respond to XML packets in the same manner. Not all TCP socket protocols respond to null bytes in the same way. Some use these as cues to terminate the session with their client. Before you attempt to adapt a Flash application for persistent socket connections you should determine whether the receiver will understand Flash's native protocol. Fortunately null byte delimiters are very common, so this shouldn't preclude the majority of applications.

The XML chat example we'll be reviewing is very simple. It's not really intended to provide a robust chat service but rather to demonstrate how Flash connects to and communicates with other applications using persistent TCP sockets. If you're interested in developing a more sophisticated chat service from this example I'd recommend going onto the Internet and taking a look at some of the public domain chat applications available. There are a good variety of chat servers using Perl, Java, TCL etc. . Once you have an idea of how to use Flash's XML socket object adapting these shouldn't prove too difficult.

The XMLSocket Object properties and methods

XMLSocket – The `XMLSocket` object constructor. `XMLSocket` is the base object of Flash 5's TCP sockets facility.

connect – The `XMLSocket` method used to establish a TCP socket connection between the local computer and a remote server. This method is expressed as `XMLSocket.connect(host, port)` where the `host` argument is the address of the target server and the `port` argument is the number of the port you'll be connecting to - this must be greater than or equal to 1024. The `host` argument should be the DNS domain of the server you'll be connecting to rather than the absolute path to the application that is managing the server's socket connections. So even if the chat script is running from http://mr_server.net/chat/chat.pl, the connection to the server will only require that you specify http://mr_server.net . `XMLSocket.connect()` will also return a Boolean value which tells you whether the connection to the server has been successful. This is either "true" or "false". The Boolean can either be read directly within a conditional statement or loaded into a variable (that is `status = XMLSocket.connect(H,P)`).

send – `send` is effective for both HTTP and persistent TCP transfers of XML data. The invocation of the `send` method can be expressed simply as `xmlObj.send`, or may incorporate arguments assigning the URL, and "window", parameters of the transfer (eg. `xmlObj.send(URL)`, or `xmlObj(URL, window)`. The `window` argument assigns the destination of an array of data received from the server. This is intended to be used within an HTML frames layout and enables the `_parent`, `_top`, and `_self` panels to be targeted selectively. Alternatively a new window can be launched by using the parameter `_blank`. These behave similarly to the `getUrl` method. When employing the send method in relation to the `XMLSocket` object no arguments are required .

onXML – The `onXML` method works as a callback function which is triggered upon the receipt of XML data from a server or peer application. It will receive this data and pass it on to whatever function is assigned as the subject of the statement (eg. `XMLSocket.onXML = function()`). For example:

```
Socket.onXML = XMLReceive ;

        function XMLReceive(xx) {
          readXML = new XML;
          readXML.parseXML(xx) ;

        }
```

You can also employ `onXML` as `XMLSocket.onXML(object)` where the `object` argument is an instance of the XML object received from the server.

close – a method associated with the `XMLSocket` object which kills the TCP session. This is expressed as `XMLSocket.close` .

parseXML – The `parseXML` method parses the XML document which is specified as its argument and passes this to the base XML object. This is implemented as `xmlObj.parseXML( xmlDoc )` where `xmlDoc` is a pre-parsed XML document. The `parseXML` method behaves similarly to the `load` method.

The Perl script we'll be using is `sockets.pl` (found in the source code). This script should be launched prior to calling it from the chat application. You can do this by simply running `sockets.pl` within the appropriate directory on your server.

The Flash movie which is negotiating this session is comprised by one frame and three buttons. The first button establishes a connection with the chat server, the second transmits an XML encoded message packet to the server, and the third disconnect the chat client from the server.

Frame 1:

The connect button

```
on (press) {
  Socket = new XMLSocket();
  Socket.connect("localhost", "2001");

}
```

This button simply instantiates a new XMLsocket object (Socket) and attempts to connect this to the server localhost on port number 2001.

The transmit button

```
on (press) {
  message = "<message><nick>"+nick+"</nick><body>"+mess+"</body>
  ➥ </message>";
  Socket.send(message);
  Socket.onXML = XMLReceive ;

}
```

With the socket established, the Transmit button sends the XML encoded string held by message through the socket. The response from the server will trigger the event handler onXML which is associated with the socket object. Socket.onXML passes this response to the function XMLReceive.

The disconnect button

```
on (press) {
  Socket.close();
}
```

The disconnect button simply kills the TCP session with the server using the close method.

The Keyframe code:

```
read = new XML;

function XMLReceive(xx) {

read.parseXML(xx) ;
nickname=read.firstChild.firstChild.firstChild;
text=read.firstChild.firstChild.nextSibling.firstChild;
line =nickname+" says: "+text+"\n"+line ;

}
```

The XML object `read` will be used to hold incoming XML strings. This object is then employed in the `XMLReceive` function through the `parseXML` method. The argument `xx` contains the XML string passed by the `onXML` event handler within the Transmit button. Each of the variables, `nickname` and `text`, are assigned elements of this XML document through a long form attribution of node properties. The `line` variable holds a concatenation of the values of `nickname` and `text` appended with a new line and the contents of the previous instance of the line variable. This produces a sequential list of messages received from the chat server within the newest message on top.

For example:

mission_control says: what ?
n.armstrong says: this is one small step for man, one giant leap for
mankind
mission_control says: oh good
n.armstrong says: landed on moon !

Again, this chat service is very primitive, but should give you an idea of how to use the `XMLSocket` Object along with its attendant properties and methods.

FlaXiMaL XML handling object

Flaximal is an original object type which assists in mapping well formed XML documents to a set of arrays. These model both the relative and absolute hierarchies of the document's node name, child node, and node value properties, as well as its attributes. It's constructed using ActionScript's prototype mechanism. A significant benefit of using flaximal is that the values used in naming these arrays derive from the node names of the subject XML document. This creates a map of the document which mirrors its own lexicon and enables multiple documents to be loaded into the same application. If a generic naming scheme were used in this situation each new document would generate arrays which displaced those of the previous document. The following will provide an example which demonstrates how flaXiMaL can be implemented to convert complex XML document into array structures that can be easily integrated into Flash applications.

The flaxReader example on the CD utilizes flaximal to present the constituent elements of several complex XML samples. Forgive the aesthetics of this demonstration, it's simply meant to show that the process is effective in mapping these documents.

The XML document we'll be working with is a section of the periodic table.

In order to load the document into flaXiMaL the following set of statements is used :

```
function loaded(){
  foo.generate() ;
}
```

The argument to flaximal will be used as the name of the base flaximal object - you can call this anything you like

```
foo = new flaximal("testXML");
foo.flaximal_obj.onLoad = loaded ;
```

The argument, example, should be replace by the name of the document you wish to load:

```
foo.load(example) ;
```

After the document has been processed, the following array structure is evident in the debugger:

```
testXML = [object #13] {
  PERIODIC_TABLE_parentof:[object #14]  [
```

The root node PERIODIC_TABLE possesses two child nodes, each of which categorize types of ATOMS:

```
        0:"ATOM",
        1:"ATOM"
    ],
    PERIODIC_TABLE_parentof_temp:1,
    ATOM:[object #15]  [
```

Because these elements only possess child nodes, and not node values, their value arrays are empty:

```
        0:"\r\n        ",
        1:"\r\n        ",
        2:"\r\n        ",
```

and so on, up to:

```
        32:"\r\n        ",
        33:"\r\n    "
    ],

        ATOM_temp:33,
        ATOM_parentof:[object #16]  [ ~
```

These are the child nodes of the ATOM Elements:

```
        0:"NAME",
        1:"ATOMIC_WEIGHT",
        2:"ATOMIC_NUMBER",
        3:"OXIDATION_STATES",
        4:"BOILING_POINT",
        5:"SYMBOL",
        6:"DENSITY",
        7:"ELECTRON_CONFIGURATION",
        8:"ELECTRONEGATIVITY",
        9:"ATOMIC_RADIUS",
        10:"ATOMIC_VOLUME",
        11:"SPECIFIC_HEAT_CAPACITY",
        12:"IONIZATION_POTENTIAL",
        13:"THERMAL_CONDUCTIVITY",
```

continues overleaf

```
            14:"NAME",
            15:"ATOMIC_WEIGHT",
            16:"ATOMIC_NUMBER",
            17:"OXIDATION_STATES",
            18:"BOILING_POINT",
            19:"MELTING_POINT",
            20:"SYMBOL",
            21:"DENSITY",
            22:"ELECTRON_CONFIGURATION",
            23:"COVALENT_RADIUS",
            24:"ELECTRONEGATIVITY",
            25:"ATOMIC_RADIUS",
            26:"HEAT_OF_VAPORIZATION",
            27:"ATOMIC_VOLUME",
            28:"HEAT_OF_FUSION",
            29:"IONIZATION_POTENTIAL",
            30:"SPECIFIC_HEAT_CAPACITY",
            31:"THERMAL_CONDUCTIVITY"
        ],

    ATOM_parentof_temp:31,
```

This value tells you how many child nodes there were:

```
        NAME:[object #17]  [
```

These are the values of each instance of the NAME node - Actinium was within the first ATOM node and Aluminum was in the second.

```
            0:"Actinium",
            1:"Aluminum"
        ],
        NAME_temp:1,
        ATOMIC_WEIGHT:[object #18]  [
            0:"227",
            1:"26.98154"
        ],
        ATOMIC_WEIGHT_temp:1,
        ATOMIC_NUMBER:[object #19]  [
            0:"89",
            1:"13"
        ],
        ATOMIC_NUMBER_temp:1,
        OXIDATION_STATES:[object #20]  [
            0:"3",
            1:"3"
        ],
        OXIDATION_STATES_temp:1,
        UNITS:"Watts/meter/degree Kelvin",
        BOILING_POINTAttributes:[object #21]  [
```

This is an Attributes array. The index values should be understood as pairs of values wherein the even value is the attribute name and the odd value is its attribute value.

The values for the rest of the child nodes are then filled in – these are omitted here due to space.

Flaximal also produces a prime array, this simply indexes all node names as they occur within the XML document. The advantage of this is that the prime array can be used to quickly iterate through the XML document structure for the purposes of searching the document or compiling its elements into an index or list. A given index value of prime can then be used as a key value of the master document array to call up the child nodes and/or node values of that element.

```
prime = [object #379] [
      1:"ATOM",
      2:"NAME",
      3:"ATOMIC_WEIGHT",
```

and so on, up to:

```
     32:"IONIZATION_POTENTIAL",
     33:"SPECIFIC_HEAT_CAPACITY",
     34:"THERMAL_CONDUCTIVITY"
   ]
```

The final array structure produced by flamimal is the Root array.

The root array works in a similar way to the prime array in that it indexes node properties in the order in which they occur within the XML document. Where the prime array presents the node names of the XML document, the root array presents their node values. Again, this type of indexing is useful when searching documents, or compiling their values into lists and the like.

```
root_PERIODIC_TABLE = [object #380] [
  PERIODIC_TABLE_parentof:[object #381] [
      0:"ATOM",
      1:"ATOM"
  ],
  1:"\r\n   ",
  ATOM:[object #382] [
      0:"\r\n      ",
      1:"\r\n      ",
      2:"\r\n      ",
```

and so on, up to

```
     31:"\r\n      ",
     32:"\r\n      ",
     33:"\r\n   "
  ],
  ATOM_parentof:[object #383] [
      0:"NAME",
```

continues overleaf

```
       1:"ATOMIC_WEIGHT",
       2:"ATOMIC_NUMBER",
       3:"OXIDATION_STATES",
```

and so on, up to:

```
      29:"IONIZATION_POTENTIAL",
      30:"SPECIFIC_HEAT_CAPACITY",
      31:"THERMAL_CONDUCTIVITY"
    ],
    2:"Actinium",
    NAME:[object #384] [
        0:"Actinium",
        1:"Aluminum"
    ],
    3:"227",
    ATOMIC_WEIGHT:[object #385] [
        0:"227",
        1:"26.98154"
    ],
```

and so on, up to:

```
      31:"\r\n         10.7\r\n        ",
      HEAT_OF_FUSIONAttributes:[object #410] [
        0:"UNITS",
        1:"kilojoules/mole"
      ],
      HEAT_OF_FUSION:[object #411] [
        0:"\r\n         10.7\r\n        "
      ],
      32:"5.986",
      33:"\r\n         0.9\r\n       ",
      34:"\r\n         237\r\n       "
    ]
```

We're going to review the flaxReader application so that you can see how these array structures can be employed within your Flash applications.

Frame 1

```
    #include "flaxObject.as"
    stop()
```

Stop the playhead so that the user can select and XML document to review. This frame also includes the compiler directive #include flaxObject.as which is the library file for flaximal.

There are several buttons presented which call sample XML files.

For example:

```
on (press) {
_root.example = "periosample.xml"
gotoAndPlay (2);

// periosample.xml is the section of the periodic table we
// reviewed earlier

}
```

The other documents available are a sample of WDDX, an archive of SlashDot headlines, and a hypothetical employee's database.

Frame 2

```
function loaded(){
   foo.generate() ;
}

c= 1
foo = new flaximal("testXML");
foo.flaximal_obj.onLoad = loaded ;
trace(example);
foo.load(example) ;
```

This is essentially the same flaximal instantiation and loading routine we looked at earlier. The only modification is the addition of the c variable, which is used to increment through the prime array of the processed document.

The Step button within this frame contains the following code :

```
on (press) {
text = prime[c]
tree = prime[c]
rn = "root_"+RootNode
children = eval(rn)[tree+"_parentof"]
nodevalue = eval(rn)[tree]
attrib = eval(rn)[tree+"Attributes"]

}
on (release) {
c++;
}
```

The c variable begins with a value of 1 and is incremented every time the Step button is released. This changes the index value of the prime array which in turn changes the values stored in text and tree. The text variable is associated with the topmost text field within flaxReader and simply reflects the node name of prime[c]. The variable RootNode in the fourth line is generated by flaximal to specify the root node of the XML document. In this example `RootNode` is appended to `root_` to construct the proper name of the base `root` array. After processing our periodic table sample the `root` array is `root_PERIODIC_TABLE` .

Once the Root array is established, and stored under the `rn` variable it is prepended to the string

```
"children = eval(rn)[tree+"_parentof"]".
```

In the case of the periodic table document this statement will resolve to:

```
children= root_PERIODIC_TABLE[ NodeName_parentof]
```

where `NodeName` is the value of the current node name. Because all `_parentof` arrays contain child nodes, the `children` variable will be loaded with a list of comma separated child node names. The flaxReader simply presents these as a list within the Children window. If you wanted to process these further you could instantiate `children` as an array, rather than a simple variable, and apply it however you like.

The `nodevalue` variable holds the node value of these same elements. Again, in the case of the periodic table example, this would resolve to `root_PERIODIC_TABLE[NodeName]` which contains an index of all node values associated with the `NodeName` element. This is also a list, which is presented in the node value window of flaxReader. The `attrib` variable receives a list of attributes from the attributes array in the same manner.

FlaxReader simply presents the arrays generated by flaximal in their string form. It's not likely that you'll employ them in this way unless you need raw lists of XML data. Each of these array structures can be employed and manipulated in the same ways that you handle any other array. You can call array values individually or as compound "multidimensional" structures. The purpose of flaximal is to provide the mapping algorithm required to translate an XML document to a native ActionScript array.

There is one aspect of XML handling which we haven't touched upon so far. This concerns the methods by which attributes are extracted from an XML element. The attributes of a node element can be extracted as an array of node attributes using the `for..in` statement. This iterates through the properties of an object and assigns these to the first argument of the `for..in` statement. Flaximal provides for the mapping of attributes, but nonetheless it's important that you understand how this is done.

The following is the routine responsible for extracting and mapping attribute arrays to the flaximal object's native array structures.

```
if (typeof(arr[arr.temp].attributes) != "undefined") {
  for (atts in arr[arr.temp].attributes) {
     var att_array = arr[arr.temp].attributes[atts] ;
     var attribute = arr[arr.temp].nodeName+"Attributes";
     flax_prop(atts,att_array);
     flax_array(attribute,atts,flax_occur);
     flax_array(attribute,att_array,atts);
  }
}
```

Here the keys of the `arr[arr.temp]`.attributes collection are successively loaded into the `atts` variable. This variable is then processed by the series of statements contained within the `for..in` construct. A simpler rendition of this process might be more useful in introducing these concepts.

Let's use the original 'the walls of my house' XML document and amend the first child node to incorporate two attributes - `color` and `plot`.

```
<the_walls_of_my_house color="periwinkle" plot="1 acre">
```

We'll assume that this document is being loaded as a string so that we can overlook whitespace problems within the context of this example. The function which will be responsible for extracting the key/ value pairs of the node attributes is below.

```
function XMLarray () {
  attArray = new Array;
  x=0;

// The keys of the attributes to "the_walls_of_my_house" element
// are assigned to the "att" variable

  for (att in XMLobj.firstChild.attributes){

// The value of "att" is then assigned to the array index
// represented by "x"

    attArray[x] = att;

// An associative array is created using the value of "att". This
// key is then assigned with its corresponding value within the
// element's attribute array.

    attArray[att]= XMLobj.firstChild.attributes[att];
    x++
  }
}


  sample="wall0house.xml";
  XMLobj = new XML;
  XMLobj.load(sample);
  XMlobj.onLoad = XMLarray ;
```

This produces the following array structure:

```
attArray = [object #41] [
     0:"color",
     color:"periwinkle",
     1:"plot",
     plot:"1 acre"
   ]
```

The `for..in` construct will only return the key value of an attribute. This is why you need to perform a subsequent operation, which will determine the value of these keys, by using the syntax `xmlObj.attributes[key]`. Because the attributes collection behaves like an array, appending the key value in this manner will return the value associate with the key.

Conclusion

What we've looked at here is a (fairly exhaustive) introduction to how XML can be handled through Flash 5.

If you're interested in learning how to design, or optimize your own XML handling applications I urge you to look at the source code provided. I've made an effort to use naming conventions which are descriptive, if somewhat abbreviated, so you should be able to follow the processes involved. Flaximal can certainly be refined and extended beyond its current functionality. If you'd like to contribute to the further development of the flaximal object feel free to contact me at semiotics@worldnet.att.net. I've posted the source code on my server and will be updating this with any contributions from the ActionScripting community.

25
Flash and XML

Section 4
Dynamic Data

24
Databases
Another Way

23
Feeding Data
to Flash
from Access

22
Introducing
Databases

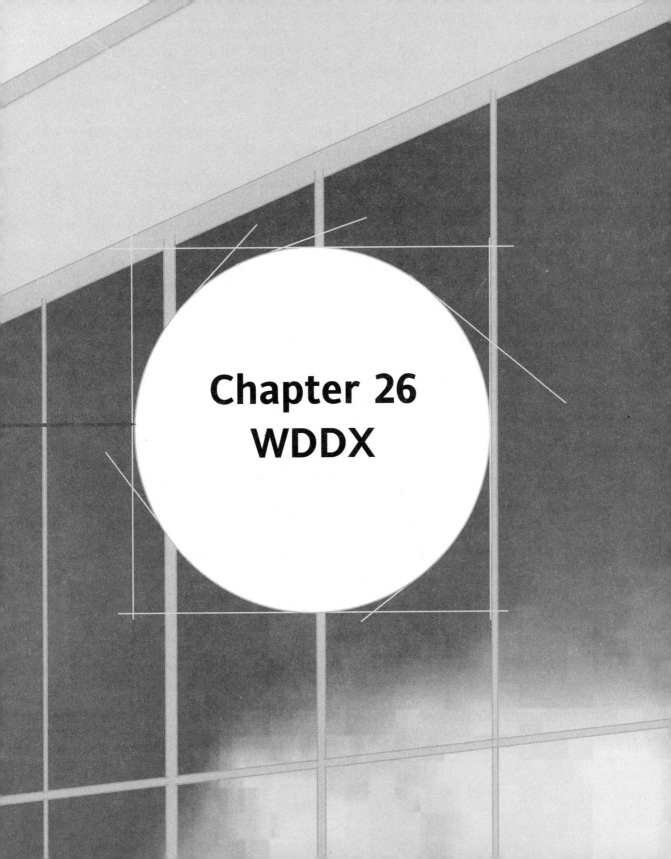

Chapter 26
WDDX

This chapter will demonstrate the power of Flash and WDDX combined, allowing for easy transfer of complex data between different programming or scripting languages, such as ColdFusion and ActionScript, using XML.

In short, it will enable Flash to 'talk' to your server, and once they've become friends, they can exchange all kinds of structured information, giving your Flash pages an added dynamic edge. Over the course of this chapter we will look at:

- The Flash Exchange – home of the WDDX extension and much, much more

- Introducing WDDX

- Demonstrating the power of serializing and deserializing your data

- Incorporating the benefits of WDDX into your data-driven Flash pages

Tips and scripts and smart clips, oh my!

One of the key features of Macromedia products is their **extensibility** – the way that they can be upgraded, enhanced or *extended* by downloading and installing new **extensions**. The Macromedia Exchange is a community where users can download or upload these add-ins and in late 2000 the Exchange for Flash was officially launched at:

www.macromedia.com/exchange/flash

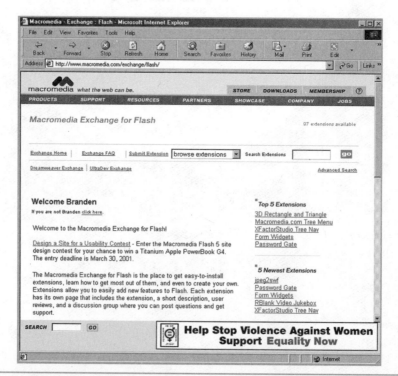

Right now on the Exchange there is everything from smart clips to code samples. There are also more meatier downloads like the JavaScript Integration Kit for Flash and even a Java server for use with ActionScript's XMLSocket object!

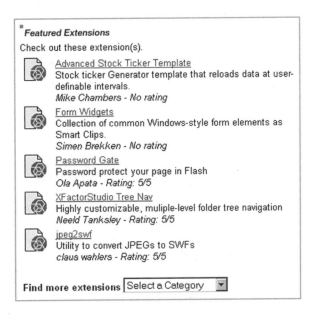

Whatever your purposes, you're bound to find something useful on the Exchange – you might even end up designing an extension yourself and submitting it for others to use. Let's take a quick look under the hood of these extension files, and then we can download the one we'll use for this chapter...

Before you can access and use these extensions, you need to register at the Exchange and then download and install the **Extension Manager**.

The Extension Manager both installs extensions for you and allows you to manage the extensions that you currently have installed across the Macromedia range. The chances are it will have been installed on your machine from the CD when you set up Flash. But in case you chose not to take it during set-up, Windows or Mac versions are available on the Exchange site.

In fact, all these extensions consist of just a single file, an MXP (**M**acromedia e**X**tension **P**ackage) file. MXP files are actually just compressed archives of any number of files. MXP files always contain one special file, a MXI (pronounced 'mixey') file. The MXI file is just an XML file that describes how to install the various files in the extension as well as the help text for the extension. If you ever decide to create your own extension for the Exchange you will be creating your own MXI file.

Now, lets go ahead and snag the particular extension that the rest of this chapter is about, the **WDDX Serializer/Deserializer** (don't worry if you don't know what it is yet!)

Finding and downloading our extension

1. If you look at the top right corner of the screen, you'll see a pink search box, which also tells you how many extensions are currently online.

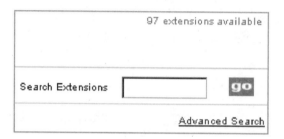

The Exchange site offers you several ways to browse for and locate extensions. Further down the page you'll see a drop-down menu from which you can browse by category, that is if the 'featured extensions' or '5 newest extensions' don't tickle your fancy.

2. Searching using the keyword WDDX should be sufficient.

3. When the Serializer/Deserializer extension is returned, click on its link to jump to the download page, which will also give you more information about what it does; you don't need to bother about this for now – we'll explain it all in a moment.

4. Download the MXP file by clicking on the PC or MAC icons, and choose to save it to disk. There is an Extensions folder in your Macromedia > Flash 5 directory.

5. Finally, all you have to do is double-click an MXP file to install it with the Extension Manager.

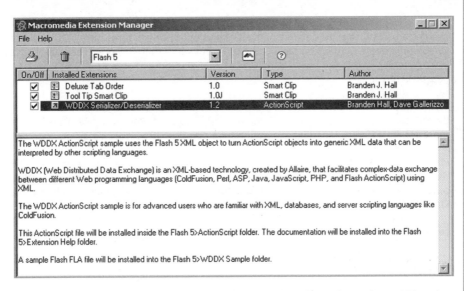

That's how easy it is to download and install extensions from the Exchange! Now, lets start digging into WDDX...

What is WDDX?

One of the reasons that XML is currently such a buzzword is because it allows for easy data syndication – which means simply that programs written in different languages can easily share data. For this to happen, however, all of the programs have to agree on the format of the XML, also known as the DTD (Document Type Definition) or schema. In fact, numerous DTDs and schemas have been created for using XML to syndicate various types of data, ranging from news headlines to real estate information.

When web-based programs need to share raw data, XML is there to fill the need. For a web program to pass and receive useful information there needs to be a mechanism that can encapsulate data and complex data structures - arrays, associative arrays and recordsets. In order to solve this problem for their ColdFusion server product, Allaire developed an XML DTD which they coined Web Distributed Data eXchange (or WDDX). The WDDX DTD defines a simple set of XML tags that can be used to describe most basic types of data structures. A data structure that is being held in a WDDX-based XML document is known as a WDDX packet.

Conversion of a native data structure to a WDDX packet is known as **serializing**, and going from a WDDX packet to a native data structure is **deserializing**.

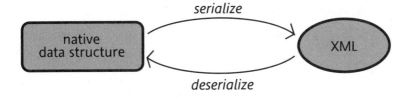

Allaire also developed a serializer/deserializer for their ColdFusion language. This special code enables a programmer to convert native ColdFusion data structures into WDDX packets and vice versa with a single ColdFusion tag - `<CFWDDX>`. But wait - there's more. The same tag easily allows a programmer to convert back from WDDX to ColdFusion and also from ColdFusion to JavaScript data structures.

Allaire also made WDDX *open*, so consequently a lot of people developed similar serializers/deserializers for other languages, including PHP, ASP/COM, Perl and Java. This suddenly allowed these totally different languages to easily share complex structured data.

Flash 5 was added to the group when Fig Leaf Software, a software development company that does extensive work with ColdFusion and Flash, made their ActionScript version of WDDX publicly available. It is now not only possible but actually very easy to exchange structured data between Flash and server-side languages.

Let's look at the equation...

Flash + WDDX = *Power*

WDDX and Flash make such a great combination for a number of reasons. First of all, if you were to forego XML entirely, you could only exchange name/value pairs using Flash's ability to **load variables**, so bye-bye any kind of structured data. Not only that, all data that comes through via `loadVariables` is interpreted by Flash as strings, even numbers and Booleans.

Now, if we were to use XML, the industrious programmer could undertake to create a custom DTD to describe data structures. However, that industrious programmer would need to know that Flash's XML parser is not a validating one, and any custom DTD that will work predictably with Flash 5 must include routines that check to make sure that loaded XML conforms to its DTD and other routines capable of translating what the loaded XML actually means!

All of this is already built into the WDDX serializer/deserializer.

Arrays are a good example of how using WDDX is superior to `loadVariables`. If you need to transfer an array with `loadVariables`, you need to send Flash each of the elements of the list as a separate name/value pair like this:

```
&name1=Hall,Branden&name2=Lee,Patricia&name3=Malkin,Grey
```

Then, once Flash received those variables, it would have to create an Array object and insert them into that array, one by one. However, if you were to use XML and the WDDX serializer/deserializer, you would simply use the server-side language of your choice to output the WDDX representation of the array. Then you would use Flash's built-in XML capabilities to load that XML into an XML object. Finally, you would simply pass that XML object to the WDDX deserializer, and it would spit back out an Array object with your data already in it!

Another reason why Flash and WDDX make a good pair is because all of the most common languages that Flash talks to also speak WDDX. From ColdFusion to JavaScript, PHP and Perl, pretty much any language that is used for server-side scripting supports WDDX. Even if the language of your choice does not currently support WDDX, given its simple nature, it is not a monumental task to write a serializer/deserializer for any language that supports XML.

Finally, since WDDX is only based on XML 1.0, Flash fully supports it. There exist other similarly purposed DTDs that have been designed to throw XML data around the web. The most notable is Microsoft's SOAP (Simple Object Access Protocol). However, SOAP and many of the other newer DTDs rely on new features recently added to the XML specification that many languages, including ActionScript, have not yet implemented.

If you would like to witness the WDDX serializer/deserializer in heavy-duty action, download the **UIKit** (originally code-named **Harpoon**) from the Exchange. It is a set of six Flash user interface objects that are instantiated and configured in ColdFusion:

- Calculator
- Calendar
- Cascading Menu
- Datasheet
- Horizontal Nav Bar
- Tree Control

Each of these industrial strength Flash movies needs to receive a large amount of configuration information and data from the ColdFusion page that instantiates it. In order to send that data, ColdFusion turns it into WDDX which Flash later loads. In fact, the whole product is dependant on the use of WDDX!

The WDDX ActionScript file

Before you do anything else, you need to first track down the special wddx.as file which the extension has automatically generated for you in the Macromedia > Flash 5 > ActionScript folder (this location is specified in the information pane of the Extension Manager). The file might look like a simple text file but will nonetheless be suffixed .as.

1. Find the file and place it in the directory that you wish to create your new movie in.

2. Next, open Flash 5 and create a new, blank movie. In order to actually have Flash import this file at compile-time, simply include it as you would any other file by inserting this line of code to the first frame of your movie:

```
#include "wddx.as"
```

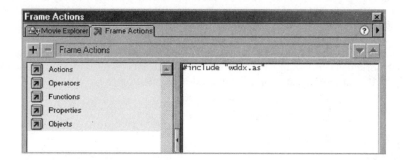

> To display this window, right-click frame 1 and choose Actions from the context menu. Also make sure you are in Expert Mode for hand-coding.

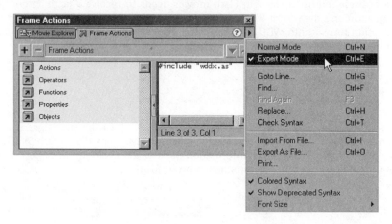

One thing to note during development is that when you are trying to fix syntax errors in your code, it may be a good idea to comment out the line of code that includes the wddx.as file. If you do not, the line numbers you get back from Flash's messages will not correspond to the line numbers in the ActionScript panel. Just make sure that when you are done, you uncomment the line!

Including the wddx.as file is all we need do to enable the use of two objects: WDDX and wddxRecordset. First we should discuss the use of the WDDX object.

3. To get started, we'll create an instance of WDDX. Our code will look like this:

```
converter = new WDDX();
```

Our converter object (as well as any WDDX object) has two methods we can use: `serialize` (this is the process of converting data into WDDX) and `deserialize` (this is doing the reverse, turning XML back into data). If you look through the code for `wddx.as` you'll see many more methods described there. The others are internal methods, not meant for us to call in our programming. The `serialize` method gets passed a Flash variable or object and returns an XML object.

4. In our code we are going to create a new array and then serialize it into an XML object called myWDDX:

```
myArray = new Array("bob", "mary", "joe", "sally");
myWDDX = converter.serialize(myArray);
```

5. Now to see what is happening, add a **trace** to print out the value of myWDDX - **trace (myWDDX)**. Your code should now match the screenshot:

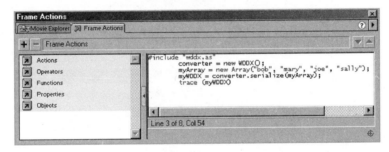

6. Test your movie with CTRL-ENTER, and in your Output window the long string of text you'll see is the WDDX packet. If we were to *pretty print* the XML (since one big line of XML is tough to read!), it would look like this:

```xml
<wddxPacket version="1.0">
      <header/>
      <data>
            <array length="4">
                  <string>bob</string>
                  <string>mary</string>
                  <string>joe</string>
                  <string>sally</string>
            </array>
      </data>
</wddxPacket>
```

7. As you can see, our array was turned into a nice little WDDX packet that contains all of the data in our array. Now, we can take that XML object and deserialize it back into

an array. The `deserialize` method of our converter object accepts an XML object and returns an object of the appropriate type. To take our XML and covert it back into a new array, we will add the following code:

myOtherArray = converter.deserialize(myWDDX);

8. Once again we will probably want to add a `trace` action so that we can make sure that the deserialized packet is indeed an array and contains our data. If we add this code our final code looks like this:

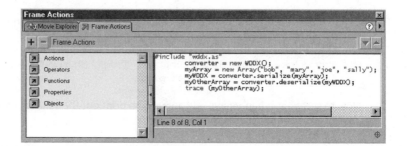

And the output will then look like this:

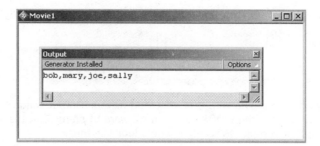

Which is *exactly* the same as what we would get had we just traced out `myArray` - it's been rebuilt exactly!

The wddxRecordset object

As mentioned earlier, wddx.as makes available an additional object, `wddxRecordset`. One of the data structures that WDDX supports is the recordset, or query object, which Flash has no way to internally represent. Thus, when the `deserialize` method of the WDDX object comes across a recordset, perhaps passed in from a ColdFusion page, it creates a new wddxRecordset object and fills it with the data from the WDDX. We will be using this object in the next section to exchange WDDX packets between Flash and other languages, but it's not the only one available. These are the other methods that come with WDDXRecordset object:

```
getRowCount()          Returns the number of rows in the recordset
addColumn("x")         Adds a column named x to the recordset
addRows(n)             Adds n blank rows to the recordset
isColumn("x")          Returns true if x is the name of a column in the recordset,
                       false otherwise
getField(n, "x")       Returns the value of the data at row n, column x
setField(n, "x")       Sets the value of the data at row n, column x
```

Making the most of WDDX

While serializing and deserializing data just inside of Flash is good for an academic exercise, it doesn't really do anything. In order to really take advantage of WDDX with Flash you have to pair it with another language that speaks WDDX. In this section we are going to cover how to toss WDDX packets between Flash and two other languages, ColdFusion and PHP.

The basic principles for these examples apply to any WDDX-enabled language, from Perl to ASP. JavaScript even has its own set of code for working with WDDX (the wddx.js file ships with ColdFusion, and acted as a code base for wddx.as). However, it's not particularly useful to shift data between two client-side technologies. In addition to that, making Flash and JavaScript talk to each other – though sometimes necessary – can be a messy exercise at best, and a number of browsers simply don't allow it.

ColdFusion, being the first language to be WDDX enabled, is an obvious choice if you need Flash to send data to a server and you want to use WDDX. Using WDDX with ColdFusion is actually fairly straightforward. There is just the one tag <CFWDDX> that does all of the serialization / deserialization. The only real problem with using ColdFusion is the fact that it tends to be very *noisy* and generate a lot of extra white space, which Flash's XML parser chokes on.

The code we will use takes advantage of two additional ColdFusion tags, <CFSILENT> and <CFSETTING> to make sure that all white space is stripped away.

Querying a database using WDDX and ColdFusion

In order to actually run the application once you are done building it you will need to have access to a server running either ColdFusion Server or ColdFusion Express (CFExpress is the free, limited functionality version of CFServer that can be downloaded from www.allaire.com/cfexpress). There is also a trial version of ColdFusion Server on the CD accompanying the book.

1. This code will simply query one of the databases that are installed by default with ColdFusion, cfsnippets. It takes the result of the query, serializes it, and prints it out. In order to try this code, create a folder in your webroot, Foed, and create an empty ColdFusion file in this location called test.cfm. The following code should go into the test.cfm file in the wwwroot/Foed directory (the comments will help you understand which part does what):

    ```
    <!-- Use a combination of CFSILENT and CFSETTING to suppress all
    white space produced by ColdFusion. CFSILENT suppresses all
    ```

    continues overleaf

```
output between its beginning and end tags.   CFSETTING suppresses
whitespace only.   -->

<CFSILENT>

<!-- Use the enablecfoutputonly attribute to suppress whitespace
(necessary).  Use showdebugoutput attribute to suppress display
of debug information (necessary). Catchexceptionsbypattern
attribute shown with default value.   -->

    <CFSETTING enablecfoutputonly="Yes" showdebugoutput="No"
➥ catchexceptionsbypattern="No">

<!-- Query database to return course information from the Math
Department  -->

        <CFQUERY NAME="qGetCourseList" DATASOURCE="cfsnippets">
            SELECT CourseList.CorName,
            ➥ Departments.Dept_Name
            FROM CourseList, Departments
WHERE CourseList.Dept_ID = Departments.Dept_ID AND
➥ Departments.Dept_ID = 'MATH'
        </CFQUERY>

<!--        Serialize query into an XML packet with the CFWDDX
tag.  Set action attribute to "CFML2WDDX", meaning "take a
coldfusion variable and serialize its contents as a WDDX packet".
Provide variable holding query results as object to be
serialized. Provide name of variable to be created, holding WDDX
XML object.  -->

    <CFWDDX action="CFML2WDDX" input="#qGetCourseList#"
    ➥ output="wddxGetCourseList">

    </CFSILENT>

<!-- Output WDDX XML packet.  When this page is called by Flash
the output will be read as text and loaded. It can then be
manipulated by ActionScript.  -->

<CFOUTPUT>#wddxGetCourseList#</CFOUTPUT>
```

Now for the Flash code. There is actually nothing particularly special in this code, and if you are familiar with using Flash's XML object it should all make perfect sense. Once the XML is loaded, it is deserialized and the contents of the third row of the data printed to the output window.

2.   Open a new, blank movie, and open the Actions panel for the first frame.

3. The first line of code includes the external file, `wddx.as`. In our example, `wddx.as` is assumed to occupy the same directory location as the FLA we are currently editing. With this file included we can use the Wddxrecordset object.

```
#include "wddx.as"
```

4. We want the very last lines of code to:

- Instantiate a new WDDX object. We will use this object for deserializing XML.

- Instantiate an empty XML object.

- Replace the default `XML.onLoad` method with a custom behavior.

- Load the contents of the `test.cfm` file into the XML object. Make sure to use the fully qualified URL to the ColdFusion file you created in the previous section.

Therefore...

```
converter = new WDDX();
myXML = new XML();
myXML.onLoad = loaded;
myXML.load("http://localhost/Foed/test.cfm");
```

5. Our next step is to write the custom method we will use to replace the default `XML.onLoad` method. We'll place this function right after our call to include `wddx.as`.

```
function loaded(valid){
    [ . . . ]
}
```

6. The `onLoad` method fires after XML has been loaded. Flash will parse the XML and report to the `onLoad` method whether the XML is correctly formatted, by passing a Boolean result. Our function casts that parameter into a variable, `valid`. We will write our function to act if `valid` is true.

```
function loaded(valid){
    if (valid){
        [ . . . ]
    }
}
```

7. The next step is to call the WDDX deserialize method, using the converter WDDX object. The converter object acts as a factory... existing only to provide a way to operate on the XML object. We will set the results of the conversion into the `table` variable, which lives on the main timeline. These results will be the Flash native format of the data that ColdFusion serialized and passed into myXML, in this case a query recordset.

```
if (valid){
        //Deserialize the WDDX
        _root.table = _root.converter.deserialize(this);

        [ . . . ]
}
```

8. Now the XML has been deserialized and is available in a native format for ActionScript to manipulate. In this application we want to use the data to print to the screen so we will call another custom function, printRow(), that we will program below.

```
if (valid){
    [ . . .]

    //Print the 3rd row (rows start at 0)
    _root.printRow(_root.table, 2);
}
```

9. To make our printRow function work, we will pass it two parameters: the object containing the deserialized XML recordset and a number that tells us which row we're targeting.

```
function printRow(recordset, row){
    [ . . . ]
}
```

10. We will need to loop over the recordset to access the complete row of data. Query recordsets are stored in ColdFusion as associative arrays, with each column of data as an individual array of information. So, to completely print a row you need to access the array representing each column at a particular index location. Below is a visual representation of a recordset we could be working with.

CORNAME	DEPT_NAME
Calculus I	Mathematics
Calculus II	Mathematics
Linear Algebra	Mathematics

And, as this would be the loop that would access the *nth* row of data, we've added a trace action to provide some debugging feedback when the code has located the correct position:

```
//Loop over the contents of the recordset
    for (i in recordset){
        //Determine if the current property is a column
        if (recordset.isColumn(i)){
            trace(recordset.getField(row, i));
        }
    }
```

11. The completed code should look like this:

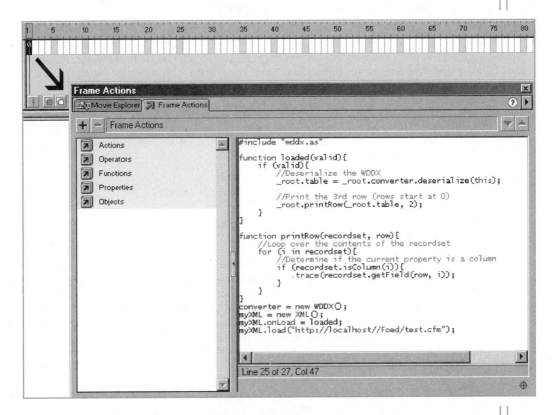

```
#include "wddx.as"

function loaded(valid){
    if (valid){
        //Deserialize the WDDX
        _root.table = _root.converter.deserialize(this);

        //Print the 3rd row (rows start at 0)
        _root.printRow(_root.table, 2);
    }
}

function printRow(recordset, row){
    //Loop over the contents of the recordset
    for (i in recordset){
        //Determine if the current property is a column
        if (recordset.isColumn(i)){
            .trace(recordset.getField(row, i));
        }
    }
}
converter = new WDDX();
myXML = new XML();
myXML.onLoad = loaded;
myXML.load("http://localhost//Foed/test.cfm");
```

Line 25 of 27, Col 47

Again, the entire block of code should be placed into the first frame of a blank movie. The URL that's called from the `myXML.load()` statement should be adjusted to match the location and name of the document on your system. Our example has the XML being created via a ColdFusion file named `test.cfm`, located in the same calling directory as the Flash movie.

To check the movie, you'll need to test from within the Flash authoring environment (Control > Test Movie). The only display we've programmed for the user is a `trace` action in the `printRow` function. Should you publish the movie to a SWF template and access it from the Web or via the Flash player you will see nothing but a blank movie.

Replacing the `onLoad` method of our `myXML` object, when the XML is loaded, the loaded function is called. This function first deserializes the XML into the `table` variable on the main timeline, then calls the `printRow` custom function which loops through the columns of `table` and prints out the second row of each.

Later, if you wanted to send the recordset back to ColdFusion, you would simply have to serialize it, and then send it using Flash's `loadVariables` action.

Creating an address book with WDDX

In order to see the benefits of using WDDX with Flash, it is best to see it in real action. Included on the CD that comes with this book is the full source code, including database, for an address book searching application that utilizes ColdFusion, Flash, and of course WDDX. It is a simple application and in fact, the next few pages describe how to build it yourself, nearly from scratch (though we won't make you recreate the database!)

In order to actually run the application you will need to install the database on the CD onto the server, which will involve uploading the database to the server and assigning it a **System DSN** name of `accessaddress`.

Creating a DSN

If you are already familiar with configuring a data source for use with ColdFusion, you should skip this section and move ahead to **How it will work**.

There are two easy ways to create a System DSN for use in your ColdFusion applications. If you are running a licensed copy of the server or a trial version, you will have access to the ColdFusion Administrator and can use it to create the data source. If running CFExpress on a Windows NT platform you will need to use the Data Source control panel. We'll go over instructions for both of these cases. The precise steps to find and manipulate the control panel do vary between versions of the Windows operating systems, but we'll be concentrating on the Windows 2000 version. If you are running CFExpress for Linux you should consult your system administrator for instructions on assigning system data sources.

Create DSN from ColdFusion Administrator

1. Locate and open the ColdFusion Administrator. By default the files are installed in your webroot: `http://localhost/cfide/administrator/index.cfm`.

2. In the left-hand navigation frame locate the section labeled data sources. The first link will be ODBC. Click on this link to jump to the **ODBC Data Sources** area. From this screen you will see a list of all, or most, of the system data sources on the ColdFusion Server. The only data sources that will not be seen here are those that have been given names including illegal ColdFusion characters. Legal characters are numbers, letters and the underscore character.

3. The database we'll be using is an Access file, so we'll need to create a data source that uses the Access Driver. Enter a name for your data source in the Data Source Name text-box, and make sure that the ODBC Driver drop-down list is displaying Microsoft Access Driver (*.mdb). Click the ADD button.

Data Source Name	ODBC Driver	
accessaddress	Microsoft Access Driver (*.mdb) ▾	Add...

4. The next screen, Create ODBC Data Source, is where you enter the database connection parameters. For our simple Access database all that is necessary is the data source name, which we have already supplied, and the path to the location of the .mdb data file on the server. The Browse Server button next to the Database File textbox will open a Java applet allowing you to visually browse the ColdFusion server's directory structure to find your file and programmatically fill in the correct path. Of the other parameters we could fill in, none are mandatory although some can significantly affect the performance of our application under user load.

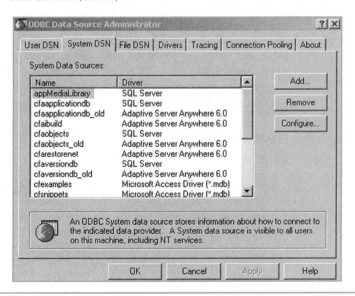

5. When finished, click the Create button. You will return to the previous screen where you'll now see your new data source appear in the list. If your information was correct you'll see the word Verified appear under the Status column of your data source.

Create DSN from ODBC control panel

1. Locate and open the ODBC Data Source Administrator control panel. On a Windows 2000 machine this can be found by navigating Start Menu > Programs > Administrative Tools > Data Sources (ODBC).

2. Click on the System DSN tab to bring it to the front. Click the Add button to begin the process of configuring a new data source.

3. Select an Access driver from the list of those installed on the system. There may be many different drivers that are associated with Access. If there is one called Microsoft Access Driver (*.mdb), select this. With the driver selected, click the Finish button.

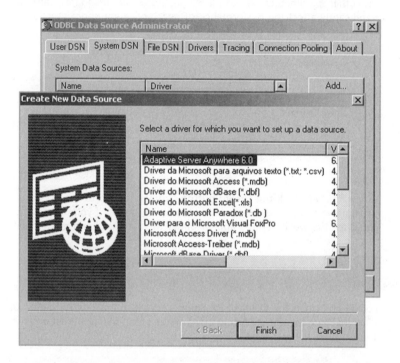

4. On this next screen, enter the name for the data source text-box. Next, click the Select button to choose the Access file to which this data source will be linked.

5.   The Select button will open a system file browser. Navigate to the directory where the `address.mdb` file is located and select it. With the file selected, click the OK button to return to the previous screen.

6.   Click the OK button. Now the configuration is complete and you will be returned to the tabbed interface of the ODBC control panel.

How it will all work

Back to our main exercise, and to start off it's necessary to understand exactly how the application will work.

- Users will initially be presented with a Flash form where they can enter the first and/or last name of the person they are searching for.

- Then, by pressing a button, the information they entered will be passed to a ColdFusion template.

- This CFM file will use this information to query the address database. It will then take those query results, serialize them into WDDX, and pass the WDDX back to Flash.

- The Flash movie will then advance to another screen where it will display a list of all of the persons matching the search criteria. If the user clicks on one of the names, further information about that person will be displayed, including the selected person's email address, role, and birthday.

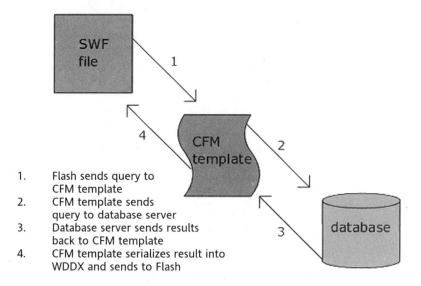

1. Flash sends query to CFM template
2. CFM template sends query to database server
3. Database server sends results back to CFM template
4. CFM template serializes result into WDDX and sends to Flash

The first thing we have to create is the CFM file.

Putting WDDX into action

1. This file has to accept two URL variables, `firstName` and `lastName`, and query the database accordingly. Also, just like our previous example with ColdFusion, it has to use `CFSILENT` and `CFSETTING` to suppress whitespace. Below is the full ColdFusion code, which you should save as `getAddress_flash.cfm`. You will notice that there really isn't much to it!

```
<!-- Use CFSILENT and CFSETTING to suppress all
white space generated by ColdFusion -->

<cfsilent>

<cfsetting enablecfoutputonly="Yes" showdebugoutput="No">

<!-- Cast the URL parameters into local variables if they have
been passed with value.-->

    <cfif isdefined('url.firstname') and
➥ len(trim(url.firstname))>
        <cfset variables.firstname = url.firstname>
    </cfif>
    <cfif isdefined('url.lastname') and len(trim(url.lastname))>
        <cfset variables.lastname = url.lastname>
    </cfif>

<!-- Query the database to bring back all values if no URL
parameters were passed with value , or bring back only  records
that match url parameters. Use 0=0 placeholder in the Where
clause of the sql statement to allow ColdFusion to dynamically
append filter statements -->

    <CFQUERY NAME="queryGetData" DATASOURCE="accessaddress">
        SELECT
                PersonID, FirstName, LastName, Role,
                ➥ BirthDate, EmailAddress
        FROM
                addresses
        Where 0=0
                <cfif isdefined('variables.firstname')>
                        AND FirstName = '#variables.FirstName#'
                </cfif>
                <cfif isdefined('variables.lastname')>
                        AND LastName = '#variables.LastName#'
                </cfif>
        Order By LastName, FirstName
    </CFQUERY>
```

```
<!—         Serialize query into an XML packet with the CFWDDX
tag.  Set action attribute to "CFML2WDDX". Provide variable
holding query results as object to be serialized. Provide name of
variable to be created, holding WDDX XML object.  —->

<cfwddx action="CFML2WDDX" input="#queryGetData#"
➡ output="wddxGetData">

</cfsilent>

<!—- Output the serialized query so Flash can call the page and
load the XML.—->

<cfif queryGetData.recordcount>
    <cfoutput>#wddxGetData#</cfoutput>
</cfif>
```

2. Now, if you upload this file to your server and then navigate to it with your web browser, you can search through the address like this:

   www.myserver.com/getAddress_Flash.cfm?lastName=Davolio

   You will get back a WDDX packet that contains a serialized result of the ColdFusion query, which returned all of the people in the address database whose last name is Davolio. Exactly what we wanted!

FIRSTNAME	LASTNAME	PERSONID	ROLE
Paul	Davolio	1	Self
Constance	Davolio	2	Wife
Kathleen	Davolio	3	Child

   Now we deal with what the user sees, the Flash movie...

3. For the sake of simplicity, the movie will exist in two scenes: one for entering the search criteria and one for viewing the search results. The first scene we'll be creating is the one for entering search criteria. First, it must include the wddx.as file. The function that will be run when the XML from the CFM file is loaded needs to be defined next. This function has to deserialize the XML and advance the main timeline to jump to the next scene. Then, instances of the WDDX and XML objects need to be created.

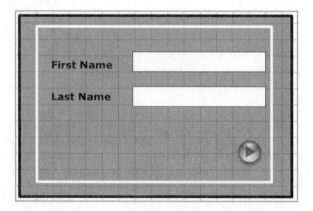

```
Frame Actions                                                              x
Movie Explorer  Frame Actions  Instance  Frame                          ?
+  -  Frame Actions                                                     ▼▲
#include "wddx.as"

function recievedResults(goodXML){
    _root.result = this.toString();
    if (goodXML){
        _root.queryResults = _root.converter.deserialize(this);
        _root.play();
    }
}

converter = new WDDX();
remoteData = new XML();
remoteData.onLoad = recievedResults;
first = "";
last = "";
stop();


◄                                                                    ►
Line 16 of 16, Col 8                                                    ⊕
```

You'll notice that we are also setting two variables, `first` and `last`, to blank strings. These are the Flash variables we will pass to the CFM file, so you will want to place on the stage two input text boxes with their variables set to `first` and `last`, respectively.

4. Finally for this scene we need to add a button that will cause the Flash variables to pass to the CFM file and put the results into our XML object.

First Name

Last Name

5. Put this code on the button:

```
Object Actions                                                             x
Movie Explorer  Object Actions  Instance  Frame                         ?
+  -  Object Actions                                                    ▼▲
on(press){
    remoteData.load("getAddressData_flash.cfm?firstName="+first+"&lastName="+last);
}

◄                                                                    ►
Line 3 of 3, Col 2
```

Now we can move onto the search results scene.

There will need to be a number of text fields on the stage that will display the results of the search. First of all, there must be a large text field on the left that will display a full list of all of the names received from the search. This text box needs to be set to render HTML and display the variable names. The reason the field should be set to display HTML is because each name will have been written with an anchor tag that passes a variable to a function in this scene. This way, when a name is clicked, the user will be able to view the details about the person they selected in the other five text fields, placed on the stage to display those details.

These five fields simply need to be single line text fields set to display the variables firstName, lastName, emailAddress, birthDate, and role respectively. The finished file on the CD also includes a back button and scroll buttons for the names field, but those are not required:

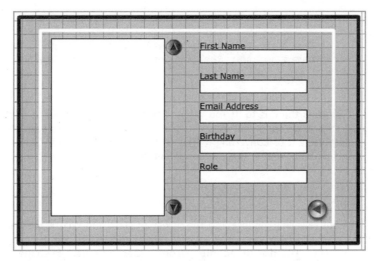

6.   Now, we just need to add the code to the first (and only) frame of this scene. This code has to take the queryResults recordset that was created by the deserialization of the XML we loaded from the CFM file. We also need to make a function that will fill in those detail fields when we click on one of the names. That function is pretty simple; it will just get passed the row from the recordset that should be displayed and then fill in the appropriate variables.

```
function displayInfo(i){
     firstName = queryResults.getField(i, "firstName");
     lastName = queryResults.getField(i, "lastName");
     bDate = queryResults.getField(i, "birthDate");
          if (bDate != ""){
               birthDate = (bDate.getMonth()
          ➡ +1)+"/"+(bDate.getDate());
          }else{
```

continues overleaf

```
                        birthDate = "Not known";
                }
        emailAddress = queryResults.getField(i, "emailAddress");
        role = queryResults.getField(i, "role");
}
```

7. Finally, we need to write the code that will fill in the names text field. We'll be taking advantage of a special thing that you can do with the anchor tag (<A>) in Flash. By specifying that the URL for the anchor tag is asfunction you can then make the link call an ActionScript function (i.e. asfunction:displayInfo). You can even pass that function an argument by appending to the function name a comma and then the desired value (i.e. asfunction:displayInfo,1). So, as you might have figured out, each name displayed in the names text field will actually link to call our displayInfo function and tell it which row of information to display.

```
names = "";
for (i=0;i<queryResults.getRowCount();++i){
    names += "<a href='asfunction:displayInfo,"+i+"'>";
    names += queryResults.getField(i,"lastName")+", ";
    names += queryResults.getField(i,"firstName")+"<br>";
}
stop();
```

8. That's all there is to it! You will notice that there is really not a lot of code involved in this application, and most of the code is devoted to displaying the data, rather than importing it or converting it. This is the power of WDDX in action; you can focus on presentation rather than data manipulation.

Summary

In this short but revealing glimpse into the power of Flash and WDDX, we learned that:

- WDDX is downloadable from Macromedia Exchange for Flash at www.macromedia.com/exchange/flash.

- Web Distributed Data eXchange uses XML as a universal language to transfer information between Flash and your server.

- Serializing data turns it into XML and deserializing data converts it back into a readable (native) form.

- WDDX does the hard work for us, allowing us to concentrate on building the front end of our dynamic web pages.

Section 5
Real World
Dynamic Content

28
Flash News Site

Chapter 27
Flash Gaming

Is it possible to create a game using Flash?

Most Flash designers will have thought about this – usually followed with "and if it is possible, where do I start"? Although not specifically designed for game development, Flash 5 combines both the programming platform and the tools necessary to develop surprisingly advanced games. So as long as you never undervalue the need for solid planning and storyboarding, yes, it's very possible. We'll look at a game development case study game in this chapter, by looking at the components of a game application (available on the CD), all the way from the frontend elements, to the ASP pages that keep track of players' scores. We'll work through it like this:

- Constructing a game environment in Flash: giving the user the information they need to get started.

- Creating the user interface: importing a neat backdrop to use for the game landscape, and converting it to a vector to use in Flash.

- Creating and animating the game's characters and the user's navigation: animated robots, the player's interactivity, and a crosshair mouse-tracker navigation system.

- And finally, linking to a database though ASP to save and display high scores.

The complete game is on the accompanying CD, so you can go right ahead and try it to get a quick feel for what this chapter will help you accomplish! Many more Flash games (and tutorials) can be found on www.flashkit.com.

The game I've developed is **Martian Mayhem**; the goal of this game being to rid the planet Mars of invading robots.... this was just used as an example, I'm sure you're more than capable of thinking up of your own tacky plots!

There are many different approaches to creating games in Flash; we will show you just one of them, keep in mind that many different techniques can often be used to achieve the same result.

Before we begin working though, you might want to see what kind of score you can get on Martian Madness. Feel free to deconstruct the FLA and examine it as much as you like – bear in mind there's a lot in there that we just don't have time to cover in the chapter. I've compromised a little between showing you the kind of game that is within your reach and the kind of game you can create in the space of a chapter!

Constructing a game environment

Let's start by taking a look at the overall game environment. A game interface often has Start and Quit buttons, together with other things you might see like high-scores, and then game-specific information like *lives left*, or *baddies killed*, or *remaining bullets*, the list goes on.

If your game is particularly long, remember you might also want a Pause button – there's nothing worse than being in the middle of a great Flash game and then the doorbell rings!

Games need to be as clear as possible about letting the user know what they can do and how, so that the player can always easily see what's going on. Let's deconstruct the game environment of the game on the CD:

OK, so what are the elements here?

- A score indicator in the top right corner. This is a simple dynamic text field with a variable called `intScore`.

- Five icons in the shape of little men in the lower left part of the screen, representing how many lives the player has remaining. Every time a robot's laser hits a player, he loses a life – it's that simple!

- Remaining ammunition is indicated at the bottom right-hand corner of the screen by five bullet icons. Each time the player fires their weapon the number of bullets is decreased by one. Once all the bullets have been used, the player must click on the Reload button to reload their weapon, and the number of bullets remaining will then be set back to five.

■   I've used a mouse-tracking crosshair for effect; I'll show you how this was done later on.

Let's investigate further, looking at the different actions and movie clips located on the main stage.

Building the foundations of a Flash game

1.   First, I created a new movie, and gave it an Actions layer, and declared the variables that I need for the movie:

```
intScore = 0;              /* player's score */
lives = 5;                 /* remaining lives */
bullets = 5;               /* remaining bullets */
strName = "";               /* name of the player */
```

Then I created two sound objects. Sound objects are useful when you need quite a lot of control over your sound files. They allow you to have full control over *how* and *when* sounds are played.

2.   To create the a sound object, you simply assign the new Sound object to a variable of your choice:

```
sndMissile = new Sound(); /* new sound object */
```

Once the sound object is initialized, you can attach a sound file to it. The name used to refer to the sound file is specified in the Symbol Linkage Properties of the sound file. Simply right-click on the sound file in the library, and then select Linkage. Click on Export this symbol and enter a suitable identifier name.

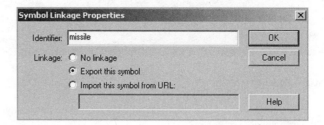

This identifier name is the name you must use to attach the sound file to the sound object:

```
sndMissile.attachSound("missile"); /* attach shooting sound to
object */
```

Remember, you'll need to do this for both the missile sound and the empty ammunition clip sound.

3. Once I'd put all of this together, my code looked like this:

```
intScore = 0;                        /* player's score */
lives = 5;                           /* remaining lives */
bullets = 5;                         /* remaining bullets */
strName = "";                        /* name of the player */
sndMissile = new Sound();            /* new sound object */
sndMissile.attachSound("missile");   /* attach shooting sound to object */
sndEmpty = new Sound();              /* new sound object */
sndEmpty.attachSound("empty");       /* attach empty ammo clip sound to
                                     /* object */
```

Once I'd got all the necessary variables declared, I started creating the different graphical elements on the main stage.

You'll normally need to create some graphics for a game environment. For this particular game, this meant producing the background, the bullets, the enemies, the buttons, the text labels, and, of course, the Martian landscape.

> *I built most of the graphics used in this example using Freehand for quicker creation, but the same effects can be achieved in Flash, Illustrator and most vector-based tools. Once I'd got it into Flash, I did some fine-tuning and made some minor modifications, like adding text and sound.*

4. On the main stage, I created a new layer called Intro Screen, putting a short text message on the first frame describing the storyline for the game:

5. Then I created a new layer called Labels to look after the different processing stages of the movie. I gave frame 1 the label Intro, and the second frame Start, and then I added a stop action to the first frame of the Actions layer.

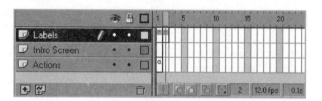

6. Then I created the movie clips that display the number of lives the player has left. I created a movie clip called lives_left containing 6 keyframes with a stop action in each of them. The 1st frame needs to display five little men, the 2nd frame four little men, and so on, until frame 6, which doesn't have any little men. I used multiple instances of the same movie for each little man, to reduce file size.

Frame one looks like this:

7. Then all I had to do was drag an instance of the new movie clip into frame 2 of another new layer, Lives on the main stage, giving it the instance name mClives.

8. I created the ammunition display in much the same way. I used a movie clip called bullets_left, again with six frames. The first frame shows five bullets, the second frame four bullets, and so on, until frame six, which doesn't have any bullets. As with the little men, I used multiple instances of the same movie. I also used a new layer underneath the bullets, inside the movie clip, in order to create 'bullet holders' that become empty as the bullets are fired. For example, frame 2 of the bullets_left movie looks like this:

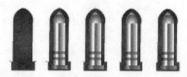

9. I put this movie clip in frame 1 of a new layer, Bullets, on the main stage, and gave it the instance name mCbullets.

> *Throughout this chapter, remember you can always refer to the finished movie to check your own work against mine. Maybe the best way to learn would be to mix building a game from scratch with taking apart and examining the final Martian Madness FLA.*

Later on, I set the movie to loop back to frame 2, so as to have continuous gameplay (looping the onslaught of Martian robots until the player is dead), and so I had to add some script to ensure that the mClives and mCbullets movie clips didn't restart from scratch every time (that wouldn't be much of a game!).

10. I added an action on frame 2 of the Actions layer that sets the mClives and mCbullets movie clip instances to the appropriate frame, depending on the values of the lives and bullets variables (as they had been defined earlier). So if the bullet count equals 2, for example, mCbullet will be told go to frame 4, which displays two bullets. Without this action, mClives and mCbullets would go back to frame one every time the movie looped.

```
if (lives == 5) {
_root.mClives.gotoAndStop (1);
} else if (lives==4) {
    _root.mClives.gotoAndStop (2);
} else if (lives==3) {
    _root.mClives.gotoAndStop (3);
} else if (lives==2) {
    _root.mClives.gotoAndStop (4);
} else if (lives==1) {
    _root.mClives.gotoAndStop (5);
}
```

And again, this time for the bullets:

```
if (bullets == 5) {
_root.mCbullets.gotoAndStop (1);
} else if (bullets==4) {
    _root.mCbullets.gotoAndStop (2);
} else if (bullets==3) {
    _root.mCbullets.gotoAndStop (3);
} else if (bullets==2) {
    _root.mCbullets.gotoAndStop (4);
} else if (bullets==1) {
    _root.mCbullets.gotoAndStop (5);
}
```

11. Then I set up a loop using a gotoAndPlay action on frame 180 of the Actions layer on the main stage:

```
gotoAndPlay (2);
```

12. Finally, I set up a dynamic text box to display the user's score, on the first frame of a new layer called Score. I gave the dynamic text-box the variable name intScore , and placed it at the top right corner.

So that's the basic infrastructure. Let's look at how I got that lovely Martian backdrop.

Creating the Martian landscape

I needed some kind of backdrop for the game. A pretty neat way of getting a plausible backdrop to your game, without creating too much work for yourself, is to take a photograph of somewhere that looks suitable, and to then use that photograph as a source to work from.

So, even if you do have a friend in NASA, you'll probably still find it easier and quicker to fake one! Just find somewhere interesting and imagine it naked – with no details or signs or complex textures.

1. I started by taking a panoramic picture of a nearby park. If you dim your eyes, you can see how this matches onto the movie, once I'd ground it down to its basic ingredients.

2. You can then use a paint or photo package to play around with the image. Elements such as planets and stars can be added, to give it an "otherworldly" effect. You don't need to make them too detailed, and you can also if necessary take out superfluous bus stations, pedestrians, dogs, lamp-posts and Coke cans that might have found their way into your photo!

3. My file was imported into Flash as a JPEG, but it could be any supported picture format. I used the Trace Bitmap command (Modify > Trace Bitmap) to convert the file into vector-based shapes (this makes the file size smaller and the image infinitely resizable – very important as you'll know in Flash).

4. You can also achieve exactly the effect you want by playing around with Corner Threshold, Color Threshold and Curve Fit options in the Trace Bitmap dialog box – these define how much detail goes into your converted image and how true it is to the original. (If you're using the local McDonald's for a game landscape, you might want your vector conversion to be as *vague* as possible.)

5. I saved this background as a button, called Background, so that it can be used to process shots that do not hit the robots. I also added an overlay, equal to the size of the background, on the hit frame of the button.

6. I put the new button on the main stage, on a new layer called Martian Terrain under the Lives, Bullets and Score layers. Then I used the on (press) event handler of the button to process shots that do not hit the robots (in other words, shots that hit the landscape).

```
on (press) {
     if (bullets > 0) {
            sndMissile.start();
            bullets = bullets - 1;
            _root.mCbullets.nextFrame ();
     } else {
            sndEmpty.start();
                }
}
```

What's going on here? Well, if there are still bullets left in the clip, then the missile sound plays, 1 is subtracted from the bullets variable, and the mCbullets movie goes to the next frame which will then display one less bullet. If there aren't any bullets left in the clip, the empty ammunition clip sound is played, indicating to the user that they must reload before shooting again.

I also implemented a flashing sequence that's triggered each time the player takes a hit from a robot's shot. To do this I just made landscape flash alternately between red and green.

7. I created a new movie clip called hit_screen, inserted a blank keyframe on frame 1 and added a stop action. I put a rectangle the size of the Martian landscape on each of the frames 2 through 6, making the color of each rectangle red or green on each alternate frame. I also made the rectangles slightly transparent to give the desired effect.

8. Then I went back to the main stage and created a new layer, Hit screen. I put the hit_screen movie clip in frame 2, and gave it the instance name `Hit_screen`.

9. To complete the game interface, I added the buttons to let the user decide what they wanted to do. I created a layer called Buttons, and put three buttons on it, labeled: Quit, Start and High Scores.

The Quit button, uses a `gotoAndStop` action pointing to the frame labeled Intro (corresponding to frame 1).

```
on (release) {
    gotoAndStop ("Intro");
}
```

The Start button action points to the frame labeled Start, which starts the game:

```
on (release) {
stop();
    gotoAndPlay ("Start");
}
```

Before we move on, remember you can check with the supplied FLA to see where you should be by now!

So, to recap, by this stage in the development of the game, I have a basic structure of layers: an intro screen, a nifty Martian backdrop, some buttons and a neat way to keep track of lives and bullets – the two things you'll definitely need if you're fighting robots on Mars!

But what about those robots?

Invading robots could be anything from simple static robots moving horizontally on the screen, to complex fully-fledged 3-D animations. I wanted to create something with some kick to it, without sacrificing the relatively small file size. I decided to use wire-frames. By designing the robots as wire-frames (practically stick figures) and with the help of some frame-by-frame animation, I could create the robots without increasing the file size too much. You'll see, if you've tested the movie, that the robots look as if they were actually walking on the Martian landscape. So let's look at that bit next.

I created the robots for this example using **Curious Labs Poser** (Curious Labs Poser was formerly known as **Metacreations Poser** - software used to easily create very realistic 3D humanoid models). It's also possible to draw them frame-by-frame directly in Flash or any other vector-based software, although the process would take longer. The kind of movements needed depend on what you want your robots to do, but basic movements such as walking left to right, right to left, and turning to face the gamer are basic requirements. Death throes are for if you're feeling confident!

After playing around with different movements and positions, as well as with the number of frames needed for smooth movement, I finally achieved a desirable result with my Martians. Building the robots as simple wire-frames meant that I could get a lower the level of detail: just enough to keep the movie size relatively low, while maintaining plausible robot figures. You can of course create your figures however you feel comfortable.

Creating the animated robots

1. So, once I'd drawn a robot, I exported the frames in a 3DS (3D Studio) format from Poser. To convert the 3D objects to vector-based objects, I used Swift 3D and exported them again, this time in AI (Illustrator) format.

2.   Back in Flash, I created a new movie clip called robot walk shoot and imported the frame sequence. I created the walking effect by placing slightly different robots one frame after the other, although the robot is walking in thin air, and on the spot at this stage.

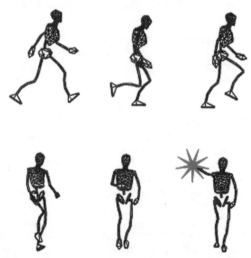

> *Frame-by-frame animations can be very nice, but the more frames you have, the larger your Flash file will be. The moral of the story is this: try to keep the number of frames to a minimum.*

My robot walks on the spot, through frames 1 to 20, facing towards the right. It stops walking and turns around to shoot in frames 21 though 38, and faces the other direction from frames 38 to 58. I used a label at frame 1 called alive, since the movements from frame 1 to frame 58 are the ones we want to use when the robot is alive (this frame comes into play later on.) I finished with a stop action on frame 58.

Although the robot is not moving an awful lot in frames 21 to 38, a lot is happening – the robot shoots three times, on frames 25, 27, 29, and plays a sound as it does.

3.   The robot needs to be able to hit or disable the player with a shot. I created this capability at frame 29, making the robot hit his target (the player) at random. I only let the robot strike once with each attack, so the three blasts only count as one hit – I had to give players a chance! Anyway, here's what the code looks like:

The script begins by declaring the `shot` variable and assigning it a random value between 0 and 2 (the random method outputs a random value starting at 0, which is why the third number is 2 and not 3). If `shot` is equal to 1, the robot hits his target and the player loses a life. If not, nothing happens. So the robot hits the player on average once in every three attacks – but of course, if the robot is blasted before it has time to shoot, the player is safe!

The code that gives the Martian skeleton robot a fighting chance breaks down like this:

```
shot = 0;
shot = Number(random(3));
```

When the robot hits his target, the player loses a life, so the value of the `lives` variable is reduced by 1, and the `mClives` movie clip on the main stage (showing the number of lives left) is moved on to the next frame, displaying one less life than the previous frame (five little men on frame 1, four little men on frame 2, etc.).

```
if (shot == 1) {
    _level0.lives = _level0.lives-1;
    _level0.mClives.nextFrame();
```

Then the hit screen (the colorful, flashing overlay that indicates to the player that he has been shot) is displayed:

```
    _level0.hit_screen.gotoAndPlay(2);
```

Finally, the number of lives left is checked. If it's 0, then the game is over and the player is forwarded to the appropriate frame (a frame labeled GameOver on the main stage), which will then allow him to save his high score.

```
if (_level0.lives == 0) {
        root.gotoAndStop("GameOver");
        }
    }
```

OK, time for another quick summary. The Martian landscape background and player buttons have been joined by a robot invader character, who walks around a bit and shoot at the player. The robot's shots have been dealt with, as have those shots that hit the player. Well, you probably know what's coming now... payback time...

The player strikes back

1. The robot needs to respond somehow when it's shot – like, well, die – so I added a new label, disabled, to frame 60 of the labels layer in the robot walk shoot movie clip. When I was building this game, I decided to represent the robot dying by using quickly flashing static (like you get on a TV with no reception) and then a fade. I used the following images for the static, and to add credibility to the overall effect, I incorporated a sound.

Frames 60 & 65   Frames 61-64 & 66-70

    Once I'd done that, all I needed was a stop action to frame 70 to prevent the movie from looping.

2. Then I created a new movie clip, called robot walk shoot moving, to make the robot advance as its legs move. If you used something other than frame-by-frame animation (in other words, just having a still picture of the robot), this is where you would put the enemy.

    I put the robot walk shoot movie clip on the timeline of the robot walk shoot moving movie clip, and gave it the instance name robot1.

    I created motion tweens for the robot's movements, to make him move according to the frame-by-frame movements. So the robot walk shoot moving movie clip had to contain at least 58 frames, because 58 frames corresponds to the length of the alive portion of the robot walk shoot movie clip.

I created two tweens, one between frames 1 and 25 that move the robot towards the right by a few inches, and another going in the other direction between frames 36 and 58.

The robot doesn't move in any direction between frames 21 and 38, (he's turning and shooting at the player!), so I left that section free of tweens and simply added a keyframe at frame 38.

3.   Of course, in the heat of the game, that simple right to left action will be seen as the invading monster cowering and fleeing from the player's onslaught of bullets!

4.   I used another variable to verify whether a robot can be shot or not. I set this at frame 1, called it `alive` and gave it the value 1. I also used a `gotoAndPlay` action to tell `robot1` to go to the first frame and play. I only had to do this when the clip loops, because the looping allows the robots to come back on the screen again and again:

```
alive = 1;
```

5.   Then I set up the player's ability to shoot and hit the robot, using a button. I created a new layer and put an empty button over the robot (one with only a hit area, the same size as the robot.) I created the same motion tweens for the button as I did for the robot, so the button always stays over the robot.

Then I added the code to the button that will process the player's shots at the robot:

```
on (press) {
     if (_level0.bullets > 0 && alive ==1) {
                 _level0.sndMissile.start();
                 stop ();
                 _level0.bullets = _level0.bullets - 1;
                 alive = 0;
                 _level0.mCbullets.nextFrame ();
                 level0.robot1.gotoAndPlay ("disabled");
                 _level0.intScore = _level0.intScore + 10;
             } else {
             _level0.sndEmpty.start();
     }
}
```

Let's walk though it. The first part says that if there are still bullets in the clip and the robot is alive, the `sndMissile` sound object will be played and the `robot1` movie clip is stopped so the robot stops moving:

```
if (_root.bullets > 0 && alive ==1) {
            _ level0.sndMissile.start();
                     stop ();
```

The value of `bullets` is reduced by one, and the `alive` variable is set to 0, so that the robot can't be shot again:

```
_level0.bullets = _level0.bullets - 1;
                        alive = 0;
```

The movie plays the next frame in the `mCbullets` movie, located on the main stage, to display one less bullet:

```
_level0.mCbullets.nextFrame ();
```

Then the robot is disabled:

```
level0.robot1.gotoAndPlay ("disabled");
```

And the player is awarded 10 points, which are added to the `intScore` variable on the main stage:

```
_level0.intScore = _level0.intScore + 10;
```

The final section of the code deals with situations when there are no more bullets loaded into the player's weapon. In this case, the `sndEmpty` sound object located on the main stage is played.

```
} else {
        _level0.sndEmpty.start ();
    }
}
```

Well, one robot with a bit of an attitude is hardly an invasion, so I'll show you how I added another robot (with slightly different behavior) to the game. I know what you're thinking, "two robots hardly constitutes the planet Mars being overrun with irate androids". Well, yes, but the fact is, it's the same methodology to create one more as it is to create a hundred more: you can use as many instances of your own robots as you want (and I'll show you how next). So, if you do want to create huge invading forces for your player to turn into bean cans, these two example robots should provide you with enough of the concept and methodology to take your player into gun-toting nirvana.

I used the second robot to walk in the background of the game, adding some depth of field to the game environment. Creating the walking robot is very simple, especially as, instead of shooting, this robot only walks in the background. I decided to make the robot smaller and faster, and as compensation for the player, award 15 points for shooting it.

Basically, I used the same imported frame-by-frame animation that I used to create the robot walk shoot movie clip but removed everything after frame 20 and just called it robot walk. The process is really pretty simple.

Building the robot invasion

1. I created a new movie clip called robot walk, and inserted the frame-by-frame walking pattern.

Then I set up the tweening, using keyframes at frame 1 and 20, and moving the robot horizontally by a few inches at frame 35. Then I set the alive variable to 1 in the 1st frame:

```
alive = 1;
```

I set the movie to loop back to frame 1 at frame 20:

```
gotoAndPlay (1);
```

2. Then I copied the disabled frames from the previous robot and pasted them in at frame 20 labeling the frame disabled.

3. Finally, I had to create a way for the background robot to be shot, so I made another new movie clip, Robot Walking, and pasted in the Robot Walk movie clip, giving it the instance name walk_robot. I added the button over the robot so that he could be shot, exactly the same way as I created the previous robot; adding a new layer to hold the button, and making sure that the button motion tweened with the robot at all times. The actions for this button are very similar to the previous one – although this time I awarded the player 15 points instead of 10.

```
on (press) {
    if (_level0.bullets > 0 && alive ==1) {
            _level0.sndMissile.start();
            stop ();
            alive = 0;
            _level0.bullets = _level0.bullets - 1;
            _level0.mCbullets.nextFrame ();
            _root.walk_robot.gotoAndPlay ("disabled");
            _level0.intScore = _level0.intScore + 15;
    } else {
            _level0.sndEmpty.start();
    }
}
```

Once I'd created the two robot types, I went back to the main stage to begin placing them.

Putting the robots on the stage

1. I created a new layer called Robot 1 on the main stage, and put an instance of the robot walk shoot moving **movie clip** at frame 2 on the left side of the screen, giving it the instance name `mCrobot1`.

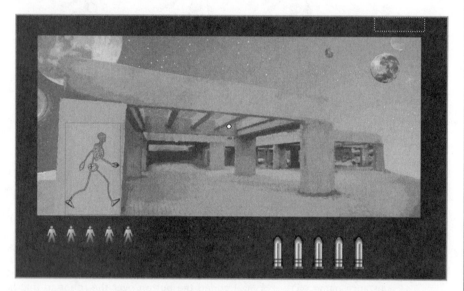

2. With the number of columns and hiding places in the Martian terrain, it seemed logical to use layer masks to give the player an impression of perspective, as the robots can then walk 'behind' columns and obstacles. Layer masks in fact work counter-intuitively, allowing viewers to see the objects only when they are, in fact, behind the mask – the mask acts as a window through which we can see the object.

    I placed my mask to the right of the Robot, like this (the robot will only appear to the player when it's under the blue square, giving the impression that it's coming from behind the column):

3. Then I created a new layer called robot2 and inserted another instance of robot walk shoot moving, this time on frame 60. I named the instance mCrobot2, and flipped the robot horizontally to make it walk in the opposite direction (Modify > Transform > Flip Horizontal), scaling it by about 70% and placing it on the right-hand side of the screen.

4. Then I created a new layer called Robot 3, making sure that the layer was under the Robot 1 and Robot 2 layers.

> *Creating a fresh layer for each robot might work out to be a bit heavy for a final game, but it's a good way of illustrating how they all work.*

I put the robot walking movie clip on frame 6, and give it the instance name mCrobot3, flipped it horizontally, and scaled it by about 40%. I put it towards the back of the scene (remember, this guy's going to be set way back in the distance; he doesn't shoot and he's worth 15 points)

> *To give your robots different colors, play with the tints in the Effects panel.*

You can add as many robots as you wish using the same process; just keep the question of computer resources in mind. If you add too many robots, the game will be sluggish and not playable at all.

Let's take a look at the final product:

Have a look at all those different game elements – they looked pretty complicated at first glance, but once you break it down into parts: the game area, the lives counter, the bullets counter, the buttons, the all-important robots, and the basic interactions that let the robots shoot and be shot – it's really not that complex.

You're probably wondering though "What about the high scores, the crosshair, the reload button – you mentioned databases!" Well, we're not quite finished yet.

Building the crosshair mouse tracker

1. I created a new layer for the crosshair mouse tracker called crosshair tracker on the main stage. Then I created a new movie clip symbol, crosshair with three layers: one for the actions, elements and lines each with about 12 frames.

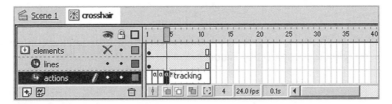

2. There are two pieces to the crosshair: a center movie clip – a small circle, about the size of a coin, with a white fill; and a movie clip called line – a line resembling a ruler.

3. Back inside the crosshair movie clip, I dragged an instance of line onto the elements layer and gave it the instance name vert. Then I put another line movie clip on the same layer, rotating it by 90° and giving it the instance name horiz. To finish off, I put the center movie clip in the middle where the two line movie clips met, and gave it the instance name center. Then I had something that looks a bit like a sniper crosshair.

4. Back on the main stage, I created a layer called coordinates and created two dynamic text fields; one with the variable name coordx (for horizontal mouse coordinates) and the other with the variable name coordy (for vertical mouse coordinates).

5. I created an invisible button, invisible button, containing a hit area the size of the main stage. I put this button inside a new movie clip, tracker. I added some code from the invisible button to inside the tracker clip, using an on (rollOver) event together with a startDrag action, to start it tracking and updating the mouse coordinates.

The button coordinates are used to update the tracker movie clip, so I set the target of the startDrag to _root.tracker (later on I put the tracker movie clip on the main stage, giving it the instance name tracker). I also updated the coordx and coordy values with the mouse position values.

```
on (rollOver) {
    startDrag (_root.tracker, true);
    _root.coordx = _root.tracker._x;
    _root.coordy = _root.tracker._y;
}
```

6. I made the tracker clip loop infinitely, so that it updates the information constantly, using a gotoAndPlay action:

```
gotoAndPlay(1);
```

At the 2nd frame, I inserted a call action to call a frame labeled tracking – and I put that frame label at frame 4.

```
call("tracking");
```

Then I used a keyframe at frame 3 to send the movie back to frame 2. This allows the movie to loop so that the variables can be updated in real-time.

```
gotoAndPlay(2);
```

7. Finally, to complete the crosshair section, I used a setProperty action to set the target to vert (remember we earlier gave that instance name to one of the Line movie clips). I set the _x value (Xposition) to _root.coordx, which records the horizontal mouse coordinates, and then did the same thing for the horiz instance (the horiz _y takes the value of _root.coordy). I used two setProperty actions for the center movie clip, one for the _y position and one for the _x position.

```
setProperty ("vert", _x, _root.coordx - 400);
setProperty ("horiz", _y, _root.coordy -240);
setProperty ("centre", _y, _root.coordy -240);
setProperty ("centre", _x, _root.coordx -400);
```

And that's it, the crosshair is complete. This type of effect can be used in any type of Flash movie, be it a game, an animation or a web site.

Saving high scores

Once the game is over, and the lives variable hits 0, the game automatically takes you to the GameOver frame.

1. I created this label at frame 181 of the main stage, and created a new movie clip called game over screen. This movie clip carries the player's score, and a button that allows him to save his score. I used a dynamic text field, with the variable name `_level0.intScore`, to display the user's score.

2. The score saving button has some actions behind it that sends the movie to the frame labeled Save on the main stage when the button is clicked:

```
on (release) {
    _root.gotoAndStop ("Save");
}
```

So then, of course, I needed that frame label, Save, which I put at frame 183 of the actions of the main scene. I also put an input box with the variable name strName at the same frame, with a save button, like so, and some text asking the user to input their name:

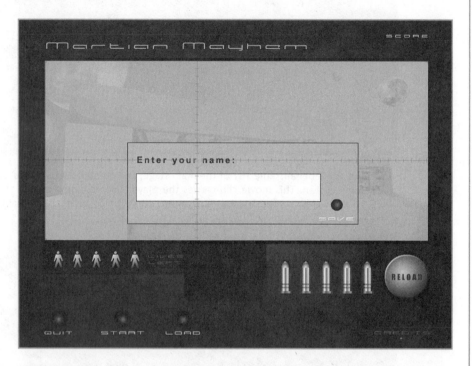

When the save button is clicked, the player's name and score are sent to an ASP page called save_score.asp, which updates the database with the information. The player is then forwarded to the frame labeled HighScores on the main stage.

```
on (release) {
    loadVariables ("http://127.0.0.1/save_score.asp", "", "GET");
    _root.gotoAndStop ("Highscores");
}
```

3. I placed the frame label Highscores at frame 194, and used a loadVariables action to populate a Top 10 high scores list, by retrieving them from another ASP page, highscores.asp:

```
stop ();
loadVariablesNum ("http://127.0.0.1/highscores.asp", 0);
```

Then I put 10 dynamic text-boxes at frame 194, with the variable name strNameX, (where X is a number from one to ten), giving me strName1, strName2, strName3, etc. up to strName10.

4. For each strName box, I created another dynamic text-box, named intScore*n* where *n* is again a number from one to ten – giving me intScore1, intScore2, intScore3, etc. up to intScore10. I finished off by labeling the highscore text fields so the player knows what they refer to.

And that's the Flash part of the game done! Now let's look at the ASP.

Building the ASP pages and the database

The ASP pages connect to an Access database called highscores.mdb. The database contains a HIGH_SCORES table with two columns, a NAME column and a SCORE column.

The first page, save_scores.asp, checks whether the variables sent by the Flash movie have a value or not, and if they don't, assigns the values of the variables of the same name in the ASP page.

Saving the player's score

1. First the code checks for a new name and score:

```
<%

DIM strName
if Request.QueryString("strName") <> "" then
    strName = Request.QueryString("strName")
end if

DIM intScore
if Request.QueryString("intScore") <> "" then
    intScore = Request.QueryString("intScore")
end if
```

2. Then the variables needed for the database connection are declared, and the connection and recordset set:

```
Dim rsScore, dbConn, strSQLScore

    Set dbConn = Server.CreateObject("ADODB.Connection")
    Set rsScore = Server.CreateObject("ADODB.Recordset")
```

3. A SQL string inserts the values of strName and intScore in the NAME and SCORE columns located in the HIGH_SCORES table.

```
    strSQLScore = "INSERT INTO HIGH_SCORES (NAME, SCORE) Values
➥('"& strName &"','"& intScore &""')"
```

4. Then the recordset is opened, so that the query can be executed:

```
    rsScore.Open strSQLScore,dbConn
```

5. And the database closed:

```
    Set rsScore = Nothing
    dbConn.Close
    Set dbConn = Nothing
%>
```

Here's the code in all its glory:

```
<%

DIM strName
if Request.QueryString("strName") <> "" then
    strName = Request.QueryString("strName")
end if

DIM intScore
if Request.QueryString("intScore") <> "" then
    intScore = Request.QueryString("intScore")
end if

Dim rsScore, dbConn, strSQLScore

    Set dbConn = Server.CreateObject("ADODB.Connection")
    Set rsScore = Server.CreateObject("ADODB.Recordset")


    dbConn.Open "Provider=Microsoft.Jet.OLEDB.4.0;Data Source=" &
➥Server.MapPath("highscores.mdb") & ";Persist Security
➥Info=False"
```

```
     strSQLScore = "INSERT INTO HIGH_SCORES (NAME, SCORE) Values
➥('"& strName &"','"& intScore &"')"

     rsScore.Open strSQLScore,dbConn


     Set rsScore = Nothing
     dbConn.Close
     Set dbConn = Nothing
%>
```

Displaying the high scores

1. This page, just like the other page, begins initializing the variables needed for the execution of the page. A variable called counter is used to assign the high score position of each player in the database:

```
<%

Dim strName
Dim intScore
Dim counter
counter = 1
```

2. The database variables are initialized and the database connection and recordset set.

```
Dim rsHighscores, dbConn, strSQLHighscore

     Set dbConn = Server.CreateObject("ADODB.Connection")
     Set rsHighscores = Server.CreateObject("ADODB.Recordset")
```

3. The database connection to the Access database named highscores.mdb is then opened:

```
     dbConn.Open "Provider=Microsoft.Jet.OLEDB.4.0;Data Source=" &
➥Server.MapPath("highscores.mdb") & ";Persist Security
➥Info=False"
```

4. Then the SQL query needed to retrieve the required information from the database is declared, and the recordset opened. The query returns all the player names and scores in descending order (in other words it lists the high scores starting with the highest down to the lowest):

```
     strSQLHighscore = "SELECT NAME, SCORE FROM HIGH_SCORES ORDER
➥BY SCORE DESC"
```

5. The recordset is opened:

```
rsHighscores.Open strSQLHighscore,dbConn
```

6. And a while loop set – this will loop until the end of the recordset is reached.

    ```
    Do While Not rsHighscores.EOF
    ```

7. The values of the strName and intScore variables are then set to the values in the database and sent back to the Flash movie. Every time this code loops, the next entry in the database is sent back to Flash, with an incremented variable name, using counter as the incremental value, for example:

    ```
    strName1=JohnDoe&intScore1=45478,
    zstrName2=Bobby&intScore2=34322).
    ```

    ```
            strName = rsHighscores("NAME")
            intScore =
    ➡rsHighscores("SCORE")%>&strName<%=counter%>=<%=strName%>&intScore
    ➡<%=counter%>=<%=intScore%>&<%
    ```

8. The counter is incremented so that the same variable name is never sent to Flash more than once.

    ```
            counter = counter + 1
    ```

9. Finally, the code moves on to the next entry in the database, and goes back to the start of the while loop.

    ```
                rsHighscores.MoveNextLoop
    %>
    ```

    Okay, so that was a lot of code. Here it is in full:

    ```
    <%

    Dim strName
    Dim intScore
    Dim counter
    counter = 1

    Dim rsHighscores, dbConn, strSQLHighscore

    Set dbConn = Server.CreateObject("ADODB.Connection")
        Set rsHighscores = Server.CreateObject("ADODB.Recordset")


        dbConn.Open "Provider=Microsoft.Jet.OLEDB.4.0;Data Source=" &
    ➡Server.MapPath("highscores.mdb") & ";Persist Security
    ➡Info=False"
    ```

```
        strSQLHighscore = "SELECT NAME, SCORE FROM HIGH_SCORES ORDER
➡BY SCORE DESC"
        rsHighscores.Open strSQLHighscore,dbConn


        Do While Not rsHighscores.EOF
                strName = rsHighscores("NAME")
                intScore =
➡rsHighscores("SCORE")%>strName<%=counter%>=<%=strName%>&intScore
➡<%=counter%>=<%=intScore%>&<%


                counter = counter + 1

                rsHighscores.MoveNextLoop

        rsHighscores.Close
        Set rsHighscores = Nothing
        dbConn.Close
        Set dbConn = Nothing


    %>
```

There you have it! Everything's in place. Of course, I've added a few finishing touches, and I'll leave you to do the same. Whether you've created your own Martian Madness, or designed your own game completely, I hope that this chapter has given you a strong foundation and a good place to start from in your own game building.

Summary

We've covered a lot of elements in this chapter, and you're probably eager to get out there and compile more of your own Flash games, but take a moment to think about how you would plan these games, before actually creating those first layers, or writing that first line of ActionScript. Planning is an extremely important part of any Flash movie, possibly more so with games, and a few hours spent sketching out what you want to do could save you days and days of reworking your layers and changing code! Once you have the big idea though, I hope you're now much more confident about turning it into a gem of a game. You now know how to:

- Create and import backdrops and design the graphic elements of your game.

- Make villains – plausible or otherwise – come to life in the game: walking, shooting and interacting with the player.

- Design buttons to keep track of lives, bullets and scores.

- And you also now know how to record those scores in a database on your server, and call up the results when you want.

Mars won't know what hit it!

27
Flash
Gaming

Section 5
Real World
Dynamic Content

Chapter 28
Flash News Site

In this section we'll be putting together a lot of the techniques we've learned in previous sections to create a latest news application. We'll be using a database to store all of the news articles that we want to display within our Flash movie. We will be using Macromedia's Dreamweaver UltraDev to actually create the ASP code for this application.

We will be taking a very Microsoft route in developing this application, by utilizing ASP pages developed in UltraDev and an Access 2000 database, both of which should be easily accessible and familiar to a lot of readers. We'll also be testing the application using Microsoft Personal Web Server.

Now, let's look at the things we'll need to develop the website, and deploy it on a web server:

- Macromedia Flash 5 - to build the front end of the application.

- Macromedia Dreamweaver UltraDev - to aid us in developing the ASP code.

- Microsoft Access 2000 - we'll store our news article archive using this.

- Microsoft Personal Web Server - will be used as... you guessed it, our web server.

- Microsoft Windows OS - go on have a guess...

Setting up Microsoft Personal Web Server

In order to test this example, we must first set up a web site on Personal Web Server, so that we can run scripts that will extract data from the database.

To do this, we we'll add a new **virtual directory** to our local web server, using the Advanced Options window of the Personal Web Manager.

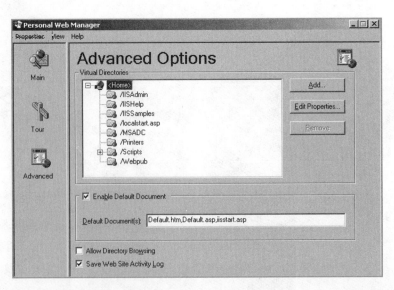

Click on the Add button, and then browse to the directory where you'll be saving your files. I'll be saving to a directory that I've created within the Webshare folder on my C: drive called C:\Webshare\newsflash. I shall also call the Alias newsflash.

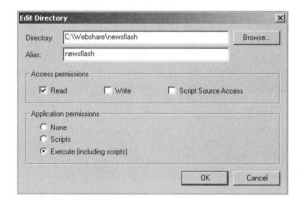

The new directory we've created can now be browsed to through our web browser at an address similar to this: http://localhost/newsflash.

Creating the news database

OK, so we've set up our virtual root, next we need to set up our Access database to store the news articles.

1.   Start Microsoft Access 2000, and select File > New. You'll be presented with a dialog box asking which type of file you wish to create. Select Database, and click OK.

     We now need to save our database file with an appropriate filename. The database file can be stored in any directory that the computer with the web server has access to. Later on in the chapter, we'll create the ODBC data source, which will tell the server where the database is actually stored. As such, I am saving the database file as news.mdb, in a directory on my desktop called Flash News Tutorial, along with all my other source files.

2.   Once the database file has been created, select Create table in Design view from the Tables node of the Objects frame.

     We'll be creating five fields in the database, with the following properties:

Field Name	Data Type	Field Size
Title	Text	200
Date	Date/Time	N/A
Link	Text	200
Article	Memo	N/A
Author	Text	100

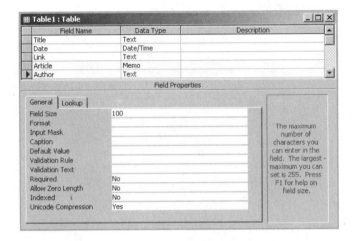

We'll be using this database to store our news articles, which we'll then display. Alongside each news article, we'll also display information relating to the article, such as the name of the Author, and the Date. There may also be an appropriate hyperlink to another site attached to the article, which we'll be storing in the Link field.

The Data Type attribute determines the type of information we'll be storing in each field of the database. Text fields can store up to 255 characters, although their default value is 50. Memo fields can store up to 65,535 characters. For the purposes of this exercise I've increased the Text data type's Field Size for the Link field to 200, and that for the Author field to 100. It's important to set appropriate values for these to optimize the database and minimize changes to its structure at a later date.

3. When you close the Design View window you'll be prompted to save the table – give it a name of News_Table. You'll then be prompted by a message telling you that a **primary key** field has not been set. It will ask you whether you wish Access to create the primary key field for you – click on Yes.

> *Do you remember what a primary key is (from the database chapters)? The primary key field is a number that is automatically generated by the database every time a new entry is added to the table. It's created in such a way that each entry has a unique value associated to it, which can then be used to identify a specific entry. Otherwise, it's very difficult to determine one entry from another!*

4. For test purposes, while we're creating this application, we're going to insert some information into the database. Open the News_Table table, and insert some example data in the appropriate fields:

News Article 1:

Title: Motion web mind food

Date: 03/26/01

Link: www.freshfroot.com

Article: A man walked into a doctor's surgery in Greater London today, with a apple in his ear, and a banana up his nose. Medical experts believe that the man isn't eating correctly.

Author: Joe Bloggs

News Article 2:

Title: Information for designers, by designers

Date: 03/26/01

Link: www.friendsofed.com

Article: In a similar incident, later on today, a man covered in gold paint attended an emergency room in Kenosha, Wisconsin. Doctors believe he was afflicted with a gilt complex.

Author: John Smith

This is just example text, which we can change at a later date. For now, it simply gives us some information to pull into our Flash movie. Close the table, and save your changes.

Setting the ODBC data source

We need to create a data source so that the ASP pages that we're going to create later on, know where to find, and how to talk to the database that we've just created. Creating such a data source is actually specific to the computer that is running the web server, although you may need to create the DSN on your development computer as well (for testing purposes). In this example, the web server is, in fact, on the same computer as the development computer, so we'll only need to set it up once. Hopefully, you've already carried out very similar operations to this in earlier chapters.

1.   Open up the Control Panel, and then select Administrative Tools > Data Sources (ODBC). You'll see the ODBC Data Source Administrator window appear. We want to add a System DSN, so click on the DSN tab. A System DSN simply means that the data source will be available to all users of the machine, and the computer itself (as opposed to being restricted to certain users).

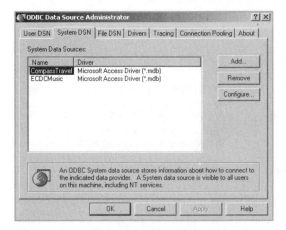

2. Click Add, select Microsoft Access Driver (*.mdb), and then click on Finish. You should then see the following window. Give the DSN the name: NewsFlash_DB, and enter a brief description in the appropriate field.

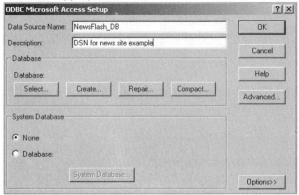

3. Click on the Select button, and browse to the Access 2000 database file that we created earlier.

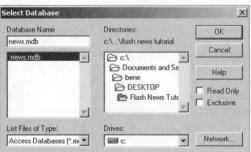

Click OK, and our Data Source will then be created. Close the ODBC Data Source Administrator window.

Creating the ASP page using UltraDev

Now that we've created the News database, and have set it up as a data source, we're now ready to create the ASP page, which we'll use to extract the news articles from the database to insert them into our Flash movie.

We must define a site in UltraDev before we can begin creating any pages.

1. Open up UltraDev, and select Site > New Site. You will be presented with a window as shown in the following screenshot. We will call the site Newsflash, and point the Local Root Folder to a directory created in Webshare, also called newsflash.

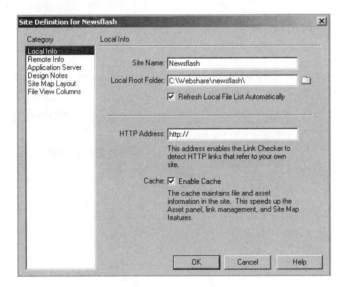

2. In the next category, Remote Info, select Local/Network for Access, as all the files will be on the same computer you're working on.

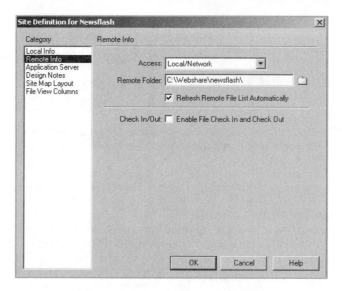

3. The last category that we need to define is Application Server, which should be set up as shown in the following screenshot:

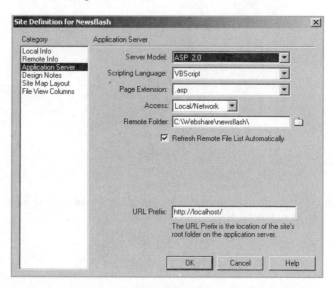

4. Click OK. Your site will then be created. You'll then see the Site window. Select File > New Window. The first line of our page will say &LatestNews=, which, as we learned in previous chapters is required so that Flash will be prompted to load the text that follows this expression, into a variable/text box called LatestNews.

5. We now need to set the data bindings for this page. To do this we go to the Data Bindings window in UltraDev, and add a Recordset (Query) as shown in the following image:

6. You'll be presented with a dialog telling us that we need to create a database connection. Simply click OK for now; we'll get around to creating the connection in just a minute. In the subsequent window that pops up, name the recordset NewsFlash_RS as shown below, then click on the Define button so that we can define a new connection.

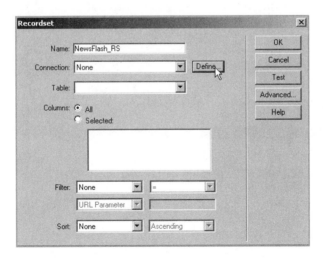

7. You will be presented with the Connections window. Select New > Data Source Name (DSN), and then configure the connection as shown in the following screenshot:

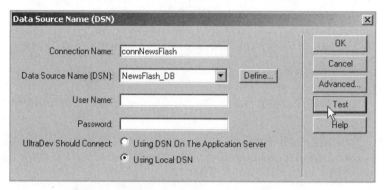

8. Click OK, and then click Done. You will then see the contents of the database in the Recordset window.

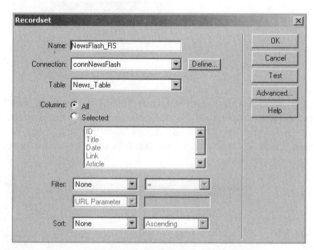

9. At this point you can click on the Test button to ensure that the connection is extracting the data correctly from the database.

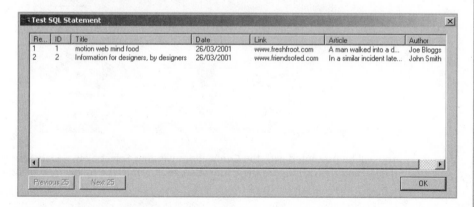

10. As it is at the moment, the data is being pulled from the database in the order that it has been stored in the database. Because we want our example to be a "latest news" feature for our Flash site, we need to sort the news articles according to date, starting with the latest article. To do this, we need to sort the data by Date, in a Descending order, so that the latest article appears first on our site, modify the Sort parameters to suit, and then click OK.

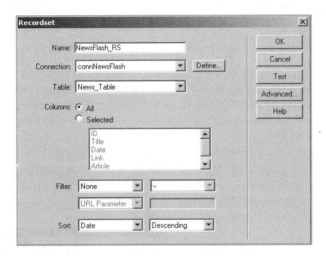

11. We can now see all of the fields from the database on our Data Bindings tab:

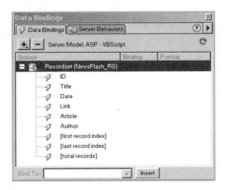

12. UltraDev enables us to drag fields from the Data Bindings window directly onto the page, into the positions required, as shown below. We're simply required to loosely lay the fields out on the page. The way we're going to go about organizing these fields to get the final display as we want it, is like this. Drag the Date field into position, and then insert a "-" character. Do the same for the Title field. Next drag the Author field into position, but don't put a hyphen after it. Instead, press SHIFT+ENTER. This will insert a carriage return, and as such will take you to the next line. Now drag the Article field into place, and then insert two carriage returns (using the keyboard combination I just mentioned).

13. To ensure that all the text appears correctly within our Flash movie, we want the server to convert the text into URL-encoded text. It's advisable to do this to all fields that contain text (although it's not a necessity), as this avoids any future problems with strange characters appearing within the text. To do this, click on the field in question, and then in the Data Bindings window, click on the Format column. From the drop-down list which then appears, select Encode – Server.URLEncode, as shown below.

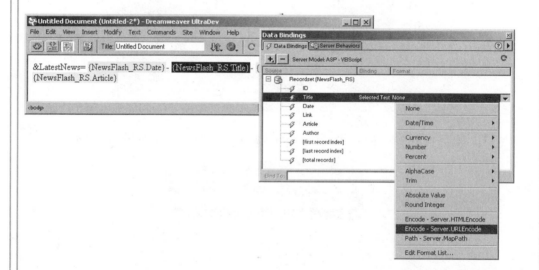

14. We can also format our text with a few basic tags. Let's make the Date, Title, and Author text bold, by clicking the Bold icon in the Properties window:

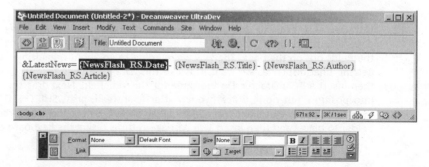

15. Let's also set the Title to hyperlink to the Link field in our database. Select the Title field on the main page, and then in the Properties window, click on the Browse icon next to the Link field.

In the Select File Name From option, select Data Sources. You will then be shown all the fields from the recordset. Select the Link field, and then click OK.

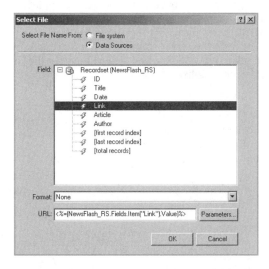

16. We now need the page to display more than just one article from the database in the page. Select all the fields on the page (make sure you also highlight the extra carriage returns we inserted below the fields), and click on the Server Behaviors tab. Add a Repeat Region behavior, as shown here:

17. At this point we have the option to display all of the database records on the page, or just, for example, the latest ten. Let's choose to have all the records in the database displayed.

18. The code for the ASP page has now been completed, so save the created page as `latestnews.asp`. This will now create a page, which when run on the web server sends HTML code back to the client's browser. If we open the page in a browser window through the server so that it processes the ASP code, we can right-click in the browser, select View Source, and we will then see the source code for this page, which will look something like this:

```
<html>
<head>
<title>Untitled Document</title>
<meta http-equiv="Content-Type" content="text/html; charset=iso-
8859-1">
</head>
<body bgcolor="#FFFFFF" text="#000000">
&amp;LatestNews=

<b>3%2F26%2F2001</b>-
<b><ahref="www.friendsofed.com">Information+for+designers%2C+by+
designers</a>
</b>- <b>John+Smith</b><br>
In+a+similar+incident%2C+a+man+covered+in+gold+paint+attended+an+
emergency+room+in+Kenosha%2C+Wisconsin%2E+Doctors+believe+that+he+
was+afflicted+with+a+gilt+complex%2E <br>
<br>

<b>3%2F26%2F2001</b>- <b><a
href="www.freshfroot.com">motion+web+mind+food</a></b>-
<b>Joe+Bloggs</b><br>
A+man+walked+into+a+doctor%27s+surgery+in+Greater+London+today%2C+
with+a+carrot+in+his+ear%2C+and+an+artichoke+up+his+nose%2E+Medica
l+experts+believe+that+the+man+is+not+eating+right%2E <br>
<br>

</body>
</html>
```

You will notice that there is obviously a lot of HTML information in there, such as the header details, and in fact, we don't need these details. As a result, we need to remove them from the ASP page. Why? Well basically, UltraDev creates an ASP page that is intended for use as a web page. So, when you view the ASP page through a server in your browser, the output is HTML. When we edit the ASP page, we're stripping the code away that produces HTML in the browser, leaving an output that is pretty much plain text that Flash will understand. I know the concept may seem a little confusing if you're new to UltraDev, or haven't programmed in ASP much... but it's quite simple when you do!!

Still not too sure? Look at it this way: most ASP pages are basically text documents, with HTML code in them, and in between the HTML code there is some ASP code. Now, when you view the page through a server in your browser, that ASP code isn't visible in the source, as the server has processed this ASP, and given some output, usually plain text, or some HTML. So, what we do is edit the page to remove any of the standard HTML output that Flash won't recognize, and we then format the page so that its output is such that Flash can understand it.

Here's what we see if we look at the ASP page's code in the code view of UltraDev:

```
<%@LANGUAGE="VBSCRIPT"%>
<!--#include file="Connections/connNewsFlash.asp" -->
<%
set NewsFlash_RS = Server.CreateObject("ADODB.Recordset")
NewsFlash_RS.ActiveConnection = MM_connNewsFlash_STRING
NewsFlash_RS.Source = "SELECT * FROM News_Table ORDER BY Date
DESC"
NewsFlash_RS.CursorType = 0
NewsFlash_RS.CursorLocation = 2
NewsFlash_RS.LockType = 3
NewsFlash_RS.Open()
NewsFlash_RS_numRows = 0
%>
<%
Dim Repeat1__numRows
Repeat1__numRows = -1
Dim Repeat1__index
Repeat1__index = 0
NewsFlash_RS_numRows = NewsFlash_RS_numRows + Repeat1__numRows
%>
<html>
<head>
<title>Untitled Document</title>
<meta http-equiv="Content-Type" content="text/html;
charset=iso-8859-1">
</head>
<body bgcolor="#FFFFFF" text="#000000">
&amp;LatestNews=
<%
While ((Repeat1__numRows <> 0) AND (NOT NewsFlash_RS.EOF))
%>
```

```
<b><%= Server.URLEncode((NewsFlash_RS.Fields.Item("Date").Value))
%></b>- <b><a
href="<%=(NewsFlash_RS.Fields.Item("Link").Value)%>">
<%= Server.URLEncode((NewsFlash_RS.Fields.Item("Title").Value))
%></a></b>-
<b><%=
Server.URLEncode((NewsFlash_RS.Fields.Item("Author").Value))
%></b><br>
<%= Server.URLEncode((NewsFlash_RS.Fields.Item("Article").Value))
%>
<br>
<br>
<%
    Repeat1__index=Repeat1__index+1
    Repeat1__numRows=Repeat1__numRows-1
    NewsFlash_RS.MoveNext()
Wend
%>
</body>
</html>
<%
NewsFlash_RS.Close()
%>
```

A couple of points to note:

The first is how on this line:

```
<!--#include file="Connections/connNewsFlash.asp" -->
```

UltraDev creates a file in a folder called Connections, which is **required** by the ASP page you create. It's worth noting this minor point, as this file would be required should you ever choose to upload your application to another server.

The second point to note is the way that UltraDev represents the ampersand character, (&), as (&amp). We must change this line of code from &LatestNews= to &LatestNews= for our page to work properly.

So, let's remove the <html> tags around the document, the header information, and amend the ampersand representation, which then gives us this code:

```
<%@LANGUAGE="VBSCRIPT"%>
<!--#include file="Connections/connNewsFlash.asp" -->
<%
set NewsFlash_RS = Server.CreateObject("ADODB.Recordset")
NewsFlash_RS.ActiveConnection = MM_connNewsFlash_STRING
NewsFlash_RS.Source = "SELECT * FROM News_Table ORDER BY Date
DESC"
NewsFlash_RS.CursorType = 0
NewsFlash_RS.CursorLocation = 2
```

```
NewsFlash_RS.LockType = 3
NewsFlash_RS.Open()
NewsFlash_RS_numRows = 0
%>
<%
Dim Repeat1__numRows
Repeat1__numRows = -1
Dim Repeat1__index
Repeat1__index = 0
NewsFlash_RS_numRows = NewsFlash_RS_numRows + Repeat1__numRows
%>
&LatestNews=
<%
While ((Repeat1__numRows <> 0) AND (NOT NewsFlash_RS.EOF))
%>
<b><%= Server.URLEncode((NewsFlash_RS.Fields.Item("Date").Value))
%></b>- <b><a
href="<%=(NewsFlash_RS.Fields.Item("Link").Value)%>"><%=
Server.URLEncode((NewsFlash_RS.Fields.Item("Title").Value))
%></a></b>-
<b><%=
Server.URLEncode((NewsFlash_RS.Fields.Item("Author").Value))
%></b><br>
<%= Server.URLEncode((NewsFlash_RS.Fields.Item("Article").Value))
%>
<br>
<br>
<%
    Repeat1__index=Repeat1__index+1
    Repeat1__numRows=Repeat1__numRows-1
    NewsFlash_RS.MoveNext()
Wend
%>
<%
NewsFlash_RS.Close()
%>
```

Our ASP page is now ready so we can now create the Flash movie that will display this information from the database. Save the newly edited page, and close UltraDev.

Creating the Flash movie for latest news

1. First, let's build the main graphics for the interface. Open up a new Flash movie. Select Modify > Movie and then modify the movie dimensions so that it measures 300x200 pixels. Rename the default layer as Main Interface, and create a large box area to the left, which will display the latest news.

2. Create a button at the top right of the stage called Scroll Button (feel free to drag a copy of the button from the library of latestnews.fla, which you'll find on the CD

accompanying this book). Add another instance of it to the bottom right corner of the stage. These two buttons will be used to scroll the news up and down.

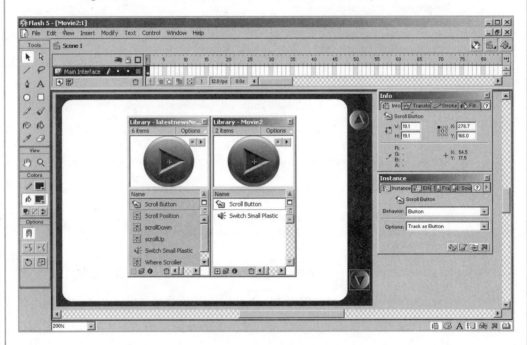

3.   In the main area, where we want the news to be displayed, we need to create a dynamic text box with the following parameters:

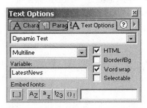

4.   To enable the top scroll button to scroll the text upwards, add this ActionScript to the top scroll button:

```
on (press) {
    _root.scrollUp.gotoAndPlay (2);
}
on (release) {
    _root.scrollUp.gotoAndStop (1);
}
```

Then add this ActionScript to the lower button for the same reason:

```
on (press) {
    _root.scrollDown.gotoAndPlay (2);
}
on (release) {
    _root.scrollDown.gotoAndStop (1);
}
```

These actions call two invisible looping movie clips, named scrollUp and scrollDown (respectively), which will scroll the text when the user clicks on and holds these buttons.

5. Create the movie clips, but don't place any graphics in the scene – this will create 'invisible' clips that users will not see in the finished movie. When you drag them onto the scene (we'll do this later) from your library (we'll do this later), they will appear as white circles. It doesn't matter where they are on the main scene, as they're invisible when the movie is compiled. However, putting them somewhere that they can be easily found is a good idea.

Add the following code to the timelines of the two movie clips:

ActionScript for frame 1 of the scrollUp movie clip:

```
stop ();
```

ActionScript for frame 2:

```
    currentScroll = _root.LatestNews.scroll;
if (Number(currentScroll)>1) {
    _root.LatestNews.scroll = currentScroll-1;
}
```

ActionScript for frame 3:

```
gotoAndPlay (2);
```

Now some ActionScript for the scrollDown movie clip. Add this to frame 1:

```
stop ();
```

ActionScript for frame 2:

```
currentScroll = _root.LatestNews.scroll;
if (Number(currentScroll)<Number(_root.LatestNews.maxscroll)) {
    _root.LatestNews.scroll = Number(currentScroll)+1;
}
```

ActionScript for frame 3:

```
gotoAndPlay (2);
```

6. Now, we're going to create another movie which will move between the two scroll buttons, displaying how far the text is scrolling, and when the maximum amount you can scroll has been reached. So, create a new movie clip and call it Scroll Postion. In this movie clip, draw a square or some other similar shape to act as you scroll indicator (you could of course copy the Scroll Position movie clip from the library of `latestnews.fla` on the CD).

7. Now go back to the main timeline, and create a new layer called Scroll Position. Drag an instance of the Scroll Position movie clip into the first frame of this new layer (putting it just below the Scroll Up button), and name it `Scroller`.

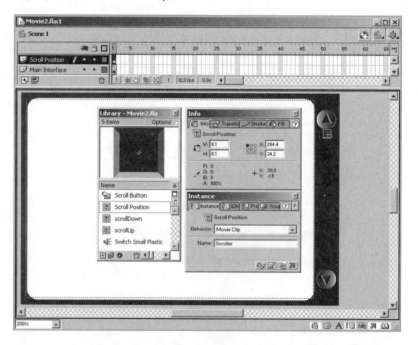

8. We'll use another looping movie clip called Where Scroller to determine the position of the Scroller movie clip. Go ahead and create this movie clip, rename the default layer as button graphics, and then add the following ActionScript to it

ActionScript for frame 1:

```
_root.scroller = _root.LatesNews.scroll;
setProperty ("_root.scroller", _y,
➡Number(((123.1/(_root.LatestNews.maxscroll-1))
➡*(_root.LatestNews.scroll-1)))+38.3);
```

ActionScript for frame 2

```
gotoAndPlay (1);
```

You're probably wondering what the values 123.1 and 38.3 refer to. Well, 38.3 is the starting y position of the clip, and 123.1 is the difference between the starting height, and the position when the movie clip is at the bottom of the scrolling line. If you're creating this movie from scratch, you may need to change these values to apply to the sizes, and positions in your movie (you'll find this easiest using the Info panel). All I'm using here is some simple arithmetic to determine the position that the user has scrolled the text to using the buttons, and then moving the position of the square movie clip accordingly.

9. Drag the Where Scroller movie clip and the other hidden movie clips onto a new layer, called Looping Hidden Clips. We do this to keep these clips separate from the other objects in the scene. Assign the instance names scrollUp and scrollDown to the respective clips.

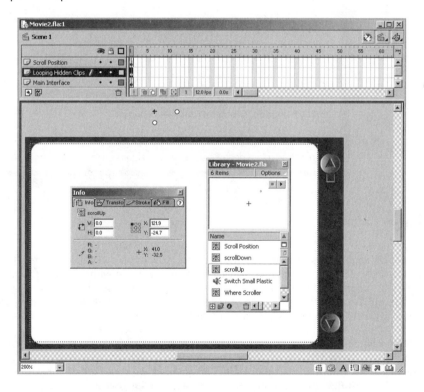

10. Now, in the first frame of the movie on the Main Interface layer, we need to add a loadVariables action to load the output of the ASP page into the Flash movie. As I'll be storing the SWF file in the same position as the ASP page, this ActionScript will look like this, on account of the relative path:

```
loadVariablesNum ("latestnews.asp", 0);
```

11. We can now test the example by publishing, copying the SWF to the same location as the rest of your site (so I copied mine to `C:\Webshare\newsflash`), and then hitting the SWF file through our browser. The movie should look like this:

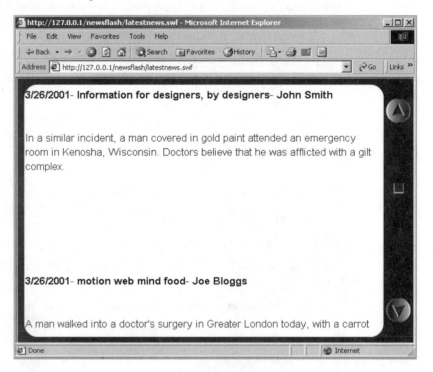

Conclusion

This application allows us to update the database, which will dynamically update the Flash movie. We can now add, edit or remove articles from the database without having to change the SWF file itself. You may want to expand the application by creating some more ASP pages which would update the database through a web browser interface as an online administration section of your website. This can also be easily created using Macromedia Dreamweaver UltraDev.

In this example we've seen how we can use an ASP page to pull data from a database into a Flash movie. Using these techniques, there are a number of other ways in which we could expand on presenting this information within Flash. For example, we could create a news ticker tape of the news headlines (just the titles) in an automatically scrolling dynamic text box (remember we saw something similar in chapter 17, Generator by Example). Try recreating the ASP file in UltraDev so that it only displays the headlines in a text box on a movie. You can modify the ActionScript in the looping movie clip that scrolls the text up so that it constantly plays, and scrolls the text without the user having to click on the button to activate it.

Remember that what we've discussed in this chapter is a way of creating a Flash movie that can have completely dynamic content pulled from a database. That way, we can update or make changes to our Flash sites without actually having to change or amend the source file, and recompile the movies as we would normally have to do.

The range of applications that we can apply this technique to is extremely broad, and many of the sites that are database driven using normal web pages can now use Flash instead so that they can be interactive and interesting rather than plain, or boring!

27
Flash
Gaming

Section 5
Real World
Dynamic World

Appendix A
Object-oriented Programming

You've probably already heard about object-oriented programming (OOP). If the concept daunted you a little at first, don't worry... most people react like that. Once you understand the core concepts of OOP, the rest is easy. We'll start with these concepts, and then look at how OOP is implemented in Flash 5.

Before OOP: procedural programming

Before OOP was invented, most programming languages followed what was called the procedural methodology. This meant that for the most part, their logic progressed in a linear fashion: identify a task, program a solution, move on to the next task, program another solution; lather, rinse, and repeat...sound familiar?

If certain steps in some procedural code are run again and again, they can be split off into what is known as a **function**. Functions are helpful because they allow you to remove large repetitive blocks of code and replace them with a single line of code that calls the function.

Functions are also great for reusing code. If you write a function to perform a certain task in one program, and you need to do that same task in another program, you can simply copy the function over to the new program and use it. Suppose, for example, I created an ActionScript virtual pet. I would have to feed the pet, a process which would entail a series of steps; figuring out if the pet needs food, feeding it, and, the nature of virtual pets being what it is, make sure I'd fed it enough to make it 'happy'. Feeding the pet would always require those same steps, and so I might create a function to perform the tasks. Then anytime I wanted to feed any pet, I would just have to call that function.

When a function is called, it can be passed arguments. The value of those arguments can then affect exactly what the function does. For example I could pass the feed function how much food I want to give to the virtual pet. Functions can also pass back a single value to the code that called it. Functions are not a thing of the past; the ActionScript function below, `lastLetter`, passes a string as an argument and then returns the last letter in that string.

```
Frame Actions
Movie Explorer  Frame Actions  Instance
+ -  Frame Actions
function lastLetter(str){
    return (str.charAt(str.length - 1));
}

Line 3 of 3, Col 2
```

There are problems with using procedural methodology, which fall into three broad categories: readability, reusability, and manageability. First of all, understanding procedural code that has been written by another programmer can be extremely difficult. This is because for the most part, in order to understand a program written in a procedural language, you would need to understand what every line of code does. It's kind of similar to opening a book written by an author you don't know, picking a chapter and page at random, and then trying to figure out the entire plot. Inline comments obviously help, but once you have enough procedural code, it tends to become very difficult to follow.

```
Frame Actions
Movie Explorer  Frame Actions   Instance                                    ?
+  -  Frame Actions                                                          ▼ ▲
function applyForce(){
    if (dragging == false){
        newSpeed.x += (_root.dTime * forces.x/mass
        newSpeed.y += (_root.dTime * forces.y/mass

    _x = _x + (_root.dTime * newSpeed.x);
    _y = _y + (_root.dTime * newSpeed.y);
    if (_y + (_height/2) > _root.floor){
        _y = _root.floor - (_height/2);
        newSpeed.x *= _root.wallBounce;
        newSpeed.y *= -_root.wallBounce;
    }

    if (_y - (_height/2) < _root.ceiling){
        _y = _root.ceiling + (_height/2);
        newSpeed.x *= _root.wallBounce;
        newSpeed.y *= -_root.wallBounce;
    }

    if (_x + (_width/2) > _root.rightWall){
        _x = _root.rightWall - (_width/2);
        newSpeed.x *= -_root.wallBounce;
        newSpeed.y *= _root.wallBounce;
    }

    if (_x - (_width/2) < _root.leftWall){
Line 49 of 49, Col 2
```

Quick, what does this code do?

Reusability of code is always important because no one wants to reinvent the wheel when it comes to code. While functions help make procedural code a little more reusable, the majority of procedural code is written to address very specific problems; therefore, unless another program is addressing that **exact** same problem (say a certain math or engineering problem), it's very difficult to reuse the code.

Finally, there's manageability. In a perfect world, a programmer would write some code and no one would ever have to deal with it again; regrettably, this isn't a perfect world yet, and you're unlikely to ever see a 'perfect' program. Managing procedural code can be a nightmare because there is no real way to divide up a procedural based program, besides functions. Once again, we come back to the same problem; every programmer that works on the code has to understand nearly all of the code to work on any of it.

Well, as you might have guessed, object-oriented programming was invented to address these shortcomings; OOP languages take advantage of something that procedural languages simply ignore, the relationship between code and data.

OOP: abstraction

In the case of the virtual pet program we mentioned, the variables that define the pet's hunger, happiness, etc. are in no way related to the actual functions that change those values. If we were to modify that program to make it object-oriented we would have to first determine what key idea or thing the code is based around. This is because one of the pillars of OOP languages is the idea of **abstraction**, representing abstract ideas (like the virtual pet) as a whole thing, rather than trying to just make the pieces work like procedural code does.

OOP: encapsulation

Well, what is this 'thing' we are defining? It's an object, and objects consist of two things, data (like the pet's hunger and color), and functions (like eating and sleeping). Wrapping the related data and code into a single handy package is another pillar of OOP languages, known as encapsulation. In ActionScript a piece of data within an object is known as a property and the functions are known as methods.

With all of that in mind let's go a little bit deeper into what we were to do if we were to create a virtual pet in ActionScript. We already know that the object we want to create is a pet object. Now we need to define what its various properties and methods will be. If you ever played with one of those virtual pets you will know that all the game really consists of is keeping the little thing as content as possible. Feeding the pet, putting it to bed, playing with it, etc. are all ways of keeping the pet happy. So, for our pet we need to keep track of its various states: to keep it simple, we will only track three things, `hungerLevel`, `tiredLevel`, and `boredLevel`. We would also need to define ways to keep those levels low, so we would need methods like `feed`, `rest`, and `play`.

Pet	
properties	methods
hungerLevel	feed
tiredLevel	rest
boredLevel	play

OOP: classes and instances

Now, here comes the really amazing part, in an OOP language, we will only have to define how a single pet works, and then we can make as many pets as we want based on that definition. This definition is known as a **class**. You can think of a class as a blueprint for an object, and this is why objects are often referred to as **instances** of a class.

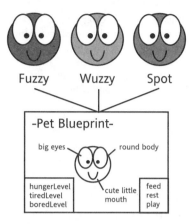

Doesn't this sound exactly like how Flash's symbols work? Well, that's actually a very apt comparison since Flash's symbol/instance relationship is exactly like the OOP class/object relationship. In fact, Flash's library symbol system was specifically designed to reflect its object-oriented methodology.

Now you understand the basics of what OOP is and does. The next step is to start getting into how to create and use objects in Flash.

Working with objects

To make use of the OOP aspects of ActionScript, we need to first create the objects that we will be manipulating. Objects themselves are declared just like any other variable in ActionScript, except that rather than create a value for the variable, we tell it what class to base its definition on. Let's first explore how this works using one of the built-in class definitions available to ActionScript, **Arrays**.

> *You might notice that the Macromedia documentation never uses the word 'class', this is because ActionScript is what is known as a prototype based OOP language, and uses prototype objects rather than classes to define blueprints for objects. However, for our purposes, this difference is minor and it makes it much more simple to call them classes rather than prototype objects.*

To create an object based on the Array class we would say:

```
tools = new Array();
```

What we are doing, exactly, is using the new operator to create a new object based on the Array class, and making the variable tools point to that object. Notice that in the statement we don't just state the name of the class, we follow it with a set of parenthesis, making it look a lot like we are calling a function. In fact we are calling a special function, known as a **constructor**. Every class, built-in or user defined, has a constructor function that initializes properties for newly created objects based off of that class. Like any other function, a class's constructor function can accept arguments, for example:

```
tools = new Array("duct tape", "screwdriver", "hammer");
```

Now the statement has been modified to initialize the tools array with its first three members.

Now that we have our object, we need to know how to access and manipulate its properties and methods. ActionScript can handle object manipulation in two ways. The first way, which is more common in OOP languages, uses the dot operator, which is quite simply a period (.).

Dot syntax

Dot syntax is written by first stating the name of the object you are talking to, then a period, and finally the method or property you wish to access. So say we wanted to set a variable called size to be the number of elements in our tools array. It turns out that the Array class has a built-in property, length, which always contains the number of elements in the array. So, we would say:

```
size = tools.length;
```

The Array class also includes a method called push, which places a new element into the array right at the very end. So if we wanted to add a staple gun to our tools array we would type:

```
tools.push("staple gun");
```

It shouldn't come as any surprise that we have parentheses after the method's name, since methods are after all, just specialized functions!

While dot notation, is fairly easy to understand and use, the second style we could use to access an object's properties and methods is a bit more complex. It is known as **array notation**, and is based on using the array access operator, which is a pair of square brackets, []. Using this method of access is more involved than dot syntax, but it does give us a very powerful new ability, which we'll look at next.

Array notation

If we wanted to access the length property of our tools object with array notation, for example, we would use this:

```
size = tools["length"];
```

Accessing methods of our tools object is very similar:

```
tools["push"]("staple gun");
```

What's going on here? Well, first of all we have our object, `tools` and we are specifying that we want to access something inside of it called `push`. Well, `push` happens to be a method of the object so we need to pass it some value, which happens to be staple gun.

You'll notice that there isn't a dot in sight. Dot notation and array notation styles cannot be mixed during a single object access. In other words, within a complete statement you have the freedom to switch access styles, but in a single call to an object's methods or properties, the access style must remain consistent.

dot notation	array notation
size = tools.length;	size = tools["length"];
tools.push("staple gun");	tools["push"]("staple gun");

So far so good, but there's more to array notation; it gives us is the ability to dynamically name the method or property we wish to access. For example, we could say something like this:

```
prop = "length";
size = tools[prop];
```

Which works exactly the same as saying:

```
size = tools["length"];
```

We can even build the name by concatenating two strings like this:

```
prop = "len";
size = tools[prop+"gth"];
```

Pretty powerful, huh? We can dynamically build the name of the property or method we want just by piecing together strings! So if we had, say an object named `foo` that had, say, four properties named `size1`, `size2`, `size3`, and `size4` we could add then up and get the result **very** easily like this:

```
total = 0;
for(i=1;i<=4;++i){
     total += foo["size"+i];
}
```

So now you know how to create and use objects. Next we'll look at extending both objects and classes so that we can add our own customized properties and methods to them.

Extending objects and classes

While the built-in classes that come with Flash are very good, sometimes you will find that they don't quite do what you need them to do. But have no fear! When this happens you can very easily extend either individual objects of that class, or the whole class.

Adding properties to an object

First of all, we'll go over how to extend a single object. It's actually pretty easy because of how ActionScript's object-oriented functionality works. ActionScript's OOP facilities are fairly 'fast and loose' compared to more strict languages like C++ and Java. In those languages objects have a lot of security built into them. The end result is that it's easier to extend classes, but difficult, if not impossible to extend individual objects. With ActionScript though, you always have full access to the internals of an object, making it quite possible to add new properties and methods to an object whenever you want. Adding new properties is the easiest. For example, if we wanted to add a new property called hat to an object named bob, with hat equal to Fedora, all we would have to type is this:

```
bob.hat = "Fedora";
```

Bang! Now our bob object has a new property. So, if we had an object based on the Array class and wanted to extend it so it would have a new property called bornOn to represent the date and time the object was created, our code would be:

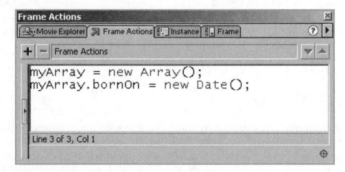

This works because when objects based on the Date class are created, they are automatically set to the date/time at which they were created.

Adding new properties to objects is pretty easy then. Extending objects with new methods is a bit more difficult, but not much.

Adding methods to an object

Before we start getting into code, you need to know what the special keyword this does. Whatever object the current code is in, this points to it. We need to use this anytime we have code inside of an object that has to utilize other methods or properties of that object. It's kind of an abstract idea, so if you don't quite get it, hold in there, our next example should help.

When you want to add a new method to an object you have to first write the method. The one thing you have to remember is that once this method is put into place, it will be inside the object; anytime you need to reference the object itself you need to use this. Now, let's say we needed to add a new method to an object based off the String class that counts the number of spaces in the string and then returns that number. We'd begin by creating a function that counts spaces in a String object like this:

```
Frame Actions
[Movie Explorer] [Frame Actions] [Instance] [Frame]                    ?
+ - | Frame Actions                                                   ▼ ▲
function String_spaceCount(){
    var spaces = 0;
    for (var i=0;i<this.length;++i){
        if (this.charAt(i) == " "){
            ++spaces;
        }
    }
    return (spaces);
}

Line 9 of 9, Col 2
```

First of all, we are defining a function called String_spaceCount. The reason we have the String_ in front is just for organizational purposes, it just reminds us that we are going to be adding this to a String object later. The first line of the function simply initializes a spaces variable. Then, a for loop is set up so that it loops from 0 to one less than the size of the String object. Next, each character of the string is examined to see if it is a space, if it is, then the spaces variable is incremented. Finally, after the for loop ends, the function returns the number of spaces it counted.

Now that we have our function, we have to attach it to our object as a method. When you attach methods to an object you state the name of the method you want to create and then set it equal to the function you have already written. If we want to create an object of the String class and extend it with the function we just wrote, we add two lines to our code that attach the function as a new method of the object, so it looks like this:

```
Frame Actions
[Movie Explorer] [Frame Actions] [Instance] [Frame]                    ?
+ - | Frame Actions                                                   ▼ ▲
function String_spaceCount(){
    var spaces = 0;
    for (var i=0;i<this.length;++i){
        if (this.charAt(i) == " "){
            ++spaces;
        }
    }
    return (spaces);
}

title = new String("This is a test");
title.spaceCount = String_spaceCount;
Line 12 of 12, Col 38
```

Now what is all of that code doing? As before, the function `String_spaceCount` creates a variable named `spaces` and then walks through the string, character by character, incrementing the `spaces` variable each time it sees another space. When it is done, it simply returns the number of spaces it finds.

Then, we created a new `String` object, called `title`. We extended the `title` object by adding a new method to it, `spaceCount`, that points to the `String_spaceCount` function.

We can now call the `spaceCount` method just like we would any other method of the `title` object. So if we wanted to trace the number of spaces in our `title` object to the Output window, we would simply add:

```
trace(title.spaceCount());
```

Now we know how to add new properties and methods to individual objects. But what if we want to extend *every* object of a given class? Well, we could extend each object individually right after their creation, but this is very inefficient in a number of ways. First of all, this would cause you to clutter your ActionScript with extra code, which is simply doing the same thing again and again. Secondly, each time you extend an individual object you are making a new copy of that property or method in memory. Now, this isn't a problem when you just have a few objects, but once you start talking about a few dozen objects, you might end up using all of the client's memory!

Well, don't worry, because there's a very easy way to extend every single object of a class in one fell swoop. This way of extending every object relies on an interesting quirk in how an object 'looks up' a property or method inside of it. Say we try to read a certain property of an object. First, the object looks to see if the property has been directly attached to it. If it finds that it hasn't been, then it looks in one more place: the prototype property (which happens to be an object itself) of the objects class. So, just by extending the prototype object inside of a class, you extend every object made from that class. The really amazing thing is that this even works retroactively! Objects that were created before their class was extended still look back onto the class's prototype object, so they are extended as well.

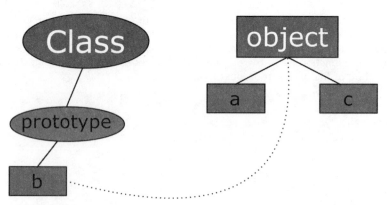

In the above schematic, **b** is a property of the object not because it was attached directly, but instead because it is a property of the class's prototype object.

Extending classes

We'll fix the `spaceCount` method that we just attached to one object, `title`, to instead extend all of the `String` objects in our movie. We simply need to extend the prototype object of its class instead of extending the single object:

```
Frame Actions
Movie Explorer  Frame Actions  Instance  Frame
+ - Frame Actions
function String_spaceCount(){
    var spaces = 0;
    for (var i=0;i<this.length;++i){
        if (this.charAt(i) == " "){
            ++spaces;
        }
    }
    return (spaces);
}

title = new String("This is a test");
String.prototype.spaceCount = String_spaceCount;

Line 12 of 12, Col 49
```

It's that final line that does the magic. It tells the prototype object to go inside the `String` class, and add to it a reference named `spaceCount` that refers to the `String_spaceCount` function.

```
Frame Actions
Movie Explorer  Frame Actions  Instance  Frame
+ - Frame Actions
String.prototype.material = "yarn";

Line 1 of 1, Col 36
```

Now each `String` object has a property called `material`, which is set to `yarn` (get it?).

Creating Classes

There are many built-in classes, and you can extend them with your own custom functionality, but sometimes this *still* isn't enough, and you need to be able to create your own class from scratch. We'll look at how you would create two new classes next, which work together to create, and keep track of, a deck of virtual playing cards.

To do this, the first thing we need to do is to define the constructor methods for our custom classes (remember, the constructor is the method that is called to create objects of a class.) To the untrained eye, a constructor method looks just like a normal function that shares the name of the class. And yes, just like a normal function it can accept arguments.

You start to build your class by first figuring out what data your class represents and what actions you need to be able to perform. When you're done, you'll have the properties and methods that your class will contain. Then, you'll need to write a constructor function to encapsulate it all. This is the beginning of a constructor function for the custom `PlayingCard` class:

```
Frame Actions                                                              x
 Frame Actions                                                          ? 
 +  -  Frame Actions                                                    ▼ ▲
function PlayingCard(name, suit){
    this.name = name;
    this.suit = suit;
    if (this.suit == "clubs" || this.suit == "spades"){
        this.color = "black";
    }else{
        this.color = "red";
    }
}

Line 6 of 11, Col 8
                                                                         ⊕
```

Now, that is pretty much it for the `PlayingCard` class, since there really aren't any methods that a playing card would need, it just needs to hold the information about itself. Since we are done with `PlayingCard` we should work on the next class, `PlayingCardDeck`. Below is its constructor:

```
Frame Actions                                                              x
 Frame Actions                                                          ? 
 +  -  Frame Actions                                                    ▼ ▲
function PlayingCardDeck(){
    this.suits = new Array("clubs", "diamonds", "hearts", "spades");
    this.names = new Array("ace", "two", "three", "four", "five",
                            "six", "seven", "eight", "nine", "ten",
                            "jack", "queen", "king");
    this.cards = new Array();
    for (var i=0;i<this.suits.length;++i){
        for(var j=0;j<this.names.length;++j){
            this.cards.push(new _root.PlayingCard(this.names[j], this.suits[i]));
        }
    }
}

Line 24 of 27, Col 1
                                                                         ⊕
```

This code will create some arrays to hold the information about the cards in a deck (suits and names) and then creates a special array called `cards`. Finally, it creates 52 new `PlayingCard` objects and puts them into that array.

Now we need to think about things you do to a deck of cards. The most obvious thing, and the one method we are going to add to our `PlayingCardDeck` class, is shuffle.

```
function PlayingCardDeck_shuffle(){
    var card0, card1, temp;
    for (var i=0; i<3*this.cards.length; ++i){
        // pick two cards
        card0 = random(this.cards.length);
        card1 = random(this.cards.length);
        // swap their positions
        temp = this.cards[card0];
        this.cards[card0] = this.cards[card1];
        this.cards[card1] = temp;
    }
}

PlayingCardDeck.prototype.shuffle = PlayingCardDeck_shuffle;
```

Now, what's going on here? First of all, we are creating three local variables, card0, card1, and temp. We create a loop next that we are going to go through three times for every card in the deck (this makes sure the deck is *good* and shuffled!). Inside each iteration of the loop we simply pick two random positions in the card array and swap those positions. By the time this little swap has been done 156 times (as it would with a normal card deck) the cards will be pretty well shuffled. Finally, just like when we were extending built-in classes, we extend PlayingCardDeck by adding our shuffle method to it.

One thing to note is that the random action is now deprecated in Flash 5 in favor of the Math.random method. To use Math.random instead, the code would look like this:

```
card0 = Math.floor(Math.random() * this.cards.length);
card1 = Math.floor(Math.random() * this.cards.length);
```

There are a few things to note about using custom classes. First of all, if you wish to create an object from a custom class on a timeline other than the one on which the class was defined, you have to explicitly give the path to the constructor function when you call it.

```
myDeck = new root.PlayingCardDeck();
```

Secondly, you will find that if you wish to use a custom class in a number of different FLAs, it's a bit of a pain to keep copying lines and lines of code between FLAs. In order to get around all of that annoying cutting and pasting, you can use Flash's special #include action. The #include action allows you to specify a text file that Flash will merge into the FLA at compile time. So, rather than copying a class's code between FLAs, all you need to do is place it into an external text file and use the #include command in each FLA that will utilize the class. If we were to place our PlayingCard and PlayingCardDeck classes into a text file called PlayingCardDeck.as, then the include command would look like this:

```
#include "PlayingCardDeck.as"
```

Finally, objects created from custom classes consume memory, as do all objects. Thus, when you are finished using an object, particularly large ones, it is best to use the `delete` operator to clear it from memory. Once we have finished using our `myDeck` object we would want to add the following to our code:

```
delete (myDeck);
```

Inheritance

As you have seen, object-oriented programming is all about keeping related properties and methods together. OOP is all about creating logical relationships and we've yet to cover one of the most interesting and useful types of relationship, **related classes**.

To understand how classes can be related, let's return to the example of the `PlayingCardDeck` class. Imagine that after we got done writing our custom `PlayingCardDeck` we realize that there are certain sub-types of playing card decks such as ones that have jokers, two decks combined, or other additions or restrictions.

In the case of a deck with jokers, we want to be able to add or remove the jokers. So, we are not only adding new cards, but also new methods. So, we want a class that can do everything that `PlayingCardDeck` can do, but with a few additions.

Well, we can do it, but we will have to implement a powerful feature of OOP languages: **inheritance**. We will create a `PlayingCardDeckJoker` class with its own methods and properties, but we will not rewrite the code it shares with the plain `PlayingCardDeck` class. Instead `PlayingCardDeckJoker` will inherit all of the `PlayingCardDeck` class's methods and properties. The first thing we are going to do is to write the code for the `PlayingCardDeckJoker` class:

```
#include "PlayingCardDeck.as"

function PlayingCardDeckJoker(){
    this.addJokers();
}

function PlayingCardDeckJoker_addJokers(){
    this.cards.push(new PlayingCard("Joker", "high"));
    this.cards.push(new PlayingCard("Joker", "low"));
}

function PlayingCardDeckJoker_delJokers(){
    var temp = this.cards;
    delete (this.cards);
    this.cards = new Array();
    for(var i=0; i<this.temp.length; ++i){
        if (this.temp[i].name != "Joker"){
            this.cards.push(this.temp[i]);
        }
    }
    delete (temp);
}

PlayingCardDeckJoker.prototype.addJokers = PlayingCardDeckJoker_addJokers;
PlayingCardDeckJoker.prototype.delJokers = PlayingCardDeckJoker_delJokers;
```

Now, we have our constructor and methods for the `PlayingCardDeckJoker` class. The `addJokers` method adds jokers to the deck and `delJokers` finds the jokers in the deck and removes them. While this is wonderful, we still haven't made this class inherit from the `PlayingCardDeck` class. Our first inclination might be to do something like this:

```
PlayingCardDeckJoker.prototype = PlayingCardDeck.prototype;
```

It won't work, though. The first problem, which you might have noticed, is that by equating the two prototype objects, we are wiping out the methods that we attached to `PlayingCardDeckJokers`'s prototype earlier. Even if we hadn't attached any methods to `PlayingCardDeck`, this idea would still be flawed. The reason is because every prototype object has a **constructor** property, which tells the class what the class's constructor function is. So, if we ran this code and tried to create an instance of `PlayingCardDeckJoker`, it will actually call `PlayingCardDeck`'s constructor, not `PlayingCardDeckJoker`'s!

No need to be concerned though, because it just so happens that Flash lets us tell any class which object that it should inherit from. The way we do this involves another special property of the prototype object, `__proto__` (two underscores, proto, and then two more underscores). This property is always set to the object that the class will inherit from. By default, this is the prototype property of the `Object` class (which is just an empty object, we'll get more into that later). What we need to do is to tell `PlayingCardDeckJoker` that it needs to inherit from `PlayingCardDeck`'s prototype:

```
PlayingCardDeckJoker.prototype.__proto__ =
➡ PlayingCardDeck.prototype;
```

That's it! Now `PlayingCardDeckJoker` will inherit everything from `PlayingCardDeck`'s prototype. But, we have not finished yet. You might have noticed that the code that actually builds the initial deck is missing. Well, again, this code is already done for us inside the `PlayingCardDeck` object; we just have to get to it. Essentially, when the `PlayingCardDeckJoker` class constructor is called, it will need to call the constructor of the `PlayingCardDeck` class in addition to its own constructor. Unfortunately, we don't have built-in access to `PlayingCardDeck`'s constructor, but we can give ourselves access with a little slick coding! What we need to do is assign a property to `PlayingCardDeckJoker`'s prototype that will point to the constructor property of `PlayingCardDeck`'s prototype. Remember, we can get a class's constructor function by looking at the constructor property of its prototype property. So, our code will look like this:

```
PlayingCardDeckJoker.prototype.super=PlayingCardDeck.prototype.
➡ constructor;
```

`super` is not a keyword or anything along those lines, it's just a good name for the property since it points to `PlayingCardDeckJoker`'s 'super class', or the class it inherits from. The final step is to add a line into `PlayingCardDeckJoker`'s constructor function that will call `PlayingCardDeck`'s constructor. The code will look like this:

```
this.super();
```

Now that we are done making PlayingCardDeckJoker inherit from PlayingCardDeck, let's look at our final code:

```
Frame Actions                                                                    X
Frame Actions                                                                  ? ►
+  -  Frame Actions                                                            ▼ ▲
#include "PlayingCardDeck.as"

function PlayingCardDeckJoker(){
    this.super();
    this.addJokers();
}

function PlayingCardDeckJoker_addJokers(){
    this.cards.push(new PlayingCard("joker", "high"));
    this.cards.push(new PlayingCard("joker", "low"));
}

function PlayingCardDeckJoker_delJokers(){
    var temp = this.cards;
    delete (this.cards);
    this.cards = new Array();
    for(var i=0; i<this.temp.length; ++i){
        if (this.temp[i].name != "joker"){
            this.cards.push(this.temp[i]);
        }
    }
    delete (temp);
}

PlayingCardDeckJoker.prototype.addJokers = PlayingCardDeckJoker_addJokers;
PlayingCardDeckJoker.prototype.delJokers = PlayingCardDeckJoker_delJokers;
PlayingCardDeckJoker.prototype.__proto__ = PlayingCardDeck.prototype;
PlayingCardDeckJoker.prototype.super = PlayingCardDeck.prototype.constructor;
◄                                                                             ►
Line 28 of 28, Col 78
                                                                              ⊕
```

There's one more important thing to understand about inheritance. It just so happens that the prototype object is just like every other object in that it inherits from the most base of classes, the Object class. This means that no matter what, every object you ever create will inherit from the Object class. This also means that if you add methods or properties to the prototype object of the Object class, every object you ever create will also have those methods and properties. So we might add some code such as below.

```
Object.prototype.creator = "me";
```

The result would be that every single object in the entire movie, every movie clip, array, custom object, etc, would have a property called creator whose value is "me".

As a final note, you might notice that in ActionScript manuals or in the Flash program, you will never see the word 'class'. Flash refers to the built-in **classes** (Array, String, Date, etc) as simply **objects**. The reason for this is that traditionally prototype based OOP languages do not have a formal structure for defining classes (unlike C++ or JAVA). What we have been calling classes are, in prototype based languages like ActionScript, called **Prototype Objects**. Don't be fooled, though. Prototype and class means the same thing.

Whew! We have come a long way! You now know what OOP is, how it works, and how to use it in Flash 5 ActionScript. You can use its most basic concepts like extending classes and some of its most complex, like inheritance. With this knowledge you will be able to not only make your own programs more readable and reusable, but also, you will be able to better understand other developers complex OOP based code.

Index

The index is arranged hierarchically, in alphabetical order, with symbols preceding the letter A. Many second-level entries also occur as first-level entries. This is to ensure that users will find the information they require however they choose to search for it.

N

Q

What's on the CD?

- Chapter Support Files

- ActivePerl from ActiveState

- Demo Software:

    - Macromedia Ultradev

    - Macromedia Generator Developer Edition

    - Macromedia ColdFusion Server Professional Edition

    - Macromedia ColdFusion Studio

    - Macromedia Dreamweaver JavaScript Integration Kit for Flash 5

    - Macromedia Extension WDDX

    - ASP Turbine

    - MySQL

    - PHP4

    - PHPEd

Trademark and Copyright Acknowledgements

ActiveState, ActivePerl, and PerlScript are trademarks of ActiveState Tool Corp

ASP Turbine - ©2000 Blue*Pacific Software

Macromedia®, Generator™, ColdFusion ®, Dreamweaver®, Dreamweaver® UltraDev™, and Flash™ are trademarks or registered trademarks of Macromedia, Inc. in the United States and/or other countries.

Macromedia Products and Screenshots - Copyright © 1995-2000 Macromedia, Inc., 600 Townsend St., San Francisco, CA 94103 USA. All Rights Reserved. Use, duplication, or disclosure by the United States Government is subject to the restrictions set forth in DFARS 252.227-7013(c)(1)(ii) and FAR 52.227-19.

PHP - Copyright © 1999, 2000 The PHP Group. All rights reserved
This Product includes PHP, freely available from http://www.php.net/